15. 00

MARLBOROUGH

BY WINSTON S. CHURCHILL

The Story of the Malakand Field Force
The River War (2 volumes)
Savrola
London to Ladysmith via Pretoria
Ian Hamilton's March
Lord Randolph Churchill (2 volumes)
My African Journey
The World Crisis (4 volumes)
The Aftermath (volume V of The World Crisis)
The Unknown War (volume VI of The World Crisis)
A Roving Commission
Marlborough, His Life and Times (6 volumes)
Great Contemporaries
Step by Step, 1936–1939
Amid These Storms
Frontiers and Wars
Painting as a Pastime
The Second World War (6 volumes)
A History of the English-Speaking Peoples (4 volumes)

BY HENRY STEELE COMMAGER

BOOKS

The Growth of the American Republic,
with SAMUEL ELIOT MORISON, 2 volumes
Theodore Parker: Yankee Crusader
A Short History of the United States,
with ALLAN NEVINS
Majority Rule and Minority Rights
The American Mind: An Interpretation of American Thought
and Character since the 1800's
America's Robert E. Lee

BY HENRY STEELE COMMAGER
(continued)

Freedom, Loyalty, Dissent
Crusaders for Freedom
The Nature and the Study of History
Freedom and Order: A Commentary on the American Political Scene
The Search for a Usable Past
The Commonwealth of Learning

COMPENDIA AND EDITED BOOKS

Documents of American History, 2 volumes
The Heritage of America: Readings in American History,
with ALLAN NEVINS
The Story of the Second World War
TOCQUEVILLE, ALEXIS. *Democracy in America*. An abridgment
America in Perspective: The United States Through Foreign Eyes
The Blue and The Gray, 2 volumes
Living Ideas in America
Official Atlas of the Civil War
*The Spirit of Seventy-Six: The Story of the American Revolution
as Told by Participants*, with RICHARD B. MORRIS, 2 volumes
The Era of Reform 1830–1860
Theodore Parker: An Anthology
The Defeat of the Confederacy
Churchill's History of the English-Speaking Peoples.
Arrangement for one volume
Lester Ward and the Welfare State
The Struggle for Racial Equality
Was America a Mistake?
Selected Writings. WILLIAM DEAN HOWELLS
The New American Nation series, with RICHARD B. MORRIS, 41 volumes
Immigration and American History: Essays in Honor of Theodore C. Blegen
The St. Nicholas Anthology, 2 volumes
Bowles, Chester. *The Conscience of a Liberal*. Selected and edited

MARLBOROUGH

His Life and Times

WINSTON S. CHURCHILL

ABRIDGED AND WITH AN INTRODUCTION BY

HENRY STEELE COMMAGER

WINGATE COLLEGE LIBRARY
WINGATE, N. C.

New York

CHARLES SCRIBNER'S SONS

Copyright © 1968 Charles Scribner's Sons

Copyright 1933, 1934, 1935, 1936, 1937 Charles Scribner's Sons;
renewal copyright © 1961, 1962, 1963, 1964, 1965 Winston S. Churchill.

Copyright 1938 Charles Scribner's Sons; renewal copyright
© 1966 Clementine Ogilvy Spencer-Churchill

ALL RIGHTS RESERVED. NO PART OF THIS BOOK
MAY BE REPRODUCED IN ANY FORM WITHOUT
THE PERMISSION OF CHARLES SCRIBNER'S SONS.

A-3.68[V]

PRINTED IN THE UNITED STATES OF AMERICA
Library of Congress Catalog Card Number 68-12353

T O

THE GRENADIER GUARDS

formerly "The 1st Guards,"
in which John Churchill,
afterwards Duke of Marlborough,
received his first commission on September 14, 1667,
of which he was colonel from the year 1704 to 1711
and from 1714 till his death,
and which served under him at the battles of
the Schellenberg, Blenheim, Ramillies, Oudenarde,
and Malplaquet,
and in all the principal sieges and other
great operations
during ten victorious campaigns,
this work is dedicated by the author
in memory of
the courtesies and kindness
shown to him by the regiment in
the great war

43457

‭ NOTE ‬

In quoting from old documents and letters the original text has been preserved wherever it is significant. Letters of Marlborough and Sarah which enter directly into the narrative have been modernized in spelling, grammar, and punctuation so far as is convenient to the reader. But the archaic style and setting has been preserved, and occasionally words are left in characteristic spelling.

Documents never made public [before the original six-volume edition] are distinguished by an asterisk (*) and left for the most part in their original form. In the case of unpublished letters to and from Marlborough preserved in the Blenheim collection no further reference is given.

In the diagrams, except where otherwise stated, fortresses held by the Allies are shown as black stars and those occupied by the French as white stars.

W. C.

METHOD OF DATING

Until 1752 dates in England and on the Continent differed owing to our delay in adopting the Reformed Calendar of Gregory XIII. The dates which prevailed in England were known as Old Style, those abroad as New Style. In the seventeenth century the difference was ten days, in the eighteenth century eleven days. For example, January 1,

NOTE

1601 (O.S.), was January 11, 1601 (N.S.), and January 1, 1701 (O.S.), was January 12, 1701 (N.S.).

The method used has been to give all dates of events that occurred in England in the Old Style, and of events that occurred abroad in New Style. Letters and papers are dated in the New Style unless they were actually written in England. In sea battles and a few other convenient cases the dates are given in both styles.

It was also customary at this time—at any rate, in English official documents—to date the year as beginning on Lady Day, March 25. What we should call January 1, 1700, was then called January 1, 1699, and so on for all days up to March 25, when 1700 began. This has been a fertile source of confusion. In this book all dates between January 1 and March 25 have been made to conform to the modern practice.

W. C.

ᶳᴅ CONTENTS ᴅᶾ

FOLLOWING THE ORIGINAL DIVISION
INTO SIX VOLUMES

(xi)

CONTENTS

CONTENTS

CONTENTS

≈ LIST OF ILLUSTRATIONS ≈

LIST OF ILLUSTRATIONS

⁊ɑ LIST OF MAPS ꭰꝫ

(xvii)

꧁ INTRODUCTION ꧂

WINSTON CHURCHILL is, beyond all doubt, that statesman who became the greatest historian, and that historian who became the greatest statesman, in the long annals of England. We do not say of him, had he not chosen to be a great public figure he would have been a great historian, for he was that, by every test. It is only because our gaze is fastened so continuously, and so intensely upon that career which has some claim to be the most splendid in two centuries of English history, that we do not concentrate more on that career which has some claim to be regarded as the most affluent in English historical literature.

Because, for half a century, Churchill played an active role in politics, we may be tempted to suppose that the writing of history was, with him, an avocation, and put him down as one of those glorious amateurs who are the specialty of English culture. There is of course some truth in this: doubtless Churchill preferred making history to writing it. The point is that he did both, and did them not as separate enterprises, but as instinctive expressions of a character of singular unity, harmony and consistency. There was no division, and certainly no conflict, between the two activities, the making and the writing of history: each nourished the other, and interacted on the other. For Churchill wrote history in order to mould it, and—so we sometimes suspect—he made history in order to write it. As he was a statesman in the familiar tradition of Cromwell, Chatham, Disraeli, and his own father, Lord Randolph, so he was an historian in the familiar tradition of Ralegh, Gibbon, Macaulay and Lecky, and to both enterprises, the political and the literary, he brought the same intellectual and moral qualities.

(xix)

It is the quality of Churchill's histories that assure them a permanent place in our literature, but the sheer bulk is no less impressive. What other major historian has written so much, so well: thirty-two volumes, no less, of history and biography, and another twenty volumes of speeches which add a not negligible dimension to historical literature. If this prodigious output had been achieved at the expense of scholarly accuracy, critical acumen, or literary polish, we might dismiss it as interesting chiefly for what it told us about Churchill himself, but the books do not shine in some borrowed light, but with their own. *The River War* is still far and away the best account of the struggle for the Sudan; *Lord Randolph Churchill* is one of the best biographies in English political literature; the *Marlborough* ranks with such biographies as Carlyle's *Frederick the Great* (a greatly under-valued work) and Freeman's *Lee*; the voluminous histories of two World Wars remain indispensable:—it is safe to say that no other leader of any of the warring nations has produced anything as sure of permanence.

We know that Churchill put a great deal of effort into his books, as he did into his speeches; but as they appear before us, they are shorn of all the machinery and all the scaffolding, and stand forth in their own comeliness and symmetry. They were, like his public papers, natural, though not spontaneous, expressions of his character. And that character was all of a piece: it is the same in whatever guise—soldier, journalist, politician, statesman, historian. Churchill wrote as he talked, and talked as he wrote; he took to the pen as he took to the sword or to the floor of the House of Commons.

As with most great historians, Churchill was self-taught and self-trained. Certainly he had no formal education for a career as historian —indeed it is accurate to say that he had no formal education for anything except soldiering. But his informal education was probably as good as that which any young man enjoyed in the whole of England. It was something to be born in Blenheim Palace, it was something to be heir to generations of Churchills, it was something to have the dazzling Lord Randolph for a father, to be connected with all the first families of politics and society, to be familiar with all the best drawing rooms—even those of royalty. As a boy he had not only read history, but seen it in the making. "I can see myself . . . sitting a little boy," he said to the students of Harrow, "always feeling the glory of England and its history, surrounding me and about me." Perhaps he did feel something of that at Harrow, but doubtless he felt even more of it in the spacious rooms and gardens of Blenheim, at the Vice-Regal Lodge in Dublin, at the house on St. James's Place. But even that was only the beginning. After Sandhurst, where he went because he was unable to pass "responsions" for Oxford, he continued his special preparation for History—and for life.

On distant Indian frontiers he immersed himself in history and philosophy. "All through the long, glistening, middle hours of the Indian day," he remembered, "from when we quitted stables till when the evening shadows proclaimed the hour of Polo, I devoured Gibbon." And not Gibbon alone, but Macaulay and Lecky and, for good measure, Plato and Aristotle too. "I approached it with an empty, hungry mind," he added, "and with fairly strong jaws, and what I got I bit." Indeed he did, and his bite left permanent marks! Circumstances, too, conspired to advance his education: he went as a journalist to Cuba, where there was a convenient revolution; he fought, and played polo, on the Indian frontier; he managed to get himself posted to the Sudan in time for the River War, whose history he wrote; he resigned from the Army, but not the military, and at twenty-one he was off to South Africa and the Boer War, a veteran now of four campaigns in four different quarters of the globe. Thus he learned of wars by fighting in them, as Herodotus had, and Thucydides, and Tacitus, and in time it came to seem that the wars were waged just so he could write the *Malakand Field Force,* and *The River War,* and *From London to Ladysmith,* to say nothing of his first, and only novel, *Savrola.*

All this preparation was, in a sense, fortuitous; the young Churchill was not really looking that far ahead. Fame was the spur, and necessity, too. Churchill had to make his way; he had to make his mark. The Army, for all its fascination, offered nothing permanent, nor assurance that it could satisfy Churchillian ambition. Torn between journalism, history, and politics, Churchill embraced all three and made them one. He was the most dashing of cavalrymen—and of polo players, too, which was important; he was the highest paid war correspondent in England; the *Malakand Field Force,* and then *The River War,* were acknowledged to be history of a high order, and if the success of *Savrola* did not beckon to a purely literary career, it was certainly nothing for a young man to be ashamed of. As early as 1898 he wrote his mother that he was planning a biography of Garibaldi, and a history of the

American Civil War, and for good measure he threw in a collection of short stories. Success intervened; he stood for Oldham, and won, and was launched on the turbulent seas of politics.

Churchill was never content to sail but one sea at a time. His father, whom he had worshipped from afar, rather than loved, had died in 1895; now that Churchill had proved himself in history, now that he had turned to politics, he launched himself upon a biography of Lord Randolph. "Once again," he said, "I lift the tattered flag lying on a stricken field." It was a splendid phrase for politics, but ominous for history. But astonishingly enough Churchill's biography of his father was not an essay in filiopietism, but judicious, comprehensive, and mature, penetrating not only to the realities of politics in those turbulent Victorian days, but of character.

It was, of course, more; it was a lifting of the tattered banner, and a mending of it, too. In a sense all of Churchill's histories were autobiographical: the early books which were history seen through the eyes of a young subaltern; the later books which were world history seen through the eyes of a world statesman; the biographies which were all family affairs. He lived a long life, every minute of it crammed with excitement, and he recorded all of it, for the benefit of posterity—and for his own benefit too, for he never overlooked that. The early books advertised his talent as a war correspondent; the books of the middle period testified to his role as a spokesman of the Churchill family; the later books were a monument to his genius as soldier and statesman. He was present in all of them: in the early histories as reporter; in the later as director. Never was there more personal history. It was Lord Balfour who called *The World Crisis*, "Winston's brilliant autobiography disguised as a history of the universe," and might not this have been said—with less justification for the touch of malice—of *The Second World War* too; while of *A History of the English-Speaking Peoples* it could be plausibly asserted that it was designed to make clear (or at any event did make clear) that the virtues which had for centuries exalted these peoples were precisely those which the whole world associated with Winston Churchill.

All of his life Churchill was fascinated with himself, and no wonder. He saw himself in his father—really a very different and much less stable character—and his description of the boy Randolph was autobiographical:

INTRODUCTION

This schoolboy, pausing unembarrassed on the threshold of life, has made up his mind already. Nothing will change him much . . . Lord Randolph's letters as a boy are his letters as a man. The same vigour of expression; the same simple yet direct language; the same odd, penetrating flashes; the same coolly independent judgments about people and laws, and readiness to criticize both as if it were a right; the same vein of humor and freedom from all affectation. . . . [*Lord Randolph*, I, 13–14]

He saw himself in the great Duke, too; like Marlborough he loved the sound of bullets, the clash of sabres, the crowded stage, the sense of power, the sporting with destiny, the applause of nations and of sovereigns, and of history, and his vindication of Marlborough from neglect and contumely was in a sense a vindication of himself. As for his histories of the two World Wars, he did not need to put himself at the center of great affairs or make clear how many threads he held in his own firm grip, for the world did that for him.

Most nearly autobiographical—and prophetic, too—was the first book that Churchill wrote (not the first he published), the novel *Savrola*. Youth excused the triteness and absurdity of its plot—it was another *Graustark*, another *Prisoner of Zenda*—and of its philosophy, too, which was half-baked Social Darwinism; but the vigorous style, the sharp characterizations, and the curiously prophetic reflections on politics, do not need excuses. The novel was about revolution, dictatorship, and, rather awkwardly, platonic love; it was about power, which always fascinated Churchill; it was about the ruthlessness and cruelty of war, the fickleness of the mob, the brevity of fame. It was, above all, about a young man who sounded and acted like Winston Churchill and who foreshadowed what he was to become. Even the oratory was prophetic:

Amid the smoke he saw a peroration which would cut deep into the hearts of a crowd; a high thought, a fine simile, expressed in that correct diction which is comprehensible even to the most illiterate, and appeals to the most simple; something to lift their minds from the material cares of life and to awake sentiment. His ideas began to take the form of words, to group themselves into sentences; he murmured to himself; the rhythm of his own language swayed him; instinctively he alliterated. . . . The sound would please their ears, the sense improve and stimulate their minds. What a game it was! His brain contained the cards he had to play, the world the stakes he played for. [*Savrola*, p. 89]

The central figure of *Savrola* was a soldier who aspired to be a states-man, or a statesman who found he had to be a soldier. If there is a common denominator in all of Churchill's histories, except the *Lord Randolph*, it is the preoccupation with the military. And if Churchill had a specialty—and now-a-days all historians must—it was military history. He is, in all likelihood, the greatest of military historians writing in English, superior to Napier on the Peninsular Wars, to Oman who wrote on the history of war, to Fortescue whose history of the British Army is curiously parochial; and the peer of the three great American masters of the history of war, Francis Parkman, Douglas S. Freeman, and S. E. Morison. For consider Churchill's claim to preëminence in military history. His first books were about wars—frontier skirmishes, to be sure, but that can be said of Parkman's histories as well; his *Marl-borough* can bear comparison with Freeman's seven volumes on *Lee* and his *Lieutenants*; his magisterial histories of two great world wars are still, for all the passage of time, the most comprehensive and schol-arly available in English. No other major military historian covered so broad a territory—India, the Sudan, South Africa, western Europe, and eventually the globe; no other chronicled so many different wars, or wars so different; no other saw the wars he chronicled from such varied van-tage points, from that of the cavalryman in the field to that of the Lord of the Admiralty and of the Supreme Commander; no other understood so fully the role of tactics, of strategy, and of grand strategy, of politics, diplomacy, and public opinion.

2.

WHAT philosophy suffused and illuminated these many histories, from *The River War* to *The Second World War?*—fifty years of history, fifty years of writing? No formal philosophy, certainly, for Churchill would have agreed with his friend George Macaulay Trevelyan, that philosophy was not something you took to history, it was something you carried away from history. Yet every historian takes some philosophy with him, inarticulate, or even unconscious—some concept of what life, and his-

INTRODUCTION

tory, are about. Churchill matured early and, for all his political maneuvering, retained, to the end of his long life, a marvelous consistency. He was, in manner, rhetoric, even in appearance, an eighteenth-century figure; he combined, in himself, something of Chatham, of Burke and, even more perhaps, of Charles James Fox; and he accepted, instinctively, the attitude towards history which that century took for granted: that history, in the words of Bolingbroke, was Philosophy teaching by examples. What is more, he was quite ready to stand there and point to the examples. Indeed we can say of Churchill what he himself wrote of Rosebery, that "the Past stood ever at his elbow and was the counsellor upon whom he most relied. He seemed to be attended by Learning and History, and to carry into current events an air of ancient majesty."

Nowhere does this appear more simply than in the "Grand Theme" which Churchill imposed upon his history of *The Second World War*: "In War: Resolution; In Defeat: Defiance; In Victory: Magnanimity; In Peace: Good Will." He read history as a stupendous moral scripture, and for him the writing was, if not divinely inspired, at least authoritative. More, it was straightforward and simple. History was a struggle between the forces of right or wrong, freedom and tyranny, the future and the past. By great good fortune Churchill's own people—"this island race," as he called them—were on the side of right, progress and enlightenment; by great good fortune, too, it was given to him to buckle these virtues onto him as armor in the struggle for a righteous cause.

If history was Philosophy teaching by examples, what lessons did it teach?

The lessons that Churchill learned from history stare out at us from a hundred aphorisms; no other modern historian has conjured up so many aphorisms or coined so many epigrams. They are explicit in scores of essays; they are implicit in fifty volumes of history and public argument. Let us summarize them.

First, History was not just the pursuit of idle hours but was, itself, philosophy and, rightly read, furnished lessons which statesmen could ponder and apply. Second, History was both memory and prophesy. It provided the counsel and the solace of the long view both to the past and to the future. The contemplation of the ages which mankind had somehow endured, and survived, infused the student with patience, with humility, and with courage; the prospect of a posterity which, a thousand years hence, might pronounce the verdict that one generation had given to a nation "its finest hour" encouraged resoluteness and hope, and strengthened the ability to confront crises that seemed insurmountable. Third, History followed great cycles: the same themes recurred, again and again, the same drama was played out, from age to age; and as men had somehow survived the vicissitudes of the past there was ground to hope that they might survive those of the present and the future. Thus four times Britain had fought to rescue Europe from the grip of a tyrant—Louis XIV, Napoleon, Kaiser William, and Hitler—and four times Britain had succeeded in saving Europe and, with it, the cause of liberty and justice. Here was a recurring pattern which augured well for the future of "this island race," and of mankind, for, as Churchill saw it, the welfare of mankind was inextricably intertwined with that of the English-speaking peoples. Fourth, History bore witness to the vital importance of national character, for character was as important to a people as to an individual, and every nation must be alert to defend and preserve it. That each nation had a special character Churchill did not doubt, and as he contemplated the long arch of centuries he was led to a fifth conclusion, that it was, above all, the English character which had lighted up the corridors of time, flickering now and then but mostly pure and clear and even luminous—the English character and that of England's daughter nations around the globe. For all his familiarity with the peoples of every continent, Churchill was the most parochial of historians. He looked out upon world history, but he looked through British spectacles, and his rallying cry was the familiar one from *King John:* "Come the three corners of the world in arms/And we shall shock them/Nought shall make us rue/if England to herself do rest but true." That was really the motto of all his histories—the *Marlborough,* when England did not stay true to herself; and the two World War histories, which recounted the famous story, how England did. All his life, Churchill's eyes were dazzled by the glory of England, and all of his writing was suffused by a sense of that glory. He never forgot that it was the English tongue that was heard in Chicago and Vancouver, Johannesburg and Sydney, Trinidad and Calcutta, or that it was English law that judges pronounced in Washington, Ottawa, Canberra and New Delhi, and English Parliamentary governments that flourished in scores of nations on every continent. It was this little island that had spread civilization throughout the globe, and what Churchill wrote, in *The River War*, could be inserted in almost all of his books:

> What enterprise that an enlightened community may attempt is more noble and more profitable than the reclamation from barbarism of fertile regions and large plantations? To give peace to warring tribes, to administer justice where all was violence, to strike the chains off the slave, to draw the richness from the soil, to plant the earliest seeds of commerce and learning, to increase in whole peoples their capacities for pleasure and diminish their chances of pain—what more beautiful ideal or more valuable reward can inspire human effort? [*The River War*, 9]

From all this flowed a sixth lesson, that the test of greatness was politics and war. Churchill knew something of the social and economic history of his people, he knew something of literature, for he had a great deal of it "by heart" which—as he said, was a good way to have it; and had he not chosen to be a soldier, a statesman, and an historian, he might have been a very considerable painter. But when he came to write history he put all this aside, and concentrated on the art of politics, the science of law, the beauty of justice, the power of government, the necessity of war.

Churchill knew the horrors of war, for he had experienced them, but he knew its exhilaration, too, and he might have said with General Lee that it is well that war is so terrible, else we might grow too fond of it. He had learned from history, and perhaps from Darwin, the law of the survival of the fittest, and he thought that England's capacity for survival was proof of her superiority. The call for "blood, toil, tears and sweat" was inspired not by the Blitz alone, but by a half century of conflict. "Battles," he wrote in the *Marlborough*, "are the principal milestones in secular history. . . . All great struggles of history have been won by superior will power wresting victory in the teeth of odds." And elsewhere he concluded flatly that "The story of the human race is War." Like those statesmen he most admired, Marlborough, Chatham, Wolfe, Clive, Washington, Lee, he was himself a war leader; alone of great war leaders he was a great war historian.

History—not least the history of war—taught a seventh lesson, and taught it not only *to* Churchill but *through* him: the vital importance of leadership. History, he asserted, was made "by those exceptional human beings whose thoughts, actions, qualities, virtues, triumphs, weaknesses and crimes have dominated the fortunes of the race." There is no record that he read Carlyle, but there is little doubt that he would have agreed with the philosopher from Cheyne Row that history "is the essence of innumerable biographies." This was the moral of the youthful *Savrola*, and it remained the moral of all Churchill's historical writing, and much of his political, for his volumes celebrated the "glorious few" who played, uncomplainingly, the role that History had assigned them—Lord Randolph, Marlborough, and that central and dominant figure of the two great war histories who so splendidly vindicated the principle of leadership.

Finally Churchill's reading of history reenforced his early education to exalt the heroic virtues. He was Roman rather than Greek, and as he admired Roman accomplishments in law, government, empire, so he rejoiced in Roman virtues of order, justice, fortitude, resoluteness, magnanimity. These were British virtues too, and, because he was the very symbol of John Bull, Churchillian. He cherished, as a law of history, the principle that a people who flout these virtues is doomed to decay and dissolution, and that a people who respect them will prosper and survive.

3.

DURING the dry years of forced retirement in the early twenties, Churchill wrote most of the volumes of *The World Crisis*. When the Conservatives were defeated again, in 1929, Churchill laid aside the scarlet robes of the Chancellor of the Exchequer which he had inherited from his father, and withdrew to Chartwell to launch himself upon an even more formidable historical enterprise, the biography of that famous Churchill who became the Duke of Marlborough. As with the *Lord Randolph* it was a filial, though not a filiopietistic work; as with the *Randolph*, too, it was a work of vindication and rehabilitation, for though Marlborough was recognized as a great soldier, his greatness of character was not acknowledged. As Churchill himself wrote, "Fame shines unwillingly upon the statesman and warrior whose exertions brought our island and all Europe safely through its perils and produced glorious results for Christendom. A long succession of the most famous writers of the English language have exhausted their resources of reproach and insult upon his name. Swift, Pope, Thackeray, Macaulay, in their different styles, have vied with one another in presenting an odious portrait to posterity."

The history of Marlborough was a theme worthy of Churchill's historical genius, and one which perhaps only he could have performed, combining as he did the advantages of access to the rich treasure of Marlborough archives at Blenheim and an experience in war and politics almost rivalling that of Marlborough himself. Churchill prepared himself for the enterprise, as he did for everything, with scrupulous care; studying all the voluminous sources, familiarizing himself with the terrain of battlefields and of marches, enlisting the aid of experts in political and diplomatic history, and deploying all his resources of narrative, eloquence, philosophy, and wit.

Here was indeed a subject worthy of the most eloquent pen in England. "It is my hope," he wrote,

> to recall this great shade from the past, and not only to invest him
> with his panoply, but make him living and intimate to modern eyes.
> I hope to show that he was not only the foremost of English sol-
> diers, but in the first rank among the statesmen of our history; not
> only that he was a Titan . . . but that he was a virtuous and benevo-
> lent being, eminently serviceable to his age and country, capable of
> drawing harmony and design from chaos, and one who only needed
> an earlier and still wider authority to have made a more ordered and
> a more tolerant civilization for his own time and to help the future.

The hero was a man after Churchill's heart: the greatest soldier in the annals of the race, ever victorious and ever magnanimous; the statesman who welded together a continental alliance; the diplomat who mediated between the English, the Dutch, the Prussians and the Empire; the Captain loved by his soldiers, trusted by his allies, respected by his enemies. But the theme was more than biographical; it was nothing less than the theme of the struggle for Europe. The battlefield was more than Blenheim, Ramillies and Oudenarde; it stretched from England to the Mediterranean, from Sweden to Savoy and enlisted all the great sovereigns of Europe.

Churchill seized upon this heroic figure and this affluent theme, and discoursed upon it spaciously. He saw its almost limitless scope, its bewildering complexities, its mighty drama; and, like a master builder he fitted them all together into a structure that was coherent and symmetrical. He quarried his facts from rich deposits of material; he grounded his volumes on the solid foundations of scholarship; he familiarized himself with the terrain and provided a background of rich verisimilitude. He interwove, wth masterly skill, the tangled skeins of a dozen nations, armies, and courts—England, France, Holland, the Empire, Bavaria, Prussia, Sweden, Spain, Savoy, even Ireland, and imposed on it all an harmonious pattern. He told his story in a language strong, muscular, rich, and resourceful, one that did full justice to its splendid drama and its glittering actors, noble and mean alike. To the study and the record of these momentous years, to the untangling of intricate webs of battle, politics, diplomacy and personalities, he brought all that he had learned in a lifetime of war politics, study and reflection.

It is, to be sure, partisan history; it is almost family history. But how few great historians, from Clarendon to Rowse, from Bancroft to Douglas Freeman, have not been partisan? *Marlborough* is an argument for the defense, all the way; but an argument not fabricated by cleverness or insinuated by chicanery, or imposed by violence, but grounded on the solid rock of evidence. It is balanced, temperate, and fair; it carries conviction.

It cannot fairly be said that Churchill is blind to the weaknesses and the flaws in Marlborough's character, but it can be said that he regards the weaknesses as venial and the flaws as superficial, and that when he casts up the balance of weakness and strength, he is content with the result. He is a skillful attorney for the defense, and if he does not convince us that Marlborough is blameless, he does persuade us that a blameless Marlborough would be uninspiring. Was the young John Churchill kept by a beautiful mistress? No doubt—but what young man could have resisted Barbara, Duchess of Cleveland? And what impecunious young soldier could have resisted her money? Did he abandon his King, James II? Yes, but that was for the well-being of England. Did he negotiate secretly with the enemy over in Paris, or Versailles? No doubt, but only to deceive them, for he played a deeper game than they did. Was he governed in all things by Sarah—her vanity, her arrogance, her imperiousness? Possibly so, but was she not the most fascinating woman in England, and how delightful that the

Iron Duke should be so romantic! Was he parsimonious, and greedy of money? Yes, but how much better to be parsimonious than to be extravagant; and as for the money, it all went to larger ends, like the building of Blenheim!

But the reader can be trusted to judge for himself the success of Churchill's vindication of the great Duke, of the wars he waged and the politics, or intrigues, he pursued. Even if he is not won over to a verdict uncompromisingly favorable to Marlborough, he can still revel in the masterly portrayal of character, the vigorous narrative, the pageantry and the roar of battle, the skillful handling of diplomatic and court intrigue; he can still rejoice in one of the great monuments of our historical literature.

But the *Marlborough* has still another interest, one which is irresistible even to those who are unmoved by the drama of the War of Spanish Succession or the spectacle of the rivalry for the affection and confidence of a Queen. It looks forward as well as backward; it is not elegiac, but, in a sense, apocalyptic.

Rarely in the history of historical writing have author and subject seemed so made for each other as were Churchill and the Duke of Marlborough. Churchill's literary skill enables us to understand Marlborough, but *Marlborough*, in turn, contributed to and advanced the education of Churchill. Surely this historical investigation which for five years absorbed Churchill's energies, may be looked upon as a providential preparation for the years ahead when he was to stand, a greater Marlborough, surveying a greater scene, presiding over a greater battle, commanding a greater coalition, whose destinies were fraught with greater significance. It is not a distortion to see in Marlborough an embryonic Churchill acting out on what seems to us a more restricted scale the role Churchill was to play with such splendor and bravura on a global scale. Like Marlborough, Churchill was called upon to rescue Europe from the grasp of a tyrant, to preside over a prodigious political and military coalition, to sustain allies who faltered and drooped, to fire the spirits of those who were reluctant, to assuage those who thought they contributed more than their share, to persuade the British people to bear, over the cruel years, the blood, toil, tears and sweat of war. Like Marlborough, on him was imposed the direction of the military, the political, even the diplomatic campaigns. Like Marlborough he had endured in silence the slings and shafts of fortune, but

(xxxi)

only to prepare himself for duties which no other could perform, and like Marlborough, too, he had shifted from party to party, never confessing to fickleness but conscious only of devotion to his sovereign and his people. Like Marlborough he was called upon, in a solemn moment of history, to save his nation and when he had done this, was rejected, only to return, at the end, to the favor and love of his people. All this may push the parallels too far, but not for Churchill, who read History as Puritans read the Scriptures.

We cannot say that without the experience of writing the *Marlborough*—an experience which was deeply personal as well as public—Churchill would not have been prepared for the great ordeal of the forties. But we can say that the writing of *Marlborough* helped prepare him for the prodigious challenge which lay ahead. And we can say that the mind and character of the man who presided over the destinies of the western world when Hitler threatened its existence, and who won through to such triumph as no other English statesman has ever known, was himself a product of a half century of conflict in which the writing and the making of History were one.

≥⊲▷≤

The only edition of the *Marlborough* heretofore available in America, is that published in the years 1933–38 in six volumes, and this has been for some time, out of print and unavailable. To make possible publication in one volume I have reduced the original text to approximately one-half its length, keeping, in the process, a large proportion of the original illustrations and maps. Nowhere, needless to say, have I taken liberties with the integrity of the text, which is precisely as Churchill wrote it. What I have done is to leave out such parts of the original as seemed to me less indispensable than others. Respect for Churchill's special talents dictated the selection of the chapters and passages included in this volume. In *Lord Randolph*, Churchill showed that he could deal, with firm hand and sure touch, with politics. But elsewhere, in his writings, he has preferred the annals of war to the story of peace, the battlefield to the cabinet, and in making the selections for this book I have very sensibly followed his preferences in the matter. Marlborough was a great political personality as he was a great warrior, but there is

INTRODUCTION

no doubt that in these volumes, at least, Churchill is at his best in telling the story of Marlborough the soldier rather than in unraveling the intricacies of Marlborough the politician or the courtier. I have therefore included almost the whole of the military narrative where Marlborough himself was in command, but merely enough of the political and the personal to brush in the background and keep the thread of the narrative, confident that while no one has told the military story in a more masterly fashion than has Churchill, others—notably George Macaulay Trevelyan—are fuller and doubtless more judicious in the analysis of the political story.

HENRY STEELE COMMAGER

Amherst, 1968

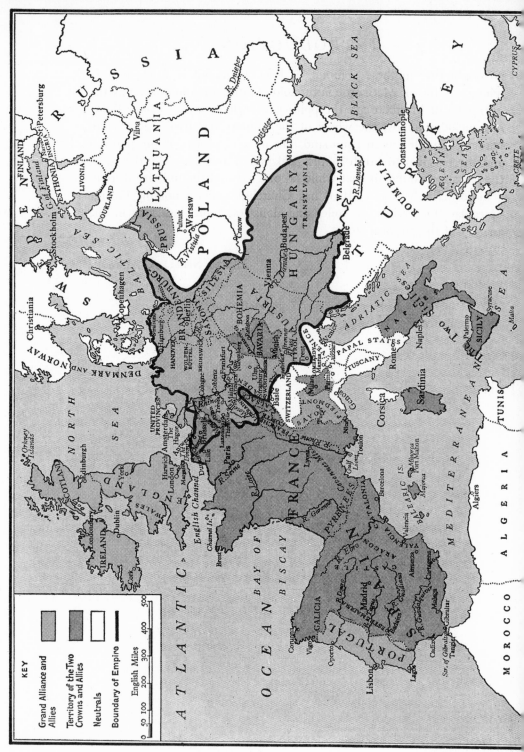

1. General Map of Europe

MARLBOROUGH

CHAPTER ONE

Ashe House

ƺɑ 1644-61 ɒƷ

IN January 1644 a Devonshire lady, Eleanor (or Ellen), widow of Sir John Drake, alarmed by the Royalist activities in the West Country, had asked for a Roundhead garrison to protect her house at Ashe, near Axminster. She was "of good affection" to the Parliament, had aided them with money and provisions, and had "animated her tenants in seven adjoining parishes" to adhere to their cause. The troops were sent; but before they could fortify the place Lord Poulett, a neighbour who commanded for the King, marched upon it with his Irish soldiers, drove out the Parliamentarians, burned the house, and "stripped the good lady, who, almost naked and without shoe to her foot but what she afterwards begged, fled to Lyme for safety."

Here she encountered fresh hardships. The Roundhead seaport of Lyme Regis was soon attacked by the Royal forces. Early in April Prince Maurice, with six thousand men and "an excellent artillery," laid siege to the town. The story of its resolute defence is a cameo of the Civil War. For nearly three months a primitive, fitful, fierce combat was waged along and across the meagre ramparts and ditches which protected the townsfolk. Women aided the garrison in their stubborn resistance, relieving them in their watch by night and handing up the powder and ball in action. Colonel Blake, afterwards the famous Admiral of the Commonwealth, commanded the town. He several times offered the Royalists to open a breach in his breastworks and fight out

(1)

the issue face to face on a front of twenty or on a front of ten men. His leadership, and twenty-six sermons by an eloquent Puritan divine, sustained the courage of the defenders. They depended for their supplies upon the sea. From time to time ships came in sight and aroused hopes and fears in both camps. Lady Drake was for a while in extreme distress. She must have watched the coming of ships with mingled feelings. The Royalist navy, such as it was, was commanded by her sister's grandson, James Ley, third Earl of Marlborough. Every week it was rumoured that her dreaded relation would arrive from the Channel Islands with reinforcements for the enemy. But he never came. The Parliament held the seas. Only Roundhead ships appeared. Eleanor endured privations, bombardments, and burnings for nearly three months. She was for her livelihood "reduced to the spinning and knitting of stockings, in which miserable condition she continued until the siege of Lyme was raised" by the arrival of a relieving Puritan army from London under the Earl of Essex, "whereof she got away and came to Parliament."

Her son John was no help to her in her misfortunes. We have been assured that he was "loyal to the King and on bad terms with his Puritan mother." But this seems incorrect. He was, on the contrary, at this time himself a prisoner of war in Prince Maurice's hands, and it was his mother who exerted herself on his behalf. Her sister, the Countess of Marlborough, stood high with the Royalists and appealed for the release of the captive. But the Parliamentary forces were now moving towards Axminster, and as the young Drake had said imprudently that he would get Lord Poulett's house burned in revenge for the burning of Ashe, his liberation was not unnaturally refused.

Lady Drake, though a resolute Puritan, continued to address herself to both sides, invoking with the Royalists her sister's, and with the Roundheads her own political merit. On September 28, 1644, Parliament ordered "that being wholly ruined by the enemy forces, she should have a furnished house in London rent free, £100 at once and £5 a week." The Westminster Commissioners accordingly four days later selected for her the house of a Royalist gentleman then still in arms—Sir Thomas Reynell; and she remained in these quarters for nearly four years, pursuing her claims for compensation through the slowly working mills of Westminster. Sir Thomas made his peace with Parliament and 'compounded for'—that is, ransomed—his house in

1646. He demanded reinstatement, as was his right; and he complained that Lady Drake during her tenancy "had digged up the ground and pulled up the floors in search of treasure." Nevertheless she continued to reside there in his despite, and perseveringly pursued her case against Lord Poulett for the burning of Ashe; and she had sufficient credit with the now irresistible Parliamentarians to carry it at last to a conclusion in the spring of 1648, when she was awarded £1500 compensation, to be paid out of Lord Poulett's estate.

It had taken Eleanor four years to secure the award. Two years more were required to extract the money from the delinquent, upon whose rents meanwhile she had a virtual receivership. In July 1650 she complained to Parliament that Lord Poulett still owed her £600. A further laborious investigation was set on foot. Six years passed after the burning of Ashe, which she claimed had lost her £6000, before Lady Drake recovered her £1500 compensation. She had need of it—and, indeed, of every penny. Hers was a family divided against itself by the wars. Her son fought for the Parliament; her son-in-law, Winston Churchill, fought for the King. Both he and his father had taken arms in the Royal cause from the early days. Both in turn—the father first —were drawn into the clutches of the Parliament. The Dorsetshire Standing Committee which dealt with the cases of the local Royalists reports in its minutes that in April 1646 John Churchill, a lawyer of some eminence, of Wootton Glanville, near Sherborne, had stated before them that he had formerly been nominated a Commissioner for the King; but he pleaded that in November 1645 he had taken the National Covenant and the Negative Oath. He had paid £300 for the Parliamentary garrison at Weymouth, and £100 on account of his personal estate. Moreover, reported the Committee, he was sixty years of age and unable to travel. In these circumstances in August 1646 he was fined £440, and a month later the sequestration of his estates was suspended.

The reckoning with his son Winston was delayed. Joining the King's army at twenty-two, he had made some mark upon the battlefields. He had become a captain of horse, and his bearing had been noted in the fights at Lansdowne Hill and Roundway Down. He was a youthful, staunch, and bigoted adherent of the King. Towards the end of 1645 he was wounded, and his plight amid the Roundheads now victorious throughout Dorset and Devon was most awkward. However, he had a refuge among the enemy. His father's house at Wootton Glanville was only a day's ride from Ashe. He was married to Lady Drake's third daughter, Elizabeth.

It is remarkable that such contracts should have been effected between persons so sharply divided by the actual fighting of the Civil Wars. We can see the stresses of the times from the fact that Winston's first child, Arabella, of whom more later, was not born till 1648, or more than five years after the date of the marriage, although thereafter children were born almost every year. No doubt the couple were parted by the severities of the war, and did not live regularly together till the struggle in the Western counties was ended. It was probable that Elizabeth lived with her mother during the whole of the fighting, and that from about the beginning of 1646 Winston joined her there. At any rate, from that time forward the two young people, wedded across the lines of civil war, lay low in the ruins of Ashe, and hoped to remain unnoticed or unpersecuted until the times should mend.

For a while all went well. But a regular system of informers had been set on foot, and, despite Winston's Roundhead connexions and Lady Drake's influence and record, the case against him was not allowed to lapse. At the end of 1649 he was charged with having been a captain in the King's army. According to the Dorsetshire records, witnesses, greedy, interested, but none the less credible, certified that as late as December 1645 Winston was still in the field against the Parliament, that he had been shot through the arm by the forces under Colonel Starr, and that he had resisted to the end with the royal garrison at Bristol. None of these facts could be rebutted.

However, the processes of law continued to work obstinately in spite of war and revolution. Beaten foes had rights which, unless specifically abolished by statute, they could assert. The delinquent captain fell back upon the law. He sought to collect debts owing to him from others. He claimed that a thousand marks given to his wife by her father, the late Sir John Drake, could not be sequestered. He laboured to put off the day when the final sentence would be pronounced. Long delays resulted. By August 1650 the Parliamentary authorities had lost patience. "Some cases," say their records,

> are sued out for no other end but to protract time, as that of Winston Churchill, who, it seems by his order, pretended his father (John

Churchill) and Lady Ellen Drake had an interest in his portion, whereas he has still a suit depending against Colonel William Fry and Sir Henry Rosewell in his own name, only for his wife's portion; had anybody else a title to it, he would not have commenced such a suit. As to his being in arms, he will surely not so far degenerate from his principles as to deny it.

The penalty was severe for a man whose estate seems to have been worth only £160 a year. Although Winston paid his fine at the end of 1651, he did not attempt to keep an independent home. Nor did he live with his father at Wootton Glanville. There may have been other reasons besides impoverishment for this. His father had married a second time about 1643; Winston was apparently on bad terms with his stepmother, and it was to his mother-in-law rather that he turned for aid. When the ultimate judgment and compassion of the Almighty, as the victors would have expressed it, had become fully manifest throughout the West Country, Lady Drake sate indignant on the winning side amid her ruins, and Ashe House continued to be a refuge from poverty, if not from destitution, for the broken Cavalier, his young wife, and growing family. They do not seem to have returned home till Winston's father died in the year before the Restoration. Thus they lived at Ashe for thirteen years, and hard must those years have been. The whole family dwelt upon the hospitality or charity of a mother-in-law of difficult, imperious, and acquisitive temper; a crowded brood in a lean and war-scarred house, between them and whose owner lay the fierce contentions of the times.

No record is in existence of the daily round of the composite Drake household. We must suppose from its long continuance that family affection and sheer necessity triumphed over unspeakable differences of sentiment and conviction. Lady Drake did her duty faithfully to her daughter's family. She fed, clothed, and sheltered them in such portions of her house as their partisans had left her. They, having scarcely any other resources, accepted her bounty. While Lady Drake, vaunting her fidelity, pursued her claims for compensation from the Parliament, Winston, with her aid and collusion, sought to escape its exactions. It may be that in this prolonged double effort to save as much as possible from the wreck of their affairs a comradeship of misfortune was added to family ties. It must, none the less, have been a queer and difficult home. We may judge of their straitened means by the fact that they could not afford to put a fresh roof over the burned-out parts of the house until after the Restoration. They huddled together all these years in the one remaining wing. The war had impoverished the whole West countryside, and to keep up the style of gentlefolk and educate children must have imposed a severe frugality on all at Ashe.

To the procreation of children and the slow excitements of frequent litigation Winston added the relief of writing and the study of heraldry. In a substantial and erudite volume, *Divi Britannici*, still widely extant and universally unread, he explored from "the Year of the World 2855" downwards those principles of the Divine Right of Kings for which he had fought and suffered. He went so far in doctrine as to shock even Royalist circles by proclaiming the right of the Crown to levy taxation by its mere motion.

He cherished the theory that all nations derived their names from their food, dress, appearance, habits, etc. He thinks, therefore, the Britons got their name from a drink which the Greeks called "bruton or bruteion, which Athinæus defined as *ton krithinon oinon*—i.e., *Vinum hordeaceum*, Barley Wine."

The preface to *Divi Britannici*, which was not published till 1675, contains in its dedication a sentence the force and dignity of which may justify the book. It was, wrote the author, "begun when everybody thought that the monarchy had ended and would have been buried in the same grave with your martyred father," and "that none of us that had served that blessed Prince had any other weapons left us but our pens to show the justice of our zeal by that of his title."

Since Arabella had been born on February 23, 1648, births and deaths swiftly succeeded one another with almost annual regularity. Mrs. Winston Churchill had twelve children, of whom seven died in infancy. The third child of these twelve and the eldest son to live is the hero of this account. It is curious that no previous biographer—among so many—should have discovered the entry of his birth. A mystery has been made of it, which Coxe and other writers have used devious methods to solve. It is still often wrongly given. We therefore offer the evidence from the parish register of St. Michael's, Musbury, in facsimile. The infant was baptized in the tiny private chapel of Ashe House seven days later.

[John the Sonne of Mr Winston Churchill,
Born the 26 Day of May, 1650.]

The first ten years of his life were lived in the harsh conditions
which have been suggested. We are here in the region of surmise.
Facts are vague and few; but it seems easy to believe that the child
grew up in a home where wants were often denied, and feelings and
opinions had nearly always to be repressed. Public affairs marched forward, and their course was viewed at Ashe from standpoints separated
by deep and living antagonisms. Blood and cruel injuries lay between
those who gathered around the table. Outraged faith, ruined fortunes,
and despairing loyalties were confronted by resolute, triumphant rebellion, and both were bound together by absolute dependence. It would
be strange indeed if the children were not conscious of the chasm between their elders; if they never saw resentment on the one side, or felt
patronage from the other; if they were never reminded that it was to
their grandmother's wisdom and faithful championship of the cause of
Parliament they owed the bread they ate. It would be strange if the ardent Cavalier then in his prime, poring over his books of history and
heraldry, watching with soured eyes the Lord Protector's victories over
the Dutch or the Spaniards and the grand position to which England
seemed to have been raised by this arch-wrongdoer, and dreaming of a
day when the King should enjoy his own again and the debts of Royalist and regicide be faithfully and sternly settled, should not have
spoken words to his little son revealing the bitterness of his heart. The
boy may well have learned to see things through his father's eyes, to
long with him for a casting down of present pride and power, and have
learned at the same time—at six, seven, and eight years of age—not to
flaunt these opinions before half at least of those with whom he lived.

The two prevailing impressions which such experiences might arouse
in the mind of a child would be, first, a hatred of poverty and dependence, and, secondly, the need of hiding thoughts and feelings from

those to whom their expression would be repugnant. To have one set of opinions for one part of the family, and to use a different language to the other, may have been inculcated from John's earliest years. To win freedom from material subservience by the sure agency of money must have been planted in his heart's desire. To these was added a third: the importance of having friends and connexions on both sides of a public quarrel. Modern opinion assigns increasing importance to the influences of early years on the formation of character. Certainly the whole life of John Churchill bore the imprint of his youth. That impenetrable reserve under graceful and courteous manners; those unceasing contacts and correspondences with opponents; that iron parsimony and personal frugality, never relaxed in the blaze of fortune and abundance; that hatred of waste and improvidence in all their forms —all these could find their roots in the bleak years at Ashe.

We may also suppose that Winston Churchill concerned himself a good deal with the early education of his children. For this he was not ill qualified. He had gathered, as his writings show, no inconsiderable store of historical knowledge. He presented in these years the curious figure of a cavalry captain, fresh from the wars, turned perforce recluse and bookworm. Time must have hung heavy on his hands. He had no estates to manage, no profession to pursue. He could not afford to travel; but in the teaching of his children he may well have found alike occupation and solace. Or, again, he may have loafed and brooded, leaving his children to play in the lanes and gardens of that tranquil countryside. The only information we have on John's education is provided by the unknown author of *The Lives of the Two Illustrious Generals* (1713):

He was born in the Time of the grand Rebellion, when his Father for Siding with the Royal Party against the Usurpers, who then prevailed, was under many Pressures, which were common to such as adher'd to the King. Yet, notwithstanding the Devastations and Plunderings, and other nefarious Practices and Acts of Cruelty which were daily committed by the licentious Soldiery, no Care was omitted on the Part of his tender Parents for a Liberal and Gentile Education. For he was no sooner out of the hands of the Women but he was given into those of a sequestered Clergyman, who made it his first concern to instil sound Principles of Religion into him, that the Seeds of humane Literature might take the deeper Root, and he from a just

Knowledge of the Omnipotence of the Creator, might have a true
Sense of the Dependence of the Creature.

It is said that famous men are usually the product of unhappy childhood. The stern compression of circumstances, the twinges of adversity,
the spur of slights and taunts in early years, are needed to evoke that
ruthless fixity of purpose and tenacious mother-wit without which great
actions are seldom accomplished. Certainly little in the environment of
the young John Churchill should have deprived him of this stimulus;
and by various long-descending channels there centred in him martial
and dangerous fires.

Besides attending to his son's education Winston in his studious leisure bethought himself often of his pedigree and his arms. His researches into genealogy have produced as good an account of the origin
of the Churchills as is likely to be required.

Students of heredity have dilated upon this family tree. Galton cites
it as one of the chief examples on which his thesis stands. Winston
himself has been accounted one of the most notable and potent of
sires. Had he lived the full span, he would have witnessed within the
space of twelve months his son gaining the battle of Ramillies and his
daughter's son that of Almanza; and would have found himself acknowledged as the progenitor of the two greatest captains of the age at
the head of the opposing armies of Britain and of France and Spain.
Moreover, his third surviving son, Charles, became a soldier of well-
tried distinction, and his naval son virtually managed the Admiralty
during the years of war. The military strain flowed strong and clear
from the captain of the Civil Wars, student of heraldry and history,
and champion of the Divine Right. It was his blood, not his pen, that
carried his message.

Although in this opening chapter we have set the reader in these bygone times, eleven years of our hero's life have already been accomplished. Ashe House, still unroofed, passes from the scene.

These scenes certainly played a curiously persistent part in John
Churchill's life. It was on the very soil of his childhood, in sight almost
of his birthplace, that he was in 1685 to lead the Household Cavalry,
feeling their way towards Monmouth's army; and three years later on
the hill across the river he was to meet the Prince of Orange after deserting James II. So much for Ashe!

But now the times are changed. Oliver Cromwell is dead. General
Monk has declared for a free Parliament. His troops have marched
from Coldstream to Hounslow. The exiled Charles has issued the Declaration of Breda. The English people, by a gesture spontaneous and
almost unanimous, have thrown off the double yoke of military and
Puritan rule. Amid bonfires and the rejoicings of tumultuous crowds
they welcome back their erstwhile hunted sovereign, and by one of
those intense reactions, sometimes as violent in whole nations as in individuals, change in a spasm from oppressive virtue to unbridled indulgence. On April 23, 1661, Charles II was crowned at Westminster, and
the restoration of the English monarchy was complete.

These memorable events produced swift repercussions at Ashe
House. Winston Churchill passed at a stroke from the frown of an all-
powerful Government to the favour of a King he had faithfully served.
The frozen years were over, and the Cavaliers, emerging from their re-
treats, walked abroad in the sun, seeking their lost estates. We need not
grudge him these good days. He had acted with unswerving conviction
and fidelity. He had drunk to the dregs the cup of defeat and subjugation. Its traces can be seen in his anxious eyes. Now was the time of
reward. Instantly he sprang into many forms of activity. In 1661 he
entered Parliament for Weymouth. In 1664 he became one of the original members of the Royal Society. Although his fortunes were much
depleted, he regained his independence and a hearth of his own. More
important than this, he stood in a modest way high in the favour of
the new régime. He was received with consideration and even intimacy
at Court. The terms under which Charles had returned to his kingdom
were not such as to allow him to bestow wealth upon his humbler adherents. His sovereignty rested on a compromise between rebels and
Royalists, between Anglicans and Presbyterians, between those who
had seized estates and those who had lost them, between the passions
of conflicting creeds and the pride of lately hostile regiments. He had
no means of meeting even the just claims which faithful subjects might
urge, still less could he satisfy the ravenous demands of long-nursed
grievances or blatant imposture.

It is remarkable that amid the crowds of hungry and often deserving
suitors who thronged the antechambers of Whitehall so much attention
should have been paid to the merits and services of Winston Churchill.
Far more was done for him than for most. There was one cheap, sure

way to please him. It was apparently well known. Accordingly an augmentation of arms and a crest unusual in a family of such standing was offered to his heraldic propensities. Nevertheless, this evidence of royal favour and affection was not in itself sufficiently substantial, in Winston's opinion at least, to repair the injuries he had suffered in pocket and skin. He remained cherished but disconsolate, blazoning on his new coat of arms an uprooted oak above the motto *Fiel pero desdichado* ("Faithful but unfortunate"). More practical reliefs, as will be shown in the next chapter, were however in store.

CHAPTER TWO

The Jovial Times

ᵴ꜠ 1661-69 ꜟᵴ

OUR readers must now brace themselves for what will inevitably be a painful interlude. We must follow the fortunes or misfortunes of a maiden of seventeen and her younger brother as they successively entered a dissolute Court. The King was the fountain not only of honour, but of almost every form of worldly success and pleasure. Access to his presence, intimacy with his family or favourites, were the sole pathway even of modest and lawful ambition. An enormous proportion of the amenities and glories of the realm was engrossed in the narrow family circle of royal personages, friends, dependants, and important Ministers or agents of the Crown. Nearly all chances of distinction and solid professional advancement went by favour. An officer well established at Court was a different kind of officer from one who had nothing but the merits of his sword. The success of jurists and divines was similarly determined. The royal light shone where it listed, and those who caught its rays were above competition and almost beyond envy, except—an important exception—from rivals in their own select sphere.

If those were the conditions which ruled for men, how much more compulsive was the environment of the frailer sex. To sun oneself in the royal favour, to be admitted to the charmed circle, to have access to a royal lady, to be about the person of a queen or princess, was to have all this exclusive, elegant, ambitious, jostling world on one's doorstep and at one's footstool. Aged statesmen and prelates; eager, ardent, attractive youths; the old general, the young lieutenant—all produced whatever treasure they had to bestow to win the favour of the sovereign's mistress, or of his relations' mistresses, and of his important friends or servants. That nothing should be lacking to frame the picture of privilege and indulgence, it must be remembered that all this was dignified by the affairs of a growing state, by the presence of upright and venerable men and formidable matrons, providing the counterpoise of seriousness and respectability. Scientists, philosophers, theologians, scholars; the mayors of cities, rugged sea-captains, veteran colonels, substantial merchants—all pressed forward on the fringes of the parade in the hope of being gratified by some fleeting glint of the royal radiance.

Such ideas seem remote to the English-speaking nations in these times. We must make allowances for the backward conditions which prevailed in England and France, to say nothing of the barbarous countries, when Charles II and Louis XIV sat upon their thrones. There was undoubtedly an easy commerce of the sexes, marked at times by actual immorality. Men and women who had obtained power were often venal, and insolent besides, to those whom they dubbed their inferiors. Even judges were occasionally, and members of the legislature frequently, corrupt. Generals and admirals were usually jealous of each other, and sometimes stooped to intrigue to gain promotion. Even brilliant writers and pamphleteers, the journalists of those primitive times, wrote scurrilous gossip to please their patrons and employers. We in this happy and enlightened age must exercise our imagination to span the gulf which separates us from those lamentable, departed days. Securely established upon the rock of purity and virtue, ceaselessly cleansed by the strong tides of universal suffrage, we can afford to show tolerance and even indulgence towards the weaknesses and vices of those vanished generations without in any way compromising our own integrity.

It is strange indeed that such a system should have produced for many generations a succession of greater captains and abler statesmen than all our widely extended education, competitive examinations, and democratic system have put forth. Apart from the Church and the learned professions, the area of selection was restricted entirely to the circles of rank, wealth, and landed property. But these comprised several thousand families within which and among whom an extremely searching rivalry and appraisement prevailed. In this focus of the nation men were known and judged by their equals with intimate knowl-

WINGATE COLLEGE
WINGATE, N. C.

edge and a high degree of comprehension. There may be more truth than paradox in Lord Fisher's brutal maxim, "Favouritism is the secret of efficiency." There was, of course, great need to seek out ability. Appointments and promotions went largely by favour: but favour went largely by merit.

The English Court under Charles II was no Oriental scene of complete subservience, where women were secluded and where men approached the supreme figures with bated breath. It had not the super-centralization of the French Court under Louis XIV. The nobility and wealthy gentlefolk could live on their estates, and though excluded from the fame of national employment, had effective rights which they used frequently against the Crown. There were always independent powers in England. This counterpoise enhanced the strength of the central institution. There were degrees, values, and a hierarchy of considerable intrinsic virtue. A great society, sharply criticized, but accepted as supreme, indulging every caprice and vanity, and drawing to itself the chief forms of national excellence, presided at the summit of the realm.

It is important to remember also the differences of feeling and outlook which separate the men and women of these times from ourselves. They gave a very high—indeed, a dominating—place in their minds to religion. It played as large a part in the life of the seventeenth century as sport does now. One of their chief concerns was about the next world and how to be saved. Although ignorant compared with our standards, they were all deeply versed in the Bible and the Prayer Book. If they read few books, they studied them and digested them thoroughly. They had settled opinions on large questions of faith and doctrine, and were often ready to die or suffer on account of them.

Rank and breeding were second only to religion in their esteem. Every one in Court or county society was known, and all about them. Their forbears for many generations were carefully scrutinized. The coat of arms which denoted the family's achievements for hundreds of years was narrowly and jealously compared. It was not easy to get into the great world in those days, if one did not belong to it. A very clear line was drawn between 'gentles' and 'simples,' and the Church and the Law were almost the only ladders by which new talent could reach the highest positions. Indeed, religion and family pride together absorbed much of the sentiment now given to nationalism. The unity of Christendom had been ruptured at the Reformation, but strong cosmopolitan sympathies prevailed among the educated classes in all the Western countries.

Although the administration of England had not attained to anything like the refined and ordered efficiency of France, there was already a strong collective view about fundamental dangers. There was already a recognizable if rudimentary Foreign Office opinion. And there were in every capital grave, independent men who gave lifelong thought to doctrine and policy. Their business was transacted by long personal letters, laboriously composed, in which every word was weighed, and conversations, few and far between, the purport of which was memorable. Government was then the business of sovereigns and of a small but serious ruling class, and, for all their crimes, errors, and shortcomings, they gave keen and sustained attention to their task.

In these days society was callous about prisoners and punishments, and frightful forfeits were senselessly exacted. But these were the ages of Pain. Pain, when it came, was accepted as a familiar foe. No anæsthetic robbed the hospital of all the horrors of the torture-chamber. All had to be endured, and hence—strangely enough—all might be inflicted. Yet in some ways our forerunners attached more importance to human life than we do. Although they fought duels about women and other matters of honour, instead of seeking damages from the courts, and although death sentences were more numerous in those days, they would have recoiled in lively horror from the constant wholesale butcheries of scores of thousands of persons every year by motor-cars, at which the modern world gapes unconcernedly. Their faculties for wonder and indignation had not been blunted and worn away by the catalogues of atrocities and disasters which the advantages of the electric telegraph and the newspaper press place at our disposal every morning and evening. Above all, they were not in a hurry. They made fewer speeches, and lived more meditatively and more at leisure, with companionship rather than motion for their solace. They had far fewer facilities than we have for the frittering away of thought, time, and life. Altogether they were primitive folk, and we must make allowances for their limitations. The one trait which they shared in common with the twentieth century was the love of money, and respect and envy for its fortunate possessors. But, then, money in those days was still mainly derived from land, and the possession of land usually denoted ancient lineage.

The Convention Parliament of the Restoration was dissolved in 1660, and the so-called Cavalier, or Pensionary, Parliament met in May 1661. This was "a parliament full of lewd young men, chosen by a furious people in spite to the Puritans, whose severity had distasted them." They were "of loyal families, but young men for the most part, which being told the King, he replied that there was no great fault, for he could keep them till they got beards." So in fact he did; for this Parliament continued to sit for eighteen years. In it Winston Churchill represented the constituency of Weymouth. During its first two sessions he was an active Member; he served on various committees, and as late as May 10, 1662, he was sent by the Commons to request the participation of the Lords in a joint committee to discuss questions arising out of an Army Bill.

Meanwhile the Restoration settlement in Ireland was proceeding very slowly. Thirty-six commissioners had been appointed and had set up an office in Dublin in May 1661. But after nearly a year's work only one claim had been settled. The King had himself blamed the commissioners, and seven new commissioners were now chosen to go over to Ireland and reopen the Court of Claims.

Among these latter Winston Churchill was named and probably sailed to Ireland to carry out his new duties in July.

Throughout 1663 Winston Churchill and his fellow-commissioners remained in Ireland. Their task was a difficult one. On March 25 they wrote to Whitehall affirming that

> Since our coming into this Kingdom, we have found so many unexpected discouragements, from those whose security and settlement was and is a powerful part of our care, that we confess we were much dejected. . . . But we have now received new life from his sacred Majesty's most gracious letters to us, by which we understand that neither our sufferings, nor our innocence, were hid from, or unconsidered by his Majesty.

Nevertheless, in December Churchill begged Arlington for leave to return home for just two months, so desirous was he of a rest from his labours. A month later his wish was gratified, for the King summoned him back to England on January 10, 1664, and twelve days later rewarded his services with a knighthood. If Winston brought his eldest son with him from Dublin on this occasion, as there is every reason to suppose, it must have been at this date that John Churchill became one of the 153 scholars of St Paul's School. His father bought a house somewhere in the City, where the fourteen-year-old boy lived while he attended school; but on September 13, 1664, Winston was appointed Junior Clerk Comptroller to the Board of Green Cloth, a minor post in the royal household, and moved into Whitehall.

About 1665 the Duchess of York was graciously pleased to offer Winston's eldest daughter, Arabella, a coveted appointment as maid of honour. Historians have inquired in wonder how a strict and faithful husband, a devoted father, and a God-fearing Anglican Cavalier could have allowed his well-loved daughter to become involved in a society in which so many pitfalls abounded. In fact he was delighted, and so was his wife, and every one whom they knew and respected hastened to congratulate the family upon an auspicious and most hopeful preferment. Who should say what honours might not flow from such propinquity to the King's brother and heir to the throne? The sanction of Divine Right descended not only on all around the sovereign, but upon all within the sacred circle of the blood royal. Power, fame, wealth, social distinction, awaited those who gained the royal favour. The association was honourable and innocent, and should any mishap occur, Church and State stood attentive to conceal or vindicate the damage. Thus it was thought a splendid advantage for a young girl to be established at Court and take her fortune there as it came.

Arabella after some delays prospered in the Duke of York's household. Anthony Hamilton, who is famous for the authorship of Grammont's memoirs, has penned some mischievous pages from which historians diligently fail to avert their eyes. There is a tale of a riding-party to a greyhound-coursing near York, and of Arabella's horse running away in a headlong gallop; of a fall and a prostrate figure on the sward; of the Royal Duke to the rescue, and of a love born of this incident. Hamilton declares that, while Arabella's face presented no more than the ordinary feminine charms, her figure was exceedingly beautiful, and that James was inflamed by the spectacle of beauty in distress and also in disarray. It is, however, certain that some time before 1668 Arabella became the mistress of the Duke of York, and that in the next seven or eight years she bore him four children, of whom the second was James Fitz-James, afterwards Duke of Berwick, Marshal of France and victor of Almanza. There is no disputing these facts, and historians may rest upon them with confidence.

Among the many stains with which John Churchill's record has been darkened stands the charge that he lightly and even cheerfully acquiesced in his sister's dishonour—or honour, as it was regarded in the moral obliquity of the age. Why did he not thus early display the qualities of a future conqueror and leader of men? Why did he not arrive hotfoot at Whitehall, challenge or even chastise the high-placed seducer, and rescue the faltering damsel from her sad plight? We must admit that all researches for any active protest upon his part have been fruitless. Nearly sixty years afterwards the old Duchess, Sarah, made her comments upon this default in terms certainly not beyond the comprehension of our own day.

By January 1666 Sir Winston was back again in Dublin, but he had left his wife and family behind him in England. By this date his eldest son, John, had left school and had been made page to James, Duke of York. The author of *The Lives of the Two Illustrious Generals* relates that James had been struck by the beauty of the boy, whom he had often seen about the Court. It may be, however, that the influence of Sir Winston's patron, the Earl of Arlington, had effected this choice. The father was well content with this: he thought it the best opening he could find for any of his sons. Shortly afterwards Arlington obtained a similar, if not so exalted, position for John's brother George, to accompany the famous Earl of Sandwich, late commander-in-chief of the Navy, to the Court of Madrid. In writing from dismal Ireland to thank the Secretary of State for this attention Sir Winston, now a civil servant, observed, "though (as times go now) it is no great preferment to be a Page, yet I am not ignorant of the benefit of disposing him (in such a Juncture of time as this) into that country where all the Boys seem Men, and all the men seem wise." And he concluded his letter by hoping that "my Sons may with equal gratitude subscribe themselves as I do," his faithful servant.

Meanwhile the annals of John are even more scanty than those of his father. Marlborough is, indeed, the last of the great commanders about whose early life practically nothing is recorded. That he was born in 1650, that he lived in his grandmother's house for nine years, that he went with his father to Dublin, that he attended St Paul's School, and that he went to Court as page to the Duke of York at about the age of sixteen and later entered the army, sums the total of our information. We know as much of the early years of Alexander the Great, Hannibal, and Julius Cæsar as we do of this figure separated from us by scarcely a couple of centuries.

THE JOYFUL YEARS

CHAPTER THREE

Barbara

ᘓ 1667-71 ᘔ

JOHN served the Duke of York as page, and, like his sister, dwelt happily in the royal household. His duties were neither onerous nor unpleasant. He had no money; but he lived in comfort and elegance. He knew all the great people of the English world, and many of its prettiest women. No one was concerned to be disagreeable to this attractive, discreet, engaging youth, who moved gaily about the corridors and anterooms of Whitehall with a deft, decided step, and never slipped or slid on those polished floors where a clumsy fall may so easily be final. He must have met about this time one of the King's pages, a young man five years his senior—Sidney Godolphin. There is a gulf between youths of sixteen and twenty-one. It soon narrowed. The two became friends; and their unbroken association runs through this story.

The Duke of York was a resolute and experienced commander. After religion the art of war claimed the foremost place in his thoughts. As Lord High Admiral he knew the service of the sea. His interest in the land forces was no less keen. It was his custom to spend a part of many days in reviewing and drilling the troops. He would frequently muster two battalions of the Guards in Hyde Park, and have them put through their elaborate exercises in his presence. His page accompanied him on these occasions.

At these parades the Duke of York noticed the interest of his page. He saw the boy following with gleaming eyes the warlike ceremonial. One day after a review he asked him what profession he preferred.

Whereupon John fell upon his knees and demanded "a pair of colours in one of these fine regiments." The request was not denied.

Besides his sister Arabella John had a tie of kinship and acquaintance with another favourite of high importance. On the eve of his restoration Charles II met at The Hague Barbara Villiers, then newly married to Roger Palmer, afterwards Earl of Castlemaine. She became his mistress; she preceded him to England; she adorned the triumphs and enhanced for him the joys of the Restoration. She was a woman of exceeding beauty and charm, vital and passionate in an extraordinary degree. In the six years that had passed she had borne the King several children. At twenty-four, in the heyday of her success, this characteristic flower of the formidable, errant Villiers stock was the reigning beauty of the palace. She held Charles in an intense fascination. Her rages, her extravagances, her infidelities seemed only to bind him more closely in her mysterious web. She was John Churchill's second cousin once removed. His mother's sister, a Mrs Godfrey, was her closest confidante. The young page, it is said, was often in his aunt's apartments eating sweets, and there Barbara soon met and made friends with this good-looking boy. Very likely she had known him from his childhood. Naturally she was nice to him, and extended her powerful protection to her young and sprightly relation. Naturally, too, she aroused his schoolboy's admiration. There is not, as we shall hope to convince the reader, the slightest ground for suggesting that the beginning of their affection was not perfectly innocent and such as would normally subsist between a well-established woman of the world and her cousin, a boy of sixteen, newly arrived at the Court where she was dominant.

John was certainly a success at Court, and his favour was not diminished by his smart uniform. Still, adolescence is a trying period both for the victim and his companions. In those days there was a feeling that young men about the Court should take their turn of service with the fleet or Army as gentlemen-volunteers. Still more was this opinion effective upon a young officer. Leave to serve abroad would readily be granted by his regiment, and all his friends and well-wishers would give their cordial approval. John found doctrine and prospect alike congenial.

Some time in 1668 he quitted the Court and sailed for Tangier. The gossip-mongers suggest that the Duchess of York herself had begun to show him undue attention: or, again, that he was getting rather old to be on such privileged terms with Lady Castlemaine. But there is no excuse for looking beyond the reasons which have been set forth. Such evidence as exists shows that his departure and prolonged absence were entirely in accordance with his own inclination. He went to Tangier, or at any rate he stayed there and in the Mediterranean for nearly three years, because he liked the life of adventure, and because the excitement of the petty warfare was refreshing after the endless glittering ceremonial of the Court. Few youths of spirit are content at eighteen with comforts or even caresses. They seek physical fitness, movement, and the comradeship of their equals under hard conditions. They seek distinction, not favour, and exult in manly independence.

He seems to have lived from eighteen to twenty the rough, care-free life of a subaltern officer engaged in an endless frontier guerrilla. That the conditions were by no means intolerable is shown by the following letter, written from Madrid in March 1670 to the Earl of Arlington by the Earl of Castlemaine, on his way back from Tangier.

> * At my arrival, I was never so surprized than to find so many officers so very well clad and fashioned that though I have been in most of the best garrisons of Europe I do not remember I ever yet saw the like, and which added to my admiration was that though necessaries are a great deal dearer, and all superfluities there four times the value of what they are in England, yet the Generality both of our Commanders and Soldiers lay up something, which argues much industry. . . .
>
> For the Town itself (if the Mole be made) all the world sees it will, as it were, command the Mediterranean, by stopping its mouth; how quick a receipt it is for the Merchants with [in] any War with Spain, what a Bridle it will be of the Pirates of Barbary, as a Constant place of our own, for our men of War, with opportunities also of revictualling and fitting as if we were at home; which bears now no small proportion with the expense of an expedition; neither is it a little honour to the Crown to have a Nursery of its own for soldiers, without being altogether beholding to our Neighbours for their Education and breeding.

The English fleet in the Mediterranean was in 1670 engaged in an intermittent blockade of Algiers. Sir Thomas Allin was setting out with a squadron of fourteen ships to renew his blockade. An Admiralty regiment, or, as we should say, a 'Naval Brigade' or Division, was being recruited and embarked as marines for the operation. It seems certain that John obtained permission to exchange his service of the land for that of the sea, and was attached to the Algiers expedition of 1670. We know that he required an outfit for the campaign and that his father bought it for him.

John's experiences with the fleet are unrecorded. All we know is that in August 1670 Admiral Allin defeated a number of Algerian corsairs, and was afterwards relieved of his command. Surveying all the facts we have been able to marshal, we may accept the following conclusions: that Churchill, still penniless and heart-whole, quitted the Court in 1668, that he served at Tangier till 1670, that early in that year he sailed with the fleet against the pirates, and served for some months in the Mediterranean. Eagerly seeking adventure by land or sea, he pulled all the strings he could to convey him to the scenes of action, and his zeal was noticed and well regarded in the highest circles.

So far all is well, and the conduct of our hero will command general approbation. We now approach a phase upon which the judgment of individuals and periods will vary. In all his journey Marlborough found two, and only two, love-romances. Two women, both extraordinary beings, both imperious, tempestuous personalities, both well-known historical figures, are woven successively into his life. Here and now the first appears. We have already made her acquaintance.

At the beginning of 1671 John Churchill, grown a man, bronzed by African sunshine, close-knit by active service and tempered by discipline and danger, arrived home from the Mediterranean. He seems to have been welcomed with widespread pleasure by the Court, and by none more than by Barbara, now become Duchess of Cleveland. She was twenty-nine and he twenty. They were already affectionate friends. The distant degree of cousinly kinship which had hitherto united them had sanctioned intimacy, and did not now prohibit passion. Affections, affinities, and attractions were combined. Desire walked with opportunity, and neither was denied. John almost immediately became her lover, and for more than three years this wanton and joyous couple shared pleasures and hazards. The cynical, promiscuous, sagacious-indulgent sovereign was outwitted or outfaced. Churchill was almost certainly the father of Barbara's last child, a daughter, born on July 16, 1672, and the ties between them were not severed until the dawn of his love for Sarah Jennings in 1675.

It is an exaggeration to speak of Churchill as "rivalling the King in his nearest affection." After ten years Charles II was already tiring of the tantrums and divagations of the Duchess of Cleveland, and other attractions made their power felt. From 1671 onward the bonds which were to bind the King and the Duchess were their children, most of whom were undoubtedly his own. None the less, the intimacy of John and Barbara continued to cause Charles repeated annoyance, and their illicit loves, their adventures and escapades, were among the most eminent scandals of the English Court at this period.

We have some indication of John's whereabouts during this year.

News-letter from London

February 6, 1671

Yesterday was a duel between Mr Fenwick and Mr Churchill esquires who had for their seconds Mr Harpe and Mr Newport, son to my Lord Newport; it ended with some wounds for Mr Churchill, but no danger of life.

Two of the adventures of the lovers are well known. The first—described by Burnet—is that, being surprised by Charles in the Duchess's bedroom, John saved her honour—or what remained of it—by jumping from the window, a considerable height, into the courtyard below. For this feat, delighted at his daring and address, she presented him with £5000.

The second anecdote is attributed to the French Ambassador, Barillon. The Duke of Buckingham, he says, gave a hundred guineas to one of his waiting-women to be well informed of the intrigue. He knew that Churchill would be one evening at a certain hour in Barbara's apartments. He brought the King to the spot. The lover was hidden in the Duchess's cupboard (she was not Duchess till 1670). After having prowled about the chamber the King, much upset, asked for sweets and liqueurs. His mistress declared that the key of the cupboard was lost. The King replied that he would break down the door. On this she opened the door, and fell on her knees on one side while Churchill, discovered, knelt on the other. The King said to Churchill, "Go; you are a rascal, but I forgive you because you do it to get your bread."

BARBARA

It is a good story, and the double-barrelled insult is very characteristic of Charles. But is it true? Barillon, who did not himself arrive in England till September 1677, probably got it from his predecessor, Courtin. He fixes the date as 1667. Burnet's story belongs to 1670. Here is a fine exposure of these gossips. There can be little doubt, as we have shown, that nothing of this kind can have occurred before 1671. It is therefore one of those good stories invented long afterwards and fastened, as so many are, on well-known figures.

We are on much firmer ground when we come to money matters. The famous Lord Halifax in the intervals of statecraft conducted a rudimentary form of life insurance. The rates were attractive, for the lives of young gallants and soldiers—the prey of wars, duels, adventures, and disease—were precarious. At twenty-four John purchased from Lord Halifax for £4500 an annuity of £500 a year for life. It was a profitable investment. He enjoyed its fruits for nearly fifty years. It was the foundation of his immense fortune. Where did the money come from? No one can suggest any other source than Barbara. Was this, then, the £5000 that she had given him when he leaped from the window, and if so what are we to think of the transaction? Some of Marlborough's defenders have disputed the facts. They point to the scanty evidence— contemporary gossip and a passing reference in one of Lord Chesterfield's letters. The Blenheim papers contain the actual receipt.

The code of the seventeenth century did not regard a man's taking money from a rich mistress as necessarily an offence against honour. It was no more a bar to social success and worldly regard than are marriages for money in these modern times. But every one has been struck by the judicious foresight of the investment. Moralists have been shocked by the fact that John did not squander Barbara's gift in riotous living. Cards, wine, and other women would seem to be regarded by these logicians as more appropriate channels for the use of such funds. They treat the transaction as the aggravation of an infamy. It may well be true that no other man of twenty-four then alive in England would have turned this money into an income which secured him a modest but lifelong independence. The dread of poverty inculcated in his early days at Ashe may be the explanation. It may be that Barbara, knowing his haunting prepossession, resolved to free him from it, and that an annuity was the prescribed purpose of the gift. However this may be, there is the bond.

CHAPTER FOUR

The Europe of Charles II

ᚦᚦ 1667-72 ᚦᚦ

It is fitting to turn from the scraps and oddities which, pieced together, form our only record of Churchill's youth to survey the vast, stately European scene wherein he now began to move and was one day to shine.

The supreme fact upon the Continent in the latter half of the seventeenth century was the might of France. Her civil wars were over. All internal divisions had been effaced, and Louis XIV reigned over a united nation of eighteen or nineteen million souls possessed of the fairest region on the globe. Feudalism, with its local warriors and their armed retainers, had at length been blown away by gunpowder, and as wars were frequent, standing armies had arisen in all the states of Europe. The possession of organized regular troops, paid, disciplined, trained by the central Government, was the aim of all the rulers, and in the main the measure of their power. This process had in the course of a few generations obliterated or reduced to mere archaic survivals the Parliamentary and municipal institutions of France. In different ways similar effects had followed the same process in other Continental countries. Everywhere sovereignty had advanced with giant strides. The peoples of Europe passed out of a long confusion into an age of autocracies in full panoply against all foes from within or from without.

But for the storm-whipped seas which lapped the British islands, our fortunes would have followed the road upon which our neighbours had started. England had not, however, the same compulsive need for a standing army as the land Powers. She stood aloof, moving slowly and lagging behind the martial throng. In the happy nick of time her Parliament grew strong enough to curb the royal power and to control the armed forces, and she thus became the cradle, as she is still the citadel, of free institutions throughout the world.

There she lay, small, weak, divided, and almost unarmed. The essence of her domestic struggle forbade a standing army. Scotland and Ireland lay, heavy embarrassments and burdens, on her shoulders or at her flank. Although there was much diffused well-being throughout the country, very little money could be gathered by the State. Here again the conditions of the internal struggle kept the executive weak. The whole population of England—their strength thus latent and depressed, their energies dispersed, their aim unfocused—attained little more than five millions.

Yet upon the other side of the Channel, only twenty-one miles across the dancing waves, rose the magnificent structure of the French monarchy and society. One hundred and forty thousand soldiers in permanent pay, under lifelong professional officers, constituted the peacetime force of France. Brilliant, now famous, captains of war or fortification, Turenne, Condé, Vauban; master organizers like Louvois; trainers like Martinet (his name a household word)—forged or wielded this splendid instrument of power. Adroit, sagacious, experienced Foreign Ministers and diplomatists urged the march of French aggrandisement. Financiers and trade Ministers as wise and instructed as Colbert reached out for colonies bound by exclusive commercial dealings, or consolidated the expanding finances of the most modern, the most civilized, and the strongest society.

Nor were the glories of France confined to the material sphere. The arts flourished in a long summer. In the latter half of the century French was becoming not only the universal language of diplomacy outside the Holy Roman Empire, but also that of polite society and even of literature. The French drama was performed and French poetry read, the names of Molière, Racine, Boileau were honoured, throughout the cultured cities of the world. French styles of architecture, of painting, even of music, were imitated in every Court in Germany. Even the Dutch, who were contributing notably to the progress of civilization in the financial, industrial, and domestic arts, accused themselves under William of Orange of being "debauched by French habits and customs." French Court theologians, their wits sharpened first by the Jansenist and secondly by the Gallican controversy, rivalled those of Rome. French Catholicism, adorned by figures like Fénelon or Bossuet, was the most stately, imposing, and persuasive form of the Old Faith which had yet confronted the Reformation. The conquest, planned and largely effected, was not only military and economic, but religious, moral, and intellectual. It was the most magnificent claim to world dominion ever made since the age of the Antonines. And at the summit there reigned in unchallenged splendour for more than half a century a masterful, competent, insatiable, hardworking egoist, born to a throne.

Since the days of Queen Elizabeth and the Spanish Armada Spain had been the bugbear of Protestant England. Many devout families, suffering all things, still adhered to the Catholic faith. But deep in the hearts of the English people from peer to peasant memories of Smithfield burned with a fierce glow which any breeze could rouse into flame. And now Spain was in decrepitude, insolvent, incoherent, tracing her genealogies and telling her beads. Her redoubtable infantry, first conquered nearly thirty years ago by Condé at Rocroi, had vanished. In their place, alike in the Spanish Netherlands, which we now know as Belgium and Luxembourg, and in the New World, stood decaying garrisons, the mockery of soldiers. The Spanish harbours were filled with rotting ships; the Spanish treasury was bare. The once proud empire of Charles V, irreparably exhausted by over a century of almost continuous war, had fallen a victim to religious mania. Layer upon layer of superstition and ceremonial encrusted the symbols of departed power. Cruelties ever more fantastic enforced a dwindling and crumbling authority. There remained an immense pride, an ancient and secure aristocracy, the title-deeds of half the outer world, a despotic Church, and a throne occupied by a sickly, sterile child who might die any day, leaving no trace behind.

Gradually the fear of Spain had faded from the English mind. In Oliver Cromwell, a man of conservative temperament, born under Queen Elizabeth, the old prejudice obstinately survived. But when, in 1654, he proposed to join France in war against Spain, his council of Roundhead generals surprised him by their resistance. Left to themselves, they would probably have taken the opposite side. The authority of the Lord Protector prevailed, and his Ironside redcoats stormed the Spanish positions upon the sand-dunes by Dunkirk. Wide circles of instructed English opinion regarded these antagonisms as old-fashioned and obsolete. To them the new menace to English faith, freedom, and trade was France. This Battle of the Dunes marked the end of the hundred years' struggle with Spain. Henceforth the dangers and difficulties of England would not arise from Spanish strength, but from Spanish weakness. Henceforth the mounting power of France would be the main preoccupation of Englishmen.

Nearest akin in race, religion, and temperament to the English, the Dutch were their sharpest rivals upon the seas, in trade and colonization. It is said that at this time one-half of the population of Holland gained their livelihood from commerce, industry, and shipping. A tough, substantial race, welded by their struggles against Spanish tyranny, dwelling, robust and acquisitive, under embattled oligarchies, the Dutch clashed with the English at many points. There was the Dutch navy, with its memories of Tromp and his broom "to sweep the English from the seas." There were the dangers of Dutch competition in the colonies and in trade as far as the coasts of India, in the East, and as far as New Amsterdam, since 1664 renamed New York, across the Atlantic. Thus the war which Cromwell had waged against Holland had broken out again in the earlier years of Charles II. Its course was ignominious to England. The sailors of the Royal Navy were in those days paid only at the end of a three or four years' commission. The crews who came home in 1666 received their pay warrants, called tickets, for three years' hard service. Such was the poverty of the Crown that when these were presented at the Naval Pay Office no payment could be made. Conceiving themselves intolerably defrauded, some of the sailors committed an unpardonable crime. They made their way to Holland and piloted the Dutch fleet through the intricate approaches of the Thames estuary. Several of the laid-up English ships in the Medway and the Thames were burned, and the rumble of the Dutch guns was plainly heard in London. But the lack of money forbade effectual reprisals. Charles and his subjects swallowed the insult, and peace was made in 1667. A great bitterness continued between the countries, and the claim of England to the unquestioned sovereignty of the Narrow Seas, though recognized by the peace treaty, accorded ill with the actual incidents of the naval war. "With the Treaty of Breda," says the historian of the United Netherlands, "began the most glorious period of the Republic."

The relations between England and Holland followed a chequered course, and many years were to pass before their grievous quarrels about trade and naval supremacy were finally thrust into the background before the ever-growing French power. It is easy nowadays to say that Charles "should have marched with the Dutch and fought the French" or "marched with the Protestants and fought the Papists." But the Dutch attitude was oblique and baffling, and many great Catholic states were opposed to France. Holland was then ruled by John de Witt and his brother Cornelius. The De Witts were friendly to France. John de Witt believed that by astute conciliation he could come to terms with Louis XIV. Louis had always a potent bribe for the Dutch in the carrying trade of France, on which they thrived. Had not France been the friend, and even champion, of the Republic during its birth-throes? And what was Belgium, that fief of Spain, but a convenient, useful buffer-state whose partition, if inevitable, offered large, immediate gains to both its neighbours? There were, indeed, two Hollands—the pacific, and at times the Francophile, Holland of John de Witt and Amsterdam, and the Holland which adhered to the memory and lineage of William the Silent, and saw in his frail, spirited, already remarkable descendant the prince who would sustain its cause. No Government, French or English, could tell which of these Hollands would be supreme in any given situation.

These uncertainties arose in part from the dubious, balancing attitude of what we now call Prussia. The Great Elector of Brandenburg ruled the main northern mass of Protestant Germany. But upon his western bounds along the whole course of the Rhine, and stretching southward to Bavaria and the Danube, lay a belt of powerful minor states, partly Protestant, partly Catholic in sympathy, whose accession to the one side or the other might be decisive in the balance of power. Beyond Prussia, again, lay Poland, a large, unkempt, slatternly kingdom, ranging from the Baltic to the Ukraine, still partly in feudalism, with an elective monarchy, the trophy of foreign intrigue, and a constitution which might have been designed for a cauldron of domestic broil. "Ceaselessly gnawed by aristocratic lawlessness," its throne a prey to all the princes and adventurers of Europe, its frontiers ravaged, its magnates bribed, Poland was the sport of Europe. There was to be an interlude of glorious independence under John Sobieski; but for the rest Louis XIV, the Emperor, and the Great Elector tirelessly spun their rival webs about the threatened state, and with each candidature for its throne put their competing influences to the test. No wonder the Great Elector, until a final phase which we shall presently reach, had to follow an equivocal policy.

On the eastern flank of Poland lay the huge, sprawling Muscovy Empire, until recent times called Russia, still almost barbarous and perpetually torn by the revolt of the Cossacks against the Tsar. Moscow was ravaged by the Cossack Hetman Stenka, who also brought "unspeakable horrors" upon an "oppressed peasantry." The possibilities of contact with Western civilization were blocked by Sweden and Poland, which together also impeded Russia from any outlet on to the Baltic. In the south the Turks shut it out from the Black Sea. The Tsar Alexis (1645–76), a peace-loving and conscientious man, entrusted a reforming patriarch, the monk Nikon, with most of the affairs of State during the early part of his reign. Later, in 1671, Stenka was captured and quartered alive, and when Alexis died, although no one yet foresaw the emergence of these eastern barbarians as a Western Power, the way lay open for the work of Peter the Great.

In the north of Europe Sweden, the ancient rival of Denmark, was the strongest Power, and aimed at making the Baltic a Swedish lake. At this time the Swedish realm included Finland, Ingria, Esthonia, Livonia, and West Pomerania; and the house of Vasa had traditional designs on Denmark and parts of Poland. The hardy, valiant race of Swedes had impressed upon all Europe the startling effects of a well-trained, warlike professional army. For a spell in the Thirty Years War Gustavus Adolphus had overthrown the troops of every Central European state. But Gustavus and his victories now lay in the past. The chief desire of Prussia was to win Pomerania from the Swedish Crown. Soon, in the battle of Fehrbellin (1675), the Great Elector with his Prussian troops was to overthrow the famous army of Sweden. The antagonism between the two countries was keen and open. Only the unfailing strength of France saved Pomerania for a time from Prussian absorption. Although the bias of Sweden was towards Protestantism, no Dutch or German statesman in the last quarter of the seventeenth century could ever exclude the possibility that her doughty soldiery would be bought by France, or rallied to her cause. All these baffling potential reactions were well comprehended at Whitehall in the closet of King Charles II.

Continuing our progress, we reach the domains of the Holy Roman Empire. This organism of Central Europe, "the survival of a great tradition and a grandiose title," signified not territory but only a sense of membership. The member states covered roughly modern Germany, Austria, Switzerland, Czecho-Slovakia, and Belgium. The ruler was chosen for life by the hereditary Electors of seven states. The Hapsburgs, as sovereigns of Austria, laying claim to Silesia, Bohemia, and Hungary, were the most powerful candidates, and in practice became the hereditary bearers of the ceremonial office of Emperor.*

Austria proper and the Hapsburg dynasty were deeply Catholic; not violent, aggressive, or, except in Hungary, proselytizing, but dwelling solidly and sedately in spiritual loyalty to the Pope. Then, as in our own age, the Hapsburgs were represented by a sovereign who reigned for fifty troublous years over an empire already racked by the stresses which two centuries later were, amid world disaster, to rend it in pieces. Confronted and alarmed by the growing power and encroachments of France, at variance often with Prussia, Vienna had fearful preoccupations of its own. The Turk under fanatical Sultans still launched in the south-east of Europe that thrust of conquest which in earlier periods had been successively hurled back from France and Spain. At any time the Ottoman armies, drawing recruits and supplies from all those subjugated Christian peoples we now call the Balkan States, might present themselves in barbaric invasion at the gates of Vienna. And there were always the Magyars of Hungary, always in revolt. In general, the divided princes of Germany faced the united strength of France, and Austria struggled for life against the Turk; but the whole vague confederacy recognized common dangers and foes, and the majestic antagonisms of Bourbons and Hapsburgs were the main dividing line of Europe.

Italy in the seventeenth century was merely a geographical expression. In the north Savoy (Piedmont) was brought out of its obscurity at the beginning of the century by the genius of Charles Emmanuel I (1580–1630). Afterwards it poised precariously between France and the Empire, deserting them both in turn according to the apparent fortunes of war. It has been said that the geographical position of Savoy, "the doorkeeper of the Alps," made its rulers treacherous. At best

* In this account we shall use 'the Empire,' 'Austria,' and 'the Court at Vienna' as more or less interchangeable terms.

they could only preserve themselves and their country from ruin by miracles of diplomatic alternation.

Such were the unpromising and divided components of a Europe in contrast with which the power and ambitions of France arose in menacing splendour. Such were the factors and forces amid which Charles II had to steer the fortunes of his kingdom.

The politics of a weak and threatened state cannot achieve the standards open to those who enjoy security and wealth. The ever-changing forms of the dangers by which they are oppressed impose continuous shifts and contradictions, and many manœuvres from which pride and virtue alike recoil. England in the seventeenth century was little better placed than were Balkan states like Roumania or Bulgaria, when in the advent or convulsion of Armageddon they found themselves bid for or struck at by several mighty empires. We had to keep ourselves alive and free, and we did so. It is by no means sure that plain, honest, downright policies, however laudable, would have succeeded. The oak may butt the storm, but the reeds bow and quiver in the gale and also survive.

It is a mistake to judge English foreign policy from 1667 to 1670, from the Triple Alliance with Holland against France to the Secret Treaty of Dover with France against Holland, as if it meant simply alternating periods of good and evil, of light and darkness, and of the influence of Sir William Temple as against that of the Duchess of Orleans. In fact, both the problems and the controls were continuous and the same, and our policy rested throughout in the same hands, in those of Charles II and his Minister Arlington. Although devoid of both faith and illusions, they were certainly not unintelligent, nor entirely without patriotic feeling. The invasion of Belgium by Louis XIV in the late summer of 1667 confronted them both with a situation of the utmost perplexity. At this stage in his life, at any rate, Charles desired to play an independent part in Europe, while Arlington, with his Spanish sympathies and training and his Dutch wife, was positively anti-French. Their first impulse was to resist the invasion of Belgium.

Strange indeed why this patch of land should exercise such compelling influence upon our unsophisticated ancestors! Apparently in 1667 they forgot or expunged the burning of their battleships in the Medway and Thames and all the passions of hard-fought naval battles because France was about to invade Belgium. Why did Belgium count so much with them? Two hundred and fifty years later we saw the manhood of the British Empire hastening across all the seas and oceans of the world to conquer or die in defence of this same strip of fertile, undulating country about the mouth of the Scheldt. Every one felt he had to go, and no one asked for logical or historical explanations. But then, with our education, we understood many things for which convincing verbal arguments were lacking. So did our ancestors at this time. The Court, the Parliament, the City, the country gentlemen, were all as sure in 1668 that Belgium must not be conquered by the greatest military power on the Continent as were all parties and classes in the British Empire in August 1914. A mystery veiling an instinct!

If resistance to France were possible, still more if it were profitable, the King and Arlington were prepared to make an effort. They sounded the Courts of Europe: but the replies which they received from every quarter were universally discouraging. Spain was utterly incapable of defending her assaulted province. Without English or Dutch shipping she could not even reach it. Yet voluntarily Spain would not yield an inch. The Dutch would not attack France. If strongly supported, they would seek to limit the French territorial gains, but would agree to many of them, and all at the expense of Spain. The Emperor, whatever his Ambassador in London might say, seemed curiously backward. He would make no offensive alliance, least of all with heretics. In fact, as we now know, he was during these very months framing a secret treaty with France for the future partition of the whole Spanish Empire. The Great Elector would not move without subsidies which the Dutch would not and the Spanish could not give him. He was nervous of Sweden, and if the French gave him a free hand in Poland he would not oppose their progress in the west. Truly a depressing prospect for a coalition against the dominating, centralized might of France, wielded by a single man.

In a spirit which it is easy to call 'cold-blooded' and 'cynical' Charles and Arlington next examined the possibility of persuading France to let England share in her winnings, in return for English support in a war against Holland. Here they encountered a sharp rebuff. Louis, who hoped to obtain Belgium without coming to actual war with Holland, was not prepared to barter Spanish colonies against an English alliance, or still less against English neutrality. Both alternatives having thus been unsentimentally explored, Charles, with natural and obvious misgivings, took his decision to oppose France. He sent Sir William Temple to The Hague to make the famous Triple Alliance between England, Holland, and Sweden. The two Governments—for Sweden was a mere mercenary—entered upon it with limited and different objectives, but both sought to extort the favour of France by the threat of war. The English ruling circle hoped to win the French alliance by teaching Louis XIV not to despise England; the Dutch thought they could still retain the friendship of France by compelling Spain to a compromise. Perverse as were the motives, flimsy as was the basis, the result emerged with startling force. Louis saw himself confronted by a Northern league, and simultaneously Arlington brought about a peace between Spain and Portugal which freed the Spanish forces for a more real resistance. The consequences were swift and impressive. The shadow of the Spanish succession fell across the world. Louis, by his aggression upon the Belgian soil so strangely sacred, had called into being in phantom outline that beginnings of the Grand Alliance which was eventually to lay him low. He recoiled from the apparition. By his Partition Treaty of 1668 with the Emperor he had assured himself by merely waiting future gains throughout the whole Spanish Empire incomparably greater than those which might now be won by serious war. He could afford to be patient. Recalling his armies, silencing the protests of his generals, he retreated within his bounds, content for the time being with the acquisition of Lille, Tournai, Armentières, and other fortresses that put Belgium at his mercy. In April 1668, under the pressure and guarantee of the Triple Alliance, France and Spain consequently signed the peace of Aix-la-Chapelle.

We now approach days fatal to the house of Stuart. The national foreign policy attempted in 1668 rested upon diverse motives and paper guarantees. The Triple Alliance must succumb to any strain or temptation. Its partners were bound to protect the *status quo* in Belgium by expeditionary forces in the event of aggression; for this they looked, and in vain, to Spanish subsidies. They were still divided by their old hatreds and recent injuries, by their ceaseless hostilities in the East Indies and in Guiana, and in their rivalry of the Channel. Charles, whatever his subjects might feel, had never forgiven the burning of his ships in the Medway. He hated the Dutch, and though he had been forced by events to side with them for a while and they with him, he yearned for a day when he could unite himself to France. In 1669 he began with Croissy, the French Ambassador, negotiations which reached their fruition in 1670.

Louis's sister-in-law, Duchess of Orleans—the "Madame" of the French Court—was also Charles's sister and his "beloved Minette." She was in the final phase the agent of France. Romance, as well as history, had played around this delightful, tragic figure, so suddenly decisive, so swiftly extinguished. No one stood so high in the love and respect of both monarchs. They cherished her personality: they admired her mind. She was to Charles the purest and deepest affection of his life. Louis realized only too late what he had lost in not making her his Queen. Minette loved both her native and adopted countries, and longed to see them united; but her heart was all for England's interests, as she misunderstood them, and for the Old Faith, to which she was devoutly attached. She presented and pleaded with all her wit and charm the case for an accommodation—nay, an alliance with the Sun King. Why condemn England to an endless, desperate struggle against overwhelming force? Why not accept the friendly hand sincerely, generously extended, and share the triumph and the prize? With France and England united, success was sure, and all the kingdoms of the world would lie in fee. It often happens that when great projects have been brought to maturity, personal touch is needed to set them in action. Minette came to England in the summer of 1670, bringing in her train another charmer, who also was destined to play her part—Louise de Kéroualle. "Madame's" husband, jealous of her political power and of his own eclipse, grudged every day of the Princess's absence from the home he had made odious with his minions. But Charles welcomed her with unrestrained joy. He met her with his Navy, and for a few sunlit days the English Court made picnic revel at Dover. Louis awaited results in eager suspense. They were all he could desire. Minette bore with her back to France—signed, sealed, and delivered—the Secret Treaty. She returned to perish almost immediately of a mysterious illness. She left as her legacy and life's achievement an instrument ruinous to all she prized.

By the Secret Treaty of Dover Charles agreed to join with Louis in an attack on Holland which aimed at nothing less than the destruction of the United Provinces as a factor in Europe, and to take all measures needful to that end. Louis agreed to respect the integrity of Belgium; to place in British keeping much of the coastline of conquered Holland, including the isle of Walcheren, with its valuable ports of Sluys and Cadsand, and the mouths of the Scheldt. Every safeguard was furnished to English naval requirements and colonial ambition. The mastery of the seas, the command of the Dutch outlets, and the exploitation of Asia and the Americas were inestimable temptations. For the young Stadtholder, William of Orange, a prince of Stuart blood, now just twenty, a dignified, if restricted, sphere would be reserved. He might reign as hereditary sovereign over the truncated domains of the former Dutch Republic, for which his great-grandfather William the Silent had battled with all that his life could give. Next there was to be money. Large subsidies, sufficient to make King Charles with his hereditary revenues almost independent in times of peace of his contumacious Parliament, would be provided. Money, very handy for mistresses and Court expenses, but also absolutely necessary to restore and maintain the strength of the Royal Navy, now decaying in its starved dockyards! Such were the secular clauses. But the pact contained what in those days was even graver matter. Charles was to try persistently and faithfully, by every means at his disposal, to bring his subjects back to the Catholic faith. Full allowance would be made for the obvious difficulties of such a task; but the effort was to be continuous and loyal. In any case, not only French money, but French troops were to be available to secure the English monarchy against the anger of Parliament or the revolt of the nation.

Such was the hideous bargain, struck by so fair a hand, upon which the execration of succeeding generations has fastened. Far be it from us to seek to reverse that verdict of history which every British heart must acclaim. It would not, however, have been difficult to state a case at Charles II's council board against any whole-hearted espousal of Dutch interests, nor to have pleaded and even justified a temporizing opportunist policy towards France, deceitful though it must be. "We cannot commit ourselves to Holland; at any moment she may outbid us with France. Spain is futile and penniless. Alone we cannot face the enmity of the Great King. Let us take his money to build our fleet, and wait and see what happens." As for religion, Charles had learned in a hard school the willpower of Protestant England. Whatever his own leanings to the Catholic faith, all his statecraft showed that he would never run any serious risk for the sake of reconverting the nation. Manœuvre, fence, and palter as he might, he always submitted, and always meant to submit, with expedition to the deep growl of his subjects and to the authority of their inexpugnable institutions.

The Secret Treaty of Dover was handled personally by Louis, Charles, and their intermediary, Minette. But, of course, Colbert and Croissy had long studied its terms, and in England Arlington's support was soon found indispensable. As the protocol began to take shape first Arlington and then Clifford and the rest of the Cabal were invited to approve its secular provisions. It was perhaps less of a turn-about for Arlington than it appeared on the surface, and we cannot measure the slow, persistent pressures to which he yielded. Ministers in those days considered themselves the servants of the King, in the sense of being bound to interpret his will up to the point of impeachment, and sometimes beyond it. The whole Cabal endorsed such parts of the treaty as were communicated to them. The religious plot—it deserves no other name—was locked in the royal breast. James had not been much consulted in the negotiations, but he learned all that had been done with an inexpressible joy. Most especially he admired the religious clauses. Here more clearly than ever before he saw the blessed hands of the Mother of God laid upon the tormented world.

If anyone in 1672 computed the relative forces of France and England, he could only feel that no contest was possible; and the apparent weakness and humiliation of the pensioner island was aggravated by the feeble, divided condition of Europe. No dreamer, however romantic, however remote his dreams from reason, could have foreseen a surely approaching day when, by the formation of mighty coalitions and across the struggles of a generation, the noble colossus of France would lie prostrate in the dust, while the small island, beginning to gather to itself the empires of India and America, stripping France and Holland of their colonial possessions, would emerge victorious, mistress of the Mediterranean, the Narrow Seas, and the oceans. Aye, and carry forward with her, intact and enshrined, all that peculiar structure of law and liberty, all her own inheritance of learning and letters, which are to-day the treasure of the most powerful family in the human race.

This prodigy was achieved by conflicting yet contributory forces, and by a succession of great islanders and their noble foreign comrades or guides. We owe our salvation to the sturdy independence of the House of Commons and to its creators, the aristocracy and country gentlemen.

We owe it to our hardy tars and bold sea-captains, and to the quality of a British Army as yet unborn. We owe it to the inherent sanity and vigour of the political conceptions sprung from the genius of the English race. But those forces would have failed without the men to use them. For the quarter of a century from 1688 to 1712 England was to be led by two of the greatest warriors and statesmen in all history: William of Orange, and John, Duke of Marlborough. They broke the military power of France, and fatally weakened her economic and financial foundations. They championed the Protestant faith, crowned Parliamentary institutions with triumph, and opened the door to an age of reason and freedom. They reversed the proportions and balances of Europe. They turned into new courses the destinies of Asia and America. They united Great Britain, and raised her to the rank she holds today.

CHAPTER FIVE

Arms

ɞ 1672-74 ɜ

THERE are two main phases in the military career of John, Duke of Marlborough. In the first, which lasted four years, he rose swiftly from ensign to colonel by his conduct and personal qualities and by the impression he made on all who met him in the field. In the second, during ten campaigns he commanded the main army of the Grand Alliance with infallibility. An interval of more than a quarter of a century separates these two heroic periods. From 1671 to 1675 he exhibited all those qualities which were regarded as the forerunners in a regimental officer of the highest military distinction. He won his way up from grade to grade by undoubted merit and daring. But thereafter was a desert through which he toiled and wandered. A whole generation of small years intervened. His sword never rusted in its sheath. It was found bright and sharp whenever it was needed, at Sedgemoor, at Walcourt, or in Ireland. There it lay, the sword of certain victory, ready for service whenever opportunity should come.

"Everybody agreed," wrote Anthony Hamilton, "that the man who was the favourite of the King's mistress and brother to the Duke's was starting well and could not fail to make his fortune." But the influence of royal concubines was not the explanation of the rise of Marlborough. That rise was gradual, intermittent, and long. He was a professional soldier. "And," wrote the old Duchess at the end of her life,

> I think it is more Honour to rise from the lowest Step to the greatest, than, as is the fashion now, to be Admirals without ever having seen Water but in a Bason, or to make Generals that never saw any action of war.

(40)

By the time he arrived at the highest command he was passing the prime of life, and older than many of the leading generals of the day. The early success and repeated advancement which this chapter records were followed by lengthy intervals of stagnation. Arabella and Barbara had long ceased to count with him or anyone else, while he was still regarded as a subordinate figure, when he had yet to make and remake his whole career. Continual checks, grave perplexities, extreme hazards, disgrace and imprisonment, constant skilful services, immense tenacity, perseverance and self-restraint, almost unerring political judgment, all the arts of the courtier, politician, and diplomatist, marked his middle life. For many long years his genius and recognized qualities seemed unlikely to carry him through the throng of securely established notabilities who then owned the fulness of the earth. At twenty-four he was a colonel. He was fifty-two before he commanded a large army.

In 1672 the slumbering Treaty of Dover awoke in the realm of action. Louis, having perfected his plans to the last detail, suddenly, without cause of quarrel, made his cavalry swim the Rhine and poured his armies into Holland. At the same time England also declared war upon the Dutch. The States-General, de Witt and his Amsterdammers, taken by surprise, were unable to stem the advance of 120,000 French troops, armed for the first time with the new weapon of the bayonet. Cities and strongholds fell like ninepins. The Dutch people, faced with extermination, set their despairing hopes upon William of Orange. The great-grandson of William the Silent did not fail them. He roused and animated their tough, all-enduring courage. John de Witt and his brother were torn to pieces by a frenzied mob in the streets of The Hague. William uttered the deathless battle-cry, "We can die in the last ditch." The sluices in the dykes were opened; the bitter waters rolled in ever-widening deluge over the fertile land. Upon the wide inundation the fortified towns seemed to float like arks of refuge. All military operations became impossible. The French armies withdrew in bewilderment. Holland, her manhood, her navy, and her hero-Prince preserved their soul impregnable.

Meanwhile the French and English fleets united had set themselves to secure the mastery of the Narrow Seas. A contingent of six thousand English troops under Monmouth's command served with the French armies. Lediard and other early writers suppose that Churchill was among them. In fact he took part in a deadlier struggle afloat. The sea fighting began on March 13, before the declaration of war, with the surprise attack of Sir Robert Holmes's English squadron upon the Dutch Smyrna fleet while at anchor off the Isle of Wight. This treacherous venture miscarried, and the bulk of the Dutch vessels escaped. The companies of the Guards in which Churchill and his friend George Legge were serving were embarked for the raid and took part in the action.

The handling of the Dutch navy under De Ruyter in this campaign commands lasting admiration. He pressed into the jaws of the Channel to forestall the concentration of the French and English fleets. But the Duke of York, setting sail from the Thames in good time, made his junction with the French fleet from Brest, and De Ruyter was glad to extricate himself from the Channel and return safely to the North Sea. The combined fleets proceeded through the Straits of Dover to Sole Bay (or Southwold), on the Suffolk coast. This was the opportunity which De Ruyter sought. On the morning of May 28/June 7 a French frigate, hotly pursued, brought the news that the whole Dutch fleet was at her heels. Every one scrambled on board, and a hundred and one ships endeavoured to form their line of battle. The French division, under D'Estrées, whether from policy or necessity or because James's orders were lacking in precision, sailed upon a divergent course from the English fleet. De Ruyter, playing with the French and sending Van Ghent to attack the ships of Lord Sandwich, fell himself upon the Duke of York's division, of which at first not more than twenty were in their stations. In all he had ninety-one vessels and a superiority of at least two to one in the first part of the battle.

Grievous and cruel was the long struggle which ensued. The Suffolk shores were crowded with frantic spectators, the cannonade was heard two hundred miles away. From noon till dusk the battle raged at close quarters. The Dutch desperately staked their superiority with cannon and fire-ships against the English, tethered upon a lee shore. The captain of the ship and more than two hundred men, a third of the complement, were killed or wounded. Both sides fought with the doggedness on which their races pride themselves. Sunset and the possible return of the French ended a battle described by De Ruyter as the hardest of his thirty-two actions, and the Dutch withdrew, having destroyed for many weeks the offensive power of the superior combined fleets.

Not one single word has come down to us of John's part in this deadly business, through which he passed unscathed. No reference to it exists in his correspondence or conversation. This was before the age when everybody kept diaries or wrote memoirs. It was just in the day's work. All we know is that his conduct gained him remarkable advancement. No fewer than four captains of the Admiralty Regiment had been killed, and he received double promotion from a Guards ensign to a Marine captaincy.

Lieutenant Edward Picks complained to Sir Joseph Williamson, Arlington's Under-Secretary, that:

> Mr Churchill, who was my ensign in the engagement, is made a Captain and I, without my Lord Arlington's kindness and yours, I fear may still continue a lieutenant, though I am confident my greatest enemies cannot say I misbehaved myself in the engagement. . . .

We do not know the details of the action. Favouritism there may have been in the double step, but it was favouritism founded upon exceptional conduct. In such rough times, when chiefs and subalterns faced the fire together, many wholesome correctives were at work. The Duke of York, coming himself out of heavy battle, would have acted in accordance with what he had seen and with what men said of Churchill's conduct.

Sole Bay for the time being knocked out the fleet, and only meagre funds were found to refit and repair it. The infantry and gentlemen volunteers came ashore, and the Guards were ordered to France. The courtiers forgathered at Whitehall to celebrate their experiences in revel and carouse, and John, fresh from danger and in the flush of promotion, was welcomed, we doubt not, in the arms of Barbara. It is believed that at this time she paid the purchase money which enabled him to take up the captaincy his sword had gained. We apologize for mentioning such shocking facts to the reader; but it is our duty, for such was the depravity of these fierce and hectic times.

In 1673 Louis XIV again made war in person. Condé with weak forces occupied the Dutch in the north. Turenne similarly engaged the Imperialists in Alsace. The Great King advanced in the centre with the mass and magnificence of the French Army. All the world wondered where he would strike. It soon appeared that he had honoured Maestricht, a strong Dutch fortress garrisoned by about five thousand men, as the scene of his intended triumph. He felt his military qualities more suited to sieges than to battles; and "Big sieges," he remarked, "please me more than the others." Maestricht was accordingly invested on June 17.

We do not know precisely what happened to Captain Churchill between the battle of Sole Bay and the siege of Maestricht. The Admiralty Regiment in which he now held a company went to France in December. Various English contingents were serving in Alsace or in garrison with the French. It seems probable that once it became clear that the centre of the war was to be in Flanders and that the Great King would be there himself, Monmouth allowed or encouraged a handful of swells and their personal attendants to leave the different units of the army and come to the bull's-eye of the fighting under his personal direction. At any rate, England was represented at Maestricht only by the Duke of Monmouth with a score of gentlemen volunteers, prominent among whom was Churchill, and an escort of thirty gentlemen troopers of the Life Guards. Louis XIV treated the distinguished delegation with the ceremony due to the bastard son of his royal brother. Monmouth was assigned his turn as 'General of the Trenches,' and ample opportunity was offered to him and his friends of winning distinction before the most critical and fashionable military assemblage of the period. Every one of them was on his mettle, eager to hazard his life in the arena and wrest renown from beneath so many jealous and competent eyes. Little did this gay company trouble themselves about the rights and wrongs of the war, or the majestic balance of power in Europe; and we cannot doubt that our young officer shared their reckless mood to the full. Comradeship and adventure and the hopes of glory and promotion seemed all-sufficing to the eyes and sword of youth.

The trenches were opened ten days after the investment, and a week later the siege works justified an attempt to break in upon the fortress. The attack, timed for ten o'clock at night, was arranged to fall in Monmouth's tour of duty. Picked detachments from the best regiments, including the King's Musketeers, formed the storming forces. The King came and stood at the end of the trenches to watch. The signal was given, and Monmouth, with Churchill and his Englishmen at his side, led the French assault. With heavy losses from close and deadly fire, amid the explosion of two mines and of six thousand grenades, the counterscarp galleries were occupied, and a half-moon work in front of the Brussels gate was attacked. Three times the assailants were driven partly out of their lodgments and three times they renewed the assault, until finally Churchill is said to have planted the French standard on the parapet of the half-moon. The rest of the night was spent in consolidating the defence and digging new communications, and at daylight Monmouth handed over the captured works to supporting troops. The Englishmen were resting in their tents, and Monmouth was about to dine, when near noon of the next day the dull roar of a mine and heavy firing proclaimed the Dutch counter-stroke. The governor, M. de Fariaux, a Frenchman in the service of the States-General, gallantly leading his men, had sallied out upon the captured works.

The episode which followed belongs to romance rather than to history or war, but the most detailed and authentic records exist about it.

Monmouth sent appeals to a company of musketeers at hand. Their officer, a certain M. d'Artagnan, then famous in the Army and since deathless in Dumas's fiction, responded instantly. There was no time to go through the zigzags of the communication trenches. De Fariaux was already in the half-moon. Monmouth, fleet of foot, led straight for the struggle across the top of the ground. With him came Churchill, twelve Life Guardsmen, and a handful of Englishmen of quality, with some valiant pages and servants. They reached the half-moon from an unexpected direction at the moment when the fighting was at its height. D'Artagnan and his musketeers joined them. The Life Guards threw away their carbines (twelve were subsequently reissued from the English ordnance stores) and drew their swords. Monmouth, Churchill, and d'Artagnan forced their way in.

Churchill, who was wounded at Monmouth's side, was also held to have distinguished himself. He was, in fact, publicly thanked upon a great parade by Louis XIV, who assured him that his good conduct would be reported to his own sovereign. Another subaltern fought in this attack whose name will recur in these pages: Louis Hector de Villars against orders joined the assault. His gallantry won forgiveness for his disobedience. We do not know whether he and Churchill became acquainted at Maestricht. They certainly met at Malplaquet.

The governor of Maestricht, satisfied with the resistance he had made and strongly pressed by the townsfolk to capitulate while time remained, beat a parley, and was allowed to march out with the honours of war. The severity of the losses, especially among persons of note in the storming troops, made a strong impression throughout the camps and the Courts concerned. Monmouth was praised and petted by Louis not only from policy, but on the undoubted merit of his performance. He and his English team received the unstinted tributes of "the finest army in the world." The brief and spectacular campaign was soon brought to a close. Louis XIV rejoined his anxious Court, who burned before him the incense of flattery with all the delicate address of which the French are peculiarly capable. The armies retired into winter quarters, and Monmouth and his hunting party were welcomed again into the bosom of Whitehall.

Meanwhile Captain Churchill and the Duchess of Cleveland continued to make the running at the Court. That a virile young officer should be the lover of a beautiful, voluptuous, and immoral woman is not inexplicable to human nature. The fact that she was a few years his senior is by no means a bar. On the contrary, the charms of thirty are rarely more effective than when exerted on the impressionable personality of twenty-three. No one is invited to applaud such relationships, but few, especially in time of war, will hold them unpardonable, and only malignancy would seek to score them for ever upon a young man's record. How disgusting to pretend, with Lord Macaulay, a filthy, sordid motive for actions prompted by those overpowering compulsions which leap flaming from the crucible of life itself! Inconstant Barbara loved her youthful soldier tenderly and followed with eager, anxious eyes his many adventures and perils from steel and fire. He returned her love with the passion of youth. She was rich and could have money for the asking. He had no property but his sword and sash. But they were equals, they were kin, they lived in the same world. She was now the mother of his child.

He was back at the front in the early autumn. The Admiralty Regiment was now with Turenne in Westphalia. There is little doubt that Churchill served as a captain with them during the rest of 1673. Although no great operations were in progress, he made his way in the Army. There is always the story of Turenne wagering, when some defile had been ill defended, that the "handsome Englishman" would retake it with half the number of troops used when it was lost; and how this was accordingly and punctually done. No one has been able to assign the date or the place, but at any rate the newly made captain in the Admiralty Regiment was a figure well known in Turenne's army and high in the favour of the Marshal himself before the year closed.

Stern, curious eyes were now turned upon the Duke of York. Rumours of his conversion to Rome had long been rife. How would he stand the Test, administered according to the Act which excluded Papists from all offices of State? The answer was soon forthcoming. The heir to the throne renounced all his offices, and Prince Rupert succeeded him in the command of the fleet. So it was true, then, that James was a resolute Papist, ready to sacrifice all material advantages to the faith his countrymen abhorred. And now there came a trickle of allegations and disclosures about the Secret Treaty of Dover. Rumours of decisions taken by the King, by his brother, and his Ministers to convert England to Rome were rife during all the summer and autumn of 1673.

Moreover, the war went ill. Like so many wars, it looked easy and sure at the outset. There is always the other side, who have their own point of view and think, often with surprising reason, that they also have a chance of victory. The cutting of the dykes had marred the opening French campaign. The Dutch defensive at sea in 1672 and 1673 was magnificent. Rupert's battles against De Ruyter were bloody and drawn. The situation of Holland had vastly improved. The Prince of Orange, Stadtholder and Captain-General, stood at the head of truly 'United Provinces,' and in August both the Empire and Spain entered into alliance with the Dutch to maintain the European balance. Diplomatically and militarily the Anglo-French compact had failed. On top of all this came the news that Charles had allowed a most obnoxious marriage between the Duke of York and the Catholic princess Mary of Modena.

A new scene, and, indeed, a new era, now opened.

Through Spanish mediation peace was signed with Holland on February 19, 1674. The Dutch, stubborn though they were, gave in their sore straits the fullest satisfaction to English naval pride. Within six years of the Medway, within two years of Sole Bay, and within a year of De Ruyter's proud encounters with Rupert, Holland accepted with every circumstance of humility the naval supremacy of England. The States-General confirmed the agreement of the Treaty of Breda (1667) that all Dutch ships should dip their flag and topsails whenever, north of Cape Finisterre, they sighted an English man-of-war. Not only were

Dutch fleets and squadrons to make their salute to similar forces of the Royal Navy, but even the whole of the Dutch fleet was to make its submission to a single English vessel, however small, which flew the royal flag. The history books which dwell upon our shame in the Medway and the Thames do not do justice to this turning of the tables. Callous, unmoral, unscrupulous as had been Charles's policy, he might now on this account at least exclaim, "He laughs best who laughs last."

There were in 1674 five or six thousand English troops in French pay; but these had to be reduced after the Anglo-Dutch treaty, and as many of the men returned home and no drafts were sent out, the strength of the various regiments soon fell, and it became necessary to amalgamate units. Thus Skelton's regiment became merged with Peterborough's. Peterborough resigned. Who was to take his place? Who should command the combined regiment but the brilliant officer who had planted the lilies of France on the parapet of the Maestricht half-moon, whose quality was known throughout the French Army, who had been thanked by Louis in the field, and whose advancement was so entirely agreeable to Charles II, to the Duke of York, and to both their lady-loves? A news-letter from Paris on March 19, 1674, says:

> Lord Peterborough's regiment, now in France, is to be broken up and some companies of it joined to the companies that went out of the Guards last summer, and be incorporated into one regiment, and to remain there for the present under the command of Captain Churchill, son of Sir Winston.

But before Churchill could receive the colonelcy he had to be presented at Versailles and receive the personal approval of the Great King. On March 21 Louvois wrote to thank Monmouth for his letter, to announce that Churchill had been accepted as a colonel in the French service by Louis XIV, and to suggest that companies not merely from Skelton's, but also from Sackville's and Hewetson's regiments, should be included in his command. On April 3 the commission was granted, and John Churchill found himself Colonel in the service of France and at the head of a regiment of English infantry. He was just twenty-four. He had skipped the rank of lieutenant after Sole Bay; he now, in the French service, skips the ranks of Major and Lieutenant-Colonel at a bound. He retained his substantive rank of Captain in the

English Army until January 1675, when he was promoted Lieutenant-Colonel in the Duke of York's regiment. He had evidently at this time impressed his personality on the French Court. He had been there a year before with half a dozen English officers on the way to the Maestricht campaign. Once again the Great King acknowledged the bows of the young Adonis in scarlet and gold, of whose exploits under the planets of Mars and Venus he had already been well informed through the regular channels. He would certainly not have allowed the royal radiance to play upon this elegant, graceful figure if there were not veils which shroud the future.

On the 16th of June the whole army marched on Sinzheim, on the left bank of the Elsatz. The battle began with Turenne's seizure of the town and the forcing of the stream. The fighting lasted for seven hours and ended in the retreat of the enemy with heavy loss. Although unaccompanied by strategic results, it is claimed as a perfect example in miniature of Turenne's handling of all three arms. Turenne after various manœuvres received reinforcements, and proceeded to ravage the Palatinate, partly to fill his own magazines and partly to impede its reoccupation by a still unbeaten enemy. This military execution of the province dictated by the needs of war must be distinguished from the systematic devastation of the same region ordered by Louis XIV seven years later as a measure of policy.

We have a letter from an old lady—the widow Saint-Just—one of the few residents who did not suffer from Turenne's severities in 1674, written to the Duke of Marlborough from Metz on July 16, 1711, in which she says:

> It would be indeed difficult for me to forget you, Monseigneur, and I have an indispensable duty to remember all my life the kindness which you showed me in Metz *thirty-four years ago*. You were very young then, Monseigneur, but you gave already by your excellent qualities the hope of that valour, politeness and conduct which have raised you with justice to the rank where you command all men. And what is more glorious, Monseigneur, is that the whole world, friends and enemies, bear witness to the truth of what I have the honour to write; and I have no doubt that it was your generosity on my account which [then] made itself felt, because the troops who came and burnt everything around my land at Mezeray in the plain spared my estate, saying that they were so ordered by high authority.

Whether this letter stirred some scented memory, long cherished in Churchill's retentive mind, which after the lapse of thirty-four years would make the shielding of this little plot and homestead from the ravages of war an incident he would not forget, we cannot tell. We think, however, that the widow is wrong in her dates. It is, of course, possible—though the evidence is against it—that Churchill was in Metz on some military duty in 1677. But it is far more likely that the letter refers to the year 1674, when indeed the troops "came and burnt everything around . . . Mezeray."

There is no dispute, however, about Churchill's presence at the head of his regiment in the battle of Enzheim in October. Here all is certain and grim. We have one of his matter-of-fact letters written to Monmouth about the action. We have also a much fuller account by the future Lord Feversham. Turenne had ten thousand horse and twelve thousand foot against enemy forces almost double. Nevertheless, he crossed the Breusch river and attacked the Imperialists by surprise. All turned upon what was called the 'Little Wood,' which lay on the French right between the armies. The development of the main action depended on who held the wood, and the fight for it constituted the crux of the battle. A competent French colonel, Boufflers by name, whom we shall meet several times in higher situations later, was sent to clear the wood with his dragoons. He could make no headway, and resigned his effort to the infantry. Both sides began to cram battalions into the wood. The French rarely stint their own, and never their allies' blood; and the brunt of Turenne's battle was borne by the hired troops. Dongan's battalion of Hamilton's Irish regiment, the third battalion of Warwick's Loyal English, and Churchill's battalion were successively thrown into the struggle. Duras (Feversham) wrote, "One and all assuredly accomplished marvels." They certainly suffered most severe losses. Churchill's battalion, which was the last to engage, had half its officers killed or wounded in the Little Wood. The rest of the island mercenaries suffered almost as heavily in this and other parts of the field. The three squadrons of Monmouth's horse charged the Imperialists who were attacking the French left and centre at a critical moment, and won much honour with almost total destruction. Turenne bivouacked on the field, claiming a victory at heavy odds, and his strategic theme was vindicated. But the battle must take its place in that large category 'bloody and indecisive.'

Feversham, reporting to the Government, wrote, "No one in the world could possibly have done better than Mr Churchill has done and M. de Turenne is very well pleased with all our nation." Turenne also mentioned Churchill and his battalion in his despatches. It was a very rough, savage fight in a cause not reconcilable with any English interest.

Even before the battle it seems likely that Churchill was well esteemed in the army. We find him selected by Turenne with five hundred picked men for an attack upon the Imperialist rearguard at a moment when it was recrossing the Rhine. But only here and there does his figure catch a fleeting gleam. Lots of others, for whom no one has rummaged, did as well. All that can be said is that he did his duty and bore a solid reputation in this hard-pressed, over-weighted, and yet victorious army. There is no doubt that he fought too in the midwinter attack on Turckheim. In those days the armies reposed from October till April, the condition of such roads as there were alone imposing immobility upon them; but Turenne, starting from Haguenau on November 19, broke into the Imperialist cantonments, and after cutting up various detachments gained a considerable success on Christmas Day. Churchill's regiment marched with him. Duras and other English officers had already been given leave to Paris, it being essential to Turenne's design to pretend that the year's campaign was over. Although a letter on December 15 states that Churchill was daily expected in Paris, he was certainly with the troops.

It is customary to say that he learned the art of war from Turenne. This is going too far. No competent officer of that age could watch the composed genius of Turenne in action without being enriched thereby. But no battle ever repeats itself. The success of a commander does not arise from following rules or models. It consists in an absolutely new comprehension of the dominant facts of the situation at the time, and all the forces at work. Cooks use recipes for dishes and doctors have prescriptions for diseases, but every great operation of war is unique. The kind of intelligence capable of grasping in its complete integrity what is actually happening in the field is not taught by the tactics of commanders on one side or the other—though these may train the mind—but by a profound appreciation of the actual event. There is no surer road to ill-success in war than to imitate the plans of bygone heroes and to fit them to novel situations.

CHAPTER SIX

Sarah

₰ 1675-76 ₯

IN the early seventies a new star began to shine in the constellations of the English Court. Frances Jennings—"la belle Jenyns" of Grammont —beautiful as "Aurora or the promise of Spring," haughty, correct, mistress of herself, became a waiting-woman of the Duchess of York. She soon had no lack of suitors. The Duke himself cast favourable glances towards her, which were suavely but firmly deflected. Fair and impregnable, she shone upon that merry, easy-going, pleasure-loving society.

Her father, Richard Jennings, of Sandridge, came of a Somersetshire family who, though long entitled to bear arms, had no crest before the reign of King Henry VIII. For some time they had been settled in Hertfordshire, near St Albans, at Holywell House, on the banks of the Ver. Her grandfather was High Sheriff of Herts in 1625, and, like his son Richard, was repeatedly returned to the House of Commons as Member for St Albans. Their property also included land in Somersetshire and Kent, and may have amounted at this period to about £4000 a year. Curiously enough—in after-light—the Manor of Churchill, in Somersetshire, was, as we have seen, in the possession of the Jennings family for a hundred years.

About Frances Jennings' widowed mother various reports exist. We find references in Somersetshire letters to "your noble mother." In *The New Atalantis* she is described as a sorceress: "the famous Mother Shipton, who by the power and influence of her magic art had placed her daughter in the Court." She certainly bore a questionable reputation, suffered from a violent temper, and found in St James's Palace, where she had apartments, a refuge from hungry creditors who, armed with the law, bayed outside.

In 1673 Frances brought her younger sister Sarah, a child of twelve, into the Court circle. She too was attached to the household of the Duke of York. There she grew up, and at the mature age of fifteen was already a precocious, charming figure. She was not so dazzling as her sister, but she had a brilliancy all her own; fair, flaxen hair, blue eyes sparkling with vivacity, a clear, rosy complexion, firm, engaging lips, and a nose well chiselled, but with a slightly audacious upward tilt. She also, from her tenderest years, was entirely self-possessed and self-confident, and by inheritance she owned, when roused, the temper of the devil.

Towards the end of 1675 she began to dance with John Churchill at balls and parties. He, of course, must have been acquainted with her ever since she arrived at St James's, but after one night of dancing at the end of that year they fell in love with each other. It was a case of love, not at first sight indeed, but at first recognition. It lasted for ever; neither of them thenceforward loved anyone else in their whole lives, though Sarah hated many. The courtship was obstructed and prolonged. Meanwhile Sarah grew to her beauty and power, and her personality, full of force, woman's wiles, and masculine sagacity, became manifest.

At Blenheim Palace there is a bundle of thirty-seven love-letters of John and Sarah covering a period of about three years, from 1675 to 1677. All are unsigned and all are provokingly undated. All but eight are his. Her contributions are short, severe, and almost repellent. She must have written many more letters, and it is surmised that these were in a more tender vein. She seems, however, only to have kept copies of her warlike missives. She asked him to destroy all her letters, and he must have done so, for none survives except this bundle of thirty-seven, of which hers are copies and his only are originals. In her old age the Duchess several times fondled and reread this correspondence. Her own letters are endorsed in her handwriting, "Some coppys of my letters to Mr Churchill before I was married & not more than 15 years old." She left a request that her chief woman-in-waiting, or secretary, Grace Ridley, should after her death be given the letters in order that she might "burn without reading them." There is an endorsement in the quivering hand of age stating that she had read over all these letters in 1736. Finally, the year before her death, "Read over in 1743 desiring to burn them, but I could not doe it."

The reader shall be the judge of the correspondence. The first batch consists entirely of John's letters.

John to Sarah

* My Soul, I love you so truly well that I hope you will be so kind as to let me see you somewhere to-day, since you will not be at Whitehall. I will not name any time, for all hours are alike to me when you will bless me with your sight. You are, and ever shall be, the dear object of my life, for by heavens I will never love anybody but yourself.

* I am just come and have no thought of any joy but that of seeing you. Wherefore I hope you will send me word that you will see me this night.

* My head did ache yesterday to that degree and I was so out of order that nothing should have persuaded me to have gone abroad but the meeting of you who is much dearer than all the world besides to me. If you are not otherwise engaged, I beg you will give me leave to come at eight o'clock.

* I fancy by this time that you are awake, which makes me now send to know how you do, and if your foot will permit you to give me the joy of seeing you in the drawing-room this night. Pray let me hear from you, for when I am not with you, the only joy I have is hearing from you.

* My Soul, it is a cruel thing to be forced in a place when I have no hopes of seeing you, for on my word last night seemed very tedious to me; wherefore I beg you will be so kind to me as to come as often as you can this week, since I am forced to wait [to be in waiting]. I hope you will send me word that you are well and that I shall see you here to-night.

* I did no sooner know that you were not well, but upon my faith without affectation I was also sick. I hope your keeping your bed yesterday and this night has made you perfectly well, which if it has, I beg that I may then have leave to see you to-night at eight, for believe me that it is an age since I was with you. I do love you so well that I have no patience when I have not hopes of seeing my dear angel, wherefore pray send me word that I shall be blessed and come at eight, till when, my Soul, I will do nothing else but think kindly of you.

I hope your sitting up has done you no harm, so that you will see me this afternoon, for upon my soul I do love you with all my heart and take joy in nothing but yourself. I do love you with all the truth imaginable, but have patience but for one week, you shall then see that I will never more do aught that shall look like a fault.

If your happiness can depend upon the esteem and love I have for you, you ought to be the happiest thing breathing, for I have never anybody loved to that height I do you. I love you so well that your happiness I prefer much above my own; and if you think meeting me is what you ought not to do, or that it will disquiet you, I do promise you I will never press you more to do it. As I prefer your happiness above my own, so I hope you will sometimes think how well I love you; and what you can do without doing yourself an injury, I hope you will be so kind as to do it—I mean in letting me see that you wish me better than the rest of mankind; and in return I swear to you that I never will love anything but your dear self, which has made so sure a conquest of me that, had I the will, I have not the power ever to break my chains. Pray let me hear from you, and know if I shall be so happy as to see you to-night.

I was last night at the ball, in hopes to have seen what I love above my own soul, but I was not so happy, for I could see you nowhere, so that I did not stay above an hour. I would have written sooner, but that I was afraid you went to bed so late that it would disturb you.

Pray see which of these two puppies you like best, and that keep; for the bitch cannot let them suck any longer. They are above three weeks old, so that if you give it warm milk it will not die. Pray let me hear from you, and at what time you will be so kind as to let me come to you to-night. Pray, if you have nothing to do, let it be the latest [earliest], for I never am truly happy but when I am with you.

We now see the falling of shadows upon the sunlit path. We cannot tell their cause, whether they come from passing clouds or from some solid obstruction. We do not know the reason, nor even the year. We must realize that these written fragments, luckily preserved, represent only a tiny part of all that happened in nearly a thousand days of two young lives.

* I stayed last night in the drawing-room expecting your coming back, for I could have wished that we had not parted until you had given me hopes of seeing you, for, my soul, there is no pain so great to me, as that when I fear you do not love me; but I hope I shall never live to see you less kind to me than you are. I am sure I will never deserve it, for I will by all that is good love you as long as I live. I beg you will let me see you as often as you can, which I am sure you ought to do if you care for my love, since every time I see you I still find new charms in you; therefore do not be so ill-natured as to believe any lies that may be told you of me, for on my faith I do not only now love you but do desire to do it as long as I live. If you can have time before you go to church, pray let me hear from you.

* I was last night above an hour in the Bedchamber still expecting every one that came in it should be you, but at last I went to Mrs Brownley's, where I found Mrs Mowdie, who told me that you were with your sister, so that you would not be seen that night; so I went to Whitehall to find out the Duke, for when I know that you will not appear I do not care to be at St James's. For 'tis you and you only I care to see, for by all that is good I do with all the truth imaginable love you. Pray let me hear from you, and I beg that I may be blessed this night in being with you. I hope you will like the waistcoat; I do assure you there is not such another to be had in England.

* My Soul, I go with the heaviest heart that ever man did, for by all that is good I love you with all my heart and soul, and I am sure that as long as I live you shall have no just reason to believe the contrary. If you are unkind, I love [you] so well that I cannot live, for you are my life, my soul, my all that I hold dear in this world; therefore do not make so ungrateful a return as not to write. If you have charity you will not only write, but you will write kindly, for it is on you that depends the quiet of my soul. Had I fitting words to express my love, it would not then be in your power to refuse what I beg with tears in my eyes, that you would love me as I will by heavens do you.

To show you how unreasonable you are in accusing me, I dare swear you yourself will own that your going from me in the Duchess's drawing-room did show as much contempt as was possible. I may grieve at it, but I will no more complain when you do it, for I suppose it is what pleases your humour. I cannot imagine what you meant by your saying I laughed at you at the Duke's side, for I was so far from that, that had it not been for shame I could have cried. And

[as] for being in haste to go to the Park, after you went, I stood near a quarter of an hour, I believe, without knowing what I did. Although at Whitehall you told me I should not come, yet I walked twice to the Duke's back-stairs, but there was no Mrs Mowdie; and when I went to my Lord Duras's, I would not go the same way they did but came again down the back-stairs; and when I went away, I did not go in my chair, but made it follow me, because I would see if there was any light in your chamber, but I saw none. Could you see my heart you would not be so cruel as to say I do not love you, for by all that is good I love you and only you. If I may have the happiness of seeing you to-night, pray let me know, and believe that I am never truly pleased but when I am with you.

Thus time slipped by, and ardent courtship must have lasted far into its second year. Sarah's sister Frances, after rejecting so many suitors, royal or honourable, was already married to Lord Hamilton, a man of charm and distinction, but of no great wealth. Sarah, approaching seventeen, was alone. She had chased away her mother, and the man she loved and who loved her so well had not yet spoken the decisive word.

Meanwhile the war continued; but such few records of John Churchill as exist for the years 1675, 1676, and 1677 are conclusive against his having fought any more on the Continent. His name is never mentioned in any of the operations. The regiment which he had formerly commanded, withering for lack of drafts, was incorporated in Monmouth's Royal English regiment in May 1675. It is therefore almost certain that he took no part in this year's campaign either with Turenne or elsewhere.

In August we read of him hastening to Paris. We can but guess at his mission. Since 1673 he had been Gentleman of the Bedchamber to the Duke of York. On August 9, 1675, the French Ambassador in England wrote to Louis XIV describing an interview with James at which the Duke had asked for an immediate subsidy from the French King to free his brother from the need of summoning Parliament. In view of the fact that four years later James was to send Churchill over to Paris to make a similar request for a subsidy, and that he was already well known at Versailles, it is not unlikely that he was sent to Paris to reinforce his master's petition. A warrant showing that in October he had permission to import from France free of duty his silver plate

(57)

seems to mark the end of his stay abroad. In September 1676 he was a member of a court-martial convened in London to try an officer for an assault on the governor of Plymouth. There is therefore no doubt that he spent these years mainly at Court, and that he was increasingly employed in diplomatic work and at his ordinary duties in the Duke of York's household.

Towards the end of this year the Duke of Monmouth expressed his dissatisfaction with the Lieutenant-Colonel of his Royal English regiment, which was serving with the French Army against the Dutch, and proposed to Louis XIV that the command should be transferred to Churchill. Justin MacCartie, a nephew of the Duke of Ormonde, who when an ensign had accompanied Feversham to the siege of Maestricht, also sought this appointment. Courtin, the French Ambassador, laid the situation before Louvois, together with elaborate and scandalous accounts of John's love-affairs. Louvois replied that Churchill appeared to be too much taken up with the ladies to devote his wholehearted affection to a regiment. He would give, Louvois said, "more satisfaction to a rich and faded mistress, than to a monarch who did not want to have dishonourable and dishonoured carpet knights in his armies." Courtin, however, considered Churchill a far abler officer than his competitor, and the post was undoubtedly offered him. It was Churchill who refused. "Mr Churchill," reported the Ambassador, whose news was now certainly up to date, "prefers to serve the very pretty sister [Sarah Jennings] of Lady Hamilton than to be lieutenant-colonel in Monmouth's regiment." Mars was quite decidedly set aside for Venus. However, the estrangement was not final.

During the same year, 1676, Sir Winston Churchill and his wife became concerned at the attachment of their son to Sarah Jennings. They did not see how he could make a career for himself unless he married money. To this, with his looks and prowess, he might well aspire. They fixed their eyes upon Catharine Sedley, daughter and heiress of Sir Charles Sedley, a man renowned for his wit and his wealth. Catharine Sedley was also of the household of the Duke of York. She exerted her attractions in her own way, and, though not admired, was both liked and feared. Ultimately, after the parental hopes had failed to unite her to John Churchill, she became, in what seemed almost rotation for the maids of honour, the Duke of York's mistress.

The news of these parental machinations must have been swiftly carried to Sarah. How far, if at all, John lent himself to them, at what point they begin to darken the love-letters, we cannot tell. Certainly the arguments which Sir Winston and his wife could deploy were as serious and matter-of-fact as any which could ever be brought to bear upon a son. We may imagine some of them.

"You have your foot on the ladder of fortune. You have already mounted several important rungs. Every one says you have a great future before you. Every one knows you have not got—apart from the annuity or your pay—a penny behind you. How can you on a mere whim compromise your whole future life? Catharine Sedley is known to be a most agreeable woman. She holds her own in any company. The Duke listens to all she says, and the whole Court laughs at her jests. She is asked everywhere. Women have beauties of mind quite as attractive, except to enamoured youth, as those of body. Sir Charles is a really wealthy man, solid, long-established, with fine houses, broad acres, and failing health. She is his only child. With his fortune and her humour and sagacity behind you, all these anxieties which have gnawed your life, all that poverty which has pursued us since your infancy, would be swept away. You could look any man in the face and your career would be assured.

"Moreover, do you really think this little Jennings could be a companion to you? Although she is only a child, little more than half your age, she has proved herself a spitfire and a termagant. Look at the way she treats you—as if you were a lackey. You have told us enough of your relations with her—and, indeed, it is the talk of the Court—to show that she is just humiliating you, twirling you round her finger for her own glorification. Did she not say only last week to So-and-so how she could make you do this, that, or anything? Even if she had all Catharine's money we would beg you for your peace of mind, with all the experience of the older generation, not to take this foolish step. It would be a decision utterly out of keeping with your character, with your frugal life—never throwing any expense on us, always living within your income—with all your prudence and care for the future. You would be committing a folly, and the one kind of folly we were always sure you would never commit.

"Lastly, think of her. Are you really doing her justice in marrying her? She has come to Court under good protection. She could never hold a candle to her sister, but she may well hope to marry into the peerage. There is the Earl of Lindsay, who could give her a fine position. He is paying her a great deal of attention. Would she ever be happy with love in a cottage? Would she not drag you down and sink with you?" "Believe me, my son, I, your father," Sir Winston might have said, "pillaged by the Roundheads, uprooted from my lands for my loyalty, have had a hard time. I can give nothing to you or your bride but the shelter of my roof at Mintern. You know how we live there. How would she put up with that? We have never been able to do more than hold up our heads. These are rough times. They are not getting better. By yielding to this absurd fancy you will ruin her life as well as your own, and throw a burden upon us which, as you know, we cannot bear. I am to meet Sir Charles next week. He is a great believer in you. He has heard things about you from the French. It is said that among the younger men none is your master in the land service. I never commanded more than a cavalry troop, but you at half my age are almost a general. But are you not throwing away your military career as well?"

How far did John yield to all this? He was no paragon. All around was the corrupt, intriguing Court with its busy marriage market. In those days English parents disposed their children's fortunes much as the French do now. Winston himself had perhaps been betrothed at fourteen or fifteen, and had made a happy, successful family life. We do not believe that John ever weakened in his purpose. Certainly he never wavered in his love. No doubt he weighed with deep anxiety the course which he should take. All the habit of his mind was farsighted. "In the bloom of his youth," says Macaulay, "he loved lucre more than wine or women." However, he loved Sarah more than all. But how were they to live? This was the cold, brutal, commonplace, inexorable question that baffled his judgment and tied his tongue.

Her situation, as she learned about the family negotiations and saw her lover oppressed and abstracted, was cruel. Already, with discerning feminine eye, she had marked him for her own. Now wealth and worldly wisdom were to intervene and snatch him from her. Already barriers seemed to be growing between them, and it was here that the vital truth of her purpose saved all. Weakness on her part in dealing with him might perhaps have been fatal. She maintained towards him a steady, bayonet-bristling front. Between perfect love, absolute unity, and scorn and fury such as few souls are capable of, there was no middle choice. Sometimes, indeed, her ordeal in public was more than she could bear. Scores of peering, knowing eyes were upon her. Her tears were seen at some revel, and the French Ambassador wrote a sneering letter about them for the gossips of Versailles.

> * There was a small ball last Friday at the Duchess of York's where Lady Hamilton's sister who is uncommonly good-looking had far more wish to cry than to dance. Churchill who is her suitor says that he is attacked by consumption and must take the air in France. I only wish I were as well as he. The truth is that he wishes to free himself from intrigues. His father urges him to marry one of his relations who is very rich and very ugly, and will not consent to his marriage with Miss Jennings. He is also said to be not a little avaricious and I hear from the various Court ladies that he has pillaged the Duchess of Cleveland, and that she has given him more than the value of 100,000 livres. They make out that it is he who has quitted her and that she has taken herself off in chagrin to France to rearrange her affairs. If Churchill crosses the sea, she will be able to patch things up with him. Meanwhile she writes agreeably to the Duchess of Sussex conjuring her to go with her husband to the country and to follow her advice but not her example.

Thus Courtin. We must make allowance for his own love of scandal, and for the palates he sought to spice: but here, at any rate, we have a definite situation. Courtin's letter is dated November 27, 1676. We see that John's relations with Barbara have ended; that his father is pressing him to marry Catharine Sedley; that he is deeply in love with Sarah, but does not feel justified in his poverty in proposing marriage; that she is indignant at his delay and miserable about the other women and all the uncertainty and the gossip. We see her magnificent in her prolonged ordeal. We see John for the only time in these pages meditating flight from a field the difficulties of which seemed for the moment beyond his sagacious strength. Well is it said that the course of true love never did run smooth. The next chapter will, however, carry the lovers to their hearts' desire.

CHAPTER SEVEN

Marriage

ᵷᵭ 1676-78 ᴅᵹ

WE now approach the delicate question of how John freed himself from the Duchess of Cleveland. Unquestionably towards the end of 1676 he quitted Barbara for Sarah. Was he "off with the old love before he was on with the new"? Or was it one of those familiar dissolving views, where one picture fades gradually away and the other grows into gleaming, vivid life? Gossip and scandal there is a-plenty; evidence there is none. Of course, a married woman separated from her husband, unfaithful to him, notoriously licentious, who has a young man in the twenties as her lover, must expect that a time will come when her gay companion will turn serious, when all the charms and pleasures she can bestow will pall and cloy, and when he will obey the mysterious command of a man's spirit to unite himself for ever, by every tie which nature and faith can proffer, to a being all his own. But Barbara took it very ill, and after a brief attempt to console herself with Wycherley, the playwright, she withdrew from England altogether and took up her abode in Paris. Here she became intimate with Montagu, the English Ambassador to Paris, with results which after a while emerged upon the stage of history.

Let us turn to the love-letters, which plead John's cause to posterity, as well as to Sarah. The deadlock in their affairs continued, and she rightly challenged him to end it or to leave her.

MARRIAGE

Sarah to John

If it were true that you have that passion for me which you say you have, you would find out some way to make yourself happy—it is in your power. Therefore press me no more to see you, since it is what I cannot in honour approve of, and if I have done too much, be so just as to consider who was the cause of it.

John to Sarah

As for the power you say you have over yourself, I do no ways at all doubt of it, for I swear to you I do not think you love me, so that I am very easily persuaded that my letters have no charms for you, since I am so much a slave to your charms as to own to you that I love you above my own life, which by all that is holy I do. You must give me leave to beg that you will not condemn me for a vain fool that I did believe you did love me, since both you and your actions did oblige me to that belief in which heaven knows I took so much joy that from henceforward my life must be a torment to me for it. You say I pretend a passion to you when I have other things in my head. I cannot imagine what you mean by it, for I vow to God you do so entirely possess my thoughts that I think of nothing else in this world but your dear self. I do not, by all that is good, say this that I think it will move you to pity me, for I do despair of your love; but it is to let you see how unjust you are, and that I must ever love you as long as I have breath, do what you will. I do not expect in return that you should either write or speak to me, since you think it is what may do you a prejudice; but I have a thing to beg which I hope you will not be so barbarous as to deny me. It is that you will give me leave to do what I cannot help, which is to adore you as long as I live, and in return I will study how I may deserve, although not have, your love. I am persuaded that I have said impertinent things enough to anger you, for which I do with all my heart beg your pardon, and do assure you that from henceforward I will approach and think of you with the same devotion as to my God.

John to Sarah

You complain of my unkindness, but would not be kind yourself in answering my letter, although I begged you to do it. The Duchess goes to a new play to-day, and afterwards to the Duchess of Monmouth's, there to dance. I desire that you will not go thither, but make an excuse, and give me leave to come to you. Pray let me know what you do intend, and if you go to the play; for if you do, then I will do what I can to go, if [although] the Duke does not. Your not writing to me made me very uneasy, for I was afraid it was want of kindness in you, which I am sure I will never deserve by any action of mine.

Sarah to John

As for seeing you I am resolved I never will in private nor in public if I could help it. As for the last I fear it will be some time before I can order so as to be out of your way of seeing me. But surely you must confess that you have been the falsest creature upon earth to me. I must own that I believe that I shall suffer a great deal of trouble, but I will bear it, and give God thanks, though too late I see my error.

Here the door is firmly closed, and then opened with a chink again.

John to Sarah

It is not reasonable that you should have a doubt but that I love you above all expression, which by heaven I do. It is not possible to do anything to let you see your power more than my obedience to your commands of leaving you, when my tyrant-heart aches me to make me disobey; but it were much better it should break than to displease you. I will not, dearest, ask or hope to hear from you unless your charity pities me and will so far plead for me as to tell you that a man dying for you may hope that you will be so kind to him as to make a distinction betwixt him and the rest of his sex. I do love and adore you with all my heart and soul—so much that by all that is good I do and ever will be better pleased with your happiness than my own; but oh, my soul, if we might be both happy, what inexpressible joy would that be! But I will not think of any content but what you shall think fit to give, for 'tis you alone I love, so that if you are kind but one minute, that will make me happier than all the world can besides. I will not dare to expect more favour than you shall think fit to give, but could you ever love me, I think the happiness would be so great that it would make me immortal.

MARRIAGE

Sarah to John

I am as little satisfied with this letter as I have been with many others, for I find all you will say is only to amuse me and make me think you have a passion for me, when in reality there is no such thing. You have reason to think it strange that I write to you after my last, where I protested that I would never write nor speak to you more; but as you know how much kindness I had for you, you can't wonder or blame me if I try once more, to hear what you can say for your justification. But this I must warn you of—that you don't hold disputes, as you have done always, and to keep me from answering of you, and yourself from saying what I expect from you, for if you go on in that manner I will leave you that moment, and never hear you speak more whilst I have life. Therefore pray consider if, with honour to me and satisfaction to yourself, I can see you; for if it be only to repeat those things which you said so oft, I shall think you the worst of men, and the most ungrateful; and 'tis to no purpose to imagine that I will be made ridiculous in the world when it is in your power to make me otherwise.

John to Sarah

I have been so extreme ill with the headache all this morning that I have not had courage to write to know how you do; but your being well is what I prefer much above my own health. Therefore pray send me word, for if you are not in pain I cannot then be much troubled, for were it not for the joy I take in the thought that you love me, I should not care how soon I died; for by all that is good I love you so well that I wish from my soul that that minute that you leave loving me, that I may die, for life after that would be to me but one perpetual torment. If the Duchess sees company, I hope you will be there; but if she does not, I beg you will then let me see you in your chamber, if it be but for one hour. If you are not in the drawing-room, you must then send me word at what hour I shall come.

Sarah to John

At four o'clock I would see you, but that would hinder you from seeing the play, which I fear would be a great affliction to you, and increase the pain in your head, which would be out of anybody's power to ease until the next new play. Therefore, pray consider, and without any compliment to me, send me word if you can come to me without any prejudice to your health.

This unkind sarcasm drew probably the only resentful reply which John ever penned in all his correspondence with Sarah. The letter does not exist; but we can judge its character by his covering note to her waiting-woman, whose support he had doubtless enlisted.

Colonel John Churchill to Mrs Elizabeth Mowdie

Your mistress's usage to me is so barbarous that sure she must be the worst woman in the world, or else she would not be thus ill-natured. I have sent a letter which I desire you will give her. It is very reasonable for her to take it, because it will be then in her power never to be troubled with me more, if she pleases. I do love her with all my soul, but will not trouble her, for if I cannot have her love, I shall despise her pity. For the sake of what she has already done, let her read my letter and answer it, and not use me thus like a footman.

This was the climax of the correspondence. Sarah's response shows that she realized how deeply he was distressed and how critical their relations had become. She held out an offended hand, and he made haste to clasp it. Some days evidently passed before he wrote again, and this time his rebellious mood had vanished.

Sarah to John

I have done nothing to deserve such a kind of letter as you have writ to me, and therefore I don't know what answer to give; but I find you have a very ill opinion of me, and therefore I can't help being angry with myself for having had too good a one of you; for if I had as little love as yourself, I have been told enough of you to make me hate you, and then I believe I should have been more happy than I am like to be now. However, if you can be so well contented never to see me as I think you can by what you say, I will believe you; though I have not other people; and after you are satisfied that I have not broke my word, you shall have it in your power to see me or not—and if you are contented without it I shall be extremely pleased.

MARRIAGE

John to Sarah

It would have been much kinder in you, if you had been pleased to have been so good-natured to have found time to have written to me yesterday, especially since you are resolved not to appear when I might see you. But I am resolved to take nothing ill but to be your slave as long as I live, and so to think all things well that you do.

This was the only surrender to which the Duke of Marlborough was ever forced. It was to the fan of a chit of seventeen. Moreover, so far as we have been able to ascertain, his courtship of Sarah affords the only occasions in his life of hazards and heart-shaking ordeals when he was ever frightened. Neither the heat of battle nor the long-drawn anxieties of conspiracy, neither the unsanctioned responsibilities of the march to the Danube nor the tortuous secret negotiations with the Jacobite Court, ever disturbed the poise of that calm, reasonable, resolute mind. But in this love-story we see him plainly panic-stricken. The terror that he and Sarah might miss one another, might drift apart, might pass and sail away like ships in the night, overpowered him. A man who cared less could have played this game of love with the sprightly Sarah much better than he. A little calculation, a little adroitness, some studied withdrawals, some counter-flirtation, all these were the arts which in every other field he used with innate skill. He has none of them now. He begs and prays with bald, homely, pitiful reiteration. We see the power of the light which sometimes shines upon the soul. These two belonged to one another, and, with all their faults, placarded as we know them, their union was true as few things of which we have experience here are true. And at this moment in the depth of his spirit, with the urge of uncounted generations pressing forward, he feared lest it might be cast away.

We now reach at least the year 1677, and with it the final phase of the correspondence. It seems plain that they are engaged. The difficulties that remain are only those of time and means. He writes of an interview with his father, of the importance of Sarah not angering the Duchess of York, and of business arrangements for their future.

Frances, Lady Hamilton, had now arrived upon the scene, and Sarah seems to have threatened him with plans for going abroad with her.

John to Sarah

When I writ to you last night I thought I writ to the one that loved me; but your unkind, indifferent letter this morning confirms me of what I have before been afraid of, which is that your sister can govern your passion as she pleases. My heart is ready to break. I wish 'twere over, for since you are grown so indifferent, death is the only thing that can ease me. If that the Duchess could not have effected this, I was resolved to have made another proposal to her, which I am confident she might have effected, but it would not have brought so much money as this. But now I must think no more on it, since you say we cannot be happy. If they should do the first I wish with all my soul that my fortune had been so considerable as that it might have made you happier than your going out with your sister to France will do; for I know 'tis the joy you propose in that, that makes you think me faulty. I do, and must as long as I live, love you to distraction, but would not, to make myself the happiest man breathing, press you to ought that you think will make you unhappy. Madame, methinks it is no unreasonable request to beg to see you in your chamber to-night. Pray let me hear presently two words, and say I shall; and, in return, I swear to you if you command my death I will die.

One by one, as in a methodical siege, he had removed the obstacles which had barred the way. He had put aside his military prospects. Barbara was gone. Catharine was gone. The parents, still perhaps protesting, had given way. Evidently he had now in sight some means of livelihood sufficient for him and Sarah. Even now she did not soften her hectoring tone. But everything was settled.

Sarah to John

If your intentions are honourable, and what I have reason to expect, you need not fear my sister's coming can make any change in me, or that it is in the power of anybody to alter me but yourself, and I am at this time satisfied that you will never do anything out of reason, which you must do if you ever are untrue to me.

Sarah to John

I have made many reflections upon what you said to me last night, and I am of the opinion that could the Duchess obtain what you ask her, you might be more unhappy than if it cannot be had. Therefore, as I have always shown more kindness for you than perhaps I ought, I am resolved to give you one mark more—and that is, to desire you to say nothing of it to the Duchess upon my account; and your own interest when I am not concerned in it, will probably compass what will make you much happier than this can ever do.

We now come to the marriage. No one knows exactly or for certain when or where it took place. For several months it was kept secret. That poverty rather than parental opposition was the cause is proved by a remarkable fact. John's grandfather had strictly entailed his estates, and Sir Winston was only tenant for life. He was heavily in debt, and was now forced to appeal to his son for help. Just at the moment when some assured prospects were most necessary to his heart's desire, John was asked to surrender his inheritance. He did so for his father's sake. Part of the property was realized, and Sir Winston's debts were paid. At his death the remnant went to the other children. John, therefore, by his own act disinherited himself. This was a singular example of filial duty in a young man desperately in love and longing to marry.

He could not keep his wife in any suitable conditions at the Court. Once the marriage was announced all sorts of things would be expected. Mary of Modena, "the Dutchesse" of the letters, was the good fairy. She was the partisan of this love-match; she used all her power to help the lovers. Evidently something had to be done to provide them with some means of living. Although Sarah had expectations, and John had his pay and, of course, his £500 a year, "the infamous wages," these were very small resources for the world in which they lived. The future Queen threw herself into the marriage, and her generous, feminine, and romantic instincts were stirred. "None but the brave," she might well have exclaimed, "deserves the fair." We have seen in the letters traces of various plans which the Duchess favoured or tried to order to make some provision for the lovers. We do not know what arrangements were made. Something, at any rate, was assured. Some time in the winter of 1677–78, probably in Mary of Modena's apartments, the sacred words were pronounced, and John and Sarah were man and wife. There is a strong local tradition at Newsells Park, Royston, Hertfordshire, then in the possession of a branch of the Jennings family, that the dining-room had been specially built for the festivities of Sarah Jennings' marriage. Probably they passed their honeymoon here.

After nearly a quarter of a century of married life Churchill, sailing for the wars from Margate quay, wrote to his wife:

> It is impossible to express with what a heavy heart I parted with you when I was at the waterside. I could have given my life to have come back, though I knew my own weakness so much I durst not, for I should have exposed myself to the company. I did for a great while have a perspective glass looking upon the cliffs in hopes I might have had one sight of you.

Sarah, in a letter certainly later than 1689, and probably when he was in the Tower, wrote:

> Wherever you are, whilst I have life, my soul shall follow you, my ever dear Lord Marl and wherever I am I should only kill the time wishing for night that I may sleep and hope the next day to hear from you.

Finally when, after his death, her hand was sought by the Duke of Somerset:

> If I were young and handsome as I was, instead of old and faded as I am, and you could lay the empire of the world at my feet, you should never share the heart and hand that once belonged to John, Duke of Marlborough.

These are tremendous facts, lifting the relations of men and women above the human scene with all its faults and cares. They rekindle in every generous bosom the hope that things may happen here in the life of the humblest mortals which roll round the universe and win everlasting sanction

> Above Time's troubled fountains
> On the great Atlantic mountains,
> In my golden house on high.

Mrs Manley, the French Ambassador Courtin, and other scurrilous writers have dwelt upon the enormous wealth which John had extracted from the Duchess of Cleveland. However, it was five years after he had married the girl he loved before he could buy her a house of his own. They shifted from one place to another according as his duties or employment led him. They followed the Duke or the drum. For five years Churchill kept on his bachelor lodgings in Germaine Street (Jermyn Street), five doors off St James's Street, and here they stayed during their rare visits to town. Meanwhile at first she lived at Mintern with Sir Winston and his wife, both now getting on in years and increasingly impoverished.

It must have been a very sharp descent for the glittering blade, lover of the King's mistress, daring Colonel of England and France, and friend or rival of the highest in the land, and for the much-sought-after Sarah, to come down to the prosaic, exacting necessities of family life. However, they loved each other well enough not to worry too much about external things. This was a strange beginning for the life of a man who "in the bloom of youth loved lucre more than wine or women."

CHAPTER EIGHT

The Unseen Rift

ᚋ 1679-82 ᚌ

THIS chapter is gloomy for our tale. While the French power grew and overhung Europe, the political and religious storms which raged in England from 1679 to 1683 concentrated their fury upon the Duke of York. His change of religion seemed to be the origin of the evils that had fallen upon the realm. There was impatience with individual conscientious processes which disturbed the lives of millions of people. That one man should have it in his power, even from the most respectable of motives, to involve so many others in distress and throw the whole nation into disorder, weighed heavily on the minds of responsible people. Even the most faithful servants of the King, the most convinced exponents of Divine Right, looked upon James with resentment. They saw in him the prime cause of the dangers and difficulties which his loving royal brother had to bear. There he was, a public nuisance, the Papist heir whose bigotry and obstinacy were shaking the throne. His isolation became marked; the circle about him narrowed severely. Forced into exile in Belgium and now to be marooned in Scotland, his lot was cast in dismal years. With all the strength and obstinacy of his nature he retorted scorn and anger upon his innumerable foes—the subjects he hoped to rule. The ordeal left a definite and ineffaceable imprint upon his character. He felt some of the glories of martyrdom. Henceforward he would dare all and inflict all for the faith that was in him.

It was in the household of this threatened, harassed, and indignant Prince that the first four or five years of the married life of John and

Sarah were to lie. The wars had stopped, and with them for John not only pay and promotion, but all chance to use that military gift of which he had become conscious. He must follow a master, united to him by many ties, but a man unlovable, from whom his whole outlook and nature diverged—nay, if the truth be told, recoiled; a master who was at times an outcast, and whose public odium his personal servants to some extent shared. Between him and that master opened the almost unbridgeable gulf which separated Protestant and Catholic. Faithful and skilful were the services which Churchill rendered to James. Many a secret or delicate negotiation with the French King or with Charles II and the Court or with English political parties was entrusted to the discreet and persuasive henchman. The invaluable character of these services and the sense of having been his patron from boyhood onwards were the bonds which held James to him. But no services, however zealous and successful, could fill the hiatus between contrary religions.

However, the joys and responsibilities of the early years of married life redeemed for John and Sarah their harsh, anxious, and disturbed surroundings. They had in their family life an inner circle of their own, against which the difficulties of the Duke's household and the nation-wide hostility with which that household was regarded, might beat in vain.

John's earnest wish was to return from Scotland to England to see his wife and baby. His hopes of coming south were not ill-founded, for on January 29, 1680, Charles sent a welcome command to his brother to return. James lost no time in taking leave of his Scottish Government, and at the end of February transported himself and his household in the royal yachts from Leith to Deptford.

Churchill on the eve of the voyage begged his wife to

> pray for fair winds, so that we may not stay here, nor be long at sea, for should we be long at sea, and very sick, I am afraid it would do me great hurt, for really I am not well, for in my whole lifetime I never had so long a fit of headaching as now: I hope all the red spots of the child will be gone against I see her, and her nose straight, so that I may fancy it be like the Mother, for as she has your coloured hair, so I would have her be like you in all things else.

The family were united in Jermyn Street in the beginning of March, and John saw his child for the first time. We do not know how long the infant lived. It may well be that the sorrow of her death came upon them almost as soon as they were together again.

James spent the summer of 1680 in England, and hoped, with the King, that the new Parliament summoned for October might be more tolerant to him. He favoured Churchill's fitness to be Ambassador either to France or to Holland. In the latter case he was warmly seconded by William. Barillon's account of May 20, 1680, may serve.

> Mr Sidney [the English Minister at The Hague] will come home soon. It is believed he will not return and I am told that Mr Churchill [le sieur Chercheil] may well succeed him. If this is done, it will be to satisfy the Duke of York and to reassure him on all possible negotiations with the Prince of Orange. He [James] distrusts Mr Sidney, and has hated him for a long time. Mr Churchill on the contrary has the entire confidence of his master, as your Majesty could see when he had the honour of presenting himself to you last year. He is not a man who has any experience of affairs. It is also said that the Prince of Orange has declared that there should be no other Ambassador of England in Holland but him, and that it is only necessary to send docile personages who let themselves be led.

But all these hopes and projects, real or shadowy, came to naught. The new Parliament was fiercer than its predecessor. Shaftesbury was at the head of a flaming Opposition. A fresh Exclusion Bill advanced by leaps and bounds. The ferocity of the Whigs knew no limit, and their turpitude lay not far behind. Their cause was the cause of England, and is the dominant theme of this tale. Their conduct was sullied by corruption and double-dealing unusual even in that age. Their leaders without exception all took for either personal or party purposes French gold, while they shouted against Papist intrigues and denounced all arrangements with France. Upon this squalid scene Louis XIV gloated with cynical eyes. His agent Barillon, presiding over the dizzy whirlpools of Westminster and Whitehall, bribed both sides judiciously to maintain the faction fight. Thus Louis stoked the fires which burned away the English strength.

One name is conspicuous in its absence from the lists of shame—Churchill's. Yet how glad Barillon would have been to have slipped a thousand guineas into the palm of this needy Colonel and struggling family man! The artful Ambassador, as we see by his correspondence, was no friend to John. Any tittle of spiteful gossip or depreciatory opinion which he could gather he sedulously reported. Churchill, this influential, ubiquitous go-between, the Protestant agent of the Duke of York, was well worth tainting, even if he could not be squared. Sarah long afterwards wrote, "The Duke of Marlborough never took a bribe." Think how these lists have been scanned by the eyes of Marlborough's detractors. See how every scrap of fouling evidence has been paraded and exploited. Yet nothing has been found to challenge Sarah's assertion.

The approaching assembly of this hostile Parliament was sufficient to force the King again to expatriate the brother of whom he was so fond. On October 20 James and his household most reluctantly again set out by sea for Edinburgh. This time both the Churchills could go together. They endured a rough voyage of five days. James was received in Scotland with due ceremony; but the famous cannon known as 'Mons Meg' burst in firing its salute, and many were the superstitious head-waggings which followed the occurrence. This time James seriously undertook the government of Scotland, and set his seal upon a melancholy epoch.

Now, embittered by ill-usage, emboldened by anger, his thoroughgoing temperament led him to support the strongest assertions of authority. When, in June 1681, Churchill brought him from London his patent as Royal Commissioner he decided to make use of the Scottish Parliament to obtain an emphatic and untrammelled assertion of his right of succession. He summoned the first Parliament held in Scotland since 1673. He set himself to demonstrate here on a minor scale the policy which he thought his brother should follow in England. He passed through the Parliament of 1681 an anti-Exclusion Bill. He developed with care the anti-national Scottish army. He used the wild Highlanders, the only Catholics available, to suppress the contumacy of the Lowlanders. The torture of the boot was inflicted freely upon Covenanters and persons of obstinate religious opinions. On these occasions most of the high personages upon the Privy Council would make some excuse to leave the room. But accusing pens allege that the Duke of York was always at his post. Dark and hateful days for Scotland!

Churchill, apart from his aversion from cruelties of all kinds, was now placed in a most difficult and delicate position. James relied on him to make every effort to secure his return to Court, and to support his claims against Monmouth and the Exclusionists; while, on the other hand, Churchill's powerful friends in London, Sunderland, Halifax, Godolphin, and Hyde, told him to keep James in Scotland at all costs. Amid these conflicting currents no man was more capable of steering a shrewd and sensible course. He carried out his instructions from James with proper diligence and discretion; but, on the other hand, his cautious temper prevented the wilder threats of his master (about raising the Scots or the Irish in his own defence) from being "attended with consequences"; for he "frankly owned" to the French Ambassador that James "was not in a condition to maintain himself in Scotland, if the King his brother did not support him there."

In August 1681 the Duke of York's affairs in England were going from bad to worse, and the King was in desperate grapple with his brother's pursuers. An intense effort was concerted to persuade James to conform at least in outward semblance to the religion of his future subjects. His appeals to be recalled to England were made use of against him. The King offered to allow him to return if he would but come to church. Every one could see what a simplification his assent would make; and what a boon to all! His first wife's brother, Laurence Hyde, afterwards Earl of Rochester, was entrusted with the difficult task of his conversion to conformity, upon which the strongest family, social, and State pressures were engaged. Hyde, Churchill, and Legge were James's three most intimate personal servants. They had been with him for many years. His partiality for them had long been proved. Legge was absent, but we cannot doubt that Churchill supported Hyde with any influence he could command. Nothing availed. James was advised by his confessor that there could be no paltering with heresy. Such advice was decisive.

This incident deserves prominence because it evoked from Churchill one of those very rare disclosures of his political-religious convictions in this period which survive. He wrote to Legge the following letter:

Sept. 12, 1681, Berwick

Dear Cousin,

I should make you both excuses and compliments for the trouble you have been at in sending my wife to me, but I hope it is not that time of day between you and I, for without compliment as long as I live I will be your friend and servant. My Lord Hyde, who is the best man living, will give you an account of all that has passed. You will find that nothing is done in what was so much desired, *so that sooner or later we must be all undone.* As soon as Lewen has his papers the Duke would have [wish to] take the first opportunity by sea and come from Scotland. My heart is very full, so that should I write to you of the sad prospect I fear we have, I should tire your patience; therefore I refer myself wholly to my Lord Hyde and assure you that wherever I am, you and my Lord Hyde have a faithful servant of [in] me.

This letter, written so secretly to his intimate friend and kinsman seven years before the revolution of 1688, must not be forgotten in the unfolding of our story.

On December 12, 1681, the somewhat lackadaisical ninth Earl of Argyll was brought to trial for treason for explaining that he took the Oath of Allegiance "as far as it was consistent with the Protestant religion," and "not repugnant to it or his loyalty." By the exertions of James he was condemned to death. On the eve of his execution he escaped by a romantic artifice and for a time lay hidden in London. When the news of his refuge was brought to the King by officious spies, the tolerant Charles brushed them away with the remark, "Pooh, pooh, a hunted partridge!" His brother had a different outlook.

Churchill had deplored Argyll's sentence. He wrote to Sir John Werden, the Duke of York's secretary, and told him he hoped on account of their old friendship that Argyll would receive no punishment; and he wrote to George Legge that he trusted Argyll's escape from prison would be looked on as a thing of no great consequence.

The leaders of Scottish society were not men of half-measures. Affronted to the core by the ill-usage of their country as it continued year after year, they devoted their lives to practical schemes of vengeance, and they turned resolutely to the Prince of Orange. The flower of the Scottish nobility emigrated to Holland with deep, bitter intent to return sword in hand. All became unrelenting enemies of the House of Stuart. In the revolution of 1688 Lowland Scotland swung to William as one man.

In 1682 the long-sought permission to come to London was granted. James, with a considerable retinue of nobles and servants, embarked in the frigate *Gloucester* on May 4, 1682, to wind up his affairs in Scotland and bring his household home.

The catastrophe which followed very nearly brought this and many important tales to an end. But another revealing beam of light is thrown by it upon Churchill's attitude towards his master. The royal vessel was accompanied by a small squadron and several yachts, on one of which was Samuel Pepys himself. Two days out the *Gloucester* grounded in the night upon a dangerous sandbank three miles off Cromer, on the Norfolk coast, known as the 'Lemon and Ore.' After about an hour she slipped off the bank and foundered almost immediately in deep water. Although the sea was calm and several ships lay in close company, scarcely forty were saved out of the three hundred souls on board.

Numerous detailed and incompatible accounts of this disaster from its survivors and spectators have been given. Some extol the Duke of York's composure, his seamanship, his resolute efforts to save the vessel, and the discipline and devotion of the sailors, who, though about to drown, cheered as they watched him row away. Others dwell on the needless and fatal delays in abandoning the ship, on the confusion which prevailed, on the ugly rushes made for the only available boat, and finally portray James going off with his priests, his dogs, and a handful of close personal friends in the longboat, which "might well have held fifty," leaving the rest to perish miserably. Catholic and Tory writers, naturally enough, incline to the former version, and Protestants and Whigs to the latter. We have no concern with the merits of the controversy. What is important is Churchill's view of it. He, like Legge, was one of the favoured few invited into the boat by James, and to that he owed his life. One would therefore have expected that he would instinctively have taken the side of his master and, in a sense, rescuer, and would have judged his actions by the most lenient standards. Instead, he appears to have been the sternest critic. Sixty years later Sarah, in her illuminating comments on Lediard's history, writes as follows:

> * Since my last account of Mr Lediard's Book, I have read the account of the shipwreck of the *Gloucester* (page 40). The Truth of which I had as soon as the Duke [of Marlborough] came to Scotland from his own Mouth: (for I was there) who blamed the Duke [of York] to me excessively for his Obstinacy and Cruelty. For if he would have been persuaded to go off himself at first, when it was certain the Ship could not be saved, the Duke of Marlborough was of

the Opinion that there would not have been a Man lost. For tho'
there was not Boats enough to carry them all away, all those he men-
tions that were drowned were lost by the Duke's obstinacy in not
coming away sooner; And that was occasioned by a false courage to
make it appear, as he thought he had what he had not; By which he
was the occasion of losing so many Lives. But when his own was in
danger, and there was no hope of saving any but those that were
with Him, he gave the Duke of Marlborough his Sword to hinder
Numbers of People that to save their own Lives would have jumped
into the Boat, notwithstanding his Royal Highness was there, that
would have sunk it. This was done, and the Duke went off safe; and
all the rest in the Ship were lost, as Mr Lediard gives an account, except my Lord Griffin, who had served the Duke long, who, when the
Ship was sinking, threw himself out of a Window, and saved himself
by catching hold of a Hen Coop. . . . All that Lediard relates to filling the boat with the priests and the dogs is true. But I don't know
who else went in the boat, or whether they were of the same religion.

There can be no doubt that this is the real story which John told Sarah
in the deepest secrecy as soon as he and the other woebegone survivors
from the shipwreck arrived in Edinburgh. That no inkling of his servant's opinion ever came to James seems almost certain. We in this
afterlight can see quite plainly where the Churchills stood in relation
to James. It is not merely want of sympathy, but deep disapproval.
They served him because it was their duty and their livelihood. He
retained them because better servants could not be found elsewhere.
But all this lay far below the surface. The whole ducal household arrived at Whitehall, for good or ill, in the summer of 1682, and
Churchill was rewarded on December 21, 1682, for his patient, astute
diplomacy and invaluable services of the past three years with the
barony of Churchill of Aymouth, in the peerage of Scotland, and the
command of the second troop of the Life Guards.

CHAPTER NINE

The Princess Anne

ᘓ 1679-85 ᘔ

FEW stories in our history are more politically instructive than the five years' pitiless duel between King Charles II and his ex-Minister Shaftesbury. The opposing forces were diversely composed, yet, as it proved, evenly balanced; the ground was varied and uncertain; the conditions of the combat were peculiarly English, the changes of fortune swift and unforeseeable, the issues profound and the stakes mortal. For the first three years Shaftesbury seemed to march with growing violence from strength to strength. Three separate Parliaments declared themselves with ever-rising spirit for his cause. London, its wealth, its magistrates, its juries, and its mob, were resolute behind him. Far and wide throughout the counties and towns of England the fear of "Popery and Slavery" dominated all other feelings and united under the leadership of the great Whig nobles almost all the sects and factions of the Centre and of the Left, as they had never been united even at the height of the Great Rebellion. Thus sustained, Shaftesbury set no limits to his aims or conduct. He exploited to the last ounce alike the treacheries of Montagu and the perjuries of Oates. He watched with ruthless eye a succession of innocent men, culminating in Lord Stafford, sent to their deaths on the scaffold or at Tyburn upon false testimony. He held high parley with the King, as if from power to power, demanded the handing over of Portsmouth and Hull to officers approved by Parliament, indicted the Duke of York before a London Grand Jury as a Popish recusant, threatened articles of impeachment against the Queen, and made every preparation in his power for an eventual resort to arms. This was the same Shaftesbury who, as a Minister in the Cabal, had acquiesced only four years before in the general policy of the Secret Treaty of Dover, and only two years before had been a party to the Declaration of Indulgence—which in the name of toleration gave to Catholics the freedom they were denying to Protestants in every country where they were in the ascendant—and the acceptance of subsidies from France.

The King, on the other hand, seemed during the first three years to be almost defenceless. His weakness was visible to all. He was forced to leave Danby, his faithful agent, for whose actions he had assumed all possible responsibility, whom he had covered with his royal pardon, to languish for five years in the Tower. He dared not disown the suborned or perjured Crown witnesses brought forward in his name to prove a Popish plot, nor shield with his prerogative of mercy their doomed victims. He had to suffer the humiliation of banishing his brother and the insult of hearing his Queen accused of plotting his murder. He had to submit to, or perhaps even connive at his beloved son Monmouth joining the leaders of his foes.

All the while he lay in his voluptuous, glittering Court, with his expensive mistresses and anxious courtiers, dependent upon the dear-bought gold of France. And meanwhile behind the wrathful proceedings of justly offended faction-fanned Parliaments, Puritan England was scandalized, Cromwellians who had charged at Marston Moor or Naseby prayed that old days might come again, and the common people were taught to believe that the Great Plague and Fire had fallen upon the land as God's punishment for the wickedness of its ruler. Vulnerable in the last degree, conscious of his peril, and yet superb in patient courage, the profound, imperturbable, and crafty politician who wore the challenged crown endured the fury of the storm and awaited its climax. And in the end triumph! Triumph in a completeness and suddenness which seemed incredible to friends and enemies alike.

The turning-point of the conflict was the King's sudden dissolution of the Parliament of 1680. After the third election both Houses were convened at Oxford in March 1681, to avoid the violent pressures which the citizens, apprentices, and the mass of London could exert. Shaftesbury, after the Royal Speech, handed the King what was virtually an ultimatum in favour of the succession of Monmouth. "My lord, as I grow older I grow more steadfast," replied the King. Confronted with the attitude of the assembly, and finding that Oxford was a camp of armed bands whom a word might set at each other's throats, Charles proclaimed the dissolution, and lost no time in withdrawing under strong escort to Windsor.

Stripped of their Parliamentary engines, the Whigs turned to conspiracy, and beneath conspiracy grew murder. Their declared purpose to exclude James from the succession broadened among many into naked republicanism. "Any design but a commonwealth," said Shaftesbury to Lord Howard, "would not go down with my supporters now." There can be no doubt that schemes and even preparations for an armed national rising were afoot; nor that some of the greatest Parliamentary personages were active in them. Behind the machinations of the famous Whig leaders darker and even more violent forces stirred. Rumbold and other grim Cromwellian figures stalked the streets of London. A design to assassinate the King and the Duke where the road from Newmarket passed Rumbold's home, the Rye House, was discussed, and to some extent concerted, by a group of plotters in a London tavern. But while projects, general and particular, germinated in the soil, the mood of the nation gradually but decisively changed; its anti-Catholic rage had exhausted itself in the shedding of innocent blood, and public sympathy gradually turned to the sufferers and against their loud-mouthed, hard-swearing, vainglorious, implacable pursuers.

By 1683 the King was as safe on his throne as on the morrow of his coronation, nearly a quarter of a century before. He had come through an ordeal which few British sovereigns, certainly neither his father nor his brother, could have survived. For all his cynicism and apparent indolence and levity he had preserved the hereditary principle of the monarchy and its prerogative inviolate. He had successfully defended his brother's right to the throne; he had championed the honour of his Queen; he had obtained a more complete control of the national and municipal organs of government and of the judiciary than had existed since the days of his grandfather. He had never lost the support of the Episcopacy. He was poor, he was a pensioner of France, he was powerless on the Continent; but as long as he avoided the expenses of a foreign war he was master in his own house.

The next three years, 1683–85, form an interlude of peace and domestic sunshine in John Churchill's anxious, toilsome, exciting life. He was reabsorbed into the heart and centre of the Court he knew so well, and in which he had lived from childhood. He enjoyed the accustomed intimate favour of the King and the Duke. We read of his being one of Charles's two or three regular tennis partners—with Godolphin and Feversham, "all so excellent players that if one beat the other 'tis alternatively"—and of accompanying the royal party on various progresses or excursions. He was promoted to the colonelcy of the King's Own regiment of Dragoons. This improved the family income, but gave rise to jealous carpings.

> Let's cut our meat with spoons!
>   The sense is as good
>   As that Churchill should
> Be put to command the Dragoons.

The appointment was, however, not ill justified by events. Otherwise no important office or employment fell to his lot. It was perhaps the only easy, care-free time he ever had. No tortuous channels to thread, no intricate combinations to adjust, no doubtful, harassing, dire choices to take! Peace and, if not plenty, a competence. But as the dangers of the State and the need for action or manœuvre ceased, he subsided into the agreeable obscurities of home and social life. Charles seems to have regarded him as a well-liked courtier and companion whom he had long been used to have about him, as a military officer of a certain standing, as a discreet, attractive, experienced figure, a cherished piece of furniture in the royal household, but not at this time at all considered in the larger sphere of public affairs. Indeed, when he heard Churchill's name mentioned as one who might be Sunderland's Ministerial colleague the King said lightly that "he was not resolved to have two idle Secretaries of State." The Court subsequently explained the rumour by cheerfully affirming that Churchill had lately been "learning to write." So all was calm and quiet, and far better than those wearing years of journeyings to and from The Hague or Edinburgh to London on errands of delicacy or distress.

John could now live a great deal with his wife. He was even able upon the pay and perquisites of Colonel of the Dragoons and Colonel of a troop of Life Guards—the latter a lucrative appointment—to settle in the country. For the first time they had a home.

The Jennings family owned an old house and a few acres close to St

Albans, on the opposite side of the town to their manor of Sandridge. It was called Holywell House on account of a well in which the nuns of Sopwell had softened their hard bread in bygone times. It stood on the road close to the bridge over the river Ver. About 1681 John seems to have bought out Frances' share in this small property, which, together with the manor of Sandridge, was then owned by the two sisters. Evidently Sarah was attached to her native town and family lands. Some time in 1684 she and her husband pulled down the old house, which was ill situated, and built themselves a modest dwelling in another part of the grounds, surrounded by well-laid-out gardens and furnished with a fine fishpond. Here was Marlborough's home for life. The pomp and magnificence of Blenheim Palace were for his posterity. Indeed, he seems to have been somewhat indifferent to the noble monument which the nation reared in honour of his victories. It was Holywell House that claimed his affections. Within it he gathered the pictures and treasures which he steadily collected, and upon its pediment in later life he portrayed the trophies of his battles. Here it was he lived with Sarah and his children whenever he could escape from Court or service. It was to this scene, as his letters show, with its ripening fruit and maturing trees, that his thoughts returned in the long campaigns, and here the main happiness of his life was enjoyed.

Meanwhile their family grew. Poor "Hariote" was gone, but another daughter, Henrietta, born on July 19, 1681, survived the deadly perils of seventeenth-century infancy. John's third daughter, Anne—note the name—was born on February 27, 1684. She too thrived.

Although to outward appearance King Charles's Court was as brilliant and gay as ever, its inner life was seared by tragedy. The executions of great nobles whom everybody knew, like Stafford on the one side and Russell on the other; the ugly death in the Tower of Essex, so recently a trusted Minister, cast their shadows upon wide circles of relations and friends. Fear and grief lurked beneath the wigs and powder, ceremonies and masquerades.

John Churchill seems at this time to have been most anxious to withdraw his wife altogether from the fevered scene, and to live with her in the country, riding to London only as required by his duties, which were also his livelihood. Sarah dutifully obeyed her husband's wish. But an event occurred which frustrated these modest ambitions.

Hitherto little has been said about the Princess Anne. Henceforward she becomes the fulcrum of our tale. And here and now Sarah begins to play her commanding part. Her first contact with Anne had been in childhood. They had met in children's play at St James's when Sarah was ten and Princess Anne was only six. They were thrown together far more frequently when Sarah came to live in the palace, from 1673 onward. From the outset Anne became deeply attached to the brilliant, vivacious being who blossomed into womanhood before her childish eyes. The Princess was fascinated by Sarah's knowledge, self-confidence, and strength of character. She was charmed by her care and devotion, and by all her resources of fun and comfort which so naturally and spontaneously came to her aid. Very early indeed in these young lives did those ties of love, kindling into passion on one side, and into affection and sincere friendship on the other, grow deep and strong, as yet unheeded by the bustling world. There was a romantic, indeed perfervid, element in Anne's love for Sarah to which the elder girl responded warmly several years before she realized the worldly importance of such a relationship. "The beginning of the Princess's kindness for me," wrote Sarah in after-days,

> had a much earlier date than my entrance into her service. My promotion to this honour was wholly owing to impressions she had before received to my advantage; we had used to play together when she was a child, and she even then expressed a particular fondness for me. This inclination increased with our years. I was often at Court, and the Princess always distinguished me by the pleasure she took to honour me, preferably to others, with her conversation and confidence. In all her parties for amusement I was sure by her choice to be one.
> . . .

The passage of time gradually but swiftly effaced the difference in age, and Sarah as a married woman and mother at twenty-one exercised only a stronger spell upon the Princess of seventeen. "A friend," says Sarah,

> was what she most coveted, and for the sake of friendship which she did not disdain to have with me, she was fond even of that equality which she thought belonged to it. She grew uneasy to be treated by me with the form and ceremony due to her rank, nor could she bear from me the sound of words which implied in them distance and superiority. It was this turn of mind which made her one day propose to me, that whenever I should happen to be absent from her, we

might in all our letters write ourselves by feigned names, such as would import nothing of distinction of rank between us. Morley and Freeman were the names her fancy hit upon, and she left me to choose by which of them I would be called. My frank, open temper naturally led me to pitch upon Freeman, and so the Princess took the other, and from this time Mrs Morley and Mrs Freeman began to converse as equals, made so by affection and friendship.

John Churchill's relations with the Princess, although on a different plane from those of Sarah, were nevertheless lighted by a growing personal attachment. To secure her safety, her well-being, her peace of mind against all assaults, even in the end against Sarah herself, became the rule of his life. Never by word or action in the course of their long association, with all its historic stresses—not to the very end—not even in the bitter hour of dismissal—did he vary in his fidelity to Anne as Princess or Queen, nor in his chivalry to her as a woman.

Anne had but to reach maturity to become a factor of national consequence. Her marriage lay in the cold spheres of State policy. By King Charles's command, and with her father's acquiescence, she, like her elder sister, had been strictly bred a Protestant. The popularity of the union of William of Orange with Princess Mary in 1677 had already helped the King to hold his difficult balances at home and abroad. Here in days still critical was the opportunity for another royal Protestant alliance.

Charles now turned to a Danish prince. Although Prince George of Denmark was, of course, a Lutheran Protestant, he represented only a diminished Continental state, and the whole transaction seemed consigned to a modest plane. Prince George obeyed the command of his brother, the Danish King Christian V; and in July 1683 Colonel Churchill was sent to Denmark to conduct him to England to fall in love with the Princess Anne and marry her forthwith. George of Denmark was a fine-looking man, tall, blond, and good-natured. He had a reputation for personal courage, and by a cavalry charge had rescued his brother during a battle between the Danes and the Dutch in 1677. He was neither clever nor learned—a simple, normal man, without envy or ambition, and disposed by remarkable appetite and thirst for all the pleasures of the table. Charles's well-known verdict, "I have tried him drunk and I have tried him sober, but there is nothing in him," does not do justice to the homely virtues and unfailing good-humour of his staid and trustworthy character. Anne accepted with complacency what fortune brought her. Her uncle the King had so decided; her father acquiesced; Louis XIV was content; and only William of Orange was displeased.

On July 28, 1683, the marriage was solemnized with royal pomp and popular approbation. Prince George derived a revenue of £10,000 a year from some small Danish islands. Parliament voted Anne £20,000 a year, and the King established the royal pair in their suite in a residence called the Cockpit, adjoining the Palace of Whitehall, standing where the Treasury Chambers are to-day.

This marriage of policy in which the feelings of the parties had been only formally consulted stood during twenty-four years every ordinary strain and almost unequalled family sorrows. Anne suffered either a miscarriage or a still-born baby with mechanical regularity year after year. Only one cherished son lived beyond his eleventh birthday. At forty-two she had buried sixteen children; and when so many hopes and grave issues hung upon her progeny, none survived her. Her life was repeatedly stabbed by pain, disappointment, and mourning, which her placid courage, strong, patient spirit, firm faith, and abiding sense of public duty enabled her to sustain. Her life, so largely that of an invalid, attached itself to grand simplicities—her religion, her husband, her country's welfare, her beloved friend and mentor, Sarah. These dominants for many years wrought the harmony of her circle, and their consequences adorned her name and reign with unfading glory. Her love for her husband was richly renewed, and she knew no bounds in her admiration of his capacities. The romantic side of her nature found its satisfactions in her strangely intense affection for Sarah. And behind, ever faithful in her service, lay the pervading genius of Marlborough with his enchanted sword.

Anne lost no time in persuading her father to appoint Sarah one of her Ladies of the Bedchamber. In a manuscript essay by Sarah, called *A Faithful Account of Many Things*, the following suggestive, impersonal, and of course retrospective account is given of their relations:

> * The Dutchess had address and accomplishments, sufficient to engage the affections and confidence of her Mistress without owing anything to the want of them in others. But yet this made room for her the sooner and gave her some advantage; and she now began to employ all Her wit and all Her vivacity and almost all Her time to divert, and entertain, and serve, the Princess; and to fix that favour,

which now one might easily observe to be encreasing towards her every day. This favour quickly became a passion; and a Passion which possessed the Heart of the Princess too much to be hid. They were shut up together for many hours daily. Every moment of Absence was counted a sort of tedious, lifeless, state. To see the Duchess was a constant joy; and to part with her for never so short a time, a constant Uneasiness; As the Princess's own frequent expressions were. This worked even to the jealousy of a Lover. She used to say she desired to possess her wholly: and could hardly bear that she should ever escape, from this confinement, into other Company.

The closing years of Charles II were calm. In the wake of the passions of the Popish Plot and on the tide of Tory reaction the country regathered something of its poise. It seemed after a while as if the executions of the Popish and Rye House Plots had balanced each other, and a fresh start became possible. We observe the formation of a mass of central opinion, which, if it did not mitigate the strife of parties, could at least award the palm of success to the least culpable. This peculiarly English phenomenon could never henceforward be disregarded. Any party which ranged too far upon its own characteristic course was liable to offend a great body of men who, though perhaps marked by party labels, were by no means prepared to associate themselves with party extravagances.

At the end of the reign we see Charles working with several representatives of this moderate Tory view. Among these, opposed to Popery, opposed to France, mildly adverse to Dissent, content with peace, and respecting the government of King *and* Parliament, the famous Halifax was preeminent. His nature led him to turn against excess in any quarter; he swam instinctively against the stream. The taunt of "Trimmer" levelled at him by disappointed partisans has been accepted by history as the proof of his uprightness and sagacity. He compared himself with justice to the temperate zone which lies between "the regions in which men are frozen and the regions in which they are roasted." He was the foremost statesman of these times; a love of moderation and sense of the practical seemed in him to emerge in bold rather than tepid courses. He could strike as hard for compromise as most leaders for victory. Memorable were the services which Halifax had rendered to the Crown and the Duke of York. His reasoned oratory, his biting sarcasm, his personal force and proud independence, had turned the scale against the first Exclusion Bill. His wise counsels had aided the King at crucial moments, and he himself often formed the rallying-point for men of goodwill. His greatest work for the nation and for modern times was yet to be done. Meanwhile he stood, a trusted Minister, at King Charles's side in the evening of a stormy day.

Halifax must have represented Churchill's political views and temperament far more truly than any other statesman. Whether or not John learned war from Turenne, he certainly learned politics from Halifax. As we watch the Great Trimmer turning from side to side, from faction to faction, from Monmouth to William, or back again to James, yet always pursuing his aim of sobriety and appeasement at home and of marshalling all the best in England against Popery, autocracy, and France, we can almost see John's mind keeping pace and threading silently the labyrinths of intrigue in his footsteps. We are sure that when Halifax fought the Whigs against perjured testimony for the life of Stafford, and fought the Crown and the Tories against packed juries for the lives of Russell and Sidney, he carried with him the heartfelt sympathies of the Churchill who had resented the condemnation of Argyll, and whose humane conduct at the head of armies the histories of friend and foe were to proclaim.

Another figure, at that time classed among the moderates, who had sat at the council board was Sir Edward Seymour. He was "the great Commoner" of those days. A fervent Tory of touchy, rancorous temper, of independent and undependable character, with great wealth and position, he marshalled a hundred members from the over-represented West Country. He could upon occasion have produced an army from the same regions for a national cause. He was the first Speaker of the House of Commons who was not a lawyer.

The King himself basked in the mellower light which had followed so much rough weather. He had overcome his enemies; and at whatever cost to his dignity or honour had restored peace at home and kept out of war abroad. He could afford to forgive Monmouth, in temporary exile following an attempt to place him on the throne. He was strong enough to bring back James. He revolved with tolerant mind Halifax's desire to summon Parliament, and might well expect that it would be loyal and serviceable. He still balanced and measured the grievous, insoluble problems with which he was oppressed: the ferocious divisions of his people, his want of money—that damnable thing—his dependence upon France, the odious state of Europe, the dangers of renewed Parliamentary strife, and, above all, the anxieties of the succession. For all his loves and troop of bastards, he had no legitimate heir. Strong and unswerving as he had been for the strict application of the principle of hereditary right, no one knew better than he the awful dangers which James's religion and character would bring upon the land. In spite of his own profound leanings to the old faith of Christendom, he had never lost contact with, and had in the main preserved the confidence of, the Church of England. He had used the laws of England and its Constitution as effective weapons in his warfare with the Whigs. He had never broken these laws in the process, nor trespassed beyond an arguable legality. He knew and loved his brother well, and foresaw how James's virtues and vices alike would embroil him with a nation as stubborn and resolute as he.

Yet where else to turn? How England would have rejoiced could he have but given her his handsome, gifted courageous by-blow—"our beloved Protestant Duke"! But never would he vitiate the lawful succession of the Crown, nor tolerate that picking and choosing between rival claims which would transform an hereditary into an elective monarchy. Had he not for this wrestled with his people and his Parliament? Was not the fate of Russell, of Sidney, of Essex, a proof of his invincible resolve?

Then there was William: the busy—nay, tireless—fiery but calculating, masterful and accepted ruler of Holland, and foremost champion of the Protestant world. The blood royal of England flowed in his veins, and Mary his wife was second heir-presumptive to the Crown. Here was a foreign sovereign, backed by a constitutional government and loyal fleets and armies, whose profound interest in the succession had never been disguised. How shrewd and patient William had been; how skilfully he had steered a course through the English storms! The Prince of Orange was sure that James would never abandon the attempt to compel the English nation to submit to autocratic rule and Catholic conversion, and equally sure that the English nation would never submit to such designs. Hence in his farseeing way he did not wish James's powers to be specially limited by law. It was better for William that James should have a free hand, and if this led him to disaster, then at least his successor would not be a king with a mutilated prerogative.

Charles comprehended this situation with a nice taste; he knew all the moves upon the board. But what more could he do? At any rate, it seemed that time might be allowed to play its part. The King was only fifty-four; his health in general at this time seemed robust. To many intimates his life seemed as good as that of his brother. He could not measure the deep inroads which continuous sexual excitement had wrought upon his vigorous frame. Another ten years, to which he could reasonably look forward, might clarify the whole scene. So he returned with cordial acquiescence to the pleasures and amusements of his Court, toyed with Halifax's proposals for a new Parliament, rejoiced that the ship of State was for the moment on an even keel, and left the baffling problems of the future to solve themselves. They did so.

Churchill was by this time in the middle thirties. He was in a position to judge men and affairs upon excellent information. It is only here and there that some record of his opinion exists. We can judge his politics chiefly by his friends. He was not accustomed to air his views upon grave matters, and such letters as have been preserved concern themselves only with private or family matters. Churchill was definitely ranged and classed with the Tories—and with the high Tories—against all interference with his master's hereditary rights. He had the best opportunities of informing himself about the King's health; he had seen him a few years before smitten with a mysterious and alarming illness. It was now certain that if James were alive at the death of King Charles, he would ascend the throne, and Churchill had every reason but one to hope for the highest favour and advancement at his hands. Yet that one adverse reason was enough to undo all. The wise, observant soldier who had dwelt so long at or near the centre of power had no doubts whatever of the clash that must ensue between his devout, headstrong, bigoted, resolute patron and the whole resisting power of a Protestant nation. Here again his course was determined. In defence of the Protestant religion he would sever all loyalties, extinguish all gratitudes, and take all necessary measures. His wife's intimate, affectionate relations with the Princess Anne, her offer to undertake the office of her Lady of the Bedchamber, must have been in full accord with his wishes and designs. The influence, daily becoming decisive and dominant, which the Churchills exerted in the household of the Prince and Princess of Denmark was steadfastly used to strengthen and fortify its already marked Protestant character, and to link the young Princess with leading statesmen and divines who would confirm her vigorous faith.

The situation had, as we have seen, arisen naturally, by the invisible impulses of friendship and custom. It had now become a definite and primary factor in the Churchills' fortunes, as it was presently to be in those of the nation. From this time forward John and Sarah began to be increasingly detached from the Duke's circle, and noticeably associated —beyond the religious gulf—with his younger daughter. Indeed, during the reign of James II Churchill was regarded by an informed foreign observer as Princess Anne's friend and counsellor rather than the trusted servant of the new King. This in quiet times meant little, but a day was soon to come when it would mean everything. A connexion had been formed around the Protestant royal personage who stood third in the line of succession, cemented by a friendship and sympathy destined to withstand the shocks and trials of more than twenty years. This union of intense convictions, sentiments, habits, and interests was soon to be exposed to the sharpest and most violent tests, and to withstand them with the strength of solid rock.

The King seemed in his usual health at the beginning of 1685. After his dinner on the night of January 26 he sat, as was his custom, with the Duchess of Portsmouth and a small company of friends. Thomas Bruce, the Earl of Ailesbury, with whom Churchill's functions must often have brought him in friendly contact—to whom we owe most delightful, if sometimes untrustworthy, memoirs—was on duty as Gentleman of the Bedchamber. He found the King "in the most charming humour possible." But

> when we came to the district of the bedchamber, I by my office was to light him to the bedchamber door, and giving the candle to the page of the backstairs, it went out, although a very large wax candle and without any wind. The page of the backstairs was more superstitious, for he looked on me, shaking his head.

The King chatted agreeably with his gentlemen as he undressed, and spoke about the repairing of Winchester Castle and the gardens he was making there. He said to Ailesbury, "I will order John" (a familiar word for the Earl of Bath, the Groom of the Stole, who was with the

King when a boy) "to put you in waiting the first time I go thither, and although it be not your turn, to show you the place I delight so in, and shall be so happy this week as to have my house covered with lead." "And God knows," comments Ailesbury, "the Saturday following he was put in his coffin."

That night Ailesbury, lying in the next room, and "sleeping but indifferently, perceived that the King turned himself sometimes, not usual for him." The next morning he was "pale as ashes" and "could not or would not say one word." A violent fit of apoplexy supervened, and after gamely enduring prolonged torture at the hands of his distracted physicians Charles II breathed his last. All untimely, the long-dreaded event had come to pass. The interlude of peace was over, and King James II ruled the land.

CHAPTER TEN

Sedgemoor

ᏹ 1685 ᎠᏮ

FOR two years past James had played an active second part in the government of the kingdom, and once his brother's approaching end became certain, he concerned himself with every precaution necessary to ensure an unopposed succession. Indeed, it was not until after he had posted the Royal Guards at various important points, and had even obtained the dying King's signature to some measures of financial convenience, that, on the promptings of the Duchess of Portsmouth, he secured Charles's spiritual welfare by bringing a priest up the backstairs to receive him into the Church of Rome and give him extreme unction. Within a quarter of an hour of the King's death he met the Privy Council, whose duty it is to recognize the new sovereign. He laboured to contradict the belief that he was revengeful or inclined to arbitrary rule. He declared himself resolved to maintain both in State and Church a system of government established by law,

> for he recognized the members of the English Church as loyal subjects, he knew that the laws of England were sufficient to make the King a great monarch and that he would maintain the rights and prerogatives of the Crown, and would not invade any man's property.

It has even been asserted he went so far at this critical moment as to say that, "as regards his private religious opinions, no one should perceive that he entertained them," but that this sentence was deleted from the official report.

These declarations were received by the dignitaries and magnates of

(94)

the realm with profound relief and joy, and as the Royal Proclamation spread throughout the land it everywhere evoked expressions of gratitude and loyalty. Charles II had died at the moment when the Tory reaction was at its highest. The sentimental nature of the English people was stirred to its depth by the death of the King, who if he had tricked them often, had not, as they now felt, served them ill, and whose personal charm and human qualities and weaknesses were pervasively endearing. In the wave of grief and hope sweeping the nation the unbridgeable differences of faith, policy, and temper which separated a new prince and an old people were forgotten. James ascended the throne of his ancestors and predecessors with as fair a chance as ever monarch had.

The summoning of a Parliament, after a lapse of more than three years, was now indispensable. More than half the revenues of the State ceased upon the demise of the Crown. The need was otherwise unanswerable, and the hour could not be more propitious. On February 9 the writs were issued, and the general election of 1685 began. On the second Sunday after his accession, near noon, when the Court was thronged, King James and the Queen attended Mass and received the Sacrament in the Queen's chapel, the doors of which were thrown open for all to see. This act of high consequence dispelled the rosy hopes of the Protestant Court and aroused immediately the London clergy. But the Royal Proclamation, striking while the iron was hot, was not overtaken in those days of slow and imperfect news. The nation voted upon its first impulse and returned a Parliament which in quality and character represented all the strongest elements in the national life, and was in temper as loyal to the Crown as the Restoration Parliament of 1660. To this new Parliament James repeated his original declaration as amended. From it he received an enthusiastic response, and the revenues, grudged and meted to his brother, were to him voted in their amplitude for life. He had only to practise his religion for his conscience' sake as a man, to observe the laws of the realm, and to keep the promises he had made respecting them, in order to receive and enjoy the faithful service of his subjects for all his days. He began his reign with that same caution and moderation which had marked his first government in Scotland, and he reaped an immediate reward. Events were, however, at hand which would impel and empower him to cast aside these wise and vital restraints.

Churchill stood in good favour with the new régime. In the list of the nine Lords of the Bedchamber his name was second only to Peterborough's. His colonelcy of the Dragoons was confirmed; and he was immediately despatched on a mission to Versailles, the ostensible object of which was to notify Louis XIV of the accession, and its substantial purpose to obtain an increased subsidy for the English Crown. For this task his negotiations in 1679 and 1681 and his full knowledge of the secret relations of the two Kings had well prepared him. But Louis, taking time by the forelock, had forestalled the request. Before Churchill could reach Paris Barillon had waited upon James with an unsolicited gift of 500,000 livres, and it was thought only becoming to express gratitude for this modest favour before asking for the two or three millions a year which the English King and Court regarded as desirable. Churchill was therefore overtaken by fresh instructions, and his mission was limited to ceremonies and thanks. On this visit Churchill seems to have committed an unusual indiscretion. "The Earl of Galway," says Burnet,

> told me that when he [Churchill] came over [to France] in the first compliment upon the King's coming to the Crown, he said then to him that if the King was ever prevailed upon to alter our religion he would serve him no longer, but would withdraw from him.

He returned to England at the beginning of April in time for the splendours of the coronation. An English peerage was conferred upon him, and he became Baron Churchill of Sandridge. Rougher work was soon at hand.

The news of King Charles's death fell like a thunderbolt on his well-loved, wayward bastard at The Hague. Monmouth by his natural vivacity had lent a fleeting gleam of gaiety to the dull, strait-laced routine of the Dutch Court. Politics apart, he had been received with genuine relish. But in the midst of dancing and ice-carnivals came the news that, instead of a father about to consummate an act of forgiveness, there ruled in England an uncle who had suffered insult and exile through his rivalry, whose last six years had been consumed in struggling against the party he led, and who hated him with all the hatred of intimacy, alike as Protestant and as Pretender.

Monmouth's mood of despair led him to seek in the companionship of his fond mistress, the beautiful Lady Wentworth, a shelter from the mischances of public life. He quitted The Hague at William's request within a few hours, and settled himself with his charming friend at Brussels. But more turbulent and daring spirits were not so agreeably soothed. Argyll—the "hunted partridge"—in his Dutch retreat brooded intently upon the sanctity of synodical as opposed to episcopal Christianity, and burned to be in the Highlands again at the head of his adoring clansmen. The plotter Ferguson, Lord Grey of Wark, Wade, and a dozen or more prominent men who had escaped from England and Scotland after the Rye House exposure, gripped Monmouth and bound him to a fatal design. Lady Wentworth herself, who loved him so well, loved also that he should be a king. She offered her jewels and wealth for his service. All these exiles had in their minds the picture of England in 1682. They could not believe in the reality of a change of mood so swift and utter as had in fact occurred since then. Monmouth yielded against his better judgment to their importunities. It was agreed that Argyll should invade and rouse the Highlands and that Monmouth should land in England. Two tiny expeditions of three ships each, filled with munitions and bitter men of quality, were organized from slender resources, and three weeks after Argyll had set out for Kirkwall Monmouth sailed for the Channel.

Monmouth tossed on the waves for nineteen days, driven hither and thither by the winds. He escaped the numerous English cruisers which watched the Straits of Dover, and on June 11 dropped anchor in the Dorsetshire port of Lyme Regis. The Duke and his confederates, who had beguiled the anxious voyage with Cabinet-making, landed forthwith. Sword in hand, they repaired to the market-place, where they were received with rapture by the townsfolk, who, like themselves, were still living in the England of the Popish Plot, and looked back with reverence to the great days of Blake and Cromwell. Monmouth issued a proclamation, drawn up by Ferguson, accusing the King of having murdered Charles II, and of every other crime; affirming also that he himself was born in wedlock, and claiming to be the champion of the laws, liberty, and religion of the realm. The rush of adherents to enlist baffled the clerks who registered their names. Within twenty-four hours he was joined by fifteen hundred men.

Meanwhile messengers from the Mayor of Lyme, who abandoned the contumacious town, were riding as fast as relays of horses could carry them to London. On the morning of June 13 they broke in upon

Sir Winston with the startling news that his constituency was in rebellion. He took them to the palace, and, summoning his son, was conducted to the King.

This must have been a great day for old Sir Winston, and one in which all the harmonies of his life seemed to merge. Here was the King for whose sacred rights and line he had fought with sword and pen, for whom he had suffered so much, once more assaulted by rebellion. The old cause was once more at stake in the old place; and here stood his son, Colonel of the Dragoons, the rising soldier of the day, high in the favour of the threatened monarch, long linked to his service—he it was who would march forward at the head of the Household troops, the *corps d'élite*, to lay the insolent usurper low. It was Sir Winston's apotheosis. There must have been a strong feeling of the continuity of history in this small group coincidence had brought together.

Instant resolves were taken. All available forces were ordered to Salisbury. That very night Churchill set out with four troops of the Blues and two of his own Dragoons—in all about three hundred horse—followed by Colonel Kirke with five companies of the Queen's Regiment.

Monmouth could scarcely have struck a more unlucky moment: Parliament was in session, the King's popularity was still at coronation height. An Act of Attainder against Monmouth was passed. The price of £5000 was set on his head. The Commons voted large, immediate supplies, and both Houses assured the King of their resolve to die in his defence. Moreover, the troops from Tangier had already landed. A prompt requisition was presented to William of Orange to send back, in accordance with the convention under which they served, the six English and Scottish regiments maintained in Dutch pay. William lost no time in complying. He had been unable to stop Monmouth's expedition from starting—it had got safely away; he could now make sure that it was destroyed. However painful it must have been to him on personal grounds to aid in the ruin of his inconvenient Protestant rival—so lately his attractive guest—he had to do his duty. The troops were dispatched forthwith; and William even offered to come over in person to take command of the royal army. This kindly proposal was declined.

Churchill marched south with great rapidity. He reached Bridport on June 17, having covered 120 miles in four days.

On the 18th he was at Axminster, and on the 19th at Chard, in country which he knew so well (Ashe House was but eight miles away). Here his patrols came into contact with the hostile forces; and here also was a messenger from Monmouth reminding him of their old friendship and begging his aid. Churchill dismissed the messenger and sent the letter to the King.

Monmouth, at the head of some three thousand men and four guns, had entered Taunton on the 18th. Here he was received with royal state and lively affection. He was persuaded to proclaim himself King, thus confirming William in his sense of duty to James. The rebel numbers rose to above seven thousand, and he might have doubled them had he possessed the arms. His handful of cavalry, under Lord Grey of Wark, were mounted upon horses mostly untrained or even unbroken. His infantry were only partly armed with muskets, and for the rest depended upon scythes fastened on broomsticks. They had neither more nor less training than the militia, out of whom, indeed, they were largely composed. Nevertheless, in their zeal, in their comprehension of the quarrel, and in their stubborn courage, they were the ore from which the Ironsides had been forged.

John, appointed to the rank of Brigadier-General, certainly hoped, and probably expected, that he would have the command of all the troops available; but in this he was disappointed. There were second thoughts. On June 19 Sunderland wrote to inform him that the Frenchman Feversham had been appointed Commander-in-Chief. This was a significant event. Here was a campaign begun which he had in his own hands, on which his heart was set, and which he knew himself more capable than anyone to direct. He did not entirely conceal his anger. "I see plainly," he wrote on July 4 to Clarendon, "that I am to have the trouble, and that the honour will be another's." One of the remaining links which bound him to James's personal fortunes may well have broken here: nevertheless, with his customary self-control he subordinated his feelings to his duty and his policy, submitted himself with perfect propriety to Feversham, and directed his wrath solely upon the enemy.

Churchill, once in contact with the rebels, never let go. His well-trained force of regular cavalry, widely spread, enveloped and stabbed the flanks and rear of Monmouth's army. He followed them wherever they moved, changing from one flank to the other as occasion served, and always labouring to impress upon the enemy, and especially upon Monmouth, whose temperament he knew well, that they were aggressively opposed by the loyal regular forces of the Crown. At the same time he endeavoured to keep the militia out of danger, to have them concentrated and as far from the enemy as possible at points where he could, with his professional troops, ensure alike not only their lives but their fidelity.

Meanwhile such parts of the regular forces as could be spared from an agitated capital were approaching. Kirke, newly landed from Tangier, with his companies of the Queen's Regiment, joined Churchill at Chard on June 21. With this reinforcement Churchill revolved the chances of a decisive action. The quality and temper of the militia was, however, prohibitive; they were prone to join the rebels rather than fight them—in fact, they went over by whole companies. Churchill did not in this event feel strong enough to bar the way to Bristol, as was desired at Whitehall. No course was open to him but to await the arrival of the royal army, and meanwhile claw the enemy.

Monmouth's only chance was swiftness and audacity; without a wide, popular uprising he was doomed. The elements existed which might make him a King, but these elements were political rather than military. He must seize towns and cities and gain their arms and supplies before the royal troops arrived in strength. Bristol, the second city in the kingdom, was full of his partisans. Here was his first obvious objective. To gain the mastery of Bristol would be a formidable advantage. It was not until June 25, a fortnight after his landing, that, with forces now swollen to eight thousand foot and a thousand horse, he stood before the decayed ramparts of Bristol. He was too late. Feversham had entered the city on the 23rd with two hundred horse. The Duke of Beaufort held the hill where the castle had formerly stood, and thence intimidated the population. The royal army was already near Bath, and Churchill lay upon Monmouth's other flank. In these circumstances, only some of which were known to him, he abandoned his design; and with his turning back from Bristol his adventure became forlorn.

Churchill followed close at his heels, cutting off stragglers, hunting his patrols, and looking for a chance to strike.

On Friday, the 26th, Churchill joined Feversham at Bath, where his brother, Charles Churchill, had also arrived, having escorted a train of artillery from Portsmouth. The next day Feversham advanced with the

bulk of his forces to attack the rebels at Norton St Philip. The affair
was ill-conducted. Five hundred of the royal foot, with some cavalry
under the Duke of Grafton, involved themselves in a narrow lane, the
hedgerows of which were lined by Monmouth's musketeers. These two
by-blows of Charles II—bastard versus bastard—were locked in semi-
fratricidal strife. Feversham and Churchill both arrived on the scene.
The rebels fought stoutly, and the royal forces, drawing off with a loss
of eighty men killed, retired to Bradford in some dissatisfaction. In spite
of this incident, Monmouth's army began to melt. Two thousand men
deserted. A convoy of arms and stores which was sorely needed was
captured near Frome. Taunton, lately so ardent, sent a deputation to
beseech him not to return to their town. Upon all this came the tidings
that Argyll's revolt had been extinguished and that he and Rumbold
had already been beheaded. Despondency and fear began to overspread
not only Monmouth's troops, but all those friendly districts which had
compromised themselves in his cause. Nowhere did they weigh more
heavily than in his own heart.

On July 3 Monmouth in the deepest gloom re-entered Bridgwater,
which he had left eleven days before. Not one man of note had joined
him. His peasant army, officered by tradesmen, was wearied and perplexed by ceaseless marches and counter-marches in mud and rain, evidently to no purpose. But those fires still smouldered in their hearts
which success would have fanned into flame and which in many only
death could quench. On the 5th Feversham, with Churchill and all the
royal forces in one body, came from Somerton and camped at Weston
Zoyland. His cavalry billeted themselves in the village of Weston, on
the right of his line; his artillery was on the opposite flank, a quarter of
a mile farther off. The militia were left out of harm's way a good
many miles behind. Not counting these auxiliaries, he mustered seven
hundred horse, including the Household Cavalry and six battalions of
infantry—in all, nearly three thousand regular troops with sixteen
guns.

The two small armies were now scarcely three miles apart, and Monmouth must choose his course without delay. Should he assault the
royal position? Should he defend himself in Bridgwater? Should he
march once again northward on the Bristol road towards Gloucester-
shire, Cheshire, and the adherents who were believed to be assembling
there? To attack the regulars in the open field was to court destruction.

To be shut up in Bridgwater was only to postpone it. But the roads to the north were still open. He could certainly march past Feversham's right and cross the Avon at Keynsham before him. Though pursued, he would advance into a friendly region and a new scene. He chose the last alternative, and during the 4th and 5th disposed and prepared his forces with that intention. To deceive the enemy he employed the inhabitants of Bridgwater ostentatiously upon the fortification of the town, and also issued orders for a retreat upon Taunton. Churchill, who digested every scrap of information, wrote on the 4th to Clarendon:

> I find by the enemy's warrant to the constables that they have more mind to get horses and saddles than anything else which looks as if he had a mind to break away with his horse to some other place and leave his foot entrenched at Bridgwater.

Monmouth, in fact, meant to march with all his force—at least, at the outset. But when, on the morning of the 5th, he quitted Bridgwater and was crossing the town bridge to join his men in the Castle Field, a local farm labourer met him with intimate news of the royal army. It lay scattered in negligent fashion without entrenchment. The last night at Somerton no proper guards had been set; and it was said that laxity, drunkenness, and roystering prevailed. From the tower of Bridgwater Church the whole camp could be seen. Monmouth returned to the town, climbed the tower, saw for the first time the loosely spread camp, and took alike the most daring and the most prudent decision of his life—a night attack!

He called a council, and his supporters agreed. The plan was less simple than plans of war by night should be. The whole force would make a march of about six miles round Feversham's right. Grey's cavalry would branch off and, avoiding Chedzoy village, cross the Bussex Rhine at one of the plungeons to the east of the royal camp, surprise the Dragoons and Blues in Weston Zoyland, fire the village, and sweep round the rear upon the camp, the artillery, and the baggage at the same time that the infantry broke into the front of the position. It was a desperate cast; but Monmouth had about 3500 brave, determined men. In the night all cats are grey; and the confusion of a hand-to-hand grapple, with all its hopes of surprise and panic, was the best chance left. Indeed, it was a good chance; and but for this, that, and the other, no one knows what might have come of it. Accordingly, a little after eleven o'clock the rebels set forth along the Keynsham road, and after shuffling along for about two miles wheeled to the right into the mist of the moor.

Serious charges have been levelled at Feversham by many historians. Burnet declares that Feversham "had no parties abroad, . . . got no intelligence, . . . and was abed without any care or order." It is certain he was asleep in bed when the musketry fire exploded all around. The royal officers spoke of their commander with contempt, mocking at his broken English and declaring that he only thought of eating and sleeping. However, though he omitted to post a guard on the plungeon beyond his right flank, he had not fallen far short of ordinary military routine. He had camped in a good position; he had posted at least five strong pickets of horse and one of foot on the approaches from the enemy; he had an inlying picket of a hundred men under arms, and he had sent Oglethorpe's troop of the Blues to patrol both of the roads from Bridgwater to the north, whither he, like Churchill, expected Monmouth to attempt escape.

Meanwhile Monmouth and his men plodded onward across the moor, with Grey, guided by Godfrey, in the van. The Black Ditch, one of the great drainage ditches called 'rhines,' had been successfully crossed. Grey, with his scraggy cavalry and part of the rebel foot, were already over the second (the Langmore Rhine), and the clock of Chedzoy Church had struck one, when suddenly a vedette of the Blues fired a pistol in alarm. Frantic excitement broke out. The assailants were now very near their still sleeping foes. Contrary to most accounts, the rebels knew about the Bussex Rhine, and Grey and his horsemen, improvidently leaving Godfrey behind, rode forward, looking for the plungeon. He struck the ditch at an impassable point. Instead of working to the left in harmony with his mission to turn the flank and rear, he swerved to his right with most of his men and rode along the edge across the front of Monmouth's infantry, whose rear was still scrambling across the Langmore Rhine in the darkness behind him. Meanwhile the royal trumpets sounded, the alarm was given, the drums beat, and the threatened camp sprang in an instant into fury and confusion. The startled Grey saw through the mist a small array of gleaming lights and moved towards them. Some say he thought they were the lights of Weston. There was a different explanation. It had not yet been possi-

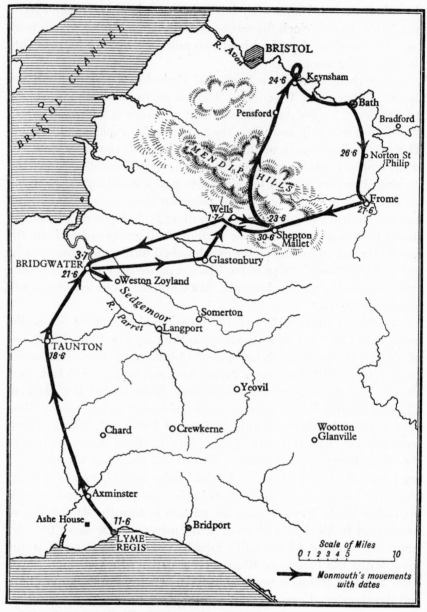

2. The Campaign of Sedgemoor, 1685

ble to rearm Dumbarton's regiment with flintlocks. The lights were their slow matches burning as the troops stood to arms. "Who are you for?" cried a voice from among the matchlocks. "The King." "Which King?" "King Monmouth, God with him!" "Take that with you," was the rejoinder, and a volley, followed at brief intervals by a second and a third as each platoon accomplished its ritual, crashed across the ditch. Grey or his untrained horses, or both, were stampeded, and scurried in complete disorder around the flanks of the infantry whom Monmouth was now leading up at the double, still in column of march. But the rest of the rebel cavalry had found the plungeon, and were only stopped at the last minute by Compton and a handful of the Blues from crossing by it.

Churchill had had a long day, but he was awake, armed, equipped, and on the spot. In the absence of his chief he instantly took command. The rebels, who halted to deploy about eighty yards short of the rhine, began to fire wildly across it, while the royal regiments were rapidly forming. The danger of their bursting into the camp had been averted; but they outflanked the royal right, and when their three cannon, under a competent Dutch gunner, began to fire at a hundred yards into the masses of Dumbarton's regiment and the 1st Guards, men fell fast. Churchill therefore rearranged the infantry. He made the two left-hand battalions march behind the others to prolong his front to the right, and summoned the artillery. These were very slow; but the Bishop of Winchester, 'Old Patch,' who accompanied Feversham as spiritual guide, took the horses out of his coach, and by these six guns were dragged successively to the critical point.

Churchill felt the injury Monmouth's artillery was working at such close quarters upon the infantry. It was probably by his orders that Captain Littleton, of the Blues, who were spread about the front, passed the plungeon, formed up on the other side, and just as the sky was paling with the first light of dawn charged and captured the rebel guns. He did not, as is usually stated, lead the charge of this small body himself. Some foot soldiers from the nearest battalion waddled across and held what the cavalry had gained.

The firing had now lasted nearly three hours without the two sides being able to come to grips, and, according to Wolseley, the rebel ammunition was running short. Certainly their wagons with the reserve of powder and ball, left two miles behind, had been deserted by the teamsters in the panic of Grey's horse. Day was breaking, and the royal artillery had at length arrived. Drear and doom-like was the dawn to Monmouth. He knew, as an officer experienced in Continental warfare, that his chance had failed and nothing could now save his little army. It is amazing he did not resolve to die on the field with all these earnest simples he had drawn to their fate. But had he been capable of that, he would have been capable of so much more that all our tales would be different. Just as the full light grew upon the plain he, with Grey, who had now rejoined him after his excursion, and about fifty horsemen, rode from the field, hoping to reach a port and seize a ship. On the rising ground beyond the moor these fugitives and deserters drew rein. There, still on the edge of the fatal ditch, stood the stubborn remnants of the Nonconformist foot. The royal cavalry enveloped them or pursued their routed comrades. Feversham's infantry, who were able to cross the ditch everywhere without apparent difficulty, advanced upon them at the charge; but the valiant peasantry, miners, and weavers, small, devout folk serving the Lord in humble station, with the butts of their muskets and their scythes met the regulars breast to breast, and closed their ranks with invincible behaviour. At last the cannon came into action upon this lump of men. All the sixteen guns had to fire for a considerable time before it was torn to shreds and the scattered survivors fled, the prey to a merciless pursuit. Of this tragedy Monmouth had but one fleeting glance. He only knew that his followers were still resisting when he quitted the field.

We must not be drawn too far from our particular theme. Enough that the charming, handsome prince was caught—drenched and starving—in a ditch; that, carried to London, he grovelled in vain for life at the knees of his implacable uncle; that he repudiated the cause for which he had fought; that he offered to turn Catholic to save not his soul, but his life; and that finally, when these discordant sounds were ended, he died with perfect composure at the hands of a clumsy and demoralized executioner. The Lady Wentworth followed him a few months later, her heart being broken. Death can be kind.

By noon on the 6th Churchill was in Bridgwater with a thousand soldiers. Unhappy town, with its rank offences, its wounded, its mobs of prisoners or fugitives, its terrified inhabitants! Feversham followed more slowly. He had the Continental view of war. To him these English peasants and common folk were but an unsuccessful jacquerie. He had to festoon the trees with hanged men. With him was Kirke, who had the Tangier outlook, and whose soldiers, newly returned from the crusade against the Moors, bore the emblem of the Paschal Lamb. He and his Lambs showed no mercy except for cash. Worse still was to come.

It is pleasant to find that the foremost man in the fighting had no part in the aftermath of atrocities. Churchill seems to have disentangled himself from the tortured West Country with astonishing deftness. The rout having been accomplished, he returned home.

The royal rewards for the victory went to Feversham; he received the Garter and the command of the first and most lucrative troop of the Life Guards. But nothing could free the public mind from the impression that Churchill had saved and won the battle. The whole Army knew the facts.

We must suppose in our attempt to revive from these fragments of history the personality of John Churchill that his treatment by James during and after the Sedgemoor campaign crystallized their private relations. John's sagacious eye weighed with precision his claims upon the royal favour. He must also have comprehended the King's point of view as fairly as he would have measured the virtues and weaknesses of any other adversary, once classed as such. But, apart from his own course and career, there were some matters which stirred his depths. To the butcheries of the Sedgemoor battlefield succeeded the horrors of the Bloody Assize. The Lord Chief Justice Jeffreys, quick to catch his master's mood and spurred by his own sadistic passions, wreaked vengeance upon Bridgwater, Taunton, and the guilty countryside. Nearly four hundred executions marked his progress. Twelve hundred rebels were sold as slaves for the Trinidad and Barbados plantations. To this day in Trinidad there exists a colony of white men who, though they have not intermarried with the negroes, toil as equals at their side. They are called the 'red-legs.' They have lost all track of their origin or family trees. Their names have perished; and few there are who know that they include the rearguard of Monmouth's army, lagging a couple of centuries behind.

CHAPTER ELEVEN

Plot and Counter-Plot

ᙓᚩ 1685-88 ᚩᙔ

In the autumn of 1687 the King made a royal progress in the West of England. Churchill accompanied him. They traversed many of the districts which two years before had been aflame for Monmouth. But the resolve of the King to extend liberty of conscience to the Nonconformists, although it was but a help for his Catholic policy, had raised hopes which for the moment almost effaced the memories of the Bloody Assize. The Catholic King received a passable welcome from the ultra-Protestants whose relations he had lately slaughtered or sold into slavery. 'Liberty of conscience' and the removal of the penal laws were war-cries which drowned even the screams and lamentations of the hideous yesterday. James felt that, with his Army dominated by Irish soldiers and Catholic officers and allied to the Dissenting masses of the Cromwellian tradition, he could afford to brave the wrath of the old, devoted friends of his house, of his line, of his person. Vain hope! Frightful miscalculation! At the best a desperate enterprise! At the least the lists were set for a destructive civil war. But was it not his duty, if need be, to tear his realm to pieces for his soul's salvation and the glory of God? Thus this melancholy zealot persevered along the road to his own ruin.

On this same progress in the West the King touched about five thousand people for the King's Evil, and at Winchester was attended in the ceremony by Catholic priests.

The provocations of the royal policy constantly increased. The publication of Dryden's *The Hind and the Panther* offers their poetical

(108)

justification. In April 1687 the King, dispensing with the law by his prerogative, issued his first Declaration of Indulgence. The spring saw his attempt to force a Catholic President upon Magdalen College, Oxford, and the expulsion of the Fellows for their resistance. In July James planned the public reception of the Papal nuncio, d'Adda. The Duke of Somerset when commanded to conduct the ceremonial objected on the ground that the recognition of Papal officials had been declared illegal at the Reformation. "I am above the law," said James. "Your Majesty is so," was the reply, "but I am not." He was at once dismissed from all his offices.

The King had, in modern parlance and now familiar style, set up his political platform. The second step was to create a party machine, and the third to secure by its agency a Parliament with a mandate for the repeal of the Tests. The narrow franchise could be manipulated to a very large extent by the Lord-Lieutenants of counties, by the magistrates, and in the towns and cities by the corporations. Upon these, therefore, the royal energies were now directed. The Lord-Lieutenants, including many of the greatest territorial magnates, who refused to help pack a favourable Parliament, were dismissed, and Catholics or faithful nominees of the Court installed in their place. The municipal corporations and the benches of magistrates were drastically remodelled so as to secure the fullest representation, or even the preponderance, of Papists and Dissenters. The Government tried to extort from all candidates a pledge to vote for the King's policy.

These measures implied a complete political and social transformation. The nobility and the country gentlemen were outraged by being either turned out of their local dignitaries or made to receive representatives of the hitherto depressed classes as colleagues. The process of setting Papists and Dissenters over, or in place of, Anglicans and Cavaliers must rupture and recast the whole social structure of English life. The purpose, character, and scope of these measures were profoundly comprehended in that incredibly rigid society from the proudest, wealthiest nobles down to the mass of the common people in town and village. The simples, like the gentles, feared the Pope, hated the French, and pitied the Huguenot refugees. They too, though voteless, counted. Their superiors could not be insensible to an atmosphere of ardour and goodwill around them.

The six English and Scots regiments in Dutch pay and service which had been sent over to resist Monmouth had all returned to Holland. James and his Ministers became apprehensive lest this fine body of men should some day pay them another and less friendly visit. For some months in 1687 James and Louis were trying to arrange for the transfer of these regiments from the Dutch service to the French. Churchill seems to have used all his personal influence—such as it then was—with James to prevent their departure from Holland, and to obtain the command of them in Holland for himself.

Churchill's desire for the appointment, the significance of which is apparent, was, as Sunderland foresaw, frustrated. But the troops stayed in Holland. William and the States-General, for reasons becoming increasingly obvious, refused point-blank to let them go. An acute tension arose between the two Governments. Their fundamental differences were exposed, and for the first time war was felt to be in the air.

The defenders of James's conduct are concerned to exaggerate the number of English Catholics. It is even claimed that one-eighth of the population still adhered, in spite of generations of persecutions, to the Old Faith. According to a return of 1689, there were then only 13,856 Catholics in the whole country, or less than one in four hundred of the people. The royal attempt to make a remarkable political spectacle of these few thousands of Papists, advanced to the headship of local and national affairs, even though supported by the Dissenters, was bound to range all the dominant national forces, incomparably stronger, against the Crown. The old Catholic families in England, apart from individuals advanced to high office, were deeply apprehensive of the headlong adventure upon which the King was launching them. They felt this sudden disproportionate favour was far from being in their true interests, and would only bring upon them the wrath and frightful passions which were being raised all about them. Still the King hardened his heart and strengthened his Army.

For many months, however, there was still parley. The parsons preached against Popery. Statesmen and divines exerted themselves by the dispersal of pamphlets throughout the country to offset James's attempt to rally the Nonconformists. Halifax issued his cogent *Letter to a Dissenter*.

Churchill had, as we have seen, entered fully into all the movements of protest against the royal policy. In December 1686 Anne had written to Mary assuring her of the strong Anglicanism of the Churchills. In March 1687 Churchill had conversed with Dykevelt. In May he wrote to William. In November he tried to get the command of the English regiments in the Dutch service, and so escape from the net which was closing round him at home. In December he supported and animated Anne in her endeavour to retain in her service Lord Scarsdale despite his refusal, as Lord-Lieutenant of Derbyshire, to obey James's orders. Finally, in January 1688 Churchill told James directly that he would not himself support the repeal of the penal Tests. A contemporary letter of January 12 states, "Lord Churchill swears he will not do what the King requires of him."

No man in all the stately company that represented the national character in these crucial days had made his opinion more plain, but James continued to rely on the intimacies and fidelities of twenty years of service on one hand and his benefactions on the other. He could not realize the truth that personal gratitude could never weigh in any great mind against the issues now presented to Englishmen. He knew Churchill loathed his policy, but fondly believed he loved his person more. At the crunch he was sure he could count on his influence, his diplomacy, and his sword. Meanwhile master and servant dwelt in all their old familiarity, and Churchill was constantly at the King's side in his bedroom, at his toilet, behind his chair at meals, and on horseback beside his carriage, just as he had been since he was a page.

How did this prolonged situation, with its many delicate, repugnant, and irreconcilable features, affect his inner mind? Was he distressed or was he indifferent about his personal relations with the King? On the surface he showed no trace of embarrassment. He possessed to a degree almost sublime the prosaic gift of common sense. His sure judgment and serene, dispassionate nature enabled him, amid the most baffling problems of interest and duty, to dwell inwardly and secretly at peace with his gravely taken decisions; and, of course, without further self-questionings to take in due season all measures necessary to render them effectual. The personalities which warm our hearts often cast much away from sentiment or compunction. Not so this man. He made up his mind with cold, humane sagacity, and a profound weighing of all the largest and smallest circumstances: and thenceforward he faced obloquy, if it were inevitable, as calmly as the ordinary chances of battle, after all had been done to prepare victory with the least loss of life. From the beginning of 1686 onward he was resolved to resist his master's designs. He saw in the Prince of Orange the agent who alone could bring in the indispensable armed power. He made his choice, if the worst should happen, to quit James and join William. He saw that the importance of his part in such a conflict would be measured by his influence over the Princess Anne and by his authority in the Army. If the hour of action should strike, he meant to use both potent factors to achieve, as smoothly and reasonably as possible, the public purpose and success of the course he had chosen.

In modern times such decisions would not be required. An officer or a courtier could resign his employments, retire to the country, and await events or the process of public reaction to his sacrifices. But for Churchill to leave the Court, to resign his command in the Army, would not merely have meant exclusion from all forms of public service and from all share in the impending crisis. No one who had been so close to the sovereign could, while he was in the full flush of manly activity and acquainted with so many secrets, retire without incurring the gravest suspicions. Instead of dwelling at Holywell with his family, he would probably have found himself in the Tower. He could, no doubt, have attempted to leave the kingdom and follow the long string of refugees and exiles who gathered in the Netherlands. But a simple flight like this would have been only to abandon simultaneously his King and his country; at once to desert the cause of Protestantism and to leave the Princess Anne, who had hitherto followed his guidance and depended so much upon him, in complete isolation.

He had certainly made two definite attempts to quit the Court under conditions which would not have entirely divested him of power, and thus to end a personal connexion with James already become false and painful. If Princess Anne had been allowed to go to The Hague, as he had planned, he and Sarah would certainly have gone with her. If he had obtained command of the British troops in Holland he would have been at William's side and in a position to exert an influence upon events. These courses had been barred: and, apart from reducing himself to a cipher and destroying all his means of service to causes which profoundly stirred him, there was nothing left but to remain and face all the dangers and peculiar reproaches of his station. All he could give the King was the faithful declaration of his opinion, and this on many occasions he made abundantly clear. If James, knowing his mind, employed him, it was at his own risk.

It was remarkable, indeed, that the King still kept Churchill about him. He made it plain to all his intimates that those who sought his favour, or still more his friendship, must embrace his faith. Many of his personal attendants yielded to the glamour of the royal smile or the fear of the royal frown. Salisbury, Melfort, Lorne, and many others thought that office was well worth a Mass. And no one needed official employment more than Churchill. He had no spacious estates in which to dwell, he lived only in the Court, at the head of his regiment, or with the prince he served; but to all attempts upon his faith he remained obdurate. He watched with silent disgust Sunderland, with whom he had many relationships and was to have more, take the plunge. The chief Minister of England, with all his wealth and high birth, bare-headed and barefooted, knelt in his shirt and knocked humbly at the door of the confessional. Churchill had only to imitate him to be the King's right arm, captain of his host, his long-cherished friend.

He never seems to have had the slightest trouble in rejecting such possibilities. Of course, he was a devout and lifelong Anglican Protestant. But we doubt if his choice, as his apologists contend, was made only upon religious grounds. He had a political opinion too. He knew England, and measured with superior accuracy the force of the passions now rising throughout the land. All the great men whose friendship he enjoyed, Halifax, Shrewsbury, Rochester, were moving in the one direction. On that same course he had launched the Princess Anne. Never mind the army at Hounslow! There would—at the worst—be two opposite factions there, and beyond the seas there was the Prince of Orange with trustworthy troops. But suppose it was the French who landed, instead of the Dutch! Still, he had chosen the part he would play.

The phrases 'religious toleration' and 'liberty of conscience' command spontaneous approval in modern times. The penal laws against Catholics and Dissenters were harsh and bitter. To create an England in which all men could seek God as they pleased and dwell in peace with their fellows was indeed a noble aim for a King. But it was not the aim of King James the Second; he sought the conversion of England to the Roman Catholic faith. He admired and applauded the intolerance of Louis XIV; he rejoiced intensely at the revocation of the

Edict of Nantes; he longed to use against the heresy in which his kingdom was sunk the secular terrors and torments which his brother sovereign could so happily apply.

Our ancestors saw, with the uncanny shrewdness which long, slow, increasing peril engenders, an endless vista of oppression and persecution, decked in a tinsel of fair-seeming toleration. They saw daily landing on their shores the miserable victims of Catholic 'toleration' as practised in France by the most powerful sovereign in the world. They knew the close sympathy and co-operation of the French and English Governments: they saw all that they cared for in this world and the next threatened, and if they failed to defend their rights and freedom, there might soon be no refuge open to them in any part of the globe. They therefore entered, not without many scruples and hesitations, but with inexorable resolve, upon the paths of conspiracy and rebellion.

If appeal is made to present-day opinion, the tribunal, while it acclaims 'religious toleration,' will at the same time inquire whether the conspiracy was only upon one side. Must the whole British nation submit, as the French people had been forced to do, to the religious convictions—whatever they might be or might become—of their anointed King? Was that King to be absolved from all reproach if night and day he concerted his plans, marshalled his adherents, trained his armies, in order to change the whole life, laws, and beliefs of his people? Was he entitled to break the solemn promises he had made, to practise every deceit and manœuvre which served his purpose, to use all the pressures of force and favour to compel obedience? Was he not guilty in his turn of conspiring against the people over whom he ruled? Was he not in rebellion against all that was most sacred, most precious, to the hearts of millions? Surely, then, it was a double conspiracy that was afoot, and must now on both sides go forward to an issue.

CHAPTER TWELVE

The Protestant Wind

↝ 1688, Autumn ↜

THE lines of battle were now slowly yet remorselessly drawing up in our
island. Everything pointed, as in 1642, to the outbreak of civil war; but
now the grouping of the forces was far different from the days when
Charles I had unfurled his standard at Nottingham. The King had a
large, well-equipped regular army, with a powerful artillery. He believed
himself master of the best, if not at the moment the largest, navy
afloat. He could call for powerful armed aid from Ireland and from
France. He held the principal sea-ports and arsenals under trusty Catholic governors. He enjoyed substantial revenues. He had on his side his
Catholic co-religionists, all the personal following which the Government and the Court could command, and, strangely assorted with
these, a very considerable concourse of Dissenters and traditional
Roundheads. He assumed that the Church of England was paralysed
by its doctrine of non-resistance, and he had been careful not to allow
any Parliament to assemble for collective action.

Ranged against him were not only the Whigs, but almost all the old
friends of the Crown. The men who had made the Restoration, the
sons of the men who had fought and died for his father at Marston
Moor and Naseby, the Church whose bishops and ministers had so
long faced persecution for the principle of Divine Right, the universities who had melted their plate for King Charles's coffers and sent
their young scholars to his armies, the nobility and landed gentry
whose interests had seemed so bound up with the monarchy: all, with

bent heads and burning hearts, must now prepare themselves to outface their King in arms.

It would indeed have been a strange war in which the sons of Puritans, Roundheads, and regicides would have marched for a Catholic and catholicizing King against Churchmen and Cavaliers, while the mass of the people remained helpless, passionate, terrified spectators. It would have been a war of the extremes against the means; a war of a heterogeneous coalition against the central body of English wealth, rank, and grit. Few there were who could truly measure the value of all these various elements and the force of their harmonious combination, should it occur. And above and beyond all lay the incalculable hazards and accidents of the battlefield.

Very fearsome and dubious must the prospect have seemed to the nobility, gentry, and clergy who embodied the life and meaning of the England that we still know. They had no army; they had no lawful means of resistance, expression, or debate. They could not appeal to the unenfranchised millions of peasants and townsmen. They saw in mental eye the King in martial panoply advancing upon them with all that royal power in whose sanctity they themselves were the chief believers, with French troops ready to descend at any moment upon their shores to quell rebellion, with the children of the Ironsides hand in hand with Jesuit priests. Never did the aristocracy or the Established Church face a sterner test or serve the nation better than in 1688. They never flinched; they never doubted. They comprehended and embodied "the genius of the English nation," they faced this hideous, fraudulent, damnable hotch-potch of anti-national designs without a tremor, and they conquered without a blow. Why they conquered and, above all, why they conquered bloodlessly, turned upon the action of no more than as many men and women as can be counted upon one's fingers.

Nearly all the preliminaries of the struggle in England were concerned with public opinion. The King could give his orders to the land and sea forces, and to all his great officers and adherents. He possessed a complete executive machine which, if it worked, was probably irresistible. But the nobility, the parsons, squires, and merchants who formed the conscious entity of England, were divided by the recent feuds of Whig and Tory and by many gradations of unorganized thought and temper. Their salvation depended upon their cohesion, and that cohesion could only be achieved by spontaneous action arising in a hundred loosely connected centres. Here lay the main risk. Unless their leaders could act together, each playing his part in his own station, their chances were precarious. Together they had to wait for indefinite and uncertain periods, together they must strike with the hour. Yet to concert action was treason.

In so wide and secret a confederacy, with scanty means of council and communication, every divergence, personal or local, was pregnant with disaster. Two main divisions of policy persisted almost to the end; each had massive arguments. The moderates, led by Halifax and Nottingham, urged caution and delay. The Ministry, they pleaded, was breaking up. Sunderland, Godolphin, Dartmouth were now striving to restrain the headstrong King. Alternatively, "Let him have rope enough!" Either things would get better or an overwhelming case would be presented upon which all could unite. No case had yet arisen to warrant actual treason. Nothing was more imprudent than a premature resort to arms. Remember Sedgemoor only three years ago, and how a standing army rallies to its duty once fighting has begun, and the soldiers see an enemy before them. "All is going well, if you do not spoil it."

On the other hand stood the party of action, headed by Danby. Danby was the stalwart. He was the first man of great position who definitely set himself to bring William and a foreign army into England. With Danby were the Whig leaders—Shrewsbury, Devonshire, and some others. These men urged that the danger was growing each day; that the King was bringing over Irish troops, that the Catholic grip upon the Army was strengthening, that the House of Lords could be watered and the House of Commons packed, and above all that no reform or mitigation could be trusted from such a bigot. The only hope lay in a disciplined Protestant army. As early as the spring of 1688 they took a most audacious decision. They invited William to invade England; and William replied that if he received at the right moment a formal request from leading English statesmen he would come, and that he would be ready by September. What followed played into the hands of these resolute men.

From April onward the party of action made good preparations. They took others into their confidence in proportion to what they needed to know. Trusty persons were informed, and their duties allotted. Efforts were made to draw in the moderates. The whole design was laid before Nottingham. At first he agreed, and then, upon misgivings in which cowardice played no part, he retracted his promise. How deadly the conspiracy had become can be judged from the story that his fellow-statesmen, leaders of a great party, Shrewsbury at their head, determined to ensure his silence by shooting him. He admitted to them that it was their right. Eventually, and with justice, they trusted to his oath. A nation-wide conspiracy was on foot by the end of May. Detailed plans were made, and a great many personal contacts established. The land was full of whisperings and of mysterious comings and goings. Sunderland, elusive, baffling to his enemies, incomprehensible to posterity, heard and understood much, not all of which was imparted to his master. Barillon knew less, but reported all he knew to both the Kings whose interests he served. Louis took a grave view. James shut his ears, pursued his course, and reviewed his troops.

Upon the troops much, though not all, depended. If the Army obeyed its orders and fought for the King, England would be torn by a civil war the end of which no man could foresee. But if the Army refused to fight or was prevented from fighting by any means, then the great issues at stake would be settled bloodlessly. It seems certain, though there is no actual proof, that the general revolutionary conspiracy had a definite military core; and that this formed itself in the Army, or at least among the high officers of the Army, step by step with the designs of the statesmen. The supreme object of all the conspirators, civil or military, was to coerce the King without using physical force. We cannot doubt that this was Churchill's long-formed intention. It is reasonable to assume that in this resolve he took every measure in his power; and, of course, these measures contemplated, if the need arose, treason and mutiny as known to the law, and personal treachery to his master. With him in secret consultation were the colonels of the two Tangier regiments, Kirke and Trelawny, the Duke of Grafton, commanding the Guards, the Duke of Ormonde, and a number of other officers.

Bishops, generals, Jesuits, and Nonconformist leaders eyed each other in a sinister silence as spring blossomed into summer. And now events struck their hammer-blows. At the end of April James issued a second and more far-reaching Declaration of Indulgence. In a reasoned manifesto he bid for the whole-hearted support of all—and they were many —who suffered—and they suffered grievously—from the penal laws. He

ordered that the Declaration should be read in all the churches. On
May 18 the Seven Bishops, headed by the Primate, the venerable Sancroft, protested against this use of the dispensing power. The clergy
obeyed their ecclesiastical superiors, and from few pulpits throughout
the country was the Declaration read. James, furious at disobedience
and apparently scandalized at this departure, by the Church he was
seeking to undermine, from its doctrine of non-resistance, demanded
that the Bishops should be put on trial for seditious libel. Sunderland,
now definitely alarmed, endeavoured to dissuade the King from this extreme step. He saw the spark which would fire the mine on which he
knew himself to dwell. Even Lord Chancellor Jeffreys told Clarendon
that the King was going too far, and had also the impudence to observe, "As to the judges, they are most of them rogues." The King persisted: the trial was ordered, and the Bishops, all of whom refused the
proffered bail, were committed to the Tower.

On June 10, while the trial was still pending, the Queen gave birth
to a son. This prodigious event produced general consternation. Until
then every one might hope that the stresses which racked English society would die with the death of the King. Till then the accession of
either Mary, the heir presumptive, or Anne, the next in order, promised an end to the struggle between a Catholic monarch and a Protestant people. Peaceable folk could therefore be patient until the tyranny
was past. But here was the succession assured in the male line to an indefinite series of Catholic princes. It was unendurable.

The conveyance of the Bishops to the Tower, their two days' trial,
and their acquittal on June 30 by a Middlesex jury, were occasions of
passionate outbursts in their favour by all classes in the capital. Enormous crowds thronged the riverbanks to watch the barges carry the
prisoners to and fro, or knelt in the streets in the hopes of being
blessed by them. The humblest citizens were swayed by the same emotions which convulsed the rank and fashion of London. The troops at
Hounslow joined in the rejoicings of the people. "What is that
clamour?" asked the King, as he was leaving the camp after a visit.
"Sire, it is nothing; the soldiers are glad that the Bishops are acquit-
ted." "Do you call that nothing?" said James. These manifestations
were repeated as the news spread throughout the country.

On that same night, while cannon and tumults proclaimed the public joy, the seven leaders of the party of action met at Shrewsbury's

town house, and there and then signed and dispatched their famous letter to William. The signatories were Shrewsbury, Danby, Russell, Bishop Compton, Devonshire, Henry Sidney, and Lumley. Of these seven Compton had long been in the closest touch with Churchill at the Cockpit, yet he did not know how far Churchill was engaged, nor exactly what he knew. Shrewsbury and Russell were Churchill's intimate friends. Though not always colleagues in office, all three acted in concert for many years.

The letter, in the sure hands of Admiral Herbert, disguised as a common sailor, sped to The Hague, and its authors dispersed throughout the island for the purpose of levying war upon the King. Shrewsbury, though brought up a Catholic, had become a Protestant in the storms of 1681. He never detached himself from his new faith. Now, after mortgaging his estates to raise £40,000, he crossed the sea to join William and thenceforward stood at his side. Danby undertook to raise Yorkshire; Compton toured the North "to see his sisters." Devonshire, who had been condemned to an enormous fine for assaulting a Court partisan in the royal palace and had lain since 1685 in rebellious obscurity at Chatsworth, raised a regiment of horse from his tenantry. William, stricken in his ambition by the birth of a male heir, exclaimed, "Now or never!" and began the preparation of his expedition.

Churchill was not of sufficient political rank or territorial influence to be a signatory. Whether, if asked, he would have signed is unknown; but there is little doubt he would have deemed it an honour. Though of secondary importance, he lay more in the centre of the web and held more threads than the larger figures. Day by day he waited on the King, and watched the temper of the troops. Night by night he sat in the narrow, devoted cluster at the Cockpit. If he was in touch with Shrewsbury and Russell and their party of action, he was also intimate with Sunderland, the chief Minister, and with Halifax, the outstanding moderate. His countenance was inscrutable, his manner bland, his discretion unfailing.

The birth of the baby Prince who set so many ponderous wheels in motion was received with general incredulity, sincere or studiously affected. From the beginning doubts had been thrown upon the belated pregnancy of the Queen. The prayers and intercessions in which the Catholics had indulged, and their confident predictions that a son would be born as the result, led to a widespread conviction that a trick had been practised. The legend that a supposititious child had been smuggled into St James's Palace in a warming-pan was rife before the ashes of the official bonfires had vanished from the streets. By a strange imprudence of the King's the majority of persons present at the birth were Papists, the wives of Papists, or foreigners. The Archbishop was absent: he had that day been conducted to the Tower. Neither of the Hydes had been summoned, though as Privy Councillors, brothers-in-law of the King, and uncles of the two Princesses whose rights to the Crown were affected, their presence would have been natural. More important perhaps than all, Princess Anne was not there. She was at Bath. The Churchills were with her, and Sarah no doubt received an authentic account from the still beautiful Frances, now Duchess of Tyrconnel, who was on the spot.

It was vital to the nation to establish the doctrine that the child was an impostor. Sincerely attached to the principle of legitimacy, confronted with the appearance of a Papist heir, the English Protestants had no other means of escape from the intolerable admission. With the characteristic instinct and ingenuity of the English people for reconciling facts, law, and propriety with public interests and their own desires, they enshrined the legend of the warming-pan as a fundamental article of political faith. It was not dispensed with until after some eventful years, and when the question had ceased to have any practical importance.

Churchill now, as the days of action drew near, renewed his pledge given fifteen months before, and wrote to William:

August 4, 1688

Mr Sydney will let you know how I intend to behave myself: I think it is what I owe to God and my country. My honour I take leave to put into your royal highness's hands, in which I think it safe. If you think there is anything else that I ought to do, you have but to command me, and I shall pay an entire obedience to it, being resolved to die in that religion that it has pleased God to give you both the will and power to protect.

Such a letter written by a serving officer, at a time when conspiracy was rife and invasion imminent, was a deadly guarantee. Its capture or betrayal would justly involve the forfeit of his life at the hands of either a civil or a military tribunal. The invitation of the seven notables had been sent in the precautions of cipher. But Churchill's letter, which survives to this day, is in his own handwriting, signed with his name. He seems to have wished to share in a special degree the risks which his friends the signatories had incurred.

All this impending struggle, so ominous for our island people, so decisive upon their destiny, was one factor, but a vital factor, in the world war now about to begin. Across the sea, watching with strained vigilance the assembling armies of France, lay William of Orange with the troops and fleet of Holland. England, in her griefs and rages, was the decisive piece on the Continental board. Profoundly Protestant, vehemently anti-French, was she, with all her resources, to be cast upon the side of Gallican intolerance and French aggrandisement? Was she so to be committed, probably with fatal effect, against the whole instinct and interest of her people by the perverse obstinacy of a single man? Protestant Europe and Protestant England alike looked to William, as the champion of freedom against the many-sided tyrannies of Louis, to break the accursed spell. William accepted the dangerous duty. In the terse words of Halifax, "he took England on the way to France."

Before the Prince of Orange could invade England he had not only to prepare and assemble his troops and ships, but to obtain freedom to use them for such a purpose. At a moment when the whole of the French Army was massed and ready for immediate advance, it was not easy to persuade the threatened princes of Germany or the anxious burghers of Holland that their best chance of safety lay in sending the Dutch Army into England upon an expedition so full of uncertainty. The Great Elector was dead, but Frederick III, who had succeeded him in April, was resolute for war and, like his father, convinced that England must be gained. He even lent William a contingent of Prussian troops under the command of Marshal Schomberg. The other German princes acquiesced in the Prussian view. Most Catholic Spain set political above religious considerations, and made no bones about an expedition to dethrone a Catholic king. The Emperor alone demurred. Although dethronement was not suggested, his religious scruples were aroused. Lulled by communications from the Vatican at William's instance, he eventually agreed to an expedition to restore harmony in England and detach her from France. Only a dominating sense of common danger could have united these diverse interests and creeds upon a strategy so farseeing and broadminded.

William had next to convince the States-General: they had agreed to an enormous expenditure during the last two years upon the Dutch armaments; their land forces were upon a war footing, their fleet decisively stronger than the English. But the decision of the Dutch, and their ruler also, must be governed by the action of France. If the French armies marched against Holland the whole Dutch strength would be needed to meet the invader, and England must perforce be left to her fate. If, on the other hand, Louis struck upon the Rhine at Prussia and Germany, then the enterprise on which the Stadtholder's heart was set could go forward. All therefore hung in suspense. Meanwhile a great fleet of transports, with all the necessary supplies, had gathered in the Texel under the protection of the Dutch Navy, and the expeditionary force lay concentrated close at hand.

Louis XIV, with whom the initiative rested, delayed his choice till the last moment. He was ready to come to James's aid if James would definitely throw England on to the French side in the impending European struggle. All through July and August he offered him money, an army of thirty thousand men, and the French fleet. The French troops would enforce discipline and loyalty upon the English Army, and together they could certainly crush all resistance to the royal will. James, partly from patriotic pride in the independence of his country, partly from fear of the resentment which a French alliance would arouse among his subjects, and under the advice of Sunderland, made light of his own dangers and dallied with the French offers. He was still absorbed in his electioneering plans to produce by hook or by crook a House of Commons favourable to the repeal of the Test Act. All prospect of this would be swept away by an outbreak of war, the announcement of a French alliance or the arrival of French troops. On September 2 Louis, with large armies straining at the leash, and compelled by the military situation, resolved to bring matters to a head. He delivered through his Ambassador at The Hague an ultimatum to the Dutch Republic. It was declared that William's military preparations were a menace to England: that "friendship and alliance" existed between England and France, and that any enterprise undertaken by the Dutch against England would involve an immediate French declaration of war on Holland.

This violent step defeated its own object in both the countries affected. The States-General were enraged by the menace. James, in the utmost embarrassment at the declaration, publicly repudiated all idea of an alliance. The rejection of his aid not only offended Louis; it aroused his suspicions. It was so contrary to James's vital interests that it seemed explicable only by some secret arrangement between James and William, or between Sunderland and the States-General. The irresolute, shifting policy of the English Government lent colour to the belief in Holland that it was tied to France, and in France that it was tied to Holland. At any rate, the die was cast. Louis abandoned the hope of procuring England as an ally; he must be content with seeing her, as he believed and trusted, torn by a savage civil war in which William would be involved, and during which the island kingdom could play no part in Europe. On September 25 all the French armies were set in motion, not against the Dutch frontier, but towards the middle Rhine. From the moment that this movement became certain the States-General eagerly granted William permission for his English descent, and James's hour was come.

As the autumn weeks slipped by, excitement and tension grew throughout the island, and the vast conspiracy which now comprised the main strength of the nation heaved beneath the surface of affairs. The King's attempt to bring in some of the regiments of Irish Roman Catholics which Tyrconnel had raised for him produced symptoms so menacing that the process was abandoned. All turned on the wind. Rumour ran riot. The Irish were coming. The French were coming. The Papists were planning a general massacre of Protestants. The kingdom was sold to Louis. Nothing was safe, and no one could be trusted. The laws, the Constitution, the Church—all were in jeopardy. But a deliverer would appear. He would come clad with power from over the seas to rescue England from Popery and slavery—if only the wind would blow from the east. And here one of Wharton's couplets, which nominally applied to Tyrconnel, gained a new and, indeed, an opposite significance.

> O, why does he stay so long behind?
> Ho! by my shoul, 'tis a Protestant wind.

The Protestant wind was blowing in the hearts of men, rising in fierce gusts to gale fury. Soon it would blow across the North Sea!

> "Lero, lero, lilliburlero!
> Lilliburlero, bullen-a-lah!"

sang the soldiers and peasants of England in endless repetition through those days, "singing," as its author afterwards claimed, "a deluded prince out of three kingdoms."

Sunderland and Jeffreys were at this moment in chief control of the Cabinet. The magnitude of William's preparations and the alarming state of feeling throughout England produced a complete change in their attitude. Confronted by impending invasion from abroad and by imminent revolt at home, these two Ministers, recently so pliable and so reckless, strenuously advised the King to reverse his whole policy. They abandoned at one stroke all the meticulous efforts to pack a Nonconformist House of Commons upon which infinite labour had been spent, and by which widespread irritation had been caused. Parliament must indeed be called without delay, and the King and his Government must face the fact that it would be Episcopalian in character. All further aggressive Catholic measures must be stopped, and a reconciliation made with the Church of England. The fact that this advice came from the two Ministers who had hitherto been the most hardy, and who were both, it seemed, committed beyond forgiveness to the royal policy and all the hatreds it had roused, was staggering. They must indeed have swept the King off his feet by their outburst of warning. He crumpled under their pressure and panic. Within a week he was persuaded that he could not make head against William of Orange without the support of the Church of England. To gain this support he must negotiate with the bishops. He must stoop to conquer—or even to escape.

On October 3, in a conference at which the Primate and most of the bishops were present, he agreed to abolish the Ecclesiastical Commission, to close the Roman Catholic schools, to restore the Protestant Fellows of Magdalen College, to put the Act of Uniformity into force against Catholics and Dissenters. Action was taken accordingly with the utmost speed. The Lord-Lieutenants who had been dismissed were invited to resume their functions. Their charters were restored to the recalcitrant municipalities. The bishops were begged to let bygones be bygones. The Tory squires were urged to take their old places in the magistracy. Too late! The adverse movement had slowly but at length gathered a momentum which was uncontrollable even by those who had started it. It was evident that this sudden, belated repentance was a proof only of the weakness of the Government in the presence of approaching peril.

Now the unhappy King began to realize that by his folly and Sunderland's advice he had lost all. At the end of October he dismissed his Minister for vacillation and lack of firmness in counsel. James had drawn upon himself the evils of all courses and gained the benefit of none. He had alienated his friends; he had united all his enemies. William was about to invade him. Louis had abandoned him. The Pope, for the sake of whose faith he had hazarded all, in aversion to whom his subjects were in revolt, was working with his enemies. Outside France he had not a friend or sympathizer in Europe; and France was marching away from him upon Germany. At home he had centered upon himself the anger of almost all the wealth and power and learning of the nation without winning support from the popular masses. He had wounded Cavaliers without gaining Roundheads. He had estranged the Church without rallying the Chapel. Although Penn and the Nonconformist organizations had naturally supported his attempt to remove the penal laws, the great bulk of their followers remained vehemently hostile to Popery, and would rather endure maltreatment themselves than join in a Catholic crusade. The Catholic gentry whose wrongs had stirred his heart were now panicstricken by the plight into which he had led them. He was not even destined to go down fighting for the cause in which he so fervently believed. In the last few months of his reign he was compelled to desert the standard he had himself set up, and to try in vain to placate the furies he had aroused, by the sacrifice of all the objectives in whose pursuit he had aroused them.

Nor has the passage of generations vindicated his efforts for Catholic toleration. Had he joined the Catholic Hapsburgs and the Protestant princes in their war against the domination of France, he would have established with his own subjects a confidence and comradeship which might well have enabled him, if not to remove, at least gradually to neglect the enforcement of the Tests. Had he allowed the incomparable soldier whose gifts he had himself so long discerned to gain for him Protestant battles upon the Continent, the English people, relieved from their fear, might well have been generous to the co-religionists of the victorious prince who had served them well. So supple a part was beyond him, and, indeed, beneath him. Instead, he set in train a movement of events which made anti-Popery and a warming-pan the foundation of a dynasty, and riveted upon the English Catholics for more than a hundred and fifty years the shackles of the penal laws.

CHAPTER THIRTEEN

The Revolution

ᚠᚢ 1688, November ᚢᚠ

ON October 19 William set out upon the seas. His small army was a microcosm of Protestant Europe—Dutch, Swedes, Danes, Prussians, English, and Scottish, together with a forlorn, devoted band of French Huguenots who had no longer any country of their own. They were embarked upon about five hundred vessels escorted by sixty warships—almost the entire Dutch fleet. The English Rear-Admiral Herbert led the van, and the Prince of Orange hoisted, together with his own arms, the flag of England, on which was embroidered his motto, "I will maintain," with the addition, "the Protestant religion and the liberties of England"; all of which was made good. Dalrymple has written of the feelings of the Dutch as they watched this impressive concourse of vessels quitting their shores:

> . . . some flattered with the grandeur of their republic, others reflecting with anxiety that their frontier on one side was in the hands of the ancient tyrants, and on the other, exposed to an army of foreign mercenaries, all the artillery of their towns carried off, only a few ships of war left in their harbours, and the whole strength of the republic sent, during the rigours of Winter, to depend upon the hazards of winds and seas, and the fortune of war.

A violent gale scattered the fleet and cast it back upon the ports of Holland. One vessel, upon which no fewer than four companies of infantry were embarked, was driven on to the English coast and captured. The numbers of troops on this single vessel, together with the size of the fleet, gave the idea that William's army was four times as large as it was. But, anyhow, it had been driven back and ruined by the storms. James saw the finger of God. "It is not to be wondered at," he said, when he received the news at dinner, "for the Host has been exposed these several days." Convinced that the divine power and Holy Church had given him his son, he thought that they would also destroy his foes; and he dismissed Sunderland from his office as First Minister for being a faint-heart. But the new Secretary of State, Preston, a Protestant, renewed to him the advice of the fallen Minister. He must call a Parliament without manipulation and without delay.

Now this was a deadly matter for the King. No such Parliament could assemble in such a situation without calling in question not only the whole prerogative of the Crown, but, far graver, the *bona fides* of his son's birth. And here, by the mercy of God, was the hostile fleet scattered. Of course he refused. On this the Lord Chancellor Jeffreys abandoned himself to despair. "It is all naught," he exclaimed, with his customary profanity. "The Virgin Mary is to do all."

It was believed that William would strive to land in the North, and thither considerable bodies of the royal troops were proceeding. But the winds decided otherwise, and William ran south under full sail. On November 3 he anchored, so as to regather his whole fleet, in the Straits of Dover, in full view of the crowded coasts of England and France. The same wind that carried him here prevented Dartmouth from coming out of the Thames in any formation fit for battle, even if the loyalty of his captains and their seamen would have undertaken it. When to doubt, disinclination, and inferior strength are added adverse weather conditions, the inaction of naval forces is to be expected. The English fleet followed tardily behind the invader, and the same Protestant wind which blew him back to Torbay when he had overshot it forced the pursuers, who had got as far as Portland, to take shelter at Spithead. On November 5 William landed at Torbay, on the coast of Devon.

James was not at first unduly alarmed at the news. It was better that the invasion should have fallen on the Western counties than upon Yorkshire. He hoped to pen William in the West, and to hamper his communications by sea. The troops which had been sent to Yorkshire were recalled to the South, and Salisbury was fixed as the point of assembly for the royal army. Meanwhile William established himself at

Exeter and awaited the arrival of adherents. For ten days none came. Danby had expected him in Yorkshire. The West had learned its lesson after Sedgemoor, and no preparations for the rebellion had been made. William was disconcerted by this apparent apathy, and thought at first he was betrayed. However, gradually some notables arrived, and Sir Edward Seymour formed an association in his support. In this lull the King still looked with confidence upon his Army, and it is thither we must turn for the next event.

Some confusion of thought is evident in the searing reproaches with which both parties and successive generations have disfigured Churchill's reputation and have singled him out to bear whatever there was of shame in the wonderful deliverance of which all stood sorely in need. No one has impugned the sincerity of his religious convictions or the wisdom of his political view. No one can dispute the proofs of his long attachment to both, or of the repeated declarations by which his position became well known to all whom it concerned. Few will urge that personal indebtedness to a prince requires behaviour contrary to a man's conscience and to the interests of his native land. Every one will repudiate the idea that Churchill—a fervent Protestant, a resolved opponent of French domination in Europe, and an adherent of our laws and Constitution as then known—should have lent his gifts and sword to the bloody task of forcibly converting his fellow-countrymen to Popery, and of setting up in England a despotism on the French model, by French arms and in French interests.

It follows, therefore, that Churchill was right to abandon King James. The only questions open are When? and How? Ought he to have quitted the King when he wrote his first letter of May 1687 to William of Orange? Surely not: the circumstances in question might never have come to pass. The King might yield to the increasing pressure brought upon him from all sides. He might reverse his policy. He did, in fact, reverse it. Was it, then, when he wrote his second letter to William, in August 1688, that he should have deserted James? But by this time he knew from Sunderland of the intended change of policy which even the most hard-bitten, self-seeking Ministers resolved to press upon their master, and of the probable summoning of a new Parliament chosen in the old way. Ought he, then, to have left the King's service, given up his commissions and appointments, and gone to his home or, if need be, to prison, when James dismissed Sunderland at the end of October and withdrew the writs for a free Parliament? But by now William was on the seas. Trusting in the solemn written promises of leading Englishmen—among which Churchill's undertakings were the most explicit—he had launched out upon the hazardous enterprise to which they had called him. Ought Churchill, then, in November 1688 to have extinguished himself as a factor in the momentous events actually impending, and left William to look for his pledged aid in vain? Surely there is more shame in a breach of faith contrary to convictions than in the severance of loyalty in harmony with them. A flight from responsibility was only treachery in another and an abject form.

It was a hideous situation into which he had been drawn by no fault of his own, by no unwise or wrongful action, by no failure of service, by no abandonment of principle. But it was a situation which had to be faced and dealt with calmly and sensibly in the manner most likely to minimize the public dangers and sufferings, and to procure a good result for his country and for himself. Moreover, in conspiracies and rebellions the penalties for failure are rightly so severe that all who are unluckily drawn into them have not only a vital need for themselves, but also a duty to others associated with them and to the cause at stake, to ensure success, and above all bloodless success, by forethought and every well-concerted measure. To lure, like Monmouth, associates and humble followers on fools' errands to their doom can find no defenders. Thus Churchill had to go through with his undertakings, and by such steps as were likely to win.

This was a dangerous time for James to have at the head of the host the Frenchman, Feversham, who had been so harshly lampooned round London and in all the garrisons after Sedgemoor. There was at the King's disposal Feversham's brother, the competent French general Roye. He certainly thought of offering the chief command to him. Roye, who had learned since his arrival of the intense feeling in the Army against France and French patronage, was well enough informed to put the suggestion aside. He could not, he said, command an army not one word of whose language he could speak. So Feversham remained Commander-in-Chief. All the more necessary was it to have Churchill almost on any terms at the royal headquarters. In the opinion of those rather loosely disciplined professional soldiers, with their brave and haughty society officers, he was without equal or rival the leading English general. The habit of soldiers to fix upon a leader who embodies to them a martial ideal and to obey him in a crisis has often been proved. Here was an hour when everything hung upon the temper of the troops. The only hope of inducing the army, and especially its officers, to fight for the King was to give the impression that the best fighting man of English blood would give or be associated with the orders they received. The misgivings which James had owned when he superseded Churchill before Sedgemoor must have recurred to his mind in an aggravated form at this juncture. But what else was there to do? Accordingly on November 7 Churchill was promoted Lieutenant-General with the command of a brigade, or, as we should now call it, a division, of the army concentrating at Salisbury.

Churchill could not consider this advancement as a mark of favour. It was, in fact, the hopeful appropriation of his military prestige to the royal cause at a moment when all title-deeds were called in question. Acceptance involved no assumption of new obligations on his part. In this important but subordinate position he had a seat at the councils of war and a voice in their decisions. He was not, however, in either nominal command or actual control of the army. His opinion was invited; his influence and authority were invoked. He was saddled before the nation with the responsibility. But the King really leaned upon the two Frenchmen. They were immune from the passions which shook England. He could count on their fidelity however his own subjects might behave. Thus Churchill was at the same moment made to fill the public eye and kept under supervision and control. In the circumstances this was probably the best course open to the King.

During these heart-shaking days many alternative solutions of the nation's problem presented themselves. When the royal headquarters arrived at Salisbury, it might well be found that the mood of the troops was such that no battle could be fought; but that, on the other hand, a negotiation would be entered into, as afterwards happened, with the Prince of Orange and his invading army. At that time none of the English conspirators had contemplated the dethronement of the King, and William had carefully dissembled his ambitions. His small, solid army was only the steel tip of the spear of a British resolve. He could not conquer six million English with fifteen thousand men. The constable had arrived upon the scene of disorder. He was helpless without the support of public opinion and of sturdy, well-disposed citizens. It might well be that a parley between the chiefs on both sides would result in an agreement. James might become a limited monarch, permitted to exercise his personal religion in private, but compelled to govern with Parliamentary institutions, to preserve the Protestant character of England, and, as part of the League of Augsburg, to make war upon France. He might even be compelled to choose between having his son excluded from the succession or brought up a Protestant. Again, there might be a regency, with William as Mayor of the Palace, with James as a powerless but much respected Merovingian king, the succession at his death assured to his daughters, the Protestants Mary and Anne. All these possibilities were still open when James left London.

The King had barely arrived at Windsor when disconcerting news was received. Lord Cornbury, eldest son of Lord Clarendon, an officer of the Life Guards, found himself for a few hours in command of the troops assembling at Salisbury. Cornbury intended to carry the whole three regiments into the Prince's army. William, duly appraised, had set superior forces in motion to surround them, and the troops would certainly have been disarmed or, if possible, incorporated. But the officers were puzzled by the length of the marches and the obvious imprudence of the operation. They demanded the production of the orders. Cornbury, seeing himself detected, rode over to William with about two hundred men, while the rest of the brigade only extricated themselves with difficulty from the trap into which they were being led.

Cornbury's desertion was the first of the successive blows. It was impossible to tell who among the officers of the Army could be trusted. It seemed certain that if they could all be trusted the Army would fight, and if it fought it would probably win.

The fact that Cornbury was intimate with his cousin the Princess Anne and was constantly at the Cockpit; the fact that the military arrangements had been so cast as to leave this young officer in chief command at Salisbury for some critical hours, and that he should have taken such audacious action, all pointed to a plot in which the superior chiefs of the Army, and Churchill above all, were engaged. There is no proof; but it may well be so. Certainly Churchill was trying to bring about the predominance of William without the fighting of a battle, and this would well have served for a preliminary move.

On November 17 the King set out from Windsor to join the army at

Salisbury. It was a strange party that fared with him to the wars. More than half were resolved, and most of these already pledged, to abandon him. Some had been for months actively conspiring with the invader. His own son-in-law, Prince George of Denmark, had actually agreed to the arrangement by which the Princess Anne should at the chosen moment leave London for William's camp. His own Household troops were honeycombed with disloyalty. His nephew, the Duke of Grafton, and nearly all his most capable officers, the leaders of many of his trusted regiments, were merely awaiting an opportunity to transfer their services to the enemy. Every decision, except those of hour and method, had been taken. Apart from his own Catholic communion and the French agents, there was no one upon whom he could depend. Even his fiercest partisans of Sedgemoor three short years before, men like Kirke and Trelawny, were now his foes. On all sides salutes and ceremony, unaffected respect and reverence for his person, and yet on all sides implacable treason, indistinguishable from public duty.

Among these men rode Churchill. None was more sure of himself than the newly promoted Lieutenant-General. His mind had long been made up, his pledge given, and his plans laid. Indeed, these evidences of design are the ground upon which censure has specially fastened. The elaborate, smooth-working preparations which are admired when they produce the march to Blenheim are repellent, though not less necessary, in a conspiracy. In London Sarah had her instructions about the Princess Anne, which she would fulfil with sure punctuality. Afloat, his brother George was working, with an ever-growing crowd of sea officers, to gain the fleet, and was himself about to carry his ship, the *Newcastle*, to William. Churchill himself was united in resolve and confederation with the principal nobles and functionaries. All—each playing his part wherever stationed—were taking day by day the steps which, should their designs miscarry, would cost them hearth and home and life itself. Ruin, exile, the scaffold—these were the stakes to which the compulsory game of politics had risen. They were already cast upon the board; there could be no withdrawal of them. Irrevocable! All grim, cold, doom-laden!

At this crisis in his fortunes King James could marshal as large an army as Oliver Cromwell at his height. Nearly forty thousand regular soldiers were in the royal pay and moving at the royal command towards Salisbury and the Dutch invader. But the Scottish troops, about four thousand strong, had only reached Carlisle, the bulk of the three thousand Irish were still beyond Chester, and at least seven thousand men must be left to hold down London. Still, twenty-five thousand men, or double the number of William's expedition, were around Salisbury when the King arrived on November 19. Here was the largest concentration of trained full-time troops which England had ever seen. What would they do?

This was the question which dominated the thoughts of all the leading figures who composed the King's headquarters or held the commands. There had been several vexatious delays and hitches in the assembly of the troops. The King and Churchill eyed each other, the sovereign in mute appeal, the servant in grave reserve: and both sought to penetrate by every channel open to them the secret of the Army. To the King, with his two French generals and the French Ambassador ever at his side, the aspect was obscure and dubious. To Churchill and the commanders banded with him it was highly disconcerting. Most of the officers were no doubt thoroughly disaffected. The Protestant regimental officers were divided and in evident distress. But the Papist officers and their men were ardent in their loyalty, and no one could be sure that the Protestant rank and file, if strongly gripped, were not capable of being led against the foreign foe or foreign deliverers. The least trustworthy regiments at James's disposal were those upon whom he should have been able to count the most. The Guards, the Dragoons and Cavalry, those officers and men who habitually surrounded the Court, who had felt the mood of London, and were aware of the political issues at stake, were known to use mutinous language. But the main body of the Line at this juncture, though Protestant in sentiment, were still governed by their discipline and their uniforms.

James, warned from many quarters, meditated Churchill's arrest. Feversham on his knees demanded it, declaring his disaffection patent. Churchill's incarceration at Portsmouth was debated. This was not a light matter to decide. His appointment had been advertised to the troops. The news of his arrest would have been not less injurious than his desertion. The shock to the Army would have been as great. So many were involved, so near, so intimate, so long-trusted and proved so faithful, that the unhappy sovereign knew not where to begin, nor, if he began, where to stop. On all sides his narrow circle of Papists, Irish, and Frenchmen encountered whisperings, averted eyes, or even cold shoulders and hostile looks. The King hesitated, delayed, put the matter off until the morrow.

We need not delve into a painful analysis of Churchill's feelings at this juncture. Lord Wolseley has drawn for us a harrowing picture of the moral and sentimental stresses through which his hero is supposed to have passed on the night of November 23, when he is represented as finally making up his mind to desert James, and how he must have balanced his duty and gratitude to his master and patron on the one hand against the Protestant cause upon the other. These well-meant efforts of a friendly biographer have certainly no foundation. All had, as we have shown, been settled long before. There never had been any process of weighing and balancing which side to take. The only difficulty had been to judge a ceaselessly shifting situation. But now all was simple. Policy and plans were settled; the last preparations had been made. The hour of action was always, to him, the least arduous of trials. That hour had now come.

A council of war was held on the evening of November 23. Churchill, supported by Grafton, when asked his opinion, advised an advance towards the enemy, while Feversham and Roye were for retreat. The King accepted Feversham's opinion. Churchill's may well have been the right advice to give on military grounds. There is a curious symmetry about his actions on many occasions which seems to range a correctness and justice of view on the event of the moment with his general designs. But it is equally arguable that he gave the right advice either because he knew the opposite course would be adopted, or because, if he had been taken at his word, that would have been convenient to his resolves. Every forward march would carry him nearer to William, would enable the two women for whose safety he was concerned, his wife and the Princess Anne, to make their escape more easily, and even his own decisive ride would be shorter. Once the Army was dispersed in its retreat, and the loyal were separated from the disloyal regiments, his arrest would be easy. All these matters are covered by the general relationship in which the chief actors stood to one another and by judgment upon the main issues.

We believe that Churchill stayed with the Army till the very last moment that he dared—and he dared much. By the end of the council on the 23rd he had convinced himself that the military plot had failed; that there was no prospect that the English commanders would be able to go to the King and say in the name of the Army, "You must open negotiations with William, and you must call a free Parliament." They had used, so far as it was possible, all their influence upon the troops without decisive results, and brought themselves into extreme peril thereby. Nothing remained but to escape with their immediate retinues and followers.

Therefore, on this same night Churchill, the Duke of Grafton, and Colonel Berkeley, with about four hundred officers and troopers, mounted their horses and rode forth from their camp by Salisbury. Some time during the 24th they arrived at Crewkerne, about twelve miles from William's headquarters at Axminster, after a march of nearly fifty miles. Churchill left the following letter to the King behind him:

> Sir,
>   Since men are seldom suspected of sincerity, when they act contrary to their interests, and though my dutiful behaviour to Your Majesty in the worst of times (for which I acknowledge my poor service is much overpaid) may not be sufficient to incline you to a charitable interpretation of my actions, yet I hope the great advantage I enjoy under Your Majesty, *which I own I can never expect in any other change of government*, may reasonably convince Your Majesty and the world that I am actuated by a higher principle, when I offer that violence to my inclination and interest as to desert Your Majesty at a time when your affairs seem to challenge the strictest obedience from all your subjects, much more from one who lies under the greatest personal obligations to Your Majesty. This, sir, could proceed from nothing but the inviolable dictates of my conscience, and a necessary concern for my religion (which no good man can oppose), and with which I am instructed nothing can come in competition. Heaven knows with what partiality my dutiful opinion of Your Majesty has hitherto represented those unhappy designs which inconsiderate and self-interested men have framed against Your Majesty's true interest and the Protestant religion; but as I can no longer join with such to give a pretence by conquest to bring them to effect, so I will alway with the hazard of my life and fortune (so much Your Majesty's due) endeavour to preserve your royal person and lawful rights, with all the tender concerns and dutiful respect that becomes, sir, Your Majesty's most dutiful and most obliged subject and servant,
>
>   *Churchill*

In the records at Blenheim a copy of this letter was found wrapped in another written by Prince George of Denmark, no doubt at the same time and under Churchill's advice. But the Prince, who, with Ormonde, deserted his father-in-law the next day, takes a view which extends beyond the island that had become his home; and for the first time we see how large a part the Protestant coalition against France played in the councils of the Cockpit.

"Whilst the restless spirits of the enemies of the reformed religion," wrote the Prince,

> backed by the cruel zeal and prevailing power of France justly alarm and unite all the Protestant princes of Christendom and engage them in so vast an expense for the support of it, can I act so degenerate and mean a part as to deny my concurrence to such worthy endeavours for disabusing of your Majesty by the reinforcement of those laws and establishment of that government on which alone depends the well-being of your Majesty and of the Protestant religion in Europe.

We have no doubt that these words expressed the deepest convictions of Churchill as well as those of the honest Prince who wrote them. James's ideal of England redeemed to the true faith, dwelling in definitely established absolute monarchy, advancing independently, but in royal alliance with the great King of France to the extirpation of Protestantism in Europe, shone for him clear and bright. In the mind of his servant there arose perhaps another picture more practical, not less dire, not less majestic. John Churchill saw the rise of Britain to the summit of Europe, curbing and breaking with the aid of William of Orange the overweening power of France. He saw himself, with the Dutchman if need be, or under England's Protestant Princess, advancing at the head of armies to the destruction of that proud dominion. He may even have seen at this early time the building up upon the ruins of the French splendour of a British greatness which should spread far and wide throughout the world and set its stamp upon the future.

To William, Churchill's arrival at Axminster was an enormous relief. Next to defeat his deadliest danger was victory. To avoid bloodshed, to avoid beating with foreign troops a British army in the field, was essential to his aim of securing the throne. He welcomed his new adherent with formal ceremony, and used his services to the best advantage.

It cannot be proved that the defection of so many important officers destroyed the possibility that the Army would fight. If a regular purge had been made, as Feversham proposed, and sergeants promoted to fill all vacancies in the commissioned ranks, if Catholic or French officers had been placed in the key commands, and if the King himself had led his soldiers to battle, it is probable that a most fierce and bloody event would have followed. But Churchill's desertion, followed as it was by that of his own relations and closest servants, broke the King's spirit. When he saw that he could not even keep the Churchill who had been till now his intimate, faithful servant for nearly a quarter of a century, he despaired. He collapsed morally, and from that moment thought only of sending his wife and child to France and following them as soon as possible. It is this fact, and the personal elements that entered into it, that have made Churchill's desertion of James at Salisbury, although compulsory and inevitable, the most poignant and challengeable action of his life.

And now revolt broke out all over the country. Danby was in arms in Yorkshire; Devonshire in Derby; Delamere in Cheshire. Lord Bath delivered Plymouth to William. Byng, a Rear-Admiral representing the captains under Dartmouth's command, arrived at his headquarters to inform him that the fleet and Portsmouth were at his disposal. City after city rose in rebellion. There was an eager rush of notabilities to greet the rising sun. By one universal, spontaneous convulsion the English nation repudiated James.

It was high time for the wives to do their part. Anne and Sarah had no mind to await the return of the indignant King. James sent orders to search both Churchill's houses, and to arrest Sarah. The Princess prevailed upon the Queen to delay the execution of this last order till the morning, and in the night the two women fled from the Cockpit.

In the dead of night they descended the wooden staircase, found the Bishop and Lord Dorset awaiting them, waded through the mud of Pall Mall, in which Anne lost her shoe, to Charing Cross, and thence were carried in a coach to the Bishop of London's residence in Aldersgate.

All search for the fugitives was vain, and when the unhappy King reached Whitehall in the afternoon, he could but exclaim in despair, "God help me! Even my children have forsaken me!"

The King, having assembled such peers and Privy Councillors as were still in London, was advised by them to enter into negotiations with the Prince of Orange and to accord an amnesty to all who had joined him. He nominated Halifax, Nottingham, and Godolphin as his Commissioners to treat with William. He did not know that Halifax and Nottingham had both been privy to William's design. Neither did Halifax know that the King had no intention to treat, and was only using the negotiations as the means of gaining time to send his wife and child abroad and to follow them himself. William, on his part, was in no hurry, and more than a week passed before the necessary safe-conducts were granted to the Commissioners, and they were conducted to his headquarters, which had now reached Hungerford. Meanwhile James had sent his infant heir to Portsmouth with orders to Dartmouth to send him at once to France. Dartmouth, for all his loyalty, refused to obey this fatal command, which he declared would render him "guilty of treason to Your Majesty and the known laws of the kingdom."

But James was not to be deterred. The baby Prince was brought back from Portsmouth, and on the night of December 9 the Queen, escorted only by Count Lauzun and Riva, an Italian gentleman, escaped, with her child, to Gravesend and thence to France. As soon as the King knew that his wife and son were safely off he prepared to follow them. Elaborate arrangements having been made to deceive the Court and the Council, the King stole from the palace an hour or two after midnight on December 11, crossed the river, and rode hard for the coast. He endeavoured to plunge his realm into anarchy. He threw the Great Seal into the Thames; and sent orders to Feversham to disband the Army, and to Dartmouth to sail with what ships he could for Irish ports. Dartmouth, stricken to the heart by his master's desertion of his post, placed the fleet under the orders of William. But Feversham, with reckless wickedness, scattered the soldiers, unpaid but not disarmed, upon the population. General consternation ensued. The King's Commissioners saw they had been befooled. The wildest rumours of impending Irish massacres spread through the land. The London mob sacked the foreign embassies, and every one seized arms in defence of hearth and home. A wild panic and terror, long remembered as "Irish Night," swept the capital. Undoubtedly a complete collapse of civil government would have occurred but for the resolute action of the Council, which was still sitting in London. With difficulty they suppressed the storm, and, acknowledging William's authority, besought him to hasten his marches to London.

But the very next day, while the Council was sitting, a poor countryman arrived at the door with an appealing message from the King. James had actually got on board a ship, but, missing the tide, was caught, mauled, grabbed, and dragged ashore by the Faversham fishermen and townsfolk, who took him for a Jesuit in flight. What followed is briefly and well told by Ailesbury, who gives unconsciously a picture which historians seem to have missed. Ailesbury had striven hard to dissuade James from his flight, and when the news that the fugitive had been intercepted at the coast was brought to the decapitated Council, he broke the prolonged silence by proposing that his Majesty should be invited to return forthwith to his post. Charged with this task, he set out by coach and a-horse to retrieve his master out of the hands of the mob at Sheerness. He was haughtily received by the royal captive. His high jack-boots prevented him from falling on his knees when entering the presence, and he could only bob his knee. Whereat James, unshaven, ill-fed, rounded up and put in the pound like an errant bull by the local townsfolk and seamen, but unshakably sure of his royal rights, remarked, "Ha! It was all Kings when I left London." To this reception at the end of his loyal and difficult journey through the turbulent, panic-stricken towns of Kent and by roadways infested with revolt and disorder Ailesbury—so he tells us—used some extremely plain language, to which his sovereign was graciously pleased to hearken. He then proceeded to collect some victuals, bake the best bread possible in the circumstances, and ask the King whether he would not dine in state. His Majesty signified his pleasure; the local dignitaries and some of the populace were admitted wonder-struck to the miserable dwelling, and the faithful Gentleman of the Bedchamber, jack-boots notwithstanding, managed (by holding on to the table) to serve him on the knee; thus restoring public confidence and decorum. At intervals throughout the day fragments of the disrupted royal household arrived in Romney. The barber, with the valets and clothes, arrived in the afternoon; the cooks a little later. The Board of Green Cloth was on the spot by dusk; the royal saddle-horses came in during the night, and a troop of Life Guards were reported approaching the next morning. Thus the Court was reconstituted, though in a somewhat skeleton state.

Ailesbury stayed by his master thenceforward. He arranged for a hundred troopers of the Life Guards to be drawn up in single file to encourage him with their acclamations. He persuaded James to drive through the City of London, where the people, perplexed and dumbfounded by the awful event of his flight, received him with relief and almost enthusiasm. He accompanied James from Whitehall when, at William's order, he was escorted by the Dutch Guard down the river to Rochester. He shared with him the peril of the "hideous shooting of the bridge" on the swift, outflowing tide. Once this danger was overcome, the royal party picnicked agreeably in the boats, the King passing food and wine to the Dutch captain of the convoying flotilla.

Ailesbury abode with the King at Rochester, and again endeavoured to prevent his leaving the island. William, who had been profoundly inconvenienced by his return and longed for his fresh departure, caused hints to reach him that his life was in danger. James, no physical coward—indeed, as we have seen, a proved veteran by sea and land—was cowed to his marrow by the overwhelming tide of adverse opinion and the wholesale desertion and repudiation of almost all on whom he had counted. After some days of painful suspense the unhappy man escaped to the river by the back door, which the Prince of Orange had taken pains to leave unguarded, and this time succeeded in leaving English soil for ever. We are told in his so-called memoirs that he expected he would be sent to the Tower, "which no King ever quitted except for his grave," and he felt it his sacred duty to preserve his royal person from such outrageous possibilities.

But though the downfall and flight of this impolitic grandson of Henry of Navarre were at the time ignominious, his dignity has been restored to him by history. Heredity, fatalism, the besetting Stuart infatuation of obstinacy, his stern religious faith, his convinced patriotism according to his lights, all combined to lead him to disaster. He was doomed alike by his upbringing, his office, and his nature. His fixed domestic ideas made an effective foreign policy impossible. His Catholic convictions left him a stubborn anomaly upon a Protestant throne. He was at once a capable administrator and a suicidal politician; a man virtuous in principle and gross in practice; a personage equally respectable and obnoxious. Yet he carried with him into lifelong exile an air of royalty and honour which still clings to his memory.

On the afternoon of December 23 William learned that the King had fled, and felt himself in one form or another undisputed master of England. He lost no time in taking the step for the sake of which he had come across the water. The French Ambassador was given twenty-four hours to be gone from the island, and England was committed to the general coalition against France.

CHAPTER FOURTEEN

Marlborough and William

ᛝ 1688-90 ᛞ

THE Prince of Orange had now become the effective military ruler of his new country; but there was no lawful Government of any kind. The Convention Parliament—assembled on the authority of the revolutionary junta—dived lustily into academic disputes, and the differences between the Whigs and the Tories, temporarily merged in their common danger, soon reappeared. Was the throne vacant? Could the throne ever be vacant? Was there a contract between the King and the people which James had broken? Had he abdicated by flight, or merely deserted? Could he be deposed by Parliament? Arising from all this, should William become Regent, governing in the name of the absent James? Should Mary become Queen in her own right? Had she not, in view of the virtual demise of the Crown, in fact already become Queen? Or should William be made sole King; or should William and Mary reign jointly; and if Mary died, should Anne forthwith succeed, or should William continue to reign alone as long as he lived? Both Houses, both parties, and the Church applied themselves to these lively topics with zest and without haste.

William's aim from the first was to obtain the Crown of England for himself alone. Until James's flight he would have been content with any solution which brought England into the coalition against France; but thenceforward he saw no obstacle to his full ambition. Years before Burnet had earned William's gratitude by inducing Mary to promise, should she succeed her father, that they should be joint-sovereigns. The Stadtholder now flew higher still. He intimated first that he would not be Regent, governing in the name and against the will of a dethroned sovereign with whom he would certainly be at war. "He had not," he said, "come over to establish a Commonwealth or be a Duke of Venice." Rather than that he would return to Holland. Mary's rights were espoused by Danby, who had been disappointed that William had not landed in Yorkshire, and that his own share in the event had not been larger. He proposed that Mary should be Queen. William disposed of this idea by putting it about that he would not be "his wife's gentleman-usher." Through Bentinck, his Dutch confidant, he bid high for the sole kingship, with his wife but a consort. Burnet was staggered by this ingratitude to Mary. The idea of supplanting her in her lawful and prior rights caused widespread anger. William's appetite found its only prominent supporter in Halifax. It was, in fact, the first shock to his popularity in England.

Churchill steered a middle course, at once independent and judicious, through these controversies. Like most of the Tories, he could not vote directly for the dethronement of James; but neither would he actively support the Tory proposal for a regency to which William objected so strongly. He stayed away from the critical division on January 29, and a regency was voted down by fifty-one to forty-nine. He voted later that James had "deserted" the throne and had not "abdicated"; but when the Lords gave way to the Commons and agreed that the Prince and Princess of Orange should be joint sovereigns, he supported their decision. Sarah, under her husband's advice, persuaded Anne to surrender in favour of William her right to succeed to the throne on Mary's death. Thus William gained without dispute the Crown for life. This was a service of the first order, and probably counted in William's mind even above the desertion at Salisbury which had prevented a battle. From the very beginning, however, and even on this subject, the King showed a definite coolness towards the Churchills. On Halifax suggesting to him that Lord Churchill "might perhaps prevail with the Princess of Denmark to give her consent" he bridled, saying, "Lord Churchill could not govern him nor his wife as they did the Prince and Princess of Denmark." Halifax, who recorded this conversation, noted in William "a great jealousy of being thought to be governed," and added, "That apprehension will give uneasiness to men in great places. His dislikes of this kind have not always an immediate effect as in the instance of Lord Churchill," but "like some slow poisons work at a great distance of time."

William accepted the arrangements made by Parliament with good grace. He confirmed Churchill in his rank of Lieutenant-General. He employed him practically as Commander-in-Chief to reconstitute the English Army. In this important task Churchill's military knowledge and organizing capacity had full scope. At the coronation in April Churchill was created an earl. The title Earl of Marlborough, so honourably borne, had since 1680 been extinct. We can understand why Churchill chose it for his own.

In May war was formally declared against France; and as William was detained in England and later embroiled in Ireland, Marlborough led the English contingent of eight thousand men against the French in Flanders. The world conflict which had now begun only gradually reached its full intensity. The French, who had a magnificent army, found eventually in Luxembourg a commander not unworthy to be named with Condé and Turenne. The allies ranged themselves along a three hundred-mile crescent from the Upper Rhine to the Belgian coast. They were more numerous than the French, and able everywhere to assume the offensive. Four separate armies advanced simultaneously, but in the leisurely fashion of those days, against the French frontiers. In the north the Spaniards and Dutch moved through Belgium towards Courtrai under the Prince of Vaudemont. Next in the line and farther south the Dutch and Swedes, together with the English contingent, sought, under the command of the Prince of Waldeck, to operate between the Sambre and the Meuse. Beyond the Ardennes the Prussians and North Germans under the Elector of Brandenburg aimed at the capture of Bonn, upon the Rhine; and farther south still the forces of the Empire, under the able leadership of the Count of Lorraine, struck at Mainz. A modest but definite measure of success rewarded all these operations.

When Marlborough landed at the end of May he found the British troops in very poor condition, and the three months which elapsed before active operations began were indispensable to their training and discipline. He made a great improvement in both. He drilled his men sedulously, saw to their pay, food, and clothing with that meticulous housekeeping from which his armies always profited, and repressed abuses of all kinds. In a few months the British force, from being the worst, was recognized as the best managed in Waldeck's army of about thirty-five thousand men.

The Prince of Waldeck was one of William's trusted leaders. His prolonged experience had made him a pedant in the art of war. Indeed, it was to him, as to most of the commanders at this time on both sides, very like a game of chess. The gambits and defences of each were well known to all players of a certain professional standing. As long as no obvious mistakes were made nor any serious risks run, no marked change in the situation was likely. Here a fortified town might be taken, there a small area of hostile country might be used as feeding-ground. But if the conventional counter-measures were taken by the opponent, these small prizes were placidly relinquished, and the armies continued to face and manœuvre against each other with the decorum of performers in a minuet. For this sedate warfare Waldeck's age of sixty-nine was no disqualification. He soon saw the improvement in the quality of the British, and took a liking to Marlborough. On August 24, having crossed the Sambre, he stood before the small ancient town of Walcourt, which rises on its hillock from an undulating and wooded landscape. Here he was well satisfied to live upon the enemy's country, sending his foraging parties out to gather supplies.

Marshal d'Humières, who commanded the opposing French army, felt bound to resent this trespass. He marched with becoming haughtiness to expel the intruders, and on the morning of August 25 fell upon the allied foraging parties and outposts about two miles south of Walcourt. It happened that Marlborough was in charge of these petty operations, and that the 16th Regiment of Foot (now the Bedfordshire Regiment), together with some three hundred Dutch horse and dragoons, formed their support. At nine o'clock the approach of large French forces was noticed, and soon after it was realized that these were the vanguard of the whole French army. Cannon were fired to recall the foragers and alarm the camps. Meanwhile the English regiment barred the advance of the French. They were heavily attacked; but under Colonel Hodges offered a stubborn resistance. For nearly two hours these six hundred English infantry prevented the hostile advance. When Marlborough learned that all was in readiness in Waldeck's army, he directed them to withdraw to the higher ground on the east of the hill of Walcourt, where other British troops and several batteries had come into line. The manner in which this single battalion effected its orderly retreat in the closest presence of very powerful French cavalry was a foretaste of the qualities which Europe was taught reluctantly to recognize in the English Army.

Meanwhile the Prince of Waldeck had occupied the town of Walcourt and had posted his army in position mainly on its eastern side. All the foragers had returned to camp, and d'Humières could take his choice whether he wanted a battle or not. It was now noon. The ground was not at all favourable to the French, but d'Humières seems to have been inflamed by the sharp fighting in which his vanguard had been engaged and did not take the trouble to reconnoitre. He ordered a strong column of French infantry, including eight battalions of the French Guard, to carry the town of Walcourt by assault. This was certainly a very difficult task to undertake voluntarily. The defences of the town were antiquated, and the walls had crumbled in several places. Still, it stood upon a hill, was partly covered by a river, and was girt about with a strong field army. Nevertheless, the French made a most determined attack upon the town, and although raked by Marlborough's flanking batteries from the eastern heights as they approached, they very nearly mastered its defenders. These were, however, reinforced by two battalions under the English Colonel Tollemache. Although the French Guard strove to burn the town gates, and everywhere fought with determination, they could make no progress, and the greensward around the ramparts was strewn with the bodies of five hundred of their men. D'Humières saw himself forced to widen the battle. He threw in his whole army in an improvised attack upon the allies' right, which had by now been extended west of Walcourt. This was the moment for Waldeck's counter-stroke. At six o'clock Slangenberg led the Dutch infantry forward from the western side. Simultaneously Marlborough attacked from the eastern side of the town. Placing himself at the head of the Life Guards and Blues, and supported by two English regiments, he charged upon the French right flank, inflicting very grave injuries upon the troops already unduly tried. The French cavalry was not only numerous, but was led by that same Villars of whom we have heard twenty years before at the siege of Maestricht, and whom we shall meet twenty years later at Malplaquet. Villars saved the French infantry from destruction, and d'Humières was able to withdraw his army as the night fell with a loss of six guns and two thousand of the flower of the French foot. As the casualties of the allies were about three hundred, the action wore the aspect of a victory. Feuquières, the French military critic, remarks severely "that this combat should never be cited save as an example to avoid." D'Humières' military reputation received a fatal blow, and in the next campaign he was superseded by Luxembourg.

The Prince of Waldeck rejoiced in his good fortune, nor was he ungenerous to those who had contributed to it. To William he wrote, "Colonel Hodges and the English did marvels and the Earl of Marlborough is assuredly one of the most gallant men I know." "Marlborough *in spite of his youth* had displayed in this one battle greater military capacity than do most generals after a long series of wars." William, being, like Marlborough, only thirty-nine himself, was not perhaps deeply impressed by this reference to the infirmities of youth. He wrote, however, in handsome terms to Marlborough:

> I am happy that my troops behaved so well in the affair of Walcourt. It is to you that this advantage is principally owing. You will please accordingly accept my thanks and rest assured that your conduct will induce me to confer on you still further marks of my esteem and friendship on which you may always rely.

Marlborough was made Colonel of the Royal Fusiliers, a regiment armed with a light musket called a fusil and employed in the special defence of the artillery. Such appointments were lucrative, and the fact that this regiment was under the Master-General of the Ordnance might encourage Marlborough to hope that this financial plum, so necessary for the support of his earldom, would some day fall into his hands. Walcourt was the only recognizable success which greeted the Dutch and English peoples in the year 1689. Thus the new King's reign opened auspiciously for him.

It happened, however, that during the summer a dispute had arisen between the King and Queen Mary on the one hand and Anne and her husband on the other, the brunt of which fell entirely on the Churchills. Up to this point all had been love between the two royal sisters, with the added thrill of conspiracy against their father. Till now Sarah had seemed to be the bond of union between them. But all things change with time, and many in a very short time. Sarah has reason on her side when she contends that her influence upon the succession settlement in the event of Mary's dying before William was used in the general interest rather than from any unworthy eagerness to ingratiate herself or her husband with the new sovereigns. For soon afterwards came the question of the Parliamentary grants to the Royal Family. And here began the rift.

Anne, who had agreed willingly to the sacrifice of inestimable reversionary rights, naturally wished, especially in the event of her sister's death, to have an independent income granted directly to her by Parliament. William resented this desire, and his wife championed his view. Both thought, moreover, that £30,000 a year was ample for the Princess's household; indeed, William expressed his wonder to Lord Godolphin how the Princess could spend so much, "though," adds Sarah, "it appeared afterwards that some of his favourites had more." Considering that Anne already had £20,000 a year settled upon her for life by Parliament, this was not generous treatment of a Princess who had voluntarily resigned an important contingent claim upon the Crown. The Cockpit household took care that Parliament was informed of the dispute, and, by way of having something to concede, suggested £70,000 as an appropriate figure. It was soon apparent that they had strong support. Mary sent for Anne and advised her to trust herself entirely to the King's gracious bounty. Anne replied sedately that "she understood her friends had a mind to make her some settlement." "Pray what friends have you," rejoined the Queen, "but the King and me?" A nasty family dispute about money matters; and not only upon money matters, but status!

Anne was found to have the House of Commons on her side. The Marlboroughs steadfastly espoused her interest. While John was fighting at Walcourt Sarah had actively canvassed the Tory Party. An independent position for the Princess Anne was held in Parliament to be essential to the Revolution settlement. Tempers rose high on both sides. Every form of pressure from ugly threats to dazzling bribes was put upon Sarah to persuade her mistress to a compromise. The figure was no longer in dispute. Shrewsbury himself undertook to win through Sarah Anne's acceptance of £50,000 from the King. Sarah was impervious. After what the Cockpit had seen of the royal generosity, they insisted upon a Parliamentary title. Sarah stood by her mistress and her friend. She cast away for ever the Queen's favour; and this at a time when there was no reason to suppose that Anne would outlive

Mary. There is no doubt that Marlborough guided the helm and faced the blizzard. But this was no Quixotism. It was his private interest that the matter should be settled so; it was his duty to the Princess; it was also the public interest, with a foreign king on the throne, and an ex-king claimant, that an English princess, heir designate, should be independently established. Again we see in Marlborough's story that strange coincidence of personal and national duties at crucial times. The new sovereigns had to accept a definite, public defeat, and the House of Commons voted the Princess Anne a life grant of £50,000 a year.

Marlborough had his own position in the country and with the King. But the Queen henceforward pursued Sarah with keen hostility, and this she soon extended to Sarah's husband. She blamed Sarah for the estrangement which had sprung up between herself and her once dearly loved sister. Repeatedly she urged Anne to remove this obstacle to their natural affection. Anne, forced to choose between the Queen and Sarah, made it plain with all the obstinate patience of her nature that she would stand by her friend, as her friend had stood by her. This choice, so deliberate and unshakable, was deeply wounding to her sister. Perhaps all this had as much to do in the future with Marlborough not getting the commands to which by rank and capacity he was entitled as had the exigencies of William's political system or his proclivities for Dutchmen. At any rate, it lay and lurked behind the daily routine of war and government.

King William was neither the first nor the last statesman to underrate the Irish danger. By May, when the European campaign was beginning on all the fronts of France, he found a serious war on his hands in Ireland. James had arrived in Ireland, was welcomed as a deliverer, and now reigned in Dublin, aided by an Irish Parliament and defended by a Catholic army of a hundred thousand men, of whom half were organized by French officers and furnished with French munitions. The Irish army was further sustained by a disciplined French contingent. Soon the whole island except the Protestant settlements in the North was under Jacobite control. William in 1690 found himself compelled to go in person with his main force to Ireland, and by the summer took the field at the head of thirty-six thousand men. Thus the French Government, at the cost only of five thousand troops, a few hundred extra officers, and moderate supplies, diverted the whole power of England from the main theatres of the war. Had Louis backed the Irish enterprise with more force, he would have gained even larger rewards.

William left the government in the hands of Queen Mary, assisted by a council of nine, four Whigs and five Tories, of whom Marlborough was one, besides being at the same time Commander-in-Chief. A most critical situation now developed. The Prince of Waldeck was encouraged by the memory of Walcourt to lay a trap for the French. But Luxembourg was no d'Humières, and at the battle of Fleurus in June he inflicted a crushing defeat upon the allies. At the same time the French fleet was stronger in the Channel than the combined fleets of England and Holland. Admiral Herbert was none the less ordered to bring them to battle. On June 30/July 10 he was defeated in a sea-fight off Beachy Head, the brunt of the action falling upon the Dutch. This was, according to Mahan, "the most conspicuous success the French have ever gained at sea over the English." It was said in London, "The Dutch had the honour, the French the advantage, and the English the shame." The French, under the energetic Tourville, now enjoyed the command of the sea. They could land an invading army in England; they could prevent the return of William from Ireland. The council of nine over which Queen Mary presided had to face an alarming crisis.

They were sustained by the loyalty and spirit of the nation. The whole country took up what arms could be found and feverishly organized the home defence. With a nucleus of about six thousand regular troops and the hastily improvised forces of the nation, Marlborough stood ready to resist an invasion for which an excellent French army of over twenty thousand men was available. William's decisive victory at the Boyne on July 1/11 threw James out of Ireland and back to France; but the English peril continued at its height. The anxious weeks of July and August slipped away, with no more injury or insult to England than the burning of Teignmouth by French troops. The French fleet was dismantled and laid up for the winter, and the English and Dutch fleets were refitted and again at sea. Thus the French opportunity was lost.

When the news of the naval defeat had been received at Queen Mary's council board, Marlborough and Admiral Russell were among the few Cabinet officers who did not volunteer to take command of the fleet. We must admire the spirit of these elderly nobles, none of whom knew one end of a ship from the other, and most of whom were devoid of military instruction or experience. They said they would sit on board the flagship and make the sea captains fight. Fortunately such desperate remedies were not required.

In the middle of August the Council was astonished to receive from the Commander-in-Chief a proposal of which he guaranteed the success, and on which he declared to the Queen that he would stake his reputation. This was to send the bulk of the regular troops out of the country upon an expedition to Ireland. Their minds, so lately exposed to the apprehensions of invasion, did not respond to his view that the danger had passed, and that the initiative should be regained.

Marlborough's plan was to seize the ports of Cork and Kinsale, which were the principal contact bases of the French in Ireland, and thus cut Ireland from French reinforcements. A double attack on the Jacobite forces in Ireland from the south as well as from the north would, he declared, be decisive. William, who was besieging Limerick, debated the matter with his Dutch generals. They, like the English Council of State, were adverse. But the King saw at once the strategic merits and timeliness of the plan. He discarded his generals' advice, overruled the Council, and placed Marlborough in charge of the expedition.

This was Marlborough's first independent command. He had not sought to go to Ireland before, and it is presumed that he did not wish to fight against an army led by King James in person. But now James was gone. The season was far advanced, and all preparations were made with the utmost speed. The expedition and its shipping were concentrated at Portsmouth, whither Marlborough repaired by August 26, and embarked on the 30th. He spread false rumours that it was intended to raid the coast of Normandy as a reprisal for Teignmouth; but the French were not deceived. Marlborough's sailing was delayed for a fortnight by contrary winds while every day was precious. The health of the troops on board suffered, and their supplies were partly consumed. But the mere rumour of the thrust produced a strategic effect. Leaving their Irish allies to their fate, Lauzun and Tyrconnel, who were tired of Ireland, and had no intention of being cut off there, retreated to France with the remainder of the French contingent.

Marlborough, very seasick, sailed on September 17, "bound (by God's assistance)," as the cautious master of the flagship wrote, "for ye coast of Ireland, Being of all Sorts about 82 Sayle." After silencing the batteries at the mouth of Cork Harbour he ran in upon the tide to Passage West and disembarked his army of about six thousand men seven miles inland during Tuesday, September 22. William meanwhile had abandoned the siege of Limerick, and returned to London. He had left orders with Ginkel to send five thousand men to join Marlborough in accordance with the plan. Marlborough had particularly asked that this detachment should consist of English troops, of whom there was no lack in the main army, and for Kirke, who was available, to command them. The Dutch general had no intention of allowing any purely English force or English commander to gain an independent success. It was with all the Dutchmen from William downward a maxim that the English were ignorant of war and must be strongly led by trained foreign officers and upheld by disciplined foreign troops. Ginkel had therefore, with many profuse apologies, selected five thousand Danes, Dutch, and Huguenots, who had now arrived on the north side of Cork under the Duke of Würtemberg.

This magnifico was junior in military rank to Marlborough, but far above him in birth. He claimed, as a prince of a royal house, to command the whole operation. A vexatious dispute, which Ginkel had foreseen with relish, arose. Marlborough displayed his commission from the Queen, and the Duke referred to his lineage and lost his temper. Meanwhile their two forces occupied the outlying works of Cork by separate action. There was no time to appeal for a decision about the command to William, and no certainty how he would have settled it. To secure unity, therefore, Marlborough was forced, not for the last time in his life, to propose the vicious expedient of antiquity that the rival generals should exercise command on alternate days. Würtemberg was with difficulty persuaded to accept this compromise. When the first day fell by lot to Marlborough he chose "Würtemberg" as the password for the troops. The Duke, surprised and mollified by this courtesy, selected "Marlborough" as the word for the second day, and thereafter made no further difficulties. Indeed, he seems to have yielded himself naturally and easily to Marlborough's guidance, once he felt it.

The governor of Cork, Colonel McElligott, returned a disdainful answer to the summons to surrender, and the attack upon the city was at once begun. Its defences were in a neglected condition, and its garrison of about five thousand men was too small to hold all the necessary works. Powerful batteries were landed from the fleet, and a breach made in the eastern wall. Marlborough was ready to assault on the evening of the 26th; but the governor beat a parley, which, though it came to nothing, allowed the tide to rise and gained him another day. At dawn on Sunday, the 27th, all was again in readiness. The batteries, supported by a frigate, which came up the river on the flood, bombarded the breach in the town. A Danish column a thousand strong forded the northern arm of the river, and at one o'clock Charles Churchill, Marlborough's brother, whom he had made a Brigadier, with fifteen hundred English infantry, headed by many noblemen and gentlemen volunteers, plunged into the estuary. The water, though ebbing, was breast-high, the current strong, and the fire from the ramparts heavy. But both Danes and English advanced undaunted and occupied the counterscarp. As they re-formed here for the final storm McElligott hoisted the white flag. In view of his trick of the day before, no terms were offered. What was left of the garrison, about four thousand men, became prisoners of war. Marlborough entered the city the next day, and sternly suppressed the looting which had begun.

From Cork Marlborough, without an hour's delay, turned to Kinsale, and the very next day his cavalry summoned the two forts which guarded the harbour to surrender. The town, which was undefended, was seized before it could be burned, thus affording the necessary shelter for the troops. Marlborough arrived himself on the Thursday, October 1, by which time considerable infantry forces had entered the town. He saw at once that the "New Fort" was much stronger than had been reported and if defended would require a regular siege. The governor, Sir Edward Scott, rejected the very favourable conditions that were offered, and, treating with contempt the threat that he would be hanged if he put the assailants to the trouble of a formal siege, addressed himself to a stubborn defence.

Trenches were opened forthwith, and by October 7 the English and Danes had sapped almost to the counterscarp. On the 11th the heavy batteries, transported with the utmost difficulty over the appalling roads from Cork, began their bombardment, and by the 15th a breach was pronounced ready for assault. The intrepid governor felt that enough was done for honour. He therefore opened negotiations, and Marlborough, whose trenches were knee-deep in water and who was worried by the approach of winter and fearful for the health of his troops, was glad to give him generous terms. Scott was allowed to march off to Limerick with his twelve hundred survivors under the customary compliments of war. But "as the enemy marched out, the Earl took a note of all their names, telling them that if ever they were hereafter in arms against King William, they should have no quarter." The siege had cost Marlborough 250 men, and the hospitals were already crowded with sick. A hundred pieces of cannon and much military supplies fell to the victors. But this was the least part of the success. The capture of these southern harbours deprived Irish resistance of all hope of French succour, and rendered the entire reduction of the country possible as soon as the winter was over. Charles Churchill was appointed governor of Kinsale, and Marlborough's army went into winter quarters. He himself landed at Deal on October 28, having accomplished what he had planned and guaranteed with complete success.

He was extremely well received in London. "In twenty-three days," says Lord Wolseley, "Marlborough had achieved more than all William's Dutch commanders had done both in Ireland and abroad during the whole of the previous year." William was most gracious: but the patronizing compliment he paid was characteristic of the Dutch attitude towards British generals. "No officer living," he said, "*who has seen so little service as my Lord Marlborough*, is so fit for great commands."

Marlborough did not return to Ireland, as some writers aver. We find him dining in January with Lord Lucas, Constable of the Tower, and ordering £100 to be distributed among "the poor Irish taken at Cork and Kinsale." He certainly desired to have the chief command in Ireland in the campaign of 1691, and public opinion expected it. But it was no part of William's policy to let English soldiers gather laurels. The closing scenes in Ireland were reserved for Ginkel, while Marlborough, at the head of the British contingent in Flanders, was to make the campaign as one of the generals of the large army William had determined to command in person. He no doubt appreciated the kindness of the King in thus repairing the deficiencies of his military education; and his experiences in this campaign must at least have had the value of showing him some methods of war to be avoided.

CHAPTER FIFTEEN

The Personal Cleavage

ᛉᚲ 1690-91 ᛈᛉ

WE have seen our England, maddened by the Popish Plot into Test
Acts and Exclusion Bills, placing after a few years a Popish sovereign
on the throne with general acclamation. We have seen her also,
angered by his offences, unseat him by an almost universal shrug of the
shoulders and set the island Crown upon the brow of a foreign prince.
And now we shall see a very strong reaction which arose against that
Prince or Parliamentary King and cast gleams of public favour upon
the true King over the water. The possibility of the return of James
could never be absent from the minds of those who had been witnesses
of the miracle of the restoration of Charles. Moreover, many of the
reasons which had led to the expulsion of James had disappeared. A
new Constitution had established the power of Parliament and limited
effectually the prerogative and authority of the Crown. No one could
doubt that if James returned it would be as the result of a bargain
which consolidated the principles of a limited monarchy and upheld
beyond the chance of challenge the Protestant character of the English
people. Those who write with crude censure of the shame of deserting
James for William or William for James seem to forget that James and
William were not ends in themselves. They were the instruments by
which the power and happiness of England might be gained or marred.
The loyalties due to their kingly office or hereditary titles were not the
only loyalties to which English statesmen had a right and duty to respond. There was, for instance, the interest of the country, to which an
increasingly conscious loyalty was due. In those days, as in these, men

were by character true or false; but unswerving fidelity to a particular king was no test of their virtue or baseness.

The events of the Revolution had created conditions in England to which no parallel exists in later times. Many of the magnates who had dethroned and expelled James still revered him in their hearts, in spite of all the Acts of Parliament they had passed, as their real, natural sovereign. Every one regarded the imperious and disagreeable Dutchman who had had to be brought in and set up for the sake of Protestantism and civil liberty as a necessary evil. They saw his dislike and contempt for Englishmen. They understood that he regarded England mainly as a powerful tool for his Continental schemes, conceived primarily in the interest of Holland. With anxious eyes they watched his unpopularity increasing with the growth of taxes and distress through long years of war rarely lighted by success. The danger of his death from natural causes, from assassination or upon the battlefield, where he so often bravely exposed himself, and the grave constitutional issues which would renew themselves upon such an event, were ever present to their minds. Devoted to the Protestant faith, and determined that the English Constitution should not sink to a despotism upon the French model, they none the less had to take into account the possible pursuance of their objects under violently and suddenly changed conditions. It was not wonderful that they should have acted upon the ancient Greek maxim, "Love as though you shall hereafter hate, and hate as though you shall hereafter love." It was an epoch of divided loyalties, of conflicting interests, of criss-cross ties, of secret reserves and much dissembling. When kings forswear their oaths of duty and conspire against their peoples, when rival kings or their heirs crowd the scene, statesmen have to pick and choose between sovereigns of fluctuating values, as kings are wont to pick and choose between politicians according to their temporary serviceableness. The conditions and standards of this period, like its tests and stresses, were different from our own. Nevertheless, as we contend, the main feature which emerges is that of steadfastness and not deceit, of patriotism above self-interest, and of courage and earnestness, rather than of craft and opportunism.

Through all these baffling changes, of which only the barest outline can be realized by posterity, Halifax seems to have threaded his way with truer hold upon the essential interest of England than any other figure of whom we have record. We have seen him a Protestant op-

ponent of the Exclusion Bill and a Minister of James II. We have seen
him an opponent of James II. We have seen him harshly conducting
that fallen sovereign to Rochester. We have seen him the trusted
counsellor of William III. He was soon to reopen his relations with the
exiled James. No one but a blind partisan of the Whig or Tory factions
of those vanished days would find it impossible to vindicate all these
successive and superficially inconsistent actions of Halifax as being both
sincere and in the public interest. On the whole throughout this long,
tempestuous period Marlborough, as we have seen, moved politically
with Halifax. His broad outlook upon affairs, his sane and reasonable
temperament, his indifference towards the two parties, his hatred of
excess or revenge, his antagonism to France, his adherence to the Protestant cause, all conform to the Halifax type, and step by step his actions
harmonize with those of the illustrious 'Trimmer.'

We must now look more closely upon the extraordinary Prince who
for good reasons and in the general interest had robbed his father-in-
law of his throne. From his earliest years William's circumstances had
been harsh and sombre. His life was loveless. He was always fatherless
and childless. His marriage was dictated by reasons of State. He was
brought up by his termagant grandmother, Amalia of Solms, and in his
youth was passed for regulation from one Dutch committee to another.
His childhood was unhappy and his health bad. He had a tubercular
lung, was asthmatic and partly crippled. But within this emaciated and
defective frame there burned a remorseless fire, fanned by the storms
of Europe, and intensified by the stern compression of his surroundings. His great actions began before he was twenty-one. From that age
he had fought constantly in the field and toiled through every intrigue
of Dutch domestic politics and of the European scene. For the last
four years he had been the head of the English conspiracy against
James.

His public hatred of France and his personal quarrel with Louis XIV
constituted the main theme of his life. All his exertions were directed
against the tyrant who had not only compassed the ruin of the Dutch
Republics, but had actually seized and dragooned the small principality
of Orange from which he had sprung, and with which his native pride
and affections were interwoven.

It was the natural characteristic of such an upbringing and of such a mission that William should be ruthless. Although he did not conspire in the murder of the de Witts, he rejoiced at it, profited by it, and protected and pensioned the murderers. His conduct in the Massacre of Glencoe was entirely unfeeling. Neither the treachery nor the butchery of that crime disturbed his cynical serenity. He was vexed and worried only about the outcry that arose afterwards. He would break a political opponent without pity, but he was never needlessly cruel, and was glad to treat foes no longer dangerous with contempt or indifference. He wasted no time on minor revenges. His sole vendetta was with Louis. For all his experience from his youth at the head of armies and for all his dauntless heart, he was never a great commander. He had not a trace of that second-sight of the battlefield which is the mark of military genius. He was no more than a resolute man of good common sense whom the accident of birth had carried to the conduct of war. It was in the sphere of politics that his inspiration lay. Perhaps he has never been surpassed in the sagacity, patience, and discretion of his statecraft. The combinations he made, the difficulties he surmounted, the adroitness with which he used the time factor, or played upon the weakness of others, the unerring sense of proportion and power of assigning to objectives their true priorities, all mark him for the highest fame.

William watched with ill-concealed disfavour the protracted wranglings of the English chiefs and parties. He was never fond of England, nor interested in her domestic affairs. Her seamy side was all he knew. He repeatedly urged Parliament to address itself to the Continental situation. He required the wealth and power of England by land and sea for the European war. It was for this he had come in person to enlist her. Although he had himself darkly and deviously conspired the undoing of his foolish kinsman, he thought little of the English public men who had been his confederates. A prince himself, he could not but distrust men who, albeit at his instigation, had been guilty of treason to their royal master. He knew too much about their jealousies and intrigues to cherish for them sentiments of liking or respect. He had used them for his own ends, and would reward them for their services; but as a race he regarded them as inferior in fibre and fidelity to his Dutchmen. English statesmen to him were perjured, and what was even worse, local-minded. English soldiers seemed to him uncouth and ill-trained by Continental standards. English generals lacked the professional knowledge which, he believed, long experience of war alone could give. The English Navy was no doubt brave and hardy, but his own sentiments naturally rested upon the traditions of Tromp and de Ruyter. The Dutch were his children; the English could never be more than his step-children, to whom, indeed, he owed a parental duty and from whose estate he was entitled during his guardianship to draw substantial advantages.

Once securely seated on the throne he scarcely troubled to disguise these sentiments.

His unsociable disposition, his greediness at table, his silence and surliness in company, his dislike of women, his neglect of London, all prejudiced him with polite society. The ladies voted him "a low Dutch bear." The English Army too was troubled in its soul. Neither officers nor men could dwell without a sense of humiliation upon the military aspects of the Revolution. They did not like to see all the most important commands entrusted to Dutchmen. They eyed sourly the Dutch infantry who paced incessantly the sentry-beats of Whitehall and St James's, and contrasted their shabby blue uniforms and small stature with the scarlet pomp of the 1st Guards and Coldstreamers now banished from London. It was a pity, thought they, that the public interest had not allowed them to give these fellows a drubbing.

Cracks had speedily appeared in the fabric of the original National Government. The Whigs considered that the Revolution belonged to them. All they had suffered since their far-seeing Exclusion Bills, all that they had risked in the great conspiracy, should now be rewarded. Their judgment, their conduct, their principles, had been vindicated. Ought they not, then, to have all the offices? Was it just they should be thrust aside in many cases for the "evil counsellors of the late king"? But William knew that he could never have gained the Crown of England but by the help of the Cavaliers and Anglicans who formed the staple of the Tory Party. Moreover at this time, as a king he liked the Tory mood. Here was a party who exalted the authority of the Crown. Here was a Church devoted to hereditary monarchy and profoundly grieved to have been driven by the crisis from the doctrine of non-resistance. William felt that Whig principles would ultimately lead to a republic. Under the name of Stadtholder he was really the King of Holland; he had no desire under the name of King to be only Stadtholder of England. He was therefore ready to break up the Convention

Parliament which had given him the Crown while, as the Whigs said, "its work was all unfinished." At the election of February 1690 "the buried names of Whig and Tory revived"; and the Tories won. Henceforward the party cleavage and party system became rigid, formal, and —down to our own days—permanent.

Shrewsbury, Godolphin, Marlborough, and Sunderland, and from a somewhat different angle Halifax, now ageing, held a middle position apart from party, and, as they no doubt thought, above it. Each of these men drew in others. "Shrewsbury was usually hand in glove with Wharton. Godolphin and Marlborough shared confidences with Russell." It was upon this central body of men, pre-eminent for their gifts, unrivalled in experience of affairs and knowledge of the Court and Parliament, that William was naturally inclined to rely either as counsellors or Ministers, and he added thorough paced Whigs or Tories in different proportions to either flank to suit the changing needs of the years.

But the King's affairs moved inevitably in a vicious circle. He could not trust high military authority to Englishmen, nor allow English soldiers to win fame in the field, without, as he thought, placing himself in their power. In all the key posts of the Army he must have Dutchmen or foreigners. Thus he angered the English officers and the English Army, and found new justification for his distrust in their resentment. Most of all this cycle prejudiced the relations between him and Marlborough. Marlborough's desire was above everything to command armies in the great war now raging. He felt within himself qualities which, if they had their chance, would produce remarkable results for himself, for England, and for Europe. But though William desired the same political ends, he feared their being gained by Marlborough. He remembered General Monk; he remembered what had happened at Salisbury. Therefore it became with him a necessary principle of his existence to bar Marlborough's natural and legitimate professional career. The abler general Marlborough showed himself, the more he must be kept in a subordinate station; the greater his talents the more imperative their repression.

Marlborough was made to realize all this, and perhaps its inevitability, at the beginning of 1691. He had rendered immense and even decisive services to the new régime both in the crisis of the Revolution and during the Revolution settlement. His had been almost the only military achievements of 1690. The charge at Walcourt, the swift seizure of

Cork and Kinsale, were outstanding episodes. It was variously rumoured in London that he would be created a Duke and Knight of the Garter, would be appointed Master-General of the Ordnance, and would be commander-in-chief in Ireland for the coming campaign. A dukedom he considered beyond his means, and he was to refuse one ten years later on the same grounds; but we know from letters which Anne and her husband wrote to the King that he desired the Garter. He wanted the Ordnance to support his title; and above all he sought an independent command in one of the theatres of war. He found himself denied on all points. The Ordnance went to Henry Sidney, a civilian who was destitute of any qualifications of which history can take notice. Ginkel had the command in Ireland, and Waldeck, in spite of Fleurus, had, under the King, the command in Flanders. Of course Marlborough ought not to have minded such treatment. He ought to have been indifferent, like our modern generals, statesmen, and financiers, to personal ambitions or material interests. However, he took it all very much amiss. He seems to have come to the conclusion that William meant to keep him down. Under James he saw his path blocked by Papists: under William by Dutchmen.

The campaign of 1691 opened in imposing style with a conference at The Hague. A league of nations assembled to concert measures against the common enemy, France. England, Holland, Prussia, the German states, the Empire, Spain, and a dozen smaller powers—all sent their representatives. Such a gathering of princes and statesmen had scarcely been seen before in Christendom. At the summit stood William in all his glory, the architect of this immense confederation of rival states and conflicting faiths, the sovereign of its two most vigorous nations, the chief commander of its armies, lacking nothing but the military art. This splendid ceremonial was rudely interrupted by the cannon. It was scarcely etiquette to begin operations before April or May; but early in March Louis XIV, with Luxembourg as his general and Vauban as his engineer, suddenly appeared with a hundred thousand men before the valuable barrier fortress of Mons. William was forced to descend from his pedestal and mount his horse. He could muster an army of barely fifty thousand, and these could only be spectators of the fall of Mons. So much for the Hague conference.

Marlborough had been left in England charged with the task of recruitment for the Army. In May the allied forces took the field with the object at least of recovering Mons. William gave Marlborough the command of the British contingent, and to make the necessary vacancy moved Tollemache to Ireland, to serve under Ginkel. Marlborough and Count Solms were sent forward to organize the assembly of the main army in the neighbourhood of Brussels. Waldeck commanded while William rested awhile in his home palace at Loo. Luxembourg, with a solid French army, barred the way to Mons. At the end of June William arrived at headquarters, and the campaign began in earnest. It was the first time since the reign of Henry VIII that a King of England had commanded in person on the Continent, and all the young bloods of quality and fashion had hurried from London to let off their pistols. But nothing happened. Luxembourg stood on the defensive in positions too well chosen for William to attack. The great armies marched and counter-marched according to the orthodox rules of war, and the precious summer months slipped away. By the end of August all was over. William, baffled and a trifle humiliated, led his armies back to their cantonments. They passed on their way the field of Fleurus, where the grisly spectacle of Waldeck's unburied corpses struck a chill through a disappointed host. William handed over the command to Waldeck and returned to Loo.

But the adversities of the campaign were not yet ended. In the middle of September, when custom should have enforced upon Luxembourg the propriety of retiring into winter quarters, he organized an outrageous cavalry attack upon the rearguard of the allied army while it was moving from Leuze to Grammont. The rising French officer Villars routed the Dutch cavalry and sabred them from the field. The confusion spread to the infantry. The sudden heavy firing rang through the autumn air. There was a tumult of scampering horses and men. Marlborough, marching in his station with the British contingent, had already passed the Catoise stream. He turned sharply back and marched towards the bridges at the utmost speed, apparently in the mood for battle. A broad flush of red and steel spread menacingly across the landscape. But Luxembourg, cool and composed in the cavalry action and content with the day, disengaged his excited army before the British brigades could deploy; and the fighting of the year ended for the allies upon this somewhat ridiculous incident, in which there were, however, above seven hundred casualties. The Prince of Waldeck led the discomfited Dutch and angry English into their winter quarters;

and in all their camps and garrisons the word ran round that King William had "entered the field too late, and quitted it too soon."

It was a heavy exertion for the states of those days, with their narrow finances, to keep such large armies in contact with an equal enemy for a whole season. The loss of a year weighed heavily on the fragile structure of the Grand Alliance. All William's skill in diplomacy had come to nothing at the point of action. John Churchill was then forty-three, in his prime. He possessed all the military knowledge and experience upon which he afterwards acted. As he watched those infirm yet stilted manœuvres, as he brooded on these wasted opportunities, as he no doubt felt how surely and how swiftly he could reshape the scene, and yet how carefully and tightly trammelled he was, can we wonder at the anger that possessed his soul? There was no prophetic spirit at his side to whisper, "Patience! The opportunity will yet be yours." His patience is almost proverbial. He had need for it all. Ten years, half of them years of war—ten years when the chances of a lifetime seemed finally to die—were to pass before he was again to exercise a military command.

CHAPTER SIXTEEN

The Jacobite Illusion

WE now approach the most unhappy and questionable period in Marlborough's life. The peccadilloes of youth, the work he had to do as confidential servant of the Duke of York, his treasonable letter to the Prince of Orange, his desertion of James at Salisbury, are all capable of either excuse or vindication. Indeed, his conduct towards James was justified not only by his religious and political convictions, but even more by the broad and long interest of England. But it entailed consequences.

Now we must record that opposition to King William, those intrigues with King James, which seem to stultify his former action, to rob it of its basis of conscientious scruple, and to arm his innumerable assailants with every weapon that indignant rectitude or implacable malice could desire. Moreover, the picture is not one to be painted in bold blacks and whites. We gaze upon a scene of greys shading indefinably, mysteriously, in and out of one another. A mere recital of facts and outlines would give no true description without a comprehension of the atmosphere.

In judging the character of Marlborough the question arises whether his actions were dictated by undue self-interest. Reasonable care for a man's own interest is neither a public nor a private vice. That Marlborough, like most Englishmen, together with all the Revolution statesmen, should become estranged from the new Government; that he should quarrel personally with King William; that he should seek to

safeguard himself in the increasingly probable event of a Jacobite restoration, are not in themselves, and under the conditions of the period,
wrongful or odious behaviour. The test is whether he was false in intention or in fact to the cause of Protestantism and constitutional freedom, and above all whether the safety of England or the lives of her
soldiers and sailors were jeopardized by his actions; and it is to these aspects that the attention of the reader will be directed.

King James and his family dwelt, refugees, by the throne of Louis
XIV. They and their shadow Court, with its handful of Irish troops
and Guards, its functionaries and its Ministers, were all dependent for
their daily bread upon the bounty or policy of their protector. The vanity of Louis was gratified by the presence in his orbit of a suppliant
monarch. He indulged to the full the easy chivalry of affluent pity.
Sometimes, indeed, his sentiments for a brother monarch, in whose
person not only the Catholic faith but even the Divine Right of Kings
had been assaulted, carried him beyond purely French interests. But, in
the main, a cool statecraft ruled. The exiled family at Saint-Germains
depended for their treatment upon their usefulness in the Continental
schemes of France. That usefulness for this purpose was measured by
the strength and reality of their English connexions. They had, thus,
the strongest inducements—and, indeed, compulsions—to magnify the
importance and the intimacy of their British ties and the general vitality of the Jacobite cause. Their supreme object was to obtain from
Louis a French fleet to carry them to England, and a French army to
reestablish King James upon his throne. They therefore, in their unhappy plight, continually represented themselves to the French Government as being in the most confidential relations with the leading
men in England, especially with the members of King William's
Council.

They developed every possible contact with English Jacobites and
friends, real or pretended, across the Channel. They put their own
gloss upon whatever news they could get, and served the result up—
more often, perhaps, than was tactful—to the French Ministers. Always they laboured to paint a picture of an England longing for their
return and ready to rise the moment a chance presented itself. Let the
French supply the army and the ships, and they would make the attempt. Once they landed, all would be well. But the French Ministers

were sceptical; they had many independent sources of information, and they had a different point of view.

As early as 1689 Marlborough was reported to James as being dissatisfied with the new régime and anxious to make his peace with the old. But nothing definite was asserted until the beginning of 1691, about which Dicconson's *Life of James* sets forth at length a series of reports by three Jacobite agents, Mr. Bulkeley, Colonel Sackville, and Mr. Floyd, or Lloyd, of conversations which they declared they had had with Admiral Russell, Godolphin, Halifax, and Churchill. That all these servants of King William allowed or invited Jacobite agents to visit them, and that conversations took place, may well be true. But Dicconson's version of what passed is at once malicious and absurd.

Dicconson has qualities of his own. We may note the ecclesiastical flavour.

> Churchill was in appearance the greatest penitent imaginable. He begged of him [Sackville] to go to the King and acquaint him with his sincere repentance and to intercede for mercy, that he was ready to redeem his apostasy with the hazard of his utter ruine, his crimes apeareing so horrid to him that he could neither sleep, nor eat but in continual anguish, and a great deal to that purpose.

No one knows, of course, what Marlborough said or did not say. Dicconson—the sole authority—can only tell us what he thought fit to record of the Jacobite agents' reports of fifteen years before. All this is one-sided assertion. Marlborough never volunteered explanations or justification. He appeared unconscious that there was anything to explain.

To what extent he deceived the Jacobite agents with the fair words and pious assurances; to what extent they boasted the value of the fish they thought they had caught; to what extent Melfort, a receiver of customs, and Nairne, under-secretary to James II during his exile, exaggerated the secret service information, the collection of which was their main duty, are mysteries; but in this case (as also with Godolphin, Russell, Shrewsbury, and others,) we certainly have at one end of the chain an important personage anxious not to be too much hated or too much overlooked at Saint-Germains, and at the other an unhappy exile in no position to be vindictive or particular in receiving friendly overtures.

Marlborough's communications with the Jacobite Court, or with his sister's son, the Duke of Berwick, or with James's son, the Old Pretender,* were no passing intrigue. They were a system. They were a lifelong policy—just so much and no more—pursued continually for a quarter of a century. Under King William there was no written correspondence. There are accounts of messages and conversations, of promises and assurances without number, many of which may be fabrications, but others which could not have been wholly invented and bear in part the stamp of truth.

In the first phase Marlborough's object, like that of the other Revolution leaders, was to obtain a formal pardon from the Exile, in the unpleasant but by no means improbable event of his restoration. This was a phase in the communications of which William was generally aware, which even had his acquiescence.

At the least William viewed all these intrigues with Saint-Germains with a tolerant eye. "With respect to the riots in Northamptonshire," he wrote on July 15, 1694,

> I recollect that not long ago I was informed that Lord Monmouth had made his peace at St Germain's. Not knowing what to believe, you must try to discover, if possible, whether he, who is lord lieutenant of the county, has fomented or interfered in those riots; and you will please to give me your opinion, whether that employment should not be given to another person.

Here we see the King, the person most affected and best informed, drawing a clear distinction between "making peace with St Germains" and overt unlawful action.

The mere "making peace with St Germains," even by one of his Lord-Lieutenants, was not regarded either by the King or the high circles around him upon the footing of treason; and since almost every prominent leader had safeguarded himself in this way it did not seem to them to be a dishonourable action. It is not our purpose to defend

---

* James Francis Edward Stuart, only son of James II and Mary of Modena, was born in 1688, taken to France with his mother, and on his father's death in 1701 proclaimed (and recognized by Louis XIV) King of England. His persistence, through a long life, in claiming to be the legitimate King of England earned him the title the "Old Pretender . . ." His son, Charles Edward (1720–1788), was the "Young Pretender."

such conduct, but only to reduce it to its proper place in the perilous, tragical politics of those days.

Under Anne we enter a region of purely military camouflage, as in 1702, when Marlborough, actively frustrating the French in the field and seeking eagerly to fight a decisive battle, received Jacobite envoys in his camp, sending them away with who shall say what cryptic or encouraging words; or as in 1708, when he is besieging Lille in circumstances of extraordinary military difficulty, and keeps up at the same time a lengthy and active correspondence with the Duke of Berwick about peace negotiations. We shall return to this later.

There is, lastly, in the long story of Marlborough's relations with Saint-Germains a phase, possibly the least insincere of all, when he endeavoured to establish some kind of amicable relationship with the Old Pretender, "James III." And there are always great civilities and protestations of devotion to the exiled Queen. All baffling; all mystifying; truth and falsehood, pity and deception, intermingled; dual loyalties deliberately exploited. Was it not important for Saint-Germains to be able to tell Louis XIV that they were in close, secret, constant relationship with the Commander-in-Chief of the enemy's army? They would be grateful for that. It was a real service. It cost nothing. It did not hamper business. It all tended to create uncertainty. The French Government, keenly interested in Berwick's peace negotiations, might have their mind diverted from the defence of Lille and its citadel. This was all part of Marlborough's war-making; and also part of his system. And so, a month or perhaps a week later—a swift march, a sudden assault, thrusting out of a cloud of honeyed words and equivocation, changed fortunes in the field. Webs of intrigue, crossings, double-crossings, stratagems, contrivances, deceit; with smiles, compliments, nods, bows, and whispers—then *crash!* sudden reversion to a violent and decisive military event. The cannon intervene.

There is no disputing the validity of the Jacobite complaint, that they never got anything out of Marlborough except promises which were not made good, and information which arrived only when it was stale. Yet there was no moment at which they could say, "He is only fooling us. He is only feeding us with trifles and smooth words." For there never was a moment when they could not nurse the hope that, if the Exile returned, the Captain-General would put him on the throne;

or when they could dismiss the fear that in the teeth of his resistance all hope of return was ended. In the upshot they were disappointed. As things turned out, they got less than nothing at all. They were mocked with false hopes; placated with counterfeit coin; smothered with empty salutations. A vast system of genuine shams, a prolonged relationship of deceits that were effective because they never excluded the possibility of being real: the whole of this prevailing over twenty-five years and expressed in terms of perfervid loyalty, with promises made, as they declare, of the highest service and of the darkest treachery. But nothing to show for it! Not a corporal's guard turned over! Not a picket conceded in the field; not a scrap of information that they did not know, or that was not public property already; but always hope and always delay, always disappointment—and then more hope. Marlborough betrayed nothing, but to the end no Jacobite agent, courtier, or Minister could ever feel sure he would not some day betray *everything* into their hands. Nor can we at this stage pursue the hypothesis of what he would have done if this or that had happened.

We must confine ourselves to what actually happened. Every account, every record, summed up, shows that the Jacobite Court were for a quarter of a century flattered, duped, baffled, and in the event ruined by an inscrutable and profound personality. They certainly had every reason to blacken the memory of the calm, deep, patient man who threaded his way almost unerringly through the labyrinth of dynastic, political, and military intrigues in five reigns, and who emerged at every decisive moment the successful champion of British interests, of Protestant interests, and of his own interests.

The long succession of historians who follow each other like sheep through the gates of error are all agreed about Marlborough's profound sagacity and that self-interest was his motive power. Let us, then, try the case by these standards. What conceivable interest could he have had in bringing back James? At the best a contemptuous pardon and a justly ineradicable distrust. Of all the notables of England he had the least to hope and the most to fear from such a restoration. How eagerly would triumphant Jacobites, proud Tories, and infuriated Whigs have combined in such an event to drive into obscurity the double-dyed arch-traitor who had presumed to be the maker and un-maker of kings! What succour from his old master could he look for against such a storm? Exile, disgrace, or at best some pittance, some sinecure, was the most that magnanimity or indifference could bestow; and James was not the most magnanimous or forgiving of men. What chance had Marlborough but the Princess Anne? There, in the narrow circle of the Cockpit, where long friendship and companionship reigned, where the bonds of union were only forged more tensely by external persecution or danger, lay the only hope. And that a great one! Why should he bring back James and his lusty son, in his own right or under a regency—under a jealous Council of State as a Catholic, or still more as a Protestant—and exclude for ever Anne from the succession? Why should he "abandon wife, children and country" for that? Never for one moment could he have entertained such inanities. We can hear him make his customary comment, "Silly! Silly!" The more sagacious, the more self-seeking he, the less harbourage such devastating contingencies could have found. From the closing years of Charles II, through the unceasing convulsions and confusions of this time, John and Sarah held on to Anne and staked their public existence upon her fortunes and her favour.

CHAPTER SEVENTEEN

The Family Quarrel

ᚠᚦ 1691-92 ᚦᚠ

At the end of October 1691 William landed at Margate from the wars, and all the way to London he was warmly welcomed by the people. They did not realize the failure of the Continental campaign, and the good news from Ireland roused their enthusiasm. Ginkel had defeated the Irish with an immense slaughter at Aughrim. Limerick had surrendered. The Irish hero Sarsfield had made terms which allowed him to carry eighteen thousand of the best Irish troops out of the country into the French service. It seemed that the Irish troubles were at an end; at least, all resistance was crushed. But the national rejoicing at the local victory was inspired by the hope of an early general peace. Of this there was no prospect. The most costly years of the first part of the world war still lay ahead.

The King brought with him in his coach Bentinck and Marlborough; apparently all were on cordial terms. At Shooter's Hill the coach overturned. Bentinck and Marlborough were hurt. Marlborough, indeed, seems to have been dazed, for he declared that his neck was broken. William, who was only shaken, reassured him that this could not be so, "since he could still speak." The party, somewhat battered, were able to make their entry into London amid cheering crowds.

Nevertheless the realities of the situation might well cause the King anxiety. The injustice done to English officers and the implied insult to the Army aroused strong feelings throughout English society. These vexations were shared by the English Ministers, through whom and with whom William was forced to govern, and especially by that central group to which he naturally inclined.

Marlborough, already offended by what he regarded as ill-usage, convinced that it was William's policy to keep him in the shade, and more excusably vexed by the futile conduct of the campaign in Flanders, did not hesitate to show his hostility. To all this movement which flared up in Parliament and the higher circles of London that winter he lent an influence which was soon found to be potent. He criticized the King openly. He welcomed the tale-bearing which carried his caustic comments to the royal ear. He said at Lord Wharton's before a company that in the previous reign James had been so eager to fill the army with Irishmen that the only question asked was, "Do you speak English?" Now all that had happened was that the word "Dutchman" was changed for "Irishman." He spoke of Bentinck as "a wooden fellow." He remonstrated with William to his face upon his gifts of Crown property to Bentinck and Zulestein. "With great grief of heart many of his faithful servants," he said,

> among whom he requested the honour to be included, saw the royal munificence confined to one or two lords and these foreigners. . . . As far as he was concerned he had no cause to complain; he was amply provided for in the post he held under his Majesty; but in duty bound he felt obliged to lay before him what he ought to know, because he could not otherwise be apprized of means to remedy the disasters that might be the result of such unpopular conduct.

Perhaps he did not express himself so elegantly; but this was the gist of it. He may, indeed, have said more. The King indignantly turned his back upon him.

William's relations with Marlborough, though strained, were not broken by mere words. When the commands for the next year's campaign were being decided, he designed to take him to Flanders as Lieutenant-General attached to his own person. Marlborough demurred to this undefined position. He did not wish to be carried round Flanders as a mere adviser, offering counsel that was not taken, and bearing responsibility for the failures that ensued. He craved leave to remain at home, unless he was required at least to command the British troops, as in the past year. But the King had offered them to Ginkel, and afterwards bestowed them, with lamentable results, upon Count Solms.

Meanwhile Marlborough began indirectly to stir the House of Commons for an address to the Crown on the subject of the Employment of Foreigners, and he proposed himself to move a similar motion in the House of Lords. Widespread support was forthcoming. It even appeared likely that the motion would be carried by majorities in both Houses. The King saw himself about to be requested to dismiss his Dutch followers and favourites from all English offices, and to send back to Holland the five thousand Dutch Guards upon whom he relied as his ultimate security. This was unmistakably a hostile proceeding. Moreover, Marlborough's activities did not end with Parliament. He was the leading British general. "His courage, his abilities, his noble and winning manner, the splendid success which had attended him on every occasion on which he had been in command, had made him," says Macaulay, "in spite of his sordid vices, a favourite with his brethren in arms." Undoubtedly many officers of various ranks resorted to him and loudly expressed their resentment at the favour shown to the Dutch. The "sordid vices" showed themselves, we are told, in the fact that he never entertained them with meat or drink. His influence was exerted on their minds, and not, as was expected in those days, upon their stomachs. In spite of this characteristic omission, he had a great public and personal following in both Parliament and the Army at the beginning of 1692.

The general unrest among the high personnel of the Court and Government could not remain secret from the King. He certainly became aware that during 1691 most of those who surrounded him, to whom he owed much and without whom he could not govern England, were in some sort of communication with the rival he had ousted, and who sought in turn to dethrone him. But he had a far better comprehension of the forces at work than any of his posthumous literary champions. He knew that he was driving England very hard, and forcing upon its Parliamentary system and society treatment to which his own Dutch oligarchy would never have submitted. He could imagine the attitude of "Their High Mightinesses" if purely Dutch offices, Dutch estates, and Dutch commands had been lavished upon Englishmen. He did not therefore resent as strongly as his later admirers have done the double-dealing by which he was encompassed. He accepted it as a necessary element in a situation of unexampled perplexity. He tolerated perforce the fact that all his principal English counsellors were reinsuring themselves against a break-up of his Government or his death on the battle-field. He continued to employ all these men in great offices of State and confidence about his person. He calculated with shrewd wisdom that, though they might turn against him as they had turned against James, yet they would not compromise the two main issues which had made them all his reluctant bedfellows; and he saw almost insuperable difficulties in their being able to dissociate the cause of James from the causes of Popery and France.

He did not, therefore, unduly trouble himself. He knew, or at least suspected, that Shrewsbury was in touch with Saint-Germains through his notorious mother; yet, as we shall see, again and again he implored Shrewsbury to take or retain the highest offices. He knew that Russell had made his peace with James; yet he kept him in command of the fleet, and was to find his confidence vindicated at the battle of Cape La Hogue. He knew that Marlborough preserved the family contacts with his nephew the Duke of Berwick, and that his wife corresponded with her sister, the Duchess of Tyrconnel. He probably knew that Marlborough had obtained his pardon from James by persuading the Princess Anne to send a dutiful message to her father. None the less he thought that the magnet of the Protestant cause and resistance to France would hold these men and others in the essentials to their duty, and that in the end it would be James, and not himself, who would be deceived. He proved right; and it may well be that his wise tolerance and prudent blind eye were the perfection of his statecraft. Meanwhile he relied on his Dutch Guards, and saw to it that no Englishman gained the control of the Army. After all, he was getting a lot out of England for his Continental schemes, of which these ignorant islanders, as he deemed them, only dimly saw the importance.

Up to this point, according to their own accounts, the Jacobites had been extremely well pleased to see all this discontent gathering against the Government. It was already whispered in their secret circles that Marlborough also had made his peace with James. They nursed the hope that this powerful man was working for a restoration. Then they suddenly remembered the Princess Anne and the small, devoted group at the Cockpit. So, then, all this movement and focus of discontent from which they had expected so much, to which they had contributed what weight their party had, was not to be for their benefit! On the contrary, if it succeeded it would exclude James for ever from the throne and would ensure the Protestant succession under Anne, with Marlborough, whose stature and force were already beginning to be understood, as her Captain-General. Their fury knew no bounds. Without consulting King James, who was dreaming that his former skilful servant of so many years would regain him his Crown, they went to Bentinck with tales of a vast and imminent conspiracy.

There is no evidence worthy of the name that Marlborough ever plotted the substitution of Anne for William and Mary. The obstacles were enormous. The risks, if not beyond his daring, were condemned by his practical good sense. It is probable that he had in view nothing more than the placing of the Princess Anne at the head of a combination of all parties, and the consequent assertion of his own power in the State for its great advantage. But though nothing so definite as a *coup d'état* had emerged in Marlborough's mind, he certainly sought to assemble and combine all forces hostile to the Government of the day, which in those days was indistinguishable from the King himself. It was for this reason above all others that he wished at this time to stand well with the Jacobites, and carry them with him as far as they would go. He thought and felt about politics as he did about war, in terms of combinations, and of forces moving up to this point or that, and then a trial of strength and skill, and a new view of the situation thereafter.

A movement in favour of the Princess Anne seemed to William far more dangerous than any that concerned James. He saw the blunt facts to which so many eminent writers have been purblind. He was never afraid of Marlborough trying to bring back James. He understood only too well where Marlborough's interests lay. He was content that James should be fooled. Of all his perils the Jacobite invasion, the most paraded in the history books, gave him the least anxiety. Quite a different mood stole over him when he saw or imagined Parliament, the Army, and the Princess Anne—a fatal trident—in the hand of Marlborough, pointed at his heart. He knew that his own policy obliged him to deny his great subject fair scope for his genius. He expected reprisals. There is a double-edged significance in the remark which the King made in the presence of a group of nobles at Court, that "he had been treated so infamously by Marlborough that had he not been a king, he would have felt it necessary to demand personal satisfaction." There are mutual injuries which efface differences of rank and station, and arouse in generous spirits the desire for an equal combat. We are to find a happier sequel for William's cause and Marlborough's fame.

These griefs on both sides—in all conscience serious enough—between the men were now to receive feminine aggravation. King William was profoundly disturbed at the suggestions of intrigue, or even plot, to transfer the Crown to Princess Anne. But his indignation was surpassed by that of the Queen. That her own sister should be made the instrument to thrust her from the throne and usurp it herself was indeed intolerable, and what step was more urgent than to preserve that sister from the influence—nay, possession—that dominated her and made her the battering-ram of such fell designs? Upon Sarah, therefore, fell the anger of the Queen.

Anne was a very real person. She was by no means the cat's-paw she has so often been depicted. She moved on broad, homely lines. She was devoted to her religion, to her husband, and to friends whose fidelity she had proved. It cannot be doubted at all that she would have faced poverty, exile, imprisonment, or even death with placid, unconquerable resolution for the sake of any of them. Once she got set, it took years to alter her. She was not very wise nor clever, but she was very like England. Now she was, as she conceived it, assailed by her sister and by her sister's husband, whose title to the throne she had willingly completed. She saw clearly what the Marlboroughs had risked and sacrificed for her. Her heart flowed out in love for Sarah and in admiration for John. All those slow, simple qualities which afterwards made her reign as glorious in the history of the British Empire as those of Queen Elizabeth and Queen Victoria now displayed themselves.

Therefore when, early in January 1692, the Queen, hot upon the news of the alleged conspiracy and the wicked intrigues of Lord Marlborough in Parliament and the Army—nay, and with Saint-Germains too, if the truth were known—summoned Anne to her presence and ordered her to dismiss Sarah, she found herself confronted with inexpugnable resistance. The Queen opened upon the enormity of Anne's giving Sarah—that mischief-maker, that breeder of dissension in the royal family, the wife of a dangerous man harassing or betraying the King—an annuity of £1000 a year from her Parliamentary grant. It was the crowning abuse. Was it for this that Parliamentary grants were made? Now we can see why the King should have been trusted to provide what was right for his relations. Sarah must be dismissed forthwith. Anne, who was expecting another baby, met the assault with silent fortitude. From time to time she uttered a few words of phlegmatic negation. In the presence of invincible refusal Mary lost her temper, raised her voice, threatened to deprive her of half her Parliamentary grant—which was certainly not in her power. The talk became an altercation, both sides having a self-convincing case. The courtiers drew back in shocked agitation. The two sisters parted in the anger of what proved to be a mortal estrangement.

The next morning at nine o'clock Marlborough, discharging his functions as Gentleman of the Bedchamber, handed the King his shirt, and William preserved his usual impassivity. Two hours later Nottingham delivered to Marlborough a written order to sell at once all the offices he held, civil and military, and consider himself as from that date dismissed from the Army and all public employment, and forbidden the Court. No reasons were given officially for this important stroke. The Court and Parliament were left to speculate whether it had been impelled by the dispute observed between the two Princesses on the night before, or whether it arose out of Marlborough's House of Commons activities, or whether some graver cause lay behind. The topic for some weeks excited all minds, and, as may be imagined, there was no lack of explanations.

Marlborough took his dismissal, and the abuse, deserved and undeserved, let loose upon him in the highest circles, with unconcern. He had deliberately courted a breach with the King. He may have been surprised that his influence, connexions, services, and ability had not counted for more: evidently he had overrated their value. But he was not the man to take a course of action without counting the cost: there is no record of any complaints, or even comments, uttered by him. His political position was not immediately affected. Parliamentary and public opinion as a whole considered that he had been ill-used, and that he had suffered for standing up for the rights of Englishmen against the Dutch and foreign favourites. His chief associates—the greatest men of the day—were offended. Shrewsbury let his disapproval be known; Godolphin threatened to retire from the Government. Admiral Russell, now Commander-in-Chief of the Navy, went so far as to reproach King William to his face with having shown ingratitude to the man who had "set the crown upon his head." William, who with some reason only trusted Russell more than Marlborough because he feared him less, preserved an obdurate silence.

Anne's distress was acute. She was convinced that the husband of her friend and guide had suffered on her account. She did not attend the Court at Kensington for three weeks, and when at length she did so, she went accompanied by Sarah. This was indeed a step of hardihood on the part of both women. The courtiers were aghast. The Queen, not unreasonably, saw herself affronted. She wrote her sister a long and vehement letter of remonstrance, appeal, and command.

> . . . Never anybody was suffered to live at Court in my Lord Marlborough's circumstances. I need not repeat the cause he has given the King to do what he has done, nor his [the King's] unwillingness at all times to come to such extremities, though people do deserve it. . . .
>
> . . . It is very unfit that Lady Marlborough should stay with you, since that gives her husband so just a pretence of being where he ought not. . . .
>
> Nor could all my kindness for you, which is ever ready to turn all you do the best way at any other time, have hindered my showing you so that moment, but I considered your condition, and that made me master myself so far as not to take notice of it then.
>
> But now I must tell you plainly Lady Marlborough must not continue with you in the circumstances [in which] her Lord is.

Anne replied firmly the next day, saying among other things:

> Your care of my present condition is extremely obliging. And if you would be pleased to add to it so far as on my account to recall your severe comment [about Sarah] (as I must beg leave to call it in a matter so tender to me and so little reasonable as I think to be imposed upon me that you would scarce require it from the meanest of your subjects), I should ever regard it as a very agreeable mark of your kindness to me. And I must as freely own that as I think that this proceeding can be for no other intent than to give me a very sensible mortification, so there is no misery that I cannot readily resolve to suffer rather than the thoughts of parting with her.

The Princess had hoped that her uncle Rochester would take this letter, but he had no intention of prejudicing his future by mingling in this dispute loaded with danger for all but the principals. By way of answer the Lord Chamberlain was directed to forbid Sarah to continue at the Cockpit. This was decisive, but in a manner different from that in which Queen Mary had expected. Anne resolved to share the banishment of her friend. Although she was every day expecting her confinement, she borrowed Sion House from the Duke of Somerset and transported herself and her household there with the utmost expedition.

The King and Queen now vented their disapproval in a series of very small actions. They endeavoured to persuade the Duke of Somerset to reclaim his house; he regretted that as a gentleman he was unable to do so. They withdrew her guards from the Princess, and deprived her of all salutes and ceremonies. Later on, when she went to Bath, they even went so far as to make the Secretary of State write to the local mayor —a tallow-chandler, Sarah calls him—that he was not to accompany her officially to church. These puerilities humiliated only their authors. Anne gained a wide measure of public sympathy, and the Queen was wounded to learn that it was commonly said that she had no natural feeling for her own kin, neither for her father nor for her only sister.

We cannot wonder that Anne, pursued in so many petty ways and seeing her cherished friends ruined, as she thought, for her sake by the malice of her sister and the King, should have used in her intimate letters to Sarah bitter expressions about William. Macaulay says that she "called her brother-in-law sometimes the abortion, sometimes the monster, sometimes Caliban," and describes this as "the style of a fishwoman." The remark is mainly interesting as contemporary evidence of the high standard of erudition among the early Victorian fishwomen. The two sisters met only once again. After Anne had been delivered of a child which almost immediately died, the Queen visited her at Sion House; but this was only to renew her command that Sarah should be dismissed. Anne, who was still weak and quivering from her labour and grieving for her dead baby, refused as resolutely as ever. These, except for some cold and formal letters, were the last words which passed between them.

Did some protecting genius of England inspire Anne's generous, faithful heart? For surely it was in these fires of adversity, and almost persecution, that the links were forged by which the smallest and the strongest executive our country has ever known in the modern age was one day to be gripped together. The Cockpit friendships were the crucible from which the power and glory of England were soon to rise gleaming among the nations.

CHAPTER EIGHTEEN

The Tower

ᕦ 1692-93 ᕤ

MEANWHILE the march of events was unfavourable both to the national and personal interests of Marlborough and to the vast Continental combinations of William. No sooner had the King set out upon the wars than the imminent menace of invasion fell upon the island he had left denuded of troops. Louvois had always been sceptical, and even scornful of a Jacobite restoration; but Louvois was dead, and Louis was freed from the trammels of his famous War Minister. Although his best opportunities had passed with the end of the Irish war and the Scottish revolts, he now planned a descent upon England. The French Channel and Mediterranean fleets, together with a multitude of transports and store-ships, were concentrated in the Norman and Breton ports. An expeditionary army of ten thousand desperate Irishmen from Limerick and ten thousand French regulars was assembled around Cherbourg. James was to be given his chance. Saint-Germains had for two years oppressed the French War Office with their assertions that England was ripe and ready for a restoration. Russell would betray or divert the English fleet; Marlborough would answer for such parts of the Army as remained at home; the Princess Anne would reassure the Church of England. The Jacobites of the northern counties were under arms; the merchants of the City were favourable; the temper of the English people was rancorously hostile to the Dutch. William was now in Flanders, and once the true King landed—with an adequate force—he would drive in his coach to Whitehall. Now was the time when all these assertions so confidently reiterated by the unhappy exiles, so buoyed up by fond hopes, so backed by distortion, fabrication, and forgery, would be put to the test. James's opportunity had come.

It was not until the middle of April, from important papers captured on a small vessel, that the French designs became known to the English Government. Feverish but vigorous preparations were made for defence by land and sea. Some regiments were brought from Ireland, others recalled from Flanders, and the English dockyards resounded with the preparation of the fleets. Despite stubborn adverse Jacobite currents, the nation had but one idea—to repel the French Papist invaders and above all the despised and hated Irish. James's declaration, framed by Melfort, "the evil genius of the house of Stuart," as he has been well called, apprised the nation of its peril. All the old arrogance, religious and political, and a new vindictiveness to pay off recent scores, were reflected in this wanton document. Large numbers of persons, ranging from the greatest nobles to the rough, ignorant fishermen who had manhandled their sovereign upon his flight to Faversham, were specifically excluded from the amnesty. Marlborough's name figured among the proscribed; but this, we are assured by the Jacobites, was only from a desire not to compromise the delicacy of his position. As upon the approach of the Spanish Armada, all England was alert. But everything turned upon the Admiral Russell. He, like Marlborough, had talked with the Jacobite agents: William and Mary feared, and James fervently believed, that he would play the traitor to his country and his profession. James was sure that the fleet was on his side, and had furnished Versailles with lists of the admirals and captains on whom he counted. Now would be proved what substance there was in all these tales. Would that every Jacobite pretension could be brought to an equally conclusive trial!

According to the Jacobites, Russell bluntly told their agent, Floyd, that, much as he loved James and loathed William's Government, if he met the French fleet at sea he would do his best to destroy it, "even though King James himself were on board." He kept his word. "If your officers play you false," he said to the fleetmen on the day of battle, "overboard with them, and myself the first." We have no doubt that Marlborough, his friend and fellow-intriguer, would have done the same with the soldiers had he had them in command. But his lot was hard. An age of revolutions and conspiracies, when all foundations quaked, had produced a tribe of professional plot-denouncers. Titus Oates, living in retirement upon his Government pension, held a veritable school for the making of bogus plots from the exposure of which much wealth and celebrity might be gained. Moreover, there was no lack of material. A rascal named Fuller had already this year from his debtors' prison offered blood-curdling revelations to Parliament, and had been exposed and convicted only by the exceptional diligence of the House of Commons. Now, at this grievous moment, came forth a disciple of Oates and Fuller named Young, also a rogue and a criminal, also in gaol, who devised a scheme to win himself riches and consideration by accusing well-known and likely men of murderous conspiracy.

Young was by his own confession an expert forger. He had obtained a specimen of Marlborough's signature by writing to him about the character of a servant. He drew up a document purporting to be a bond of association between certain persons to take the Prince of Orange, dead or alive, and to restore King James. He forged the names of Marlborough, Cornbury, Archbishop Sancroft, and the harmless Bishop of Rochester, Sprat, with some others, as signatories. His confederate, Blackhead, hid this poisonous evidence in a flowerpot in the house of the unwitting Bishop of Rochester. Young then warned the Cabinet of their peril and where the proof could be found. Above all things, he said, they must search the Bishop's flowerpots. Under the threat of invasion, on the eve of fateful battle with the fleet commanded by a suspected admiral, a panic-fierce mood ruled at the council-board. Marlborough and one or two leading Jacobites were arrested out of hand and sent to the Tower.

Three members of the Council, Lords Devonshire, Bradford, and Montagu, kept their heads; they declined to sign the warrant upon the evidence of a single witness of whose credibility the most that could be said was that "he had not yet had his ears cropped." But Marlborough slept the night of May 4 a prisoner of State upon a charge of high treason.

Stringent search was now made of the Bishop's palace, and almost every flowerpot was examined. But there was one which, because it stood near the servants' quarters, was overlooked. In this lay the paper which, if discovered at that moment, might have cost not only the Bishop but our hero his life. The officers of the Crown returned to

Whitehall with the Bishop in custody, but no evidence. Young then procured from his prison cell the recovery of the document, and sent it with another legend to the Council.

But meanwhile a fortnight had passed and great events had happened. On May 19/29 the English and Dutch fleets, which had effected their junction before the French were ready, encountered Tourville with the main French naval power off Cape La Hogue. The forces were impressive in their number, but Russell's armada, which carried forty thousand men and seven thousand guns, was the stronger by ninety-nine ships to forty-four. Both sides fought hard, and Tourville was beaten. His flagship, *Le Soleil Royal*, named in honour of Louis XIV, was first battered and then burned to the water's edge. The French fleet was scattered and driven into its ports. But this was not the end. Russell and his admirals, three of the most daring of whom were counted on the Jacobite lists as pledged and faithful adherents of King James, followed the beaten navy into its harbours. For five successive days the fighting continued. The fugitive warships were cut out under the shore batteries by flotillas of hardy English row-boats; the store-ships and many of the transports were burned; and the whole apparatus of invasion was destroyed under the very eyes of the King it was to have borne to his native shore.

The battle of Cape La Hogue, with its consequential actions, effaced the memories of Beachy Head. More than that, it broke decisively for the whole of the wars of William and Anne all French pretensions to supremacy at sea. It was the Trafalgar of the seventeenth century. We invite the reader to judge whether fact is not stronger than fiction; whether substance is not more solid than shadow. Because Russell had flirted with the Jacobite agents; because these agents had vapourized to the Court at Saint-Germains; because James had wanted to believe all his agents told him, and made the most of it to Louis; and because the Jacobite writers have invented and written whatever they pleased about him, Russell stands convicted before history as a "villain" and a "traitor." This shattering victory and noble feat of arms counts for nothing in his favour. Macpherson, Dalrymple, Macaulay, and the docile flock of scrap-nibblers who have browsed upon their pastures, have managed hitherto to twist history and reality to his condemnation. We submit to modern judgment two propositions about him: that he was wrong and foolish to have trafficked with the Jacobite agents, but that he was quite right to beat the French and ruin King James's cause, which was on the whole rather more important.

The fears of the Council and the excitement of the public were calmed by the victory. Lords Huntingdon and Scarsdale, who had been arrested on other grounds at the same time as Marlborough, were set at liberty. William, who had been perturbed by the irregularity of these arrests, wrote to the Council expressing his doubts about such serious steps. Nevertheless, so strong were the feelings of the Queen that Marlborough was still kept a close prisoner in the Tower. Sarah came from Brentford to London in order to be near him, to help in his defence, and to agitate for his release. No one was allowed to visit him except upon the authority of the Secretary of State, and we have consequently a series of orders signed by Nottingham giving Sarah and some others access to him. Among the few who faced the displeasure of the Queen, Lord Bradford was conspicuous. As is usual with people in such a position, the Marlboroughs found few friends. Other nearer trouble fell upon them. On May 22 their younger son Charles died.

There is little doubt that the King and Queen, heating each other in their anger, explored the question of curtailing Anne's Parliamentary grant. They encountered a steady resistance from Godolphin at the Treasury. Moreover, the House of Commons would have resented any such proposal. Rumours, however, of the project reached Sarah through a sure channel. She continued to suggest that she should relieve the tension by departing—at any rate, for a time. The Princess's attitude was magnificent:

> I really long to know how my dear Mrs Freeman got home; and now I have this opportunity of writing, she must give me leave to tell her, if she should ever be so cruel to leave her faithful Mrs Morley, she will rob her of all the joy and quiet of her life; for if that day should come, I could never enjoy a happy minute, and I swear to you I would shut myself up and never see a creature. You may easily see all this would have come upon me, if you had not been. If you do but remember what the Q. said to me the night before your Lord was turned out of all; then she begun to pick quarrels; and if they should take off twenty or thirty thousand pound, have I not lived upon as little before? When I was first married we had but twenty (it is true indeed the King [Charles] was so kind to pay my debts), and if it

should come to that again, what retrenchment is there in my family I would not willingly make and be glad of that pretence to do it? Never fancy, dear Mrs Freeman, if what you fear should happen, that you are the occasion . . . ; therefore rest satisfied you are no ways the cause; and let me beg once more, for God's sake, that you would never mention parting more, no nor so much as think of it; and if you should ever leave me, be assured it would break your faithful Mrs Morley's heart.

Meanwhile Marlborough had recourse to the Council. To Danby, the Lord President, he wrote:

Having been informed that it is now publicly discoursed in Westminster Hall to-day that a letter under my hand was to be produced to the grand jury, to induce them to find a bail against me, I beg leave to assure your Lordship, upon my honour and credit, that if any such letter be pretended, it must and will, upon examination, appear so plainly to have been forged, that as it can be of no credit or advantage to the Government, so I doubt not but your Lordship's justice will be ready to protect me from so injurious a proceeding, who am, etc.

He also used his rights under the law, invoked the Habeas Corpus Act, and demanded admission to bail. To Halifax he wrote:

My Counsel being to move the Court of King's Bench for my Habeas Corpus the beginning of next term, and [I] being very certain of my own innocence, and that no instance can be shewn why I should not be bailed, I desire the favour of your Lordship to be there and be one of my Sureties for my appearance, not knowing yet how many they may require to be found for me; I shall be unwilling to give your Lordship this trouble without a necessity, and in that case I shall always own it as the greatest obligation to your Lordship's most obedient

Marlborough

On June 11 Young and his accomplice, Blackhead, were brought before the Privy Council. The event was dramatic. Confronted with Bishop Sprat and under the stern eyes of the Council, Blackhead, who had already weakened, broke down completely, and confessed his crime.

The forged document was produced. As we have to deal in Marlborough's life with other charges equally elaborately presented, we give it here as Sprat recollected it.

> That we, whose names were subscribed, should solemnly promise, in the presence of God, to contribute our utmost assistance towards King James's recovery of his kingdoms; that to this end, we would have ready to meet him, at his landing, thirty thousand men well armed; that we would seize upon the person of the Princess of Orange, dead or alive; and take care, that some strong garrison should be forthwith delivered into his hands; and furnish him with a considerable sum of money, for the support of his army.

> March 20, 1691

Marleborough	*Salisbury*	*W. Cant.*
		*Tho. Roffen.**
		Cornbury
Basil Firebrace		*John Wilcoxe*

The Bishop was startled at the perfection of the forgery. "I am very much amazed," he said, "to see my hand so well counterfeited; all the difference is they have done me the favour to write it finer than I can: otherwise I acknowledge it is so like that I verily believe I myself, had I seen it in another place, should have been apt to doubt whether it were of my writing or no. I am confident it might, upon the first blush, deceive the best friends I have."

Here Godolphin intervened, and his friendly purpose is easily discernible. "My Lords," he said, "I am very well acquainted with Archbishop Sancroft's hand, and here it is almost exactly counterfeited." He added that the Earl of Marlborough's hand had been so well feigned in a letter that had been written by Young himself that it was very difficult for his most intimate friends to observe any distinction.

Young was now brought before the Council.

> EARL OF NOTTINGHAM (*taking up the association and showing it to Young*): Did you not give this paper to Blackhead and order him to put it in a chimney in the Bishop of Rochester's house, and into a flowerpot, if there were any?
> YOUNG: No, I never desired him to carry it thither, or to put it into a flowerpot.
> EARL OF NOTTINGHAM: What say you, Blackhead?

* This is Sprat's signature, as Bishop of Rochester.

BLACKHEAD: Mr Young did give me that paper, and directed me to leave it in the Bishop's house; and if I could, to put it in a flowerpot in some room; which I did, in the parlour.

YOUNG: There is no such matter. I absolutely deny it.

EARL OF NOTTINGHAM, LORD SYDNEY, AND OTHERS OF THE COUNCILLORS: Why, then, did you give us such express directions to send and search the flowerpots among other places in the Bishop's house?

YOUNG: I said nothing of flowerpots. I bid you take care that the Bishop's person should be exactly searched; because when he went abroad he carried the association about him; when he was at home, he put it in some private place, for fear of surprise. Perhaps I might say, in the chimney.

THE COUNCILLORS: Nay, we all well remember, you particularly mentioned the flowerpots.

There was now no case of any kind against Marlborough. Not even one of the two witnesses necessary to sustain a charge of treason was available; and the document which incriminated him was a proved and exposed forgery. On June 15, after an imprisonment of six weeks, he succeeded in bringing his case before the Court of the King's Bench on a writ of Habeas Corpus. The Government demanded sureties and bail for £6000. Halifax did not fail him, neither did Shrewsbury. Both these lords, with two other persons, became his sureties. Their action was resented by the Queen. These two famous builders of our constitutional history were forthwith struck off the Privy Council. Marlborough's name was found still, apparently by oversight, upon the roll. The oversight was repaired.

Marlborough was now free, and the Cockpit group reunited at Berkeley House in a companionship of wrath and misfortune. The ordeal had been severe, and escape narrow. The forgeries of Young had been so perfect that Marlborough admitted himself when shown the document that he could have hardly believed that it was not his own autograph. Such a plot, had it not miscarried, might well have sent him during the invasion panic to the scaffold. Moreover, he might expect that at any moment some one or other of the Jacobite agents with whom he had consorted and through whom he had communicated with Saint-Germains might come forward with confirmatory revelations. However, his nerves were steel, and neither imminent peril nor prolonged strain affected his poise and serenity. Nor did he in any respect alter his course. He continued through various secret channels to preserve exactly the same shadowy relations with King James—neither less nor more—as before his disgrace. He persisted in his opposition to the King by every means open to him.

And now from the war came news which must have gnawed his soul. As in 1691, the campaign had opened with a brilliant French success. Louis XIV had laid siege to the hitherto inviolate fortress of Namur before William, through the tardiness of his allies, could be ready. Vauban, under Louis, conducted the siege, while Luxembourg with an army of eighty thousand men stood between William and its relief. Once again the unlucky head of the Grand Alliance and his army watched impotently the fall of one of their most important fortresses. But worse was to come. In August William marched by night with his whole army to attack Luxembourg, whose forces were somewhat divided. The French were surprised near Steinkirk in the early morning. Their advanced troops were overwhelmed and routed, and for an hour confusion reigned in their camp. But Luxembourg was equal to the emergency, and managed to draw out an ordered line of battle. The British infantry formed the forefront of the allied attack. Eight splendid regiments under General Mackay charged and broke the Swiss in fighting as fierce as had been seen in Europe in living memory. Luxembourg launched the Household troops of France upon the British division, already strained by its exertions, and after a furious struggle fought mostly with sword and bayonet beat them back.

Meanwhile from all sides the French advanced, and their reinforcements began to reach the field. Count Solms refused to send Mackay the help for which he begged. A Dutch general on the opposite flank, the valiant Overkirk, brought two battalions to their aid with remarkable effect. But for this, that British force of which Marlborough had been so proud the year before would have been cut to pieces. As it was they escaped with a loss of their two best generals, Mackay and Lanier, and of half their number, more than three thousand being killed or wounded. William seemed unable to control the battle. Witness of this cruel disaster, we are assured that he shed bitter tears as he watched the slaughter and exclaimed, "Oh, my poor English!" But what was the good of that? By noon the whole of the allied army was in retreat, and although the losses of seven or eight thousand men on either side were equal, the French proclaimed their victory throughout Europe.

The wheel of fortune spins with infinite caprice, and no one can tell whether it was Marlborough's good luck or bad that tied him in England unemployed and a prisoner of State while Count Solms cast the English away at Steinkirk. He had sunk now to the minor and unpleasant position of being a critic of mishandled affairs with whose main intention he agreed. This condition was to rule him for a long time, as our short lives go. The Court guerrilla against Anne continued, and she was subjected to many petty impertinences and something very like what we should now call a society boycott. Marlborough presented his general case to Parliament when it met in November. He found support which in modern times might be decisive. The House of Lords ignored the Royal Speech and proceeded to examine the causes why certain of their members had been unlawfully imprisoned. It was argued that once the charges were dropped the retention of bail and the refusal to discharge recognizances were infringements of privilege. Acrimonious debates ensued. The Constable of the Tower, the Treasury Solicitor, even the judges of the High Court, were summoned. William found himself in the presence of one of those tensely wrought, sternly measured constitutional movements towards which he had been taught in the days of Charles II that English kings should not be unbending. He used the royal prerogative to discharge Marlborough from his recognizances. This grievance removed, both Houses turned to the war.

The Lords carried an address praying that no English general should be subordinated to a Dutchman, whatever his rank. In the Commons the Court, or, as we should now say, Ministerial, orators inculcated precepts of humility. In the end the Commons pressed less strongly upon the King than the Lords. The conspiracy of Grandval, a Jacobite enthusiast set on by Saint-Germains to murder the King, had rallied strong English sympathies in his behalf; and the power of the Crown proved overwhelming. If William's government could bear the odium of Solms at Steinkirk, it could bear anything. The King returned brief answers to the addresses, and supplies were voted for another mismanaged and disastrous year of war.

In July 1693 was fought the great battle of Landen, unmatched in its slaughter except by Malplaquet and Borodino for two hundred years. The French were in greatly superior strength, having 96 battalions and 210 squadrons to William's 65 battalions and 150 squadrons. Nevertheless the King determined to withstand their attack, and constructed almost overnight a system of strong entrenchments and palisades in the enclosed country along the Landen stream, within the windings of the Geet. After an heroic resistance the allies were driven from their position by the French with a loss of nearly twenty thousand men, the attackers losing less than half this total. Nevertheless William rallied the remnants of his army, gathered reinforcements, and, since Luxembourg neglected to pursue his victory, was able surprisingly to maintain himself in the field.

Of all these stirring events, which at so many points touched him intimately, Marlborough continued to be a mere spectator.

CHAPTER NINETEEN

The Fenwick Trial

ᚷᚨ 1694-1697 ᛞᚦ

WE now reach one of the turning points of this story. At the end of
1694 the Queen was stricken with smallpox. Anne wrote a sisterly letter
and asked to be allowed to come to her bedside. A civil answer was returned by Lady Derby, then Lady-in-Waiting, declining the visit for the
moment on the very natural ground that it was "so necessary to keep
the Queen as quiet as possible." The Postscript was added, "Pray
madam present my humble duty to the Princess." Sarah's shrewd eye
read into this "that the disease was mortal," and so in a few days it
proved to be. On December 28 Queen Mary died, beloved and mourned
by her subjects and bitterly missed by her husband.

This unforeseen event produced profound changes in the prospects
and relations of those with whom this story is concerned. Hitherto the
natural expectation had been that Mary would long survive her husband, upon whose frail, fiery life so many assaults of disease, war, and
conspiracy converged. An English Protestant Queen would then reign
in her own right. Instead of this, the Crown, thanks in part to the surrender which Anne had made of her rights, devolved on William alone
for life. Thereafter it must come to Anne. Any day, any month, certainly as it seemed in a few years, the Princess to whom the sentinels
had been ordered to deny their salutes, whom the Mayor of Bath had
been forbidden to attend to church, who dwelt quietly with her family
and intimate friends in the unfashionable chambers of Berkeley House,
would be Queen of the three kingdoms. And at her side, linked by ties
which the whole power of the dual reign had been unable to break,

would stand the redoubtable couple without whom even in their darkest fortunes it had been impossible to reckon. No wonder Berkeley House, lately so deserted, was thronged with "people of all sorts flocking," in spite of Sarah's ironical smiles, "to pay their respects to the Prince and Princess."

It was no longer Marlborough's part to raise an opposition to the King. From the moment that the Queen had breathed her last his interests were the same as William's. He shared William's resolve to break the power of France. He agreed with the whole character and purpose of his foreign policy. His patience enabled him to wait with contentment for that "sunshine day" of which Anne had written. By the mediation of Sunderland and Somers a formal reconciliation was effected between William and Anne. She was received with her proper ceremony when she waited upon the King at Kensington, and St James's Palace was prepared for her use. Thither in due course she carried Sarah. But the wounds of the quarrel still rankled. The relations between the sovereign and the heiress-presumptive, if correct, were also frigid, and Marlborough remained excluded for four more years from all employment, military or civil, at the front or at home. This, however, did not sway his course of action. Although William treated him with such prolonged and marked personal hostility, he became his steady supporter, and used his graceful arts to prevent anything like a rivalry or open breach between St James's and Whitehall. He continued from time to time to receive the Jacobite agents and preserve his connexion with King James. This was an easy task, since his imprisonment and continuing disgrace at the hands of William pleaded for themselves at Saint-Germains.

Europe believed that the death of Queen Mary would greatly weaken William, and the Jacobites at home and in France looked forward to his speedy downfall. But in fact, owing largely to the concord reestablished in the royal circle, he appeared at first even to be strengthened by his loss. His principal Ministers and advisers had long been Marlborough's friends, and were united with him by many open and some secret ties. The death of the Queen only consolidated the general accord of this strong and powerful group. Well was it so, for a new danger was already approaching.

The campaign of 1695 brought William his one success in the European war. He besieged and retook Namur in the teeth of the French armies, which now that Luxembourg was dead could find no better leader than a certain Marshal de Villeroy, destined afterwards to a more serious reverse.

The year 1695 was filled with activities of the Jacobites. The connexions of their party spread throughout the country. In their political clubs, in elegant society, in lonely halls and manor-houses, in the taverns and on the village greens, they held their heads high and exchanged confident salutations. They could not believe that William, deprived of his English Queen, could stand alone. Beneath all their froth upon the surface there grew at a hundred points preparation for armed rebellion, if and when the hour should strike; and beneath this again, as so often happens in movements of this character, at the root of all, there festered a murder plot. King James was privy to both designs, though it cannot be said he directly or specifically commissioned the assassins. In the autumn he sent Berwick into England to concert the insurrection. For several months this daring young man moved about the country in disguise or lay hidden in London. He saw all the leading Jacobites, and endeavoured to bring their plans coherently to a head and fix the occasion.

If Berwick had seen Marlborough he would certainly have recorded it in his *Memoirs*, not written until the events of his mission possessed only historical interest. No such idea ever seems to have occurred to him. Yet his father would surely not have sent him on so mortally perilous a mission without letting him know the full extent of his English connexions. The truth is that James in his inmost heart only placed limited reliance upon the friendly assurances that reached him from the Revolution leaders. They might serve to impress Louis XIV with the strength of the Jacobite movement, or as a basis for history; but James would not risk the life of a well-loved son, nor Berwick his own life upon them.

Berwick found the resources of the conspiracy were by no means inconsiderable. As many as two thousand horse, "well appointed and even regimented," were ready to take the field on the first notice, and "several people of the highest distinction were also engaged in the business." But here came the deadlock. The English Jacobites were "unanimously agreed not to throw off the mask before a body of troops was actually landed in the island." Louis XIV was willing to supply these troops, but only on one condition. After his experiences in 1692 he was determined not to launch an expedition until after a rising had actually begun. Thus on both sides of the channel the potential rebels and the contingent invaders were in suspense, and waited each on the other.

Meanwhile, independently of Berwick, James had sent over a Sir George Barclay with instructions, written throughout in his own hand, authorizing him in comprehensive terms to commit such acts of hostility against William as he might think right and practicable. At the same time by various routes about twenty resolute members of James's bodyguard at Saint-Germains made their way into England, and by secret signals got into touch with Barclay in London. The most deadly and resolute plot since the Gunpowder Treason was now hatched. Every Saturday King William was wont to go a-hunting, and it was designed on his return from one of these excursions to fall upon him, overpower his guards, and kill him. Turnham Green, where on his homeward journey he recrossed the river by boat and was taken up by a new coach with a new escort, was chosen for the ambuscade. For this desperate deed forty men were needed. Twenty had come from Saint-Germains. Twenty more must be found in England. In this delicate recruitment Barclay and his confederates next engaged themselves.

The conspirators had fixed the afternoon of Saturday, February 15, 1696, as the moment for their onslaught, and forty determined men, mounted and armed to the teeth, were gathered hard by the landing-stage at Turnham Green. The Rye House Plot of the Whigs had got no farther than tavern talk: the Jacobite desperadoes had come to the very verge of well-concerted action. A fire was even prepared on the Dover cliffs to carry the news to the anxious party at Calais. But two of the forty, one from fear, the other from scruple, had given warning to Bentinck, and at the last moment William was with difficulty persuaded not to hunt that day.

The Government, having got some threads in their hands, speedily drew out the rest. Many of the conspirators were seized, the alarm was given, and the plot in all its gruesome reality and imminence was exposed. The nation was roused to fury. All classes rallied round the King. Parliament suspended the Habeas Corpus Act, and the vast majority of its Members swore themselves into an association to defend the King's person and revenge his death. It was also resolved that Parliament should not be automatically dissolved upon a demise of the

Crown from any cause, and that the succession should be instantly ensured in accordance with the Declaration of Right. Thus the confusion following the death of the King, on which James's party counted, would be effectually prevented. The trials and executions of the conspirators were speedy and not too numerous. Never had William enjoyed such popularity since the first days of his reign.

Even if the plot had not miscarried, James had no chance of regaining his lost Crown across the murdered corpse of William. The leading Ministers were in the closest contact with Marlborough, and long forethought had taught them to link their future with Anne. No panic or disorder would have followed the bloody deed. Within the compass of a single day, swept upward by a wave of national indignation, Anne would have mounted the throne and Marlborough would have gripped the Army. Not a shot would have been fired. Not a dog would have barked. The new organism of government would have presented itself far stronger than the former combination.

The murder plot brought in its trail a great Parliamentary drama. Sir John Fenwick was no assassin, but he was deeply involved in the preparations for rebellion. Warrants were issued for his arrest, and after some time by chance he was caught. Well born himself, he was through his wife Lady Mary, daughter of the Earl of Carlisle, connected with several of the greatest families. To save himself from swift condemnation and to gain time for powerful influences to come to his aid, he wrote a confession in which he charged Marlborough, Russell, Godolphin, and Shrewsbury with treasonable correspondence with Saint-Germains. The accusation against Marlborough was that he had sent a message by Floyd to King James asking for his pardon. "The answer to my Lord Marlborough," wrote Fenwick, "was, that he was the greatest of criminals where he had the greatest obligations, but if he did him extraordinary service, he might hope for pardon; and a little after he did a considerable piece of service, of which we had an account by one sent on purpose by King James." It was also alleged that King James relied on Marlborough to bring over the Army to his cause. Fenwick betrayed none of his confederates, the real Jacobites who had been waiting with arms and horses for the signal of revolt. He selected only those "false Jacobites" who were or had been employed in the greatest stations round King William, and who had mocked the royal exile with vain promises and deceitful homage. William was in Holland. His action when he received his confession casts a revealing light upon the politics of his reign. The King saw through Fenwick's manoeuvre at a glance. He learned from it nothing that he had not known for years and discounted at its proper value. He had no intention of destroying the system upon which he ruled or of deranging the structure of his Government by tearing the heads off both great parties. He therefore sent the paper home to his Council with assurances to its incriminated members that his confidence in them was utterly unaffected by such nonsense. This for the moment sufficed.

But when Parliament was apprised of the confession a graver situation supervened. Nobody would have been surprised at the intrigues of Tories with the Jacobites. It was in their blood. But here were the immaculate Whigs aspersed. The House of Commons was determined to test the truth of Fenwick's accusations. Brought to the bar, he refused to amplify or prove what he had written. One Member, Colonel Godfrey, the husband of Arabella, no doubt at Marlborough's desire, specifically invited him across the chamber to state fully all he alleged against Marlborough. But Fenwick excused himself. Brought at the request of Parliament before the King, he persisted in his refusal. We must presume that, like the historians, he had no proofs, and, like them, was merely repeating the secret talk of the inner Jacobite circles. He was sent back to prison. The charge under which he lay was in any case grievous. Still, since it was not concerned with the actual murder plot, it might not have entailed the forfeit of life. But now he had drawn upon himself the wrath of both great parties, and particularly of the Whigs, who saw two of their most famous leaders impugned without proof or reason. He had also aroused the enmity alike of the powerful men he had accused, and of others whom he might have accused. He had deeply angered the King by what to William was an obvious attempt to rupture his Government. Meanwhile one of the two witnesses indispensable to the treason charge had been bribed or terrorized out of the country, and it seemed that the law stood dumb before him. It was at this stage that the Commons fell back upon the last reserve weapon of the State—an Act of Attainder.

There is no need here to describe the many vehement debates, narrow and exciting divisions, and Parliamentary situations which marked the two months' passage of the Bill through both Houses. They have been so often brilliantly told. We are not concerned with the fate of Sir John Fenwick, but only with the effects of his charges upon Marlborough and the other aspersed statesmen. None of them had been in any way concerned either in the assassination plot or in the projected rebellion. All of them had at some time or other conversed or trafficked with Jacobite agents and thus easily, in King William's phrase, "made their peace with Saint-Germains." Their prolonged ordeal was most severe. When, in a moment of intense public feeling and widespread suspicion, men have to defend themselves from terrible charges, the fact that they have been guilty of comparatively venial conduct of the same kind, compromising in essence and still more in appearance, may shake the strongest nerve and wear down the boldest spirit.

"Every one of the accused persons," says Macaulay,

> behaved himself in a manner singularly characteristic. Marlborough, the most culpable of all, preserved a serenity, mild, majestic, and slightly contemptuous. Russell, scarcely less criminal than Marlborough, went into a towering passion, and breathed nothing but vengeance against the villainous informer. Godolphin, uneasy, but wary, reserved, and self-possessed, prepared himself to stand on the defensive. But Shrewsbury, who of all the four was the least to blame, was utterly overwhelmed.

This fell short of the facts. William knew more from the Jacobite talk of the day. But the King set himself to comfort Shrewsbury. "In sending you Sir John Fenwick's paper," he wrote,

> I assured you, that I was persuaded his accusation was false, of which I am now fully convinced, by your answer, and perfectly satisfied with the ingenuous confession of what passed between you and Lord Middleton, which can by no means be imputed to you as a crime. And indeed you may be assured, that this business, so far from making on me any unfavourable impression, will, on the contrary, if possible, in future, strengthen my confidence in you, and my friendship can admit of no increase.

But Shrewsbury was inconsolable. He buried himself in the country. He declared that a fall out hunting had rendered him unfit for public business. Certainly his health broke down completely. He repeatedly but in vain besought William to allow him to resign. Meanwhile he seems to have left Marlborough to watch over his interests, for we have one of Marlborough's very rare letters in this period to him:

December 2, 1696

Wednesday night—

Although I have not troubled your Grace with my letters I have not been wanting in inquiring constantly how you did. I did about a fortnight ago write a letter to acquaint you with what I had observed of some people, in hopes Mr Arden would have called upon me as he promised, but I did not care to send it by post, and so it was burnt. We had yesterday Sir Jo. Fenwick at the House, and I think all went as well as you could wish. I do not send you the particulars, knowing you must have it more exactly from others; but on this occasion I should be wanting if I did not let you know that Lord Rochester has behaved himself on all this occasion like a friend; and in a conversation he had with me he expressed himself as a real servant of yours, and I think it would not be amiss if you took notice of it to him. . . .

Wharton also wrote to Shrewsbury describing what happened when Fenwick came before the Lords:

. . . after the reading of the paper, my lord Marlborough first stood up and spoke to this purpose: "that he did not wonder to find a man in danger, willing to throw his guilt upon any other body; that he had some satisfaction to be owned in such good company; but that he assured their lordships that he had [had] no sort of conversation with him, upon any account whatsoever, since this Government, which he said upon his word and honour." . . . After which my lord Godolphin said, "that he found himself named in two places, first, as having been looked upon as being in King James's interest, from the beginning, and afterwards, as having entered into a negotiation, as was expressed in the paper. As to the first, he confessed he was one of those that had, to the last, continued in King James's service, and he did not know, but from that, King James and his friends might imagine him to continue in that interest, but as to the latter part, there was nothing in the world so false."

In the course of these proceedings a peculiar complication had arisen. Mordaunt, already mentioned as Monmouth, and afterwards Earl of Peterborough, although himself an alleged Jacobite, impelled by his mischievous instincts and the hope of throwing the Government into disorder, endeavoured secretly to persuade Fenwick through his wife to point and elaborate his charges, especially against Marlborough, assuring him that this was the path to safety. Fenwick pondered anxiously upon this suggestion. Ailesbury was a fellow-prisoner in the Tower. Though never a serious rebel, he was an avowed Jacobite and had been drawn unwitting into dangerous company on more than one occasion. Fenwick endeavoured to persuade Ailesbury to join with him in pressing his charges. Ailesbury probably knew as much as Fenwick of all that had been whispered for some time past in the ranks of the English Jacobites. His appearance beside Fenwick at the bar with corroborative allegations would, in the then temper of both Houses, and still more of the public, have created an ugly situation for Marlborough and the impugned Ministers. Ailesbury, however, was, as we have noted, a friend of Marlborough's. They had been thrown together at Court in the days of Charles II. He therefore sought Marlborough's advice through channels which were open. The counsel he received was to have nothing to do with Fenwick and to remain quiet till after the execution, when he would soon be released and all would be well. He had the wisdom to act accordingly, and ever afterwards believed that he had rendered Marlborough an important personal service. Fenwick, unsupported by Ailesbury, rejected Monmouth's suggestions. Monmouth, angered at this, turned against him with extreme bitterness. Lady Mary Fenwick then in revenge exposed Monmouth's conduct to the Lords. There was general indignation at this mischief-mongering. He was stripped of his offices and sent to the Tower, from which he was released only upon abject apologies. But this was not the end of him.

The process of attainder crawled remorselessly forward stage by stage. Marlborough, entirely unaffected by the strain which had broken Shrewsbury and intimidated Godolphin, comported himself with the confidence and vigour of a man conscious of his own innocence. He actively pressed forward the Bill, and voted for it in the important divisions. Calmly and inexorably he threw his whole influence against Fenwick, and it was publicly remarked that he was zealous for his condemnation. His brother George Churchill, who had commanded a ship at the battle of La Hogue with credit and was a member of the House of Commons, observed less decorum. "Damn him!" he exclaimed, with brutal frankness, in the Lobby; "thrust a billet down his throat. Dead men tell no tales." But in truth Fenwick had no tales to tell. He had founded his charges on nothing but hearsay; he had no proof of any kind.

Marlborough sternly pursued his course as if his conscience were clear of any shameful or deadly deed. Perhaps it was. Sir John Fenwick was beheaded on Tower Hill on January 28, 1697.

CHAPTER TWENTY

Avarice and Charm

THERE is no virtue so universally unpopular as frugality. Every one likes the handsome spender who offers lavish hospitality and eases his path through life by a shower of money. In the days of which we are writing all who held high public appointments were accustomed and expected to live in fine style and at a profuse expense. Public opinion was more critical about how important people spent their money than about how they acquired it. Graft, pilfering, and corruption, unless too flagrant, were leniently judged in the governing circle; stinting and saving were resented as peculiar. It does not, however, follow that those who are the most extravagant and easy with their money are the most unselfish, nor that those who are the most niggardly are the most mean. There is a happy medium which can only be defined for each individual by the general opinion of the society in which he lives.

Judged by this standard, Marlborough lay under reproach. He was at once highly acquisitive in the gaining of money and extremely careful in the spending of it. In those days, when almost the only other form of wealth was landed property, public appointments all had a recognized money value. An officer without means could not take his promotion. An officer who had reached high rank was a substantial proprietor, carrying with him in his own person and his appointments the cumulative and reinvested savings of his career. In all but extreme cases these vested interests were respected. There was nothing secret or corrupt about them. They were the system and the custom, and it is only within living memory that the principle of purchase was abolished in the British Army. In the seventeenth and eighteenth centuries those who had no money had no standing. Instances there were to the contrary; but in the main it was not until the French Revolution that the glorious principle of *la carrière ouverte aux talents* was proclaimed or even comprehended.

Marlborough's childhood had been lived in penury. But to Marlborough's early years there was an added sting. He learned almost as soon as he could walk and speak that he and his father and mother were dependants upon the charity and goodwill of his grandmother. As he grew older he saw the straits to which the impoverishments of a Cavalier had reduced his father. He heard the talk of the exactions of the Roundheads and of the frequent litigation for quite small sums in which all the grown-ups of the household were engaged with the Government or with the other members of their family. When, for his father's services and his own good looks, he was taken as a page at Court, he was penniless. He might be finely dressed and well fed, but he was penniless among those who monopolized a large proportion of the entire wealth of the kingdom. On every side his seeming equals were youths of noble fortune, heirs to vast estates and splendid titles. He was the earthenware pot among the iron ones. This was his second strong impression of life.

Before he was eighteen he realized that, unless he could make and save money, he could neither have a career, nor a bride nor a home, nor even a modest independence. It is therefore not at all surprising, however unromantic, that his first preoccupation was the gathering of money. In his twenties and thirties his temper was very similar to that which we have attributed to the French nation—always more generous of life than treasure, ready to encounter every personal hazard, prodigal of blood, but deeply concerned about money. His thrift was not without a certain grandeur, a habit of self-denial differing altogether from a miser's sordidness. We have seen how when, after heartbreaking postponements, he married a girl almost as poor as himself he could offer her no home. We have seen him at twenty-eight marrying for love, and at the same time helping his father out of debt by resigning his own reversionary interest in the small family estate. In all supreme matters his actions were those of a generous spirit. His need and desire to possess a competence and not to be crippled in his career did not outweigh—nay, were cast aside by—true love and family duty.

But these great decisions only made thrift and circumspection more imperative. He could not afford to gamble and carouse with his equals. He could not indulge in the slightest personal extravagance. He ate sparingly, drank little, always more readily at the expense of others than his own, and eschewed all kind of display in dress. He was always strict and punctilious in money matters. He paid his bills with the utmost promptitude. He condescended to keep careful accounts in his own handwriting about quite small household affairs, and generally behaved more like a tradesman whose livelihood depends upon his honesty and solvency than like a gay and gallant courtier and fine gentleman. Even now, fifteen years later, after having held several lucrative posts, he was by far the poorest man in the high circle in which he had taken his natural place. He was an Earl, but the most impecunious in England. He was the first Lieutenant-General, but unemployed. He had braved the displeasure of the Crown. It might well be that his career was closed for many years. The slightest financial imprudence would be fatal to his future. Thus he continued those habits of strict and austere personal economy which had been ingrained in childhood and youth, and without which he would certainly have been submerged.

All this was very deplorable, and no doubt the historians are right to mock and sneer at him. But their taunts are only an echo of the gibes and jokes of his contemporaries. Probably many stories of meanness were fastened on him, once he had that reputation, which are not true. But, true or false or merely exaggerated, they must be accepted by his biographer as representing the impression of the society in which he lived. He had, we are told, in 1692 but three coats ("depuis trois ans il n'a fait que trois habits modestes"), one of which he wore only on the greatest State occasions. "He was," wrote Sarah, "naturally genteel, without the least affectation, and handsome as an angel, tho' ever so carelessly drest." He would walk home from the Palace through the muddy streets to save the hire of a sedan chair. He entertained very few. Even when he wished to gain officers of the Army to his faction, he spent nothing on their meat and drink. Macaulay is no doubt right in stating gleefully that when he was robbed of five hundred guineas by a highwayman it was a bitter blow. There is the story on which Swift founded the scathing insult "that he had risked his life for a pair of stockings." When as Commander-in-Chief the gaiters he wore were so drenched that they had to be cut off him, he gave meticulous instructions to his orderly, before a number of officers, apparently without any proper sense of shame, to rip them up the seams, so that they could be resewn.

It seems undeniable that when he planned the celebrated march to the Danube he also scheduled which brigades and divisions of his army he would dine with at the different dates, without, of course, disclosing the places where the camps would lie. The splendid silver wine-flasks, or pilgrim bottles—as big as small barrels—which have been so much admired travelled with him in his campaigns; but they and other luxurious trappings were used only on State occasions when it was his duty to entertain the princes and generals of the Grand Alliance, or for some special rejoicing.

Ordinarily, instead of keeping, as was the custom of generals in the field of those days, a sumptuous open table to which a fine company sat down every night when war permitted, Marlborough lived very simply with his immediate personal staff. This, again, was a grievous fault in a General at the beginning of the eighteenth century. Brigadiers and even Colonels were attended by sumpter-horses and wagons suitable to their dignity. Although hard fare was recognized to be the lot of the private men and subordinate officers, and such as their station required, it was most inappropriate that the Commander-in-Chief of the main army of a European coalition with princely revenues at his disposal should not travel and dine in the luxury of his august position.

Marlborough seems to have regarded war merely as a serious business in which he was interested to the exclusion of pleasures and personal indulgences. All this puts his admirers to shame. One feels that virtues, valour, and victories alike are tarnished by such traits. We blush; but we must not conceal these shocking facts or legends. The truth is that from his upbringing and the pressures of his life he had acquired a hatred of waste of money in all its forms, and especially of frittering away comparatively small sums. He resembled a certain type of modern millionaires, who accumulate wealth unceasingly, spend hardly anything upon themselves, and use their fortunes for the well-being of their families and the endowment of their children, or apply them to great buildings or public objects.

He was like them in other ways. He had that curious mixture of business capacity and Imperial vision which in our own day excited the admirers and the critics of Cecil Rhodes. In 1666 two French-Canadian Protestants who had opened up the fur trade around Hudson Bay, but had found no support from their own Government either in Quebec or Paris, came to England and obtained an audience of King Charles II. After a successful voyage a permanent company was formed. In 1670 the King granted a charter "to the Governor and Company of adventurers of England trading into Hudson Bay." Prince Rupert, twelve times re-elected till his death, was the first Governor. In 1683 James, Duke of York, was elected to succeed him. On James's accession John Churchill was chosen. He thus became the third Governor of the Hudson's Bay Company. "The new governor," we are told, "threw himself heartily into the work of the Company." In 1688 it declared a dividend of 50 per cent; in 1689 a dividend of 25 per cent was paid; in 1690 of 75 per cent; and in that year it was decided to triple by a share-splitting operation the value of its original stock. Nor was the expansion of the original £10,500 capital unjustified. The stocks in the warehouse were alone worth that sum; the trapping of the year was expected to bring in £20,000 worth of beaver; and a claim for damages against the French for £100,000 was to be made. The Company then decided to increase its trade and widen the scale of its operations. The river running into the west side of the bay far to the north was named, in honour of the new Governor, Churchill River, and at its mouth in 1686 a new port and trading centre for the north and west of Canada was founded. This project is alive to-day. Many instances are given by the historians of the Hudson's Bay Company of the energy and helpfulness of Lord Churchill.

Churchill's part in the Revolution gave the company a good position in the new reign. In June 1689 he sent out instructions for William and Mary to be proclaimed in the posts on the shores of the bay. "He was able shortly after to report to his Company that a hundred marines had been detailed to protect the Company's ships." The enthusiasm of the directors and shareholders at this mark of consideration obtained through the influence of Lord Churchill was very great, and we learn from the minutes that profuse thanks were given to the governor, and a piece of plate of solid gold worth a hundred guineas was presented to him for his distinguished services. His arrest and imprisonment in 1692 cut through these happy proceedings. It was indispensable to the Company that its monopoly and its charter should have a governor with great influence at Court. Churchill's dismissal from the Army and all official employments, which we have already described, carried with it this private loss as well. In November 1692 Sir Stephen Evance was elected governor in his place.

His habit of personal economy extended to the whole control of Marlborough's armies. He was always worrying about the cost of things in a manner that seemed most petty and unbecoming. It was remarkable, indeed, that he was so popular with the troops; but, then, of course, he always took care that they got their rations and pay punctually, and the country people were always paid promptly for their supplies, so that the rank and file did not feel his cheeseparing at all, and only saw the victories. This naturally prevented their making a true judgment of his meanness. These simple common soldiers only noticed that they were well looked after and never once led to failure of any kind. Little did they know about the gaiters story. Little would they have cared if they had—so defective was their sense of proportion. Indeed, they might only have made jokes about it, and loved him all the more. But history cannot be thus easily satisfied; and we must record the truth. Both Frederick the Great and Napoleon were remarkable for the economy with which they managed their armies. But Marlborough made money go farther in the field than either, or, indeed, than any commander then or since, except perhaps Sir Herbert Kitchener, who kept the accounts of his reconquest of the Sudan as if he had been the manager of an emporium.

We have tried, however painful it may be, to set this out with naked candour. There are, on the other hand, a few mitigating features which may also be mentioned. Paget says:

> His declining, when in poverty and disgrace, to accept the generosity of the Princess Anne; his repeated refusal of the government of the Netherlands, with its princely income of £60,000 a year; his generosity to young and deserving officers; his application of all the money at his private disposal amongst the wounded officers of the enemy after the battle of Malplaquet; his liberal provision during his own lifetime for his children. . . .

are all to be counted in his favour. When to these are added his early imprudences of marrying for love and paying his father's debts at the expense of his inheritance, it may perhaps be recognized that he was not wholly base and sordid. We do not venture to press the point too far.

It is said that, though Marlborough was stingy in small matters—tips and the like—which may well be taken as proved against him, he was uncommonly courteous and considerate to his subordinates and inferiors in the social scale, and a most kind-hearted man. "For his natural good temper," says Ailesbury, "he never had his equal. He could not chide a servant and was the worst served possible, and in command he could not give a harsh word, no not to the meanest Sergeant, Corporal, or soldier." We have found a new confirmation of Ailesbury's testimony that Marlborough, for all his sagacity in large matters, and ridiculous small personal economies, was gentle to the point of laxity with his servants.

These qualities also played their part in European history. "Of all the men I ever knew," wrote Lord Chesterfield,

> the late Duke of Marlborough possessed the graces in the highest degree, not to say engrossed them. Indeed, he got the most by them; and contrary to the custom of profound historians who always assign deep causes for great events, I ascribe the better half of the Duke of Marlborough's greatness to those graces. He had no brightness— nothing shining in his genius. . . . His figure was beautiful; but his manner was irresistible either by man or woman. It was by this engaging graceful manner that he was enabled, during all the war, to connect the various and jarring Powers of the Grand Alliance, and to carry them on to the main object of the war, notwithstanding their private and separate views, jealousies and wrongheadedness. Whatever Court he went to (and he was often obliged to go to restive and refractory ones) he brought them into his measures. The Pensionary Heinsius, who had governed the United Provinces for forty years, was absolutely governed by him. He was always cool, and nobody ever observed the least variation in his countenance; he could refuse more easily than others could grant; and those who went from him the most dissatisfied as to the substance of their business, were yet charmed by his manner, and, as it were, comforted by it.

The Dutch Deputy Sicco van Goslinga, whose hostile opinions we shall encounter later on, has left on record what is on the whole the best word-picture of him as he was a few years later.[1]

> Here is his Portrait, drawn to the best of my insight. He is a man of birth: about the middle height, and the best figure in the world: his features without fault, fine, sparkling eyes, good teeth, and his

[1] Sicco van Goslinga, *Mémoires*, pp. 42–44, *sub* 1707.

complexion such a mixture of white and red as the fairer sex might envy: in brief, except for his legs, which are too thin, one of the handsomest men ever seen. His mind is keen and subtle [*il a beaucoup d'esprit, et délicate*], his judgment very clear and sound, his insight both quick and deep, with a consummate knowledge of men which no false show of merit can deceive. He expresses himself well, and even his very bad French is agreeable: his voice is harmonious, and as a speaker in his own language he is reckoned among the best. His address is most courteous, and while his handsome and well-graced countenance engages every one in his favour at first sight, his perfect manners and his gentleness win over even those who start with a prejudice or grudge against him. He has courage, as he has shown in more than one conjuncture: he is an experienced soldier, and plans a campaign to admiration. So far his good qualities. Now for the weak points which if I am not mistaken I have found in him. The Duke is a profound dissembler, all the more dangerous that his manner and his words give the impression of frankness itself. His ambition knows no bounds, and an avarice which I can only call sordid, guides his entire conduct. If he has courage—and of this there is no question, whatever may be said by those who envy or hate him—he certainly wants that firmness of soul which makes the true Hero. Sometimes, on the eve of an action, he is irresolute, or worse; he will not face difficulties, and occasionally lets reverses cast him down: of this I could adduce more than one instance as an eye-witness. Yet I saw nothing of the kind either at Ramillies or Malplaquet, so it may be that some constitutional weakness, unfitting him to support fatigue, has something to do with it. He does not know much of discipline, and gives too much rein to his men, who have now and then indulged in frightful excesses. Moreover he lacks the precise knowledge of military detail which a Commander-in-Chief should possess. But these defects are light in the scale against the rare gifts of this truly great man.

There is no doubt that Marlborough took from the various offices which he held everything to which he was entitled either by warrant or recognized custom. But no one has ever been able to prove that he took more. The House of Commons was vigilant in those days, and charges of corruption and peculation were constant features of its debates. Danby's second and final disgrace in 1695 is a remarkable instance of the zeal and fearlessness with which Parliament discharged its duties. Both Churchill's brothers, George and Charles, were in a single year sent for a while to the Tower for financial irregularities and abuses, and there are numerous other cases on record. No one was more jealously watched than Marlborough. He had numerous enemies. As he was never a strong party man, he had not the protection which others enjoyed. Yet, although allegations, gossip, and slander pursued him, as they did most prominent people, no charge was ever brought against him till the famous charges of 1712, and these were, as will be seen in due course, completely exploded. It might be supposed that a man who was known to be poor and fond of money, and who was for a long period viewed with extreme hostility by the King and by powerful people at Court, would, if his misconduct was flagrant, as is alleged, have certainly been called to account. In that ruthless age he was the last man to receive exceptional licence.

It is probably a just conclusion that Marlborough's conduct was above and not below the standards of his time; that though he took all the emoluments, perquisites, and commissions which belonged to his offices and appointments, he never took bribes or any money that was not his by usage or law. Although he always recognized the claims of natural love and affection, as in choosing his wife, in helping his father, or providing for his children, and set these far above riches, his own deep-rooted habits of personal thrift and self-denial were carried to a point which drew upon him the mockery of his envious contemporaries and of malicious historians. Yet these habits, unpleasing though they may seem, were an essential part of his character as a gatherer, as a builder and a founder. They were mitigated or often baffled by the pervasive kindness of his nature. They arose from the same methodical, patient, matter-of-fact spade-work which characterizes all his conduct of war, and formed the only basis upon which the great actions for which he is renowned could have sprung. His handling of his private affairs was as grave, as strongly marked by common sense, and as free from indulgence or unwisdom as his conduct of politics and war. His private fortune was amassed upon the same principles as marked the staff-work of his campaigns, and was a part of the same design. It was only in love or on the battlefield that he took all risks. In these supreme exaltations he was swept from his system and rule of living, and blazed resplendent with the heroic virtues. In his marriage and in his victories the worldly prudence, the calculation, the reinsurance, which regulated his ordinary life and sustained his strategy, fell from him like a too heavily embroidered cloak, and the genius within sprang forth in sure and triumphant command.

CHAPTER TWENTY-ONE

Peace and Reconciliation

☜ 1696-98 ☞

IN its eighth year the so-called War of the League of Augsburg came to an inconclusive end. The Maritime Powers and Germany had defended themselves successfully, but were weary of the barren struggle. Spain was bellicose, but useless. After the withdrawal of the English fleet from the Mediterranean the Duke of Savoy made peace with France, and the Emperor and the King of Spain were constrained to accept the neutralization of Italy. Only the Emperor, with his eyes fixed on the ever-impending vacancy of the Spanish throne, was earnest to keep the anti-French confederacy in being. But this same reason dictated an opposite policy to France. Louis had no mind to see the Spanish empires in the Old and New World become the prize which should inspire all the banded enemies of France with renewed comradeship and ardour. He understood the numerous strains which were rending the Grand Alliance. He saw that it was falling to pieces under the pressure of so many fruitless campaigns. Once resolved into its component parts, the reconstitution of so ponderous and complicated an engine might well be impossible. He believed that no hand but William's could reassemble it; and how long would William last? Peace would dissolve the hostile coalition. Many of its members would lay aside their panoply and go their several ways disarmed. But the great central Power which had hitherto withstood them all, albeit narrowly, would under his absolute sovereignty refit her armies, revive her strength, and pursue her aims better at the moment by peace than by war. Moreover, the long struggle against all Europe had seriously affected the strength of the

French nation. Louis therefore at the end of 1696 made overtures of peace to William. It gradually became clear that France would restore all her conquests in the Low Countries and on the Rhine made since the Peace of Nimwegen except only Strasburg; and for Strasburg she would give an ample substitute.

William, with his lifelong knowledge of Europe, comprehended perfectly the meaning of these proposals. But the pressure for peace, especially in England, convinced him that he had not the power to reject them. The negotiations, opened under Swedish mediation at Ryswick, were protracted. The French, who had been able to draw fifty thousand of their troops from the Italian theatre for the northern front, were in no hurry to close the campaign. The differences between the allies, an elaborate ceremonial, and the necessary adjustments of points of dignity and honour occupied the rest of 1697. The Emperor, who wanted Strasburg, protested strongly. Considering, however, that he had himself made a separate agreement neutralizing the Italian front and liberating the French army operating there, his position was not morally strong. The Spaniards were tamed by disasters at Barcelona and at Cartagena, in the Indies. The English Parliament clamoured for a settlement.

It was not till October 1697 that the group of treaties bringing back peace to the whole world was completed. Apart from the territorial arrangements, Louis agreed tacitly and under curious reserves to recognize William as King of the three kingdoms. He refused to abandon James II by name, but he contracted not to support any enemies of England, adding the words "without any exception," which, since they covered the Prince of Wales as well as the exiled King, were by no means unacceptable. He also withdrew his demand that the mass of the Jacobite refugees apart from the Royal Family should return under an amnesty to their native land. He restored the principality of Orange to its redoubtable owner, stipulating only that no French Huguenots should reside there. William on his part abated his claim that James and his Court should leave French soil, and by a provision which casts a revealing light upon the cool mood of the times undertook to pay to Mary of Modena a jointure ultimately fixed at £50,000 a year. Thus all the polite society of Europe bowed and scraped amicably to one another, and all its harassed peoples rested from their painful strife.

The five-year interlude between the first nine and the last ten years of this world war is commonly viewed as a mere truce. In fact, however, the situation after the Treaty of Ryswick contained many elements of peace. Certainly all its signatories sincerely hoped to accomplish their aims without further resort to arms. All were weary of costly and desultory strife. The great antagonisms of Europe remained; the perils of the Spanish succession impended; but there was an earnest resolve, shared in various degrees by sovereigns, Governments, and peoples, to exhaust every method of diplomacy and bargaining before again drawing the sword. The Peace of Ryswick left in Europe two great figures instead of one. Louis XIV recognized in William III almost an equal. Nicely chosen terms of honour were interchanged between them. William expressed his "veneration and admiration" for Louis, and Louis his "high respect" for William. Both potentates yielded themselves for a space to the sensation that together with goodwill they could settle the problems of Europe and give repose to Christendom.

William was now at the height of his glory. He seemed about to outshine even the Sun King himself. In the east, in the north, and now in the south and west of Europe he seemed about to lay, after generations of religious, dynastic, and territorial wars, the foundations of a lasting peace for the whole world. But at this very moment when all that the hearts of men desired was coming within their reach through his exertions, he was woefully and even fatally weakened by the action of the House of Commons. To deal with Louis XIV as an equal—the only key to safety—it was imperative that he should be strong. Not only must he marshal all his influence in Europe, not only must he wield the overwhelming sea-power of England and Holland, but he must have at his back a considerable British Army.

Very different were the mood and outlook of the Tory country gentlemen and Whig doctrinaires who assembled at Westminster. The wars were over; their repressions were at an end. They rejoiced in peace and clamoured for freedom. The dangers were past; why should they ever return? Groaning under taxation, impatient of every restraint, the Commons plunged into a career of economy, disarmament, and constitutional assertiveness which was speedily followed by the greatest of the wars England had ever waged and the heaviest expenditures she had ever borne.

England came out of the war with an army of eighty-seven thousand regular soldiers. The King considered that thirty thousand men and a large additional number of officers was the least that would guarantee the public safety and interest. His Ministers, in contact with Parliament, did not dare propose more than ten thousand, and the House of Commons would only vote seven thousand. The Navy underwent a less severe compression. The picture is complicated by a considerable garrison which all admitted must be kept in Ireland, by two thousand men in the West Indies, and by three thousand marines borne as sailors, though actually infantry. A new Parliament only reiterated more stridently the demands of its predecessor. Its Members had vowed on the hustings that they would cut the expenses to the bone and break up the standing army. They ingeminated economy. The reductions were carried out in the most brutal manner, the war-bitten veterans and the Huguenot refugees who had fought so well being summarily flung on the streets and treated as rogues and vagabonds on the first provocation. The process was only tempered by the half-pay granted to the officers as a retaining fee, and delayed by the inability of Parliament to pay the arrears due to the men before discharge. An orgy of insult and abuse in which all classes of the civil population heartily joined began around all uniformed men, the half-pay officers, and especially those who had already been disarmed and turned adrift and had no means of support. The roads and countryside became infested with desperate, starving footpads who had lately grappled with the French Guard and shed their blood for King and country. The days of Robin Hood returned, and what was left of the English cavalry was largely occupied in hunting down their old comrades-in-arms now driven into outlawry. The gibbet and the lash were meted out with ruthless vigour on all who fell into the clutches of the law. Such was the process of demobilization in the seventeenth century.

A new and in many ways a singularly modern figure whom every one nowadays can understand had appeared in the House of Commons. Robert Harley was born and bred in a Puritan family and atmosphere a Whig and a Dissenter. In the process of opposing the Court he gradually transformed himself from Whig to Tory and from Dissenter to High Churchman, so that eventually he became the chief of the Tories both in Church and State. Already in 1698 he had become virtually their leader in the House of Commons. He it was who conducted the reckless movement for the reduction of the armed forces. He it was who sought to rival the Bank of England with the Land Bank. He appealed to moderate opinion even when heading the attack. He kept in touch with the Whigs, while delighting the Tories. He made the Court feel that, though he was their most serious enemy, he might also some day, perhaps, become their best friend.

Behind Harley, Seymour, the pre-eminent 'sham goodfellow' of the age, cheered on his West Country pack with all the zest of a huntsman on a good scenting day. The Tory squires roared about the expense of useless and insolent popinjays; and the Whigs joined them in descanting upon the menace to freedom inherent in a standing army. The King was aghast at these furious manifestations. His heart bled for the officers and men with whom he had marched and fought during the long, sombre campaigns. Every fibre in his nature revolted at the baseness, cruelty, and ingratitude with which his faithful troops were treated, and at the same time he felt his whole European position undermined by the blotting out of England as a military factor. But he was powerless. Moreover, it was resolved that such troops as must perforce be retained should not comprise a single foreigner. The Dutch Guards must forthwith quit the island. Accordingly this well-trained, devoted brigade began its march to the coast.

Can we wonder that the unhappy prince, insulted in the hour of his greatest triumph, hamstrung in the full stride of his most beneficent activity, outraged in his honour and comradeship as a soldier, wished to quit the insensate and ungrateful people whose religion, whose institutions he had preserved, and whose fame he had lifted so high? He would abandon the odious and intractable race. He would retort their hatred of foreigners with a gesture of inexpressible scorn. Europe might clatter again into confusion so that insular ignorance should reap its harvest. That he mastered these emotions is a measure of his quality. It was the hardest of his victories, and without it his life's work must have perished. Yet if we reflect on his many faults in tact, in conduct, and in fairness in the earlier days of his reign, the unwarrantable favours he had lavished on his Dutchmen, the injustices done to English commanders, Count Solms' maltreatment of the English troops at Steinkirk, his uncomprehending distaste for the people of his new

realm, their relegation to be mere pawns on his Continental chess-
board—anyone can feel that all the blame was not on one side. His
present anguish paid his debts of former years. As for the English, they
were only too soon to redeem their follies in blood and toil.

Few features in Marlborough's long life are more remarkable than
the manner in which he steadily grew in weight and influence through
the whole of the six years when he was banished from favour and
office. The Whigs were jealous of Shrewsbury's honour, and the Tories
felt a strong interest in Godolphin. But Marlborough had no party to
take care of him, and he alone bore the weight of the royal displeasure.
He took a regular share in the business of the House of Lords. Apart
from the attainting of Fenwick, he preserved a conciliatory attitude towards the Jacobites. He remained the trusted friend of the Princess
Anne. For the rest he lived in tranquil retirement, seeming not to fret
at the great war-opportunities which were slipping away, or at the years
of his prime which were being consumed. He was happy with Sarah
and his children, and his equanimity was perfect. He rarely wrote letters, except to Sarah when he was parted from her, or on public business when he was employed. We have, therefore, only the scantiest
records of his daily life during these years or of his public actions. Still
he grew, and at the end of this lengthy period of eclipse was felt by
every one around the summit of affairs to be one of the greatest Englishmen of the day.

William was very slow resuming relations with him. After the death
of Queen Mary in 1694 he had been readmitted to the Court, but to
no employment. At last, however, the barrier fell to pieces. Anne's
eldest son, the Duke of Gloucester, was now nine years old. It was
thought fitting to provide the future heir-apparent to the Crown with a
governor of high consequence and an establishment of his own. Parliament in voting the King a Civil List of £700,000 a year had foreseen
such an arrangement. William's first thoughts turned to Shrewsbury,
who was still brooding in the country and constantly asking to be relieved of his office. He had, as we have seen, more than once pressed
Marlborough's claims upon the King. He now declined the appointment for which his friend seemed the obvious choice. Nothing could
be more agreeable to the young Prince's parents. Still the King hesi-

tated, and a current of Tory opinion brought Rochester's name forward. Sunderland seems to have exerted his still potent influence in Marlborough's favour.

It may well have been, however, that a new associate of Marlborough's carried the greatest weight. William had become deeply attached to the young Dutch courtier Keppel. He had advanced him in a few years from being a page to a commanding position in the State. He had newly created him Earl of Albemarle. There was an affinity between them—honourable, but subtle and unusual. The lonely, childless monarch treated Keppel as if he were a well-beloved adopted son. The King's old faithful intimate, Portland, had long been Marlborough's enemy. He had not perhaps forgotten a description of him as "a wooden fellow." But Portland was now on his embassy in Paris, and Keppel had supplanted him in the King's heart. The rivalry between these two Dutchmen was hot. In fact, Portland was soon to cast off all his offices for a ludicrous cause. Keppel in his absence abroad had installed himself at Newmarket in the rooms next to the royal apartments which Portland had long occupied; and William would not eject him. It sufficed that Portland was Marlborough's enemy for Keppel to become his advocate. Thus those obstacles against which merit and policy had so long pressed in vain were smoothly removed by the deft and tactful addresses of a youthful counsellor.

In the summer of 1698 William invited Marlborough to be governor of the boy Prince. When he kissed hands upon his appointment William uttered the gracious but discriminating words, "My lord, teach him but to know [? be] what you are, and my nephew cannot want for accomplishments." At the same time Marlborough was restored to his rank in the Army and to the Privy Council. The King announced his decision in remarkable terms in the *Gazette* of June 16, 1698:

> His Majesty has been pleased to appoint the Right Honourable the Earl of Marlborough to be Governor of His Highness the Duke of Gloucester, as a mark of the good opinion His Majesty has of his lordship's zeal for his service and his qualifications for the employment of so great a trust. . . .

The miniature Court of the Duke of Gloucester was formed with expedition in the summer of 1698. His parents and the Marlboroughs had their own ideas about its composition. The King shied at their clear-cut plans. "The Princess Anne," he exclaimed petulantly, on the eve of sailing to The Hague, "should not be Queen before her time." Marlborough made no difficulties. He sought only to know the royal pleasure; and Keppel, who was inseparable from his master, promised to guide it into proper channels. In the end the list was accepted very much as it had been planned. William had chosen Bishop Burnet to be the young Prince's spiritual guide, and in addition to educate him in history, politics, and the lesser arts. A Tory governor must be balanced by a Whig preceptor. William may also have been glad to get Burnet, "the blabbing Bishop," of whom he was tired, out of his way. However, Marlborough and Burnet became close friends. The Bishop yielded himself to the charm and courtesy of his chief. He fell so much under his attraction that he even rewrote the passages in his history dealing with Churchill's desertion of James. Improvidently he forgot to destroy the original version, which has been unearthed to his posthumous mockery. Lord Churchill, Marlborough's only surviving son, aged twelve, was appointed Master of the Horse and no doubt 'playmate in chief.' A son of Bishop Burnet became a page, and an impoverished gentlewoman named Hill was put in charge of the laundry.

Among fleeting shadows the name of Hill is significant. In 1689, shortly after the Revolution, Sarah discovered that she had poor relations. Her grandfather, Sir John Jennings, had produced no fewer than twenty-two children. His estate, though substantial, could not bear such subdivision. One of his daughters, with hardly £500 for her dowry, had married a Levant merchant named Hill. Having prospered for some years, he was ultimately ruined by speculation. When Mr and Mrs Hill died they left four children, two sons and two daughters.

> The elder daughter [Abigail] . . . [writes Sarah] was a grown woman. I took her to St Albans, where she lived with me and my children, and I treated her with as great kindness as if she had been my sister. . . . As for the younger daughter (who is still living) I engaged my Lord Marlborough, when the Duke of Gloucester's family was settled, to make her laundress to him, which was a good provision for her. And when the Duke of Gloucester died, I obtained for her a pension of £200 a year, which I paid her out of the Privy Purse. . . . The Queen was pleased to allow the money for that purchase [an annuity] and it is very probable that Mrs Hill has the annuity to this day, and perhaps nothing else, unless she saved money

after her sister had made her Deputy to the Privy Purse, which she did as soon as she had supplanted me.

The elder son was at my request put by my Lord Godolphin into a place in the custom-house; and when, in order to his advancement to a better, it was necessary to give security for his good behaviour, I got a relation of the Duke of Marlborough's to be bound for him in two thousand pounds.

His brother (whom the bottle-men afterwards called "honest Jack Hill") was a tall boy whom I clothed (for he was all in rags) and put to school at St Albans. . . . After he had learnt what he could there, a vacancy happening of Page of Honour to the Prince of Denmark, his Highness was pleased at my request to take him. I afterwards got my Lord Marlborough to make him Groom of the Bedchamber to the Duke of Gloucester. And though my Lord always said that Jack Hill was good for nothing, yet to oblige me he made him his aide-de-camp and afterwards gave him a regiment. But it was his sister's interest that raised him to be a General and to command in that ever memorable expedition to Quebec; I had no share in doing him these honours. To finish what I have to say upon this subject:—when Mr Harley thought it useful to attack the Duke of Marlborough in Parliament, this Quebec General, this honest Jack Hill, this once ragged boy whom I clothed, happening to be sick in bed, was nevertheless persuaded by his sister to get up, wrap himself in warmer clothes than those I had given him, and go to the House to vote against the Duke.

Here, then, is a succinct account of the Abigail Hill who afterwards, as Mrs Masham and Harley's confidante, saved France from destruction as surely, though scarcely as gloriously, as Joan of Arc. It was an annoyance of peculiar rankle to Sarah to the end of her long life that she, by indulging her most generous sentiments of compassion, should have prepared her own undoing and her husband's fall at the moment when the consummation of all his victories and toils seemed so near. In her strong, domineering, bustling life Sarah did many actions both bad and good, but her charity to the Hills was her special benevolence. She was, indeed, for many years their patron saint. Nepotism apart, her kindliness to them shines brightly. Yet this was one of the traceable causes of her catastrophe.

Thus we see Marlborough picking his steps warily and with foresight through all the perplexities and hazards of the times, while at the same time his devoted wife by one of the best deeds in her life sets in train, all unwitting, the series of events which amid his glories shall lay him low.

> The young disease, that must subdue at length,
> Grows with his growth, and strengthens with his strength.

It is a classic instance of how far romance lags behind reality.

CHAPTER TWENTY-TWO

Marlborough in Politics

₰ 1698-1700 ₰

MEANWHILE Marlborough's family had grown up, and in the years 1698 and 1699 his two eldest daughters both married. The eldest, Henrietta, became engaged to Francis, Lord Godolphin's son. The lifelong friendship between both the Marlboroughs and Godolphin is a factor in history; but this was no marriage of political or worldly calculation. It was a love-match between very young people—Francis was only twenty and Henrietta eighteen—who were thrown together by the intimacies of their parents, to whom it gave the keenest pleasure. Godolphin's wife had died after giving birth to Francis a generation earlier. The Treasurer was too deeply attached to her memory ever to marry again. In that corrupt age, when public office was almost the only road to riches, Godolphin was for more than thirty years and in four reigns in control of the national finances. He was, however, a man of stainless integrity in money matters. At his death in 1712 he left but £14,000, somewhat less than what he had inherited forty years before. He could therefore at this time give only the smallest competence to his son. But the fabulous avarice of John and Sarah seems to have slumbered on this occasion, as it had when they themselves plighted their penniless troth. Marlborough's notorious greed for lucre had so far left him at forty-five the poorest of his rank. Nevertheless he provided a dowry of £5000. The Princess Anne, whose enthusiasm was kindled by this cementing of friendship in her circle, wished to bestow £10,000 upon the young couple. But the Marlboroughs, no doubt from some base motive, would only accept £5000. The marriage took place on March 24, 1698.

The bride was beautiful and accomplished. Her graces were the theme for the rhymesters of the day. The union was lasting.

The marriage of Marlborough's second daughter, Anne, in January 1700, was a theme of greater importance. We have seen how long and varied had been the relations of Marlborough and Sunderland and the political association that had always subsisted between them. A close friendship had grown between their wives.

Sunderland's heir, Lord Spencer, who was a widower, was a remarkable personality. He had none of the insinuating charm and genial courtesy of his incomprehensible father. He was an ultra-Whig of the straitest and most unbending type. He did not trouble to conceal his republican opinions. He was so conscious of the rights of his order and of Parliament against the Crown that he had little sympathy left for the commonalty. According to his philosophy, citizens of the worst republic were free, while subjects of the best king were slaves. He was a keen book-lover, and the Sunderland Library remained for many generations his monument. The Whig Party took a lively interest in the development of his mind. It was thought that experience would mellow his orthodox severity, and they already saluted him as the future champion of the cause for which "Hampden had died in the field and Sidney on the scaffold."

Sarah, that sturdy Whig, may have shared these hopes; but Marlborough's temperamental Toryism was repulsed by the harshness alike of Lord Spencer's doctrine and disposition. Anne was his favourite daughter, and by every account was a brilliant and fascinating creature. Intimate and subtle as were his relations with Sunderland in State affairs, important as were the reciprocal services which might be rendered, magnificent as was the inheritance, he was disinclined to mingle that wayward blood with his own, or to countenance a marriage which might not bring his daughter happiness. He was therefore very hard to persuade. However, he gradually yielded to Sarah's persuasions, and, being at length convinced of Lord Spencer's sincerity, he finally consented. Once again Princess Anne, who was the girl's godmother, matched the family dowry with a gift of £5000. Sunderland, who seems to have longed for the marriage, wrote in a remarkable letter:

If I see him so settled I shall desire nothing more in this world but to die in peace if it please God. I must add this that if he can be thus happy he will be governed in everything public and private by my lord Marlborough. I have particularly talked to him of that and he is sensible how advantageous it will be to him to be so. I need not I am sure desire that all this may be a secret to everybody but Lady Marlborough.

These expectations were not fulfilled, and Spencer's personality and conduct were to become after his father's death a cause of serious political embarrassment. It is, however, by this marriage that the Marlborough blood, titles, and estates have descended to posterity, for his only surviving son, Lord Churchill, Master of the Horse in the Duke of Gloucester's household, had almost as short a span to live as the little Prince he served.

The ice of a long frost being broken, the King felt the comfort in his many troubles of Marlborough's serene, practical, adaptive personality, which no difficulties found without resource, which no dangers disturbed. In July 1698, when the royal departure for Holland rendered a Council of Regency necessary, Marlborough was nominated one of the nine Lords Justices to exercise the sovereign power. From this time forth William seemed to turn increasingly, if without personal friendship, towards the man of whose aid he had deprived himself during the most critical years of his reign. He used in peace the soldier he had neglected in war; and Marlborough, though his prime bent was military, though stamped from his youth with the profession of arms, became in the closing years of the reign a shrewd and powerful politician.

This new relationship of William and Marlborough requires close examination. The King seemed speedily inclined to trust him implicitly and to make common cause with him in great matters. We have Somers' letter of December 29, 1698, to prove that in his grief and wrath upon the dismissal of the Dutch Guards he confided to Marlborough, although he was not in the Cabinet, his secret resolve, withheld from some of his Ministers, to abdicate the Crown.

We have no record of what Marlborough advised; but there can be little doubt he urged the King to abandon his design. William's abdication at such a juncture might as easily have been followed by a republic as by the accession of the Princess Anne. He must surely have counselled upon the King the patience he practised himself. His comprehension of Europe at this time was second only to that of William.

Both regarded with much detachment, both viewed with a distaste which it was politic to conceal, the violent passions and prejudices of the English political parties, and both were prone to use them alternately for their own purposes, which included also the greatest purposes of the age. Thus for the next two years, if he did not wholly trust Marlborough, William leaned on him. Marlborough felt the weight, and understood and discounted the cause. He did not give himself wholly to the King. The royal confidence was only half-confidence: the rest was the need of help. Hence he preserved his independence and carefully guarded the sources of his own personal power.

Lord Wolseley has not comprehended Marlborough's conduct during the closing years of William III. He is shocked to find his hero, although employed by the King in many great matters while war drew nearer, voting on all test party issues with the Tories in their savage faction fight.

If Marlborough had cut himself adrift from the Tory Party and become a mere adherent of the Court he would soon have lost all influence upon events. His own power would have been reduced to his own personal ability, while at the same time his usefulness to the King would have vanished. William knew England almost as well as he knew Europe, but he despised the ignoble strife of its parties, and underrated the factor of party as an element in his vast problem. In his embarrassments he would turn from Whig Ministers who could not manage and would not face the House of Commons to the turbulent Tories, only to find them ignorant of world facts and with a view of national interests which was at that time wrong-headed and utterly at variance with his own purposes. The Whigs at least saw what was coming, and would help him to meet it. Marlborough, who understood the public interest as clearly as his own, knew that the Whigs could never carry England through the approaching ordeal in the teeth of Tory opposition: he knew that the Tories were by far the strongest faction in the State. Except in the most general way he did not share their prejudices, but he knew their power and that the credit he had with them was one of the main foundations of his own position. Marlborough was in close friendly relations with Harley, and through him with the House of Commons. He wielded himself great influence in the House of Lords. Through Sunderland, now linked to him by the marriage of their children, and through Sarah, he was in contact with the

Whigs. And always he stood by the Princess Anne, dominated and inspired her circle, and championed her interests, in which also the future lay.

These incomplete relationships were the King's own fault, and a misfortune to his reign. If in 1689 and 1690 William, with two kingdoms to govern and the diplomacy of half Europe in his hands, had treated Marlborough fairly and had not denied him his rightful opportunity upon the battlefields, he might have found that talisman of victory without which all his painstaking, adroit combinations and noble exertions could but achieve a mediocre result. He might have found across the differences of rank that same comradeship, never disturbed by doubt or jealousy, true to the supreme tests of war and fortune, which later shone between Marlborough and Eugene.

A tragical event supervened. The little Duke of Gloucester was now eleven. King William's interest in this child casts a pleasing light on his somewhat forbidding character. He saw and petted him repeatedly. At the time of the Fenwick trial, Gloucester, when but seven years old, caused one of his boy soldiers to write out the following address which he signed: "I, your Majesty's most dutiful subject, had rather lose my life in your majesty's cause than in any man's else, and I hope it will not be long ere you conquer France." To which his juvenile army and household appended, "We, your majesty's subjects, will stand by you while we have a drop of blood." In this same year he went with his mother to Tonbridge in order to study fortification "under the care of his clerical tutor." We may readily believe that with such propensities the young Prince rejoiced to have so martial a governor. It is, however, probable that Marlborough, far from encouraging this precocious militarism, inculcated habits of courtesy, gravity, and above all a judicious care of pounds, shillings, and pence.

The hearts of Englishmen and the eyes of Europe were turned towards this child. The Whigs drew from his games the hope of a sovereign who would make valiant head against France. The Tories, on the other hand, repeated with gusto some of his alleged disrespectful interruptions to Burnet's constitutional discourses. A warrior prince, an English prince, a prince with Plantagenet blood and the necessary Parliamentary education—a good match for any warming-pan impostor, however clad with Divine Right!

These hopes were blasted; other solutions awaited the problems of the English people. On July 30, 1700, the Duke of Gloucester died of smallpox so swiftly that his governor reached his bedside only as he breathed his last. His playmate Churchill survived but three years, before he fell beneath the same fatal scourge.

Immense, far-reaching interests were opened by this new gap in the succession. Anne's health amid her repeated miscarriages and stillborn births was precarious. William's days were plainly drawing to a close. The Crown of England, and with it not only all those issues of religion and Constitution which obsessed men's minds, but also the part which the British Isles would play in the destiny of Europe, was once again adrift on a dark, tempestuous ocean. There were many alternatives and many weighty objections to all of them. No one seems to have hankered for James II; but naturally many thoughts turned to the Prince of Wales. The warming-pan myth had lost its primal power. Why should he not be brought up under William's care in Holland? A Protestant, if possible; a Catholic, if it must be, but none the less with his constitutional duties engrained in him.

Historians have debated whether William did not at this time of amity with France dwell upon this solution. He certainly played with it. Had James II died one year earlier and the rightful heir been left alone, freed from the antagonisms which centred upon his father, our affairs might have decided themselves differently. Then there were the children of Victor Amadeus of Savoy, who had married the daughter of Charles II's sister, the famous 'Minette.' But the house of Savoy was under a cloud. Its Duke had so recently deserted the Grand Alliance in the face of the enemy. Thirdly there were the rights of the house of Hanover, at this time represented by the aged Electress Sophia. This solution seemed likely to renew all the difficulties which had arisen in England through the importation of a foreign king. All monarchical sentiment longed for a prince of island character and English speech. But there was another sentiment which suddenly surged up stark and logical. Why should the nation be tormented by these riddles of a disputed succession? Why should not William III be the last King in England? The expense of a Court was in those days sufficient to maintain powerful additions to the Navy or afford longed-for reliefs of taxation. The sudden advance of the republican idea made it imperative that a decision should be reached without delay. This mood dictated the Act of Settlement, and gave the Crown to the house of Hanover in a statute which was virtually a reproach upon the reign of King William. The sovereign must be an Anglican—neither a Catholic nor a Calvinist. He must never leave the country without the permission of Parliament (as some had done so often). He must be advised not by any secret Cabinet or closet about his person, but by the Privy Council as a whole; and the Privy Council must be governed by the preponderating authority of an elected assembly wielding the money power. Thus the reign of Anne would be an interlude; and all would be in readiness at her death to give a dutiful and chilling reception to a Hanoverian prince.

We have no doubt where the Marlboroughs stood in these dominant matters. They must have been unswervingly hostile to any plan of the Prince of Wales intervening between Anne and her declared rights of succession. After Anne they felt themselves free to choose. It was unwise to peer too far ahead.

The untimely death of the Duke of Gloucester deprived Marlborough of his office; but he was by now so strongly established in the centre of English politics that, in spite of his recent difference with the King, his personal position was unimpaired.

In October 1700 Brydges, who had called upon him, noted down in his diary, "My Lord [Marlborough] told me, he believed the Parl: would not be dissolved, and that for Secretary of State the King had not disposed of it, not denying it might be given to himself." A Dutch envoy reported home, "On dit toujours que le comte de Marlborough sera fait secrétaire d'état et le Lord Godolphin, premier commissaire de la trésorerie, mais ces deux icy ne sont pas encore declarez." These anticipations were reduced to irrelevance by wider events.

CHAPTER TWENTY-THREE

The Spanish Succession

·〈 1698-1701 〉·

No great war was ever entered upon with so much reluctance on both sides as the War of the Spanish Succession. Europe was exhausted and disillusioned. The bitter aftermath of eight years' desultory conflict had turned all men's minds to peace, or at least to a change of experience, and to economic instead of military expansion. The new-found contacts which had sprung up between William and Louis expressed the heartfelt wishes of the peoples both of the Maritime Powers and of France.

There is no doubt about the sincerity of William III in the peace effort. It did not only arise from his own nature. He could not conceive how England could be brought again into the field. She seemed to have shot her bolt for at least a generation. He saw the turbulent pacifism of the Parliament; he bowed to the irresistible pressure of disarmament; he understood, while he resented, the insularity and detachment of his acquired subjects. Holland might yet resist any menace to her frontier; but England was cloyed with the Continent, and saw in a strong navy and a strict neutrality a sure escape from the deadly labyrinth. Without the aid of England the States-General must submit to almost anything short of subjugation. War against France without the power of Britain was impossible. Therefore William was in earnest. He must keep peace at almost any price.

The feeble life-candle of the childless Spanish King, known to his country as Charles the Sufferer, flickered, smoked, guttered, but still burned. At any moment it might have gone out. Yet it kept alight for

(229)

nearly a third of a century, and one by one the great statesmen of Europe who had watched for its extinction had themselves been overtaken by the darkness of night. But now the candle burned low in the socket. To the ravages of deformity and disease were added the most grievous afflictions of the mind. The royal victim believed himself to be possessed by the devil. Every sign and symptom betokened the end. What then was to happen to half the world, and what would the other half do with it? A score of claimants, ranging from a successful usurper in Portugal to the Emperor Leopold, confident in his vague, but to his mind paramount, dynastic right, would come forward to demand a greater or lesser share of the mighty heritage. But could not William and Louis, incomparably the most skilled and experienced diplomatists in Europe, lords of the strongest armies and fleets in existence, both of whom saw and shrank from the danger of a renewal of the European conflict, devise some solution to which every candidate would be forced to bow?

England and Holland, who lived by seaborne trade and dreamed of colonies and wealth beyond the oceans, could not bear that the control of Spain, the Indies, Mexico, South America, and the Mediterranean should fall into the competent hands of France. They saw themselves shut out by prohibitive tariffs, mercantile laws, and indefinite naval expansion, alike from their daily bread and their future. The independence of Belgium from France was a vital interest which England and Holland shared in common. The Protestant states shivered at the prospect of the Government that had revoked the Edict of Nantes being united with the Government that had devised and enforced the Holy Inquisition. The Emperor, that Catholic despot without whose aid Protestantism and Parliamentary institutions would be imperilled, advanced proud and impracticable claims. Unless a settlement could be reached between him and France there must be general war. Still, if Louis and William could agree upon a settlement, they would together have the power to impose their will on all concerned.

The peace so earnestly desired could only take the form of a new partition of the Spanish Empire. Very secretly—breathing not a word to Spain nor to the Emperor—the two leading princes set about this task. There were three claimants, each of whom could advance important pretensions. The first was France, represented by the Dauphin. Next there was the Emperor, who, as the widower of the younger

Spanish princess, claimed as much as he could, but was willing to transfer his claims to the second son of his own second wife, the Archduke Charles. Thirdly there was the Emperor's grandson by his first marriage, the Electoral Prince of Bavaria.

Only one conviction dominated the Castilian aristocracy—the Spanish Empire must not be divided. It was intolerable to their patriotism —indeed, to their good sense—that the empire their ancestors had gathered should be parcelled out in fragments. Accordingly Spain plumped for the Electoral Prince. Where the trunk of their empire was, there the limbs should also go. On November 14 Charles signed and declared a will by which the whole of the Spanish domains passed intact to the Electoral Prince.

But now a startling event occurred. The will of Charles II was made public on November 14. On February 6 the little Prince of Bavaria, the heir to these prodigious domains, the child in whose chubby hands the greatest states had resolved to place the most splendid prize, suddenly died. Why did he die, how did he die? A coincidence so extraordinary could not fail to excite dark suspicions. But the fact glared grimly upon the world. All these elaborate, perilous conversations must be begun over again.

Ultimately William and Louis arranged a second Treaty of Partition on June 11, 1699. To the disgust of Harcourt, his Ambassador at Madrid, Louis consented to the Archduke Charles being heir-in-chief. To him were assigned Spain, the overseas colonies, and Belgium, on the condition that they should never be united with the Empire. The Dauphin was to have Naples and Sicily, the Milanese, which was to be exchanged for Lorraine, and certain other Italian possessions. The terms of this provisional treaty allowed the Emperor two months in which to decide whether he would or would not be a party to it. But his heart was set upon Italy; and he finally refused.

On March 13, 1700, therefore, the treaty was ratified only by France and the Maritime Powers.

From this point onward the guile of Louis becomes obvious. During the greater part of 1700, while he was negotiating with William, his Ambassador in Madrid was using every resource, especially money, to win the Spanish Court to the interests of a French prince. At one and the same time he was signing with William the treaty which favoured the Archduke Charles, fomenting a party in Madrid in favour of his grandson, the second son of the Dauphin, Philip, Duke of Anjou, and gradually moving a considerable army towards the Spanish frontier. Since the Emperor would not accept the Partition Treaty, and war between France and the Empire seemed certain, it was natural that, if he must fight anyhow, Louis should fight for the maximum rather than for the minimum claims of his dynasty. Moreover, the weakness of England's pacific mood and the consequent incoherence of the Maritime Powers became continually more apparent. He therefore soothed William with his treaty, and shook Madrid with his propaganda, resolving to seize what fortune should offer.

The event was decisive. Charles II was on his deathbed. Within that diseased frame, that clouded mind, that superstitious soul, trembling on the verge of eternity, there glowed one imperial thought—unity. He was determined as he lay prostrate, scarcely able to utter a word or stir a finger, with his last gasp to proclaim that his vast dominions should pass intact and entire to one prince and to one alone. In the nick of time the French gold in Madrid and the French bayonets beyond the Pyrenees triumphed. The influence of the Holy See under the new Pope was transferred to the side of France. A palace revolution occurred. The Archbishop of Toledo, with a few other priests, established himself in the sick-room and forbade the Queen to enter. The King was then persuaded to sign a will leaving his throne to the Duke of Anjou. The will was completed on October 7, and couriers galloped with the news from the Escurial to Paris. On November 1, Charles II expired.

Louis XIV had now reached one of the great turning-points in the history of France. Should he stand by the treaty, reject the will, and face a single war with the Empire? Should he repudiate the treaty, endorse the will, and defend his grandson's claims in the field against all comers? Apart from good faith and solemnly signed agreements upon which the ink was barely dry, the choice, like so many momentous choices, was nicely balanced.

The news of the death of Charles II reached Paris on November 8, and no further delay was possible. A conference was held in Madame de Maintenon's rooms at which the King, his brother, Pontchartrain (the Chancellor), the Duc de Beauvilliers, and Torcy were present. The will had it. On November 12 Louis wrote to Madrid accordingly.

On November 16 a famous scene was enacted at Versailles. After the

Great King's levee he brought his grandson and the Spanish Ambassador, Castel des Rios, into his Cabinet. To the latter he said, indicating the Duke of Anjou, "You may salute him as your King."

We must now return to England. William was dining at Hampton Court when the news arrived. He bent his head in vain attempt to conceal his feelings. He saw the work of his lifetime was to be shattered, yet he was powerless. He knew it would be futile to appeal to Parliament. King William bowed to the awful logic of circumstances. On December 22 Tallard was able to report that the English and the Dutch would recognize Philip V. They would merely demand certain safeguards. William could only trust that from the discussion of these safeguards a Grand Alliance against France would emerge.

But now Parliament began to realize that the language and attitude of the French King about the essential separation of the Crowns of France and Spain was, at the very least, ambiguous. In February 1701, indeed, Louis XIV had expressly reserved his grandson's right of succession to the French throne, an action which seemed fatally significant to the Maritime Powers. Then came the news—keenly disturbing to all the British commercial interests represented by the Whig Party as the champions of civil and religious liberty—that the Spaniards had handed over to a French company the entire right of importing negro slaves into South America. But the supreme event which roused all England to an understanding of what had actually happened in the virtual union of the Crowns of France and Spain was a tremendous military operation effected under the guise of brazen legality. Philip V had been received with acclamation in Madrid. The Spanish Netherlands rejoiced in his accession. The bonfires blazed in the streets of Brussels in honour of their new sovereign. The fortresses of Belgium constituted the main barrier of the Dutch against the French invasion. After the Peace of Nimwegen * the most important had been occupied by Dutch garrisons who shared with their then Spanish allies the guardianship of these vital strongholds. But now the position was reversed. The Spaniards were the allies of France, joined not by a scrap of paper, but by

---

* The various treaties constituting the Peace of Nimwegen were signed during the autumn of 1678. Louis had come off with solid advantages; nevertheless, Nimwegen registered in his mind an unmistakable sense of being checked. He had widely extended the boundaries of France; but he had felt the thrust of definite and formidable resistances to his onward career.

kindred Crowns. The European states which had fought against France in the late war were still undecided. But everywhere the storm signal had been hoisted. Preparations were being made; officers and soldiers were being recalled from penury to their old formations. Louis, knowing that his enemies would fight if they could muster strength and courage, resolved to make sure of the barrier fortresses.

Citadels defended during all the years of general war, the loss or capture of any one of which would have been boasted as the fruits of a hard campaign, were swept away while a moon waxed and waned. Every one of these fortresses had to be retaken by Marlborough before he could even reach the position established at the Peace of Nimwegen. Only Maestricht, by the accident of an exceptionally strong Dutch garrison which guarded enormous supply depots, escaped the general landslide. Thus all that the Grand Alliance of 1689 had achieved in the Low Countries in eight years of war melted like snow at Easter.

Europe was roused, and at last England was staggered. Some of Louis's admirers condemn him for this violent measure. They argue that when all was going so well for his designs, when his grandson had been accepted as rightful King by every part of the Spanish Empire in the Old World and the New, when his adversaries in their lack of union seemed utterly impotent, he should have displayed all the virtues of quiescence and restraint. But, like William, he knew that the storm was gathering. He had launched himself upon an audacious voyage; and he knew the value of the fortresses. The nations were now arming fast, and we may imagine with what a glow of hope and salvation all those poor, neglected, despised, professional soldiers saw again the certainty of employment, of pay, of food, of shelter, and the chance of fame. Once more fighting men would come into their own. Once more the drums would beat, and the regiments in their brilliant uniforms would march along the highways. Once more the smug merchants and crafty politicians would find they could not do without 'popinjays.' Once more they would flatter the martial class and beg—though so lately ungrateful—for its renewed protection.

In the early summer of 1701 the Whig Party, a minority in the House of Commons, mobilized its pamphleteers to convert the electorate. But the Tories were slow. They were still hunting William III and planning retrenchment. They were still dreaming of detachment from Europe when the nation awoke beneath them. On May 8, 1701, the freeholders of Kent presented a petition to the Commons, begging the House to grant supplies to enable the King to help his allies "before it is too late." The militant pacifists were for punishing the freeholders for the presumption. They actually imprisoned their leaders; but the ground crumbled beneath their feet. The insular structure in which they sought to dwell crashed about their ears. The mass of the Tory Parliament had already moved some distance. On June 12, when they had extorted from the King his assent to the Act of Settlement, Parliament had also authorized him to "seek allies." Ten thousand men, at any rate, should be guaranteed to Holland. William felt the tide had set in his favour, and on the flow he prorogued Parliament, well knowing that their hour had passed.

The same processes which undermined the Tory factions and all their reasonings, so weighty to modern minds, united William and Marlborough. They joined forces, nor was their partnership unequal. For while King William now saw that he could once again draw the sword of England, he felt the melancholy conviction that he himself would never more wield it. This was no time on either side for half-confidences or old griefs. Some one must carry on. In his bones the King knew there was but one man. On May 31 he proclaimed Marlborough Commander-in-Chief of the English forces assembling in Holland. On June 28—the day of the Prorogation—he appointed him Ambassador Extraordinary to the United Provinces. The instructions to Marlborough show the far-reaching character of his powers. Discretion was given him not only to frame, but to conclude treaties without reference, if need be, to King or Parliament. But the King would be at hand and would maintain the closest contact possible. On July 1 the royal yacht carried them both to Holland. Though the opportunities of the reign had been marred or missed by their quarrels and misunderstandings, the two warrior-statesmen were at last united. Though much was lost, all might be retrieved. The formation of the Grand Alliance had begun.

CHAPTER TWENTY-FOUR

The Grand Alliance

⅔ 1701-2 ⅔

THE duties at length confided to Marlborough were of supreme importance. He was to make one last effort to avert the war. If that failed, he was to make an offensive and defensive alliance against France between the three great Powers, England, Holland, and the Empire; thereafter to draw into the confederacy by subsidiary treaties Prussia, Denmark, and as many of the German states and principalities as possible, and to make a treaty with Sweden ensuring at least her friendly neutrality. The King was at hand, usually at Loo, but in practice everything was left to Marlborough and settled by him. Meanwhile through Godolphin he vigilantly watched the tempestuous Parliamentary situation at home, the movement of English opinion, and the reactions which these produced upon King William. In this press of affairs he passed the next four months, and for the first time we see him extended upon a task equal to his capacity.

At this moment also two men who were to be his closest intimates and to continue at his side in unfailing loyalty through the whole period make their appearance. They were already his old friends. William Cadogan, the son of a Dublin lawyer, had won Marlborough's confidence at the taking of Cork and Kinsale. He was now serving in Ireland as a major of the Royal Irish Dragoons. Marlborough appointed him Quartermaster-General in the Low Countries, and he came to Holland with the twelve battalions transported thither from Ireland. He was in the van of all the battles and in numberless operations. Nothing disturbed his fidelity to his chief or the mutual comprehension between them. He shared Marlborough's fall, refusing to separate himself from "the great man to whom I am under such infinite obligations." "I would be a monster," he added, "if I did otherwise."

The second was his military and political secretary. Adam de Cardonnel, the son of a French Protestant, had entered the War Office at an early age, rose to be a Chief Clerk, and came in contact with Marlborough at the beginning of William's reign. From the early part of 1692 he had acted as his secretary, and was in his closest personal friendship and confidence. He too made all the campaigns with Marlborough. He conducted the whole of his correspondence with the sovereigns, princes, and commanders of the Grand Alliance and with the English political leaders, drafting the letters himself, writing from Marlborough's dictation, or copying what his chief had written, to the very great advantage of its grammar and spelling. Thus when the occasion came to Marlborough he was not only ready himself, but he had at his disposal both a military and a civilian instrument which he had long selected and prepared, and which were so perfectly adapted to his needs that they were never changed.

At this moment also appears upon our scene Marlborough's famous comrade. During the spring the Emperor, with the encouragement of King William, had gathered an army of thirty thousand men in the Southern Tyrol. At the head of this stood Prince Eugene.

Prince François Eugene of Savoy was born at Paris in 1663, but from the age of twenty, for just over fifty years and in more than thirty campaigns, he commanded the armies and fought the battles of Austria on all the fronts of the Empire. When he was not fighting the French, he was fighting the Turks. A colonel at twenty, a major-general at twenty-one, he was made a general of cavalry at twenty-six. He was a commander-in-chief ten years before Marlborough. He was still a commander-in-chief, fighting always in the van, more than twenty years after Marlborough's work was done. At the end of his life of innumerable and almost unceasing perils, toils, checks, and triumphs, his skinny body scarred with many wounds, he could still revel in his military duties. He never married, and although he was a discerning patron of art, his only passion was warfare. His decisive victory over the Turks at Zenta in 1697 made him at this moment in our story "the most renowned commander in Europe."

Eugene was a grandson of Duke Charles Emmanuel of Savoy and

son of Olympe Mancini, a niece of Cardinal Mazarin and one of the most beautiful women at the Court of Louis XIV. As a youth, his weakly frame, turned-up nose, and short upper lip gave him, despite his fine eyes, a vacant appearance and caused him to be considered unfit for a soldier. Against his will he was forced to enter the Church, and the King nicknamed him *le petit abbé*. Intrigue at Court twice brought about his father's exile. His mother's grief at this misfortune weighed deeply upon the young mind of the Prince, and he is said to have sworn to leave France and never to return except with his sword in his hand. He became the persistent enemy of France throughout his life. After the early death of his father, Eugene, with two of his brothers, migrated to Vienna. His lack of frivolity, which had injured him at Versailles, was a positive advantage to him at the sombre Court of Leopold I. His earliest experience of war was in the fateful year of 1683, when the Turks reached the gates of Vienna. Here his eldest brother was killed. But Eugene made his mark in a strange land. The Emperor liked and admired him. He saw warfare in its most ruthless forms, and fought under the leadership of the famous Charles of Lorraine. After he had become a colonel Eugene abandoned his desire for a principality in Italy, and fixed as his sole ambition the command of the Imperial Army.

In essence the second Grand Alliance was bound to become another Partition Treaty. Hard pressure had to be put upon the Emperor to reconcile his extortionate demands with the claims of Holland, and thereafter English interests had to be sustained against both Powers. Marlborough, with the angry debates upon William's Partitions in his ears, was intent to study the susceptibilities of the House of Commons, and also to secure due prominence for the particular kind of buccaneering warfare on the sea and across the oceans which was alone acceptable to Tory hearts. In the end he presented results which reconciled the pride of the Empire, the cautious obstinacy of the Dutch, and the commercial and colonizing appetites of the English.

Although French and Austrian troops were already fighting fiercely in Italy, the last hopes of a general peace were not abandoned. Marlborough had been given a separate set of instructions to enter into negotiations with the Ministers of France and Spain at The Hague. He demanded once again on behalf of the Maritime Powers the withdrawal of the French garrisons from the barrier fortresses, the surrender of "cautionary towns" by the Spaniards to Anglo-Dutch control, and the guarantee of "a reasonable satisfaction" for the Emperor out of the Spanish heritage. He seems to have thought it just possible that Eugene's victories in Italy, the process of forming the Grand Alliance at The Hague, and the evident resolve of the Allies to proceed to extremities would oblige Louis to agree in August to the terms he had rejected in March. The French King refused to consider the Emperor's demands, or even to admit to a conference the Ambassador of a Power with whom, though not formally at war, his troops were already engaged.

When, on the 18th, Marlborough learned that Villeroy had left for Italy he felt sure that France had abandoned any thought of opening a campaign in Flanders during the autumn of 1701. Forthwith he allowed Sarah to come over for the greatest day his life had yet seen. On September 7, 1701, he signed alone for England the main treaty with the Empire and Holland by which the three Powers bound themselves to exact their terms from France by negotiations or arms. Sarah was present at his side in his hour of triumph. She was fêted by the brilliant throng assembled for the famous event.

Great moderation characterized the stipulations of the allies. They acquiesced in the rule of Philip V over Spain and the Spanish Indies, provided that the Crowns of France and Spain should never be united. The Emperor was to secure Milan, Naples, Sicily, the Spanish Mediterranean islands, together with Belgium and Luxembourg. But these last two, under the sovereignty of Austria, were to be so organized as to serve "as a fence and rampart, commonly called a barrier, separating and keeping off France from the United Provinces." This basis being settled, the minor states were urged by subsidies provided by England and Holland and by other inducements to join the alliance, and with each a separate agreement was made. The recognition of the Elector of Brandenburg as King of Prussia was the price reluctantly paid by the Emperor in return for his adhesion.

The territorial objectives of the war having been at length agreed, the three principals proceeded to discuss the *dénombrement*. It was finally settled that the Empire should bring into the field against France 82,000 men, the Dutch 100,000, and the English 40,000, together with an equal number for the fleet.

It will be seen that Marlborough's fear of offending Parliament by finally deciding the treaties without their approval was even more acute where the quota of British troops was concerned.

On October 3 he writes to Godolphin:

> *. . . You will excuse me that I trouble you again about the *dénombrement*. I have made use of the argument, that is very natural for England, which is that their [England's] expense at sea must be great. This argument is of more use to me when I speak to the Imperialists, than with the Pensioner; for the latter tells me, that they shall be willing to furnish at sea the same proportions as they did the last war, which was three in eight; and since their land forces are greater than they were the last war, the people here might reasonably expect that ours might not be less. I continue still of the opinion that it would be fatal to have this settled anywhere but in Parliament; but on the other hand I ought to say some thing to them, and I should be glad to know if I might not endeavour to make them not expect more than one half of what they had the last war. For aught I know, this may be more than England will care to do; but I hear no other language here, than that this war must be carried with more vigour than the last, if we ever hope to see a good end of it; and I confess it is so much my own opinion, that I hope we shall do our utmost; what that is, you and 16 [Hedges?] are much properer judges than I am. When the King speaks to you of this matter, I beg you will be positive in the opinion that it is of the last consequence [not] to do any thing in it, but in Parliament. That which makes me the more pressing in this of the *dénombrement* is that the Pensioner is inclined to have it done before the Parl meets; which I think would be destruction.

While all these preparations resounded upon the anvil of Europe, both sides, though yielding nothing further, nevertheless still hoped against hope for peace. As so often happens in world affairs, and particularly in English affairs, a sense of dire necessity grows in men's minds and yet they shrink from action. The atmosphere is loaded with inflammable gas: but a flash is needed to produce the explosion.

On September 16, 1701, James II died. Louis visited in state his deathbed at Saint-Germains. While the unhappy exile was in the stertorous breathing which often precedes the flight of the soul, the Grand Monarch announced to the shadow Court that he recognized his son as King of England and would ever sustain his rights. Chivalry, vanity, and a recklessness born of the prolonged suspense had impelled Louis to this most imprudent act. He upheld it in face of the solid opposition of his Cabinet. Its consequences surprised him beyond measure. All England was roused by the insult to her independence. The Act of Settlement had decreed the succession of the Crown. The Treaty of Ryswick had bound Louis not only in formal terms, but by a gentleman's agreement, to recognize and not to molest William III as King. The domestic law of England was outraged by the arrogance, and her treaty rights violated by the perfidy, of the French despot. Whigs and Tories vied with one another in Parliament in resenting the affront. Was England, then, a vassal of France on whom a king could be imposed and despite all plighted faith? The whole nation became resolute for war. Marlborough's treaties, shaped and presented with so much Parliamentary understanding, were acclaimed; ample supplies were tendered to the Crown. King William saw his moment had come. Forthwith upon the news he recalled his Ambassador from Paris and dismissed Tallard from St James's. Now also was the time to rid himself of the Tory Party, which had used him so ill and in their purblind folly had tied his hands till all seemed ruined. Now was the time to hale before the bar of an awakened nation those truculent, pigheaded Commoners who had so provedly misjudged the public interest. The King saw his way to a sound Whig Parliament for the vigorous waging of war. Whispers of Dissolution pervaded the high circles of Court and politics.

Marlborough watched the King attentively. He read his mind and dreaded his purpose. The expulsion of the Tories in a disastrous war-fever election would undermine all the power and credit he had acquired in these spacious months. Moreover, he judged better than the King the inherent strength of Tory England. Even taken at so great a disadvantage, the Tories would be strong enough to wreck, if they could not rule. Only the peace party could draw the sword of England. A Whig triumph at the polls threatened a divided nation in the war. He used all his arts to dissuade William from the course upon which he saw him bent. The King, though filled with admiration at the capacity of his lieutenant, discounted his advice as interested, and held to his design.

He did not mean to be persuaded. "I have but just time to tell you," wrote Marlborough about September 18, "that as the king went into his coach he told me that he would write to me, by which I understand that I am not to stir from hence till I hear from him. . . ." The King quitted Holland suddenly, leaving Marlborough thus chained to his post. Several weeks passed before the efforts of Godolphin and Albemarle secured him permission to come home. On the very day his letter of recall arrived Marlborough learned that Parliament was dissolved and that Godolphin had resolved to resign.

The election belied King William's hopes. Although a cluster of his personal assailants and many Jacobites lost their seats in the Whig attack, the Tories were found to have, as Marlborough had predicted, a very solid core. They actually carried Harley back to the Speaker's chair in the new Parliament by a majority of four. The two parties were so even that, for all their hatred, they could scarcely maul one another. This in itself was a gain; but, on the other hand, the Tory rage against the King was mortal. They held that he had flung them to the country wrongfully within a year of their return at a time when they were giving him loyal and resolute support. He had played a party trick upon them, and the trick had failed. They never forgave him; they longed for his death. Nevertheless they joined with the Whigs in supporting his war.

The turn of affairs had brought about a sensible change in Marlborough's political position. In spite of Godolphin's demand to resign, the Tory Ministry had been kept by the King till he could see the election results. From his point of view this half-measure was a mistake, for the party in power had great influence upon the poll. After the results were known, the King felt himself strong enough to get rid of the Tories. He sent Rochester packing and released Godolphin. Marlborough's case was that of a man all of whose colleagues had been dismissed, but who has himself become detached from their fortunes by the importance of a foreign mission for which all parties judge him supremely fitted. Moreover, although he had worked consistently in the Tory interest and kept all his labels unchanged, he had become in fact the mainspring of the Whig policy in Europe. Thus both parties looked to him with regard and recognized, however grudgingly, that he was above their warfare. This was not the result of calculation on his part, for the happenings had been often contrary to his wishes and almost entirely beyond his control. Events had detached him from his party and left him, without partisan reproach, independent on the hub of affairs. Henceforward he ceased gradually to be a party man, though still of Tory hue. We shall see him try long and hard to keep this neutral footing until he is driven through coalition to the Whigs and finally destroyed by the revengeful Tories.

The gathering together of so many threads and resources in the hands of a single man of known abilities and ambition aroused fierce jealousies in that world of proud magnates; and all foresaw that the King's death and the accession of Anne would make Marlborough virtual master of England. To the Tories this was not unwelcome. They thought they saw in it the ascendancy of their party. For this very reason the Whigs were alarmed. Although they realized that Marlborough held the Whig view of foreign policy, although his wife was an ardent Whig, although Sunderland probably laboured to reassure them, yet the Whigs could not regard the arrival of Marlborough at the supreme direction of affairs as other than the triumph of a Tory chief serving a Tory Queen. Some of their leaders entertained the idea of passing over the Princess Anne and of bringing the Elector of Hanover to the throne. Marlborough, whose sources of information were extensive, heard of this. He questioned Dartmouth, who replied that he knew of the proposal, but did not regard it seriously. Marlborough declared that the plot existed, and, with a fierce flash unusual in him, exclaimed, "But, by God, if ever they attempt it, we would walk over their bellies!" This unwonted violence may well have been calculated. He was so situated that he could certainly have used the Army as well as the Tory Party to resist any such design, and he no doubt wished this to be well understood. The prize long awaited was near, and he would not be baulked of it.

The second Grand Alliance now formed must have seemed a desperate venture to those whose minds were seared by the ill-fortune of William's eight-years war. How vain had been that struggle! How hard to gain any advantage over the mighty central power of France! Hardly a trophy had been won from all that bitter toil. France, single-handed, had fought Europe and emerged wearied but unbeaten. In the six years of peace she had regained without a shot fired all the fortresses and territory so stubbornly disputed. But now the widest empire in the world was withdrawn from the Alliance and added to the resources of its antagonists. Spain had changed sides, and with Spain not only the Indies, South America, and the whole of Italy, but the cockpit of Europe—

Belgium and Luxembourg—and even Portugal. Savoy, the deserter, still rested with France. Cologne was also now a French ally. Bavaria, constant to the end of the last war, was to be with France in the new struggle. The Maritime Powers had scarcely a friendly port beyond their coasts. The New World was almost barred against them. The Mediterranean had become in effect a French lake. South of Plymouth no fortified harbour lay open to their ships. They had their superior fleets, but no bases which would carry them to the inland sea. On land the whole Dutch barrier had passed into French hands. Instead of being the rampart of Holland, it had become the sallyport of France. Louis, occupying the Archbishoprics of Cologne and Trèves, was master of the Meuse and of the Lower Rhine. He held all the Channel ports, and had entrenched himself from Namur through Antwerp to the sea. His armies ranged through the region east of the Meuse to the Dutch frontier. His winter dispositions disclosed his intention in the spring campaign to renew the invasion of Holland along the same routes which had led almost to its subjugation in 1672. A terrible front of fortresses, bristling with cannon, crammed with troops and supplies, betokened the approaching onslaught. The Dutch cowered behind inundations and their remaining strongholds. Lastly, the transference of Bavaria to the side of France laid the very heart of the Empire open to French invasion. In every element of strategy by sea or by land, as well as in the extent of territory and population, Louis was twice as strong at the beginning of the War of the Spanish Succession as he had been at the Peace of Ryswick. One final adverse contrast must be noticed. The Papacy had changed sides. Clement XI had abandoned the policy of Innocent XI. He espoused the cause of the Great King. He sent his congratulations to Philip V, and granted him subsidies from Spanish ecclesiastical property. He lived to repent his error. The scale of the new war was turned by the genius of one man. One single will outweighed all these fearful inequalities, and built out of the halved and defeated fragments of William's wars a structure of surpassing success under the leadership of England.

"The little gentleman in black velvet," the hero for a spell of so many enthusiastic toasts, now intervened. On February 20, William was riding in the park round Hampton Court on Sorrel, a favourite horse said to have once belonged to Sir John Fenwick. Sorrel stumbled in the new workings of a mole, and the King was thrown. The broken collarbone might well have mended, but in his failing health the accident opened the door to a troop of lurking foes. Complications set in, and after a fortnight it was evident to him and to all who saw him that death was at hand. He transacted business to the end. His interest in the world drama for which he had set the stage, on which the curtain was about to rise, lighted his mind as the shadows closed upon him. He received the reports of his gathering armies and followed the business of both his Parliaments. He grieved to quit the themes and combinations which had been the labour and the passion of his life. They were now approaching their dread climax. But he must go. He had his consolation. He saw with eagle eye the approach of a reign and Government in England which would maintain the cause in which his strength had been spent. He saw the only man to whom in war or policy, in the intricate convolutions of European diplomacy, in the party turmoil of England, or amid the hazards of the battlefield, he could bequeath the awful yet unescapable task. He had made his preparations deliberately to pass his leadership to a new champion of the Protestant faith and the liberties of Europe. In his last years he had woven Marlborough into the whole texture of his combinations and policy. In his last hours he commended him to his successor as the fittest man in the realm to guide her councils and lead her armies. William died at fifty-two worn out by his labours. Marlborough at the same age strode forward upon those ten years of unbroken victory with which our future chapters will be mainly concerned.

CHAPTER TWENTY-FIVE

The Sunshine Day

๕ 1702, March ฿

THE accession of a sovereign is rightfully an occasion for rejoicing; but seldom has a great and virtuous prince been so little mourned as King William III. The long foreign compression of his reign was over. A personality always dominating and active, but never likeable, was gone. A queer, unnatural interlude in English history had reached its end. Bishops and courtiers who watched the couch upon which William of Orange gasped and choked on his journey into silence vied with each other in sending or carrying accurate bulletins of his death-agony to his successor. In the morning of March 8 Anne had become ruler of the three kingdoms. There was a sigh of relief throughout the capital, and then, with scarcely the pause which decorum enjoined, a very general jubilation for Her Majesty Queen Anne.

Little cause had she or her friends, the high personages with whom we are concerned, to cherish the memory of William. Anne had been at one time almost persecuted by him, often vexed in petty ways, and always excluded from the slightest share in public affairs. She "should not," he had reminded her, "be Queen before her time." He had treated her husband with cordial, unspoken contempt. Marlborough, though in the end handed Elijah's mantle, had been imprisoned in his reign and denied a fair part of the war while he was in his military prime. Godolphin, who stood next to Marlborough in experience and authority, had been newly driven from office as the result of the wanton dissolution of 1701. All these three, certainly Anne and Marlborough, were conscious of the lifting of a great weight. The whole of the

Tories, smarting from their recent but partial defeat, reviled the late King's memory, and the Whigs were deeply conscious of the national reaction against him and all his works.

But far beyond the bounds of the ruling political circles there was satisfaction throughout the country at the disappearance of an alien ruler who, though he had faithfully discharged his duties to England, had scarcely troubled to conceal his dislike for her and his preference for his native land. Dignified ceremonial but no public funeral was accorded to the corpse of the world-famous prince by the island he had saved. His Dutch favourites—Bentinck, Keppel, and the rest—were brushed out of English affairs. All the policies of his reign were searchingly called in question. Although a more correct, if frigid, demeanour was observed by the Court, and the customary verbal tributes were paid, the vindication of King William's memory was left to history, which has not failed him.

The Privy Council repaired to the new Queen, and for the first time her subjects heard in official declaration that melodious, well-trained voice which always charmed and often thrilled. She spoke of the Protestant Succession, of the Church of England, of resistance to France, of her resolve to do her constitutional duty and to fulfil the obligations entered into by her predecessor for the common good of Europe. She was acclaimed. By the time she met the Houses of Parliament on March 11 the feeling of the nation was revealed to the London world. We are told that the Queen repeated "more copiously" to Parliament what she had said to the Privy Council. But there were some significant additions. "I know my own heart to be entirely English," she declared, and added in marked and challenging repetition of her father that "you shall always find me a strict and religious observer of my word." The royal attire was also deemed remarkable. She wore a robe of red velvet lined with ermine and edged with gold galloon, and over it a royal mantle of the same materials, and around her neck a heavy gold chain with the badge of St George hanging on her bosom. Upon Anne's head was the red velvet cap surmounted by the Crown of England. On her left arm she bore the ribbon of the Garter. It was said that she had used a portrait of Queen Elizabeth as a model. The impression produced by her declarations, her voice, and her appearance was profound. Many, taking the cue, spoke of a second Queen Elizabeth, and felt the presage of great days to come.

MARLBOROUGH

To Marlborough belongs the responsibility for the impulse given to the whole policy of the State and for the note struck by Queen Anne. In these first momentous hours and days he was not only the chief but the sole guide of the Queen, and the decisions to which he obtained her assent shaped the future. Anne relied on Marlborough. Moreover, in the main she agreed with him. She liked his innate Toryism. She admired his strong religious strain. His high, tolerant outlook upon the fierce factions of the times, his desire for national unity, all seemed to her to harmonize with her own duties as sovereign. There was the wise, great, and good man who had always stood by her; the captain who had steered her ship through so many storms and shoals, who always knew what to do, and never made a mistake. He would protect her from "the mercyless men of both parties." He understood all about Europe and this terrible war into which she must now plunge. And was he not also the husband of her dearest personal friend? So Queen Anne and her ablest subject, the man whom she knew best and liked and trusted most, sat down together to bring prosperity and glory to the realm.

The new reign opened amid a blaze of loyalty. It was the "sunshine day" for which the Princess Anne had waited with placid attention. In her mind were a number of particular things she had long wished but lacked the power to do. She hastened to appoint her husband General-issimo and Lord High Admiral. She made the Earl of Marlborough Captain-General of her armies at home and abroad. More than ten years had passed since she had begged in vain a Garter for him from William. She was now, on the fifth day of her reign, able to confer it herself. For nearly ten years also Henry Sidney, now Lord Romney, had enjoyed by William's favouritism the lucrative position of Quarter-master, or Master-General of the Ordnance, which Marlborough had needed and too much desired. Upon the death of his patron Sidney was stripped of his unmerited, though not ill-borne, advantages, and Marlborough put in his stead. An emblem from the Sidney family arms, the Broad Arrow, has, however, left its mark upon our country.

At every point we see intermingled the policy of Marlborough and the wishes of the Queen. It was the Queen's wish to load him and his wife with honours and wealth; and we need not suppose that either of the recipients made much objection.

Anne gratified many special desires. Marlborough had one general purpose. No sooner had the Queen met the Privy Council on March 8 than he informed the Imperial Ambassador, Wratislaw, that the Queen, like the late King, would support unswervingly the interests of the Emperor. He also authorized the Ambassador to make this public by every channel. That night he sent a personal message of the same character to the Grand Pensionary of Holland. Wratislaw seems to have urged Marlborough to go to The Hague forthwith himself. For the moment this was impossible. He could not leave the Queen. But after the Queen had met Parliament and announced the broad lines of her policy Marlborough turned immediately to Holland. On the 13th he visited Wratislaw again, bringing Godolphin with him. He announced that the Queen had instructed him to proceed as soon as possible to The Hague. If the wind were favourable he would start the next day. Lord Godolphin would act for him in all matters during his absence, and Wratislaw should have recourse to him.

The personal influence of Anne upon history has been much disputed. The modern impression of the important part she played is due to foreign rather than national historians. The portrait of a weak, feeble-minded, narrow being, managed by her female intimates or by Marlborough has never been recognized abroad. Nor does it represent the character of one of the strongest personalities that have reigned in these islands. The politics of England, in fact, revolved around Queen Anne. Her intellect was limited, but her faith, her conscience, her principles, and her prejudices were for ten years a factor in the life of England and in the fortunes of Europe which held its own with the growing power of Parliament and the victories of Marlborough. She was a simple, brave, constant woman, and she formed a fairly stable pivot upon which the passions and the fortunes of the parties turned. Anne cared about some of the largest and some of the smallest things, and for the sake of these she was ready to make exertions and run risks which might shake the realm. Anne cared about the Church of England, the Tory Party, Marlborough, her faithful servant, guide, and champion, and Sarah, her dear bosom friend from childhood onward. Besides these she cared intensely about the glory of England, which mattered a great deal, and about her husband Prince George, who mattered very little except to her.

Nothing ever stirred her mind more deeply than her right and duty to wear the Crown. At heart she was a Protestant-Jacobite. While in her person and in her policy she barred the return of the rightful heir, she embodied the claims of blood and affirmed the Divine Right of Kings. She reverenced the principles the overthrow of which had brought her the Crown. But she did not mean to give up the Crown. She desired to have it, to keep it, and to transmit it to an heir of her own body. There was therefore an innate discordance in the bosom of this virtuous and pious woman. She had grieved for her exiled father. She had sought his forgiveness. At the same time she had taken every step in her power to turn him out and keep him out. From the very beginning she had disputed the legitimacy of the Prince of Wales. Like the England she typified so closely, she clung to the warming-pan. She held it between her and the pricks of conscience. But the warming-pan was wearing thin. By 1702 it was regarded throughout Europe as a fraud, and in good society in England as a salutary fiction. Anne could not escape the atmosphere which she breathed. But never for a moment even in her fullest self-revelations did she lay down her defence and she found sanctuary in the Church of England. Was she to betray the holy instrument to Roman idolatry? Was she to deliver her realm to civil war? Above all, was she, as Sarah put it bluntly, to give up her Crown? No—a thousand times no! She would make the conscientious sacrifices which her public duty required, and she would take every step to make them effective. She gave the fullest expression to her people's will, which was also her own. But at the same time she hated the Whigs for being the driving-force of such ideas, and she clung all the more tightly to the Church of England, whose sacred mission alone could preserve her from self-reproach, and to the Tories, who guarded that Church from agnosticism or Dissent. Thus it followed that the Queen had a sentiment for the Jacobite cause, against which she warred, and a liking for the Tories, who felt as she did; and she nursed a resentment against the Whigs, because if there had not been such people there never would have been such problems. As long as she lived she meant to reign. She had already buried many children. But she still prayed, and invoked the prayers of the Church of England, for an heir. If that failed—and miracles were rare—then it must be an open question who should succeed her at her death. Certainly above all things she was determined that, however ill the fates might lie, the detestable Hanoverian who for reasons of State had spurned her youth and maidenhood should not obtrude himself within her bounds. Conscience and kinship, in revolt from such possibilities, turned to Saint-Germains. After all, "maybe 'tis our brother."

Among the sympathies which united the Queen to Marlborough and Godolphin was their mysterious respectful attitude towards the exiled house. Like her, they seemed to wish for forgiveness without making reparation. Like her, while waging ruthless war, they laboured to preserve not only polite relations but some human contact with the opponent they were destroying. Never was such sincere deceit, such studied effort to enjoy both sides of the argument, such airy indulgence of sentiment, while purpose and action flowed inexorably down the opposite channel.

But Sarah was different, and the changes in her position from the beginning of the reign deserve close study. Anne on her coming to the throne still loved Sarah fondly. Nothing gave the Queen more pleasure than to bestow honours and wealth upon her friend and those who were dear to her. Sarah was at once made Groom of the Stole, Mistress of the Robes, and Comptroller of the Privy Purse, and both her married daughters became Ladies of the Bedchamber. William's death deprived the Earl of Portland (Bentinck) of the Rangership of Windsor Park, and a few weeks later, in May, the Queen, remembering that Sarah had often admired the Lodge, wrote:

> Mentioning this worthy person puts me in mind to ask dear Mrs Freeman a question which I would have done some time ago; and that is, if you would have the Lodge for your life, because the warrant must be made accordingly; and anything that is of so much satisfaction as this poor place seems to be to you, I would give dear Mrs Freeman for all her days, which, I pray God, may be as many and as truly happy as this world can make you.

Nevertheless we must not overrate the influence of Sarah upon national affairs. On the contrary, her relations with Anne were definitely, though at first insensibly, impaired. At the accession the ties which joined them were of nearly thirty years' growth, and their differences of political opinion and temperament were frankly and sympathetically recognized on both sides. But these differences were fundamental. Sarah's logical mind and downright character offered no shelter for the internal dualism which oppressed the Queen. She was not troubled by spiritual conflict. She despised the warming-pan myth as much as she abhorred the Church of Rome. England would not have Popery or Absolutism, and the sooner kings and queens were taught this, the better for them and their subjects. Sarah was an inveterate Whig, with a detached, disdainful, modern outlook upon life, except where her interests were touched, and a tolerance and rationalism on religion which would now class her as an agnostic. Her salt common sense, her pithy conversation, and her pungent judgment of men, women, and politics, had long fascinated, fleetingly convinced, and at times terrified the Queen. The two women had hitherto lived in the most sincere and natural comradeship possible between persons of the same sex. Till now they had dwelt in a small society in the Cockpit or at St James's, generally under an official cloud and without responsibility or power. The sharp contrasts in politics and religion between Mrs Morley and Mrs Freeman had not been of much importance so long as they lived together in private life. But now Anne was Queen. She was forced from day to day to make grave choices of men and things: and here immediately opened a constant discordance and friction between the two by which in the long run their wonderful friendship was slowly but surely worn away. Indeed, it is amazing that it survived for several years.

From the outset and for nearly six years Marlborough through one agent or another managed nearly everything. Anne yielded herself gladly and often unconsciously to his guidance; and thus the main direction of British, and presently of European, affairs came to reside in Marlborough's hands. The Queen had always her own wishes, and these had almost invariably to receive satisfaction. Often they centred upon minor matters, and did not touch the supreme needs of the State. The more clear-cut and vital decisions of war and policy were largely beyond her comprehension. Great actions in the field, the webs or clashes of politics, the long, deep furrows of strategy, were necessarily outside her sphere. But Queen Anne knew without the slightest doubt what she wanted, and where she wanted to go, and she knew still better where she would never be made to go.

We must at the outset establish her relations with Marlborough. They were always the relations of mistress and servant. Never, in private or in public, in the dark times of William and the Tower, or in the European glories of Blenheim and Ramillies, never on the flowing tide of overlavish favour, or in the hour of injustice and dismissal, did

John Churchill lose for one moment the instinct of submission to the august personage he served. A servant confronted with impossible tasks or subjected to undue strain might claim to retire; a mistress might beseech him to remain—or might not; but the relation was dominant, tacit, and immutable. We must recognize this, for it is the keynote of the reign. The Queen was the crowned embodiment of the nation, and she often interpreted in a shrewd and homely way to a degree almost occult what England needed and, still more, what England felt. We portray her as a great Queen championed by a great Constable.

Thus was inaugurated the age of Anne. A gulf in national life separates it from the times of Charles II. That gulf had been traversed almost unperceived during the alien interlude of William III. Many unspoken conclusions had gathered in these fourteen years which now emerged as the accepted facts of society. We have entered a period less antique, less harsh, less grim, but with more subtle complications. The struggle of parties continued in the midst of war with an inconceivable bitterness and vigour. The personal stakes for which sovereigns and their Ministers were forced to play were more limited. It was now only nominally that their heads were brought into question. Their property and even their liberty stood on a more assured foundation. All men breathed a gentler air. All classes rose together in the rapid expansion of England. The nobility were recovering an almost feudal splendour after a century and a half of eclipse. The Parliamentary Constitution and the Cabinet system developed with extraordinary speed. The City merchants and financiers became a factor in world affairs. Science, learning, architecture, literature, and painting continued to herald all along the line the general advance of the islanders. Public opinion and national consciousness moved forward hand in hand. The masses of the people shared in the national gains.

We may claim this period as on the whole the greatest in our history. In ten years England rose to the leadership of Europe. She gained the mastery of the seas, including the control—never since lost—of the Mediterranean. The ocean roads to trade and empire in the New World were opened. Her soldiers, according to their enemies, were the best in Europe. Her wealth and prosperity seemed for a while to rise upon the tide of war. By the union with Scotland the island became one. The might of France was abated, and a balance was established in Europe to correct her exorbitant power. The Dutch ally, crippled in the long war, ceased to be a rival at sea, and, weakening under the financial strain, soon ceased to be a rival in trade.

The foundations were laid of that power which fifty years later enabled Lord Chatham by the victories of Wolfe and Clive to drive all challengers alike from America and India.

CHAPTER TWENTY-SIX

The Republic of the Dykes

ᖷᕯ 1702, April ᕲᖸ

THE accession of Anne had raised Marlborough to the first position under the Crown in England, but across the Narrow Seas, in the Dutch Republic, he gained a domain of power and influence which was hardly less important and proved at the end of ten years more durable. Always, in spite of everything that vexed or tempted, Marlborough was true to the principle of the Anglo-Dutch alliance, and always the statesmen of the Republic trusted him as their anchor and salvation. At the very end, when he was hounded out of his own country and stripped of every vestige of power or favour, the fathers of the Republic and the populace of its cities treated him with the honours of a sovereign prince. The union thus formed in his person, as formerly in that of William of Orange, of the two Great Powers of the sea, of trade, and of the money market, was found capable of breaking the ambition of Louis XIV and humbling the might of France. It thus preserved that freedom for the Protestant religion and those rights of Parliamentary government which lighted and guarded the Age of Reason and prepared the civilization of the nineteenth century.

This was the great period of the Dutch Republic. The Seven Provinces, which had been forged in the fires of Spanish persecution and tempered by heroic warfare against France on land and England by sea, were now become a wonderful instrument and force in Europe. They embodied a victory over suffering, tyranny, and dead-weight bulk which was of precious consequence to the future of mankind. But the very freedom which had preserved them, and the strength and tradition of the resulting organism, bore all the marks and characteristics of the protracted ordeals which had brought them forth. The Dutch Republic perhaps was the most perfect manifestation of obstinacy—constitutional, moral, temperamental—which has ever been known. Obstinacy, stolid, valiant, harsh, even brutal, dwelt in every fibre of the nation; and the humblest burghers and the smallest villages confronted the problems of Europe and the puzzles of men with their own narrow, potent, and unyielding convictions. Their service to the western world was at once sublime and matter of fact. They wished to be free, by which they meant—Protestant and democratic; prosperous, by which they meant—masters of seaborne commerce; and above all safe, by which they meant—behind a dyke, well guarded. The dyke embodied the national idea. On the one side it kept back the hungry seas; on the other the French armies. Behind their dykes they would dwell, and from this shelter they would trade. These and no more were their aims, and for their sake they gave forth over a prolonged period an immense volume of sacrifice and toil.

By the death of William of Orange the entire structure of the Dutch oligarchy and republic was riven or shaken. Who would lead the armies against the gathering foes? Who would preserve the common action of the Sea Powers? All seemed in dissolution and jeopardy. Hard upon the news of William's death came the message from Marlborough to the Grand Pensionary Antony Heinsius promising in the name of the Queen the resolute prosecution of the war and adherence to the treaties. This caught the mood of the assembly at its most tense phase. Sorrow, perplexity, and alarm all took the channel of stern action. Through the long debate there resounded the unanimous determination to march forward unitedly upon the path the dead Stadtholder had opened and prescribed.

A few days after their debate Marlborough was in their midst. He was received in Holland at this juncture almost with worship. He was already trusted as a friend, and here was a friend in need. The Dutch instinctively regarded him as their champion and deliverer, and much of the loyalty and trust they had given to William of Orange was directed almost unconsciously to this gleaming English figure which appeared in a dark hour so suddenly among them, speaking in accents of comfort and command. "The only change resulting from the death," said Marlborough, "is this, that the Queen does not take the field. In all the remaining conduct of affairs the general business against France will lose nothing. The Queen will be loyal to the alliances which have been formed."

About Naples and the Italian provinces Marlborough reversed William's policy. "I may now assure you that England will strain every nerve to secure that all the Spanish possessions in Italy without exception shall fall to the Emperor's share. That is the constant thought of the Queen in accordance with the opinion and interest of the English people. If the Emperor can provide the necessary forces England will stand loyally by his side and the Republic must follow our lead."

In those words, "the Republic must follow our lead," we have the first indication of the change wrought by the death of William III upon the relations of England and Holland. William was a Dutchman to the core. He regarded England as a valuable auxiliary which his birth, marriage, and achievements had gathered to the Republic. The arrival of Marlborough in power meant that the combination would continue—nay, it would become more forceful than ever. The same main objects would be pursued even more vigorously. England would make a greater and not a smaller contribution. But the predominance would lie in the island rather than among the dykes. The alliance would be of England and Holland, instead of the old reversed form. The declaration had yet to be made good by the weight of the English effort and by events in the field. The Dutch Republic was for some time unconscious of the altered emphasis and priority, and they learned it only through the agreeable channel of aid and victory.

The most interesting and most powerful figure in the Dutch federation was Antony Heinsius, the Grand Pensionary. Even under the august authority of William of Orange, with the Crown of England upon his brows, Heinsius had been in fact Chancellor of the State. Upon the death of the Stadtholder and as long as that office remained unfilled he became naturally and inevitably the citizen-sovereign of the Republic.

Heinsius was a lonely man, a bachelor of simple, austere habits whose whole life was one long round of official business. The discharge of his office was the tale of his existence, the unity and safety of the Republic his sole purpose. The Stadtholder, when he became King of England, induced Heinsius to undertake the office of Grand Pensionary, with all that accession of responsibility which resulted from the prolonged absences of the ruler. The influence of Heinsius had helped King William to combine the headship of the two nations. His aims, if narrow, were definite. In his own nature he embodied the national conviction or obsession of the dyke. All his life-work was devoted to building an invincible fortress-barrier between his fatherland and France.

His sincerity was felt by all who came in contact with him. Although a man of high courage and indomitable perseverance, he carried soberness of judgment to the point of pessimism. Nor did he care if friends who visited him in his modest dwelling in times of crisis found him in tears amid his papers over the perils of the State. His patience in discussion, his kindliness, his probity won universal respect. It was obvious to all that he must fill a large part of the void which had opened. Upon him descended the responsibility for maintaining the treaties of the Grand Alliance, and above all the special relations with England, which William's double office had enshrined. And in this his friendship with Marlborough and their mutual confidence were decisive. Heinsius looked upon Marlborough as his link with England. It was as a statesman and diplomat rather than as a soldier that the foundations of Marlborough's influence in Holland were laid. The military command was a second stage.

The practical and vital question of the command of the armies of the Sea Powers was not brought to an issue during Marlborough's visit; yet it was in every one's mind. Even before Marlborough had reached The Hague some steps had been taken by the Dutch Government. They apprehended, not without good information, that Queen Anne would propose Prince George of Denmark to them. The Queen was sure that her beloved husband was the very man for this responsibility and power. She was alone in her view, and, as one might say, biased; but her view was none the less important. It was well known in Holland that the Prince Consort's intellect and ability were extremely modest.

No one can ever tell from the records which have survived whether at this time Marlborough expected to obtain the supreme command for himself. But it is certain that he pressed Prince George's claims in such a manner that if they had not been absurd they must have been accepted. He did not on this occasion make a direct proposal. According to the Imperial Ambassador Count Goes, he said he was not authorized to raise the question formally. If, however, the proposal were made from the Dutch side, it would seem the best way of binding the two armies together as closely as before, and he stated that as the English Captain-General he would then readily serve under Prince George as Commander-in-Chief.

Certain it is that he employed every argument in favour of Prince George. The extraordinary feature is that in his advocacy of Prince George's claims lay the surest route to the attainment of his own.

We do not think he was at all sure at this juncture that the command would fall to him. In that patient, persistent, contriving mind, long accustomed to inferior solutions, there must have arisen a practical plan by which Prince George would hold the supreme command while Marlborough, from the second place, would nevertheless govern the event. Nor did he recoil from such expedients. The best obtainable was nearly always good enough for him.

Here, then, this all-important matter rested uncomfortably for the time being. Its solution must be sought in the inherent prejudices of the Dutch. They disliked a royal Commander-in-Chief. They feared even more a combination of Marlborough plus a royal prince whom he dominated. They were seeking the impossible; they wanted a general who would be strong against the enemy, but weak and submissive towards themselves. Their ideal was a deferential dictator, a docile champion. They therefore looked with favour upon a foreigner who was not a prince, because he would be the more controllable. Subject to this condition, they were agreeable to his being competent. Thus from the first in those very quarters where the sharpest opposition might have been expected there was a definite inclination towards this Englishman, of no great rank, but undoubtedly a remarkable person.

Marlborough allowed all this to simmer. When we consider the dazzling prize, as it must have seemed to an ardent soldier, which dangled aimlessly in the air, we must be astonished at his composure and seeming detachment. If he had lifted his hand to grasp it, a hundred voices of authority would have been raised against him. Yet can we believe that he was indifferent? Could so powerful a mental mechanism of schemes and action be combined with perfect self-effacement? However this may be, Marlborough quitted The Hague without having exposed by even the twinkle of an eye the slightest personal interest in the question of command, while at the same time there grew throughout the high circles of the Republic the general feeling that no one would suit all purposes so well as he.

Not until after he had reached agreement upon the main lines of policy with Heinsius and Goes did Marlborough present himself to the States-General. He had wished to preserve an informal and private status. But the public temper would not be satisfied without a demonstration. Accordingly at Heinsius' insistence he assumed the character and style of an Ambassador-Extraordinary, and went to the Assembly in full pomp. He was received with the utmost honour. He addressed Their High Mightinesses in French.

"Her Majesty . . . is firmly resolved to contribute all that lies in her power towards the advancing and increasing union, friendship, and correspondence, and to make that a constant maxim of her government. . . . She will not only exactly and faithfully observe and execute the treaties and alliances made between the Kings her predecessors and your High and Mighty Lordships, but . . . is likewise ready to renew and confirm them; as also to concur with you in all the measures which have been taken by the late King of glorious memory, in pursuance of the said alliances. Her Majesty is likewise disposed to enter into such other stricter alliances and engagements, which shall most conduce to the interests of both nations, the preservation of the liberty of Europe and reducing within just bounds the exorbitant power of France."

Dykevelt, now President of the Assembly, in welcoming these bold, plain offers with thanks and "with a flood of tears," turning to Marlborough, added "that his person would be highly acceptable to them not only for the Queen's choice of him and for the sake of King William who first invested him with that character, but for his own merit."

These declarations, carried as fast as the posts could ride into every capital, consolidated the Grand Alliance. All the temptations, bribes, and threats which French diplomacy was offering to every signatory Power lost their potency. Marlborough restored the vast structure which King William's death had seemed about to dissolve.

Marlborough's mission was therefore entirely successful. In ten days he had rallied all the signatories of the Grand Alliance and expressed all their engagements in strict terms. All that had threatened to fall to pieces was now gripped together more strongly than ever; where all had been doubt and despondency there was now resolve and confidence.

THE REPUBLIC OF THE DYKES

The Dutch rejected with scorn the peace proposals of Louis XIV. The three Great Powers bound themselves together secretly to declare war upon France on May 4/15. The additional article, with the word *prœtensus*, was duly signed, and the English political situation was for the time being consolidated for the most vigorous action. Nothing remained when Marlborough returned to England for King William's funeral but to choose the commander, make the plans, and begin the fighting. But these were matters not to be so swiftly settled.

CHAPTER TWENTY-SEVEN

Queen Anne's First Government

ƒɑ 1702, May ɒƷ

QUEEN ANNE and Marlborough had not waited to begin their political studies until after the death of King William had been formally announced. They both knew what they wanted to do, and their aims, though different, were not in the main incompatible. The Government of England had passed by lawful succession to Princess Anne and her Cockpit group. There they were, this tiny circle, bound together by common interests and by the anxieties and partisanship of many years —the Queen, sacred and at the moment of accession almost omnipotent; Marlborough, master of politics and diplomacy, and certainly the leading English general; Sarah, the much-loved link; and Godolphin, the faithful friend of the Queen and kinsman of the Marlboroughs. Here was a close confederacy which had been slowly and tensely wrought. Anne had insisted upon the equality of their intercourse, but this privilege was strictly limited. Mrs Morley, Mr and Mrs Freeman, and Mr Montgomery—there could not be a tighter thing. They formed a group as integral and as collectively commanding as anything of which there is record in our annals. Outside, beyond their privacy, prowled the magnates of the Whigs and Tories with their strident factions and the formidable processes of Parliament. Outside lay the Church of England in the highest state of effervescence, and the finances of the country, already drained and overtaxed by a long war. Across the seas loomed the European coalition and the mighty armies of France, already on the march. With all these the Cockpit must now deal. It must have seemed an unequal struggle; but the result showed them completely triumphant, and had they held together to the end it is certain that they could have continued to enforce their will in every direction.

Below this personal organism of the Queen and the genius of Marl-borough came the constitutional Ministry of the realm. This had now to be formed. It must surely be Tory. The phrases of the Queen's Speech which had chilled the Whigs had made this fact public. The Queen was a Tory and a High Tory at heart. Marlborough was a Tory by origin, sentiment, and profession. But he was quite cool about whether the Government was Tory or Whig. What he sought was a political system that would support the war. He shared none of Anne's strong feelings about the High Church or Low Church bishops. Unity at home and in Parliament to sustain, with the combined resources of the nation, the war abroad against the power of France was his sole and only end. When all deference had been shown to the Queen's wishes Marlborough secured from her the larger necessities of his policy. He was still convinced that the war against France could only be waged with success by a united nation. The Tories were the peace party. Their opposition would rend the State. But if the responsibilities of office would compel them to face the task themselves, then they could make the war truly national. The Whigs would have no choice but to support them, and no wish but to do it themselves instead. It was therefore certain that, though the Whigs had a narrow majority in the existing House of Commons, the emphasis of the new reign and the character of the Queen's first Government would be Tory. Anne de-sired to gather Tory Ministers round her, and Marlborough sought a solid Parliamentary foundation for the war.

Both sovereign and counsellor wished by the retention of some Whigs in the less important offices to make the Government broad-bottomed, and to tinge it with a national beyond a party complexion. The Tories were moreover made aware that if they received the favour of the Crown and were entrusted with the conduct of public affairs, it must be upon the basis that they would support and prosecute the war with the whole of their party forces. These undertakings their leaders were ready to give, though with many unspoken reservations which will presently emerge about the character and scale of England's war effort. This Tory allegiance to the war was the foundation of the politics of the first half of the reign. However fierce the faction fights might be, however bitter the rivalries of the parties or the discontents of deposed Ministers, it was definitely understood that the waging of the war and the voting of the necessary supplies were above and beyond political strife. This dominant condition was on the whole punctiliously fulfilled.

By the time Marlborough returned from The Hague the Queen's intention to rest upon the Tories was known everywhere, and the principal figures in the new Administration could be plainly discerned. It is certain that Marlborough used his influence sparingly. He reserved it for essentials. Of these the first was Rochester's demand to be Lord Treasurer. If Marlborough was to lead the Army with any prospect of success he must be sure of the money for pay and supplies. He must have some one at the Treasury, and near the Queen at home, whom he could trust. We cannot doubt that before he went to Holland the Queen had promised him that Godolphin should have this key-post.

At the desire of his Mistress Marlborough continued to press upon the Dutch Prince George's claims to the supreme command of the armies. The more Tory appointments they saw in the new English Ministry the less they were inclined to such a plan.

The Dutch took refuge in the folds of their quaint but sometimes serviceable constitution. Even the threats conveyed by the English agents that England might stand out of the land war did not move them. All the towns of Holland except Dordrecht resolved that no Captain-General should be appointed; and Dordrecht bowed to the general view.

The Queen and her husband had to accept such an unmistakable decision. For months Marlborough had used all his influence upon the Dutch in favour of an appointment which must certainly run counter to his dearest wish and greatest need. He had failed. But it was not his fault. Certainly he had done more than could have been claimed from mortal man.

The character of the Government was not changed violently in a day. The transformation, which was ceaseless, was complete in about three months. Whig officers of the Household were replaced with Tories. Jersey became Lord Chamberlain, and Sir Edward Seymour, ailing and grumbling, with his solid block of West Country members behind him, became Comptroller. On May 2 Nottingham, in spite of his recalcitrance to the avowed main objects of the Government—namely, the maintenance of the Grand Alliance and the prosecution of the war—became publicly Secretary of State in charge of Southern Affairs at a council board which already included Rochester. Moreover, Rochester and Nottingham brought with them as their colleague in the Secretaryship of State (Northern Affairs) Sir Charles Hedges, a pleasant, adaptable man, who owed his preferment to their patronage. Soon the notorious Jack Howe of the Gloucester address, the defamer of King William, received a petty but challenging post. Marlborough had the greatest difficulty in inducing Devonshire to remain Lord Steward. Almost the only other Whigs in office were the Duke of Somerset, Master of the Horse, and Boyle, a friend of Harley, Chancellor of the Exchequer, an office then, and sometimes since, of subordination. All this was Anne. Marlborough waited for the main issues as a general should do on a battlefield. There were two of these. The first was the appointment of Godolphin to be Lord Treasurer and, as we should now say, Prime Minister. On this Marlborough had from the first been resolved. Against him stood Rochester with the whole Tory Party at his back. To the political world the matter seemed long in suspense.

Godolphin had proved his devotion in the days when Anne was under the scowl of "Mr Caliban," when Sarah was barred from the farthest limits of the Court, and Marlborough was in the Tower. He had been Anne's friend when Rochester would not even carry her letter to Queen Mary. Godolphin had always obstructed with the power of his office every attempt of William and Mary to reduce the Parliamentary grant by which the Cockpit household was sustained. Like the Churchills, Godolphin had not been driven in terror from Princess Anne's home and circle by the ban of the ruling Court. Like Marlborough, he had taught the future Queen a great deal about public affairs. Above all, he was an old friend. In the Queen's eye, therefore, Godolphin was of a different order altogether from the proudest dukes and greatest party leaders of the day. He was dignified in her mind by a title far above the common nobility. He was "Mr. Montgomery." She had conceived and bestowed this honour herself from her own heart, without the aid of the College of Heralds or the forms of the English Constitution. Historians have fallen into tangled arguments through failing to understand the intense responses of Anne's warm heart and cunning mind.

A new sovereign was to be crowned: most of the Ministers of the late King were out of favour with her. Not so Godolphin. He had been turned out of office barely a year before King William's death. He represented just in time the incoming Tory tide. There must have been a great dexterity, and there must have also been an enormous fund of serviceableness. We remember Charles II's pithy description of him— "never in the way, never out of the way." Thus all the turns and surprises of party politics and changes of rulers left Godolphin eminently agreeable to every Administration and sovereign. He had held the Treasury as one of Charles II's "chits." He had voted for excluding the Duke of York from the throne; he had been that King's Minister. He had accompanied him in unreproached loyalty almost to the beach. He had been one of King William's principal assistants, while making no secret of his sentimental devotion to the exiled Mary of Modena. He was never able to mount more comfortably into the saddle than upon the accession of Anne. Yet the bridging of all these gulfs did not seem a masterpiece of calculation. Each transaction had been smooth and natural, almost inevitable. Nor did he display at any time any keen appetite for office. He had resigned several times, and more often still had threatened to do so. He always had to be pressed to resume official service, and invariably declined with almost invincible obstinacy every post which was sure to be forced on him.

Godolphin, of course, made his habitual objections. He did not wish to take office—there were so many other more amusing things to do. Of all offices the one he would least like was the care of the finances. How well he knew that arduous and thankless task! Surely after all these years he might be spared. He pressed this resistance to so sharp a point that we cannot tell at this distance of time, in spite of all research, with any certainty whether he wished to have the place or not. Certainly Marlborough had to use all his various influences to persuade him. The Captain-General declared in repeated letters that he would not attempt to conduct the war and direct the armies unless Godolphin were Lord Treasurer. No one else could he trust. With no one else would he enter the struggle. He knew and foresaw many of the obstacles he would have to overcome before he could ever reach the enemy. He knew the Queen; he knew the Dutch; he knew the German Princes; he knew the English Parliament. Unless he could count on the Lord Treasurer to pay the British troops and their hired contingents, to pay for the supplies in the theatre of war and the munitions from home, he would not mount his horse. Sufficiently pushed, Godolphin yielded with dignity and on the best of terms, and thus in due course was opened the historic Marlborough-Godolphin Administration which through six years of general war led England and Europe triumphantly.

Marlborough had one other thought about the formation of the Government; and he urged the Queen to call Shrewsbury to her side. Here was the great Whig who would establish the national character of the Government. Shrewsbury was the Whig he wanted. No partisan could impugn his orthodoxy. No aristocrat could surpass his magnificence. But here Marlborough failed, and his failure condemned him to less good arrangements at home. He had to do without Shrewsbury. Shrewsbury, with many expressions of goodwill, excused himself behind several lines of personal fortification. He preferred an elegant dalliance by the Tiber, and soon fell in love with a widow—an Italian lady of experienced charm—whom he met by its banks. The fact that, although on the friendliest terms with Marlborough, he would not come home and do any work was untoward.

The Queen conceived that she knew as much as anyone about the Church of England, of which she was the supreme head, and was resolved to protect and rule it according to her lights. Godolphin was now undisputed master of the public finances. The armies and the Grand Alliance fell evidently into Marlborough's sphere. But there remained Parliament, and especially the House of Commons, with which the Cockpit must establish a direct relationship. It is noteworthy that the elective assembly was already recognized as the dominant factor in the State. Robert Harley, the Speaker and also, as we should say, Leader of the House, was a man of the middle. He was a Nonconformist who had become a mouthpiece of Anglicanism, without repudiating his original sect. He was a Tory leader who had begun as a Whig and still preserved friendly Whig connexions. He was a strident pacifist and disarmament-monger who now thought that there was much to be said for vigorous participation in the European war. He understood the House of Commons from every angle. At thirty-nine he had been chosen Speaker and in a sense Leader of the House. The Tories considered him their future candidate, and the Whigs would rather have him than any other Tory.

But Harley embodied much more than the contradictions of his career; he was a man of broad and solid ability. He was no seeker for small or near prizes. We may picture him in the Chair hearing confidences from both sides, persuading the one to concede and the other to forbear; and giving when asked advice which suited his general purpose, withal preserving agreeable relations in every quarter. In his desire to dwell at the hub of Parliamentary opinion he had necessarily to use much artifice.

His frequently disconcerted opponents dubbed him trickster and sharper. They said that his political creed reached its pinnacle in the conviction that power, fortune, and influence were identical with enjoyment. When the factions of the day rose to such extravagant heights a man in a central position needed to protect himself from their fury by an entire scaly apparatus of ruse and ambiguity. That Harley was false to every cause and every man was in a certain sense true; but he was not false to himself, nor to his persistent purpose of steering a middle course for England between many alternating extravagant attitudes and perils. At this juncture he presents himself in his youthful prime as at once the most massive and most artful Parliamentary figure.

Harley was the man whom Marlborough and Godolphin needed in 1702. Here was the means by which they would form a direct contact of their own with the House of Commons. Here was the expert who could advise them upon what the House would or would not do in any situation. Here was the agent who heard everything, and could sway decisions. From the very beginning both these super-Ministers saw in Harley the means of making themselves independent of the ordinary party channels. Rochester and Nottingham might pose and fulminate in the Lords, but Harley could cover a very large body of sober Tory and Whig opinion. It may be said that Marlborough and Harley had this in common, that in their different spheres they deflected and deceived enemies or wild people into courses which kept England safe. It was certainly upon this basis that they came together.

Harley had already an admiration for Marlborough, and was well content to be drawn by him into the elevated circle around the Queen and into the majestic chaos of Europe. He knew, however, that all his value depended on his ability to control or at least sway the Commons and to induce the Tory Party to follow paths of sanity and patriotism.

From his unique Parliamentary position he soon became, though not actually in the Government, superior in importance to any of the ordinary great office-holders, and Marlborough and Godolphin reached out to him across the Tory Ministers and drew him into their private confidences. Harley was not joined in the Cockpit by those deep ties of personal friendship or family connexion which bound the rest; but he soon became an independent and almost indispensable partner. His own central following in the House of Commons could henceforward feel themselves more closely associated with the conduct of the State through the Speaker working with the great Ministers than by their regular party chiefs in office. For all the toilsome discharge of business Marlborough, Godolphin, and Harley were gradually to become a triumvirate, and were so described by their contemporaries.

We may suppose that the Queen and Marlborough delayed the announcement of Godolphin's appointment until the Tory Ministry was complete. Rochester was allowed to indulge his hopes to the very end. Another great issue had to be settled before they could afford to render him desperate. By solemn pact Marlborough, with the Queen's authority, had bound England, simultaneously with the Empire and the States-General, to declare war upon France on May 4/15. This secret was in England known only to these two and Godolphin. But now May was at hand. The new Cabinet must be confronted with the decisions of supreme power. Not only must the question of peace or war be settled, but also the kind of war England must wage. Was she to be an ally, playing a full part upon the Continent, or was she to be an associated Power, joined, indeed, to the confederacy against France, but limiting her exertions to picking up what she could overseas on the outskirts of the struggle? Here the collision between Marlborough and Rochester was direct. Rochester seemed to have made much headway with the Queen. He was leading her steadily forward on Tory and party courses. He felt strong enough to meet Marlborough foursquare upon the issue that England must intervene as only an auxiliary.

But Marlborough was found armed with an argument which was judged conclusive in those times. He remarked that by the commands of the Queen, following upon the resolves of Parliament, he had procured the assent of the allies to the additional article denouncing the claim of the pretended Prince of Wales. Here, then, was a major purpose of exclusively English interest to which the other partners in the Grand Alliance had agreed reluctantly at English insistence. England was therefore formally involved as a principal, and must contribute her whole power to the common cause. This contention cut the ground from under the Tory chiefs; for it was they, as we have seen, who in the hope of shattering King William's plan by disgusting the Emperor had brought forward this additional article and made it a test of faith at home and abroad.

The new Tory Cabinet seem to have been quelled or even rallied by this deployment of their former party demands. Behind lay the growing realization that the Queen, if really forced to choose, would throw her whole weight upon the side of Marlborough and Godolphin. In the end the Queen was not troubled with the dispute. It was agreed that England should throw her whole weight into the war.

On May 4, at one o'clock in the afternoon, the King-at-Arms rode out from the Queen's palace splendidly adorned and surrounded by the heralds and the guards. From St James's he went by way of Charing Cross and the Strand to the City, where he proclaimed the declaration of war against France to the clash of cymbals and the blare of trumpets. His challenge to Louis XIV was everywhere cheered by the masses and the poorest citizens, the genius of whose race had taught them that their freedom and the greatness of their country were at stake. Two days later, all being now committed to the struggle, Godolphin received the White Staff of Lord Treasurer, and Rochester saw himself finally relegated to his Irish Viceroyalty.

CHAPTER TWENTY-EIGHT

The Tory Ferment

₤ 1702, August ₯

WITH the death of William and with the accession of a Tory Stuart Queen, Jacobite sentiment, which lay low and deep throughout England, and stirred in so many hearts and consciences, surged forward and became the fashion and temper of the hour. These emotions found their expression, curiously enough, in loyalty to the new monarch, who in her own person and in the most effective manner barred the return of the lawful Prince, and but for the warming-pan—now much battered—made a mockery of all the theories of Divine Right. However, an indifference to logic where it is likely to lead to serious trouble is one of the strongest of English characteristics. Here at last was a sovereign of Stuart blood, of Tory inclinations, and happily a fervent adherent of the Church of England. All Tory England was ready to make the best of that.

At this moment in our history, therefore, all the Tory forces, from those who regarded Anne regretfully as a usurper to those who acclaimed her as a supreme blessing vouchsafed by heaven, swelled together in an incongruous yet not unexplainable harmony. Throughout every circle and degree Toryism was bitter and aggressive; while the Whigs, for their part, were thrown into the embarrassing position of being roughly assaulted by the Government whose main policy on the greatest issues of the age—Europe and the war—was their own.

We have therefore this Tory Party, so intractable and unyielding in character, so unreasoning and narrow in outlook, equally conscious in the highest degree of their grievances and of their power. This is the first great political fact in the reign of Queen Anne. By the Acts passed on the morrow of the Fenwick Plot, Parliament was prudently no longer dissolved on the demise of the Crown, but continued automatically for six months and no more. Whig hopes that the House of Commons elected in 1701 would be allowed to run its normal course never had any foundation. The law prescribed and the Queen desired a dissolution. In the late summer there must be a general election, and the Tories, already possessed of office, eagerly looked forward to overthrowing their Whig antagonists, who stoutly prepared for resistance. The Government of the day, enjoying the fresh flush of royal favour, had a marked advantage at the polls. The character of the Ministry made it unmistakably plain that the Queen wanted a Tory Parliament. The Tories were seen to be favoured; the Whigs were obviously under a cloud. Moreover, this inclination of the royal will corresponded with the natural sentiment in favour of change and against the agents of the late unpopular King.

The party fight shaped itself as the dying Parliament drew towards its end. The parties girded at each other, and marshalled the points of malice and prejudice upon which they relied at the impending trial of strength.

In Marlborough's absence at The Hague, Rochester, venerable, furious, absentee from Ireland, wove the Queen into Tory electioneering. On May 25 she dismissed King William's Parliament with the blistering passage, "I shall be very careful to preserve and maintain the Act of Toleration and to set the minds of all my people at quiet. My own principles must always keep me entirely firm to the interests and religion of the Church of England, *and will incline me to countenance those who have the truest zeal to support it.*" To the Whigs this was a declaration of war upon them by the Sovereign. All the popularity and prestige of the new Queen Anne, with her English heart, were to be marshalled at the hustings against them. At the same time their Tory opponents before the election proclaimed a measure against Occasional Conformity which would make every Dissenter a political outlaw. What had they done, the Whigs exclaimed, to be treated as public enemies? They were the force which had made the Revolution of 1688. They were the men who by the Act of Settlement had placed the Queen upon the throne. They were the traditional champions against the Jacobitism and Popery which everybody condemned, or affected to condemn. They were the party which earnestly supported the war Lord Marlborough had gone abroad to wage. And the Whigs were half the nation! Wherein had their conduct failed the Queen and Constitution? The future and the freedom of England rested in their midst. Why, then, was their loyalty so spurned? Because, said they, there was some dark intrigue to bring in the pretended Prince of Wales and subjugate England to Rome and France. But the Tories replied that the Whigs were all republicans and atheists at heart, who paid lip-service to the Crown in order to devour it, and took the Holy Sacrament to qualify for positions from which they could the better destroy, not only the Church of England, but all faith of man in God. On these agreeable platforms Whigs and Tories proceeded to the polls.

However, the fibre of both parties was tough. The election of August 1702 was no landslide. Just as the Tories had come through the election of February 1701 much better than they themselves expected in the circumstances, so now the Whigs made a stubborn fight and were perhaps not more than a hundred behind the Tories in the first Parliament of Queen Anne. Harley, the Tory leader, was again elected Speaker; this time unanimously. His Parliamentary gifts and ascendancy commended him to the House as a whole. His moderation comforted the Whigs. His party colouring just held the Tories. Across the gulfs of a Tory majority and Government and the disfavour of the Crown the Whigs could regard him as a link with Marlborough and Godolphin, the national Ministers above the ebb and flow of party. For the rest they remained effective, weighty—almost half the nation —organized with a grip inconceivable to-day. Moreover, they were still entrenched in strong positions both in Church and State.

During the whole of the reign Church politics was the strongest theme at home. The cry "The Church in danger" represented all the sentiments, principles, prejudices, interests, and tactics of Toryism.

Under the laws of England as they had been administered in King William's reign no attempt had been made to persecute Nonconformists for worshipping as they pleased, and a very wide measure of practical toleration existed for the people. Even Papists were not molested, if they behaved discreetly. But where the holding of public office was concerned it was argued that no one ought to be trusted to enforce the laws who disagreed with them on grounds of conscience. Officeholders of all kinds from the highest Minister to the smallest revenue officer—Lord-Lieutenant, magistrates, all who would be concerned with elections, every one who sat in either House, the heads of all colleges and universities, nearly every one charged with the education of youth —all these must by law be communicant members of the Church of England. The Corporation Act and the Test Act prescribed that no one could hold any of these key-posts without taking the sacrament according to Anglican rites. But the wealthy, influential Dissenters who formed so valuable a part of the Whig forces, who by their standing, substance, and capacity were qualified for public office, were not so easily to be ejected or shut out from power by the manœuvres of their political and religious opponents. With the full assent of Whig and Nonconformist opinion, they had been accustomed by King William's goodwill to turn the flank of the Test Act by taking the Anglican sacrament as required by law, and thereafter continuing in their Dissenting tabernacles.

The Tories, on the wave of Jacobite, Stuart, and Church emotion evoked by the accession of Queen Anne, and not unmindful of the vacancies which would be created, determined to bring this fraudulent abuse, as they regarded it, to an end. The whole Tory Party thought the practice wicked, blasphemous, deceitful, an outrage upon the body and blood of Christ, and also extremely inconvenient at election times, and their pertinacious, passionate, ruthless exertions to root out Occasional Conformity and punish those guilty of it, far outstripping the world war and Marlborough's victories, became during the opening years of Queen Anne's reign the main issue and topic of English political life.

After the Church the second great party cleavage of the reign was upon the character of the war. The Tories obstinately championed the policy that if we were drawn into a war we should go as little to the Continent, send as few troops, fight as near to the coast as possible, and endeavour to secure territory and traffic across the oceans. Whigs, on the contrary, dwelt upon the theory familiar to us as the doctrine of "the decisive theatre," and sought, with the largest army that could be maintained, to bring the war to an end by a thrust at the heart of France, the supreme military antagonist, arguing that thereafter all the rest would be added unto them.

It should be noticed that the Tories favoured the popular idea that the Navy should be the stronger and the Army stinted. This gave them a good constitutional position as against the Whigs, who, though equally opposed to a standing army, had to have one if they wished to fight on the mainland. Here was a new cause of confusion. As the reign of Anne continued these opinions organized themselves, to a degree almost unbelievable, in hard-and-fast party principles about the kind of strategy and operations which should be adopted. The Tories were prone to judge every action not so much by whether it was successful as by whether it was in accordance with their party doctrine. Thus taking a town near the coast was more to be applauded than taking one farther inland. Thus an action at sea was preferable to one ashore. The Tory policy leaned to operations against Spain and the liquidation of the Spanish colonies as a prize of war, and to the entry of the Mediterranean with all the exploitation of trade in the East that would come with the command of the sea. Marlborough's march to Blenheim was therefore, as we shall find, the greatest violation of Tory principles which could be conceived. Even dazzling success could hardly redeem such a departure from the orthodox and conventional party method of waging war.

Marlborough throughout his campaigns was bound, apart from military facts and the enemy, to consider the character of any operation by the effect it would have on Tory opinion in the House of Commons. Both parties could use powerful and capacious arguments in support of their dogmas, and neither hesitated to turn the fortunes and accidents of the war to its special account. From this it followed again that not only were victories in the field or afloat classified as Whig and Tory victories, but the officers concerned in specific operations became coloured with the party hue. Generals and admirals were encouraged to have strong party affiliations, and each faction had its favourites whom it praised and defended through thick and thin. Indeed, neither side in Parliament hesitated to foment rivalries and jealousies among the commanders and to set one against another, or against their commander-in-chief. From this again we see how vital it was to Marlborough that he should have Godolphin at the Treasury; otherwise he might find his strategy in the face of the enemy hamstrung by money being granted for one operation and refused for another. It was equally necessary to him that no one serving under his command should be appointed except by and through his authority. The slightest weakening of the principle that he alone governed all promotions and appointments would in the party commotion have thrown the whole of his forces and of his plans into disorder.

CHAPTER TWENTY-NINE

The Structure of the War

ᎷᎯ 1701-12 ᏴᎴ

ALTHOUGH Eugene's brilliant campaign in Italy had opened the War of the Spanish Succession in 1701, no shot had been fired in the northern theatre. In Flanders, upon the Rhine, and upon the Moselle armies had assembled, and each of the great combatants was busy securing smaller allies. Louis XIV had acquired partial control of the Archbishopric of Cologne and the Bishopric of Liége at the same time as he had occupied the Belgian fortresses. The first overt act of the Germanic states was the coercion of the Duke of Brunswick-Wolfenbüttel. This prince was a mere figurehead whose younger brother had collected in his name, but with French gold, an army of twelve thousand mercenaries, and was forming a league of French supporters in North Germany. The Elector of Hanover at length intervened. During the night of March 20 the younger brother was driven out by Hanoverian troops, and the mercenaries agreed to serve henceforth under the Emperor. This was the first war news which reached Queen Anne after her accession.

Marlborough had arranged that on May 4/15 war should be simultaneously declared upon France by England, the States-General, and the Empire. This event finally reassured the Dutch, who hitherto, despite Marlborough's firm assertions, had feared that their island ally intended only to act as an accessory—i.e., to pick up what was good for herself at the expense of friend and foe. The causes of England's quarrel were set forth in a proclamation which is a model of forceful historical compression. Its conclusion should be noted.

(276)

We henceforth strictly forbid the holding of any correspondence or communication with France or Spain or their subjects. But because there are remaining in our Kingdoms many of the subjects of France and Spain, We do declare our Royal intention to be, that all the subjects of France and Spain, who shall demean themselves dutifully towards us, shall be safe in their persons and estates.

This passage will jar the modern mind. We see how strong was the structure of Christendom in these times and with what restraints even warring nations acted. Of course, nowadays, with the many improvements that have been made in international morals and behaviour, all enemy subjects, even those whose countries were only technically involved, even those who had lived all their lives in England, and the English women who had married them, would, as in every other state based on an educated democracy, be treated within twenty-four hours as malignant foes, flung into internment camps, and their private property stolen to assist the expenses of the war. In the twentieth century mankind has shaken itself free from all those illogical, old-world prejudices, and achieved the highest efficiency of brutal, ruthless war.

We shall see that the same kind of archaic conduct ruled in the field. After the fury of battle was spent both sides, and especially the victors, laboured to rescue the wounded, instead of leaving them to perish inch by inch in agony in No Man's Land. If in their poverty they stripped the dead of their clothing, they also exchanged prisoners with meticulous accounting. The opposing generals paid each other every compliment and courtesy which did not hamper their operations, and in the winter season issued passports to prominent officers to traverse hostile territory on their shortest routes home. Although the great causes in dispute were stated with a robust vigour and precision which we have now lost, no hatred, apart from military antagonism, was countenanced among the troops. All was governed by strict rules of war, into which bad temper was not often permitted to enter. The main acceptances of a polite civilization still reigned across the lines of opposing armies, and mob violence and mechanical propaganda had not yet been admitted to the adjustment of international disputes.

Since from this time forward military affairs must play a main part in our story, the reader should survey the whole scope of the war, and consider the governing conditions under which it was fought. Two great European countries, one much weaker than the other, found themselves lapped about and almost encircled by a numerous alliance of which England was the mainspring, and by the sea, of which she was already the mistress. The kingdoms of France and Spain were in a central position in 1702 similar to that of Germany and Austria in 1914. They had the advantage of interior lines and could strike outward in various directions. They could throw their weight now against this opponent, now against that. All their fortunes depended upon an army, incomparable in power, numbers, organization, and repute, and upon the authority of its War Lord. Spain throughout followed the guidance of Louis XIV in the same subordination that in our days Austria observed to Germany. Louis XIV at the beginning could choose for each campaign where the decisive theatre should lie. He could perfect his plans in secrecy, and execute them without any domestic hindrance. The allies, so loosely and precariously joined together, among whom communication was slow and slender, were liable to be struck down one after the other.

The command of the sea rested throughout in the hands of England and Holland. Queen Anne had above two hundred ships of war—half of them of over fifty guns and "fit to lie in the line"—manned by forty or fifty thousand sailors and marines. To these the Dutch joined three ships to every English five. The French were scarcely half of this combined strength. They never attempted seriously to dispute the Narrow Seas or the Channel. Their frigates and privateers maintained themselves upon the oceans; but for the rest their aim was to preserve the control of the Mediterranean. Until the allies could alter this King Louis was only partially enveloped, and still had the advantage of striking where he chose. On the other hand, the fact of having to defend simultaneously so many ports and potential landing-places from amphibious attack was a serious drain on French man-power.

If the allies were to rid themselves of the peril of being attacked in detail they must wrest the initiative from Louis XIV, and by dominant action at one point or another rivet the attention of the central mass. The paths by which France could be invaded were not so numerous as might appear. Roads were few and bad, and in the absence of railways all the natural obstacles of forests, mountains, and barren regions asserted their full power. Armies of from sixty to a hundred thousand men could only live by moving constantly through fertile lands or where their supplies could be brought them by fresh or salt water. The

great rivers were the railways of this war. The control of the long, uninterrupted course of rivers and canals enabled armies to operate in
their full power, drawing their food and ammunition easily to them
week by week and moving their siege trains. But for this very reason
every river and canal, especially the confluences and junctions, was
barred by strong, elaborate fortresses, each of which had to be separately captured. The value of every fortress and the cost of taking it in
time, life, and money were measured with high exactness on both sides;
two months for this, a month for that; a fortnight for a small place,
and three or four days for a mere castle. Thus the rivers represented
the lines of railways, and the stations on them were forts barring all
traffic to those who held them not.

The shipping resources of the two Maritime Powers, relatively large
though they were, their harbours, quays, and port accommodation,
were never sufficient to make the invasion of France possible by any sea-
borne army likely to overcome so mighty and war-like a state.

There were three or four practicable lines of invasion open to the allies. In the south there was the Riviera road. An army might work its
way slowly from Italy into France along the coast, being fed and
helped by its ships from port to port. This was a plan which several
times attracted Prince Eugene. A second line of invasion was offered in
the gap between the Jura Mountains in the north of Switzerland and
the southern spurs of the Vosges. North of this gap France was protected for a hundred miles by the triple obstacles of the Black Forest,
itself almost a mountain-range, the Rhine, and the Vosges Mountains,
one behind the other. The third route was through Northern Alsace or
along the Moselle, converging on the French fortress group Saarlouis,
Thionville, and Metz. This was generally believed to be the surest and
most deadly, and, if Marlborough had found it possible to marshal the
effective strength of Germany behind him, it was the pathway he
would certainly have made his own.

Lastly there were the plains of Flanders, fertile, populous, intersected
by their great and magnificent rivers and canals, offering every facility
to the movements of the largest armies and enabling the two Maritime
Powers to act in the closest harmony. But this area was covered by immense systems of fortification. More than thirty large fortresses of the
first class, complete from outworks to citadel, and perhaps fifty fortified
towns and strongholds, the work of two generations, formed artificial

barriers between France and Holland. At the time when Marlborough's campaign began nearly all these fortress-towns were in the hands of France. All the fortresses of the Spanish Netherlands had been seized by Louis XIV in 1701. All the fortresses on the Meuse and Rhine, with one remarkable exception, had passed to the French by the seduction of the priestly rulers of Cologne and Liége. Thus the Dutch began the war deprived of virtually the whole of their barrier and of all the strong places they had held in the time of King William. They had a few fortresses like Nimwegen and Bergen-op-Zoom in their own land, but for the rest they must rely solely upon the manhood of their armies.

The exception was Maestricht. This very large fortress on the Meuse lay in an enclave of Dutch territory. It had not been affected either by the transfer of the Spanish Netherlands or by that of the Bishoprics of Cologne and Liége. It was a fortress of the first order, of historic fame and modernized defences. Within its earthworks the Dutch had gathered immense supplies, very considerable stores, and a trustworthy garrison of no less than fourteen thousand men. The French, on the other hand, had as their second line the great fortresses within the French frontier, and thus enjoyed both their own defences and those which should properly have belonged to their opponents. Thus at the outset of the new war the French had the control of the Scheldt and all its tributaries, of the Meuse (excepting Maestricht), and of long stretches of the Rhine and the Upper Rhine. Finally, Louis had constructed in 1701 a continuous line of fortifications along a seventy-mile crescent from Antwerp to Namur. These "Lines of Brabant" had been sited under Vauban's supervision by the best French engineers; and entrenchments, palisades, and inundations, all vigilantly watched, offered an unbroken defensive position, on any sector of which the French field army could confront an assailant from the north.

During 1701 the attitude of the Germanic princes was ill-defined. They were taking precautions and raising forces; but they were for the most part indisposed either to succour the Emperor, as their antiquated feudal fealty required, or to declare war upon France. In these circumstances the Margrave of Baden, whose domains around Rastadt, between the Upper Rhine and the Neckar, were very near the conflagration, was a personage of high importance. At the head of the Imperial armies he had gained several notable victories over the Turks in bygone years. He was reputed an accomplished soldier, and was certainly a man of proved physical courage. As a ruling prince he was prepared to lead troops of his own against the French. It was natural, therefore, that he should receive the command of whatever Imperial armies should be assembled to defend Germany. He thus appears at the outset of the war as the first general of the Empire.

During the autumn and winter of 1701 the Margrave busied himself with the defence of the Black Forest and the valley of the Upper Rhine. He aroused considerable enthusiasm among the German populations threatened by French invasion, especially in the circles of Swabia and Franconia. He organized local militias, supported by the inhabitants of the towns and villages, to aid the regular troops which were gradually coming into the field. For further protection he constructed a number of fortified lines barring the least difficult tracks through the Black Forest. But the most important strategic task which he accomplished was the creation of the celebrated Lines of Stollhofen. These fortifications ran from the river to the wooded mountains, and barred a French advance from the Strasburg bridgeheads down the Rhine valley on the right bank of the river. A frontal attack upon the fortifications, if they were adequately garrisoned, seemed a hazardous and certainly a very costly major operation. It was not until 1707 that Marshal Villars captured them by a brilliant and almost bloodless surprise. Thus the Lines of Stollhofen played a most serviceable part throughout the early critical years of the war, and their construction must be regarded as a military measure of rare discrimination and of the highest value.

The task of the commander in Marlborough's wars was direct. There were no higher formations like divisions and corps. Even the brigade was an improvisation adopted for the campaign. The armies were often divided into wings. There were for each wing generals of cavalry and infantry. Each, like the Chief, was assisted by lieutenant-generals. These high executive officers were available either to carry out particular tasks assigned to them often in the heat of action, or to see that the main plan, with which they were made acquainted, was carried out. The control of the battle was maintained on each side by eight or ten superior officers who had no permanent commands of their own, and were virtually the general staff officers of modern times, working in a faithful subordination. It was with and through these that the commander-in-chief acted, and it is astonishing how smoothly and effectu-

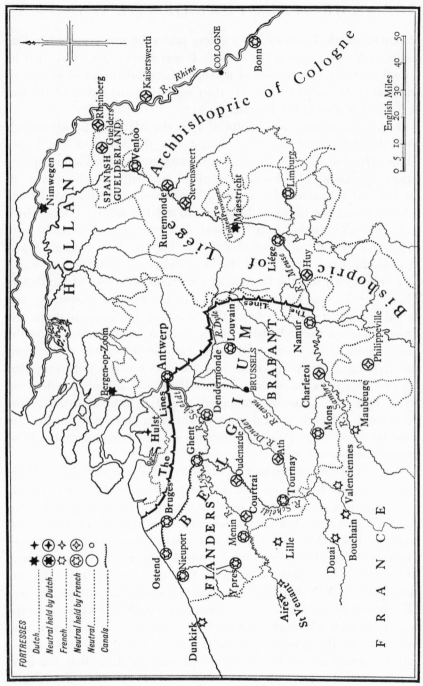

FORTRESSES
Dutch............
Neutral held by Dutch...
French............
Neutral held by French
Neutral............
Canals............

COLOGNE
Bonn
Kaiserswerth
R. Rhine
Rheinberg
Guelders
SPANISH
GUELDERLAND
Nimwegen
Venloo
HOLLAND
Stevensweert
Ruremonde
Limburg
Maestricht
To
United Provinces
Liège
Huy
Liège
R. Meuse
The Lines
Namur
BISHOPRIC
Bergen-op-Zoom
Antwerp
R. Dyle
Louvain
BRABANT
Charleroi
Philippeville
R. Senne
BRUSSELS
Dendermonde
The Hulst Lines
R. Scheldt
Ghent
Bruges
Oudenarde
R. Dender
Ath
Mons
R. Sambre
Maubeuge
Ostend
BELGIUM
FLANDERS
Menin
Courtrai
Tournay
R. Scheldt
Valenciennes
Bouchain
Nieuport
Ypres
Lille
Douai
Aire
St Venant
Dunkirk
FRANCE

Archbishopric of Cologne

ENGLISH MILES
0 5 10 20 30 40 50

3. The Barrier Fortresses in April 1702

ally the troops were often handled and great changes of plan and formation effected even in the stress of action.

In the midst of the scene of carnage, with its drifting smoke-clouds, scurrying fugitives, and brightly coloured lines, squares, and oblongs of men, he sat his horse, often in the hottest fire, holding in his mind the position and fortunes of every unit in his army from minute to minute and giving his orders aloud. We must picture him in those days when the Signal Corps was non-existent, attended not only by three or four generals of high rank, but by at least twenty young officers specially trained and specially mounted, men who were capable of following the event with intelligent eyes, who watched the field incessantly, and who knew where to find the subordinate commanders, their brigades and regiments. For short distances or less important orders the runners we see in the tapestries with their long brass-headed staves of authority were used. Thus in the space of four or five hours perhaps thirty or forty thousand men were killed or wounded on the two sides, and another fearful but glorious name was inscribed in the annals of war.

In the times of which we tell the great commander proved in the day of battle that he possessed a combination of mental, moral, and physical qualities adapted to action which were so lifted above the common run as to seem almost godlike. His appearance, his serenity, his piercing eye, his gestures, the tones of his voice—nay, the beat of his heart—diffused a harmony upon all around him. Every word he spoke was decisive. Victory often depended upon whether he rode half a mile this way or that. At any moment a cannon-shot or a cavalry in-rush might lay him with thousands of his soldiers a mangled bundle on the sod. That age has vanished for ever. Other trials are reserved for the human spirit. New and vaguer problems overtop such minds as are available. But let us not pretend that modern achievements can be compared, except by million-tongued propaganda, with the personal feats which the very few great captains of the world performed.

CHAPTER THIRTY

The Heaths of Peer

1702, Summer

QUEEN ANNE's Cabinet under Marlborough's impulsion formed immediately resolute war plans by land and sea for the opening campaign. Marlborough would go to the Low Countries—it was hoped in command of the armies of the Sea Powers, or at least of all the troops in English pay—and would strive by every means to obtain a major decision in the field. Sir George Rooke, the Admiral of the Fleet, and the Duke of Ormonde would conduct a large naval and military expedition to capture Cadiz. From this base it would be possible, certainly in the following year, to take Minorca and thus dominate the Mediterranean. Meanwhile, in 1702, after the capture of Cadiz, the fleet was to cruise along the Riviera coasts for as long as possible in the summer months and bring brief but possibly important aid to Prince Eugene.

To both these bold designs violent opposition arose from all concerned. We shall see presently the impediments to the campaign on land, but the obstruction of some of the high authorities in the Cabinet and of Sir George Rooke to the naval expedition was vehement. He incited the merchants to cry out that the Channel would be at the mercy of the French. He persuaded Sir Cloudesley Shovell, who was to be in charge of the Channel, to complain that his force was inadequate. All this resistance and the arguments which sustained it were beaten down by the leading men in the Cabinet, and the main Anglo-Dutch fleet in overwhelming superiority to the enemy sailed for the coast of Spain and the attack on Cadiz at the end of July. They carried besides marines eight thousand soldiers under the Duke of Ormonde, and were thus capable of seizing this all-important harbour by an amphibious descent.

For the year 1702 Louis had decided to set his strongest army against Holland. He knew the divisions and uncertainty into which the Republic had been thrown by the death of King William. He believed that the links which joined it to England had been at the least gravely weakened. He counted upon a period of hesitation and loss of contact which, if turned to good account by military action, might break the Dutch and scare off the English. The prejudices of the Tories against heavy war on the Continent and their sympathy with Jacobite sentiment were well known at Versailles, and indeed throughout Europe. Their preponderance in Queen Anne's Administration was widely accepted as opening a period of English detachment from the main struggle. It was quite natural for friend and foe to reckon without Marlborough. How could foreigners measure the real relations of the Cockpit group? How could they know what Marlborough was or foresee what he would become?

According to the treaties of the Grand Alliance, the Emperor should have ranged ninety thousand troops out of his quota of a hundred and twenty thousand in the field against the French. Actually he was unable by midsummer to place more than forty thousand in Italy under the command of Prince Eugene, and could only muster twenty thousand upon the Rhine under the Margrave Prince Louis of Baden.

The evident failure of the Empire to make any serious concentration upon the Upper Rhine led the French to leave that theatre in suspense while they used their principal armies against Eugene in Italy, and against the formidable Anglo-Dutch forces which were now on a war footing in the Netherlands. Two Marshals of France, Villeroy and Vendôme, with sixty thousand men, were assigned to the Italian theatre. Marshal Boufflers, with sixty thousand men, comprising the first army of France, confronted the Sea Powers in the Low Countries. Marshal Catinat, with twenty thousand men, watched the Margrave about the confluence of the Neckar with the Rhine, and guarded Alsace. By the beginning of June both sides had placed about two hundred thousand men upon the fighting fronts, with large and growing establishments in the rear.

Marlborough had reached the Dutch capital on May 26 to find every one in distress and everything in dispute. The supreme command was still unsettled. In June the Prussian King arrived to press somewhat half-heartedly his claim. There is little doubt that Heinsius and his colleagues meant by now to have Marlborough; but the actual announcement was embarrassing. In these circumstances they requested him to remain at The Hague as long as Frederick I was there. The foreign princely candidates, including the Prussian King, had all been ruled out by Queen Anne's opposition. The Dutch, with the French bayonets glistening at their very throats, were sure that Queen Anne's husband would not do. Indeed, since May they had made it clear that for their part they would never consent. Still they hesitated, and the tension on the front grew. On June 30 Marlborough, judging the moment opportune, announced that he must leave for Nimwegen, presumably to command the British troops and those in English pay. This apparently clinched the matter; for when he started for the front the next day he was in possession of a patent which conferred on him the title of Deputy Captain-General of the Republic. Cardonnel wrote to say, "The States have given directions to all their Generals and other officers to obey my Lord Marlborough as their General." Thus we may say that from the beginning of July 1702 Marlborough assumed command of all the Dutch, British, and hired German forces and became the principal general of the Grand Alliance. This post, with its authority varying according to events and the different signatory Powers, he held continuously till the end of 1711. His own discretion and frequent submissions, combined with the shattering military events which he produced, preserved to him, if often only in a ghostlike form, a vague but majestic primacy. He could at no time have asserted a claim to be Generalissimo without widespread repudiation; but there was never an allied demand for anyone else.

The Dutch, when at last they gave Marlborough the command of their armies and to enforce their authority paid him a salary of ten thousand pounds a year, had very definite intentions about the kind of warfare he should wage. They thought he was the best man for the command, and, indeed, the only one who could hold it. But their confidence did not go so far as letting him fight a battle. By the Constitution of the Republic two members of the Government were bound to accompany their Captain-General throughout his operations, and no important action could be fought or town besieged without their assent. They now provided Marlborough with mentors and censors in the Baron Heyden and Mynheer Geldermalsen. Geldermalsen, a Zeelander and a former Ambassador to England, soon succumbed to Marlborough's arts, and stood up vigorously for the rights of the English general, even against his own fellow-countrymen.

When the news of Marlborough's appointment as Commander-in-Chief reached the camps, indignation rose high among the Dutch generals at their supersession. Ginkel had to the last contended for the command upon alternate days. Opdam, Overkirk, and Slangenberg deemed their military records and experience superior to those of this foreigner. He had, they argued, never grounded himself in the theory of war by professional study. Court favour, diplomatic influence, political intrigue, a chain of accidents, the mutually destructive claims of better men, had given him the coveted distinction. There was truth in much of this; but there was other truth besides.

Upon his arrival at Nimwegen Marlborough at first remained in considerable seclusion. He sat through the councils of war silent and observant. He took his great position sedately. He treated the Dutch generals with respect and reserve. He seems to have spoken more intimately to the captains of the foreign mercenary contingents. These soon gained the impression that the new Commander-in-Chief did not approve of the cautious methods of making war which reigned in the allied camp. He seemed dissatisfied with the idea of passively protecting the frontier, and possibly capturing some Belgian fortress in the course of the campaign. He was reported to hold strange doctrines about war. England was not attracted by small warfare or limited objects. It was not this town nor that which she sought. The annihilation of the French army in a great battle and the humbling of Louis XIV in the open field were the purposes which had brought the English troops to the Netherlands. He would not agree to be responsible to the Queen if the allied army tethered itself at the gates of Nimwegen, and allowed the enemy to live at its side on friendly soil between the Meuse and the Rhine. He had not been a week at headquarters before it was known that he was demanding drastic decisions from the Dutch Government.

His attitude caused excitement in the camp and perturbation at The Hague. Heinsius felt so insecure in his authority, and all parties in Holland were in such lively alarm, that it was only with extreme difficulty that they could be persuaded to entertain any offensive operation. They clung to the strong army which now stood between them and the enemy, and sought to prevent any movement which would uncover Nimwegen. They could not bear to "lose sight of the Army." But Geldermalsen supported Marlborough.

The discussions were protracted both in the capital and in the camp. Meanwhile Marlborough was drawing in reinforcements from every quarter, and by July 6 had concentrated in front of Nimwegen at Duckenberg an army which, though somewhat smaller than the French, gave him the assurance that he was master. He held a grand review, and sixty thousand well-trained soldiers, equipped and furnished in every way and led by experienced or veteran officers, paraded before him. On the 15th he marched with his whole force directly towards the enemy and camped upon the Meuse about Grave. Here only seven miles separated the two armies.

The ostensible object of the advance had been the siege of Rheinberg, but Marlborough intended, once the army was in motion, to substitute a larger design. The challenging movement of the army and its magnificent appearance freed the troops from the sense of weakness and irresolution by which they had been oppressed while they huddled around Nimwegen. His perfect self-confidence, although he was for the first time at the head of a great army, spread itself throughout the ranks.

Sixty miles behind the menacing French front lay Maestricht, strong and unsubdued, with its ample supplies, beckoning its friends from the north. The advance of a strong army towards Maestricht would immediately bring Boufflers hurrying back to Brabant and to a safer line of communications. He would have to abandon the Meuse or—fight and win a battle. Without alarming the Dutch by dwelling unduly on this second possibility, Marlborough pressed for permission to march south from Nimwegen. Even for this limited movement he had a wearying struggle. He had to persuade not only generals who, like Ginkel, resented his command, but a crowd of anxious Dutch functionaries and magnates. He took a number of these upon a reconnaissance towards Boufflers' camp, and, pointing to the long lines of French tents, remarked, "I shall soon rid you of these troublesome neighbours."

At length after the loss of ten precious days his patience and the sense of confidence he inspired around him prevailed. The Dutch still disbelieved that the march he proposed would have the result of forcing Boufflers to retire, but they consented to the experiment. At last on July 26 Marlborough crossed to the left bank of the Meuse with about fifty thousand men, including the English. That night and on the following days he marched steadily southward. On the 31st he captured a small frontier garrison and three hundred men in the castle of Gravensbrück, and reached Lille Saint-Hubert the same night. Here he halted, having covered forty miles. What would the enemy do?

They did what Marlborough had promised. The results were immediate. He obliged the enemy, in Captain Parker's homely words, "to quit their camp and dance after him." He gained the initiative.

On the 30th Boufflers, seeing no other chance open, turned westward and began his perilous march. The two armies were now approaching each other almost at right angles and a serious battle might be fought. Boufflers was at a grave disadvantage, because he had, in slipping past, to expose during the whole day his right flank to Marlborough's downward spear-thrust. He had to make a flank march across the front of an army which he must presume would attack him in the midst of the awkward manœuvre. He could not know what troops, if any, Marlborough had been obliged to leave behind to soothe the Dutch. There might well be seventy thousand men on top of Boufflers when he was most ill-arranged to receive them. Moreover Maestricht, that hostile fortress with its large garrison, was already obtruding itself upon his movements. The gap between Marlborough's army and Maestricht was now only twenty miles. Boufflers decided to run the risk. Meanwhile Marlborough was joined by the English artillery, escorted by two battalions and comprising thirty-four cannon and four "Hawbitzers," or half the artillery of the army.

Marlborough had from the beginning intended to bring matters to a point where both the French, in spite of their disadvantage, and the Dutch, in spite of their misgivings, would be compelled to fight. Once on the move and in contact with the enemy he began to assert his authority. He hoped that once the Dutch were presented with a rare war-chance of taking the enemy at a marked disadvantage he would be able to swing them into the battle. But he reckoned vainly. On the night of August 1, at Little Bruegel, he saw that the moment had come. He exposed to the Dutch Deputies his intention to attack Boufflers with his whole army the next day. We do not know how long he wrestled with them: in the end they agreed. All the baggage was sent back, and the allied army was set in battle array. Dawn broke, and Marlborough was on horseback, meaning to order a general attack upon the French, the heads of whose columns were to be seen approaching from the southward, about to cross his front. But then ensued a painful scene. The Deputies had given their consent: the decisive commands were about to be issued: and now they withdrew it. They were conscious of their weak position. They did not dictate—they besought him not to put the army of the Republic upon the cast of the die. He might have been right about the strategy, but no one could tell whether he would be victorious in a battle. There was the risk of defeat and the certainty of heavy loss. Besides, they had now heard what he had known the day before, that Tallard was close behind Boufflers and that the enemy's army was thus superior in numbers. They implored him to let them off their over-night resolve.

Anyone acquainted with war will realize that this was a very hard trial for a general. But the armies of a coalition cannot be handled like those of a single state. Swallowing his feelings, the Commander-in-Chief bowed to their appeals. There should be no battle: but he exacted a condition. They must, he said, ride out with him to see what might have happened. They did so, and beheld during the whole of the morning of the 2nd the French army, in imposing numbers but considerable disorder, streaming across their front with their whole flank exposed. As this spectacle told its own tale, the Deputies admitted that a grand opportunity had been lost. But another immediately recurred. After their long march the French were forced to camp on the night of August 2 at Zonhoven, still in a most dangerous position. Marlborough, hopeful that his demonstration in the morning would win him freedom to give the necessary orders, again urged an attack the next day. Again the Deputies could not bring themselves to do such violence to their instructions.

Upon the opportunity we have confirmation from the other side. Berwick, with his military instinct, measured the position as well as Marlborough.

> The Earl of Marlborough proposed to march up to us, by passing the defile of Peer, by which a battle on the heaths would have been unavoidable; but the Deputies of the States-General would never consent to this, any more than to attack us in our camp at Sonoven. This was very fortunate for us; for we were posted in such a manner that

we should have been beaten without being able to stir, our left being very high, and our right sunk into a *cul-de-sac* between two rivulets.

The retreat of Boufflers from the Meuse had enabled Marlborough to draw six thousand men, nine battalions, to his army from the troops extorted from him to cover Nimwegen. When these joined him he was again definitely the stronger. But the veto on battles continued. Thus Boufflers, so recently aggressive and menacing, was able to make his escape into Brabant. He had lost no battle, but he had abandoned the whole Meuse with its fortresses and two out of the three areas which he had been told by Louis XIV it was his duty to guard. Here was the first crux of Marlborough's campaign of 1702.

Boufflers, animated by Berwick and spurred by the King, tried to interrupt Marlborough's communications with the north. Accordingly, on August 9 and 10 he marched to Riethoven, sending Berwick forward to Eindhoven.

Marlborough withdrew south and used General Opdam as the bait. He kept Opdam and his tempting detachment just far enough behind him to attract the French.

Boufflers, with his back towards Holland, now followed for three days, Marlborough retreating towards France. Where armies are equal the general who is retiring can always turn and fight, and as he can choose the moment, so he can choose the ground. For three days the French had the exhilaration of apparently driving the enemy before them and away from his home and his communications. On the afternoon of the third day they began to emerge from difficult country on to the Heath of Helchteren, a wide expanse well suited to the action of cavalry, in which arm Marlborough was superior. Here they saw the allied army suddenly drawn up in full array and evidently about to strike. Now even the Dutch Deputies were converted. Any plain man could see the advantage they would have in attacking the French while they were but half-debouched from defiles, scrub, and morasses. They gave their assents, and the Commander-in-Chief, so called, issued his orders. The cannonade opened from both artilleries, and several hundred men were stricken in each of the armies.

At five o'clock Opdam on the right, reinforced to ten thousand men, was ordered to begin the battle by attacking the French left, whose difficulties and disarray could be plainly seen. But after the Dutch Deputies the Dutch generals. Opdam, alleging the state of the ground, consumed three vital hours without making any appreciable movement. The advance of the rest of the army depended upon Opdam. Night fell and under its cover the French were able to complete their deployment.

The next day, the 24th of August, although the battle would have been much more even, Marlborough still wished to engage. But now it was the Deputies who jibbed. They could see the advantages which might have been seized yesterday, but to-day the issue seemed balanced. Surely it was wiser to wait till to-morrow. If Boufflers attacked he must be encountered; but if he did not attack the matter could be reconsidered on the morrow. "To-morrow," said Marlborough, "Monsieur de Boufflers will be gone." And so he was. "The French lofty army," wrote Sergeant Millner, "immediately withdrew from their attempt and fell backward." A pursuit by the English cavalry yielded only minor advantages. Here was the second crisis of the campaign. Here was the second lost opportunity.

Marlborough repressed his wrath at the obstructions by which he was hampered. It has been said of him that he had so many plans all thought out in his mind, and could change so easily from one to the other, that he suffered less by the frustration of his combinations than would a general whose heart was set on some particular scheme. He always felt that if he was not allowed to win one way, he could find another.

One thing, however, was beyond endurance. He could not bear that his kinsman Berwick, whose merit he divined, and Marshal Boufflers should suppose that he had himself thrown away glorious chances and shrunk from carrying his combinations to the point of battle. His professional pride and instinct asserted themselves above all things. We have the strange spectacle of a Commander-in-Chief apologizing to his antagonists for not attacking them upon two occasions when they knew he would have been technically right to put all to the test. He actually sent a trumpet with letters to Boufflers and Berwick to assure them with compliments that the failure in coming to battle was none of his fault. There is no doubt from their movements at many crucial passages in this and the next campaign that they believed him. Whether his candour was wise or not can never be decided. It is certainly curious.

CHAPTER THIRTY-ONE

The Fortresses of the Meuse

ᘒ 1702, Autumn ᘔ

MARLBOROUGH was forced to recognize for the time being that even under the most favourable circumstances he would not be allowed to fight a battle. No one can measure the internal stresses of the general who has to conduct war against an equal enemy under such paralysing control. Now Marlborough must reconcile himself to the conventional warfare of the end of the seventeenth century. He must content himself with parades, manœuvres, the sieges of fortresses, and the control of foraging areas. This was not his kind of war. But if it was the only one permitted, he would make it serve. The fortresses on the Meuse were within his grasp. But in this project he had already encountered many disappointments.

Marlborough to Godolphin

Everbeeck

August 21, 1702

* It is now eight days since we made the detachment for Venloo, and last night we received a letter from Monsrs Geldermalsen and Cohorn from the Grave which says that for want of powder and other necessaries they can't begin the siege till the beginning of the next month. Notwithstanding the great conveniency and desire the States have to have Venloo, yet their Government at this time is so very negligent that I am afraid at last they will not be able to attack it by which all the frute of this campaign will be lost. I have written very pressing letters to The Hague and have endeavoured to make them sensible how scandalous it would be if this siege should miscarry for want of necessary preparations. They promised that everything should be ready by the 2nd of this month. What I say of Venloo and the Dutch you will see is fit only to be known by the Queen and [the] Prince; for a friendship with these people is absolutely necessary for the common cause and her Majesty's service, and I am in hope that the prudence of the Pensioner this winter may order matters so that their parties may unite, and then there can be no doubt but everything will go better.

All authorities were agreed upon the siege of Venloo. The Dutch and the French attached equal importance to it; and Marlborough himself had perforce to describe it as the "frute of this campaign." Venloo was much the strongest of the three fortresses which the French held on the Meuse north of Maestricht. On August 29 Venloo was regularly invested by the Prince of Nassau-Saarbrück, reinforced by Opdam to a total of 32 battalions and 36 squadrons. Marlborough, with the rest of his army of about forty-five thousand men, took post at Asche. Here he covered Maestricht and could, if need be, draw supplies from it for a time. Here he was on the flank of any effort by Boufflers to relieve Venloo. Once again the value of Maestricht became evident. Marlborough could afford some risk to his communications with Holland because of the fortress and its exceptional supplies, but Boufflers, moving north past Marlborough's right, would run the gravest risks both of battle and interception. If alternatively he recrossed to the right bank of the Meuse and sought to rescue its fortresses by a turning movement through Limburg and Aix-la-Chapelle, he would expose the whole of Brabant to immediate invasion. One has only to study the map to admire the choice of Asche for all purposes.

The siege of Venloo at first went very slowly. Marlborough's secret letters complain of the Dutch. For weeks preparation had been ordered for this deeply desired event; but after the investment had been made everything was late. The arrival of the heavy batteries and their munitions, the opening of the trenches by civilian labour, and all the necessary sapping and mining, were many days behind the schedule prepared and counted upon for this operation. Cohorn as the expert engineer, the specialist in sieges, was soon in quarrel with the Dutch generals, each party blaming the other for the delay. Now that so many allied troops were at the siege Marlborough was a good deal weaker than Boufflers. He had to watch him from hour to hour, and be always ready to fight. On September 13 Boufflers moved to Tongres, where he was but ten miles from Liége, and Marlborough, moving south, placed himself between him and Maestricht. Here he was well supplied both from the north and from the district.

On September 18 a surprising feat of arms was performed at Venloo. The Royal Regiment of Ireland, later the 18th, with two English battalions, had been ordered as one of the processes in the siege to clear the glacis of Fort St Michael and drive the enemy from the covered way. However, Lord Cutts assembled the officers and told them that he assigned no limit to their attack. If they could get farther, all the better. This unusual order produced astonishing results. The Anglo-Irish brigade rushed forward, and, having chased the enemy from the covered way, followed them over the drawbridge and across the open ditch so closely that "the loose planks were not slipped" and the whole crowd arrived together on the actual ramparts of the fort. By more good luck the governor had omitted to mow the grass, and all the redcoats scrambled up the steep slope by hand and foot, mingled with the flying French, and tumbled pell-mell into the interior of the fort, where after some slaughter the whole garrison of fifteen hundred men surrendered to fewer assailants. Thus was the mad escapade rewarded by astounding success.

The loss of Fort St Michael broke the spirit of the defence, and preparations were pressed forward for the final attack. On September 22 the news arrived that the fortress of Landau, far off in Germany, had been taken by Prince Louis of Baden. A joy-fire of musketry and of all the cannon was ordered in celebration of this event. The defenders of Venloo, not knowing the reason of these loud explosions, deemed them the prelude of the assault. They therefore displayed white flags, beat a parley, and forthwith capitulated. Altogether we had much good fortune in the siege of Venloo.

These were days of strain for Marlborough. He had 55 battalions and 110 squadrons against Boufflers' 70 battalions and 86 squadrons. He might any day, almost at any hour, be forced to fight a battle at considerable odds; but he was better placed than Boufflers to receive supplies or to manœuvre. Thus days grew into weeks, and weeks passed while the two armies stood bristling at each other—the stronger seeking a chance to strike, the weaker always offering baffling propositions. Meanwhile, by Marlborough's orders, the captors of Venloo had advanced up the Meuse towards him. They took Stevensweert in four days and Ruremonde in nine. By October 7 Marlborough had the whole line of the Meuse clear behind him, and was about to be joined by a force which would make him much stronger than Boufflers. The Marshal and his officers had foreseen with dread this new situation. Evidently Liége itself was in the gravest danger. Already, in the third week of September, Boufflers had inspected the fortress and reinforced the citadel. But as he also feared for Bonn, which might alternatively be attacked, he felt bound to detach Tallard to strengthen it. Boufflers' only uncertainty now was what further punishment he would receive. "The King," writes Berwick, "seeing the ill turn affairs took in this campaign, recalled the Duke of Burgundy [who had arrived to 'learn the art of war' under Boufflers] from the army to save him the mortification of being merely a spectator of the Earl of Marlborough's victories." The Royal Duke made no difficulties. Indeed, he may himself have invited the recall. Anyhow he quitted his pretended command of the army in deep disgust.

Marlborough's letters show that he would formerly have been content with clearing the Meuse up to Maestricht. October was now a third spent, and it was deemed hard service to keep the troops in the field so late. But now a new favourable prospect opened before him. He tried again to win the Dutch consent to a battle to break up the French army. The Council of War again refused, and would go no further than the siege of Liége. This was certainly far bigger "frute" than Venloo, and would crown the campaign. Liége was the only remaining passage by which the French garrisons on the Rhine, at Rheinberg, Düsseldorf, Cologne, and Bonn, could be rapidly aided or rescued. The Dutch Government, knowing the importance the French attached to Liége and what a large part it played in their affairs on the Rhine, feared that an advance on that place would lead to a battle. All had gone so well without incurring that awful risk and expense. Why jeopardize it? Why not take their profits and settle into winter quarters? But here was this English commander who was able to transform everything at his touch, who seemed as he moved to and fro about the countryside invariably to impose his will on the formidable French; here was this unproved man, whom they had with such difficulty withheld from fighting battles which he declared he could win (and perhaps he could—no one could tell), who now wanted more. Still, their generals were all in favour of the siege. Their own hearts were cheered by everything that had happened. How gloriously different was their situation in October from what it had been in June! Their confidence had grown. Marlborough got leave to move.

Boufflers had orders from Paris on no account to allow Liége to fall into the hands of the allies. Easy to say: but he was now definitely weaker than Marlborough. He therefore sent reinforcements into Liége and withdrew behind the Jaar stream, a tributary of the Meuse, fortifying himself at Tongres and hoping by threatening Marlborough's right to cover Liége and also to prevent a movement into Brabant, should that be Marlborough's purpose.

Marlborough received permission to act on the 12th. At midnight precisely on the 13th he marched all night to the southward, crossing the Jaar before dawn between Boufflers and the Meuse. He could now besiege Liége; but he wanted to attack Boufflers. The proposed battle was, of course, vetoed, and the siege of Liége began. Boufflers, feeling his rôle exhausted, withdrew behind the Lines of Brabant. The burghers of Liége opened the gates of the town to the allies, and the siege was confined to the citadel and to the Chartreuse fort, a detached work of considerable strength. These were stern operations. The full bombardment of the citadel began on the 20th, and by the 22nd the destruction of both ramparts and magazines was such that the engineers reported that the breach was fit to be stormed. Marlborough offered the governor honourable terms for immediate surrender. M. de Violaine replied that "it would be time to think of that six weeks after." Whereupon, on the afternoon of the 23rd, the British troops headed the general assault. Without firing a musket till they came to the closest quarters, the allies pierced the counterscarp and the covered way, passed the ditch, mounted the breach, and took the place "by dint of sword." The governor was taken prisoner in the breach. His officers beat a parley, "but the victorious allies, being already in the place, would hear none of it, and had killed all they met, if the French had not thrown down their arms and begged quarter, which they obtained." More than one-third of the defenders were destroyed. The rest of the eight thousand men were given 'quarter at discretion.'

The three battalions defending the Chartreuse had been eyewitnesses of the fate of the citadel. Nevertheless their commander resolved to abide the bombardment. It took six days to carry the heavy batteries across the river and plant them opposite the Chartreuse. Then, after four hours' bombardment, the garrison begged for terms. They were refused the honours of war (drums beating, flags flying, bullet in the teeth, etc.), but accorded 'honourable terms,' and marched out disarmed, "with their hands in their pockets." This episode cost the French in all nearly ten thousand soldiers, and in those days soldiers were hard to come by and valuable. An unpublished letter of Marlborough's reveals the rigour of the fighting.

> This has been an action of much vigour, so that it is impossible to say too much of the bravery that was shown by all the officers and soldiers. The governor and great numbers of their officers are already brought to my quarters.

The strategic consequences of the capture of Liége were of higher importance than the heavy losses of the enemy. The French had been expelled from the Meuse and the lower Rhine. The Archbishopric of Cologne and the Bishopric of Liége had been recovered from their hands. Already by the end of the campaign an ally of the Great King, the priestly Elector of Cologne, was wandering through the Netherlands without territory, army, or revenue. The navigation of the two great rivers was now open to the allies, and to the allies only. Their garrisons occupied Kaiserswerth, Venloo, Ruremonde, Stevensweert, Maestricht, and Liége. Marlborough arranged for the winter siege of Rheinberg, which fell eventually on February 9, 1703. The new campaign could be begun under favourable conditions. The Dutch, who when they gave Marlborough the command were crouching in the deep anxiety of valiant, puzzled men under the guns of Nimwegen, were now, less than five months later, masters of a territory many times greater than all that King William had gained in eight campaigns. They no doubt plumed themselves that all had been done without fighting a battle. They were equally satisfied with their general and with themselves. The least contented man in the allied army was Marlborough. He might rejoice at what had been gained, but he also knew what had been lost. He had not been allowed to strike one of those crashing blows in the field which he believed would have given him the necessary control of the war, and might have led swiftly to its victorious end. He had not been allowed to make war, but only to play military chess. Undoubtedly he had won the game.

In the first week of November the armies, except the troops besieging Rheinberg, dispersed into winter quarters, and their commander set out upon his journey for England, home, and the political crisis. And now we must describe the hazardous adventure which befell him.

Much the best way to The Hague was to be towed down the Meuse. On November 2 the Commander-in-Chief embarked in a 'yacht' at Maestricht. It was arranged that fifty horsemen should reconnoitre the country, and keep pace along the banks with the vessels by day and protect them at night. These seemed ample precautions against any French raiding parties which might be abroad. But after passing Venloo, where a new cavalry escort took charge, various accidents occurred. The French still held the fortified and marsh-protected town of Guelders, far behind the allied front. A trap was laid for persons of high consequence descending the river from the armies, and above all for the Commander-in-Chief. The lieutenant chosen for this service had special knowledge of the country. In the darkness of the night this desperate man led his troop with stealth to that point on the river where the cavalry escort would be forced to diverge. They pounced upon the 'yacht,' drew it to the bank by the towrope, fired a volley, and threw a bouquet of hand-grenades on board. Before any resistance could be set up they had Marlborough, Opdam, and his two colleagues in their hands.

Catastrophe! Here Fortune sported with Destiny, and many great tales might have perished unborn. However, the raiders proceeded according to the customs of war. They knew the two Deputies; but all the Dutchmen had passes signed by the Duke of Burgundy to free them from annoyance on their voyage. Marlborough had no pass; not caring to be beholden to his enemies, he had trusted to his escort. But Fortune was at heart his faithful friend. While the Deputies' papers were being scrutinized in the lantern-light of the cabin one of his secretaries, or clerks rather, Stephen Gell, slipped into his hand a pass accorded to his brother, General Churchill, which had not been used. This was one of the situations for which Marlborough's gifts were well suited. With perfect calm and in the most natural manner he tendered the pass to the leader of the raiders.

A prolonged parley followed. The validity of the passport was argued at length. No one knows what was said on either side. It seems that the lieutenant chose at last to release Marlborough upon the pass which was made out for his brother Churchill, which was out of date and did not cover transit by water; or alternatively he allowed this English general, evidently of the highest rank, to count as one of the two servants or secretaries allowed upon the pass of Field Deputy Geldermalsen. The yacht floated on down the stream and soon overtook Cohorn and his armed guard.

Meantime what had happened to Marlborough's cavalry escort? They heard the firing and soon learned the facts. The officer in command seems to have become panic stricken. But perhaps he was told that any attempt at rescue would mean the immediate slaughter of the captives. He did nothing but report what had happened. The news, distorted, outsped the current of the river. By daybreak the alarm was general. Marlborough had been captured! He had been carried into Guelders! It would have been easy, says Ailesbury, to have conveyed him on horseback through the disturbed country into France. The news was received in Paris on the morning of the 10th that Marlborough and the others, all named, were taken. Directions were at once given by Louis XIV that Marlborough was to be well treated. Confirmation arrived by a second messenger from Boufflers' headquarters. It was not till the 11th that a third messenger reported that the lieutenant had let the prisoners go by mistake.

During the 4th the news reached The Hague. The States-General assembled; they ordered all troops within reach to join the forces marching upon Guelders. They sent couriers as fast as men could ride to the Emperor at Vienna to warn him to hold Marshal Villeroy, who had been captured by Prince Eugene two months before, as a hostage for exchange. Villeroy was an intimate friend and favourite of Louis XIV. We cannot tell how the Great King would have chosen, but certainly much would have depended upon his choice. However, while horses galloped, and columns of soldiers marched, and the commander of Guelders found himself threatened by trumpet with appalling penalties, Marlborough and his party arrived peacefully in the evening at The Hague. When it was known he was safe and approaching the city a spasm of relief and joy shook all classes. The whole population was on the bank and in the streets to receive him. In those days the populace were sparingly admitted to great affairs. The spectacle of cheering, weeping, caressing crowds was one Marlborough had never seen before; nor did he see it again until twelve years later, when he returned from disgrace and exile and was acclaimed by the Londoners. Both the peril and the welcome made a deep impression upon him: indeed, it is said he was moved to tears in the throng. "It was not without great difficulty he could get through them to his lodgings, to such a degree was he beloved, and of so high esteem was the name of Marlborough, with people of every condition."

CHAPTER THIRTY-TWO

The Occasional Conformity Bill

ᛤ 1702-3, Winter ᛞ

QUEEN Anne was overjoyed by all she heard from Europe. Here was the admirable Mr Freeman, long the unfailing friend and champion of "poor unfortunate, faithful Morley," of whom every one now at last spoke so well. Her chosen Captain and Minister had returned home with laurels from the wars very different from those which "Mr Caliban" had ever gained—he who had never even acknowledged our congratulations upon Namur. And what was Namur compared to Venloo, Ruremonde, Liége, and all the others; not to speak of the French being smitten and chased time after time; and both Houses of Parliament so pleased about it all? Nothing would content her but that he must be made Duke, and £5000 a year must be settled upon him and his descendants for ever. Thus only could he maintain the station she had accorded him. Surely the House of Commons would not object to that. And dear, beloved Mrs Freeman—how proud she ought to be of her lord! How the Queen wished she could do more for them! Thus in the goodness and gratitude of her heart thought Queen Anne. But both Sarah and the Parliament were a good deal cooler. Sarah manifested a violent opposition to the dukedom; and the Commons would have nothing to do with the perpetual grant. Both have left their reasons on record.

The Queen prepared her reward for Marlborough with all that love of a surprise with which a mother would surround a birthday present to her child. She contrived it with her Ministers in secret, and only on October 22 wrote to Sarah:

(302)

Lord Treasurer intends to send you a copy of the address of the House of Lords which is to be given me to-morrow, and that gives me an opportunity of mentioning a thing to you that I did not intend to do yet. It is very uneasy to your poor unfortunate, faithful Morley to think that she has so very little in her power to show how truly sensible I am of all my lord Marlborough's kindness, especially at a time when he deserves all that a rich crown could give. But since there is nothing else at this time, I hope you will give me leave as soon as he comes to make him a duke. I know my dear Mrs Freeman does not care for anything of that kind nor am I satisfied with it, because it does not enough express the value I have for Mr Freeman, nor nothing ever can how passionately I am yours, my dear Mrs Freeman.

In after-years Sarah described her feelings on receiving this gracious, charming letter—every sentence poised to enhance the gift—the like of which the highest in the land might covet in vain.

When I read the letter first . . . I let it drop out of my hand and was for some minutes like one that had received the news of a death of one of her dear friends. . . . I was so easy for [indifferent to] anything of that kind, having before [already] all that was any use, by which it is plain I have no great taste for grandeur.

This might pass for affectation if it were not confirmed by facts. It is evident that she wrote at once to her husband urging him to refuse the dukedom. Her letter does not exist, but we can easily reconstruct her arguments from his reply. He, on the contrary, was greatly pleased.

John to Sarah

The Hague
November 15

You know I am very ill at compliments but I have a heart full of gratitude; therefore pray say all you can to the Queen for her extraordinary goodness to me. As you have let me have your thoughts as to the dukedom you shall have mine in short, . . . but be assured I shall have a mind to nothing but as it may be easy to you. I do agree with you that we ought not to wish for a greater title till we have a better estate. Your other objection is also very just that this promotion may bring great solicitations upon the Queen which I am sure I would not give occasion for. The Queen's goodness in being desirous to establish my family answers the first, since that may be done this winter; for I agree with you that it should be done before the title.

As for Sarah's point, which Marlborough repeated,

> that I should make a worse figure in England by being a duke than as I am till I had the estate for it, he [Heinsius] said the Queen's kindness was such that I need not doubt a fortune, and that whatever was done at this time for my fortune as well as the title would be quite without envy since all the people were pleased with what I had done.

Weighing the matter dispassionately, he ended by deciding that it was his duty to comply with the Queen's desires and his own.

The new Parliament met on October 20, and the Lords congratulated the Queen. The Commons added that "the vigorous support of Your Majesty's Allies and the wonderful progress of Your Majesty's arms under the conduct of the Earl of Marlborough have signally retrieved the ancient honour and glory of the English nation." This affront to the memory of King William was intended by the Tories to irritate the Whigs, and for this purpose was well devised. Accordingly the House divided on the word "retrieved," "all who had any favour at Court, or hoped for any, voting for it." Only eighty Whigs could be mustered against the Tory majority. A solemn thanksgiving was appointed; and on November 12 the Queen, with Sarah at her side, and attended by both Houses of Parliament, proceeded in state to St Paul's amid the tumultuous acclamations of the London crowds.

A Government is naturally shy of proposing a grant of money to its leading member, who must, however indirectly, be involved in the advice given to the sovereign. Godolphin's letters to Harley tell the tale in modern times. On December 9 the Treasurer writes to the Speaker that Marlborough, having been given a grant by the Queen for the support of his dukedom during her life, had been encouraged by his friends "to think it will not be difficult at this time to get this latter grant confirmed by Act of Parliament to him and the heirs of his body." It seemed that the Government was agreed and the House agreeable. The Queen sent her message to the Commons, announcing that she had granted the Duke of Marlborough and his heirs a pension of £5000 a year upon the revenues of the Post Office for the support of his title during her lifetime.

But here immediately began animated and unpleasant debates. Permanent alienations of the public revenue to individuals had long been one of the best targets of Tory attack. How bitterly had they inveighed against King William's grants to his Dutch favourites! Upon all the hustings of the recent elections they had denounced such practices. Must the new Parliament begin its life by so incongruous an act? The Tory veteran, Musgrave, Clerk of the Ordnance, Marlborough's direct subordinate, from whom he had had "great professions," dwelt in a sour-sweet speech upon the pay and allowances the Captain-General was already receiving from British and Dutch sources. These certainly amounted to £60,000 a year, and little imagination is required to understand the feelings which were excited among much poorer people.

Godolphin asked the Speaker for his "direction and help in what is fit to be done." Evidently the next day these two Parliamentarians had a long talk. It was certain that the Commons would not agree to the permanent grant, and the only question was how to withdraw the proposal without humiliating Marlborough, with whom all were so pleased, or distressing the Queen, to whom all were so loyal.

Marlborough was both vexed and surprised at the position into which he had too easily allowed himself to be drawn. He agreed with Godolphin and Harley that "the chief thing is to avoid a division in the House because the consequence of that will be . . . that men will look upon themselves to be listed." This would have involved a disastrous crystallization. He therefore urged the Queen to "forgo her message on his behalf, since it might embarrass her affairs and be of ill consequence to the public." On December 15, therefore, the Queen informed the Commons that the Duke of Marlborough had declined her Message to them. She was deeply offended by the rebuff, and not at all inclined to forget it.

Marlborough had only accepted the dukedom in the belief that provision would be made for its maintenance. His emoluments as Commander-in-Chief might be swept away at any time by a cannon-ball, or by loss of favour or a demise of the Crown. The idea of a poor duke seemed ridiculous and unnatural to that age. It was one of the main objects of his life to found a family whose wealth and magnificence would long survive him down the generations. Nor did this seem a vain desire in a society where rank and property were so deeply ingrained and seemed secure and permanent.

It would have been more agreeable to the Muse of History if Marlborough had refused all honours and rewards, and had met the addresses of the Commons by saying that owing to the heavy charges upon the public he had resolved to fight the next campaign on half-pay. But then he would not have been the Marlborough who gained the victories. For certain it is that this same matter-of-fact care for his own interests and desire to found a powerful family in an enduring State was an inherent part of his great deeds. He was a builder for England, for posterity, and for himself. No one of these purposes could be removed without impairing the others, and part of his genius lay in their almost constant harmony.

Meanwhile the new Parliament was aglow with Church and Tory fervour. Dr Sacheverell, a young and vigorous Fellow of Magdalen, had preached an election sermon which had inspired the political campaign. The majority were determined to root out the humbug of Occasional Conformity and at the same time possess themselves of many desirable places of influence and profit. In solemn conclaves, in ardent tavernings, the Members inflamed one another.

There were not wanting men to see in this burning question a path which might lead them far. Here a new actor, destined to play one of the decisive parts, makes his entry upon our stage. Henry St John (later the Viscount Bolingbroke) had been elected as a Tory in 1701 to William's last Parliament. His father had been mulcted £16,000 for a pardon from Charles II for killing a Sir William Estcourt in a brawl in 1684, and bore besides a drunken, rakish reputation. But the fortunes of his house were still substantial, and Henry, after undergoing the usual treatment at Eton and on a foreign tour, arrived in London well furnished with money and representative of the family borough of Wootton Bassett. He reproduced his father's traits, and now at twenty-four was a roysterer and hard-drinker, who lived notoriously with a Miss Gumley, described as "the most expensive demirep in the kingdom." It was said that, impelled by liquor or a wager, he had run naked through the park. But he had besides other qualities of which his father had given no sign. He was from his earliest efforts a most brilliant Parliamentary speaker who always commanded the attention, if not the agreement, of the House of Commons. He had elevation of thought, breadth of view, and rare distinction in his use and comprehension of the English tongue. He also spoke French exceedingly well, and had read discursively but widely in English and European history. Clever, apt, and audacious in the highest degree, he was possessed by ambitions which no scruples were ever seen to hamper. He picked his early steps in politics shrewdly. He chose both a Patron and a Question. The Patron was Harley, and already in 1702 Henry St John by his charming, vivacious assiduity had personally ingratiated himself with that eminent politician. The Question was Occasional Conformity.

The Occasional Conformity Bill was first brought forward in the autumn of 1702. It sought to destroy the abuse by imposing fines on any public official who, having attended Anglican communion presumably for the purpose of qualifying for office, had afterwards reverted to his non-conformist manner of worship. The fines were so heavy as to be prohibitive, and the aid of the 'common informer' was invoked for their enforcement. This measure passed the Commons by a large majority, and was carried by an excited mob of two hundred Members to the Lords. Here the Bill encountered a small but resolute Whig majority, composed in part of King William's thirty peers and his Broad Church bishops.

An immediate conflict between the two Houses arose. Great stresses also showed themselves in the Cabinet and above it, which cast a revealing light upon the politics of the whole reign. The Queen was for the Bill. She felt that the utilizing of the sacrament for the purpose of gaining a place of profit or influence was a malpractice from which the Church she loved and deemed she understood so well should be protected. Her uncle Rochester, the Lord-Lieutenant of Ireland, who remained in London and would rather have been Lord Treasurer, felt both as a Churchman and as a "Highflyer" a strong and sincere indignation, which was in no way lulled by the vehement support which the Bill had gathered in the House of Commons.

So at the outset the Queen, the Commons, the dominant Tory Party, and the characteristic Tory Ministers—the men that the party could trust—were all hot for the Bill. Against it was the barest majority of the Whigs and bishops of the House of Lords. Out-of-doors such an act of hard, calculated aggression by one half of the nation upon the other spread consternation and anger in every shire and town.

This schism was deeply embarrassing to Marlborough and Godolphin. As Tories they found it difficult to repel the arguments for the Bill. Nor did they care to begin their administration by a quarrel with their own party in full career. They did not wish to distress or upset the Queen, nor to consume their influence in persuading her against her will on a Church question, above all others. But if England were to be rent and infuriated by the same kind of passions which had reduced her to impotence in the days of the Popish Plot, how was the war to be carried forward?

Marlborough, viewing the situation with military eye, had no intention of being brought to battle on ground which was so suited to his enemy. He and Godolphin therefore presented an oblique front to Rochester's formidable advance. They avoided his thrust by a practice, which even in our own reformed days is not unknown, of affirming their support for the principle of a Bill while taking steps to get it killed behind the scenes. They shielded Nonconformity from political ruin and preserved the national strength from a mad injury by dissembling their opinions and tricking their party.

Upon the second reading of the Occasional Conformity Bill in the House of Lords Marlborough and Godolphin marched with Rochester. The Queen's ardour can be measured from the fact that she compelled her husband, whom the Bill would have disqualified from public life, to vote for it. But as he filed into the Aye lobby the poor Prince, who suffered many vexations in his comfortable life, was heard to exclaim to the Whig teller, Wharton, of whom Queen Anne so sternly disapproved, "My heart is vid you." The second reading was carried only by twelve votes. Under the promptings of Wharton the Whigs in the Lords pursued sagacious tactics. They carried an amendment, represented as a compromise, reducing the fines to levels where they no longer deterred. Wealthy Dissenters, having already paid something in conscience, would not find it impossible to pay a little more in cash. Thus Occasional Conformity would be brought within the means of any man of reasonable substance likely to be affected.

The time had now come to deal with Rochester. Rochester was the Queen's uncle. She agreed with him in Church and party. He was the lay head of the Church of England which the Queen loved. He was in many ways the leader of the Tory Party which she favoured, and which was master in her new Parliament. But none of this availed Rochester at all when once Marlborough, choosing his moment, finally decided they could work no more together. Many and grievous were the provocations which Rochester gave. He was jealous of Marlborough, and prepared to dispute his ascendancy: but he thought Godolphin was the more vulnerable. Against Godolphin, therefore, he marshalled his influence and his faction. He would pull him down. Godolphin gone, Marlborough would be alone. He did not hesitate to criticize and oppose unpopular measures of the Government of which he was a leading member or to reveal its secrets in damaging debate. He strove ever to increase his authority in both Houses of Parliament at the expense of the Ministry and of public business. When every effort to rally him had failed Marlborough resolved that he should go. Then was seen Anne's loyalty to the old Cockpit days. What use had her uncle been to her when Mr Caliban and her own sister had tried to chase Sarah from the Court, and when Sarah's lord was in the Tower? What had he done when she had wanted her letter carried to Queen Mary? He had failed her in her darkest hour, and he had failed her in order to curry favour with the ruler of the day. But that ruler was no more; and the Princess who had vainly sought his good offices in her distress was now the Queen. Who was he to set himself against her dear and faithful friends—friends who, even against their inclinations and better judgment, as she realized, had newly obliged her by voting for the principle of the Occasional Conformity Bill? Mrs Morley, Mr and Mrs Freeman, and Mr Montgomery, joined in familiar conclave, had no doubt that the dismissal of Rochester would add to their difficulties, of which they already felt the weight. But once Mr Freeman said that it was no good trying to work with him any more, and that he was less dangerous outside than in, the matter was settled.

Early in February 1703 Rochester was astonished by receiving the Queen's command to go to Dublin and discharge his duties as Lord-Lieutenant of Ireland. He took a week to measure forces, and then intimated that it was his higher duty to remain in London. Forthwith his resignation was demanded, with no choice but that of dismissal. He quitted the Queen's Government accordingly, and without a day's delay appeared at the head of the High Tories who sought to wreck it.

In the midst of these activities almost the greatest sorrow that can come to man fell upon Marlborough. His only surviving son was now sixteen. We remember him as a playmate of the poor little Duke of Gloucester. He had been at Eton and had already gone to Cambridge, where Dr Hare, afterwards celebrated as Marlborough's chaplain, whom we shall often meet during his campaigns, and eventually Bishop of Chichester, guided him in religion, morals, and learning. "Notwith-standing his high birth, splendid prospects, and courtly education," ob-serves Archdeacon Coxe ingenuously, "he set an example of affability, regularity, and steadiness, above his years." Life began early in those days, and this handsome, eager youth wanted, of course, to go with his father to the wars. Bred in a martial atmosphere, he was thrilled by camps and soldiers, and especially by reviews and processions. His fa-ther would have liked to have him with him at the front; but his mother thought he was too young. In those days an officer on the staff of the Commander-in-Chief must be frequently under fire, and might be required at any moment to ride with a message into the hottest of the fighting. Sarah could not bring herself to let him go so young— while still a child. Let him stay one more year at Cambridge and finish his studies. Thus was it settled. But Death knows where to keep his appointments.

During the autumn of 1702 Lord Blandford (Marlborough's son) of-ten came over from Cambridge to stay with Lord Godolphin close by at Newmarket, and apparently made the best impression upon the Treas-urer. There was smallpox in the town, but Godolphin thought that he, "going into no house but mine, will I hope be more defended from it by air and riding, without any violent exercise, than he could possibly be anywhere else." Meanwhile the boy was making plans of his own to join the Army, and with a friend was intriguing for commissions in a cavalry regiment.

It was at the end of his long visit to Godolphin that the infection fell upon him. He had scarcely returned to Cambridge in February when he was struck down by virulent smallpox. Sarah was there as fast as horses could bear her, nursing him herself and invoking all that the medical knowledge of those days could do. The Queen hurried her own physicians into the royal coach and sent them posting to Cambridge. It was less than three years since the same scourge had carried off her own child. She wrote to Sarah:

Thursday morning

I writ two words to my dear Mrs Freeman yesterday, and could not help telling her again that I am truly afflicted for the melancholy ac-count that is come again this morning of poor dear Lord Blandford. I pray God grant he may do well, and support you. And give me leave once more to beg you for Christ Jesus' sake to have a care of your dear precious self, and believe me with all the passion imaginable your poor unfortunate faithful Morley.

"I wish," she added in another letter, "that the messenger who carries the medicines which my dear Mrs Freeman sends for could fly, that nothing may be wanting the moment there is any occasion."

Till all hope was abandoned John was kept away. He wrote to Sarah:

Thursday night

I wrote to you this morning, and was in hopes I should have heard again before this time, for I hope the doctors were with you early this morning. If we must be so unhappy as to lose this poor child, I pray God to enable us both to behave ourselves with that resignation which we ought to do. If this uneasiness which I now lie under should last long, I think I could not live. For God's sake, if there be any hope of recovery, let me know it.

Shortly after writing these words he received his summons and, hurrying to Cambridge, arrived as his son expired. On the morning of Saturday, February 20, John and Sarah crept off to Holywell to endure their pangs. The Queen wrote:

St James's
Tuesday night

It would have been a great satisfaction to your poor unfortunate faithful Morley, if you would have given me leave to come to St Albans, for the unfortunate ought to come to the unfortunate. But since you will not have me, I must content myself as well as I can, till I have the happiness of seeing you here. I know nothing worth writing; but if I did, I should not trouble you with it, being sure no sort of news can be agreeable to your dear, heavy heart. God Almighty bless and comfort my dear Mrs Freeman, and be assured I will live and die sincerely yours.

This blow not only cut at the natural feelings of John and Sarah, but seemed to ruin their future. Both were dynasts. To gather wealth and fame and found a family to run on down the ages was their dear— indeed, their over-dear—ambition. Now it was ended. The Duke had to make a fresh will, leaving his already large properties to Sarah in trust for his eldest daughter's husband, Mr Godolphin, to whom he desired that his titles should pass. But he was already overdue at the front. The Dutch awaited him, and the armies were entering the field. He sailed for Holland with a leaden heart in the early days of March. The will, which had not yet been engrossed, was sent after him, and his letters show the anxiety which he felt when the packet-boat containing it was reported captured by a French privateer. To Ailesbury, whom he met at The Hague, he said, "I've lost what is so dear to me, it is fit for me to retire and not toil and labour for I know not who. My daughters are all married." It was in this sombre mood that he began a most harassing campaign.

CHAPTER THIRTY-THREE

"The Great Design"

ʧɑ 1703, Summer Dʒ

MARLBOROUGH arrived at The Hague on March 17 and began forthwith to draw his forces into the field. This year he could concentrate the "grand army" eighty miles south of Nimwegen, around Maestricht. He reviewed his troops and garrisons, beginning with the English at Breda, and inspected all the fortresses of the Meuse from Venloo up to Maestricht. While he marshalled the troops and set all things moving with the utmost activity he argued with the Dutch about the plan of campaign. The evident intentions of Louis XIV to make his effort against the Empire, and to stand on the defensive against the Anglo-Dutch armies, could be countered either by sending large reinforcements to the Moselle or the Upper Rhine, or by decisive action in Flanders. The Prussian King had offered an extra corps of eighteen thousand men for service in the northern theatre, provided that it served as an independent command. Marlborough would have welcomed this, but the States-General, fearing political designs, rejected the powerful aid. There remained the resource of a battle gained among the fortresses, the consequences of which would instantly make Flanders and Brabant the decisive theatre. But Marlborough knew already too well that the Dutch Government and command would never commit themselves to this in cold blood. They might be drawn into a great decision of arms by the force of events, but they would not agree to it beforehand. He did not press them, therefore, to allow him to seek the enemy in the field under the best conditions. Within the limits and in the theatre to which he was restricted there were, however, opportunities of producing

(313)

dominating results. For this purpose he had set his heart on the capture of Ostend and Antwerp. Ostend would give him a new direct communication with England: Antwerp was not only the northern keystone of the French lines, but, more important still, controlled the whole waterway system of the Scheldt, the Lys, and the canals, which with the Meuse formed the principal lines of advance through the fortress zone. These two great trading centres, if won, would open up Belgium to the commerce of the allies. The fall of the city and seaport of Antwerp would offset the success which the French must certainly gather elsewhere, and it seemed almost certain that they would fight a battle in its defence. Moreover, the Tory Party would approve a campaign in which the Navy would play an important part, directed against the coast ports and with promising commercial reactions. It was not only good strategy, but good politics.

The States-General, like Louis XIV, were not averse from sieges. Sieges seemed the safest way of making war; but they looked in the opposite direction. The fortress of Bonn, midway between Cologne and Coblenz, was now the sole barrier to the navigation of the Rhine for three hundred miles from its mouth to Philippsburg. The capture of Bonn would seem to succour the Empire, with which it opened a sure communication. This enterprise had been prepared during the winter, and the Dutch had undertaken to have all in readiness before the end of March.

Marlborough deferred to the Dutch opinion on the understanding that the siege of Bonn should be begun early, pressed with extreme vigour, and disposed of in the early stages of the campaign. Ostend and Antwerp could follow later, if no time were lost. Leaving Overkirk between Maestricht and Liége to guard the line of the Meuse, he marched in the middle of April to the Rhine, forming with the Prussian, Hessian, and Hanoverian troops an army of 40 battalions and 60 squadrons for the siege of Bonn. So backward were the preparations that Cohorn, the expert on whom the Dutch were relying, at the last moment advised that the siege of Bonn should be put off till the autumn. But Marlborough would have none of this.

The siege of Bonn while the armies were still assembling was a serious undertaking. The obvious counterstroke for the French was Liége. Overkirk with the partially formed main army guarded against this danger, but was himself largely outnumbered meanwhile. Bonn was resolutely defended, and the garrison even sallied out upon their assailants. But Marlborough, commanding in person on the spot, used all his power. The Dutch and Germans who composed his army were stout troops, and the artillery was overwhelming. Never before had been seen such a concentration of cannon and munitions as shattered the defences and, indeed, the town of Bonn. Ninety large mortars, many of them six and eight inches in bore, with as much as thirty rounds a day each, five hundred smaller mortars, and over five hundred guns bombarded the doomed fortress. Its outlying works were broken and stormed in fierce fighting, and when the ramparts of the citadel were no more than one great breach the governor averted the final assault by an appeal for terms.

Meanwhile the two French Marshals, Villeroy and Boufflers, had, as expected, been instructed by the King to recapture Liége as a relief, or at the worst an offset, to the siege of Bonn. They too had made large preparations before the campaign opened, and fifteen thousand workmen and three thousand pioneers, together with the necessary stores, were already gathered behind the main French army around Saint-Trond. They had hoped, indeed, to begin the military year by this attack upon Liége. But Marlborough had provided for its solid defence. They now saw in Overkirk's army which lay between Maestricht and Liége an even more tempting prize. Villeroy had in his hand forty thousand men. Overkirk for some time had but fifteen thousand. Probably because of the stringency of supplies, Marlborough had left the English in their cantonments till April 30. He realized the French menace in sufficient time, and ten thousand English, well drilled and in the finest fettle, reached Overkirk on May 9, just before they were needed. On the same day Villeroy marched upon him, and his vanguard attacked Tongres, an entrenched post held by a Dutch and a Scottish battalion in Dutch pay. This handful of allied troops resisted for twenty-four hours the onslaught of the French army. They were not only brave, but lucky. Though forced to surrender at discretion, they fell into the hands of Berwick, by whom they were kindly treated. He hastened to assure the Scots that they were his countrymen and that "no man shall do you wrong." The delay gave time for Overkirk to arm and entrench a strong position under the walls of Maestricht and for Marlborough on the 12th to send a further reinforcement. On the 14th the whole French army drew up in order of battle: but after inspecting the defences and bethinking themselves of their general strategic instructions from Versailles the two Marshals decided not to try conclusions, and withdrew, somewhat abashed, towards their own lines.

Marlborough had measured carefully, and, as was proved, justly, all the factors; but we should not underrate his anxieties sixty miles away at Bonn. The fortress was at its last gasp, but meanwhile a disaster at Maestricht would be ruinous. The crisis at Maestricht arose on the 13th. It was not till the 15th that Bonn surrendered. He certainly passed an unpleasant forty-eight hours. This was the kind of situation he had to gauge many times over in his campaigns, and it is astonishing how almost invariably his summing-up of facts, times, and risks was right.

Marlborough returned to the Meuse not only with relief at the ending of a crisis, but full of ardour to begin the campaign as he had always wished. With the fall of Bonn and the retreat of the Marshals wide prospects opened, and he unfolded to his generals and to the Dutch Government what he called "the Great Design."

Marlborough to Godolphin

Maestricht
May 19

I shall to-morrow send an express to The Hague to see how far they have prepared for what I call the great design; so that we may not lose time in endeavouring to put it in execution. Before I left Bonn, measures were taken for the embarking 20 battalions of foot, if it be possible to get boats enough, and 21 squadrons of horse are to march the nearest way to Bergen-op-Zoom, where they are to join the 20 battalions that go by water. These troops are to take the most advantageous post near Antwerp, after which there will be care taken to join more troops to them. If this design of Antwerp can be brought to perfection, I hope we shall make it very uneasy for them to protect Brussels and the rest of their great towns. I am speaking as if we were masters of Antwerp, *but as yet the two marshals threaten.*

Since this was one of his most cherished and most complicated schemes, and since it miscarried, it is worth some attention. The field armies were almost exactly equal in units, but the allied units were the stronger. The Sea Powers had a superiority of perhaps 73,000 to 67,000 men. But these numbers are uncertain because behind each of the

1. John Duke of Marlborough. BY PERMISSION OF EARL SPENCER.

2. Barbara Duchess of Cleveland. BY PERMISSION OF VISCOUNT DILLON.

3. Sarah Jennings before she married, by Simon Verelst. This portrait always hung in her dressing-room at Holywell. BY PERMISSION OF EARL SPENCER.

4. James II. NATIONAL PORTRAIT GALLERY.

5. The Earl of Marlborough, by John Closterman. NATIONAL PORTRAIT GALLERY.

6. Louis XIV. BY PERMISSION OF THE DUKE OF MARLBOROUGH.

Francis Earl of Godolphin.

7. The Earl of Godolphin. BY PERMISSION OF THE DUKE OF MARLBOROUGH.

8. William III: The Last Phase, by Godfrey Schalcken.
BY PERMISSION OF THE DUKE OF MARLBOROUGH.

9. Sarah Countess of Marlborough. BY PERMISSION OF EARL SPENCER.

10. Robert Harley, by Sir Godfrey Kneller. BOARD ROOM, BRITISH MUSEUM;
BY PERMISSION OF THE TRUSTEES.

11. The Mauritshuis at The Hague: The Banquet to Charles II on the Eve of the Restoration. On Charles's left is his sister Minette; on his right are his mother, Henrietta Maria, and his brother, James, Duke of York; in front is the young Prince of Orange. Marlborough lived in the Mauritshuis from 1701 until its destruction by fire in 1707. FROM A PRINT IN THE POSSESSION OF MR. ERNEST POULTER.

12. Marshal Villeroy, from an engraving after the painting by Hyacinthe Rigaud. BRITISH MUSEUM.

13. Cadogan and Marlborough. BY PERMISSION OF EARL CADOGAN.

14. Sarah Duchess of Marlborough, by Michael Dahl. NATIONAL PORTRAIT
   GALLERY.

15. Queen Anne, by Edmond Lilly. BY PERMISSION OF THE DUKE OF MARL-
BOROUGH.

16. Prince Eugene of Savoy,
by Jacob van Schuppen.
RIJKSMUSEUM, AMSTERDAM.

17. Marshal Tallard.
BY PERMISSION OF
DAVID MINIORE, ESQ.

armies were the garrisons. The French, for instance, had no fewer than 63 battalions spread in their fortresses, and the allies a much smaller number. It depended upon the tactics employed to what extent these garrison reserves could be used. The Dutch were eager to undertake another siege, and Marlborough as usual wished to fight a battle. Although this looked more hazardous, it offered really a larger safety. A siege lasted for weeks and a battle only for a few hours. The margin of allied superiority was scarcely sufficient to undertake a siege, because the moment they had divided their armies for that purpose the French could draw freely from all their garrisons. On the other hand, if the initiative were retained and a number of French fortresses simultaneously threatened by an aggressive field army it would be the French who would have to disperse, and Marlborough could strike at their remaining army. Thus a siege was in fact to risk both the initiative and the superiority.

Forced by the Dutch to adopt the least favourable measure, Marlborough had devised a plan which cast siege warfare in an offensive form. To this end he used the waterways at the delta of the Scheldt to move troops and stores quickly and secretly to the northern front while still keeping his main army in the south. The transportation of twenty battalions from Bonn, on the Rhine, to the neighbourhood of Bergen-op-Zoom, near the coast, was favoured by the current of the rivers, which carried the troop-barges forward night and day far quicker than men on the march; while the necessary cavalry rode swiftly across country. Thus the first phase of the operation was the unexpectedly rapid concentration in the north, while all the time the main armies faced each other at the other end of the theatre. All this was easily accomplished.

The second phase was to force the dispersion of the French troops in the north. For this Cohorn, assisted by the fleet, was to attack and lay siege to Ostend. Ostend is sixty miles from Antwerp. Bedmar, the Spanish-French commander in Antwerp, would thus be compelled either to divide his forces out of all supporting distance or to lose the highly valued seaport. Marlborough foresaw that nothing less than the fear of losing Ostend would tear him asunder.

The third phase depended upon the timing and upon the strict obedience of the secondary commanders. On zero day Marlborough would move first towards the French main army to pin it and then north-west towards Antwerp. Two days later Cohorn would attack Ostend, and

Spaar west of Antwerp. This should produce the division of Bedmar's forces, while Marlborough held the two Marshals so closely that no help could be sent him. On the sixth day Opdam would advance against Antwerp from the north-east. Spaar would attack from the west, and Marlborough would be close at hand near Lierre with the main body. If Bedmar did not divide his forces Ostend would fall, an important prize would be gained, and further combinations would become possible. If, on the other hand, Bedmar defended Ostend, Opdam and Spaar would have a good superiority against him at Antwerp, and no help could come to him from the main army facing Marlborough. The French could choose between losing Ostend or Antwerp or both, or as an alternative weakening their main army, which Marlborough could then attack.

But Marlborough would have required the authority of Napoleon to compel this accurate execution of his intricate plan. Actually the Dutch commanders were not at all interested in Ostend. They were not attracted by opening any new line of communication from the sea to the English forces. They preferred English drafts and stores to pass through Holland. Cohorn used his influence at The Hague to substitute for the siege of Ostend a pillaging excursion into the Pays de Waes (the region between Antwerp and Ostend), from which his office entitled him to receive 10 per cent of any contributions exacted. Now, this diversion was not sufficiently remote from Antwerp to make Bedmar divide his forces beyond the power of swift recovery; and consequently Marlborough's combination would not become operative.

While the forces were taking their new positions in the north, and while Cohorn was busy at The Hague, Marlborough sought to draw Marshal Villeroy southward farther away from Antwerp, hoping that by manœuvres he could place himself nearer Antwerp than the French main army. For this purpose he pretended with many elaborate refinements a siege of Huy. But the French had the advantage of their lines, behind which they could move in safety and along which they had stores of food and forage. Moreover, these lines, following the course of the Demer, bulged out convexly. Thus Marlborough must traverse the arc while Villeroy could follow the chord. Marlborough therefore required a considerable start to win a 'race to Antwerp.'

By the end of May Villeroy was lured down towards Huy, and almost as far from Antwerp as was Marlborough, and the Dutch army which was to begin the operations was gathered to the north of Antwerp and along the seaboard. But already at his camp at Thys Marlborough received the disconcerting news that Cohorn had obtained permission to substitute for the siege of Ostend the raid into the Pays de Waes. The Duke saw at once that this change of plan would spoil his combination: and that his elaborate attempt to make siege and manœuvre warfare serve the purpose of battle, or bring about a battle which neither French nor Dutch could avoid, would not succeed.

Almost the whole of June thus passed in a tense immobility, the two principal armies facing each other at a few miles distance, or sidling this way or that in constant readiness for battle. But now the Dutch began to carry out as a disconnected operation and in the wrong way the northern part of Marlborough's design. On June 26 the attack from the seaboard began. For some days their movements had puzzled Bedmar. He felt himself about to be assailed, but at which point on his lightly guarded sixty-mile front from Antwerp to Ostend he could not tell. On the 27th Cohorn and Spaar fell from opposite directions upon the north-western salient of his lines and pierced them, Cohorn with scarcely any loss, Spaar after hard fighting. The Pays de Waes thus lay open to Dutch incursion, pillage, and contribution. The unwisdom of the Dutch action now became plain. The mere raiding of the countryside and the levying of a contribution, though pleasing to Cohorn and his troops and vexatious to the enemy, failed to make Bedmar change his general conceptions. He remained rightly concentrated in Antwerp. Cohorn's action was only a flourish, and a feint which did not deceive.

There was a second more disastrous error. Opdam, who was to attack Antwerp from the direction of Bergen-op-Zoom, should never have moved until the Cohorn-Spaar operations had had time to draw some reinforcements from Bedmar, nor above all until Marlborough and the main army had come near enough to support him. Nevertheless, the next day, June 28, Opdam, with 13 battalions and 26 squadrons, advanced in this faulty combination to Eckeren, four miles from Antwerp. Here he was in great danger. The three Dutch forces were widely separated from one another, and the French and Spaniards were concentrated in superior strength in the city close to Opdam. His subordinates, Slangenberg at their head, pointed out to him that he might be attacked by the enemy with fifty battalions, or at least three times his numbers. They prevailed on him to send his baggage to the rear. But for the rest he stood his ground, seemingly unconscious of his peril.

No positive information of their offensive had been sent by any of the Dutch generals to Marlborough, still sixty miles away at Thys. But evidently he had news of their movement; for on the 27th he suddenly broke his camp before daybreak and marched in the direction of Antwerp. Villeroy within a few hours was keeping pace with him within his lines along the road Landen-Diest. There could be no doubt that Villeroy could reach Antwerp before Marlborough. But if Opdam took care of himself the allied armies could still concentrate before Antwerp for battle with somewhat superior forces. However, on the 29th Villeroy learned of the Dutch incursion into the Pays de Waes, and also of the arrival of Opdam at Eckeren. He perceived at once that Opdam could be destroyed. On the night of the 29th he sent Marshal Boufflers, with 30 squadrons of cavalry and three thousand Grenadiers, helping themselves forward by holding on to the horsemen's stirrup-leathers, to join Bedmar, with orders to pass through the city of Antwerp and fall upon this exposed Dutch force. Villeroy, weakened by sending this detachment, marched the next day in anxiety lest Marlborough should attack him. But Marlborough did not know what he had done, and in any case was forbidden to seek a battle without specific authority from The Hague. During the 30th both armies were marching on parallel lines towards Antwerp through ceaseless rain and terrible mud. The French had every advantage of the short-cut and the stores of forage behind their lines. Marlborough, without knowing all the facts, was already deeply alarmed about Opdam. On the 29th he had sent him a most urgent warning of his danger and advised his immediate retirement towards Bergen-op-Zoom. But before this message could reach Opdam the blow had fallen.

Early on the morning of July 1 Boufflers, reinforcing Bedmar with his cavalry and Grenadiers, who had marched nearly forty miles in twenty-fours hours, debouched from Antwerp in four columns, and fell upon Opdam. Boufflers had nearly forty thousand men against ten thousand. Luckily for the allies, this large force did not immediately strike its quarry. Berwick says they had "to beat about the country for several hours as hunters would seek a boar." It was not till the evening that the surprise became effective. Opdam found himself enveloped by swiftly approaching superior forces. His line of retreat lay along a causeway to Lillo; but the French cavalry and dragoons, sweeping around his left, cut across the causeway, and had they promptly dug themselves in upon it would have caught everybody. Fierce fighting began. The French troops, strained to the utmost by their march, were met by the stubborn Dutch foot, and several brigades were not only repulsed, but fled in panic back into Antwerp. The ground was divided by dykes and watercourses, and a soldiers' battle began.

Opdam had a humiliating personal experience. With a few officers and horsemen he got separated from his troops, and, believing all was lost, galloped off to Breda. From here he sent two letters, one to Marlborough and one to the States-General, reporting that his army was destroyed. The messenger to Marlborough was captured by the French. The other letter reached The Hague after nightfall. The Council of State met together at Heinsius' house in consternation. Their action was worthy of their greatest national qualities. They at once sent Deputies to organize a front before Bergen-op-Zoom. At the same time they resolved to fill the gap in their forces which the destruction of Opdam's corps seemed to cause by hiring further contingents from Germany. Trusted emissaries took the roads to Münster and Berlin forthwith upon this quest. But meanwhile the Deputies who were on their way to the army met other tidings.

When darkness had fallen on July 1 the fighting was at its height. It continued in much confusion throughout the night. Opdam had disappeared, but on the bloodstained dyke stood Jacob Hop, Treasurer of the Republic. Strengthened by his authority and determination, General Slangenberg took command. Under his orders the Dutch, tough and desperate, beat off the superior numbers of the assailants, stormed and overwhelmed the French cavalry who lay across their line of retreat along the causeway, and when morning dawned were marching in stubborn array towards safety and Lillo. The hand-to-hand fighting in the afternoon and night had been so violent and disordered, and the Dutch at bay had shown such discipline and fury, that Antwerp was full of fugitives, and the French thought at first they had lost not only their prey, but the battle. It was not until daybreak that they realized they at least possessed the field. They hastened to proclaim their victory, set themselves in imposing array, and advanced with drum and trumpet. They had indeed, if they had known it, finally ruptured "The Great Design." But Slangenberg, with the bulk of the Dutch troops, was beyond their reach.

This was the joyful news which met the Deputies as they hurried towards Bergen-op-Zoom, and they returned at once to report to the States-General that, although Opdam had run away and reported his army lost, Slangenberg had not despaired of the Republic and had cut his way out with heavy losses but in good order. Actually each side had lost about two thousand men killed and wounded, and the French had captured six cannon, nine hundred prisoners, and the Countess of Tilly, who was visiting her husband in male attire. (Berwick says "disguised as an Amazon.") The French boastings of victory and of their trophies did not mar the thankfulness of the Dutch at so narrow an escape.

We must now remind the reader of General Slangenberg. We met him last ten years ago at Walcourt when he and Marlborough from the two opposite flanks had fallen upon Marshal d'Humières's imprudently exposed army. Slangenberg's career had not been cheered by success. He had fought his way through William's wars, but his rancorous temper and vicious tongue had marred his fortunes, and he was still only a subordinate. Now in the hour of disaster he had emerged, a stern, embittered man, as the saviour of his country's honour. He was acclaimed with the wildest enthusiasm by both the oligarchy and the mob. His dispatches from the battlefield were modest, but upon this wave of national applause and in his just sense of his own deserts, the hatreds and jealousies which had long festered in his breast burst forth from him in a passion. All the reputation he had gained in that grim night he used to assail not only the conduct but the loyalty of the English Commander-in-Chief. He declared that Marlborough out of spite had left Opdam exposed and unsupported; that when Opdam's jeopardy was apparent he had neither sent him reinforcements (which was physically impossible) nor attacked Villeroy's army (which he was forbidden to do). Opdam, though his personal position was weak, seemed also inclined to associate himself with Slangenberg's charges. We can imagine the unpleasant character of these reproaches from such a man at such a time. But Marlborough's authority in Holland was deeply founded. His friendship with Heinsius, his hold upon the confidence of the Dutch, his position as the Queen of England's Captain-General, were immediately found to be unshakable. There was a storm of criticism. The Dutch pamphlets during this summer are full of bitter references to the "foreign Commander-in-Chief" and his "unheard-of" maxims of war.

But all this abuse recoiled as a wave from the rock. It was Slangenberg who suffered. In Lediard's words, "he lost by his tongue what he had gained by his sword."

This melancholy miscarriage reveals Marlborough's qualities as a general as well as any of his victories. He foresaw the uselessness of Cohorn's raid. He knew at a distance, with almost uncanny prescience and far better than Opdam on the spot, the danger in which that strange military personage stood. He received the news of the downfall of his own plans without discouragement, and instantly formed others to restore the position. All the time while bearing the brunt of responsibility, and vexed by every kind of senseless obstruction, his vigilant, tireless mind has plenty of room for family affairs and for love-letters to Sarah. Afflicted by the most trying provocations, hampered and blamed, the sport of jealous and foolish rivals, the first army of France on his hands, battle possible any day at a few hours' notice, he only shows the more plainly his massive superiority alike over events and men, and over friend and foe.

CHAPTER THIRTY-FOUR

"*Victorious Without Slaughter*"

ᛄ 1703, Autumn ᛞ

THERE was such good Parliamentary support in England for a campaign designed to capture Ostend and Antwerp that Marlborough, despite Slangenberg's virulence and the perturbation in Holland, was able to press hard for the second attempt. Marlborough's letter to Heinsius of July 3 had put the question of a main trial of strength in its most direct form. A council of war of all the Dutch commanders was ordered by the States-General to meet at Bergen-op-Zoom. Marlborough did not at first attend; and at this moment the feeling among the Dutch generals was hot against him. His proposal to force and attack the lines between Antwerp and Lierre was rejected. He refused to accept the first rejection. He repaired in person to the council. Again and again he reiterated his request. At last he actually wrung an assent, in form at least, from this unfavourable tribunal. It was at length resolved to "come to an engagement." The decision of the experts at Bergen-op-Zoom was thereupon remitted to the statesmen at The Hague.

Marlborough did not delude himself. He was gloomily certain that Villeroy would retire behind his fortifications as soon as the whole allied army advanced upon him, and that the Dutch would refuse to attack him there. The event warranted these misgivings. Before daylight on July 23 Slangenberg marched from Lillo to join Marlborough, and the whole army of the Sea Powers advanced upon the French camp. "I take it for granted," wrote Marlborough to Godolphin the night before, "that as soon as they know of our march they will retire behind their lines . . . I think it is one thousand to one they do not stay, for they can be behind their lines in one hour's march."

As soon as the heads of the allied columns were discerned Villeroy burned his camp and stores and swiftly retired within the fortifications of Antwerp and the Lines. Further councils of war ensued. After hours of fruitless discussion Marlborough could only end the conclave by asking all the members to express their views in writing. "I see enough, I think, to be sure the Lines will not be attacked and that we shall return to the Meuse. I intend to go out to-morrow morning with a body of horse in hope to get near enough to view the lines."

The reconnaissance confirmed the Dutch generals in their opinion. What they saw of the strength of the works produced the worst impression upon them. Marlborough was still earnest for a general assault, and we do not know how he proposed to deliver it. But all the others resisted obdurately. Whether he or they were right was not proved. It would certainly have been a frontal attack upon a fortified position defended by an army four-fifths as strong as his own. It was then agreed to abandon the attempt upon Antwerp, and nothing remained but to return to the Meuse and lay siege to the minor fortress of Huy as a consolation.

On August 2 the allies, leaving Cohorn, who had quarrelled with Slangenberg, sulking on the seaboard, marched back southward. Villeroy kept pace with them inside his lines. On the 14th they arrived at Turinne. A corps under the Prince of Anhalt invested and began the siege of Huy, while Marlborough moved to Val Notre-Dame to cover the operation. The investment was completed on August 15.

While the Dutch were effectually paralysing Marlborough in the Low Countries, and frittering away the months in which they had a local superiority, the course of the general war turned sharply and sourly against the allies. The grand conception which the recent treason of the Elector of Bavaria and the progress of the Hungarian revolt had enabled Louis XIV to form was being brilliantly executed. In Italy Vendôme held the flower of the Imperial troops, twenty thousand veterans under Starhemberg, fully occupied. For the whole course of the summer the Austrians were confined in their entrenched camps by overwhelming opposition. Meanwhile the main resources of France were concentrated in Alsace, and acted from Strasburg. The combination of Tallard and Villars completely dominated this theatre. While

Tallard pinned the Margrave to the defence of the Lines of Stollhofen, Villars plunged deep into Germany to join the Elector of Bavaria. On March 11 he had captured his bridgehead, the fortress of Kehl, opposite Strasburg. A choice was open to him. He could join with Tallard in driving the Margrave from his lines, and then take the easy valleys round the north of the Black Forest; or he could attempt to traverse the lonely passes to the south. He chose the mountain road. His vanguard had left Offenburg on April 27, and he followed with the main army on April 30. The Margrave could not believe that Villars intended to lead thirty thousand men through the heart of the Black Forest. Villars was therefore opposed only by the local German militia, and on May 8 he dined with the Elector at Riedlingen, on the Danube. The long-sought-for junction had at last been effected. A Franco-Bavarian army far stronger than any force of which the Empire could dispose stood in the centre of Germany with power to move in any direction.

The French plan unfolded step by step. In June Vendôme, leaving Starhemberg blockaded in his camps, began to move upon the Brenner towards the Tyrol. At the same time the revolt in Hungary assumed a new importance. It had begun as a rising of Roman Catholic peasants against Protestant landlords. Under the influence of French gold and the pressure of French diplomacy it had now become a national Hungarian rebellion against the Emperor. The Protestant landlords armed their Catholic tenantry against a common foe. There then began those disastrous forays in which at times before the end of 1703 the rebels plundered and burned almost to the gates of Vienna. Under these triple thrusts the entire structure of the Empire threatened to dissolve. The exertions of 1702 had ruined its finances; the disasters of 1703 broke its military power. Of what use was it to think of campaigns of the Rhine, of conquests in Italy, or of the Spanish inheritance, when the Austrian Hereditary Lands were the prey of the rebel and the spoiler; and when the venerable capital of Central Europe, Vienna itself, might in a few months witness the triumphal entry of Max Emmanuel, or endure the ravages of the outlaw Rakoczy? Here was this great power of the Empire, which was pledged to place ninety thousand men in the field against France, now completely absorbed by its own perils and internal stresses, able only to cry aloud for help from those allies which it had so woefully failed. Yet the downfall of the Empire meant the loss of the war.

The dyke-mind of the Dutch was possessed by the desire for a strong fortress barrier defended by the largest possible army. Huy commended itself to them as a preliminary to the capture of Limburg and, in a future campaign, the regaining of Namur. These seemed to their statesmen and their generals objectives at once practical and satisfying. But Marlborough felt the war in every theatre. He suffered with the Margrave on the Rhine or on the Danube, with Eugene now trying to quell or appease the Hungarian rebels, with Starhemberg marooned in Italy. He held the nominal command of the largest and finest armies on either side in any quarter. A battle won by these armies even in the fortified zones of the Netherlands would "in three or four hours" change all the values, and the impingement of all the forces throughout Europe. How shameful to sit idle in superior strength at such a time! How horrible to comtemplate the penalty which 1704 would exact for the sloth of 1703!

The Dutch Field Deputies and all the generals gathered round him at Val Notre-Dame, the headquarters from which he covered the siege of Huy. A vehement council of war was held on August 24. Once again he proposed a plan of battle. He demanded a general attack upon the lines, which in this part of the country between the river Mehaigne and the minor fortress of Léau he considered "contemptible." The nature of the country on this sector would allow the whole allied army to be employed. In a battle upon a six-mile front the advantage would rest with the larger army and the heavier fire. The French Marshals would not be able to meet such an assault upon an equal front. Either they would retire, or a trial of strength under favourable conditions would ensue. In Flanders the defeat—perhaps destruction—of the French army and the rupture of their vaunted lines would open fine prospects. In Europe it would stem and turn the tide.

Again the discussions were interminable. This time all the generals except the Dutch—even the commanders of their own mercenaries —agreed with Marlborough. But the Dutch were solid, and the deadlock was complete. Both sides drew up their reasons in writing for submission to The Hague. Marlborough's paper, which was signed by the generals of the English, of the Danes, of the Lünebergers, and of the Hessians, thirteen persons in all, declared:

> If we do not attack the enemy in this place, with the finest troops
> that can be seen, and such superiority as we cannot expect to have

next year, it will be evident, not only to our Allies (to their great discouragement), but the Enemy may with reason boast that these lines, which they will make stronger every day, are an invincible barrier against the troops of the Allies.

. . . The Enemy being superior in Italy, and in the Empire, and being out-numbered no where but here, the Eyes of all the Allies are fixed upon us, and they will have cause justly to blame our conduct, if we do not do all that is possible to relieve them, by obliging the Enemy to call back such succours into these parts, which is not to be done but by pushing boldly.

Against this the Dutch generals contended that the choice lay between attacking the lines or besieging Limburg. "Without doubt the first would be the more glorious attempt, but. . . ."; they then proceeded to elaborate the difficulties of the ground to be attacked, and all the many dangers and obstacles that would be encountered, even if the first assault were successful. For this purpose they enlarged upon the strength of the various positions in rear of the lines. There was one position to which they drew particular attention. "For instance, that of Ramillies, where, their right being extended to the Mehaigne, near Taviers, and their left towards Ramillies, and Autréglise, they will have a narrow aperture of but 1200 paces to defend." The attack upon the lines was forbidden. The siege of Limburg was prescribed.

Even the most hostile Continental historians are struck by Marlborough's resiliency. Every action that he thought vital to the success of the war was denied him. His opinion as Captain-General and deputy Captain-General of the two armies was brushed aside, as though he were a suitor with a doubtful case before some small tribunal. He preserved an imperturbable demeanour.

But his stress of soul and inward vexation were so great as to make him physically ill. To be thus continually thwarted and forbidden to carry out what his genius told him was right, and what his knowledge of the whole war declared vital to the Common Cause, roused passions in his breast, the more tormenting because borne with apparent composure. He burned with suppressed anger; he was wracked with headaches; a profound loathing for the conditions of his task possessed him. He spoke no word of complaint or menace before subordinates, but he resolved to be quit of such stifling responsibilities. This should be his last campaign. He would serve no more under intolerable conditions.

He bore all the responsibility before Europe and before his professional opponents, and yet was constantly prevented from doing justice to his task.

Not so far away across the narrow seas the peaches were ripening in his garden at Holywell. The trees he had planted were growing up, and the trout stirred in the fish-ponds. He had affluence now, the highest rank, and a name already famous. The formidable enemy was the least of his troubles. All his strength was consumed by his friends, allies, and subordinates. On every side—in the field, at The Hague, in Parliament—opponents, rivals, detractors, plied their arts with bristling diligence. Was it strange that home, peace, rest, his children, Sarah, presented themselves in irresistible contrast? But then, the Queen—the Common Cause—the unbroken might of France! A deep longing to retire possessed him. He would not act in haste. At least he would wait until he had calmed his spirit and recovered his health. But he must have relief: he must break away from futile, interminable disputations with jealous or obstinate subordinates. He would go somewhere where he would not see their faces for a while. If all they would do was to besiege Limburg, at any rate he would have this excursion for himself. On September 6 he announced that he proposed to conduct the siege of Limburg in person. Directing the siege, planting the batteries, mingling with the troops, tramping the trenches, in the fresh air and under fire, he regained in a fortnight his poise and good humour.

The capture of Limburg ended the campaign. As the fastness of Guelders, protected by its morasses, had also been starved out during the summer, Spanish Guelderland and the whole of the Bishopric of Liége had been restored to the allies. The capture of Limburg and Guelders raised issues which shook the structure of the Grand Alliance to its foundations, and were of the same nature as those which finally dissolved it. Guelders had been taken by the Prussian general Count Lottum. Louis XIV had already offered Spanish Guelderland to the new Prussian monarchy as a bid for an alliance. Frederick I had with many backward glances spurned the temptation. He not unnaturally claimed as good payment from the allies for his loyalty as he would have received from France for his desertion. But the Dutch wanted Guelders for themselves. It was to be part of their barrier. The States-General demanded that the stronghold should be placed in their charge, and their Commissioner thrust himself forward with warrant and proclamation. But the Prussians said that the fortress captured by Prussian blood must be garrisoned by Prussian troops. They did not care whether it was counted as part of the inheritance of the house of Hapsburg, or whether it fell within the disputed sphere of the Dutch compensation claims. There they were, and there they stayed.

Limburg raised in an even more acute form the rival claims of Holland and the Empire. Here the Empire had the law and the Dutch the force. The Empire was failing in all its obligations to the Alliance. Barely a fifth of the troops it had engaged to march against France were in the field. The Emperor had already craved and received succour. Marlborough had prevailed upon the States-General to send their General Goor and twelve battalions to aid the Margrave between the Rhine and the Danube. While, however, the Hapsburg Empire revealed month by month its awful collapse as a fighting unit, its rulers abated no jot of their titular and sacred rights. Limburg was a part of the Spanish Netherlands—no mere Guelderland or Bishopric, but undoubted Belgium. By all the causes for which the war was being fought it belonged to the Spanish monarchy. But the Dutch, who maintained in their solid persevering manner over 100,000 troops in operation against the enemy, meant to have for themselves Limburg and all the Belgian fortresses Marlborough might take as part of the Dyke, and also for their commercial profit. And here force was on their side. This direct collision between the Empire and the Republic, both indispensable allies, confronted Marlborough with a crucial task. Perhaps one of his reasons, apart from temperamental self-indulgence, for taking the siege into his own hands was the need for him to be in physical control at this diplomatic storm-centre. The representatives of the Empire, strong in their indefeasible right, proceeded to assume the government of Limburg; and the Dutch, with brawn and bayonets, and that kind of rough justice which asserts itself among allies in war whatever the parchments say, pushed the Imperial Commissioner from their path with complete indifference to all the consequences.

Here Marlborough acted the statesman as decisively as he ever acted in the field. He met the pretensions of the Dutch, the appeals of his invaluable friend Heinsius, and the physical obtrusiveness of the Dutch agent, with uncompromising resistance. No one knew better than he the strength of the Dutch and the weakness of the Empire. But if the Grand Alliance was to continue, this seizing of territory as booty wherever the armies marched, without regard to treaties and hereditary rights, must be stopped. He stopped it. The municipal administration of Limburg was transferred to the Imperial Ambassador. It is true that the Dutch, in default of Imperial troops, garrisoned the place, and collected the revenues, but the title-deeds were preserved intact for a future peace conference.

The Dutch alliance was creaking. Parliament had only consented to provide an additional ten thousand men in the beginning of 1703 on the condition that the Dutch abandoned their habit of trading with the enemy. The States-General had agreed to this, but had not kept their word. Pressed as they were for money to carry on the war, they could not in practice deny themselves the earnings of the lucrative French carrying trade; and all their wealthy citizens who lived by this brought, as may well be imagined, every kind of pressure to bear upon the assembly. But the House of Commons was indignant at this process of nourishing France with the one hand while fighting her with the other.

Meanwhile the year 1703 drew to a grievous conclusion for the allies. The two Marshals had successfully discharged their minor part in the Low Countries. They had maintained themselves against superior armies with only the loss of three lesser fortresses out of more than thirty which they held. Elsewhere France had triumphed. The French were dominant in Alsace and upon the Upper Rhine. Their bridgehead from Strasburg to Kehl opened the road to Bavaria. Villars had traversed the Black Forest and joined the Elector. Vendôme, advancing upon the Brenner, had isolated Starhemberg in Italy. The genius of Prince Eugene was absorbed in the distracted war councils of Vienna or in attempting to placate or crush the Hungarian insurgents. The Empire, unyielding in its legal rights, unbending in its ceremonial, was at the last gasp.

Meanwhile elsewhere the position grew steadily worse. At the end of July the Margrave joined his other lieutenant, Count Styrum, who confronted Villars on the Danube. Crossing this river in August, he entered Bavaria and laid siege to the free city of Augsburg. His position exposed Bavaria to ravage. The Elector, drawn by these needs in front, and impelled by the vigorous Tyrolese at the rear, hastened home. His arrival with his well-trained Bavarians transformed the scene. He was able, on the one hand, to besiege Ratisbon, and, marching with his main body, joined Villars opposite Count Styrum on the Danube. Styrum lay across the French communications with a force of eighteen thousand men. He posted himself before the town of Höchstadt, of which we shall hear more in another year. Villars and the Elector, crossing the Danube by the bridgehead fortress of Donauwörth, marched upon him with combined forces. On September 20 Count Styrum, taken between two fires, was defeated in a severe action at Höchstadt and retreated in disorder upon Nördlingen. The Margrave was now himself in turn cut off at Augsburg, but he managed to escape across the Danube and retired into the Black Forest north of Lake Constance. Thus it was the Elector who took the free city of Augsburg; and Ratisbon, the seat of the Imperial Diet, also fell into his hands. The result, therefore, of these complicated marchings and counter-marchings was grievously adverse to the Empire.

In spite of these successes the quarrel between Villars and the Elector grew to a height. The Marshal felt that his grand design against Vienna had been sacrificed for minor and disjointed operations, one of which had been a grotesque failure. His breach with Max Emmanuel became irreparable. Louis XIV had no doubt where his interest lay. He discarded his Marshal in favour of his ally. He deemed the Elector the ablest German prince of the age, with the best army. He regarded the Bavarian alliance as the keystone of his policy in Germany. He foresaw decisive results by this agency and channel in the coming year. He recalled Villars to Versailles, and sent him to cope with the rising in the Cevennes. Marshal Marsin succeeded Villars in the command of the French army in Bavaria.

Marlborough had put the bulk of his army into winter quarters, and was forced himself by the political situation and the insistent appeals of Godolphin to return to England.

The Dutch were well satisfied with the campaign of 1703. They struck a medal with Queen Anne on the obverse, and on the reverse Marlborough on horseback being presented with three keys in a basin by a nymph adorned with a mural crown. The inscription was truthful. "Victorious without slaughter, by the taking of Bonn, Huy, and Limburg."

We can imagine with what measured words and gestures and inward scorn and sorrow Marlborough received these local tributes. He never ceased to think of the war as a whole. To him the wide scene of strife and struggle, which spread through so many lands and involved the fortunes of almost all the nations, was but one. He saw himself only an actor in a single theatre without power, yet the presiding mind of the entire confederacy. These three fortresses were all that could be gained in the Netherlands during a year of definite superiority. Meanwhile what had happened in Germany? What ruin impended upon the Empire? And what chance, if the Empire fell, for the allied cause? While the sturdy, obstinate, short-sighted Dutch clapped their hands and struck their medals, Marlborough and Louis XIV were agreed in their measure of 1703. Versailles knew the year had been disastrous for the allies. France had run risks in the Low Countries in order to lay broad and deep the foundations of future conquests in Germany and Austria. In the Northern sphere they had not even lost Antwerp. Of what avail would Bonn, Huy, and Limburg be compared with the fall of Vienna and the destruction of the Hapsburg monarchy, for which all was now prepared? What would be the fate of the Dutch? What would be the value of the petty successes of an English adventurer, not even a prince, a mere Queen's favourite, the son of a country squire, when the large armies, which would force a separate peace upon the Empire in 1704, turned their victorious bayonets upon the Netherlands? Let him strut in his new dukedom; let his Queen be flattered with ill-founded praise; let them have their medals! The year was approaching when the long, profound designs and strategy of the Great King would bear their golden fruit—absolute victory of the French armies in the East. Then might the Republic and England beg for such terms as the magnanimity of Europe's master would accord.

Our General saw all this as clearly as his foes. It was with the deepest feelings of grief and fear for the public cause and a distaste for the part he had to play that he took leave of his Dutch admirers. He saw that this fleeting hour of "victory without slaughter" was probably the prelude to slaughter without victory. The attitude of the States-General and the Dutch oligarchy towards him was that of loving masters to an indispensable servant, without whom they would suffer disaster, but whom they nevertheless were determined to control. "No battles" was still their rule; and how well it had answered! The illustrious Duke, the dauntless commander, the link of the Alliance, so skilful, so reasonable, so reassuring, was the man of all others they needed. If only they could keep his fighting propensities within bounds! And had they not suc-

ceeded during two whole years? Had they not reconquered wide territories and important fortresses? Was not the hostile cannonade driven
now far to the southward? Was not the Republic relieved from all
danger of invasion? Not even could they hear the sound of guns. And
might not all have been cast away "in three or four hours" if they had
let him fight a battle—he who had never fought a battle in his life?
They were equally grateful to him for what he had done, and for what
they had compelled him not to do.

But he had tempted them so often, pressed them so hard, coaxed
them so much, and his reasonings on the general war were so grave,
that in their hearts were serious misgivings. Marlborough was plain with
Heinsius and his colleagues. They were deeply conscious of the unspoken reproach which his sombre reception of their compliments conveyed. Perhaps he had been right after all. It would be awful if the
Empire fell. How wonderful if the lines had been forced and the army
of the two Marshals had been broken up in the field! Was this
Ramillies position really so strong as their generals had declared? Thus
the Dutch searched their hearts as they conducted their Deputy Captain-General to the quay.

CHAPTER THIRTY-FIVE

The Queen's Commands

ᒡ 1703, Winter ᒣ

SINCE the days of Job no man's patience has been more tried than Marlborough's in 1703. The year had begun with the death of his only son. It was to end in a melancholy breach with his beloved wife. We have seen how his campaign had been spoilt by the Dutch, and the endless vexations which the "many-headed Republic" inflicted on its own servants. He returned to England heartily sick and weary of his command, and determined, whatever might happen, never to exercise it again under similar conditions. But the situation awaiting him at home was not less baffling and distasteful.

The violence of the High Tory attacks upon the conduct of the war put the Whig Party in an awkward plight. Although the Whigs were angry because they had no larger share of the offices, they had hitherto most loyally voted the supplies and sustained the policy of a great land war; but they expected results. Without victories and solid gains they saw themselves stultified and pilloried in the party fight. They were the war party. The Tories said it was *their* war. As the year closed under its succession of heavy blows—as the French grip closed on the Upper Rhine and the Moselle, as the Empire broke down everywhere, as the Dutch would venture nothing, and Marlborough came home with little to show, the Whigs felt that as a party they must reconsider their position.

There was much to be said for their leaders making a triple arrangement with Marlborough-Godolphin and the Dutch. Such a combination might plough its way through the less highly wrought substances;

but would Marlborough agree? Would or could the Dutch play the part assigned? The Lords of the Junto—eminent, wealthy, powerful, uplifted above the crowd, masters of their party, the famous Ministers of King William's reign, nursing the wounds and insults they had received from the new régime; convinced that they had the secret of British greatness and British freedom in their keeping—coldly and massively reached a definite decision. There must be an end to the friendly relations they had preserved with Marlborough and Godolphin. The Whig Party—its strength in the Commons, its majority in the Lords, its landed magnates, its City financiers, its chapel-going folk of every class, the entire Dissenting interest, all their orators, pamphleteers, and newspapers—must turn their fire in a new direction. Marlborough must be accused of military incompetence. Marlborough and Godolphin must be charged jointly with the malevolent wasting of the subsidies and with a deliberate frustration of the projects of the war amounting to malignant treachery against the State. Language of this kind, it was felt, would outstrip all Tory abuse of Marlborough and Godolphin, and save the Whig Party from the reproach of having drawn the nation into a disastrous war. The war was right: the policy was good: King William was a true prophet; but his majestic designs were being cast away by corrupt, incapable, and malicious Ministers who fattened upon the cruel misfortunes of the times and feared lest even victory might put an end to their evil reign. This seemed the most promising line; and the whole Whig Party worked themselves up on it. Both parties therefore delivered their full blast of competitive calumny against Marlborough and Godolphin.

Accordingly Marlborough was assailed by the Whigs in speech and pamphlet as a supporter of the Occasional Conformity Bill, as a suspected Jacobite, and as a bigoted defender of the Prerogative of the Crown. They accused him—of all men—of acting defensively in Flanders, while wasting national strength upon useless naval expeditions. The Tory attack took exactly the opposite form on nearly all points. The Whigs were angry because he had not allowed them a larger share of the offices: the Tories because he would not let them drive out what Whigs there were. The Tories made no scruple of working with Rochester, and the mass of their party outside, against Godolphin and Marlborough. Not only did they oppose their policy, but they revealed their secrets, and sought to cast the blame for every misfortune and difficulty upon them. Opposed by conviction and party tenet to England's large share in the Continental war, they laboured to make it unpopular, and recked little if it were unsuccessful.

Many methods lay to their hands: of these, the first was to become strong critics of the Dutch. Every shortcoming of the Republic in its obligations as an ally—its tardiness in supplying ships or money; its underhand trading with the enemy; nay, its interference with Marlborough's military plans—was used to prove the unwisdom of being so deeply involved with so perverse and selfish a State. They did not care what ill-will was bred between the two countries. Why should England be dragged on to the mainland to waste her life and treasure and the splendid opportunities which offered overseas, to gratify the selfish desires of an individual? When Ministers set on foot such propaganda their followers could hardly be blamed for spreading it.

During the whole of the summer Godolphin had been worried out of his life by incessant attempts to isolate him from his own party and supplant him in the Queen's favour. He repeatedly appealed to Marlborough to allow him to resign. Marlborough, burning inwardly against the Dutch Deputies and generals, who thwarted him on every occasion, brought his plans to nought, and sullenly forbade the battle which would have cleared the air and established his authority, had, nevertheless, to bear all this in silence, lest his enemies at home should use his complaints to mar the alliance. There is no doubt that the two "Great Ministers," with the weight of the war and the Grand Alliance on their hands, were now strained to breaking-point.

When they turned their gaze from the fierce feuds and intrigues of English and Dutch politics to the general war, it was only to encounter an even darker scene. For the new campaign Louis XIV was placing in the field eight separate armies, each commanded by a Marshal of France. Nor could there be much doubt where the fatal blow would fall. The Empire was the prey, and Vienna the prize. The contingents from different German states paid by the Sea Powers were still available for the defence of Southern Germany; but a further advance of the French and Bavarians would recall them all, in accordance with their subsidy treaties, for the local defence of their own home lands. The defeat of the Empire spelt the ruin of the confederacy and the final triumph of France. Meanwhile, as we have seen, the States-General had little thought beyond gathering the largest numbers of

Dutch, auxiliary, and English troops for the defence (without battles) of the approaches to their own frontiers; and the English Parliament was moving powerfully towards leaving them to do this by themselves.

Marlborough realized with sombre conviction that the general defeat of the allies was approaching. The components of the confederacy would make separately what terms they could with the conqueror: a supreme Catholicizing monarchy of Gallican stamp would be erected upon the Continent by French bayonets; and Protestant England, little England with its six million people, with its trade and newly planted Empire, would be left alone to face the wrath and appetite of this enormous rival.

Since no coherent plan for common action could be devised; since even his sword-arm in the field was fettered; since his every movement was baulked by clinging hands and censured by shrill voices; since responsibility with odium, but without power, was all that was offered, and even that dreary situation grudged—why should not the Captain-General and the Lord Treasurer yield these awful burdens to those who coveted them so ravenously? Why not retire from "these uneasy and troublesome broils"? Why struggle further for the privilege of being involved in a vast catastrophe? Their would-be successors pressed avidly forward. Why not let them have their wish? He and Godolphin had done their best. It was not that Marlborough feared the task: the task was not confided. It was not that he felt unequal to it. Indeed, part of his trials consisted in seeing so clearly what ought to be done, and was prevented. Give him a reasonably free hand to direct the war-policy even only of the two countries of which he was Captain-General, even only for a year, and he felt sure he could transform the scene. But to be at once burdened, paralysed, and abused was more than could be endured.

But now Queen Anne struck her blow for the victory and the greatness of her country. She had reigned barely two years, but far behind her, it seemed, lay the "sunshine day," that brief space after the weight of Caliban had been lifted from her shoulders and before the weight of his cares was fastened there instead. She felt the distress and rising temper of those about her, the servants she knew best and trusted most. She resolved to draw them together around her in a new endeavour. Putting aside for the time being all her feelings about Whigs and Tories and her honest, inevitable differences with her bosom friend, she wrote Sarah a letter, magnificent and momentous, which ranks her with Queen Elizabeth and the greatest sovereigns of the English line.

> Windsor
> Saturday

> The thoughts that both my dear Mrs Freeman and Mr Freeman seem to have of retiring gives me no small uneasiness, and therefore I must say something on that subject. It is no wonder at all that people in your posts should be weary of the world, who are so continually troubled with all the hurry and impertinencies of it; but give me leave to say you should a little consider your faithful friends and poor country, which must be ruined if ever you should put your melancholy thoughts in execution. As for your poor unfortunate faithful Morley, she could not bear it; for if ever you should forsake me, I would have nothing more to do with the world, but make another abdication; for what is a crown when the support of it is gone. I never will forsake your dear self, Mr Freeman, nor Mr Montgomery, but always be your constant faithful servant; and we four must never part, till death mows us down with his impartial hand.

Sarah's letters throughout the year give no sign of her appreciating the nobility of the Queen's gesture. But Marlborough was moved in every fibre of his being. Under the captaincy of his mind and the smooth surface of his manners his soul flamed within him. He would endure all things and dare all things: he would not despair: he would not lose patience: he would find a way to make the Queen victorious, or perish in the attempt.

With regard to the command of the armies the Whigs had a definite plan. Marlborough must be removed. The country could run such risks no longer. Moreover, his resolve never to take the field again under the Dutch restrictions of the 1703 campaign was widely known. Through King William's old friend Portland the Whig leaders discussed with the Grand Pensionary whether the supreme command might not be transferred to the Elector of Hanover, the lawful heir to the English throne. Thus the Prince who was to preserve the Protestant succession and restore the Whig supremacy would be at the head of the armies, leading the English troops, and ready, should the Queen's health fail, to claim his Parliamentary rights with all the advantages of armed force. It was hoped that Marlborough would consent to advise the proposed new Commander-in-Chief. This scheme was duly brought before him. Through Sarah and Sunderland, wife and son-in-law, he had contact with the Junto and must have received early and accurate accounts of their designs. To the astonishment of every one in the secret Whig circles, Marlborough agreed at once to the plan. He declared himself ready as commander of the English Army to serve under the command of the Elector, and to use his best endeavours. "Marlborough himself," write Portland to Heinsius, "seems to be *very strongly* drawn to this plan, and will be relieved and contented to be under the Elector's orders."

There is scarcely any doubt that Marlborough meant what he said. Not only was he sickened of his treatment by the Dutch and wearied by the clatter of eloquent malice directed upon him in England, but also he saw a way of procuring a better direction of the war as chief of the staff under a royal head than as titular commander. He lent himself fully and frankly to the scheme. That it failed was no fault of his; and here again we see the unfathomable mystery which Marlborough's character presents. Did he know all the time that the Dutch would never agree to the transference of the command to so considerable a prince of the German Empire who himself provided a substantial mercenary contingent? Was he always sure that this Whig proposal would be choked in the inundations of Dutch obstinacy? There is no telling. We think that he had reached a point in human endurance when he did not care what happened to his own career; that at this moment ambition was utterly quenched. He would serve the Queen wherever it would help most.

The Dutch executives were staggered at this development. They had conceived themselves throughout the year in imminent danger of a widespread domestic revolt against their authority and the continuance of the war. They knew their generals hated Marlborough. All their experts said his notions of war were unprofessional and unsound. But the more the men who knew him thought about losing him the less they liked it. And how would they enjoy this German prince at the head of their armies? So they took no decision. Once again their natural obstructiveness stood them in good stead. They let the weeks slip by, and the campaign of 1704 drew near in its appalling panoply.

The increasing gravity of events at home, and the imminent resumption of the war along all its fronts, weighed heavily upon every one who was not diverted by the excitement of party politics. Harley not only was the best judge of House of Commons opinion, but took great pains to inform himself of public feeling throughout the country. He had a number of agents of remarkable quality and discernment, who prowled to and fro in the land from Cornwall to Scotland sending him their reports. Daniel Defoe was one of these; Paterson was another. It is in one of Paterson's letters that we find the best epitome of the situation:

> The face of affairs both at home and abroad requires another kind of resolution and vigour than, perhaps, ever yet appeared in the councils. *Two or three choice men should show another sort of courage and resolution than you and they have done yet in this reign.*

It was in this temper that Marlborough now revolved the strategic problems of 1704.

CHAPTER THIRTY-SIX

The Genesis of Blenheim

୫ 1704, Spring ଽ

IN a war involving nearly the whole world it was natural that each campaign should offer to both sides a wide choice of plans, for and against any one of which there was much to be said. Each plan had to be weighed not only on its own merits, but in relation to all the others in the general setting of the war. The wonderful results which followed Marlborough's march to the Danube have led historians and biographers to hail the idea as if it were in itself an inspiration of genius. In fact, however, it was only one of the more daring moves upon the board which must have been present in the minds of all the chief authorities carrying on the war, and the only questions open about it were: Was it the best, and could it be done? But these were the riddles of the Sphinx.

The Empire had been crying for help throughout the whole of 1703, and as its plight grew worse it cried the louder. Wratislaw was the principal mouthpiece of the appeal. In him the Emperor had an agent of tireless activity and the highest persuasiveness and tact. He knew the desperate straits to which the Empire was reduced; he had the whole picture of the war in his mind; he saw deep into the politics of London and The Hague, and he had the confidence of Marlborough and Heinsius. In his importunity he moved to and fro between all the Courts and headquarters of the confederates emphasizing the peril of the collapse of the Hapsburgs and its imminence, and begging for troops and money. He further urged that, to avert the defeat and break up of the alliance, the main effort of the allies in 1704 must be made outside the Netherlands. A successful offensive upon the Moselle by an Anglo-Dutch army would have advantages. It would set free the Imperial forces under the Margrave of Baden to make head against the Elector of Bavaria. An offensive on the Upper Rhine would be better; for then the allied armies would be nearer together and able to help one another more. But most of all he pressed for the gathering together of all available troops to strike down the Elector and close the awful gap which exposed the heart of the Empire. All this was the natural, obvious point of view for the Emperor's representative to take. But Wratislaw rendered fine service to his master in pressing upon Marlborough the boldest course of all, in choosing the occasions of his advocacy, in preserving the best contacts, and in smoothing away difficulties and misunderstandings. If Eugene, now head of the War Council in Vienna, did not ask Marlborough to come to Bavaria with an army, it was not because he did not desire it above all things; but because he thought it was beyond hope. Wratislaw, in personal relation with Marlborough, and comprehending the pressures to which he was subjected, did not despair. Nor did he risk anything by asking for the best: it might be the surest way of getting at least the second best.

As early as February 1703 the Imperial Envoy had urged upon Marlborough the dispatch of an auxiliary corps to meet the Bavarian danger. Marlborough did not oppose this, but, being then absorbed in "the great design" against Antwerp and Ostend, and hoping for a decisive battle in Flanders or Brabant, he only induced the States-General to spare twelve Dutch battalions.

Marlborough was, of course, pondering how he would fight his campaign of 1704, if, indeed, he were called upon to do so. He had come home in November determined that he would not repeat his odious experiences of the late campaign in the Netherlands. Upon this his decision was final. If he were to command it must be upon the Moselle or the Upper Rhine, and the Dutch must give him proper control of the army.

Whether he was, at this time, weighing the chances of a campaign on the Danube can never be known. He conferred with Wratislaw at the end of January on the eve of a visit to The Hague to discuss the war plans for the year with the Dutch. Marlborough then said, "It is my intention to induce the States-General to decide upon a siege of Landau, or a diversion on the Moselle. I should be very glad to march there myself, but as it is difficult to move the Dutch to a defensive, which would at the same time be an offensive, I should be able to get at most only 45 battalions and some 60 squadrons for that purpose. Should I take Landau I would supply the Margrave of Baden with as many troops as possible, so as to enable him to overthrow the Elector of Bavaria." He authorized Wratislaw to report this statement both to the Margrave and to Prince Eugene, as well as to the Emperor. He strictly enjoined that nothing should be said to the Dutch; he would deal with them himself.

There were three important points in this statement. He was resolved, first, to fight outside the Netherlands; secondly, to have an independent army (for the numbers he specified corresponded exactly to the troops in English pay); and, thirdly, he sought the overthrow of the Elector Max Emmanuel. Of these the second is the most remarkable. The Anglo-Dutch forces had been so long intermingled under King William and in the present war that the separation of those paid by the Queen from those paid by the States-General would be a startling departure from the ingrained habits of the two allies. Marlborough had been forced to this decision by the treatment we have described, which rendered military success impossible. He must have a separate army under his own orders, and he would perhaps go himself as far as Landau. More than that could not then, and cannot now, be said of his intentions up to this time.

The Duke started for The Hague in very severe weather on January 26. The winter had been so bitter and tempestuous that his yacht was the first vessel which "for six weeks had ventured to navigate the German Sea." He landed at Rotterdam three days later. He found opinion and affairs equally unpromising. There was great anxiety about the peril to the Emperor and the Empire, combined with an obstinate helplessness to take any steps to avert it.

We must suppose that by this time Marlborough had examined in very considerable detail the possibilities and methods of carrying the war to the Moselle, to the Upper Rhine, or to the Danube, and that the essential features of all these three plans were marshalled in his mind. It is impossible to fathom the working of his mind from his manipulation of the different factors. Whether he intended by this move to bring matters to a head, or whether his schemes as yet went no farther than the Moselle, cannot be stated. At any rate, this movement increased the alarm, and should spur the efforts, of the Empire and of the German princes, and it presented the idea of a campaign on the Moselle to the Dutch in the agreeable form of some of their troops actually coming nearer home.

Marlborough left The Hague for his brief return to England seriously concerned by all that he learned there. He wrote to Sarah (February 20 or 21):

> For this campaign I see so very ill a prospect that I am extremely out of heart. But God's will be done; and I must be for this year very uneasy, for in all the other campaigns I had an opinion of being able to do something for the common cause; but in this I have no other hopes than that some lucky accident may enable me to do good.

The German princes, headed by the Elector Palatine, now joined their appeals for the succour of Germany to those of the Emperor. Marlborough's orders to the Hanoverian and Cellian troops to descend the Rhine tortured the Empire.

Meanwhile Wratislaw continued almost daily his entreaties to Marlborough to "come to the aid of the distressed German fatherland"; and more and more he urged that he should come in person. The astute Ambassador seems to have felt that here he was pressing the Captain-General where he wanted to be pressed. He gave important assurances that if Marlborough would come, the Emperor would "meet all his wishes." The Margrave of Baden and the other Imperial commanders would defer to his judgment. The whole authority of the Imperial Crown would be cast against the Elector of Bavaria. His destruction would be the sole object of the campaign. On the other hand, he declared that if the Commander-in-Chief allowed the large English army to be used only to guard the Dutch frontier, while the Emperor, the faithful ally of England, was overwhelmed by superior force, the fortunes of the Empire would not fall alone, but would in their collapse bring down the whole. And if Marlborough, out of deference to the Dutch, confined within the narrow ambit of their supposititious patriotism, failed to rise to the occasion, on his head before Europe and the English Parliament would the blame fall. Thus Wratislaw wrestled with Marlborough during the whole of March, and thus Marlborough, continually obtaining conditions, consented to be wooed.

He had serious need to explore the ground thoroughly. The politics of the German princes made a strange embroidery of half-friendships and hungry ambitions. The attitude of Frederick I also deserved deep study. The new Prussian kingdom was voracious. By the treaty in which the Emperor had recognized his new kingship Frederick I was bound to provide eight thousand men for the Grand Alliance. Now that Franconia was menaced by the advance of the Franco-Bavarian army towards Nördlingen and Nuremberg, the Prussian King offered nearly double this quota. As before the campaign of 1703 he had been willing to send eighteen thousand Prussians to join the Anglo-Dutch army on the Meuse or the Moselle *provided they constituted an independent command,* so now he offered fifteen thousand men to protect Franconia on the same condition.

These examples suffice to illustrate the dangerous web of German affairs. Marlborough was aware of these shifting, indeed sinister relations. He had to measure the potential movements of his allies with as much care as those of the enemy, or his own marches and the supply of his own troops. Whether these evil tendencies would become dominant in 1704 turned upon belief or disbelief in the victory of France. The Grand Alliance quivered at this moment in every part of its vast fragile organization. Marlborough saw that without some enormous new upholding force it must come clattering down. Could he impart that force, or would he, if he tried, only be buried in the ruins? No wonder as he listened to Wratislaw's advocacy he weighed all things carefully in his massive scales.

When Marlborough returned to The Hague in the third week of April two most important points were established. The leading personages in Holland had made up their minds that some kind of campaign on the Moselle was inevitable, and that they would have to play their part. The second was that, unknown to the Dutch, Marlborough had procured from the Imperial Court satisfactory conditions for a campaign on the Danube. The Dutch authorities had taken a big step forward without suspecting any ultimate desire, and the Empire spread a carpet of welcome at his feet. We cannot pronounce how far these advantages were the result of the designs of Marlborough or of the course of events. He must by now have studied in hard detail the elaborate mechanism of a march to the Danube and also of the campaign in Bavaria if he got there. This comprised, first, the military disengagement from the Dutch of whatever army he could gather; secondly, the safety of the Netherlands in his absence; thirdly, the movement of his army up the Rhine and through the German states; fourthly, the movements which the French would make when they saw what he was doing; fifthly, the supply and financing of his army and its re-equipment through Germany as might be necessary at every stage; sixthly, the opening of a new and natural line of communications into Germany once he had entered the Danube basin; and, seventhly, how to coerce or crush the Elector of Bavaria. None of these matters could be left vaguely to chance, and, as we shall see from the marvellous smoothness with which everything was executed, all must have been foreseen and prepared.

It was, of course, indispensable to have some authority from the Queen and the Cabinet. Godolphin certainly knew henceforward what Marlborough meant to do. No one can ever know what Marlborough, or Sarah—so far as she was instructed—said to the Queen, and Anne certainly would not have greatly concerned herself with the strategic significance of the various theatres mentioned. But it may be taken as certain that she knew that her army was to be sent very far into Europe to save the Empire, and that she meant that it should go, and desired to bear the consequences, whatever they might be.

We have thus examined the genesis of the Blenheim campaign. It will be seen that Wratislaw, going beyond his instructions, pleaded for it; that Marlborough, at a moment which cannot be fixed, undertook it; that Godolphin shared the responsibility; and that the Queen, trusting in her devoted servants, issued the commands they desired of her.

Sarah had been smitten to the core by the death of her son. It affected, said one observer, "not only her heart, but her brain." It had "near touched" her head, wrote another. The hope to which she had clung of bearing another son had failed in the summer, and she underwent not only grief, but those profound changes which mark the sad climacteric in a woman's life. Some time at the end of the year she persuaded herself that John had been unfaithful to her, and was obsessed with the idea that he was intriguing with, or "sending to," some lady upon whose identity Time has cast a decorous veil. It would seem from the letters that Lord Sunderland had made mischief in family, as well as in political, affairs. He had said something to his mother-in-law which had thrown her into paroxysms of rage and distress. Husband and wife had been happy in a brief spell together at Holywell, and this trouble fell upon them when they came back to London to meet the insistent demands of public affairs.

John to Sarah

London
[April 1704]

* When I do swear to you as I do that I love you, it is not dissembling. As I know your temper, I am very sensible that what I say signifies nothing. However, I can't forbear repeating what I said yesterday, which is that I never sent to her in my life, and may my happiness in the other world as well as in this depend upon the truth of this. If there be aught that I could do to let you know my innocency I should be glad to do it, tho I am sensible you can never esteem me: so that long life is not what I wish for, but after my death you may have juster and kinder thoughts of me than is possible for you to have of me whilst I am living. You say that every hour since I came from St Albans has given you fresh assurances of my hating you, and that you know I have sent to this woman; these two things are barbarous, for I have not for these many years thought myself so happy by your kindness as for these last five or six days, and if you could at that same time think I hated you I am most miserable. And for the last which you say you are sure of, may I and all that is dear to me be curs'd if ever I sent to her, or had anything to do with her, or ever endeavoured to have.

Marlborough sailed again for the wars on April 8. With him were Wratislaw, his brother General Churchill, Cadogan, Orkney, and many other officers, and, of course, Cardonnel. A fleet of transports carrying four infantry regiments and several thousand drafts convoyed by battleships and frigates accompanied him. He must have bade a grim farewell to England. Sarah was at the waterside. The breach between them was not closed. She knew that he was going upon a high and dangerous enterprise, that there was desperation in his mood, that he would be in the forefront of great battles, that she might never see him again. Yet he was her whole life.

His feelings about his own affairs and his country's fortune were sombre. The national and political situation was dangerous and hateful. On every side were jealousy and baseness. The Tory Party was still harrying the Dissenters. The Whigs and Tories hated each other worse than the foreign enemy. The Lords and Commons were at bitter variance. Scotland seemed to be moving, not to union with England, but to a separate peace with France and a neutrality which could only mean civil war. The Cabinet struggles were burning swiftly into crisis. The old arrangement had broken in pieces, the new had not yet been established. Even the throne of the Queen seemed to quiver. Beyond the cold, rough sea bristled all the obstinate, intricate confusions of Dutch politics, and the cracking structure of the Grand Alliance; and beyond them all—if only he could reach them—stood the foe.

CHAPTER THIRTY-SEVEN

Trepanning an Army

❧ 1704, April ☙

MARLBOROUGH and Wratislaw arrived in Holland on April 21. "With Marlborough's journey," wrote Johann Philipp von Hoffmann, the Imperial Minister Resident in London, to his master the Emperor, "the conduct of foreign affairs will be transferred from London to The Hague."

Unfortunately at this juncture Heinsius was ailing. Marlborough in fact was now acting in sole responsibility. He found the Dutch in the worst of moods, resolved to keep all their forces in Flanders, except, as a great concession and for the sake of agreement, to allow fifteen thousand men to go to the Moselle. He warned the Deputies for Secret Affairs at the outset that Louis XIV would open the campaign by sending another French corps to reinforce the Elector in Bavaria. It would therefore be wrong to recall the troops paid by the Maritime Powers which were already on the spot. His first trial of strength was taken upon this, the easiest issue. The four provinces of Guelders, Groningen, Zeeland, and Utrecht argued none the less for the recall of the troops; but Marlborough, aided by the Pensionary, gained the support of the Deputies of Friesland and Overyssel, and, above all, of the Deputy for the predominant province of Holland. After many hours the decision was reached not to withdraw the troops from Germany for the present. This marked a first and definite success.

The Duke then proceeded to argue for a strong campaign upon the Moselle. The fifteen thousand troops suggested were useless; they bore no proportion to any plan. A good army must be formed there which he would command. As the anxious debate rambled on Marlborough disclosed day by day a little more of his intentions. It became clearer to his audience that he had made up his mind. Presently he mentioned that, if opportunity offered, he would join battle with the enemy without consulting the States-General or the Field-Deputies. A hum of disapproval swept the crowded council chamber.

There must be an end to all this. The hostile armies were now coming into action in every theatre. On May 2 he struck his decisive blow. Having put his views to the three Dutch Generals with whom he could work best, Overkirk, Dopff, and Goor, he requested a meeting with the heads of the Government in the house of the Grand Pensionary. Here the Dutchmen saw a different Marlborough. Hitherto their valued Deputy Captain-General had always submitted to their final judgment. This day it was otherwise. Marlborough declared that he meant to march with the whole of the English and English-paid troops to Coblenz. He displayed upon the table the Order in Council he had obtained, in circumstances already described, from the Queen. When the Ministers sought to continue the argument he silenced them with hauteur, the more impressive because unwonted. He observed that, this being the definite order of the Queen, he could not permit himself to criticize or discuss it. He charged them so to inform the States-General.

The full conference the next day met in a tense atmosphere. The Deputies besought the Duke to explain his plan more precisely. On this he took up a position difficult to assail; the plan must be reserved for settlement with the Margrave of Baden. It was not for him alone to prescribe its tactical features before he had even met the eminent soldier at whose side he was to serve. And then in the pause which followed he added with alarming irrelevance, "Care must be taken about the necessary supplies of powder." At this the resistance of the assembly gave way. What else could they do? The only choice open was a campaign on the Moselle in which they would be consulted, or one in which they would be left to themselves. It was the shock they needed. The Captain-General's firm decision "deprived the governing classes of the Netherlands of the will to resist." Having yielded, they gave, like the robust folk they were, the Duke their heartfelt blessing, and promised whatever aid was in their power.

Nothing, of course, had been proposed to the States-General but the

Moselle. The arguments about the impending fall of the Empire and ruin of the confederacy were addressed solely to the proposition that Marlborough should transport an army to Coblenz. If anyone had blurted out the Danube or even the Upper Rhine, the course of history might have been deflected. Marlborough had already set on foot many preparations for supplies, and the necessary agencies of finance centring upon Coblenz and Frankfort, all of which would be necessary to carry a main thrust of the allies up the Moselle. Much of this was bound to leak out. In fact, Marlborough did not seem to care very much if it did. His customary secrecy and reserve seemed to break down upon this aspect. He had already written a letter to the King of Prussia imparting to him the outline of the Moselle operation, going so far as to name dates and places where collisions might occur, and inviting his royal and military opinion thereupon.

While this decision was being extorted from the Dutch, Marlborough had required Wratislaw to secure most explicit pledges from the Emperor that he would proceed against his rebellious vassal with the utmost rigour. He required an Imperial order to the Margrave, "in his own hand or that of the King of the Romans; to put all other schemes aside and to operate with Marlborough against the Elector." He asked also for the presence of Prince Eugene.

On May 6, Wratislaw wrote to the Margrave to inform him that Marlborough would advance by way of Coblenz and the South. "I assure your Highness," he added, "that Marlborough sets out with the fixed intention of taking a hand in that great enterprise. His own words are: *The issue in this matter is victory or death*." These were very unusual expressions for the sober-spoken and matter-of-fact Marlborough. Assuredly they did not go beyond the naked truth.

The Emperor for his part had already on May 15 agreed to the sending of Prince Eugene:

> From this decision on my part there should readily be deduced the eagerness with which I take part in this matter, and how greatly I hope for a happy issue, inasmuch as in the present state of affairs I am sending away from myself and my supreme war council a person that I value so highly.

Further, he wrote to the Margrave on May 14:

> On the fortunate result of this stroke depends the salvation of us all and the desired object of this war. Because of our paternal anxiety

for the Empire, and in accordance with the obligation of the Alliance, *I will not consent to any other operation at the opening of this campaign.*

Before we set forth on the famous adventure it will be convenient to take leave of English politics for a time. The resolve which Marlborough had taken before leaving England to have done with Nottingham, who was "doing her majesty all the hurt that he is capable of," had now borne fruit. Nottingham did not underrate the quality of his opponents, nor the probable accuracy of Marlborough's information of his designs. He doubtless knew that Marlborough and Godolphin were preparing to drive him from power, and he now resolved to forestall them. Shortly after Marlborough sailed for the Continent Nottingham presented to Godolphin, and afterwards, to the Queen, a very direct ultimatum. It was impossible, he intimated, to continue with a hybrid Ministry. Either it must be Tory or it must be Whig. If it were Tory he and his friends would form a united Administration to serve the Queen and carry on the war as they thought fit. If it were Whig they would oppose the Government by every means in their power. The Queen must choose, and to prove her choice he demanded the immediate dismissal of the Whig Dukes of Somerset and Devonshire from their offices and from the Privy Council. Unless these requests were complied with, he would tender his resignation.

Such language coming from a Minister who commanded a majority in the House of Commons necessarily brought all political affairs to a crisis. But Nottingham did not rightly measure Queen Anne. He counted too much upon the respect and liking which the Queen had for him and, like Rochester the year before, on her personal sympathy with his principles in Church and State. He did not understand that Anne more than anything else wanted her England to win the war, and was prepared to suppress her dearest convictions for that purpose. He did not even now realize that, compared with Mr Freeman and Mr Montgomery, he was only a great noble and a high functionary. Moreover, his challenging procedure and the criticism which his party had permitted themselves to direct against the Queen were bound to rouse her slow but massive combativeness and engage her royal pride, her sense of duty to the nation and of loyalty to her general and the army he was leading so far. We may also suppose that Marlborough, Godolphin, and Mr Speaker Harley had a well-concerted plan of action, and knew where they stood with the sovereign.

When Nottingham tendered his resignation the Queen desired him to reconsider the matter. But a few days later, instead of parting with the Whig Dukes of Somerset and Devonshire, two Tory Ministers, Sir Edward Seymour and the Earl of Jersey, Nottingham's immediate adherents, were summarily dismissed from their offices. They hastened indignant to vaunt their wounds to their startled party.

Nottingham was so staggered by the rough dismissal of his friends that he seemed inclined to leave his own resignation in abeyance. The mood of the Tory Party left him no choice. He renewed his request to retire, and was at once shown the door. Officially the Tory Party now went into opposition. But it was soon apparent that there was a considerable body of Tory Members who were indisposed to violent faction in the midst of an adverse war. These Members clustered around the Speaker, and a rift soon opened between them and the main body of their party. It was evident that the immediate sequel to the dismissal of Nottingham must be a system based upon Harley and the moderate Tories, or 'Sneakers,' as they were unkindly called by all true 'gentlemen of England.'

Marlborough must have had a good understanding with Harley before he left England, and he pressed upon Godolphin his prompt appointment to the vacant Secretaryship of State. The new system for the House of Commons pivoted on Harley. The replacement of Nottingham must be made without delay. Any interlude would be not only detrimental, but dangerous. The political foundation must be made as solid as possible in view of the stresses to which it would soon be exposed. "By what you say to me," Marlborough wrote to Godolphin from Vorst on May 7, "I take it for granted by the next post to hear Lord Nottingham has given up the Seal, which makes me beg you will take no excuse from 46 [Harley] but that he must immediately come in."

Harley showed a becoming diffidence, and even affected repugnance to accepting the seals. His scruples were overcome, and on May 18 he added the principal Secretaryship of State to his far-reaching duties as Speaker of the House of Commons.

Thus there was constructed another 'National' Ministry in which Whigs and Tories found their places. But the real Tory Party, dominated by the country clergy, was embattled against the Government, and in direct pursuit of Marlborough and Godolphin; while the Whigs were not sufficiently represented to bind them as a party. The new Ministry had no majority in the House of Commons. But the supply for the year had already been voted, Parliament was about to be prorogued, and before it met again the war would be lost or won.

CHAPTER THIRTY-EIGHT

The March to the Danube

&d 1704, May D&

THE annals of the British Army contain no more heroic episode than this march from the North Sea to the Danube. The strategy which conceived, the secrecy and skill which performed, and the superb victory which crowned the enterprise have always ranked among the finest examples of the art of war. But a brighter and truer glory shines upon the Man than can be won by military genius alone. Never did lifeboat captain launch forth to the rescue of a ship in distress with more selfless devotion to duty. Not Wolfe before Quebec, not Nelson before Trafalgar, nursed a purer love of his country's cause than Marlborough in this supreme passage in his career. The profound calculations which he made, both political and military, could only present a sum of dangers against which forethought could make no provision. All that gallant army that marched with him risked life and honour: but he alone bore the burden. It was for them to obey the lawful authorities. For him the task was to persuade, deceive, and defy them for their own salvation.

Marlborough felt the greatest compulsion that can come to anyone —the responsibility of proprietorship. It had become his war. He was the hub of the wheel. He was bound to function. He had made the treaties. He had accepted William's bequest. He must discharge it faithfully. He must bring it all to success and safety. The task was his. These foolish-frantic Parliaments, jealous princes, hungry generals, and bitter politicians were all, as he conceived it, in his care. He alone knew the path which would lead them out of their tangles and tribulations, and he was bound to force or trick them to salvation if he could.

Although none of the dangers of his enterprise had been surmounted and its hazards were necessarily imponderable, Marlborough's spirits were high as his coach bore him eastward. He had gathered his army, and wrested it from the Dutch trammels. At last he had an army of his own to command. The Government he left behind in England was no doubt weakened and its foes increased by the purge of the High Tories, but at least it was united and coherent. The Lord Treasurer should be able to hold his own till the autumn, and before then the die would be cast in the open field, and the fate of Europe and the war settled one way or the other. Without a victory of the first order and the signal destruction of one of the main armies of France, all was already lost. But he knew himself and he knew his men, and longed earnestly for the ordeal. Moreover, though the sword was in his hand and battle was his quest, there was peace in his heart, for Sarah was kind. One crashing blow to restore the allied cause and then home and quiet, leaving "a good name behind." Thus he mused while the coach rumbled on towards the magnificence of Keppel's country seat, where he would "lie one night" on his way to the army on the Meuse.

Louis XIV had prepared himself to renew the war on all his eight fronts. He and his Marshals in the north and east took it for granted that the initiative rested with them, and from January to March they indulged in the agreeable exercise of choosing where they should throw their weight, what regions to invade, and what fortresses to capture. They surveyed with satisfaction the results of 1703. Trèves and Trarbach, now in their hands, gave them the control of the Moselle. The capture of Landau secured the Upper Rhine. The capture of Kehl and Old Brisach gave them good gateways into Germany. Thus many alternatives were open.

Very long letters were written by the Marshals Villeroy, Tallard, and Marsin to each other and to Chamillart, the Minister of War, and from time to time these letters were answered at equal length by the King. The longest of all were written by Marshal Tallard. In an easy, graceful style, observing the fullest etiquette of old-world gentlemen to one another, and with the profound ceremony due to the first of gentlemen and the first of kings, they discoursed agreeably upon the forthcoming operations. It was a pity the letters took so long to go to and fro; but when one is controlling such great events there should be time for calm procedure. There was no doubt that Max Emmanuel must be

(357)

reinforced. Marsin's army had received neither recruits nor remounts for nearly a year. He needed strong drafts for all branches, including especially armourers with their flints, etc., to repair the muskets and technical stores. Thus replenished, he and Max Emmanuel believed that they could attack Nördlingen and Nuremberg in the early summer and thus make secure the foundation for an advance which would eventually carry them to Vienna. It was settled that Villeroy should stand on the defensive in the Low Countries, and that Germany should be attacked both by Tallard down the Upper Rhine and by Marsin and the Elector down the Danube. The strong combined offensive in the Italian theatre already proposed should at the same time be launched by Vendôme, by his brother, the Grand Prior, and by La Feuillade upon the Duke of Savoy. The first step of all these operations was the reinforcement of Marsin and the Elector. For this Marshal Tallard assumed the responsibility.

Thus the campaign opened in the south. The Elector of Bavaria, with Marshal Marsin, had constructed a strong entrenched camp astride the Danube below Ulm. Here, almost surrounded by ramparts and flowing water, they lay with a Franco-Bavarian army of forty thousand men, representing the depleted units of a much larger force. The first step in the main French design was to raise this army to its proper strength. For this purpose Marshal Tallard had collected drafts of ten thousand men at Strasburg. It was arranged that he should try to pass these troops through the Black Forest towards Ulm under the protection of his own army of eighteen thousand men, and that the Elector should meet them on the way with an adequate force and ample supplies. Accordingly on May 4 the Elector and Marsin, leaving fourteen thousand men around Ulm, marched westward with thirty thousand men and an enormous convoy of wagons, intending to take over the reinforcements from Tallard near Villingen. The army of the Margrave, Prince Louis of Baden, also about thirty thousand strong, was spread along the Upper Rhine mainly in the lines of Stollhofen, while his lieutenant, Count Styrum, with ten thousand men, watched the Elector at Ulm. Styrum thought he had a chance, in spite of his small numbers, of striking at the Elector as he wended westward, accompanied by his heavy convoy. But the Margrave, wishing to make sure, set out from Stollhofen with two-thirds of his force to join him, and forbade the attack till he arrived. He united with Styrum on May 19; but it was then

too late. The Elector had already reached the neighbourhood of Villingen, and was in touch with Tallard. That Marshal had started from
Strasburg on the 13th. He had slipped by the fortress of Freiburg, running the gauntlet of its cannon at six hundred yards in the darkness of
night without loss of life. He had brought the drafts safely through the
Black Forest, and during the 19th and 20th handed them over to the
Elector and Marsin.

The united Franco-Bavarian army was now somewhat superior to
that of Margrave, forty thousand against thirty thousand. But the new
drafts were not yet incorporated, and the convoy was a burden. The
Margrave therefore planned to strike at the Elector while his long columns were passing through the defile of Stockach, in the difficult country north of Lake Constance. This promised great results, for the Bavarians were short of food, and the pass narrow. He was, however, again
too late, and after their rearguard had been engaged in a brisk cannonade on May 24, the Elector and Marsin returned successfully with
their reinforcements to their stronghold north of Ulm. Thus by the
end of May Tallard had succeeded in reinforcing the Franco-Bavarian
army to a total of fifty thousand men. The Margrave was blamed for
his double failure to interfere with this concentration. He continued
with his main force opposite Ulm, while Tallard, his mission accomplished, resumed his station on the Upper Rhine. The first move in the
French plan was thus completed.

Meanwhile, however, in Flanders, two hundred and fifty miles away
to the northward, something had happened which immediately attracted and thenceforward dominated the attention of all the French
commanders. A scarlet caterpillar, upon which all eyes were at once
fixed, began to crawl steadfastly day by day across the map of Europe,
dragging the whole war along with it.[1] During the early part of May it
became apparent to the French that Marlborough was dividing the allied forces in Flanders into two armies, one of which, under Overkirk,
lay around Maestricht, while the other was assembling at Bedburg and
might amount to twenty thousand men, and certainly included the
bulk of the English. On May 19, the same day when at the other end
of the theatre Tallard was passing his reinforcements to the Elector,
this new army began to march towards the Rhine. On the 21st it was

[1] This epithet is justified by the variety of tints in red, scarlet, and crimson prevailing in the British uniforms of the period.

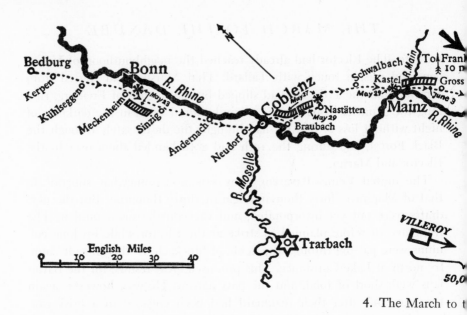

4. The March to t

at Kühlseggen. On the 23rd it was at Sinzig, and evidently moving towards Coblenz. It was also known that Marlborough was at its head. The natural conclusion of the French High Command was that he intended a campaign on the Moselle, with the fortresses of Trarbach and Trèves as his immediate targets. The very moment that his movement up the Rhine had become apparent Villeroy, leaving Bedmar with twenty-five thousand men to face Overkirk, started with twenty-one thousand men through the Ardennes for the new scene of operations. He wrote to Versailles explaining that "there was only danger at the point where the Duke in person stood at the head of the allied troops." On May 27 the Marshal was at Arlon, forty miles from Trèves. Tallard was also returning to Strasburg from the south. The French thus conceived themselves not ill-arranged to meet Marlborough along the Moselle; but obviously Tallard could not quit the Rhine until Marlborough was definitely committed to the Moselle. Nor, of course, could the Elector and Marsin begin their march upon Nördlingen and Nuremberg while everything had been thrown into such uncertainty in the north.

The French plan of campaign which had opened propitiously must now be held in suspense. Marsin on the Danube, Tallard on the Rhine, Villeroy on the Moselle, Bedmar on the Meuse—all stood still, waiting with strained attention upon Marlborough's movements. From

nube May 23–June 25

the very outset, therefore, the initiative had passed from the whole line of French armies to the English commander. The pressure upon Overkirk had been relieved by Villeroy's departure, and Flanders was safe. A respite had been gained for Franconia. But the French hoped that this disconcerting check to their plans would not last long. The Englishman was marching fast, and would surely turn up the Moselle at Coblenz. At this stage we may leave the French Marshals and the Great King waiting and guessing while precious days slip by, and return to Marlborough and his army.

On May 16 Marlborough had set out from Maestricht to overtake his troops. On the 18th, near Bedburg, he passed them in review. The force which began the famous movement comprised at this outset, and for the greater part of the march, 14 battalions, and 19 squadrons, representing England, Ireland, Scotland, and Wales, and the English Artillery, with 20 foreign squadrons, in all about nineteen thousand men.

Few cities in Europe are more strikingly placed than Coblenz. It stands opposite the majestic rock-fortress of Ehrenbreitstein on the long tongue of land formed by the confluence of the Rhine and the Moselle. No one can visit this spot and watch the gleaming Moselle mingle in the broad, swelling flood of the larger river without feeling its geographical significance. Captain Parker and Sergeant Millner both

(361)

describe the dramatic moment when after marching thus far with the Rhine on their left hand, and crossing the Moselle by the stone bridge, they saw that, instead of turning to the right up the tributary towards France, the long column held on by the Rhine for another mile, and then lo! on the left lay two bridges of boats across which the battalions were swiftly filing deeper into Germany. All day long the passage of the Rhine continued, and by nightfall on the 29th the British foot and cannon had been swallowed up in the hills and gorges upon the farther side. Marlborough and the cavalry were already two marches ahead.

In those days espionage was easy and we must suppose that the French agents mingled with the Coblenz crowds on this day. They had seen the bridges built across the Rhine. They had seen the cavalry pass over, but these might be merely pretences. What they had to report was which turning the infantry and artillery took. Now they knew. In the hostels of backstreets men mounted their horses and rode westward into the night along the Moselle. Ride, horsemen, ride! Ride to Villeroy, to Tallard, and on to Paris, bearing news of high consequence. "There will be no campaign upon the Moselle. The English have all gone higher up into Germany."

Once across the Rhine the scarlet caterpillar progressed amid flowers and blessings. Now it was no devastated region but the beautiful, smiling Rhine valley in the glory of summer which welcomed the marching columns of horse and foot with every sign of gratitude and admiration. Then, as in later times, the costly excellence of the British equipment attracted attention. Bouquets and waving of ribbons, friendly helpful hands, and bands of smiling women and girls—"some of them much handsomer," says Captain Pope characteristically, "than we expected to find in this country"—cheered the long marches. High and low, from prince to peasant, the Germans greeted their rescuers. And around all an embracing forethought, at once sure and easy, provided for all their needs.

Thus a complete outfit of new shoes for the whole army had been secretly prepared at Frankfort for issue to the troops. The saddlery of the cavalry was similarly kept in the highest condition, and in every particular the British and all other forces in the Queen's pay were maintained as they deserved. These continual evidences of design unfolding day after day bred in all ranks that faith in their commander which, once rooted, is hard to destroy, while at the same time the eyes of a grateful population convinced the soldiers of the righteousness of their cause.

Thus this march is remarkable among military operations both for the detail in which it had been prepared and the secrecy and mystery in which it was shrouded from the enemy. Alike for its audacity and forethought, alike for its strategic swiftness and day-to-day comfort, it was a model which in those days had no copies. We wonder how it was done when organization by our standards was so primitive, and the staff employed so small. None of those large departments of A (Adjutant-General), G (General Staff), and Q (Quartermaster-General) existed. In fact, the full classification was not to be made for two hundred years of military history. Four or five men, each with no more than as many clerks and officers around them, handled the whole affair. Cadogan, Cardonnel, Davenant, the English agent at Frankfort, stand out almost alone at this stage as Marlborough's managers. He had picked them all carefully and tried them long. He must have kept the whole central grip in his own mind largely without any written record. All were men of high quality in their different functions, and each accepted without question the orders they received from their chief.

Thus the columns rippled along the roads as the scarlet caterpillar beat the ground rhythmically with its feet. Up the hills and down the hills, through the forests and gorges, across the Main and across the Neckar, always wending on, while the Great King and his Marshals readjusted their views from week to week, and Europe from one end to the other became conscious of an impending event.

On June 3 Marlborough's cavalry, now reinforced by various allied contingents from the German states to eighty squadrons, crossed the Neckar at Ladenburg by the floating bridge and encamped on the other side. Here he halted for three days to allow Churchill with the infantry and cannon to overtake him. It was not till the 7th, when his brother was only two marches away, that he moved again, this time in the direction which finally revealed his purpose. He turned sharply east to Sinzheim, which no doubt he remembered from the days of Turenne, and headed openly for the Danube. Once again the messengers sped to the French headquarters.

The news that Marlborough had crossed not only the Rhine but the Main created a profound sensation at Versailles. While the Marshals had waited and wondered, while they interchanged anxious messages with Paris, while they canvassed every possibility, the strategic situation had been gradually but remorselessly transformed. All Marlborough's calculations had been justified. Villeroy had not attacked the weakened Dutch, but had been drawn south, first to the Moselle and then to the Upper Rhine. The Dutch had been obliged by the force of facts to accept and condone Marlborough's movement and to reinforce him against their wishes up to the limits he required. He was now in Swabia with the power to concentrate nearly fifty thousand men, and in sure and easy contact with the Margrave, whose forces at Stollhofen and opposite Ulm, together with various detachments, were of about the same strength. Allied armies of about a hundred thousand men stood in harmonious relation in a central position between the Rhine and the Danube, while the two enemy armies, though not much inferior in numbers, lay at opposite sides of the circle, separated from each other by distance and stronger forces, and able to reinforce or join each other only by long and painful détours; and each was liable meanwhile to be attacked by overwhelming strength. Finally, Marlborough could soon, if need be, discard the whole of his communications by the Rhine and establish a new direct line of communication north-east behind him into Germany.

It was with consternation that the French chiefs felt the weight of these facts upon their well-trained military minds. Villeroy and Tallard understood plainly the peril in which the army of the Elector and Marsin lay. That army, gathered for the march to Vienna, was now exposed to attack within a fortnight by very much stronger forces, many of whom had marched across Europe for that express purpose. Bavaria, the deserter state, lay open to invasion by the confederates her ruler had so grievously wronged. The two Marshals saw how easy it would be for Marlborough to leave one-third of the combined forces to hold them off on the Rhine, while he threw his main weight against their comrades on the Danube. But what to do?

The story of the next fortnight is one of futility and paralysis in the French High Command. The Marshals thrust their burden back upon the King. They sent him not one plan, but four, each with its own memorandum setting forth the grave or destructive objections to it. In mid-May they had been choosing between prizes: now there was only a choice of evils. Tallard began his covering letter with a disconcerting sentence. "In view of the superiority of the enemy forces between the Rhine and the Danube, assistance to Bavaria is so difficult as to appear almost an impossibility." In short, the Marshals avowed themselves completely baffled.

Thus the tables were completely turned, and nearly all the strategic advantages the French had enjoyed in the middle of May had been transferred to their opponents by the end of June. And this by manœuvres of almost equal forces without a shot fired in either siege or battle.

As early as June 5 the Elector had heard that Eugene was in the field. He immediately divined that he had been sent from Vienna to attack him. He even foresaw the exact plan of campaign which would be used against him. That same day he wrote his supplication for help from Louis XIV. Marshal Marsin supported him by a more explicit letter two days later. It was no longer a question, said the Marshal, of strengthening the Franco-Bavarian army for offensive action, but of saving the Elector from being forced out of the war and the French troops with him from being cut off and destroyed. If the King did not send a new army to help him, but, on the contrary, his enemies received one, Max Emmanuel would in despair embark his wife, children, and treasure on the Danube to seek safety with the Hungarian rebels. "Monsieur," wrote Marsin, "judge of the condition of a prince who can fall back on no other resource to save his family!"

On this the King made up his mind. He consulted the Marshals, who were shirking their responsibilities no further. On June 23 he sent his orders to Villeroy.

> It is then my intention that you, Marshal Tallard, and General Coigny should divide all my troops which you and they command in Alsace into three corps. That of Marshal Tallard is to advance over the mountains. . . .
>
> The second army which you command should advance to Offenburg, observe the enemy, retain them in the lines of Stollhofen, follow them into Alsace, or join Marshal Tallard with the whole or a part if they move all their troops towards the Danube.
>
> The corps which Coigny is to command will safeguard Alsace. The Swiss regiments, even my Swiss Guards, will form part of this corps, as I have no intention of forcing them to cross the Rhine against their will. . . .

The Marshals had asked for orders, and now they had got them. But when on June 27 they sat over these orders at Langenkendal, they were filled with deep misgivings. Villeroy was deprecatory, but Tallard was outspoken. His complaint was bitter. The superior armies of the enemy between the Rhine and the Danube, he protested, would at any time be able to join together, while the French and Bavarian forces would be "always separated, in the air, and dependent on what the enemy decides to do." The infantry assigned to him was perhaps sufficient, but with only 50 squadrons of cavalry he declared his task impossible. Fifty more squadrons were required, and also the presence of an army in the Rhine Valley strong enough to prevent Eugene from leaving it. Unhappily, these forces did not exist.

Nevertheless both the Marshals obeyed. Tallard crossed the Rhine at Kehl, and began his southward march around the long curve to Villingen on July 1. Villeroy followed him and took up his station at Offenburg. Thus at last a decision had been wrung from the French. But Marlborough had also moved.

CHAPTER THIRTY-NINE

Marlborough and Eugene

⊰ 1704, June ⊱

MARLBOROUGH at Wiesloch credited the enemy with more clarity of view and decision than they possessed. He thought it probable that their answer to his march would be either a violent attack upon the Lines of Stollhofen or that very bridging of the Rhine and thrust into the valley of the Neckar towards Stuttgart that Louis XIV had favoured but had not resolved. He must set up a shield upon the Upper Rhine strong enough to give him time to come to conclusions with Bavaria. Moreover, his own position was complicated because the Danish reinforcements which the States-General had sent after him, without which he had not enough strength, were still nearly a fortnight behind him.

Towards the end of May Prince Eugene had left Vienna for the Margrave's headquarters at some distance before Ulm. Marlborough now sent Wratislaw to the Imperial camp to explain the situation and procure compliance with its needs. It is plain that he wished to have Eugene with him on the Danube, and that the Margrave should undertake the defence of the Rhine. But one or the other must go to the Rhine at once.

On June 8 Wratislaw reached the Margrave's headquarters at Aermingen. Prince Eugene had already arrived, but the conversation was begun between Wratislaw and the Margrave alone. The Margrave agreed at once that the army on the Upper Rhine must be strengthened. On the question of who should go there he remarked casually but decisively, "You will have great difficulty in persuading the Prince of Savoy to take the command." At this moment Eugene entered the

(367)

room: Wratislaw began his story over again. Marlborough, he said, considered that the army on the Upper Rhine must forthwith be reinforced. Either the Margrave or Prince Eugene must take command of it. Here the Margrave broke in, "Try to persuade the Prince to do so. For in the army he is the only man who could be entrusted with a command so responsible *and subject to so many risks.*" The reference to the "many risks" was shrewdly calculated. Eugene's temperament and sense of military honour were evidently well known to the Margrave. He knew he was leaving no choice open. Eugene answered as a soldier: "The Emperor has sent me into the Empire to serve under the command of his Lieutenant-General, and as I have never made difficulties about going wherever duty called me, I am quite ready to carry out the order of the Lieutenant-General. But I must remind you that, as our weakness and the enemy's strength there are quite well known, I must have left with me sufficient troops to put me in a position *to attack* the enemy."

The Margrave, having secured his main point, made no difficulty about distributing the forces. He transferred to Prince Eugene all the Würtemberg troops in Dutch pay and offered the whole of the Prussian corps of eleven battalions and twenty squadrons, if they were found willing to go. What followed shows the curious conditions of these times. The Margrave sent for the Prussian commander, Prince Leopold of Anhalt-Dessau, and tendered him the choice of serving with the main army or with Eugene. If he opted for the main army, he was warned that he might be sent into districts where it would be impossible for the Margrave to guarantee his troops a daily bread-ration. Anhalt-Dessau put this issue bluntly—"Starve or obey"—to his generals. They decided to go to the Rhine. The fortresses and garrisons in the Black Forest, Freiburg, Villingen, Rothweil, and some smaller places also passed to Eugene.

The command and the partition of the forces being thus determined, the Margrave opened a third topic. He mentioned that he had received approaches from the Elector. This roused the suspicions of Wratislaw and Eugene. So he had been in personal touch with Max Emmanuel during all the abortive operations which had enabled the French and Bavarians to combine their armies. The Margrave explained the nature of the Elector's proposals: how he "wanted to play Ulm into the hands of the Empire," to join the allies with sixteen thousand men and "treat the French if they would not agree in such a way that they would never forget it," always provided that the conditions offered to him were "sufficiently good."

The Margrave said that the negotiations would first of all be concerned with a personal meeting between him and the Elector; and the Elector had said he would welcome at this meeting the presence of Prince Eugene. His two colleagues were stiffly reserved and adverse. Wratislaw wrote to the Emperor, ". . . we are of the opinion that the Margrave is unwilling to attack the Elector vigorously or to do him injury."

In the evening of Tuesday, June 10, Eugene with Wratislaw reached Marlborough's camp. The Duke received his illustrious comrade with the highest military honours, and after a banquet described as "magnificent" the two generals spent several hours in each other's company. Then at once began that glorious brotherhood in arms which neither victory nor misfortune could disturb, before which jealousy and misunderstanding were powerless, and of which the history of war furnishes no equal example. The two men took to one another from the outset. They both thought and spoke about war in the same way, measured the vast forces at work by the same standards, and above all alike looked to a great battle with its awful risks as the means by which their problems would be solved.

Both, moreover, possessed the highest outlook on the war; for Eugene, though in the field, was still head of the Imperial War Council, and Marlborough was not only Commander-in-Chief of the English and Dutch armies, but very largely a Prime Minister as well. They could therefore feel towards the whole problem a responsibility different from that of the leaders of individual armies, however large. It must have been very refreshing to Eugene after his toilsome discussions at Vienna and with the Margrave, and to Marlborough after the long, paralysing obstructiveness of the Dutch, to find themselves in such perfect harmony upon the essentials of their task. Each felt the relief which comes from the shadow of a great rock in a thirsty land. In the midst of the intrigues, cross-purposes, and half-measures of a vast, unwieldy coalition trying to make war, here was the spirit of concord, design, and action.

Strangely different were they in appearance and manner; the Englishman with his noble, symmetrical features and pink-and-white complexion, with his languid courtier air and quizzical smile, and with that sense of calm and power which was his aura: the French-Austrian-Italian death's head, vibrant with energy, olive-dark, fiery like a banked furnace; Marlborough bland, grave, affable, cool: Eugene ardent, staccato, theatrical, heroic. Nor was the contrast of their lives less marked. Marlborough, the model husband and father, concerned with building up a home, founding a family, and gathering a fortune to sustain it: Eugene, a bachelor—nay, almost a misogynist—disdainful of money, content with his bright sword and his lifelong animosities against Louis XIV. Certainly quite different kinds of men; yet when their eyes met each recognized a kindred spirit in all that governs war. They were in action, as has been well said, "two bodies with one soul."

The two men were together from Tuesday till Friday, and the more they talked over what they had to do the better they understood and liked one another. The fullest confidences were interchanged between the two chiefs. Here and now they resolved one way or another to bring matters to a supreme trial with the French before the campaign ended, and, although they must at first be separated for a time, to combine for that purpose. This desultory but costly and possibly fatal warfare of sieges and manœuvres of nicely balanced forces, advancing and retiring according to the rules of war, exercising strategic influences upon each other with many bows and scrapes at the public expense, could only lead to destruction. It must be made to give place to a bloody punch and death-grip; and on this they would stake their lives and honour, and the lives of all the soldiers they could command. Surveying the general war, we can see that matters had now come to such a pitch that, without a great victory in two or three months, the Grand Alliance was doomed. Something had to be produced outstanding, and beyond the ordinary course of events, which would transform the scene. Safety and self-preservation demanded the stake of all for all. On that day they must be together.

Meanwhile the Margrave was approaching. He was, as arranged, reinforcing the Rhine front at Stollhofen from his army opposite the Elector, with 9 squadrons and 15 battalions, perhaps twelve thousand men. On the morning of the 13th he was a day's journey from Heppach. No pains were spared to gain his good-will.

The three generals met before the Lamb Inn at Gross Heppach under a great tree still distinguishable in the nineteenth century. Marlborough was the eldest: he was fifty-four. Prince Louis was fifty, and Eugene not yet forty-one. In military rank the Margrave stood first, next Marlborough, and then Eugene. Marlborough was the only one who was not a royalty. He was the only one who had never gained a battle. He could not compare in military renown with Prince Louis, still less with the famous Eugene. Still, there he was, the Englishman, with his commanding personality, his redcoats, and the army he had led so far to aid the Empire. Thus he counted for something. Indeed, he became naturally and at once the presiding authority: and this was virtually implied in the conditions he had exacted before he committed himself to the adventure.

It was agreed at Gross Heppach that the Margrave, with his army north of Ulm, should hold the Elector; that Eugene, with less than thirty thousand men, should at Philippsburg or Stollhofen confront the Marshals, who were found to have sixty thousand on the Upper Rhine, and that Marlborough should traverse the mountains with his whole force, and join the Margrave as quickly as possible.

And so, in Marlborough's words to Godolphin, "After we had taken the necessary resolutions for putting in execution what had been projected against the Elector of Bavaria, yesterday in the afternoon Prince Eugene went for the Rhine, Prince Louis to his army, and your humble servant to his place."

Meanwhile Marlborough's march had produced its reactions both in Holland and England. The States-General had, it is true, promptly acceded to his request to allow their troops and reinforcements to go to the Danube. But they naturally felt entitled to throw the whole responsibility for what might happen upon the commander. By concealment and stratagem he had forced their hand. He had created a position in which they had no choice but to wreck the campaign or support him against their wishes and judgment in an obviously most disputable adventure. Heinsius had been glad to see the decision ultimately carried in Marlborough's favour, but under-currents of resentment and alarm ran through the whole Dutch oligarchy and its military advisers. "On his head be it," was the general view.

In England these feelings were even more intense. The Tories were outraged in their party principles by this carrying of the war and of the Queen's troops into the heart of the Continent. Such measures were contrary to their whole theory of British policy. No authority had been given by Parliament for any such surprising transference of the army to a new and remote theatre. The influential ex-Ministers threatened fury and retribution upon the Captain-General, who had broken loose not only from prudent methods of warfare, but from proper Parliamentary control.

It was lucky indeed that Parliament, with its Tory majority in the Commons and hostile Whigs, was not in session. The chiefs of the Opposition consoled themselves meanwhile with the belief, or even secret, subconscious hope, that a disaster was impending. It was worth while to wait for the supreme opportunity which would probably come their way. They could not bring Marlborough back now before some awful trial of strength occurred. An overwhelming case would come into their hands when the famous, invincible armies of France baffled, defeated, or destroyed the presumptuous general and lukewarm Tory.

These tidings and doubtless many others came daily to Marlborough's headquarters as they rolled forward, march by march, and formed a background to his thoughts while he pondered upon the impugned loyalty of the Margrave, strove to conciliate and work him, and measured from hour to hour the anxious, obscure strategic scene.

The first step was to join the two armies. Marlborough had still to traverse the hilly country of the Swabian Jura before he could enter the Danube basin. This required enormous exertions from Churchill's foot and artillery. The defile of Geislingen, through which he must pass, was narrow, and even in good weather extremely difficult for wagons. Of course it poured with rain for ten days. Men and horses floundered and struggled forward. Meanwhile the Margrave's army was well placed to cover the exits from the mountainous regions on to the Danube plain. But the Margrave was greatly weakened by the departure of the troops he had sent to Eugene for the Rhine. There was always the danger that the Elector and Marsin would attack him before Marlborough could get clear of the hills and join him in the plains. While this task was at its worst the States-Generals were led to believe that Villeroy was returning to the Netherlands, and demanded a part at least of their force for the defence of Holland. They did not get them.

Because we have turned aside to discuss strategy and politics, the reader must not lose the sensation of a continuous march. Marlborough could ride on ahead and have two or three days to transact his affairs. But the scarlet caterpillar crawled onward ceaselessly. It averaged about ten miles a day for six weeks. Napoleon's march a century later from

Boulogne to Ulm over much better roads was considerably faster. But Marlborough's aim was not entirely speed. The Danes anyhow were lagging behind him. Everything depended upon the timing of passing successive critical points in relation to the knowledge and movements of the enemy, and on the fitness and spirit of his troops at the end of their march. All his strategic requirements were satisfied by the pace they made. To Versailles and to the French Marshals, as from time to time they received their news, it seemed that Marlborough was marching with "great strides" to the Danube, and that nothing could intercept or overtake him.

CHAPTER FORTY

The Storm of the Schellenberg

ஜ 1704, July 2 ஜ

THE junction of the two armies was effected on the 22nd at Laun-
sheim, and their full concentration was complete by the end of June. It
was the largest and strongest force of cavalry and infantry yet massed in
Europe in all these wars. After providing the army for the Rhine the
line of battle was formed of 177 squadrons and 76 battalions. Its weakness was in artillery. Marlborough had only been able to bring field-
pieces with him in his six weeks of marching, and the Imperialists were
woefully deficient even in the lighter guns. Together they could muster
but forty-eight cannon. However, three-quarters belonged to the English Artillery, which, under Colonel Blood, was of exceptional quality
and mobility. Siege train as yet there was none, and only twenty-four
pontoons were available for throwing bridges.

But the long, delicate flank march was now over, and he was independent of the middle Rhine, with its many points of weakness. To
subsist and be secure he must at once move east and pick up his new
line of communications with Franconia. All this had been duly prepared. Under cover of the Margrave's army at Ulm he had been for
some weeks past forming large magazines and hospitals at Nördlingen,
whence his line of supply stretched back to Nuremberg and its fertile
regions. His financial base at Frankfort was already linked up with the
new area, and his agents and contractors were actively purchasing supplies and hiring transport throughout the whole valley of the Pegnitz.
It was necessary to draw the allied army from the broken, barren foothills of the Swabian Jura and place it at the head of these far safer

communications. It was, moreover, urgent to force the Danube and seize a fortified bridgehead upon it. There was only one place which suited both these requirements. On June 8, the day before he had met Eugene and four days before Prince Louis had arrived, Marlborough had written to Godolphin, "I shall in two days after the junction [of Marlborough's and the Margrave's armies] march directly to Donau-wörth. If I can take that place, I shall there settle a magazine for the army."

The capture of Donauwörth would give crossings for both the Danube and the Lech and direct entry into Bavaria. Its fortified posses-sion would enable Marlborough to bestride the Danube and manœuvre on either bank as events might require. From Donauwörth his new line of communications, and if necessary of retreat, would run back natu-rally into Franconia almost at right angles to his front.

The Duke was therefore only awaiting the arrival of his infantry to do what he had for some time intended. He now replied that "he would ask the Margrave to make him a present of Donauwörth, and until this had been done not to think of a separation or of any other design." He added that "he must confess to the Margrave that his troops had this failing, that they could not remain in the field without bread. It was therefore necessary to capture some place where maga-zines could be formed." The discussion was continued on the 27th. The Margrave remarked that he had information that the enemy intended to fortify the position on the heights of Donauwörth, and to this end had already collected a great many peasants from the district. Now Donauwörth had assuredly been mentioned in the conference of the three generals at Gross Heppach, and it seemed odd to both Marlbor-ough and Wratislaw that the Elector should have gained such timely intelligence. He replied sternly that the Schellenberg, the fort above Donauwörth, must be stormed even if it cost ten or twelve thousand men. Here was a clash of wills. There was therefore not only the sharp-est difference of opinion between the two commanders, but Marlborough and Wratislaw had the deepest misgivings about the Margrave's good faith.

Wratislaw then proposed to the Emperor to strip the Margrave of his two most trusted officers, Baron Forster and the Comte de Frise. The one was to be sent to Vienna and kept there, *"once you have got him,"* dur-ing the whole campaign. The other was to be sent to the Rhine.

Amid these various tensions Marlborough remained serene, calm, patient, efficient, and good-humoured as ever. His repose and conviction were imperturbable. His letters to Sarah show his care of his troops, his poise, and his resolve.

Giengen
June 29

Since my last, I have had the happiness of receiving yours of the 30th of the last month, and the 1st and 2nd of this. It is not only by yours, but by others that I find that there are several people, who would be glad of my not having success in this undertaking. I am very confident, without flattering myself, that it is the only thing that was capable of saving us from ruin, so that whatever the success may be, I shall have the inward satisfaction to know that I have done all that was in my power, and that none can be angry with me for the undertaking, but such as wish ill to their country and their religion, and with such I am not desirous of their friendship.

You will easily believe that I act with all my heart and soul, since good success will in all likelihood give me the happiness of ending my days with you. The Queen's allowing you to say something from her is very obliging. I shall endeavour to deserve it; for I serve her with all my heart, and I am very confident she will always have the prayers and good wishes of this country.

Meanwhile the allied army waited at Giengen, opposite the entrenched camp and at an equal distance from Ulm and Donauwörth. Thus the enemy was still left in doubt where they meant to strike. After the argument of the 27th the Margrave resisted no further, and resigned himself to an attack on Donauwörth with united forces. Marlborough waited at Giengen till Churchill came in with all his infantry and cannon, and had a good day's rest. On June 30 the whole army was moved eastward downstream, parallel to the Danube, to Balmershofen, within four miles of the Lauingen-Dillingen lines. The march was resumed the next morning, Marlborough taking sixty squadrons as flank guard. Though the cavalry rode as close as possible to the enemy's works, the defenders lay low, and not a shot was fired. The allies camped near Amerdingen, fifteen miles from Donauwörth. Marlborough sent out a reconnaissance of four hundred horse with officers of high rank to view the Schellenberg and learn what was happening there. With this went the quartermasters of the army with orders to choose a camp behind the Wernitz stream about four miles from Donauwörth, and also to report on the roads, bridges, and tracks. The officers reported strong enemy camps on the Schellenberg, and that the troops were working hard on their entrenchments. During the afternoon various peasants and deserters came to Marlborough's tent and were carefully examined.

The Elector had felt bound to delay the reinforcement of the garrison of Donauwörth until he could learn clearly the intention of his more numerous opponents. But as soon as he saw the continuous procession of the allied army across his front during the 30th he sent Comte d'Arco with fourteen thousand men to defend Donauwörth and complete the fortification of the Schellenberg. He had no reason to suppose that Donauwörth could be attacked before the morning of the 3rd. His enemies had still two fifteen-mile marches to make, and even their advance guard could hardly reach their objective before the evening of the 2nd. They would certainly not attack so late in the day and with wearied troops, and by the 3rd d'Arco should be strongly entrenched. In spite of having delayed so long to fortify the Schellenberg, the Elector had good reason to hope for success.

During the afternoon of the 1st Marlborough issued orders which could only portend action the next day. One hundred and thirty men were to be drawn from every battalion of his own army to form a special force nearly six thousand strong of what would now be called 'storm troops.' When darkness fell and while all this was going on, Marlborough visited the Margrave. There is no record of the details of their interview, but it is certain that he procured the agreement of his colleague, for we know that at 10 P.M. an officer was sent to Nördlingen with a letter from the Margrave to the local authorities to collect surgeons and prepare for the reception of a large number of wounded. Moreover, three battalions of Imperial Grenadiers were added by the Margrave to Marlborough's 'storm troops,' evidently to make it plain that the two commanders were united. The special force of infantry with 35 squadrons and strong parties of pioneers for road- and bridge-making were ordered to march at 3 A.M. under Marlborough's personal command. A forlorn hope of eighty volunteers led by Lord Mordaunt, Peterborough's son (one of the suitors of Lady Mary), was formed to head the assault. The rest of the army was to follow with the Margrave at daylight.

Every one learned from these orders the desperate character of the operation and the unusual measures which were to be adopted. It seemed to many a plan of hardihood. The army was still fifteen miles from Donauwörth. They had to cross the Wernitz stream in their march and deploy for battle at the end of it. They could not hope to come to grips before about six o'clock in the evening, and there would only be two hours' daylight left. There is no doubt that nearly all the generals on both sides, friend and foe, thought it inadmissible for the allies to fight a battle before the 3rd. But by the 3rd d'Arco would be well entrenched and the Elector would be moving to his aid. Victory was more than doubtful on the 3rd; failure was certain on the 4th, or later. Nothing could avail unless the battle were set forward a day. Marlborough saw that exceptional risk must be run if the campaign was not to miscarry. A supreme effort must be demanded of the troops; a bloody price must be paid by them; and their commander must stake his reputation upon the outcome. To the questionings which arose he replied, "Either the enemy will escape or will have time to finish their works. In the latter case the delay of every single hour will cause the loss of a thousand men." There was little sleep that night in the allied camp. The thrill of excitement and the stir of preparation ruled the few remaining hours. A stern effort was required of the English and Dutch, who had travelled a long way to make it and upon whom the brunt was evidently to fall. The hour was come, and they were ready.

Early on the morning of July 2 Marshal d'Arco, with Count Maffei and other general officers, was a-horse upon the Schellenberg watching the working parties of troops and labourers entrenching the hill. On the left of Marshal d'Arco, and five hundred feet below him, lay this star-shaped Donauwörth, bristling with roofs and spires, traversed by the silver ribbon of the Danube, across which the all-important bridge lay like a buckle. On his right, reaching almost to the summit of the hill, lay a dense wood. It was an impenetrable obstacle. Individuals could push their way through, but at the worst could only fire a shot or two before they would be killed with bayonet or sword. It was true that beyond the wood, farther to the right, there was more than a mile of open ground stretching down to the river. But in this space the lines had been completed and could be occupied easily while the enemy were making the necessary détour. Therefore Marshal d'Arco was at this moment concerned with the thousand-yards stretch between the low fortress and the high wood.

The old fort of Gustavus divided this space again into two. The cannon of Donauwörth gave considerable protection to the ground in closest range. There only remained from three to four hundred yards between the Donauwörth cannonballs and the obstacle of the wood. Here, then, was the place to fortify and where to mass the troops and field artillery (sixteen guns). It was on this space that all d'Arco's men were digging and binding together the long faggots called fascines which held up their breastworks. How many men d'Arco had is much disputed. Marlborough's estimate after the battle gives him fourteen thousand men, including 5 good French regiments and 16 battalions of the cream of the Bavarian infantry, besides 9 to 15 squadrons: evidently a very tough proposition.

About eight o'clock in the morning enemy horsemen, many in red coats, began to appear at the edge of the woods and scrub, five or six miles away on d'Arco's left front to the north-west. They were probably the advanced cavalry of the great army marching against him, or perhaps they were only another reconnaissance. As the hours passed more and more horsemen made their appearance, trickling out of the woods, and forming into squadrons upon the heaths and meadows. Then the perspective glasses disclosed rivulets of infantry flowing down the hillsides. So it was the army, as expected, that was coming. But about ten o'clock a very familiar sign became apparent. The allied quartermasters were marking out a camp. They could be seen four miles away beyond the Wernitz stream setting up all the flags upon which the tent lines of the various regiments would presently be pitched. This confirmed d'Arco and his staff in their most reasonable expectation that the enemy after a full march would sleep behind the Wernitz, and deliver their attack the next day. Dig then, like moles, and make this narrow strip between the gunfire of the fortress and the tangles of the wood impregnable! Having reached these well-grounded, serious, but not unsatisfactory conclusions, Marshal d'Arco and his principal officers rode down about noon into the town of Donauwörth for their midday meal. To-morrow fateful battle; to-day dig, and meanwhile dine. However, between two and three o'clock reports arrived that the enemy had not stopped at the marked-out camp. They had thrown several bridges and plankways across the Wernitz, and were moving steadily across these and the old stone bridge into the cup-like space beneath the Schellenberg. It was surely too late to make so grave an attack before sundown; but anyhow one must ride out and see. The horses were brought, and the Command clattered up the hill to their toiling troops. The scene was now much changed. The whole of the opposite slopes descending to the foot of the Schellenberg were crowded with brightly clothed regiments and brigades, horse, foot, and guns all moving forward as fast as they could and with an air of resolute aggression. Large numbers were already across the Wernitz, and long columns were streaking towards that very space between the wood and the fortress cannon which Marshal d'Arco and his assistants admitted was the most likely point of assault.

The fringe of Bavarian outposts and covering troops came hurrying back before the advancing tide. They set light before retiring to the village of Berg and other hamlets and dwellings spread in a half-circle beneath the Schellenberg. The smoke drifted across the landscape, and as it died down at five o'clock a battery of ten guns opened fire from below Berg upon the deadly passage near the wood. All work had been abandoned for an hour past, and the defenders had drawn themselves up in battle order behind their unfinished breastworks. The heavy blue and scarlet columns hugging the wood and just out of range of the fortress were already massed in a dip in the ground—easily recognizable to-day—only two hundred and fifty yards away. The tips of all their standards could be seen, suggesting the number of battalions crammed together in this small space. Behind them, subtending both the fortress and the intervening ground, were certainly more than forty thousand men moving forward, line behind line in battle array. They were willing to pay the price for what they meant to have. Well, let them pay it.

Marlborough had come on the scene about nine o'clock, and directed the advance of the army. He reserved the old bridge which still stood across the Wernitz for the march of the storm troops. He had three pontoon bridges thrown for the main army. He sent the bulk of the cavalry into the thickets to cut fascines with which the infantry could fill any ditch that the enemy might have had time to dig in front of the breastworks. The storm troops, delayed by the soft, miry track, did not cross the river till noon. He then rode out with the Margrave and the generals concerned in the attack, and, as was his custom, personally reconnoitred the whole of the enemy's position. Their escort having driven in the enemy's outposts, they were able to examine the whole front minutely. So close did "the high generality" press that the fortress guns and even the field batteries opened a lively cannonade upon them which was continued during the whole of their inspection. The Duke had hoped that he could pass some at least of his troops through the dense wood, and thus extend his attack beyond it. But what he saw of the wood at close quarters convinced him that this was not practicable. The fortress cannon-balls bounding along among the staff showed how narrow was the space upon which the first and main assault must be delivered. He also saw how densely the enemy were gathered upon this threatened point.

It was nearly four when the generals joined their troops and the enemy's guns became silent. The main body of the army was now about to pass the bridges, and the storm troops were approaching the foot of the Schellenberg. The formidable aspect of the position had become only the more apparent at close quarters, but when Marlborough looked across the Danube beyond Donauwörth he could see the considerable camp marked out for the enemy's reinforcements. The tents of the cavalry were already pitched on either flank, and between them a broad space was reserved for infantry who would certainly arrive during the night. To-day the price would be heavy. To-morrow the Schellenberg might be unpurchasable. There are no signs that Marlborough had any second thoughts, for the advance and deployment of the army continued at the utmost speed.

In this action Marlborough used the same method which he afterwards, with modifications, pursued at Blenheim and at Ramillies. He thrust a mass of English infantry, conspicuous by their scarlet coats, soon to be dreaded for their prowess, upon what the enemy felt was the key of their position; and he pressed these attacks with a disregard of human life unusual in these prolonged and stately wars. By this means he attracted disproportionate forces of the enemy to the threatened point, and strove with might and main to crash through them. Success here meant victory. If he did not succeed, the dislocation of the enemy's forces produced by this ferocious effort gave him the battle elsewhere upon the denuded portions of their front. Surplus troops from his feints could in every action carry his ultimate attack. By five o'clock the striking-force was already close to the wood half-way up the Schellenberg. To their right upon all the approaches the lines of battle were formed, and extending as the main army came up. The cavalry delivered a short fascine to every officer and soldier in the assaulting infantry. Leaving the Margrave to direct the advance of the army, Marlborough rode to the storming column, the infantry of which was now deployed about three hundred yards broad, in the dip a furlong from the hostile breastworks. Behind the six thousand picked men in three dense lines he had brought eight battalions in support and eight more echeloned right-handed in reserve. These large bodies were sustained by 35 squadrons, including all the English cavalry, formed close behind and somewhat farther to the right of the storm troops. The Margrave's army was now also partly formed, and growing every minute as the marching columns deployed. At about a quarter-past six the drums beat, and Lieutenant-General Goor, who commanded the assault, preceded by Mordaunt and the forlorn hope, led the English infantry up the hill. The battery which d'Arco had posted in the angle formed by the wood and the works fired with deadly effect, while the fortress cannon galled the other flank. The leading troops of the 1st Guards; Ingoldsby's, now the Royal Welch Fusiliers; two battalions of Orkney's, now the Royal Scots; and Meredith's, now the 1st Hampshires, fell by scores; but the whole array rolled forward at a slow step, the soldiers with shouldered arms and clasping their fascines with their left hands.

When half the distance was covered the Bavarian guns fired case instead of ball and tore long lanes through the ranks, while at the same time the breastworks began to blaze with musketry. At the first volley General Goor fell dead. Undaunted, all the English now raised cheers, heard everywhere above the firing, and shouts of "God save the Queen!" as they broke into the charge. But an unlucky accident cost them dear. A deep, unexpected gully, dry though made by water, ran across the enemy's front about fifty yards from the breastworks. Mistaking this for the actual ditch, the troops cast their fascines into it, and thus the survivors of the first line reached the breastworks without the means of crossing them. The rest of the assault coming steadily on behind them, the whole force was brought to a standstill in the unfinished ditch while the exultant Bavarians fired into them from the par-

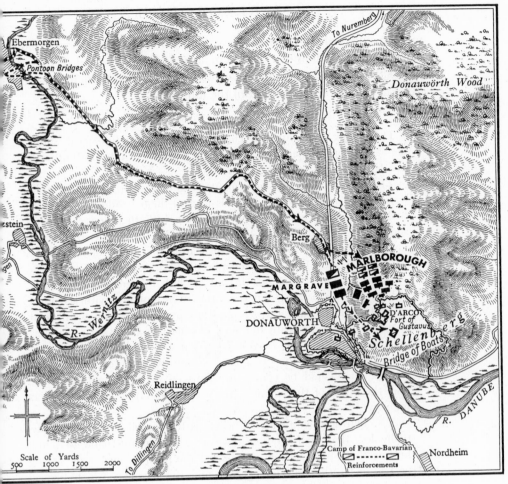

5. The Storm of the Schellenberg

apet. A protracted struggle followed. By all reports nothing like the fury of the musketry-fire had ever been heard before. "Incredible" is the word which occurs in various foreign accounts. And all at a few yards' distance into solid masses! At length the assault slackened. Men began to double to the rear, the Bavarians leaped out in counter-attack, and a panic began. But the 1st Guards, who had now lost half their men and nearly all their principal officers, turned, faced the foe, and drove the Bavarians back to their trenches.

We must now introduce a new character to our readers. M. de la Colonie, whose *Memoirs of an Old Campaigner* afford by far the most modern and vivid picture of these wars from the enemy's side, commanded the battalion of French Grenadiers whom Marshal d'Arco had personally posted behind the breastworks at the point where the wood came to an end on the summit of the hill.

He says:

> The enemy broke into the charge, and rushed at full speed, shouting at the top of their voices, to throw themselves into our entrenchments.
>
> The rapidity of their movements, together with their loud yells, were truly alarming, and as soon as I heard them I ordered our drums to beat the 'charge' so as to drown them with their noise, lest they should have a bad effect upon our people. By this means I animated my grenadiers, and prevented them hearing the shouts of the enemy, which before now have produced a heedless panic.
>
> The English infantry led this attack with the greatest intrepidity, right up to our parapet, but there they were opposed with a courage at least equal to their own. Rage, fury, and desperation were manifested by both sides, with the more obstinacy as the assailants and assailed were perhaps the bravest soldiers in the world. The little parapet which separated the two forces became the scene of the bloodiest struggle that could be conceived. Thirteen hundred grenadiers . . . bore the brunt of the enemy's attack at the forefront of the Bavarian infantry.
>
> . . . During this first attack, which lasted a good hour or more [actually less than half an hour], we were all fighting hand to hand, hurling them back as they clutched at the parapet; men were slaying or tearing at the muzzles of guns and the bayonets which pierced their entrails; crushing under their feet their own wounded comrades, and even gouging out their opponents' eyes with their nails, when the grip was so close that neither could make use of their weapons. I verily believe that it would have been quite impossible to find a more terrible representation of hell itself than was shown in the savagery of both sides on this occasion.

It is probable that more than three thousand of the assailants had fallen in this first attack, and lay in a space perhaps three to four hundred yards square. Marlborough immediately ordered a second attempt. And now the generals, brigadiers, and colonels dismounted from their horses, and, with the remnants of Mordaunt's forlorn hope, formed a glorious front line. At the head marched Lieutenant-General Count

Styrum, soon mortally wounded; but this renewed effort, though nearly as bloody, was repulsed more easily than the first. Most of the generals and colonels were soon shot down, and the wave recoiled a second time from the terrible defences. But General Lumley brought his squadrons up in close order within musket-shot, thus heartening the infantry and preventing all retreat.

Wratislaw, watch in hand, was spectator from the opposite slope behind Berg. According to his timing, the Margrave's attack began only a quarter of an hour after Marlborough's. At about seven o'clock the Margrave, advancing valiantly at the head of his troops, was already in close action. The Duke in the dip, unmoved by the bloody disaster around him, sent an officer with a platoon of infantry to test the defences farther to the right of those he had attacked. They were found to be almost empty, the bulk of the defenders having been drawn into the struggle by the wood. Marlborough therefore directed the eight battalions of his reserve to attack in the new direction more to the right, in conjunction with the Margrave's general advance. At the same time he called upon his shattered battalions for a new attack over the same deadly ground. Most of the high officers were now killed or wounded, but at about a quarter-past seven a new onset was organized and began to move forward, though less confidently than its precursors. So obstinate was the temper at this point that Lumley ordered Lord John Hay's regiment of dragoons, now deathless as the Scots Greys, to dismount and attack with the infantry.

The defenders still resisted with the utmost constancy. But at last Fortune, who had remained insensible to sacrifice, began to declare herself on the side of numbers. Marshal d'Arco had told the governor of Donauwörth to spread two French battalions along the covered way, and had assigned to two Bavarian units the task of guarding the curtain of entrenchments which joined the fortress to the scene of the struggle. But the governor had withdrawn all his troops within the ramparts, and the others were too few to defend their front against the forces now coming into action. The Margrave's horse was shot under him, and he himself was wounded; but the enemy's fire, whether from the trenches or the fortress, could not cope with the crowds of troops which now pressed upon them. The ditches were filled with fascines, and about the same time as Marlborough on the left was organizing his third attack large bodies of German infantry pierced the centre of the entrenchments with little loss. D'Arco was on the spot. The intruders were charged by his cavalry, but they were already too many to be driven out. The cavalry charge failed, and the Imperialist infantry, pouring through the gap and spreading to the right and left, advanced upon the flank of those who had so bravely and successfully defended the summit of the hill.

What followed is best told by La Colonie.

> . . . About 7.30 . . . I noticed all at once an extraordinary move-
> ment on the part of our infantry, who were rising up and ceasing fire
> withal. I glanced around on all sides to see what had caused this be-
> haviour, and then became aware of several lines of infantry in greyish-
> white uniforms on our left flank. From lack of movement on their
> part, their dress and bearing, I verily believed that reinforcements had
> arrived for us, and anybody else would have believed the same. No in-
> formation whatever had reached us of the enemy's success, or even
> that such a thing was the least likely, so in the error I laboured under
> I shouted to my men that they were Frenchmen and friends. . . .
>
> Having, however, made a closer inspection, I discovered bunches of
> straw and leaves attached to their standards, badges the enemy are in
> the custom of wearing on the occasion of battle, and at that very mo-
> ment was struck by a ball in the right lower jaw, which wounded
> and stupefied me to such an extent that I thought it was smashed.

This was the moment when Marlborough's final attack began to struggle forward across the shambles. All resistance now became impossible. The ten battalions, exhausted by their ordeal, and finding their left flank turned and their retreat menaced by overwhelming numbers of fresh troops, retreated a few hundred yards in order, and then broke and ran as hard as they could down through the cornfields towards the river and a pontoon bridge across it. But this had already been broken asunder by the flight of the wagon-train, and the Margrave's forces separated all these men from Donauwörth. Marlborough, entering the captured position with the leading squadrons, had his dazed infantry stopped and re-formed while he launched all the 35 squadrons of English and Prussian cavalry, including the Greys (now remounted), after the fugitives. The pursuit was merciless. The troopers, infuriated by the slaughter of their foot, gave no quarter. "Kill, kill and destroy!" was the word. So they rode them down and killed them all, or chased them into the Danube.

The battle was over and the allies had won. When the Margrave came riding up to the bloodstained summit he called out to Marlborough, "I am delighted that your proposal has proved such a success." The Duke replied, "I am thankful that you have supported me so well with your troops, and relieved the pressure on me." Of Count d'Arco's fourteen thousand men scarcely five thousand rejoined the Elector's army. The capture of the Schellenberg involved the surrender of Donauwörth, which could not be held for many days against the fire of batteries planted on the hill. The governor did not await this trial. During the night of the 3rd he quitted the fortress in such haste that he failed either to burn the town or effectively destroy the bridge as ordered. The allies now had their bridgehead on the Danube, and valuable stores found in Donauwörth formed the nucleus of the magazines Marlborough had planned to establish there. The prize had been gained, but the cost of nearly six thousand casualties, fifteen hundred killed outright, was shocking in an age when soldiers were hard to find, and human life narrowly valued. The resources of Nördlingen were overwhelmed by the wounded. All who could walk or crawl were dispersed in the surrounding villages with only the most primitive arrangements. Marlborough's correspondence of the 3rd and 4th is full of directions for their care.

The English were the hardest hit. Out of four thousand in action fifteen hundred were killed or wounded. Many weary, faithful feet that had trudged from the Thames to the Danube here came to rest. The proportion of loss among the senior officers was beyond compare. Six lieutenant-generals were killed and five wounded, together with four major-generals and twenty-eight brigadiers, colonels, and lieutenant-colonels. The gazettes and news-letters of Europe were adorned with the names of those notables, including princes and commanders long celebrated in the wars.

Various reflections may be made upon this action. That it was vital to the army and the campaign to secure this bridgehead on the Danube is obvious. But Marlborough admitted in a letter to Overkirk that the prize *a coûté un peu cher*. It is arguable, though by no means provable, that if he had waited till the 3rd and brought the whole army into play on both sides of the wood, the enemy even though reinforced could not have held so extended a line, and possibly life might have been spared. But the fear of the reinforcements was decisive upon him.

CHAPTER FORTY-ONE

The Devastation of Bavaria

⟨ 1704, July ⟩

FAME and fortune, which had hitherto journeyed with Marlborough, halted on the frontiers of Bavaria and awaited his return. The month which followed the battle of the Schellenberg is gloomy for his record. It would seem that his vision and calculation had carried him no farther than this. He had foreseen with uncanny accuracy all the milestones of his long march and the reactions upon friend and foe which would be imposed as each one was passed. He had marked Donauwörth as the gateway by which he would enter the promised land. He was there. The European situation, military and political, was for the moment transformed. But what was he to do next? He had always made it plain that he meant to compel the Elector to return to his allegiance under threat of destroying his country. Accordingly when, on the 8th, the allied army crossed the Lech, they began to burn and lay waste all within their reach. In vain did the despairing inhabitants offer the largest sums of money they could scrape together to placate the wrath of the invaders. Marlborough could have enriched himself vastly by such a process. The precedent of Cohorn in the Pays de Waes only a year before was but too well known to him. He does not seem to have thought of it. His military needs conquered both his avarice and his humanity. He replied—"nobly," says Lediard—"The forces of the Queen of England were not come into Bavaria to get money, but to bring their prince to reason." Thus the army advanced to Aicha, which they reached on the 22nd, spreading terror on all sides and leaving a blackened trail behind them.

The Elector had not awaited the forcing of the rivers. To tarry was to be cut off. As soon as the news of the Schellenberg reached him he evacuated his entrenched camp beyond the Danube and retreated to Augsburg. He fortified himself in a strong position partly protected by the Lech and under the cannon of the fortress. Here he hoped to maintain himself until a new French army came to his aid. He had in fact no other military choice. However, his retreat had carried him forty miles farther from his hoped-for succours, and his weakness prevented him from protecting the country. Simultaneously he gave up Neuburg and withdrew its garrison to Ingolstadt, the sole fortress remaining in his hands on the long course of the Danube from Ulm to Passau.

Marlborough, who had promptly occupied Neuburg, had now a satisfactory technical position, at the head of his communications with Nuremberg, astride of the Danube and the Lech, and with enough fortified bridges to enable him to manœuvre with ease on either side of both these rivers. The defended triangle Donauwörth—Rain—Neuburg was the central structure upon which all his movements depended. He could hold out his right hand for a junction with Eugene, and with his left he dominated Bavaria. He could concentrate for battle on either side of the Danube. It is important here to notice also that as soon as the Elector had quitted the Lauingen-Dillingen lines Marlborough had them levelled by local labour, and placed small garrisons in the towers of Dillingen and Höchstädt. This foresight was later rewarded.

The threads of negotiation with the Elector had not been severed. Marlborough earnestly desired a settlement. The transfer of Bavaria from the party of the Two Crowns to the Grand Alliance was the hinge on which the whole war seemed at this time to turn. He did not trust the Margrave as an intermediary, and still less would he trust Frederick I. Heinsius had long opened to him, and had recently warned him of, the Prussian designs. But a direct negotiation in the field with the faithful, accomplished Wratislaw as the agent at once of the Empire and the Maritime Powers, even if it led to nothing, must certainly be tested to the end.

It was Max Emmanuel's interest to bargain with the allies for peace, and with France for help. No appeal to France could be so potent as the open threat to change sides. There was besides the hope of gaining time from the enemy. The plight to which his ambitions had led him was unenviable. Huddled around Augsburg with no news of succour, he was condemned to watch the torment of his country. The confederate generals had, as we have seen, agreed from the outset that while they treated with him seriously for a separate peace they would not relax or alter the course of their military operations. They proceeded to ravage Bavaria before its ruler's eyes. From many points of the horizon rose pillars of smoke. By every pathway open his terrified subjects implored from their prince either protection or peace. At the same time Wratislaw, sceptical but persuasive, offered grand bribes. If Max Emmanuel would return to the loyalties from which he had been seduced by the lure of the Imperial Crown there should be full forgiveness. He might resume his place among the Germanic princes of the Empire. His dominions should be restored to him. Nay, they should even be increased. Pfalz-Neuburg and Burgau would be added to his hereditary lands upon the guarantee of the Queen of England, the Emperor undertaking to compensate the lawful owners. Two hundred thousand crowns would be paid to repair the damage—which was, however, increasing daily. Marlborough, now duly empowered from London, added the promise to hire twelve thousand Bavarian troops for service in Italy at the current rates of pay. On two points only was the Emperor insistent. "You must and shall at all times reject the claim to the title of King, and also refuse the French troops permission to depart freely."

On the other hand stood Marshal Marsin and the French army. Under the duress of rapine the Elector had dispersed his own troops throughout his territory to guard towns and properties, especially his own. In Augsburg the French were far the stronger. The Great King had sent them there at his request. If he made his peace with the Emperor what would Marlborough do with them? He asked through his secretary, Reichard, who had been in touch with the allied headquarters since June 6, that they should be granted safe-conduct home. The most that Marlborough would allow was that he should not be compelled himself to fight against them. Nevertheless, the negotiations went forward, and by July 12 what was virtually a draft agreement had been framed. The Elector had even fixed the Monastery of Fürstenfeld as the place, and the 14th as the date, when he would himself personally meet Wratislaw to sign the bond.

But now Marsin in dire straits used his power. He suggested to Max

Emmanuel that the allies might well seize his person and make him a prisoner of State. Further he declared that if he went to the rendezvous, the French troops would burn their baggage, march at once towards the Rhine, and shake the dust of Bavaria off their feet. It is possible even that these threats did not stop there. Certainly the feelings of the French officers can be understood. Under their weight the Elector yielded. He would not go himself. But in the absence of any further help from France he insisted that the parleys should be kept alive. Marsin and his generals held a council of war at which the Elector was present. Each gave his opinion. Here it appeared that the main anxiety of the French was to get out of the country safely. One of the generals, Blainville, whom we shall see for the last time on the field of Blenheim, voiced a latent opinion that the best that could now be hoped for by Louis XIV was the neutrality of the Elector and the escape of the French army. Max Emmanuel seized upon this as ground for continuing to treat, though not in person. He had meanwhile been confronted with the menace that Marlborough would systematically burn and destroy the whole of Bavaria, which lay open to his cavalry, unless he came to terms.

On the 13th the Electress, daughter of the hero King of Poland, John Sobieski, came to Augsburg. She cared little for the French and much for Bavaria. She implored her husband to make peace. Marsin spent the day in fierce anxiety. But on the morning of the 14th, when Wratislaw was already waiting at the Monastery of Fürstenfeld, came the longed-for letter from Tallard. Written on the 8th, it announced that Tallard and his whole army of 40 battalions and 60 squadrons were marching through the Black Forest upon Villingen. This was decisive. The Elector, unstable, unprincipled, but torn by strains which few could bear, saw once again his dream of empire revive. He decided that Bavaria must burn. He sent Reichard to the monastery to explain to Wratislaw that Marshal Tallard was coming to his aid with thirty-five thousand men, and that therefore his 'honour'—this had not arisen before—precluded him from entertaining the proposals, which were otherwise satisfactory.

Meanwhile the negotiations, in a broken-backed condition, still lingered on. The threat of burning all Bavaria still hung over the Elector, and Tallard, though nothing further had been heard of him by either side, was presumably approaching. His arrival would bring about a crisis. Tallard had only to move along the north bank of the Danube against Marlborough's communications alike with Eugene and with his Nuremberg supplies to bring about a battle somewhere between Ulm and Donauwörth. If the Elector joined himself to Tallard Marlborough must recross the Danube with an army strong enough to fight them both. In either case the reign of the allies in Bavaria was limited. What could be done must be done quickly.

Thus the month in Bavaria passed. These precious days gained by toil and daring slipped swiftly by. Tallard was drawing near, and, more dominating than Tallard, winter was but three months away. Parliament must meet in November. London and The Hague would inquire why their troops were so far afield; what authority had there been for this excursion; and what had their Captain-General to show for it all. The shock of the Schellenberg had passed. The helplessness of the Empire to provide the promised siege train had robbed that victory of its natural fruits. Neither Munich nor Ulm could be taken. The Elector had been neither crushed nor gained. We see Marlborough for a while in the flicker of that baleful sunlight which was to play at Moscow upon Napoleon, who also sought a treaty or a battle at the end of a long march far from home.

There was no longer goodwill between the commanders, nor even a pretence of it between their circles.

Marlborough's correspondence shows a real dislike of the Margrave and a repulsion from his military outlook. It was increasingly difficult to come to any agreement with him. Prince Louis now made objections to all Marlborough's proposals. He longed to divide the armies and escape from this tutelage and interference. When it was seen that there was no use in remaining any longer at Friedberg, Marlborough and the Margrave at last agreed that the siege of Ingolstadt was the best measure still open. This had been Prince Louis's wish ever since the capture of Rain on the 16th. The siege train, such as it was, was assembling at Neuburg.

Before making what was obviously a retrograde movement from Friedberg Marlborough demanded a renewed and far more extensive devastation of Bavaria. The Margrave again objected. He would not make war "like a hussar," but only "like an experienced general." He did not on this date, July 28, know that the Emperor had expressed the strongest abhorrence of the policy. Marlborough was insistent. Wratislaw, who agreed with Marlborough, challenged the Margrave fiercely. Hard words passed between them. Was this another instance of his pro-Bavarian sympathies? Under this pressure the Margrave gave way. More than this: Marlborough required that the Imperial cavalry should do the work. The Margrave again submitted. Sixty squadrons were now sent forth upon this lamentable duty. Not only on either side of the great Munich road, but as far as they could reach in the countryside, all villages and townships were destroyed. All grain which could not be collected was burned. By an ingenious refinement the personal properties of the Elector, which were numerous, were scrupulously spared, in order no doubt to prejudice him with his subjects.

The object of the first burnings had been to torment the Elector into compliance. Though there had been much smoke, no great harm had been done. Anger at the Elector's proved bad faith in the negotiations, disappointment and anxiety at their having come to nothing, had no doubt caused exasperation at Marlborough's headquarters. But these were not the motives for his action. Now that he was being forced to leave Bavaria, the military need of denying the whole region and its supplies to the enemy is plain. But there was another reason not noted by English writers which seems far more important. The proposed ravaging of the country, and the threat to destroy it entirely wherever a cavalry brigade could ride, had already induced the Elector to disperse a large part of his army in protecting valuable places, and among these particularly his own estates and salt-mines. Out of 35 battalions and 60 squadrons at his disposal he had at the end of the first week in August only 5 battalions and 20 squadrons to combine with the French in Augsburg. We shall see presently what Tallard, when he arrived, thought of this squandering of vital forces at the climax of the campaign. The fact in itself affords a military explanation of Marlborough's action. It was not senseless spite or brutality, but a war measure deemed vital to success and even safety. But to the wretched sufferers it made no difference what the motive was.

Although perhaps four hundred villages were burned, the devastation of Bavaria was neither so sure nor so widespread as that which France had inflicted upon the Palatinate a quarter of a century before. It was, of course, incomparably less efficient than the destruction wrought by the Germans in their withdrawals from France and Belgium in our own times. But we must make allowances. Explosives were then in their infancy, and fire often leaves cottage walls standing. Moreover, Marlborough would not allow the beautiful trees to be cut down, as was systematically done in the orchards of Northern France in 1917. Thus the policy was not applied with the thoroughness which our broader civilization has achieved. Still, in those days when the civil population was as far as possible kept out of the war, when the habitations and property of mankind were on so humble a scale, when often a house was a welcome sight, when a mill or granary betokened riches, when a spread of cultivated fields was a cheerful relief to the landscape, the measure meted to Bavaria seemed most grievous. The French, forgetting the Palatinate, of course proclaimed that this barbarism was worthy only of the Turks. Its military usefulness cannot be disputed.

CHAPTER FORTY-TWO

Marshal Tallard

ϟɑ 1704, July ϙϟ

On June 28 Tallard's army had begun to move towards the Strasburg bridges. On July 1 it crossed the Rhine, and, turning away from the lines, wended southward up its valley with obvious intention of marching towards the Danube. The Marshal, his army crawling on its belly, being fed with great difficulty along the broken tracks which threaded the Black Forest, arrived on July 16 before the town of Villingen. He had brought some siege cannon ahead with him, and he planned to reduce Villingen with his vanguard while the rest of his troops and their supply-trains trickled forward through the gorges and caught him up.

The garrison proved stubborn. They resisted with spirit. The French batteries were awkwardly placed, and suffered severely from the fortress fire. Red-hot shot set light to the town; but the German inhabitants extinguished the flames. Meanwhile Eugene in considerable force had appeared at Rothweil and threatened to intervene. For Tallard to pursue the siege to its conclusion was probably to be involved in a festering local crisis; and meanwhile no aid to the hard-pressed and faltering Elector. Tallard decided, no doubt rightly, to abandon the particular for the general situation. He therefore on the 22nd, after four days' bombardment, raised the siege of Villingen, put his army on short commons, and made for the Upper Danube, whence he reached Ulm, hungry, tired, but essentially intact, on July 29. He was disturbed to find in that fortress only six thousand sacks of flour.

Eugene's movements after Tallard skirted round Villingen and took his plunge are easy to understand, now that we know the whole story.

From Rothweil, where he was joined by 40 squadrons sent from Marlborough's army, he could come to Donauwörth and link up with the Marlborough triangle at least four days before Tallard could reach Ulm, and a week before he could join the Elector at Augsburg. But Eugene had to think constantly of Villeroy and the Lines of Stollhofen. He wished therefore to give the impression to the enemy by spies and deserters, who were numerous, that he was moving back to his old position. Accordingly, after repairing Villingen he marched with ostentation twenty miles northward to Tübingen, which he reached on the 27th of July. At that point he vanished from the French view among the desolate hills of Swabia.

Eugene had fulfilled both his objects. He had deceived Villeroy: he was about to join Marlborough, and Villeroy, gaping at the half-vacant Lines of Stollhofen, need no longer be considered as a factor in the fateful decisions impending upon the Danube.

Much foolishness has been written of the sudden surprising arrival of Eugene to the rescue of Marlborough, and how he appeared in the nick of time where he was most needed. But that all these operations were most closely concerted between the two commanders is evident, not only from the common sense of the matter, but from Marlborough's official correspondence.

Eugene knew that, whatever might miscarry behind him on the Rhine, or in Würtemberg, he must arrive on the Danube somewhere between Ulm and Donauwörth at the same time that Tallard joined the Elector. Marlborough in all his conduct counted upon him to do this, and his own arrangements made the junction sure and certain.

We are commonly assured that Marlborough and Eugene planned together to send the Margrave out of the way to besiege Ingolstadt while they themselves sought battle upon the Danube. One must beware of trying to find a pattern everywhere among the facts of history. It is only sometimes that design is truly present, and even then there are often many events happening unexpectedly or disjointedly from day to day which are inconsistent with it.

Marshal Tallard reached Augsburg on the 5th, and the next day the full concentration of the Franco-Bavarian army was effected at Biberbach. The two hostile armies lay about twenty miles apart. Simultaneously the army of Prince Eugene had appeared on the Danube at Höchstädt, in the tower of which, it will be remembered, Marlborough had a post. The confederate position was at this moment thoroughly sound. The enemy could not advance towards Donauwörth or Rain, where all the crossings were fortified against them. Unless they wished to force a battle at a disadvantage, their only offensive movement was against Eugene beyond the river. By this also they would assail Marlborough's communications through Nördlingen with Nuremberg. There could be little doubt they would take this course. Marlborough and the Margrave could join Eugene in front of Donauwörth in time to meet such a menace with their three armies united. But they would only just have time; for there was only one day's march in favour of the allies. Marlborough—for he was in fact the directing authority—had superior forces, interior lines with well-prepared roads and fortified bridges within them, and satisfactory communications with his advanced base, Nördlingen, and even better *via* Neuburg with his ultimate base, Nuremberg. The enemy would have to march round and see what part of this closely wrought structure they would attack; and all the while they would be courting a battle with perhaps sixty thousand men against more than seventy. So far prudence and advantage rested with the allies.

On the afternoon of the 6th Eugene had arrived at Schrobenhausen. He was welcomed by Marlborough alone. The Margrave had already started from Neuburg to inspect the siege train and make arrangements for the siege. That night he wrote to Marlborough that he had found everything ready, and had therefore given orders to invest and isolate Ingolstadt by a cavalry brigade. Marlborough and Eugene had twenty-four hours together, with Wratislaw at hand. The Margrave returned on the evening of the 7th, and the three commanders discussed the situation. They decided that the arrival of Tallard should not deter them from the siege of Ingolstadt. Marlborough then stated he would prefer to serve with the covering army. Before Eugene could speak the Margrave declared that he was ready to conduct the siege, and pointed out that his troops were nearer to the fortress than those of Prince Eugene. The latter therefore remained silent, and the Margrave had his wish. After the battle Prince Louis viewed the story in a different light; but he had surely no ground for complaint. His was the decision, and that it was agreeable to the two superior minds with whom he was working is not a fact for which they can be reproached.

Early on the 7th Marlborough and Eugene with a large escort rode forth to examine for themselves all the country between them and the enemy. A battle might be fought here, and they must know the ground thoroughly. They did not return till nightfall. On the 8th they moved to Sandizell. On the 9th Prince Louis's besieging force of 20 battalions and 15 squadrons, or fifteen thousand men, most of whom were camped along the Neuburg road, marched across the river towards Ingolstadt. Eugene returned to his command at Höchstädt, and Marlborough set the main force on a short march to Exheim, five miles nearer to Donauwörth and his military triangle. He had not gone far when news arrived that the whole Franco-Bavarian army was in motion towards the Danube at Lauingen. A similar report met Eugene just as he had got through Donauwörth. He immediately turned his horse and rode back to Marlborough at Exheim.

Now comes the surprising event. Marlborough, with Eugene's agreement, allowed the Margrave to continue his march to besiege Ingolstadt twenty miles in the rear. He thus discarded his numerical superiority. He left himself with only thirty-eight thousand men (who could, indeed, join or be joined by the eighteen thousand under Prince Eugene on either side of the Danube before a battle) but opposite to more than sixty thousand Franco-Bavarians. The chronicles of disaster no doubt afford innumerable precedents, but we know of no similar defiance of the sound principle of gathering all forces together for a battle by any of the successful captains of history. We have therefore a new situation deliberately created by Marlborough and Eugene in which the odds in numbers were turned against themselves. They could certainly unite, but when united they would have to fight with about five men to six and barely half as many guns. Judging in the after-light, we may admire the confidence of these masters of war in themselves and in their soldiers.

But their decision was scarcely complimentary to the Margrave. His military epitaph for all time must be that the two greatest captains of the age, pre-eminent and renowned in all the annals of war, rated, by actions more expressive than words, his absence from a decisive battle-field well worth fifteen thousand men. And this before a Europe whose military society, evolved by twenty years of war, measured all the facts and values with professional eye. No wonder Prince Louis never forgave them!

The sun was setting on Marlborough's camp at Rain when an officer galloped in with a decisive letter from Prince Eugene.

MARSHAL TALLARD

* Monsieur,

The enemy have marched. It is almost certain that the whole army is passing the Danube at Lauingen. They have pushed a Lieutenant-Colonel whom I sent to reconnoitre back to Höchstädt. The plain of Dillingen is crowded with troops. I have held on all day here; but with eighteen battalions I dare not risk staying the night. . . .

While I was writing sure news has reached me that the whole army has crossed. Thus there is not a moment to lose and I think you might risk making the march by the Lech and the Danube. That will shorten it a good deal, and the road is better. I await your answer, milord, to make my dispositions. It is above all important not to be shut in [? cramped] between these mountains and the Danube.

Much praise has been bestowed upon the smoothness and celerity of the concentration which followed. But the divisions of Marlborough's army lay conveniently at the moment when the sudden but expected call came, and the distances were short. Part of his cavalry had already joined Eugene. Starting at midnight on the 10th, they could both be at Donauwörth during the next morning by marches of only seven miles. A further four miles would bring the combined army into the line behind the Kessel stream. Knowing that Churchill and Marlborough were on the march and close at hand, Eugene at daybreak on the 11th led his infantry back to join his cavalry, who were watching the enemy. He thus laid strong hands upon the position and freed the roads for the movement of Churchill's twenty battalions, followed by Marlborough and the main body. Of course, when so large a force is marching by a single road, as after Donauwörth, the rear must be a day behind the van. But the last of the cavalry and infantry were closed up and came into line by 10 P.M., after a total march of only eleven miles. The enemy by a fifteen-mile march from their bridgeheads might have drawn up before the allies' position at the same time, but not sooner, and neither army would have had their artillery for a battle till the next day.

The enemy moved forward to Höchstädt on the 11th. During this day they learned that Marlborough was joining Eugene. They did not know whether the Margrave was with them both or not. The initiative, they conceived, rested with themselves. The allies would naturally retreat upon Nördlingen and along their communications. The only

(399)

question open was whether they could not maul Eugene's rearguard as he and Marlborough withdrew into the hills.

It was decided as a compromise to move three miles farther forward to the open ground in front of Höchstädt. On the 11th and the next morning they captured the small posts of eighty and a hundred men respectively which the allies held in the towers of Dillingen and Höchstädt. They marched into their new camp on the morning of the 12th. It never entered into their minds that they might be attacked themselves. In this warfare of marches and counter-marches battles were so rare that if reasonable precautions were taken, and the military movements were correct, they might almost be ruled out. They had been so long accustomed to the war of manœuvre and of engagements with limited risks that the idea of a ferocious death-grapple, where the destruction of the whole of one side or the other was at stake, did not present itself. For three years a world war had raged without any decisive battle having been fought. That the armies before which they were grimacing in the orthodox fashion would suddenly fall upon them and try to kill them all or perish in the attempt, seemed as unlikely as that a chess-player should knock over the board and seize his opponent by the throat. These experienced generals in no way contemplated such violent behaviour. They therefore passed the 12th in great composure. They lay behind a marshy stream. Their front was covered by a line of loop-holed and defended villages. Their right lay upon the Danube; their left upon the wooded mountains. They felt safe and comfortable, and when Tallard proposed to build a few redoubts, the Elector begged him not to break the soil.

On the morning of the 12th, as they were moving into their laid-out camp behind the Nebel stream, they could plainly see the enemy six miles away in considerable numbers at the mouth of the gorge between the hills and the river. And they were struck by the fact that, instead of a retirement while time remained, a broad expanse of tents began to spring up at the beginning of the plain. Evidently the allies were not in a hurry. What did this mean? They caught four prisoners or deserters, who were subjected separately to sharp examination. Each of these men told the same tale. They one and all declared that the Margrave and his troops had arrived. And secondly that the whole allied army was going to move off towards Nördlingen the next morning. This intelligence seemed to be confirmed in the first part by the reports of the

French cavalry scouts who had watched the dust clouds above Marlborough's baggage column marching the day before from Rain to
Donauwörth, and in the second part by the rumours which came in
from the countryside. Thus the two Marshals and the Elector were all
in the end agreed, first that they should not attack so strong an army,
and secondly that it was naturally responding as might be expected to
the strategic compulsion of their move. Of course these prisoners or deserters had been 'planted' upon them in order to deter them from making any attack on the 12th, which would have deranged the deployment of the allied offensive on the 13th.

During this day Marlborough and Eugene from the church tower of
Tapfheim had gazed long and intently at the French camp, and both
had ridden out with their cavalry to drive back the French reconnaissance. With pride and pleasure they rejoiced in each other's companionship and in their conviction that the whole war must be put to
the test at dawn. But in the French and Bavarian camp no one expected anything of importance to occur on the morrow, and generals
and soldiers went untroubled to their rest.

The Count of Mérode Westerloo, a Flemish officer of distinction
who commanded a Belgian contingent in the service of Spain forming
part of Marshal Tallard's army, has left us sprightly memoirs of this
and other campaigns. He dined that night in Blenheim village with
the generals and colonels of his division. Never was he in better spirits
than when, having eaten and drunk excellently, he returned to his
quarters. These were in a grange which overlooked the Nebel. His
retinue had carpeted the floor and set up his bed. "Never I believe
have I slept a sleep more sound and tranquil than this night." He was
still sleeping profoundly at six o'clock in the morning when his trusty
valet, all out of breath, entered the barn. "Milord, the enemy are
there!" "Where," said the count, mocking him; "there?" "Yes, there,
there," reiterated the servant, and, throwing open the door of the barn
and the curtains of his master's bed, he revealed a brilliant and astounding spectacle. The wide plain, bathed in the morning sunlight,
was covered with hostile squadrons and battalions, already close at
hand and steadily marching on. But behind this magnificent array, if
the count could have discerned them, were the shapes of great causes
and the destinies of many powerful nations. Europe protested against

the military domination of a single Power. The Holy Roman Empire pleaded for another century of life. The ancient rights of the Papacy against Gallicanism and the ascendancy of a Universal over a National church—despite the mistaken partisanship of the reigning Pope—were, in fact, fatefully at stake. The Dutch Republic sought to preserve its independence, and Prussia its kingdom rank. And from across the seas in England the Protestant succession, Parliamentary government, and the future of the British Empire advanced with confident tread. All these had brought their cases before the dread tribunal now set up in this Danube plain.

CHAPTER FORTY-THREE

The Battle of Blenheim
౪౮ 1704, August 13 ຈ౺

MARLBOROUGH had spent some of the night in prayer. He received the sacrament from Dr Hare. "The religion he had learned as a boy" fortified his resolution and sealed his calm. While the advance guards were moving into the night he visited Prince Eugene, whom he found writing letters. They mounted their horses.

The army filed off at three o'clock in eight columns, preceded by 40 squadrons, along tracks which had been carefully marked and prepared, through darkness intensified by the gathering mists of dawn. As day broke they crossed the watercourse by Tapfheim, and here the advance guards were merged in their respective columns. Here also a ninth column was formed close to the river. The artillery and the pontoons marched by the main road with the Duke's six-horse coach at their tail. The whole force numbered 66 battalions, 160 squadrons, and 66 guns, or about fifty-six thousand men. Daylight came, but at first the sun only drew more vapours from the marshes and shrouded densely the crawling masses. Thus the heads of the columns arrived in line with Schwenningen village, scarcely two miles from the enemy's camp, about six.

Here Marlborough and Eugene remained together for some time. The plan of the two commanders was that Eugene should attack and hold the enemy's left wing while Marlborough overwhelmed his right. If Marlborough succeeded he carried forward Eugene's battle with him. The more decisively Eugene could attack, the greater the chances of Marlborough's success. If both allied wings were defeated, retreat would be difficult, especially for Eugene, most of whose troops could only have fallen back into trackless wooded heights. On the other hand, the advance of Marlborough along the Danube and towards Höchstädt would not only conquer the enemy in his own front, but would threaten the retreat of the whole of the French opposite Eugene.

The mists began to thin as the sun rose higher, and the enemy outposts became aware of large numbers of men gathering along their front. They sent back speedy warnings, and at the same time the mists dispersing revealed from the French camp large forces covering the whole space from the Danube to the hills. Even now the Marshals and the Elector held to their prepossession that the confederate army was retiring under a bold display through the shallow valley which led back to Nördlingen. Tallard had finished a letter to the King, but before dispatching it he added the following postscript:

> This morning before daybreak the enemy beat the *général* at 2 o'clock and at three the *assemblée*. They are now drawn up at the head of their camp, and it looks as if they will march this day. Rumour in the countryside expects them at Nördlingen. If that be true, they will leave us between the Danube and themselves and in consequence they will have difficulty in sustaining the posts and depots which they have taken in Bavaria.

Incredible as it may seem, the Marshal penned these words about seven o'clock or even a few minutes afterwards, *and sent off the messenger*. We see that the possibility of the allies forcing a battle did not even enter his mind. This also gives us the measure of the audacity of Marlborough and Eugene in relation to the military conventions of the period as understood by the French High Command.

However, the columns still moved forward, and when, shortly after seven, they began to deploy into a long wall of blue, red, and buff, gleaming with steel, the truth broke suddenly upon the French and Bavarians. They were about to be attacked! There was no time to retire, even if they wished to do so, without abandoning their camp and baggage. They must now prepare to fight for life and honour. This sudden revolution of ideas had an effect not only upon the commanders, but upon their troops. It was a moral surprise. The camps sprang into activity. Aides and messengers galloped to and fro, the soldiers hustled out of their tents, formed in their companies, battalions, and brigades, and moved forward to their appointed places in the order of battle.

This had, of course, subject to the final dispositions of the commanders, already been prescribed. The allied army, whose formation developed and broadened continually, was soon within cannon-shot, and at half-past eight the powerful French artillery which covered their front opened fire upon them. The English field batteries began to reply as they came into range, and the cannonade became general. Its thunders rolled down the Danube Valley. The Margrave, forty miles away in his camp before Ingolstadt, was writing to the Emperor. His officers drew his attention to the distant thudding which loaded the air, and he inserted in his letter the words, "The Prince and the Duke are engaged to-day to the westward. Heaven bless them."

The French position had been selected for its military advantages. Its flanks rested securely on the Danube and the wooded hills. Its four-mile front was shielded by the rivulets of the Nebel. Along it were three considerable villages. On the French right, a furlong of water-meadows from the Danube, stood Blenheim (locally Blindheim), about three hundred houses, many of stone, with the usual South German gardens and enclosures, clustered round a solid church and stone-walled graveyard. Two miles or more away in the centre rose the roofs and church-tower of Oberglau, and a mile and a half beyond, nestling under the hills, the spire of Lutzingen. Here were three strong points on which to hang the front. From the marshes of the Nebel the ground rose almost imperceptibly but steadily in about a mile to a grassy upland, upon which the four or five thousand French and Bavarian tents were spread in well-drawn rows. On the allies' side the slopes were slightly more pronounced; and here the villages of Weilheim and Unterglau with several smaller hamlets had served as the French outpost line. These had already been set on fire by the retiring pickets and were burning briskly.

Tallard, Marsin, and the Elector met in Blenheim at about nine o'clock to concert their plans of defence. They were somewhat staggered by the stern aggression of which they saw themselves the objects. They assumed that the Margrave had joined the allied army, and that they were to be assaulted by superior forces. But they were not ill-content with their position, and they had time to occupy it advisedly. The generals climbed up the church-tower, whence the whole scene was revealed. From this modest height it appeared as a large, flat plain, framed by the mountains and the river. The cannon were firing busily on both sides, and between the bulges of dense white smoke which sprang into being and drifted towards them, and the dark clouds which arose from the conflagrations, long columns of the enemy were seen slowly making their way through the scrub of the foothills towards the head of the valley opposite Lutzingen. Not far away, before Blenheim, four heavy lines of infantry, among which the English redcoats predominated, and two of cavalry were deployed. In the centre, opposite the long, too long, space between Blenheim and Oberglau, the main force of the allies was drawn up in four dense lines.

Tallard placed 12 dismounted squadrons of dragoons behind a barrier of carts from the Danube to Blenheim. He assigned 9 battalions to the defence of the perimeter of Blenheim, with another 7 immediately behind them and 11 more battalions a few hundred yards back in reserve. He drew up 68 squadrons, supported by 9 battalions of infantry, and he sent his two remaining battalions to join twelve of Marsin's command in Oberglau. Marsin and the Elector arrayed the remainder of the French and all the Bavarian cavalry from Oberglau towards Lutzingen; and massed their infantry on either flank, posting Count d'Arco with 12 Bavarian battalions in front of Lutzingen with their flank resting 'refused' upon the hills. In all they marshalled 84 battalions, 147 squadrons, and 90 cannon, or about sixty thousand fighting men, against the allies' 66 battalions, 160 squadrons, and 66 cannon, or fifty-six thousand men.

Prince Eugene, with the troops he had brought from the Rhine and the cavalry which had joined him three weeks before at Rothweil, was meanwhile toiling through the rough and broken country in front of the Elector and Marsin. His progress was slow, and all the time he was harassed by the enemy's artillery, to which his own cannon, being still on the march, could for some time make no reply. At ten o'clock his leading British brigade, having expelled the enemy from two watermills upon the Nebel, crossed the marsh and lay within a hundred and fifty yards of the outskirts of the village. Here they endured for the next three hours with fortitude the severe fire of a heavy six-gun battery posted on a small eminence near Blenheim and to their right. The rest of Marlborough's army sat or lay in their ranks on the forward slope, the horse dismounted, and they too endured the cannonade of an artillery nearly twice as strong as their own. Marlborough's pioneers and working-parties, protected by infantry from the first line, repaired a stone bridge across the Nebel, and with the planks of the pontoons and seven hundred fascines which had been cut by the rear line of cavalry, constructed five additional bridges or causeways across the marsh between Blenheim and Oberglau. The artillery fire caused serious losses in both armies, but by far the heavier to the allies. The cannon-balls struck, bounded, and shore their way through the lines of men and horses on the plain, and caused nearly two thousand casualties before the attack could even be begun. Divine service was held at the head of every regiment, and the prayers and psalms rose to a grim accompaniment of crashes and cries of pain. But no unwounded man stirred from his place.

The services being ended, the waiting soldiers, unsheltered from the fire, ate their midday meal. Marlborough, resplendent in scarlet, wearing his Garter ribbon and riding his white horse, paced slowly in front of his harassed lines. A roundshot, striking at his horse's feet, enveloped him in a cloud of earth, and wrung an anxious gasp from the watching troops he had led so far from home. But he continued his progress uninjured. He had found the time to choose the sites for the field hospitals, such as they were, and had posted every battery himself. He spent the dragging hours in watching their shooting or conversing with the commanding officers. After a while he dismounted and lunched with his attendants, probably on the rising ground behind Unterglau village. In these conditions, where every man's bearing could be so closely scrutinized, he seemed entirely free from care; yet a grave anxiety was growing in his heart. What had happened to Eugene? He should have been in position by eleven. It was now nearly noon. Messengers had gone and returned with vague reports. The columns were struggling on as fast as they could. At length he sent Cadogan to find the Prince, and to see for himself. Cadogan returned shortly after twelve with the news that Eugene was nearly ready. All the bridges were now finished, and so far the enemy opposite Marlborough showed no mind to dispute the passage. But the day was wasting. Each minute now acquired a value. At last an aide-de-camp arrived at a gallop. "His Highness will give the signal for attack at half-past twelve." Marlborough rose, called for his horse, and mounted, saying to the group of officers, "Gentlemen, to your posts." All the troops stood up and dressed their ranks. The infantry fixed their bayonets, and Cutts launched his attack upon Blenheim. At the same time the first line of General Churchill's infantry began slowly to move towards the Nebel.

High and proud was the bearing of these regular soldiers as they strode into battle. "All," says Hare, "advancing cheerfully showed a firm and glad countenance and seeming to be confident to themselves of a victorious day."

The British brigade of five battalions which had been sheltering as much as possible in the stream-bed from the artillery now rose up and marched upon the palisades and enclosures of Blenheim. Their brigadier, General Rowe, had ordered that there should be no firing till he struck his sword upon the pales. The distance was perhaps a hundred and fifty yards, and almost immediately, owing to the ground, the troops passed out of the fire of the hostile battery. They marched in silence and perfect order to within thirty yards of the defences. Then the French fired a deadly volley, and General Rowe, who was still unscathed, struck the palisade with his sword; whereupon the survivors of the leading companies fired in their turn, and came to grips with the French through the palisades and across the obstacles which they tried by main force to tear to pieces. Their efforts were vain. Although here and there small parties penetrated, the French, who so greatly outnumbered their assailants, repulsed the attack, inflicting a loss of one man in three.

Lord Cutts now extended his line to the left with Ferguson's English brigade, and with Rowe's brigade, which had reformed, and the Hessians who still covered the right, delivered a second and even more costly attack. Here the troops broke at various points into the enclosures and pressed the defenders back upon the actual fronts of the houses and the barricades across the streets. More than this they could not win.

Shortly after midday Marshal Tallard, conceiving that there would be another two hours' delay before the attack, decided to visit the left of the Elector's line to survey the situation there. He had not been with the Elector long when the heavy firing around Blenheim recalled him to his own army. He noticed that M. de Clérambault, who commanded all the troops in Blenheim, had drawn the reserve into the village, but he took no steps to alter this decision. As he sat his horse upon the gentle rise on which his cavalry stood his attention was riveted by an episode which made a disconcerting and profound impression upon his mind. Marlborough's first line of infantry was already crossing the Nebel and drawing up in solid bodies on the firm ground. His first line of cavalry were now leading their horses continuously along the causeways. Five English squadrons from Lumley's command who had scrambled across near the burning mills were actually formed in the low ground on the edge of the plain. The eight squadrons of Gendarmerie, some of which had already been sharply engaged, were ordered by General Zurlauben to charge these intruders. They swept down upon them in an enveloping formation. But the five English squadrons, under Colonel Palmes, charging outward in three directions, broke the wings of the charge, and then, wheeling inward in perfect discipline and horsemanship, fell upon the centre of the Gendarmerie, completely routed them, and pursued them three hundred yards behind the Maulweyer brook, which flows through Blenheim. It was true that these squadrons, carried away by their zeal, came under tremendous fire from the outskirts of the village, and themselves recoiled with many empty saddles to their starting-point. But what Tallard had seen struck a chill into his soul. In the account which he eventually wrote in December of the battle he remarks that, "although there were eight squadrons on our side, the five enemy squadrons sustained their shock and made them recoil." He explains the loss of the battle "first, because the Gendarmerie were not able to break the five English squadrons." Well might Marlborough say, "The troops I carry with me are very good."

While these exciting incidents attracted unduly the attention of the hostile High Command, Marlborough's main body was gradually but ceaselessly forming beyond the Nebel. Already the first line of the infantry had advanced far enough to enable the first and a good part of the second line of cavalry to draw up in good order. Tallard now directed a cavalry charge upon the left of this array. Through confusion or neglect only a part of the squadrons he designed to use committed themselves to the charge. Much disorder was caused to the left of the allied line. Four or five English squadrons were rolled up from the flank. It was a dangerous moment, but the fire of the infantry repulsed the horsemen, and General Lumley made good the line by bringing across several fresh Danish and Hanoverian squadrons. Nothing could more plainly illustrate the delicate and hazardous character of the great operation which Marlborough was conducting in his centre, so long as it remained incomplete.

The whole front from the Danube to the hills was roaring with fire and conflict. "From one end of the armies to the other every one was at grips and all fighting at once—a feature very rare in battles." Marlborough, who had lately been watching the battle from the rising ground behind Unterglau, attended by his retinue, now came quickly forward, passed the burning villages, crossed the Nebel by a causeway, and took personal control at the danger-point. He led forward three Hanoverian battalions from Holstein-Beck's reserve. He made Colonel Blood bring a battery of cannon across the streamlet. With these he threw the Irish back some distance towards Oberglau. In this breathing-space the rest of Holstein-Beck's command began to form a line on the firm ground. This was the moment for Marsin's cavalry beyond Oberglau to renew their charges, and strenuous efforts were made to gather a strong force and set it in motion.

But meanwhile Marlborough had sent a personal message to Prince Eugene asking for the use of Fugger's brigade. Eugene was himself in an intense crisis. His second attack was quavering on the verge of repulse. Marlborough's aide-de-camp found him in the front line. He made his request. Without a moment's hesitation Eugene gave the order. The Imperial Cuirassiers changed front and advanced towards Oberglau. At that moment Marsin's cavalry advanced to the charge. But Fugger's cuirassiers charged at the same time and, striking at a favourable angle and on the bridle hand, threw back Marsin's squadrons in disorder. Marlborough, planting his battery to rake Blainville's line, was now able to move forward again with the three Hanoverian battalions, supported by the growing masses of Holstein-Beck's command. The struggle around Oberglau rose to a climax, both sides being closely engaged and their cannon firing grape and even case. But by three o'clock Blainville's troops were driven in upon the village, and Marlborough, nearly one thousand yards beyond the Nebel, was able to pen them, as Cutts was penning the much larger masses in Blenheim. This was the second crisis in the passage and deployment of Marlborough's centre.

A lull now descended upon the battlefield. The firing had lasted more than six hours and physical contact for nearly two, and everywhere it seemed that the armies reeled. Indeed, many an experienced officer in Europe, impartially surveying the scene, would have pronounced the allies defeated. They had failed with ghastly slaughter to take Blenheim. Nothing but deadlock existed there. They had equally failed to take Oberglau, and only narrowly escaped a severance of their wings. The whole of Prince Eugene's attack had come to a standstill. For nearly three-quarters of an hour the two lines of cavalry in this quarter stood facing each other at sixty yards' distance, neither of them able to move forward or strike another blow. In vain did Eugene on one side and the Elector on the other ride along the ranks animating, commanding, entreating, and taunting their exhausted and shaken soldiers to a renewed effort. At no point, it seemed, could the allies move forward. Yet it was certain they could not stay where they were. If they could not advance they must soon retreat. If they retreated they were lost.

Nevertheless at this moment Marlborough was sure of victory. Shortly after three o'clock he sent one of his aides, Lord Tunbridge, to Eugene, announcing that all was well in the centre. From the tumult of battle his design was now emerging. Although his total army had at the beginning been several thousands fewer than the French, and although it had suffered up to this point perhaps double their losses, he was now in a position of overwhelming strength. By four o'clock the whole of the cavalry and the whole of Churchill's infantry were formed in good order on the farther side of the Nebel opposite the French centre. The cavalry now formed the first two lines and the infantry the second pair. The English field batteries were moving forward to join them. Upon the two-mile stretch from Blenheim to Oberglau he had now nearly 80 squadrons, only a few of which had yet charged, against 50 or 60 French, many of whom had been several times engaged. Upon the same front he had 23 battalions against only 9. Leaving the bloody local fight around Oberglau, he now rode to conduct the advance of this formidable array.

The pause in the battle continued for a while. The reason for it is plain. Marlborough wished to concert the attack upon the whole front, and Eugene after his second repulse required time to reorganize. At half-past four, when the Danish infantry had worked their way round the Bavarians on the extreme left of Lutzingen, the battle was renewed at all points. The Prince of Anhalt-Dessau, carrying a regimental colour in his hand, led forward for the third time the redoubtable Prussian Foot. Eugene advanced again at the head of the Imperial cavalry. And now between Blenheim and Oberglau Marlborough's long lines, horse and foot together, were set in motion. The impact of so great a body of troops, comparatively fresh, upon the weakest part of a wasted front everywhere closely engaged, after so many hours, might reasonably be expected to be decisive.

Meanwhile Marlborough's attack was almost abreast of a line drawn from Blenheim to Oberglau, and so far there had been no collision. Tallard, who now saw doom outstaring him, ordered his first line to charge; and they became intermingled with Marlborough's squadrons, who do not seem at this time to have quickened their pace beyond a walk. The French were pressed back; but the allied horse as they advanced now came into the fire of the nine battalions who caused a good deal of disorder in Marlborough's first line, and compelled it to halt and then to retire a distance estimated by several observers at about sixty paces. The Marshal called upon his cavalry for a further effort. He met with no response. Marlborough now brought forward not only infantry but cannon to rake the devoted French battalions, some of which were formed in square. A battery of nine guns, which was following up the main advance under Colonel Blood's personal direction, fired upon them with grape, while at the same time the German infantry, coming to the front through the horse, opened a devastating musketry at close quarters. As the French squares would not give way, they had to be very largely destroyed where they stood.

We cannot pretend to unravel the details of this uneven struggle, but enough has been said to expose the delusion that the battle of Blenheim was gained by a cavalry charge. It was gained by the onset of a largely superior force of all arms working in close accord with one another at a decisive point. At least an hour elapsed between Marlborough's advance from the foot of the slope, before the moment of the final charge was reached. And by that time the result could hardly be doubtful. At about half-past five Marlborough re-formed both his lines of cavalry in front of the foot. He had time to ride along their ranks, and, being now satisfied that the masses of French infantry and cavalry which still held the field before him were disorganized and could resist no more, he drew his sword and ordered the trumpets to sound the charge. Now for the first time the whole body of the allied cavalry broke into a trot, and sword in hand rode forward upon all who barred their path. The French squadrons did not await the shock. Discharging their pistols and carbines in ragged, ineffectual volleys, they broke and fled, leaving the remnants of the nine battalions to their fate. Of course, when we read of troops being 'cut to pieces' we may be sure that the greater number usually escape somehow. But these poor soldiers of France behaved so bravely that the positions they had held could be plainly seen the next day upon the battlefield by their corpses lying in ranks.

In this part of the field all serious resistance now came to an end. Tallard, who redeemed as a soldier his shortcomings as a general, rallied a body of his cavalry behind the tents of his camp. His one hope and duty was to procure the retreat of the infantry in Blenheim. He sent messages to them to retire, and to Marsin to come to his aid. But all control had passed out of his hands. Marlborough, with Lumley and Hompesch, the Prussian, and over seventy squadrons, was upon them. The French ran in two directions, some towards Marsin's army and the rest towards the Danube. Sending Hompesch to the right with half the cavalry, the Duke with Lumley pursued those who were making for the river. The spectacular tragedy which followed has attracted the attention of many historians. The bank of the Danube near Sondenheim falls very steeply as much as fifteen or twenty feet. A mob of French horsemen, jammed knee to knee and variously computed at thirty squadrons or two thousand men, were driven headlong over this drop into the marshes and the deep, swift river; of whom the greater part were drowned. Mérode Westerloo, who after much hard fighting was caught in this rout, says that for three hundred paces he was so jammed in the crowd that "his horse never put its feet on the ground," until suddenly he was precipitated "the depth of two pikes" into a marshy meadow and buried beneath several falling cavaliers. Marshal Tallard, trying to make his way into Blenheim, recognized by his Order of the Saint-Esprit, was taken prisoner with several of his staff not far from this point by a Hessian regiment. He was conducted to Marlborough, who with salutes and courtesies placed his coach at his disposal.

This was the moment when John wrote the letter to Sarah. Borrowing a piece of paper, actually a bill of tavern expenses, from an officer, he traced in pencil his well-known message:

August 13, 1704

I have not time to say more but to beg you will give my duty to the Queen, and let her know her army has had a glorious victory. Monsieur Tallard and two other Generals are in my coach and I am following the rest. The bearer, my aide-de-Camp Colonel Parke, will give Her an account of what has passed. I shall do it in a day or two by another more at large.

Marlborough

The destruction of Tallard's army involved the instant retreat and possible capture of Marsin and the Elector. It was now six o'clock. Eugene's cavalry had failed in their third attack. The Prince, infuriated at a courage not equal to his own, is said to have shot two fugitives with his own hand. Certainly he was himself in the direst peril—his coat clutched by the enemy, and his life saved only by the devotion of his troopers. When the collapse of their charge was apparent he left his cavalry with bitter words, saying that he would fight and die with the gallant infantry and not with cowards. Indeed, the Danes and Prussians had made remarkable progress. With only two squadrons of cavalry to aid them, they had driven the enemy's extreme left back more than two miles, scrambling over the spurs and valleys amid the rocks and bushes of the foothills. From these slopes the Prince could see the result of Marlborough's main attack. He saw the whole centre of the enemy break into disorder, and knew that the battle was won. Soon the smoke and flames rising from Oberglau and Lutzingen proclaimed the retreat of the army which had so valiantly withstood him. He set to work to organize his troops for pursuit.

When Marshal Marsin saw Tallard's line broken and the wide plain between Oberglau and Blenheim occupied by Marlborough's troops advancing in solid formations, he resolved to retreat. The Elector and the other generals were all in agreement. The disengagement and withdrawal were effected with skill and discipline, and the army of the French left wing marched in the direction of Lauingen in admirable order. This was indeed necessary, for they must expect to have to fight hard to gain the exit between the hills and the marsh of Höchstädt. Marsin's army was by no means exhausted. They had no reason to

(414)

boast about their battle. With more squadrons, with nearly double the battalions and more than double the cannon of Prince Eugene, they had been hard put to it to defend themselves. They had even ceded important ground to the attack of far less numerous forces. They had fought a self-centred battle, and had been able to give no help to their friends on the right, with whose defeat their own was now involved. These facts attest the glory of Prince Eugene, whose fire and spirit had extorted the wonderful exertions of his troops; who after contending all day against very heavy odds held the initiative and the offensive to the end; and who, moreover, in the midst of local disaster had not hesitated to answer Marlborough's call for the Cuirassier brigade. By seven o'clock the whole of Marsin's army, escorting their prisoners and rescuing on their way two of Tallard's battalions who had already surrendered, were making for the gap above Morselingen, followed by all the troops that Prince Eugene could muster.

Meanwhile Marsin's army in three columns, the outer ones of cavalry, was drawing near, and Hompesch was about to charge, when another large body of troops in good formation came in sight from behind Oberglau village. These were thought to be Marsin's rearguard. They were so disposed as to take in flank such a charge as Hompesch was about to make. They were in fact the leading brigades of Prince Eugene following the French, and themselves seeking a chance of attack. Marlborough, in no mood to compromise his victory, sent out patrols to make sure of the truth, and meanwhile waited. Eugene in his turn mistook Hompesch for a part of Tallard's cavalry, and likewise paused to assure himself. By the time these mistakes were discovered Marsin and the Elector had made such progress across Marlborough's front that a new attack meant a new battle. The Duke surveyed the scene against the setting sun. He observed the firm attitude of the enemy and their superior numbers. He knew that he had the bulk of Tallard's infantry—how many he could not tell—behind him in Blenheim, still to be mastered. He decided to break off the pursuit of Marsin, and in all the circumstances his judgment should be accepted.

Meanwhile the twenty-seven battalions in Blenheim were attacked on every side. The fire of the surrounding troops, which were constantly reinforced, shattered the heads of every formation. The three British Generals, working in spontaneous combination, all realized the tremendous prize they had in their grip. A French brigade which had

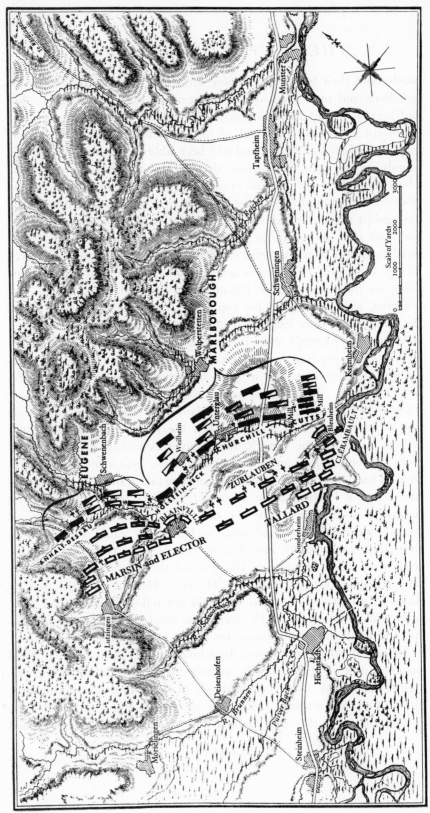

6. The Battle of Blenheim

actually debouched was brought to parley, and its commander allowed himself to be sent in to bring the rest to reason. Agitated argument began about capitulation. Resistance was impossible. All must surrender at once as prisoners of war. The one concession granted by Churchill, to whom the issue was referred, was that the officers should not be searched.

The grief and fury of these unbeaten troops have often been described. The regiment of Navarre burned its standards, and many officers refused to sign the convention; but this could hardly avail them much. Before nine o'clock the surrender was complete. It was not till then that Marlborough's orders arrived. The Duke, concerned at the very great numbers he now knew to be in the place, would run no risks. All the troops were to lie on their arms, and by morning he would bring the entire army. But the work had already been completed by his competent lieutenants. "Without vanity," wrote Orkney, "I think we did our pairts." And so had they all.

CHAPTER FORTY-FOUR

The Consequences of Victory

ξα 1704, August ϸξ

COLONEL Parke rode fast across Europe, spreading the good tidings through the German and Dutch cities as he passèd. On the morning of the 10th/21st he delivered his note to Sarah at St. James's, who sent him on with it at a gallop to Windsor. Queen Anne sat in the big bay-window of the long gallery overlooking the Terrace, and serious must have been her thoughts. Here, at the summit of England's war effort, many grievous pressures met in a sovereign's breast. She knew that far away in Germany Mr Freeman meant to strike some blow that should kill or cure. Rulers in constitutional states hear tales from many quarters, and the Queen understood only too well that the entire political system of her reign was under grave and pent-up challenge. She could read the stress of the times in Mr Montgomery's anxious eyes. With all her patient courage—and, let us add, Stuart obstinacy—she had sustained the men she trusted against the gathering antagonism of Parliament and society, and amid the growing degeneration of her affairs both at home and abroad.

A scarlet horseman has crossed the river: news of battle is in the air. They bring the weary messenger to her presence. He falls on his knee, but before he speaks she knows that all is well. He hands her Marlborough's note to Sarah, and tells her that with his own eyes he has seen the first army of France broken into flight and ruin, and the celebrated Marshal Tallard led off prisoner by the Duke's officers. As the Queen read its pencilled lines she knew that something very great had happened to her country and to the world.

(418)

Meanwhile from Whitehall Godolphin spread the news throughout the town. The cannon of the Tower were fired; the bells were rung; copies of Marlborough's note, struck off upon the presses, passed from hand to hand. A wave of enthusiasm swept all classes. The streets were filled with cheering crowd. Bonfires and illuminations disputed the night. "Never were such demonstrations of joy since the laying of London stone." Nor were these rejoicings unwarranted. Indeed, they arise from the smallest part of what had happened. Every one could understand that the Grand Monarch had had a drubbing, and that Marlborough had caught his famous general, old Tallard, the Ambassador, well known at St. James's, and packed him in his coach. But few could measure the consequences, and none could foresee how the fortunes of Britain would now broaden through the centuries.

The news of Blenheim came also to Versailles. A few days before the battle there had been a splendid evening fête at the Court. The most brilliant society in Europe was assembled, and the warm, delicious night favoured the festivities. Upon a triumphal car attended by warriors and nymphs the God of War was drawn past the daïs on which the Great King sat, and Louis XIV displayed a lively pleasure in accepting his dutiful salute. Then followed an allegorical representation of the state of Europe, in which all its rivers played their parts. The Thames, the Scheldt, the Rhine, the Meuse, the Neckar, and also the Danube made their submission to the assured pre-eminence of the Seine. The festival culminated in a prodigy of fireworks designed to bring home to the numerous and exalted company a vivid picture of modern war.

One afternoon rumours began to spread of something ugly which had happened in Bavaria, and presently it was known that a courier from one of the armies in the field had been conducted by Chamillart to the King. They all had something else to talk about after that.

We must return to the Danube.

Sergeant Millner sets forth with careful pride the full tally of the slain, the wounded, and the captives. The sergeant's catalogue of grisly spoils, although a little sanguine, has not been seriously challenged by the estimates of later times. The casualties of the allies were certainly not less than the 12,700 which he has recorded. Indeed, the later details of the British losses would seem to raise this figure considerably. The confederate army had lost by fire and steel nearly a quarter of its numbers. Six thousand lay dead upon the field, and the thirty-five or forty thousand hale men who stood to arms on August 14, worn out by their prodigious exertions and sleepless nights, had, besides their own six or seven thousand wounded and an equal number of the enemy wounded, twelve thousand prisoners on their hands: in all twenty-five thousand to tend or guard.

Meanwhile the victors triumphed. A solemn thanksgiving service was celebrated with joy-fire of musketry, and triple discharges of cannon. Marlborough's bearing towards the captives won general admiration. "Whereas Prince Eugene was harsh," wrote Saint-Simon, "the Duke of Marlborough treated them all, even the humblest, with the utmost attention, consideration, and politeness, and with a modesty perhaps more distinguished than his victory. . . ." The rank and file of the prisoners reserved to him received by his orders every possible comfort and favour. Some of the interchanges have been preserved:

> MARLBOROUGH: I am very sorry that such a cruel misfortune should have fallen upon a soldier for whom I have had the highest regard.
> TALLARD: And I congratulate you on defeating the best soldiers in the world.
> MARLBOROUGH: Your Lordship, I presume, excepts those who had the honour to beat them.

All the Frenchmen of every rank showed the keenest admiration for the Great Twin Captains, as they were already regarded, and clustered round them in curiosity. The soldierly bearing of a French private to whom Marlborough spoke drew from him the remark, "If the King of France had many men like you, he would soon be victorious." To which the soldier, somewhat unkindly to his superiors who stood around, rejoined, "It is not men like me he lacks, but a general like you."

Every one could see, as Lediard says, that "the Face of Affairs was wholly changed." The first decision of Marlborough and Eugene was to bring in the Margrave. There was no sense in besieging Ingolstadt when the whole of Bavaria must almost certainly fall into their hands by a treaty. Augsburg and Memmingen had already been abandoned by their

French garrisons, and their deputations were at Marlborough's head-quarters imploring government and protection. Ulm was obviously the first objective; and for that siege the cannon deployed before Ingolstadt was required.

Marshal Marsin and the defeated French made haste to quit Ulm. They left a garrison of nine weak French and Bavarian battalions in the fortress for the sole purpose of bargaining an honourable capitulation which would safeguard the future of the several thousand grievously wounded officers and men who could accompany them no farther. On the 20th they retreated to Tuttlingen, reduced to no more than sixteen thousand men. All the French had but one thought—to return to France. But for the Elector of Bavaria the question was more difficult.

On the night of the battle when he met d'Arco in the market-place of Leipheim (a village behind the field), he had cried out to him, "The devil take me if I know what to do now." Indeed hard choices lay before Max Emmanuel. Should he make peace with the Emperor and return chastened to his country, or should he cast in his lot as a soldier with France, and as a throneless prince with the Grand Monarch? Honour, frequently embarrassed, now pointed to Versailles; but his interest was more evenly divided. He sent to inquire from Marlborough whether the conditions which he had rejected before the battle were still open. He was answered that the accretions of territory could no longer be offered, but that if he would desert the French and furnish a contingent of eight thousand men, he should be restored to his dominions, and receive an annual subsidy from England and Holland.

The spectacle which was next presented of the Elector refusing the favourable terms which were pressed upon him, separating himself from his country, from his family, and from his home, at the imperious call of honour, was impressive. In fact, however, the position was not so simple. As Vicar-General of the Spanish Netherlands, Max Emmanuel had another sphere of action in the North. All the Spanish troops in Belgium were subject to his orders. He could bring with him his own handful of Bavarians. He still believed that France was invincible; but if he were mistaken there was always another possibility. He might make an arrangement with the allies, and especially with the Dutch, to whom the independence of the barrier state was an idol. To come to terms with the Emperor about Bavaria at this juncture was certainly to sacrifice the interests he prized so dearly in Belgium: whereas a treaty with the Dutch about Belgium would naturally carry with it the restoration of his own Hereditary Lands.

The best—indeed, almost the only possible—route for Marsin and the defeated army lay through the Black Forest and by the tracks around Villingen along which Tallard had journeyed to his fate a few weeks before. They hoped that Villeroy as soon as he learned of the disaster would come to their assistance, and they hesitated to enter the forest-defiles of the mountains without hearing from him. They counted upon him not only for the protection of his army, but, what was even more vital, for the organization of the supplies without which they must have starved.

On August 17 Villeroy at Erlach was at length advancing against the Lines of Stollhofen in pursuance of the King's orders. That night the first reports reached him of an awful disaster upon the Danube. So far he had received no message from Marsin or from Versailles. What he heard was enough to arrest his movement. He waited in suspense during the next two days: but on the 19th, when Marsin's courier arrived, he resolved, without waiting for orders from Versailles, to march forthwith to the rescue of his defeated comrades. The decision does credit to his strategic comprehension. Only a Marshal enjoying his high favour would have dared to abandon the task so insistently prescribed by the King. Forthwith he set to work to bake bread and collect biscuit and transport, and marched with all his force along Tallard's old route towards Villingen. The fortress was still held by the Germans, but the neighbouring tracks were open. He arrived on the 23rd, and the next day the beaten army fell into his arms and upon his provision-trains. They were a tragic remnant. The Elector had but three thousand Bavarians and Marsin thirteen thousand French. Their horses were devoured by contagious disease; their officers and men were infected with the not less dangerous virus of defeat and sense of hopeless inferiority which they had contracted upon the Höchstädt battlefield. Their despondency and lack of discipline spread throughout the ranks of their rescuers, and only a passionate wish to return to France held them all together. They marched by Freiburg, Hornberg, Offenburg, and Kehl, and crossed the Rhine at Strasburg on the last day of August.

Thus ended finally the design of Louis XIV against the Empire, and his far-reaching Bavarian intrigue. The sixteen thousand war-broken men who trudged across the Strasburg bridges represented the fragments of three powerful armies: first, the Bavarian army of 35 battalions and 55 squadrons; secondly, the army of Villars (afterwards of Marsin) of 60 squadrons and 50 battalions, together with Tallard's reinforcements, equal in themselves to 20 battalions; and, thirdly, Tallard's own army of 40 battalions and 50 squadrons. The total effort in the two campaigns could scarcely be measured by less than 150 battalions and 170 squadrons, or upward of a hundred and fifty thousand men. For all this and the vast ambitions and policies involved nothing remained but the dispirited sixteen thousand who gasped with relief when their weary feet touched again the soil of France. The Scarlet Caterpillar had not traversed the map of Europe in vain.

Blenheim is immortal as a battle not only because of the extraordinary severity of the fighting of all the troops on the field all day long, and the overwhelming character of the victory, but because it changed the political axis of the world. This only gradually became apparent. Even a month after all the facts were known, measured, and discounted, scarcely any one understood what transformations had been wrought. Until that August day the statesmen of every country must contemplate the prospect of the Elector of Bavaria supplanting the House of Hapsburg in the Imperial Crown, with Munich instead of Vienna as the capital of Central Europe. Yet this Prince, should he become so bright a luminary, would be himself a planet only in the system of the Sun King. Spain and Italy would have their appointed orbits around the parent of light. The vast new regions opening beyond the oceans to the consciousness of man, those distant constellations, would shine with brightening gleams upon a French Monarchy of Europe and a dominant Gallican Church. The sullen and awkward Dutch and boorish English would perforce conform to the august design. Their recalcitrancy would be but the measure of their sufferings.

All this glittering fabric fell with a crash. From the moment when Louis XIV realized, as he was the first to realize, the new values and proportions which had been established on August 13, he decided to have done with war. Although long years of bloodshed lay before him, his object henceforward was only to find a convenient and dignified exit from the arena in which he had so long stalked triumphant. His

ambition was no longer to gain a glorious dominion, but only to preserve the usurpations which he regarded as his lawful rights, and in the
end this again was to shrink to no more than a desperate resolve to
preserve the bedrock of France.

On the field of Blenheim also sank the fortunes of the House of
Stuart. The collapse of the Grand Alliance and the hegemony of
France in Europe must have brought with them so profound a disintegration of English political society that for perhaps a century at least
vassalage under a French-imposed King might well have been our fate.
However, a different tale was told by the good behaviour on August 13
of Cutts, Churchill, Orkney, Cadogan, Blood, Lumley, Ingoldsby,
Rowe, many Captain Blackadders, and Parkers and Sergeant Millners,
with their dauntless rank and file, marching onward behind the swords
of Marlborough and Eugene.

The terror of the French armies was broken. Forty years of successful
war, the invasion of so many countries, few and minor reverses, and
these repaired by victory upon a hundred fields, had brought a renown
before which, even while they still resisted, the most stubborn opponents bowed their heads. French generals and French troops believed
themselves to be, and were largely accepted throughout the Continent
as, a superior military order. All this was changed by the Danube battle. Here was defeat, naked, brutal, murderous; defeat in spite of numbers; defeat by manœuvre and defeat by force. The prolonged severity
of the fighting and the extraordinary losses of the victors proved the
reality of the test. But to all this was added the sting of disgrace and
ridicule. A surrender in mass of the finest infantry of France, the most
famous regiments disarmed wholesale on the battlefield, the shameful
confusion and collapse of command in Blenheim village, the overthrow
of the French cavalry front to front by sword against pistol, their flight
while their comrades perished—all these hideous disillusionings had
now to be faced. And with them also arose the red star of the island
troops. Their discipline, their fighting energy, their readiness to endure
extraordinary losses, the competence and teamplay of their officers, the
handiness of their cavalry and field artillery, their costly equipment and
lavish feeding, their self-assured, unaffected disdain of foreigners, became the talk of Europe. There was a quality in their attacks upon the
Schellenberg and the village of Blenheim, earnest, downright, and violent, which seemed to raise the fierceness of the war to a new degree.

Few they were, but thenceforward they were marked men. Soon we shall see Louis XIV writing special instructions to his marshals that in any order of battle "the best troops should be placed opposite the English."

And their Chief! Here indeed was a portent. "The day at Höchstädt," wrote Napoleon's historian, "froze with horror the Party of the Two Crowns. Thenceforward the name of Marlborough became as it were a new power which entered into the confederacy and upheld it by a terror, the profound marks of which the passage of a century has not effaced."

*In September, 1704, the British captured Gibraltar, and in a naval battle off Malaga drove off the French fleet and took command of the western Mediterranean.**

After Blenheim there were still three months left of the campaigning season. Marlborough had no doubts how to use them. He wished to take Ulm, and neutralize and pacify the rest of Bavaria by a treaty. Having thus completely mastered the Danube valley and freed the Empire from all immediate danger, he proposed without a day's delay, except for supplies, to carry the entire army of the confederacy to the Rhine and thence to the Moselle. There he would establish the strongest possible forces in winter quarters for an advance towards Paris in the spring. Meanwhile he urged the Emperor to send substantial and speedy aid to the Duke of Savoy, who was penned around Turin, and above all to make terms, involving some kind of Federal Home Rule, with the Hungarian insurgents. But the victory had seated the Emperor securely upon his ancient throne. He saw no reason to give in the days of regained strength what he had denied even in his worse straits and weakness. He and the proud incapables who surrounded him resented the interference of an English Parliamentary Government and a Dutch Republic in the domestic concerns of the Holy Roman Empire. All these Western ideas of constitutional right and self-determination for subject nationalities were subversive of the very foundations of his House. He was grateful to Marlborough for the deliverance he had brought; but he was also grateful to that Providence without whose blessing men's nob-

* By H. S. C.

lest efforts are vain, and whose strong arm required no reward but praise, for which the Church made regular provision. Moreover, the Emperor felt that he himself had contributed to the success of the allied army. Had he not prescribed the three days of solemn intercession on the very eve of the Danube cannonade?

On August 25 the allied forces began their march for the Rhine. For the convenience of supply the three generals moved by separate routes through Würtemberg. The English and the Danes regained at Gross Heppach the road by which they had come, and on the 31st were overtaken at Mondelsheim by Marlborough. For a second time the redcoats were welcomed in these German towns, and surely they might feel that this time the tributes were deserved. In June they had come as rescuers: in August they returned as victors. They had certainly made good their untactful promise "to lend spirit to the Empire and spurs to the French." Joy, gratitude, and jubilation hailed their homeward path. But little more than half of them were there to tread it.

The concentration of the allies along the Rhine in the Philippsburg area was effected smoothly and punctually. Marlborough and Eugene arrived together, and the Margrave a few days later. Eugene had collected all the troops which had hitherto guarded the Lines of Stollhofen. At this stage it was only the enemy who would have need of defensive systems. The open field belonged to the allies. Marlborough summoned the heavy artillery furnished by the Landgrave of Hesse, which he had been forced to leave at Mannheim and had used as a feint on his original march. The total strength of the confederates on the Upper Rhine now amounted to 92 battalions and 181 squadrons. At this late period in the campaign all the units on both sides were much reduced in numbers. "Above one half of our battalions," wrote Marlborough (September 8) to Godolphin, "are extremely weak, so that if we come to action I intend to make the fourteen English battalions but seven, and to do the same thing to the Danes and Hessians, which will bring our battalions to seventy-eight." The numerical and moral superiority of the confederates was, however, not disputable. During the 6th, 7th, and 8th, after personal reconnaissances by Marlborough and Eugene, the army crossed the two floating bridges which had been thrown by Philippsburg, and drew out on a seven-mile front before the Queich river, along which lay the French main forces.

Early on September 9 Marlborough, Eugene, and the Margrave marched south against the Queich with all their forces in battle array, resolved to force the passages by general battle on the following day. Villeroy felt himself unequal, in the despondent mood of the army, by which he was himself affected, to meet the attack. He ordered a retreat of twenty miles to the next tributary of the Rhine, the Lauter. The alacrity with which this command was obeyed exposed to the confederates the remarkable disorder of the French. Marlborough followed them with the united army, and Villeroy thereupon retired another twenty miles to Hagenau and the line of the Moder.

Landau was now isolated and exposed. The Margrave undertook the siege, and Marlborough and Eugene covered him along the Lauter. For greater convenience in supply one of the floating bridges at Philippsburg was towed upstream, and established close behind the junction of the Queich and the Rhine. The fortress of Landau contained a garrison and nine battalions under a resolute governor, Laubanie, and before retreating Villeroy had thrown into it a mass of munitions and twelve months' victuals. In the preceding year it had yielded to a French siege in thirty days, and it was therefore hoped that the same allowance would now be sufficient. If so there would still be time for Marlborough to develop his projects upon the Moselle. But the Imperial army was found deficient in all the apparatus of a first-class siege. It was said of them that they "undertake sieges without cannon, ammunition or engineers with as much assurance as they did a war without money, credit or troops." Besides this a singular lethargy seemed to have overcome the Margrave, whose foot, bruised at the Schellenberg, had begun to trouble him; and the progress of the works was judged by all observers to be unaccountably and unwarrantably slow.

The King of the Romans, an agreeable youth inspired by the keenest admiration for Marlborough, now arrived in great state from Vienna to take nominal command of the operations. Although this was a formality, it aggravated the Margrave's already festering internal griefs. He saw, with an irritation he scarcely troubled to conceal, that his reputation was eclipsed by the glory of Marlborough and Eugene. He had been kept out of Blenheim; he had been recalled from Ingolstadt; and now an obsequious world would ascribe the honours of the capture of Landau to the heir to the Imperial throne. As the poet fulsomely sang of the young King:

MARLBOROUGH

What tides of Glory to his Bosom ran,
Clasped in th' Embraces of the GODLIKE MAN.

The Margrave could hardly be expected to see Marlborough in so rosy a light. He resented both the domination and the bland dissembling of the English upstart, whom he conceived he had saved from disaster at the Schellenberg, and who had shown no gratitude even for that. Well, let him wait upon the siege, and wait also for his preposterous campaign on the Moselle. Imagine opening new operations at this season of the year! Was the man's ambition insatiable? Thus, we suppose, not without much evidence, did the Margrave chew his bitter cud.

General Thüngen's batteries had opened upon Ulm on September 8. The governor beat the chamade on the 10th, and the next day was allowed to march out with the honours of war. The Bavarians dispersed to their homes. Sickness and desertion were such that only nine hundred Frenchmen reached the Rhine. A great supply of munitions, including two hundred and fifty cannon and twelve hundred barrels of powder, fell to the captors; and the whole attacking force, with its much-needed siege train, set out for the Rhine and Landau.

On October 10 John wrote to Sarah:

> For thousands of reasons I wish myself with you. Besides I think if I were with you quietly at the lodge, I should have more health, for I am at this time so very lean, that it is extreme uneasy to me, so that your care must nurse me this winter, or I shall certainly be in a consumption. I am very sorry to hear you have so often returns of your illness, and I do with all my heart thank you for the resolution you have taken of letting the physicians try to cure you, which I hope in God they will, and that you may live many years after me, which both by my age and constitution you must do.

Sarah was distressed by her husband's accounts of his health. She evidently urged him to wind up the campaign and come home. When could there be a better moment than after so great a victory? Godolphin too was insistent. Parliament was meeting. The Captain-General's presence was necessary in England to use the full political effect of his success while all were dazzled by it. The advantage of his return was not lost upon the practised statesman. The sound maxim, "Leave off a winner," occurred to the gambler of Newmarket and the Whitehall card-tables. Why worry about Landau, and still more about the Moselle? Enough had been done for the Germans. Let them go into winter quarters, as, indeed, they desired. Embark the Queen's troops at some handy place, and let the Rhine current bear them swiftly and easily back to Holland.

A supreme desire to bring the war to a victorious end by the surest and speediest means now possessed the general who was constantly accused of prolonging it for his own advantage. After the capture of Gibraltar and the battle of Malaga the combined Anglo-Dutch fleet might well control the Mediterranean. By this means the Italian front could be effectually restored to an activity which would exact exhaustive efforts from the French. For this purpose the Duke of Savoy must be strongly reinforced, both overland from the Empire and from the sea, by troops and naval action. The highest possible pressure must similarly be exerted along the front in Flanders. With these two wings rigorously engaging the enemy's strength, the conditions would be created for the main advance of the confederate centre by Thionville and Metz towards Paris. An army of a hundred thousand men must be concentrated on the Moselle, based principally on Coblenz, at the very opening of the new campaign. He must have forty thousand Germans, twenty thousand Dutch, and his own forty thousand in the Queen's pay ready to take the field by April, so as to have the full year's fighting before him and reach the result. Considerable forces must winter upon the Moselle, with the command of the river behind them. He must have Trarbach; he must have Trèves, and he must have Saarlouis. This structure of fortresses and magazines, held in force during the winter and filled continually with supplies, would be the foundation from which he could move in the spring as the first step upon Thionville. There was no surprising novelty in such a conception. In fact, so far as the Moselle was concerned, it was the plan which the Margrave had proposed at the end of 1703. But for the first time the rescue of the Empire and the ascendancy, as might have been hoped, of one mind in the allied war direction, together with the injury which France had received in 1704, the improved balance of forces, and the command of the Mediterranean, had made it feasible.

For this end every effort must be made. This was no time for triumph or repose. Was the war to drag on in costly, bloody gnawings around the frontiers of France until perhaps it died down in disastrous futility, until the Alliance, reforged on the anvil of Blenheim, broke again to pieces? For a thrust at the heart, the chance, the means, the time, and—might he not feel?—the man had now come. Beyond the battle-smoke of a terrible year he saw peace rising out of an otherwise endless warfare, and order emerging from chaos, with England the glorious deliverer at the summit.

On September 19 Louis XIV wrote a very fine and discerning letter to Villeroy. The Marshal had been much disquieted by the silence which his master had observed upon his hurried abandonment of the lines on the Queich and Lauter. This had lasted for no less than ten days. It must have been with relief that he read the generous, cheering message which reached him probably upon September 21.

> Raise yourself above the talk of the public. Do not look upon yourself as the victim of Höchstädt day. You have done your duty as a true man. You have taken the steps which you thought best for my interest. In disregard of a false pride which would have been ill-founded, you have been more concerned in preserving my army and my State than with your personal reputation. Nothing could convince me more of your devotion to me.

The next day the King showed that he and his experts had penetrated Marlborough's future designs.

> I have reason to believe . . . four battalions are being sent from Overkirk's army to the Moselle. . . . It looks very much as if Monsieur de Marlborough will send at the same time cavalry, and perhaps even infantry to strengthen this corps to occupy Trèves if they can, and even to attack Trarbach in order to develop their plan and besiege Thionville at the beginning of the next campaign.

This warning was written from Versailles on September 20, and it exactly embodied Marlborough's intentions.

We may be sure that Villeroy pondered deeply upon it. He had long conferences with Marsin, who lay crippled in Strasburg. Both Marshals decided that Marlborough would not be able to attack the Moselle before Landau had fallen, and all the troops fastened around it were released. They were therefore content to strengthen M de Coigny, who commanded in the Moselle valley, to about three thousand horse, composed of their weakest squadrons. They must after all contemplate, at least as a possibility, that they would perhaps themselves be the objects of a major attack as soon as the fortress was taken. They could not tell what was happening at Landau, from which they were quite cut off.

The siege dragged on. "Our people," wrote Marlborough to Harley on October 6, "are advancing by the sap [*i.e.*, by sapping], in order to make a lodgment on the counterscarp. This method may save a few men, but will cost the more time, and, it may be, a great many more men in the end by sickness." The cavalry captain Pope, writing a month later, expressed the common talk of the English regiments.

> The Prince of Baden is now sufficiently revenged for our robbing him of a share of the glory of the victory of Blenheim. He has spun out this siege till the left wing of the horse, to which that action was chiefly owing, is entirely ruined. We have not above twenty horses a troop left.

At length Marlborough could watch this process no longer. It was not in his power to coerce or remove the Margrave. He determined to make a personal effort of his own. He was fairly sure the Marshals would not expect him to quit the main army before the capitulation of Landau. He therefore began from October 13 onward to build up secretly a force at Homburg, thirty-five miles to the westward. The defences of this place, as we have seen, had been recently dismantled by the French; and to Villeroy its occupation and repair might seem to be a natural precaution for the right flank of the confederate army covering the siege of Landau. On the 19th the Duke sent Colonel Blood with fourteen guns and four howitzers, escorted by 3 battalions, to this strong post. Twenty-two battalions marched thither on the 20th, 48 squadrons on the 21st, and he himself joined them on the 24th. This little army in its shrunken state amounted to twelve thousand men, but all lively. Eugene agreed to be left on the Lauter with no more than twenty-five thousand men against Villeroy, twenty-seven miles away, with forty thousand.

On the 25th the Duke plunged into the wild Hunsrück mountain region. In those days when roads were but tracks, and scarcely a dwelling pleaded with primeval solitudes, the march seemed forlorn and sombre to the troops. Marlborough with the horse reached St Wendel at the head of the passes on the 26th. But it was only with a hard struggle that the foot traversed the twenty miles in three days. He had

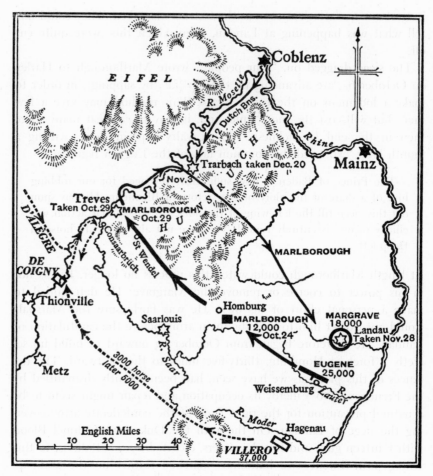

7. Marlborough Secures the Moselle

to wait at St Wendel till they came up. He could not tell how many French he would find in the valley of the Moselle. His usually excellent information reported ten thousand reinforcements approaching Trèves, but there might be more. No retreat was possible. Unless he could establish himself upon the Moselle and gather the Dutch troops now coming from Coblenz, he must "throw his cannon into some river"; for back they could never go.

All went well. "We have had," wrote Cardonnel, who lost all his kit and baggage by a fire, "a most horrible march hither day and night, but

I thank God it has had all the success we could desire." Villeroy was not sure of Marlborough's movements till the 26th. He dispatched d'Alègre, a capable officer (Coigny having succumbed), with a reinforcement of five thousand men. They were within six miles of Trèves when Marlborough's vanguard, urged on by appeals from the inhabitants, came within sight of the ancient city. The handful of French in the fort fled without having time to burn the place as Marlborough, judging by his own severities in Bavaria, feared and expected. Instead of being a French fortress held by a skeleton force, Trèves now became a well-garrisoned confederate stronghold. Six thousand peasants were set to work night and day to repair the extensive but ruined fortifications, and they were covered by Marlborough's cavalry at Consaarbrück. The seizure and fortification of Trèves left the much more strongly defended fortress of Trarbach isolated and open to attack. The twelve Dutch battalions had now arrived from Holland. Marlborough could entrust the siege to the Prince of Hesse. He had to abandon his hopes of taking Saarlouis. Having neither the time nor the strength for this, he returned with his staff to Landau, the King of the Romans, and the Margrave. The campaign was now drained to the very dregs. Landau was not taken till November 28, and even so the garrison marched out under the honours of war. Laubanie, although blinded at the outset by a bomb, had made a fine defence of more than seventy days. The Margrave had to ascribe what there was of credit to the King of the Romans.

This winter effort of Marlborough's will-power deserves admiration. The whole feeling of the armies after Blenheim was that they had done their part for the year. Their commanders longed to parade their laurels before their countrymen, and to receive the tributes they had so well deserved. But Marlborough was deaf to all appeals, even the most seductive. He yielded neither to success nor exhaustion. He was dominated by his theme, or, as might be said, his duty. He was driven forward against longings for home and bodily discomfort by an overriding desire to achieve his purpose. His physical symptoms did not reduce his continuous output of hard work and thrustful energy, and ever he set himself new tasks and dared new hazards in his thorough, painstaking way. It is these moral and soldierly virtues which made Marlborough the greatest servant, who remained a servant, of any sovereign in history.

CHAPTER FORTY-FIVE

The Conquering Hero

৳ 1704-5, Winter ৳

THE labours of the year were not over. The campaign of 1705 which might end the war could not be fought without the vigorous and punctual aid of Prussia and the German states. The only chance of obtaining this was that the hero of Blenheim, now the cynosure of Europe, should in person visit the Courts of Prussia and Hanover. Eight hundred miles in the lumbering coach with its six horses and cavalry escort, splashing along the uneven roads in the depth of winter, interspersed by arduous ceremonial, by official festivities, and by intricate negotiations, before he could even reach The Hague and wait for a fair wind! "The ways have been so bad," he wrote to Sarah from Berlin (November 23), "I have been obliged to be every day 14 or 15 hours on the road, which makes my side very sore; but three or four days I shall stay here will make me able to go on." He had a great welcome in Berlin. He was treated as the Prince he now was, and gazed upon as a marvel. The King was gratified by his visit, and by his tributes to the bravery of the Prussian troops.

But Marlborough's task was one from which, as he approached it, anyone might have recoiled. The northern war had entered upon an extraordinary phase. In their fear of Prussian domination both the Czar and the King of Saxony had adopted the most desperate expedient open to statecraft. They had deliberately courted defeat at the hands of Charles XII so as to bring Prussia and Sweden face to face. Only a fortnight before Marlborough's arrival reinforcements were kept back from the Saxon and Russian armies. Charles XII had won his victory at

Punitz, and Poland lay open to the Swedes. Should Prussia intervene? This was the paramount question in Berlin. The Prussian army was being rapidly recruited and enlarged. Upon what fields would it seek fame and booty? Patkul, the Livonian weaver of anti-Swedish coalitions, had hastened secretly to Berlin at the first news of Marlborough's impending visit.

It was Marlborough's aim to prevent this vast extension of the northern war, which by diverting German energies would so seriously aid Louis XIV; and also to secure a large additional contingent of the Prussian Army to fight against France in Italy. No wonder he thought it an unhopeful quest. The language which he was authorized to use was hard. The best account of his discourse is given in Frederick I's letter to Augustus II, in which the Elector-King states that Marlborough went so far as to intimate that if Prussia stirred up this new trouble she would *"be dealt with as Denmark had been in 1700,"* when the English fleet had carried the Swedish Army to the neighbourhood of Copenhagen. To prevent such an ugly out-turn, Marlborough urged the Elector-King either to disband his newly recruited troops or transfer them to the Grand Alliance on favourable terms.

Marlborough caught Frederick I and his Ministers at a most timely moment, when they were already cooling from the projected triple alliance against the formidable Swede, and when the troops that had been raised in that intention might become superfluous. The Elector-King therefore hearkened to a voice which offered threats and bribes with equal smoothness, and set himself to make upon the best terms a bargain for farming out a part of the desirable Prussian Army. Three days later Marlborough concluded in the Queen's name a treaty, to which he undertook that the States-General and the Empire would accede, whereby eight thousand Prussians would forthwith march to Piedmont to the help of the Duke of Savoy in return for an annual subsidy of two hundred thousand thalers from England, one hundred thousand from Holland, and bread-rations from the Empire.

He set out from Berlin in a blaze of goodwill, with results far beyond his expectations or those of the Government he served. He had been greatly favoured, we now know, by unforeseeable events. But the effect produced upon the Courts of Europe was as if a magic wand waved in Berlin had changed the policy of the Prussian King, prevented the spread of the northern war, and turned the sharpened bayonets of

Prussia from the shores of the Baltic to those of the Mediterranean. Without this succour the Italian front against France could not have been sustained during the year 1705. But Marlborough also deeply interested the King in his schemes along the Moselle. He carried away with him the King's gift of "a hat with a diamond button and loop and a diamond hatband valued at between twenty and thirty thousand crowns and two fine saddle-horses with rich furniture."

The compliments and courtesies of Berlin were repeated in Hanover. He was received with the greatest honour. Here he trod the delicate ground of the succession to the British Crown, and he well knew that every step would be jealously scrutinized by both the great English parties and by Queen Anne. The Electress Sophia was at first prejudiced against Marlborough. We have seen her disparaging reference to "the great general Marlborough" in her letter to Leibnitz about the Schellenberg. Blenheim had effaced these impressions and contact with Marlborough transformed them. "Never," she wrote, "have I become acquainted with a man who knows how to move so easily, so freely, and so courteously. He is as skilled as a courtier as he is a brave general." This comment travelled far.

She declared him as sensible in politics as pleasant in manner, and presented him with a piece of tapestry. To this the reigning prince added a jewel reputed to be worth twenty-five thousand thalers, which we may be sure he accepted with grace and pleasure.

The city of Amsterdam had long been the focus of pro-French sentiment, and if its powerful magistracy had favoured Marlborough's appointment as Deputy Captain-General, it was, as we have seen, largely for the purpose of keeping the 'Royalist' office of War Lord in abeyance. But now the Amsterdammers wished to throw up their caps for Marlborough. They sent a special delegation to press him to visit their city, and received him with remarkable enthusiasm. On the 12th he reached The Hague. He had deceived the States-General; he had purloined a part of their army; he had carried it far from the frontiers of Holland. Many sturdy Dutchmen lay by the Danube and the Upper Rhine. But his judgment had been right. He had stemmed the tide of adverse war; he had reconstituted the Grand Alliance in all its parts; he had saved the Empire; he had broken the military prestige of France. He was indeed their protector, and a champion worthy to hold—as deputy, of course—the military office of the great Stadtholders. The

Grand Pensionary and seven Deputies received him on behalf of the Republic. He was presented with a basin and ewer of solid gold. The assembly listened with profound respect to his account of the general situation. The States of Holland immediately endorsed his Berlin treaty. All rejoiced that they had him safely back. They hoped and prayed that he would never go so far, nor run such risks again. They exulted in the past; they remained blind to the future. They did not understand that the destinies of Holland might be enlarged or restricted according as they used or spurned their new opportunities. Amid their blessings Marlborough sailed from Rotterdam to England, having been absent eight months, during which he had moulded Europe in a form which was not broken till the French Revolution.

Tory politicians found the victory of Blenheim hard to welcome. Not only did it crown with success the policy of Continental enterprises, but it had been gained by a General, also a kind of Prime Minister, who was well known to be lukewarm, if not indeed by now actually hostile, to the Occasional Conformity Bill. No doubt the success of the British arms and the allied cause was desirable and even necessary, but the party disadvantages resulting therefrom were obvious. The Tories were therefore torn between their relief and a good deal of uncontrollable pride as Englishmen, and their annoyance as partisans. In fact, there was much truth in Sarah's caustic remark that one would think from their demeanour that "the battle of Höchstädt had been gained over the Church of England and not over the French." The Tory chagrin was, however, restrained not only by their patriotism, but by a lively sense of the joy of the nation.

The estimates for the year guaranteed the still more vigorous prosecution of the war by land and sea. The Army was to be enlarged to fifty thousand men for Flanders and ten thousand for Portugal, and to be fully recruited. The Navy was raised from forty to forty-five thousand seamen, including marines available for landing purposes. All the subsidies to allies and for the hiring of mercenary troops at the joint expense of the Maritime Powers were continued. The expense amounted to more than nine millions, three-quarters of which must be raised by taxation. The whole of this unprecedented supply was voted speedily and unanimously by the House of Commons.

On December 14, Marlborough landed at Greenwich, and hastened to pay his duty to the Queen. He had brought with him to the Thames a shipload of thirty-six French officers of the highest distinction. At their head was Marshal Tallard; sixteen of them were generals; none was below the rank of lieutenant-colonel. He also deposited in the Tower all the standards and colours captured by his wing of the army at Blenheim. The next day he repaired to the House of Lords, where he was solemnly thanked by the Lord Keeper in the name of the Peers. "Your Grace," said the Lord Keeper, "has not overthrown young, unskilful Generals, raw and undisciplined troops; but . . . has conquered the French and Bavarian armies; armies that were fully instructed in all the arts of war; select veteran troops, flushed with former victories, and commanded by Generals of great experience and bravery. . . ."

In the first days of the new year (January 3, 1705) all London crowded to a pageant the like of which England had never seen. A long procession of the household troops and footguards bore the captured standards and colours from the Tower to Westminster Hall amid the salutes of the 'great guns' and the cheers of the people. The thirty-four French standards were borne by the gentlemen of the Blues, and the hundred and twenty-eight French colours by the pikemen of the Guards. Through the city, down the Strand, along 'the Pall-Mall,' before St James's Palace, through St James's Mews, they marched into the Park, where two salvos of forty cannon were fired. Queen Anne had let it be known that she would see them pass, and did so from Lord Fitzharding's lodgings in the Palace. These banners of mighty France, that nation of twenty millions, whom men in middle age could remember as England's disdainful paymaster, were received and set up in Westminster Hall for all to see. But more significant than this well-organized ceremonial was the temper of the masses who lined the route or thronged behind the procession. The foreign Ambassadors, bred in countries where Courts, nobles, and magnates counted for all, were struck by a manifestation of a national self-consciousness unique among the nations. Here was a society which did not end with the powerful and the rich, which descended through every class of citizen down to the very poorest and most humble, all of whose hearts responded to the feeling that it was *their* victory, that *their* cause had triumphed, and that *their* England was growing great. Even while foreign observers cavilled with some reason that the London populace claimed for themselves a victory in which their troops had formed but a quarter of the army, they admired the integral force and comprehension of the vigorous islanders, who could quarrel so fiercely with one another and yet rejoice together in national glory.

Now this complex society, laid aside for the moment their feuds in order to do Marlborough honour beyond what any absolute monarch could bestow. The applause, the admiration, the gratitude of equals has a ring more true and more comforting than the favour of a prince, however mighty, however gracious. It was common ground among the whole society which then expressed the English nation that some magnificent and unprecedented reward should be bestowed upon the Duke of Marlborough, and the only question was what form it should take.

It was on all sides agreed that the gift should be, if possible, unanimous. The danger of one proposal being matched against another was avoided by framing the address of the House of Commons in general terms. Accordingly they solicited the Crown to consider proper means of perpetuating the memory of the great services performed by the Duke of Marlborough. The Queen replied, "I am very well pleased by this address, and will take it into my consideration and send you my thoughts upon it in a little time." Anne now gave full rein to the generosity which had been frustrated to her annoyance after the campaign in 1702. On February 17 she informed the Commons that in conformity with their address she proposed to convey to the Duke of Marlborough and his heirs the Royal Manor and Park of Woodstock, and desired "the assistance of the House upon this extraordinary occasion" for the purpose of clearing off various encumbrances upon the estate. The grant comprised about 15,000 acres, and was reported to be worth about £6000 a year.

The necessary Act was speedily passed without opposition.

At the same time the grant of five thousand a year upon the Civil List, which was valid only for the Queen's lifetime, was made permanent by Parliament. The Queen appointed him Colonel of the First Guards, in which he had originally received his commission; and finally she set herself to plan and build at her expense at Woodstock a splendid palace which, in memory of the victory, was to be called the Castle of Blenheim. She selected Sir John Vanbrugh as the architect, and interested herself keenly in the model which she had had constructed.

Marlborough was highly gratified by the splendid possessions which descended upon him. Although the pressure of great affairs absorbed almost the whole of his mind, his strength, and his time, he liked at odd moments to reflect upon his growing fortune and the princely setting in which his heirs and successors would dwell. He regarded the raising of his family to the first rank in England as second only in importance to raising England to the first place in Europe, and he saw no reason why these two processes should not be combined. His tireless industry and exertion, his profound sagacity and calculation, his constant readiness to stake not only his life, but all he had gathered in reputation and wealth, upon the hazards of war and of well-chosen battle, were faithfully offered in his country's service. But a time was to come when England needed for her guidance some high qualities beyond the constructive and acquisitive genius with which he was born, and when through the lack of these Queen, country, and servant were to taste griefs they had not deserved. The pursuit of power with the capacity and in the desire to exercise it worthily is among the noblest of human occupations. But Power is a goddess who admits no rival in her loves.

CHAPTER FORTY-SIX

The Margrave's Toe

⊰ 1705, Spring ⊱

THE consequences of Blenheim governed the war in 1705. Louis XIV resolved to stand on the defensive upon all the fronts. Strenuous efforts were made during the winter to repair the losses of France in man-power and equipment. The regular troops were brought to full strength not only by compulsory recruitment, but by large drafts from the militia. The destruction of the cavalry, probably by the disease we now call glanders, was made good by enormous purchases of horses in Switzerland. Severe sacrifices were exacted in taxation, and the clergy alone were induced to contribute a free-will offering equal to six million pounds. To the astonishment of Europe the French armies in the spring were reported to be "more numerous and more brilliant" than ever. Actually, besides maintaining the war in Spain, the Great King was able to place in the field 100 battalions and 100 squadrons under Vendôme in Italy, and 200 battalions and 260 squadrons upon his northern frontiers. These latter were divided into three armies: 80 battalions and 100 squadrons commanded by Villeroy under the nominal orders of the Elector in Flanders; 70 battalions and 100 squadrons under Villars upon the Moselle; and 50 battalions and 60 squadrons in Alsace and upon the Upper Rhine. These Marshals were made aware that the entire forces in the north must be considered as a single group of armies, capable of reinforcing each other in accordance with the enemy's attack. To make this easy the lateral roads behind the front were brought into the best condition, and supplies were distributed along them, as well as in all the fortresses concerned. The Elector during the absence of Villeroy from Brussels had prepared a minor offensive along the Meuse, having for its object the recapture of Huy and Liége at the outset of the campaign. He was, however, told that he must await the development of the allied attack. This was expected along the Moselle, but no final opinion could be formed until the movements of the English were known. As these were now regarded as the best troops of the allies, it was thought that they would certainly be used for the main offensive. Accordingly it was upon them that the chief attention of the French headquarters was fixed.

It was believed at Versailles that the Grand Alliance would be able to place sixty thousand men in Flanders under Overkirk, sixty thousand on the Moselle under Marlborough, thirty thousand on the Rhine under the Margrave, thirty thousand in Italy under Prince Eugene, and fifteen thousand in Portugal under Galway, in addition to the thirty thousand absorbed by the revolt in Hungary. Besides all these there were the forces of the Duke of Savoy and the King of Portugal, and the immense fleets by which England and Holland maintained what had now become the complete command of the seas. Actually, when the campaign opened, the confederates had, as we shall see, by no means achieved such totals. Nevertheless it may be broadly computed that the allies marshalled for 1705 field armies of nearly a quarter of a million men, and that the Two Crowns resisted them with about two hundred thousand. If we double these figures so as to comprise the garrisons, depots, and all the services in the rear, apart from the manufacture of munitions, we obtain a fair measure of the war effort which Europe now made, prodigious in proportion to its wealth and manhood and to its primitive organization.

Unity of command was imposed by Louis XIV upon the three French armies in the north. But Marlborough, although he tried to manage the whole war and to provide for every theatre, had in fact a lamentably defective control. He could, indeed, lead the dreaded English and the troops paid by the Queen where he pleased. But every movement of the Dutch Army must still be settled both beforehand with the States-General, and at the time with the Dutch Deputies and commanders; and his influence upon the Imperial armies was exerted only through his correspondence with Wratislaw and Prince Eugene. Louis XIV was absolute Commander-in-Chief: Marlborough was only an informal chairman of a discordant committee. In this lies the explanation of the war in 1705. Moving painfully through obstructed channels and pulling many tangled strings, he was, however, able during the winter and early spring to prepare an allied front in the north, so as to leave himself a choice of action and impose uncertainty upon the French. Great magazines were established in the frontier fortresses of Trèves, Coblenz, Liége, and Maestricht, and large masses of horse and foot were gathered in Holland. Numerous flotillas of boats and barges were assembled and fitted which could carry all the material down the Scheldt for a siege of Antwerp, up the Meuse for a siege of Namur, up the Moselle for that of Thionville or Saarlouis, or along the Rhine towards Fort Louis, Kehl, or Old Brisach. He had no doubt himself which was the true line of advance.

While the siege of Landau had dragged on Marlborough had agreed with Eugene, and, as they both thought, with the Margrave too, upon the general plan. Marlborough had taken all the preliminary steps. He had recaptured Trèves and Trarbach, and put them in the strongest state of defence. He had made every arrangement in his power with the German princes and the Dutch agents to gather immense magazines in both those fortresses, and had obtained from all the German states concerned the promise that their contingents in the pay of the Sea Powers would be in readiness during April. He had himself visited the Courts of Berlin and Hanover. He had procured the assent of the Dutch Government and the reinforcement of the English army. Making allowances for the slowness of communication and the difficulties of supervision, he had reason to expect that he could take the field about the middle of May.

His plan was to stand upon the defensive in Flanders and on the Upper Rhine, and advance upon Saarlouis and Thionville, through Lorraine into France, with over ninety thousand men. These would be formed in two armies; the smaller, embodying the main war effort of the Empire, would operate under the Margrave from the area about Landau, westward towards the Saar; the larger he would lead himself, south-west up the Moselle. It was the essence of this plan that these two armies should work together within manœuvring distance, so that neither could be overwhelmed. The arrangements which he had made in Italy, and the action of the English fleet in the Gulf of Lyons, should enable Prince Eugene at least to hold the French in that theatre, if not, indeed, to press an advantage. Modern military opinion would endorse these conceptions.

Everything was behindhand at The Hague and on the Rhine, and everybody in the worst of moods. Marlborough with great labour obtained the consent of the Dutch Government to the concentration of the main army of the Sea Powers round Trèves, and of the second army at Maestricht. He found in the Dutch command an attitude of jealousy and envy towards himself and his astonishing success.

As early as February 6 the Duke had written decisively to Prince Eugene at Vienna. He expressed his disquiet at the lack of care in making the necessary preparations in the Imperial army which was reported to him from all quarters. He asked for an exact statement at the earliest moment of the artillery and powder which the Empire would supply and of the strength of the Margrave's army. He requested that the fortifications of Landau should be repaired forthwith to prevent the field army being weakened by having to find a large garrison. Lastly he spoke of

> the necessity that the two armies should act in concert on the Moselle and that they should be able to aid each other as the need required. In that case we may be sure that as we advance towards Thionville the enemy will draw their last man out of Alsace to oppose us . . . ; instead of which if the two armies act separately and are not near enough to support each other *it will only cost a stroke of the pen to France to throw her whole force on one or the other,* thus bringing about its ruin or at least rupturing all our plans.

In consequence of Prince Eugene's advocacy the Emperor on February 25 called on the Margrave for his plan of campaign, but gave him at the same time the strongest hint that the two armies should work together. However, Prince Louis, at Rastadt, had formed a different plan. In his view it would be a mistake to concentrate so much force upon a central thrust. It would be better for Marlborough to work along the Moselle, while he would separately advance up the Rhine towards Hagenau and threaten Alsace. He wrote to Vienna a considerable memorandum upon the advantages of disconnected over connected operations. But all this discussion took time, and meanwhile the Margrave adhered to his view. He was building himself "a noble palace with beautiful gardens" at Rastadt. He did not wish to run the slightest risk of opening Würtemberg, Swabia, and Baden to French raids. He dwelt upon the importance of preserving the confederate conquests in Alsace. He was in his heart determined not to serve under Marlborough, or even with him—for that, according to his experience, was the same thing. His antagonism to Prince Eugene in the councils of the Empire continued; but it was dwarfed by his jealousy, now nakedly exposed to Europe, of the laurels which Marlborough had gained at Blenheim. Besides all this, the wound in his foot which he had sustained at the Schellenberg, though slight at the moment, had become troublesome. It broke out again, was no doubt infected, and often became inflamed. Thus Prince Louis developed a resistance, expert, moral, and physical, to the great campaign which proved invincible. In those days, when every objection took at least a week to be answered, such a wealth of reasoning or pretext could not be overcome. On May 5 the Emperor Leopold died. He was succeeded by his son Joseph. This prince was extremely well disposed to Marlborough and an ardent admirer of his military qualities. There were therefore good hopes of support from Vienna.

The Margrave had by now received definite orders from Vienna to co-operate with Marlborough, and he expressed his willingness to do so, but at the same time he unfolded the lamentable weakness and ill-equipment of his command. Marlborough had been entitled to expect the aid of an Imperial army of 50 battalions and 80 squadrons. He had for some time realized that this would not be forthcoming. All the recruits from the Hereditary Lands had been sent to Prince Eugene in Italy, and the Imperial regiments on the Rhine stood at little more than half their strength. A great part of the military effort of the Empire was absorbed in Hungary; even some Prussian battalions in the pay of the Sea Powers, which were due to join the army in Trèves, were still detained in Bavaria. Artillery, food, ammunition, and horses were all woefully scarce. In sending a field-state of the Imperial forces to Godolphin on May 4 Marlborough had written, "You see what a miserable thing a German army is."

The Margrave now made the most of his weakness. It was evident that the plan of working in two armies must be abandoned. One army alone must be formed at Trèves. The Margrave promised to join it. He could only bring 20 battalions and 40 squadrons, or less than half what had been prescribed in the winter. Of these only 12 battalions and 28 squadrons could reach the rendezvous by June 10—the rest must follow as they were ready. But the Margrave agreed formally, and in writing, to lead these forces himself to join Marlborough upon that day. With this the Duke had to be content.

After a week of ceaseless travel Marlborough arrived at Trèves on May 26.

His whole plan depended upon a certain speed of execution. He could not keep his army, with its mass of cavalry, stationary in any place for long. The herbage that year was scanty, and the delays had given Villars time to denude the Moselle valley and to fortify his position. The magazines at Trèves were but half full. Before leaving for England in the previous winter the Duke had arranged contracts with trustworthy agents for this essential supply; but after his departure the Dutch had accepted a lower tender from a commissary of less repute. This worthy had failed in his undertakings and, conscious of his guilt or neglect, now deserted to the enemy. The seven thousand Palatine mercenaries were already three weeks late, and still ten days distant. The twelve thousand Prussians were more than a week behind them. The troops under Marlborough's command, and in the pay of the Sea Powers, which were assembled round Trèves, were in excellent spirit and condition, well furnished, well disciplined, and eager to fight. In all, they amounted to 83 battalions and 94 squadrons, or about sixty thousand men. The delay had eaten up the local supplies, and even this partly formed army must now either advance or retire. It could not wait at Trèves for the Elector. Twenty-five miles to the southward lay Villars, with 100 battalions and 160 squadrons or nearly seventy thousand men.

Moreover, strategic success depended upon Marlborough being able to make the Moselle attack so dominant upon the enemy that they would have to draw reinforcements both from Flanders and from the Rhine, and so remove any danger of attack in those theatres. If he were able to deal Villars a heavy blow, Villeroy in Flanders would be paralysed. If he were able to invest Saarlouis, the fertile land of Lorraine would nourish the largest armies. The Duke of Lorraine, though nominally neutral and sending envoys to both headquarters, was at heart friendly to the allies, and his people generally shared his feelings. With one hundred thousand men it would have been easy to reach this vantage ground, and thenceforward the whole campaign would have been governed therefrom. But to move through the dangerous gorges with little more than half that number, with the chance of being brought to a standstill, even if not defeated, was a very hardy project. Prudence should have counselled Marlborough to abandon his design. Almost every element in it had already miscarried. The breakdown of the Empire, the reluctance of the Margrave, the tardiness of the Palatine and Prussian contingents, the half-filled magazines, and lastly the failure of the various Electors along the Rhine to supply the three thousand draught-horses needed to draw the siege artillery, provided ample justification. But Marlborough's unrelenting will-power and his confidence in himself and his own proved army led him into a most daring perseverance. He determined to traverse the defiles and confront Villars. He hoped that his very weakness might be made the means of victory by tempting the Frenchman to a battle.

At two o'clock on the morning of June 3 the Duke began his advance. At six in the evening both the columns began to deploy on a broad front in the plain of Sierck. The troops had marched nearly twenty-one miles across uneven ground, and now was the moment for Villars to fight the battle which Marlborough courted. But such was the impression which Blenheim had produced upon the French High Command, and such was the surprise of this arrival, that as soon as the heads of Marlborough's columns and detachments were seen emerging at numerous points from the hills all the enemy advance troops, including a powerful corps before Sierck, hastily retreated into their fortified position, with a loss of some hundreds of prisoners, and the weary English and Dutch infantry lay upon their arms in battle order, unmolested through the night.

The next fortnight was terrible. Villars wisely refused battle. No supplies of any kind could be found in the district. Everything for man and horse must be brought through the defiles from Trèves by convoys requiring strong escort, until the communications could be picketed, and the seven fords of the Moselle properly guarded. Marlborough had sent Cadogan, his Quartermaster-General, far back to appeal to the Margrave to come on. He seems to have managed the supplies himself. In the meanwhile he held himself ready for battle at any moment.

And almost daily he sent trusted officers back to the Margrave, and to Prussia and to the Rhine Princes, to hasten the fulfilment of their promises.

Marlborough fixed his headquarters in the castle of Elst, high on the hills opposite Villars' position, and from here surveyed the situation and the scene. "I am placed," he wrote to Eugene on June 11, "so that by a slight movement and without any obstacle I can come between the enemy and Saarlouis, to which we aspire to lay siege." The Palatines had arrived on the 5th, but were mostly required for the communications. The Prussians still lagged on the road. The Würtembergers and Westphalians were only now approaching. As for the Margrave, he had never meant to come. He started as agreed with about nine thousand men from Landau towards the end of May. Instead of marching across to Trèves by Homburg and St Wendel along the route which Marlborough had traversed in the winter, he made a détour of sixty miles by Kreuznach which secured another five days' delay. When Cadogan had ridden through Birkenfelt on the 15th even his cavalry were still two marches away. The Quartermaster-General found the longed-for reinforcements at Kreuznach. But the Margrave was no longer in command. By the advice of his doctors he had repaired to Schlangenbad, a rest by whose waters it was hoped would allay the undoubted inflammation of his wound. The Comte de Frise, who was now in command, manifested no zeal. He moved sluggishly forward. It was certain he would not arrive, if he could help it, before the 20th. But meanwhile what had been happening elsewhere?

Marsin from the Rhine had already reinforced Villars by a larger force than the Margrave had promised to bring. But even more serious news came from Flanders. Villeroy had taken the offensive. On May 21 he advanced upon Huy, and laid siege to this small but significant place. Overkirk, who was but half his strength, was forced back into his entrenched camp under the walls of Maestricht. Villeroy entered the town of Liége on the 18th, and planted heavy batteries against the citadel. From the moment when the French offensive began the Dutch demanded 30 battalions and 30 squadrons from Marlborough for the defence of the Meuse. Deputies were sent, and finally Hompesch, with the most insistent commands and appeals. It is important to notice the threat with which the Dutch backed their demand. It was a threat to make a separate peace.

Marlborough had foreseen such a development. Before leaving Trèves he had hinted to the States-General that he would not be averse from receiving a request to return. This he had done to secure himself a good reason before Parliament and the Alliance for abandoning his plan, if he should find himself unable to execute it. Now real emergency had arisen on the Meuse, and only the prospect of immediate and decisive action against Villars could absolve him from neglecting it. He had stood for fifteen days in a position of extreme difficulty, and, as it seemed to Europe, of much danger; and during that period he had not been joined by a single soldier not in the pay of the Maritime Powers. Of these several important contingents were still absent, and a month late in their concentration. His plan had failed. The combination he had designed had broken down in respect of every factor not under his direct control. He had hoped against hope, unreasonably perhaps, that his forward movement and dangerous station would draw to him from all quarters the help on which he had counted. He had forced the hands of doubting and obstinate allies the year before, and had dragged them all to victory and safety at Blenheim. He had vainly counted on repeating this process. He now resolved to extricate himself while time remained.

After darkness had fallen on the 17th the confederate army folded their tents and repassed the gorges under pouring rain in a long night march. They were safely across the rivers by noon. Daylight informed Villars that the tented city he had watched for an exciting fortnight had disappeared. Later his trumpet returned to the French camp, bearing an astounding verbal message from Marlborough. "Tell Marshal Villars that I am in despair because the Margrave has broken his word, and that I can hold only him responsible for the breaking up of all our plans." A less trustworthy account has added, "Be assured that my contempt of him does not equal my respect for you."

We must not imagine when we survey this ill-starred episode that Marlborough's hard-bitten professional critics were always wrong about his operations. A solid case can be set forth against his attempt upon the Moselle. No doubt it was the true road into France, and if he could have planted his armies in unravaged Lorraine the highest prizes were within reach. But before he left Trèves he must have known that nearly all the conditions which would render such a movement possible were lacking. He required not only an army or armies of a hundred

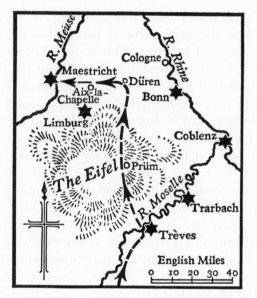

8. Marlborough Returns to the Meuse

thousand men, but also to be able to make a speedy advance into the fertile regions. He could not hope to maintain armies of the size required for more than a few weeks in denuded districts upon any magazines which could have been created. But with less than these numbers the great thrust at the heart of France would not become dominant. It would be brought to a stop, and then immediately diversions would begin. Yet he persisted. To use his own phrasing, he "opiniatred" the matter. He tried to compel events beyond any fortune that men may hope from the gods. A battle at heavy odds with all the penalties of defeat at their highest and the rewards of victory severely curtailed was the most he could have expected at Sierck. This was all he sought, and even this he was denied.

Marlborough had no need to offer excuses to the States-General for his failure upon the Moselle. They had nothing but gratitude to utter for his swift return. Yet their thanks were wounding. "How often," said the Dutchmen in effect, "have we begged Your Grace not to go so far from home to help these unworthy and ungrateful allies? Did we not warn you they would fail you? Never let yourself be put in such an unfair position again. Stay here with us and we shall all be safe, so long as we do not fight any battles. After all, you have a splendid army, and there are many fine fortresses to take." This absolute stultification of all Marlborough's conceptions of war only increased the bitterness of his disappointment. He wrote and spoke openly of his resolve to resign his command and quit the service. But of course at this time there was no chance of his being indulged. Such language expressed his feelings, and at the same time strengthened his power. He still hoped "some accident," by which he meant a battle, might enable him to rescue the campaign from failure. But further tribulations were in store. He was to find that he had exchanged the delays and excuses of the Margrave for the open insolence and mutinous obstruction of Slangenberg. He had been deserted in Germany: he was to be fettered in Holland.

CHAPTER FORTY-SEVEN

The Lines of Brabant

⪪ 1705, Summer ⪫

THE famous Lines of Brabant covering the sixty miles from Antwerp to Namur have been frequently mentioned in this account. Then as now the best military opinion accorded only a secondary value to such systems of defence. The obstacles of ramparts, dammed-up streams, entanglements of felled trees, palisades with forts and redoubts at intervals, could easily be traversed, if no one was there to defend them. They were therefore only regarded as affording a series of carefully considered fortified battlegrounds upon which the defending army could meet its presumably stronger assailants. For this purpose all the sideways roads behind the lines were carefully developed; food, forage, and ammunition were stored under guard in strongholds at convenient intervals; and as the lines, following the course of the river Demer, curved outward towards the enemy, it seemed probable that with proper dispositions the defending army would arrive and man the ramparts before any large force could attack them. If so they would have a very great advantage. The method of the assailants was, of course, to deceive the enemy by feints into sending his field army in one direction while they themselves marched under the cover of night in the other.

There had not been any difficulty in making minor surprise attacks upon portions of the lines, and we have seen how Spaar at the beginning of 1703 and Overkirk during the winter of 1704 had without much loss made themselves masters for a time of sections of the defences. In 1704, while Marlborough was on the march to the Danube, Overkirk had been disconcerted by the ease with which a portion of his own army had penetrated the lines south of Merdorp, and had made haste under the orders of the Republic to abandon such audacious gains. But the intention to carry the main army across the defences not only made surprise more difficult, but was tantamount to seeking battle either during or after the passage of the barrier. The Dutch had always shrunk from this as partaking of the nature of gambling with armies and contrary to their methods of warfare.

Marlborough, chafing over his disappointment on the Moselle, saw in forcing the lines the only means now open to rescue the whole campaign from failure. He saw no insuperable difficulty in the operation. There were a dozen ways of doing it—here or there; and as he was above all things anxious to fight a battle, about which he also felt confident, he was not alarmed by the risk. According to the principles which had gained acceptance during so many years of war, an army attacking under these conditions ought to have had substantial superiority over the whole force of the enemy. In fact he was somewhat weaker, having 92 battalions and 160 squadrons to Villeroy's 100 battalions and 147 squadrons, or say seventy thousand men in the open against seventy-three thousand behind their defences. This did not deter him. He had studied the country and the lines profoundly over many years, and their aspect was to him an open book. He therefore in the first days of July formed a plan nicely conceived in times and distances and garnished with the appropriate feints and deceptions whereby the lines could be forced. The novel feature, apart from his being numerically weaker, was his selection of the point to be attacked. Instead of seeking the weakest part of the defences, he chose one of the strongest. He argued to himself that because it was the strongest it would be the least considered, and probably defended by the fewest covering troops. He would feint therefore at a weak part of the lines, to which the enemy would have to hurry their main forces, and then by a very long night march in the opposite direction his men would assault the earthworks where the defenders were but few.

His greatest difficulties, as usual, were presented by his own friends. The Government and States-General of the Republic cherished and admired him, but they trembled at his reckless and ruthless habit of mind. He seemed constantly to leave a great deal to chance. They felt that almost all his exploits would have ended badly if events had taken a slightly different turn. There was no general then alive except

Eugene—and even Eugene was judged more correct—who appeared to trouble so little about taking what any experienced officer knew was a very dangerous course. It is marvellous indeed that during all these ten campaigns he was never made to pay any forfeit. He certainly ought to have been punished scores of times for his unprofessional temerity. The Dutch felt in their bones that they were always in jeopardy when they rode with him. It was only after Ramillies that they gave up thinking about it, and forgot for a while to clutch at the reins or the brake.

But with the generals of their army other complications appeared. Slangenberg, the hero of Eckeren, veteran of forty years of war, hated Marlborough as a foreigner, as a rival, and as a man. He had formed a low opinion of his tactics at Blenheim. He would not bow to the imposture of their success. No experienced, well-trained commander would have attempted such an operation. It was his duty and should be his care to prevent any such hare-brained gambling with the army that guarded the frontiers of Holland. Besides this he was personally annoyed by the fact that the Duke's brother, General Churchill, had through accelerated English promotion become senior to him as General of Foot. Finally, he had a poor opinion of Overkirk, whom he thought too old for active service, too subservient to Marlborough's insidious influence, and personally obnoxious because he held the chief command which another might better have discharged.

For all these reasons it was not deemed expedient to make Slangenberg privy to the design. Indeed, Marlborough seemed inclined to deal only with the Veldt-Marshal Overkirk as responsible chief of the Dutch army. At the council of war the plan of forcing the lines was not presented in the form in which he intended to carry it out. The proposal put forward was that the attack should be made on the weaker sector between the Mehaigne and Namur. The Dutch generals pointed out that they must expect to find the main French army behind the fortifications. They were all opposed to such a costly attempt. But Marlborough persisted, and Overkirk seemed to be with him; and after several days of confrontation rather than discussion the Council agreed to a manœuvre for forcing the lines, provided that no undue risks were run, and that no battle was fought without a further council of war, if peradventure the enemy should be found in force at the point of attack. Marlborough, impassive, inscrutable, endured this protracted ordeal, and accepted the grudged and limited authority offered to him. Since he had come back from the Moselle he had not merged the armies into one as had been the custom in the earlier campaigns before he went to Blenheim. On the contrary, he seemed bent on keeping all the English and the Queen's troops separate in his own hand, and he dealt with the Dutch army only through Overkirk, who seemed to Slangenberg and other brave Dutch officers willing to be his tool or his dupe. In fact Overkirk had become increasingly silent; yet it was he to whom above all the malcontents looked to lead a revolt.

Marlborough now acted. He had a twofold plan: he had to deceive both the Dutch, excepting Overkirk, and the French. Ten miles in front of Villeroy's lines northward and away to the confederate right lay the well-known and convenient camping ground of Saint-Trond. The allied troops who had been besieging Huy arrived on the 16th. Marlborough had let it be believed that he would pretend to be occupying Saint-Trond and then move southward across the Mehaigne river to attack the weakest point of the lines on the sector between that river and Namur. Slangenberg and his colleagues did not believe that Villeroy would be deceived. They predicted that he would ignore any feint at Saint-Trond and concentrate his army in the trenches between the Mehaigne and Namur. And they were right. Early in the morning of July 17 Overkirk, with the whole of the Dutch army, crossed the Mehaigne and began his southward march. His patrols and advance parties pressed far on ahead even to the verge of the lines. Overkirk had passed the river by four bridges, but the French scouts and watchers from the lines reported that no fewer than eleven bridges in all were being constructed. Thus it was concluded that Marlborough's army would cross rapidly during the night, and that the whole force would advance together to the attack on the 18th. Villeroy therefore with the utmost speed concentrated forty thousand men upon the threatened front. Overkirk camped after a short march about six miles distant from the lines. The fact that the allied armies were divided by the Mehaigne led Slangenberg to make a written protest that the Dutch were being exposed to grave danger. To meet this criticism and for other purposes Marlborough built no fewer than twenty bridges across this little river, until, in the words of Orkney, "it was all one, as if there were no river." The last thing seen as darkness fell was Overkirk's dragoons marching southward beyond the Mehaigne towards

Namur. It seemed almost certain that there could be no surprise, that the lines would be fully guarded, and that therefore the promised council of war would be able to forbid the battle. But when the stars shone in the sky and night's curtains fell upon the undulating plains sudden orders, equally unexpected by friend and foe, were issued. The Dutch broke camp and their columns were turned to the right-about. They counter-marched to the north. They recrossed the Mehaigne very swiftly by the numerous bridges. Whereas during the day there had seemed to be no hurry, and they had only moved four miles beyond the river before halting, now in the night the march was pressed with the utmost severity. Overkirk was evidently carrying out a definite plan. Argument was useless. Councils of war were impossible. Every general was with his command, and no collective representations could be made. On, then, through the night toiled and trudged the sturdy troops. Whither—no man knew.

They were not the only troops who were moving north. At four in the afternoon Marlborough had ordered his whole army to be ready to march, the baggage to be assembled by six. These preparations disquieted the field Deputies. They were, however, assured that only a reconnaissance was intended. At seven Count Noyelles, with twenty battalions and thirty-eight squadrons, started upon the road which leads through Landen to Saint-Trond. Six hundred pioneers with their tools and bridging-material were attached to the advance guard. Great pains had been taken about the numerous guides, and Noyelles and his principal officers knew the country well. As the making of fascines would have aggravated the suspicions of the enemy, each trooper carried instead a truss of hay which might either serve to cross a marshy stream or as forage for a long march. Marlborough himself started at ten with the rest of his army. The whole of the confederates were thus marching steadily towards Landen through a very dark night.

Marshal Villeroy did not lack vigilance. He was aware that the allies were on the move. He remained, however, in total uncertainty. Numerous conflicting rumours had reached him. The most trustworthy pointed to a general attack the next day upon his lines south of Merdorp, and for this he was well prepared. Even when reports came in during the night that allied horse were moving northwards he concluded that their objective was Saint-Trond. Meanwhile he enjoined a strict alertness along the whole front. All his infantry and cavalry with their general officers slept on their arms at the head of their camps. Constant patrols were ordered out, especially from the posts on the left. He himself passed the night at Merdorp.

In spite of all precautions Noyelles' corps had much difficulty in finding its way through the black night. They toiled and stumbled across the battlefield of Landen, where thousands of skeletons had long lain unburied. They were nearly two hours late in reaching Landen itself. Up to this point their aim might well have been Saint-Trond. But now Noyelles in three separate columns marched towards the passages of the Little Geet, behind which ran the French fortifications. The distance was but three miles.

In fact Noyelles broke into the entrenchments at three points—at Elixem, Wangé, and Orsmael. The Little Geet here is but a marshy stream three or four yards wide. Storming parties of grenadiers waded through the water or rushed the stone bridge at Elixem. The French posts, suddenly aware of overwhelming numbers swarming upon them through the morning mists, fell back amid a splutter of firing. The three dragoon regiments in Orsmael fled at full speed into the fortress of Léau without even giving an effective alarm. There is no moment in war more thrilling than a surprise attack at dawn. The confederate pioneers threw themselves diligently into bridge-making; but the infantry would not await their efforts. They knew too much about the war not to realize how precious was every moment. In their ranks were veteran officers and sergeants who had fought at Landen twelve years before. It had been the talk of the camp for weeks that the lines would cost ten thousand men. Here were the lines empty and undefended. To the impulse of adventure was added the sharp spur of self-preservation. Everywhere, forgetting eighteenth-century drill, they splashed through the Geet, scrambled up the bank, down into the miry ditch beyond, and hand and foot up the ramparts of the bugbear lines. From 4 A.M. onward they were pouring into the fortifications and forming up in good order on the farther side. Every house and every hedge they seized or lined. By five o'clock at least six thousand men were inside the French position. Meanwhile bridges and passages had multiplied behind them, and Noyelles' horse, almost equal to two modern cavalry divisions, were passed over. Behind the Geet the ground rises into fine open, down-like country, stretching to Tirlemont, perhaps fifty feet higher than the river-bed. Between Elixem and Tirlemont they had formed between half-past five and six a double line of horse at right angles to the entrenchments, facing south and with their left upon their ever-growing infantry. And now the enemy appeared in force.

The French had reason to complain of the way in which their outposts served them. Small posts cannot resist armies; but at least they are expected to cry "Alarm." It was not till after five o'clock that d'Alègre, only three miles south of Elixem, learned what was happening. He mounted thirty-three squadrons of Bavarian, Spanish, Cologne, and French cavalry, and sent for the eleven infantry battalions under Caraman, who were four miles farther off. By six all these troops were moving forward. With them hastened ten guns of a new design. These were the triple-barrelled guns which could either fire three cannon-balls in quick succession or three at once. High hopes and much mystery had enveloped this invention, the last word in modern artillery. By half-past six collision was imminent.

Towards Tirlemont from the Geet there run two sunken roads. The northern, near Elixem, which can be seen unaltered to this day, is a remarkably deep ravine with sides so steep that anyone would hesitate even to lead a horse up and down them. The hostile cavalry halted on their own side of this obstacle. They were already galled by fire from the houses, roads, and hedges by the Geet. The leading brigade of allied infantry advanced and seized the sunken road, and by their volleys forced the enemy to draw back out of shot. It happened, or Marlborough had arranged, that the sixteen squadrons that had first come across comprised the whole of the British cavalry. These, shielded by the infantry, either crossed the sunken road where it was practicable, or else, coming round where the road shallowed into the upland, continually stretched out to their right towards Tirlemont.

The matter stood thus when Marlborough, a little before seven, came on the scene. He saw before him two lines of hostile cavalry and, more than a mile away, Caraman's infantry deploying. He resolved to attack the horse while they were still separated from their foot. He had now already on the ground over fifty squadrons, but not more than half of these were clear of the sunken road or prolonging the line towards Tirlemont. He rode to the right centre of the line and ordered the charge. All the English cavalry, with the Scots Greys on the extreme right, rode forward upon the enemy in echelon at a trot which it is believed, in parts of the line at least, broke into a gallop. The Bavarians were magnificent to see. They were nearly all cuirassier regiments. Between their squadrons appeared the triple-barrelled guns, which opened a remarkably rapid fire. But the result was never for a moment in doubt. The Bavarians where they met the shock were overthrown, and for the rest driven into flight. On the right the Scots Greys broke four squadrons without losing a single man. The guns were taken.

Marlborough led the charge himself. He rode with the front rank like a trooper. The routed horsemen made no bones about galloping across the second and much easier sunken road. Arrived here, the Duke again became a General. Caraman's division was close at hand in line of battle. The left of the English cavalry was checked by infantry in the hedges and ditches along the Geet. Five fresh squadrons, including the Cologne Life Guards, reinforced the enemy. They rallied and attempted a charge. There was a moment of confusion. But by now the second line of the allied horse had also come upon the scene. A second charge was delivered by both lines of the allied horse, certainly no faster than a trot. Marlborough again rode with the English squadrons. This time the rout of the enemy's cavalry was final. They galloped off the field, leaving their pursuers face to face with the musketry of Caraman's infantry, who had at length arrived. According to Orkney,

> My Lord Marlborough in person was everywhere, and escaped very narrowly; for a squadron, which he was at the head of, gave ground a little, though [it] soon came up again; and a fellow came to him and thought to have sabred him to the ground, and struck at him with that force, and, missing his stroke, he fell off his horse. I asked my Lord if it was so; he said it was absolutely so. See what a happy man he is.

It was now eight o'clock. Marlborough, with his retinue and staff again about him, could survey the scene. Practically his whole army was inside the lines and advancing southwards between the Little Geet and Tirlemont. Overkirk, with all the Dutch, was approaching the bridges and river-crossings, now good and numerous; but it would be at least two hours before they could form in order of battle. Where was Villeroy? That was the question. The upland ridge rose in a gentle slope, and tended to narrow to the southward. Beyond the skyline, two miles away, all was unknown. If the alarm had been promptly spread, the Marshal at Merdorp should have learned before six o'clock that the allies had forced the lines between Orsmael and Elixem. Merdorp was only seven miles away from the second sunken road. It might well be that forty thousand men were approaching just "on the other side of the hill." It was the peculiar quality of Marlborough that his moods of awful gambling sprang from cold calculation, and were followed by sudden sober caution. Certainly when all were aflame he now pulled up with a snap.

Marlborough dealt separately in daring and in prudence. Sometimes he was over-daring and sometimes over-prudent; but they were separate states of mind, and he changed from one to the other in quite definite phases. Having ruptured the lines and routed the counter-attack, the thought that dominated his mind was to concentrate the whole confederate army upon the conquered ground. We can express his feelings in the characteristic phrases of the Cockpit circle. "The army must be gathered with all speed imaginable. Until then I shall be most uneasy." There is no doubt that upon the knowledge which he had this was the right decision; and yet in fact, if he had given way to the general ardour around him, he might have had a greater success. Perhaps this extraordinary quality of using audacity and circumspection as if they were tools to be picked up or laid down according to the job is the explanation of his never being entrapped in ten years of war. His mind was a weighing-machine for practical affairs as perfect as has ever been known. Infallibility is not for mortals. It is enough to say that no one could do more than he could or try harder and more continuously.

It is on this morning field of Elixem that we see him as he should be remembered. It was one of the very few moments in his life when he came in contact with spontaneous mass affection. As he rode up sword in hand to take his place in the cavalry charges, the troopers and their officers broke into loud acclamations, quite unusual to the military etiquette of those formal times. And afterwards, as he moved along the front of his army, the soldiers, mostly Blenheim men, cast discipline to the winds and hailed him everywhere with proud delight. Here were the dreaded lines pierced and broken so easily, and the enemy baffled and put to flight, not at the cost of thousands of poor soldiers, but by the sleight of a master-hand and by the Queen's troops alone; and here was Corporal John, who could do it every time if only he were set free, who was so careful of their food and pay and so just in his government of the army, who thought for all as their commander and fought in the scrimmage as a private man—surely for once they might show him what they felt! Yet these soldiers were judges of war, and many knew the country well. Amid their cheers were mingled the cries, "Now, On to Louvain," and "Over the Dyle."

It was ten o'clock before Overkirk's army was across the lines. Marlborough, returning from the pursuit of the determined Caraman, was greeted by Slangenberg with the remark, "This is nothing if we lie still here. We should march on Louvain or Parc." The Duke would have demanded no better. He had, however, already heard from Overkirk that his troops must camp at once. Considering that they had marched twenty-seven miles in the last thirty-one hours, no complaint could be made of this. Still, as Colonel Cranstoun, who commanded the Cameronians, wrote:

> Those who know the army and what soldiers are know very well that upon occasions like this where even the common soldier is sensible of the reason of what he has to do, and especially of the joy and success of victory, soldiers with little entreaty will even outdo themselves, and march and fatigue double with cheerfulness what their officers would at other times compel them to.

Marlborough replied to Slangenberg, "I am very glad . . . to find you are of my opinion, for this is my judgment of it too; I think we should march on, and I entreat you to go back and dispose your generals to it." Slangenberg, completely stultified by the event and furious at not having been a party to it, was only establishing somewhat cheaply a controversial position for the future. He rode off to Overkirk, but he never returned to Marlborough; and as the Dutch tents rose continuously upon the plain it became certain that they would not move that day.

That a fine opportunity had been lost, and whose was the fault, was long the subject of acrimonious discussion in the army between the two wings of the army. Marlborough had lost a chance.

An event of capital importance had, however, occurred. The piercing of the Lines of Brabant marked an important stage in the world war. The stalemate in the northern theatre was ended, and henceforward much might happen there. The French abandoned Aerschot and Diest. They left Léau to an inevitable and speedy fate. The battalion of Monluc which garrisoned Tirlemont surrendered at discretion. Fifty miles of the lines, including the technically important salient, passed into the power of the allies. From Aerschot to the purlieus of Namur the famous front which had so long scared off attack and guarded the whole of Belgium was left for the conquerors to demolish. The tide of war flowed thirty miles farther to the west. These gains far exceeded the material prizes of action. But several notable leaders of the enemy and all the cannon on the field were captured, and the French forces were weakened by perhaps five or six thousand men. Counts d'Alègre and Horn, both lieutenant-generals, were prisoners of the English. But most important of all were the moral effects. The French knew themselves beaten and outmanœuvred. All the difficulties of their defensive were worsened and multiplied, and the advantages of the assailants proportionately improved. The destruction of the Lines of Brabant was an event which Europe recognized had definitely altered conditions in the main theatre of the war.

CHAPTER FORTY-EIGHT

The Unfought Waterloo

↔ 1705, August ↔

OUR General resolved to make a final effort before the campaign ended. A peculiar quality of his manœuvres is the ease and exactness with which they can be explained to the lay reader. From the moment of his return to the Meuse, Villeroy, although slightly the stronger, had yielded him the initiative. He had used it to pierce and render useless the Lines of Brabant. All the more after that did he enjoy the right to move; all the more were the French obliged to wait on his movements. In a country studded with fortresses the concession or loss of the initiative imposed grievous disadvantages upon the defenders. They could not tell where they would be hit. Therefore they had to garrison all their threatened fortresses and weaken their field army accordingly; while on the other hand Marlborough, master of the proceedings, could gather nearly all his troops into a striking force. His new plan was to advance deeply and suddenly into the enemy's country, so as to menace equally and at once a number of important places, and then, when Villeroy had been forced to detach troops for these, to fall upon his weakened army and destroy it in a battle.

After being baulked by Slangenberg and the Deputies at the Dyle, he sought freedom to carry out a fresh design which he had formed. He wrote to Godolphin:

Meldert

August 3, 1705

I have sent Lieutenant-General Hompesch once more to The Hague. . . . You will see that I have a mind to serve them if they please; but if they should not allow of what I propose, it is impossible to act offensively; for besides the danger of resolving everything that is to be done in a council of war, *which cannot be kept so secret, but that the enemy must know it time enough to prevent it, as we had the experience of in our last undertaking,* so monsieur Slangenberg, though he is a brave man, his temper is such that there is no taking measures with him. I am so tired that I cannot answer yours at this time.

Hompesch returned with an absurd compromise. The field Deputies were instructed to permit the Captain-General to make two or three marches without summoning a council of war. At the same time Marlborough was not to bring the army to any serious engagement without the approval of both Overkirk and the Deputies.

In spite of these insensate restrictions, Marlborough determined to persevere. He hoped by his three free marches to create a situation in which either the enemy would make a battle inevitable, or his advantage over the enemy would be so obvious that even the Dutch could not deny him. On this basis therefore he decided to take this hampering chance over and above the deadly hazards of war. On August the 15th he marched southward to Corbaix, with Overkirk keeping pace with him on his left. On the 16th he moved on to Genappe, crossing the headstreams of the Dyle. On the 17th he turned north along the Brussels road towards Waterloo. The three marches "in scorching hot weather" totalled thirty-three miles.

Villeroy and the Elector, encamped between Louvain and Brussels, saw with astonishment this movement of the whole confederate army across and round their front. They had heard from sure sources that the convoy of biscuit had been kept loaded on the wagons, and that Marlborough was carrying with him the batteries for besieging fortresses. They saw that he had let go his communications with Liége: these were now exposed to their attack if they cared to pay the price of battle. They preferred to await events. They must now be concerned for the safety of five fortresses, Namur, Charleroi, Mons, Ath, and above all the weakly defended Brussels. A report, based on the intercepted letter of a member of the States-General, had also reached them that Marlborough intended to pass the Senne at Hal and march right round them to the attack of Dendermonde, thus placing himself between them and Antwerp. Both Villeroy and—when they were informed—the main headquarters at Versailles were unable to understand the purpose and hardihood of such manœuvres. That a commander should be prepared to sever his communications and move so large an army encumbered by a siege train and heavy convoy across their front into their fortress zone was a departure from every canon of the military art deserving the severest punishment. However, since Marlborough was known to be seeking a battle and they were not anxious to fight, they did not try to exact the forfeits which they conceived were their due. Instead, as he had expected, they submitted to his will. They assigned a strong garrison to Louvain and detached Grimaldi with eighteen battalions, twelve squadrons, and ten guns to support a Colonel Pasteur, who with a small force was barring the road from Waterloo to Brussels. They moved their main army slightly to its right in order to be nearer Grimaldi. They still remained in their central position between Louvain and Brussels; but they were completely mystified about Marlborough's intentions, and the dispersion of their army was far advanced.

During the night of August 17–18 the confederate advance guards were found to be still moving along both the roads to Brussels. Pasteur, though he returned during the night to his position at Waterloo, was roughly thrown back. When the morning of the 18th broke, the reports which reached the French command from all quarters convinced them that Marlborough was striking at Brussels with his whole force. The high road was crowded with his advancing infantry, while the French army was, it seemed, only to be 'amused' by a cavalry flank guard. This revelation of what they conceived to be Marlborough's true purpose confronted Villeroy and the Elector with a grievous dilemma. "I confess to Your Majesty," wrote the Elector of this moment,

> that the choice was very difficult, because a single false step drew with it the loss of the Low Countries, and I believe that for centuries there has not been a more thorny hour. To march to Brussels was to abandon the position which up to this time has saved Louvain and all Brabant; to stay in it was to lose Brussels, and by that the larger part of the country as well. To divide the army was impossible; for we should not have been strong enough for either purpose and by that we should have lost the army into the bargain; *and through being forced to guard so many open places at once there were already 27 battalions and 20 squadrons detached from Your Majesty's army*: de-

lay also, even the slightest, would have lost all upon the instant.
. . . It was necessary to choose . . . between the loss of Brussels or
of Louvain, there being no middle course.

They decided to sacrifice Louvain. About seven o'clock they prepared
to march by their right to join Grimaldi, who was at the same time
moved nearer to the main army while still covering both roads to
Brussels.

This resolve was hardly taken when the whole scene was transformed. "The order was no sooner given," says the Elector, "than there
appeared before our eyes a column of hostile infantry which we could
well recognize to be the English, thus revealing from this moment that
their main design was not against Brussels, for the English infantry
came from that quarter."

These masses began to debouch upon the French right from the
Forest of Soignies. Great numbers of the allied cavalry advanced towards the French centre beyond the Ysche stream between Overysche
and Neerysche. Behind them heavy columns of infantry could be discerned. It was not Brussels, then, that Marlborough sought: it was
BATTLE! They were about to be attacked; and for all their vigilance they
were as much astonished as Tallard had been a year before, almost to a
day, at Blenheim. Marlborough had, in fact, quitted the Brussels road
during the night, and was rapidly building up a front to his right which
continually grew along the French position.

All this was grave. But there was one factor they did not know, or
could not measure. At 2 A.M. Marlborough had sent his brother Churchill
with 20 battalions and 20 squadrons from Hulpen, where he had bivouacked, to march upon Groenendaele. This powerful detached corps
found the roads obstructed by felled trees. They had nevertheless made
good progress, and at ten o'clock were established across and beyond
the Ysche near Groenendaele and in a position where they could turn
not only the French right flank, but by persisting traverse his rear and
assail his retreat on Brussels. Meanwhile Grimaldi remained tethered to
the protection of the Brussels roads, and was as much out of the impending battle as Churchill was in it. This use of a large detached
corps of manœuvre as an integral part of the main battle was hitherto
unexampled in the European war.

All the rest of the confederate forces were meanwhile rapidly approaching and deploying. But let us see what were the armies now, it

seemed, to be matched together in decisive conflict. With the reinforcement he had already received from the Moselle, Villeroy had
under his command 103 battalions and 147 squadrons. Of these he
could now only marshal (including Grimaldi) 76 battalions and 127
squadrons. All the rest had been drawn from him piecemeal by the
various pressures and anxieties we have described. Marlborough had, on
the other hand, concentrated 100 battalions and 162 squadrons; or
more than four men to three for the operation, and much more upon
the actual front of his attack. We have seen him eager to fight Villars
with four men to five, and victorious at Blenheim with ten men to
eleven. Later both at Ramillies and at Oudenarde he was slightly inferior. Always he welcomed a trial on equal terms. This was the only battle except the Schellenberg which he planned or fought where he had a
large superiority in numbers. His combinations had been entirely successful. Every forecast he had made of the psychological effect which
his marches would produce upon the enemy was vindicated. First he
had compelled their strategical dispersion throughout the theatre of
war; and secondly their tactical dispersion on the chosen battlefield.
Not only had they been forced to weaken their army to guard so many
threatened points, but now, at the moment of action, they were drawn
out on a front larger than their force could cover, their main position
divided by a dangerous ravine, and with an important part of their
army under Grimaldi completely out of joint. Superiority of numbers,
the confusion visible in the French lines—troops moving forward,
backward, now here, now there—the proximity of the Dutch, and
above all the death-dealing position in which Churchill and his corps
stood, all encouraged a just confidence. Marlborough had still eight
days' food in his wagons and could manœuvre or pursue with exceptional freedom. It was with a glow of inward satisfaction that he began
about nine o'clock his customary close, personal reconnaissance of the
hostile front.

When Villeroy and the Elector understood that they were about to
be assaulted by the violent Duke at the head of a much larger army,
their first impulse was to retreat to Brussels. Considering the dangers of
combining a flank march and a rearguard action, they decided to fight
it out. Forthwith they began to fortify the villages behind the Ysche
and to array their troops for a dire struggle. Marlborough meanwhile
had discerned four practicable points of attack, between Overysche and

Neerysche. Prying closely at one of them, he was fired upon by a battery, and when the cannon-balls sang through the air or smote the ground amid his staff, he remarked complacently, "These gentlemen do not choose to have this spot too narrowly inspected."

By the time he reached the end of the front Overkirk arrived, and Marlborough, bound first of all to convince him, took the old Dutchman over the dangerous ground. Overkirk agreed to fight. Thus the first condition of the States-General was established. Indeed, Marlborough had actually issued orders for his infantry to seize the weakly defended passage near Holberg, when he learned that his artillery had been delayed on the march, and forbore pending its arrival.

The deployment of the army was steadily proceeding when, at about noon, Marlborough met the Field Deputies. He greeted them with confidence. "Gentlemen, I congratulate you on the prospect of a glorious victory." He invited their assent to an immediate attack. They curled up. "Your Highness will doubtless allow us to request the opinion of our generals." Although this demand was outside the resolution of the States-General, Marlborough had foreseen that it would be made. He bowed to it. Strong in the support of Overkirk, the Dutch Commander-in-Chief, and in the splendour of the opportunity, he braced himself for confrontation with subordinates. It was some time before they could be assembled on the high ground opposite Overysche. His words have been recorded by Dr Hare, who was at his side. "Gentlemen, I have reconnoitred the ground, and made dispositions for an attack. I am convinced that conscientiously, and as men of honour, we cannot now retire without an action. Should we neglect this opportunity, we must be responsible before God and man. You see the confusion which pervades the ranks of the enemy, and their embarrassment at our manœuvres. I leave you to judge whether we should attack to-day or wait till to-morrow. It is indeed late, but you must consider that by throwing up entrenchments during the night, the enemy will render their position far more difficult to force."

There was a sullen murmur, and then Slangenberg—"that beast Slangenberg," as Hare calls him—broke out, "Since I have been led to this place without any previous communication of the design, I will give no other opinion than that the passage at Overysche is impracticable. However, I am ready to obey the orders which I may receive." Marlborough fastened on the last sentence. "I am happy to have under my command an officer of your courage and skill, and I flatter myself that in a situation which requires instant decision you will start no difficulties." It is sometimes possible to induce a contumacious person to act by giving him charge of the action to which he objects. Accordingly Marlborough proposed to Slangenberg that he should himself direct the attack upon Overysche. Slangenberg was not to be cajoled. "Murder and massacre!" he muttered in audible tones. Of course it would be the Dutch who would be sacrificed. "No," replied Marlborough, "I will place two English battalions at the side of every Dutch one." This must have involved a considerable dislocation of the front. But Slangenberg only rejoined that he did not understand English. "German battalions then," replied the Captain-General. Slangenberg fell back upon his assertion that the attack was impracticable. "Then I will lead it myself," said Marlborough. "I will not send troops to dangers which I will not myself encounter." To this there could be no answer.

He then appealed again to the Deputies. The Deputies turned obdurately away and formed a circle with the generals, where they all stood growling together for about two hours, while the French dug and the day wore on. There is hardly any picture like this in war annals. This cluster of men, shame-faced but stubborn, shifting from one leg to the other, shaking their heads and repeating their arguments while their so-called Commander-in-Chief, humiliated, defied, stood or paced up and down a little way off, now breaking in with words of conciliation and then with words of wrath. But they all knew that if they talked long enough the matter would settle itself as they meant. And here surely Overkirk, from whom history will not withdraw a friendly regard, ought to have made his authority felt by his own Dutch officers. He had agreed to the attack. Should he not have said, "I have given my opinion to the field Deputies, and I cannot allow my officers to contradict me"? But Overkirk, though worth the lot, was old. He was alone among his fellow-countrymen. Faithful in thought and action, he lacked personal dominance. He subsided. If the Duke could not persuade them to it, who could?

The afternoon was now far advanced. Some of the generals had safeguarded themselves by saying that they could not pronounce a final opinion without inspecting the actual points of attack themselves. Slangenberg then proposed that a delegation should make a personal reconnaissance. It was agreed that Slangenberg, Salisch, and Tilly should compose it. The chance of the day was now gone. To-morrow the line of the Ysche would be a fortification. Still, Marlborough named three of his officers to accompany them. Count Noyelles could not trust himself to ride in courtesy with Slangenberg. But Bothmar and Starck complied. As they toured the line the Dutchmen dwelt at every point upon the dangers and difficulties of the attack. Slangenberg claimed that Starck admitted the position to be three times as strong as Höchstädt. But this is denied. Slangenberg then made the offensive re- mark that "the attack at Höchstädt had been regarded as an impru- dence and censured as such by many." Upon this Marlborough's two officers without a word turned their horses and rode away. The remain- der of the delegation returned to make their report. Slangenberg seems to have expected that Marlborough would be anxious to renew the argument with him. In this he was disappointed. ". . . And as we came to make our report to the Veldt-Marshal, of what we had seen," he wrote in his justification, "and came into the road which was bor- dered on both sides by tall hedges behind which the Veldt-Marshal had camped, the Duke of Marlborough passed before us without speaking to us." He added a reference to Overkirk which did himself harm in Holland when the account was published. "After that we came to the Veldt-Marshal, *whom we found sleeping in his coach,* to whom we made our report, and heard no more talk that night nor the following day of attacking the enemy."

What followed is well told in Marlborough's letters.

Marlborough to Godolphin

Lower Wavre
August 19, 1705

You will see by the enclosed to the States that after four days' march, I found the enemy encamped as I expected, so that I thought we should have had a very glorious day. But as the Deputies would not consent without first consulting the generals, who were all against it, except M. Overkirk, we have been obliged to retire from the en- emy, notwithstanding we were at least one-third stronger than they, which I take to be very prejudicial to the common cause, and scan- dalous for the army. I think this will shew very plainly that it is next to impossible to act offensively with this army, so governed as they are; for when their general and I agree, as we did in this, that it shall be in the power of subaltern generals to hinder the execution, is against all discipline. This last action of the Dutch generals has given us great mortification; for the enemy will see very plainly that they have nothing to fear on this side, nor can I ever serve with them without losing the little reputation I have; for in most countries they think I have power in this army to do what I please. I beg you will give my duty to the queen, and assure her that if I had had the same power I had the last year I should have had a greater victory than that of Blenheim, in my opinion; for the French were so posted that if we had beat them they could not have got to Brussels.

On the same day he sent his formal report to the States-General:

. . . Yesterday we were in motion before daybreak and after passing several defiles we came into fairly open country [*une assez grande campagne*] having found the enemy as we expected them between Overysche and Neerysche with the little stream of the Ysche before them. At noon or a little afterwards all our army was ranged in battle, and, having examined with M. Overkirk the four posts which I wished to attack, I flattered myself already, in view of the goodness and superiority of our troops, to be able soon to congratulate Their High Mightinesses upon a glorious victory. But at the last moment when nothing remained but to attack, it was not judged advisable to seek a decision [*pousser l'affaire*]. . . . I am sure that the Deputies will explain to Your High Mightinesses the reasons which were presented to them on both sides, and at the same that they will do justice to M. Overkirk in stating that he shared my feeling that the occasion was too good to throw away. I submitted however, although with much regret.

He added a postscript of severe protest.

My heart is so full that I cannot refrain from representing on this occasion to Your High Mightinesses that I find myself here with far less authority than when I had the honour to command Their troops last year in Germany.

Thus set the star of the Dutch Republic. It is vain to plead that nine months later, only a score of miles away, the victory of Ramillies destroyed Villeroy's army and regained Belgium, and that still the war went on. Time is inexorable. Had Marlborough won the unfought battle of Waterloo in August 1705, all the French power in the Netherlands would have been thereby annihilated. The French stood with their faces towards France, just as the Dutch looked towards Holland. In such a situation there could have been no recovery in the Low Countries for the defeated side. Marlborough would have acquired that supreme authority which he always lacked to plan the campaign of 1706. He would have been there to execute the great projects which we shall presently unfold, unless even better had presented themselves. The year of victory, 1706, might also have been the year of peace. But the Dutch wore out Fortune with their sluggish precautions. Six or seven separate times, for reasons which no instructed modern soldier would tolerate, they "feared their fate too much," and paralysed the genius which could have delivered them. Not all their courage, their sacrifices, and their dauntless constancy could appease the insulted gods. Long and bloody years of struggle lay before them. They were to see their cherished Blue Guards mown down under their own prince at Malplaquet. Their Deputies were even to beg Marlborough to fight a battle against his better judgment in 1711—and beg in vain. They were to exhaust their wealth in a seemingly interminable series of campaigns. Their sea-power and their share in the New World were to pass insensibly, but irresistibly and soon, to England. In the end Marlborough, serviceable, grand, helpful, would fall victim to the English parties, and England, now so fierce and ardent, would sicken of an endless war, desert her allies, and leave them to their fate. But if the valiant Republic, to whom Protestant civilization owes an inestimable debt, was to be deprived of its fruition in modern times, condemned for ever to be a minor Power while rivals grew so great, this was the fatal scene. Here by the cross-roads of bodeful Waterloo, as earlier upon the heaths of Peer, the destinies of Holland turned; and upon that milestone there may well be inscribed the not otherwise noticeable name of Slangenberg.

CHAPTER FORTY-NINE

The Mortified Adventurer

ᏓᏍ 1705, September ᏋᏗ

MARLBOROUGH's wrath and protest caused widespread commotion. A long swell rolled across England. Marlborough knew that in fastening a reproach upon the Dutch he would find a ready response. The Whigs, the advocates of vigorous war, were bound to support it. The Tories marched up eager for a quarrel with those Continental obstructionists and shirkers for whom English citizens had sacrificed too much already. The Queen shared these sentiments with spontaneous warmth, and the Cabinet responded. Harley, as Secretary of State and Speaker, gave full vent to the national mood. For the Dutch formal processes were prepared. A nobleman of the highest standing should be sent as Envoy Extraordinary to the States to protest before the world at the treatment the Captain-General of the joint armies had received. Lord Pembroke was actually selected for this grave mission. The feelings of the magnates and legislators were voiced in rough form and to a most unusual degree, not only by the well-to-do citizens and country gentlefolk, but by the populace. Blenheim sunk throughout the year ever deeper into the national mind. Here was this accursed war which they must fight and which they must win or else be made "slaves and Papists." Here was their own English General who had the secret of victory, whose sword could deliver them from the toils. And here were these pinchbeck princes of Germany and money-grubbing burghers of Holland who would not allow him to strike the blow that would free them all from the heavy, harsh yoke.

On September 1 there arrived a letter from Harley expressing his sympathy. "The queen upon reading your grace's letter," he wrote, "ordered the lords immediately to be summoned; they were all of opinion to advise the queen to take notice of this to the States, in regard not only to the public service, but also what is due to your grace's great merit, to which such usage is very inconsistent." He then explained the plan of Lord Pembroke's mission of protest. Marlborough saw in a moment that this would be regarded throughout Holland as a national insult. He was at the height of his vexation, but he kept his head even in anger. He rejected the proposal at once.

Meanwhile the recriminations in the Army had risen to a dangerous height. Marlborough's letter of August 19 to the States-General, with its accusing postscript, was published even before it was considered by the Assembly. The disclosure was traced to the English Mission at The Hague, and there is little doubt that the Minister, Stanhope, had acted upon Marlborough's instructions. The anger of the British Government and the proposal to protest by a special envoy also became known throughout Holland. There was a crisis of public opinion, and for some days the preponderance was not clear. The peace party naturally took the side of the Dutch generals and Deputies, and the States-General gave prominence to peace talk as an effective counter to the grievances of their ally. Nevertheless, for a space Marlborough did not restrain the resentments which burned within him. Nor was this without a definite purpose. Slangenberg must go. If he remained with the army after what had happened the authority of the Captain-General was at an end. Unless an example were made it was vain to persevere in the campaign. Slangenberg was a national hero in Holland, and he had the whole weight of the Dutch generals and field Deputies on his side. For a fortnight the tension was extreme.

To be rid of Slangenberg Marlborough assigned to him the siege of Léau with fifteen battalions and as many squadrons. Slangenberg, apparently sure of his position, refused unless he were given thirty battalions. The duty was therefore entrusted to General Dedem. The fortress surrendered a week later as soon as the batteries were planted. The publication of Marlborough's protest drew from Slangenberg and the Dutch Deputies lengthy explanations of their conduct, some of which were widely circulated. But now the voice of the Dutch people was heard from many quarters. They declared themselves on Marlborough's side and against their fellow-countryman. Rotterdam led the popular movement: Amsterdam, where the peace party at first was strong, underwent a swift change. The burghers beset the council house with demands "that more attention should be paid to the Duke of Marlborough's advice." Feeling was not less vehement at The Hague. Shrewsbury, who passed through Holland that winter, used that grim phrase which every functionary in the Republic understood only too well. He wrote that if Slangenberg had been seen in the streets he would have been "de-Witted." The storm grew among the masses of the common people, and the magnates bowed to it. Slangenberg, astonished and abashed, withdrew on the plea of ill-health to Maestricht and afterwards to Aix-la-Chapelle.

The departure and downfall of Slangenberg appeased the injured commander. By September 14 he had evidently gained his point. He had appealed against the functionaries to the people. Satisfied upon the essential, he was among the first to be alarmed by the vehement response. No one saw more plainly than he the peril with which the passions he had been forced to unleash threatened the Grand Alliance. He could probably have withdrawn the British Army from the Continental war and returned home amid the plaudits of an angry and short-sighted nation. But this was the conclusion which he most feared and hated. He had tested his strength in England and found it superabundant. All this foreign talk of his being a rash general who had had a lucky fluke, and set his somewhat amateur opinions against the experts of European warfare, counted for nothing in his native land. Queen, Parliament, and people brushed it aside with an instinctive gesture. Slangenberg was gone. The Duke now exerted himself to allay the storm he had aroused. That wind had been felt in every allied Court from The Hague to Vienna. His authority prevailed. The Queen was soothed, the Cabinet was cooled, and Parliament and the people were allowed to simmer down.

There is no doubt that the Dutch were deeply distressed. It was true that Louis XIV was busy with proposals for a separate peace. Terms most favourable to the Republic were offered. Barriers, securities, trade—lucrative trade—were laid before them. Why should they, the French whispered, exhaust themselves for this bloodthirsty island and for the vanity and ambition of a single man, risen from nothing, who wished to make awful experiments in war? But the cause held good. The Dutch were as much alarmed by the French blandishments as by the English anger. They, like Marlborough, realized that their road lay together. There had grown up around Marlborough a curious affiliation in Amsterdam. Those who would not deal with Heinsius would work for Heinsius' policy through him. Buys, the Pensionary of Amsterdam —so lately a leader of the peace faction—volunteered, and was eagerly chosen, to wait upon Marlborough in his camp and offer him satisfaction for the past and assurances for the future. There must be a reconciliation: after all, no one doubted that the Captain-General was the appointed guide. No one could express their affection and his worth to them. If only he did not demand such horrible and dangerous gambling warfare!

The care which Marlborough had taken to strengthen the Rhine secured the Margrave a substantial superiority over the French. Nevertheless Villars, reinforcing and later replacing Marsin, developed a vigorous campaign. He stormed Kron-Weissemburg and regained the line of the Lauter. He reoccupied Homburg and rebuilt its fortifications. The Margrave continued to nurse his foot, against which his debilitated constitution could make no headway, and to supervise the laying out of his gardens at Rastadt, the blooming of which he was never to see. Meanwhile his conduct was under critical review at Vienna. The new Emperor was almost resolved to face the grave embarrassments of removing him when, at the end of August, the ailing general made a vigorous effort to retrieve his reputation. With a superiority of nearly seven to five he advanced suddenly across the Lauter, and recaptured Hagenau and the whole line of the Moder. This exploit was worthy of his former career. It quashed the adverse proceedings on foot against him at the Imperial Court. Villars, arriving after the misfortune, drew out in full array and offered battle. But the Margrave was content with what had been achieved. He treated the French demonstrations with a contempt which the historian Klopp assures us was well-founded, and rejoiced in the fact that, while the enemy were thus vaingloriously parading, a large provision train had been successfully received. The relative strengths of the opposing armies show the different standards by which Villars measured Marlborough and the Margrave.

The forcing of the Lines of Brabant had produced a deep impression upon the Great King. He lost faith in a purely defensive policy. On July 21 he wrote Villeroy a letter which was afterwards to prove of the highest importance.

Although I am convinced of your vigilance and the pains which you have taken to be carefully informed of the movements of the enemy, is it none the less most disagreeable to see them in the middle of the Low Countries masters of the lines and several important posts, and my army compelled to retire precipitately before them to avoid its entire defeat. . . . The disorder which has befallen you springs from the disposition of your army, which is consequent upon the great stretch of country you have to guard. I blame you in no way for what has happened; but, our affairs having definitely changed their character, we must forget a kind of warfare which is suited neither to the genius of the nation nor to the army you command—at least as numerous as that of the enemy. . . . You should not in the future avoid them with too much care; you should make war as we have made it in the past; hold the field, take full advantage of the strength of the positions which you may occupy. Do not expose yourself to a general engagement without need, *but do not avoid it with too much precaution*; because if the enemy perceive this they will take advantage of it.

Villeroy felt that he had escaped so far by a miracle. He protested vehemently to Chamillart against sending any substantial reinforcements from his army to Villars. In his letter of September 30 he uses expressions which in boastful phrases reveal his secret fears.

Would God that the King's interests could be served by my renouncement of command. I would reduce myself with pleasure to dwelling only in a flying camp [*camp volant*], so as to send all the troops to Marshal Villars; but I must point out to the King that the Duke of Marlborough *against every principle of war* wished again to attack the King's army in the last camp which we have just left. His journey to Turnhout was for the sole purpose of obtaining permission from the States. We have *an adventurer mortified with the scanty success of his campaign* who seeks only to stake all; he is within striking distance, in the same mood, and will be so to the last day of the campaign. *We have miraculously saved Flanders*. Would it be prudent to expose it to its fate, when it is only a question of waiting for twelve or fifteen days? . . .

These painful words bring home to us the sense of domination and almost terror with which Marlborough had inspired the soul of his adversary. Villeroy felt himself face to face with a furious wild beast. True, it was caged by the Dutch veto, but it was tearing at the bars, and at any moment might break out in frightful strength and rage. Mercifully in another fortnight winter would come. The monster would have to hibernate. There would be a breathing-space. Meanwhile with a larger army, the first army of France, in an area fortified from end to end, he had "miraculously saved Flanders."

But the King in the tranquillity of Fontainebleau adhered to the robust views he had formed after the piercing of the lines; and his resolve reached its conclusion when a few months later Villeroy met the "mortified adventurer" on the field of Ramillies.

CHAPTER FIFTY

The Whig Approach

⟡ 1705 ⟡

THE General Election which began in May 1705 produced changes in English politics which at first seemed only slight and beneficial, but which set in train events of decisive importance to Marlborough and his fortunes. The Captain-General was capable of enduring endless vexations and outfacing extreme hazards. But he had one sensitive spot. In the armour of leather and steel by which in public affairs he was encased there was a chink into which a bodkin could be plunged. He sought not only glory but appreciation. When according to his judgment he had done well he yearned for the praise of his fellow-countrymen, and especially of those Tory squires—'the gentlemen of England,' as they styled themselves—to whom he naturally belonged, but with whom he was ever at variance. They were the audience whose applauses he sought to compel; and when instead of admiration he received their sneers and belittlings his indignation was profound. "Blenheim indeed!" quoth they. "What was that? A stroke of luck, and the rest the professional knowledge of Eugene." Rooke was the man and the sea war the theme. The campaign of 1705, was it not a failure? All this Continental exertion and expense were follies which should be stopped. How much longer must the blood and treasure of England be consumed in European struggles while rich booty glittered neglected across the oceans and the Church was in danger at home? Thus the Tories. On the other hand stood the Whigs, logical, precise, resolute, the wholehearted exponents of the great war on land and of England rising to the directing summit of the world.

Sarah, as we can judge from John's replies, must have confronted him with this contrast in many a letter. She saw, with a woman's unsentimental discernment, that his illusions about the Tories were vain. They would ever be his foes, and would in the end work his ruin. Her hatred of them ran bitter and strong. With deft hand she picked and shot at him the Tory taunts that would sting him most; and others no doubt wrote in the same strain. Usually the Duke was proof against all minor assaults; but when the Moselle campaign was ruined by the desertion of the German princes and his fine conceptions in Brabant were one after another frustrated by the obstinacy and jealousy of the Dutch commanders, many shafts got home, and he palpably winced under the pangs.

The Parliamentary manœuvre of the Tories in trying to 'tack' the Occasional Conformity Bill to the main supply of the year was undoubtedly a breach of the solemn unwritten convention by which Whigs and Tories were alike bound—that, however party strife might rage, the national war effort must not be weakened. Reluctantly but remorselessly during 1705 Marlborough took the resolve to break with the Tories.

Even before the scandal of the 'tack,' not only Marlborough and Godolphin but Harley too seem to have made up their minds to lean upon the Whigs, as Sarah ceaselessly urged. On the night of March 28, 1705, when Buckingham retired, Portland wrote exultingly to Heinsius, "The liaison is thoroughly effective between the Whigs and 22 and 23 [Marlborough and Godolphin]." A more significant step was the supersession of Admiral Rooke in the command of the Fleet. This ran directly counter to the resolution which the Tories had carried in the Commons, coupling his victory of Malaga with that of Blenheim, and may well have been the royal and ministerial rejoinder to it.

At the beginning of April the Lord-Lieutenancies, so important in elections, were shuffled in favour of the Whigs. On April 7 [1705], two days after the dissolution, political society was astonished to see the Queen sit down to luncheon with Orford (Admiral Russell) and other Lords of the Junto. These steps showed, and were meant to show, the electorate which way the royal favour inclined.

Yet it is remarkable with what restraint Marlborough and Godolphin tried to measure the blow which must now be struck. There was no sense in weakening the Tories only to fall into the hands of the Whigs.

Enough force must be used to beat them, but not so much as to produce a Whig triumph; for then the balance would be deranged, and the two super-Ministers and the Queen would but have exchanged the wrong-headed grumblings and intrigues of the Tories for the exacting appetites and formulas of the Whigs. Marlborough wrote to Sarah from The Hague (April 19/30):

> [Neither] You nor anybody living can wish more for the having a good Parliament than I do, but we may differ in our notions. I will own to you very freely mine; which is, that I think at this time it is for the Queen's service, and the good of England, that the choice might be such as that neither party might have a great majority, so that her Majesty might be able to influence what might be good for the common interest.

Such nicely calculated plans rarely stand the rough tests of action. The rank and file cannot fight hard to win only half a victory; and once the party forces were launched to the attack they strove with might and main. Everywhere the Tories proclaimed the Church in danger. The highflying Tories were furious at what they called the Queen's desertion of the Church. They marshalled all the prejudices of the Old England against the fighting effort of the New. But the vision of the English people was not clouded. Out of the brawl and clatter of the polls one dominating fact emerged—the battle of Blenheim. From the depth of the national heart surged up a glow of pride and of desire for British greatness. Mighty France, four times as populous, the Grand Monarch, tyrant of Europe in all his splendour, cut to the ground by island blades and English genius; his proudest regiments led off captive in thousands by the redcoats, his generals and nobles brought home in droves and tethered about the countryside; conquest, glory, the world to win and the man to win it—these scenes and thoughts stirred the English imagination.

Thus, although the Tories fought with deep-rooted local strength, it was apparent by the beginning of July that the voting would carry their defeat beyond the calculations of the Ministry. The Whig Party had been but one-fifth of the old House of Commons. They were now nearly equal to the Tories. Hitherto, with their ascendancy in the House of Lords, they had been able to maintain themselves vigorously in the State. Now, with the Commons so much more evenly divided, their predominance became apparent. If they joined with the extreme Tories in a general opposition the new House of Commons would be unmanageable. If they supported the Government what price would they ask in return? This now became the crux.

The Lords of the Junto surveyed the scene on the morrow of the elections with cool and determined eyes. They might well have been tempted to claim their rights with the same pedantic rigour with which they held their doctrines. Their turn, they felt, was coming. Why should not the war party wage the war? They had the strength, they had the talents, they had the experience, they had the Cause—why should they be proscribed? Why, indeed, should they not have the Government? Their wishes were no more than the workings of the Constitution would nowadays automatically concede. But at the beginning of the eighteenth century the Crown was still the prime factor in actual politics. The Queen might not be able to choose the policy of the State, but she could still choose the agents to conduct it. To entrust her beloved Church to the freethinking Whigs and their Dissenter supporters, to surround her person with men who in their hearts, as she believed, were the inveterate enemies of monarchy, to part with faithful Tory Ministers and household friends under Parliamentary pressure, was all against the grain to her.

The conflicts and disputations between Lords and Commons which had lasted since 1698 were now ended by Whig control and influence in both Houses. But in its place there opened a wearing struggle in which the Whigs, using all the resources and pressures of Parliamentary government, sought to force themselves upon the Queen. The Tory Party was splintered into four sections: the Jacobites, who claimed to be the only true exponents of the Tory creed; the anti-Jacobite Tories, generically dubbed the Sneakers, or more courteously "the Whimsicals"; the Tackers, whose embittered opposition was led by Rochester and Nottingham and found a new and eloquent mouthpiece in the converted Whig, Haversham; and the placemen, the "Queen's Servants" and independent moderate forces who followed Harley and St John, deferred to the Court, and sustained the Government. Although the whole party had an underlying sense of unity, and felt alike on many questions of peace and war, they were for the time paralysed by their feuds. Indeed, in the Commons they could not find a single man of sufficient distinction and aptitude to be their leader.

Their opposition was effectively vocal only in the Lords. Yet, resting as they claimed upon the Land and the Church, commanding as they did the support of the squires and parsons, they constituted the strongest political force in the realm. If at any moment Tory divisions were healed, their inherent power would assert itself.

The five Whig nobles, on the other hand, had the advantages of unity and leadership. They controlled a disciplined party, inspired by broad and logical principles, which in its most active branches, interests, and classes accepted their guidance with almost military obedience. They knew well the prejudices of the Queen against them. They acted at first with the utmost moderation and with admirable adroitness. They decided to put forward Sunderland, their youngest member —the only one who had not held high office under King William—as their candidate for official favour. Sarah, as usual, was ardent in their cause. Her influence both with the Queen and with her husband was regarded as irresistible. How could that influence be more easily and more naturally exerted than in pressing the claims of her own son-in-law? Sunderland would be the thin end of their wedge. Behind it were the sledgehammers of action in both Houses of Parliament.

The impact of all this fell, as the months passed, upon Godolphin. He had to procure a Parliamentary majority to carry on the war. From this there was no escape. It must be there, on the benches and in the lobbies of both Houses, from day to day. Without it there would be no Supply, the armies would wither, the Grand Alliance would crumble, and the war would be lost. Since he had broken with the Tory Party and the Queen was increasingly reluctant to admit the Whigs in numbers, his task soon became arduous and ungrateful to the last degree. His days were spent in begging the Whig Junto to forbear and the Queen to concede.

It was inevitable that this long, unceasing, day-to-day friction should destroy the relations between Anne and Sarah. The Queen's friend became no more than the advance agent of the Whig Party, so ardent for tangible proofs of royal favour. She not only overrated her influence on public matters with the Queen, but she mistook its character. She sought to win by argument, voluble and vociferous, written and interminable, what had hitherto been the freehold property of love. She undertook to plead every Whig demand with her mistress. For Sunderland, her son-in-law—that might be understood. There the Queen could suppose a personal desire which in old friendship she still wished to meet. But the acceptance of a Whig Lord Keeper, guardian of the Queen's conscience, adviser upon the Church patronage, seemed to Queen Anne not a matter for the judgment of her favourite and confidante. As for all the propaganda of Whiggery of which Sarah made herself the advocate, this only encountered an obstinacy, and in the end wore out a patience, which in conjunction were unique.

The result of the elections and its effect upon the Government manifested themselves as soon as Parliament met on October 25, and the House of Commons proceeded to choose a Speaker. The Tories put forward the pious 'tacker' Bromley, Member for Oxford University, long identified with the Occasional Conformity Bill. The Whigs found a respectable figure in a certain John Smith. Smith was elected by 249 votes to 205 for Bromley.

The Queen's Speech dwelt upon the now familiar theme of Marlborough and Godolphin—"war abroad and peace at home."

In every point both Houses of Parliament cordially sustained the sovereign. The addresses of the Lords and the Commons repeated the sentiments of the Queen's Speech about the war in even stronger language. They overflowed with praise for the Queen's person, her zeal for the Church, and her devotion to the harmony of her subjects. The Commons then proceeded to vote unprecedented supplies of money for the war, and to make large additions to the armed forces by land and sea.

Their resentments now betrayed the Tory leaders into further acts of extreme unwisdom. Once again they tried by an insincere manœuvre to entangle the Whigs, and once again they were themselves upset. Their spokesman, Haversham, put forward in the Lords a proposal that, in order to ensure the Protestant succession, the Electress Sophia should be invited to take up her residence in England. No one knew better than Rochester and Nottingham that this suggestion was insupportable to the Queen. Yet it seemed a plan for which no Whig could refuse to vote without repudiating the whole doctrines of his party. If the Whigs endorsed it, they made a new breach with the Queen. If they refused it, they falsified their principles, and staggered their party. Such was the plan upon which the Tories were led into the enemy's lines masquerading in their uniforms.

The political sagacity of the Junto and the discipline of their party enabled them easily to defeat the fantastic assault, and to turn it to their own advantage. They supported the Government in meeting Haversham's motion with a plain negative. The Queen herself was encouraged to be present 'incognito,' as it was called, in the House of Lords during the debate. She heard the Tory orator putting forward the project most deeply repugnant to her. She heard the Whig debaters, whom she had so long regarded as her enemies, displaying all their brilliant gifts of argument and rhetoric upon her side. Never had the Whigs more nearly won the heart of Queen Anne than on this occasion. The motion was rejected by an overwhelming majority. The Queen returned to St James's with the feeling that her lifelong friends had outraged her, and her lifelong foes had come to her rescue. How profoundly shaken she was alike in her faiths and her prejudices can be judged by the letter which she wrote to Sarah.

> I believe dear Mrs Freeman and I shall not disagree as we have formerly done; for I am sensible of the services those people have done me that you have a good opinion of, and will countenance them, and am thoroughly convinced of the malice and insolence of them that you have always been speaking against.

One final exhibition remained. The Tories came forward with their cry, "The Church in danger." Rochester, Nottingham, and the newly dismissed Buckingham set forth their threefold case. The Act of Security—which in that dark hour before the victory of Blenheim brought new life Godolphin had advised the Queen to sign—authorized the Presbyterian Government in Scotland to arm a fierce, fanatical antiepiscopalian peasantry. The Occasional Conformity Bill had been for three sessions handspiked. The invitation to the Electress Sophia had been rejected. Thus (moaned the Tories) Presbyterians and Dissenters had gained the upper hand both in England and in Scotland.

CHAPTER FIFTY-ONE

The War in Spain

⁊ɑ 1705-6 ᚦ

THE curtain must now rise upon a scene where striking episodes and personages play their part. In Spain from the summer of 1705 to the autumn of 1706 the cause of the Two Crowns [Spain and France] fell to so low an ebb that the War of the Spanish Succession seemed to be settling itself in the country primarily concerned. The failure of the large Franco-Spanish army under Marshal Tessé to recover Gibraltar at the end of 1704 had been followed by a complete lull in the Spanish war. It was throughout a war of petty armies, occasionally fighting small, fierce battles and making long marches about an enormous country in the main stony and desolate. The fortresses, ill-protected by defences or garrisons, easily changed hands. The sympathies of the countryside, however, played a serious part in the fortunes of the wandering armies, and a surge of national feeling was almost immediately decisive. So far the Allies, advancing eastward with the Portuguese, had made little or no progress. The Marquis de Ruvigny, who commanded there, was one of King William's generals, a French Huguenot refugee raised to the English peerage. The Earl of Galway, to use the title by which he was henceforward known, was an heroic figure in the resistance to the tyranny and persecution of Louis XIV. He had been Deputy-General of the Huguenots. Connected by marriage to the Russells, he had acquired English nationality as early as 1688. He had commanded for King William in Ireland. He had fought in his Continental campaigns. Saint-Simon has recorded the moving story of his adventure at the battle of Landen. His French captors, knowing that his life was forfeit, in the heat of battle refused with soldierly magnanimity to hold him prisoner. They found him a horse and set him free. He was a gallant and faithful man, and a skilful, experienced professional soldier. A contemporary record describes him as "one of the finest gentlemen in the army, with a head fitted for the Cabinet as well as the camp; is very modest, vigilant, and sincere; a man of honour and honesty, without pride or affectation; wears his own hair, is plain in his dress and manners." His right hand had recently been shattered by a cannon-ball at the siege of Badajos, and he had henceforth to be lifted on to his horse like a child.

Marlborough had known him long and held him in the highest esteem. He had himself chosen him for the command of the Portugal expedition. Without approving some of his operations, he upheld him through the worst misfortunes. He defended his military character in strong and even passionate terms when Galway was censured by Parliament in 1711.

But now a far more brilliantly coloured personality was to enter upon the Spanish scene. Early in 1705 the English Government decided, under Marlborough's impulse, to use their sea-power in the Mediterranean. A wide latitude was necessarily accorded to the commanders of the fleet and army. Their prime purpose was to assist the Duke of Savoy upon the Riviera coast. Their second was to act in Spain, as they might decide upon the spot. The preference of the Cabinet was for the succour of the Duke of Savoy. Already Marlborough hankered for an attack upon Toulon. As early as April 1705 he described Toulon to Briançon, the Savoy envoy in London, as a main English objective. The slow, precarious communications forbade them to prejudge the issue from Whitehall. In order to avoid repeating the naval and military discordances which had wrecked the Cadiz enterprise in 1702, it was resolved that the general should not only command the troops, but should have equal power with the admiral in the strategic movements of the fleet. Sir Cloudesley Shovell was appointed to the naval command, and Charles Mordaunt, Earl of Peterborough, became Commander-in-Chief in Spain with additional commission as Admiral, jointly with Shovell. Peterborough's appointment was delayed till Parliament had separated, as it was known to be unacceptable to both political parties.

We cannot attempt here to appraise the character and quality of one who is called by his admirers "the great Earl of Peterborough," but merely to present the reflections cast upon his memorable deeds and misdeeds by Marlborough's judgment and actions. Hoffmann reported to his Government upon him, "He is of such a temperament that he cannot brook an equal. He is a thoroughly restless and quarrelsome character, incapable of dealing with anybody, . . . and on top of that he has had no war experience on land or sea." This seems to have been well informed. John and Sarah had known Peterborough all his life, and had tasted his malice and mischief as far back as the trial of Sir John Fenwick in 1696. In the closing years of King William, and since the opening of the new reign, friendly and even cordial relations seemed to have subsisted between the Marlborough and Peterborough families. We have seen how Peterborough's intrepid son, the hero of the forlorn hope at the Schellenberg, had wooed but not won Marlborough's youngest daughter, Mary. Peterborough certainly regarded the Marlboroughs, especially Sarah, as friends who rated him at his own valuation. He corresponded with the Duchess in terms of gay affability, and with the Duke with almost obsequious respect. Sarah, whose sure scent for genius had led her in her youth to marry the penniless John Churchill, and was to lead her in old age to bestow ten thousand pounds upon the great Pitt, then equally undistinguished, was evidently conscious of the Peterborough spell. Certainly she sang his praises to Marlborough during 1705, and Marlborough bears responsibility both for the appointment and for its exceptional conditions.

It is strange that he should have chosen a commander for Spain whose character, qualifications, and methods were so utterly different from his own. Peterborough had, as Hoffmann reported, no training as either soldier or sailor. He lacked patience, reserve, and persistency. He was quarrelsome and boastful. His caprice, or inspiration, was incalculable. His recklessness, his violence and profusion, were well known. How far, then, did Marlborough act upon his own judgment and how far did he trust himself to Sarah's instinct? At any rate, at the end of May 1705 an armada of sixty-six British and Dutch battleships, with many smaller vessels and 6500 soldiers, sailed from Portsmouth to Lisbon under the command of Peterborough and Shovell.

In issuing their orders to an expedition which once launched passed almost completely out of control the English Cabinet, guided by Marlborough, had pondered deeply upon their past experience. Although there was much friction, upon which historians have dilated, the arrangement at first worked well, and the results were splendid. All the leaders of the Allies for the war in Spain met at Lisbon in the last week of June 1705. Charles III, with his handful of personal officers, awaited them. Das Minas, the Portuguese general, and Galway rode in from the front a little beyond the Portuguese boundary. The valiant Prince George of Hesse-Darmstadt, an Imperial Field-Marshal at thirty-six, came in an English frigate fresh from his six months' defence of Gibraltar. To these were now joined Peterborough, with Stanhope at his side, and Shovell, with Leake his second-in-command. This symposium of forceful, competing personalities was gathered to debate problems offering many alternatives. Their subsequent quarrels have led historians to dwell upon their differences. But the outstanding fact at the beginning is their agreement and its successful execution. Peterborough, fresh from Whitehall, leaned to the succour of Savoy. The Archduke, the Allies' King of Spain, naturally regarded this as desertion of his cause. He had been sent by the Allies to fight for the Spanish crown in Spain. What was this talk of Italy?

Darmstadt, as we may call him, seems first to have recommended a march on Madrid through Valencia; but he was also agreeable to an attack on Barcelona. He had defended Barcelona against the French in 1697. He had been Viceroy of Catalonia. The Catalans regarded him with gratitude and admiration. He had played a decisive part in the capture of Gibraltar, and was the soul of its defence. Whether under his influence or not, the Lisbon Council chose Barcelona as their goal. Their discussions and the necessary preparations were protracted, but at length the great fleet resumed its progress. Galway authorized the exchange of the seasoned regiments at Gibraltar for the raw English and Irish recruits, and contributed two regiments of Dragoons. All were confirmed in their resolve by a dispatch from London giving the Queen's permission for a landing in Catalonia. Marlborough had learned from the English envoy with the Duke of Savoy, Richard Hill, that an attempt upon Toulon was not to be contemplated. He therefore relaxed his dominating control, and was content to see a Spanish venture in 1705.

On the voyage along the eastern coast of Spain the fleet touched at Denia, in Valencia. They were received with enthusiasm by the people. The magistrates of Philip V made immediate submission. All reports declared the acceptance by Valencia of the Hapsburg claim. Peterborough was excited. He saw the merit of Darmstadt's first suggestion. "Land here," he urged, "and march directly upon Madrid." The distance was but a hundred and fifty miles through easy, unravaged country. In a fortnight, he suggested, King Charles III would be enthroned in the Spanish capital. This was widely different from his previous counsel; but no one can say it was wrong. However, Darmstadt had now been rallied by Charles III to the capture of Barcelona. He believed and protested that all Catalonia would rise to welcome him. Ultimately what he said proved true. The youthful sovereign, with the proved officer whose name seemed to be magic upon these doubtful coasts, prevailed. Peterborough, the Commander-in-Chief, submitted, and the fleet sailed northward to Barcelona. By this time there was sharp disagreement in this hydra-headed enterprise. Probably if Marlborough had been in Peterborough's shoes in the Lisbon discussions he would have refrained from advocacy of any course. He would have been content if all were agreed that the fleet, having on board the strongest possible force, should pass the Pillars of Hercules and enter the Mediterranean. He would have left the partisans of various plans to exhaust each other and so gradually transform a nominal command-in-chief into effective control. But Peterborough struck with all his force in one direction, and now, valid reasons having arisen, with equal vehemence in another. Thus he lost much power.

In the third week of August the armada anchored before Barcelona. This was the most populous and wealthy city of Spain. It was a fortress of no mean repute, tested within a decade by siege. Its fortifications could not compare with the wonderful creations of Vauban in the Low Countries. But they comprised a complete perimeter of bastioned ramparts and ditches, and the most vulnerable quarter was guarded by the strong stone star-fort of the Montjuich upon its dominating height three-quarters of a mile south of the city. The Spanish Governor, Don Velasco, was a resolute, vindictive champion of the Bourbons. He had about three thousand trustworthy soldiers under his command. On August 22 Charles III landed north of Barcelona, and was greeted and acclaimed by the Catalans, who flocked to his banner. The sympathies of Catalonia were manifestly favourable. Crowds of countryfolk and local nobility assembled to welcome him. Of armed forces only fifteen hundred Miquelets, as the Catalan rebels were called, presented themselves.

Velasco saw in the local hostility a military advantage for the defence of Barcelona. The Allies could not afford to destroy their popularity with the Catalans by starving the citizens or bombarding their dwellings, still less by delivering them to storm and sack. With all these facts present in their minds also, the councils of war upon Sir Cloudesley Shovell's flagship became distracted. Charles, animated by Darmstadt, demanded a siege. Shovell supported him. No one has ever been able to plumb Peterborough's mind. Whether he was actuated by caprice and day-to-day events, or whether he prepared a profound design with all Marlborough's dissimulation, may well be indefinitely disputed. Certainly he could exert his influence most strongly by urging his Lisbon proposal to proceed at once to Italy. The armed support which Darmstadt had predicted—nay, promised—in Catalonia was lacking. The Council had rejected his own bold plan of a march from Valencia on Madrid. What hopes were there of capturing a fortified city which could not even be bombarded for fear of alienating local sympathy? Peterborough played his card for all it was worth. Thus, with a shrewdness unusual in him, he forced all his colleagues to try to conciliate him. From weakness or from craft he yielded to their wishes, but he stipulated—and all agreed—that eighteen days was to be the limit of the siege.

Accordingly the guns were landed and siege approaches made from the north side of the town, supported by sixteen thousand soldiers and sailors, mainly British. The ground was marshy and difficult, and Governor Velasco protected his ramparts at the threatened point by a preliminary lunette. No practicable breach appeared, and Peterborough continued to baffle the council of war by the alternatives of a march to Valencia and thence to Madrid, or preferably an immediate departure for Italy. After a fortnight when everything was thus in the most perfect confusion he suddenly emerged with an audacious surprise. He informed Darmstadt that he was about to assault the Montjuich. The Prince, who, according to some, had already pressed this course, was delighted. Neither of them told Charles III or the admirals of their plan till the troops were already marching.

On the evening of September 13, 1705, a thousand men, of whom eight hundred were English, set off under Peterborough and Darmstadt ostensibly for Tarragona, the first stage in a march southward to Valencia. A reserve of twelve hundred men under Stanhope followed later. The fleet cannon had already been re-embarked, and Governor Velasco was preparing his celebrations. Peterborough and Darmstadt marched all night by a circuitous route and at daybreak appeared from the contrary quarter upon the most accessible side of the Montjuich. There followed a comedy of chance which was also an epic. The assailants stormed the outer works. They placed their ladders in the stone ditch, but these proved too short by seven or eight feet, and they found themselves stopped. The scanty garrison sent frantic messages for help to the city. Governor Velasco dispatched at once a hundred dragoons, each with an infantryman riding pillion. The garrison, seeing this help approaching, raised a cheer which Lord Charlemont, who commanded the British brigade, mistook as the signal for surrender. Thereupon the English leaped into the covered way, assuming themselves the victors. In this exposed situation they received a series of deadly volleys from the cannon and musketry of the fort. Many fell and two hundred surrendered. Darmstadt, hastening to intercept Velasco's reinforcement, was wounded. A bullet severed the major artery in his thigh, and in a brief space he bled to death. Aghast at this catastrophe, Charlemont's remaining men retreated. They had already abandoned the action when Peterborough, arriving, behaved in a most becoming manner. Seizing a half-pike and declaring he would conquer or die, he rallied his surviving soldiers and led them back to the outworks. This would have availed him nothing but for a curious turn of luck.

The two hundred prisoners were being hustled down the hill towards Barcelona, three-quarters of a mile away, when they met virtually the whole garrison of the city advancing to the rescue of the Montjuich. Interrogated, they admitted that both Peterborough and Darmstadt were assaulting the fort. The officer in command of the relief was staggered by the presence of these great personalities. He concluded that the bulk of the allied army must be with them; he therefore returned to Barcelona, and sealed its fate. By extraordinary exertions ships' cannon, relanded, were dragged into the captured outworks, and from this deadly position launched a bombardment which after three days compelled the commandant of the fort to surrender. The fall of the Montjuich broke the spirit of Velasco. He agreed to capitulate unless relieved within four days. Hostages were accordingly exchanged, Stanhope representing the Allies. The terms could not however be executed. The excitement of the Barcelona populace rose to an uncontrollable pitch. The Miquelets from the surrounding hills penetrated the city. The massacre of Bourbon adherents without respect to age, sex, or quality was imminent. The Governor invoked the aid of his hostage, Stanhope. Peterborough with strong forces entered the city while it was in wild confusion, and had the crowning and romantic satisfaction of personally saving a beautiful and terrified duchess from the fury of the mob. Even the King, who suffered so much from his arrogance, wrote to Queen Anne that Peterborough had saved the city from "a veritable blood bath."

However it happened, Barcelona was captured. Whosoever's conception it was, whether it arose from accident, caprice, or profound design, the glory belongs to Peterborough, who lost no time in claiming it. Forthwith he sent Stanhope to England with dispatches couched in a grandiloquent vein, with letters to the Ministers, and to all his friends and his family, clamouring for praise, reinforcements, and appointment as commander-in-chief of all the forces in Spain, with sole control of the fleet.

Conflicting accounts reached Marlborough from Barcelona. On September 29 he wrote to Hedges, the Secretary of State for the Southern Department:

> When the Duke of Savoy receives these dispatches, and sees how earnest the Queen is in giving him all the assistance that is possible, it will encourage H.R.H. to continue firm in the interest of the Allies, which, I believe, he must needs be sensible is his own too, though he may suffer for the present. And if the good news we have from Catalonia be confirmed, no doubt but it will have a great influence upon our affairs in Italy, and likewise in Portugal. By letters I received yesterday I am advised that the whole country had owned King Charles, and that even at Barcelona the inhabitants had taken arms to oblige the garrison to surrender, so that it was not doubted but H.M. was in possession of the city likewise.

And three weeks later:

> A great deal will depend on what we do in Catalonia, from whence the news you send me is the freshest we have that we can depend

upon. The last letters from Paris of the 16th pretend that Barcelona held out still, but we have no reason to doubt our affairs going well on that side, since they tell us nothing to the contrary. We were still in hopes, till the receipt of your letters, that the news of the Prince of Darmstadt's death might not be true.

The news of the capture of Barcelona had been hailed in London with unbridled enthusiasm. The highest opinion was held of King Charles's conduct. Godolphin was impressed by his detailed report to the Government. The English bias, especially Tory bias, was so strong for Spanish operations and for using the naval power that the capture of a fortress in Spain was judged at double the far stiffer similar prize in Flanders. Stanhope's mission met with the warmest response. Parliament presented addresses acclaiming the prowess and conduct of Peterborough. Five thousand British infantry and two hundred and fifty thousand pounds, together with a strong squadron under Byng, were eagerly devoted to the Peninsular campaign of 1706.

Success, however, had not assuaged the quarrels of the allied commanders. Everybody hated Peterborough, and Peterborough struck at all. His differences with "the Germans," or "the Vienna crew," as he described Charles III and his Imperialist advisers, soon made even formal relations difficult. "If another general," wrote Prince Lichtenstein, one of Charles's Austrian counsellors and his old tutor (November 5, 1705), "had been in command, it would have been easy to take Majorca or Minorca, and to conquer the whole of Aragon and Valencia." He added, "All the officers under Lord Peterborough seek to leave for home. But I see no hope they will send us out a better general from England." On the other hand, Peterborough himself was vociferous. "God protect this land," he wrote to Stanhope (November 18), "from even the best of the German Ministers." Peterborough's vanity, his violence, his giddy shifts of view and of mood, made him quarrel with the young King, with the allied generals and the English admirals. Shovell had sailed for home with most of the heavy ships. But Leake, who remained upon the coast, regarded this human firework with equal dislike and distrust. In December Charles appealed to London to send Galway from Portugal to take the command.

The effects of the fall of Barcelona and the ardour of the whole province enabled the small allied forces to become speedily masters of every stronghold in Catalonia and on the Aragon frontier. At the same

time the Spanish officers whom Darmstadt with sure knowledge had selected to uphold King Charles's causes in Valencia met with unbroken
success. Peterborough after several minor successes entered Valencia at
the end of January 1706, and Charles was then in effective possession
of all Eastern Spain with the overwhelming support of its inhabitants.
These conquests—easy come and easy go though they were to prove—
threw a glowing light upon the Spanish scene at the end of the year,
when all else was black or grey.

Yet beneath the surface of success were causes of deep anxiety.
Charles III, writing to Marlborough from Barcelona (October 22,
1705), described his condition in gloomy terms:

> *. . . We are in want of everything necessary for the war, having
> neither the money nor the ammunition required to defend Catalonia,
> which is all for us, except Rosas, . . . but the country very devoted.
> . . . We are in great danger, whatever Lord Peterborough's efforts
> may be, without prompt and extraordinary succours. . . .

And Peterborough, amid his gay diversions in Valencia, was himself
under no illusions.

Peterborough to Marlborough

Valencia
3 February, 1706

* My Lord,

How long we can resist such odds I know not. It is very uncomfortable to receive no letter this four months. My Lord, it is a hard
shift I am put to to sustain a war against French Generals and
French troops with a Spanish horse—the best that be seen anywhere
—without troops, without baggage, without money, in a country
without an Officer speaking the language but myself. . . . The greatest honours imaginable have been paid in Valencia to the Queen, and
we have been received with unexpressible marks of joy. I think we
have deserved to some degree the kindness they have expressed. Under all fatigues I endure and dangers I undergo my comfort is that I
have done my duty and that I am confident I shall continue to do so.
I wish My Lord a happy campaign. I believe Your Grace has had a
good winter one, and I hope whenever we are overpowered the enemy
shall pay a reasonable reckoning. It is a great pity, My Lord, that we

should have made such false steps as those I have given much account of, and that we must languish so long without relief or support.

The active prosecution of the war in the Peninsula had really sprung from English Parliamentary circles. The Cabinet and Marlborough became conscious of a strong impulse of support for this theatre. They yielded somewhat easily to a genial breeze. Many writers have censured the dispersion of forces as improvident and unorthodox. There is no doubt that Marlborough was influenced by politics rather than by strategy in the tolerance, and more than tolerance, which he showed to the Spanish venture. Still, he could have cited facts and figures in deprecation if not in defence. The English expenditure in the Low Countries in 1706 was £1,366,000 and in Spain no less than £1,093,-071. The number of English troops, apart from those in English pay, sent to Spain was above ten thousand. On the other hand, the French had at least fifteen thousand regular troops in the Peninsula during 1706, and eighteen thousand in 1707. Whether, if there had been no war in Spain, Marlborough could have gained these troops for Flanders is more than doubtful. Probably if they had not fought there they would never have been granted him. Fighting there, they actually contained through the ups and downs of three critical years superior numbers of the enemy. We feel sure that he regarded all troops sent to Spain as a concession to London opinion. He would have rejoiced to have them in his own hand. Nevertheless, they were by no means wasted in the general application of available forces. A substantial military compensation, apart from political convenience, could be adduced in the grim account. When we deplore the absence of ten thousand redcoats from the campaigns of Ramillies and Oudenarde, and all the extra weight that this would have given to Marlborough's control over the main confederate army, we are by no means entitled to assume that this alternative was ever open to him.

The attitude of the Emperor Joseph was different. He had a natural sympathy for his brother in his trials. But the sending of the young Archduke to the Peninsula was a London and not a Vienna plan. It was not until after the capture of Barcelona that a surge of enthusiasm for the effort in Spain rose in the Emperor's heart. Certainly thenceforward he was deeply moved. In a dispatch to Gallas in London (December 23, 1705) he offered to provide troops for Spain, and urged that transport, and of course money, should be furnished by England. He would even, so Gallas was instructed to state, pawn his own jewellery rather than allow Charles's life and honour to be cast away.

But—and on this point all opinions converged—Peterborough must be removed, and if possible Galway appointed in his stead.

CHAPTER FIFTY-TWO

The Tottering Alliance

⟨ 1705-6 ⟩

EVER since the disaster of Blenheim Louis XIV had been anxiously seeking by this road and that for a peace based on compromise. He no longer sought victory; but until the beginning of 1709 he hoped to escape a treaty of absolute defeat. In its military and financial weakness the Empire claimed the most from the war; in its strength and ardour England sought the least. The Dutch occupied the decisive position; they maintained the largest army in the field; they made a substantial money contribution; they played their part at sea. Nevertheless, their aims were practical and compact. They wanted their barrier of Belgian fortresses, with as many French fortresses to broaden it as possible. They hoped for a barrier on their southern and south-eastern frontiers stronger than that which they had so incontinently lost in 1701. The article of the original treaty of the Grand Alliance, while deliberately vague upon the question of the sovereignty of Belgium, was explicit about its strategic destiny. The Spanish Netherlands must be recovered "to the end that they may serve as a dyke, rampart and barrier to separate and keep France at a distance from the United Netherlands." After Blenheim at various times, through successive agents, Louis XIV intimated secretly to the Dutch that he was willing to partition Belgium and divide its fortresses with them.

At the end of 1705 the French negotiations, hitherto intangible, took a more definite form. The Marquis d'Alègre, a French Lieutenant-General, had been captured by the Scots Greys in Marlborough's cavalry charge after the forcing of the Lines of Brabant in July 1705. To this high personage the Duke granted a parole of two months to settle his affairs in France, and charged him to convey to Louis XIV a message of ceremony. Arrived at Versailles, d'Alègre was taken into Torcy's confidence and became a secret emissary of peace. On his return to Holland he was to seek out Marlborough, express the pleasure with which the King had received his compliments, and, if permitted, open decisively the question of peace. D'Alègre was to dwell upon the vexations Marlborough was bound to suffer at the hands of the Dutch, upon the hazards of war, and the many shifts and insecurities of private fortune. How success, however brilliant, brought envy in its train; how often ingratitude alone repaid the efforts of great servants; how peace would consolidate the glories which Marlborough had gained; and how earnestly the King desired that just and lasting peace. If these overtures were well received by Marlborough, d'Alègre was to broach a very delicate topic. So ardent was his Majesty for peace that he would bestow a kingly reward on anyone who could bring it about. "It might perhaps have been wished," d'Alègre was instructed to say,

> that the Duke of Marlborough had not already received all the honours which have been bestowed upon him, in order that there might be room for his Majesty to offer him, after the peace, rewards worthy of a man of his standing. Since he possesses them all, the King has no resource but munificence: but whatever benefits he had received from his own sovereign, two millions of French livres [about £300,000] would raise him above the dangers to which eminence is always exposed in England, if not sustained by great wealth.

It was further suggested that the payments should be spread over the first four years after the Peace. If all this went down well with Marlborough, and d'Alègre sustained no rebuff, he was then to outline the actual terms on which the King would treat.

These were curious, and widely different from all later versions. Philip V was to keep Spain and the Indies, also the Milanese. Charles III was to become, as an Archduke, Elector of Bavaria, thus strengthening the house of Hapsburg exactly where it had been most imperilled. Max Emmanuel was to be indemnified for the loss of his native land, Bavaria, and for abandoning his Vicar-Generalship of the Spanish Netherlands, by becoming king of the "Two Sicilies." France was to hold all the bridgeheads on the Upper Rhine. Holland was to have

(499)

her Barrier fortresses, to be held by Swiss garrisons, and the full possession of Guelders and Limburg. The Duke of Lorraine, whose balancing attitude during the campaign of 1705 had been noticeable, was to be consoled for French acquisitions on the Rhine by the Vicar-Generalship of such parts of the Spanish Netherlands as remained after the Dutch claims had been met. This French proposal contemplated for the first time since the outbreak of the war the division of the Spanish inheritance. Nevertheless, it was a French peace. The Great King paid his debt to Max Emmanuel, but held him in his power. He maintained his grandson in Spain. He kept his grip on Northern Italy.

We have no record of what passed at d'Alègre's interview with Marlborough. It is, however, certain that the Duke allowed the captive peace agent to unfold the whole story. Imperturbably he listened to the proposal of a vast bribe to himself, and thereafter to the French terms for a general peace. He must have been all smiles to d'Alègre, who departed without an inkling of where Marlborough stood. Clearly Marlborough was not at all attracted by the French peace proposal. He did not think that the French power was as yet sufficiently broken to give England the security which she needed and deserved. He doubted the French sincerity in view of their great remaining military strength and the disappointing close of his late campaign. He suspected a manœuvre to spread disunion between the Allies. He was resolved to continue the war and bring France low. When d'Alègre unfolded four days later his peace terms to Heinsius, Marlborough set himself to discredit and frustrate them. He was neither offended nor seduced by the personal bribe. He put it by in his mind as something which might be of interest some day, but which could not in the slightest degree affect his judgment or his action.

Now the new, fierce campaign was about to begin. The eight French armies were already almost gathered upon their respective fronts. Every promise of the German states had been at the best half kept; all the contingents were weaker and later than arranged. Every single ally had his special complaint. The Empire, the most helpless, the most failing, was the most arrogant and querulous of all. The Margrave maundered over a mouldering army on the Rhine. The King of Prussia held all his troops back from the fighting fronts to which it had been agreed they should march. The Danes, even after their Eutin incursion had been adjusted, were set upon their arrears of pay. England was the milchcow of all, and Parliament was already voluble upon that pregnant point. But England, detached yet dominant in the distracted Continent, was still resolved upon war and victory. She was to have both.

CHAPTER FIFTY-THREE

Fortune's Gift

⧼ 1706, May ⧽

MARLBOROUGH had reached The Hague full of a great military design. Our chief source for this is in the letters which he wrote after it had been decisively prevented. But there is ample evidence how far he had carried his plan for marching all round France into Italy. For months past he had been setting everything in motion to that end. There were the eight thousand Prussians who were anyhow to stay in Italy. There were the seven thousand Palatines and three thousand Saxe-Gothas. There was the English Government subsidy of three hundred thousand crowns, there was the £250,000 loan, both of which were payable only to Prince Eugene's account in Venice. Well-equipped in the Italian theatre would stand Eugene, and thither Marlborough would march with the renowned redcoats and such other contingents as he could scrape. He had procured the assent of the Cabinet, and was now strong enough to have his plan embodied in a solemn commission from the Queen authorizing him to act, if he thought fit, independently of the Dutch.

Armed with this vigorous document, he now opened the matter boldly at The Hague. The States-General showed much more imagination and confidence than they had done in 1704. Their terms were simple. If he went he must take no Dutch troops: that would cost them their lives at the hands of the Dutch populace. But for the rest they would run all risks to help him. He had already directed eighteen thousand men upon the Italian theatre. If with twenty thousand English, who were to make another long pilgrimage, and certain auxiliaries of quality he could reach Lombardy, he and Eugene might do a deed the fruits whereof would be inestimable and the fame immortal.

To take the pressure off the Dutch, while he was fighting in Italy, Marlborough had resolved upon an important diversion. A French refugee, the Comte de Guiscard, a man whose dark and explosive nature was armed with much address, had for many months past pressed upon the London Cabinet a plan for the landing of a strong force upon the coasts of France far behind the fortress barrier of the Low Countries. St John was much impressed with Guiscard. He wrote of him to Marlborough in the highest terms: "His conduct had been full of zeal, very discreet and very moderate." Guiscard proposed that a number of battalions should be raised from the Huguenot refugees, and that these, reinforced by several brigades of British infantry and regiments of dragoons, should be landed by surprise somewhere between Blaye and the mouth of the Charente. Xantes was to be occupied and fortified, and the French Huguenot officers were from thence to rouse the Cevennes and reanimate the Camisards, carrying rebellion supported by invasion into these smouldering regions. Marlborough thought well of the venture and of the part it would play in his general strategy.

The Italian scheme was destroyed by the earliest events of the campaign of 1706. The French forestalled the Allies in the field both on the Rhine and in Italy. In March Vendôme, unseasonably mobilized, inflicted at Calcinato a savage minor defeat upon Reventlau, who commanded the Imperial forces in Eugene's absence at Vienna. Eugene arrived, not indeed to stem the rout, but to reorganize and reanimate the beaten army when they reached the Trentino. Here was a loss in capture, and still more in desertion, of ten thousand men. In Germany Villars fell upon the Margrave, who with feeble forces was blockading Fort Louis, and on May 3 chased him over the Rhine. The blockade of Fort Louis was abandoned, and the blockaders were thankful, or even proud, to have made their escape. Hagenau and Duremberg were captured with their garrisons, and almost all those conquests which the triumphant Allies had made on the left bank after Blenheim were lost.

All this time the French armies were steadily concentrating, and further rude shocks impended on all European fronts. In these circumstances the States-General made Marlborough another simple offer. They would approve the sending of an extra ten thousand men to the aid of Prince Eugene, provided that he would himself command the

Dutch armies on the Flanders front. Moreover, he should not be hampered in any way by Deputies or generals. If he, their Deputy Captain-General, would stay to guard the Dutch homeland, he should be master in the field, and he might send this further substantial aid to his comrade Eugene. Marlborough closed with this. Assuredly the Dutch kept their word. Slangenberg smouldered in sullen obscurity. Three new field Deputies were appointed with instructions to obey the Duke and with no prohibitions against fighting a battle, which however seemed most unlikely.

It was with melancholy thoughts that Marlborough began his most brilliant campaign. "I cross the sea," he wrote to Wratislaw, "with sufficiently sad reflections." "The little concern of the King of Denmark and almost all the other princes give me so dismal thoughts that I almost despair of success." These expressions can be multiplied. But this was his dangerous mood. Just as he had written before starting upon the Blenheim march that he saw no prospect of doing any good that year, so now he was in the deepest gloom. It was not the abysmal despair into which he was plunged in the two or three days before Oudenarde, but it was black as night. Yet he had his consolations, and his poise remained perfect. There is a letter of his which we like as much as any he wrote to his wife.

John to Sarah

May 4[/15], 1706

* I am very uneasy when Your letters do not come regularly, for without flatterie my greatest suport are the thoughts I have of your kindness; hether too I really have not had tim to write to my Children, but when I do, be asur'd that I shal let them know my heart and soul, as to their living dutyfully, and kindly with You, and let mee beg for my sake of my dear Soull, that she will passe by litle faults and consider thay are very Young, and that thay cant do other then love you withal their hearts, for when thay consider how good a Mother You have been to them, thay must bee barbariens if thay did not make a kind return; You will see by my letters to Lord Treasurer that *in all likelywhode I shal make the whole Campagne in this country, and consequently not such a one as will please mee, but as I infinitely vallu Your estime, for without that You cant love me, let mee say for my self, that there is some merit, in doing rather what is good*

for the publick, then in prefering ons private satisfaction and Intirest,
for by my being here in a condition of doing nothing that shal make
a noise, has made me able to send ten thousand men to Italie, and to
leave Nyntien thousand men on the Rhin til the Mareshal de Marsin
shal bring back his detachement to this country; the ffrench are very
possitive that thay must succed at Barcelone but I trust in God our
ffleet will releive it, and then we may end this Campagne so as that
the ffrench may have nothing to brag off, for I fflatter my self that
the ten thousand men we are sending to Pr. Eugene will put him in a
condition of acting offensively; for Garmany I expect nothing but ill
news, and for this country I do not doubt but You will be so kind as
to beleive if I have an opertunity I will do my best; the decent [de-
scent] is what I have also a great opinion off.

This is the most splendid period in Marlborough's career. Every
personal need urged that he should win a battle for himself. At home
the wolves, though temporarily baffled, were always growling. Already
Sarah was losing her influence with the Queen: already her contacts
were becoming a hindrance, not a help. His dream of another epic
march across Europe and an Italian "Hochstädt" won side by side with
the man he loved had faded. But there still remained the duty of a soldier and the dominating responsibility of the working Head of the Alliance. Not without pangs, but certainly without the slightest hesitation,
Marlborough divested himself of troops which would have secured him
a large superiority in the Low Countries and the chance of some deed
"that shall make a noise." We know of no similar instance in military
history where a general-in-chief, thus pressed, has deliberately confined
himself to a secondary rôle while furnishing colleagues, who were also
rivals, with the means of action.

The Captain-General quitted the endless discussions at The Hague
and set out in his coach for Headquarters on May 9.

The mental processes of a general should lead him first to put himself faithfully in the position of his enemy, and to credit that enemy
with the readiness to do what he himself would most dread. In the
next stage idiosyncrasies of the hostile commander, the temper and
quality of his troops, and the political background come into play. But
these are secondary. The safe course is to assume that the enemy will do
his worst—*i.e.*, what is most unwelcome. With that provided against,
lesser evils can be resisted. Marlborough, surveying the campaign of

1706 as if he were King Louis's adviser, was convinced that the true French effort should be made in Italy and in Spain. If more force was available it should be used against the Margrave on the Upper Rhine. A period of sieges in the fortress zone of the Low Countries might lead to a few French strongholds being lost, but would gain much precious time for action elsewhere. Accordingly, in various letters Marlborough had formally advised the Dutch Government that no French offensive in the Low Countries need be expected.

He was wrong only because the French were wrong. He judged their hand as he would have played it himself. Hence the despondency with which he resigned himself to a difficult, wearisome, and limited manœuvring among the fortresses. His costly Intelligence service could give him no clue to the personal reactions which his operations of 1705 had produced upon Louis XIV, nor to the pressures which the King was putting upon his Marshal. Up till May 18 we see Marlborough sombrely resigned to the path of duty, having cleansed his heart of personal ambition, and acting solely in the common cause.

King Louis's dispositions for the northern front comprised an army of forty thousand under Villars to operate against the Margrave on the Upper Rhine, and an army under Villeroy of sixty thousand to confront Marlborough in Brabant. Marshal Marsin, with 25 battalions and 30 squadrons, lay so as to operate in either theatre, and likewise the famous Maison du Roi was so posted as to be capable of intervening either way, but with a strong bias towards Brabant. The King's plan was that both these important forces should join Villeroy, and thereafter seek Marlborough, and put him to the test.

The reader will remember the minor fortress of Léau, which surrendered to the Allies after the Lines of Brabant were forced in July 1705. Louis XIV held, and was advised, that the siege of this place would either inflict painful humiliation upon Marlborough or force him to a battle at odds and disadvantage. Villeroy's instructions were therefore definite. Moreover, that Marshal had newly lighted upon one of Marlborough's many intrigues. A prominent citizen of Namur was believed to be in treacherous correspondence with the Captain-General for the purpose of delivering that important fortified city into the hands of the Allies. This was no more than the truth. Villeroy's counterstroke to such designs was well expressed in an aggressive siege of Léau, and he became most anxious to forestall his opponent. He knew that none of the Prussians had passed the Rhine. He learned that the Danes would be absent from any immediate concentration Marlborough might make. It therefore seemed necessary to reckon only with the Dutch and the English, and over these the Marshal conceived he had an ample superiority.

On May 18 the Intelligence service reported heavy French assemblings on the left bank of the Dyle between Wavre and Louvain. On the 19th decisive news arrived. The French army had crossed the Dyle and advanced to within four miles of Tirlemont. This could only mean that they courted battle. The situation was instantaneously transformed. Doubt and despondency vanished; all became simple and dire. All the allied contingents were ordered forthwith to concentrate. Marlborough's first thought was for the Danes of Würtemberg.

Marlborough's topographical memories went back to the wars of King William. The whole area had been thoroughly mapped by English and French engineers. Maps of those days reached a high level of information and accuracy, and we must imagine besides that Marlborough could visualize the whole of these areas and their military potentialities in exceptional clarity and detail. Moreover, though in no way he expected the French advance, he would mark the Ramillies position as one which the French might be inclined to occupy if he could not get there first, and where a battle might very well be fought. This knowledge, his eye and memory for country, together with his belief in his own troops and in his own capacity, explain the amazing wave of confidence which swept over him as soon as he divined the purpose of the French advance, and the spontaneity of his subsequent action on the battlefield.

We now see him, with all doubts and fears swept away, in the full, joyful plenitude of his powers. He seemed wrapped in a perfect serenity. Purged from all dross and self-seeking, his genius flying free, he was in these days and those that followed sublime. In all his circle of high personages there was but one from whom the coming shock was hidden. Sarah had no inkling.

And now Fortune, whom Marlborough had so ruefully but sternly dismissed, returned importunate, bearing her most dazzling gift.

CHAPTER FIFTY-FOUR

The Battle of Ramillies

৳ৢ 1706, May 23 ৢ৳

THE Confederate army was concentrated around Corswaren by the evening of the 22nd. The English had joined the Dutch the day before, and the Danes were only a league behind. Marlborough mustered 74 battalions and 123 squadrons, with exceptionally strong artillery and pontoon trains (100 guns, 20 "hawbitzers," 42 pontoons). The suddenness with which the campaign had opened found the Dutch with four hundred officers absent; but otherwise the army was in excellent condition, and comprised about sixty-two thousand men. Marlborough's intention was to march through the gap of firm ground between the headstreams of the Geet and those of the Mehaigne in order to occupy the plateau of Mont Saint-André, which formed a part of the Ramillies position. He purposed thereafter to seek Villeroy in the neighbourhood of Judoigne and bring him to battle or drive him across the Dyle.

An hour after midnight he sent Cadogan and the quartermasters, with an escort of six hundred horse, to scout ahead of the army and if unopposed to mark out the new camp. The prescribed march was about twelve miles. The whole army, in four columns, started at 3.00 A.M. in dense fog and darkness. The organization by which these large masses found their way across country deserves respect; but of course their progress was very slow. Three hours after daylight, at about eight o'clock, Cadogan, far ahead of them, reached the high ground beyond the hamlet of Merdorp, and here in thick mist his escort struck into advance parties of French hussars. There were shots and scamperings. Cadogan halted. The mist lifting a little, he was able to see moving objects on the farther side of the valley; this was the Mont Saint-André plateau, upon which it seemed the enemy also had designs. He sent word at once to Marlborough. The Duke had already started, and, passing through his marching troops, joined his trusted and treasured lieutenant at ten o'clock. Almost at the same moment the mist curtains rose, and the whole western horizon was seen to be alive with men whose armour and weapons flashed back the bright sunshine from ten thousand sparkling points.

Marlborough could not know at this moment whether the enemy would fight or retreat. He resolved forthwith to attack them in either event. If he was in presence only of a rearguard, he would fall upon them with all his cavalry; if, on the other hand, they were prepared to defend the Ramillies position, a general battle would at once be fought. Orders were sent back to all the columns, and especially to the cavalry, to press their march; for the enemy awaited them. At about eleven the allied army were traversing the Lines which Marlborough had demolished in the autumn, and here they subdivided into eight columns preparatory to forming the line of battle. The Danish horse was already close to the Dutch cavalry on the left wing.

We must now recur to M. de la Colonie, the "Old Campaigner," who at the head of his Franco-Bavarian brigade had marched with the French army from Judoigne in the morning:

> So vast was the plain at Ramillies that we were able to march our army on as broad a front as we desired, and the result was a magnificent spectacle. The army began its march at six o'clock in the morning, formed into two large columns, the front of each consisting of a battalion; the artillery formed a third, which marched between the two infantry columns. The cavalry squadrons in battle formation occupied an equal extent of ground, and, there being nothing to impede the view, the whole force was seen in such a fine array that it would be impossible to view a grander sight. The army had but just entered on the campaign; weather and fatigue had hardly yet had time to dim its brilliancy, and it was inspired with a courage born of confidence. The late Marquis de Goudrin, with whom I had the honour to ride during the march, remarked to me that France had surpassed herself in the quality of these troops; he believed that the enemy had no chance whatever of breaking them in the coming conflict; if defeated now, we could never again hope to withstand them.

About eleven o'clock the Duke began his personal reconnaissance. There rode with him only Overkirk, Dopff, Cadogan, a couple of ex-Spanish officers (Belgians) who knew every inch of the ground well, and the new Deputy, Sicco van Goslinga, whom it was so important to captivate. We are indebted to Sicco for a naïve account. As they stood on the slopes opposite Ramillies the ex-Spanish officers said boldly and positively to the Duke "that the enemy's left could not be attacked with any prospect of success: for the hedges, ditches and marshes were a complete barrier *to both sides:* that therefore the whole of our cavalry should be massed on our left, even if they had to be three or four lines deep: and that all thereabouts was fair open plain." The Duke listened impassively; but, adds Goslinga, "he left the order of battle as it was with an equality of cavalry on each wing."

The new field Deputy saw the mistake at once, and, writing years afterwards, pointed it out to his children. In spite of the advice which he had received that the cavalry could only act upon his left, Marlborough supinely let them remain equally divided according to the conventional order of battle. Luckily, notes Goslinga, "the enemy made the same mistake as the Duke did, and did not remedy it as he did during the combat." These inane comments should strip Goslinga of any military credential except that of being a stout-hearted Dutchman. We can see Marlborough, bland, inscrutable, on his horse at the head of this small group, making the great mistake of dividing his cavalry more or less equally upon each wing, so that Villeroy fell into the same error and kept no fewer than fifty squadrons massed upon this impracticable flank. No doubt Marlborough did not at this moment forget that the French occupied the well-known crescent position of which he commanded the chord. However, he said nothing. He deceived Goslinga. The poor man missed the whole point. He deceived Villeroy, which was, of course, more important.

Meanwhile the eight columns had arrived on the rolling upland of Jandrinol and were deploying into line of battle, eating their dinners as they arrived at their preparatory stations. A little after one all along the line the French artillery began to fire. The Allies replied a few minutes later with far heavier metal. Whereas at Blenheim the French had used a 50 per cent. superior artillery, the case was almost reversed at Ramillies, for Marlborough had not only more guns, but nearly thirty 24-pounders. Although artillery in those days was not a decisive

weapon, the fact should be noted. The roar of the cannonade resounded, and the smoke clouds drifted across the broad undulations of
a battlefield unchanged and unobstructed to this day.

Contact between armies began about half-past two. The Allies advanced in magnificent array on a four-mile front; but at both ends of
the main line, and nearly half an hour ahead of it, two separate attacks
of pregnant consequence projected like horns. Towards the extreme
French right, now lodged in the villages of Franquenay and Taviers, a
column of Dutch infantry rapidly advanced. Next to them, but nearly a
mile behind, all the cavalry of the left wing, Dutch and Danish, approached the gap between Taviers and Ramillies, where eighty-two
French squadrons, including the long-renowned Maison du Roi, stood
to receive them. The main allied infantry attack, comprising forty
thousand men ranged in two heavy lines, advanced slowly towards the
enemy's centre between Ramillies and Autréglise. The massive onset
of the whole army, drawing momentarily nearer with intent to kill and
destroy, made its impression upon Marshal Villeroy and his troops, as
it had upon Tallard and Marsin at Blenheim. The French command
observed the scene from the high ground to the north of Offus, and one
fact riveted their thought. This was the northern horn of Marlborough's
line of battle led by Orkney. Against their left, towards the village of
Autréglise, considerably ahead of the Allies' general line, there steadily
developed a Red Thing. The two scarlet columns of this flank had now
formed into lines, and were rapidly descending the slopes about Foulz.
Already their skirmishers were paddling and plodding in the marshy
bottom, using bridging equipment, finding tracks, and wending their
way across. Intermingled with this infantry were considerable bodies of
red-coated cavalry, also plashing forward mounted or leading their
horses towards Autréglise.

When in contact with immeasurable events it is always dangerous to
have fixed opinions. Villeroy's opinions had been fixed for him by the
Great King. "It would be very important," Louis XIV had written a
fortnight earlier, "to have particular attention to that part of the line
which will endure the first shock of the English troops." With this the
Marshal was in full agreement. He had therefore no doubt what to do.
He saw with satisfaction that this dreaded attack, which also threatened his line of retreat upon Louvain, was about to fall upon that part
of the French army which was most strongly protected by the accidents

of the ground. A fine opportunity offered itself. Forthwith the sector between Autréglise and Ramillies was heavily reinforced by troops brought up from the rear or transferred from the French right and right centre. The choice battalions of the French Guards and the Swiss were urgently brought into the line to meet, under the most favourable conditions, the impending collision with the redoubtable islanders. The whole of the cavalry of the French left wing, about fifty squadrons, was held in close readiness for the decisive moment. That moment would come when this red attack was half across the sloppy meadows of the valley, and enough British had breasted the upward slope to make the prize worth taking. That moment could not be long delayed. Evidently the marsh was not so grievous an obstacle as the French engineers had deemed it. Not only had considerable bodies of British infantry made their way across it and formed on the farther side, but several squadrons of the same kind of horsemen could be observed in order at the foot of the slope. A definite line of battle, much inferior to the troops who awaited them, was already moving upward towards Offus and Autréglise. The Marshal judged his presence necessary at this dominating point. By his side rode the Elector, Max Emmanuel, who, summoned at the last moment from his pious exercises of Pentecost, had just arrived at a gallop from Brussels. For all that they counted in the main decision, we may here leave the French High Command. This we must regard as Act I of the battle of Ramillies.

But three or four miles away, at the other end of the line, there had been an overture. It was essential to the French occupation of the Ramillies position that the village of Taviers, to which Franquenay formed an outwork, on the extreme right, should be strongly held. A mile and a half of perfect cavalry country separated Taviers from Ramillies. Here must be the scene of the great cavalry encounter. The cannon of those days could not effectively sweep so wide a space with crossfire, but the position of both these strong villages would make the intervening ground most adverse to his assailants. Thus Villeroy had occupied Franquenay and Taviers with five battalions, but not apparently with artillery. Against Taviers a little after 2.30 P. M. there marched four battalions of the Dutch guard, under General Wertmuller. Behind them to their right, opposite the cavalry gap, the solid masses of Dutch and Danish cavalry could be plainly seen.

Almost everything about the battle of Ramillies is clear, but none of

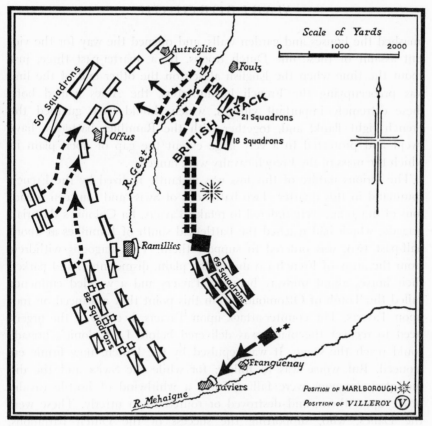

Scale of Yards

9. The British Attack

the accounts explain how these four battalions managed so swiftly to storm the villages of Franquenay and Taviers, and expel the larger number of French troops from their houses and enclosures. An ancient map throws light on this. This map was drawn for General Overkirk, probably under his personal directions, a year after the victory. It throws a sharp gleam of light upon this operation. The two cannon were apparently brought forward in the very van of the Dutch attack. So unusual was the employment of artillery in those days in the front line, and so remarkable was the effect of these pieces, that a special reference in the explanatory table is devoted to them—a departure from the whole proportion of the map. Evidently these two cannon were attached to the Dutch Guards by orders of the supreme command, probably by Overkirk himself. Brought into action at close range, they

(513)

smashed the houses and garden walls, and opened the way for the violent assault of these fine Dutch troops. By a quarter-past three, just about the time when the English attack on the other end of the line was preoccupying the French headquarters, the Allies gained both these extremely important villages, which should have guarded the French right flank, and, together with the Ramillies batteries, have swept and protected to a very large extent the gap of open plain in which the mass of the French cavalry were ranged.

The serious nature of this loss was instantly realized by the French command in this quarter. Two battalions of Swiss and fourteen squadrons of dragoons, were ordered to retake Taviers. La Colonie's Bavarian brigade, which had reached the battlefield south of Ramillies at about half-past two, was ordered to support them. The dragoons withdrew from the array of French cavalry in the plain, dismounted, and parked their horses about midway between Taviers and a wooded eminence called the Tomb of Ottomond. From this point they advanced on foot upon Taviers. The counter-attack upon Taviers, because of the urgent need to recover the place, was delivered before La Colonie's brigade could reach the scene. It was repulsed by the Dutch, now firmly ensconced. But worse was to follow; for while the Swiss and the dismounted dragoons were falling back, a whirlwind of hostile cavalry broke upon them, and destroyed or routed them utterly. These were the Danes, who, supporting the success of the Dutch battalions, slipped in between Taviers and the French right, and, already reaching forward round the French right, exacted this cruel forfeit. The dismounted dragoons never saw their led-horses again. Thus, before the main cavalry shock occurred the French cavalry in the plain had been reduced from eighty-two to sixty-eight squadrons, while losing all security for their right.

At this point we must return to the Old Campaigner. The orders he had received "to reinforce the village of Taviers" drew his Bavarian brigade across the front of the Maison du Roi under long-range cannon fire to which he replied, ordering

> flourishes upon our hautboys, to entertain us the while; but the booming of the guns that went on all round so startled our musicians that they disappeared like a flash before anyone noticed it, and transported the melodious sounds of their instruments to some quarter where the harmonies were not quite so discordant. However, we set out, and

passed along the right of our line to reach the marsh without knowing if any other troops had preceded us, or if others were to follow us.

Arrived near this point, the Old Campaigner became sharply conscious that a mishap had occurred. Not only had the troops originally sent to occupy Taviers been driven out of the village, but the Swiss and dragoons who had been thrown in to recapture it

came tumbling down upon my battalions in full flight, just at the time when I was re-forming my men after their crossing; they brought such alarm and confusion in their train that my own fellows turned about and fled along with them. It appeared that they had attacked the village without waiting for us, and had been repulsed with much loss by the fourteen [actually four] battalions the enemy had there, which were well posted, and outnumbered them by two to one. The Swiss perished almost to a man, and it is not surprising that a small body of troops attacking others more than double their strength in an advantageous position should have been vigorously repulsed and driven back in disorder. M. d'Aubigni was killed, and his lieutenant-colonel and many others wounded. The runaways threw themselves amongst my men, and carried them off with them, and I was never more surprised in my life to find myself left standing alone with a few officers and the colours. I was immediately filled with rage and grief; I cried out in German and French like one possessed; I shouted every epithet I could think of to my grenadiers; I seized the colonel's colour, planted it by me, and by the loudness of my cries I at last attracted the attention of some few of them. The officers who had stood by me rushed after the fugitives, also shouting and pointing out the colonel's colour, which I still kept in my hands, and at last they checked the stampede. I gradually rallied my French grenadiers and several companies of the Cologne regiment, making in all four small battalions, very much shaken with the manœuvres they had just gone through.

With this small force behind the marshes the colonel maintained himself throughout the afternoon, and from this point had a fine view of the tremendous cavalry battle which was now about to begin.

The second act of the drama opened. Overkirk, with the Dutch cavalry and twenty-one Danish squadrons well forward on his left, advanced against the Maison du Roi and the mass of the French forces between Taviers and Ramillies. At the same time the infantry of Marl-

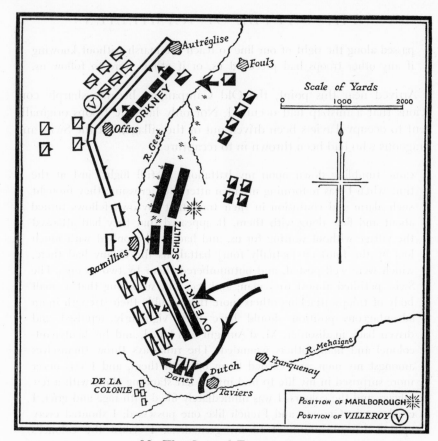

10. The General Engagement

borough's centre began to come into close contact with the Ramillies
defences. The main fronts of both armies were now in action. Marlborough with his staff and retinue must at this time have been on the
high ground before Offus and Ramillies. Indeed, he was practically opposite to Villeroy and the Elector, though somewhat farther south. But
whereas Villeroy's gaze, fascinated by the advance of the English, was
turned to the northern flank, Marlborough was watching the cavalry
struggle beginning in the contrary quarter. It is probable that he had
no certain knowledge of what had happened in Taviers; but he could
see plainly the surge and shock of Overkirk's resolute advance, and that
this was not impeded by any cross-fire. He saw the forty-eight Dutch
squadrons crash into the Maison du Roi. Measuring and timing the

forces now launched, he was entitled to the same assurance of success as he had felt before the final attack at Blenheim.

Forthwith he began the simple yet superb manœuvre to which the preliminaries had led—namely, the transference of all his cavalry to the left wing. He sent peremptory orders to Orkney to break off the attack on Offus and Autréglise and retire, and to withdraw the British to the high ground behind Foulz. Casting aside his veil of secrecy and deception, he exclaimed, "I have five horses to two." Actually he now had the power to bring first four to three, and finally five to three; but it was enough. Leaving Cadogan to enforce Orkney's withdrawal and to rearrange the right, he ordered eighteen squadrons from the cavalry of that wing to trot across the rear of his infantry attack on Ramillies to the support of Overkirk's cavalry attack. He galloped on ahead of them with his personal staff. He arrived at a crisis. The Dutch, knee to knee in a solid mass, had charged the Maison du Roi. These splendid warriors, the pride of the French nobility, advanced in countercharge to meet their foes. Where their squadrons engaged front to front they conquered, but the Dutch, penetrating the intervals between the French squadrons, assailed them in flank and even in rear. In this mêlée the French cannon could not meddle; and the horsemen were free to fight it out alone. Nevertheless, such was the vigour of the French cavalry that they drove in the Dutch right, and were about to fall upon the left flank of the allied infantry now engaging upon the outskirts of Ramillies.

It was at this moment that Marlborough arrived with his handful of English officers and orderlies. The long column of eighteen squadrons was still traversing the front, and had not yet assembled. The Duke sent instant orders to bring from his right the whole remaining cavalry except the English, twenty-one squadrons more, and, riding himself with his personal attendants into the whirlpool, he rallied the nearest Dutch squadrons. Transported by the energy of his war vision and passion, he led them himself again to the charge. This lapse from the duty of a commander-in-chief nearly cost him his life, and might well have cost the Allies the war.

The mile and a half space between Ramillies and Taviers had now become the scene of the largest cavalry battle of which there is any trustworthy account. In all nearly twenty-five thousand horsemen were brought into collision hand to hand, charging and countercharging with varying fortune for two hours. If we can imagine seven or eight modern cavalry divisions fighting in close order on such narrow ground, we shall realize that it was densely thronged with solid masses of flesh and blood in every stage of symmetry or dissolution. Wave after wave of charging horsemen, each trooper seeking with his sharp sword to slay his foe, were hurled in mob violence one upon another. Here numbers told. Where nearly all did their duty bravely the last reserves prevailed. The finest troops of France and the pride of French society, all the military splendour of the Court and age of Louis XIV, met the onslaught of the stern, tough Dutch in a white heat of disciplined passion. But then came Marlborough, with his inspiration and new lines of formed squadrons crashing in; and on the Taviers flank the twenty-one Danish squadrons, lapping round till Taviers village was at their backs, outflanked and rode down all in their path. The fourteen squadrons of French dragoons who had been dismounted to help retake Taviers and had been repulsed therefrom sought in vain to regain their led horses near the Tomb of Ottomond. These had stampeded in the tumult and galloped riderless about the countryside, some even finding their old winter quarters twenty miles away. Their masters, running away on foot, fell victims to the swords of the Danes.

Still more waves of allied cavalry rolled upon the Maison du Roi as Marlborough's orders to bring all the cavalry, except the English, from the right wing were obeyed. Twenty-one fresh squadrons fell upon the harassed, over-pressed cavalry of France. The odds against them were now five to three. In vain were their glorious golden banners, the royal emblems, the lilies of France, borne forward in sublime devotion. Nothing could withstand the hammer-blows of repeated and seemingly inexhaustible reinforcements. The whole of the French cavalry of the right wing was shattered by superior numbers of very good troops who attacked them in front, in flank, and at the end almost in rear, and thus set about them from all sides.

It is difficult in this grand confusion to settle what actually happened to Marlborough himself. That he regarded the struggle at this point as decisive for the whole battle, that he led two charges by the Dutch in succession, that he remained trying to dominate events within a few hundred yards of the left of his infantry attack upon Ramillies, and was in the cavalry mêlée for about twenty minutes, is indisputable. Upon details, as would be natural, all accounts conflict. But certain definite impressions emerge. Marlborough charged for the second time against the victorious left flank of the Masion du Roi at between a quarter and half-past three. The Dutch squadrons which he led or which he succoured were broken. There was a pell-mell to the rear. Amid these blue- and grey-coated troops the scarlet uniforms of the Commander-in-Chief and his personal retinue were conspicuous. The French troopers recognized him; they fired their long pistols at him, and individuals breaking from the ranks rode at him and overthrew him. Or, again (a better account), he turned his horse with the crowd of fugitives and tried to jump a sunken pathway or ditch. His horse pecked, and he fell to the ground. He was ridden over by the throng. Napoleon's historian, perhaps under direction, makes this point:

> Here we see how important it is to a general to be loved by the soldiers he leads. At the very sight of the danger which threatened their commander his squadrons thought above all of making themselves his rampart. They returned upon their own impulse to the charge. They hurled back the French who had penetrated their ranks, and the rescue of Marlborough was identified with a military success.

More grim versions are found in the letters of British officers, actors in and eye-witnesses of the drama.

It is clear that Marlborough had to run in the scrimmage some considerable distance on his feet towards the friendly Swiss battalions. His devoted aides-de-camp were about him, thinking only of saving him. Captain Molesworth got off and gave him his horse—"we got the Duke mounted again." He reached Major-General Murray's battalions a few minutes later. Behind their bayonets he was able to resume the control of the battle—at least in the centre. He must have remained at this point for more than an hour. It was under the close and continuous fire of the French batteries in Ramillies; but it was well placed for watching both the end of the cavalry conflict and the infantry onslaught now about to break on that village. Marlborough's staff, scattered in the fray, gradually rejoined him here. Presently his equerry, Colonel Bingfield, arrived with his second charger. The Duke changed horses. Bingfield was holding the off-side stirrup, and as Marlborough threw his leg over the saddle a cannon-ball cut off the faithful colonel's head. Orkney, who was on the other flank and no eyewitness, but had the view of the senior officers, writing the next day, said:

Milord Marlborough was rid over, but got other squadrons which he led up. Major Bingfield holding his stirrup to give him another horse was shot with a cannon ball which went through Marlborough's legs; in truth there was no scarcity of 'em.

We must now return to the British on the right. Orkney's attack upon Autréglise had made unexpected progress at the moment when Marlborough had ordered its recall. Ten or twelve British battalions, including the 1st Guards, had crossed the morass, and their first line had already broken into the houses and enclosures of the village. Lumley, with several English squadrons, made a show of covering their right. The French advanced large bodies of troops from their main line to resist the assault, but always retired as it advanced, with the purpose of drawing it into the open country where their overwhelming numbers of cavalry would be decisive. Fighting became severe. "Indeed," wrote Orkney the next day, "I think I never had more shot about my ears —both musketry and cannon."

It was at this moment, when the British were advancing in the highest confidence, that an aide-de-camp from the Duke brought an order to retire. Marlborough, in order to impart the more reality to this attack, had not informed his valiant lieutenant that it was a feint. Orkney thought that the order had been sent him in the belief that it was impossible to traverse the marsh, whereas he had in fact traversed it and was in full action. He therefore persisted. Messenger after messenger reached him in quick succession, but his blood was up and his vigorous infantry seemed to be driving all before them. Autréglise was in his grip. "But as I was going to take possession, I had ten aides-de-camp to me to come off." Last of all came Cadogan himself. The two generals argued in the storm of shot. Orkney urged that the High Command did not know how good were the prospects. Cadogan explained that the Duke had gone to the left with all the cavalry of the right wing, and that there was no horse to sustain the British foot. It was, he said, impossible to attack everywhere at once. It took all this to recall the vehement assault once it had been launched. When Orkney at length obeyed, he had to make a similar exertion to force his troops to retire. Many of them, in spite of the victory, nursed the grievance for years. They would not believe that the orders had come from the Duke; Cadogan, they grumbled, had relied too much on maps and theory, and acted on his own responsibility and thus baulked them of their prey. However, the whole line was made to retire. Slowly and indignantly they withdrew, the Guards covering the harassed retreat. Once again they floundered through the marsh—re-formed and ascended the slopes of Foulz.

Then followed under Cadogan's eye a manœuvre which we cannot doubt was part of Marlborough's original design. When the two red lines reached the summit of the hill from which they had started, the original first line faced about and stood displayed upon the crest, while the second, which had not been engaged, descending into the dip in the rear, wheeled into column, and began marching towards the centre of the battle to form an additional reserve for the main attack on the Ramillies-Offus front.

The battle moved at such a pace that all the troops of both sides on the northern flank were left behind its headlong course. Marshal Villeroy and the Elector were still ardently awaiting the climax of the British assault upon the French left when grave news reached them from their right. The cavalry of the right wing had been broken; the Maison du Roi was defeated. Moreover, the flank was turned. Forthwith they spurred their horses from Offus along the main line of the army to the rear of Ramillies. They encountered a tide of fugitives, and were soon involved in the rout. Half an hour earlier they had been expecting the battle to begin. They now saw that it was lost beyond repair. They set themselves to form a new front bent back from Ramillies at right angles to their original line. At the same time they ordered a general retreat upon Judoigne. Ramillies was the pivot upon which all this turned. Here Count Maffei, a Bavarian general, commanded a strong brigade.

Marlborough's central conception of the battle had been the storm of Ramillies by the mass of his infantry; and his feint with Orkney on the right, the capture of Taviers, and his onslaught with the whole of his cavalry on the left were but to be the preliminary and ancillary phases of this crowning result. In fact they had already decided it. The main infantry struggle had been growing in severity during the cavalry battle in the plain. Long lines of foot, backed by the whole reserves of the army, including now the British second line from the right, all aided by the fire of twenty heavy cannon and the bulk of the allied artillery, impended upon the enemy's centre.

With the destruction of the French right wing and the flower of their cavalry the third phase of Ramillies began. A series of decisions was taken by Marlborough and Overkirk, evidently working in full comprehension and harmony. About five o'clock the immediate pursuit of the French horse was stopped, and the whole of the victorious cavalry was ordered to attack and roll up the French army from their exposed flank. Just as at Blenheim, Marlborough delayed his final attack until Eugene could re-form and strike at the same time, so now the infantry advance on Ramillies was suspended or slowed down until the cavalry got into their new position.

We have no record of these orders. We only see them in execution. The allied infantry, who had begun their advance at about three o'clock, had little more than a mile to cover. Their leading brigades were on the outskirts of Ramillies by half-past three. Since then they had been in heavy action, attacking and counter-attacked. On the other hand, the allied cavalry, victorious at about five, did not resume their advance until they were completely formed upon the new front. This marked pause in the battle, in order to deliver a final blow in thorough combination, when Marlborough must already have felt assured of victory, gives us a measure of the way in which his mind worked on the battlefield. Neither the dazzle of success nor the ordeal of personal combat, neither the fall from his horse nor the breathlessness of his run, affected in the slightest degree his sense of proportion, or his perfect comprehension of the whole problem—at least from the moment when he was once again in his saddle. He had wrongly descended from his high station upon an immediate local need. He emerged from this violent personal experience, and instantly, as after the charge at Elixem, resumed his normal poise.

It was now six o'clock. Marlborough and Overkirk had reformed the whole of the allied cavalry almost at right angles to their original attack. They stretched in overwhelming strength from behind Ramillies to the Tomb of Ottomond. Both generals must have been brilliantly served by their staffs and subordinate commanders; for the feat of wheeling the whole front of more than a hundred squadrons, disordered by fierce action and triumphant pursuit, although it flowed naturally from the course of the battle and the Danish turning movement, is remarkable in cavalry history. This grand array now began a second resolute and orderly advance. Villeroy and the Elector by their personal exertions had managed to form a new cavalry front facing south against them, composed partly of rallied squadrons from the plain, but mainly of the fifty fresh squadrons hitherto idle upon the French left. This new front rested upon the remnants of Maffei's unlucky brigade, which now clung to the rear of Ramillies, also facing south, and manning a sunken road. Thus the French army was re-formed in a right angle, one side of which comprised the whole of their cavalry remaining on the field; and the other (from Ramillies to Autréglise) of their infantry. Behind this evidently shaken screen the Marshal hoped to withdraw his artillery and transport wagons and make a respectable retreat through Judoigne across the Dyle.

This picture was no sooner created than it was dissolved. The advance of the allied cavalry was not resisted. The fifty squadrons from the French left, appalled by the disaster to their comrades in the plain and to the whole army, would not face the coming charge. They turned their horses' heads and melted from the field. Count Maffei at the angle or hinge of the position suffered the same shock as the Old Campaigner had sustained at the Schellenberg.

> I then saw coming towards us a line of hostile cavalry who, having broken our right, were advancing to surround the village; but as this cavalry was coming from the side from which I naturally had expected our own to arrive, I thought at first that they must be our people, and I had not even the slightest suspicion to the contrary when I saw that they stopped two or three hundred paces from us without doing anything, although they could have attacked us from the rear. I did not notice the green cockade which they wore in their hats, which was indeed so small that it could hardly have been discerned at the distance. Thus convinced that they were our friends, I made up my mind to collect all the infantry I could to [complete the front]. . . . I went towards the nearest of these squadrons to instruct their officer, but instead of being listened to was immediately surrounded and called upon to ask for quarter.

This he was compelled to do at the point of sword and pistol, and thereafter became prisoner of war. The hinge was broken.

And now the whole of the allied infantry, including several English battalions from Orkney's command, crashed into the French line between Ramillies and Offus, and to the north of Offus. Lumley, with the British cavalry, hitherto inactive on the extreme right, at length got across the Geet, followed by Orkney, and, piercing the crumbling front, cut directly on to the line of the French retreat.

We have the definite record from numerous witnesses of that almost unknown feature in European warfare of that epoch, charges at the gallop. The King's Dragoon Guards and the Royal Scots Greys compelled whole battalions to lay down their arms. The infantry Régiment du Roi, caught at the moment they were picking up the knapsacks they had discarded for the battle, were cut to pieces or captured almost to a man.

Now the whole French army broke and collapsed together. Their left drew off northward across country in fair order. Orkney relates how Lumley asked him to hurry on with his infantry, as the cavalry could not deal alone with that part of the French infantry which was unbroken. "If," says Orkney, "I could only have got up in time we should have taken eight or nine battalions." The main part of the French centre fled along the road to Judoigne, but this road was blocked by the transport of the army. The remaining troops, impeded by the obstacle, dispersed and scattered over the countryside, for the main part throwing away their arms to hasten their flight, which achieved itself by its rapidity. Another long stream fled panic-stricken westward towards Wavre. The Old Campaigner behind Taviers found himself completely cut off by the floods of allied cavalry which covered the plain as far as the Tomb of Ottomond, and were everywhere charging and pursuing the flying French. He was by no means at a loss. As the shadows fell upon the battlefield he marched off with his four battalions and many fugitives who accompanied him, or whom he had rescued from the swamp, in the opposite direction towards Namur, which he reached the next morning.

Thus, in the space of four hours, between three and seven o'clock, the entire magnificent French army was shattered and scattered into utter rout and ruin. All their baggage, their cannon, trophies innumerable, five thousand unwounded prisoners, fell to the victors. The pursuit for a considerable time was merciless, and thousands of flying men were denied all quarter and cut down. So rapid had been the transformation, and the day was already so far advanced, that darkness fell without the full realization of their victory coming home to the allied commanders. Nearly all the accounts of Ramillies written immediately after the battle give the impression that their writers only very imperfectly understood the completeness of their triumph. Under the burden of their long march to the battlefield, worn by the excitement of the day, baffled by the rapidity with which the French recoiled and ran before them, scattered and unlinked by the sudden collapse of the hostile front, they fell forward as through a suddenly opened door in very great disorganization. The orders and the urge of every one were to press forward into the night; and when each brigade or regiment halted they had only vague ideas of their own whereabouts, and still less of that of their friends and foes. "We might have been a defeated army," says Orkney, "for the confusion we were in." They had, in fact, fought a great battle and marched twenty-five miles across country in as many hours.

The pursuit roared away to the north. At midnight Marlborough and his headquarters staff, with a heavy column of cavalry, was near Meldert, more than twelve miles beyond the field of battle. He still wished to press on, but his guide was lost, and he was forced to a brief halt. He had been nineteen hours in the saddle. He was bruised and shaken by his fall, and worn by his physical exertions. He knew he had gained one of the greatest battles of history. His cloak was spread upon the ground, and he was about to throw himself upon it for a few hours' sleep, when one more thought—eminently characteristic at this moment—occurred to him. Goslinga, the field Deputy, who might be either so great a help or hindrance in future operations, was at hand. Marlborough saw the opportunity of paying him the finest compliment that could be conceived. He invited him to share the cloak of the Commander-in-Chief on the night of victory. However, as the reader will learn, this pearl was cast in vain.

CHAPTER FIFTY-FIVE

The Conquest of Belgium

ᛪ◌ 1706, June ◌ᛩ

UNRELENTING pursuit magnified the victory of Ramillies. No battle in the eighteenth century produced comparable direct results. The fortress-barrier was for a while shorn away like grass before the scythe. As Blenheim saved Vienna, so Ramillies conquered the Netherlands. Cities and towns, the masterpieces of Vauban, any one of which would have been the prize of a campaign of King William, capitulated on all sides. The rout and temporary destruction of the French field army led to a collapse so far-reaching and so unexpected that it dwarfed even the shock of battle. To measure rightly this prodigy we must recall the mile-by-mile methods of those days, the limited means of offence and movement, and the habits of thought engrained in military minds by a generation of this kind of war.

Before midnight of May 24 Orkney's British and the leading brigades of Dutch infantry under General Churchill had orders to force the Dyle. The pontoon train and all available cannon were pressed forward along the crowded roads. The British cavalry were soon upon the head-streams of the river. As he knew he had captured all the French artillery on the field, Marlborough was sure he could not be withstood. In fact there was no resistance. By noon on the 25th his advance-guards appeared before the gates of Louvain. This stronghold, which he had longed to possess in the autumn of 1703 and in the summer of 1705, surrendered to the trumpet. At midnight after the battle Marshal Villeroy and the Elector had held haggard, dishevelled council by torchlight in the marketplace. Fugitives of high distinction, veteran leaders of so many years of strife, gathered as they rode in, stained and seared. Survivors of the Maison du Roi clustered about them. There was no difference of opinion among the generals. All were agreed that neither the Dyle nor even the Senne could be held. The French army could only be rallied behind the Scheldt—if there. In that direction all formed bodies of troops remaining were ordered to retreat with the utmost speed. Of the brilliant army of sixty-three thousand men which had set out so confidently in the morning to seek a decision of arms, barely fifteen thousand were under control. Twelve thousand had fallen killed or wounded in the clash. Nearly six thousand were prisoners of the Allies. The rest had dispersed to every quarter of the compass, seeking the gates of some friendly town. For more than a month no semblance of a French army could keep the field.

Marlborough could not know all this. Indeed, his standard of values, inculcated by so many years of war in this obstinate theatre, expanded itself only day by day. At first no one realized how overwhelming had been the victory, still less its reverberations. But the Duke thrust forward with every scrap of moral and physical energy he could extort from himself or from his soldiers. In this temper, but always with considerable precaution and always against the stubborn drag of supplies, he traversed Louvain on the 25th, and encamped on the heights of Bethlehem with above fifty thousand men. On the 26th his headquarters stood upon the Senne at the castle of Beaulieu, midway between Malines and Brussels. Both these places were summoned to surrender. On the 28th the army halted for two days, having since the 23rd advanced fifty miles. Detachments were sent forward to secure the crossings of the Dender and the Scheldt.

Intent upon these new gains, and especially of the capital, Marlborough had already forgotten Ramillies. The French cannon lay where they had been abandoned among the dead; and while the allied army rolled forward on its irresistible career the French command in Namur had the enterprise to send out teams of horses and drag them inside their ramparts. The heave of Marlborough's advance and the exclusive intensity of his forward impulse cannot be better judged than from this curious lapse. This was no time to count or even collect spoils and trophies. The dominating military objectives lay ahead: to drive deep into the fortress zone and to keep the French from the sea flank; to isolate and perhaps soon besiege Antwerp; to strike at Ghent and

Oudenarde on the Scheldt, were prizes which threw past triumph into twilight.

And now a political revolution in Belgium supervened. Spectators of the French disaster, confronted by the massive invasion of the allied army, dazzled by the sword of the Captain-General, not only the magistrates of Brussels and the Estates of Brabant, but the whole Spanish authority in the Netherlands deserted the cause of the Two Crowns and declared their allegiance to Charles III. The prolonged French occupation, with its insolences and exactions, not less than the fear of hostile armies, sustained the decision of the rulers with the ardent support of the entire population. In a trice the conquest of Belgium by the Allies became the act of its deliverance from the thraldom of Louis XIV.

Marlborough was not furnished with formal powers to deal with so surprising a transformation. There was no time to communicate with London or even The Hague. He therefore took everything upon himself. Keeping in close accord with Goslinga and the other Deputies, he received on the 27th at Beaulieu a joint delegation from the Brussels magistracy and the Estates. He accepted their change of allegiance. He guaranteed all religious and civil rights. He renewed the famous charter of "La Joyeuse Entrée"; and in an order to the allied army he threatened "death without mercy" to any officer or soldier found guilty of plundering or molesting the inhabitants. These measures were far-reaching, and not only the citizens but the whole countryside came over to the Allies. The Spanish garrisons in several fortresses turned the French out of the citadels, and held them for Charles III. Food and forage poured in from the farms in response to British and Dutch cash. French stragglers were caught and brought in by the peasantry. French detachments hurried to disentangle themselves from the hostile population, and overtake the general retreat. Meanwhile the Allies were able to draw troops from their garrisons. The Prussians, Lunebergers, and Hanoverians began to move forward from the Rhine, and Villeroy was justified in reporting that Marlborough was soon to be at the head of ninety thousand men. Early on the 28th Charles Churchill took possession of Brussels, and that evening Marlborough made his public entry into the city. The magistrates received him with the pomp of ancient ceremonial, and the populace welcomed him with hectic enthusiasm and every sign of gratitude. Flanked by his own garrisons in Brussels and Malines, he could now march forward to the Scheldt.

Villeroy and the Elector had hoped to halt near Ghent, behind the Lys and the Scheldt, whence they could cover Bruges and Ostend and thereby flank any allied movement on Antwerp. Up to this point, and especially while the French were under immediate shock of the battle, the pursuit had been direct. Now Marlborough moved across Villeroy's communications with France. His impending passage of the Scheldt at Gavre threatened these to such an extent that Villeroy withdrew to Courtrai.

Marlborough's letter to Sarah after the battle is a moving document.

> Monday, May 24, 11 o'clock
>
> I did not tell my dearest soul in my last the design I had of engaging the enemy if possible to a battle, fearing the concern she has for me might make her uneasy; but I can now give her the satisfaction of letting her know that on Sunday last we fought, and that God Almighty has been pleased to give us a victory. I must leave the particulars to this bearer, Colonel Richards, for having been on horseback all Sunday, and after the battle marching all night, my head aches to that degree that it is very uneasy to me to write. Poor Bringfield, holding my stirrup for me, and helping me on horseback, was killed. I am told that he leaves his wife and mother in a poor condition. I can't write to any of my children, so that you will let them know that I am well, and that I desire they will thank God for His preserving me. And pray give my duty to the Queen, and let her know the truth of my heart, that the greatest pleasure I have in this success is that it may be a great service to her affairs; for I am sincerely sensible of all her goodness for me and mine. Pray believe me when I assure you that I love you more than I can express.

On the 27th he wrote to Godolphin:

> Since my last we have not only passed the Dyle, but are masters of Louvain, Malines, and Brussels; you will see by what I send to Mr Secretary Harley what has passed between me and the states of Brabant, which I found assembled at Brussels. As there could not be time for orders from England, I hope her Majesty will approve of what I have done. . . . *The consequence of this battle is likely to be of greater advantage than that of Blenheim; for we have now the*

whole summer before us, and with the blessing of God, I will make the best use of it. For as we had no council of war before this battle, so I hope to have none this whole campaign; and I think we may make such a campaign as may give the Queen the glory of making an honourable and safe peace; for the blessing of God is certainly with us. . . .

On June 3 to Sarah:

Every day gives us fresh marks of the great victory; for since my last, which was but two days ago, we have taken possession of Bruges and Damme, as also Oudenarde, which was besieged the last war by the King, with sixty thousand men, and he was at last forced to raise the siege. In short there is so great a panic in the French army as is not to be expressed. Every place we take declares for King Charles. . . .

You are very kind in desiring I would not expose myself. Be assured I love you so well, and am so desirous of ending my days quietly with you, that I shall not venture myself but when it is absolutely necessary; and I am sure you are so kind to me, and wish so well to the common cause, that you had rather see me dead, than not to do my duty. I am so persuaded that this campaign will bring us a good peace that I beg of you to do all you can that the house at Woodstock may be carried up as much as possible, that I may have a prospect of living in it.

Twelve of these letters reporting the victory are printed in the *Dispatches*. They were as important a part of his warfare as the military movements. They are in the main variants of one another. Cardonnel was a master of correspondence; but to the Emperor and ruling sovereigns the Duke wrote in his own hand, and the labour of scribing must alone have been severe. These personal letters from this extraordinary English general announcing his victories fortified the whole Alliance. To Eugene he sent a detailed account of the battle and its preliminary movements. He had marched on the Saturday "to seize the gap between the Mehaigne and the Great Geet" and at two o'clock

we attacked the village of Ramillies, which sustained the right of their infantry and where they had their strongest battery *avec beaucoup de monde*. The fight warmed up and lasted for some time with very great fury, and at last the enemy were compelled to bend. We there took their cannon and made many prisoners and having continued the action with the same vigour, infantry as well as cavalry, up to four or five o'clock, when the enemy began to retreat, we pursued them continually till long into the night. . . . We halted for only two hours in the night and were on the march before daybreak to gain the Dyle, of which we had determined to force a passage to-day at dawn. But the enemy have spared us the trouble, having retired last night towards Brussels, so that we have already occupied Louvain and our whole army has passed the river without any opposition. . . . Your Highness can judge from this the losses of the enemy and the consternation in which they lie. We propose to march to-morrow upon Brussels to exploit their disorder and try to close with them or compel their further retreat. Nothing could justify making such demands upon the troops after so violent an engagement except the need of pushing them to extremes before Marshal Marsin can join them, as he might do in four or five days.

The account which he gave to the Margrave mentioned that "the Maison du Roi has been almost all cut to pieces," and he added, "I am sure Your Highness will soon feel the advantages of our success by the detachments which will have to be drawn from the Rhine, and that will give you a chance of acting on your side."

The return messengers from England brought a flood of congratulations. The Queen wrote (May 21/June 2) a letter which gains from being printed in its original form:

> * The great Glorious Success wch God Almighty has bin pleased to Bless you wth, & his preservation of your person, one can never thank him enough for, & next to him all things are oweing to you; it is impossible for me ever to Say or doe much as I ought in return of your great & faithful Services to me, but I will endeavour by all ye actions of my life to Shew you how truly Sensible I am of them. The account you Send by mr Pitt of ye great progress you have made since ye Batle is astonishing, the Blessing of God is Sertinly with you, may he Still continue to protect you, & make you the happy instrument of giveing a lasting peace to Europe; I never durst venture to Send ye enclosed by ye post for feare of any accident but Stanhope going to see her father I would not miss yt opertunety it being what may be usefull on some occasions, I intended to have made use of this opertunety to writt my mind more freely then I can by ye post, but I have bin in Such a Continual hurry these three or four days & am Soe still yt I can only now desire you to forgive all ye faults in my letter of

fryday last wch was writt when I was soe Sleepy I could hardly keep my eyes open, & to be assured yt I Shall ever be wth all truth your humble Servant.

It was not until he woke on the morning of May 26 that Louis XIV learned that his finest army had suffered disaster in Flanders. No formal dispatch conveyed the details, but the courier from Louvain brought a short letter from Marshal Villeroy to Dangeau, the Court Chamberlain, telling him how bravely his son had fought, and that he would surely recover from the scalp wound he had received from a sabre. Thereafter there was a silence of six days. "I was at Versailles," says Saint-Simon. "Never has one seen such anxiety and consternation. . . . In ignorance of what had happened and of the consequences of such an unfortunate battle, and amid every one's fears for their kith and kin, the days seemed years." The King was reduced to asking his courtiers what they had heard. At length, finding suspense intolerable, he astonished Versailles by sending Chamillart in person to Villeroy's headquarters, thus leaving the Ministries of War and Finance headless. Chamillart reached Lille on the 31st, and found Villeroy, reinforced by Marsin, around Courtrai. He had retired successively from the Dyle, the Senne, the Dender, and the Scheldt; he had abandoned the whole of Spanish Flanders. He was content if he could hold the French fortress line along the Lys. Chamillart spent three days in long separate discussions with the Marshal and the Elector, and heard versions of the battle and the retreat from all quarters. He found Villeroy dominated by the sense of Marlborough's power; but equally convinced of his own blamelessness, and, indeed, that he had saved the remnants of the army by his prolonged, rapid retreat.

To the King he wrote with dignified assurance. Three main criticisms were focused upon him by his generals: first, that he had accepted battle without knowing the strength of the enemy, and without waiting for the troops of Marshal Marsin; secondly, that he had not reinforced his right and held the village of Taviers in superior strength; and, thirdly, that he had so marshalled his army that the battle had been lost without its main strength being engaged. To all these points the Marshal addressed himself pertinaciously, observing, however, that as a man of the world he knew well "that good reasons are no explanation for catastrophe." He finished his lengthy justification, "I have said more than enough. I end by taking the liberty of telling Your Majesty that the only happy day which I foresee in my life will be that of my death."

It was resolved to remove the Marshal from his command. The feelings of his army and even such public opinion as the French Court could nourish made this step imperative. But Villeroy was a personage of high consequence. He was a veteran general; he was a great gentleman. He was also the personal friend both of the King and of Mme de Maintenon. The King's egotism, which now wore the guise of magnanimity, led him to treat Villeroy, who enjoyed the privilege of being in his inmost circle, with an extreme consideration. Elaborate procedures were accordingly used towards the defeated Marshal. He was offered alternative appointments, and for several weeks discreetly urged to resign. But when he continued as obstinate in holding his command as he had been in retreating from the enemy, patience was at length discarded. He was dismissed. Yet, even when forced to abrupt action, Louis practised the utmost politeness. "At our age," he said to Villeroy when he received him, "we must no longer expect good fortune."

The next measure was to re-create the field army. The resources of France seemed inexhaustible. Marlborough has given his own account of this process.

> The method the King of France has taken to make good his word to the Elector of Bavaria, of putting him at the head of an army of 80,000 men, are the 18 battalions and 14 squadrons which came with the Marshal de Marsin; the detachment that is now marching from Alsace, of 30 battalions and 40 squadrons; and 14 battalions, which the Comte de Gassy commanded in the lines, which were not at the battle. These, joined with the troops that were at the battle, would make above 100,000 men. . . .

Thus, after making provision for garrisons, there was speedily built up the largest French army with which Marlborough had been confronted. In that hour only one man was deemed capable of leading it. The Duke of Vendôme was recalled from Italy.

The strategic pursuit had lasted nearly a fortnight, had cleared all Brabant and much of Flanders, and had rendered the French army for the time being wholly ineffective. The easy gains of panic now ceased. The French were withdrawing into the main fortress zone and towards France. Further advance by Marlborough, especially if any siege was involved, depended upon the waterways. The rivers were still blocked by the French possession of Antwerp and Dendermond. Their fortresses at Ostend and Nieuport controlled the entrance to the canals leading to the Lys and the Scheldt. Marlborough was compelled to suspend his advance in order to clear the communications. He could take whichever fortress he wished and no one could gainsay him, but every siege took time and strength, and it was soon plain that half a dozen captures would be the limit of the campaign in Flanders and Northern France. On June 5 the allied army crossed the Scheldt and the Lys and camped at Arsele, where it could cover any siege necessary to open the communications.

The joyous news here reached Marlborough that Antwerp had capitulated. Summoned by Cadogan, the Spanish grandee in command declared for Charles III. The burghers endorsed his action; the Spanish and Walloon regiments came over to the Allies, and the French troops marched out upon terms. The gaining of this great prize, with all its strategic and commercial attributes, without the firing of a shot was deemed a wonder. "The hand of God," wrote Marlborough to the States-General, "appears visibly in all this, spreading such fear among the enemy as to compel them to surrender so many strong places and whole districts without the least resistance."

Overkirk, deflected from Nieuport by the opening of the sluices at the mouth of the Yser, conducted the siege of Ostend. Admiral Fairborne blockaded the harbour with a squadron of battleships from the main fleet and small craft from the coast flotillas, including the bomb-ketches *Blast* and *Salamander*. The citizens of Ostend adhered to the French garrison, and for three days both the fortifications and town were subjected to severe bombardment from land and sea until, according to contemporary accounts, "the place was near reduced to a heap of rubbish"—not for the last time in its history. On the second day, July 4, a Dutch battalion, preceded by a storming party of fifty British grenadiers, formed a lodgment upon the counterscarp, and after a vigorous sally by the besieged, Ostend surrendered. The French garrison, undertaking not to serve for six months, marched out "without marks of honour," and the Spaniards mostly joined the Allies. Two Bourbon men-of-war of seventy and fifty guns and a quantity of smaller shipping, together with many colours, ninety cannon, and much ammunition, were captured with the fortress, the casualties of the Allies being five hundred men. Ostend deprived the enemy of a hitherto useful port for their galleys and privateers; it gave Marlborough a base nearer to the army than the Dutch rivers, and it placed in his hands the chief port of entry for English cloth into the reopened markets of Belgium.

Meanwhile French soldierly admiration of Marlborough rivalled their fears. Upon a nation so responsive to chivalry, valour, and prestige the genius of the English leader exercised an abnormal fascination. His courtesy to the captured nobles, his humanity to the wounded, the care he took about the well-being of the humbler prisoners, find testimony in all contemporary records. It was noted that he allowed no distinction between the treatment of the French and allied wounded. The Duke always showed the utmost attention to his prisoners. "Marlborough treated his prisoners of mark," writes Saint-Simon, "with an infinite politeness and set many of them at once at liberty for three months upon their parole." He was most careful to shield the aristocracy of France from any reflection upon their courage. French historians of successive generations cherish and repeat his words of praise. They are probably not authentic, but this was the strain in which he spoke: of Villeroy's army, "With thirty thousand men as brave as that I could go to the end of the world"; of the Maison du Roi, "These were more than men, and I knew them so well that I was forced to set six men against each one of them." Thus we see to what perfection he carried the art of conquest, and while inflicting the most terrible injuries made the vanquished grateful for his praise. Thus he created the hold upon the French mind which lasted for generations after English contemporary politicians and writers had done their worst.

Marlborough cannot be robbed of the laurels of Ramillies. The Schellenberg, his detractors said, had been won by the Margrave. Blenheim was the conception and achievement of Prince Eugene. But neither of these explanations covered the amazing event of May 23. Here the world saw Marlborough alone, without a council of war, achieving a military masterpiece seldom equalled and never surpassed. This was his victory and his alone. Ramillies belongs to that rare class of battles fought between equal forces of the highest quality wherein decisive success at comparatively small loss is gained through the manœuvres of a commander-in-chief. It will rank for ever with Rossbach and Austerlitz as an example of what a general can do with men.

CHAPTER FIFTY-SIX

The Reverse of the Medal

❦ 1706, July-October ❧

THE consequences of Ramillies rolled forward in every quarter. Louis XIV, responding to the event, stripped all other fronts to make head against Marlborough. The distresses and perils of Flanders dominated the enemy mind. The King of France was not incapable of taking the sweeping decisions required at intervals from the head of a mighty state assailed upon every side by a coalition. All his orders were obeyed. Indeed, if the French military power had not been so highly organized in the person of its ruler, France might have escaped the disaster which was to befall her in Italy. Marlborough, after all, was still only half-way through the fortress zone. More than twenty fortresses of the first order barred all the roads, rivers, and canals by which he could enter France. Every one of these would, if resolutely defended, count in the recognized schedule of weeks and days, of life, money, and gunpowder, before capture. The temporary dispersion of the French field army enabled them to receive ample garrisons. There is such a thing in war—it must be stated with all reserve—as over-precision of thought and action. Probably the King's best plan was to take his punishment among the fortresses with phlegm, and to finish the war in Italy by defeating the Imperial army under Prince Eugene and destroying the Duke of Savoy. A less highly sensitive organism or an even more comprehensive mind might have taken this chance.

But Louis XIV felt in his own bosom the shock of Ramillies, the overthrow of his household troops, the slaughter or capture of his intimate courtiers, the stigma of rout upon the armies of France. Thus

(536)

he devoted every effort to rebuilding his Flanders army. He drained the Rhine and the Moselle of French troops. He resigned his successes at Hagenau and on the Lauter, and all prospects of recapturing Landau. Here the Margrave, defeated, broken, and now dying in his half-finished palace and gardens at Rastadt, might remain unmolested at the head of the hungry, ragged, dispirited remnants of the Germanic armies. All the weight was taken off them. But in Italy, where final French victory was already in sight and where the allied cause seemed hopeless, an even greater submission to the battle was enforced. The whole flow of French reinforcements was stopped. Considerable forces were actually withdrawn, and Vendôme, who thought he had all the fruits of success in his hand, was ordered to the north. Thus did the victory of Ramillies prepare the rescue of Turin.

The effects upon the Allies were not less pronounced. Prussian loyalties returned to the allied cause, and the Prussian troops hitherto dawdling at Wesel had already marched to join Marlborough's army. All the German princes were heartened to make at least a renewed gesture of putting their shoulders to the wheel. But there were other less favourable reactions. The Court at Vienna was confirmed in their mood that all the Empire had to do was to lean heavily upon these marvellous Sea Powers, to be prompt in asserting its judicial rights to any conquests they might make, and as a prime endeavour stamp out the Hungarian revolt. In Holland the evil went much farther. The victory, the revolution in the Spanish Netherlands and their reversion to the Allies, created a new European situation which hinged directly upon Marlborough. The reconquered lands and cities were by every principle of the Grand Alliance a province of the monarchy of Charles III. That prince, now planning a march upon Madrid, had left behind him in Vienna, on the chance, however remote, that the French would be driven out of the Low Countries, a series of blank commissions for their government. These were in the hands of his brother, the Emperor, who since correspondence with Spain was slow and irregular had plenary powers to act in the general Hapsburg interest. Besides this, Count Goes, the Imperial Ambassador at The Hague, had lawful authority to take possession in the name of Charles III of any territory or fortresses that might be recovered. The major part had now suddenly fallen into the hands of Marlborough's army; and the Emperor and all his agents made haste to claim them.

On the other hand, the Dutch regarded Belgium as their longed-for Barrier, their indispensable dyke against France and Louis XIV. Here was their means of self-preservation, their prime objective of the war, as they saw it, in their grip. Moreover, Ramillies was to them above all a Dutch victory. Their native troops had borne the brunt. They had lost more blood than all the allied contingents together. It was the Dutch guards who had stormed Taviers against surprising odds. Dutch troopers had ridden down the Maison du Roi. The English had been but lightly engaged. The Prussians had stood aloof. The gallant Danes were the mercenaries jointly of the two Sea Powers. The Dutch acknowledged cordially that the battle had been won by the genius of an English Commander-in-Chief. But was he not also Deputy Captain-General of the Republic? Was he not their salaried officer? Had they not had the foresight to choose him and sustain him when the Queen of England would have set some ninny in his place? As the broadening tale of glory and of conquest flowed in to The Hague and Amsterdam, accompanied by lengthening lists of the Dutch killed and wounded, the States-General and every warlike element in Holland felt that the prize was theirs.

Far gone were the days of 1702, when their army crouched under the ramparts of Nimwegen, and when this new English commander, whom, to bind the English to their cause and keep out more overweening servants, they had made their Deputy Captain-General, had invited them to take the offensive, sword in hand. The Meuse was clear to the gates of Namur. The whole course of the Rhine, and all its strongholds, were in allied hands. Brussels had fallen. Antwerp, the greatest prize of all, for which the utmost sacrifices might well have been made, had surrendered without a siege. Bruges, Ghent, Oudenarde, Ostend, even Tournai and Mons, were already theirs or were within their grasp, and Nieuport, Ypres, Menin, Ath, might well be gained. Behind these bristled the fortresses of the French frontier—Dunkirk, Aire, Saint-Venant, Lille, Valenciennes, Douai, Bouchain, Maubeuge, and Phi-lippeville. But were these trophies essential to the preservation of the Republic? They wanted to humble the power of France. Surely it was humbled already. Were not the great King's envoys busy through half a dozen channels with proposals for a separate peace, based primarily and without question upon a good Barrier for Holland? And what of England? Her schemes ranged far. While with one hand she animated and led the armies of Europe to the invasion of France, with the other she calmly took possession of trade, of the oceans, and of the fabulous regions that lay beyond. How far should Dutchmen be drawn by this island incantation? If Marlborough wielded a glorious sword, did he not also wave a magician's wand? They might be grateful; they must not be bewitched.

The majestic events of history and the homely incidents of daily life alike show how vainly man strives to control his fate. Even his greatest neglects or failures may bring him good. Even his greatest achievements may work him ill. If Marlborough had merely won the battle of Ramillies, taken Louvain, and perhaps entered Brussels, the campaign of 1706 might have carried the allied cause to victory in 1707. But he now began to experience a whole series of new resistances and withholdings from the Dutch, as well as their grabbings and graspings, all of which were destined to bring the fortunes of the Allies once again to the lowest ebb.

In the middle of June the Emperor filled in and signed one of the blank commissions which his brother sovereign had confided to him. He appointed the Duke of Marlborough Viceroy of the Netherlands. In the instructions to Goes the Court of Vienna gave their reasons. Marlborough would be acceptable to the Belgians. His appointment would bind the English more closely to the interests of the Empire. His prestige both in England and Holland would alone preserve the Netherlands intact for Charles III. He controlled "the heart of the war," and would, they thought, also control the peace negotiations. On its merits this was a fine stroke of policy. It offered far the most agreeable arrangement to the Belgians, and safeguarded in the highest degree possible Hapsburg interests. Who else but Marlborough had a chance of persuading the Dutch? The courier bearing this important news reached Marlborough's headquarters on June 28. The proposal confronted him with one of the testing decisions of his life. It was no doubt the best military and political arrangement conceivable. Combining the command of the army with a virtual sovereignty in the theatre of war, his control would for the first time be perfect. It would, if adopted, adjourn the rending question within the Alliance till peace was gained. It invested him with almost royal status, and offered him a revenue of sixty thousand pounds a year.

From every point of view, personal and public, British and European, it met all needs. There is no doubt that Marlborough greatly desired to accept it. Nothing in his whole career shows in more striking fashion how far he could rise on great occasions above all those private advantages which in the ordinary swing of life he counted so carefully. Here was the greatest prize ever within his reach. Moreover, it was the best arrangement. Let us see how it weighed with him in comparison with what was now already a hackneyed phrase, but none the less to him a grand reality—the common cause.

It happened that the Dutch Treasurer, Hop, was in his camp at Rousselaer almost immediately after the Emperor's letter had been received. The Duke laid it before him. Hop said at once that it would raise ill-humour in Holland. The States-General would say that the Emperor wished to make use of Marlborough and the Queen of England to keep the wealth of Belgium out of the hands of the Dutch. This only confirmed Marlborough's own opinion. He saw that his acceptance of this great and lucrative office might deeply injure the Allies. If that were so he would have none of it.

Every one consulted in England was delighted. Not only Godolphin but the Whig leaders, Somers and Sunderland, whom he apprised, accepted the proposal cordially. England would have Belgium in her hands. What could be better, whether for the war or for the peace? The Queen, still under the impression of Ramillies, was entirely content that Mr Freeman should have this great honour which he had won with his sword. She was glad when her Ministers moved her to authorize him to decide the matter as he thought fit.

Meanwhile Count Goes brought the dispatches he had received from the Emperor to the notice of the Dutch authorities. Certainly Goes, smarting under his rough usage from the Dutch, took the worst way. Instead of submitting the documents to the Pensionary in due routine, he handed them, as we may suppose with some air of triumph, to the President of the States-General for the week. The letters of the Emperor were read out to the Assembly. There was general astonishment. The Pensionary, assailed by a storm of questions, was completely unprepared. The Dutch view was overwhelmingly expressed that the Emperor had no right to dispose of the Government of Belgium without previous consultation with the Republic, whose Barrier it must be. Pensionary Heinsius quitted the stormy meeting, indignant at having been thus inconsiderately exposed. He fell upon Count Goes, and reproached him vehemently with not having warned him beforehand. Heinsius addressed himself by letter to Marlborough. He complained of the proposal; he complained of the procedure. Marlborough replied in terms of the utmost goodwill. He would on no account allow any question of his personal interest to impair the unity of the Alliance. Never was disinterested renunciation more forthcoming or more complete.

Marlborough hoped that his renunciation of great advantages would give him all the more influence in inducing the Dutch to abate their own ambitions.

Thus we see this man, described by so many historians as the most self-seeking and avaricious of his generation, rejecting without apparent mental hesitation a personal advantage of the greatest magnitude. It came to him as the fruit of his victory. He longed to have it. The Emperor wished it. The English Government warmly approved. The plan was good in itself. There was no obstacle but the Dutch. But if the Dutch disagreed, if the structure of the Alliance were thereby endangered, Marlborough was ready at once to discard the whole scheme.

He was also ready to make another personal sacrifice. His intense military exertions after Ramillies were accompanied by a remarkable diplomatic intrigue equally designed to exploit the victory. While he could not meet his wishes, he sought by every means to establish a personal and friendly contact with Prince Max Emmanuel who seemed marked on every occasion to be the nearest victim of his sword. On the morrow of Ramillies came a new occasion.

Marlborough appointed an agent, one Sersanders, a distinguished Belgian functionary, to visit the Elector. There was a secret interview at Mons on August 3. Sersanders urged Max Emmanuel to desert the cause of France. He cited the example of the Duke of Savoy. In Marlborough's name he offered the fugitive Elector the full restoration of his hereditary Bavarian lands. He held out the hopes that these might be stretched across the Brenner Pass to include the Milanese. Lastly, to clinch the matter and to prove Marlborough's sincerity, Sersanders was authorized to throw in the principality of Mindelheim which Marlborough had gained at Blenheim and by laborious negotiations with the Emperor. It was the trophy which had most tempted his vanity. But now in a larger grouping of ideas it might play a different part. Sersanders in Marlborough's name offered the Elector "all his Bavarian estates without any exception, not even that of the principality of Mindelheim."

If ever there was a bribe it was here. But one item remained: the four key-fortresses which Marlborough could not see his way to conquer within the limits of the campaign—namely, Namur, Mons, Charleroi, and Luxembourg—at this moment garrisoned by the Elector's troops, were to be surrendered to the armies of the Sea Powers.

Here were the four vital fortresses, by which alone the sail of France could be defended, about to be betrayed. The French, taking no avoidable risks, replaced all Max Emmanuel's Spanish garrisons with their own troops, and the campaign was ended only by the winter.

Fate with sardonic smile ordained that the most brilliant victory gained by Marlborough for the Dutch Republic should raise new hindrances to his action in their name; and that his most generous of personal sacrifices should leave behind it in Dutch hearts only embarrassing suspicions. From the day on which the Emperor offered him the Vice-royalty of the Netherlands a sense of divergent interest arose inevitably and irresistibly between the Dutch leaders and their Deputy Captain-General. Henceforward, whatever Marlborough might declare, they could not help believing, first, that he owed them a grudge for having been the obstacle, and, secondly, that he still hoped to obtain the prize. Henceforth they must regard him as an interested supporter of Hapsburg and Imperial claims rather than of their own. It is no reproach to Marlborough that persisting elements of truth underlay the Dutch misgivings. His conduct had been spontaneous, high-minded, and scrupulously correct. He bore no grudges; he pursued no conscious designs. But of course he was gratified by the offers of the Emperor and of Charles III, and hoped, indeed, that a day might come when without prejudice to the common cause he might accept and enjoy them. How far in the deep springs of human action this fact influenced his policy and counsel no one can measure; but certainly in every negotiation about the Barrier, in every overture for peace with France—nay, almost in every march of the Confederate army—Dutch opinion sought to trace a prevailing and personal motive; and from this cause his influence throughout Holland suffered a partial but none the less profound and incurable decline.

Ramillies, with its prelude and its sequel, was the most glorious episode in Marlborough's life. Whether as the victorious commander, the sagacious Minister, or the disinterested servant of the allied cause, his personal conduct was noble. Before the battle he had sacrificed as he believed his prospects of a fine campaign in the Low Countries for the sake of the armies in other theatres, and especially for Prince Eugene. He had gained a great battle by consummate art. He had used the military pursuit and the political consequences to such deadly profit as to drive the French out of the Netherlands. After the victory he had handsomely renounced his own interests in order to preserve the harmony of the Alliance. To procure from Max Emmanuel the four French key-fortresses he had not hesitated to throw his own principality of Mindelheim into the scale. How vain are those writers in so many lands who suppose that the great minds of the world in their supreme activities are twisted or swayed by sordid or even personal aims. These, indeed, may clog their footsteps along the miry road of life; but soaring on the wings of victory all fall away. It is Marlborough's true glory that the higher his fortune, the higher rose his virtue. We must at a later stage present the reader with some contrasts, and show how Marlborough's conduct contracted with his power. But in 1706 he shines as genius and hero, wise, valiant, and stainless, striving only for the best for England and the best for all.

*Meantime, while the campaign of 1706 had gone badly in Spain, Prince Eugene had, in a masterly campaign, relieved the siege of Turin and driven the French from Italy.**

When we recount the famous victories of 1706 and set forth the long tale of captured cities and conquered or reconquered lands which built up the allied triumph, it seems amazing that all this good fortune should not have prompted the comparatively small effort of good comradeship needed to bring the war to a successful conclusion. The victories of Ramillies and Turin; the relief of Barcelona; the capture of Antwerp and a dozen famous fortresses in the Low Countries; the French expelled from Italy; Charles III entering Madrid; the complete suppression of France upon the seas and oceans—all these prepared a broad, an easy road along which the signatory states of the Grand Alliance, who had striven so hard against misfortune, could walk to peace and plenty. But by the mysterious law which perhaps in larger interests limits human achievement, and bars or saves the world from clear-cut

* By H. S. C.

solutions, this second revival of the allied cause led only to a second decline. Twice now the genius of Marlborough and Eugene had lifted the weary, struggling signatory states to the level where their will could be enforced, and most of their needs secured. But again, in despite of their champions, they were to cast themselves down into peril and distress. The Empire represented nothing but moral and military decay and legal or territorial appetite. The German principalities and the strong kingdom of Prussia cast off their responsibilities and sponged for subsidies upon their Anglo-Dutch deliverers in proportion as they were relieved of their dangers. The Dutch themselves, with their Dyke at their fingertips, were "unaccountable." In Spain the incursions of the Allies, especially the Portuguese, had roused a national spirit similar to that which a hundred years later wore down Napoleon. The Hapsburg king imposed by foreign troops had become to Spanish eyes usurper and invader; while the Bourbon claimant, though more alien, seemed to embody the continuity and grandeur of the Spanish past.

In England, now the hub of this Juggernaut wheel, not only party strife, but the prejudices and failings of a handful of men and women, including and circling round the Queen, were to crack and splinter the inefficient but still august league of nations which hitherto had successfully defended the liberties of Europe against the intolerance of totalitarian monarchy. Thus success bred failure, and prosperity prepared collapse, by which again new, larger, and more painful efforts were extorted.

CHAPTER FIFTY-SEVEN

Marlborough and Charles XII

ᛏᛞ 1707, Spring ᛞᛉ

DISASTER is the name affixed by history to the Allies' campaign of 1707. On the Rhine, on the Riviera, and in Spain the French won or even triumphed. In Flanders, the main theatre, where the best and far the largest armies faced each other, where Marlborough commanded, no victory was gained. At the same time the slow, subtle processes by which Marlborough's foundations in England were sapped made steady progress, and grew from an intrigue into a crisis. At the end of 1706 the Grand Alliance was once again found incapable of enduring success. Each partner was balancing the hopes of extortionate gains against the risks of a separate peace. Ramillies and its companion Turin had removed from short-sighted Governments the fear of general defeat at the hands of France. The war was hard and long. Why pursue the theme of victory farther? The cruel need which had called into being the disjointed federation of so many states, kingdoms, republics, empires, principalities, had been banished by the swords of Marlborough and Eugene. The temptation to rush for the spoil, to grab and depart, was strong. The Dutch could have their dyke; Austria saw herself mistress of Italy; Prussia was sure of important satisfactions in status and in territory; Germany, incoherent and ineffectual, at this time felt scarcely less fear of Charles XII than of Louis XIV. Thus every common impulse was relaxed, every contribution was neglected, and every preparation for 1707 delayed.

But the power of France was still unbroken. Louis XIV was forming his armies for the new campaign. Twenty-one thousand militia were drafted into the front line. Vendôme and the Elector in Flanders, Villars on the Upper Rhine, Noailles in Roussillon, Tessé in Dauphiné, and Berwick and the Duke of Orleans in Spain confronted the Allies. The Great King sought peace, but still only a French peace: and at any moment a turn of fortune would revive his full claims. Between equals and similars there always is much to be said for peace even through a drawn war; but to a wide, numerous, disconnected coalition, faced by a homogeneous military nation and a grand autocracy, a drawn war embodied in a treaty spelt permanent defeat. One man, still carrying with him the British island in its most remarkable efflorescence of genius and energy, stood against this kind of accommodation. Marlborough, harassed and hampered upon every side, remained unexhausted and all-compelling.

After the day at Blenheim had shifted the axis of the war he planned the decisive invasion of France by the Moselle. In the sunshine of un-hoped-for prosperity the German states had failed him. The surest, easiest road into France would never be trodden by the Allies. The chance had fled. But now 1706 had restored the Blenheim situation, and once again he formed a plan which if it were executed—as with ordinary loyalties it could be—would bend or break France to the will of England. This plan lay in that high region of strategy where all the forces are measured and all the impulsions understood. Since it had proved impossible to lead Germany into France directly by the Moselle, a wider operation was required. His conception was now a double invasion from north and south. This used the resources, the war-will of England, and above all her supreme naval power, at the highest pitch. With his present ascendancy in Holland, with his redcoats and the British-paid contingents and subsidies, Marlborough and the Dutch would hold and press hard upon the principal army of France in the fortress zone of the Netherlands. Simultaneously Eugene, with the forces of the Empire sustained by the allied mercenaries and the whole strength of the English and Dutch fleets in the Mediterranean, and based upon sea-borne supplies and munitions, would invade France from the south. For this purpose they must first of all seize a safe fortified harbour through which the amphibious power of England could exert itself to the full, and also animate the Imperial armies. The mighty French monarchy would be taken between hammer and anvil. This he deemed would be irresistible and final.

This scheme, for which Marlborough toiled and ran great and drawn-out hazards, reveals to us his true views about the Spanish theatre. We have seen him repeatedly and genuinely supporting the war in Spain, always ready to send trusted generals and good, sorely needed troops from England or from Flanders to the Peninsula: always ready to accept this large, costly, and disconnected diversion. Although, as has been shown, there were substantial offsets, such a policy cannot easily be reconciled with the canons of true strategy. Political and commercial factors had launched the Allies into a great war in Spain. Not only the Tory Party, but on the whole the bulk of English opinion, preferred an alliance with Portugal and an expedition to Spain to the grim ding-dong in Flanders. To Parliament Spain seemed the easy and clever road. It was in fact an additional détour on a journey already only too long. Why, then, did our great commander acquiesce so tamely in this questionable exertion? Did he agree or did he submit? There is no doubt that he submitted. He paid off at great cost Tory and English prejudices, and did the best he could with what was left. Otherwise even that might have been lost.

But now we shall see how truly he measured the war in Spain. The capture of Toulon and a real thrust up towards Lyons into the vitals of Southern France would, in his judgment, instantly clear Spain. The French, no matter how few there were to drive them, would flow out of the Peninsula as naturally as water flows out of a cistern when its bottom tap is opened. Therefore in the winter of 1706–7 Marlborough's central aim became the siege and capture of Toulon.

The victory at Turin had roused Victor Amadeus to a high degree of war vigour and of territorial desire. He hoped to have the concessions he had been promised in Lombardy endorsed by treaty with the French, and to spread his sovereignty in Provence by conquest. He was therefore eager to invade Southern France. All his ideas and efforts were in harmony with Marlborough's plans. The Empire, on the other hand, had contrary ambitions. After the rough treatment they had received from the Dutch in Belgium, and with the proofs of extreme Dutch claims about the Barrier before their eyes, they were resolved to take physical possession not only of Lombardy, but also of the Kingdom of Naples. They were not interested in aiding the general victory by carrying the war into Southern France. They developed an obstinate resistance even to the transfer to Savoy of those parts of Lombardy which had been specifically promised to Victor Amadeus in the original treaty by which he had joined the Grand Alliance. Naples, as a conquest or at least as a counter for the peace treaty, now became their supreme desire. The whole urge of the Imperialist policy was therefore divergent from the purpose of common victory which Marlborough steadfastly pursued.

It was impossible for the Imperialists to march on Naples unless the English Fleet by its command of the sea prevented French sea-borne reinforcements forestalling the long, slow overland expedition. This potent factor, added to the menace of the withdrawal of the troops of the Sea Powers, forced the Emperor to transfer some of the fortresses of Lombardy to the Duke of Savoy, and to agree to the Toulon plan. But nothing could persuade him to abandon the design upon Naples. Early in February Marlborough made a detailed written agreement with Victor Amadeus for the attack upon Toulon. England would furnish forty ships of the line to sustain the advance along the Riviera of the Savoyard and Imperialist troops. The fleet would supply money, powder, and food upon a very large scale. It would land cannon and sailors in strong force for the siege and the preliminary operations. Article XV was laconic and precise: "The proposed expedition to Naples is excluded, being judged at the present time impracticable, and harmful to the interests of the campaign in France."

Confronted with a virtual ultimatum, the Imperial Court behaved in the worst manner. They persisted in their plans against Naples. They were taking a far more disloyal and selfish step. They entered ardently into a military convention with France which resulted in the Treaty of Milan. This amounted to a separate local peace. The Emperor agreed with Louis XIV to close down the Italian front altogether. The twenty thousand French troops who were blockaded in the various fortresses of Northern Italy and must in a few months have become prisoners of war were accorded free passage to rejoin the main hostile armies. Portions of them reinforced Vendôme in Flanders; the rest strengthened Marshal Tessé, who was guarding the passes of the French southern front.

The history of all coalitions is a tale of the reciprocal complaints of allies; but the conduct of the Imperial Court at this juncture stands forth remarkably as an example of wanton, reckless self-seeking. If the

Dutch were too narrowly set upon their Barrier, if English ambitions sought a disproportionate humiliation of France, at least the Sea Powers backed their aims with enormous and generous exertions for the common cause. But the Empire, saved from disaster in Bavaria in 1704, restored to success in Italy in 1706 by the resources of England and Holland, dependent upon them not only for the inestimable prizes to which it aspired, but also for its very existence, stands guilty of folly and ingratitude of the basest kind.

Marlborough's faith was in Eugene. In 1706 he had provided him with the core and substance of the army which had conquered at Turin. In 1707 he placed at his disposal overwhelming naval power, and encouraged him by every practical means to strike another equally glorious and possibly final blow for the allied cause at Toulon. "I not only esteem, but really love that Prince." To arm him for another splendid achievement he would be himself content to face Vendôme with a smaller army and to conduct a campaign in Flanders under most unpromising conditions. Never mind! He would manage it somehow, and far to the south his great comrade would gather the fruits which would make amends for all.

During the successes of 1706 the Northern War encroached ever nearer to the main quarrel. Charles XII was now at his zenith. His triumphs over the Russians were followed at the beginning of 1706 by his crushing defeat of King Augustus of Poland, also Elector of Saxony, at the battle of Fraustadt (February 13). At the head of his veteran and victorious Swedish army Charles marched into Saxony. Encamped in the heart of Germany at the head of forty thousand devoted, ruthless, athletic, disciplined Swedish co-adventurers whom no troops had yet been able to withstand, he became the object of the most earnest anxiety, and solicitation from all parts of Central Europe. He recognized no law but his grand caprice; and Christendom, divided against itself, competed for his sword. To which quarter would Charles XII turn his fierce and as yet invincible bayonets? Throughout all Germany in the winter of 1706 this was the main preoccupation. To the Sea Powers it was a monstrous irrelevance. But there he poised, with the choice of plunging into the Russian wilderness or marching into the very heart of world affairs.

Marlborough was alarmed at Charles XII's attitude as early as September 1706. "I am very much afraid," he wrote to Heinsius, "that this march of the Sweeds [sic] into Saxe will create a great degree of trouble. . . . Whenever the States or England write to the King of Sweden, there must be care taken that there be no threats in the letter, for the King of Sweden is of a very particular humor."

In February he wrote again to the Pensionary:

> If you thought it might be of any advantage to the Public, I should not scruple the trouble of a journey as far as Saxony, to wait on the King, and endeavour, if need be, to set him right, or at least to penetrate his design, that we may take the justest measures we can not to be surprised. I have mentioned this to nobody here, neither will, till I have your opinion. . . .

There was a general feeling in the shuddering Courts of Germany and in the dour Cabinets of the Sea Powers that Marlborough, with his military glamour and almost equally renowned diplomatic arts, was the man who of all others could penetrate the King's designs, could tip the balance, if it were possible, and cushion this formidable, romantic, ruffianly genius and his grim phalanx into the Russian wastes. Accordingly on April 20 the Captain-General set off in his coach from The Hague through Hanover to the tent of Charles XII. Many picturesque accounts have been given of their meeting, which fascinated contemporary Europe as a "topic of wonder" to all men. They met as commanding generals each fresh from glowing victories. Whatever effects could be produced depended upon personal contact. Biographers of Marlborough usually claim that his mission at once transformed the purposes of Charles XII. This seems unreasonable. It established a relationship upon which Marlborough negotiated all the summer with results which eventually reached their conclusion in 1709 upon the battlefield of Pultawa.

When Marlborough arrived at Altranstädt from his tiring journey through Hanover he went to see Count Piper, who was a kind of Prime Minister to Charles XII. The Count, for reasons which are not worth examining, sent out word to say that he was engaged, and kept Marlborough in his coach waiting half an hour behind his appointment. Then the Swede, having asserted his dignity, came down the steps of his house to the gate to receive Queen Anne's envoy. Marlborough got out of the coach at the same moment and, putting on his hat, walked past Count Piper without recognizing him or saluting him, and turned aside on to the grass "as if to make water." After a delay more protracted than would have seemed necessary he came back into the path, and with courtly gestures and ceremonious phrasing began his embassy. Count Piper meanwhile had stood embarrassed in the roadway.

Charles XII and Marlborough were interested in each other—the first a knight-errant pursuing glory through all hazards, at all costs, and irrespective of reward; the other the statesman and commander, trying to shield large public purposes from capricious disturbance. Charles stands for all time as an example of the firmness of the human soul under every freak of fortune. John was a monument of practical sagacity. The young King, since he leaped from his throne at the throat of Europe at seventeen, had only experienced measureless triumph. The elderly General, reared as a courtier, with all the ups and downs of a lengthening life behind him—a little heavy with the weight of all that weighed upon him, and webbed by the combinations of which he was the motive power—had a different status and outlook. But War and Victory were a theme, a basis, and a bond. At their meeting Marlborough presented a letter from Queen Anne: "Had her sex not prevented it, she would have crossed the sea to visit a prince admired by the whole universe. I am in this particular more happy than the Queen, and I wish I could serve in some campaign under so great a commander that I might learn what I yet want to know in the art of war." Charles XII appeared to accept the compliment, and it was frequently repeated by his devoted army. He was not to be easily flattered, and it is said that he deemed it overdone. He thought, we learn from Voltaire, that Marlborough in his scarlet uniform and Garter star and riband looked less like a soldier than he himself in his austere dress and with his studied abhorrence of all show.

The meeting was both memorable and important. The two men had a long talk about what they understood best. Marlborough spoke French, which the King understood but did not speak, and the Reverend John Robinson, the envoy to Sweden, translated the Royal replies. Charles XII, with the reports of Blenheim and Ramillies in his mind, asked whether, and if so why, Marlborough thought it necessary to charge at the head of his troops. Marlborough replied in effect, "Only because otherwise they would not think so much of me." The King agreed with this. They were together for about four hours, until, in fact, his Majesty's "kettledrums called him to prayers."

The King expected Marlborough to make him proposals upon the international situation, but all accounts show that Marlborough kept entirely upon personal and professional ground. He did not even, though he had been pressed to do so, presume to intercede on behalf of Patkul. Voltaire in his romantic but none the less profound *Histoire de Charles XII* wrote:

> Marlborough, who was never in a haste to make his proposals, and who, by a long course of experience, had learned the art of diving into the real characters of men, and discovering the connexion between their most secret thoughts and their actions, gestures, and discourse, studied the King with close attention. When he spoke to him of war in general, he thought he perceived in his Majesty a natural aversion to France, and noticed that he talked with pleasure of the conquests of the Allies. He mentioned the Czar to him, and observed that his eyes always kindled at the name, notwithstanding the calm tone of the conversation. He remarked, besides, a map of Russia lying on a table. He wanted no more to convince him that the real design and sole ambition of the King of Sweden was to dethrone the Czar, as he had done the King of Poland. He divined that if Charles remained in Saxony it was only to impose some hard conditions on the Emperor of Germany. He knew the Emperor would make no resistance, and so the whole affair would be wound up without difficulty. He left Charles, therefore, to follow his own bent; and, satisfied with having read his mind, made him no proposals.

The day after the talk of the two warriors Charles XII set off according to his custom (and Napoleon's) at full gallop for Leipzig, where he had arranged to meet Augustus, dethroned King of Poland and vanquished, but still ruling, Elector of Saxony. More than that, Stanislaus, Charles XII's nominee and actual holder of the Polish Crown, was in attendance. Queen Anne had not recognized this usurping pawn of the Swedish victories. Charles therefore asked Marlborough, whom he kept at his side, whether he could meet him. The Duke made no difficulty, and when Stanislaus arrived through the double doors he bowed and addressed him as "Your Majesty," which committed England to nothing, but was received with evident gratification by both the conqueror, Charles, and his puppet, Stanislaus. Apart from compliments he was careful to hold no intercourse with the unrecognized sovereign. The King of Prussia did not wish to be left out of these conversations, and Marlborough on the next day therefore repaired to Charlottenburg, where he met King Frederick. He thus, according to the biographers of his day, "met four kings in four days." His comment to Sarah is the instructive "If I was obliged to make a choice, it should be [the] youngest [Charles XII]."

He returned by hard stages from Leipzig to Brussels to meet the news of the worst disaster which had yet befallen the Allies.

CHAPTER FIFTY-EIGHT

Almanza and Stollhofen

⇥ 1707, April and May ⇤

[On April 25 Galway, at the head of some fifteen thousand men, only five thousand of them British, met the greatly superior army of Berwick on the plains before the walled town of Almanza. At the first onset of the French, Galway's Portuguese troops fled. Exposed on both flanks the Allied army was all but destroyed, and Galway retreated with the survivors to the frontier fortress of Valencia.]

"This ill success in Spain," wrote Marlborough stubbornly (May 23), "has flung everything backwards, so that the best resolution we can take is to let the French see we are resolved to keep on the war, so that we can have a good peace."

* * * *

On May 21 the Duke had assumed command of the army which had assembled under Overkirk near Brussels, and advanced at once to the south of Hal. He drew out 97 battalions and 164 squadrons with 112 guns, in all about ninety thousand men. Vendôme had assembled around Mons 124 battalions and 195 squadrons—say, about a hundred and ten thousand men, not including the detached cavalry (16 squadrons) of La Motte. Vendôme was operating from a frontier well guarded by many fortresses of the first class; and his instructions were not to hazard a battle without urgent need. Marlborough, on the other hand, had to cover several important but poorly fortified towns, especially Brussels. He had thought earlier of making a dash for Mons or Tournai before Vendôme was ready. His journey to see the King of Sweden had prevented this, and the moment had now passed. He was too far outnumbered to undertake a siege, and must content himself with covering Brabant, hoping for a chance of battle on favourable terms. All his letters show him anxious for battle, though not at undue risk. The Dutch had instructed their field Deputies that they were not to allow a battle. He was careful "not to let the army know that the Dutch are not willing to venture, since that must have an ill effect." Marlborough was thus thrown back into the conditions he had found intolerable in previous campaigns. He had to create a situation where the superior enemy were at great disadvantage, and where at the same time the Dutch had no option but to fight. This double problem was incapable of solution. Thus unhappily circumstanced, he took the field.

At midnight on May 25, after he had ordered the army to march the next day to Soignies, his spies reported that the French were also to move forward at daybreak. These movements brought the two great armies into critical relation. On the 27th Marlborough, taking with him the field Deputies, made a reconnaissance in force towards the enemy but failed to find them. They had in fact moved eastward to Gosselies, where they formed a strong camp. This was not known till late in the day. The French movement deliberately uncovered the fortress of Mons, as if to challenge its siege. Had the Allies attempted this, Brussels, Louvain, and, indeed, all Brabant would have been exposed. The choice remained of moving eastward across the Senne to converge upon the enemy with the chance of battle, or of retracing the marches along the Brussels road and standing between him and Brabant. A council of war debated the question. Marlborough proposed to remain where he was, and send a detachment to demolish the abandoned French lines before Mons. Evidently he wished to lead Vendôme to believe that he was about to commit the error which the Marshal's movement had invited. Upon this pretence he would await Vendôme's next move. The general opinion was against this apparent adoption of an unsound policy.

According to Goslinga, Marlborough then proposed to retire on Brussels. At this the Deputies, supported by many of the generals, Dutch and English, raised an outcry.

We have Marlborough's letter written to Godolphin on May 30, while the facts were well known to the principal officers of the army:

This caution of mine is absolutely necessary; for instead of coming to this camp I would have marched yesterday to Nivelles, but the Deputies would not consent to it, telling me very plainly that they feared the consequence of that march might be a battle. So that unless I can convince the Pensioner that I am not for hazarding, but when we have an advantage, they will give such orders to their Deputies that I shall not have it in my power of doing good, if an advantage should offer itself. . . .

The explanation of Marlborough's decision seems plain. Had he possessed the powers which are the right of every commander of an army, he would have marched to meet Vendôme through Nivelles after encouraging him to commit himself more deeply by a feint by Mons; and perhaps the chance of battle would have come. But it was not primarily against Vendôme that he was in this instance manœuvring. He hoped that this super-prudent retreat, and the heart-burnings it caused to the Dutch field Deputies and generals, would convince Heinsius of his extreme cautiousness, and procure him the freedom without which it was not possible to handle an army with success. If he gained that freedom from his friends, and if the enemy, inflamed by his apparent weakness, would "grow insolent," then something might be made of the campaign. Meanwhile he had no intention of forcing the Senne and bringing about a situation where he could offer battle, when he knew that at the culminating moment the Deputies would produce their written instructions to veto such hazards. As the somewhat crestfallen confederates passed by Brussels and their columns bent eastward towards the Dyle and their former fighting-grounds, the news of a second major disaster reached Marlborough. The Lines of Stollhofen had been captured by Marshal Villars.

Prince Louis of Baden was dead, and the Margrave of Bayreuth, appointed by Vienna because, though a bad general, he was a good Catholic, led the armies of Germany in his stead. Prince Louis had left behind as his monument that renowned system of defences upon the Upper Rhine known as the Lines of Stollhofen. It had become a joke in the armies that the late Prince's whole conception of the world war was the defence of the Lines of Stollhofen. He had originally expected to command on the Rhine the hundred and twenty thousand Imperial troops which had been promised by the old Emperor in the treaty of the Grand Alliance. These had not appeared; but as the successive campaigns passed with their twists of fortune Prince Louis when in doubt had always persevered in the fortification of his lines. In fact, it was said that in exact proportion as the military strength of Germany diminished so his fortifications grew. They had never been more impressive than in the spring of 1707. From the impassable mountains of the Black Forest to Fort Louis stretched the double and triple lines of bastions, redans, redoubts, trenches, strong points, inundations, marshes, which had hitherto in the War of Succession effectively prevented all invasion of Germany along the Rhine valley. Now, after the Margrave had been driven out of Alsace, the defences had been perfected along the whole course of the river to the fortresses of Landau and Philippsburg. Counting round the angle of Fort Louis, these fifty or sixty miles of elaborate earthworks and water-shields constituted the finest manifestation of passive defence which war in those times had seen. Within them stood the ragged remnants of the Emperor's Rhine army, recently stripped and stinted for the sake of the expedition to Naples. Behind them lay Germany, defenceless, disunited, but, thanks to the Sea Powers, to Blenheim and Ramillies, hitherto unravaged. But behind them also had risen at Rastadt the magnificent palace and gardens of the late Margrave, on which he had lavished hundreds of thousands of pounds, and by which he proclaimed his confidence that his lines were inexpugnable. The mercy of God, manifested through his toe, had laid him in his tomb before the striking of the fatal hour.

On the night of May 22 Marshal Villars gave a grand ball at Strasburg. This festivity and its date had become widely known. The news had crossed the gulf between the armies, and upon the staff of the new Commander-in-Chief, the Prince of Bayreuth, entire confidence prevailed. But while Villars arranged his general officers in the minuet, their troops, mobilized with the utmost stealth, were marching fast, and when they received their orders from him in the ballroom they rode off to play their parts in a great surprise. The famous lines which for five years had protected the German Fatherland were overrun at numerous points without loss of life, almost without the firing of a shot. The most impregnable section, between the river and the mountains, was the first to fall. The French clambered in succession over tiers of permanent defences. The Reich troops fled in disorder towards Durlach, and Villars fixed his headquarters in the palace and castle of

Rastadt on the evening of the 23rd. By then the entire system of defence which had hitherto served Central Germany in the place of an army was in French hands. The roadway into Germany was now barred neither by ramparts nor soldiers. The dyke had broken, and the bitter waters flowed onward in a deluge. This was no more than the Germanic states deserved for their meanness to the Empire, and the Empire for its incompetence. Fortune committed an injustice when the main penalty was paid by the Circles of Swabia and Franconia, which had done the most to defend their country.

Such was the opening of the campaign of 1707. In a trice the entire face of the war had changed. In Italy an improvident separate peace; in Spain a shattering defeat; in Germany unstemmed invasion; in Flanders deadlock and veto. There remained Marlborough's hope: Eugene and Toulon.

CHAPTER FIFTY-NINE

Toulon

ᕷ 1707, Summer ᕷ

THE attack upon Toulon in 1707 was one of the greatest naval enterprises ever undertaken by England. Marlborough's power and the whole authority of the Government sustained the Fleet. They found in Sir Cloudesley Shovell an admiral who brought to the enterprise a strong surge of his own. Admiral Shovell was from the outset as keen and convinced as Marlborough about taking Toulon. He saw the profit to the naval war of securing this excellent Mediterranean base. He saw from his quarterdeck across the short, wind-whipped seas of the Gulf of Lions exactly what Marlborough saw in his headquarters at Meldert —the destruction of the French fleet and its base, and the command of the Mediterranean for England during the war and perhaps longer. Both Shovell and Admiral Norris, his representative in the Duke of Savoy's army, also comprehended the strategic consequences upon the whole struggle of the organized invasion of Southern France from a conquered Toulon and an English-dominated Mediterranean.

Marlborough ceaselessly urged the attack upon Toulon. The disasters at Almanza and Stollhofen only increased its importance in his eyes. To Noyelles he wrote, June 3, "Our greatest hope is on the Italian front, although the expedition to Naples in which they [the Imperialists] are persisting with so much obstinacy may cause much difficulty." To Wratislaw, "England and Holland base all their hopes on the Italian plan and are convinced that the whole future of the campaign and even of the war depends upon it." To Sinzendorf, the Imperial Ambassador at The Hague, on June 6, "The maritime powers have set their hearts upon the entry into France, and it is there that they expect the greatest fortune that can come to the high allies to restore our affairs."

Although the nominal command rested with the Duke of Savoy, everything turned upon Eugene. Eugene was a land animal, a denizen of Central Europe. He did not understand the sea; what he knew of it he disliked and distrusted. He had no comprehension of amphibious strategy. But the attitude of the Vienna Government with which he was himself bound up also reacted upon him. He knew they had been forced into the plan by Marlborough. The Empire had no army of its own worthy of the name in Italy. It was as feeble and ragged on the Po as on the Rhine. But twenty-eight thousand Germanic troops, to be revived by the Sea Powers with nearly fifteen thousand recruits, were a force upon which they might ride, if not to victory in the South of France, at least to annexation in the South of Italy. The threat of withdrawing these twenty-eight thousand northern soldiers had compelled them to consent to the Toulon enterprise. They resented both the menace and the task; and Eugene to some extent shared their mood. Thus we see before Toulon a Prince Eugene different from any of the gleaming pictures with which he illuminated the warfare of his age. We shall show how in 1708 Marlborough, worn down, leaned upon Eugene and was in a dark hour sustained by him; but now in 1707 it must stand on record that the ever-glorious prince and warrior who with his own dauntless heart constituted the fighting power of the Holy Roman Empire allowed himself to fall below the level of the event.

We therefore have the spectacle of Marlborough inspiring Shovell, and Shovell trying to animate Eugene: of a half-hearted military command and an overflowing fleet stimulus. Shovell was obliged by the agreement to furnish large specified quantities of powder and shot. But he never considered these limits. He would land more than a hundred guns for the siege. Most of his marines had been dropped in Spain to plug the gap of Almanza; but he proffered his seamen. Forty rounds a gun was considered the lowest reserve tolerable in an English fleet; Shovell cut it down to thirty-five without express authority. Acting on Marlborough's suggestion, he sent to Leghorn and Genoa to purchase ammunition. He pledged his own personal credit pending sanction from the Treasury. Throughout the operation the Navy never failed to give more material aid than was contracted beforehand or asked under necessity. The spirit of the Admiral and his stubborn, audacious counsels thrust themselves upon the Duke of Savoy and still more upon Prince Eugene. At every moment he was at hand to aid, to encourage, to reassure. In our history the Navy has sometimes stood by to watch the Army do the work. Here was a case where a navy tried by its exertion and sacrifice to drive forward an army. It did not succeed.

Marlborough's wish and endeavour were to begin the advance against Toulon in early May. But many insuperable obstacles intervened. The snow melted late upon the passes; both the Imperialists and the Duke of Savoy were behindhand with their preparations; and even the allied fleet, delayed in Spain, did not "come on to the coast" till the middle of June. In spite of this and of the lengthy and embittered discussions between the Allies, no hint of the Toulon plan had reached Versailles till June 10, when it was reported that Eugene would shortly march on Nice. It was the end of the month before it was recognized that Toulon was the allied aim, and that Provence and not Dauphiné was threatened. Toulon was at this moment an easy prey. Its defences were neglected; its garrison less than eight thousand men. Forthwith Marshal Tessé, leaving the forces on the coast to delay the advance, began to concentrate all his available troops upon Toulon, and set to work to fortify an extended position north-east of the city.

Eugene, having feinted at Susa, began his march on June 30 with about thirty-five thousand men. Of these scarcely a sixth were provided by the Empire. Over eight thousand Imperialists under General Daun, the defender of Turin, were slowly wending their way down the leg of Italy towards Naples amid the protests of the Papal States. The first charge on whatever recruits, supplies, and transport the Empire could procure had been for Naples. All the engagements which the Imperial Ministers had signed with the Sea Powers, particularly England, about the supplies of food, powder, shot, mules and horses, had hopelessly collapsed. Every attempt to borrow money on the Imperial credit had failed. Eugene's letters to the Emperor are a painful exposure of military and financial prostration. On his side, however, stood the redoubtable German mercenaries of the Sea Powers. There were the ardent Savoyards who followed their Duke; and there was the fleet and Sir Cloudesley Shovell, upon whom all burdens could be thrown, and by whom nearly all were accepted.

It was under these depressing auspices that Eugene came down through the Alps, reached the sea, and marched along the Riviera through Nice and Cannes. The picture presented to modern eyes of shores lined with endless pleasure cities, villas, and gardens, and striped with mighty causeways at every level, affords no suggestion of the stern country that confronted Prince Eugene. Only one ill-kept road wound its way across the innumerable spurs and watercourses with which the mountains meet the sparkling sea. Primitive hamlets of goatherds or fisher-folk offered neither food nor shelter to an army. Small, impoverished coastal towns, few and far between, scowled from amid their fortifications upon open roadsteads, with here and there perhaps a jetty or a quay; and the Mediterranean, for all its smiles, afflicted a sailing fleet with constant uncertainty and frequent peril.

On July 11 Eugene came in contact with the French delaying force in redoubts behind the Var. The English fleet with its Dutch squadron had kept pace with the army. Shovell now stood in, and four ships of the line, one of seventy guns, sailed into the mouth of the river and bombarded in flank the seaward works. These, speedily abandoned, were occupied by landing parties of seamen, while at the same time the advanced troops of Eugene's army forced the passage inland.

After the Var only seventy miles now stood between the Allies and Toulon. For an army whose artillery and supplies were largely carried by sea a week's marching should have sufficed. Actually a fortnight was consumed. "It was the opinion of almost every officer," wrote Chetwynd to Marlborough a month later, "that if before coming to Toulon, we had not been so dilatory and cautious, we might have done a great deal." It was not until July 26 that the allied army and fleet arrived before Tessé's new lines at Toulon. The Marshal had managed to gather about twenty thousand men for their defence, the last of whom only reached their position some days after the Allies.

Now came the crux. The Admiral proposed the immediate storm of the newly constructed and still only partially garrisoned defences. Victor Amadeus appeared favourable, but, though nominally in chief command, he threw the burden upon Prince Eugene. A year before he and Eugene with barely twenty thousand men had not hesitated to attack the French lines before Turin, although there were on the spot or in the neighbourhood more than fifty thousand enemy troops. At Toulon these proportions were almost reversed. There were the same

Prussians, Hanoverians, and Saxe-Gothas—all at their full strength. There was now besides the mighty fleet: fifty battleships with a score of ancillary vessels. Moreover, every day's delay meant the arrival of French reinforcements and the strengthening of their fortifications. Should the signal be given?

Eugene refused. All the dislike he had for the enterprise, all his misgivings, broke forth. The place was no longer lightly defended. The enemy were there in strength. Surprise had miscarried. Prudence commanded immediate retreat before the army was cut off from Italy by a French descent through a choice of passes upon its communications. A council was held at headquarters. Shovell reacted vigorously. He renewed the assurances he had already given at Nice. Why fear for the line of supply? He would feed the army from the sea. Why fear for the line of retreat? The cavalry could ride away, and he would embark all the infantry in his ships and land them on the Italy side at any intercepting position which the French might occupy. Grave, tense debate! Finally a compromise; no grand onslaught, but an attack upon the lines by bombardment and local assaults. Trenches were accordingly opened, and a dead-lift effort began.

The section of the defences resting upon the height of St Catherine was stormed on July 30, not without severe casualties, and a first parallel of the attacking works was completed by August 7.

Properly speaking, it was no siege, but only an attack by the fleet and one field army upon the fortified position of another.

For a while the fierce and costly fighting for the outworks of Toulon flowed forth and back as the days drew into weeks, and all the bombardments of Shovell's landed cannon of the fleet could not master the adverse tide. The strategic excellence of the Toulon design made itself only the more intelligible. Louis XIV and those who sat around him could not see the deep divisions and underlying despondency in the allied camp before Toulon. What they weighed with increasing clarity were the consequences of its fall. They saw, in fact, what Marlborough had seen. They put the same value upon it as he did. Both the high centres from which the war was directed now measured with the same rod. The Versailles Council, through the difficulties of communication, were from three weeks to a month behindhand in their power of intervention. But as soon as they knew that a violent struggle was proceeding on the heights to the east of Toulon, and that the fate of the harbour hung in the balance, they laid their hands on every other theatre and clawed troops away even from the most urgent need. Exactly what Marlborough had foreseen and predicted happened. First of all they denuded Spain. Marshal Berwick in the full exploitation of Almanza was ordered on August 18 to gather his troops and quit the Peninsula, recross the Pyrenees, and march to the succour of Toulon. The foolish descent, prayed for by the Empire, of five thousand men at Barcelona would not have shifted a French battalion out of Spain. The attack upon Toulon denuded Spain of French troops. The remnants of the allied forces were suddenly conscious that everywhere pressure upon them was relieved.

On August 15 a French counter-stroke expelled the Allies from the heights of St Catherine, which they had gained on July 30. The gallant Prince of Saxe-Gotha, who had led the right wing at Turin a year before, was killed. By the 20th it was resolved to retreat. There were the recriminations usual in failure.

But all was over.

The fleet embarked the sick, wounded, and artillery in its transports. Before he sailed away Shovell determined to attack the French fleet in the dockyard basins from the sea. Battleships had already prepared the way for bombardment: they had cannonaded the batteries that prevented the approach of their vulnerable bomb vessels, and had landed men to spike the deserted guns. On August 21, the first day calm enough for bombarding, Rear-Admiral Sir Thomas Dilkes anchored the flotilla of bomb-ketches near the shore. That afternoon and throughout the night under his direction they hove shells and explosive carcasses over the neck of land into the dockyard, setting ships and storehouses alight. What was thought in those days to be immense damage was done, and Toulon was shrouded in the smoke of many fires. That same night the army retreated along the coast in five columns. They were neither pursued nor intercepted. They crossed the Var on the 31st, reached Pignerol about the middle of September, and with the object of securing a more favourable line of advance in another year wound up the campaign with the siege and capture of Susa.

Thus ended the memorable effort against Toulon. The design and will-power were Marlborough's and the impulse English: but nothing could prevail against the selfish divergencies of the Empire or the signs of oppression which seemed to rest throughout upon Prince Eugene.

No one must ignore the estimate of the difficulties presented on the spot by so sincere and noble a warrior as Eugene. He may well have been right that the task was impossible. It does not look in retrospect so hard as many of the feats of arms which he performed both before it and after. But it had failed, and with it failed the best hope of redeeming for the Allies the year 1707. Nevertheless good strategy even in failure often produces compensations. The secondary evils of the defeat at Almanza were avoided, and the Allies regained a fleeting control of the Peninsula. The results afloat were decisive and enduring. The French had scuttled their fleet in shallow water to save their hulls from the Allies' fire. When the time came to raise these ships again, all but a few were found to be past repair. Others were burned or fatally injured by the English and Dutch bombardment. The dockyard, its cordage-stores and factories, were largely destroyed. Never again in the War of the Spanish Succession did France attempt to dispute the English command of the Mediterranean, which has been maintained with occasional interludes up till the present day. "The war of squadrons is finished," wrote the French naval historian. "Toulon is safe; but our Fleet is defunct."

CHAPTER SIXTY

Marlborough in Trammels

ᛤᛃ 1707, Summer ᛃᛤ

It is hard across the gulf of time to represent the magnitude of the effort which the siege of Toulon cost Marlborough. Upon this enterprise he staked all his power to plan the next move which the Ramillies campaign had won him. It was his design. His wishes had been obeyed by the Cabinet in London, by the States-General at The Hague, by the princes of Germany so far as they were concerned or were capable of action. Even Vienna had conformed sullenly, disloyally, but still decidedly. So far as lay in his power, then so far-reaching, he had set all things moving in one direction. Was he right or wrong? Would the fall of Toulon have been the deathblow of France? Marlborough's own authority and conviction must carry the chief weight; but Louis XIV and his military circle thought the same as their opponent; and Charles XII from his entirely different standpoint arrived secretly and spontaneously at a similar conclusion. Thus the three supreme exponents of the military art were in accord upon the merits of the plan. But the cost was measureless. A year's campaign must be used; a year of political attrition at home; a year of waning comradeship throughout the Alliance. High stakes for Toulon!

Nothing remained for Marlborough at Meldert but to await the result, and meanwhile to hold the main French army close gripped upon the Flanders front. His smaller numbers prevented him from making a siege; the Dutch veto forbade him to force a battle. There was only the faint hope that Vendôme, like Villeroy, would himself seek a decision. But Vendôme, although from his fortified camp at Gembloux he pressed various projects upon Versailles, was himself restrained from running any serious risks by Louis XIV.

The need for a victory in Flanders became only the more apparent. Marlborough continued to coax and persuade the Pensionary Heinsius to grant him the necessary freedom to fight, without which he could only manœuvre up to a fiasco. Geldermalsen had by this time returned to the army, apparently with Marlborough's consent. His colleague Goslinga continued to cavil and malign.

Thus we see Goslinga blaming Marlborough for sluggishness and lack of zeal against the enemy, while at the same time he had in his pocket the explicit orders of his "masters" to avoid every occasion where there would be a "risk of coming to an action" till news was received of the upshot of Toulon, which might not be for two or three months. It may be thought hard upon a general to be blamed for not fighting, and foully aspersed in his motives, by the very man whose highest function was to prevent him.

The repercussion of the attack at Toulon had been protracted. Marlborough used language which spread over the high circles of the confederate army an expectation that presently Vendôme would be ordered to send troops to Toulon. Even Goslinga records this impression. It was justified. By August 1 Louis XIV had sent peremptory orders to Vendôme to dispatch thirteen battalions and six squadrons to the southern front. As soon as this news reached Meldert Marlborough declared that the hour for action had struck. Vendôme was weakened. His superiority was gone. Marlborough demanded the right to attack him in his fortified camp at Gembloux. He appealed to The Hague. The Hague referred the matter to its Deputies and generals. Goslinga may speak for himself. "The Duke of Vendôme having at last received the order to send a large detachment to France, Milord appeared anxious to use the chance to attack the camp of the enemy, whose strength was still about equal to ours." This should surely have been Goslinga's moment to spur the hitherto recreant Captain-General out of his lucrative inertia. But alas, all he remarks is, "This seemed risky" (*C'est ce qui paroissoit téméraire*). Therefore he, Geldermalsen, and the Dutch generals with whom they consorted unleashed their veto. "Nothing remained," says Goslinga, "but a secret sudden march which might compel him [Vendôme] to quit his unattackable camp. This is what the Duke resolved. I may say without vanity that I encouraged him in it as much as possible, and that when he made up his mind it was to me and Geldermalsen that he first told the secret."

Here was, in fact, the march which Marlborough had for six weeks past been suggesting to The Hague, to the Deputies and the generals. He was almost certain, through his Secret Service and from his calculations, that Vendôme would resist nothing but a frontal attack, and that a movement upon his communications would send him scurrying back towards his main fortress line. He did not hope for a decisive battle. That could only be obtained by paying the high price of a direct assault. Still, there was the chance of mauling his rearguard or his flankguard, and once these clashes began no one could fix their limits. The Deputies deemed an attempt of this kind not barred by their instructions. After all, they could always recur to them if undue risk threatened by ordering the Dutch troops to halt or retire at any moment, which would effectually arrest the confederate army. It seemed a good opportunity for a spirited gesture with restricted commitments. Thus on the late afternoon of August 11 the splendid army of the Sea Powers, the best and largest that Marlborough had yet commanded, sending its baggage by daylight towards Louvain as a feint, broke camp at dusk.

There ensued the second brief series of rapid movements by the great armies which marked the campaign of 1707. Marlborough, marching south-west through Wavre, reached Genappe in the afternoon of August 11. Here he threatened to attack the left flank of Vendôme's position, or alternatively to cut him off from Mons and his fortified lines and feeding-base. Vendôme, realizing at midnight (10th/11th) what his adversary was doing, abandoned his strong camp and retreated instantly by Gosselies towards Seneffe. The two armies therefore marched all day, converging in the same direction. But Vendôme by his promptitude in retiring kept ahead of Marlborough. The former distance of ten miles between the armies was perhaps halved, but in spite of their greater exertions no contact could be made by the Allies. The weather had suddenly become frightful; torrents of rain descended, making the few roads by which these large masses were moving most painful. Marlborough, who had intended to march early, postponed his further advance till noon to give his tired troops a rest. He reached Arquennes at 6.00 P.M. on August 12. Vendôme, who had halted when his pursuer halted, moved on again as soon as the chase was resumed, and thus kept a lead. Still the armies converged, and when the Allies reached Arquennes the French were but three miles away.

Both generals were under veto of the Dutch and French Governments respectively against wilfully fighting a battle. Marlborough's only chance was to stamp on the French rearguard. Such an event might have involved a general action. On the other hand, Vendôme, who might, if well posted and entrenched, have been ready to withstand an onslaught, was bound by his orders from Versailles to avoid this contingency if possible. Marlborough tried during the night of the 12th/13th to compromise Vendôme's rearguard. This operation miscarried, not only because of the general intentions of the French, but also by an accidental delay in the pursuit.

Marlborough sent written orders to Count Tilly to march with forty squadrons and five thousand grenadiers and attack the French rearguard. Count Lottum, with thirty squadrons and twenty battalions, was to support him. Tilly reached the point upon which he had been directed and opened his orders.

> It rained heavily, was pitch dark, and no house near, so that it was an hour before a light could be got for him to read and know his orders, and no guides being there who knew the country and many defiles before him. It was another hour before guides were found, and, it still continuing dark and raining the whole night, he was shy to venture to march the detachment so near the enemy in the dark, so that in reasoning upon this the night was spent.

Two allied squadrons who pushed on through the darkness reported at daylight the French army already in retreat under a strong rearguard of twenty-five squadrons and two thousand grenadiers. Tilly's men doubled for six miles; but the rearguard, using sunken roads to delay the pursuit, and withdrawing as fast as possible, got themselves out without serious ill-treatment. Thus the attempt to pin the French tail failed, and with it the last chance, if ever there had been a chance, of bringing about a battle under the limited conditions prescribed. The next two marches could not alter the relations of the armies. Vendôme moved through Haine-Saint-Pierre and on to Saint-Denis, where he was close to his fortified lines about Mons and where further chase was useless. In terrible weather Marlborough moved on August 14 to Soignies; and Vendôme, resting his right wing on Mons, continued a little farther to the westward towards Ath. Both armies, exhausted and dripping, then settled down in almost the same positions they had occupied in May. Vendôme now drew reinforcements from Charleroi and Namur. Marlborough remained about Soignies, being only able in the continuous heavy rain to feed himself by the stone-paved turnpike from Brussels.

It was with sorrow that the Captain-General surveyed the results of 1707. The recovery of France seemed complete in every theatre. Grievous defeats had overtaken the allied arms at Almanza and Stollhofen; cruel disappointment at Toulon. His own campaign had been fettered and ineffectual. The Empire pursued its woebegone, particularist ambitions. Southern Germany had allowed itself to be ravaged without any rally of the Teutonic princes. The Dutch, angry and disappointed, hugged their Barrier, and their grasping administration had already cost the Allies every scrap of Belgian sympathy. There had been no lack of political malice in England even after the glories of 1706. What would be the temper now when there was nothing to show but vast expense and general miscarriage? In this adversity the confederate armies sought their winter quarters; and Marlborough returned home to face a Cabinet crisis, the Parliamentary storm, and, worst of all, a bedchamber intrigue.

The first Parliament of Great Britain met on November 6/17, 1707. The forty-five new members from Scotland were solidly favourable to the Government, and the re-election of Mr Speaker Smith was uncontested. The Commons replied dutifully and without demur to the gracious Speech. When the management of the Navy was arraigned they listened contentedly to the cogent defence presented by a young Minister—Robert Walpole by name—who had lately been appointed to the Admiralty Board. Not so the Lords: on the contrary, while the Commons were voting even larger Supplies than in the previous year and increasing the army from fifty to sixty thousand men, the Upper House opened a series of debates on the most thorny questions of the day. They declined to acknowledge the Queen's Speech until the state of the nation had been reviewed. They actually delayed their reply for six weeks. Never had such action been taken by the Peers. It seemed, as the Queen said, to deny her "even ordinary politeness." The Whig lords led the way in the attack on the Admiralty, and no sooner was this launched than the Tories came in behind it. The Government was

called to account by both the great parties. Marlborough, reaching England on November 16/27, found Godolphin in dire straits.

*　*　*　*

It may be remembered that as far back as 1689 Sarah had discovered
with some surprise that she had a poor relation named Hill, a Levantine
merchant ruined by speculation, who had four children, among them a
daughter, Abigail. When the parents died Sarah became the benefactress
of the orphans, and provided for all of them in various ways. Abigail, the
eldest, lived at St Albans with the Churchills and their children, and
Sarah treated her as a sister. Thus the years passed. When Anne came
to the throne Sarah introduced Abigail into the royal household, and
during the course of 1702 she became one of the Queen's dressers. She
figured in the list of bedchamber women of 1704. In this post of humble
intimacy Abigail faithfully and tenderly waited upon the Queen in her
daily life and frequent illnesses. To beguile the long hours, she played
with skill the harpsichord, greatly to the Queen's enjoyment. But at
first and for some time their relations were those of mistress and servant,
or of patient and nurse. There is a curious letter of Anne's in 1703 in
which she chides Sarah, with a touch of jealousy, for her friendship for
"Mrs [Mistress] Hill," as Abigail was called.

> Dear Mrs Freeman hates writing so much I fear, though she would
> stay away two or three days, she would hardly let me hear from her,
> and therefore for my own sake I must write to get a line or two. I
> fancy now you are in town you will be tempted to see the opera, which
> I should not wonder at, for I should be so too, if I were able to stir,
> but when that will be God knows, for my feavor is not quite gone, and
> I am still so lame I cannot go without limping. I hope Mrs Freeman has
> no thoughts of going to the Opera with Mrs Hill, and will have a care
> of engaging herself too much in her company, for, if you give way to
> that, it is a thing that will insensibly grow upon you. Therefore give
> me leave once more to beg for your own sake, as well as poor Mrs
> Morley's, that you would have as little to do with that enchantress as
> 'tis possible, and pray pardon me for saying this.

Gradually, however, an attachment grew in the Queen's heart towards
one who rendered her so many small offices.

We have noticed the change in Sarah's relations with Anne which
followed the Queen's accession. They were no longer united by common
dislike of King William, and they had widely different feelings about

politics and religion. We have traced the growing tension and estrangement which Sarah's advocacy of Whig interests produced between her and her royal mistress. At the same time Sarah's habits also changed. She had now become a great lady—after the Queen the greatest in the land. She dwelt at the centre of politics, and with her strong, clear-cut views, powerful, practical mind, and caustic tongue was bound to play a prominent part in all the business transacted by Ministers with the sovereign. In her husband's absence at the wars she was his link with the Queen. Her relations with Godolphin were those of an indispensable Cabinet colleague. Courted by all, besought on every side for favours, united to the Queen by what the world believed to be a tie of lifelong and undying affection, Sarah seemed endowed with power to make or mar. To do her justice, she set singularly little store by the dispensation of patronage and favours. Her interests were in the great spheres of war and affairs; her pride was to manage the Queen for the glory of the realm.

But Sarah had also her own four daughters to guide. She had her pleasant home at St Albans; she had her loving life with John in his fleeting visits, and her daily correspondence with him when he was at the wars. Can we wonder that now she found her constant attendance upon Anne, their endless privacies, the dull, exacting routine of the palace, a companionship almost stifling? Insensibly she began to bring Abigail forward to bear some of the burden of entertaining the Queen. Abigail showed herself apt in this, and Anne made less difficulty about being separated from her beloved Mrs Freeman as the early years of the reign slipped by. There was no doubt, up to 1705 at least, that Anne would much rather have had Sarah with her than anyone else in the world except her husband. Nor can we doubt that had the Duchess of Marlborough continued the same assiduous and unceasing attentions which had been for nearly twenty years Sarah Churchill's task in life she would have kept her strange dominance over the royal heart. However, as the splendid reign unfolded and Marlborough's triumphs raised him to the pinnacle of Europe, Sarah saw less and less of Anne, and Anne increasingly leaned on Abigail.

By the summer of 1705 Anne had become at least as dependent upon Abigail as upon Sarah. Till about this time Abigail never seems to have "talked of business" to the Queen; but she gradually became conscious of the reality of her influence. She was the witness on many occasions of hot disputes about politics between Sarah and the Queen. She saw Anne's distresses; she comforted her after stormy scenes. Presently she began not unnaturally to make comments upon public affairs which pleased the Queen. She always said what her mistress liked to hear. This process became pronounced as the divergence between Harley and Godolphin developed, and here we must note, though Sarah appears to have been long unconscious of it, that Abigail stood in about the same family relation to Harley as she did to Sarah. She was bound by a cousinly tie to both. She would naturally see the Secretary of State in his audiences and on many occasions. She cultivated this intimacy, as well as that with the Queen.

It is not till June 2, 1707, that the name of Abigail figures in Marlborough's correspondence. Evidently Sarah had become aware of a marked change in the demeanour of her poor relation. She felt herself in contact with a new power, hesitating, tentative, furtive, undefined, but in all senses real. She wrote in alarm to the Duke. Marlborough, into whose category of values Abigail had not yet swum, replied, "I should think you might speak to her with some caution which might do good; *for she is certainly grateful and will mind what you say.*" This optimism did not last long.

Sarah was deeply disturbed. Instead of increasing her attendances upon the Queen, using all her arts upon her, and acting as if she were entirely at her ease, she indulged in the haughtiness of offended friendship. She stayed away from Court, and taxed the Queen roundly in letters with departing from their old affection and talking politics with her chambermaid. Sarah's eyes ought surely to have been opened by Anne's letter of July 18.

Anne to Sarah

Friday, five o'clock, July 18 [1707]

I give my dear Mrs Freeman many thanks for her letter, which I received this morning, *as I must always do for everything that comes from her,* not doubting but what you say is sincerely meant in kindness to me. But I have so often been unfortunate in what I have said to you that I think the less I say to your last letter the better; therefore I shall only, in the first place, beg your pardon once more for what I said the other day, which I find you take ill; and say something in answer to your explanation of the suspicions you seemed to have concerning *your cousin Hill,* who is very far from being an occasion of feeding Mrs Morley in her passion, as you are pleased to call it; *she never meddling with anything.*

I believe others that have been in her station in former times have been tattling and very impertinent, but she is not at all of that temper; and as for the company she keeps, it is with her as with most other people. *I fancy that their lot in the world makes them move with some out of civility, rather than choice;* and I really believe, for one that is so much in the way of company, she has less acquaintance than anyone upon earth. *I hope, since in some part of your letter you seem to give credit to a thing because I said it was so,* you will be as just in what I have said now about Hill; for I would not have anyone hardly thought of by my dear Mrs Freeman for your poor unfortunate but ever faithful Morley's notions or actions.

This evidently was not one of Anne's genuine, forceful, effusions. It is, indeed, a masterpiece of sarcasm and polished hostility. It may well be that two or three people sat together upon this and chuckled in exclusive comradeship over its many stabs and gibes. We have little doubt that Harley pointed the pen with which the Queen wrote. Such a letter nowadays would chill relations between equals. Between Sovereign and subject it wore a graver aspect. The relations could not be ended. The sword of Marlborough upheld Britain and the Grand Alliance. His authority and connexions at home were on a vast scale, not easily to be measured. Sarah was his wife. Her office of Mistress of the Robes was as important as that of the Lord Keeper. She and the Queen were bound together and had to bicker it out. All political forces converged upon the point. Besides, in the Queen's heart there still perhaps sometimes lurked a fading wish to kiss, and let old days come back.

At the end of July 1707 Sarah learned that Abigail had been married some months previously to a Mr Masham, one of the Prince's gentlemen. Abigail, taxed with the concealment of this important fact from the author of her fortunes, admitted it with her mutinous deference. It was not until Sarah learned that the Queen had been present at the ceremony and had made a substantial dotation that she realized how closely organized was this inner world from which she was excluded.

* * * *

When we review the situation which the two friends had to face after the year of disaster one must admit that it required strong nerves. The

Queen, estranged from Godolphin, severed from Sarah, bridling at the Whigs, loyal only to the Admiralty; the High Tories in Church and Parliament intent to smash the Government and the war; the Whigs resolved to use the public difficulties to assist their constitutional claims and oust and humble their party foes; the maturing of Harley's profound schemes, St John at his side, Abigail in his hands! But Marlborough's weight and fame were immense. In spite of his own barren campaign and the many misfortunes that had befallen the Allies, he seemed to bulk even larger in men's minds than after Blenheim and after Ramillies. The very fact that things were going wrong restored him an authority denied on the morrow of his victories. When he landed at Dover all eyes were turned upon him. We have glimpses of him at this time from contemporary pens. His levees were thronged as if they were those of a sovereign. He seems to have fallen into the habit, used by the greatest personages of those days, of receiving in his bedroom as he did in his tent. Like the kings of France, though he did not carry it to the same extremes, he made his toilet in public. "Every morning when he is in London he has in his antechamber gentlemen of the first quality including ambassadors and Ministers of foreign princes; he dresses, even shaves and puts on his shirt, in public; yet he behaves in a manner calculated to offend no one, at least by words, and affects a gentle and gracious air with all."

Marlborough's conception of the campaign of 1708 was, in fact, a renewal of the double invasion of France which had failed in 1707. If he could have ordered it, Prince Eugene, with the Duke of Savoy, would have broken into Dauphiné at the head of the forces, brought up again to full strength, which had attempted Toulon in the previous year. He was extremely set upon this, and the reports which Brigadier Palmes brought back showed Victor Amadeus well disposed to the scheme. Marlborough was resolved to stand on the defensive in Spain and make the main effort in the Low Countries. Eugene, for his part, was more inclined to come round to the northern theatre and fight upon the Rhine or the Moselle in conjunction with Marlborough. However, English politics and Parliamentary strategic fancies complicated the problem. Many Whigs, as well as the Tory Party, were unduly fond of the Spanish scene. They had worked themselves up year by year to the exorbitant principle "No peace without Spain," thus vastly extending the aims of the war. They supposed that the conquest of Spain could best be achieved on the spot. They wearied of the severe fighting in Flanders, and imagined the Iberian peninsula the shorter and easier road. They wished to avenge the defeat at Almanza locally.

Stanhope ranks high among the heroic and brilliant figures of the age of Anne. He was an accomplished soldier. He had gained the entire confidence of Marlborough when serving under him in the campaign of 1705. He was one of the Duke's most trusted informants upon Spanish affairs. With his already acknowledged force and ability, he now urged upon Marlborough and the Cabinet a halt in Flanders and a decisive campaign in the Peninsula.

Such strategy found no foothold with Marlborough. He was inflexibly resolved not to shift the axis of the war to Spain. He was willing to recruit the English forces already there sufficiently to enable them to mark time without collapse. He was willing that the Empire should send new contingents; but the bulk of the drafts and all the reinforcements under British control must be reserved for the main army in Flanders. One grievous concession he would make if absolutely forced: he would consent to Prince Eugene going to Spain.

He had written to Wratislaw (November 21), "One sees that the last resource of the King is in the presence of Prince Eugene at the head of the army next year." The English Cabinet was ardent for such a decision. Nothing could be more popular in London. Marlborough therefore lent himself to suggestions of this character which were freely made during the late autumn to the Emperor and to his glorious general. Nevertheless we do not believe that Marlborough ever thought there was much likelihood of Eugene consenting to go. Obviously, if the whole burden of the Spanish theatre was to be thrown upon him, Eugene would stipulate for a strong, effective army. Indeed, he had already written that he would not serve without "a real army, not on paper, capable of acting offensively."

Marlborough was sure that with his authority in London and his influence at The Hague he could prevent any large diversion of forces. Thus there would be no army to satisfy Eugene. Meanwhile, if necessary, great play could be made in England with the Prince's name, and the Cabinet could safely go all the way with Parliament in asking for Eugene's services, which would almost certainly not be granted. This seems to be the key to Marlborough's inner policy and to the voluminous correspondence which arose between the Allies. On November 29 the

Queen wrote to the Emperor asking that Eugene should be sent to Spain. On December 9, however, we know that Marlborough said in great confidence to Primoli, a secretary of Count Gallas, the Imperial Ambassador, that he "did not intend to send troops into Catalonia for the new campaign." This is the decisive fact.

The second debate in the Lords on Peterborough's conduct drew from Marlborough his most memorable Parliamentary performance. It is the more remarkable because, although he had made up his mind what ought to be done and what he meant to do, his handling of the debate was at once spontaneous, dissimulating, and entirely successful. As on the battlefield, he changed his course very quickly indeed and spread a web of manœuvre before his opponents. He made candour serve the purpose of falsehood, and in the guise of reluctantly blurting out the whole truth threw his assailants into complete and baffling error. Under the impulse of an emotion which could not have been wholly assumed, he made a revelation of war policy which effectively misled not only the Opposition but the whole House, and which also played its part in misleading the foreign enemy, who were of course soon apprised of the public debate. He acted thus in the interests of right strategy and of the common cause as he conceived them. He was accustomed by the conditions under which he fought to be continually deceiving friends for their good and foes for their bane; but the speed and ease with which this particular manœuvre was conceived and accomplished in the unfamiliar atmosphere of Parliamentary debate opens to us some of the secret depths of his artful yet benevolent mind. But to the scene!

Rochester opened the debate. The Queen was present incognito in her box "till five of the clock in the afternoon." The high Tory leader embraced the interests of Peterborough the Whig, who had thrown himself upon the good offices of his party opponents. He dilated upon Peterborough's courage and skill. He recounted his services. Was it not usual and fitting that an officer of such rank and achievement, recalled from the front, should either be thanked by Parliament or called to account for his conduct? Halifax, speaking for the Whigs, took a line which would enable his party to throw its weight for or against the Government as they might later decide. He supported the demand for a full inquiry. Several Tory peers, headed by Haversham, followed with open attacks upon Galway as an incompetent foreigner responsible for a British defeat. Then Rochester rose again. He broadened the issue. In the temper of the House he felt able to impugn the whole principle of a major offensive in Flanders: "We seem," he said, "to neglect the principal business and mind only the accessories. I remember the saying of a great general, the old Duke of Schomberg, 'that the attacking France in the Netherlands is like taking a bull by the horns.'" He proposed that we should stand on the defensive in Flanders, and send from that army "fifteen or twenty thousand men into Catalonia." Nottingham, the other Tory ex-Minister, followed in the same strain: "Spain, the principal object of the war, is almost abandoned."

Marlborough had certainly not expected this development, nor the evident swing of opinion with which it was received. He rose at once. Every eye was upon him, and his anger was apparent to all. He spoke of "undigested counsel." He declared that the need was to augment rather than lessen the armies in Flanders. He gave two reasons, blunt and solid. The first "which induces me to object to this proposal is that in Spain most of the enemy's strong places may be kept with one battalion in each, whereas the great towns of Brabant which we have conquered require twenty times that number of men for their preservation." This implied that relaxing pressure in the main theatre would liberate incomparably more French troops for the struggle in Spain than any allied reinforcements which could be spared. His second reason was: "If our army in the Netherlands be weakened and the French by their great superiority should gain any considerable advantage, which is not improbable, the discontented party in Holland, who are not a few, and who bear with impatience the necessary charges of the war, will not fail to cry aloud for peace." These massive truths delivered tersely did not stem the tide. Spain was uppermost in all minds, and Marlborough had not even mentioned Spain.

For the third time Rochester rose. He declared himself astonished that "the noble peer, who had ever been conspicuous for calmness and moderation, should now lose his natural temper." The House was set upon the succour for Spain. "Would not his Grace oblige their lordships by apprising them how they might attain troops to send thither for that purpose?" "The obligation," he added, "is the greater as Lord Peterborough has reported the opinion of Prince Eugene that the Germans would rather be decimated than be sent into Spain."

Thereupon Marlborough resolved to make public the idea of sending Prince Eugene. He excused himself for his warmth. Such a vital issue could scarcely be discussed without profound concern. He would take the House into his confidence:

> Although it is improper to disclose secret projects in so numerous an assembly, because the enemy will not fail to be informed of them; yet I am authorized by the Queen to gratify your lordships by the assurance that measures have been already concerted with the Emperor for forming an army of forty thousand men, under the command of the Duke of Savoy, and for sending succours to King Charles. *It is also to be hoped that Prince Eugene may be induced to take the command in Spain,* in which case the Germans will gladly follow him. The only difficulty which may be objected to this scheme is the usual tardiness of the Court of Vienna; and it must be admitted that if the seven thousand recruits, which the Emperor promised for Piedmont, had arrived in time, the enterprise against Toulon would probably have been attended with success. But I dare engage my word that for the future his Imperial Majesty will punctually perform his promises.

The peers were staggered by his declaration. They felt they had been made party to the secrets of the Cabinet and of the Captain-General. They rejoiced to find how much they had misjudged the policy. The opposition collapsed. Rochester even said, "Had we known sooner how well all things had been managed, this debate might have been spared." Somers clinched the matter for the Whigs by moving "That no peace could be reasonable or safe either for her Majesty or her allies if Spain and the West Indies were suffered to continue in the power of the house of Bourbon," and a resolution was passed unanimously thanking the Queen for pressing the Emperor to send a considerable force to Spain under the command of Prince Eugene. The action of the House moved so rapidly that the Whigs had to be very agile in adding a rider-resolution in favour of also "reinforcing the Duke of Savoy and strengthening the army on the Rhine," and further setting up a committee to cast this resolution into the form of an address, upon which Marlborough, Godolphin, and Peterborough were named to serve, but no Tory except Rochester. Thus was affirmed the Whig thesis, "No peace without Spain," but at the same time there was safeguarded the main effort in the main theatre. The long-delayed acknowledgment of the Queen's Speech embodied these conclusions.

When the Ministers met to consult on the morrow of this memorable debate they set themselves to implement Marlborough's declaration, with which they themselves were in hearty accord. The idea of Eugene conquering Spain for the Allies captivated London opinion. Accordingly solemn appeals were renewed to the Emperor to send him there. Marlborough joined in these. He wrote letters to Wratislaw. He held conversations with the Imperial Ambassador which presented the view of the British Parliament. But all the time he had continued obstinately and calmly to strengthen the main theatre, to prepare for the double invasion of France, and to withhold all reinforcements from Spain except a meagre draft of eighteen hundred men. He submitted as little to the strategic conceptions of the Lords and Commons in 1707 as he did during the march to Blenheim.

On December 22/January 3 the hopes of the Cabinet were dashed by a dispatch from the English Ambassador at Vienna, in reply to their earlier requests, stating that the Emperor could not consent to send Eugene to Spain. The Ministers, with the assurances given to Parliament only three days before vivid in their minds, and the general applause which had greeted them ringing in their ears, were consternated. Indeed, they were furious. Hoffmann, the Imperial Ambassador, was summoned before them. His excuse was blunt: there were not enough troops in Spain to make a worthy command for Prince Eugene. "I must admit," he reported to his Government, "I have never seen the English Ministers in such a state of excitement as over this refusal." Marlborough appeared to share the general feeling, and he lent his weight to their appeals both orally to Hoffmann and, three days later, in a strong letter to Wratislaw. Inwardly, we may suppose, he was able to bear the disappointment with his customary composure.

Eventually, in February, for it is convenient here to anticipate, the Emperor made a counter-proposal. He had recourse to one of those expedients which even now have not gone entirely out of fashion. He suggested a conference at The Hague, where the war leaders of England, Holland, and the Empire should settle among themselves the final plan of campaign. This was found acceptable by all. In the first place it seemed to put everything off for a time. The Ministers could feel that the question of sending Prince Eugene to Spain was still open, and as it gradually appeared that the conference could not assemble until April, Marlborough saw that there was very little prospect of his going. In fact, the procedure adopted after all the political storms left everything in Marlborough's hands under the exact conditions which he desired. Little wonder, then, that on the very day (February 17/28) when Hoffmann received his instructions from Vienna Marlborough saw him, and personally urged him to frame his proposals for a conference in a formal memorial to be presented to the Queen. From that moment he never said another word about sending Prince Eugene to Spain. There can be no doubt that he got what he had wanted all along. But he had certainly been guilty of dissimulation.

The first month of Parliament had been dominated by the Whig attempt to link Supply with the attack on Admiral Churchill. This did not prove so formidable as Marlborough and Godolphin had feared. The Tories gave it only partial and lukewarm support. The more the Whig agitation prospered the cooler the Tories became. Their sympathies were more easily aroused by the distress of the Queen's husband than by that of the City merchants who had lost their trading ships. In the end Parliament was made content by the passing of an Act "for the better securing the Trade by Cruisers and Convoys," which regulated the service of trade defence on the lines which had been proposed by Admiral Churchill, among others, fifteen years before. Prince George's Council had in fact followed these principles so far as the means allowed after providing for the offensive function of the main fleet abroad. After the passing of this Act in March 1708 the losses of merchant shipping diminished sensibly; but this may well have been because the state of the war, especially after the destruction of the French fleet at Toulon, no longer required so great a force in the Mediterranean, and thus more cruisers could be found for the North Sea and the mouth of the Channel.

Both Houses seemed glad when in the fifth week of the session the Spanish question, with all the exciting scandals about Peterborough and the Almanza disaster, came upon the scene and diverted attention from what threatened to become a very dangerous Whig electioneering cry. It seems probable that both Godolphin and Harley, for opposite purposes, were favourable to this development. At any rate, it was from the Ministerial bench that on December 9/20 the matter was originally opened in the House of Commons. The first phase of the conflict of the session was ended on December 19/30 by Marlborough's triumphant speech. The Address had been voted in the Lords; the Supplies had been given by the Commons: the Ministry still held together; and it seemed that the crisis was past. Exhausted, as one may readily believe, by all they had gone through, Marlborough and Godolphin retired to Woodstock and Newmarket for Christmas, and both remained in the depths of the country for a full fortnight.

When in the middle of January Godolphin and Marlborough came back to town they felt strong enough to consider definitely Harley's expulsion from the Government. Godolphin, with Marlborough's assent, discussed with the Whig leaders the promotion of the moderate-Whig Chancellor of the Exchequer, Boyle, to the Secretaryship of State in Harley's place. Thus in the middle of January the whole blast of these internal passions was concentrated upon Harley, already somewhat smitten in public opinion and under grievous personal imputation. Such was the power of the Queen's support and his own following that he maintained an equal and now open war within the Cabinet and in Parliament for nearly a month.

Harley, at bay, marshalled his forces. He assembled the elements of his alternative Government. He drew the Duke of Buckingham into his combination. He persuaded the Queen directly, and through Abigail, to encourage the Tories with the near prospect of a moderate Tory Administration.

Harley's attempt to overturn the Government developed very rapidly. It is to be distinguished both in nature and form from the previous Whig and Tory party manœuvres. These had aimed far lower— points of prejudice for the election, a working agreement with the Ministry, perhaps Cabinet rank for one or two of the leaders. Harley's was a deliberate attempt to upset the whole Government, to detach men from both parties, and to form an entirely new Ministry of the middle. Shocking!

During the week of January 29 the Government majority, even upon a financial measure, fell to twenty-nine, and then to fifteen. On the Saturday a majority of fifty-one was recorded "against the Court." Finally a hostile resolution about the numbers at Almanza was carried "without a division." The House of Commons was completely out of control. In the Lords the Whigs were still pressing the Admiralty. Following this week of Opposition triumph, the Queen "told Mr St John that she was resolved to part with the Lord Treasurer [Godolphin]. She sent him with a letter to the Duke of Marlborough which she read to him to that purpose; and she gave him leave to tell it about the town, which he did without any reserve."

Harley was now sure he had won. He spoke openly of his new Administration and of the favour of the Crown. Nothing remained but the supreme trial of strength. All that royal intrigue and Parliamentary manœuvre could do was achieved. Against it stood Marlborough, virtually alone. No one outside the circle of Harley's most daring adherents had faced what the nation, Europe, and the Queen would do if he were overthrown. It was generally believed, or at least hoped, that he would consent to the sacrifice of Godolphin, and serve the Queen at home and abroad in the new combination. All this was now to be put to the test.

On January 29, the very night of St John's disclosure, Godolphin instructed the Attorney-General to tell Harley officially that he no longer possessed the confidence of the Lord Treasurer. Harley met this formal and final challenge with imperturbable effrontery. He professed himself at a loss to understand what complaint could lie against him. He volubly defended his loyalty and good faith as a colleague. He declared himself the victim of a conspiracy. He demanded an interview with Marlborough. He appealed to him as his patron and protector. But Marlborough had slowly been brought to regard him as an inveterate liar and a mortal foe. He showed that he did not believe a single word that Harley uttered, and he cited with particularity a number of odious but now established details. Even after this Harley wrote Godolphin one of those dishonest letters of injured innocence which have but to be read in the light of the established facts to prove him a base and hardy hypocrite. Godolphin's answer stands upon its own simplicity:

> I have received your letter, and am very sorry for what has happened, to lose the good opinion I had so much inclination to have of you; but I cannot help seeing, nor believing my senses. I am very far from having deserved it of you. God forgive you.

Marlborough meanwhile had been at grips with the Queen. Those who depict Anne as a weak woman should reflect upon the marvellous tenacity of her will-power, right or wrong. Upon her lone head and worn, ailing frame descended the whole weight of the quarrels of her realm. The mightiest men of that brilliant age contended for her verdict. The passions of great parties, inflamed by faction and impelled by real needs, collided in her bosom. The storms which now exhaust themselves over enormous electorates beat upon her. Alone she had to face in personal confrontation the reason, knowledge, and appeal of her most famous servants and counsellors. We can see from her vigorous letters the skill with which she selected her lines of resistance. When these became untenable she fell back on woman's tears. But she would not yield. At all costs she would stand by Harley. When Marlborough declared that he would not sit again in Council with such a man she made no response. When he made plain his determination to resign she answered that "he might as well draw his dagger and stab her then and there as do such a thing." But she would not dismiss Harley. She wept convulsively, she seemed about to suffocate; but never would she agree. Such were the scenes inseparable from the discharge of public business in these antique conditions. Marlborough, with his tenderness and chivalry to women, his romantic, almost mystic reverence for the Queen, must indeed have felt that life was not worth living.

Marlborough to the Queen

Madam,

Since all the faithful services I have endeavoured to do you, and the unwearied pains I have taken for these ten days to satisfy and convince your Majesty's own mind, have not been able to give you any such impressions of the false and treacherous proceedings of Mr Secretary Harley to Lord Treasurer and myself, but that your Majesty is pleased to countenance and to support him, to the ruin of your own business at home, I am very much afraid it will be attended with the sorrow and amazement of all Europe, as soon as the noise of it gets abroad. And I find myself obliged to have so much regard to my own honour and reputation as not to be every day made a sacrifice to falsehood and treachery, but most humbly to acquaint your Majesty that no consideration can make me serve any longer with that man. And I beseech your Majesty to look upon me, from this moment, as forced out of your service as long as you think fit to continue him in it.

No heart is fuller of duty to your Majesty than mine; nobody has more sincere wishes for your prosperity, nor shall more constantly pray for your Majesty's long life, and for your happiness both here and hereafter.

But Queen Anne was determined to see the quarrel through. On February 9 in a brief, tense audience she received the resignations of her illustrious servants. She made some final entreaty to Marlborough but showed herself glad to let Godolphin go. The two Ministers who had raised her strength so high at home and carried her fame so far abroad quitted her presence, entered their coaches, and drove away from St James's. The scene which followed at the Cabinet Council is well known. The Queen seated herself in her State chair at the head of the table. Harley rose with a confident air to open the first business of the day, which happened to relate to his department. "The members at first," says Coxe, whose account is based on Swift and Burnet, "appeared as if absorbed in reflection: half-smothered murmurs were then heard, and the Secretary paused. A momentary silence ensuing, the members turned to each other, with looks of surprise and uneasiness, till the Duke of Somerset arose, and, with warmth, exclaimed, 'I do not see how we can deliberate, when the Commander-in-Chief and the Lord Treasurer are absent.'" Swift gives a rougher and probably truer version. "If your Majesty suffers that fellow," pointing to Harley, "to treat of affairs of the war without the advice of the General, I cannot serve you." It was plain that every one agreed with him except Harley and the Queen. Harley faltered. The Duke repeated his remark, and neither the Queen nor her favourite said another word. The Council broke up in confusion. The Queen was assisted from her chair half stifled with anger and distress amid the bows of her agitated advisers. But even now—this is the measure of her grit—she did not abandon Harley. She showed in that hour in magnificent fashion the quality which had sent her grandfather to the scaffold and her father to Saint-Germains. She would not have shrunk from either fate. Absolute deadlock gripped the Government of Great Britain at a time when London was the dominating centre of world affairs.

The news spread far and wide that Marlborough and Godolphin had been dismissed by the Queen. The effect was devastating. The calculations of adroit intrigue, the hot blood of partisanship, suddenly seemed of no account. The larger values asserted themselves in a sobered London. Both Houses of Parliament—the Commons by a definite resolution—decided to conduct no business till they were better informed of these transactions. The City, with its vast new financial power, was in consternation. George of Denmark, appalled by what he heard and saw of the public mood, and strengthened by what he felt himself, implored his wife to bow to the storm. Even then it was Harley, not the Queen, who gave way. During the afternoon and evening he succumbed to the fury of pressures which bore in upon him from every side. He furled his standard for a better day. He advised the Queen to accept his resignation. She wept; and he departed.

Anne was now absolutely alone; apart from Abigail, with the pillows, with the harpsichord and the Tory gossip, she could find no one to whom she could turn. Then, and then only, did she yield. On the 10th she summoned Marlborough to her presence, and after bitter lamentations and reproaches informed him that he had his way. The dismissal of Harley was announced on February 11.

The injuries given and received in this struggle were of the kind that men do not forget. They seared and destroyed all fellow-feeling and comradeship between the antagonists. In this bitter month will be found the explanation of the ruthless ill-usage which Marlborough was to receive four years later at the hands of Harley and St John.

Thus ended one of the decisive constitutional conflicts of our history. The authority of the Crown was once more definitely restricted. The public interest, the power of Parliament, the force of party organization, all combined might not have prevailed against the will and courage of this wrong-headed Stuart sovereign. For her part, in pursuance of her conviction, she would have squandered Marlborough, the Grand Alliance, and all that was bound up in their cause. But she was beaten by Marlborough's prestige without the slightest distortion of the Constitution, without a vote, without even an address. She submitted only with undying resentment. She never forgot and she never forgave. Henceforth she set herself to plan revenge. If we have called her a great queen, it is not because of her benevolence or her understanding, though both were considerable; certainly not because of her right judgment—but because of her toughness and will-power, and the part they played both for good and for ill in this expansive and glorious period.

CHAPTER SIXTY-ONE

Eugene Comes North

ᘓ 1708, Spring ᘔ

PRINCE EUGENE, according to Schulenburg, said of the campaign of 1708, "He who has not seen this has seen nothing." This remark is typical of the accounts of eyewitnesses of all ranks on either side. The captious Goslinga ends his tale with the words, "Thus ended this dangerous and remarkable campaign, one of the most glorious which was ever made." Indeed, it is not easy to find operations more novel and suggestive to the student of military affairs. We have the two greatest commanders of the age at the head of troops from many confederate states, surmounting the vices of coalitions, beginning under a serious misfortune, courting undue risks to gain victory in the field, and undertaking the greatest siege till then recorded, with their communications cut. We see besiegers besieged while still besieging; preserving existence from day to day only by the narrowest margins and chances; isolated and invested in the midst of enemy territory, yet never relinquishing their prey; fighting on in defiance of custom and season till the end of December; finally overcoming every obstruction and succeeding in every detail against the forces of a homogeneous French army, which never outnumbered them by less than six to five.

It is worthwhile, in order the better to recognize the sequence of events, to set forth the major episodes beforehand: namely, the loss of Ghent and Bruges; the battle of Oudenarde; the investment of Lille; the convoy of the siege-train from Brussels; the French attempt to raise the siege; the severance of the communications with Brussels; the opening of new communications with the sea; the critical action of Wynendael; the bombardment and assaults of the city of Lille; the inundations and aquatic warfare for supplies; the total isolation of the allied armies; the timely surrender of the city of Lille; the opening of a third line of communications from the sea; the French diversion against Brussels; the forcing of the Scheldt and the relief of Brussels by Marlborough and Eugene; the fall of the citadel of Lille; the final recapture of Ghent and Bruges by the Allies.

Encouraged by his success in 1707, Louis XIV resolved, as Marlborough had predicted, to gain the mastery in Flanders. By a hard effort he brought to the field the most numerous army which the world had seen for centuries. Nearly a hundred and ten thousand men, forming 131 battalions and 216 squadrons, assembled during May around Mons. His intention was to give the effective command against Marlborough to Marshal Vendôme. His eldest grandson, Fénelon's pupil, the blameless Duke of Burgundy, having, however, expressed a desire to serve, was placed nominally at the head of the army, and the Elector of Bavaria was constrained to transfer himself to the Upper Rhine. Vendôme favoured the change, thinking that the inexperienced prince of the blood would hamper him less than the able, war-toughened Elector.

Max Emmanuel, on the other hand, was loath to leave Flanders. What Marlborough had foretold in 1706 had come to pass. The cities of Belgium were seething with discontent under the rule and exactions of the Dutch. The Elector felt himself possessed of real influence with the Belgian people. Moreover, he feared lest his removal should be the prelude to peace negotiations with Holland at his expense. The French Court, however, consoled him with the prospect of so strong an army upon the Upper Rhine that by a brilliant campaign he might even regain his own Bavaria. "On account of the disgust that subsisted" between the Elector and Villars, the latter was made to exchange commands with Berwick, who had already been appointed to the southern front (Dauphiné). Berwick, when he arrived on the Rhine, like Vendôme in Flanders, was held responsible commander, with the extra duty of keeping a royal or exalted figurehead out of mischief and in good humour, and of securing to such personages the glory to which their birth entitled them. Neither of them was, however, willing to be a puppet or even a passenger. When we dwell upon Marlborough's troubles with the Dutch field Deputies and recalcitrant allies, it must not be forgotten that similar vexations often afflicted the marshals of

France. Not only had they to endure a divided authority, but also a persistent interference by almost daily couriers from the Great King himself, to whom all decisive issues were referred.

Indeed, once Eugene had joined Marlborough their perfect comradeship and pre-eminence established a higher unity of command than had ever been seen in the war. "The Princes," as they came to be called in the confederacy, settled everything between themselves. Neither ever allowed a whisper of disagreement to circulate. They were apparently immune from any kind of jealousy of each other, were proof against every form of mischief-making or intrigue, and in the field at any rate were in practice absolute. The councils of war were frequent, and many opinions were heard. But once "the Princes" had finally spoken all bowed to their judgment. Without this new fact at the allied headquarters the extraordinary operations which these chapters describe, so intricate, so prolonged, and contrary on many occasions to the accepted principles of war, could never have been achieved.

Marlborough, Eugene, and Heinsius met at The Hague on April 12 to concert the general strategy of the year. It immediately became obvious that Eugene would not go to Spain. The Emperor would not agree; Eugene did not want to go; Marlborough did not mean him to go. Thus the pet project of the British Parliament and Cabinet which had been referred to this conference was promptly dismissed. The theatre was judged minor, and the policy should be defensive. Who, then, should command? This also had been largely settled by Marlborough. A fortnight earlier Stanhope had been appointed Commander-in-Chief of the British forces there. He had travelled to The Hague in Marlborough's company. He attended all the meetings. But it was not Marlborough's policy to send any important British detachment to Spain. Only about two thousand British troops were actually capable of taking the field. Marlborough therefore had procured from the Cabinet authority to pay the expense of a considerable reinforcement of Imperial troops. He also proposed that the Palatine contingent in Italy, seven thousand strong, under General Rehbinder, hired jointly by England and Holland, should be sent to the Peninsula. This was the most he could do; it was also the least. The great preponderance of Germanic troops made it necessary that an Imperial commander should also be appointed. Starhemberg, reputed "the best General of the age for the defensive," was at that time commanding against the Hungarian rebels. It was decided to transfer him to Spain. This implied that Stanhope's military rôle would be minor or nil. However, as he was entrusted with the payment of £10,000 a month from the British Government to Charles III, he was assured of some attention; and his instructions from the Cabinet charged him to "enlarge the bounds" of the operations in Spain by land and sea. To console the British Parliament upon the withholding of Eugene from Spain special emphasis was laid upon the naval aspect of the campaign—namely, the need of capturing a safe sea-base.

It was already plain that no forces could be provided for an important offensive in Dauphiné under Victor Amadeus. Marlborough, serenely unmoved by the Titian hangings, acquiesced at once in this restriction of the southern front. Every one at The Hague welcomed the idea that Eugene should fight in the north. But a further complication remained.

The Elector of Hanover had with great difficulty been at last induced to accept the Rhine command as Imperial Generalissimo. He had viewed the arrival of Prince Eugene in the north with disfavour. He saw himself eclipsed in reputation, and feared—with justice, as it proved—that his troops would be diverted or that his rôle would become subsidiary. Not only because of the difficulty of finding an Imperial commander-in-chief, but as a substantial ally, and heir to the British throne, Elector George Lewis of Hanover was a figure of the highest importance throughout the confederacy, and especially to Marlborough. Nevertheless, when Marlborough and Eugene came together their war-thought prevailed over all other considerations. Eugene at first proposed to Marlborough that the main allied effort should be made along the Moselle and also across the Rhine. Thirty thousand men should be withdrawn from Flanders to Coblenz, making a Moselle army of seventy thousand, which Eugene would command. In conjunction with the Elector of Hanover's Rhine army of forty thousand men, Marlborough's abortive plan of 1705 would be tried again under more hopeful conditions. But the States-General would not agree, in the face of the heavy French concentration proceeding daily on their front, and magnified by rumour, to strip themselves of so large a part of their defence. Marlborough was unwilling to weaken the Flanders army. He could use the frustrated invasion of Scotland against moving his forces away from the sea. He warned Eugene from his own bitter experience that the assembly of the German contingents upon the Moselle would be fatally delayed; and the French would seize the initiative in Flanders long before the Moselle army could be assembled.

Accordingly he proposed to Eugene that, although the three armies should be formed, and every pretence made of an invasion of France by the Moselle, yet at the proper moment secretly and suddenly Eugene should carry whatever troops had gathered on the Moselle to join the main army in Flanders; and that in the few days before the French could bring similar reinforcements from the Rhine he and Eugene should fall upon them with the superior strength of a hundred and twenty thousand men, and force a decisive battle. This idea of a super-Blenheim commended itself to Prince Eugene. The two agreed to confine their secret to the narrowest circle. By these plans the French were remarkably deceived. With the impressions of Toulon strong in their minds, they still feared a major offensive in Dauphiné. Everything that leaked out from Briançon's office in London about such schemes misled them. Completely mystified in this theatre by the allied strategy, they provided a substantial army to guard their southern front and sent Marshal Villars to command it.

As a part of his main scheme Marlborough was still attracted by the idea of a "descent." He believed that practically all the French regular troops were engaged on the various fronts, and that nothing but encampments of militia guarded the long coasts of France. Even if a serious landing was not made he hoped that the appearance of a substantial force in transports, escorted by a fleet, now here, now there, would draw far more than its own numbers from the main armies. We have seen the fate which awaited the troops of the first "descent." Now, at the beginning of 1708, a second force under General Erle of eleven English battalions was assembled in the Isle of Wight with the necessary shipping and escort, to be used on the Belgian coast or against the French Channel ports in conjunction with Marlborough's operations as he should direct. This, as we shall see, played a decisive part.

Thus it was settled that Starhemberg and Stanhope should stand on the defensive in Spain; that Victor Amadeus should play a minor rôle in Dauphiné; that Eugene should concentrate upon the Moselle, as if to work with the Elector of Hanover on the Rhine, but that suddenly thereafter he should join Marlborough for a surprise battle in Flanders;

and, lastly, that an amphibious descent should be prepared as a contributory diversion.

It was understood between the princes that Marlborough might have to fight a battle before the junction of the armies could be made. "We are assured," he wrote to the Queen (May 9),

> that the Duke of Burgundy is coming to the head of this army with the King of France's leave and orders to venture a battle. I shall be so far from avoiding it that I shall seek it, thinking it absolutely necessary for your service, so *that God only knows whether this may not be the last I may have the honour to write you.* . . .

This histrionic note mingles more than once in Marlborough's later letters to Queen Anne. It marks the decline in their relationship. He never wrote like this in any campaign before 1707. Its lack of reserve is excusable only by the crises of the Queen's personal attitude and the political factions at work around her. But the same conditions that prompted the Captain-General to strike the note led the Queen to disregard it.

The months of May and June were one of Marlborough's periods of silent stress. In England the impact of the Whigs upon the Queen had produced a dangerous deadlock. All Holland, especially the burghers of Amsterdam, lent themselves to the demand for peace negotiations, even negotiations to be opened by the Allies. All Belgium was utterly wearied of the Dutch, and its great fortress towns were alive with conspiracy. Eugene's army, as Marlborough had foreseen, had scarcely begun to assemble. The French were ready to take the field with about a hundred and ten thousand men collected around Mons, and Marlborough faced them with 112 battalions and 197 squadrons, or almost ninety thousand, in his camps to the south of Brussels. Indeed, Louis XIV announced to his Court on May 24 that his reports from the armies led him to believe that a general engagement would be fought before the end of the month.

A wealth of alternatives presented themselves to the French High Command. Vendôme persuaded Louis XIV to approve the siege of Huy as a provocation to battle. It was a small undertaking, and if Marlborough sought to interrupt it the whole army could meet him in country favourable to the more powerful French cavalry and offering no helpful enclosures to the much-respected confederate foot. Burgundy wished to march directly towards Brussels to threaten the Dutch Barrier and test the alleged disaffection of the Belgians. Marlborough himself apprehended a third plan towards the coast, beginning with a siege of Ath and aiming at Ghent, Bruges, and Antwerp. His instinct proved sound. For the moment Vendôme agreed with Burgundy's view, and on May 26 the French army marched suddenly by night to Soignies. Marlborough advanced to Hal to confront them, and a battle seemed imminent. On June 1, however, the French moved eastward towards Nivelles, threatening Louvain; whereupon Marlborough repeated his retreat of the previous year by a very long march (thirty-six miles in thirty hours and drenching rain). He passed around Brussels, and reached Terbanck, behind the Dyle, on June 3. The French, again confronted, halted between Genappe and Braine l'Alleud. In these positions both armies lay for the rest of June, the French in doubt what to choose, and Marlborough waiting on their choice and for Eugene. The Deputy Goslinga deemed Marlborough's retirement pusillanimous, and recorded his usual calumnies upon it. But the Duke pursued his strategy with phlegm. At Terbanck he was safe. There he covered Brussels and Louvain, and thence he could move by his many prepared routes to parry attacks so divergent as upon Huy on the Meuse or Ath on the Dender. Meanwhile he contained a superior hostile army; but time was precious.

One discerning eye had early pierced his secret. Berwick had ridiculed the airy plans of an invasion of Germany with which the French Court had soothed Max Emmanuel.

He therefore thought it his duty "principally to watch the movements of the enemy," in order to send the Duke of Burgundy "troops in proportion as detachments should be made by them."

Marlborough was soon conscious, from the way Berwick disposed his troops, of his nephew's suspicious vigilance. Gradually prospects of making a superior concentration against Vendôme faded.

To Eugene he wrote:

June 11, 1707

You will have learned on your arrival that the Elector of Bavaria [advised by Berwick] has sent a strong detachment towards the Moselle, which will doubtless march forward, in proportion as your troops advance, so you will easily judge that for a beginning we can rely only on the cavalry, *with which I request you to hasten in all dil-*

igence; for we can only reckon on a surprise which will depend on the little time you may take for your march between the Moselle and the Meuse. *If the Palatines are not now arrived, you will please not to wait for them;* and as soon as I know the day you will be at Maestricht, I will send some one to meet you, and acquaint you with my projects.

If you can gain only forty-eight hours, I will make my dispositions for the moment of your arrival, and with the blessing of heaven we may profit so well by these two days as to feel the good effects of it the rest of the campaign. *You will order the infantry to hasten as much as possible to Maestricht, where they will receive directions for their further march.*

The two armies have remained in their present camps, and there is no appearance of a change, till I have the news which I expect from your Highness. I have employed this time in making an exact review of the troops, which are in so good a condition that it would gratify your Highness to see them.

This letter is interesting because it shows the relations between Marlborough and Eugene at this time. We see Marlborough giving the definite orders of a superior commander. Moreover, Eugene fully accepts the position. "Your Highness," he wrote, "may be convinced I will omit nothing to press on my march from Rheinfels. I will give you due notice by courier, being myself extremely impatient to assure you in person of my respect. . . ."

On June 29 the Prince started on his 150-mile march from Coblenz with forty-three squadrons and eighteen battalions—only fifteen instead of the originally hoped-for forty thousand—but still a formidable reinforcement. But Berwick was also hastening to Flanders with fifty-five squadrons and thirty-four battalions (twenty-seven thousand men), and Eugene could not hope to be more than two or three days ahead of him even with his cavalry. The impending climax was apprehended in the secret circle at home. Sarah evidently bent beneath her anxieties, but who should reproach a soldier's wife in such an hour?

"You are so kind," wrote Marlborough (June 25), "as to be in pain as to what may happen when Prince Eugene comes. Put your trust in God, as I do, and be assured that I think I can't be unhappy as long as you are kind."

The moment (July 2) had now come to inform the States-General that the whole Moselle army was marching to Flanders.

Having reflected on the situation of our affairs in this country, and considered those on the Moselle, and observing the little probability of supplying the army of Prince Eugene with all the requisites, so as to act offensively and with vigour . . . I have imparted to Prince Eugene and to Count Rechteren my opinion that it will be more advantageous to the interests of the common cause for the army on the Moselle to join us in Brabant without delay, and entreated them to begin their march as soon as possible. These measures being taken in conformity with the approbation of the field Deputies, I doubt not but they will give notice to your high Mightinesses. Nevertheless, I would not fail to inform you that I have just received from Prince Eugene intelligence that his army commenced their march last Friday, the cavalry advancing by long forced marches, while the infantry rapidly followed; and that it was his intention to arrive in our camp on the 5th or 6th, to concert with me the operations, according to our arrangement; that as soon as the cavalry shall approach we shall move directly upon the enemy, and bring on a battle, trusting in God to bless our designs, and hoping that I shall soon have an opportunity of sending you good news.

The ink was scarcely dry upon this letter when news arrived that the French army was about to move.

CHAPTER SIXTY-TWO

The Surprise of Ghent and Bruges

ᛄ 1708, July 4-10 ᛚ

THE hatred which the Dutch occupation had aroused in the Belgian people in the two years since Ramillies had made the former French yoke seem light by contrast. Count Bergheyck, a Flemish noble of high repute, headed and organized a widespread pro-French conspiracy. His partisans prepared themselves to deliver the great fortress towns of Belgium to the French at the first favourable opportunity. In May Marlborough had detected and nipped in the bud the plot to surrender Antwerp. He had grave reasons to be anxious about the feeling in Brussels itself. He was under no illusions about Ghent and Bruges. Indeed, he had stationed Major-General Murray in that region with a whole brigade for the express purpose of giving timely aid to any threatened garrison.

During July Count Bergheyck unfolded a design for delivering Ghent and Bruges to France. The plan was considered immediately both by the French headquarters and at Versailles. Burgundy himself resolved upon the sudden flank march across the Dender towards Ghent. Vendôme thought it too hazardous, and advised a longer détour to the south. But the young prince took the plunge. On July 4 his strong advance forces under Grimaldi, ostensibly foraging to the westward, crossed the Dender at Ninove, and moved fast on Ghent. Simultaneously a flying column under the Comte de la Motte moved from the French lines at Comines to summon Bruges. The French Grand Army broke camp at 7.00 P.M. They marched all night and all through the day of the 5th. At 3.00 A.M. La Motte entered Bruges without opposition. At dawn the French army was crossing the Senne at Tubize. At eight in the evening, having thrown out strong detachments under Albergotti to cover their right flank, they were crossing the Dender at Ninove. Here they learned that the town of Ghent had surrendered, and that the governor had agreed to yield the citadel by July 8, if not sooner relieved. This continuous march of more than thirty miles, part in heavy rain, had exhausted the army. The baggage and artillery could not cross the Dender till dawn on the 6th. They lay protected only by their rearguards.

Late on July 2 Marlborough learned that the enemy were preparing to move, and on the night of the 4th at about ten o'clock he heard that they were marching westward, having sent strong detachments forward towards the Dender. He gave immediate orders to strike the camp and stand to arms. His first concern was to reinforce the garrison of Oudenarde, and thus make sure of a bridgehead on the Scheldt. He sent the following significant instructions to Murray, whose mobile brigade was near Ghent:

> Camp at Terbanck
> July 5, 1708
> Two in the morning

> The enemy detached yesterday in the afternoon five thousand men towards Ninove. We are told since that their whole army is marched, of which we only expect the confirmation to begin ours, all things being in readiness for it. In the meantime I desire that immediately upon receipt of this you cause Sir Thomas Prendergast to march with his regiment to Oudenarde, there to remain till further orders.

Marlborough began to move his army towards Brussels at the same hour.

After a march of eighteen miles the Allies came into camp about Anderlecht, on the south-western outskirts of Brussels, during the afternoon. Their advanced troops, the right wing, lay as far west as Lombeek. We have here a picture which, although drawn by a spiteful pen, is too rare to omit. It shows us the rough side of the tapestry. Goslinga arrived at about half-past six at Marlborough's headquarters.

> We found him ready to mount his horse. He had received an hour earlier a report from the right that they were in touch with the enemy and there was a chance of striking at their rearguard. . . . It was

upon this message from the generals of the right that the Duke had got up from his bed, pale and worn out and disconsolate, to go and reconnoitre for himself the situation of the enemy. We had scarcely ridden a couple of miles when he said that there was no use in going further, that it was too late to begin an operation, and thereupon he turned his horse and rode back to his quarters.

Goslinga followed him thither, and urged an attack next morning upon the French rearguard, which must be exhausted by an extraordinary march. The Duke replied that the ground was not favourable. However, upon further reports that the whole French army was before him in position and might even itself attack at daybreak, he reinforced his right or advanced wing with thirty battalions and thirty squadrons of his weary troops, only just camped after their heavy march. "I was wakened at one in the morning," continues Goslinga,

> by Milord's adjutant, who told me that the Duke was getting up to go to the right wing. I dressed forthwith and presented myself before two o'clock at his quarters. I found him at prayers. These finished, he got into his carriage. M. Dopf and I followed him. It was at the first gleam of dawn that we arrived at the mill of Tombergh [Lombeek]. We there found Bulow with other generals of the right. All were under the strong conviction . . . that we should find the enemy army in battle array ready to fall upon us. Several even in the dawn and darkness, when no objects could yet be distinguished, imagined that they counted squadrons and battalions. But at length broad daylight dissipated these phantoms, and we found not one living soul before us.

A detachment sent in pursuit captured a French baggage column and two or three hundred prisoners, but thereafter came in contact with the infantry of the enemy's rearguard posted in hedges and enclosures, and returned with their booty to camp about noon. It was evident that the French, by a sudden and extremely daring forced march, had carried their whole army beyond the Dender, and that they stood between the Allies and Ghent. They were thus in a position to adopt the third alternative plan, which Marlborough had always apprehended, and to attack the allied fortresses and bridgeheads on the Scheldt and the Lys, including particularly Oudenarde and Menin.

The worst was to come. On the march to Assche the news he must inwardly have dreaded of the loss of Ghent and Bruges arrived. To

Marlborough this seemed for the moment disastrous to the whole campaign. Ghent was, in Berwick's words, "the key to all the rivers and all the waterways of Flanders." It seemed to govern the movement of siege artillery. Bruges was only less important. By its loss the direct line of communication with England by Ostend was destroyed. The fruits of Ramillies could be torn away piecemeal. The climax of the new campaign seemed ruined. What wonder if the Captain-General yielded to an hour of gloom? He was only a man.

Brigadier Grumbkow, the Prussian commissary at the British headquarters, wrote to Frederick I:

> The blow which the enemy dealt us did not merely destroy all our plans, but was sufficient to do irreparable harm to the reputation and previous good fortune of Mylord Duke, and he felt this misfortune so keenly that I believed *he would succumb to this grief early the day before yesterday, as he was so seized by it that he was afraid of being suffocated.*

It was in this mood that Eugene found him. They met at Assche. The Prince, escorted by a hundred Hungarian hussars, had driven on in his post-chaise four days ahead of his cavalry, and here he was fresh and gay with Cadogan at his side. Now for the first time the Army of the North saw the hero of the Empire in their midst. "Eugene had," we are told, "at first to live down the disappointing impression given by his stunted frame, his slouch, and the pock-marked cheeks which sagged in his pale face. Although thirteen years younger than Marlborough, he was called the 'old Italian Prince.' At headquarters and in the heat of the fighting, in deliberations and bold, calculated deeds, in his domination of councils of war and his irresistible power of command, he revealed his worth as a man and a soldier."

Marlborough was overjoyed to see his heroic comrade. He was also very glad to have Cadogan back from Ostend. He had noticeably missed his Quartermaster-General and Intelligence chief during these exhausting days. He "tenderly embraced" Eugene, saying, "I am not without hopes of congratulating your highness on a great victory; for my troops will be animated by your presence." But this was for the public. The two shut themselves up together for some hours with their maps. No one knows what passed. Eugene was certainly surprised at Marlborough's depression. ". . . I did not remain in Brussels, but passed straight through the town to the army in order to discuss with the Duke of Marlborough what is to be done. I have found him also in full march and pretty consternated."

Eugene's Austrian biographer says that

> the Prince was astounded to see such despondency in a general like Marlborough over a misfortune not relatively very important. They were closeted together for several hours, and Eugene succeeded in convincing the Duke that his affairs were not in anything like so bad a state as he saw them.

Eugene's encouragement to Marlborough at this moment is a bright feature in their comradeship. He brought a draught of new life to a hard-pressed man. But Marlborough had summoned Eugene from the Moselle for the express purpose of fighting a battle, and no other thought but procuring it was ever in his mind. It was obvious that a movement across the French communications was the effective answer to their daring march, and the best way of bringing on the long-sought decision. When "the Princes" emerged, their plans were made. Their original design of joining forces and attacking in superior strength had failed. It was resolved to rest the army at Assche for two or three days until Eugene's cavalry could reach Brussels and his infantry come into the theatre. Then they would strike south and west across the Scheldt to prevent or interrupt any siege of Oudenarde or Menin, to attack the French communications along the Belgian coast with France, and if possible to force a battle and to fight it *with Marlborough's army alone.* These clear-cut decisions were endorsed by the council of war.

On the evening of the 7th Marlborough collapsed. He was forced to abandon business. His doctor advised his removal to Brussels. He refused to quit the camp, but the orders of the 8th were issued from Overkirk's tent. "His Grace," wrote Hare, "has been confined to his bed to-day by a hot fever fit, but something he took in the afternoon carried it off with a gentle sweat and he was much mended." Cadogan. with a strong detachment, started south at dusk with pioneers to make sure of the ways. At 2.00 A.M. on Monday, the 9th, the army marched in four columns, two of infantry in the centre, with cavalry on either flank. Thirty squadrons under Albemarle covered their rear and interposed as long as possible between the enemy and Brussels. Marlborough's condition improved greatly in the night, and he was able in the morning to ride his horse in the sight of all men. "In all appearances," says Hare, "he was very well." The army reached Herfelingen, where Eugene overtook them, before eleven o'clock, having marched fifteen miles, and the Duke ordered a halt and camp to be pitched.

Meanwhile the French had not been able to make any use of their leisure since the 6th. They had received the surrender of the citadel of Ghent, they had rested their army, they still lay in the angle of the Scheldt, and obviously believed themselves to have the advantage. After sharp discussions it was decided to besiege Oudenarde rather than Menin, to attack it only from the western bank of the Scheldt, and to cover the siege from a strong position at Lessines. The investment of Oudenarde began early on July 9. About three o'clock it was learned that the Allies had camped at Herfelingen. This seemed to the French command to portend a movement on Namur or Charleroi. For precaution they decided to move at once upon Lessines. By midnight their vanguard had reached Voorde, ten miles short of it. But at four o'clock on the afternoon of the 9th Cadogan, with eight battalions and eight squadrons, had set off quietly from the camp at Herfelingen, and by midnight eight hundred of his men had actually crossed the Dender and occupied Lessines. By four in the morning the rest of Cadogan's forces had come up. They spent the night building bridges for the army and establishing themselves in the naturally strong Lessines camp. Marlborough moved throughout the night with the whole army, and reached the Dender at Lessines at 11.00 A.M. on the 10th, having marched in extremely good order over thirty miles in thirty-three hours. All day long his columns were crossing the bridges and closing up. In the early morning from Cadogan's outposts he saw with pleasure the steel flashes of the French troops still on the heights before Voorde. The corner was turned and the Dender passed.

Finding themselves forestalled at Lessines, the French held a council of war. They could, of course, have marched to the attack, in which case the battle would have been fought a day earlier and upon the Dender instead of the Scheldt, with the difference that Cadogan already occupied a strong position, and the allied main army was deployed or close at hand. But neither Burgundy nor Vendôme, although numerically stronger, was thinking of an offensive battle. They were constrained to raise the siege of Oudenarde. The investing cavalry was ordered to return, and their great army of over a hundred thousand men turned right-handed, withdrew northward by an easy march, and lay for the night near the crossings of the Scheldt which they were preparing at Gavre. Their general intention was to hold the line of the Scheldt, and establish a thoroughly secure communication with Lille, and eventually with Berwick's army. Their sense of security was enhanced by the fact that Marlborough had left some of his tents standing at Ghislenghien. They had no idea that his main body was already at Lessines. None of the experienced French commanders expected a serious event. They might wrangle about future action, but all thought themselves in control of the situation.

Certainly many choices lay open to them. The normal position of the great armies was reversed. The French looked towards France, the Allies towards Holland. Each might threaten the communications of the other. Each could count upon powerful reinforcements. Eugene's cavalry had reached the outskirts of Brussels. Berwick's advance guard was already at Namur. Whichever side could combine its whole force first would enjoy for some days a decisive superiority. Burgundy's stroke on Ghent and Bruges had been crowned by substantial and sensational success. The price of the long French marches to the north and west was, however, that Marlborough and Eugene could now certainly join forces a week before Burgundy could be strengthened by Berwick. In fact, the armies of Marlborough and Eugene were already in strategic relation, while the recent French movements had left Berwick on the balance six marches farther from the decisive scene. The realization of this potent fact explains the hesitancy of the French behaviour. They wanted to guard their stolen prizes in the north; but vital safety enjoined them to come nearer to Lille and to Berwick's approaching army. This they thought easy to achieve from their central position in the angle of the rivers. They held the chord, while the Allies to forestall them must move around an arc three times as long. It was therefore with complacency that they lay on the night of the 10th within a few miles of the Scheldt, over which their bridges were a-building. Even if Marlborough's advance troops were holding Lessines, they had plenty of time to blockade the bridgehead of Oudenarde from the west and thus put themselves behind a secure river line and within two marches of Lille.

But they had no idea of the astonishing speed with which Marlborough's army was moving.

CHAPTER SIXTY-THREE

The Battle of Oudenarde

ᨑ 1708, July 11 ᨒ

As the campaign of 1708 opened new conceptions of the art of war, so
its decisive battle was quite different in character from any previously
fought. Apart from the primitive types of firearms and the slow movements of the artillery, Oudenarde was a twentieth-century battle. The
chance encounter by forces of unknown strength, the gradual piecemeal broadening of the fighting front, the increasing stake engaged
willy-nilly by both sides, the looseness and flexibility of all the formations, the improvised and wide-ranging manœuvres, and, above all, the
encircling movement of the Allies, foreshadowing Tannenberg, present
us with a specimen of modern war which has no fellow in the rest of
the eighteenth century. This was no set piece of parade and order. The
troops fought as they came up on the unknown ground where they collided. There was no fixed plan nor formal array. Opportunism and
hardy pugnacity led the victors. The French High Command never
understood what was happening till they realized they had sustained a
most grievous defeat. And thereafter, also in accordance with modern
practice, they lied zealously to prove that nothing had happened. Yet
the day at Oudenarde reversed the fortune of war, upset the odds, and
dominated the whole campaign.

When the Allies sank into their bivouacs about Lessines, as they arrived during July 10, the soldiers scented battle in the air. Men deserted their duties as escorts of the baggage wagons in order stealthily
to take their places in the fighting ranks.

At 1.00 A.M. on the 11th Cadogan set off along the Oudenarde road with sixteen battalions, eight squadrons, strong detachments of pioneers, thirty-two guns, and the whole of the pontoon train. Although Marlborough's rear had hardly crossed the Dender before dark on the 10th, he marched after Cadogan with the whole army at seven. Goslinga, judging backwards, snarls at Marlborough for not starting even earlier. Those who ride in carriages have their own point of view. Eugene's diary, on the contrary, says, "The army could not follow until the roads had been repaired." "We marcht at dawn," said Private Deane, and that no doubt was how it seemed to him. In fact, not a moment was lost in this surprising march.

This was the greatest day in Cadogan's splendid military career. It was nine o'clock when he reached the high ground overlooking the Scheldt below Oudenarde. His scouts could see that the great masses of the French army six miles away were still east of the Scheldt. He instantly sent this all-important news back to Marlborough, and proceeded with his engineers to pick the sites of the bridges. At 10.30, while his infantry columns were closing up, his pontoons arrived, and the throwing of five bridges began. There were also two stone bridges inside the fortress of Oudenarde. These were supplemented by two temporary bridges in order that if necessary the whole of the Dutch, who formed the rear and left wing of the army, could cross thereby. In all, nine bridges for eighty thousand men.

Meanwhile the French, in complete ignorance of these activities, had begun to cross the Scheldt in a leisurely fashion. Lieutenant-General Biron, a nobleman of the highest repute, had been ordered to command the advance- or flank-guard of twenty squadrons and seven Swiss battalions. He was delayed for some time because the French bridges were still unfinished; but during the morning he made his way into the plains beyond, occupied the village of Heurne with his infantry, four battalions of which, apparently in error, moved on a mile farther to the village of Eyne. He remained himself with his cavalry astride of the Ghent road, and his foraging parties scattered themselves about the peaceful fields.

As soon as Cadogan's news reached Marlborough at about ten he advanced, with Prince Eugene, at the head of the cavalry of the right wing as fast as possible to the river. Indeed, the two generals, with twenty squadrons of the Prussian horse, made a large part of the way at the gallop.

Marlborough disposed the whole cavalry of the left wing as a flank guard to the northward in case the French should advance against him instead of crossing. He ordered the whole army to press on with the utmost diligence. The troops were told that they could surely pass the river before the French. This aroused an intense excitement among all ranks. Forgetting the fatigues of their tremendous marches, the infantry columns strode out manfully. Many intelligent men and veteran soldiers in every rank understood what was at stake. They were also deeply angered by what they considered the treacherous filching from them of Ghent and Bruges. Their exertions were wonderful. "It was no longer a march," says Goslinga, "but a run." A fierce enthusiasm, noted by all observers, and most unusual in those times, inspired the private soldiers. The strictest orders had been given against the baggage of high personages being intermingled with the troops. Such breaches as occurred were punished out of hand. The soldiers hurled the wagons from the track, scattering or pillaging the contents, and overtook their marching comrades with hoarse cries of satisfaction. Never was a battle more consciously fought by the rank and file. Trust in Marlborough, admiration for Eugene, and hatred for the enemy filled their sturdy hearts. "Towards 12 o'clock [actually 12.30] the head of our cavalry of the right wing reached the bridges and crossed by the pontoons at a brisk trot; but the infantry took longer to move and it was several hours later that they began to cross."

Cadogan's bridges had been completed shortly before noon, and all his troops assembled near them. Leaving four battalions to guard the passage, he crossed the river with the other twelve, and, with his eight squadrons under Rantzau, the general in command of the Hanoverian cavalry, guarding his left, moved cautiously towards the village of Eyne. Rantzau's patrols almost immediately brushed into Biron's foragers. Shots were fired, and some foragers were captured. Others carried the alarm to the rear. Biron thereupon advanced sharply with twelve squadrons, and Rantzau fell back behind the left of Cadogan's infantry, now in line and approaching the Diepenbeck rivulet and the village of Eyne. Biron, advancing under the belief that he had only a raiding party in front of him, suddenly saw a little after one o'clock a considerable force of hostile infantry already deployed for action. Conspicuous among these was a brigade of redcoats. The presence of allied infantry in such a place at this time was most surprising to the French generals.

They were nearly seventeen miles beyond Lessines, where the allied vanguard had been reported the previous evening. But much more broke upon him. Advancing to the windmill of Eyne, he saw the bridges and the battalions guarding them. He saw an endless column of cavalry streaming down the hillside above Eename, crossing the bridges at a trot, and swiftly forming on the near bank. Above all, on the opposite uplands he saw dust-clouds of an approaching army. Evidently something very serious and totally unexpected by the French command was in progress. He sent a succession of messengers spurring back to the French headquarters as these successive apparitions confronted him.

His aide-de-camp found Vendôme and the royal princes already over the river, dismounted and lunching by the roadside. Vendôme at first refused to believe the news. He thought it incredible that strong enemy forces, especially of foot, could have crossed or even reached the Scheldt at this hour, still less that the allied generals would attempt to carry any large proportion of their troops across the Scheldt within such close striking distance of the whole French army. A study of the distances on the map will show that there were solid reasons for this opinion. After all, it was but two days since Marlborough had been located at Assche, nearly fifty miles away. But successive messengers amplified Biron's facts, and it is with facts that soldiers have to deal. The Marshal, whose temper had been rising under the pressure of unwelcome news, at length got up furiously from the improvised table and mounted his horse. "If they are there," he exclaimed, "the devil must have carried them. Such marching is impossible!" But when he looked across the rolling plain to the southward he too saw the dust-clouds from Marlborough's marching columns. These showed the heads of the allied main body only a mile or two from the bridges. So far, however, it seemed that only their vanguard had crossed. He sent Biron's aide-de-camp back with an order to attack at once, adding that he would come himself and support him with ample forces. Telling the princes to follow gently with the main body now across the river and close at hand, he rode in no great haste to the head of the leading columns, composed of the cavalry of the right wing, and turned them in Biron's direction.

It must have been at least half-past one before Biron's third aide-de-camp aroused Vendôme to his danger. By that time Marlborough and Eugene had crossed in person with the Prussian horse, and the Duke himself was posting a six-gun battery on Cadogan's left behind the village of Schaerken.

When Biron received Vendôme's order he was hardly in a position to execute it. The hostile front had broadened; it now extended almost to Schaerken village, behind which the battery of cannon was now visible. It was protected by the marshy rivulet of the Diepenbeck. The enclosures and hedgerows behind Eyne and about Schaerken were lined with enemy infantry. Their strength across the river was increasing every moment, and large bodies of cavalry were now formed on the slopes above Bevere. Biron did not know the ground, and was evidently outnumbered.

After another quarter of an hour Vendôme was seen approaching along the Ghent road at the head of considerable forces of horse and foot. He asked why Biron had not attacked as ordered. Puységur, a Lieutenant-General of high reputation, intervened. He declared that a morass lay between them and the enemy, and as he was supposed to have unique personal knowledge of the ground his judgment prevailed. Vendôme, still more angry, submitted. He withdrew his reinforcement west of the Ghent road, leaving Biron's seven battalions in Eyne and Heurne unsupported.

While this was passing Burgundy, "following gently" at the head of the main body of the army, began to descend the slopes towards the Norken stream; and, seeing that no action was in progress, and that Vendôme's squadrons were halted or moving westward, he and his advisers decided not to cross the Norken, but to draw up the army in order of battle along the high ground behind it with the centre about Huysse. This was accordingly done. In the circumstances, with no special instructions and having regard to the ponderous masses moving steadily behind him, this seems to have been a prudent measure. It must have been half-past three before the movement was completed. Vendôme, who was certainly no more than a mile away, does not seem to have made any attempt to prevent this deflection of the army. It was, however, essentially a refusal of battle, and inconsistent with any idea of driving the allied vanguard into the Scheldt. Moreover, it left Biron's seven battalions, particularly the four in Eyne, most perilously detached and exposed to Cadogan's assault.

It was a quarter to three. Although the Allies were morally they were not yet physically committed to the hazardous operation of crossing the deep, broad river, and forming on the other bank in the face of a superior enemy. There was still time to withdraw Cadogan. But the moment of final choice had come. Argyll and the leading corps, including all the British infantry, had reached the bridges. The hesitating movements of the French, their unaccountable delays, their deployment behind the Norken, confirmed Marlborough's resolve. With Eugene at his side in resolute accord, he allowed his dusty, ardent redcoats to trample across the pontoons. At this moment, when the main action was about to begin, these infantry had marched over fifty miles in sixty hours. For the Allies the die was cast; but even now the French could refuse battle. If they were content to let Marlborough dominate the region between the Scheldt and the Lys, and themselves to stand where they were to cover Ghent, no general attack could be made upon them that day. But their great opponents were playing confidently and high.

No record exists of any order sent to Cadogan; but it is certain that he acted in the very closest concert with his chief. He now called up his fourth brigade, no longer needed at the bridgehead, and at 3.00 P.M., with his whole force of sixteen battalions and Rantzau's cavalry guarding his left, advanced to storm the village of Eyne.

Sabine's British brigade was in the centre opposite the village. In perfect order, with shouldered arms, they moved slowly forward without firing a shot; nor did they bring their bayonets to the charge until they were within twenty yards of the Swiss who lined the enclosures. There was a roar of musketry, and the battle of Oudenarde began. The Swiss brigade, feeling themselves forgotten or abandoned by the French army, now nearly three miles away, left alone far from any help, made practically no resistance. Three battalions out of four surrendered at once. The fourth sought to retreat along the road to Heurne. But Rantzau's squadrons, circling around the western outskirts of the village, rode in upon them, broke them up, and cut them down. At this grisly spectacle the three battalions in Heurne, who had advanced some distance to support their comrades, fled in disorder beyond the Norken.

Rantzau now saw before him in the open plain Biron's twelve French squadrons. With him was the young Electoral Prince, the future King George II, and a group of daring notables. Rantzau charged the twelve French squadrons. These good troops, oppressed by the destruction of the Swiss, feeling no firm grip behind them to counter the aggressive will-power of the enemy, were broken and scattered by the Hanoverian charge. They all fled towards the main French army. The cavalry of its left wing, or rearguard, was slowly defiling across the front to take their positions in the battle array drawing up beyond the Norken. Into their left flank suddenly drove a disorderly crowd of fugitives, and behind them Rantzau and his eight squadrons still in hand and in good order. In hot blood no doubt, but as a definite military decision, Rantzau charged into the whole cavalry of the French left wing. There was a wild confusion. Prince George's horse was shot. The squadron commander with whom he rode, Colonel Loseke, gave him his own, and was himself killed as he helped the Prince to remount. Many French squadrons, unable under the impact to wheel left into line, were thrown into disorder. Numbers speedily prevailed. A French battery between Mullem and the Ghent road came into action. A dozen squadrons advanced at the gallop. Nevertheless Rantzau got out of the mêlée with surprisingly small loss, carrying with him a mortally wounded colonel, numerous officer prisoners, ten standards, kettle-drums, and horses.

This audacious and affronting exploit, much of which was plainly visible to the proud army of France, brought on the general battle. It was an insult not to be borne. Those who had previously favoured caution now clamoured for revenge. The mood was valiant, but the hour was late, the ground unstudied, the plan unformed, and the leadership divided.

At four o'clock the French, more from impulse than design, began to advance from behind the Norken to the attack. Burgundy sent sixteen squadrons under Grimaldi to reconnoitre the approaches to Cadogan's left. This movement, if the prelude to a general attack, was most dangerous to the Allies. Fortunately the ground was difficult and broken. Farms and enclosures, small woods, avenues of poplars, and above all three rivulets, of which the chief was the Diepenbeck, with their surrounding thickets and boggy patches, arrested Grimaldi, who reported that the ground was unfit for cavalry, and was held in strength, and that infantry alone would serve. He withdrew towards the mill of Royegem. From the ladder-ways of this large structure, which itself stands on a small eminence, a fair view of the country towards Oudenarde is offered. Here Burgundy and his younger brother, Berri, and the Pretender, the Chevalier de St George, gathered with their staffs and suites.

Practically the whole of the French infantry of the right wing had now crossed successfully the Norken and were now entering the entangled country on a broad front. This formidable movement was necessarily slow, but at present there were no troops to resist it. Unless it could be stopped it would be fatal. Burgundy ordered six battalions to drive the Prussians from Groenewald. A fierce fire-fight at close quarters along the hedgerows began. The Prussians made good their defence against heavy odds. The six French battalions recoiled in some disorder. The loud, increasing fusillade drew Vendôme to the spot. He would better have discharged his duties as a commander had he joined the princes on the steps of Royegem mill. Instead he plunged into the local conflict. He rallied the six battalions; he brought up another six, drawn from the French centre, along the road from Mullem, and ordered a renewed attack.

All Cadogan's sixteen battalions were now in line about Groenewald and behind the rivulet towards Schaerken. Cadogan found time before the second attack to occupy the avenues leading to Herlegem, even to seize that hamlet. When Vendôme's troops came forward again they found themselves unexpectedly galled and delayed by the flanking fire from this advanced position. After a fierce encounter they were again repulsed. Marshal Vendôme was now in a fighting frenzy. The violence of his nature, which so often cowed or quelled his equals and superiors, determined him to have Groenewald whatever the cost. He drew lavishly for that purpose upon the French centre. Brigade after brigade was hurried forward, arriving breathless. Many battalions were even sent into the fire- and bayonet-fight as they arrived in column. A very heavy mass of troops was crowded upon Cadogan's front. He was outnumbered and hard pressed. His men fought with devoted courage, helped by the congestion of the enemy and the broken ground, to every feature of which they clung tenaciously.

At five o'clock Vendôme sent orders to Burgundy to bring the whole of the left wing into action by attacking to the east of Groenewald and across the Ghent road. Here, where Marlborough had posted them, stood Natzmer's twenty squadrons of Prussian horse and Rantzau's eight squadrons, reorganizing after their charge. That was all. Not a single infantry battalion was available. The ground thereabouts was favourable for cavalry, but cavalry alone could not have withstood very long the thirty thousand men—horse, foot, and artillery—constituting the French left wing.

Vendôme's order reached Burgundy at the mill a few minutes after five. The Prince was assured by his staff and Puységur that the ground was obstructed by a morass. He therefore did not endorse or pass on Vendôme's order. He sent Captain Jenet, an aide-de-camp who had brought it, back to Vendôme to explain the reason. Jenet was killed before delivering his message by the heavy fire under which the Marshal stood. In consequence Vendôme did not know that the French left would not co-operate in the renewed attack he was about to make upon Cadogan. Had he known that his order was countermanded and the reason he could in a few minutes have reassured Burgundy about the ground, for, as Vendôme stridently repeated ever afterwards, he had himself ridden over it with considerable forces only two hours before.

We must regard the paralysis of the French left wing at this moment as most fortunate for the Allies. No one can pretend to measure what would have happened had Cadogan been driven, as he surely would have been, back upon Eyne by the concerted onslaught of overwhelming numbers. But ill-luck does not exculpate Vendôme. He should not have indulged himself by entering the local fight around Groenewald unless he could keep a sense of proportion and a comprehensive grip of his great army. Half an hour later it was apparent that the left wing was still motionless; but by that time he was fighting with a pike, like a private soldier rather than a marshal of France charged with the supreme control of ninety thousand men.

Another mortal danger confronted the heroic Cadogan. Overweighted in front, his right flank threatened, he was now momentarily being overlapped and turned on his left by the advance of the French right wing. This alone rendered his situation desperate. But help was at hand. The Duke of Argyll, with twenty battalions of British infantry, advancing in perfect order, now came into line on his left, and met foursquare the masses of French infantry, who assaulted along the whole front from Herlegem to Schaerken.

The first main shock of the battle now began. Along the rivulet upon a mile of front Cadogan and Argyll, with twenty British and sixteen German battalions and the single battery which Marlborough had posted, fought nearly fifty battalions of the French right and centre. The intensity of the musketry fire was said to have surpassed all previous experience. The troops repeatedly fought hand to hand. Each side advanced and recoiled several times in the struggle, and every battalion had its own tale to tell.

Marlborough and Eugene remained together between Groenewald and the Ghent road. They were in equal anxiety both for their right and their left. But the immediate peril was on the left. All the bridges were now disgorging infantry in great numbers. Lottum's corps of twenty battalions was already close at hand, fully formed in line, and as the weight and breadth of the French right wing began to lap round Argyll's left, this powerful reinforcement advanced in its turn to meet the extending attack. Cadogan's action had long been flaring. Argyll was in deadly grip. The inn at Schaerken was captured by the French about 5.30, and the enemy were everywhere across the Diepenbeck. Here they were within a mile of the pontoons. Lottum became heavily engaged at 5.45, and by six o'clock his counterattack drove the French back over the Diepenbeck and recovered Schaerken. To and fro swayed the struggle. Always the French brought up superior numbers and reached round the allied left. Always Marlborough's infantry poured across the bridges and advanced to make new head against them.

Hitherto Eugene had sat by Marlborough's side discharging, as was said, the functions of a counsellor, staff officer, and aide-de-camp. The critical situation in the centre and on the left required Marlborough's immediate personal control. Lottum's fight was hanging in the balance. But there was another reason which made Marlborough's presence at the other end of the battlefield indispensable. Overkirk, with the flower of the Dutch army, all their national troops, horse and foot, was now crossing by the Oudenarde bridges. This force of nearly twenty-five thousand men seemed likely to come into action exactly where and when they were most needed. They could deliver the decisive stroke of the battle. The fighting front was now developing fast in both directions. Marlborough wished to be on the spot to concert Overkirk's entry into the field. On the other hand, his main preoccupation was still the attack which he must expect at any moment from the French left wing, whose great intact masses of cavalry and infantry could plainly be seen a mile away beyond the Norken. There was a crisis at each end of the line. The "two bodies with one soul" must now separate. At six o'clock, therefore, Marlborough placed Eugene in command of the whole right of the battlefront, including Cadogan and Argyll, Natzmer's twenty squadrons of Prussian and German horse, and Rantzau's Hanoverians. Eugene henceforward conducted the main action and commanded all the British troops. Marlborough galloped to the centre of Lottum's front, and concerned himself with this, and with bringing Overkirk and the allied left wing into action.

Overkirk, with the whole of the Dutch horse and foot, was engaged in crossing by the two stone bridges through the town of Oudenarde, and it was evident that if he could debouch in time he would reverse the position in this quarter of the field, and turn the French right decisively. But Marlborough still feared that Eugene would not be able to support an attack by the French left. Lottum's successful entry into the action and his advance had given a precious breathing-space. A new corps of eighteen Hanoverian and Hessian battalions was already in line behind Lottum.

We now witness one of those intricate manœuvres in the height of action of which Marlborough's battles afford several notable examples. There is no evidence that Eugene asked for further help. There is undoubted proof that he needed it. Vendôme's third attack was actually at its height. At 6.15 he drove Cadogan from both Herlegem and Groenewald. Eugene was at full strain. His comrade felt his burden as if it were his own. At this very moment, therefore, Marlborough brought up the eighteen Hanoverian and Hessian battalions as if to reinforce Lottum's attack, and then ordered Lottum to withdraw through the intervals of these fresh battalions, and march to the right to strengthen Prince Eugene. We remember how in the crisis of Blenheim Eugene instantly parted with his one remaining cuirassier brigade at Marlborough's call. Now Marlborough repaid this glorious debt. There was, indeed, also a high economy of force in the manœuvre. Lottum's troops, which had been fighting heavily, would now march to the right, and be out of the fire for a space before they came again into action. The Hanoverians and Hessians, who had marched so far and fast but not yet fought, would come for the first time into action. The presence of both these forces simultaneously in Marlborough's array gave the enemy the impression of double weight on this sector. Discipline and drill enabled this complicated evolution to be executed with precision under Marlborough's eye. It took Lottum over twenty minutes after coming out of the line to reach Eugene on the right flank a mile away. The arrival of his twenty battalions stemmed the adverse tide. At this moment, therefore, Marlborough had placed Eugene in command of fifty-six engaged battalions, while keeping only eighteen under his own hand for the hard fight on his immediate front. Of this, while waiting for Overkirk, he now assumed personal direction.

At six o'clock Overkirk's intervention in force had seemed imminent. There were still two and a half hours of daylight, and Marlborough might feel, as he did before the final charge at Blenheim, that very great results lay surely within his grasp. On the Danube he had broken the hostile centre. On the Scheldt he could roll the French up from their right flank. But now a misfortune fell upon him. The supplementary bridges in Oudenarde, for some reason not explained to us, broke down, and the two narrow stone bridges could not secure the passage of Overkirk's great force at the rate expected. Overkirk, with most of his cavalry, was already by 6.15 upon the slopes of Mooregem. There was grievous congestion in the fortress, and the delivery of the infantry into the plain behind Mooregem was delayed for at least an hour. Marlborough found himself hard pressed and overlapped in his turn. It was necessary to attack with the first troops available, and Overkirk received orders to do so at 6.45 P.M.

A high control of the battle is evident at this moment. For the first time the whole allied fighting front advanced together. Overkirk sent his two leading infantry brigades under General Week through a gap in the woodlands to strengthen Marlborough's left. Marlborough with his eighteen battalions drove the French across the brook as far as Diepenbeck village. On Eugene's front Lottum arrived with his twenty battalions in the nick of time, and the French were driven from Groenewald and Herlegem. The musketry fire of all the infantry engaged at close quarters in the enclosed, broken country was now perhaps the most intense that had yet been heard anywhere. But a third of the French army had not yet been engaged. Their reserves were enormous. Large masses could be seen moving to reinforce their right, while the greater part of their left wing and all its cavalry still overhung Eugene. The Captain-General could no longer expect the supreme results he had hoped for from Overkirk's intervention on his left. But neither need he any longer fear defeat in that quarter, for the Dutch infantry were now flowing fast out of Oudenarde, and their leading columns, undeployed, were already beyond Mooregem. His dominant thought was for Eugene. The whole of the British cavalry, seventeen squadrons under Lumley, were now at Bevere. Once Overkirk was in action they were no longer indispensable to the safety of the army. Marlborough therefore at seven o'clock sent his second great reinforcement to Eugene. The brilliant regiments which had charged so finely at Elixem trotted swiftly across the field, and drew out behind the Ghent road to strengthen Eugene's right flank against the expected onslaught of the French left wing.

Thus we see Marlborough, himself in the height of action only a few hundred yards behind the swaying, quivering infantry fighting line, having also a momentous hope in his heart, depriving himself first of Lottum and then of Lumley for the sake of the general battle. It is these qualities of perfect comprehensive judgment, serene in disappointment or stress, unbiased by the local event in which he was himself involved, this fixing with untiring eye and absolute selflessness the problem as a whole, that deserve the study and respect of soldiers of every age.

Just as Lottum had arrived in time to throw back the French assault and recover the villages of Groenewald and Herlegem, so did Lumley and the English horse reach their new station on Eugene's right when they were needed. The strain upon Eugene was, as Marlborough had truly felt, almost overwhelming. So bitter was the struggle, and yet so good the hopes that a further advance could be made, that Eugene a little before seven at Count Lottum's appeal launched the whole of his available cavalry upon a desperate charge. "It was only an hour before dark," records Eugene in his diary,

> when the Prussians and Hanoverian cavalry managed to reach the small plain in a little valley, to the left of which they formed into ten or twelve squadrons [actually twenty] on the flank, after the infantry ranks had been opened and room had been made by two battalions.

General Natzmer, with the Prussian gendarmes, had time to draw up in strict array before leading the charge against very superior numbers. He broke the French squadrons. Behind them lay intact battalions of French infantry. The Germans rode straight at these and were received with a deadly fire. Swerving to the right, they encountered more infantry lining the hedgerows. The Prussian gendarmes broke two battalions, capturing their colours; but the command was now dispersed. The Maison du Roi, "rich in scarlet with silver facings," arriving in force, fell upon these remnants. Natzmer, left quite alone in the midst of the enemy, received four sabre-cuts, and escaped only by leaping a broad ditch, "full of water in which a half-dead horse was lying." Survivors of his twenty squadrons found refuge behind the ranks of Cadogan's and Lottum's battalions. Three-quarters of the gendarmes perished. The twenty squadrons existed no more as a fighting force; but precious time had been gained. The initiative had been held. The charge of the gendarmes, as we can see from Marlborough's dispatches and from many Continental records, was long deemed memorable throughout the armies. The cavalry of the French left wing, deranged by the incursion, now saw before them in the distance the seventeen English squadrons in perfect order in their path. Ill-led by their chiefs on this day, they forbore to attack them. Lumley's regiments, now the only shield on Eugene's right, remained by the Prince's order motionless till darkness fell.

Marlborough, with his small numbers all now heavily engaged and without any reserves, could do no more in the centre than hold the line of the Diepenbeck against a renewed attack. But Overkirk's great operation upon the left was now in full swing. Week's brigades were in hot action against the French right flank. The old Veldt-Marshal was already in possession of the high ground called Boser Couter, and a whole division of his infantry, sixteen battalions, occupied the hill of Oycke. From this point the entire field was visible. He saw himself in a position almost to surround the French army. He wheeled to the right and, having received an express order from Marlborough, advanced from Oycke towards Royegem. This deadly attack was delivered by four brigades of Dutch infantry, sustained by twelve squadrons of Danish cavalry. At the head of the Dutch, commanding for the first time the troops of the Republic, rode the young Prince of Orange. He was but nineteen years of age. This was his first battle. Down the slopes before Royegem he marched irresistibly. The French infantry in his path were swept away. The Maison du Roi failed to stop him. At the same time upon the other flank Cadogan attacked successfully from Groenewald. The entire French right and a great part of their centre were now almost surrounded. The straight line had become a vast horseshoe of flame within which in a state of ever-increasing confusion, were more than fifty thousand Frenchmen. It was now half-past eight. But for the failure of the bridges in Oudenarde this situation might have been reached an hour earlier.

For more than two hours the enemy princes had clustered around or upon the mill of Royegem. With them was the numerous train of military courtiers and nobility who enjoyed the coveted privilege of personal attendance. The slopes about the mill were crowded with several hundreds of orderlies, grooms, and valets, holding the led horses of the royal circle and of the headquarters staff. The Duke of Burgundy and his younger brother, with the pathetic figure of the English Pretender neglected in the background, gazed with anxious, fascinated eyes upon the battle which was raging along a wide crescent a mile away to the south-east. They could see from Herlegem, on their left, almost to the castle of Bevere, on their right, the infantry of the two armies in the meadows between the thickets and woodland, locked together in fierce fight, swaying forward and back, charging and counter-charging amid a ceaseless roar of musketry and drifting wreaths of smoke. They had witnessed the confusion and surging masses of horsemen which had marked the charge of Natzmer's cavalry division. Reassuring reports had arrived. The assailants had been driven back and cut to pieces. But the left was none the less receding. The line of smoke and flame was now drawn nearer than the villages so lately captured. Masses of enemy infantry could be seen advancing across the open spaces behind Groenewald, while out on the slopes beyond the Ghent road long lines of scarlet horsemen sat motionless upon their horses as if at a review.

Sombre reflections held the mind of Fénelon's pupil, and gnawing anxiety. Here was the army of France, at whose head he had been marching a few hours before, short of ammunition and in increasing disorder, locked in deadly grapple with an enemy whose strength seemed inexhaustible, whose numbers were growing every moment, and whose confident aggression proclaimed the presence and the genius of Marlborough and Eugene. This was the battle which he, heir to the crown of France, had been sent forth to win. War, yesterday the jaunty boon-companion, now glared upon him with lineaments of fury, hate, and doom. Where was Vendôme? Where was that brutal, bestial, but none the less tremendous warrior who had been placed at his side to win him military glory, whose advice he could lean upon, whose decisions in the end he had been directed to obey? The Marshal was in the cauldron fighting hand to hand, organizing and reorganizing attacks, sending messages which were incomprehensible and orders which were obsolete by the time they arrived. The one thing the Great King had always forbidden, and which Burgundy had above all others resolved to avoid—namely, an infantry battle in enclosed and broken country—was now burning away the grand army of France. Such is the chastisement of those who presume to gain by easy favour and pretence the glories which the gods reserve for their chosen heroes.

But what is this stir close at hand? Why has every one about him turned so suddenly their backs upon the battle? What is this at which they are all staring in the opposite quarter? Who are these troops in ordered lines and masses who are crowning the skyline by Oycke village, and now already rolling forward down the grassy slopes less than a mile from the mill? Horse and foot in great numbers far behind the French flank—nay, upon its rear, driving all before them, their volleys flashing red in the fading light! Messengers gallop up with terrible news, followed by fugitives and riderless horses. The Maison du Roi in the fields by Chobon hamlet can be seen wheeling to the rightabout to meet this new appalling peril. A wave of panic swept the courtly group; the royal princes scrambled to their saddles. The troops of the French right, says Saint-Simon, "gave ground so fast that the valets of the suites of all who accompanied the princes fell back upon them with an alarm, a rapidity, and a confusion which swept them along with extreme speed and much indecency and risk towards the main battle on the left." But here too they met masses of French infantry retreating and dispersing in disorder before Cadogan's final effort. Unhappy princelings, far astray from the mirrored halls and obsequious glitter of Versailles! We are assured by those who attended them that they behaved with courage and composure, that they encouraged the troops, praised the officers, asked the generals they met what ought to be done, and told Vendôme when they found him what they thought themselves. This may well be so. But over their actions, as over the carnage of the field, night and the increasing dissolution of the army now cast an impenetrable cloak.

It is this phase of the battle of Oudenarde which suggests so strongly the German victory at Tannenberg. But with weapons that shot no more than a hundred yards there was no means of covering the many gaps between the encircling brigades. The fish were in the net, but the meshes were large enough to let the greater part of the catch escape. Nevertheless, the circle was in fact completed. The Prince of Orange and Cadogan from the opposite ends of the line of battle actually fired into each other near the mill of Royegem. Total darkness descended upon the wild confusion of the field. Marlborough at nine o'clock ordered all allied troops to cease fire, halt where they stood, and lie on their arms till daybreak.

It must have been nearly ten o'clock when the defeated leaders met in the village of Huysse on the high ground behind the Norken, and on horseback a tragic council of war was held. Two-thirds of the army were in a welter, surrounded by the enemy, and to a large extent beyond control. No one knew how to lay hands upon the remaining third which had not yet been engaged, including all the cavalry of the left wing. Vendôme, habitually careless of his appearance, now dishevelled with the sweat and dust of physical combat, arrived furious with the enemy, with Burgundy, and above all, for good reasons, with himself. What should be done? Burgundy sought to speak, but the Marshal, drunk with authority and anger, told him to hold his tongue. "Your Royal Highness must remember that you only came to this army upon condition that you obeyed me." We have to transport ourselves into that vanished age to realize what Saint-Simon calls the "enormity" of these words, spoken as they were before a score of officers of all ranks. They seem, moreover, important in judging Vendôme's responsibility for the misconduct of the battle. If this was the relation established between him and Burgundy by the King, nothing can relieve Vendôme's military reputation. He had without purpose or reason delayed crossing the Scheldt. He had been completely surprised by Marlborough's march. He had flung the army piecemeal into a disastrous action; he had abandoned the functions of commander; he had quitted the centre, from which alone they could be exercised. He had crashed about in the front line like an enraged animal, squandering the strength and cohesion of the troops, and upon his head rested, and rests, the burden and shame of an easily avoidable disaster.

The Marshal was for fighting it out. A little more than half of the army, he said, had been engaged. Let them spend the night in reorganizing the front. Let them bring up the intact reserves from the unused left wing. Let them fall to at dawn and see what was left at the end of the day. But this personal ardour did not correspond with the facts. No

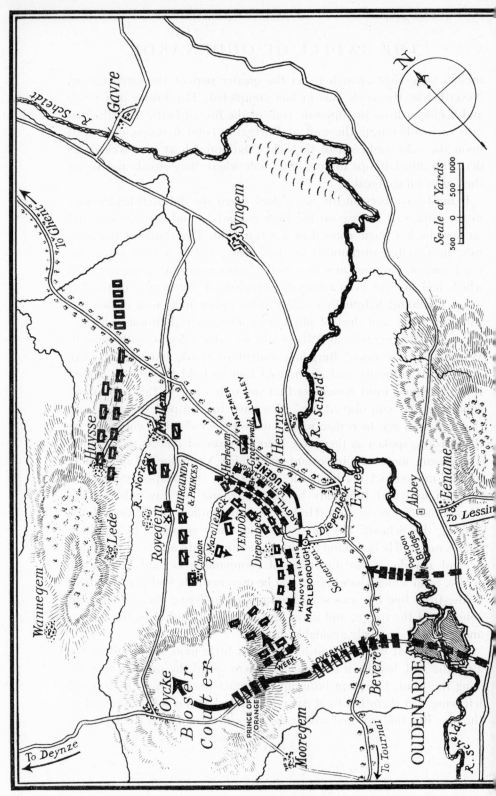

11. The Battle of Oudenarde

one dared outface him, but the silence struck its chill. Officer after officer, Puységur, Matignon, Cheladet, arrived in succession. All declared that the army was in total disorder, and that to await the onslaught of the Allies at daybreak was to court certain destruction. The only course was an immediate retreat upon Ghent. The consensus was overwhelming. It was also right. If the French had engaged little more than half their army, the Allies had fought during the greater part of the day with scarcely a third of their strength. Another third had hardly been in action for two hours; and, according to Prince Eugene, "there were still troops crossing the Scheldt late on into the night."

When Vendôme saw himself alone in opinion, and was also probably himself shaken in his own mind, he relieved his passions in the most cowardly manner. "Very well, gentlemen," he said; "I see you all think it best to retire. And you, Monseigneur," fixing the Duke of Burgundy, "have long had that wish." With this crowning insult he gave the order to retreat to Ghent, and disappeared into the night. Once this signal was given the French army fled from the field of Oudenarde. The brave troops still in close contact with the enemy were left to their fate. The masses imperfectly surrounded could take their chance. All the rest set off along the highroad at their best pace. There had been some discussion whether the princes should be taken in their carriages under escort to Bruges, but Vendôme had dismissed this as shameful, and the royalties jogged along on horseback with the rest. No one knew the whereabouts of General Rosen and the cavalry of the left wing. However, they were in fact marching off with the rest in the darkness. The Maison du Roi had cut their way through the encircling Dutch, many squadrons of dragoons being sacrificed to secure their retreat. Ghent became the only thought for the great majority; but large numbers broke out through the thin cordon of the Allies in all directions. Some fled to Courtrai. Nearly ten thousand men struck across the Scheldt towards the French frontier.

Meanwhile the Allies could do no more in the pitch dark but stand their ground and arrest all who collided with their front. Many regiments and battalions surrendered. Stragglers in great numbers were collected. By a stratagem of Eugene's, Huguenot officers in the allied service were sent into the darkness calling out the names of famous regiments, "A moi, Picardie," "A moi, Roussillon," etc., and taking prisoner those who rallied to these calls. It had now begun to rain, and the victors sank worn out upon the ground and slept on their arms. Marlborough and Eugene remained on horseback throughout the night. Reinforcements were brought up, and at least twenty thousand weary troops, who had not yet been engaged, were guided to their places for a general attack at dawn. But dawn disclosed the battlefield occupied only by the prisoners, the wounded and the slain.

CHAPTER SIXTY-FOUR

The Morrow of Success

ᚻᚨ 1708, July ᚦᚩ

BATTLES are the principal milestones in secular history. Modern opinion resents this uninspiring truth, and historians often treat the decisions of the field as incidents in the dramas of politics and diplomacy. But great battles, won or lost, change the entire course of events, create new standards of values, new moods, new atmospheres, in armies and in nations, to which all must conform. The effects of Oudenarde, both moral and material, transformed as by magic the campaign of 1708. The hasty retreat of the French did not stop at Ghent. They did not feel safe until they had crossed the canal from Bruges beyond the town. Some one—the honour is disputed—had organized an effective rearguard, and forty squadrons which Marlborough sent in pursuit met with a stiff resistance. Dismay and disorder none the less gripped the French troops, and their leaders resigned themselves to waiting upon the Allies. Marlborough and Eugene were united: Burgundy and Berwick were widely separated, the former behind his canal, the latter now the sole defence of France. The French army never recovered during the whole of 1708 from the shock, and the remarkable operations of the Allies are only to be explained by this fact.

When Marlborough rode into the fortress of Oudenarde about 9.00 A.M. on the 12th the fine old square—which stands little touched to this day—was already filled with French prisoners, and they continued, as Hare says, "to come in by droves for many hours." He sent Lord Stair, with whom he had contracted a friendship, to London with the news.

He summoned a council of war for four o'clock and meanwhile, after snatching a few hours' sleep, discussed and decided the next moves with Prince Eugene. The council met in Governor Chanclos' house. Marlborough and Eugene in preconcerted agreement proposed to march westward at once across the Lys, and threaten the French frontier and its fortresses. The strategic situation was peculiar. While Vendôme continued at Ghent he paralysed the whole water communications of the Lys and Scheldt by which the siege-train could reach the allied army. The French frontier was protected by a strong line of fortifications which ran from the fortress of Lille through Warneton and Ypres, and was thence prolonged to the sea by the water defences controlled from Dunkirk. To pierce and level these lines before they could be occupied by Berwick's army was to lay bare the path in France. Such a menace, it was hoped, would force Vendôme to evacuate Ghent and Bruges and bring his army to the defence of France. Such was the advice of "the Princes."

Every effort to minimize the defeat was made by Burgundy and Vendôme to the King and by the Paris *Gazette* to the world. There had been, it was alleged, a partial and indecisive combat, and the losses had been moderate but equal. These absurdities find repetition even in the instructed pages of Pelet. It was some weeks before Louis XIV himself realized the gravity of the event. His army had left six thousand killed and wounded on the field. Nine thousand prisoners, including eight hundred officers, were taken. At least another fifteen thousand men were scattered about the countryside and separated from the main army. Many of these, however, eventually returned to their duty, or were put to some other service. "It is most certain," wrote Marlborough a fortnight later,

> that the success we had at Oudenarde has lessened their army at least 20,000 men, but that which I think our greatest advantage consists in the fear that is among their troops, so that I shall seek all occasions of attacking them. But their army is far from being inconsiderable, for when the Duke of Burgundy's army shall join that of the Duke of Berwick, they will be at least one hundred thousand men. If it had pleased God that we had had one hour's daylight more at Oudenarde, we had in all likelihood made an end of this war.

CHAPTER SIXTY-FIVE

The Thwarted Invasion

✠꠷ 1708, July-August ꠷✠

MARSHAL Berwick had reached the Meuse at Givet on the day of the battle. His army of 34 battalions and 56 squadrons was still toiling by forced marches; but on the 12th its head lay on the Sambre. Here he learned from the governor of Mons that "there had been an engagement on the 11th near Oudenarde . . . , that the enemy had had the advantage, and that our army was retreating towards Ghent in great disorder." In spite of the need of resting his troops and allowing his rear to close up, the bad news determined him to hasten forward to Mons, which he reached on the 14th with twenty squadrons. He found great numbers of stragglers and small bodies who had escaped south and homeward from the battlefield, streaming in upon the fortress. He collected and organized these into a force of nine thousand men, with which he reinforced the garrisons of Tournai, Lille, and Ypres. None of these troops were found capable of further service in the field, and in the French accounts of the campaign they are frequently referred to as "*débris* of the Grand Army." Here we have another measure of the gravity of Oudenarde.

Berwick's sure instinct made him fearful for Lille. Ordering his army to concentrate upon Douai, he went himself to Lille on the 14th to prepare for the coming shock. "I took care to supply the fortresses with all sorts of stores, and as my infantry came up I distributed it among them, in order that, which way soever the enemy should take, they might meet with opposition."

Marlborough's army lay during the 12th on the battlefield recovering from its immense exertions; but at midnight on the 13th, in accordance with the decision of the council of war, the Duke dispatched Count Lottum with thirty battalions and forty squadrons to seize and level the French lines about Warneton and Comines. He followed himself with the main army the next day.

The pathway into France was now laid bare and open. During the afternoon of the 15th Marlborough arrived at Werwicq, which became for some time his headquarters.

Vendôme believed that by holding his key position he could prevent any important siege. He certainly showed remarkable constancy in his opinion, and it was his willpower that kept the French army at Ghent in spite of every strategic pressure or moral provocation that the Allies could apply. Marlborough, however, with his knowledge of the resources of Holland, conceived it possible to undertake a first-class siege, although deprived of the Belgian waterways. Immense masses of munitions and stores and more than a hundred heavy cannon were moved towards Brussels from Antwerp and Maestricht through such canals and rivers as the Dutch controlled. From Brussels all must be drawn forward by road. Two great convoys would be required merely to begin the operation. Marlborough's army had been separated from its heavy baggage since the first movements in July, and to transport this to them and replenish the field parks was urgent. The second and far larger convoy would carry the siege-train and the heavy projectiles. The process of collecting the necessary sixteen thousand horses from Holland and from the armies, and of extorting them from the countryside and from French territory, must take several weeks, and was at once begun.

Both these convoys had very nearly seventy-five miles to traverse through a region in which they could be attacked from the opposite sides by both French armies separately or in combination; Vendôme could descend from Ghent, and Berwick could strike north from Mons. The securing of each of the convoys was therefore a major operation of war requiring the use as escort of all the troops at the disposal of the allied command. The passage of the first was accomplished during July 22–25. Eugene covered the wagon-train to the Scheldt with his army; and Marlborough advanced to receive it from him at the bridgehead he had prepared near Pottes. Berwick, who wished to attack Eugene on the way, was by the King's order held at Douai to safeguard France, and

Vendôme, in spite of Berwick's timely and repeated warnings, remained obdurately behind the Bruges canal.

Critics have asked why Marlborough did not march directly upon Lille, into which place Berwick was daily sending troops and supplies. The first and sufficient answer is clearly that he did not wish to involve himself in a premature attack upon any one particular fortress, until he knew the siege-train could come through from Brussels. He could not have encircled Lille for at least a week, and once the factor of uncertainty had gone the whole French effort and succour would pour in through its open gorge. By moving to Werwicq and levelling the Comines line he threatened equally Ypres, Lille, and Tournai.

This advantage had to be balanced against the undoubted strengthening of the defences and garrison of Lille which was in progress. Suppose Marlborough had tried to carry the town of Lille by assault without artillery, suppose even that he had succeeded, everything in the theatre of war would have become quite clear, and all the French commanders could have acted upon certainties. There is no reason to believe that he could have stormed the fortifications on July 17 or 18 with his field troops. But if he had achieved this questionable venture, he would have been obviously tethered to the citadel of Lille without any of the means of carrying the operation through. Goslinga, furious at the rejection of his plan to blockade the French army at Ghent and Bruges, pours out his calumnies. This needless levelling of the lines of Comines was, he asserts, in part the revenge of prolonging the war which Marlborough was taking upon the States-General for having baulked him of his desire to be Governor of Belgium in 1706, and the rest was sordid love of his pay and allowances. During the next ten days, he declares, no doubt with much truth, the resisting powers of the fortress of Lille were enormously strengthened. Marlborough and Eugene decided to face this disadvantage, but Marlborough had yet another reason for not entangling himself prematurely in the siege of Lille.

In the days following Oudenarde he imparted to Eugene his greatest strategic design. The whole combined army should invade France, ignoring the frontier fortresses and abandoning all land communication with Holland. A new seabase of operations should be seized and formed in French territory. Abbeville was in every way suitable. General Erle, with his six thousand men, would descend upon it from the Isle of Wight. The English and Dutch sea-power would be used to escort and ferry round from Holland in the calm summer weather the whole mass of stores, cannon, and equipment required for the armies, and thereafter would maintain a constant flow of supplies. From Abbeville Marlborough and his illustrious comrade would march on Paris through unravaged country at the head of a hundred thousand men, and bring the war to a swift and decisive close. This movement Duke believed would irresistibly draw in its train all the French armies and fortress garrisons. It would free Holland from the menace of Burgundy's army. It would avoid the cost, labour, and peril of reducing the great fortresses on the French frontier. It would clear or render impotent Dunkirk, Calais, and all fortresses, naval bases, and garrisons on the sea-coast. Such was the secret project of the general who was represented by his detractors as prolonging the war for his own ends.

Marlborough had convinced the London Cabinet. He had, of course, expected a stubborn resistance from the Dutch. He hoped that with Eugene's aid he might overcome this. But, as we have already observed, Eugene was a land animal. He was staggered at the proposal. The dangers of leaping forward to a new base to be formed from the sea, with the terrible fortresses and strong hostile armies barring all return, seemed to this prince of tireless audacity to involve an unnatural hazard.

Without Eugene there was no hope for the plan. "By what I hear from Buys," wrote Marlborough to Godolphin (July 26),

> it is plain that they [the Dutch] think enough is done for peace, and I am afraid they will not willingly give their consent for the marching of their army into France, which certainly, if it succeeded, would put a happy end to the war. . . . I have acquainted Prince Eugene with the earnest desire we have for our marching into France. He thinks it unpracticable till we have Lille for a *place d'armes* and magazine, and then he thinks we may make a very great inroad, but not be able to winter, though we might be helped by the fleet, unless we are masters of some fortified town. . . .

While all this was being debated Marlborough from his headquarters at Werwicq sought by every means to torment Vendôme out of Ghent. He sent cavalry detachments northward to cut off all supplies which Berwick might try to send to the main French army. He ordered the governor of Ostend to impede the communications between Bruges and Nieuport by opening such sluices as were under his control. Strict injunctions deterred the Belgian population from offering their produce to the enemy's camp. By these means he subjected Vendôme to scarcity. It was beyond his power to invoke famine. The French communications along the coast were never effectually severed. But Marlborough's greatest hope lay in raiding the French provinces which now lay open and exposed. He repeated in Artois, and to some extent in Picardy, the same severities, though greatly modified, which he had inflicted upon Bavaria in the month before Blenheim. Using fifty squadrons, sustained by infantry and guns, he entered many French towns whose names have hallowed memories for our generation. On July 23 he occupied Armentières; on the 26th La Bassée, and his cavalry burned the suburbs of Arras; on the 27th Lens. From these positions during a whole week the allied horse ravaged Artois. Crossing the Scarpe, they harried the countryside, molesting Doullens, Guise, Saint-Quentin, and Péronne. In the last week of July he had at least twenty-five thousand men in Artois gathering food, booty, and hostages. Louis XIV, unable to protect his subjects, authorized the unhappy province to compound for a contribution of fifteen hundred thousand livres. Picardy was also summoned. Following the precedent set by Villars in the previous year in Germany, they were invited to fix their indemnity, having regard to the arrears due from 1702. Burning and pillage enforced these extortions, and many violent deeds were done. Berwick, with such forces as he could spare from the fortress line, resisted with energy; there was sharp cavalry fighting, but the French were everywhere outnumbered.

All that happened shows how easily the first stages of Marlborough's strategic adventure could have been achieved. He might have moved at this time the whole allied army into France behind the fortress lines, fed himself comfortably upon the country, and received his munitions and reinforcements through Abbeville. Such an invasion would have dominated the war. The lesser processes to which he was confined, although yielding immediate necessary supplies, did not procure the strategic result. Wrath and panic rose in Paris. Here was war, so long fought in foreign lands, now raging upon French soil. The Great King, who had for more than a generation laid his rod upon his neighbours, must now endure the same measure for his own people. But Vendôme stubbornly insisted that so long as he held the waterways at Ghent and strangled the Scheldt-Lys no great siege could be undertaken by the

Allies, nor any lasting invasion. He induced Louis XIV to bear the woes of his subjects with fortitude. He clung to his invaluable position. He could even retaliate to some extent by harrying the Dutch province of the Pays de Waes, which was in his grip. If the siege of Lille was to be attempted Marlborough's incursion could only be temporary. He would need all his troops to bring the convoys through. By the early days of August therefore this bitter phase of the war subsided. Marlborough's garrisons still held La Bassée, Armentières, and Lens, but his whole strength was required to receive the great convoy from Eugene.

We must regard the refusal of the Allies to accept Marlborough's scheme for the invasion of France at this juncture as one of the cardinal points of the war. Although Louis had borne the injuries and humiliations which Marlborough had thus far inflicted upon him, the strain was near breaking-point. He forbade Berwick to quit Douai and attack the convoy. He warned Burgundy on July 30, "If the enemy resolve to cross the Somme or the Authie you should not hesitate for one moment to march towards them, taking none the less all proper measures in concert with Marshal Berwick."

Thus it is certain that the spell would have worked had Marlborough been allowed to use it. If his strategy had prevailed, not only would Ghent have been freed, but all the French armies and garrisons would have been recalled to defend the capital and to confront the invasion. Great battles would have been fought in the heart of France, and victory would have provided in 1708 that triumphant peace which after so much further bloodshed the Grand Alliance was still to seek in vain.

The question arises, ought not Marlborough to have been able to enforce his conception upon Eugene and the Dutch? He had the English Cabinet behind him. The Whigs were ardent to carry the war into France. Godolphin, faithful and trusting, was still at the helm. If Eugene had been gained the Dutch could hardly have demurred. But Marlborough's admiration for Eugene, his respect for his vast experience and mastery of the art of war, made it impossible for him to force Eugene beyond his will. In the previous year he had tried to press him unduly about Toulon. It had not succeeded. Indeed, when Eugene differed from him he may well have questioned his own instinct. His infinite labours, the stresses to which he was being subjected at home, and the physical weakness and weariness which lay heavy upon him in this campaign constrained him to acquiesce, and the supreme opportunity was gone, as fate decreed, for ever. " . . . As I think," he wrote sadly on another miscarriage at this date (August 2), "most things are governed by Destiny, having done all that is possible, one should submit with patience."

The great convoy had now assembled at Brussels. The sixteen thousand horses had been procured. Every district of Belgium and France in Marlborough's control had been compelled under threats of fire and sword to deliver every suitable horse or vehicle. In vain had Berwick ordered all horses to be brought into the French fortress. The threat of military execution was decisive upon the country folk, who were under the hard impression of the ravages in Artois and Picardy only a week before. They had to choose between yielding their horses and having their homes burned. Louis XIV could not ask this sacrifice of subjects he could no longer protect.

At length the moment came.

On August 4 Eugene left Marlborough's headquarters at Werwicq for Ath, where the bulk of his own army was concentrated. Marlborough sent him in addition twenty-five squadrons and twenty-five battalions. Together with the escort of the convoy numbering thirty-five squadrons under the Prince of Hesse-Cassel, who guarded the opposite flank to Eugene, and a powerful rearguard, Eugene disposed of more than fifty thousand men. Thus covered, the convoy started; eighty heavy cannon, each drawn by twenty horses, twenty mortars drawn by sixteen horses, and three thousand four-horse munition wagons, formed two columns, each fifteen miles long, marching by separate roads. They took the direction not of Lille but of Mons, thus keeping as far as possible from the main French army, and incidentally deceiving Berwick, who, thinking Mons was after all the objective, reinforced that garrison by seven battalions from his field forces. By nightfall on the 7th the convoy reached Soignies unmolested. Here they found Eugene with a fighting force of forty thousand men.

On the 8th before dawn the convoy turned at right angles on to the road to Ath, and marched throughout the day under shield of Eugene's army and Hesse-Cassel's cavalry. They had slipped away from Brussels "on the sly," and Vendôme could scarcely reach them during their first two marches. But the 8th, 9th, and 10th were the critical days. Upon this stage of the journey Vendôme and Berwick could combine by the shortest route. Marlborough's forty-two squadrons near Oudenarde

were, however, a screen against Vendôme, and would have given timely
warning to Eugene had he moved to strike the convoys between Ath
and the Pottes bridgehead. The Dender was crossed at Ath on the 9th,
and the march towards the Scheldt began the next morning. Had Vendôme moved south in force he could have been encountered on this
day by the whole of the allied armies. The Oudenarde squadrons would
have fallen back before him, and Marlborough from Werwicq could
have reached the battlefield as soon as he. But Vendôme had no
thought of moving. He remained deaf to the appeals of Berwick. He
suppressed Burgundy. He declared himself incredulous that any great
siege could be undertaken while he held the Ghent waterways. He
affected to disbelieve all reports about the great convoy. At the root of
this attitude lay the fact that he did not mean to fight a battle. In this
resolve he was right. He measured truly the havoc Oudenarde had
wrought in the Grand Army. Thus the convoy crossed the Scheldt at
Pottes in tranquillity during the 10th. Here they were in the midst of
Marlborough's army. Thirty battalions and thirty-four squadrons under
the Prince of Orange masked the fortress of Lille, while thirty squadrons at Petegem guarded the northern flank. The Duke himself
marched with his remaining troops to Helchin on the 12th, and that
night the siege-train safely entered the allied fortress of Menin.

This operation was watched with intense curiosity by the soldiers of
all countries. Certainly no general of those days, studying the positions
of the armies upon the map, would have pronounced it possible.
French military historians have criticized with extreme severity the negligence of Vendôme. Berwick roundly condemns him. Nevertheless,
the terror of Oudenarde and the combined skill and prowess of Marlborough and Eugene were facts which maps and documents cannot
convey. On the 13th—Blenheim Day—Eugene, crossing the stream of
the Marque, joined both hands with the Prince of Orange, and the
investment of Lille was complete.

Marlborough wrote that night to Count Maffei: "The Prince of
Savoy has invested the town of Lille on all sides, and the cannon has
arrived at Menin within reach of the siege, which will be pressed with
all possible vigour, and this may at last convince the enemy that they
have lost the battle of Oudenarde."

CHAPTER SIXTY-SIX

The Siege of Lille

ᘿ 1708, August-September ᘾ

AFTER Paris Lille, the capital of French Flanders, was the greatest city of France. It was almost the earliest, and certainly the most splendid fruit of Louis XIV's lifelong aggressions. For forty years it had been the monument of his military fame. It was also the staple of all the trade between the Netherlands and France. Its wealthy merchants financed and profited by the privateering from Dunkirk. Its name, Lisle, sprang from its secure position amid the pools and swamps of the Deule. Since the most ancient times it had been a stronghold and refuge. All the art of Vauban, unhurried by time, unstinted in expense, had been devoted to the fortifications. Broad double moats filled with water, massive masonry of covered ways and galleries, surmounted by enormous earthworks armed with heavy cannon, and an intricate system of outer defences made the town itself as strong as a citadel. But, besides the fortifications of the town, a large and wholly independent pentagon-shaped fortress afforded the garrison the means of standing what was virtually a second siege. These defences would have been formidable in the last degree if manned only by six or seven thousand troops. But Berwick, with the King's cordial agreement, concentrated a miniature army of fifteen thousand men within them, including twenty-one battalions; and Marshal Boufflers, Marlborough's old comrade of Maestricht days, had claimed the honour of commanding the resistance. It was evident that Lille would be the greatest siege operation since the invention of gunpowder. All Europe watched with wonder what seemed to those times a prodigy of human effort. That it should be undertaken by armies inferior in numbers to the French forces actually in the field, whose water communications were cut by fortresses in their rear, whose road communications seemed to lie at the mercy of Vendôme and Berwick, constituted an act of temerity only possible when allied to the authority and fame of Marlborough and Eugene. Vendôme, among his many miscalculations of 1708, declared that "so wise a commander as Prince Eugene would not venture upon such an enterprise," and the French Court boasted that "without striking a blow they would oblige the Allies to abandon the siege."

All these facts are cited by historians to extol the indomitable firmness of the Allies in choosing such a trial of strength. They were, indeed, the very reasons which had made Marlborough earnest to find some other course. Compared with the perils of the siege of Lille and the limited objects obtainable by its capture, the hazards of a new sea-base and of a march to Paris seemed attractive. Nevertheless, Marlborough, anticipating Lord Kitchener's dictum, "One cannot wage war as one ought, but only as one can," addressed himself with zeal and confidence to the inevitable step.

John to Sarah

Helchin
August 16

. . . The siege of Lille, which was begun on Monday last, is of that consequence to France that I nowise doubt of their drawing all the troops that is in their power together, to give us what disturbance they can. I pray God to bless this undertaking, and all others that may tend to the bringing of us to a safe and lasting peace. . . .

But I think we are now acting for the liberties of all Europe, so that, . . . tho' I love the Queen with all my heart, I can't think of the business of England till this great affair is decided, which I think must be by another battle; for I am resolved to risk rather than suffer Brussels to be taken, tho' the number of this army is very much diminished by the siege. But I rely on the justness of our cause, and that God will not forsake us, and that He will continue to keep our troops in good heart, as they are at present. I beg you to be so kind and just as to be assured that my kindness for you is such that my greatest ambition is bounded in that of ending my days quietly with you.

The Great King was vehemently stirred by the siege of Lille. Like Vendôme, he had not believed it would be begun. He was resolved that it should be prevented. He ordered that Marshal, and, of course, Burgundy, not to hesitate to fight a decisive battle to relieve the city. Weariness of war lay heavy upon this old monarch. For more than forty years he had been the scourge of Europe. But war had lost its glamour with its laurels. One final, supreme battle to rescue Lille or lose the war; and then peace—peace now become dear and precious even on the worst terms. Such was his mood. But the French army and its generals, with the doubtful exception of Vendôme, whose conduct we shall examine later, did not find it so easy to court such dire decisions. They still felt the mauling of Oudenarde. Marlborough judged the facts with perfect accuracy. The siege was a grave hazard and might fail, thus spoiling the campaign, but that the enemy would fight a decisive battle for its relief was too good to be true. Only one movement would force a decisive battle—the march on Paris. That the army he commanded would win any pitched battle he was sure; but he did not think it probable that any decisive result would be reached in the field in 1708.

Marlborough to Godolphin

Helchin
August 20

By the threatening of M. de Vendôme I did not think we should have continued thus long in this camp; but as yet he is not marched from behind the canal. But the Duke of Berwick is drawing to his army, with all the troops he can, from their several towns. M. de Vendôme declares in his army that he has *carte blanche*, and that he will attempt the relief of Lille; that when the Duke of Berwick joins him, they shall then have 135 battalions and 260 squadrons, which he flatters himself will be much stronger than we can be. If we have a second action, and God blesses our just cause, this, in all likelihood, will be the last campaign; for I think they would not venture a battle, but that they are resolved to submit to any condition, if the success be on our side . . . If God continues on our side, we have nothing to fear, our troops being good, though not so numerous as theirs. I dare say, before half the troops have fought, the success will declare, I hope in God on our side, and then I may have, what I earnestly wish for, quiet; and you may be much more at ease than when you writ yours of the 31st of the last month, which I received yesterday.

The attack was delivered from the north. Prince Eugene commanded the fifty battalions, of whom ten were always in the trenches which were assigned to the task. Of these thirty were provided from Marlborough's army. Lines of circumvallation were drawn, and the work of mounting the batteries began.

The magistrates of Lille, by Boufflers' leave, sent a deputation "with compliments and refreshments" to Prince Eugene, appealing to him to spare the burghers as much as possible. But he answered

> that a besieged town ought to be kept very close; so that he could not yet admit of their civilities; but when he should be master of the place, the burghers might be assured of his protection, provided he should be satisfied that they had endeavoured to deserve it, by their impartial carriage during the siege.

So strong was the garrison that fierce fighting developed upon the approaches. The chapel of St Magdalen and the neighbouring mill were scenes of carnage. However, on the 21st the lines of contravallation and circumvallation were perfected. Thus Eugene and his besiegers dwelt in a double ring of earthworks several hundred yards apart and nine miles in length, facing outward and inward around the city, and Marlborough with the field army protected them from interference. Trenches were opened on the 22nd, and five days later the heavy batteries began to play with eighty-eight pieces. The object of this process in a siege was to shatter the masonry and crumble the earthworks, so that as they fell in ruins they filled up the moats, and made a breach in which hand-to-hand fighting proceeded till the moment of assault was ripe. The large cannon-balls of those days and primitive shells from the mortars, after a certain number of days of firing, which could usually be accurately estimated, were capable of producing such a result. But all depended upon the powder and ball. By the early days of September deserters reported that the breach was very wide, that the ditch was almost full with the ruins of the wall, and that Marshal Boufflers had ordered a good part of his best cannon to be withdrawn from the ramparts into the citadel. The assault of the counterscarp was accordingly fixed for the 7th. But now the French grand army, united with that of Marshal Berwick, arrived upon the scene.

18. Tapestry of the Schellenberg. BY PERMISSION OF THE DUKE OF MARLBOROUGH.
PHOTOGRAPH BY PERMISSION OF THE VICTORIA AND ALBERT MUSEUM.

20. Marshal Villars, from an engraving after
the painting by Hyacinthe Rigaud.
BRITISH MUSEUM.

19. Tapestry of the Battle of Blenheim. BY PERMISSION OF THE DUKE OF MARL-
BOROUGH. PHOTOGRAPH BY PERMISSION OF THE VICTORIA AND ALBERT MUSEUM.

21. Sicco van Goslinga,
from an engraving
after a painting by
Bernard Accama.

The Battlel of Ramillies where y D of Marlbo
roug. &c took 26. Standards & 63. Enfigns the
French lobsing 20000 men all their Baggage
Amunition &c.

22. The Ramillies Playing-Card.
ROYAL LIBRARY, WINDSOR;
BY PERMISSION OF HIS
LATE MAJESTY KING GEORGE V.

23. Robert Harley, Earl of Oxford,
from an engraving after the
portrait by Sir Godfrey Kneller.

24. Sidney, Earl of Godolphin,
from a copy of a painting
by Sir Godfrey Kneller.
NATIONAL PORTRAIT GALLERY.

25. Tapestry of the Lines of Brabant. BY PERMISSION OF THE DUKE OF MARL-
BOROUGH. PHOTOGRAPH BY PERMISSION OF THE VICTORIA AND ALBERT MU-
SEUM.

26. Tapestry of the Battle of Oudenarde. The tapestry illustrates Eugene receiving the command of the right wing of the army from Marlborough; but the
background of the general characteristics of the battle of Oudenarde does not
represent the hour and place of the incident. BY PERMISSION OF THE DUKE OF
MARLBOROUGH. PHOTOGRAPH BY PERMISSION OF THE VICTORIA AND ALBERT
MUSEUM.

27. Sarah Duchess of Marlborough, in 1708, by Sir Godfrey Kneller.
BY PERMISSION OF EARL SPENCER.

28. Marlborough, from a copy of a painting by Sir Godfrey Kneller.
NATIONAL PORTRAIT GALLERY.

29. Prince Eugene of Savoy, by Sir Godfrey Kneller. BY PERMISSION OF THE
DUKE OF MARLBOROUGH.

30. Marlborough, from an engraving after a painting by Sir Godfrey Kneller.

31. The Old Pretender, by A. S. Belle. NATIONAL PORTRAIT GALLERY.

32. Thomas Wentworth, Third Earl of Stratford, from an engraving after a painting by C. D. Agar.

34. Robert Walpole, by J. M. Rysbrack.
BY PERMISSION OF THE MARQUIS
OF CHOLMONDELEY.

33. Tapestry Showing Marlborough at Bouchain. BY PERMISSION OF THE DUKE OF MARLBOROUGH. PHOTOGRAPH BY PERMISSION OF THE VICTORIA AND ALBERT MUSEUM.

35. Blenheim Palace.

In a letter to reassure Sarah Marlborough forecasted with perfect comprehension the future action of the enemy. His power of putting himself in the enemy's shoes, and measuring truly what they ought to do, and what he himself would most dislike, was one of his greatest gifts. He was only wrong in his anticipations when the enemy made a mistake. But this also had compensations of its own.

After protracted discussions and long letters to and from the King, Burgundy and Berwick marched towards each other at the utmost speed on August 27. They joined, as Marlborough had forecast, at Grammont on the 29th, and reached the Scheldt at Tournai together on September 1. Berwick, who refused to serve under Vendôme, resigned his command, and became Burgundy's rival adviser. It was learned that Marlborough had left Helchin on the 31st and that he was moving on an inner circle between them and Lille, which, they heard, had been since the 27th under the heaviest bombardment by Eugene. They spent September 2 in crossing the Scheldt, camped at Orchies on the 3rd, and reached Mons-en-Pévêle during the 4th. Here they were joined by their heavy cannon from Douai. Burgundy and Vendôme climbed the heights behind the camp, and thence saw the allied army spread in a wide arc before them. Their best chance was to draw out their line astride of the Lille-Douai road, and begin the battle that very evening. Although all their troops had not come up, they had on the spot or close at hand nearly double Marlborough's strength. Berwick's account agrees with Vendôme's view that the hour was too late. It was, however, earlier than that on which Marlborough had stormed the Schellenberg. Thus night fell in silence. But all seemed set for battle on the 5th. The fate of Lille and of the campaign was at stake. The orders of the King to fight a decisive engagement were imperative and reiterated.

Marlborough's concentration was effected with precision. Before dawn on the 5th Eugene, with seventy-two squadrons and twenty-six battalions, arrived from the siege and took his station on Marlborough's right. General Fagel, with seven battalions, by "incredible" marches from Dutch Brabant reached the battle front as the sun rose. The Captain-General drew out 209 squadrons and 109 battalions, between seventy and eighty thousand men, to face the combined French army of a hundred and ten thousand.

As this was the only occasion when Marlborough seemed prepared to fight a defensive battle on a large scale, his dispositions are of interest. The position he had selected permitted the French to attack only on a narrow front. He narrowed the gap further by strong infantry bodies on either flank supported by cavalry. In the gap he placed his cavalry in two lines, covered by guns and backed by infantry. To prevent the enemy capturing Ennetières village on his front and so breaking the cohesion of his cavalry attack, and also to disrupt the French cavalry attack, he occupied it with a brigade of infantry. He clearly intended to disorganize the more numerous French cavalry by artillery fire, and then to charge them down-hill with cavalry supported by infantry, trusting to the training and morale of his cavalry as proved at Blenheim, Elixem, and Ramillies. The position he had selected was four miles outside the lines of circumvallation. He made no attempt to impede the approach and deployment of the enemy. In order to leave himself full freedom to counter-attack early in the action, he did not at first entrench. When Eugene proposed this Marlborough answered that "since he had commanded he had never accustomed his army to entrench in the presence of the enemy." Eventually he allowed digging to begin at Ennetières; but he kept the whole of the rest of the field open to a gigantic manœuvre-battle once the enemy had committed themselves to the attack. Thus we may measure his confidence in his troops and in himself, and his readiness to risk all upon the stroke of the day.

A different mood held the French High Command. At daylight their chiefs began a prolonged reconnaissance. Vendôme wished to attack at once. Berwick pointed out the particular marshes and woods which would interfere with the advance. Burgundy decided that the approaches must be improved before the attack could be made. This work was accordingly begun, and it soon became apparent that there would be no general battle on the 5th. Boufflers, as prearranged, took advantage of Eugene's absence from the siege to make a vigorous sortie upon his denuded lines. We are told by several authorities that as early as 10.00 A.M. orders were issued to Eugene's troops to return to the siege. But this is absurd. Even the infantry did not move off the field till darkness fell; and the cavalry not till the next day. Marlborough, although now only half the strength of the enemy, but with confidence confirmed by their indecision, was still reluctant to entrench. Bidding high for battle, he was prepared to run what seemed desperate risks to tempt the enemy. But the opinion of Eugene, and, indeed, of all the allied generals, was so strong that during the evening of the 5th he began to break the ground, and by the 8th important works stretched from Noyelles to Fretin. As he was now confined to defensive action, he reorganized his array, the infantry being in two lines behind the trenches and the cavalry massed in rear of the wings. The difference between these dispositions and those of the 5th reveals very clearly the kind of battle he had hoped to fight.

The three French marshals spent the 5th and 6th in personal reconnaissance. All day they examined the hostile front with a curiosity which frequently drew the fire of its field batteries. All night they argued in Burgundy's tent. Vendôme still had no doubts; he urged an immediate onslaught, first upon the allied left and then extending to their centre, which lay across a wide plain. Berwick took the opposite view. The allied flanks were secure. It could only be a frontal attack in a country "where ten thousand could stop thirty thousand." Burgundy, torn between these conflicting views of eminent commanders, resorted to his customary habit of consulting his grandfather. So on the night of September 6 they all wrote letters to the King.

Faced with this grim decision, Louis XIV showed no weakness; he resolved to play the stake. He expressed his surprise that his positive orders had been questioned, and renewed his commands to Burgundy to attack even at the risk of "suffering the misfortunes inseparable from failure, less dishonouring however, both for his person and for the army than to become spectators of the capture of Lille." He sent Chamillart to the camp to enforce his will.

In the midst of this tension the Allies found themselves strong enough to prosecute the siege. The assaults upon the counterscarp were delivered on the prescribed day, although upon the opposite side of the city at this very moment the largest battle of the war seemed imminent. On the south of Lille Marlborough faced Vendôme at heavy odds. On the north side the great assault was launched. Fourteen thousand men reinforced the troops in the trenches, and at half-past seven in the evening attacked the whole front from one hornwork to the other. Four great mines exploded under the feet of the assailants, "which destroyed abundance of men." All through the night the struggle raged with varying fortune in the intricacies of the fortress system. The counterscarp was stormed; but, owing to the engineers who were to direct the second phase being all killed, and the workmen in their charge "departing under the Favour of the Night," the enemy were able to retire to their capital works, from whence they maintained a terrible fire for some hours. It was impossible to advance beyond "the Angles of the Glacis of the two Hornworks and of the Tenaille." The slaughter among the allied troops in this assault by all accounts was nearly equal to their loss in the battle of Oudenarde. The French claimed that five thousand men had fallen. Certainly between two and three thousand, of whom the most part perished, covered the few acres of the saps and breaches with their gay uniforms and mangled bodies.

Had the French grand army forced a general battle on the morning of the 5th, as Marlborough hoped, every scrap of force at the disposal of the Allies would have been cast simultaneously into the fateful scales. The interest of these operations to posterity, and to military annals, consists in the odds against which Marlborough and Eugene preserved their ascendancy, and the absolute conviction with which they acted upon narrow and impalpable margins. Marlborough courted the decisive battle. He was ready to face with less than sixty thousand men the possible onslaught of a hundred and ten thousand. Yet at the same time five miles away Eugene involved himself in the tremendous and necessarily bloody assault of the breaches. The two captains were disappointed in both respects; the assault did not capture the capital works, and the French army did not face a battle. Even more difficult trials lay ahead.

While the siege was thus at its crisis and great numbers of troops involved in deadly grapple in the *débris* of the ramparts, the quagmire of the ditch, and the labyrinth of the counterscarp galleries, Vendôme threatened again to force a battle. Very heavy cannonades and the deployment of the whole French army once more aroused the Allies' hopes. Eugene rejoined Marlborough on the south front with his cavalry and spare troops. But this time battle was no longer offered in the open field, and it was hardly to be conceived that the enemy would pay the price of demanding it against entrenchments. The only effect of the French demonstrations and bombardments of the 11th was to divert Eugene from the siege for a few hours, and to supply the Allies with a large quantity of cannon-balls, which were diligently collected and fired into Lille. On this day also an important munitions convoy which had left Brussels on the 8th was escorted into camp by Albemarle.

All French Society—indeed, France itself—waited in protracted suspense. A freezing hush fell upon the Court. The card-tables, the supper parties, were deserted. The churches were thronged with rank and fashion praying for the life of husband, lover, son. It was known that Chamillart had been sent to the army for the express purpose of compelling its leaders to fight. This had seemed a very plain and obligatory course amid the galleries of Versailles and in the presence of Louis XIV. He arrived clear and decided. On the spot, in contact with the realities and the atmosphere of doubt which infected the French command, the War Minister soon lost heart. He watched the desultory cannonades. He heard the talk. He saw the ground and the defences along which flaunted the standards of the Allies, and behind which the shapes of Marlborough and Eugene seemed crouched to spring. On the night of the 14th Vendôme was left alone in his opinion; Burgundy, Berwick, Chamillart, and almost all the generals were for retreat. At this point it cost Vendôme little to persist in valorous opinions. No one would take him at his word. Were there not other methods of succouring Lille? They knew the besiegers were short of powder. Although two convoys had lately arrived, a third was urgently expected. Any prolonged interruption of the supplies must be fatal. All the communications were exposed. If the main French army were used, it should be possible to cut Marlborough and Eugene both from Brussels and the sea. There is little doubt that the painful and humiliating decision was right. Comforting themselves with these hopes, the French army fell back by Orchies to Tournai.

Marlborough to Godolphin

September 20

. . . It is impossible for me to express the uneasiness I suffer for the ill conduct of our engineers at the siege, where I think everything goes very wrong. It would be a cruel thing, if after we have obliged the enemy to quit all thoughts of relieving the place by force, which they have done, by repassing the Scheldt, we should fail of taking it by the ignorance of our engineers and the want of stores; for we have already fired very near as much as was demanded for the taking of the town and citadel; and as yet we are not entire masters of the counter-scarp; so that to you I may own my despair of ending this campaign, so as in reason we might have expected. I beg you to assure the Queen that my greatest concern is on her account; for as to myself, I am so tired of the world that were she not concerned my affliction would not be great.

When the fate of Lille is once known, we shall endeavour all we can to bring the French to a general engagement; *but as that is what we shall desire, I take it for granted it is what they will avoid. . . .*

This just reflection was fully confirmed by events.

CHAPTER SIXTY-SEVEN

Wynendael ✓

ᛞ 1708, September-October ᛞ

A GREAT battle being denied him, Marlborough, as he had foreseen, must face a far more harassing attack. The siege batteries were firing at full blast. The defence of Lille had been already maintained for nearly three weeks beyond the scheduled time. The bombardment was living from hand to mouth. To suspend it even for a few days was to take the pressure off Marshal Boufflers, who, for his part, watched with anxiety the daily diminution of his own limited magazines. Unless he could continue his counter-battery, the front would clearly break. The King had prescribed a proportion of powder to be reserved for the defence of the citadel. The losses of the garrison had been severe. If Eugene's bombardment and the progress of his saps continued, Boufflers must within a definite time retire to the citadel. But if the cannonade ceased he could stand where he was indefinitely. All therefore turned upon the convoys. Now upon the communications with Brussels came the main French army. In the last fortnight of September Vendôme and Burgundy occupied the whole line of the Scheldt from the Lille approaches to Ghent. They held and fortified every crossing. They made a curve around Oudenarde, at which point their defences became more like a fortress than field entrenchments. By this means they cut absolutely all communication between the Allies and Brussels, and beyond Brussels with Holland. Marlborough and Eugene were thus isolated. They were separated both by road and river from their base, from the homeland, and from all supplies, while they had the greatest siege of modern history on their hands, and when any slackening in their attack

(643)

meant almost certain failure. From this time forward the siege of Lille became a desperate operation.

Only one resource lay open. Marlborough's eyes turned to the sea-coast. The fortress and harbour of Ostend were in his hands. But on either side of this life-line lay the hostile fortresses of Ypres, Nieuport, and Bruges. From Nieuport the French controlled the sluices of the Yser, and could flood a large and indefinite area. The road from the coast was now alone left to the besiegers of Lille, and the French gathered heavy forces on both sides of Ostend, but especially from the north, to attack the convoys. Possessing the command of the sea, Marlborough had directed large supplies of munitions upon Ostend. On September 21 General Erle with his six thousand British infantry was brought under a strong escort of the fleet from the Channel into Ostend. Marlborough sent a trusted officer to him with full instructions, and set him to work to prepare a heavy convoy.

Meanwhile the siege and bombardments proceeded with all possible vigour in the teeth of an obstinate defence. Eugene prepared for another major assault on the St Andrew and St Magdalen sectors. This was delivered on the evening of the 21st by about fifteen thousand men. At first good progress was made, and it seemed that the grand breach would be carried. But a violent sortie from the city robbed the assailants of most of their gains. In this savage night they lost at least a thousand men. Among the wounded was Eugene. With Hesse-Cassel at his side, he conducted the attack at close quarters. Seeing the grenadiers repulsed, he advanced into the deadly fire to rally and animate his troops. He was soon struck by a musket-ball which grazed his forehead above his left eye. The force of the blow was broken by his cocked hat, which was "beat off" his head. Hesse-Cassel gave him his own hat, already pierced by a bullet. Eugene, according to his usual habit when receiving a wound, made light of his injury and insisted upon remaining in action. But as it was apparent that he was half stunned and dazed his officers prevailed upon him to withdraw. He was led or carried to his headquarters while the struggle at the breaches was at its height. Although his injury was bloodless, he was suffering from severe concussion of the brain. It was clear to all about him that he would be incapacitated for some time. This serious news was carried to Marlborough during the night. Early the next morning the Duke arrived at Eugene's headquarters. He found his comrade, among an expostulating staff, preparing to go up to the trenches. He was only prevailed upon to return to his couch by Marlborough's undertaking to conduct the siege himself, as well as to cover it, till he was restored.

From September 21 till the end of the month the double burden was borne by Marlborough. This was a period of incredible strain. The besiegers were in extremities. The batteries were approaching the end of their ammunition. The engineers were scandalously at fault in their estimates. Around Lille all was in arrears and in confusion. A critical and hazardous operation was required to bring the convoy through from Ostend in the face of superior forces and ever-spreading inundations. Riding to and fro between the covering army and the siege, Marlborough effectively "sustained the weight of the command." He looked narrowly into the siege-stores and munitions, and was shocked at his discoveries. On the 23rd he renewed the assault on the fortifications. He directed it himself from the trenches, and after hard fighting a substantial improvement was achieved. In these days he reorganized the siege operations like a careful housekeeper. The bombardment and trench-grapple were ceaselessly maintained. Meanwhile Eugene began to throw off his concussion.

The remorseless attack and heavy firing reduced Marshal Boufflers' magazines to very near the last reserve for the defence of the citadel.

This emergency provoked a dramatic enterprise. The Chevalier de Luxembourg, a Major-General, with about two thousand dragoons, who "besides their arms carried each a fusee and a bag of sixty pounds weight of powder," set out during the night of the 28th along the Douai road. In order the better to conceal their identity in the darkness they wore green boughs in their helmets, as was often done by the Allies on battle occasions. They arrived at the lines of circumvallation at a point near Pont-à-Tressin held by the Palatine troops. Their officers pretended to be Germans carrying prisoners to the camp. In this war of many nations and all languages spoken indifferently on either side they were suffered by carelessness—other accounts say by corruption—to pass the barrier. Several hundred were already safely over when a subaltern officer, "having some distrust, advanced to examine them." There was a challenge, an altercation, shouts, shots, and pandemonium. The whole two thousand galloped along the road towards the city. About half got through, the rest turned back in disorder. The road from Douai to Lille was paved with cobbles. Horses slipped: sparks struck out from their hoofs, or fire from the muskets, ignited powder-bags. A succession of loud explosions alarmed the camps and covered the road with scorched fragments of men and horses. About thirty prisoners were taken, but Luxembourg brought into Lille nearly sixty thousand pounds of powder for the fortress batteries. Marlborough's and other allied accounts minimized this grave annoyance, but it was regarded throughout Europe as a brilliant feat of arms.

During this last week of September the fate of Lille hung in the balance. At several agonized councils the raising of the siege was debated by the allied commanders. Goslinga, as usual, declares that he and his colleagues were for fighting it out, and that Marlborough was in despair. All accounts agree that Eugene, rising from his sickbed, declared "that he would be responsible for the success *provided he was supported with ammunition.*" But this begged the question. It is certain that Marlborough, who was engaged in the important operation of bringing in the convoy, allowed it to be known that, unless the convoy came through, the siege must be abandoned.

General Erle, whom Marlborough had reinforced at Ostend till he had perhaps seven thousand British infantry and a large number of vehicles and horses, in spite of his gout behaved with zeal and skill. He succeeded in draining a large part of the inundation between Nieuport and Ostend. He occupied Leffinghe, and there built a bridge over the canal. Communication was thus for the moment restored with the main army. Marlborough had sent twelve battalions and as many squadrons towards Leffinghe to receive the convoy. But now Vendôme ordered La Motte to advance southward from Bruges with no fewer than twenty-two thousand men, a small army, and seize the prize. Marlborough had early information of this movement, though he underrated its strength. On the 25th he sent twelve more battalions and some horse to reinforce the convoy guard. The command of these troops was confided to General Webb. We are familiar with this picturesque personage through Thackeray's malicious pages. Webb was a High Tory, at heart a Jacobite, a man as vain as he was brave, but also a competent and experienced veteran of the long wars. He was now to fight a most brilliant and glorious action, no small part of whose lustre falls upon the British infantry.

Early on the morning of the 28th the precious convoy was trailing along the road from Leffinghe to Thourout when the news came that La

Motte, rebuffed by the allied defences at Oudenburg, was advancing at right angles upon it. His pathway to strike the convoy led him between two thick woods a thousand yards apart. It is contended that his great numerical superiority—far beyond what Marlborough had expected —should have been used to outflank one or the other of these woods. But La Motte felt that the thickets on the one hand and the Château de Wynendael on the other debarred him from this. Accordingly he advanced between the woods, and about 2.00 P.M. found himself confronted by General Webb with twenty-four battalions drawn up in the gap, and, as he was soon to learn, in the woods on either side. He deployed his whole force, line behind line, and after three hours' cannonade advanced to the assault, being in superior strength of at least two to one. His troops found themselves fired upon not only by the British infantry on their front, but by strong forces hidden on both their flanks. The slaughter was heavy, and for those days unusually swift. His leading lines, largely composed of so-called Spanish infantry—that is to say, Belgian battalions adhering to the French—melted under the fusillade, and the rest refused to renew the battle. Here was a striking instance of the superior fire-discipline which was so marked a feature of Marlborough's infantry training. Three or four thousand men lay killed or wounded in the narrow space, and none would face the allied line, which stood unbroken and invincible. In the intense fire which preceded this decision Webb himself lost nearly a thousand men. But the repulse of the French was utter. Marlborough, who had come with strong forces of the main army to Roulers, had the day before sent Cadogan with twenty-six squadrons and infantry support to strengthen Webb. Cadogan arrived with a handful of squadrons as the victory declared itself. He offered Webb to charge the defeated French corps. Webb thought the odds were too great, and did not ask this effort of his comrade. Meanwhile the convoy had slipped safely past the point of intersection and was coming within the ambit of Marlborough's main army. The victory of Wynendael had sealed the fate of Lille.

Great if haggard rejoicings saluted the arrival of the new convoy in the camps before Lille. Above two hundred and fifty thousand pounds of powder, with cannon-balls and shells sufficient in those days for a fortnight's bombardment, had reached the besiegers. Besides this Eugene, now fully recovered, began to appear among the troops, and in the early days of October resumed the conduct of the siege, which was prosecuted night and day. However, a new and even more dangerous attack impended upon the communications. Vendôme, stung by the disgrace of Wynendael, came down on October 3 through Bruges to Oudenburg with thirty thousand men. He reinforced Nieuport and threatened Ostend and Leffinghe. He broke the dykes, opened the sluices in all directions, and "drowned the country." The French were still capable of moving freely all along the coast across the allied communications, which now seemed finally cut. This mortal challenge was instantly accepted. On the morning of the 7th Marlborough divided his army. He left twenty battalions and as many squadrons to aid Eugene in case of need, and with sixty battalions and 130 squadrons, or about forty-five thousand men, marched at daybreak directly upon Vendôme. At Roulers he learned that Vendôme was still at Oudenburg, and there seemed to be good prospects of pinning him against his own inundations. The expectation of battle ran high. King Augustus hastened from the siege to see the day. In an intercepted letter Vendôme had assured Louis XIV that "he engaged his honour the Allies should have no further communication with Ostend." Indeed, the Marshal was disposed to stay and fight. This hardihood was not shared by his generals. Finding remonstrance useless, they adopted, according to Berwick, a more compulsive argument. They opened the sluices higher up the coast, and before it was too late flooded him out of his camp. Marlborough, arriving on the field of Wynendael with his vanguard, heard that the French had retreated to Bruges, laying the countryside under water to the utmost extent. He accordingly halted his army at Roulers.

Ostend was now completely isolated by the floods. Another heavy convoy of munitions, brandy, salt, and other necessaries had been transported thither by sea from Holland and England. Eight or ten miles of flood-water, rising with the full-moon tides, stretched between these supplies and the ravening batteries and straitened army before Lille. Hitherto the want of food had not been felt. The forays into France had provided for men and horses. The convoys had been reserved almost entirely for powder and ball. In the third week of October, however, Marlborough was forced to reduce the bread ration by one-third, four days serving for six. He ordered the other two days to be paid in money. "Particular care," he wrote to Cadogan, "must be taken that the officers pay the two days in money, that the soldiers have less rea-

son to complain." He had in the middle of October to push his foraging parties ever more deeply into France around Armentières and La
Bassée. Both besiegers and besieged were in dire straits. All hung on
the passage of supplies. Marlborough now took possession of the region
round Dixmude with strong forces. Erle on one side of the floods collected a flotilla; Cadogan on the other procured high-wheeled vehicles.
By these means the powder and shot was ferried across the inundations, drawn through the shallow waters by Cadogan's high wheels, and
finally transferred to Marlborough's supply wagons. Every day and
night small quantities came through. The Duke's letters record each arrival, and give instructions for drying any bags of powder which were
wetted. Thus the cannon and the siege were fed literally by handfuls.

The siege batteries were now entrenched amid the ruins of the fortifications. "They have mounted nearly fifty pieces of cannon, besides a
battery of mortars," wrote Marlborough, "upon the counterscarp, and
hope to begin to fire from them to-morrow." This intense fire at close
quarters marked a well-known phase. The breaches gaped. Boufflers
had already withdrawn most of his cannon into the citadel. The hour
of summons and of general storm drew near.

On the 22nd, all the troops being at their stations for the final
assault, which if successful would deprive the garrison of quarter and
expose the city to sack, Marshal Boufflers beat a parley and offered to
surrender the town. The hostages and courtesies were immediately exchanged. Eugene imposed upon Boufflers the task, difficult and exacting to an accomplished soldier and a man of honour, of fixing himself
the terms of capitulation. "Whatever you think right I will agree to."
Boufflers asked for a three days' truce to withdraw to the citadel, leave
to send his movable sick and wounded into Douai, and that the attack
upon the citadel should not be directed from the town side. Eugene,
sending presents of wine and fresh provisions for the Marshal's table,
subscribed to these conditions without demur. Little was lost by these
gestures of chivalry. Every inducement was offered to Boufflers to state
his terms for the surrender of the citadel, and when the old Marshal
deprecated the raising of such unseasonable questions, Eugene began
the opening of his trenches and moving his cannon even before the
three days had expired. There was an unpleasant difference of opinion
as to whether or not the truce precluded this. Of the garrison of fifteen
thousand who had defended the fortress three thousand burghers laid

down their arms upon parole, four thousand sick and wounded were carried to Douai, and between four and five thousand men retired to the citadel. The rest had perished. Besides the casualties of Wynendael and upon the communications, the Allies admitted 3632 men killed and 8322 wounded, of whom in those days about half died. The French asserted that they had inflicted more than double this loss. The price of Lille, although less than King William had paid for Namur twenty years before, was regarded as terrible throughout Europe.

CHAPTER SIXTY-EIGHT

The Winter Struggle

₤ɑ 1708, Winter ɒ₹

WHILE their success was reverberating throughout Europe Marlborough and Eugene were for a space completely cut off from the outside world. The city had no sooner been surrendered than the communications with Ostend were finally closed. The garrison of Leffinghe, who had distinguished themselves by their stout resistance, were relieved on the 24th by an English, Dutch, and Spanish force. The newcomers proceeded forthwith to celebrate the joyous news in such a fashion that both officers and men were surprised drunk and incapable by a French attack during the night of the 24th, many being put to the sword. The gateways to the sea were shut, but luckily too late. The situation of the allied armies was nevertheless still precarious. In every direction lay the French fortified positions and lines. Not only the seacoast but the entire line of the Scheldt was sealed against them by superior forces. In their midst bristled the citadel of Lille with its ample garrison, its powerful artillery, and sacredly hoarded separate reserves of ammunition. On the other hand, the greatly contracted lines of circumvallation liberated more than half the besieging army for service in the field, and both siege-works and bombardment were upon a far smaller scale.

The fall of Lille wrung further efforts from Louis XIV. He drew reinforcements both from the Rhine and Dauphiné to the Flanders theatre. Grave differences of opinion, aggravated by personal bitterness, distracted the French headquarters in the field. Berwick, without a command, had established his ascendancy over Burgundy. His keen eye and military sagacity detected every fault in Vendôme's successive projects. That Marshal was throughout very loud for battle. Whether, if he had exercised the sole command, he would in fact have fought is doubtful. But as he knew the bulk of the generals would not agree with him, that Berwick and Burgundy would overrule him, and together had greater influence at Court, he ran little risk in assuming an heroic rôle and forcing every one else to hold the only brave man back. Certain it is that Marlborough wished for nothing better on three or four separate occasions than that Vendôme should have his way. It is difficult, therefore, to believe that Vendôme's attitude, if sincere, was right.

At any rate, the French command had him well restrained. On November 3 there was a council of war at headquarters. Vendôme, as usual, clamoured for battle. His plan to attack Marlborough was vetoed. He then proposed to hold all canals and rivers from Nieuport and Bruges through Ghent round to Tournai, in order to reduce the Allies to the alternative of being "starved to death or suing for peace." He might have added "or fighting." But the ill-reception of his first proposal warned him of the unwisdom of dwelling on this theme. Chamillart favoured the scheme, but Berwick mercilessly pointed out that the Allies had enough ammunition to reduce the citadel, and that, as for food, they could live far better on the plenty of Artois and Picardy than the French in war-worn Flanders. Berwick advised that serious garrisons should be left in Ghent and Bruges while the whole of the French army concentrated to cover the rich French provinces. The council decided to hold their ground and wait events. The relations of Vendôme and Berwick were now so intolerable that Berwick quietly allowed himself to be withdrawn from the main army to his original command on the Rhine. Thus a fortnight passed during which Eugene battered and bored into the citadel of Lille.

In the third week of November the Elector of Bavaria returned from the Rhine, where the armies had gone into winter quarters, and joined the princely circle at the French headquarters at Saulchoi. He had no command, but he had a plan. A renewed attack should be made upon Brussels, and he would lead it himself. The inhabitants, he declared, were his devoted subjects, and would rally to his call. The garrison was thought to be meagre, and the defences were certainly weak and defective. With a small force drawn from various neighbouring fortresses he would capture the city. The idea caught fire; it prevented other plans.

THE WINTER STRUGGLE

The Elector, at the head of fourteen battalions and eighteen squadrons with a minor siege-train, camped at Hal on November 21, and presented himself before Brussels the next day. Marlborough's unfailing Secret Service, although he lay surrounded by the French forces, gave him warning of this enterprise almost as soon as it had been conceived. He had already some weeks before reinforced the garrison of Brussels. It now consisted of ten battalions, comprising about six thousand men. He enjoined a spirited resistance upon the governor, Colonel Pascal, an officer of exceptional quality.

The sanguine hopes which the Elector, Max Emmanuel, had nourished about Brussels proved ill-founded. He summoned Colonel Pascal in imperious terms to surrender.

Colonel Pascal proceeded to animate his troops. He ordered a pound of flesh, two quarts of beer, and four glasses of brandy to be distributed every day gratis to each soldier. Thus fortified, the garrison resisted with vigour; and the inhabitants remained mute and motionless. The Elector, instead of making a happy pounce, found himself committed to a grievous assault, if not, indeed, to a regular siege. He clamoured for reinforcements, and, the business having been started, these perforce had to be supplied. Bloody fighting ensued, and for a week the attempt to break into Brussels—siege it could not be called—became the feature of the campaign.

Although the French command were reassured by the news they had of Marlborough's preparations to move into winter quarters, Burgundy harboured misgivings about his own power to defend the line of the Scheldt if heavy forces were brought against him. Vendôme, on the other hand, appeared to be serenely confident, and had the misfortune to assure the King, in a letter dated the 26th, that the French positions were impregnable. The piercing of long lines by selected attacks was familiar to Marlborough and Eugene. Nevertheless, the decision to force the fortifications of the Scheldt defended by the French main army was deemed most serious in the small circle of veteran officers who were privy to it. It was a major operation which might entail heavy slaughter even if all went well. During the 26th Marlborough marched upon the river at three widely separated crossings, Gavre, Oudenarde, and Kerkhoff, while Eugene, leaving only the barest screen before the citadel, moved on Hauterive. The fortified line was seventy miles long, and the four attacks covered twenty miles of front.

By the afternoon of the 27th the whole French army was chased from the fortifications of the Scheldt. Some fell back on Ghent and the rest on Tournai. The position of the Elector of Bavaria at Brussels became at once forlorn. Saving himself at the loss of all his artillery, and leaving eight hundred wounded behind him, he escaped to Mons. Meanwhile the strong post of Saint-Ghislain, which he had denuded of its garrison for the siege of Brussels, was captured by a raid of the governor of Ath, and many troops and much time and trouble were required to recover it for France. The moment the passage of the river was known to be secured Eugene hastened back to reinforce his scattered cordon around the citadel of Lille. The whole of this swift and fine operation marks the ascendancy which the Allies under Marlborough and Eugene had gained over the still numerically superior French armies. The fate of the citadel was now only a question of days. By this operation Marlborough had not only relieved Brussels, but had reopened the eastern line of supply to the besiegers of Lille and to the country in which his troops must winter. The morale of the French army had suffered a further shock. On December 9 the citadel of Lille capitulated. Boufflers marched out with honours of war, never more justly earned, and with the remnants of his garrison retired into France.

When the news of the loss of the Scheldt, of the failure before Brussels, and of the surrender of the citadel of Lille reached Louis XIV, he was so mortified that he incontinently ordered his armies to abandon the field and disperse into winter quarters. To protract the campaign further into the depth of winter no doubt meant a severe disorganization of all the recruiting and recuperative processes upon which the efficiency of his armies must depend in the new year which scowled upon France. It was believed at Versailles that Ghent and Bruges could stand prolonged sieges, and that the Allies would find it impossible to continue fighting incessantly. They too would have to break up, and by the late spring of 1709 the grim board might be set afresh. But this decision took little account of the forfeits which must be paid when one side ceases fighting and the other continues. Vendôme protested violently. The King remained obdurate. Berwick makes the pithy comment, "It is astounding that the King should have agreed to all the Duke of Vendôme's extraordinary proposals during the campaign, and should then have persisted in rejecting the only reasonable one he had made."

One final, vital stroke was required to complete this glorious, remorseless campaign. The French must be driven from Ghent and Bruges. With a piercing eye Goslinga discerned the obvious. "While we were in this camp [on the Dender] to cover the convoys, I said to the Duke one day that I feared very much that, if the enemy remained in possession of Ghent," the opening of the next campaign would be impeded. "The Duke listened to what I said with attention; he said that he would ponder over it maturely and asked me to come back the next day to thrash it out anew." When on the morrow at eight o'clock the Deputy repaired to the Duke's quarters, he was received by Cadogan, who seemed very ready to be convinced in favour of the project. Thus fortified, Goslinga pressed the plan upon the Commander-in-Chief as soon as he emerged from his bedroom. If Marlborough was a good general, he was also a consummate actor. Like Cadogan, but more slowly, he yielded his mind gradually to Goslinga's audacious plan; and finally he adopted it. Goslinga, thrilled, full of having given this important turn to strategy, hurried off to write enthusiastically to The Hague in its support, leaving Marlborough and his Quartermaster-General to exchange smiles and confidences which can readily be imagined.

Having long held these intentions, it was no doubt most agreeable to Marlborough to see the officious Deputy going forward with the plan as if it were his own, and to make him its spontaneous advocate with the Dutch. No doubt it was a help for him to be able to say to the members of the Dutch Government or the States-General, "Goslinga's plan is sound. We should be culpable if we neglected it."

Within an hour of Boufflers' surrender at Lille Marlborough began his concentration against Ghent. The French garrison consisted of thirty-four battalions and nineteen squadrons well supplied. The population of eighty thousand dreaded the siege, declared they would observe neutrality, and begged Marlborough not to bombard the city. The Duke could give them no comfort. On the 11th he approached; but in view of the strength of the place and its garrison he decided that Eugene must aid and cover him. Accordingly on December 16–17 Eugene marched north to the neighbourhood of Grammont, and sent his infantry forward to the siege. On the 18th Ghent was invested. The weather was obliging. Hitherto the frost had been intense, but now a sudden thaw without any rain freed the waterways for the barges carrying the siege cannon. On the 24th the trenches were opened; on the 27th Fort Rouge, on the north, was captured, and by this time the batteries were planted. There was no reason why Ghent should not have stood a prolonged siege, but the disheartenment of the French armies produced a surprising collapse. To the indignation of the King, Count de la Motte on the 29th opened negotiations. In his justification before a French court-martial he pleaded that his supreme duty was to preserve his army. Marlborough's judgment was thus expressed: "I believe Monsieur de Lamotte will not be able to give good reason for what he has done." Following La Motte's example and orders, Grimaldi evacuated Bruges, Plassendael, and Leffinghe. All the French troops withdrew along the coast upon Dunkirk. The very next day the weather broke completely; it poured, and Marlborough dispersed the allied armies to their winter quarters.

Marlborough to Godolphin

Ghent
January 3, 1708[9]

I was yesterday from ten in the morning till six at night seeing the garrison of Ghent and all that belong'd to them march by me. It is astonishing to see so great numbers of good men to look on, suffer a place of this consequence to be taken at this season with so little a loss. As soon as they knew I had possession of the gates of this town, they took the resolution of abandoning Bridges. *This campaign is now ended to my own heart's desire,* and as the hand of the Almighty is visible in this whole matter, I hope her Majesty will think it due to Him to return public thanks, and at the same time to implore His blessing on the next campaign. I can't express enough to you the importance of these two towns, for without them we could neither be quiet in our winter quarters nor have opened with advantage the next campaign. I shall to-morrow give the necessary orders for the separating the army, so that in two days they will be all on their march for their winter quarters. I must go with Prince Eugene for some few days to The Hague, after which I shall take a little care of my health. . . .

Thus ended, according to his "heart's desire," Marlborough's grand campaign of 1708. Throughout the supreme command had rested unquestioned in his hands. He often deferred to Eugene's advice, and the two commanders always presented themselves in full agreement. Marlborough's decisions, supported by Eugene, were accepted invariably by the councils of war. The noble Prince not only served and aided, but inspired Marlborough in anxious days. But the responsibility and authority rested with the Duke, and five-sixths of the troops in the field were under his own command. Success was joyously shared between the two, but failure would have fallen upon Marlborough alone. Constantly ailing in health, reduced once to despair, gnawed by his political anxieties at home, harassed by every kind of pressure and appeal from Godolphin, Sarah, and the Whig leaders, conscious of his waning favour with the Queen, pursued by the inveterate malice of the Tory Party, he nevertheless continuously took great risks, and wished to take more.

The answer to the innumerable criticisms passed upon his operations must be their complete success. While always audacious, in every case he made the most careful plans based upon wonderfully accurate information. He had studied attentively the character of his chief opponent, Vendôme. He realized quickly the divergence of view among the French commanders, and played upon it. From the battle of Oudenarde onward he was sure that the morale of the French army was broken. Weighing all these factors and making his plans, he did not allow himself to be distracted by the closing of his communications or converging superior forces. He was unaffected by the terrible appearance of the war-map. Although baulked in his design of marching into France, he contrived to produce outstanding success by a second alternative. He persevered, undaunted by hazards, unsatisfied by victory, until every antagonist and almost every adherent was worn down by physical and mental strain, and he was left unchallenged master of the whole theatre of war. "I think," he wrote to Sarah on December 10, "we may say without vanity that France will with terror remember this campaign for a long time."

CHAPTER SIXTY-NINE

Culmination

❦ 1708, Winter ❧

ENGLAND had now been raised by Marlborough's victories to the summit of the world. Many living men could remember the island as a paid dependant of France. The Constitution and the religion of the nation had repeatedly lain under mortal challenge. Only twenty years before, with Ireland in rebellion and Scotland separate and estranged, the English people, led by the aristocracy, had been reduced to the desperate remedy of bringing in a foreign ruler and foreign troops to protect them against betrayal by their own sovereign and invasion by Louis XIV. Even after the wars of William III, as it seemed but yesterday, the nation, disarmed by an insensate economy, had quaked to see the Grand Monarch occupying without the firing of a shot all the fortresses of the Spanish Netherlands, and adding, apparently without opposition, the mighty empire of Spain and the Indies to the already paramount and overweening power of France. Protestantism and Parliamentary institutions crouched behind the dykes of Holland or stood ill-guarded and downcast beyond the Strait of Dover. The discordant petty states of Germany could make no headway against the gleaming arms and all-embracing diplomacy of France. Not only European hegemony, but even the dominion of the whole world seemed about to fall to a glorified, triumphant, Catholic ruler, as intolerant as he was cultured, as cruel and ambitious as he was strong, and sole autocrat of twenty million Frenchman.

One man and three battles had transformed all. The Grand Monarch was beaten to his knees. His armies would no longer face in the open

field the men who had conquered at Blenheim, Ramillies, and Oudenarde, or the Commander who led them. The whole of the Netherlands,
all their fortresses, had been regained, and now stood as the barrier of
salvation for world causes dear to Dutch and English hearts. The three
parts of the British Isles were united under one Queen and one Parliament. The French fleets had been driven from the seas. The Mediterranean had become an English lake. The treasures of the ocean, the
wonders of the New World, seemed to be the appointed inheritance of
the islanders.

We have seen by what narrow margins, against what adverse
chances, the Grand Alliance had three times been rescued by Marlborough's war and policy from ignominious collapse. The external
difficulties were now virtually at an end. With Eugene at his side, his
military command was undisputed. The princes and sovereigns of the
Grand Alliance had in general yielded themselves to his leadership.
From The Hague, from Hanover, from Berlin, from Vienna, from
Turin, from Barcelona, all roads led to his tent. The Russian excursion
of Charles XII had removed that formidable irrelevancy from the
scene. To dictate terms of peace to France, either upon her frontiers or
in Paris itself, seemed a prospect near and sure. But now a new and
fatal burden was bound upon those shoulders which had borne so
much. The Queen's heart, it was said, was changing. The Captain-
General and his wife were losing—nay, had lost—the favour they had
used to such effect. The Tories, the peace party, the Jacobite party,
were gaining in royal favour. Henceforth the Court of Louis XIV pondered the question, If reasonable peace is denied, can France hold out
till Marlborough falls? Thus every scrap of gossip about Queen Anne,
about her relations with Sarah and Abigail, about Mr Harley and the
back stairs, about Whig obtrusiveness and Godolphin's helplessness,
exercised its influence both upon the conduct of the war and every
peace negotiation. Queen Anne was the axis upon which the fate of
Europe turned: and Queen Anne had now become her own worst
enemy.

As the meeting of Parliament approached the Whigs professed
themselves highly discontented with the exertions which Godolphin,
Marlborough, and even Sarah—who had broken herself in their interests—had made to bring them into office. Sunderland was deputed to
inform the Duchess that unless Lord Somers received promotion, and

unless Law Officers more agreeable to their party were appointed, they would withdraw their support. Sarah passed this on to Marlborough, besieging Lille, and did her best herself. When it was seen that she no longer had any influence with the Queen some of the Whig lords even stooped to make their court, with poor success, to Abigail. They realized that Marlborough alone still possessed exploitable credit with the Queen. They therefore sought to spur him to their service by renewing the attack upon his brother, which had been called off at the beginning of the year. Whether or not Admiral Churchill was vulnerable in his financial record, or in his naval administration, he was certainly obnoxious to them as a politican. The Admiral had during the year stimulated the Toryism of his chief, Prince George of Denmark, and given full vent to his own. Sarah became deeply incensed against him. In vehement letters she importuned her husband to free himself of a brother who had become an encumbrance. For a long time Marlborough resisted. He was attached to his brother George, through whom he controlled naval strategy.

It was not till October that Marlborough was finally convinced that his brother must go. Then he wrote him a truly devastating letter.

Marlborough to Admiral Churchill

October 19, 1708

Finding you still continue in the Prince's council, and the Parliament now so near, I cannot be so wanting either to you or to myself as not to tell you plainly, with all the kindness of a brother and the sincerity of a friend, that if you do not take an unalterable resolution of laying down that employment before the Parliament sits, you will certainly do the greatest disservice imaginable to the Queen and Prince, the greatest prejudice to me, and bring yourself into such inconveniences as may last as long as you live, and from which it is wholly impossible to protect you. Whereas, on the other side, if the considerations of making the Queen's affairs more easy next session, of avoiding a great deal of trouble and disagreeableness to the Prince, and of real danger to yourself, as well as prejudice to me, prevail with you to comply with my earnest desire in this thing, I think I could be answerable to you that you could not fail of finding your advantage in it, doubly to what you do now, both in profit and quiet. These motives being all of them as strong as it is possible for me to suggest, I hope you will give me the satisfaction of letting me know very soon, that my mind may be at ease in this matter, and that you have virtually laid down before my coming over.

Both Marlborough and Godolphin hoped that the sacrifice of the Admiral would placate the Whigs and spare the Queen the distress of a Parliamentary attack upon George of Denmark. All through this summer the Prince had lain grievously ill in the little house the Queen had occupied at Windsor. Here she and Abigail nursed him with every care. The poor Prince "had his astma, a spitting of blood, a lethargie, a hidropsie and something of a palsie." The summer of 1708 was hot, and the Prince suffered much in the small house from the weather, from his maladies, and no doubt from the remedies of those days. The house was backed upon the park, and, according to Sarah, gave easy access to Harley, who was frequently admitted by Abigail to the Queen.

Who can wonder at Anne's hatred of the Whigs, whose cruelty and greed of employment sought to hound her stricken husband out of place and reputation. Her sorrow as a wife, her wrath as Queen, were flames that fed each other. Heedless of this, and, indeed, of every decency, but strong in their sense of constitutional injustice, the Whig lords expanded their claims. The Whigs struck at Marlborough through his brother and at the Queen through her husband. Their calculations were proved correct, their methods efficacious. To spare her husband's last days from pitiless public attack, Anne flung the hungry Whigs their offices. What she would not give to Marlborough's wise and loyal counsel, to Godolphin's entreaties, and to the obvious facts of the Parliamentary situation, she yielded to this peculiarly mean form of personal pressure.

The Junto were indignant to find that after the promise had been extorted its fulfillment was delayed. On October 28 they learned the cause. Death had discharged the Lord High Admiral from his office. " . . . Nature," wrote Godolphin,

was quite worn out in him, and no art could support him long. The Queen's affliction and the difficulty of speaking with that freedom and plainness to her which her service requires, while she has so tender a concern upon her is a new additional inconvenience, which our circumstances did not need, and will make it more necessary than ever that you should not delay your return to England; for I really foresee that unless that can be compassed very, very soon, it will be next to impossible to prevent ruin. . . .

The crisis had, however, passed. The Whigs obtained their posts. The office of Lord High Admiral was put into commission under Pembroke. Wharton, from whom Anne had once so summarily demanded his staff on account of his evil character, went to Ireland as her Lord-Lieutenant; and Somers became Lord President. Thus in the teeth of the Queen, somewhat to the concern of the country, but in accord with the will of the House of Commons, a characteristically Whig party Administration was installed in power. The events of the next four years were to make this expedient the rule for the future. A memorable milestone in British constitutional history had been passed.

On October 27 Sarah, who had driven all night from Windsor when she had heard that Prince George's condition had become critical, presented herself at Kensington. She was, as she records, received "very coolly, and like a stranger," by the afflicted Queen. She returned, however, the next day and was present at the moment of the Prince's death. Archdeacon Coxe, writing for the England of 1820, says:

> She again waited on the Queen the ensuing morning. With affectionate zeal she removed her royal mistress from this sad spectacle to her closet, and desiring the other attendants to withdraw, she knelt down, and endeavoured to soothe the agonies of her grief, continuing in that posture till the first emotions had subsided.

Such rigmarole probably does justice to what occurred. Sarah was in a false position. She would have been universally condemned if she had abandoned her mistress and former beloved friend in her grief; yet her presence could only be an intrusion. One person alone in the whole world could be of any comfort to Anne. It was to Abigail she turned. She suffered herself to be led and advised by Sarah, whose duty it was; but she only wanted Abigail. Sarah directed affairs with her customary precision. The Queen must leave Kensington for St James's in order that the funeral arrangements should be made. Anne, reluctant to quit her husband's body, resisted feebly for a while and then submitted. The Duchess, putting aside the Queen's requests for Abigail by saying, "Your Majesty may send for her at St James's, when and how you please," conducted her in her own coach to that palace.

CULMINATION

No fault can be found with Sarah's behaviour on this difficult occasion. It was correct, capable, and considerate; but on neither side was there a spark of loving companionship. All that was dead. Even its afterglow ended with the breath of the poor Prince. He had always been a good friend to Sarah and a staunch admirer of the Duke. Now he too was gone. Sarah in her memoirs wrote of her relations with the Queen in the succeeding weeks:

> She would make me sit down as formerly and make some little show of kindness at night when I took my leave; but she would never speak to me of anything, and I found I could gain no ground, which was not to be wondered at, for I never came to her without finding Mrs Masham had just gone from her, and I went to her seldomer.

Sarah's behaviour would lie under no reproach but for her subsequent writings upon these events. She thought fit to record that the Queen, in spite of her grief, "ate a very good dinner" on the day of her husband's death. When Anne took the habit of sitting alone for long hours in her husband's little workroom at St James's Palace, she made a reflection which does only herself discredit. "But the true reason of her Majesty choosing this closet to sit in was that the backstairs belonging to it came from Mrs Masham's lodgings, who by that means could secretly bring to her whom she pleased." These aspersions, uninspiring as thoughts, unpleasant as statements, recoil upon their author when contrasted with one of Anne's scribbled notes to Sarah:

> I scratched twice at dear Mrs Freeman's door, as soon as Lord Treasurer went from me, in hopes to have spoke one more word to him before he was gone; but, nobody hearing me, I wrote this, not caring to send what I had to say by word of mouth; which was, to desire him that when he sends his orders to Kensington he would give directions there may be a great many Yeomen of the Guards to carry the Prince's dear body, that it may not be let fall, the great stairs being very steep and slippery.

Low, low lay the Tories in the trough of misfortune after Harley's fall. Harley's ordeal, until William Greg's dying breath had exonerated him, had been shattering. That at least was over; but he had quitted office and the Court to find his party split into at least three sections, each abusing the other, and all laying the blame of their plight upon him. The Jacobite attempted invasion ruined Tory prospects at the polls. Mauled and diminished, they awaited the meeting of a Parliament where, for the first time during the reign, the Whigs would be masters. St John, seatless, buried himself in the country. Harley was returned; but to a scene how changed! For nearly a decade he had practically led the House of Commons, either from the Speaker's Chair or as Secretary of State. All that time he had been its principal figure. Now, stripped of his official trappings, without a majority to support or even a party to cheer him, and lacking the power of dramatic and eloquent speech by which an individual position can be maintained, his prospects seemed at first forlorn.

But Harley's political knowledge taught him that a healing process would soon begin in the Tory Opposition. Common misfortunes would beget a common partisanship. He felt sure the party would come back to him. He knew its great strength if united. Meanwhile, as was notorious—and notorious to his advantage—he was, through Abigail, in the closest contact with the Queen.

Apart from his hopes in Court intrigues and party strife, Harley might at any time receive a valuable windfall from abroad. Oudenarde, indeed, had been a heavy blow, setting the town agog again with Marlborough's fame. But as the autumn advanced it seemed almost impossible, if one took a map and studied the positions of the armies and Marlborough's communications, to believe that he could capture Lille. Expert military opinion was predominantly adverse throughout Europe.

Harley and the leaders of the Tory Opposition watched the heart-shaking drama of the famous siege run its course, and awaited with equal eagerness bad news from the front and the meeting of Parliament.

Thus, while the Queen and Abigail had been holding the fort against the Whigs and obdurately resisting the advice of her two great counsellors, Harley quietly and deftly rallied the Tories. The spectacle which greeted the new Parliament of a purely party Whig Administration monopolizing all the important offices, though certainly not the favour of the Crown, was all that was necessary to unite the "gentlemen of England" into a solid opposition. To whom could they look but Harley, who had suffered for resisting Whig pretensions, and whose relations with the Queen gave him the key to the spacious patronage of any new Administration?

CULMINATION

The intense constitutional struggle recorded in the letters between the Queen and Marlborough had proceeded unknown to Parliament or the nation. It was fought out sternly in secret. To the outer world the Constitution seemed to work with perfect smoothness. The Queen was seen to extend her gracious favour increasingly to those statesmen who had the greatest influence with the new Parliament. The new Parliament extolled its happy relations with the Crown; and the Commons voted ever larger supplies for the prosecution of the war, even before the campaign of 1708 reached its long-drawn, glorious conclusion. Such was the world parade. But underneath how strangely different! The victorious General broken and begging to retire; the faithful Treasurer a blackmailed agent of the Junto; the world-revered Sovereign working by the backstairs with the publicly discredited leader of the Opposition against the Parliament which sustained her throne and the great Ministers who had made it safe and almost all-powerful!

We have now reached the culmination of the eighteenth-century world war, and also of this story. The foundations of Marlborough's authority in England had been destroyed, and the national and European cause which he served was triumphant. His power had gone, but his work was done. We have witnessed a spectacle, so moving for the times in which we live, of a league of twenty-six signatory states successfully resisting and finally overcoming a mighty coherent military despotism. It was a war of the circumference against the centre. When we reflect upon the selfish aims, the jealousies and shortcomings of the Allies, upon their many natural divergent interests, upon the difficulties of procuring common and timely agreement upon any single necessary measure, upon the weariness moral and physical which drags down all prolonged human effort; when we remember that movement was limited to the speed of a marching soldier or a canal barge, and communication or correspondence to that of a coach, or at the best of a horseman, we cannot regard it as strange that Louis XIV should so long have sustained his motto, "Nec pluribus impar." Lying in his central station with complete control of the greatest nation of the world in one of its most remarkable ebullitions, with the power to plan far in advance, to strike now in this quarter, now in that, and above all with the certainty of implicit obedience, it is little wonder how well and how long he fought. The marvel is that any force could have been found in that unequipped civilization of Europe to withstand, still less to subdue him. In Marlborough the ramshackle coalition had found, if not its soul, its means of effective expression, its organic unity, and its supreme sword. Thus the circle of quaking states and peoples, who had almost resigned themselves to an inevitable overlordship became a ring of fire and steel, which in its contraction wore down and strangled their terrible foe.

This result had in fact been achieved. Behind the lines of the French armies, beneath the glitter of Versailles, all was exhausted, all lay in ruin. The Grand Monarch still stood magnificent at bay; but his heart was broken. When he looked out upon his wasted realm, upon the depleted manhood of France, upon his pillaged treasury and half-tilled fields, upon his cowed armies and sunken fleet, despair and re-morse swelled upon him in a dark flood, and peace at any price became his dearest, all-compelling wish.

Marlborough, Heinsius, Eugene, the Triumvirate of executive action, could not as yet see the dust and ashes which lay behind the fortresses, the rivers, and the mountain-chains of the French front. They saw that front was still unbroken; they were sure it was crumbling. One more campaign, one effort stronger than any yet made, and the prize of their long toils would be won. This was their conviction at the fall of Ghent and Bruges. They could not foresee the crowning calamity of the great frost which was to fall on France in the winter of 1708. Neither, on the other hand, were they or any of their generation conscious of the new strength which the French people could supply if a war of monarchical aggrandizement should be transformed into a war of national survival. They all three underrated both the present prostration and the latent final resources of France. None of these facts presented themselves to the breathless actors in this struggle in the clear light, shape, and pro-portion in which we now see them. They could not tell how soon or with what exertions they were going to win. But that they were win-ning, and had only to hold together and drive on, was their absolute conviction.

But when they looked behind them to their own countries they saw themselves at the last gasp. The Empire, including Austria and all Ger-many, could not put forty thousand men in the field, apart from the troops paid for by the Sea Powers. The Dutch were worn to the bone by the endless struggles of the Republic. Their Barrier was in their

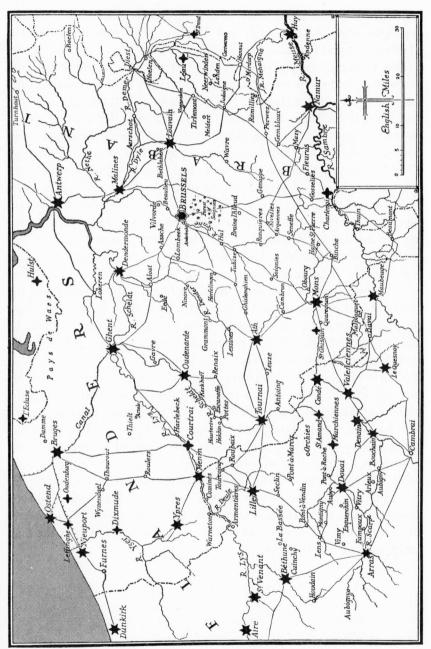

12. General Map of the Western Netherlands

hands to take and hold. They longed for peace. All future war-effort depended upon Marlborough and England, and from this moment Marlborough and England were no longer one.

The Captain-General and the Lord Treasurer, Marlborough and Godolphin, had spent upon the seven campaigns all their political capital. The Queen was estranged. Instead of being their strength, she was henceforth their bane. Sarah and Godolphin were her aversion, Marlborough a splendid but oppressive fact. The Tories, banished from power, united by misfortune, nursed revenge. The Whigs had arrived. They had forced their way into what the Queen regarded as her own apartments. They had gained control of all the great offices and assets of State, including the services of Marlborough. They had the majorities of the Lords and Commons at their backs. They cared nothing for Sarah and Godolphin; for these were blunted tools which could be thrown aside. They knew they owed nothing to Marlborough. He constantly vowed that he would align himself with no party. In so far as he had used his influence in their behalf upon the Queen it had been in vain. He had not only had no part in their success, but had even been grievously offended by the actual methods by which they had succeeded in gaining their ends. They recognized him as their greatest possession. They were sure he was in their hands, or at least that without them his power was at an end. He knew this too. He was inflexibly resolved not to play the game of any party. From the bottom of his heart, and with forty years' experience in court, camp, and council, he despised both Whigs and Tories with a cordiality which history has readily understood. Henceforward he regarded himself not as a leader, but as a functionary. He would serve the Government as a soldier or as a diplomatist. He would not be answerable for their relations with the Queen or with Parliament. He would lead such armies as they provided, and negotiate such treaties as they prescribed. In this humbler guise he might still procure the means to fight the final campaign and march to Paris.

CHAPTER SEVENTY

"OO" ✓

⚜ 1708-9, Autumn and Winter ⚜

THE whole of Europe was now weary of the almost unceasing wars which had ravaged its peoples for twenty years. Peace was desired by all the warring states. It was in all men's minds. The Allies wished to reap the fruits of victory. Louis XIV, resigned to the decision of arms, sought only a favourable or even a tolerable escape. The enormous quarrel had been fought out, and the exorbitant power of France was broken. Not one of the original objects of the war was not already gained. Many further advantages were open. Why then was this peace not achieved in the winter of 1708 or the spring of 1709? Upon Marlborough has been cast the responsibility for this lamentable breakdown in human affairs. How far is this censure just? The issue is decisive for his fame. Before it can be judged his authority and the foundations on which it stood in Holland and in Britain must be measured.

From the day in 1706 on which the Emperor had first offered him the Viceroyalty of the Netherlands a sense of divergent interest had arisen between the Dutch leaders and their Deputy Captain-General. Although Marlborough had at a very early stage refused the offer, the Dutch could not help suspecting first that he owed them a grudge for having been the obstacle, and secondly that he still hoped to obtain the prize. It was known in Holland that both the Hapsburg brothers were intent upon this plan. After Oudenarde Marlborough had been sent a patent for life of the Governorship of the Netherlands. In August 1708 King Charles had written, "I do not doubt but that you will never allow the Netherlands, under the pretext of that pretended Barrier, to suffer any diminution either in their area or as regards my royal authority in them, which authority I wish to place in your hands."

In reporting the arrival of the patent to Godolphin Marlborough had written, "This must be known to nobody but the Queen; for should it be known before the peace, it would create inconveniences in Holland." But, he had added, if when the time came Anne "should not think it for her honour and interest that I accept of this great offer, I will decline it with all the submission imaginable."

During the summer of 1708 a correspondence sprang up between Heinsius and Torcy, the French Foreign Minister, the tendency of which was a separate understanding between Holland and France which might well bring about a general peace conference. Louis XIV also was obstinately convinced that the path to peace lay through an initial and separate understanding with The Hague. At the end of May 1708, even before the battle of Oudenarde, Torcy had invited the Pensionary's servant Petkum secretly to Paris, and in August, with the knowledge and approval of Heinsius, he had conversations with Torcy at Fontainebleau.

It was not proper nor did it prove possible to keep all this from the vigilant Captain-General. During August the news of Petkum's Paris visit leaked out in high circles at The Hague, and it cannot be doubted that it soon reached Marlborough. In fact, at the beginning of 1709 his Secret Service obtained the whole file of the current Torcy-Petkum correspondence. He was not willing that Heinsius should pursue separate negotiations behind his back or that of the British Government, and in his turn he sought contact with France.

Throughout the long campaigns Marlborough had maintained correspondence, written in English and under his secret sign "OO," with his illustrious nephew Berwick. In the main this had been concerned with the courtesies of war, and cherished kinship amid national quarrels. It was not till 1708 that the correspondence touched any serious matter. To and fro went the messengers with their trumpets and flags of truce, bearing letters of routine, and other letters also, in their sabretaches. Marlborough took every possible precaution. He enjoined secrecy. He requested Berwick to return each of his letters with the answer. He seems to have trusted him absolutely, and as it proved rightly. Nevertheless, he ran a very high degree of risk in confiding himself to those upon whom he was inflicting such grievous injuries when, without consulting the Queen or the Cabinet, Sarah or Godolphin, Heinsius or

Eugene, he at last, in mid-August 1708, definitely set on foot a peace negotiation.

Marlborough to Berwick

August 24

OO. I would assure you that no one in the world wishes for peace with more sincerity than I. But it must be stable and lasting, and in conformity with the interests of my country. Circumstanced as I am, I am inclined to think that the best way to set on foot a treaty of peace would be for the proposal to be first made in Holland, whence it will be communicated to me, and then I shall be in a better position to help, of which you may assure the King of France. And if there is anything which he wishes me to know upon this, I beg him that it may not be by other hands than yours, for then you may rest assured that I will tell you my opinion frankly. OO

It will be seen that Marlborough's intervention took the form, not of superseding any negotiations already in progress between France and Holland, but rather of broadening their basis, and bringing himself and Britain into them. Berwick replied cordially to this letter, and sent it to the King. Louis and his advisers Chamillart and Torcy were all set on dealing with the Dutch alone. They did not welcome the intervention at this stage of Marlborough, and still less of Britain. They also inclined to regard Marlborough's letter as only another of his innumerable traps and stratagems. The answer which Berwick was at length directed to send reflected these views. "It is not now for his Majesty to make such overtures, but for the Dutch." He invited Marlborough to continue to use him as a channel. Marlborough could only reply, "The King is alone the judge of what is best for his honour and his interest. . . . If ever the King wishes to let me know his intentions about peace, I desire that it should be by your agency, for I shall have no reserve with you, being sure of the care you will have for my safety and my honour."

During the next two months Petkum continued his activities. By the end of October the Duke feared that the Dutch were about to quit the Alliance. No answer had been returned to his urgent request for an augmentation of their army for the campaign of 1709, and he saw that the fall of Lille would encourage the Dutch to a quick separate negotiation. Confronted with a grave menace to the Alliance and to British interests, he made a renewed and far more direct effort to gain control of the peace negotiations, and to bring London and Vienna into them.

On October 30, the night that the capitulation terms of Lille were finally agreed, and the day after receiving Heinsius's refusal to increase the Dutch army, he wrote again to Berwick. This time he proposed that France, counting on his aid, should ask for an armistice and openly seek a peace.

Marlborough to Berwick

October 30

. . . You know that I have formerly assured you of my desire to contribute to peace whenever a favourable occasion should present itself. In my view it is at this moment in our power to take such a step as will produce peace before the next campaign. . . .

My opinion is therefore that if the Duke of Burgundy had the King's permission to make proposals by means of letters to the deputies, to Prince Eugene, and to me, requesting us to communicate them to our masters, which we should be bound to do, that would have such an effect in Holland that peace would certainly ensue.

There follows this remarkable passage:

You may be assured that I shall be wholeheartedly for peace, *not doubting that I shall find the goodwill [amitié] which was promised me two years ago by the Marquis d'Alègre [i.e.,* the *douceur* of two million livres]. If the King and the Duke of Burgundy do not feel that this time is suitable for peace proposals, I beg you to have the friendship and justice to believe that I have no other object than to end speedily a wearisome war.

As I trust you without reserve I conjure you never to part with this letter except to return it to me.

It is indeed amazing that any man should have the hardihood to write such a letter to those who regarded him as their most terrible foe—indeed, their only foe. Marlborough is justified before history in pursuing these unauthorized negotiations. In his supreme position, both military and political, he was entitled, on his own judgment and at his own peril, to act for the best for his country, for the Alliance, and for

Europe, all bleeding and ravaged by interminable war. It is often inevitable that the first overtures of peace should be made by secret and informal means. Marlborough, for his part, combined all the qualities both of the military and the civil power; he was the soul of the war, and if he thought it was time to make peace he was right before God and man to do so. But to introduce into this grave and delicate transaction a question of private gain, a personal reward of an enormous sum of money, however related to the standards of those times, was, apart from moral considerations, imprudent in the last degree. Yet this conduct has a palliative feature curiously characteristic of several of Marlborough's most questionable acts. It served interests national, European, and personal at once and equally. It was the one thing capable of convincing the French King and Cabinet of his sincerity. It affected Berwick in this sense immediately. "Although naturally," he wrote to Torcy on November 2, "I am not taken in by all he says, nevertheless I am inclined to believe in his good faith on this occasion, *all the more because he speaks in it of a certain matter by which you know he sets great store.*"

It certainly shook the advisers of Louis XIV. "If he is sincere," wrote Chamillart to Torcy (November 2), "use should be made of his goodwill, which would not be bought too dearly at Monsieur d'Alègre's figure." The dreaded conqueror placing himself in their hands in this way, and revealing his personal weakness so nakedly, went far to sweep away their inveterate suspicions. They addressed themselves with renewed concern to his proposal. In the course of their anxious confabulations a memorandum was written, assembling all the arguments for and against the project, which throws a revealing light upon the inmost thoughts of the hard-pressed yet mighty monarchy.

> The Duke of Marlborough must amidst all his prosperity fear the envy and antagonism of his own class, the general hatred of his countrymen, whose favour is more inconstant than that of any other people, the fickleness of his mistress and the credit of new favourites, perhaps the death of the Princess [Queen Anne] herself, the resentment of the Duke of Hanover and the residence of his son in England, and lastly the breaking up of the Alliance. . . . If the war could last for ever, a man like Marlborough, who rules absolutely the councils of the principal European Powers and who conducts their armies, might have to make up his mind whether the fear of the fu-

ture should induce him to abandon so fine a personal position. But in one way or another the war is drawing towards its end. . . .

He might well be satisfied with his glory if he could win peace for his country. . . . He will be no less satisfied upon the point of possessions, which the war has procured him in plenty. It is not just that peace should deprive him of all the advantages which the command of the armies brings him. We might well, therefore, give him to understand, and that without undue circumlocution—scarcely necessary, indeed, with him—that if he worked sincerely for peace he would be rewarded on its conclusion with a sum of two or even up to three million livres, payable at the earliest date, which would be a matter of arrangement.

The influence which Cardonnel has upon his mind is such that it is absolutely necessary to persuade the secretary in order to succeed with the master. The sum of three hundred thousand livres would be usefully employed to this end, and the King agrees to the Duke of Berwick proposing this by the person whom he chooses to speak to the Duke of Marlborough.

In the end, however, King Louis and his councillors could not bring themselves to take the momentous step which Marlborough required. They still saw plainly the shattering effects upon French prestige and French means of resistance which were involved in suing for an armistice or initiating a peace proposal to Holland on the morrow of the fall of the city of Lille. It spelt defeat, acknowledged for all time in letters of fire. Well might they believe that Marlborough was sincere; for what better conclusion could the war hold for him? His sword would have struck the final blow. They would have surrendered beneath its impact, and he would quit the field of war loaded alike with glory and booty. More grievous distresses were needed to bring them to their knees. So, hearkening principally to Chamillart and his false ideas about the immediate military situation, clinging to the hope that the French armies could winter on the Scheldt and that Lille could be regained in the spring, the King directed Berwick to say in reply:

November 5, 1708

You know that the Kings of France and Spain desire peace. . . . You are aware that so far [the Allies] have made no response indicating a genuine desire for a settlement. Their situation, although most brilliant in appearance, cannot prevent those who have experience of war from perceiving that it is strained in all sorts of ways, and may at any moment be so transformed that even if you took the citadel of Lille you might be thrown into extremities which would destroy your armies and put it out of your power to supply with munitions and food the strong places you occupy beyond [*depuis*] the Scheldt, to recruit and re-establish your forces, and to put your armies in a state to resume the war in the next campaign.

I cannot but think that these reflections, joined to the desire which you have always shown me to contribute to a peace, have led you to write me the letter which I have received from you, which I will send you back if it has no happy results, and which I would return with great pleasure if it proved to have hastened the moment for me to thank you for the part you have allowed me to play in this important negotiation. . . .

Marlborough felt himself violently rebuffed. He does not seem to have minded at all asking the King of France to give him a fortune if he brought all things to a happy conclusion. He had no consciousness of how disdainfully posterity would view this incident. But he was deeply angered that the other side should dispute his opinion upon the military situation. He was sure he could beat their armies wherever they chose to stand. His peace proposals had been sincere. He had made the French what he deemed a fair offer. They had rejected it. Let them, then, since they were so proud, learn the consequences. In a few weeks he had broken their lines along the Scheldt, recaptured Ghent and Bruges, and driven Burgundy and Vendôme helter-skelter into France. "I am much mortified," he wrote to Berwick,

to see that you believe I had any other motive for my letter except a wish for peace and the promise which I had given to let you know when I thought the proper time had come to take the steps necessary to secure it.

He would, he added, continue to do his best to reach a just and lasting peace before the next campaign, "and meanwhile the two armies will be free to make the best use of the advantages which they each suppose they possess. Please send me back my letters with your next."

So failed Marlborough's personal effort for peace. That it was wisely and justly founded at the time few can doubt. It is tarnished for us by the alloy of a sordid pecuniary interest. But this, indeed, in that age added to its chances of success. It reflects more upon Marlborough as a man than upon Marlborough as a worker. He was a greater worker than man. No personal interest or failing turned him from his work. He toiled and schemed with all his power for a reconciled and tolerant Europe, a chastened France, and a glorious England to inherit the New World. As a part in these purposes he delighted in military success. All these conditions being satisfied, and without prejudice to their achievement, he would take pains and stoop for a commission. Supreme sanity, profound comprehension, valiant, faithful action, and if all went well large and punctual money payments!

At this time one would suppose Marlborough and Godolphin had all they could ask in Britain for themselves or for their policy. Yet their intimate letters reveal their profound misgivings and discouragement. Godolphin harps again on vexations to which "the life of a slave in the galley is paradise in comparison." Marlborough replies that nothing but his loyalty to his colleagues and his duty to the Queen would make him endure the burden and hazards of his command. There is so much bewailing in the Marlborough-Godolphin correspondence, written for no eye but their own, that many writers have questioned the sincerity of these tough, untiring personalities who, in the upshot, held on with extreme tenacity and to the last minute to every scrap of power. It was surely, then, no mere desire to keep up appearances before each other, but rather to fortify their own minds for action by asseverating their own disinterestedness, that made it worth while to set all this on paper? It is certain that neither was deceived by the favourable surface which British politics had assumed. Both knew too much of what was hidden from Parliament and even from the foreign envoys in London. They knew Queen Anne with the knowledge of a lifetime. They knew the Tory Party to its roots. They had enjoyed the best opportunities of measuring ex-Secretary of State Harley. Thus their eyes were necessarily fired upon Abigail and the visitors she brought to the Queen by the back-stairs.

The Whigs could not bring to the peace negotiations the real force of a national decision. A Whig Government might in 1707 and earlier years have been most helpful to vigorous war. In 1709 their peculiar qualities, prejudices, and formulas were a new obstacle to the peace now within reach. England had little to ask for herself. The recognition of the Protestant Succession, the expulsion of the Pretender from

France, and the demolition of the harbour and fortifications of Dunkirk seemed modest requirements for the State and nation which had formed, sustained, revived, and during so many years led to victory the entire coalition. But upon the general objective of the war the London Cabinet was implacable. The whole of the original Spanish Empire— Spain, Italy, and the Indies—must be wrested from Philip V, the Duke of Anjou, and given to Charles III. As early as 1703 Rochester and the High Tories, intent upon colonial acquisition, had raised the cry "No peace without Spain." The Whigs, while holding a different view about strategy, were for their part more than willing to associate themselves with this sweeping demand. What had become for years a Parliamentary watchword was now to be made good. This was not only an extension of the original purposes of the war; it was a perversion of them. The first aim had been to divide the Spanish inheritance; now it was to pass it in a block to the Austrian candidate, himself the direct heir to the Imperial throne of the Hapsburgs. From the rigid integrity of this policy there was not to be even the slightest concession. Nothing was to be offered to the Duke of Anjou. Nothing was to be offered to Louis XIV. In order to carry into history their English Parliamentary slogan, the British Government, with Parliament behind them, were ready to shoulder all the demands of the Empire upon the Rhine, including Strasburg, all the demands of the Duke of Savoy, and almost all the demands of the Dutch for their Barrier.

There is no doubt that responsibility for the loss of the peace in 1709 lies largely upon England, and that the cause arose unconsciously out of her Parliamentary stresses. In Parliament the Spanish theatre always commanded vivid and abnormal interest. Money for Spain; troops for Spain; ships for Spain; a base for the fleet in Spanish waters; war in the Peninsula; no peace without its entire surrender—these were phrases and ideas popular not merely for a session but year after year, and enlisting a very general measure of active support. Marlborough throughout regarded the whole of this Spanish diversion as a costly concession to wrong-headed but influential opinion. By one device or another he had contrived to reduce it to the least improvident dimensions. He scraped away troops and supplies on various pretexts. He sought his results in Flanders or at Toulon. Nevertheless, as in the famous debate of December 1707, he found it necessary to his system to humour Parliament in these ideas which were so strangely cherished by them. No doubt he found it convenient to gather support for the general war by adopting and endorsing the watchword "No peace without Spain."

Indeed, at this juncture in 1709 we find Marlborough mouthing this maxim, to which he had become accustomed, as fervently as its ill-instructed devotees. He was committed to it by the shifts to which he had been put to gain supplies from precarious majorities in former years. It had become a sort of drill, a parade movement, greatly admired by the public, of doubtful value on the battlefield, but helpful in recruiting. So now, at the culmination of the war, Marlborough marched along with the Cabinet and Parliament upon this Spanish demand; and the whole influence of England, then paramount, was used to compel the Dutch and incite the Empire and German states to conform. The Whigs in the brief morning of their power invested this demand with their own sharp precision. Upon it was placed an interpretation which certainly had not been adopted by any English party at an earlier stage. 'Spain' was made to include not only the Indies, but Italy. The interests of the City and of the Whig merchants in the Levant trade now found full expression in the Cabinet. "Let me tell you," said Sunderland in April to Vryberg, the Dutch envoy, "that any Minister who gave up the Sicilies would answer for it with his head." There could be no compromise with the Whigs about Sicily and Naples.

It has been remarked as curious that each side in the great war, while remaining in deadly conflict, had in fact largely adopted the original standpoint of the other. The English, who under King William had seen their safety in the partition of the Spanish Empire, now conceived themselves only served by its transference intact to the Hapsburg candidate. The Spanish nation, which at the outset cared little who was their king so long as their inheritance was undivided, were now marshalled around their Bourbon sovereign, and were almost indifferent to what happened outside the Peninsula. The insistence by England upon her Parliamentary formula destroyed the victorious peace now actually in her grasp. The incidents of the negotiations which will presently be recounted followed inevitably from this main resolve. But although England with her wealth and Marlborough's prowess could, as the event showed, over-persuade the Allies to her point of view, her resulting position was unsound and even absurd. Neither the Dutch nor the

German states had the slightest intention of making exertions to conquer Spain after they had made a satisfactory peace with France. Austria, at once famishing and greedy, was impotent for such a purpose. Upon England alone and the troops she paid must have fallen the burden of conquering not only Spain but, as it had now become, the Spanish nation. It is certain that this was a task of which she would soon have been found incapable.

The Dutch demands were more practical, but no less serious. They had fought hard and long for their Dyke against France. It was now certain they would gain it. Exactly which fortresses, how many of them, where the flanks of the line should lie, were to be matters of sharp discussion with the French, with the English, with the Prussians, and still more with the Empire. But in all that concerned military security friend and foe were agreed that the Dutch rampart should be established. During the course of the war the Dutch trading interests had come to regard the conquest of the Barrier of fortress towns as carrying with it control over the commerce of the whole countryside between the fortresses. The Empire, the Allies, King Charles III, several of the most important German states, and also England had rights or interests which this Dutch demand affronted. In those days the wishes of the local population, with their charters and long-established customs, also counted. The Belgian people, Flemings and Walloons alike, were no friends of France. They were prepared in the circumstances to be ruled by Charles III of Spain, by the Elector of Bavaria, or, if that could be brought about, by the Duke of Marlborough. The one solution which was abhorrent to them was the intimate exploitation of their Dutch neighbours. A hundred and thirty years later the severance of Belgium from Holland arose from the very same antagonisms which surged within the victorious Grand Alliance and beat upon the head of Marlborough.

The divergence between Marlborough and Heinsius was thus inevitably serious. The Pensionary had been vexed by Marlborough's obstruction of the Barrier negotiations in 1706. He had for months been conducting secret parleys with France on the basis that Marlborough was not to be told about them. Already in December 1708 Heinsius had gone so far as to instruct Vryberg to discuss the Barrier Treaty directly with Somers and to appeal to the new Whig Ministers apart from Marlborough. In December Vryberg reported that he had done so, and had found the Whig leader very desirous of a settlement with Holland on the basis of a reciprocal guarantee about the Barrier and the Succession. Godolphin wrote to Marlborough that he agreed with Somers. The formal proposals for a Barrier Treaty which he was expected to negotiate reached Marlborough on his way from Ghent to The Hague, and on arrival he was officially told about the French peace offers through Petkum. Thus at the outset of these all-important negotiations Marlborough found himself to a large extent isolated. He was divided both from the Dutch and from his own Government upon large issues of principle and procedure.

His main wish was to convince the Dutch that he cared more for their confidence in the conduct of the war than for the Viceroyalty of the Netherlands. For this he conveyed through Stanhope, with whom he had relations of close confidence and friendship, an account of the difficulties which prevented him from accepting the Viceroyalty and in the middle of 1709 took a decisive step to exclude himself. At all costs to himself he must regain the confidence of the Dutch. A letter from Charles III to Wratislaw on June 30, 1709, shows how far he went. Not only did he three times specifically refuse this magnificent office, but he urged that it should be conferred upon Eugene. He thought that only by the substitution of another name for his could the misunderstandings between him and the Dutch be finally removed. Reluctantly he had reached the conclusion that only this sacrifice would preserve that Anglo-Dutch unity, the keystone of the whole Alliance, which was now in jeopardy.

Charles III to Wratislaw

June 30, 1709

[As to] what concerns the person of the Duke of Marlborough, to whom I alone upon the advice of Moles [Charles's principal councillor] have given the patent of the Governor in the Netherlands, which he has three times resigned and bidden me rather to name another 'actualen' [in order] to placate the jealousy of the Dutch. He has also written about this matter to the Emperor to ask if he does not think that it would be better to send Prince Eugene himself there, for he is very popular with the Dutch, and it is at the moment very necessary to bring order into the whole Barrier affair, and thereby to animate the Dutch further.

It would no doubt have been agreeable to Marlborough, since he was resolved not to accept the Viceroyalty himself, to have it conferred upon his friend and comrade Prince Eugene. With Eugene in control of the Spanish Netherlands, he could be sure that the treatment of the Belgian inhabitants and the general course of the Government would be no hindrance to the military operations. But to propose Eugene for the appointment was by no means to secure it for him. The question became a burning one as soon as Eugene reached Vienna. The Prince himself was anxious to accept. He had been baulked by internal jealousies in 1706–7 of his desire to remain Viceroy of the Milanese. Here now was the opportunity of gaining a finer kingdom, where he would be more closely knit with Marlborough for any further campaigns in the Low Countries. His enemies, however, were as persistent as ever against him. They were now reinforced by the apprehensions of his friends, who saw themselves likely to be deprived in the future of his leadership and protection in Vienna. Thus Marlborough's proposal was never made public by the Emperor or by Charles III, and it was only after a lapse of a hundred and fifty years that the fact became known.

CHAPTER SEVENTY-ONE

The Great Frost

ƨɑ 1709, January-April ɒƷ

THE campaign of 1708 had ended according to Marlborough's "heart's desire," and although it had been protracted beyond all custom into the depth of winter and over the end of the year, his warlike energy was entirely unabated. "This has been," he wrote to Godolphin (January 31, 1709), "a very laborious campaign, but I am sensible the next will be more troublesome; for most certainly the enemy will venture, and do their utmost to get the better of us; but I trust in the Almighty that he will protect and give success to our just cause." Neither his own fatigues and worries nor his deep desire for peace had slackened his preparations for 1709. While peace negotiations regular or secret, now by this channel, now by that, made The Hague a whispering gallery, Marlborough had already for two months past been concerting with Godolphin, the British Cabinet, and throughout the Grand Alliance the marshalling for 1709 of the largest armies yet seen in Europe. In order that the whole movement of the Alliance towards its goal should be unfaltering, it was planned that he and Eugene should take it in turns to remain in Holland driving forward the gathering of men, munitions, food, and forage, and making sure that no signatory state fell out of the line. Eugene's presence in Vienna being judged at first indispensable, Marlborough stood on guard in Holland during January and February. As soon as the fall of Ghent liberated the confederate armies for what remained of the winter he repaired to his headquarters at Brussels, and thence, with occasional visits to The Hague, began to

(682)

pull all the levers of the vast, complicated, creaking machine of which he was still master.

He seems to have quartered himself when at The Hague upon the Prussian commissary, General Grumkow, who wrote some droll accounts to his master:

> My lord Duke has obliged me to take a furnished house opposite the Orange palace and is living there himself. This costs me twenty louis d'or a month, and as I have very good Tokay, *qu'il aime à la fureur*, I gave his Highness a supper yesterday, which was attended by Prince Eugene, my lord Albemarle, Cadogan, and Lieutenant-General Ros. They were all in the best spirits in the world. I recommended the matter of exchanging the prisoners to my lord Duke in the most pressing manner yesterday; he was almost angry and said to me, "I will stake my fortune on what you want; you will have your people before the end of this month." "Good," I said; "I will wager you ten pistoles." "Done," replied the Duke, and soon afterwards, with a violent gesture, "Mordieu, if these people make me lose this money I will make them suffer so much that they will have cause to regret their surliness." Prince Eugene laughed loudly over the effect which a bet of ten pistoles had upon the spirits of my lord Duke, and I cannot help assuring your Majesty that if I had foreseen that my lord Duke would take this matter so much to heart I should have offered him fifty pistoles and gladly lost them so that your Majesty should be more certain of getting back two battalions and two squadrons. The bet has at any rate resulted in the Duke's sending precise and threatening commands to the French commissary over the matter.

Marlborough lavished his flatteries and persuasions upon the King of Prussia, using exactly the kind of arguments which were most likely to appeal to a military monarchy.

> Brussels
> February 17

> Yesterday, while at table with My lord Albemarle, My lord Duke received letters from Berlin and told me with great joy that he was informed that your Majesty had allowed the Crown Prince to serve in the campaign; in his view, he added, your Majesty could do nothing more glorious for yourself or more advantageous to your interests than to send the Crown Prince to the school where great men are formed

and princes are only esteemed so far as their valour and good conduct make them worthy of it. All good Englishmen, he added, would be enchanted, and he for his part would give a good example and exert himself to let your Majesty see by his devotion and attention to the Crown Prince the extent of his sentiments in this direction for the sacred person of your Majesty yourself. If your Majesty would permit it he would himself undertake the duties of a father from time to time, giving his Royal Highness the best advice of which he is capable in order to effect the purpose which your Majesty has laid down— that is, to make the Crown Prince ever more and more fitted for the time when he has to rule, and enable him to follow the noble examples of his father and his great and illustrious ancestors.

These attentions produced remarkable results. Frederick I was more amenable to Marlborough's solicitations than to any other. But here is another odd illustration of Marlborough's attitude towards money. Because of the need for reinforcements, he gave up the 2½ per cent. commission on the pay of the contingent to which he was entitled by the Queen's warrant and which formed the fund under his unchecked control by which his Intelligence and Secret Service were maintained. How this was applied is not recorded, but it turned the scale at Berlin, and King Frederick by an addition of 6210 men raised the Prussian troops to the magnificent figure of twenty-two thousand for the coming campaign.

It was not until the Prussian negotiations were completed, and he had also made his arrangements for the Würtembergers and the Palatines, that he once again addressed himself to the Dutch. He was now in a position to display to them the powerful succours which he had obtained, and the States-General were threatened with the reproach of being the sole defaulter. Thus spurred, they in the end produced an increase of six thousand hired troops, and this, added to the ten thousand expansion sanctioned by the British Parliament, would raise the confederate army to an unprecedented strength during the currency of the peace negotiations. We must admire the dual process to which the Allies were now committed of earnestly seeking peace while at the same time preparing for war on an ever greater scale. Nearly always Governments which seek peace flag in their war efforts, and Governments which make the most vigorous war preparations take little interest in peace. The two opposite moods consort with difficulty in the human mind, yet it is only by the double and, as it might seem, contradictory exertion that a good result can usually be procured.

Everywhere except in Spain the military misfortunes of France were numerous and heavy. The disastrous campaign in Flanders has been recounted. The Hungarian revolt, mortally smitten by Rakoczy's defeat at Trentschin, was dying down. Turkish intervention against Austria was no longer likely. The Empire, freed from these distractions, must be regarded as a less feeble enemy in the future. The capture of Port Mahon confirmed upon a permanent basis the absolute English command of the Mediterranean. Nevertheless, Louis XIV prepared indomitably to meet in 1709 the onslaughts of the Allies, and from every quarter troops were gathered to face Marlborough and Eugene. Intercepted letters in January confirmed the reports that the French Grand Army would reach a total of a hundred and fifty thousand men by the early summer, that Villars would command it, and that the objective would be Lille. At the same time by Marlborough's exertions there were gathering over a hundred and fifty thousand men around the Allies' standards in the Low Countries. The campaign was therefore planned by both sides upon an unexampled scale.

But now there fell upon France a new and frightful misfortune. Since the beginning of December there had been a hard and almost unbroken frost. On January 6, after a brief thaw, it set in again with a bitterness so intense that two days later the rivers of France, even the Rhône, one of the most rapid rivers in Europe, were almost completely covered with ice. All the canals of Venice were frozen, and the mouth of the Tagus at Lisbon. Masses of ice appeared in the Channel and the North Sea. Communications between England and Holland were suspended; Harwich and the Dutch ports were ice-bound. Olives and vines split asunder. Cattle and sheep perished in great numbers. The game died in the forests, the rabbits in their burrows. From January 25 to February 6 there was an interval of snow followed by a few days' thaw, and then another month, until March 6, of extraordinary cold. Thereafter gradually the weather became less severe. Thus this almost glacial period had lasted into the fourth month. On February 4 it was known at Versailles that the seed corn was dead in the ground. The English fleet, now active in the Mediterranean and in the Baltic throughout the winter, intercepted supplies of grain from Africa, the Levant, and Scandinavia. After more than sixty years of his reign, more than thirty years of which had been consumed in European war, the Great King saw his people face to face with actual famine.

Their sufferings were extreme. In Paris, the death-rate doubled. Even before Christmas the market-women had marched to Versailles to proclaim their misery. In the countryside the peasantry subsisted on herbs or roots or flocked in despair into the famishing towns. Brigandage was widespread. Bands of starving men, women, and children roamed about in desperation. Châteaux and convents were attacked; the market-place of Amiens was pillaged; credit failed. From every province and from every class rose the cry for bread and peace. Meanwhile the northern horizon darkened continually with the menace of impending invasion.

The peace discussions wended onward. A secret meeting between Dutch and French agents had been arranged in February under the authority of Heinsius and Torcy. In March the burrowings of Petkum were replaced by public negotiations which originated in another quarter. Philip V had, apparently on his own impulse, in the early days of the New Year sent an agent from Spain with full powers to make peace offers on his behalf. The Dutch had replied that a minimum offer of Spain, the Indies, Milan, and Belgium, and a favourable treaty of commerce were the essential basis of conversations. Louis XIV saw in this reply the possibility of compensating and consoling his grandson with Naples and Sicily, and grasped the opportunity. In January he had been vigorously preparing for a new campaign pending negotiations. But during February, appalled by the full realization of the calamity which had befallen France, he resolved upon peace at all costs. In March he sent Rouillé, one of his ambassadors, the President of the Parlement of Paris, to meet the two Dutch plenipotentiaries at Moerdyk, an obscure village within the Dutch frontier.

It was several weeks before the Allies understood this change of mind and the extent of the disaster which had enforced it. Marlborough sailed on a flying visit to England on March 8. He was still under the impression that another campaign must certainly be fought, and that it would open early in Flanders with unexampled fury. "I think the only good step that we can make towards a peace is to get early into the field. I have given my orders for all officers to be at their commands by the end of this month, and I beg the Queen would show a dislike of any that should stay after that time."

Before he reached London on March 14 the Whig leaders Somers and Halifax had carried an address in the Lords defining the minimum terms of an English peace. The purpose of this address was to proclaim the main outlines of the Government policy, and to rouse and reveal its support in Parliament and the country. It was in essence a vote of confidence in Whig foreign policy, emphasizing the popular side and putting foremost the guarantee of the Protestant Succession. There was no mention of Spain. Somers and Halifax knew that the public were indifferent to this Parliamentary counter. It was better to dwell on the guarantee of the Protestant Succession, which every one understood, and in which the Whigs and the majority of the nation was one. The loud demand by the Commons for the razing of Dunkirk was a warning signal to the Dutch negotiators. "The Pensionary," wrote Petkum, "is scarcely pleased by the latest address of the English Parliament, or the Queen's reply. He let me know in confidence that he suspects that the Duke of Marlborough is the author of both."

Marlborough on his arrival in England was conscious of a somewhat restrained welcome, especially from his colleagues. He was expected in many circles to be the bearer of definite peace proposals. He had none. He had not sought to have any. His position was sensibly undermined. William III's old friend Portland, who was an extremely well-informed Dutch agent in England, and Vryberg had been equally successful in convincing the Whigs of the Duke's obstruction and the Dutch of his loss of influence. When the news of Rouillé's apparition and the details of the first Moerdyk conversations reached London, the startled Whig leaders looked askance at Marlborough. How could this detrimental situation have arisen without his knowledge?

Rouillé's coming caused equal alarm in Vienna. It was, of course, believed that Marlborough was behind it. His disclaimers to Wratislaw, although true, did not convince. "It seems almost incredible," replied Wratislaw, "that you should not have been informed." Marlborough's position was further prejudiced. Hitherto his influence with the Dutch had helped him with the British and the Empire, and his influence with these had helped him with the Dutch; now the British and Dutch began to talk together directly, and the Empire still held Marlborough responsible.

Meanwhile Marlborough's Secret Service had intercepted Rouillé's correspondence describing the conversations at Moerdyk. The Dutch seemed prepared to go very far to meet France upon the crucial issue of Naples and Sicily. The French proposal was not only that Naples and Sicily should be guaranteed to Philip V, but that the guarantee should be enforced if necessary by a Franco-Dutch (and possibly English) expedition. It is noteworthy that this is the first appearance in the negotiations of the idea of enforcing peace terms upon recalcitrants by war, and that it came from France. Clearly the French envoy was suggesting to the Dutch hostilities in the last resort against the Empire. It also appeared from Marlborough's intercepts and decipherings that the Dutch were not prepared to go so far as that.

The new instructions with which Marlborough reached The Hague on April 20 emphasized among other matters "that no negotiations for peace should be concluded with France until preliminaries were adjusted between England and the States." This sealed the fate of the Rouillé mission. Eugene had arrived from Vienna the day before. "My lord and I are agreed," wrote Eugene, "that we should press for the dismissal of Rouillé out of the country." The last formal interview took place between the Dutch and the French envoys at Bodegraven, another obscure village by the banks of a small, remote canal where the French envoy had been deposited by Heinsius. Rouillé was informed that there could be no guarantee of the use of allied force to procure the cession of Naples and Sicily to France. The very idea was impossible, and ought never to have been suggested. The French envoy then asked for an armistice. Such a request exposed the weakened will-power of France, but the Dutch delegates had no authority to grant it. This was the end of Rouillé's mission. He brushed from his shoes the dust of the Dutch pothouses to which he had been relegated, and set off for the challenged splendours of Versailles.

Heinsius was now resolved that Marlborough should face the definite Dutch demands which he had so long staved off, but upon which he had been instructed by his own Government to negotiate. On April 19, when Eugene was away at Amsterdam, a deputation of the States waited on Marlborough and with all ceremony unfolded their claim. They opened their mouths very wide. "You will see," reported Marlborough afterwards, "it encloses what might be thought a great kingdom." In the course of the discussion it was plainly hinted that if Marlborough objected too much or dallied too long the rumour would be circulated that personal aims—for instance, the Viceroyalty—were his motives. The Duke listened urbanely. When at length he spoke he criticized only the two points which his instructions from the Whigs authorized him to resist. He protested against the inclusion of the coast towns, particularly Ostend, in a military Barrier against France. He drew attention to the weight of the contribution demanded from the Belgians to maintain the Dutch garrisons. He could not resist at the end asking what was to be left to King Charles III of his possessions in the north. Having thus met the attack on ground which even the Whigs must occupy, he dismissed the subject with the soothing remark, "The matter is not yet ripe for discussion." Thus he had broken the Rouillé mission by invoking the priority of the Barrier, and now put the Barrier once again for the moment upon the shelf.

During March and April the allied Governments became convinced that Louis XIV was finally defeated. The reports which poured in upon them seemed to show that France was incapable of fighting another campaign. To the lamentable tales of the frost havoc, of the widespread famine, of the desperate condition of the French troops, without bread and forage, had been added the bankruptcy of the great French banker Bernard of Lyons, whose efforts to found a French State Bank with an official paper currency had been remarkable. Whereas the Allies had previously overrated the remaining resources of their antagonist, they now set them as far beneath the truth. Marlborough was not immune from this process. Apart from his manœuvring against Heinsius, he was now sure that the French would grant the whole allied demands. All the more had it been right to drive away Rouillé! Why prolong these partial local chatterings when Louis XIV was forced to beg before all the world for armistice and peace? To drive away Rouillé was not to drive away peace. A far fuller offer was impending.

But how long would it be before France made a new proposal of peace, not secretly to Holland, but publicly to the Grand Alliance? Evidently the Duke thought it was a matter of days. But days were now very important. Heinsius was demanding the Barrier. The Whig Cabinet was set upon the Barrier and Guarantee Treaty as a preliminary to peace. But if the French opened a general peace negotiation all preliminaries between the Anglo-Dutch allies would be superseded. The discussion would be with the three great allied Powers. Marlborough's instructions were to negotiate the Barrier, and he knew that

within a few days of Rouillé's departure Heinsius would force him to a
decision. That decision must cause great dissensions among the Allies.
"I tremble," he wrote to Godolphin on April 19, "when I think that a
very little impatience may ruin a sure game."

Heinsius at length felt himself certain of his preliminary Barrier
treaty. Marlborough was convinced that much larger events were at
hand. The question was whether Heinsius would corner him upon the
Barrier before France publicly appealed for a general peace. In order to
gain time he returned to London. No one could stop him. While
Heinsius and the Deputies were arranging their plans, their Captain-
General was at sea on one of the "yahcts," sailing for home. How
could he have negotiated the Barrier Treaty? He did not agree with it.
He thought the Dutch demands monstrous in themselves, ruinous to
the Alliance. Besides—here he turned the argument which had dam-
aged him against those who used it—the Dutch would never believe he
was impartial after the offers of the Viceroyalty had been made to him.
The Whigs must appoint a colleague to deal with the Barrier question,
some one who felt as they did and commanded their entire confidence;
some one who was not hampered as he was by all that had happened
in the past and by all that might happen in the future. So Marlborough sailed from the Brill to Margate, leaving Heinsius to extract
what consolations he could from the frosty, sepulchral glitter of Eugene.

CHAPTER SEVENTY-TWO

The Fatal Article

᚛ᚄ 1709, April and May ᚃᚌ

WHEN Louis XIV read in Rouillé's report the "hard replies" which were the sole fruit of peace efforts he had never dreamed he would be forced to make, he broke into tears before his Ministers, and with a gesture of despair said he would give up all—yes, even Lille and the Sicilies. To this point, then, had he been reduced by Marlborough's seven campaigns and the terrible frost. After the Council had been dismissed, Torcy loyally offered himself to carry the humiliating acceptance to Holland. Upon the mood of the moment this offer was accepted.

The sending of the French Foreign Minister into Holland to sue for peace was a signal acknowledgment of defeat by France. Marshal Villars, when he heard of it, was convinced that peace was already agreed; for otherwise how could so devastating an admission have been made? It was a proof of sincerity and of stress which none could mistake. Henceforth no longer would there be merely attempts to make sectional treaties with the Dutch, but a grand negotiation for a general peace on the part of a Power which could, it was apparent, no longer continue the war. "Had not Torcy come himself," wrote Petkum, "the Allies would never have asked for such preliminaries." On May 4 Eugene reported to the Emperor that an unknown man with the passport of an ordinary courier had passed through Brussels, where the Prince lay, and that rumour said he was Torcy. Most writers suppose that Heinsius had no previous notice. It is certain, however, that when on that May night the Pensionary heard Torcy's knock at the door he was already expecting him. Thirty years before Heinsius, acting in Paris too zealously in the interests of the Dutch Republic, had been menaced by Louvois with the Bastille. The Great King had in his long reign patronized as well as maltreated the Dutch. This small Republic of the Dykes now found mighty France suppliant upon its threshold.

Heinsius received Torcy with courtesy, but informed him that he could only confer with him by the authority of the States-General; and thereafter the States-General declared "that the States did bind themselves to nothing until they knew the sentiments of the Queen of Great Britain by the return of the Duke of Marlborough." The second stage of the parleys thus began, but on a footing entirely different. An excessive admission of weakness had been made, disastrous to France, but destined in the long swing of events to be fatal to the Allies.

Torcy's plan was first to gain the Dutch by extreme concessions upon their Barrier, then to induce them to bring pressure upon Marlborough, and at the same time to win Marlborough's goodwill by a colossal bribe. He believed that "at the present conjuncture Marlborough holds the key and that there are means of making him choose peace." Marlborough had just left the second time for England, and the French Minister anxiously awaited his return. In the meanwhile he received the detailed assent of the King to his proposed procedure. He was to tell Marlborough how astonished the King was that he should be making efforts to break off the negotiations after his previous overtures for peace. The King would be glad to see Marlborough receive the reward which had been promised him. A precise tariff was set up. If Philip V received Naples and Sicily, or even in extreme necessity Naples alone, two million French livres; if the fortifications and harbour of Dunkirk were spared, or Strasburg was left to France, two millions: a total, if all these objectives were obtained, of four millions. Such was the view which the French took of their conqueror. They can hardly be blamed for doing so after his letter to Berwick. However, as we shall see, Marlborough was not to be bought for money. He would accept it as a reward, but not as an inducement. There is no doubt a real distinction between the two cases; but it is not one of which the French could be aware, nor upon which posterity will bestow any large measure of respect.

But Marlborough was in England. His second visit to London taught him further how his power had declined. The Whigs had full control of the Cabinet and both Houses, while the Queen was cool with him and hot against Sarah. The Whigs, and Godolphin with them, were convinced that France was at her last gasp, and would submit to whatever terms were imposed. Marlborough, upon whom the reports of the ruin wrought in France by the frost had made their impression, did not contest the general view. He understood only too well that henceforward in all negotiations he was no longer to be executor of his own policy, but only spokesman of the Cabinet. His keen instinct and knowledge of men must have apprised him of the little goodwill which his new colleagues bore him; but whether he had any inkling of the ingratitude of his son-in-law may be doubted. He did not make a quarrel with the Whigs because he had been overruled or because he found himself in a strait-jacket. He set himself, as usual, to bring about the best results possible with the means at his disposal. But he was determined not to become responsible for the kind of Barrier Treaty which the Dutch demanded. Already on April 24 he had written to Godolphin asking for a colleague plenipotentiary representing the view of the Whigs and accountable to them.

The Whigs deferred to the logic of facts. Their first choice fell upon Halifax, who was still fuming out of office, and for whom they wished to provide. He refused his friends' offer with a taunt directed at Marlborough. "If the Duke had anticipated that the treaty to be concluded with the Republic would be to the satisfaction of the English people, he would not share it with anyone else; but the fact that he is asking for a colleague shows that he wishes to push off some of the odium upon this colleague."

The Cabinet next considered Sunderland, and all were speedily agreed that he would never do. So the choice fell upon the young Lord Townshend. He was an amiable and well-informed politician, a recent convert to the Whig Party, and a friend and protégé of Somers. He was a student of foreign affairs, and had much personal charm. Townshend was prepared to serve as Marlborough's colleague, and the Junto were able to conceal themselves united in the background. Hoffmann said of him, "He is pliant and manageable." Marlborough announced Townshend's appointment at once, treated him with the greatest ceremony, and made him bear the responsibility for those parts of the Cabinet policy to which he himself had from the beginning been inveterately opposed.

(693)

Meanwhile in Holland the negotiations had made great progress. According to his discretion, inch by inch Torcy yielded to the Dutch demands about their Barrier. Heinsius was able to announce to Eugene that the Dutch were content with the terms so far as they concerned themselves alone; they had only to consider their allies. The mood of the Pensionary had changed considerably since the early months of the year. As the desperate plight of France became every day more understood, both he and his countrymen stiffened towards the French and warmed towards the Allies.

Buys now raised the question of what guarantee the French could offer that the Spaniards would accept the terms. Torcy answered that Philip would be given three months to submit on pain of the complete withdrawal of French support. Heinsius also continued to demand, though without great enthusiasm, the entire Spanish monarchy for Charles III. Even this was no longer to be resisted by the French. But now every one hastened to put in his claim.

When we look back on the long years of terror and spoliation to which these princes had been subjected from the might of the Great King, it would be surprising if they had acted otherwise. Moreover, the allied armies were now gathering in the field. Contingents, in former years so tardy, were this time hurried to the front by rulers who saw the prey in their grasp, and were anxious to be in at the death and establish their rights to a handsome share. Marlborough's exertions for five months to have large forces at his disposal during the negotiations had succeeded beyond his hopes. "All the facts," wrote Eugene to the Emperor, "go to show that France is quite unable to prolong the war, and we can, therefore, if we wish obtain everything we ask for. We have only to hold together and preserve a good understanding among ourselves." Even those Dutchmen who at the beginning of the year were willing to make a separate peace were now convinced that France was at their feet. Van der Dussen, the leader of the Dutch peace party, himself wrote, "The policy of this province [Holland], the largest of all, depends upon more than five hundred persons, most of whom regard France as brought to bay, and who are so embittered by the memories of the past that they are resolved without compunction to make an end once and for all of their puissant foe." In this mood van der Dussen had advised Torcy not to hesitate or wait for the arrival of Marlborough, which would only create fresh complications. Let him now, while time remained, concede all that was demanded. But Torcy still had hopes of Marlborough, and one remarkable reason for those hopes.

On the 18th the two Englishmen arrived.

The situation had simplified itself and vastly improved. The French were ready to submit; the Dutch had no thought of a separate treaty; Heinsius was content to shelve the idea of preliminaries with England. Marlborough saw all going as he had wished, and evidently thought the peace as good as made. Torcy, who was staying with Petkum, asked at once through his host to see him. Marlborough met the French envoy that very night. Torcy has given his own account of the discussion. Marlborough was all smiles and blandishments. He protested profound respect for Louis XIV, and presently mentioned Berwick. Torcy replied that he was familiar with the correspondence and that the attitude of the King had not changed. He would have enlarged upon the details, but Marlborough at once dismissed the subject. So far from suggesting any mitigation, he asked, in accordance with his instructions, for the restoration of Newfoundland. This was a fresh demand, and Torcy was shocked by it. To ease the situation they talked about Saint-Germain. Torcy had spoken of the Pretender as "the King of England." Marlborough referred to him always as "the Prince of Wales." He expressed an earnest desire to do some service to the Prince as the son of a king for whom he would gladly have sacrificed his blood and life. Speaking of Townshend, he said, "He is here to keep watch over me [en surveillant] in person. He is a very good fellow, whom I chose myself, but he is a Whig party man. Before him I must speak as an obstinate Englishman. But I wish with all my heart it were in my power to serve the Prince of Wales, and that your good offices may give me an opportunity." Marlborough went on to emphasize his desire for peace, and how he longed to end his days quietly. Torcy, who knew how fast the armies were gathering, was not comforted. He saw that there could be no hope of saving any part of the Spanish monarchy through Marlborough. He had that morning received permission from the King to drop Naples and Sicily if need be. He now announced this to Marlborough. The Duke, gratified, assured him that this was the only way to make peace. The interview ended. Torcy went to the Pensionary and informed him of the fresh sacrifice he had been prepared to make for the sake of peace.

The culminating phase in the negotiations was now reached. Together Marlborough and Townshend drafted their report for the Cabinet. Torcy had admitted willingness to concede not only Spain but Italy. He had, however, in telling Heinsius used a phrase which had attracted immediate attention.

> . . . As far as in him lay, by which expression it seems as if he thought the King would not be able to do it of himself in the manner we expect, or that he has some further reserve.

Here was the first glimpse of the rock on which all was in the end to split. It was not immediately approached.

On May 20 the three leaders of the Alliance met Torcy and Rouillé in formal conference. The Dutch and English demands were discussed first. These were easily conceded by the French plenipotentiaries. But then Prince Eugene began to say that France had given way to England and Heinsius in order to gain them to her interest. He took his stand for Germany on the terms of the Treaty of Westphalia, which had ended the Thirty Years War in 1648. He must now on behalf of the Emperor ask for Strasburg and Alsace. At this Torcy appeared to lose patience. "We were practically at one with Torcy," wrote Eugene to the Emperor, "but when mention was made of the lands of the Holy Roman Empire he began to stutter, and answered he must leave, and demanded to depart and asked for his passports, so that without any further resolution the conference broke up." Neither Eugene nor Marlborough thought that Torcy was in earnest, The Frenchman saw himself faced by united enemies. Later on in private van der Dussen warned him that the war spirit was rising in Holland, and there was no more hope from the pacifists. Torcy returned to the conference when it met again next day. He had powers to abandon Strasburg, but not Alsace. He fought for both, and no agreement was reached. There was a similar dispute over the claims of Savoy. In the end Torcy offered to dismantle Strasburg; but Eugene still continued to demand Alsace, and the Dutch and English supported the claims of Savoy. The deadlock continued.

Alone with Marlborough, Torcy made a final effort to seduce him. We have only the French Minister's account. Marlborough, who had himself proposed the interview, urged submission. He used all his most obsequious arts. If the peace was made he would earnestly desire the favour and protection of the King. He spoke again with sympathy about the Pretender. He referred to his desire for peace, to his uprightness, to his conscience, to his honour, and frequently to God. Torcy, thinking his moment had come, renewed his offer of a vast bribe. He received at once the same rebuff. We are left wondering why Marlborough should have wanted to repeat this unpleasant scene. Did he wish to expose Torcy to a second rejection of his offer? Did he wish to convince Louis XIV how vain it was? Did he, perhaps, take a personal relish in being offered these immense sums of money and seeing himself reject them? No one can tell, but the fact remains that this hardy, avaricious man, who could at this juncture without the slightest injury to the interests of England have helped the French towards the peace he himself desired, and gained an immense sum thereby, proved incorruptible. There is nothing to boast of in this.

When the conference met again on May 22 the two questions, Alsace and the claims of Savoy, were still in dispute. The Allies complained of the inadequate security which was offered for the surrender of Spain. They asked that they should not have to carry on the war in Spain while France was enjoying peace. They demanded guarantees. It had been realized at Versailles for some weeks that security for the fulfilment of the peace treaty would be required.

King Philip was established in Spain. His kingship was championed by the Spanish people. His armies were victorious. He had declared to his grandfather, "I will only give up my crown with my life." He had created his one-year-old son Prince of Asturias, and the Cortes had acclaimed the infant as heir to the monarchy. Here were grave realities. Louis XIV was not necessarily able to answer for the King of Spain. He may have been aware of the strong feeling of the Dauphin against any desertion of his son, who had fought successfully at odds amid perils.

Torcy violently opposed the idea of any guarantee. The Pensionary on behalf of his colleagues asked as proof of good faith for three French and three Spanish fortresses actually still occupied by French troops over and above all that had been conceded. Eugene, the land animal, wanted permission to march the allied armies into Spain through France. During the conference Marlborough sat silent. But on the night of the 23rd he expressed his doubts upon the possibility of forcing Louis XIV to act against his grandson. "Marlborough even suggested schemes to turn the article so as not to commit his Majesty to war against Spain."

"The French Ministers absolutely refused," wrote Townshend, "an amendment which might, they sayd, possibly engage their master to a condition so unnatural as to make a war with his grandson. . . ."

For two days the discussion turned around this crux, and as it became the ultimate cause of the disastrous breakdown it is necessary to realize its importance. Many writers think it monstrous that, when these immense issues were so nearly settled, all should have been wrecked on such a point. It is certain that the Allies would have been wrong and unwise to break upon it, and without doubt they did not mean to do so. None the less it was a matter of far more importance than many of the terms over which both sides haggled so long.

The allied chiefs were convinced that King Philip would obey the orders of his grandfather if these were given to him *in earnest*. Torcy was evidently of the same opinion. All that was necessary, therefore, was for the King to give gages that he would issue these orders in good faith. It never occurred to anyone on either side at this moment that Louis XIV was really to be compelled to use armed force to expel his grandson from Spain. The allied leaders were surprised and shocked at a later stage that this colour could be put on their requests. The alternative for them was a new war, perhaps a very grievous war, a war of conquest and subjugation in Spain. It might impose enormous expense in blood and treasure on the Allies, already exhausted, while defeated France, whose ruler could by a word have prevented it, would rebuild her prosperity in peace.

Marlborough had his plans ready for a Spanish war. It would have been on the largest scale. The great armies would be transported to the Peninsula. One army under Marlborough would advance from Portugal, and the other under Eugene from Catalonia. They would meet in Madrid. Marlborough himself considered that a single campaign would suffice. It may well be that he greatly underrated the resisting power of a nation, and thought of it in terms merely of professional armies. He might have fallen into the same trap as was a hundred years later to ruin Napoleon.

As no agreement could be reached on the outstanding points and no solution was forthcoming of the guarantee problem, Torcy invited the

Allies in their turn to put their whole proposals in the form of a memorandum. Heinsius undertook to draw it up. The days following were occupied with the final drafting of the preliminaries. The Dutch statesmen worked throughout the nights of May 24 and 25 to frame the project. During that time the memorable Articles IV and XXXVII were drawn up.

> IV. . . . But if it should happen that the said Duke of Anjou does not consent and agree to the execution of the present convention, before the expiration of the term aforesaid, *the Most Christian King, and the Princes and States concerned in the present treaty, shall in concert take convenient measures to secure the full execution thereof.*
>
> XXXVII. . . . *In case* the King of France executes all that is above mentioned, *and that the whole monarchy of Spain is delivered up and yielded to King Charles III as is stipulated by these articles, within the limited time,* 'tis agreed that the cessation of arms between the parties in war shall continue till the conclusion and ratification of the treaties which are to be made.

On the morning of May 27 Heinsius laid what were called the "preliminaries" before the Frenchmen. Invited to comment upon it, they made various reserves, but it is remarkable that they made no specific objection to Articles IV and XXXVII, which, read together, obliged France, under penalty of losing the cautionary towns, to procure the submission of Philip V. The document must, of course, be sent to Versailles for the King's final decision. Would the French envoys sign it first themselves? Torcy refused point-blank.

The French were requested to give an answer by June 4. Thus the "memorandum" acquired the character of an ultimatum. This had not been the original intention. Into this position the Allies had been manoeuvred by Torcy's skill. The document he had obtained presented the issues to his master in such a way as to enable him to refuse, should he choose to do so, on the broadest grounds.

CHAPTER SEVENTY-THREE

The Lost Peace ‿

ᵫ 1709, May and June ᵭ

"YOUR MAJESTY," wrote Torcy on May 28 in sending the preliminaries to Versailles, "is thus entirely free to reject absolutely these conditions, as I trust the state of your affairs will permit; or to accept them if unhappily you conceive it your duty to end the war at any price." If the King decided to break, his Minister advised that the odium should be thrown upon Alsace and the claims of Savoy, rather than upon the methods of ensuring the surrender of Spain. It is thus clear that Torcy had in no way taught the allied negotiators to recognize that Article XXXVII possessed a fatal character. On the contrary, it is evident that he took it for granted that Philip V would obey his grandfather without the slightest hesitation. Indeed, he had even remarked in the conference that the King of Spain would very likely be at Versailles before him. With heavy heart the unhappy Frenchman followed the woeful ultimatum he had sent forward to his master. On the journey he passed through Villars's headquarters at Douai. He showed the terms to Villars. The Marshal, mortified, indignant, indomitable, conjured him to tell the King that he could count upon the army.

London and The Hague, as well they might, made haste to ratify the preliminaries. Vryberg reported that he had never seen Godolphin so cheerful. There was not even a Cabinet meeting. Every one was confident that peace was made. Marlborough began to arrange for the transport home of the British troops after the paying off of the foreign contingents in Flanders. "Everything goes so well here," he wrote to Sarah, "that there is no doubt of its ending in a good peace." Nevertheless, he found the suspense irksome, and from time to time he had misgivings about this Article XXXVII. It is recorded that he said privately in these trying days, "I fear Article XXXVII may spoil everything." Certainly, to be prepared for either event, he put the armies at twenty hours' notice to march.

Torcy reached Versailles on the evening of June 1, and made his report to the King in the apartments of Madame de Maintenon. All next morning the Council sat. The highest dignitaries of France swelled the throng of courtiers in the anterooms, and although they were nourished only upon rumour, the sharpest division prevailed. Peace was the cry of the realm. But did they know what peace meant? Meanwhile behind the closed doors Louis, his son, and his councillors faced the awful alternatives. In 1855, the publication of the memoirs of Rakoczy's agent, the Hungarian Vetes, who might well have been in a position to know, threw a light upon this grim debate. Vetes attributes the decision entirely to the action of the Dauphin. This Prince, usually so tranquil, appeared to be transported with wrath at the idea of his son, the crowned King of Spain, at that time idol of the Spanish people, being abandoned, even dragged from his throne, by Louis XIV. He bitterly reproached the Council with the shameful deed they were about to commit, and apostrophized his father the King himself in terms so little marked by respect that the listeners were petrified. Furiously he reminded the Ministers who had spoken for peace that one day he would be their master, and that if the King by their advice abandoned his son they should render a long account to him. He rose from the table and left the room. The doors closed behind him, and there was a lengthy interval; but presently Torcy emerged, and, pursuing the indignant Dauphin, told him and the whole Court that the resolve had been taken to stand by the King of Spain. Rouillé was sent post-haste to tell the Allies that their ultimatum was rejected.

Marlborough's spy was as well informed as Vetes; and Marlborough within a few days had knowledge of the Dauphin's intervention.

Advices from Paris

June 3, 1709

* Monsieur de Torcy arrived Saturday evening at Versailles, and found the King at Madame de Maintenon's. The King at supper said nothing, and seemed sad and gloomy. Yesterday from eleven o'clock till half-past one the Council dealt with the peace proposals of the Allies, which were found very hard. *The Dauphin opposed them with heat*, and so did the Duke of Burgundy, and a general assured me on good grounds that the Council did not think fit to accept them, and letters from Versailles state that the negotiations are broken off. However, the Council meets again to-day or to-morrow on the same subject. I am told that Monsieur de Beauvillier [tutor to the Duke of Burgundy's sons] will ask for peace on behalf of all his followers.

"Is there, then, no counter-proposal?" asked Marlborough, when he learned the staggering news. He was deeply shocked. For some days he nursed a project for some compromise upon Article XXXVII. In much despondency he set out for the front.

He wrote to Godolphin (June 7):

> The Marishall de Villars has given his advice to the King for the venturing a Battel. There is no doubt a Battel in the plains of Lens wou'd put an end to this Warr, but if that shou'd happen, and God Almighty as hethertoo bless with Success the Armes of the Allyes, *I think the Queen shou'd then have the honour of insisting upon putting the ffrench Government upon their being againe govern'd by the three Estates which I think is more likely to give quiet to Christendome, then the taring provences from them for the inriching of others.*

This is one of the most revealing insights which we have into Marlborough's statecraft. The idea of substituting for the despotic rule of France a Parliamentary régime had long commended itself to him. It is a strange speculation how the course of history would have been changed if he had been able to enforce his policy upon France. The French Revolution might have accomplished itself gradually and beneficently in the course of the eighteenth century, and the whole world have moved on to broader foundations without paying the awful price in war and horror. There might have been no Napoleon! To pursue such thoughts beyond their earliest suggestions is vain; but Marlborough's words show how far in this respect he stood ahead of his times —and our own.

The question which is capital for Marlborough is whether he strove for peace or war. The immense tangle of the negotiations and the multitudes of letters written by the principal actors baffle history by their bulk and by their contradictions. A full account from day to day of all that passed would carry little meaning. Sometimes we see Marlborough rupturing what looks like a pacific move. Often he is arguing a minor point. Sometimes he presents himself in sharp opposition to Dutch, Prussian, or Imperial desires. Sometimes he is their champion. At each of the numberless phases of the negotiations the attitudes of the various principals shift. At one moment it is the Dutch who are sincere, at another the French; and always when there is agreement between any two, friend or foe, it is because the interests of others have been put in the shade.

But there can be no doubt where Marlborough stood. To Heinsius, to Godolphin, to Torcy, he wrote a series of urgent and at times impassioned appeals, the only aim of which was peace with France, leaving Spain, if necessary, to be dealt with separately and later. These appeals and warnings began from the moment when the XXXVIIth article, or, in other words, the question of guarantees, became crucial. He was the first to state in open conference, in the presence of the enemy representatives, that Article XXXVII ought not to be pressed. Torcy bears witness to this. When, to Marlborough's consternaton, the negotiations were ruptured and the French envoys took their departure he tried to intercept them, and his first thought, in harmony with Eugene, was to condemn the obstinacy on this point which had led to disaster. His letters to Heinsius, and above all their secret postscripts "For Yourself Only," are the pith of the whole debate and the revelation of his inward mind. And he revealed his convictions on this point at any rate to Townshend with perfect candour.

Tournay
August 31, 1709

*. . . As I never shall have any other thought of acting in this or any publick business, but agreeable to the orders I shall receive from England, I beg as a friend you will assure everybody where you think it may do good, that my judgment is entirely guided by the orders you received from England; *but to you as a friend I will own very freely, by all the observation I can make, I do not think it in the power of the French King and his ministers to recall the Duke of Anjou. On the other hand I do think it very practicable to force him out of Spain in less than six months if just and vigorous measures are* *taken by England and Holland.* This opinion of mine I desire should be known to nobody but yourself; and be assured that I will be directed and guided in this whole matter by yourself and the Pensioner.

Although at the beginning of the conferences Marlborough recognized his own weakness unduly, although he affected an extreme deference to the London Cabinet and the Whig power, although his letters dutifully breathe the form and spirit of his instructions, although no doubt he made wrong estimates of the forces at work, and used many arguments which were not his own, nevertheless it can be proved that at every stage he threw the whole of his weight upon the high personages with whom he was in the most intimate relation in favour of a settlement.

The far shrewder criticism has been launched that he failed to assert his authority and his genius.

We are told by later writers that he had become so used to conciliating divergent interests, to finding a middle course, to avoiding awkward points, to submitting to the mistakes of others and devising new expedients to achieve his own plans, that now, at the culminating moment in his career, he gave in fact no clear, real guidance, and resigned himself with sombre complacency to the drift and sequence of events. Marlborough, say these critics, had become an institution rather than a man, a function rather than an actor. To keep the Grand Alliance united, and himself at the head of it, till final victory was secured had so long been his duty that he thought it his sole duty. In a certain degree he had become the creature of his task. He had gained so often by being patient that he had lost the quality of revolt. He had conducted so many ill-assorted, antagonistic forces through endless toils and hazards to safety and success that the Common Cause had become more to him than the rightful cause. If his countrymen and colleagues, if the States-General, if the Empire, chose to frustrate the French desire for peace, and conjured him to lead the strongest armies yet known to the invasion of France and the march to Paris, he would willingly, too willingly, be their servant and commander.

The great decline in Marlborough's personal power must not be ignored by those who censure him. He had since 1700 woven together a Grand Alliance and carried it forward by management, tact, and great victorious battles to mastery. At every stage he had had to hold in check divergent and competing aims. The fear of being defeated and destroyed had joined the Allies together. Now his own victories had destroyed that fear. Thus at the moment when his work should have given him the greatest authority, and when that authority might have been most beneficently exercised, he found himself alone, with no party and no country at his back. In England he was the servant of a Queen with whom his favour was gone, and the agent of a Government to whom he was in one aspect the survivor of a period during which they had been excluded from office. In Holland Heinsius and the leaders of the Dutch Republic were convinced that he was no longer their advocate. The Empire and the Hapsburg brothers still hoped to bind him to their cause and to sever him from the Dutch by proffering him almost a kingdom.

Whereas up to this point Marlborough has been leading forward the whole Alliance for the most part along paths which he had chosen, we now see a cluster of magnificos bearing him shoulder-high on their own courses, but in great difficulty in deciding, and still more in agreeing, what those courses shall be. We see also efforts and manœuvres by Marlborough to free himself from these ceremonious maulings and to regain independent authority.

In the process everything was lost. Marlborough did not regain his control, and the Allies did not secure their terms. Europe was long denied the peace so sorely needed. Confusion and disaster were destined to cloud the end of this triumphant war. Peace was achieved only after further years of waste and torment, and then at the price to Britain of an act of desertion and dishonour. And Marlborough, who had performed a prodigy of loyalty, skill, valour, and effort, was condemned to be the scapegoat of universal disappointment. He had won the war. Some one, somehow, had lost the peace—his peace—and lost it for ever. Between them all they had let the splendid opportunity slip through their fingers. There were too many powers and potentates engaged, and no commanding leadership was tolerated. No one can be convicted of malice. All wanted peace. At the end two great Captains were still striving for it. They all failed. They all suffered for their failure.

The disappointment of the Allies found vent in a vain and furious clamour that they had once again been tricked and fooled by Louis XIV. The drums beat in the allied camps, and the greatest armies those war-worn times had seen rolled forward to the carnage of Malplaquet.

CHAPTER SEVENTY-FOUR

Darker War

⟨ 1709, June ⟩

WHEN Torcy had declared at the peace congress that Louis XIV could not wage war upon his grandson to dethrone him Marlborough had replied at once that he agreed with that. But now the die was cast to fight it out, and for the first time in his reign of more than sixty years the Great King appealed directly to French public opinion. In a circular letter addressed to the governors of his provinces, but intended for the widest audience possible in those days, he fastened the blame of the broken negotiations upon this cruel and unnatural demand. It had not been made, but there was enough appearance of it in the excessive claims of the Allies and in the protracted discussions upon them. Many famous verbal manœuvres have been less justly founded.

From this time the character of the war was profoundly affected. Justice quite suddenly gathered up her trappings and quitted one camp for the other. What had begun as disjointed, tardy resistance of peoples, Parliaments, and Protestantism to intolerant and aggressive military power had transformed itself for some time gradually, and now flagrantly, into invasion and subjugation by a victorious coalition. From this moment France, and to a lesser degree Spain, presented national fronts against foreign inroad and overlordship. Many generations had gone since Joan of Arc had struck this gong, and three were to pass before its harsh, reverberating clang was heard again. In those days, when all the large populations were controlled and their life expressed only by a few thousand notables and educated persons, there was, of course, no conscious movement of the masses. Nevertheless the governing classes throughout France, and also in Spain, derived a strange invigoration from the national spirit. The French people reverenced and almost loved their monarch; and a strong unity reaching far beneath the official hierarchies now made itself felt. A new flood of strength, welling from the depths which the early eighteenth century had not plumbed, revived and replenished an enfeebled nobility, exhausted professional armies, and a ruined treasury. The Spanish were already fighting a national war on behalf of Philip V. Now the French nation moved against foreign oppressions with some rude foretaste, even at that time formidable, of the passions of 1792.

The King's circular letter invoked a haggard but none the less genuine surge of indignation through all the circles upon which the French Government was accustomed to rely. "I cannot express to you the wrath of this nation," wrote Vetes, "against the Allies at the news of their stiff demands, and the general joy at the King's resolve to sustain his grandson, the King of Spain." In Court circles there was a wave of emotion. Marshal Boufflers sent his plate to the Mint. The royal Princes and the aristocracy followed his example. Louis XIV melted down his gold dinner service and made efforts to pawn or sell the Crown Jewels. His example was followed by the Duke of Grammont and all the Ministers. No one in Paris dared to dine off silver.

Much of the exaltation was on the surface and short-lived. The King and his morganatic wife set no great store by it. "When it became known that the King refused the shameful terms of peace," wrote Madame de Maintenon to the Duke of Noailles (June 9), "every one cheered and called for war; but this impulse did not last, and people soon fell back into that prostration which you saw and despised." There was also a fierce temper around.

In July there were serious riots at Dijon and Rouen. At Rouen the mob cried, "Vive Marlborough." In the capital bitter tongues repeated a new Lord's Prayer. "Our Father which art at Versailles, unhallowed is thy name. Thy kingdom is no longer great. Thy will is no more done on land or sea. Give us this day our daily bread, which we are short of on all occasions. Forgive our enemies who have beaten us, but not your generals who have allowed them to do so. Do not fall into all the temptations of the Maintenon, but deliver us from Chamillart." This appeal was answered. Chamillart's obstinacy, it was declared, had lost the chance of peace. His improvidence had neglected the preparations to resume the war. In June he was replaced by Voisin. For the eighth campaign the French armies assembled. Money drawn from every recess trickled into the military chest. Rations, though not enough, were gathered into the magazines, and in the old hero Boufflers, and even more in the ardent, indomitable Villars, the army of France found leaders worthy of the greatest nation in its greatest need.

The unfolded map of history now shows us that Louis XIV was right in rejecting the peace terms and renewing the war. He wavered long; but the outcome vindicated his final plunge, and in the after-light his grandeur amid appalling stresses shines forth. Here is another triumph for perseverance against the enemy. His decision was condemned at the time by some of the clearest minds in France. Fénelon has left his reasoned censures upon record. Moreover, the final result of the war was not determined by the fortitude of the sovereign, nor by the magnificent efforts of the French armies. It was settled by the obscure intrigues upon the backstairs and around the couch of Queen Anne and by the consequent reversal of British policy which produced and followed the fall of Marlborough. None of this was guessed or even dreamed of by Louis XIV at the time. It was unknown and unknowable. Who could foresee that in little more than a year the dominating Whigs would be hurled from power or that England, so long the implacable soul of the confederacy, would become the active agent of its destruction? All the more must the moral be drawn—"Fight on."

The allied army was already assembled about Ghent, and Marlborough and Eugene set out thither along the causeway road on June 12 under an escort of two hundred horse. As reports had been received that French raiding parties were in the woods near Alost with intent to seize the High Commanders, considerable detachments of allied troops were drawn out in this direction. The army at Ghent was the most powerful yet known, and more numerous than Europe had seen for many centuries. The order of battle comprised 194 battalions and 320 squadrons. Of these 152 battalions and 245 squadrons were already marshalled, amounting to between 110,000 and 120,000 men for active operations, apart from a much larger number in garrisons and on the communications.

The cruel winter was followed by a cold, wet spring. The fields were sodden. Even by June the grass could scarcely support the cavalry horses. The magazines which Marlborough had sought to establish at

Ghent and Lille were only half filled. "The account we have concerning forage is so terrible," he wrote to Godolphin (June 9), "that I fear *that* much more than the Marshal de Villars's gasconading." Even if there had been no peace conference the campaign could not have begun sooner. Moreover, it was plain from the state of the French countryside that famine-stricken regions alone awaited the invader. Not only did the campaign open late, but it was already obvious that it would have to end early. There was no chance of repeating in 1709 the winter struggle of 1708. A mighty, well-equipped army, the best-fed community in Europe, stood at the orders of the renowned Chiefs. But the time at their disposal was short, and the fortress barrier of France after all these years of siege and battle, though worn thin, was still unbroken. If forecasts were to be made upon the military facts only, the prospect to those who had lost so good an opportunity of peace was certainly bleak. But we find at this time an overwhelming conviction among all the allied leaders, soldiers and statesmen, that the economic and internal misery of France would compel a peace. Merely leaning the weight of the great army upon the enemy would, it was believed, confront them with stresses they could in no wise sustain. The blockade was rigorously enforced.

When Marlborough and Eugene reached Ghent several councils of war were held. The headquarters of the confederates had now become an assembly of the leading warriors of Europe after nearly thirty years of war. So many states had sent their contingents to Marlborough's army that his own British redcoats actually in the field army were barely a seventh of the international force which now awaited his orders. The commanders of all these forces, and representatives from all the countries from which they came, made a gathering of notables and potentates at once imposing and top-heavy. Nevertheless, so nicely were the distinctions drawn and so unquestionable was the authority which flowed from Marlborough, acting with Eugene, that it was not only possible to discuss the war measures in a considerable body without leakage, but for sudden and surprise action to be taken. The councils of war surveyed the situation, and many alternatives were examined or aired, but afterwards orders were issued by Marlborough which embodied what he with Eugene decided. Only in this way can the repeated deceptions of the enemy be explained.

Apparently both Marlborough and Eugene at first spoke freely of their disapproval of the way in which the negotiations had been conducted; and to such an extent that offence and some alarm were caused at The Hague.

Public opinion in England expected that a great battle and a victorious advance to Paris would follow the impudent rejection of the Allies' peace terms. This was not unreasonable, considering the mood of Ministers.

At the front the matter was less easy, although the strategic issues were simple. Could the confederate army defeat the French, no longer in the open field, but behind entrenchments amounting almost to fortresses? If so the march would lie forward into the heart of France. But if these lines and the troops which held them were judged too strong for frontal assault, then they must be turned on one flank or the other. The approaches to both these flanks were protected by fortresses—on the north Ypres, on the south Tournai. The reduction of either of these places would probably occupy a large part of the all too brief campaigning season which was open. It was therefore first of all necessary to decide whether a frontal attack should be made or not. Great reconnaissance was made of the whole of Villars's front during the latter part of June. Cadogan and Dopf not only pressed at this point and at that with powerful escorts, but also it is said that the former, descending from his high position as Marlborough's Chief of Staff and Quartermaster-General, traversed at the peril of his life, disguised as a labourer, a large section of Villars's front.

On June 24, in the light of all information procurable, the question of frontal attack was put to the council. There was no doubt about the conclusion. Villars supposes that Marlborough and Eugene were overruled by the Dutch Deputies. But there is no truth in this. Marlborough's letters show that he accepted Cadogan's view that a frontal attack would not be justifiable. It was unanimously resolved that the French lines were too strong to be attacked. The only question in dispute was whether Ypres, on the one flank, or Tournai, on the other, should be besieged. Considering how France had begged for peace and the terms which could have been obtained, it was a poor and damaging outcome that the main effort of the Allies could compass no more than a siege. Indeed, Villars by his lines, by his forays, by his gasconades, had already gained an unfought victory when he compelled his indignant enemies to content themselves with such local and stony fare.

Which, then, should it be? The allied commanders debated in deep conclave. Marlborough still hoped to pursue his design of the previous autumn. He wished to advance along the coast by Boulogne upon Abbeville and then up the Somme to Amiens and towards Paris. As a preliminary to this it would be necessary to besiege Ypres. We know now from Villars's memoirs that this was the movement which he dreaded most. It would be difficult for him to feed his own army in opposing it; and he saw as clearly as Marlborough that here alone could the Allies make use of their command of the sea in supplying their forces or in establishing a new base. There seems little doubt that Marlborough's view was right. But Eugene opposed it. He advocated the attack on Tournai, and he found great support. On political grounds the whole inclination of the German states and the Dutch was to draw the British away from the sea and carry the war as far inland as possible.

"The Duke," says Goslinga,

> did not set forth his reasons, except [the Goslinga touch] for mentioning the considerable revenues of the Châtelainie of Ypres. I believe, however, that his principal motive was to get nearer the sea, and once Ypres was taken to begin another siege on the coast, preferably that of Dunkerk, in order to put it into the hands of England; he took care, however, not to let this come out; on the contrary, he submitted without hesitation to the views of the Prince [Eugene].

Thus we see Marlborough deferring as easily to the opinions of Eugene and the Deputies in the field as he had to those of the Whigs in council. In the one case, as in the other, he was evidently conscious of diminished authority. Besides this, it had become a habit with him to try to get everybody together and yield to majority opinion in the hope that at some moment or other a situation would be created out of which his ingenuity might draw some great event. He was ageing and worn with incessant exertions, and perhaps unduly conscious of the decline of his power in England. He could not well, when the British contingent was so modest, force the commanders of the confederate army into courses which were unwelcome to them. It was rash even to persuade them against their will. He believed at this time that the state of France was so desperate and the war so nearly over that unity among the Allies was more important than true strategy. He underrated the remaining strength of France. He perhaps still more underrated his own strength, ebbing though it now was. He thought the Grand Alliance would gain an inevitable victory if only it kept together; and this was no doubt true if it had kept together long enough. Lastly, he was in favour of a siege of Tournai if the other alternative was excluded. The rapidity and precision of the operation which follows makes it certain that there was no friction in the allied High Command.

CHAPTER SEVENTY-FIVE

Tournai

₰ 1709, Summer ₫

THE decision to besiege Tournai was taken on June 24. The operation was executed with masterly precision, and, according to Pelet, "with such extreme secrecy that no one was able to divine the true objective." Marlborough, in pursuance of his Ypres plan or alternatively as a feint, had brought all the siege-train down to Menin. Its position there was known to Villars, and seemed to him proof that it was his left that was about to be attacked. At tattoo the allied camps were struck, the baggage loaded, and the whole army stood to arms ready to march. Once it was dark the heavy baggage started back to Lille, and the mass of Marlborough's and Eugene's forces moved in the opposite direction south-west towards La Bassée. By these manœuvres Marshal Villars was convinced either that he would have to face a frontal attack upon his lines at daybreak, or more probably that a feint at La Bassée was to cover the turning of his left. Accordingly, he reduced the garrison of Tournai, reinforced those of Saint-Venant and Aire, and proceeded himself to Béthune with five hundred men, who lighted fires along three leagues of the front as if he had moved his main army towards his left. Finally he sent a detachment toward La Gorgue with orders to spread the tale that they were the vanguard of the French army.

At 11.00 P.M. on June 26, after marching southward towards La Bassée for about two hours, Eugene turned north-west and later east towards Tournai. At the same time the long strings of barges carrying the siege-train and its ammunition began to float down the Lys back to Ghent, in order to be towed up the Scheldt. Marlborough's right and centre, moving at first south through Seclin, turned simultaneously in the same direction, while his left, which had not yet quitted camp, marched due east directly upon Tournai. Agreeably with these changes, the Prince of Orange with 30 squadrons and 10 battalions moved against Mortagne and Saint-Amand, on the Scarpe before it joins the Scheldt above Tournai.

The confederate troops, whose wagons carried six days' rations, did not know where they were going, and at first expected to be called upon for a general assault on the lines in the morning. But the turns in the darkness completely mystified them as well as the enemy, and when day broke they were astonished to see the towers of Tournai Cathedral rising at no great distance before them. Dompré, from the north, arrived simultaneously on the eastern side of the Scheldt, where he was soon joined by Lumley with 30 squadrons, including the British cavalry, and 10 battalions. Marlborough's army deployed during the day, facing south with its right on the Lille-Douai road. Mortagne and Saint-Amand were captured without opposition by Orange; and Eugene, coming in later, filled the gap between Marlborough's left and the Scheldt. By nightfall on the 27th Tournai was invested in force on all sides. The surprise was complete, and the fortress was caught with barely five thousand men, or half the proper number to man its defences. It was well supplied with munitions and had some bread, but the hostile apparition was so sudden that Surville, the commander who had distinguished himself at Lille, had no time even to drive in the cattle from the surrounding fields. The attempts by Villars on the 29th to throw in seven or eight hundred horse from Mons and Condé, and on the 30th by Luxembourg, who had orders to repeat his brilliant exploit at Lille with a thousand dragoons each carrying a foot soldier behind his saddle, were effectually frustrated.

Although the pretence of French historians that the Allies had been forced to alter their plans by Villars's nocturnal measures cannot be maintained, the Marshal had nevertheless no serious ground for self-reproval or disappointment. It was beyond human wit to guess which way the cat would jump. It had jumped in the least dangerous direction. The siege of Tournai, begun as late as midsummer, meant, even with the favour of surprise, the indecisive consumption of the greater part of the campaigning season. Villars was relieved that the danger of operations against his left in conjunction with the naval power of the Allies might now be definitely set aside.

Marlborough's letters to Godolphin speak repeatedly of the hardships of the troops and of the misery of the countryside. "All the wheat is killed everywhere that we have seen or heard of." "It grieves my heart to see the sad condition all the poor country people are in for want of bread; they have not the same countenances they had in other years." To Sarah: "It is not to be imagined the ill weather we have, insomuch that the poor soldiers in the trenches are up to their knees in dirt, which gives me the spleen to a degree that makes me very uneasy, and consequently makes me languish for retirement." "If we have not peace, I shall be sooner with you this year than any of this war, for in all likelihood we shall not find forage to enable us to make a long campaign, and that is what I fear the French know as well as we." And: "The misery of all the poor people we see is such that one must be a brute not to pity them."

The strains were increasingly hard in all directions. Godolphin wrote to Marlborough (July 4):

> * I am glad to find you continue to have so hopeful an opinion of the siege of Tournai; the people are a good deal prejudiced against it here, but if it succeeds . . . we shall be as sanguine as ever, which is too necessary; for unless our credit be not only supported but also augmented by successes abroad, our provision in Parliament for the expenses of the present year will fall short before the end of it by at least twelve hundred thousand pounds.

Meanwhile the vessels carrying the battering-cannon had passed through Ghent and were being towed up the Scheldt. The French had blocked the fairway by sinking barges filled with stone, and it was necessary to cut a new channel. The first thirty barges passed the obstruction on the 8th, and by the 10th the whole of the siege artillery had arrived. The work of constructing the batteries and mounting the cannon absorbed the energies of the besiegers. Marlborough, with sixty battalions, undertook the siege. Eugene commanded the covering army. Thus the rôles at Lille were reversed. Three separate attacks were launched against the town: Lottum the Prussian against the citadel from the Valenciennes road; Schulenburg the Saxon against the Sainte-Fontaine gate from the left bank of the Scheldt; Fagel the Dutchman against the Manville gate. Keen rivalry existed between these commanders, and wagers were laid as to which would win the prize. The difficulties of the siege were vastly increased not only by the unseasonable rains, but by the enemy's control of the sluices of the Upper Scheldt, which enabled them to flood the siege works suddenly in various places. The Town Ditch opposite Fagel, which was in fact a branch of the Scheldt, was filled with a deep stream running so fast that it washed away the débris as fast as the bombardment cast it down. To this was now added an intensity of mining and countermining novel and horrible in that age. "The great quantity of waters," Marlborough wrote to Godolphin (July 25), "which this garrison are masters of gives us great trouble now that we should pass the Fosse, so that our being masters of the town is retarded for some days."

On the 19th Marlborough had determined not to press Fagel's attack, but to concentrate upon the other two. The garrison, although active and frequently successful with their mines, were clearly saving themselves for the defence of the citadel, and on the 28th, when preparations for a general storm were far advanced, Surville hung out a white flag and beat the chamade on the fronts of all three attacks. The terms of capitulation resembled those of Lille. Eight hundred French wounded and invalids were allowed to proceed to Douai. The town was yielded, and Surville after dining ceremonially with Prince Eugene withdrew into the citadel with about four thousand men. Taking the town cost the Allies over 3200 men—800 in Lottum's, 1800 in Schulenburg's, and 600 in Fagel's attack.

The hardest part was yet to come. The citadel, a five-bastion fortress of earthworks and masonry, was reputed "one of the best fortify'd Places by Art that is in the World." The garrison was sufficient for the defence of their reduced lines. Powerful as were the visible defences, the underground works were soon found by the assailants to be even more formidable. A bitter subterranean warfare began. "We have to fight with moles," the British complained. Mining parties met each other below the surface and fought with picks and shovels, and, as the process developed, with sword and musket. The men in the batteries and trenches heard the ceaseless tapping of the miners beneath their feet. Explosions where soldiers were buried thirty or forty at a time, and one in which no fewer than four hundred men perished, made the siege terrible in the memories of veteran troops.

Private (afterwards Corporal) Matthew Bishop, whose moving life-story is too little known, writes:

> I remember after our Army had completed twelve Saps, we mounted the Trenches, and sat upon the Foot Banks, when of a sudden the Enemy sprung a Mine, which made the Earth tremble under us; but it ceased in a Moment. We were surprised it had not taken us up into the Clouds; for, comparatively speaking, it ascended like unto a Cloud.

Surville was prepared to make a resolute defence of the citadel, and his underground works gave him great advantages. He had, however, been guilty of the fatal neglect of not laying in sufficient provisions. His resistance was limited to little more than a month by his food. He therefore proposed to Marlborough that the citadel, unless relieved before September 5, should then be surrendered, and that in the meanwhile the siege operations should be suspended. He asked leave to send an officer through the lines to obtain the King's approval. Marlborough was agreeable to this, "since it will save the lives of a great many men, and we cannot hope to take it much sooner."

Villars, when he heard of the shortage of food, vented his wrath upon Surville in cruel terms. He alleged that the proposal for a local armistice had come from the Allies. He advised the King to reject it. Louis XIV accepted his view. It seemed to him unwise not to compel the Allies to spend their munitions upon the siege. Surville was, therefore, sternly forbidden to go forward with his proposal, unless the allied commanders would consent to a general armistice throughout the whole of the Flanders theatre. This, of course, was in turn rejected.

The siege went forward in a severe and bloody style. Nothing like the mining and counter-mining had ever been known. On August 5 a hundred and fifty besiegers who had gained a footing upon the defences were blown into the air. Through the nights of the 16th and 17th there was fierce fighting in the mining galleries, ending in the expulsion of the French. On the 20th the blowing up of a wall smothered thirty or forty Ally officers and men. On the 23rd the besiegers discovered a large mine when it was about to destroy a whole Hanoverian battalion. But while they were rejoicing in this good fortune another mine below it was sprung, causing very heavy losses. On the 26th a townsman of Tournai offered to reveal one of the principal mines of the citadel on condition that he should be made head gaoler of all the prisons in Tournai. His offer was accepted, and the mine gallery was occupied by three hundred men. The French, however, again sprung a mine below this gallery, and the whole three hundred were destroyed, and a hundred more besides.

In the face of grievous losses and ordeals the Allies persevered remorselessly in their attacks. On August 31 Surville, almost destitute of food and exposed to imminent storm, when no quarter would be shown, hung out the white flag of capitulation. Marlborough demanded that the garrison should be prisoners of war, and on Surville refusing another two days' bombardment ensued. On September 3 it was agreed that the garrison should march out with the honours of war and be permitted to return to France on condition of not serving again until duly exchanged. On September 5 the Allies were masters of Tournai.

CHAPTER SEVENTY-SIX

The Investment of Mons

ᔓ 1709, August and September ᔓ

THE fall of Tournai was followed by an explosion of war-fury strangely out of keeping with the policy and temper in which the campaign had hitherto been conducted. Up to this moment the French had been virtually forbidden by Louis XIV to fight a battle. Villars was told that their interest enjoined a strategy of delay. On the other side, Marlborough, Eugene, and the Dutch Deputies, convinced that France must collapse under the weight of the war through economic and financial pressure, had also been wedded to caution. Repeatedly they had examined Villars's lines, and always it had been decided that to incur the risks and costs of forcing them was not warranted in the favourable position of the allied cause. Thus the campaign seemed relegated to the sphere of manœuvre, with no more serious objective than making a further inroad upon the French fortress line.

Now suddenly, upon the capitulation of Tournai, an access of mental rage seems to have taken possession of both sides simultaneously. They discarded their cold calculations. They flung caution to the winds. The King gave Villars full freedom. The Marshal used it to court an encounter battle. Marlborough and Eugene two days later assaulted him frontally in a position already strong by nature, and now fortified by serious entrenchments and defences. The contagion of this mood swept through both armies like a fever. A terrible ardour inspired all ranks. They thirsted to be at each other's throats, and slay their foes. The soldiers of every nation, national and mercenary alike, fell upon each other with a ferocity hitherto unknown to the age, and in the largest and bloodiest battle of the eighteenth century quarter was scarcely asked or given.

But the source of this new temper is to be found in the allied Governments even more than in their troops or their generals. A hitherto unpublished letter of Marlborough's shows that his own instinct was against a supreme trial of strength, but that both the Empire and the Dutch were pressing him to it. In this letter is revealed for the first time the origin of Malplaquet.

Marlborough to Heinsius

August 18, 1709

* I am sure you do the Pr. and myself the justice to beleive that we shall neglect no opertunity of undertaking what we can judge practicable, and as a friend I own to you that I think our affaires are in so good a postur, and that of the Enemy in so very ill condition, that I shou'd think wee aught not to ventur, but where in reason wee shou'd hope for success; but if you Judge otherways, and that the temper of your people are such, that thay will not be satisfied unless there be action, we must then take our measures agreable to that; for what ever is in my power You may comand, for I have a Confidence in your Judgement, besides you know the temper of England is always for action; but I can't think it for the service to attempt, without hopes of success.

As the fall of Tournai citadel approached the next step was considered by the Allies. It was realized that the situation would not be greatly changed by its capture. On the one hand, the course of the Scheldt would be open up to Saint-Amand; on the other, Villars's army was better organized, his supply was less stringent, and his defences more complete. The season was far advanced, and no important invasion of France could be made that year. There remained, as it seemed, only the possibility of prolonging the pressure upon the French to renew the negotiations, or, if that failed, to secure a good start for the army in 1710. An advance in the centre between the Lys and the Scarpe would be confronted by the French prepared positions. Eyes therefore turned again to the flanks. In the west Ypres, Aire, and Saint-Venant offered themselves as costly prizes. Ypres was strong and well prepared, and Marlborough and Eugene judged the country round it bad for manœuvre late in the season. On the other flank lay the fortresses of the Sensée—Condé, Valenciennes, the entrenched camp at Denain, or perhaps Bouchain.

A wider turning movement would be facilitated by the capture of Mons. But this fortress of the first order controlled no river communication. High ground stood between it and the valley of the Sambre. There is no account of the discussions which took place. Mons may have been chosen because it completed the occupation of the Barrier required by the Dutch. There was always the chance that Villars would fight a battle for the sake of Mons; but neither Marlborough nor Eugene counted upon his doing so. Actually the Marshal does not appear to have considered the likelihood of an attack on Mons. Thus quick movement and surprise were necessary to Marlborough.

The first step was to seize the fort of Saint-Ghislain, on the Haine. Orkney was entrusted with this task. French accounts record his arrival in front of Saint-Ghislain at 1.00 A.M. on September 3. He was followed on that day by Hesse-Cassel with sixty squadrons and four thousand foot. They were to help Orkney take Saint-Ghislain, and if successful to cross the Haine and invest Mons from the south-west. If Saint-Ghislain could not be taken, both forces were to pass round the north of Mons and capture the line of the Trouille to the eastward. After dark on the same day Cadogan with forty squadrons followed Hesse-Cassel. At midnight the main army marched to Brissœil. The operation was hazardous and Goslinga was full of misgivings. "This is only to tell you," he wrote to Heinsius on the 4th, "that the army marched this night [i.e. the 3rd]. They aspire to invest Mons, but, according to my humble view, it is impossible to succeed. We are going to follow to-morrow and join the army on the march. If all goes as wished, Mons will be invested to-morrow; but, as I had the honour to tell you, I doubt myself whether even our leaders are convinced that the thing is possible. . . ."

Saint-Ghislain had been reinforced from Condé, and resisted Orkney. He therefore turned northward. On September 5 the main army marched to Sirault, where Orkney rejoined them. On the 6th, at 2.00 A.M., Hesse-Cassel crossed the Haine at Obourg, driving a small French force before him. At 7.00 A.M. he formed his line south of Mons, and at noon crossed the French lines on the Trouille. Three French regiments of dragoons withdrew back into Mons. Luxembourg, with thirty squadrons, arriving too late for an action, retired to join Villars at Quiévrain. By nightfall Hesse-Cassel held the heights south of Mons on the line Frameries-Jemappes. That same night (the 6th) Marlborough reached Obourg, and marched south at dawn to support Hesse-Cassel. By these swift operations, which won Hesse-Cassel much praise, Mons was effectually cut off and invested.

Villars, awaiting at Quiévrain the arrival of part of his infantry under D'Artagnan, spent the 7th in a reconnaissance in force towards Hesse-Cassel's position. Boufflers had arrived, bearing with him in his person the proof of the King's willingness for battle. During the evening Villars advanced with his army, and lay ten miles from the Allies on the front Montrœul-Athis. The fact that Boufflers had joined the French army reached Marlborough within a few hours. He therefore continued his southward march, and halted for the night on Hesse-Cassel's left on the line Ciply-Quévy. The armies were now eight miles apart in gently undulating country. Between them lay a broad belt of forest, through which there were but two passages (*trouées*). If Villars wished to attack elsewhere than through one or the other of the gaps, he must make a long march round, and eventually attempt the river lines of the Haine and the Trouille.

On the morning of the 8th a council of war was held at the allied headquarters at Quévy, in which it was decided that to cover the siege of Mons Eugene should block the exit of the Gap of Boussu, and Marlborough that of the Gap of Aulnois. As Villars on that day faced the former gap Marlborough must keep close to Eugene. Accordingly during the afternoon Eugene occupied the heights of Quaregnon, while Marlborough camped between Genly and Quévy. A French general captured by the patrols stated openly that Villars had the King's leave to fight.

Marlborough seems to have had at this moment no fixed plan of action. His letters show no expectation of battle. He and Eugene were waiting upon events. If they had been content merely to make the siege of Mons they could during the 8th and 9th have constructed a line of circumvallation either in the woods and across the gaps or behind them. But this was not their object. They wanted to bring about a battle in the open, and to hold themselves loose so as to be able to encourage and accommodate Villars, if such was his purpose. No attempt was therefore made to take up a defensive position. Such a step would have prevented a battle. They cherished the hope that Villars would advance through one or other of the gaps, and that then they could fall upon him. They did not want to do anything which would deter him from this. Still, we can hardly think they believed he would do so. The heroic Marshal, while breathing fire and slaughter and inspiring his troops with the spirit of the offensive, never had any such intention. He was only doing what he had done several times before, and was to do afterwards on notable occasions—namely, advancing to close proximity in the hopes of finding a weak body of the enemy in his clutches, or some other exceptional advantage. Marlborough and Eugene during the 8th were evidently tempting him; and for the sake of doing so they allowed him to occupy the forward edges of the woods by the Gap of Boussu—that is to say, they would let him without dispute make of this gap a gateway which he could open when he chose, and through it debouch and deploy for battle. But this was too good to be true.

Villars, who had to halt for supplies, and fed his troops with the greatest difficulty, contented himself again with a cavalry demonstration. His patrols and squadrons came in contact at many points with the cavalry of the Allies, and the numerous sharp minor collisions which took place showed the tension of the great masses now brought so close together. He had seen the Gap of Boussu left open to him on the 8th. During the night which followed he sent Luxembourg with a strong force of cavalry to seize the forward edges of both the gaps, thus securing to himself the power to debouch at either. It cannot be supposed that Marlborough and Eugene, watching the scene on horseback from hour to hour during the preceding day, permitted him to do this by negligence. Evidently they meant deliberately to leave both doors open for him to come through either into a battle arena. At dawn on the 9th Villars learned that both the gaps were in his possession. He marched forthwith to his right in four columns ready for immediate deployment, and occupied the Aulnois gap with his whole army.

Early on the morning of the 9th Eugene was writing a letter.

Eugene to the Emperor

His Imperial Majesty will have learned from other sources how the armies have remained stationary. But I am this instant about to mount my horse. . . . In fact, the enemy is near, although up to now he has hazarded nothing, and remains behind his fortresses and entrenchments. . . . From our side, since we do not know well the lie of the land, we dare even less take any risks. The terrain is very uneven, and cut up by many small brooks and ponds swollen by the bad weather, and is full of water and gullies, paths and defiles, so that one cannot march directly forward. But I am about to go off with my lord Duke under heavy escort to review the situation thoroughly, so that we can come to such a decision as will be to the benefit of the Common Cause. . . .

At this moment the news that Villars was moving came in and Eugene arrived at Marlborough's camp. Marlborough's horse was brought, and, with an escort of thirty squadrons and four hundred grenadiers under the Prince of Auvergne, the two commanders rode out to the Mill of Sart to reconnoitre. They reached this point about eight o'clock. As the fringe of their cavalry patrols approached the village of Malplaquet, in the Aulnois gap, they came in contact with Luxembourg's outposts. Auvergne with a heavier force brushed through the hostile screen and found himself confronted by strong bodies. To the westward he or his officers discerned the French army marching towards the Aulnois gap and the plateau of Malplaquet. As far as they could tell, the enemy seemed to be about to advance through the forest clearing into the open country towards Mons. Thereupon Marlborough ordered the concentration of the Allies. Only his left, composed mainly of the Dutch under Dopf, could immediately come into line. The right could not come up for several hours, and Eugene's army lay six miles farther to the north. The concentration, according to Orkney, was delayed by "prodigious dusty rain," through which the troops marched incessantly. At 2 P.M. the French batteries, which had now gathered in strength about Malplaquet, began to cannonade Marlborough's left, who, as they were without artillery, could not reply.

This situation has been represented by several writers as critical for the Allies. It is suggested that if Villars had advanced through the gap and deployed his forces he could have beaten the confederate army in detail; but this is nonsense. Marlborough's left, unencumbered by artillery, could have fallen back as fast as the French could advance, and as they receded would have accelerated the concentration of the allied army. Villars himself could not have forced them to battle till they were willing. Nothing could have prevented them from reoccupying, for instance, their former position from Genly to Quévy with their whole united strength. It is certain that this was exactly the kind of situation which Marlborough and Eugene desired. They could then, at dawn on the 10th, have fought that general battle in the open which had never been offered to them since Ramillies. The whole of the allied movements on the 8th and 9th show beyond all question that Marlborough and Eugene had only one object and hope—namely, to entice Villars to go through one or other of the gaps into the plain of Mons, and then fall upon him.

But Villars was far too good a soldier to be caught in that way. He never for a moment contemplated attacking the Allies, or even the risk of an encounter battle, in the open. Under such conditions his ragged, ill-found army, however brave and trained, was no match for the perfectly equipped veteran forces of the Allies. He saw, as well as we see to-day, that the great Captains opposed to him had left these gaps open because it suited them that he should go through them. It is, indeed, surprising that Marlborough and Eugene should have even appeared to take Villars's offensive seriously. Allowance must be made for the atmosphere of excitement which rises to explosion-point when great masses of armed, eager men are manœuvring in close contact with one another, and when the fall of the thunderbolts is expected and even longed for by all. Accordingly Villars sat down in his gap. His troops were marching up all day. His artillery continued to fire on Marlborough's left, which stood in position against his front. During the afternoon the English and Dutch batteries came up, unlimbered, and began to reply in increasing numbers. Thus night fell. During the night Villars began to fortify his position across the gap. He dug the deepest ditches and built the highest parapets that time allowed. The woods on either side he defended by successive lines of smaller trenches, and with abattis.

Early on the morning of the 10th it was seen that Villars had already begun entrenching himself, and all prospect of his attacking faded. The allied Commanders had now to decide first whether they would themselves assault his position, and whether they should do so at once or wait until the next day. On the one hand, the French defences were growing hourly; on the other, General Withers with nineteen battalions and ten squadrons was marching from Tournai, and could not join the army until very late that night. In the outcome, "the Princes" resolved to wait until their whole army was assembled, and to hold a council of war that night to decide the question of battle. Such a council was necessary in view of the constitution of the army and the stipulations of the Dutch. The Dutch Deputies had remained behind at Tournai, and Goslinga alone reached the army.

All through the 10th the cannonade continued in the centre of the army, and several hundred casualties were inflicted on either side. Marlborough and Eugene spent the day examining the French position. Breastworks were constructed for the attacking batteries. Towards evening the guns fell silent.

In the meanwhile the measures which Marlborough took had all been directed to a battle on the 11th. Instructions were sent to Withers to press his march. In order to have an uninterrupted line of retreat upon Tournai in the event of a repulse, Marlborough determined to take Saint-Ghislain by storm. About two thousand men, collected under General Dedem from the battalions blockading Mons, marched accordingly upon this post. Its garrison had been reduced by Villars to two hundred men, and about nine in the evening it was carried "sword in hand," the garrison being accorded quarter. Withers actually passed through Saint-Ghislain after its capture, and camped four miles beyond the Haine.

At the council of war Marlborough and Eugene urged a general attack the next day. Goslinga, who represented the Republic, vigorously supported them. Such a combination of authority was not questioned by the other generals present, and the momentous resolve was taken unanimously. There was no obligation upon them to fight. They had only to sit still and let Villars watch them choke Mons into surrender. There had been half a dozen situations in the war when a great battle could have been fought on no harder terms—nay, on terms less hard —and several others were to occur afterwards. Both sides wanted to fight. Villars made the greatest contribution in his power by coming forward into the gap. Marlborough and Eugene, pressed by their Governments, were in the mood to accept his challenge. How many times of which we know nothing had they perhaps found it impossible to procure an agreement upon decisive action? Now they had the pugnacious Goslinga with them, and alone. Never might such an opportunity return. Now was the time to end the war at a single stroke. Even if conditions were not entirely favourable they believed they were strong enough to beat and ruin the last remaining army of France.

Eugene's diary records:

> Orders to attack the enemy to-morrow in the name of God. My lord Duke of Marlborough's armies, the Imperial Troops, and the corps from Tournai, which is to make a special attack, are to be let loose upon the enemy. . . . All attacks to begin at daybreak, when everything must be in readiness. The signal will be a salvo from the entire British artillery, which will be taken up by the Dutch cannon.

CHAPTER SEVENTY-SEVEN

The Battle of Malplaquet

ξᴆ 1709, September 11 ᴆξ

Bʏ the first light of dawn all the troops were already under arms and in their stations. But with the sun a dense fog rose from the fields and marshy places, shrouding the loaded woods and the two hundred thousand men who awaited the signal to fall upon one another. In the allied army of many nations the ministers and priests of almost every communion known to Christendom—Church of England, Presbyterian, Dutch Calvinist, Huguenot, Lutheran, Roman Catholic—performed their solemn offices at the heads of the regiments. So perfect was the harmony which the ascendancy of Marlborough and Eugene exercised upon all minds that these soldiers of different races, creeds, and Governments—English, Scots, Irish, Danes, Prussians, Hanoverians, Hessians, Saxons, Palatines, and Dutch—acted together as if they were the army of a single nation. Opposed to them was the greatest Power of that age, at length brought low, but finding in desperation new, unmeasured sources of strength from its valiant people. The French stood at the gateway of France—almost along the line where the frontier runs to-day—prepared to dare all to shield their land from invasion. With the French army were a few brigades of Irish exiles, and of troops driven out of the Electorates of Bavaria and Cologne, but all were united in the Catholic faith and in long military comradeship. While they ate their meagre bread, they mocked the plenty of the allied camps and the rum and brandy rations customary there on battle days. The standards of the Maison du Roi bore Louis XIV's challeng-

(728)

ing motto, "Nec pluribus impar." Never was it more bravely sustained than at Malplaquet.

During September 10 the French line had been minutely studied by "the Princes" and the allied Command. Marlborough's conception was in principle the battle of Blenheim adapted to a new field. The enemy's wings were to be assaulted until Villars was induced by this pressure to weaken his centre. The centre was then to be pierced by the reserve of the infantry (in this case mainly the British), and its earthworks occupied. Out of a hundred guns no fewer than thirty-seven were assigned to move and work with the attacking infantry. The enormous cavalry army, nearly thirty thousand strong, was then to pass through the gaps in the defences, and fight a sabre battle with the French cavalry in the plain beyond. If the French cavalry were routed, all their troops drawn into the two flanks would be cut off, as had happened to the French right at Blenheim. But Marlborough, and still more Eugene, had behind him a vast experience of war. If they had a plan it was to be no rule. The measureless chances of action would certainly create better or worse situations with which they felt competent to deal. Whatever they may have said or written, both looked out upon the day with zest and thrill, and, casting care aside, rejoiced in the intensity of risk, will, art, and action which lay before them. Moreover, here must be the end of the long war, and rest and glory after toil. All should be staked. Nothing should be neglected, and nothing should be withheld.

The curtain of fog by all accounts was regarded as highly convenient for the drawing up of the allied troops. For the main attack of the right wing the lines of battle were three deep: for the secondary but still heavy attack by the left wing, two deep: and in the centre, where it was hoped to give the decisive stroke, only a single line. To this centre, covering a third of the front, Marlborough assigned only nineteen battalions out of a hundred and twenty-eight. But these battalions, which he kept under the strictest personal control, were thirteen English, two foreign, and four Prussian, and constituted his only infantry reserve. He himself would stand near the redcoats and use them for the culminating stroke. Behind this slender infantry line were massed over two hundred squadrons of cavalry and the main artillery of the confederate army.

As the sun gained power the mist dispersed. Broad daylight lapped the field, bright with symmetrical masses of uniformed men and the sparkle of standards and blades. On both sides the famous leaders presented themselves to their soldiers. In the well-known figures of Marlborough and Eugene the confederates saw the assurance of certain victory. In Villars and in Boufflers the French army recognized the two foremost heroes of France. The artillery began to fire about half-past seven, and gradually grew far louder than on the previous days, until at nine o'clock Marlborough ordered the Grand Battery to fire the signal salvo, and the battle began.

The Wood of Taisnières points north-eastward a projecting tongue. This salient, the scene of the fraternization of the day before, held by the five brigades of Albergotti, was Marlborough's first objective. Upon the edge of this his forty-gun battery concentrated its fire. Schulenburg, with forty battalions, three lines deep, marched against its northern face; and Lottum, with twenty-two battalions, after moving as if to attack the French centre, was to change direction to his right, and assault it from the eastward. When Lottum turned to his right Orkney with his fifteen battalions would cover Lottum's left shoulder, which might otherwise have been exposed. At the same time, beyond Schulenburg's right, the detachment of nineteen hundred men from Mons entered an unoccupied part of the wood, and upon the extreme right Withers, with nineteen battalions and ten squadrons, began to march through the forest in the direction of the La Folie farm, with the object of turning the left of the whole French army. Thus eighty-five allied battalions were simultaneously launched upon or into Taisnières Wood, of which more than sixty attacked the comparatively small tongue-shaped salient. The allied forces outnumbered the French in the Wood of Taisnières by four to one, and Marlborough might well have expected a speedy result.

Marlborough and Eugene in their battles understood one another so well that each exercised a supervision over the entire field. But although there was no formal division of spheres, Eugene assumed the direction of this great operation upon the right, while Marlborough, with his headquarters staff, conducted the general battle from a slight eminence about half-way between the Grand Battery and the village of Blaregnies. From this dangerous but convenient spot, a little behind Orkney's corps, he was able personally to ensure the safety of Lottum's exposed flank, thus preserving his contact with Eugene, and at the same time to survey, or receive information from, the rest of the front.

Schulenburg's Germans marched firmly to the assault. This oblong mass of over twenty thousand men had eight hundred paces to cross before they came to grips. The five brigades of Albergotti met them according to the tactics of their commanders and the nature of the ground. Here the French charged forward; there they stood behind their entrenchments and reserved their fire till pistol range. But, however it befell, the clash was savage and the slaughter heavy. Two of the three major-generals and all the colonels of Schulenburg's first line were killed or wounded as they led their men inexorably forward till they were stopped by lead or steel. The opposing battalions grappled with each other. The fringe of the wood blazed with fire and smoke. The survivors of Schulenburg's first line recoiled, rent and ragged. But the second, following at two hundred paces under Eugene's personal direction, bore them forward in a double wave.

La Colonie, the "Old Campaigner," to whom we have often recurred, was posted with his Bavarian brigade behind the redans, and watched the advance of Lottum's twenty-two battalions.

> As soon as this dense column appeared in the avenue, fourteen guns were promptly brought up in front of our brigade, almost in line with the regiment of Garde Française. The fire of this battery was terrific, and hardly a shot missed its mark. The cannon-shot continued to pour forth without a break, plunged into the enemy's infantry, and carried off whole ranks at a time; but a gap was no sooner created than it was immediately filled again, and they even continued their advance upon us without giving us any idea of the actual point determined on for their attack. At last the column, leaving the great battery on its left, changed its direction a quarter right and threw itself precipitately into the wood on our left, making an assault upon that portion which had been breached.

The French under Albergotti resisted with the utmost tenacity, and the defences proved their value. Sheltered behind the breastworks, they fired steadily into the great numbers of assailants, who struggled through the abattis and tried to re-form a fire front at close quarters. To the surprise of the allied generals, the first onsets of both Schulenburg and Lottum were brought to a standstill either on the fringe of the wood or in the open ground before it. Their second and third lines bore them forward again. Generals and colonels sacrificed their lives with the highest devotion. Eugene, riding into the severity of the fire, reorganized and forced on the attack by weight of numbers, regardless of losses. On the other side Albergotti's reserves were thrown into the struggle.

The attack by the allied left was timed to start half an hour later than that of the right. It had originally been intended to reinforce the Dutch in this quarter by Withers' nineteen battalions from Tournai. The fatigue of these troops after their long, rapid march from the fortress, the late hour on the 10th at which they approached the main army, and the advantage of turning the French left flank by a wide movement had induced a change of plan. Withers was to act upon the right, and the Dutch attack was to become secondary in importance. For this reason it was ordered to halt just outside the range of grapeshot for half an hour after Schulenburg and Lottum had begun. All the officers in the Dutch army looked with pride and loyalty to the gallant figure of their young Prince. Those elements in Holland which wished to keep the house of Orange in the shade were represented by the aged General Tilly. About half-past nine, therefore, the Prince of Orange, without waiting for the consent of General Tilly and accompanied by the fiery Deputy Goslinga, led forward thirty battalions of the Republic with several batteries, the Scots brigade being up on the left. As the left of the attack skirted or penetrated the Wood of Lanières a withering fire burst upon them. Here, in line with the Highlanders, fought the redoubtable Dutch Blue Guards, the flower of their army. The Prince of Orange had most of his staff shot around him. General Oxenstiern fell dead at his side. The Prince's own horse collapsed, and he advanced on foot. The entrenchments before him, three lines deep, were held by some of the finest troops in French service—men of Picardy, of Navarre, of Piedmont, and the French Royal Marines. These considerably outnumbered their assailants. In fact, on this wing the French had sixty battalions against thirty Dutch.

As the Dutch attack advanced in magnificent order it passed on its right hand the salient of the French line on the spur south-west of the Wood of Tiry. Beyond this wood there is a long, shallow trough of ground, about two hundred yards wide, which strikes obliquely across the path the Dutch took. Concealed at the head of this trough was a nest of French batteries mounting twenty cannon. From these there now burst a horrible flanking fire of cannon-balls and grape-shot which tore through the Dutch and Scottish ranks, killing or wounding thousands of men as they moved in faultless discipline towards their goal. The ground was soon heaped with blue uniforms and Highlanders, over whom the rear of the attack moved forward steadfastly, paying their toll. Nevertheless the young Prince, his surviving generals, and Deputy Goslinga arrived, with the mass of the Dutch and the Scots, before the French entrenchments, endured their volleys at close quarters, tore away the abattis, stormed the parapets, and captured the works. But they were now too few. The reserves of Navarre and Picardy charged forward in counterattack, not only upon the front of the Dutchmen, but out of the Wood of Lanières on their left flank; while always around them the scourge of the French batteries smote upon their right and upon the troops advancing in their support.

A retreat in good order began. The generals set the highest example. Spaar was killed; Hamilton wounded. Tullibardine fell amid his clansmen; General Week was killed. The Swiss general Mey was hard hit. The whole allied left wing fell back slowly, receiving terrible punishment, over the ground which they had traversed, now thickly strewn with the corpses or writhing bodies of their comrades. They might have fared even worse, for the French pursued them with vigour, but for the fact that the Prince of Hesse-Cassel, with the twenty-one squadrons of cavalry assigned to this flank, was perceived by the enemy, drawn up and seeking the moment to charge. Thus covered, the Dutch halted their deliberate retreat, and faced about. They had lost in half an hour at least five thousand men. Among the Scots there was an equal carnage. But the Prince of Orange would not be denied. His second horse shot under him, he seized the standard of the wounded Mey, ordered a second attack, and led it forward in person on foot. Once again the faithful battalions ran the gauntlet of the batteries firing along the trough. Once again they reached the French entrenchments. Foremost of all their heroic prince planted his standard upon the parapet. Once again the counterattack swept them backward, this time in grave disorder. Once again Hesse-Cassel with his cavalry checked the pursuers.

On the right of the Dutch attack Baron Fagel with Pallandt's seven battalions stormed the defences of Bléron Farm; but they in their turn were driven out by the French counterattack. Rantzau commanded the four Hanoverian battalions on the right of the Dutch. Although he did not belong to the left wing and was in Marlborough's reserve, he had sent two of his battalions to assist them. They had suffered severely in the slaughter. "Monsieur de Goslinga," he wrote when his conduct was afterwards questioned,

> passing at full gallop, came to me and asked me if I did not wish to advance; I answered that he could see quite well that I was advancing, that it might please him to order the Prussians on my right to make the same movement, and to march forward like me, considering I had too little with two battalions to carry through the affair alone. Monsieur de Goslinga thereupon stopped a moment, and in his confidence of victory, or perhaps seeking to encourage the soldiers, shouted, "La bataille est gagnée, ha! Les braves gens!" After which [says Rantzau somewhat maliciously] he departed, all the more quickly since the enemy had forced our left [i.e. the left of Fagel's assault] to abandon the entrenchment.

Thus upon the left there was a complete and bloody repulse. This is the moment when the French consider that Boufflers, who was on the spot, should have ordered a general advance of their right wing, which he commanded. It was certainly not from want of spirit that he did not do so. He did not feel entitled to make so great a change in the plans of the Commander-in-Chief without consultation, and for this there was no time. The opportunity passed without being tested.

At ten o'clock, while the Dutch were in their agony, Schulenburg and Lottum renewed their onslaughts upon the Taisnières salient. This time Schulenburg broke into the north face of the wood, and his whole command vanished into it. Lottum's corps also fell on, but were again brought to a standstill "torn and exhausted." Their position in the open, almost at right angles to the French centre, harassed by artillery fire from both their front and left flank, became critical. Orkney, who, though not himself actually engaged, was close at hand, sent two more British battalions to support and extend Lottum's left. While these troops were making their way through the marshy ground, Chemerault, the French general commanding the left of the line of redans, saw a chance. He formed a counter-attack of twelve battalions, and was about to launch it upon Lottum's exposed left flank. But meanwhile Marlborough had himself ridden forward with the Prince of Auvergne's thirty squadrons of Dutch cavalry, whom he placed in readiness to charge the French counter-attack. Marshal Villars, who on the other side had also reached this crucial point, seeing the redcoats extending to their right, and this large cavalry force, which Chemerault had not noticed, ready to charge, stopped the counter-stroke and ordered the twelve battalions back—but not to their redans. "I saw," he declares, "that our infantry was losing ground in the wood, and I posted these twelve battalions to receive them when they came out of it." The denudation of the French centre had begun.

With conspicuous zeal Argyll's brigade and Orkney's two battalions plunged into the Wood of Taisnières at the root of its tongue. Thus they drew forward with them in their movement the whole of Lottum's corps, which, like that of Schulenburg, now disappeared among the trees and undergrowth. The conditions inside the salient were indescribable. Within a triangle, no side of which exceeded six hundred yards, there were at least seven thousand men lying killed and wounded, more than thirty thousand allied infantry in almost solid masses, and four or five thousand French survivors. More than half the superior officers had fallen. The wounded of both sides, officers and men, were bayoneted and plundered. The screams of the injured, the roar of the mob of combatants, the crash of musketry, resounded from this smoking inferno, in which half the allied foot had become engulfed.

Argyll's brigade sustained heavy losses—in fact, Sir Richard Temple's regiment lost more men that day than any other single British battalion. They performed prodigies; but their high spirits took a savage form. "They hewed in pieces," wrote a German observer, "all they found before them, . . . even the dead when their fury found no more living to devour."

Such was the situation which Marlborough from his post a furlong behind the Grand Battery surveyed upon his right. Here amid the cannon-balls he sat his horse, waiting for the moment to strike at the French centre. He must for some time have felt serious concern at the numbers of his troops which were being absorbed in the Taisnières Wood, and by the carnage and chaos which reigned there. Towards half-past ten he began to feel uneasy also about his left. He knew that the first attack of the Dutch had been repulsed. He had not intended this attack to be pressed to the same extremity as that of his right. It was, however, an essential part of his plan that the fighting even on the left flank should be serious and heavy. Only by these brutal pressures would the two French Marshals be forced to denude their centre. He had not, however, prepared himself at all for the catastrophe which now broke upon him.

He had already begun to ride towards the left wing when Goslinga, indignant, excited, stained with battle, met him a little short of the Wood of Tiry, before which Rantzau and his battalions were posted. The brave, vehement Deputy told his tale. To anyone who had been through that double repulse it must have seemed that the Dutch corps was virtually destroyed. Goslinga added that the Prince of Orange was organizing a third attack. He demanded immediate reinforcements for the Dutch. Apparently he complained of the change of plan which had deprived them of Withers' corps. It is very likely that he also reported that when he had urged Rantzau to advance with his two remaining Hanoverian battalions Rantzau had not complied. The Captain-General bore the tidings with his usual composure. He calmed the passionate Deputy, and brought him along with him. About this time Eugene, warned of what had happened on the left, overtook Marlborough. Together they reached the point where Rantzau was in action.

Marlborough, Eugene, and Goslinga rode on through the streams of Dutch wounded staggering from the battle, or returning bleeding to resume their places in the ranks, to the point where the survivors of the Dutch command gathered around the indomitable Prince. They found consternation both at the appalling losses and at the young Prince's resolve to renew the attack. Together they forbade the further effort, and ordered the left to stand still under the protection of Hesse-Cassel's squadrons.

Then the two Chiefs returned to the centre and the right. Perhaps they galloped, for the crisis of the battle approached. Eugene hastened back to the Wood of Taisnières. Marlborough resumed his former position behind the Grand Battery. It was now half-past eleven of the clock on a fine summer's morning.

Eugene found that progress had been made in Taisnières Wood. Weight of numbers had prevailed over both the obstacles and the

French resistance. The French had been driven out of their second position behind the tongue, and the allied line was rolling forward yard by yard, extending as the wood broadened. General Withers with his separate corps, including three British battalions and the Royal Irish, who were some way behind, had entered the wood on the extreme right and encountered little resistance. Eugene had sent him ten additional squadrons, which with his own ten were making their way by a wide circle round the woods and also moving towards La Folie. This movement as it progressed tended to turn the whole hostile position.

A combination of forces was thus developing against the left of the French army which if not broken would be fatal. Marshal Villars watched this with deepening anxiety. He felt the left of his centre was about to be exposed. He responded to this dire pressure exactly as Marlborough had planned and expected. First he sent to Boufflers for reinforcements, but that Marshal, in grapple with the Dutch, could send him none. Villars then resorted to the desperate expedient of taking the remaining troops out of the redans of his centre and throwing them against the Wood of Taisnières to stem the allied advance. He, or others acting on his authority, drew first the Irish brigade, the Champagne brigade, and later La Colonie's Bavarians, and sent them to reinforce Albergotti's remnants. Some of these troops, as will presently be seen, ranged widely in the wood, but their main attack fell upon Lottum. Both Lottum and Schulenburg were heavily checked. The dense but much disordered allied line wavered and recoiled. Eugene was at hand. He rode forward into the front line rallying the German Imperialist troops. It was now that a bullet grazed him behind the ear. He was not disabled. He refused to withdraw. "If we are to die here," he exclaimed, "it is not worth dressing. If we win, there will be time to-night." Step by step, with hideous losses, all the allied nations fighting in the wood resumed their advance, and shortly before noon arrived in a ragged but heavy line at the edge of the plain.

"The wood being forced," says Schulenburg, "I found myself on the other side towards the enemy's lines, where I managed to bring up by a kind of miracle seven big cannon which I had with me, by which I did not fail to do great harm to the line of French cavalry." This battery began to fire with highly disconcerting effect from the southern flank of the line. At the same time the twenty squadrons of cavalry in Withers' force were making their way round the western edge of the Taisnières Wood towards the French extreme left flank behind it. The remainder of Albergotti's corps, driven out of the wood, formed on a prepared line and on their reserves three or four hundred paces from its farther edge. For a space of perhaps an hour all the forces on this wing were occupied in rearranging their disordered lines and preparing for a further clash.

By noon Schulenburg's troops were reassembled and drawn up beyond the wood "where one saw the open country." Their front stretched from the village Chaussée du Bois to La Folie, and the enemy's line stood before them at a distance of two to three hundred yards. In the depths of the wood, by one of the strange coincidences of history, the Royal Irish met and defeated the French Royal Irish Regiment—famous in the war as the "Wild Geese."

Marlborough was still uncertain of the position in the centre. He doubtless knew that the Wood of Taisnières was cleared of the enemy. But more than four-fifths of his infantry were either repulsed with the Dutch or so deeply committed on the right as to be beyond manœuvring control. He now resolved to ride swiftly through Taisnières Wood to where Schulenburg's battery was heard to be firing, in order to see the condition of his right wing, and above all from this new angle the state of the enemy's centre. As he picked his way through the terrible wood, encumbered with slain, filled with the groans and piteous cries of the wounded, he met Eugene. Schulenburg describes how the two Commanders both joined him on the inner edge of the wood at about a quarter to twelve.

A great situation disclosed itself. Beyond the wood to the southward, perhaps three hundred yards away, a strong French line of battle of apparently forty or fifty battalions had been formed to deliver the supreme counter-attack on the remaining forces of Lottum, Schulenburg, and Withers. The forces now facing each other in array at a few hundred paces in this part of the battlefield amounted to perhaps twenty-five thousand men on each side. But the vital fact lay in the centre.

Once again the moment had come when, the whole of the enemy's infantry being fully engaged and their centre naked, Marlborough still had under his hand a decisive reserve of fresh troops of the highest quality. Much is contradictory and most things uncertain in this vast, dark battle; but we know definitely that Marlborough was with Schulenburg at the edge of the wood somewhat before noon, and that a few minutes after twelve he was back at his former post behind the Grand Battery giving a series of orders which snatched victory from the jaws of defeat. He ordered Orkney to advance with the British corps and several Prussian battalions upon the line of redans. He rearranged the artillery in the centre so as to bring cross-fire to bear upon these works. He ordered Auvergne with his thirty squadrons to follow immediately behind Orkney. He summoned Hesse-Cassel from the left to keep pace with Auvergne. He ordered the whole mass of the cavalry to be ready to advance. He must now have felt, as in the afternoon at Blenheim, that in spite of all mischances and disasters victory was in his hands.

The British and Prussian infantry had hitherto stood in array under severe cannon fire, close to the battle-front. On Marlborough's order Orkney led them forward in a single line of battalions upon the redans of the French centre, from which they had noticed for some time neither smoke nor fire had come. Now their Hussar patrols cantered forward, and here and there got round or into some of the works and signalled that they were empty or weakly held.

"It was about one o'clock," says Orkney, "that my thirteen battalions got up to the retrenchments, which we got very easily; for as we advanced they quitted them and inclined to their right. . . . We found nothing to oppose us, however. Not that I pretend to attribute any glory to myself (for it was the nature of our situation), yet I verily believe that these thirteen battalions gained us the day, and that without firing a shot almost." But this advantage had not come by chance to the gallant Orkney. It was the gift of Marlborough's genius dominating at last the confusion of the battle.

The French Guards, resplendent in their new uniforms, who were posted some distance behind the redans, did not attempt any counter-attack, incurring thereby bitter ridicule and reproach from the French army. Only upon the British left was there any resistance; and all the entrenchments in the enemy's centre were captured with small loss. The Dutch infantry on the left, torn by their fearful losses but with undaunted spirit, were led for the third time to the attack on the corpse-strewn triple entrenchments by their Prince and their surviving generals. All accounts speak of the ardour of these troops, who had to be restrained rather than incited. "As at the beginning of the battle, so now, the Dutch bought with their blood every step of the broad earth, and in the end the French right wing had to abandon the field to such death-defying courage." Hesse-Cassel with his twenty-one squadrons was already passing the gaps upon the left of the line of redans, and unless arrested would speedily take the hitherto victorious French right wing and their defences in flank and rear.

By a quarter-past one the British battalions held the front face of all the redans. The intervals between them became so many gateways through which the allied cavalry could debouch and endeavour to form line on the plain beyond. The cross-fire of their supporting batteries afforded them some measure of protection during this critical opera-tion. The Prince of Auvergne, with his thirty Dutch squadrons, had followed close behind the British infantry, and began to pour through the gaps and deploy for the charge. Close behind came General Wood with the whole of the British cavalry. Rolling forward behind them again marched the heavy columns of the Prussian and Hanoverian horse under General Bülow, and the whole body of the Imperialist cavalry under the Duke of Würtemberg and Count Vehlen; in all, pressing forward at this point, more than thirty thousand horsemen, the equivalent of seven or eight modern cavalry divisions. This com-bination of horse, foot, and guns recalls the central attack at Blenheim. The perfect execution of these complicated manœuvres in the roar and crash of the great battle, the discipline and mutual loyalty of all these troops of different nations, justly won the admiration of their enemy, and deserve the proud glance of history.

Marlborough with his staff had ridden forward to a point near one of the redans where he could regulate this new and decisive phase. The struggle of the infantry was mainly over, and a cavalry battle, far larger even than Ramillies, the greatest, in fact, of which there is any ex-ample, was about to begin.

While all this was in progress in the centre the much diminished and somewhat disorganized forces of Lottum, Schulenburg, and With-ers, in line beyond or along the southern edge of Taisnières Wood, faced the counter-stroke which Marshal Villars had prepared at so heavy a cost to his army. The Marshal had collected upwards of fifty battalions, composed of the remains of Albergotti's five brigades, all the troops he had withdrawn from his centre, and the French reserves which had hitherto been posted in this quarter of the field. The two lines along a mile of front faced each other, often at no more than two hundred yards' distance. Beyond La Folie, and in full view of the greater part of the French left wing, a cavalry episode cheered the arms of France. General Miklau, with the squadrons of Withers, had at length made his way round the forest belt, and his leading squadrons were already deployed to attack the left flank of the hostile infantry. Upon him fell eight squadrons of French carabineers. They caught Miklau in flank in the act of deploying. At least six squadrons of the allied horse were cut to pieces, and the rest driven from the field, the bulk taking shelter in the woods. No mercy was shown by the victors, and the wounded were slaughtered on the spot.

As the whole French line braced themselves to attack there arrived from the centre the veteran artillerist Saint-Hilaire. The tale he told to Villars was terrible. The redans were empty. Masses of the English were already breaking into them. He had only by minutes saved his guns from capture. The Marshal, resolute as ever, saw no remedy but to lead forward twelve battalions which were at the moment in his hands as part of his general counter-stroke. Opposite to him at the edge of the wood was Eugene, who, with all the troops he could control, prepared to meet the French in full career. The whole front came into close, intense fire action, quivering and writhing under the effect of the volleys, while the dead and wounded sank upon the ground. Marshal Villars and his staff, riding forward, caught a blast of fire. His horse fell dead, and a bullet smashed his left leg below the knee. At the same moment Albergotti fell from the saddle with a broken thigh, and General Chemerault was killed. Aides-de-camp and a surgeon ran to the prostrate Marshal. He refused to quit the field. A chair was found in a cottage hard by. Seated in this, he endeavoured to conduct the battle, but the agony of his wound was over-powering. He swooned, and remained so long unconscious that they carried him away. He did not recover consciousness until he was in the hospital at Quesnoy. In his own words, "That is all I know about the end of the battle."

There is no doubt that the fall of the illustrious Commander-in-Chief and the simultaneous loss of Albergotti and Chemerault disorganized the French command at the supreme moment of their counter-attack. It is natural that French writers, then and afterwards, should claim that but for this they would have won the battle. But the troops who stood before them were tough and bitter, certainly as numerous, infuriated by their losses, flushed by success, and with Eugene at their head. They would not easily have been driven back into the wood, certainly not through it.

After an interval of paralysis Puységur, the staff officer whose reputation after Oudenarde still stood high, assumed direction of the French left wing. He organized and ordered a methodical retirement. Some regiments marched to within twenty yards of the Allies to fire their final volley before retreating, but within a quarter of an hour of Villars's wound the fifty battalions with their supporting cavalry had retired in good order out of all contact. The Allies, still clogged by the confusion of their passage of the wood, were in no condition to pursue. Eugene himself ordered them to remain halted, and to consolidate, and hastened to join Marlborough in the new focus of the battle.

From early morning onward the French cavalry on the plain behind the centre had suffered severely from the allied cannonade. The slopes of the ground were such that many cannon-balls which ricochetted from the crest of the redans flew onward, cutting cruel gaps in the closely formed squadrons. The allied cavalry did not suffer in this way, for the ground on which they had waited was not exposed to this glancing fire. Nevertheless, the French horse was almost as numerous as the Allies'. The French also had the advantage of being able to attack in superior strength an enemy while forming. It was indeed with relief and pent-up wrath that the brilliant squadrons, which had so long borne their punishment from the cannon, found at last a foe to strike. Marshal Boufflers, learning that the supreme command had devolved on him, placed himself at the head of the Maison du Roi, and as soon as Auvergne had formed twenty squadrons beyond the redans, charged him with these splendid troops.

Orkney, whose battalions now manned the whole line of redans, watched the scene at close quarters. "Before we got thirty squadrons out they came down and attacked; and there was such pelting at one another that I really never saw the like." Auvergne's Dutch squadrons were driven back upon the redans, and through the intervals between them. But here the pursuers were stopped by the steady fire of the British infantry and guns. As they recoiled the allied cavalry poured forward again through every gap. General Wood came up with the British cavalry. The fighting was now almost entirely with the sword. Orkney's

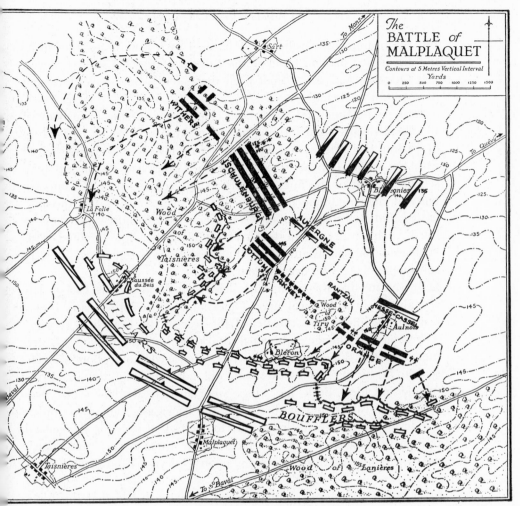

13. The Battle of Malplaquet

laconic, veteran style reveals how deeply he was stirred: "We broke through them, particularly four squadrons of English. *Jemmy Campbell, at the head of the Grey Dragoons, behaved like an angell, broke through both lines.* So did Panton, with little Lord Lumley at the head of one of Lumley's and one of Wood's." The struggle ebbed and flowed. The Maison du Roi, with Boufflers fighting sword in hand at their head, again drove back the Dutch, British, and Prussian horse, and repeatedly prevented them from deploying in sufficient numbers.

(743)

But the triumphant cavaliers were brought each time to a standstill by the disciplined platoon firing of the British infantry. "I really believe," says Orkney, "had not ye foot been there, they would have drove our horse out of the field."

Six separate times did the French charges prevent the main body of the allied cavalry from forming on the plain. Marlborough had led up in person the British and Prussian squadrons. Now Eugene arrived with the whole Imperialist cavalry. Hesse-Cassel had established himself on the left of the line. Boufflers, at last convinced of the impossibility of charging home and producing decisive results against the well-posted and well-trained infantry on the redans, withdrew the mass of the French cavalry to the heath of Malplaquet, a few hundred yards farther to the southward. Here the cavalry conflict renewed itself in continuous charges for over an hour.

But meanwhile the main battle had been decided. The French left was already in full retreat upon Quiévrain. On the other flank Hesse-Cassel's squadrons now threatened the rear of the French right wing. The Prince of Orange in his final attack led his heroic fellow-countrymen over the three lines of trenches. The aged, noble Boufflers, unshaken by his prodigious exertions, did not forget his duty as Commander-in-Chief. Both his wings were in retreat. His centre was pierced, his cavalry outnumbered, pressed backwards, but still in order. He devoted himself with his cavalry to the task of covering the general retirement which was now in progress. By three o'clock the French were marching in three directions upon Quiévrain, Bavai, and Maubeuge.

So severe and sternly contested had been the battle that the Allies could not pursue. The infantry of both wings were fought to a standstill. The intact British battalions in the centre were the sole link between the two disorganized wings. The cavalry pursued as far as the Hognon stream, but the French had organized strong rearguards of infantry, and their cavalry, though worsted, was still formidable. Marlborough and Eugene were both convinced that they could ask no further sacrifices of their troops. The battle was won, and the victors camped upon the bloody field. Marlborough sat down in his tent near the Mill of Sart and finished the letter he had been writing to Sarah at intervals since the morning of the 9th. The intense strain of the two days' manœuvre and battle, the long hours at close quarters under the cannonade, the tumult and collision of the cavalry masses, the thirty or forty thousand killed and wounded men who cumbered the ground, the awful stake which had been played, left his sober poise undisturbed, his spirit calm. He reread what he had written the day before, took up his pen, and added:

Sept. 11, 1709

I am so tired that I have but strength enough to tell you that we have had this day a very bloody battle; the first part of the day we beat their foot, and afterwards their horse. God Almighty be praised, it is now in our powers to have what peace we please, and I may be pretty well assured of never being in another battle; but that nor nothing in this world can make me happy if you are not kind.

CHAPTER SEVENTY-EIGHT

The Ebb-Tide

⟨ 1709, Autumn and Winter ⟩

EUROPE was appalled at the slaughter of Malplaquet. The battle of
Landen, to which its features have sometimes been compared, had not
been nearly so bloody. The losses of the Allies were returned at twenty-
four thousand officers and men; those of the French were not fewer
than twelve thousand, and probably nearer fifteen thousand. Not until
Borodino in 1812 was the carnage of this day surpassed. Our modern
mass minds, brutalized by the tenfold figures of the Great War, spread
over wider fronts and often weeks of fighting, measure only with some
difficulty the shock which the intricate polite society of the old world
sustained. Upon no one was the impression of the slaughter more deeply marked than upon Marlborough. It disturbed his mind; it affected
his health; it changed his sense of values. As he rode through the
ghastly woods of Taisnières, or up the trough across which the Dutch
had attacked, the heaps of stripped corpses affected him profoundly.

"It is melancholy," he wrote to Godolphin, "to see so many brave men
killed, with whom I have lived these last eight years, when we thought ourselves sure of a peace." He was unmanned by the plight of the wounded,
of whom at least fifteen thousand of all nations and both armies were left
upon his hands. "I have hardly had time to sleep, being tormented by
the several nations for care to be taken of their wounded." His resources and the science of those days were hopelessly inadequate. For
days the woods were crawling with shattered beings. From all sides it is
testified that he did his utmost to succour them. He invited Boufflers
to send wagons without formality or delay to take back all French

(746)

wounded, officers or men, upon the simple promise not to serve again. He sent back the wounded Irish himself. He took all the money in his military chest and spent it on relief. His behaviour at this time was greatly respected in all countries. It was known how hard and well he had fought in the battle, and also that his compassion for the wounded was sincere.

Marlborough, like his army, was morally and physically exhausted by the battle. He had fought it with all the skill and vehemence he had shown at Blenheim. His plans had proved successful. He had won at every point. The enemy had been beaten out of all their defences and driven from the field as a result of the heart-shaking struggle. But they had not been routed: they had not been destroyed. They had got off as an army, and, indeed, as a proud army. They retreated, but they cheered. They were beaten, but they boasted. Unable to face the Allies in the open, Villars contrived to bring about the main trial of strength under conditions which were most costly to them. Resting his wings upon the woods and covering his centre with intermittent entrench-ments, he presented a front which no army but that commanded by Marlborough and Eugene, with superior numbers and eight years of unbroken success behind them, would have dared to attack. He exacted from the Allies a murderous toll of life by his entrenchments and abat-tis; but all the time he fought a manœuvre battle around and among these created or well-selected obstacles. By a prodigy of valour, tactical skill, and bloodshed they drove him from the field. The victory was theirs; but not one of the allied generals, if he could have gone back upon the past, would have fought the battle, and none of them ever fought such a battle again.

England was inured to victory, and France to defeat. The Allies were discontented at not having gained all. The French were elated at hav-ing escaped with so much.

The Dutch bore their losses with fortitude. The "High and Mighty Lords" wrote their acknowledgments and thanks to Marlborough in the most flattering terms. Their leaders did not play false to their own responsibility in pressing their Deputy-Captain-General for action. It is strange, when the strength of the Peace Party in Holland in earlier and easier years is remembered, that it seemed to lose its influence now. Whereas for some years it had been Marlborough's preoccupation to keep the Dutch from making peace, we see them during the last four years of the war the most steadfast and unrelenting of all the Allies.

No one disputed that a great victory had been gained, and that nothing that the courage of soldiers and the skill and devotion of Chiefs could give had been withheld. But equally no one doubted that it had cost more than it was worth, and that it cast a lurid reproach upon the failure to make peace in the spring, when all was so near. For a month the impression of triumph was strong in London. There were loud rejoicings, and every one believed that peace was at hand. But the Tories soon recovered from their setback. They sought to represent the battle as a positive disaster.

But the Whigs used their party and Parliamentary power to the full. They declared Malplaquet Marlborough's signal and culminating triumph. They voted him the thanks of both Houses of Parliament. They celebrated the battle with all the resources and ability of their party and all the machinery of State. The Tories, outmatched by this exuberance, could but look down their noses and mutter insults and calumnies.

After Malplaquet the French retired behind the line of the Rhonelle, which formed a part of Villars's defensive lines. The Allies were free to open the siege of Mons. Boufflers began to extend his defences from Valenciennes to the Sambre with a view to protecting Maubeuge. Marlborough wished to forestall him in the interests of a future campaign. He therefore, as he tells us, would have preferred to leave Mons and besiege Maubeuge. However, he convinced himself that this was impossible until Mons was taken. French writers assert that the Dutch were inclined to abandon the siege of Mons. Marlborough and Eugene insisted upon its prosecution. The battle had been offered by Villars in order to save Mons, and Mons must fall, if only to prove that Villars was beaten. Besides this, it was of real importance to maintain the pressure upon France to the end of the campaign in the interests of the peace negotiations. Accordingly it was decided to persevere. The siege-train had been ordered before the battle to descend the Scheldt from Tournai to Brussels and thence journey by road to Mons. It could not, however, arrive till September 25. Meanwhile the siege-works were completed and all preparations made for the attack.

Marlborough exchanged eighteen battalions which had suffered the most at Malplaquet for twenty-four others drawn from the various garrisons. The numerical strength of his army was thus restored. Boufflers managed to slip two battalions into Mons before the investment finally closed. He also reinforced the garrisons of Condé, Maubeuge, Charleroi, Douai, and Landrecies at the expense of Ypres and Aire, and strengthened his weakened formations with men drawn from all his garrisons. Even so his strongest battalions could muster only four hundred men each. Eventually he collected forces under Luxembourg in the neighbourhood of Charleroi to threaten the communications of the Allies with Brussels and to harry their foragers. Eugene, Orange, and Hesse undertook the siege with 31 battalions and 31 squadrons, another 27 battalions being added later. Marlborough with the covering army lay to the south and south-west. The siege-train arrived safely, and on the 25th the trenches were opened.

Marshal Boufflers wished to make an effort to break the siege, but Louis XIV was more concerned for the safety of Maubeuge. He and his military advisers agreed with Marlborough upon the importance of this place. The King told Boufflers that he might risk another battle if necessary to save it. Boufflers thought Maubeuge was strong enough to last out the campaigning season. Meanwhile the siege of Mons progressed steadily, and the breaching batteries performed their remorseless task. At the end of September Berwick, who had been sent to assist Boufflers, personally reconnoitred Marlborough's covering position. He reported that it was too strong to be attacked. On October 20 Mons capitulated. The French army concentrated to protect Maubeuge, but Marlborough had already decided, owing to the bad weather, the hardships of the siege, and the lack of forage, to disperse the army into winter quarters. "I am glad to tel You," careful as ever, he wrote to the Treasurer, "that we have sav'd this Yeare above one-third of the Monys given by Parl: for the additional ten thousand men."

Although war had been resumed upon the greatest scale, negotiations for peace were unceasing. The new discussions played around various alternatives to the obnoxious Article XXXVII. In principle, the French were prepared to give some cautionary towns in France, but were neither ready nor able to give similar cautionary towns in Spain. The Whigs and the Emperor, bringing the Dutch along with them, continued to insist upon Spanish towns being yielded. A further obstacle was the French demand that there should be an immediate armistice, which the Allies would by no means entertain. Thus both before and after Malplaquet the summer and autumn passed in futile interchanges.

Marlborough felt convinced of the French insincerity. Both at The Hague and in London tempers rose, and declarations were made of the allied resolve to continue the war with the utmost vigour in 1710. On December 14 the Dutch sent a bellicose message to Queen Anne. In face of this attitude the French became more conciliatory. Their hopes of the Northern distraction proving effective had faded, and in January they made a definite offer to agree to all the preliminaries provided that the difficulties of Article XXXVII were first of all surmounted. The allied chiefs debated this in stormy session at The Hague. The Dutch peace party, headed by Buys and van der Dussen, put extreme pressure upon Heinsius to bring about a conference, and even declared that neither the Province of Utrecht nor the city of Amsterdam would vote the supplies for the new campaign unless this was accomplished.

We have only fleeting glimpses of Marlborough's part in these debates. It is certain, however, that while helping Heinsius to moderate the vehemence of Buys and the Dutch peace party, he also desired to give them satisfaction in the main. He, in fact, sponsored the proposal that should the conference be reached Buys and van der Dussen, the two chief advocates of peace, should themselves conduct the negotiations. This would give the greatest opportunity for obtaining a settlement if one were to be had, and if not, would satisfy the peace party that all possible had been done to procure it. This course was eventually adopted.

Whatever disputes there might be about the consequences of Malplaquet, one fact was certain: peace was no nearer than in June. A far more potent current than any that set from that battlefield was now flowing. It was becoming evident to the world that Marlborough's authority was being undermined. The effect of this conviction upon the fortunes of the war was instant and constant. The French began to feel that they could afford to wait. Marlborough's need was to create for himself an independent position at the head of the Alliance before his authority vanished at home. It was a grim race.

As early as May 1709 he had sent Craggs to London to make a quiet search in the Privy Seal offices. He hoped to find a precedent for a life-appointment as Captain-General.

Nothing could have appeared less auspicious. Both authorities consulted were independently adverse. For some months the matter slumbered. The urgency of the European situation in the autumn led him to thrust it forward again. In October he applied directly to the Queen, and when she refused his request he made a strong protest against the adverse influences which he declared had been used against him. Continental historians have complained that Coxe has not published these letters in his voluminous Marlborough correspondence. But, in fact, no one has been able to trace them. Considering how regularly all correspondence with the Queen was preserved by the Duke or Sarah, it is a fair assumption that these records were destroyed. Certainly the request could not have been made in worse circumstances nor at a worse time. It was just the kind of demand which Marlborough's enemies would have wished him to prefer, and which Harley could safely advise the Queen to refuse.

The Queen to Marlborough

Windsor
October 25, 1709

I saw very plainly your uneasiness at my refusing the mark of favour you desired, and believed from another letter I had from you on that subject you fancied that advice came from Masham; but I do assure you you wrong her most extremely, for upon my word she knows nothing of it, as I told you in another letter; what I said was my own thoughts, not thinking it for your service or mine to do a thing of that nature; however, if when you come home you still continue in the same mind I will comply with your desires. You seem to be dissatisfied with my behaviour to the Duchess of Marlborough. I do not love complaining, but it is impossible to help saying on this occasion I believe nobody was ever so used by a friend as I have been by her ever since my coming to the Crown. I desire nothing but that she would leave off teasing and tormenting me, and behave herself with the decency she ought both to her friend and Queen, and this I hope you will make her do. . . . Whatever her behaviour is to me, mine shall be always as becomes me. Since I began this I have received yours by the Duke of Argyll, and have told him he shall have one of the vacant Garters, and have enjoined him secrecy.

The Queen added:

* I am very sorry for ye resolution you have taken of quitting my service when ye War is ended but I hope when you have talked with your best friends here you will be prevailed with to alter it.

From the terms of this refusal it is clear that Marlborough's request to be accorded the Captain-Generalcy for life was coupled with a declaration of his resolve to retire at the end of the war. There is no reason to doubt the sincerity of this intention, and in any case the Queen could have held him to it. There is not, nor has there ever been, power in a sovereign to make an irrevocable grant. Crown and Parliament together cannot be bound by any law. If, then, a future revocation of the grant were to turn on the question only of fair dealing, Marlborough's expressed resolve to retire would have afforded the fullest justification to the Queen. Therefore, the request which Marlborough was making, however unseasonable, was by no means improper. It might have given him the authority which he needed to bring the war to a satisfactory end. It would have largely re-established his credit among the Allies and his prestige with the enemy. It could only conduce to national and international advantage. Yet, on the other hand, what doors it opened to malice! It not merely exposed the Duke to a direct and painful rebuff, but it afforded Harley fertile occasions of working on the Queen's fears and of convincing her that she was losing her rights and prerogatives by needless subservience to an insatiable family.

In the Tory coffee-houses the story was spread that Marlborough sought to subvert the Throne. "General-for-life" was but the stepping-stone. He would be King. "King John II" was the latest term of abuse cast upon him.

While freeing Marlborough from all the graver imputations, it is impossible not to be surprised that he should have exposed himself to such dangers. How could he not have foreseen the fate of his request? His surefooted judgment had gone for once astray. Was this a proof of his inordinate pretensions, or was it a measure of the difficulties by which he was being overcome, and of the forlorn expedients to which he was reduced to carry through his task in the dusk of his power?

Not only were the Tories inclined to peace, but several eminent Whigs, who were watching all the Queen's motions, might be easily gained upon this line. Of these the greatest was Shrewsbury, at this time a sincere advocate of peace. He was in the opinion of all men a prize of the first order. Finally an agitation for peace enabled the whole propaganda against Marlborough to be used to the fullest advantage. The General—thus it ran—was prolonging the war for his own profit. Military men raised by the luck of battle to dizzy heights were naturally prone to preserve the conditions upon which their authority and affluence alike thrived. How many good opportunities of obtaining all the objects of the war by sagacious and even glorious peace had not Marlborough burked! He could have had a good peace after Ramillies; he could have had a better peace before Malplaquet. Even now everything could be obtained by a sincere negotiation. But nothing could be expected except a continuance of the slaughter and taxation, and the ever-mounting indebtedness of the landed gentry to the money-power, while the General ruled all. Here, then, was Harley's political campaign, and to it he devoted himself with slow-burning zeal and shuffling skill.

However, the peace movement encountered obstacles none the less serious if submerged. First, the Tories, for all their party spite, were powerfully affected by the impression of England leading Europe, of redcoats beating the French, and some, politics apart, could scarce repress a cheer for the Duke of Marlborough. Secondly, the Ministry presented an oblique front to the peace talk. They too, so they declared, were striving for peace. Indeed, indefatigable negotiations, fathomless to outsiders, were unceasing. Discussion must therefore turn, not upon a vague desire to escape from war burdens or hardships, but upon particular points of the Treaty. And who had cried loudest for "No Peace without Spain" but Rochester and his Tories? Many Tories prided themselves upon being what Marlborough called "good Englishmen." War under Marlborough, however costly, had spelt glory. No would-be Minister dared openly cast away the fruits of eight dazzling years. Evidently this part of the case had to be stated by the Tory leaders with discretion.

Thirdly, there was the Queen. It was engrained in Anne that her security upon the throne depended upon the stunning defeat of France. All her reign she had pursued this course and had prospered. If she felt her own position greater, more solidly founded, if she found all the princes of Europe attentive to her slightest mood, it was because of her wonderful success in war which Marlborough had unfailingly brought to her. True the Queen was tired of the ordeal. She was galled by the submissions to Marlborough, and still worse to the Whigs, which it required. Had she not exclaimed on the day of the Oudenarde dispatch, "Lord, when will all this dreadful bloodshed cease?" None the less she remained deeply conscious that her sovereignty and British national greatness were founded upon undoubted victory in the war, and that this victory in one form or another, as long as Marlborough was her servant, was almost certainly within her grasp.

Therefore Harley, working steadily through the whispering Abigail, found that his peace talk gained only a lukewarm, doubtful, and hesitating response. The Queen made difficulties about backstair audiences. Abigail flitted to and fro with explanations that "my poor Aunt" was "short of ready money [courage]," and that she allowed herself to be overborne by the cruel pressures of her Ministers and General.

Even the slaughter of Malplaquet did not affect the Queen, nor, indeed, her people, as deeply as might have been hoped by the Tories. British troops had been few and their losses comparatively small. It was the Dutch, the Prussians, and the mercenaries whom England set in motion and directed who had shed their blood. The British casualties at Malplaquet had been under eighteen hundred. Marlborough's fame, his influence upon the Continent, his comradeship with Eugene, had compelled the tremendous event. The war was not all loss or waste to the British realm, and it was no use for Mr Harley to pretend the contrary.

The end of 1709 marked the zenith of Britain in Europe, of the Whigs under Queen Anne, and of Marlborough's career. Thereafter all fell with odd rapidity. The victorious Alliance moved forward with ever-growing disunity and ever more unreasonable pretensions. The Whigs were driven from office; Marlborough was hounded down; and glorious England turned renegade before all men. But the winter sun shone with fitful brightness.

CHAPTER SEVENTY-NINE

The Queen's Revenge

ᘒ 1709, Autumn and Winter ᘒ

QUEEN Anne brooded and planned revenge upon the Whigs. Her power, founded upon Marlborough's victories, was immense. The Courts of Europe studied her whims; the fierce parties in Britain competed for her smile. But there is a cruel sketch of her about this time, oppressed with sorrow and physical suffering, struggling under her burdens, which commands sympathy and mocks pomp. "She appeared to be the most despicable mortal I had ever seen in any station. The poor lady as I saw her twice before, was again under a severe fit of gout, ill-dressed, blotted in her countenance, and surrounded with plaisters, cataplaisma, and dirty-like rags." From the autumn of 1709 onward the Queen felt herself capable of driving out the Whigs if she could take her time and have good advice. Thereafter she thought about little else. These Whigs had forced themselves upon her. They had intruded into her Council of State. They had used without scruple the power they had from majorities in both Houses of Parliament to override her sovereign pleasure about the personages she thought fit to employ. Not only were her wrath and prejudice directed against the Whigs, but they fell upon Godolphin, her Lord Treasurer, who had been their tool. Marlborough, although not upon this plane, had lent his weight to the Lord Treasurer and shared his disfavour. As for Sarah, the Queen was utterly worn out by her arguments and admonitions. She desired above all things never again to hear her voice or see her handwriting. Nothing remained of that remarkable partnership except the opportunities of quarrel; and these were nearing their end.

When they met at great functions, or when Sarah's offices required her attendance, appearances were preserved. Sarah was a State and political personage. Her dismissal might be followed by Marlborough's resignation and a crisis in Parliament and throughout the Alliance. Even the rumours that she was in disfavour stirred Europe. The Queen did not feel strong enough to face such contingencies in the autumn of 1709. Had Sarah discharged her duties with respectful formality, avoided all intimate or controversial topics, and remained in the country as much as possible, a tolerable relationship between the two women might have been preserved. But Sarah's judgment was warped by her hatred of Abigail, and she was tormented out of all prudence or proper self-respect by jealousy of her triumphant rival. She obtruded herself upon the Queen; she protested her party views; she asked for petty favours, and attributed the refusals to the influence of Abigail. Abigail Masham had become an obsession to her, and she acted as if it were possible to tear the Queen away from her by force. Thus what might have been a dignified if frigid association became a violent and protracted annoyance to the Queen. At every rebuff or repulse Sarah wrote of her grievances to her husband, and urged him, as he loved her, to take up the cudgels on her behalf. All the advice he gave was sound. He begged her to stay away from Court, not to accost or write to the Queen, to remain as quiet as possible and ask no favours. This was advice which Sarah could not bring herself to follow.

The accomplishment of the Queen's political purpose was by no means easy or free from risk. The Government commanded the ability of the great Whig lords, and behind them lay the force of the Whig organization. This included not only the City, with its mysterious power of manufacturing credit, but also the Dissenters, who might upon occasion become the Ironsides. Besides this both Houses of Parliament—the Commons but one year old—were capable at any time of taking sharp and measureless action against the Court, of refusing supplies to carry on the war, of arresting and impeaching friends of the Queen, or having her gentlewoman, the comforting Abigail, dismissed or sent to the Tower. Above all, Marlborough stood at the head of the armies of the Grand Alliance, apparently invincible, indissolubly wedded to Godolphin, to the Whigs, to the Parliamentary system, as well as to Sarah.

This was a great combination for the Queen to confront. Such was her confidence in herself and in her majesty and prerogative that she set herself without hesitation to overthrow it.

The successive steps by which the Queen sought and compassed the destruction of her Ministers were calculated and timed with remarkable address. At every stage her action was measured by the growing Tory strength in the country. This process continued remorselessly through the autumn of 1709 to the winter of 1710. This gradual but persistent change from Whig to Tory was only possible because the doctrine of collective Cabinet responsibility was in its infancy. The Lord Treasurer had many of the duties but few of the powers of a modern Prime Minister. His colleagues at the council table felt little loyalty to one another or to him. The Queen had no thought of loyalty to her Ministers, nor to the Parliament which voted her great supplies by their majority. To break and turn them out upon the advice of secret counsellors and by intrigue, veiled under deceitful protestations of confidence and regard, was her unswerving aim. She pursued it with almost total disregard of the consequences to the war, upon which she had spent so much of her subjects' blood and treasure, or to the princes of the Grand Alliance, to whom her royal faith was pledged. Queen Anne conceived herself as entirely within her rights in cleansing herself from the Whigs whom she detested, and also in punishing the two great super-Ministers who had helped to force the Whigs upon her. In behaving thus the Queen violated every modern conception of the duties of a constitutional monarch, and also most of the canons of personal good faith. Nevertheless, neither she nor her subjects felt the same repugnance to these methods as we do to-day. Royal favour was like the weather. It was as useless to reproach Queen Anne with fickleness and inconstancy as it would be to accuse a twentieth-century electorate of these vices.

So complete a transformation in little more than a year of Government unquestionably sustained by majorities in both Houses could not have been effected if the threatened Ministers had stood together and acted resolutely in their own defence. It would probably have been possible in the early stages to confront the Queen and her secret advisers with an issue. Marlborough, with his sure instinct, was, as we shall see, most anxious for a decisive trial of strength on well-chosen ground. But at every stage the timidity of Godolphin, and the jealousy and selfishness of the Whigs towards one another, prevented any combined front from being formed.

Two main methods were pursued by Harley. The first was a villainous propaganda against Marlborough, or what was more easy, 'the Marlboroughs.' Here was the pair and their offspring holding the Queen in bondage, engrossing to themselves all the sunlight of the realm. Here was this General gathering with his covetous hands filthy lucre in fabulous quantities. He was prolonging the war for his own advantage. He had prevented a triumphant peace in order that he might batten on the public fortunes at the head of the army, which, it must be admitted, he sometimes conducted with diabolical skill, but—as Harley did not shrink from hinting—with doubtful courage. Even to this level did he sink. The General had now at Malplaquet contrived a battle, which for its brutal slaughter was without compare, in order that he might line his pockets with the profits of favouritism and corruption, through filling the commissions of those he had led to death. Now this ogre, in base ingratitude to the Queen to whom he owed all, in treason against the kingdom and Parliament, was secretly aiming at the Crown. A new Cromwell dictatorship was his goal. See how the mob cheered him when they had the opportunity. Parliament itself must be on its guard against an ambitious adventurer, who had betrayed in turn every party and every prince he had served. Such, in insidious forms, was the nourishment which Harley fed to Abigail, and which Abigail fed to Anne.

For the rest there were the Whigs, the party foe, a cabal of wealthy nobles, an obsolete expression of the forces which had cut off the head of King Charles the Martyr, now allied with the profiteers and money-lenders of the City and the Bank of England. These were piling up ceaselessly a gigantic debt, of which they were the usurers, which soon would equal in its dead weight and in its interest the whole value of the land and annual food of England. These same Whigs were at heart not only republicans but atheists. It might be going too far to suggest they were the only evil-livers in the land; but still, their standards of morality were drawn at a level which, if accepted for a generation, would destroy the Church of England and debase the British breed.

Ought not the Queen to count for more? Ought she not to be mistress in her own realm? Could she not free herself with loyal aid from the trammels in which Whig majorities in the Commons and the Lords had entangled her? Then England might also be freed from the recreant, self-seeking, and blood-sucking allies who sheltered behind her sword—victorious no doubt—who pursued aims which had no longer any interest for the British Isles. Let the Queen use her undoubted rights and power, let her throw herself with confidence upon the love of her people; and the hateful toil of war would end, peace could be made upon unchallenged victory, and plenty would cheer manor house and vicarage alike. Such was the propaganda, a mixture of fact and malice, pressed upon Queen Anne from many quarters, urged by Harley in his backstair consultations, and counselled by Abigail at the Queen's bedside as she smoothed the pillows and removed the slops.

Side by side with all this lay a plan of action profoundly studied and step by step brought into execution. Fortified by the unfailing favour of the Queen, Harley now began to tamper with the Whig weaklings. The Duke of Somerset was a Cabinet Minister. Although a duke and wealthy, he had never reached beyond a secondary sphere in national politics. A searching process of reciprocal canvassing and criticism proceeded within the ranks of the aristocracy. Society and politics coincided through the entire field. In that keen, well-informed atmosphere personal defects were soon descried. Somerset's intelligence was limited, but he was independent, ambitious, bold, and could upon occasion be both violent and forcible. The insulting manner in which he had driven Harley from the Cabinet in 1708, when Marlborough and Godolphin had stayed away, had played its part in history. His wife was becoming the Queen's close friend. The seduction of the Duke of Somerset from the Whigs and his separation from Marlborough and Godolphin were objects of high political importance.

Harley knew all about the Duke of Somerset. He measured shrewdly both his smaller qualities and his large potential usefulness. For more than a year Somerset was led to believe that he might become the head of some great Ministry, truly national, combining the best in all parties, for causes with which, until they were defined, none would disagree. No records are available of Harley's approaches to Somerset. But we know that the Queen—no doubt by Harley's guidance—began to show him exceptional favour from the end of 1709. She was repeatedly

closeted with him. She listened with unwearied patience to all the advice he had to give. He basked resplendent in the royal grace. Godolphin wrote drily to Marlborough that Somerset seemed to be more
hours each day with the Queen than away from her. Already because of
his airs he was spoken of in the Court as "the Sovereign." We are wit-
nessing an early eighteenth-century example of the process, familiar to
twentieth-century democracy in every land, by which a pretentious, imposing mediocrity can be worked up into a national leader. The Duke
of Somerset enjoyed the treatment, and while sitting at Council with
Marlborough, Godolphin, and the Whigs, upon the assumption of
amity and good faith, he actively, crudely, and obviously played Harley's game. Lord Chancellor Cowper has passed a severe judgment on
him. "On the whole he appeared a false, mean-spirited knave, at the
same time he was a pretender to the greatest courage and steadiness."

The Houses met on November 15, 1709. The Queen for the first
time since her husband's death opened Parliament in person in royal
and war-time pomp. Her speech from the throne, though read, as some
noticed, in faltering tones, was all that a Whig Parliament could wish.
French duplicity had used the peace negotiations in an attempt to provoke dissension among the Allies. Their design had failed. The war
had been renewed with greater resolution. A splendid victory had been
won, and peace was now only the more needed by the enemy. But the
war was still going on, and the final effort was required. The Queen
appealed for generous supplies.

The Whigs excelled in Parliamentary stage-management. Under
their influence the House of Commons resolved, contrary to all custom, to present the Address to the Sovereign on the very same day.
Both Houses then proceeded to extol Marlborough. Never in the whole
course of the war had the Commons expressed thanks to their General
in such glowing terms. They exalted the victory of Malplaquet. They
praised his skill and valour. Fifteen of the most distinguished members
of the House were deputed to wait upon him with the thanks—against
which no single speech had been made—of the most powerful assembly
in the world. The Lords vied with the Commons. When Marlborough
returned and came to the Upper House on November 17 Lord Chancellor Cowper outstripped all the eulogies he had earned in eight years
of invincible war. Klopp rightly says, "This day may be called the su-

preme and also the last pinnacle of Marlborough's career." Barely two years were to pass, and two more unfailing campaigns to be fought, before he was to be dismissed from all his offices, his faithful generals superseded or cashiered, and he himself charged with peculation and eventually driven from his native land in obloquy.

CHAPTER EIGHTY

The Ninth Campaign

ƨɑ 1710, March-September ɒƷ

ONCE again the great armies assembled, and now more numerous than ever. Although the plans of the Allies contemplated converging inroads upon France from the Rhine, from Dauphiné, and upon the coast, all gravitated irresistibly to the main theatre. Apart from the separate, self-contained war in Spain, all the subsidiary operations languished. Marlborough's diminished authority was incapable of infusing vigour into them. The Elector of Hanover threw up the command of the Imperial forces on the Rhine on the ground that they were relegated to a minor rôle. Even with superiority of three to one he had only gaped at his opportunities in 1709. Victor Amadeus of Savoy felt that this was a season for politics rather than for war; and M. de Seissan, a French refugee of some mark, who had undertaken to raise the Cevennes, never found himself provided with the means to undertake this task.

All lay in the north and among the fortresses. Here Marlborough and Eugene would war with Villars supported by four other marshals; and every scrap of force that could be gathered by the war-wearied combatants was hurried to their respective camps. The confederate army marshalled 155 battalions and 262 squadrons, with 102 cannon, 20 howitzers, and 40 pontoons. France, rightly judging the impotency of the minor theatres, claimed to have available for Villars's command no fewer than 204 battalions, 308 squadrons, and a full proportion of artillery and pontoons. There is no doubt that the allied armies were far better equipped and supplied and thus stronger in warpower than their opponents, and all the movements of both sides were based upon this fact.

European and English public opinion expected that the two great commanders, superior in skill and in the numbers at their command, would soon bring the war to an end; but the task was not so easy. The dangers and cost of assaulting bravely held entrenchments were rated at a new high level after Malplaquet. The campaign still lay in the second and third lines of the French fortress zone, with all the obstinacies and time-losses that must be encountered there. The problem of feeding and foraging their enormous armies in ruined, famine-stricken regions confronted these lords of thirty or forty thousand cavalry with rigorous limitations. Eighteenth-century warfare had reached its maximum and its culmination as a result of squandered opportunities both of victory and of peace, and of a will-power on both sides which was alike unreasoning and indomitable. Meanwhile at Gertruydenberg the diplomatists and plenipotentiaries, surrounded by a host of agents and busybodies, official and unofficial, manœuvred sedately around the clauses of the peace treaty, incapable as were the armies of reaching a decision.

Two alternatives offered themselves to the Allies for the final penetration of the French fortress zone. The first, which no doubt Marlborough would have favoured because of the use he could make of British amphibious power, was near the coast, down the Lys by Saint-Venant and Aire, aiming at the creation of a new reinforcing base at Abbeville. This movement would turn the left and cut in behind the principal fortresses of the French barrier. It would also avoid the fortified line which Villars was preparing from La Bassée to Douai. A right-handed operation of this kind, however, though very agreeable to English interests and to the true strategy of a combination possessing the command of the sea, exposed the whole of Brabant to a northward thrust by strong French forces. The other choice was to punch at the French centre up the Scarpe to Douai and towards Arras, with further inclination towards Cambrai. Advance by this route was the most direct invasion of France. It covered Brabant and the Spanish Netherlands from French counterstrokes, and it threatened simultaneously five or six fortresses essential to the French defence, any of which might be attacked, all of which must be heavily garrisoned. Both routes led into unravaged regions where the advancing armies could feed themselves for many weeks. Both were sustained by good waterways. Marlborough controlled the Lys up to Armentières, and the Scheldt to beyond Tournai. By either of these rivers he could draw through Ghent the whole resources of the confederacy, and carry forward supplies, siege-trains, and munitions with ease and sureness. Upon the whole, the central punch, if successful, would lead into better ground for the operation of all arms, and especially the cavalry, then so dominant a factor. Thus the strategic choice was evenly balanced; but the political needs of the Dutch to have the main allied army between their regained territory and the enemy was decisive. There is no evidence that Marlborough at this time pressed seriously for the coastal movement. The councils of war were guided by him and Eugene towards the French centre. This meant the siege of Douai, followed if successful by that of Arras. There was complete agreement upon this.

The French placed four armies in the field—in Roussillon under Noailles, in Dauphiné under Berwick, on the Rhine under Harcourt, and the great mass under Villars, when he was fit enough, in the Netherlands. Owing to the stringency of food, forage, money, and equipment, these armies were to stand everywhere on the defensive. In the main theatre the winter was spent in strengthening the fortresses and collecting supplies. In March Berwick was offered the command till Villars had recovered sufficiently. Berwick demanded authority to assemble and forestall the impending attack. As this was contrary to Louis XIV's general conception of a defensive campaign, he was not encouraged, and proceeded, as originally proposed, to his command in Dauphiné. Marshal d'Artagnan, who had succeeded to the title of Duc de Montesquiou by which he was in future to be known, was therefore placed in charge of the preparatory phase. He reinforced La Bassée and Ypres, with some difficulty persuaded Louis to let him use men and money to strengthen the lines about La Bassée, and clamoured for everything needed for war. Montesquiou as yet could only feed 40 battalions and 40 squadrons upon this front, and that for a short time.

Marlborough, arriving at The Hague, decided to take the field at the end of March. He ordered Albemarle, who had been in command of the British troops in Flanders during the winter, to seize Mortagne and Saint-Amand, on the Scheldt, so as to open the water communications for a siege of Douai. Albemarle captured Mortagne on April 14. It was retaken the next day by Luxembourg, and finally mastered by the Allies

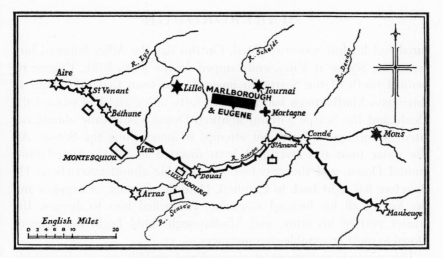

14. The Situation in April 1710

on April 18. The confederate army began to assemble around Tournai, and in the third week of April Marlborough and Eugene arrived together from The Hague at that fortress. In spite of the late spring and the consequent shortage of forage, they had decided to begin operations at once without waiting for all their troops to arrive or for the grass to grow.

To besiege Douai it was necessary first of all to pierce the French defensive lines. Only half the allied army had yet assembled; sixty thousand men were still to come, but it was known that the French would be largely immobile for some weeks, and a great operation to pierce their lines was planned, albeit with incomplete forces. On the 20th the Allies advanced. The next day Würtemberg, accompanied by Cadogan, entered the French lines at Pont-à-Vendin. The defenders retired without fighting. Feltz failed at Pont-Auby, but Eugene, coming up in heavy force, crossed at Courrières and Saut, and the main army followed across these captured bridges and pressed on to the south of Lens, where it halted before the Vimy Ridge after a thirty-mile march. Montesquiou, who was evidently not expecting so early an attack, and could not in any case command the means to resist it, was caught foraging, and retreated across the Scarpe at Vitry, breaking his bridges behind him. On the 22nd the advance continued. Montesquiou, now joined by Luxembourg, withdrew precipitately, his front ruptured and his forces overweighted. On this day the Allies followed him across the Scarpe at Vitry, and camped on the south bank. Eugene remained north of the Scarpe to invest Douai from that side. Thus in three days Marlborough had advanced forty miles, and had crossed the Deule and the Scarpe without fighting. Douai was already almost isolated. Montesquiou could not attempt to stand along the Sensée. All the water from this river had been diverted to fill the inundations around Douai, and the river-bed was passable almost everywhere. He therefore fell right back to Cambrai. Here the shortage of supplies and the loss of all his forward magazines compelled him to disperse the greater part of his army, and Marlborough could begin the siege of Douai in most favourable circumstances.

This masterly movement of extraordinary rapidity was made possible only by dry forage brought by water. It succeeded because it was launched before the enemy could feed on the ground enough troops to man their extensive lines. All these fortifications, upon which so much labour had been spent, proved perfectly useless. They were simply walked over, and a very great tract of country, which might well have been disputed for the whole campaign, passed at a stroke into Marlborough's possession. We are often told of the leisurely and ceremonious methods of eighteenth-century war. Here are movements of large armies as swift and sudden as any in military annals.

Douai was a fortress of the first order, well prepared and supplied for a siege. Water played a great part in its defences, and the inundations severely limited the sectors open to the attackers. General Albergotti commanded the fortress with a garrison of over eight thousand men, comprising 17 battalions in Douai and 3 in Fort Scarpe.

Forty battalions and as many squadrons under the command of the Princes of Anhalt and Orange conducted the siege, which Marlborough and Eugene covered. It was generally hoped that the town would be reduced before the grass grew and Villars could assemble an army strong enough to attempt relief; but the siege-train of two hundred guns, including 80 heavy pieces, did not reach the camp till May 9. The fact that the French had control of the sluices made water communications difficult. They were also able, by galleys from Condé operating down the Scheldt, to threaten water convoys moving south from Tournai. Marlborough therefore collected large quantities of wagon transport, and also developed the water communications up the Deule from Lille. The heavy batteries began to play on May 11.

Louis XIV hoped that by this time Montesquiou would be strong enough to impede the task of the besiegers. He was answered that the Allies, even after undertaking a siege, were still superior, and that the French army could not yet take the offensive. Villars arrived at Péronne on May 14, and took command. His army could not be fully assembled till the end of the month. Although strategically the Great King was upon the defensive, the idea of a battle to relieve Douai, if a good chance offered, was cherished. Berwick, recalled from Dauphiné, joined the army for the same purpose as Boufflers before Malplaquet. Commanders-in-chief fought so hard in the battles of those days that it was indispensable to have a recognized understudy fully versed in the part. The gallant Villars was still suffering from his wound. His knee discharged, and from time to time threatened an abscess. He had had a steel "machine" made which held the joint rigid on horseback. He could not ride for more than two hours without fatigue and pain. But he was none the less overflowing with vitality and what in any man less brave and skilful would be called braggadocio. His army began to draw together around Cambrai. Far from minimizing his forces to safeguard his reputation, he declared that he was at the head of 160,000 men. Actually he had a little over 100,000.

Innumerable sieges took place in these long wars, and most of them were merely matters of routine. But the siege of a fortress as strongly garrisoned as Douai, with the two main armies in close contact around it, created a situation in which on any day one of the decisive battles of the world might explode. The fact that no great battle was fought does not mean that an intense trial of strength and skill was not proceeding between these armies, upon whose interplay all European eyes were fixed.

According to Villars, Berwick and Montesquiou deprecated a battle, and Villars admits in his memoirs that he did not mean to fight one. He thought, however, that it would do his army good to march up to close contact with the enemy, and that if they were found well posted he could easily retire. He presented his manœuvre from the outset to his colleagues as a reconnaissance with the whole army. Announcing by word and manœuvre that he intended to attack from Bouchain, he concentrated forward in that direction, brought in all the troops from Arras, and advanced north-westward full of menace. The Ally cavalry patrols detected, as Villars desired, the eastward march of the Arras detachment. Marlborough and Eugene personally reconnoitred all the possible battlefields between Douai and the front Valenciennes-Arleux, and the confederate army was deployed in that direction. Only 30 battalions were left at the siege and 12 squadrons at Pont-à-Rache. The whole of the cavalry, which had been feeding its horses from the Deule barges south of Lille, were also brought across the Scarpe by Vitry.

As this confrontation developed day by day both sides received strong reinforcements: Villars from the Rhine and Dauphiné; Marlborough of the Hessians on the spot, of the Palatines coming into Brabant, and of several cavalry regiments which Eugene had summoned from the Rhine. By May 22 the armies faced each other, Marlborough and Eugene being astride of the Scarpe. These two Commanders, acting as ever in the most perfect harmony, of course realized that Villars might only be making a feint, and one fine night would move suddenly back to the west. They therefore built no fewer than twenty bridges across the Scarpe between Vitry and the lines of circumvallation, so that their whole army, moving on interior lines, could swing round to the new quarter of the compass without the slightest impediment.

On May 25 Villars made this move. Under the cloak of darkness he crossed the Scarpe by eight bridges just east of Arras, and debouched into the plain of Lens. On May 27 the three French marshals, Villars, Berwick, and Montesquiou, reconnoitred the allied right wing and, not liking the look of it, continued their left-handed movement towards Lens. Simultaneously Marlborough and Eugene extended their right, drew in the bulk of the siege troops, and formed a front facing west, leaving only the Dutch under Tilly south of the Scarpe. On May 30 Villars advanced directly to within barely two miles of the confederate line, which was now covered by a chain of redoubts. Simultaneously Albergotti began a series of vigorous sorties from Douai. Marlborough none the less brought up Tilly and the Dutch troops, and battle from all appearances seemed imminent.

All day the great masses watched each other within cannon, and at some points within musket, shot. The French marshals, including Villars, were agreed that the Allies were too strong to be attacked, and in the evening the French withdrew out of immediate striking distance. This was no doubt a wise decision. The question arises, however, why if the numbers of men were approximately equal, as Marlborough writes, he and Eugene did not themselves advance and attempt to force a battle. The answer must be that they did not intend at this time to run any supreme risks. They thought the war was certainly won, and that they need only continue to conduct it successfully to compel a peace. Time, they believed, was on their side. There was no warrant for staking the overwhelming advantages that had been gained. This reasoning was no doubt sound upon all the military facts. Perhaps Marlborough was not himself satisfied with it. His mind was oppressed by the hostility of the Queen and the growing power of his foes in England. He did not feel that confidence in victory which had inspired him at Blenheim and Ramillies. "I am not so fully pleased with those sanguine thoughts as formerly, that God would protect and bless us," is a sentence which shows that the strains and stresses to which he had been so long subjected had worn him down. Had he felt the same need and urge for battle as in his campaign of 1705 it is by no means certain that Villars could have paraded and promenaded north of the Scarpe with impunity.

The siege of Douai was strongly contested. Albergotti is said to have made no fewer than thirty-two sallies during its course. But the Prince of Anhalt's attack in particular progressed steadily. The covered way was mastered by the middle of June, and on the 19th two important ravelins of the inner defences were stormed in a bloody assault. During the night of the 24th the besiegers were so much the masters that they were filling up the 'capital ditch' and building galleries across it. On the morning of the 25th Albergotti beat a parley, offering to surrender Douai but not Fort Scarpe. This was refused, but after some haggling he yielded, and on the 26th articles of capitulation were agreed.

The losses of the siege had been severe. Albergotti had lost a third of his men. The Allies had paid eight thousand casualties for the acquisition of the fortress; but, what was even more costly, they had consumed the whole of May and June, and their campaign, which had started so early and so brilliantly, was now a month behind their plans. Marlborough's depression was extreme.

Not only the resistance of the fortress but the ravages of typhus had smitten the besiegers. "My last quarters," wrote Marlborough to Godolphin (June 16),

> infected a great many of my servants, by which I have lost Groffy, my steward, and poor Turliar [his dog]; but the rest are recovering. It is impossible, without seeing it, to be sensible of the misery of this country; at least one-half of the people of the villages, since the beginning of last winter, are dead, and the rest look as if they came out of their graves. It is so mortifying that no Christian can see it but must with all his heart wish for a speedy peace.

The flow of Ally reinforcements was continuous. Marlborough replaced the weakened regiments from his numerous garrisons, and in the first week of July he and Eugene stood at the head of 182 battalions and 284 squadrons, all in good strength, a total 120,000 men. It was still their intention to strike at Arras, the keystone of the last line of the French fortress barrier. On the 12th the Allies moved forward past and over the Vimy Ridge, and lay along the Scarpe with Arras in full view. Villars, denuding the French garrisons not immediately threatened, had concentrated an even larger army in his new lines stretching along the Crinchon stream from Arras to the Somme. These fortifications, held in force by the main army of France, offered bluntly to the Allies another Malplaquet. Upon the acceptance or refusal of this challenge the decisive character of the campaign depended. Afterwards, as will be seen, Argyll attacked Marlborough for timidity in not having besieged Arras, as he had already attacked him for temerity in fighting at Malplaquet; but at the time the allied high command was united in declining to play so high a stake as the great frontal attack upon the whole French army in its entrenchments which was the needful preliminary. All were agreed that the French position was too strong to assault. Marlborough revolved deeply an attack upon Calais and Boulogne. Political deterrents were added to the military difficulties. He wrote to Godolphin (August 2):

> You may be assured that the King of France is so encouraged by what passes in England that he has taken a positive resolution for the continuation of the war, and reckons upon my not being employed this next campaign. The little consideration that the Queen has for you and me makes it not safe for me to make any proposal for the

employing those regiments now in the Isle of White; though, if things were formerly, I could attempt a project on the sea-coast that might prove advantageous. But as everything is now, I dare attempt nothing, but what I am almost sure must succeed; nor am I sure that those now in power would keep my secret.

Béthune, which was defended by fifteen battalions, was invested on July 15, and capitulated on August 29. The siege was bloody, and cost 3500 men, apart from sickness and desertion. Villars continually threatened a battle for its relief, but he, like the allied commanders, was not prepared to "venture." Once again, after the capture of Béthune, Marlborough and Eugene pondered the question of a general assault upon the French entrenchments, and once again they decided not to try. Although there had been no battle, the losses of the campaign had been heavy: eight thousand at Douai, 3500 at Béthune, and fourteen thousand sick or deserted. Nevertheless, while resigning the main objective, and in spite of "a very unlucky accident," they felt strong enough to attack two fortresses at once.

On September 6 Anhalt with forty battalions and as many squadrons besieged Aire, and Nassau-Friesland (the Prince of Orange) with twenty battalions and five squadrons Saint-Venant. Of the two towns Aire was incomparably the stronger, and held a garrison of fourteen battalions, double that which defended Saint-Venant. Marlborough stood midway between his sieges and Arras. Saint-Venant fell on September 30. Aire made a more obstinate and formidable resistance. The slaughter was heavy, and the weather terrible. "Our poor men," wrote Marlborough, "are up to their knees in water." It was not until November 9 that the capitulation was signed. The garrison had lost more than a third of its strength, and the Allies nearly seven thousand men, apart from sickness. Villars, whose wound required repeated attention, had handed over the command of his army to Harcourt after the fall of Béthune some six weeks earlier. It was now too late to attempt an advance on Abbeville and the creation of a new base there, and both armies dispersed into winter quarters.

Although this campaign, so costly in casualties and disease, was conducted impeccably by Marlborough, and the results achieved were substantial, it was nevertheless a disappointment. That Marlborough and Eugene with 120,000 men should not have been able to bring the enemy to battle or take Arras seems surprising in view of the achievements of their great years. Reasons other than military must be invoked in explanation. Marlborough, ageing rapidly, undermined at home, uncertain of the loyalty of some of his principal officers, could bring himself to do no more than play military chess with his accustomed skill, and wait for the enemy to make some fatal mistake. If he had run the supreme risk, if he had hurled his army upon the French entrenchments, or if, repeating his manœuvre of 1705 and carrying eight days' supplies in his wagons, he had marched through the intervals between the French fortresses and forced a crisis, he might have ended the war at a stroke, or, on the other hand, have ruined all. No one can pronounce. The authority of the twin Captains cannot lightly be set aside by posterity. What they deemed imprudent must certainly have been perilous. What they declared to be impossible was probably beyond the reach of mortal man.

CHAPTER EIGHTY-ONE

Sunderland's Dismissal

1710, April-July

HITHERTO the forces gathering against the domestic system and foreign policy of Marlborough and Godolphin had been numerous and powerful, but disunited. Now there emerged the same group of powerful nobles loosely attached to either party which had played its part in 1708 and was to do so again in 1714. But this time their weight was cast on the Tory side. The encouragement which the Queen gave to almost all elements hostile to her own leading Ministers offered prospects of favour and power to both honest antagonism and selfish aims. To control the Government of Britain, which Marlborough's sword had raised so high, was an attraction captivating the great nobles and magnates of the day. At the root lay Harley with the Tory Party, and now, somewhat incongruously, with the Church. The jealous or disaffected officers in the Army found their leader in the Duke of Argyll. In the Cabinet the Duke of Somerset was incited by the craft of Harley and the smiles of Anne to pursue his dream of heading a Government. He found support at this time from the Duke of Newcastle, Lord Privy Seal. He saw himself upon the high road to mastery; he did not hear the slighting comments which those whom he aspired to lead, and whose interests for a time he served, were accustomed to make upon him behind his back. Already, as has been described, Shrewsbury had begun in his cautious manner to work with Harley. All these men in the months following the Sacheverell fiasco 'entered into measures'—to use their dignified expression—with one another. Harley, in close touch with St John, guided from the House of Commons; Argyll glared in the camp; Somerset flaunted himself at the Court; and Shrewsbury lent an aspect of prudence and disinterested moderation to the whole cabal. A novel term now came into British politics. The five Whig lords had been called the Junto. The new group was nicknamed the Juntilla. "There is a Juntilla in imitation of the Junta," Count Maffei wrote to Victor Amadeus, "and the Duke of Somerset, who is called by the nickname of 'the Sovereign,' plays the figure of a chief, although the others, who are of his society, make him depend on their counsels, and only make use of him to inspire the Queen with what they think proper."

Harley's combination, however disreputable and clandestine in its methods, is not to be dismissed as mere intrigue. It represented powerful forces in the land, and stood for a definite and arguable policy both at home and abroad. Harley had never diverged from the principle on which he had accepted the Secretaryship of State before Blenheim, of a broad-based centre administration to serve the Queen and make her independent of the extremists of either faction. This had also been the conception of Marlborough and Godolphin, but they had been forced to abandon it, and had become the agents or prisoners of the Whig Junto. They had done this against their will and better judgment; but the fact remained that they had done it. Neither had the Queen altered her general position of wishing to reign above either party with the assistance of leading statesmen from both sides. Nor could the Jacobites be disdained. They proffered their goodwill to a movement which promised to them the disintegration of the European coalition which had so long waged successful war against their true King—as they saw it—and against the chivalrous French monarch who had sheltered him, and who championed the Catholic faith.

But apart from self-interest and the wish to acquire control of the State the main bond between all these diverse elements was a common desire for peace. Harley's policy was to stop the war. Shrewsbury was convinced not only that it should stop now, but that it might have been stopped in the spring of 1709. The Tory Party wanted peace, but peace with British profit. The Queen was the least convinced upon the peace. Her chief desire was to free herself from the Whigs, and now from the Marlboroughs, and to reign—to quote the phrase by which she was allured—"as Queen indeed." But she had been too long in the war to think lightly of the abandonment of its aims. She was convinced that only by unquestionable victory could her throne be safe; and she saw no means of accomplishing this end but through Marlborough.

In the winter of 1709 the leading members of the so-called Juntilla believed that a good peace was procurable at will. They continued to nurse the conviction in the spring of 1710; but although they remained eager for peace, they became, as the summer wore on and they approached nearer to direct responsibility, increasingly doubtful whether it could now be obtained on any terms which the nation would accept. They were not blind to the fact that as they weakened Marlborough, and as the shadow of his approaching fall spread across Europe, the goal they sought receded. They were in close enough contact with affairs to feel the stiffening of the French attitude. At length they realized that there was no chance of their being able to present a good peace to the nation before the election. To present a bad peace was to ruin their chances. Therefore, like the Queen, they reached the conclusion that the war must be continued for the present, and this in its turn imposed a certain restraint upon their action.

In this, rather than in any lack of power, lies the explanation of the gradualness with which the change of Government was effected.

Sarah had retired to Windsor Lodge after her parting from the Queen in April. She was now disillusioned of the Whigs, and impatient at their weakness and vacillation. She despised the individual attempts they made to stand well with Somerset at the expense of Godolphin. She remained convinced that there was no comfort to be drawn from Shrewsbury. With sure instinct, she distrusted his affabilities, she recognized him throughout as an enemy. She was disgusted when the Whigs in their distress suggested even that she should seek a reconciliation with Abigail. Sunderland had toyed desperately with the idea of joining forces with Somerset. He had a three hours' conversation with him, as between colleagues, and reported hopefully that Somerset had spoken with great coldness of Shrewsbury, and had declared that he had only met Harley once at Argyll's house. Sarah was sure that her son-in-law was allowing himself to be deceived.

She now became the object of Whig solicitations to return to Court. We have need of "a good advocate with the Queen," wrote Lady Cowper (May 14). Godolphin frequently advised her to come to town, and Maynwaring constantly warned her of the dangers of leaving the field open. But Sarah at this time followed Marlborough's advice to keep clear of the Court and leave the Queen alone. She shared to the full his prescient pessimism.

Unknown as yet to Marlborough, Shrewsbury had taken his first important step. He had brought together Harley and Somerset, and he provided easy access for Harley to the Queen. At the head of the Juntilla a powerful triumvirate had come into being. A further attack could now be launched against the Whig holders of office. Sunderland was to be dismissed, and the hostile forces also felt themselves strong enough for another affront to Marlborough, which should produce a separate trial of strength.

After the campaign Marlborough had submitted a series of promotions to encourage the Army. He had, however, stopped on the roster only one short of the names of Mrs Masham's brother, Colonel Hill, and of her husband, Colonel Masham. Harley and Somerset were not slow to point this out to the Queen. They saw, and so did she, an opportunity of renewing under more favourable conditions the rankling issue that had been fought out earlier in the year. The Queen invited Marlborough to propose both names, and meanwhile she delayed signing the whole list of promotions. Marlborough immediately complied in the case of Masham, but raised objections to Hill which were certainly justified on military grounds; for even in those days of favour such an appointment would create a scandal in the Army.

While Cardonnel was at the front Walpole acted as Secretary-at-War. The Queen sent for him. She remarked that if the promotion list were stopped only one short of Mrs Masham's brother it would be thought by all the world to be done out of prejudice to him. She then told Walpole "to notify her Secretary of State for three more commissions of Brigadiers." She consented at length not to order the three extra commissions until Walpole had been able to write to Marlborough about them. Till then, however, she would sign none of the other commissions.

The busy circles at Court were soon astir with this new mischief. We may admire the cleverness of selecting a point which at the same time enlisted the Queen's affection for Abigail, revived her vexation over the January dispute, and threatened Marlborough with a thrust which must, if it went home, humiliate him before his army. Moreover, this was the very point on which it had already been found

(776)

impossible to marshal Whig resistance. It seemed to the Whig leaders no more, one way or the other, than a petty piece of patronage—of which there was plenty—and a chance of pleasing the Queen cheaply. They were concerned that Marlborough should take it so seriously. They did not see that it would rot the Army, and treated it entirely as a matter to be smoothed.

Meanwhile Marlborough, in reply to Walpole, gave reasons which might seem unanswerable.

> Camp before Douay
> May 29th, 1710

> . . . The trew reason for my restraining the promotions of brig-adiers to the 25th of March, was not only from the numbers and confusion it must have occasion'd amongst the queen's subjects, but also have given great disatisfaction to all the forainers, this army being compos'd of eight different nations, and next to the blessing of God, we owe all our success to our unanimity, which has been hethertoo, as if in reallity we were but one nation, so that I beg her majesty will be pleas'd to allowe of its stoping at the 25th of March; and as soon as a promotion can be made with any coullor of reason, I shall be sure to take care of those mention'd by the queen.

Anne was conscious of the weight of these reasons which Walpole urged resolutely upon her. "The Queen was," wrote Walpole to Marlborough, using ciphers for names,

> not a little at a loss what to do and seemed both unwilling to comply or deny; at last desired it might be done, but in the softest manner that was possible. The commission is therefore to be taken out by me and sent over to you to be delivered at the end of the campaign or when he shall think fit. The Queen promised to write this night to you to assure you that no mortification was meant; and I must say that in this and the last conference there seem'd a great struggle betwixt the desire of doing the thing and not putting a mortification upon you.

Marlborough, painfully aware of his lack of support at home, was so far mollified by these expressions that he published the commission at once. Colonel Hill became a Brigadier. The Army did not, however, receive any immediate benefit from his military skill. He repaired at once to Spa to undergo a thorough cure before subjecting himself to the rigours of active service.

The Triumvirate at the head of the Juntilla found the Queen very ready to get rid of Sunderland, and relieved that they thought it could now be safely done. By June 1 Godolphin was certain of Sunderland's coming dismissal, and that the question of a successor alone caused delay.

Marlborough allowed nothing to disturb his duty to the Army. The military facts alone could render a battle possible. He was coming increasingly to regard his military fame as all that might soon be left him. "I am with drawing my self," he wrote to Godolphin (June 5), "as fast as the Service will permit, out of all that sort of intelligence with the foraine Courts, so that it may naturally fall into the hands of the two Secritarys." Isolated and unsupported, Marlborough awaited the impending blow. That it might injure his authority with the Army to the utmost, Argyll spread through the camp that the Queen was weary of Marlborough's services, "which would quickly appear by the removal of Lord Sunderland." Sad, toiling, prescient, the Captain-General watched narrowly the operations of the great armies, never being drawn by one hair's-breadth from his professional art.

John to Sarah

June 19

If I were to make the choice, I had much rather be turn'd out, than that Ld. Sund: shou'd be remov'd, so that I hope all my friends will struggle with all their might and power, for if this point be carry'd there nothing disagreable and ruinus but must be expect'd.

To please Godolphin Marlborough wrote him one more letter (June 9/20) which the Treasurer could read to the Queen.

I am sorry Lord Sunderland is not agreeable to the Queen; but his being, at this time, singled out, has no other reason but that of being my son-in-law. When this appears in its true light, I am very confident every man in England will be sensible that my enemies have prevailed to have this done, in order to make it impossible for me, with honour, to continue at the head of this glorious army, that has, through the whole course of this war, been blessed by God with surprising successes.

There was no response. The choice had at last been made. On the morning of June 14 Boyle was sent by the Queen to take the seals from Sunderland.

England was still at war and at the head of the Grand Alliance. All from the Queen downward showed themselves under extreme anxiety. What would Marlborough do? Veritable entreaties from every side were made to him not to give up the command. The Whig leaders feared the danger of his instant resignation. On the day of Sunderland's displacement they and Godolphin held a meeting at Devonshire House and drafted a joint letter beseeching him to stay at his post. This was now their only hope, both for themselves and for their Cause. This was signed by Cowper, Godolphin, Somers, Newcastle, Devonshire, Orford, Halifax, and Boyle.

Heinsius added his appeal.

June 21/July 2

* I beg you not to give way to vexation, but on the contrary to prove by the continuation of your service that you take the common cause more to heart than the resentment you feel in yourself.

The Emperor was the most insistent of all. "Illustrious Cousin and most dear Prince," he wrote (July 16),

. . . can your affectionate heart, even for a moment, indulge the thought of such terrible calamities, both to the public weal and yourself? by which the whole fruits of the war, acquired with such labour and glory, would be exposed to the utmost peril; and the almost desperate cause of the enemy, to the eternal reproach of your name, would resume new strength, not to be overcome by future exertions. I am willing to believe, on the contrary, that you will continue firm to the public weal; and be convinced, that whatever aid, favour, or authority, I can ever confer, shall be given to you and yours, as the Prince of Savoy will tell you more at large.

Marlborough had never doubted, as we know, that he must hold his post till the end of the campaign. At Godolphin's request he had once again threatened resignation. It had been of no avail. All the time his own mind was clear: Sunderland would be dismissed, and he would have to stay. A collapse in the field and the break-up of the Alliance might have been the consequences of his retirement. No one then or since has ever doubted that it was his duty to stay. But with what melancholy feelings did he face the closing circle of jealousy and malice which after so many glories, with full success in view, and while all the world wondered, was to be his reward.

CHAPTER EIGHTY-TWO

The Fall of Godolphin

ᘓ 1710, June, July and August ᘔ

THROUGHOUT this summer the eyes of Europe were fixed upon London in hope or fear. It was realized at Versailles, as well as in every allied capital, that a profound change in the government and policy of England was in progress, and that Marlborough's power was passing. For nine years, in a world war on the largest scale yet known, he had been the central managing force against France. He had struck the main blows himself, and in his hands Britain had become the keystone of the confederate arch. Now, as the result of processes which to friend and foe alike were mysterious and, apparently, irrational, the will-power of the Islanders, for so long the supreme factor in the struggle, seemed about to fail, or even to be exerted in the contrary direction; and this at the moment when all that it had sought was in its grasp. "The fearful carnage of Malplaquet," says Klopp, "was less important to the development of the peoples of Europe than the bloodless change of the Ministry in England which began with the dismissal of Sunderland."

The conference at Gertruydenberg had begun with the Dutch, represented by their peacemakers, more stiff than they had been at any previous time. It continued during the whole of the siege of Douai, but thereafter a potent tide carried the French into marked recalcitrance. Louis XIV became increasingly convinced that Queen Anne's heart was changed, that the Whig power was menaced, and above all that Marlborough was no longer master of events.

The larger calculations of Versailles were based upon domestic affairs in England. Time would bring them the ultimate victory. In July, al-

(780)

leging that the Dutch were impossible, Louis XIV brought the conference to an end. In replying to Petkum's shrill remonstrances the French envoys at Gertruydenberg revealed their true motive. "We see things quite differently," they wrote; "we are convinced that in a short time you will see the English commander dismissed in disgrace, or treated in such a way that he will be unable to continue to serve with honour, and that further the present Ministry will fall, and Parliament will be dissolved."

Their calculations were not belied.

During the whole of Anne's reign members of both parties had sat together in the Government. The proportion varied with the complexion of Parliament. Hitherto the assumption had been that they worked together for national purposes. At this juncture we see one set of men holding the great offices, and at their side or close at hand another set, encouraged by the Queen, whose whole purpose was to drive out the Ministers, and become themselves the masters of the Government, and if possible of Marlborough's services.

The position of Godolphin had now become entirely devoid of strength or dignity. The Queen still listened to him on great business, but no longer allowed him the slightest influence on patronage of any account. He had submitted to Shrewsbury's being appointed Lord Chamberlain without his having been consulted. He had protested, and his protest had been ignored. He had striven hard to save Sunderland, but Sunderland had been dismissed. Even in minor offices under the Treasury his nominations were not accepted. Any step which he might wish to take to placate hostile colleagues or opponents was barred by the backstair counsellors, who were resolved not to allow him to strengthen or even mitigate his position. He knew that all about him was intrigue, that the Queen no longer valued his advice, and that his dismissal was so constantly discussed that even British ambassadors abroad reported the tale in their dispatches to London. Yet after nearly a lifetime of high office he still held stubbornly to his post. This was not from any base or small motive. He believed that only by his control of the Treasury could Marlborough receive the regular supplies without which neither his army nor the war could be maintained. For the sake of his friend and of the allied cause he endured every conceivable humiliation, and was resolved to persevere to the end, hoping that it would not be distant. "But," he wrote to Marlborough, "it will be no great surprise to you to hear in some very short time that I am no longer in a capacity for doing you any further service."

Both sides now looked abroad. Harley and what was now being called the Court party had for some time felt the need of giving Hanover favourable impressions of their views and intentions. The opportunity came during the summer. Mr Howe's successor at Hanover must be a fit person to prepare so important a Court for coming changes. Accordingly the Queen wrote (June 25) to Godolphin:

> * You spoke to me some months ago that Sir Philip Meadows might be sent to Hanover. There being a man who is known to everybody in that court, I think it more proper to send him thither at this juncture than one who is a stranger to them—Cressit. I would not give my orders to Mr Secretary Boyle in this matter until I had first acquainted you with my intentions.

Godolphin, though fully aware of the purpose of the appointment, perforce acquiesced, and a few days later Cresset was made envoy to Hanover. He wrote to the Elector that his mission was one of goodwill. He was, however, going as an envoy not so much of Great Britain as of Harley and the Juntilla. He was to carry with him from the Tory leaders pledges of loyalty to the house of Hanover. But the pith of his task was to propose to the Elector that his Highness should succeed Marlborough as Commander-in-Chief of the main armies. Although these experienced politicians did not share the fears they excited in the Queen and expressed in the Court and the clubs that Marlborough might become "a second Cromwell," yet the shadow of his renown lay heavy upon them. While he stayed his power was massive; if he went the void would be grievous. In that case what could better convince the nation that no Jacobite restoration was intended than the appointment of the Hanoverian heir to the highest command; and what could better commend the unofficial rulers to him than the offer? It was well known that the Elector had been offended by Marlborough's secrecy before Oudenarde. It was hoped that he was jealous of his fame. If so this proposal, made with so little concern for the public interest, might be tempting.

But on July 25 Cresset, whose plans for sailing were not noticeably aided by the Whig-controlled Admiralty, suddenly died.

On the other side as early as June Walpole had suggested to Marlborough that pressure might be brought to bear by the allied Governments upon the Queen to save the Ministry and the Parliament. Formal occasion was given for such intervention by the Queen's voluble assurances, after Sunderland's dismissal, that no further alterations in the Ministry would be made. Marlborough saw the objections to this course. Knowing the Queen as well as he did, he feared that she might easily be led to resent such interference in her affairs. Still, all the Allies were extremely alarmed: they wished to take advantage of the opening offered to them, and Marlborough lent himself to the process. If it were to be done at all it must be done thoroughly. He therefore communicated with all the Courts with whom he was in close contact. In particular he addressed himself to Eugene, who wrote at once to the Emperor (July 23):

> The confused state of affairs in England has come to a head. The Queen cannot any longer put up with the Whigs and the Marlborough party, although she still has a certain, though less, consideration for the person of my lord Duke himself—which may perhaps be a reason for hesitating and postponing the issue. Otherwise Parliament will be dissolved, and the said Whigs, together with all those friendly to Marlborough, will be removed from their offices. . . .
>
> We have learned from my lord Duke and elsewhere that the situation in England is of such danger and consequence that a [Ministerial] revolution is without doubt to be feared this coming winter, or else the Queen must undergo a complete change of front. . . . The Tories intend absolutely to bring about peace.

As a result of these representations Joseph I wrote a personal letter to the Queen, and also ordered Gallas to act directly under the control of Eugene and Marlborough.

Similar replies to the Queen's assurances were drawn up in all the Courts concerned. The Dutch were the first, on July 15, to present their version to the Queen at Kensington.

The Elector of Hanover was the next to reply. His language was extremely blunt. He wrote through Bothmar, his Ambassador at The Hague, that he hoped the Queen did not intend to make any further changes in a Ministry which deserved so well of her, and in a Parliament which was so excellently disposed. It was no part of Harley's politics to become involved in an argument with the heir to the throne;

and the Hanoverian reply was left unanswered. The King of Prussia wrote far more ceremoniously. Frederick I confined himself to thanks for the assurances, and disclaimed any idea of judging the Queen's internal policy. He notably avoided all references to a dissolution of Parliament.

Now an incident occurred which brought the whole matter to a head. Gallas had received from the Emperor the letter which Joseph I had written on the lines suggested by Eugene in replying to the Queen's assurances after Sunderland's dismissal. The Emperor, writing with his own hand, allowed himself great freedom in commenting on the Ministerial changes and deprecating the dissolution. Gallas was so apprehensive of its effect that he did not present it until Eugene and Marlborough, as well as Godolphin, had approved it. Their advice was wrong. This was just the kind of letter which Harley had been waiting for. A foreign potentate, the most backward of all in discharging his obligations to the Alliance, had intruded upon the prerogative of the Queen of Great Britain! It was decided to follow exactly the opposite course from that urged by the Emperor, and to dismiss Godolphin.

The Treasurer was aware that the Court party were plotting his dismissal and disputing about his successor at the busy, furtive conclaves in the Queen's apartments. There was a slender hope that she would desist for fear of the effect abroad of such a change. Indeed, for some days she seemed to wish to deceive him by a return to her former cordiality. She spoke of the importance of "a moderating system," and even hinted vaguely that he should be reconciled with Harley. That this was designed to draw Godolphin from the Whigs is suggested by the report which Shrewsbury conveyed through Halifax to Godolphin that the Queen was resolved to make him and Harley agree. Amid these lures and traps the Treasurer held his head high and transacted his business as usual. But the end had come. There seems to have been a Cabinet on the 6th at which he had an altercation with Shrewsbury, reproaching him with "French counsels." The Queen intervened on Shrewsbury's side, and Godolphin continued to argue, and this time with her. On the morning of August 7 he called upon the Queen, and afterwards penned a perplexed note to Marlborough: "I think the safety or destruction of the Parliament remains still under a good deal of uncertainty." In the evening he again sought the Queen's presence, and for two hours he harangued his Sovereign upon the evils of government by

THE FALL OF GODOLPHIN

secret cabals, and closed by asking, "Is it the will of your Majesty that I should go on?" The Queen replied without hesitation, "Yes." The next morning one of the Queen's servants brought Godolphin a letter.

The Queen to Godolphin

Kensington
August 7, 1710

The uneasiness which you have showed for some time has given me very much trouble, though I have borne it; and had your behaviour continued the same it was for a few years after my coming to the crown, I could have no dispute with myself what to do. But the many unkind returns I have received since, especially what you said to me personally before the lords, makes it impossible for me to continue you any longer in my service; but I will give you a pension of four thousand a year, and I desire that, instead of bringing the staff to me, you will break it, which, I believe, will be easier to us both.

Thus ended an association which had lasted for more than thirty years of Anne's life, had been a prop to her in times of trouble both under King James and King William, and in her own reign had helped to make her throne unsurpassed in Europe. Mr Montgomery took a few hours to sign and settle a good many minor things; then he broke his staff and cast the fragments in the grate. He had stood by Marlborough to the end. Harley became Chancellor of the Exchequer and in all that mattered First Minister.

It would be idle to portray Godolphin as a powerful and dominating personality, fitted for the contentions of a tumultuous period. He was an honest servant of the State, loyal and faithful to his friends and to his duty. He had unrivalled knowledge and experience of affairs. He was a most able and circumspect finance Minister. The means by which he provided the immense sums required for the war, at a time when taxation was narrowly limited in character and degree, and when the credit system was in its mysterious infancy, must be regarded as a splendid public achievement. In that lax age his personal integrity shone as an example. He more nearly corresponds to the great civil servants of the present day than any of his contemporaries. He quitted his nine years' administration of war-time finance, with all the opportunities of self-enrichment by speculation or by taking presents, apart altogether from direct corruption, without reproach and with barely a thousand pounds a year. In days when a Paymaster-General, by merely using according to custom the interest on the moneys which passed through his hands, could amass an enormous fortune Godolphin walked out of the Treasury poorer than he had entered it. Although addicted to cards and betting and a passionate lover of the Turf, he always played for modest stakes and lived at the height of power with admirable frugality. Queen Anne's offer of a pension of four thousand pounds a year was never implemented. It is uncertain whether she did not give it or he would not have it. But by a curious coincidence his immediate family wants were provided for. He was dismissed on August 7, and ten days later the death of his elder brother brought him an inheritance of four thousand pounds a year.

John and Sarah regarded themselves as responsible for his well-being. Their houses were at his disposal. He spent a good deal of the remaining two years of his life at Holywell. His chief concern was to prevent Marlborough from giving up the command of the army, and to try to help him through his influence with Boyle and in other ways. He was not, however, able to play any strong part in Parliament. He left the defence of his finance in the competent hands of Walpole, in whose qualities and future he had unbounded belief. In every respect his conduct after his dismissal was a model of good temper and disinterested care for national interests.

CHAPTER EIGHTY-THREE

Dissolution

ᚫ 1710, August-October ᚦ

ᘜ

THE last hope of the now ignominious band of Whigs lay in averting the dissolution. To the end they continued to flatter themselves that this would not be forced upon them. Their very apprehension might in itself have confirmed their opponents. Harley knew well from the beginning that without a dissolution he could do nothing, and, indeed, that his path was perilous. The Whig Parliament had no opportunity of coping with the situation created during the summer. They had separated in May. Harley did not dare to let them meet again. Parliaments were dangerous instruments in those times, and rarely had a House of Commons more just grounds for complaint against the Crown. They must therefore be prorogued until they could be dissolved. Harley had no choice in this. It is remarkable that he persuaded so many of the remaining Whig Ministers, now become his colleagues, that the issue still stood in doubt. Then, when the moment was ripe and none could resist, the final blow was struck. Somerset woke up to the fact that he had been fooled, as he deserved. The scales of illusion fell from Somers's eyes. Newcastle had for some time taken refuge in absence. Halifax had become futile and even contemptible. The old Admiral, Orford, and the sharp-tongued libertine Wharton were ripe for the sickle. All this proceeded behind the back of Parliament and through advice tendered to the Queen by a man who, having no constitutional right to advise the sovereign, tampered with her through her dresser.

Sunderland, inveterate optimist, wrote to Marlborough (August 10), "By all accounts from the counties there is like to be a good election."

"The stocks fall so much," wrote Godolphin to Seafield, a Scottish peer (August 10), "and our people suffer to that degree that they begin to be enraged at what is doing. . . . I have great hopes we shall have a good Parliament here." Marlborough responded a little to the combative mood. He wrote to Sarah (August 11), "*What has been said by the Duke of Shrewsbury, that he knows the way home, he may by it cheat himself; for a ruined people may be angry.*" He gave precise directions about the return of Cadogan for Woodstock, but on the general result he had no illusions. He warned Sarah (August 18), "My intelligence is very positive, that there will be a new Parliament, and that you must not flatter yourself, but expect everything that can be disagreeable personally to yourself; for there is no barbarity but what you and I must expect." And (August 25), "The Queen will risk England rather than not vex you. She has at this time no resentment but to you, me, Lord Treasurer, and our children. God knows how little I have deserved this, and his will be done." And to Heinsius (September 8), *"A New Parl. is so sure that all the officers that have interest to be chosen have desired leave of me to goe for England to take care of their Elections. . . . My Lord Godolphin assures me that the chief member of the Bank has promised him that they will lend moneys for the subsistance of this army during this campaigne." He had evidently obtained a new source of secret information.

Marlborough to Godolphin

Aug. 16, 1710

. . . I am informed that Mr Harley, in his conversations, keeps no sort of decency for you or me, by which it is plain that the Queen has no design of reconciling you and Mr Harley, as was mentioned to me in a former letter. . . . When I see you, you shall have the particulars, how I came to be informed of this business. . . . I beg you will never mention this to anybody; for though I think I shall have the glory of saving the Queen, she must know nothing of it; for she certainly would tell so much of it to Mrs Masham and Mr Harley, that they would for the future order it so that I should not come to know, which, *otherwise, I shall know, all that passes.*

Our extravagant behaviour in England has so encouraged the French that they take measures as if the war were but just beginning; so that our new Ministers will be extremely deceived, for the greater desire they shall express for peace, the less they will have it in their power to obtain it.

Towards the end of September the Queen, emboldened, yielded herself finally to Harley's political management. For some days her blandishments to Somers had ceased. The Lord President was conscious of a disdain, perhaps not undeserved. On the 19th under evident pressures he resigned. The next day the Council met to swear the new Ministers. No sooner was this ceremony completed than the Queen declared that she had determined upon a dissolution. She caused a draft proclamation to be read. The Lord Chancellor, Cowper, got up to protest. Orford, Lord High Admiral, and Wharton, Lord-Lieutenant of Ireland, veteran chiefs of the Junto, were ready to support him. But before Cowper could even begin the Queen rose to depart, and the sitting came to an end.

The passion of the election exceeded anything that had been known since the days of Charles II. Indeed, old men thought the savagery of the Civil War had returned. "By the accounts you give," wrote Godolphin to Seafield (October 12), "and by what we find, all the most arbitrary proceedings in the elections are to be expected, but how anybody can think that is long to be maintained in our country and in this constitution is to me, I confess, a very great riddle." "There never was so apparent a fury," Craggs reported to Marlborough (October 13), "as the people of England show against the Whigs and for High Church. Those that voted for Mr Stanhope at Westminister were knocked down; Sir Richard Onslow has lost it in Surrey, and I believe in Parliament they will exceed two to one."

The Tory Party, united and inflamed, proved itself, as Marlborough had for years believed, definitely the stronger part of the nation.

Two hundred and seventy Members lost their seats. In the new Parliament the Whigs were not a third of the House of Commons. It was proved, indeed, that "the Whigs had no bottom." When this was realized the stocks fell by 30 per cent., and the Bank refused to discount any foreign bills.

Thus was ended, by the power of the Queen and, as it now appeared, by the will of the electorate, the ever-famous Administration of Marlborough and Godolphin, which for eight years had led the league of European nations to victory against the exorbitant power of France, which had made the British Island one United Kingdom, and had raised Great Britain from despondency and weakness to the summit of world affairs. The old Treasurer had retired to Newmarket. Marlborough, entangled in the war, wedded to the Army, claimed by the Allies, remained to struggle on, like a weary, baited bear chained to the post. The Continent, which had long yielded itself to the strong impulse of the island Power, without comprehending the causes of its inspiration and mysterious strength, was now staggered by what seemed to be a meaningless disintegration, the result of a bedchamber intrigue.

Queen Anne, after the intense personal stresses of the conflict which had raged about her, and perhaps also in her own conscience, and in which her will-power had played the decisive part, withdrew to Hampton Court to recover her strength and balance. By all accounts she was enormously relieved and gratified by the results of her exertions. She was not the only sovereign to rejoice. Louis XIV knew that at the eleventh hour he had been saved from utter ruin. When he heard that the Queen had dissolved the Parliament he sent for Mesnager, his former agent at The Hague, to read him the news. "It is impossible," wrote Mesnager,

> for me to describe the transport of joy the King was in upon reading that part, [viz.] the dissolving of Parliament; "Well," says the King, "if Monsieur Harley does that, I shall say he is un habile homme, and that he knows how to go through what he has undertaken. . . ."

Marlborough had measured rightly the whole sequence of events from the beginning. He lent himself to various requests made to him by Godolphin and other Whigs. From time to time he wrote letters to the Queen or to Shrewsbury. But at no moment did he deceive himself. As far back as the summer of 1709, when he saw that Abigail had supplanted Sarah in the Queen's favour, he knew that, unless some extraordinary step was taken, his system was doomed. When the Queen was instigated to make the Hill appointment, he chose that moment and that ground, unsatisfactory though they were from some points of view, for the decisive fight. If Godolphin and the Whigs had rallied to him when he quitted the Cabinet and retired to Windsor, the Queen would in all probability have been compelled to amend her courses. Parliament was in session, the campaign was about to begin, the Government was intact. Then was the chance, which never recurred, of bringing everything to a head. It would not have been necessary, in

Marlborough's opinion, to proceed against Abigail by a Parliamentary address, and neither he nor Sarah advocated that course. The pressure which the whole Ministry could have brought upon Anne to choose forthwith between her responsible Ministers and her backstairs advisers would almost certainly have been irresistible. Abigail could have been chased from the Court, and Harley exposed before Whig majorities in both Houses.

As things fell out, the Ministry suffered the worst of both courses. The Queen was filled with fear and resentment at the rumour of a Parliamentary address against her cherished Abigail. When this menace proved to be unfounded her fears passed, but her resentment remained. Nothing that had ever happened before had smitten her so deeply as this. All her quarrels and scenes with Sarah, all the interminable correspondence, all the political stresses attending the dismissal of Harley in 1708, and the forcing upon her one after another of the lords of the Junto—all these were upon a lower plane. The alleged attempt to set the House of Commons upon Abigail, and upon her for sheltering Abigail, was, she felt, a mortal affront. Repeatedly in this long-drawn crisis we find the rancour which this episode aroused, hardening her against her Ministers, and severing the last personal ties which united her to Marlborough. It enabled Somerset week after week to pour into her eager ear tales of this outrageous design to rob her of her own personal friend and attendant. How easy for Harley to warn her of Marlborough's alleged desperate ambition! Her grandfather had perished on the scaffold; her father had died in exile. Marlborough, at the head of the armies and of the Grand Alliance, was far greater in power than Cromwell before he became Lord Protector. Deposition in favour of the detested Elector, a republic of the Whigs, a dictatorship of Marlborough, were all bugbears which could be used to aggravate her anger and her alarm. And, on the other hand, what alluring prospects had been unfolded to her, not only by Harley, but also by the unwitting Somerset, and perhaps by Somers! The over-mighty subject should be put down; a Government above party, of her own choosing, should be established; the royal prerogative should be erected again on a new foundation. She would be Queen indeed.

CHAPTER EIGHTY-FOUR

∨ *The New Régime*

⳥ 1710, October-December ⳤ

"You may venture to assure everybody," declared St John, the newly chosen Secretary of State, "that credit will be supported, the war prosecuted, the Confederacy improved, and the principle in which we engaged preserved as far as possible. Our friends and enemies both will learn the same lesson, that however we differ about things purely domestic, yet we are unanimous on those points which concern the present and future happiness of Europe."

Behind these words of high resolve and reassurance the new Ministers were intent upon making peace. But even before they had obtained power they had become convinced, though with much reluctance, that the war would go on for some time, and that peace was more distant than before their intervention. In these circumstances they found it convenient to upbraid the Allies upon their many obvious shortcomings. They proclaimed that England would show even greater vigour in the war than under the late Administration. All the more was it necessary that her allies should act up to the highest standard of their obligations, and should be made to, at all costs. "The most popular thing for England," wrote Harley, with much candour, "is to press all the Allies to keep exactly to what they have agreed to do in their Treaties. The partiality to them has been much complained of, and the pressing relentlessly to their exact performing is the likeliest way to obtain peace."

This certainly was a sound policy for men who did not care very much what kind of peace it was. Nevertheless, the complaint of England against her allies, especially the Empire, was only too well founded, and a certain tonic was administered to them by the attitude of the new Government. England had got into the position of begging them to follow her. The change of government, which occasioned so much waste of power, at least reversed this process: the Allies now begged England not to desert them. St John was especially anxious to whip up the Empire. His mood towards Austria was always hostile, and his language harsh. He found it more congenial to harry the Allies than the enemy.

Upon universal appeal and overwhelming reason Marlborough had retained his command under the new Administration. He had every proof that they hated him and the cause which he upheld; but they also at the same time feared and needed him. In his headquarters, from which he was conducting the sieges of Aire and Saint-Venant, he awaited their orders. At first these were expressed very roughly. St John in particular seemed to find a strong satisfaction in displaying himself as master of the great man who had favoured his early career, admitted him to his comradeship, helped him with his debts, and, indeed, almost adopted him as his son. All his letters about Marlborough at this period are of a scornful and often spiteful character. He wished at once to patronize him and to make him feel the humiliation of his new position. We shall see that some months later, under political strain, he changed his note and flattered, proffering his false friendship, as if he were back in the buoyant days of the Blenheim campaign.

The new Ministry, however, pursued contradictory and ambiguous courses towards their General. They would have rejoiced if they could have flung him out, and set the Elector, George Louis, in his place; but that could not be done. They were conscious of serious danger in dismissing Marlborough before finding a substitute whom England and the Allies would accept. On the other hand, they wished to bend him, break him, tame him to their yoke. They sought to foster a faction against him among his generals and colonels. They laboured to show the Army that his political power was gone. They took the whole business of promotion out of his hands. They set up a board in London under the Duke of Ormonde, his political opponent and professional competitor, to scrutinize and decide the claims of all officers for promotion. They dismissed or removed from their special appointments his most trusted and competent brigadiers and rising officers. They appointed in their stead those who had been personally disloyal or offensive to him in the campaign, or who had insulted him in Parliament. If there was anyone on whom he specially relied they removed him. If a man could be found who was particularly obnoxious they thrust him forward as near to the Commander-in-Chief as possible. They even made a virtue of this by pretending that Marlborough was making by favouritism an army to subvert the Crown and Constitution. The Queen herself, they hinted, was in danger from his favouritism. Above all, Abigail's brother and husband, Brigadiers Hill and Masham, sailed forward upon this breeze.

If Marlborough endured this treatment his authority with the Army must, they thought, be fatally wounded. If, on the other hand, he found the treatment intolerable, let him resign. They saw that if he resigned he would put himself in the wrong. To dismiss him was dangerous: to provoke his resignation comparatively safe. Then they could have filled England with the cry that he had deserted his post on party grounds, that he had cast away the cause of the Allies, that he had ruined the peace which otherwise was in their hands. Any disaster in the field which followed his withdrawal they could lay on him. In fact, their conduct towards him during their first months exceeded in malice and in meanness anything which is known—and it is a wide field—in the relations of a British general with a British Government. In all this the most poisonous was St John.

Marlborough, though he writhed and groaned under the ordeal, was in no mood to yield his enemies any advantage. He held on to his position with the tenacity with which he had fought the siege of Lille two years earlier. Surrounded upon every side by foes, the worst—his own countrymen—at his back, exposed to all the hazards with which war between equal armies confronts a general, feeling the French spirit rise every day as his political weakness became known, watching the peace which would have released him steadily recede, he repressed all impatience, and disdained or ignored every insult. But can we wonder that in such distress he would have welcomed serving under the Elector of Hanover, or transferring the command in the best conditions to him?

In his steadfast attitude he gained comfort from the great companions with whose aid he had waged the long war. Heinsius usually presents himself to us as a prosaic, austere, and even bleak personality; he had been in conflict with Marlborough over the Barrier since 1709; but we now see him showing every sign of personal sympathy. The Elector of Hanover, recognized future master of these arrogant Ministers, and the King of Prussia gave him unswerving support. The Elector declared publicly as a member of the Grand Alliance that unless Marlborough remained in command of the armies he would withdraw his troops. Frederick I spoke in a similar spirit. Eugene, who was not the master of armies, could only publish his resolve not to serve in Flanders except with Marlborough. As for the Dutch, their remonstrances on Marlborough's account had already strained their relations with our queer Queen and her new circle.

It was a reasonable expectation that Marlborough's treatment at this time by the Queen and Government would have rendered his position impossible by destroying his credit with the Army while heavy operations were proceeding. He himself certainly feared that this would be the result. Curiously enough, the reverse happened. Never in the height of his success was there such a rally to him throughout the allied armies as in these winter months. Apart from the group of intriguing officers round Argyll, all ranks sought occasion by the strict performance of their duty to prove their discipline, and show their respect for their General. In that glorious army of veteran soldiers drawn from eight nations, welded together by so much war for causes which for the most part they comprehended and espoused, the malignant time-servers and backbiters became lepers. Dutch Deputies and foreign generals now supplied Marlborough by their alacrity with the support hitherto forthcoming from home; and, far beyond the Army, there spread through all the signatory states of the Grand Alliance a vehement resolve that he should not be taken from them before the fruits of their efforts were gathered in.

One has a sense at this time of the magnitude of the power which was being wantonly destroyed. The British oak had struck its roots so deep in Europe, its branches spread so far, that even the lopping off of tremendous limbs and the undermining or severing of one root after another still left it erect, the feature of the landscape. Marlborough's faults and limitations have not been, need not be, concealed; his misfortunes now crowded upon him; but he remained the champion of Europe against the military dictatorship of Louis XIV; and, apart from his enemies in England and France, all the nations looked to him.

As the weeks passed those who had risen by the methods we have described found themselves, in their turn, oppressed by the weight of official cares, and disturbed by the temper of their own new-found Parliament. The landslide of the elections had carried affairs far beyond that moderate, middle dispensation which Harley and the Queen, to say nothing of Marlborough and Godolphin, had always desired. The year 1708 had produced a sultry Whig House of Commons: 1710 showed a red-hot Tory domination. From the backwoods of England, from the acres which they cultivated with hard authority and exemplary skill, came in unforeseen numbers and in uncontrollable temper the backbone of England, the Tory squires, blessed by the Church they had sworn to defend. Their hatred for the Whigs was at once instinctive and religious. The process of electioneering had, however, exercised an educative function. They had catered for the Nonconformist vote; they had boasted that the national credit would be safe in their hands; and though they disapproved of Marlborough's tactics and strategy, as well as his character and politics, they were at first genuinely anxious to beat the French, and not to show themselves less competent than their opponents.

We can see how irresistibly the character of the new House of Commons impressed itself upon the Queen and her advisers. All ideas of co-operation with moderate Whigs, upon which Harley had traded so successfully before the election, had been swept to limbo by one stroke of the national wing. All plans for an equipoise of parties, and their impartial control by the Queen's favourites at the Court, vanished like the smoke of a quenched fire. This was not Harley's Parliament. St John felt far more at home with the new majority. When Sarah saw St John in a large company just before he became Secretary of State, she said "in her manner which was often the reverse of polite," "There goes an ungrateful rogue." St John seemed resolved to prove that this was true. He availed himself of Harley's apparatus for collecting dispassionate information from many quarters through trusted agents. In Holland Harley had an agent, one John Drummond, a Scottish merchant and resident of high standing, very shrewd at finding out facts, and blunt in reporting them. Drummond, who was used as a channel between the Ministry and Marlborough, wrote to both Harley and St John.

THE NEW RÉGIME

John Drummond to Harley

Amsterdam
November 1/12, 1710

What is it are we to imagine that hinders or will hinder their [the French] new proposals, but what they write us every day, viz. the hopes they have of the divisions in England and that the Duke of Marlborough will be made so uneasy as to be obliged to retire and abandon the army, who they know has been no less instrumental in keeping the Allies together than in his success in the field? It is not for his person, but for the public good that I argue or presume to meddle in so important an affair, for well do I know all his vices as well as his virtues, and I know as well that though his covetousness has gained much reproach and ill-will on this side of the world, yet his success in the field, his capacity or rather dexterity in council or in the Cabinet, and his personal acquaintance with the heads of the Alliance and the faith they have in him, make him still the great man with them, and on whom they depend. I can tell you with certainty what I meet in daily conversation, that you will have little money to expect from this [Government] if he stay at home, that they wish with all their hearts almost any sort of peace before he be taken from them, that there is no Englishman who they have any opinion of for the command of an army but himself, that his agreeing so well with Prince Eugene is one of their greatest contentments and to make a new acquaintance and intimacy of such a nature with any one is what they fear and abhor the thoughts of.

Pensionary Buys came to me two days after Lord Rivers left this place almost with tears in his eyes, saying "Lord! what shall become of us. Lord Rivers would give me no satisfaction that the Duke shall return. For God's sake write to all your friends, let him but return for one campaign till the French but once make new proposals, let the Queen afterwards do with him what she pleases, but must the safety of us all be put in the balance with personal pique which perhaps may be reconciled if rightly gone about?" I hope the Queen will forbear her farther resentments till a better occasion, though justly deserved by him and all who belong to him. Baron Gersdorff was last day here: he is Envoy at The Hague for the Elector of Saxony or King of Poland; he assured people in a general assembly or society that his master would recall his troops if the Duke was not to command.

This letter smote Harley. For all his love of dissembling, artifice, and intrigue, to which was soon added inveterate drunkenness, he was nevertheless a man built on a large scale and of a nature not wholly divorced from the life of Britain. He was not at all like St John, a brilliant, fugitive rascal, prone to bully or grovel with equal facility according to circumstances or mood. Also Harley felt himself the man responsible. On him lay the burden. He had been wronged. He had resented his injuries. He had avenged them. But he felt himself morally as well as constitutionally accountable to Parliament and in some degree to history. One is at first astonished at the freedom with which this powerful Minister unbosoms himself to the outspoken John Drummond at Amsterdam. But, of course, this letter was meant for Marlborough.

Harley to John Drummond

Amsterdam
November 7/18, 1710

. . . As to any reconciliation between me and the [Duke of Marlborough], give me leave to say that I were unworthy the Queen's service should I not live with anyone that her service or the public good requires. I do solemnly assure you I have not the least resentment towards him or anyone else. I thank God my mind puts me above that. I never did revenge injuries. . . . In one word I do assure you, I can live and act with the Duke now in the same manner and with the same easiness as the first day that ever I saw him. . . .

I have upon many occasions since shewn by actions relating to his particular affairs of Blenheim that I am far from resentment. But this I find by experience, those who have done injuries are more difficult to be reconciled than those who have received injuries, and hatred, the more groundless and unreasonable it is, the more durable and violent it most times proves. Now I have opened to you my heart upon this subject and do again assure you that no resentment of mine shall ever obstruct the public service or hinder the co-operating with any one for the good of the common cause. . . .

Negotiations were therefore set on foot with Marlborough, with the object of reaching a basis upon which he should command the armies in the now inevitable campaign of 1711.

THE NEW RÉGIME

John Drummond to Harley

. . . Mr Secretary St John will have acquainted you with what I wrote him of my discourse with [Marlborough]. . . . He has faithfully promised both to the Grand Pensionary and to Buys that he is resolved to live with you if you will make it practicable or possible for him; he will not enter into the heats of party debates, but will go heartily and sincerely into all the measures that may be esteemed proper for carrying on the war, but for other votes he will be at his free liberty. . . .

Marlborough stayed as long as possible at The Hague, and kept the seas between him and his ferocious fellow-countrymen. Here, at least, he found a friendly and grateful Government. Here he remained a European figure, whose gleams were not yet extinguished in the British fog.

Harley and St John—for these are the two who now counted—pursued their policy of bargaining and affronts, of baits and insults, of compliments and threats, and neither they nor anyone else knew what Marlborough would do.

CHAPTER EIGHTY-FIVE

The Death of the Emperor

ꜩ 1711, April and May ꜩ

IN April an event occurred which cut to the tap-root of the European quarrel. The Emperor died of the smallpox.

All military plans were cast into the melting-pot. *"It would be very necessary," Marlborough wrote to Heinsius (April 29), "for me to *know from England* as well as from *Holland* how far this death of the Emperor is to have any influence on our operations. . . . [One should] lose no time *in sending a Deputation to the Queen in order to regulate everything with that end.* . . . No siege can be ventured till this is settled."

By the death of the Emperor Joseph his younger brother, the Archduke, now fighting for the Crown of Spain as Charles III, became sovereign of the hereditary dominions of the house of Hapsburg, comprising Austria, Hungary, Bohemia, and Silesia. It was presumable that he would be elected Emperor of the Holy Roman Empire by the German Electoral princes. The Imperial Office had usually gone to the heir of the hereditary Austrian dominions. Although Prussian ambitions might stray in this direction, they were never to be achieved. The other potential rival, the Elector of Bavaria, expelled alike from Bavaria and Belgium, was a fugitive from Marlborough's sword. There does not seem to have been any serious doubt throughout Germany, or, indeed, at The Hague or in London, that Charles III would be elected Emperor in natural succession to his brother. The exertions of Prince Eugene, in fact, procured the support of all the Teutonic Electors.

But how had this affected the Allies and the war into which they

(800)

had all become welded? Many British historians or writers have suggested that the prime cause of the quarrel had disappeared, and that there was no further reason for pursuing it. The Crowns of Spain and the Empire were now united in a single person, who would from Vienna rule half the world. Where, then, was the balance of power? Was not this aggrandizement of the Hapsburg family an evil of the same order as the union of the Crowns of France and Spain? Was the Grand Alliance—and in particular were Holland and Britain—to continue fighting to bring about this result? It has therefore been generally argued that the death of the Emperor Joseph was an overwhelming justification for a speedy peace.

But these fancies ignore the practical facts as they impinged upon the actors of that day. First, Charles III was King of Spain only in name, and ruler of the Indies and controller of the Mediterranean only by the navy of Britain. Secondly, if he should ever acquire these titles in a treaty of peace, he would be no menace to the Sea Powers. They were not afraid of him. All too plainly they had seen the weakness of the Empire. They had carried it on their backs; they had kept it alive with their money. Blenheim had saved Vienna. Marlborough in Flanders had gripped the main military power of France for eight campaigns. Even so the Empire, which was to have been the mainstay of the original Alliance, had barely preserved a coherent existence. Therefore the spectacle of nominal unions of states and dominions under the Vienna Court and the Imperial Crown caused no real alarm to the Allies. They all accepted the prospect with hardly a tremor. The Germanic states naturally did not object to the Holy Roman Emperor of their choice becoming possessed of whatever Spanish dominions he could seize and rule. The Dutch never seem to have feared a union of Spain and Austria or regarded it as comparable to the control and exploitation of Spain by France. Even the Tory Ministry in England, already involved in their secret negotiations with France for a separate peace, never hesitated to accept the amalgamation under one Crown of Vienna and Madrid if it could be obtained. On the first day that the news was received in London the Imperial Envoy, Gallas, received immediate and explicit assurances that the British Cabinet would support the election of Charles III to the Empire and in no way abandon his claims to Spain and the Indies.

Nevertheless the death of the Emperor, so far from bringing peace nearer, drove it farther away. It completely ruptured, as we shall see, all plans for a decisive campaign in Flanders. It stimulated Louis XIV, and furnished him with a verbal argument against the logic of the Allies. It convinced him that he would be able to defend his northern fortress-line through the whole of 1711, and therefore that his remaining strength would outlast Marlborough's dying favour.

One of the by-products of the Emperor's death was to furnish Harley and St John with a specious argument for their secret negotiations with France. If the Allies' candidate for the Spanish throne was simultaneously driven out of Spain and translated to the summit of the Empire, was there not a lively prospect of his making a direct settlement with France on the basis of his keeping the Milanese, Naples, and Sicily—in fact, Italy—together with the Netherlands, and leaving the Duke of Anjou (Philip V) in form, as well as in fact, ruler of Spain and the Indies? The French had offered these terms to Charles in 1706, and again in January 1711. He had remained loyal to the Alliance. This was just the solution which Tories as well as Whigs in Parliament had been brought to regard as most abhorrent to British interests. The strong naval power of France would assert a real authority over the Spanish Indies, and an estranged Hapsburg monarchy at Vienna would from its Italian dominions obstruct British trade in the Mediterranean and all that movement to the East which was to flaunt a vision of fabulous wealth before the eyes of a triumphant generation. Thus it could be urged that England too must be in secret parley with Versailles.

Such arguments enrich debate, but darken counsel. The sole remedy for the embarrassments of the Allies at this juncture was a remorseless punching at the heart of France, the shattering of her remaining armies, and the deep invasion of her territories. A continuance of this pressure, upon the proclaimed decision that Marlborough would be upheld to the end, would at any time have re-created the opportunities lost at The Hague at the beginning of 1709, and again at Gertruydenberg in 1710. But the Tory Government were now furnished with a supply of convenient words, which they could parade as a substitute for necessary deeds.

Most commentators, including especially Tory apologists and later pacifist writers, treat the question as if England could have had peace for the asking. She could, indeed, secure peace by the sacrifice of most of what she had gained and by the desertion of her Allies. But the Court of France, and even the aged Monarch at its head, were now once again thinking in terms not of peace, but of victory. It was not, indeed, to be such a victory as seemed already gained in 1701; but they saw before them a treaty incomparably superior to anything attainable in 1706 or 1709 or 1710. This realization imposed itself by successive severe gradations upon these new British Ministers who in the previous summer and autumn had thought that all was for them to take or leave. Now Harley, St John, and Shrewsbury understood that they had got to go on fighting. The Queen, if indeed she had ever wavered, had never lost that conviction. They might negotiate underhand with France, but fight all the time they must. Thus we see during the summer of 1711, and when the campaign opened, a remarkable smoothing over of their differences with Marlborough. Only by the power of his sword could they extricate themselves, without arousing British fury, from this wearisome war. We therefore witness a series of overtures of goodwill to Marlborough which were sincere because they corresponded to a real need. Marlborough's advice was asked upon the international scene. It was intimated that the building of Blenheim would be resumed. The indispensable General must be kept in good humour. "Thou shalt not muzzle the ox when he treadeth out the corn."

The good relations thus temporarily re-established between Marlborough and the Government formed a basis at home upon which the campaign could be conducted. But the balance now leaned heavily against the victorious Allies, and Marlborough's letters to Godolphin show his gloom and despondency. His health was poor. The news of Rochester's death, which occurred suddenly at this time, aroused sombre thoughts. (May 25) *"I see Ld. Rochister is gone where wee must all follow. I believe my journey will be hastn'd by the many vexations I meat with. I agree intierly with You that men are never want'd. I am sure I wish well to my country, and if I cou'd do good I shou'd think no pains to much, but I find my self dekay so very fast, that from my heart and soull I wish the Queen and my Country, a Peace. . . . I have already told You that wee are very considerably weaker and the Enemy much stronger then the last campagne, so that God only knows how this may end." And (May 4), "Since constant success has not met with approbation, what may I not expect when nothing is done!" But with that sense of resolve which so often emerged from his depression, and was the prelude to great exploits, he added, "As I rely very much on Providence, so I shall be ready of approving all occasions that may offer."

CHAPTER EIGHTY-SIX

Ne Plus Ultra

♯◁ 1711, March-August ▷♯

"I ONCE heard the Duke of Wellington asked," wrote the historian Stanhope in 1836, "whether he thought Napoleon or Marlborough the greater general. 'It is difficult to answer that,' he replied. 'I used always to say that the presence of Napoleon at a battle was equal to a reinforcement of forty thousand men. But I can conceive nothing greater than Marlborough at the head of an English army. He had greater difficulties than I had with his allies; the Dutch were worse to manage than the Spaniards or the Portuguese. But, on the other hand, I think I had most difficulties at home.' "

Chroniclers must measure justly the immense efforts necessary to mount and sustain the campaign of 1711. It involved the final consumption of Marlborough's power. In spite of the savage party antagonisms in England, in spite of secret negotiations, in spite of exhaustion and war-weariness, the Common Cause and the Captain-General once again had the strength to draw the great armies to the field. A lull imposed itself on faction. The whispers of intrigue were for a space stilled. Indeed, even the doubters felt that France would not be able to withstand the persistent force and culminating momentum of the Grand Alliance.

Before the end of March the movements of the French and the news from the frontier seemed to indicate a design to besiege Douai before the Allies could take the field. Marlborough countered this by sending Cadogan with a covering force of twenty thousand men to the plains of Lille and strengthening all his positions along the Scarpe.

This done, he plunged into the business of bringing the army into the field at the highest strength. He wrote repeated personal letters to all the signatory states about their contingents. He made arrangements for the pay of the troops and auxiliaries, for the accumulation of food and transport, for the posting of recruits and drafts, and for the armament of the fortresses taken in the last campaign. Fifty pages of his letters during the six weeks he remained at The Hague are printed in the *Dispatches*. He also opened the cordial correspondence with the new Ministers which he maintained throughout the campaign. Every few days he wrote at length to St John in terms of deference and goodwill. In fact, he gave the new Secretary of State far fuller accounts of this campaign than he had ever sent to his predecessors. His further correspondence with Robert Harley (now Earl of Oxford) will require to be studied later. Like his letters to Shrewsbury and Poulett, it shows the enormous pains he took to conciliate those who had been his opponents but under whom he had agreed to serve, and to create a basis of mutual confidence upon which he could act. The Ministers for their part replied in the most complimentary terms, and anyone reading by itself the correspondence of this summer would have no inkling of what had happened at the beginning of the year, or of what was to happen at its close.

In February the Queen was moved to send a letter to the States-General in which she commended Marlborough to them in high terms, and affirmed her unswerving confidence in his skill and her resolve to support him. Consideration was also shown to Marlborough's position at the head of the Army; and the clique of officers who had gained favour by backbiting him in 1710 were given higher but other employment. Argyll had been sent to Spain. The Earl of Orrery was withdrawn from the Army and ousted Cadogan in diplomatic functions at The Hague. We find him almost immediately in polite and ceremonious relations with the Duke. A working basis, at any rate, was formed for the purposes of the war between Marlborough and his political opponents. Thus the campaign of 1711 shows Marlborough as General only. Could he under these conditions succeed?

The capture by the Allies in 1710 of Douai, Béthune, Aire, and Saint-Venant had marked a further piercing of the French fortress barrier. At the point of maximum penetration only Arras and Cambrai stood in the way of the long-sought allied march into the heart of France. Their command of the sea enabled the Allies, if they should invade upon a narrow front, to replenish their advancing armies by opening new bases on the sea-coast at Abbeville or even at Havre. The conclusion of peace between the Empire and Hungary promised to free Imperial troops for the main theatre. The adjustment of the differences between Victor Amadeus and the Imperial Court made it likely that the crafty and powerful Duke would act with vigour in Dauphiné.

Marlborough longed for the arrival of Eugene. In repeated letters he begged him to hasten his journey. On March 9 there is a postscript in his own handwriting: "Au nom de Dieu, mon prince, hâtez votre voyage autant qu'il sera possible." Amid all the relaxations of success, when none of the Allies was frightened any more, the spectacle of Marlborough and Eugene within the French frontier at the head of a hundred and forty thousand men seemed once again to bring an absolute decision within reach.

Marlborough took the field at the beginning of May with 120,000 men, facing Villars's line from Arleux to Bouchain. This was the most interesting part of the front, for the conquest of Cambrai or Bouchain would effect the deepest inroad into France. Moreover, the inundations of the Sensée were traversed here by two causeways at Arleux and Aubencheul-au-Bac. The strength of the French position was obvious. "The enemy," he wrote to St John on the 7th, "are very busy fortifying and securing all the passages of the rivers, and are being obliged to send a good part of their horse to some distance for the conveniency of forage." "Our chief business at present," said Marlborough, "is to subsist." He fed himself by the Scarpe through Douai, and was at the same time concerned in passing a heavy convoy of munitions to the newly captured fortresses on the Lys. The French garrison of Valenciennes were but ten miles from the Scarpe, and made several successful raids upon the barges, in one of which they destroyed not only many laden barges but two escorting battalions.

Eugene had joined Marlborough on May 13. The Duke was facing the enemy in the neighbourhood of Douai. The Prussian dispute was at its height, and none of their troops had reached the army. He welcomed Eugene with heartfelt pleasure. But the death of Joseph had disconcerted all plans. The two comrades were to be together only for a few weeks. The Imperial Diet was to meet at Frankfort for the election of the new Emperor. Louis XIV saw that by threatening an invasion he could convulse all German affairs, and with a comparatively small detachment frustrate the impending onslaught from Flanders. He ordered Villars on June 3 to send 15 battalions and 15 squadrons to the Rhine. This shrewd stroke was immediately effective. On June 14 Eugene, with the whole of the Imperialist troops, was forced to march off to the Rhine. At the same time the Dutch, feeling themselves isolated, insisted upon strong garrisons in all the conquered fortresses.

Whereas in March Marlborough had, with his remaining strength and by many personal submissions, begun to concentrate 140,000 men, counting also on the comradeship of Eugene, he now saw himself left alone with but 90,000 men, opposed by a French army certainly 30,000 stronger. His vehement efforts to resist or repair this denudation, both with Vienna and The Hague, exhibited him as a beggar on all sides. His distress could not be concealed. Everything had gone wrong. In the British Government and around the Queen there was an air of singular detachment. Ministers shrugged their shoulders about the war, and threw the burden on Marlborough. He and his Whig friends wanted the war to go on. The Tories had always wished to quit. Out of their patriotism they had deferred to the policies of their opponents for this one more campaign. With what noble superiority to party wishes had they not played their part! Against their better judgment—so they presented it—they had given Marlborough a final chance. If he failed, how right they would be proved. All the time Harley and St John knew that upon his exertions in the field depended their means of making any peace tolerable to the British nation.

Marlborough, in order to divert attention from the departure of Eugene and his troops, and also to pin Villars to the defence of Arras, marched westward, crossing the Scarpe between Vitry and Douai, and formed his front towards Lens, his right wing resting on the Vimy Ridge. He was now definitely weaker than Villars, and he lay in these broad plains for more than a month reviewing his troops, and drawing them out in line of battle to tempt Villars to an attack, which he had no intention of making. Villars, far from attacking, on June 2 sent 42 battalions and 26 squadrons, including all Max Emmanuel's troops, to meet Eugene on the Rhine, and moved the rest of his army to the neighbourhood of Arras. This still left the French with a small superiority, and ten weeks of the campaign had passed in futility.

Marlborough's conduct of the war at this time is in strong contrast with the aggressive method of his earlier campaigns, and also with the extraordinary exertions he was shortly to display. He was not only depressed by all he heard from England, but he had serious and alarming symptoms of illness. His headaches and earaches were severe. He suffered again from "giddiness and swimmings in my head, which also gave me often sickness in my stomach," and it may well be that he was not much removed from the stroke which five years later fell upon him. By all accounts he had greatly aged, and was, in fact, worn down by the long, exacting war.

All the time he set his mind upon the problem of how to end the war by military means. In his camp at Lens he formed an elaborate strategic and political plan. He sent his friend Lord Stair upon a confidential mission to Oxford. In the first place he was to unfold to the Lord Treasurer, as he now was, a military scheme whereby the bulk of the allied army would, instead of dispersing, spend the winter concentrated upon the frontier. This involved a heavy additional expense in the provision of food, dry forage, and also shelters for the troops and stabling for the horses. It would cost about double as much as the ordinary winter quarters. On the other hand, it would cost the French incomparably more; indeed, they could not match it. It would keep the pressure upon them at its height, and would enable the campaign of 1712 to be begun at the earliest moment and at great advantage.

The military project was easily settled. But the political overtures which Marlborough made to Oxford encountered an insuperable obstacle. Oxford knew that he could not carry Marlborough with him in his peace plans, and if they succeeded he would not need him.

There is little doubt that what Marlborough proposed to Oxford through Lord Stair was that they should work together *à deux* to fight the war to a finish. Oxford weighed this matter long and anxiously. If the war must go on in 1712 an arrangement with Marlborough seemed indispensable. But the progress of negotiations made in secret gave Ministers increasing confidence that the armies would not be forced again to take the field. Nevertheless, amicable relations were maintained between the Treasurer and the General. These might ripen into close co-operation or wither into antagonism.

Since the changes in London had first been perceived by the French Court, the whole policy of Louis XIV had been to gain time for the downfall of Marlborough and an English defection to break up the

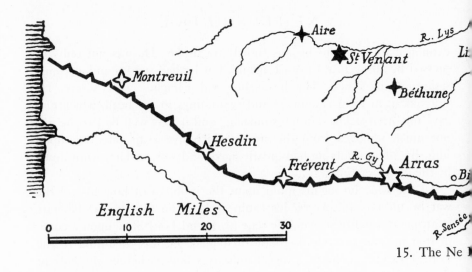

confederacy.Thus, and thus alone, could France be saved. Hence Marshal Villars was forbidden to risk any battle in the open, and only allowed to fight behind parapets. After the siege of Douai in June 1710 the French had begun to construct an immense new line of fortifications and inundations behind and through which they could stand or manœuvre. This line ran from the sea by the Canche river through the fortresses of Montreuil, to Upper Scarpe, west of Arras. It followed the Scarpe to Biaches, turned along the valley of the Sensée to Bouchain on the Scheldt, and thence to Valenciennes. The whole of this ninety-mile front was fortified, not for a siege defence, but for the effective manœuvring of a field army. The many marshes of those days were multiplied and extended by numberless dams, which spread broad sheets of water, or quagmires, more impassable still. The watersheds between the rivers were held by strong ramparts with deep ditches, often doubled, in front of them, and frequent redoubts or strong points. Behind the line, which ran east and west and was almost straight, was a thorough system of lateral roads and bridges, and food and ammunition depots for use in emergency were established.

Beyond Valenciennes the fortifications ran through Quesnoy to Maubeuge, on the Sambre, and thence down that river to Namur, beyond which lay the natural barrier of the Ardennes. But this sector was not likely to be involved in the operations of 1711. The Allies could only approach the lines to attack the strong fortress of Arras in their

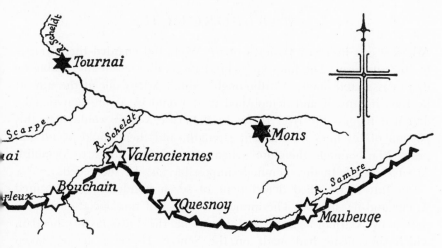

Lines

centre by the riverways of the Lys and the Scheldt, which join at
Ghent. They could accumulate supplies in the four fortresses captured
in 1710—Aire, Saint-Venant, Béthune, and Douai—and operations on
a great scale were almost certainly to be confined to the twenty-five
mile sector Arras-Bouchain. During the whole of the winter great numbers of peasants were employed by the French in perfecting this defensive system, every mile of which was studied with the utmost care. By
the spring of 1711 Villars was so pleased with his lines that he began to
boast about them in his usual exuberant style. It was a joke in the
armies that Marlborough had bought himself a new scarlet coat of a
cut which the tailor described as *ne plus ultra*. Villars, fastening upon
this phrase, applied it to his lines, and it was soon on every lip.

✳   ✳   ✳   ✳

The forcing of long lines was a standard operation until the Great
War of 1914. In the old days, when the defence was not greatly superior to the assault, the attacking army feinted one way, and made a
forced march by night the other. The interest of Marlborough's campaign of 1711 consists in the artifices and stratagems which he used,
and the perfection and true sense of values with which he combined
and timed all parts of his schemes. He weighed every factor justly, but
most of all he read the character and temperament of Marshal Villars.
The causeway across the Sensée by Arleux has been mentioned.

Arleux was a French fort north of the river, and guarded the entrance to the causeway. The lines lay behind the Sensée, itself impassable by its morasses and floods. Marlborough wanted Arleux out of the way. If he took it himself and demolished it, it would be a sure sign that he designed to pass the river there. In that case Villars would man this portion of his lines in sufficient strength, and there could be no surprise. Marlborough therefore sought to induce Villars to demolish Arleux himself. In this seemingly impossible task he succeeded.

On July 6 an allied detachment of seven hundred men captured Arleux and its garrison. The immediate object of this operation was reported by Marlborough to St John to be the breaking of the dam which the enemy had made on the Sensée. However, having taken Fort Arleux, Marlborough proceeded, not to demolish it, but to fortify it, and on a much larger scale. He placed a strong force under Hompesch on the glacis of Douai, five miles away, to cover this work. Hompesch was certainly careless, for on July 9 Villars counter-attacked the fort and Hompesch's camp. The fort held out, but Hompesch was seriously cut up and lost nearly a thousand men killed, wounded, and prisoners. Villars exulted publicly, and in his letters to Paris, upon the affront he had inflicted upon his opponent. Marlborough persisted in the fortifying of Arleux; but when these extensive works were completed he assigned only a small garrison of six hundred men to their defence. This clearly wears the aspect of design. Moreover, the Duke now displayed considerable irritation at Hompesch being surprised, and it got about in the allied army, and spread to the French, that he was much upset and very angry. On July 20–21, having recalled Hompesch, he marched his army twenty miles farther to the west, and camped south of Lillers; at the same time he reinforced his garrisons in Douai, Lille, and Tournai, so that he had an exceptional number of troops unnoticed thereabouts. He left his pontoons at Douai. These were certainly definite steps in his plan. They deceived Goslinga, who wrote a letter of protest to Marlborough, complaining of his "remaining so long with folded arms inactive at the head of so fine an army."

More important, they deceived Villars. He too moved his main army a march farther to the west, but at the same time detached a force under Montesquiou to capture Arleux. Villars now viewed Fort Arleux in a new light. He had wished to keep it as a toll-gate to the causeway on Marlborough's side of the river. But now it appeared that Marlborough, far from wishing to demolish it, desired to keep it to prevent an incursion by Villars. If Marlborough had demolished it, Villars would have refortified it. As Marlborough had greatly strengthened its fortifications, Villars thought it would be right to destroy them. This was precisely the reaction which Marlborough had foreseen. With his main army forty miles away, and quite a lot of his troops dispersed within easy reach of Douai, Arleux and its weak garrison was a bait: and the bait was taken. On July 22 Villars attacked Arleux. Instead of using any of the troops which he had within reach of Douai, Marlborough dispatched Cadogan with thirty squadrons and all the Grenadiers from the camp near Lillers to the rescue. Cadogan was too late. Arleux was captured by the French, and its garrison were made prisoners of war. Marshal Villars trumpeted to the world this new gross humiliation he had inflicted upon Marlborough, and proceeded to level the peccant Arleux to the ground. At the same time, feeling comfortable about his right, he sent Montesquiou on with his detachment to reinforce Maubeuge and threaten Brabant.

The effect upon Marlborough of this second rebuff was noticed by all. His customary urbanity and composure deserted him. "He was," says General Kane, "very peevish publicly." He was known to be ailing in health, worried out of his wits by politics, and now deeply angered by the severe pinpricks he had received. Spies were everywhere, and his demeanour was reported to the enemy. It was a natural reply to Montesquiou's advance to Maubeuge that Marlborough should send a similar force to the eastward. Accordingly he ordered Albemarle, with twelve battalions and twenty-four squadrons, to Béthune. The French staff saw nothing unusual in this, nor did they notice that, mixed up with Albemarle's movement, much of the baggage of the army and the heavy artillery with a strong escort moved on towards Douai. It now became known that Marlborough had resolved to attack Villars and his lines with the main army in the neighbourhood of Arras. He had for some time past been writing, even to his most intimate friends, that battle would be necessary. On July 26, escorted by two thousand horse, he made a personal reconnaissance of the French lines west of Arras about Avesnes-le-Comte. He took a large staff with him, and rode close enough to have a brush with the French light cavalry. It is noticeable that, though the French force from Maubeuge moved towards Brabant, Albemarle moved no farther east, and Marlborough contented himself with sending a small reinforcement to Brussels. The stage was now set.

Count Tilly, whom Goslinga describes as a brave and loyal man, had his wife with him in the camp. This lady was not only talkative, but suspected, by Goslinga at least, of illicit correspondence with the enemy. Marlborough visited Count Tilly and informed him of his decision to attack Villars in two or three days. Goslinga, who was now in the secret, lunching with an abbé near by, committed the calculated indiscretion of drinking to the great event which would happen two days later, and was pleased to see a young stranger at the table leave very rapidly after the meal. Thus Villars by the end of July was convinced that Marlborough meant to attack him. It was now too late to recall the French troops sent to Maubeuge, and his Intelligence informed him that Albemarle was still at Béthune, near enough to join the main allied army for the battle. The fact that Albemarle had not moved to protect Brussels seemed to prove that he was needed by Marlborough for a general engagement. Villars thereupon concentrated all his forces upon the sector of the lines west of Arras. His men worked night and day to strengthen the already formidable defences. He drew in all cannon and detachments and drained the garrisons of all the fortresses in reach. The ardent spirit of the Marshal was highly elated by the prospect of an attack upon his lines. As he surveyed their immense strength and the superior numbers of the army he had arrayed behind them he proclaimed on all sides his confidence in the result. He even wrote a letter to the King, for which he was afterwards ridiculed, declaring that he had brought Marlborough to the *ne plus ultra*.

On the 2nd and 3rd of August the Duke moved forward again and halted abreast of Villers-Brulin within striking distance of the French. He ordered the cavalry to make the thousands of fascines which were needed to fill in the double ditches in front of the French entrenchments. Every preparation was made for battle in both armies. All his commanders, except four or five who were in the secret, were thoroughly misled and deeply alarmed. Defeat was probable; a frightful slaughter certain.

On the 4th Marlborough, protected by a large force of cavalry and attended by a numerous staff, reconnoitred the enemy's lines at close quarters. While all eyes were attracted by this spectacle, the field artillery moved off to the eastward in successive detachments. Captain

Parker, who was posted with his company, heard of this reconnaissance, and thought there was "something extraordinary in it."

Cadogan, with an escort of forty Hussars, galloped off to Douai. Here he found Hompesch. As darkness fell troops from Lille, Tournai, and Saint-Amand joined the Douai garrison, the whole forming a corps of twenty-three battalions and seventeen squadrons. During the morning, while Marlborough's pioneers were all out preparing the approaches towards the French left, the whole of the field artillery—this certainly seems a great risk—began to move in the opposite direction, and at nightfall Albemarle, instead of being summoned west to join Marlborough, was ordered to march with the utmost speed to Douai. Thither the heavy baggage with its exceptional escort was also proceeding.

That day in the allied camps there was a solemn hush. All were ready to do their duty and pay its forfeits if these were demanded of them. Still, the memories of Malplaquet, and the close survey of the enemy's lines which so many officers had been able to make, led experienced men to wonder whether the Captain-General was in his right mind. There can be no doubt of the readiness of these hard-bitten professional troops to make the frontal assault, and their faith in Marlborough's hitherto infallible skill mastered their misgivings. But when during the afternoon the orders for battle were circulated bewilderment was general. The sun set upon two hundred thousand men who expected to be at each other's throats at daybreak. Villars moved about his army, animating his soldiers for an ordeal which would decide the fate of France. As he considered the position he must have felt, with Cromwell at Dunbar, "The Lord hath delivered them into our hands." All the enemy accounts show that the French soldiers braced themselves in the highest spirit of devotion to conquer or to die, and that their High Command was well content that the supreme stake, decisive for the long war, should on these terms be ventured. As night approached a large body of light cavalry was sent out on the right flank of the allied army, as if to portend some movement towards the west. This was the last thing the French saw before darkness fell.

"At length," says General Kane, "tattoo beats, and before it had done, orders came to strike our tents immediately." The troops stood to arms. Soon staff officers arrived to guide the four columns, and in less than half an hour the whole army was on the march to the left. All through the moonlight night they marched eastward. They traversed those broad undulations between the Vimy Ridge and Arras which two centuries later were to be dyed with British and Canadian blood. The march was pressed with severity: only the briefest halts were allowed; but a sense of excitement filled the troops. It was not to be a bloody battle. The "Old Corporal" was up to something of his own. On they strode. Before five o'clock on the morning of the 5th they reached the Scarpe near Vitry. Here the army found a series of pontoon-bridges already laid, and as the light grew they saw the long columns of their artillery now marching with them.

At daybreak Marlborough, riding in the van at the head of fifty squadrons, met a horseman who galloped up from Cadogan. He bore the news that Cadogan and Hompesch, with twenty-two battalions and twenty squadrons, had crossed the causeway at Arleux at 3 A.M. and were in actual possession of the enemy's lines. Marlborough now sent his aides-de-camp and staff officers down the whole length of the marching columns with orders to explain to the officers and soldiers of every regiment what he was doing and what had happened, and to tell them that all now depended upon their marching qualities. "My lord Duke wishes the infantry to step out." One must remember that he was dealing with an army composed primarily of men many of whom, though only privates, had for several years, some for ten years, had no other life but the service, and who were keen critics of every move in war. He knew that their comprehension of what he was doing, and what he was saving them from, would gain him their utmost efforts. The whole army marched with every scrap of life and strength they had. As the light broadened and the day advanced, the troops could see upon their right, across the marshes and streams of the Sensée, that the French were moving parallel to them within half cannon shot. But they also saw that the head of the French horse was only abreast of the allied foot. "It was," says Parker, "a perfect race between the two armies, but we, having the start of them by some hours, constantly kept ahead."

Marlborough, putting his fifty squadrons to the trot, hastened on to join Cadogan. His infantry followed with a superb endurance and devotion. Men marched until they dropped, fainting or dying by the road. The track was lined with stupefied soldiers, of whom scores expired from their exertions. Little more than half stayed the course. It was like the rush upon Oudenarde, but far longer. In sixteen hours the infantry of the army marched thirty-six miles, and by four in the afternoon considerable masses had arrived in the new position behind the enemy's lines from Oisy towards the Scheldt.

Villars had not learnt that Marlborough was marching till eleven o'clock that night. All his troops were in the trenches, ready to stand to arms at a moment's notice. He had received a message from Montesquiou, near Maubeuge, that he expected to be attacked at dawn. This was, of course, a delusion. He began to be uncomfortable about the Cambrai-Bouchain area, which, as he says, "was no longer defended." It was 2 A.M. before he was sure where Marlborough was going. He knew at once that he had been forestalled. He ordered the whole of his army to march eastward, and hurried on himself at the head of the Maison du Roi. He was met on the way by the news that the lines had been crossed by an allied advance from Douai, and that large hostile forces of cavalry and infantry were already across the Sensée. On this he pressed forward so rapidly that he arrived on the scene at about eleven o'clock with two or three hundred men. He found Marlborough at the head of a veritable army, long past his lines, and ready to receive him. The impetuous Marshal lost a hundred of his men, and was within an ace of being captured himself, before he accepted what had happened.

During the 5th of August the bulk of the allied army was crossing the Sensée and drawing up inside the enemy's lines. The whole of the cavalry of the right wing, which acted as rearguard, was employed in bringing in exhausted soldiers, their muskets, and their packs, with which the route was littered, as they had fallen by the way. Villars's main body, after a forced march, was now approaching. The night of the 5th fell on these exertions.

We are indebted to Goslinga for an invaluable sketch of the next morning's proceedings. "Milord," he records, "said to me out loud, so that every one could hear him, 'Now we shall make our siege' (meaning Bouchain): 'our hands are free. I shall use these five or six days which we need for the preparations, in trying to bring the enemy to action.' I loudly applauded this generous resolve," says Goslinga, "and animated the Duke to it. Hompesch did the same." Meanwhile the cavalcade, with its escorting squadrons and patrols, reached the hamlet of Framegies. Here they met two peasants, who declared that the French army was close at hand and advancing. Cadogan and Goslinga climbed the church tower, and even before they reached the top saw a couple of miles away several heavy French columns marching forward and already in the act of deploying. They could even see the colour of their flags. Most of the High Commanders, including Hesse and Würtemberg, had now come up, and all sat their horses awaiting Marlborough's decision. Not so Deputy Goslinga. With all his faults, right or wrong, he was always for fighting; which is something. "Ought you not," he said to Marlborough, "to make all the troops stand to arms, and harness the Dutch artillery, and bring the English artillery as fast as possible across the Sensée?"

Marlborough was a model of politeness and patience in personal relations. Up to now the Deputy had always received bland and even deferential treatment from him. Long night marches, early rising, endless vexations, intense military issues, had not hitherto worn down Marlborough's ceremonious manner. However, on this occasion Goslinga was conscious of a very definite change. "I found him freezing; he answered me dryly that there would be time for that, that the first thing was to find out whether the ground made a general attack possible. I answered him," says Goslinga, "that it was always right to be ready," and on this the Deputy turned to Cadogan, looking for his support. "I couldn't get a word out of him." Hesse offered to reconnoitre with his cavalry. Marlborough contented himself with ordering forty squadrons to stand by. Goslinga, the privileged civilian in the midst of these military men, let himself go.

> As for me, seeing this coldness of Milord, and of Cadogan, so ardent by nature but now ice in this rencontre, I said that I should go and warn Count Tilly; and if Milord was agreeable, I would in passing by the left give the order for the army to stand to arms, and to harness and to bring up our artillery: and at the same time recall by a cannon-shot all the foraging parties which were afield.

Goslinga records that Marlborough said to him most coldly, "All right—you may do it," and that he added as the Deputy rode off, "I shall expect you for dinner at noon." Was this good manners, or was it ridicule? Certainly it dismissed very curtly Goslinga's wish for a battle. Across the centuries one can almost hear the titter that ran round the circle of high, proud military men, with lifetimes of war behind them, as the important and self-important Deputy galloped off to issue his commands. "Don't be late for dinner!"

Meanwhile Goslinga hastened from one general to the other. "First I tackled Hompesch, and tried to make him stimulate Milord, but he put me off [*mais il battit froid*]." Goslinga turned to Natzmer. All that the Prussian cavalry general, a hard, fierce man of war, hero of the charge at Oudenarde, would say was, according to Goslinga, "We shall have to examine the ground." Natzmer in his own account says, "I supported my lord Duke." Then Tilly arrived with the other Dutch Deputies, and a sort of council of war was held in the open, and it seems on horseback. Goslinga remembered that once, in 1707, Marlborough in a burst of confidence had said to him in effect, "When I don't want to do a particular thing I call a council of war." The Duke now asked for opinions in the reverse order of seniority. All were for battle if the ground permitted it, but the English generals Orkney and Lumley, and Anhalt the Prussian, declared that the ground was too favourable to the enemy, and that the best thing was to cross the Scheldt. Albemarle hedged. Hesse and Würtemberg, according to Goslinga—and the story is taken as he tells it—were for the attack. Thereupon Marlborough spoke for the first time.

He said that there was no possibility of bringing the enemy to decisive battle except by attacking at great disadvantage, and that the only thing to do was to cross the Scheldt and besiege Bouchain. Count Hompesch and the Dutch general Fagel, and even the other two Dutch Deputies, thereupon supported Marlborough. Goslinga protested at length and aloud. "But I spoke in vain," he writes. "Milord held to the resolution which had been taken." It was settled that at sunset the army should cross the Scheldt by four bridges covered by a rearguard of forty squadrons. The generals then dispersed. Marlborough again asked Goslinga to dine with him. "But," says this irate civilian, almost alone among chiefs of war,

> my heart was too full of wrath against his damnable politics, which
> by avoiding battle only sought to prolong the war.

Let us now judge this episode in the light of modern knowledge. Marlborough had hoped that Villars would be stung into attacking him during the 6th, and, in spite of the severe forced march, he had the army well in hand for this. But it had not been his purpose to fight an offensive battle himself after forcing the lines. His intention was always to move to his left, cross the Scheldt, and besiege Bouchain. All his dispositions on crossing the Sensée and the lines—the roads, the bridges, and the bivouacs of his troops—were arranged for such a movement. Of course, if Villars had committed some grave fault, either by attacking or exposing himself to be attacked at a disadvantage, he would have turned aside to deal with him. Villars himself considered that his position was very strong. A modern study of the ground confirms this view. By the afternoon of the 6th he had a substantial superiority in numbers. He had been entrenching his front and preparing abattis in Bourlon Wood since about eight o'clock.

Both armies were tired, but the French had marched along their prepared lateral roads, and the Allies for the most part had tramped across country. Being on outer lines, they had had nearly ten miles farther to go. The allied generals who were consulted had complete confidence in Marlborough, and if he had said "Attack" they would have fallen on in good heart. They would certainly not have wished to venture against his better judgment. The decision was obviously his. It was convenient in the controversy of that time to cite the agreement of all these eminent warriors, but Marlborough alone bears the responsibility. Apart from the natural desire which we all have to witness miracles, there is no doubt he was right. The Allies were under no call to fight a desperate battle. As far as they knew, they had the game in their own hands, if they did not throw it away. Moreover, at this particular juncture Marlborough, although at the head of a smaller army, had gained all his strategic objects. He had ruptured the long-vaunted Ne Plus Ultra line, and was now in a position, albeit inferior in numbers, to undertake a siege. Villars must submit to his will; Bouchain was in his grip.

Villars had now for the moment a choice of evils. He could only protect Bouchain and Valenciennes by moving his army to the right bank of the Scheldt. If he did so Marlborough could besiege Arras. There was no doubt which would be the greater loss. He resigned himself to a siege of Bouchain, and hoped from his safe and near base at Cambrai to interrupt it. In the afternoon of the 6th the allied army marched to its left towards the Scheldt, and by evening eight bridges had been thrown by Etrun. During the night the whole army passed over in heavy rain. Goslinga dilates and gloats upon the confusion of this night march, and tells us that ten thousand men could have routed all. In fact, however, Villars could not pierce the strong cavalry screen, and rested in complete ignorance of what was happening; and the passage of the Scheldt and the investment of Bouchain were accomplished without the slightest loss or even interference. The whole operation was acclaimed at the time, and has since been held to be, an unsurpassed masterpiece of the military art. Indeed, not only in the army but throughout Europe it was regarded as Marlborough's finest stratagem and manœuvre.

CHAPTER EIGHTY-SEVEN

Bouchain

ᵷɑ 1711, August and September ᴅᵹ

BOUCHAIN was an amazing operation. Marlborough, having passed the Scheldt during the night of August 6–7, moved round the east side of the fortress and threw a number of bridges across that river by Neuville. He made his main camp between the Scheldt and the Selle, but he immediately pushed his right hand across the Scheldt to the westward, so as to encircle Bouchain. At the same time Villars in superior strength, with at least a hundred thousand men, came to sit down with him at the siege.

On August 8 the Marshal, finding his suddenly captured lines abandoned, and Marlborough committing himself to Bouchain, moved into the angle formed by the Scheldt and the Sensée and established himself there, barely two miles away from the besieged fortress.

Marlborough's communications ran through Douai, nineteen or twenty miles to the west. They were within easy striking distance of the French in their entrenched camp at Wavrechin. The Scheldt was blocked above him by the fortress of Valenciennes. He had to bring in a siege-train now at Tournai, and also all the supplies and munitions for the siege and for his own army of about ninety thousand men, from Tournai down the Scarpe to Douai, and thence by wagon convoy from Douai, or, as was arranged later, by a short cut from Marchiennes. Villars could at any time cross the Sensée and march north-ward, traversing all Marlborough's communications. Marlborough's only remedy in that case would be to come round north of Bouchain and fight a battle. As he must keep at least twenty thousand men in the trenches of the

(822)

siege, he would have to fight at odds of seventy thousand against a hundred thousand or even more. During the whole of the siege he accepted and often courted this possibility. He must have foreseen all these dangers before deciding on the siege. No wonder even his most faithful followers and admirers in the High Command thought the siege impracticable.

As soon as Marlborough heard on August 8 that the French were crossing the Sensée in force he concluded that Villars meant to cut his communications and bring about a battle. This was, indeed, an obvious move for Villars to make, and it would immediately have forced an encounter in the open field, which Marlborough above all things desired, even at serious numerical odds. He did not mean to fight another Malplaquet, but would have welcomed another Ramillies. He therefore, before finally engaging in the siege, multiplied his bridges below Bouchain, and began moving his main army round to meet Villars somewhere between Bouchain and the Scarpe.

However, Villars had apparently a move either way. If Marlborough came round to the west the Marshal could cross the Scheldt instead of the Sensée by a right-handed instead of a left-handed movement, and once he was ensconced there the siege of Bouchain would become impossible. On the other hand, Arras would be uncovered. Marlborough could then march through Douai direct upon that place. Therefore when Villars began feinting across the Scheldt his gesture did not carry conviction. As long as Marlborough was ready to fight a battle in the open plains west of Douai at heavy odds his plan was sound, and he was master. On any other basis the siege of Bouchain was absurd.

It seemed at first essential to the siege to drive Albergotti out of the Wavrechin position. Dopf had already crossed at Neuville with 30 battalions and 40 squadrons to complete the investment which at Wavrechin was obstructed. Dopf was reinforced during the night of the 8th by sixteen battalions under Fagel; and Cadogan, that trusted Eye, went with him. In this force was the whole of the British infantry. On the morning of the 9th they were ordered to assault Albergotti in such fortifications as he had been able to construct overnight. Here Captain Parker may take up the tale.

> I must confess I did not like the aspect of the thing. We plainly saw that their entrenchment was a perfect bulwark, strong and lofty, and crowded with men and cannon pointed directly at us: yet did

they not fire a shot great or small, reserving all for us, on our advancing up to them. We wished much that the Duke might take a nearer view of the thing. . . .

But while I was thus musing, the Duke of Marlborough (ever watchful, ever right) rode up quite unattended and alone, and posted himself a little on the right of my company of grenadiers, from whence he had a fair view of the greater part of the enemy's works. It is quite impossible for me to express the joy which the sight of this man gave me at this very critical moment. I was now well satisfied that he would not push the thing, unless he saw a strong probability of success; nor was this my notion alone: it was the sense of the whole army, both officer and soldier, British and foreigner. And indeed we had all the reason in the world for it; for he never led us on to any one action that we did not succeed in. He stayed only three or four minutes, and then rode back. . . He had not been longer from us than he stayed, when orders came to us to retire. It may be presumed we were not long about it, and as the corn we stood in was high, we slipped off undiscovered, and were a good way down the hill, before they perceived that we were retiring; and then they let fly all their great and small shot after us: but as we were by this time under the brow of the hill, all their shot went over our heads, inasmuch that there was not a single man of all the grenadiers hurt.

This episode reveals Marlborough's soldierly qualities as a model for all commanders of British troops. It was because his soldiers felt he was watching over them, and would never spare himself where their welfare and honour were concerned, that they were deeply attached to him. His "attention and care," as Corporal Matthew Bishop wrote, "was over us all."

Perhaps it would have been better if the French had recognized the Captain-General as he rode along the front in the high corn within seventy paces of their entrenchments. One volley, and he would have ranked in our national affections with Wolfe and Nelson. He would have been spared the detestable indignities and maltreatment which his Tory countrymen had in store for him. But there was nothing morbid about Marlborough. He liked living, and was content to take whatever came. It was all in the day's work. Still, if the French had had sharper eyes, the pens of Swift, Macaulay, and Thackeray would have been blunted.

When it was found impossible to dislodge the French from their Wavrechin position, Marlborough consulted the engineers of the army upon whether Bouchain could be taken, and whether it was practicable to persevere in the siege. All answered in the negative except one, Colonel Armstrong, who declared it could be done, and that "he was ready himself to undertake the most difficult part of it." Under the cover of five thousand British troops there was raised in the darkness of the night opposite the French entrenchments a series of "most noble and indeed surprising redoubts with double ditches in which were mounted twenty-four large pieces of cannon, over which at daylight the British standard was flying."

Marlborough now proceeded to wall himself in upon all sides. On August 12 he demanded from the Dutch Council of State six thousand pioneers, or workmen, with their tools, raised by compulsion from the provinces of Flanders, Brabant, and Hainault, and seven hundred additional wagons. The Dutch immediately produced all these men for him. With their aid and by the labour of the army he constructed lines of circumvallation around the whole of Bouchain, except on the side of the southern marsh and along the Selle and the Scheldt, and also double entrenchments from these lines to the Scarpe, making a protected area about seven miles long north-west of the siege, through which he could draw all his supplies, conveyed by water to Marchiennes. He also entrenched the whole of his camp on the east of Bouchain, and fortified the Scheldt southward against Villars. The total length of these lines, which were, of course, additional to all the siege-works, amounted to over thirty miles. Thus he constructed not only one fortress around another, but a fortified feeding-area joining him to his waterways, fortresses, and supplies. These prodigious works, which came into existence very rapidly during August, could, of course, only be very lightly held by an army of ninety thousand men. One may imagine how intense was the effort required to make sure that whatever section was attacked would be reinforced in time from the general reserve. At no period in his service was Marlborough more active than at this siege. At all hours of the night and day he moved about the astonishing labyrinth which he had constructed for his protection while he strangled Bouchain.

The severing of the Cow Path through a great bog—the only path left there—was a prime essential. Accordingly the besiegers set out into the morass from both sides, building fascinades—swiftly copied—step by step till they got near enough for an attack. Marlborough came himself to direct this curious operation, and examined its possibilities with scrupulous care. The water in the marsh was in places up to the necks of the four hundred grenadiers who assaulted on the 17th. A short officer had himself carried, a particular target, high on the shoulders of his men. The fortress cannon fired heavily upon the wading and splashing soldiers as they struggled slowly forward; but the French defenders fled when their advance continued. The Cow Path was taken, and the town completely isolated. "Our greatest difficulties," wrote Marlborough to Godolphin (August 20), "for the siege of Bouchain are over. . . . They are now shut up on all sides."

The spectacle of a siege proceeding with two great armies so closely interlocked was unique in the wars of the eighteenth century. It was watched by all Europe with profound interest. The actual reduction of the fortress proceeded with great rapidity. By September 12 the long ordeal reached its end. The governor hung out white flags upon all attacks. He offered to surrender the fortress if he could march out with the honours of war. Marlborough usually accorded such conditions. But on this occasion he determined to inflict upon Villars, under whose eyes the drama proceeded, a rebuke which would be everywhere noticed. He demanded that the garrison should yield themselves prisoners of war. The governor refused, and a terrible bombardment was resumed. The defenders then proposed they should become technically prisoners of war, but should be allowed to reside in France on parole, because the Dutch fed their prisoners so badly. A second time the bombardment was resumed, and after some hours unconditional surrender was made. Two thousand five hundred men marched out of the place into captivity. The Allies had sustained four thousand casualties in the siege. Marlborough was master of Bouchain. It was his last conquest and command.

The project of wintering on the frontier had moved forward slowly. The Dutch were reluctant to promise their contribution. They had become with reason deeply suspicious of the English Government. Marlborough still hoped to persuade them, and might well have succeeded had he been able to return to The Hague immediately after the fall of Bouchain. This was, however, impossible. The English Ministers received the Dutch objections with inward satisfaction. They found themselves in the agreeable position of obliging Marlborough and making a show of favouring his schemes without having to make any substantial exertion.

Oxford seemed genuinely disappointed. "Ours is a very unlucky situation," he wrote to Marlborough, "that every one is shrinking from the war, and at the same time casting the burthen upon Britain, and yet unwilling to let her have the least advantage. I would to God that our Allies would resolve either to make a good war or a good peace."

Marlborough allowed himself to indulge the illusion that a friendly basis had been established between him and the Cabinet under which he was serving. He seems to have relied too much upon the Treasurer's professions of goodwill.

After Bouchain Marlborough, still hoping to carry out his plan for the advanced winter quarters, had wished to attack Quesnoy. He rode out with the cavalry and reconnoitred the intervening country. He persuaded Oxford to support this further operation. But once again the Dutch in their uncertainty were disinclined to spend more life and treasure. They made no effort to provide the forage and supplies which Marlborough required, and after garrisoning Bouchain and repairing its fortifications he withdrew upon Tournai, and in October sorrowfully dispersed the Grand Army to its normal winter quarters.

He now set out for home. He wrote Oxford a letter so conciliatory and submissive as to be painful for his admirers to read, but for which there was justification in the tone of Oxford's correspondence.

October 1711

But, my lord, as you have given me encouragement to enter into the strictest friendship with you, and I have done nothing to forfeit it, I beg your friendly advice in what manner I am to govern myself. *You cannot but imagine 'twould be a terrible mortification to pass by The Hague, with our plenipotentiaries there; and myself a stranger to their transactions; and what hopes can I have of any countenance at home, if I am not thought fit to be trusted abroad.* I could have been contented to have passed the winter on the frontier, if the States had done their part; but, under my present circumstances, I am really at a loss what part to take. My lord, I have put myself wholly into your hands, and shall be entirely guided by your advice, if you will be so kind as to favour me with it.

We can see the answer he received from his letter to Sarah of October 22.

The intelligence You have had as to the particulars of the peace having been sent to me, is without foundation, and I know the intentions of those that now govern is that I am to have nothing to do in the peace. This is what I am extreame glad off, but thay must not know it. . . . As I am now convinced the peace will be conclud'd this Winter, I shall take my measures for living a retier'd life, if it may be in England I shall be glad of it, *if not my business shall be to seek a good climate*, for my Constitution is extreamly spoilt.

"Thus," wrote General Kane, "ended the Duke of Marlborough's last campaign, which may be truly reckoned amongst the greatest he ever made." Natzmer goes even farther. "The year 1711," he wrote, "was certainly the most glorious for my lord Duke. . . . Next to God this success [the passing of the lines] must be attributed solely to his wisdom, and he can be justly given credit for it as a *coup-de-tête*."

In after-years Marlborough always looked back to the campaign of 1711 with pride. The Blenheim tapestries made under his directions assign to the capture of Bouchain a prominence over any of the great battles he had won. To understand this one must weigh the facts and figures. An army of perhaps 130,000 opposed by 90,000 could normally undertake a first-class siege, and provide a covering force which at any time could fight a battle behind entrenchments, or even at a hazard in the open. But for an army of 90,000 to effect the conquest of a fully garrisoned fortress in the face of at least 96,000 was an overturning of all the rules and experience resulting from twenty-five years of continuous war.

Thus ended the ten campaigns of the Duke of Marlborough, during which he had won four great battles and many secondary actions and combats, and had taken by siege thirty fortresses. In this process he had broken the military power of France, and reduced the first of military nations to a condition in which they were no longer feared by any country. He had practically destroyed the French barrier with the exception of some fortresses of the third line, and at any time a road into France could be opened. During the whole of these ceaseless operations of war on the largest scale the world had seen, or was to see for several generations, confronted by the main armies of France and their best generals, he had never sustained a defeat or even a serious check. Hardly a convoy had been cut up or a camp surprised. The aspect which these affairs wore to friend and foe alike was that of certain victory in any battle, siege, or foray he might undertake. The annals of war contain no similar record.

CHAPTER EIGHTY-EIGHT

Hanover Intervenes

❦ 1711, June-November ❧

THE tale of these times should not be told as if it were wrong for an Opposition to seek to become a Government, or for Ministers at the head of the State to labour diligently for peace. The stigma upon them lies somewhat differently. Just as they had obtained power, not by free debate in Parliament, but by a backstairs intrigue with the Queen, so they sought a peace by a greedy and treacherous desertion of their allies. In the first case, they infringed every principle of Parliamentary government as accepted in Great Britain to-day. In the second, they violated the whole structure of personal and international good faith, of which British Governments have so often prided themselves on being the architects and defenders. All this, however, was but the starting-point. The career of deliberate bad faith for special national advantage, pursued by Ministers whose personal interests were also engaged, had but begun. It was now confined to the words of documents and the mutterings of Cabinet conclaves. Presently we shall see it translated into action in the field and in the face of the common enemy; and few who study it with attention will be surprised at the old French taunt, "Perfidious Albion."

On October 8 three documents relating to the English claims, to the interests of the allies, and to the special interest of Savoy, were signed between England and France, and approved by the Queen.

England and France were now agreed upon the preliminaries, and the special interests of England were only too well protected. St John next addressed himself to the task of reconciling the allies to the Anglo-French basis. He thought at first this would be easy. The Dutch, who had hitherto only been shown Torcy's letter of April 11, had passed the summer in uncertainty and suspicion. They had perhaps been inclined to follow the British example of direct and separate contact with France. They had not made any formal complaint upon the terms of the Torcy letter; and St John might reasonably claim that they were not disturbed by it. None of the other allies had been informed at all. Now in October the preliminaries, *apart from the secret Anglo-French agreement,* were circulated to the allied Courts. Vehement opposition developed at once from two quarters. The first was, of course, Vienna. The Emperor protested by every means in his power—and there were many—against the proposal to deprive the house of Hapsburg of Spain and the Indies. On this, as Charles VI or as Charles III, he had a strong case against England. Was it not at the English request that he had gone to Spain to fight so long and hard for the Peninsular monarchy? Had he not twice been proclaimed King of Spain at Madrid? Had not the English Parliament above all other bodies or powers in Europe proclaimed and ceaselessly ingeminated "no peace without Spain"? Yet now England appeared ready to turn her back on all this. Why? Was this the whole of the transaction? Were the so-called French proposals for dicussion in fact a bargain already struck between England and France? What lay behind?

Continental historians like Klopp naturally dwell upon the ill-usage of the Emperor Charles; but there is another side. No allied Power had more at stake in the war than the Empire. None had made greater promise to contribute to it. But what had been the performance? Where had been those ninety thousand men whom in the original treaty the Empire had bound itself to maintain upon the Rhine and in the Northern theatre? Where had been that support which the Hapsburg Emperor professed to enjoy from the Germanic states? The feeble, ill-paid armies, never rising above forty thousand, which under unhelpful or incapable commanders had appeared upon the Rhine had been the laughing-stock of friend and foe. The contingents which the Germanic princes should have sent to their supreme liege lord had only appeared in the guise of mercenary troops paid and maintained by the Sea Powers. Nothing had been given freely to the Empire. That decrepit body, paralysed from the outset by the Bavarian desertion and the Magyar revolt, had utterly failed in all its engagements. Vienna itself had been saved by the battle of Blenheim, gained in Central Europe by British soldiers and by contingents maintained by England and Holland. Even the troops which Eugene had led with quenchless valour and unsurpassed skill had been largely provided by the Sea Powers. His Turin campaign was sustained almost entirely by British money and allied contingents. His attempt on Toulon was similarly founded, and there remained much reproach about the ineffectual use of these resources. The Empire had shown itself quite unmindful of the Common Cause, which now played so large a part in their protestations, when they weakened the Toulon expedition for the sake of acquiring territorial gains at Naples. The military convention which they had made with France at the end of 1706 had shown no consideration for allied interests, and had liberated large numbers of French troops, cut off and invested in the fortresses of the Milanese, to face Marlborough in Flanders in 1707.

Klopp, while admitting the woeful facts of physical failure, still claims that the Empire had acted loyally and correctly. This loyal and correct attitude had, however, been maintained while they were carried shoulder-high by the Sea Powers. Perfidy among allies is justly odious, but failure to fulfil solemn undertakings and make adequate contribution to the common cause is not distinguishable, in its consequences at least, from perfidy. No British Government was therefore unprovided with an answer to the Austrian reproach. To bring all this to a point St John had at the end of June asked that eight thousand of the Imperialist troops released from Hungary should be sent to reinforce the Duke of Savoy and encourage his offensive. It was a request which courted a refusal, which the Secretary could turn to good account. "We must look upon a refusal," he wrote with characteristic cant (June 12), "*as an absolute desertion of the Common Cause.*" He could write this while he was corresponding with Torcy upon the basis that the allies were the "common enemy."

It was not from the Empire but from another quarter that the real thrust against the new British policy was delivered. The Elector of Hanover held a far stronger position in everything that concerned England than the Emperor. His troops had fought well throughout the war in the main theatre and in Marlborough's battles. His son had risked his life in the charge at Oudenarde. But far more important than such actions or gestures was the fact that he was the proclaimed constitutional heir to the British throne. All party politics in England revolved around him. We have seen the perfervid attempts of Oxford, Shrewsbury, and St John to gain his good graces. Well might they try; for the Queen's health, for many years precarious, gave no assurance of a lengthy reign. At any time a recurrence of her gout or some other of the maladies by which she was afflicted might remove her from the scene. Where then would be those proud Ministers who had obtained power by her favour and Abigail's intrigues if they now set themselves in direct hostility to the sincere desires and the treaty rights of their future sovereign? Although two generations had passed since the axe had fallen upon an English Minister as the result of impeachment for policy apart from rebellion, no one could say that the practice might not be revived. The fate of the great Lord Strafford was still vivid in men's minds. The weapons of impeachment and attainder remained in full existence. They were perhaps blunted by the insensible but ceaseless march of culture and civilization which distinguished this great period in our history. But it would not take long to sharpen the axe on the Tower grindstone. That these possibilities were never forgotten by the public figures of the age of Anne is revealed by innumerable references in their letters. Marlborough certainly never had the assurance that even his victories could protect him from impeachment. The dispossessed Whigs from now onward never ceased to declare of Harley that they "would have his head" should they regain power. The Hanoverian accession would give them power. A quarrel with the sovereign designate upon the high issue of the abandonment of the war might easily inspire power with vengeance.

The attitude of the Court of Hanover became at once vehemently hostile to the peace and to the new advisers of Queen Anne. This was even so marked as to show a very considerable detachment on the part of the Elector from his prospects of gaining the British throne. Evidently by his antagonism to the Tory Ministers, who would presumably be in office on a demise of the Crown, he tempted them for their own sakes to look elsewhere for a successor, if that were possible. They might well face the perils of such a course if it became the only escape from other equal dangers. Hitherto they had hoped that the lure of the Crown of Great Britain would far outweigh any pride in the Electoral Hat. It now appeared that the Elector was at heart a Hanoverian prince rather than a candidate for the British throne, and that he did not hesitate to base his chances of succession upon the Whigs and upon Whig policy at home and abroad. These developments intensified severely the passions of the British parties during the last years of Anne, until at times they seemed almost to revive in a gentler period the merciless hatreds of Charles II's reign and of the Popish Plot.

During these months the whispers had grown in Whitehall. The allied ambassadors in their anxiety obtruded themselves on Ministers and asked awkward questions. Oxford was not handy at replying. He lied obdurately without convincing. Sometimes he talked confusedly for an hour without creating any impression but that of mistrust. On October 5, meeting Hoffmann at Court, he said, "I beg you to see that no time is lost in submitting the plan of campaign for Spain, which has already been asked for a number of times. I am afraid it may arrive too late." Hoffmann smiled sardonically at him. "Have we really got to make a plan of campaign for Spain, when every one here knows that a peace is concluded, or at least certain? Indeed, if rumour is to be trusted, I should not like to carry the news to King Charles." "I should, though," replied the Treasurer genially. "How is that, when Spain and the Indies are to be given to the Duke of Anjou?" "There is no question of that," asserted Oxford, turning sharply away to end the conversation.

St John throughout this interval had been more artistic. He diffused ceaselessly an atmosphere of defeatism and uncertainty. He threw out a continuous stream of hints that the Alliance was breaking up. Every one was playing for his own hand. Only the Queen, of course, as he made out, was faithfully, laboriously, quixotically, adhering to the Common Cause. When Brigadier Palmes, of Blenheim day, returning from Vienna, suggested that opportunity was favourable for capturing Sicily, St John replied, "How do you know that the Court of Vienna is not at this very moment secretly negotiating with France?" To the Savoyard envoy he said, "Are you sure that negotiations are not proceeding in Holland?" And to the Hanoverian he remarked, "I don't say that we have anything in hand, but if we had we should be doing nothing more than what others have long been doing." In this way he rocked and shook all the foundations of the Alliance, and sought to encourage the signatories to break their bond and shift for themselves, well knowing he and his colleagues had stolen the decisive march upon them all. It is an astonishing proof of the basic strength of the structure that it did not collapse entirely during the summer.

It was the peculiar quality of St John to be able to brand in the most caustic terms in others the exact conduct which he was himself pursuing. To criticize a Government of which he was a member was "to attack the Queen." His opponents were always "a shameless faction." The allies were always guilty of the basest duplicity. He was unfeignedly indignant at the espionage and corruption by which he felt himself surrounded, and to which he made a notable contribution. He could use all arguments and all rhetoric on all sides of all questions, and he did it with a zest and pith which almost enlists us in the cause he championed at the moment. He had good reason to be annoyed when, the day after the French note had been sent in secrecy to the allies, its text appeared in the Whig news-sheet. There was a great sensation. "Both Whigs and Tories in the coffee houses were so astonished at the terms that they looked at each other without speaking. The stocks on the exchange fell several points."

The Ministry asserted that Gallas had disclosed the secret. They may well have had conclusive but unpublishable proof at their disposal. Anyhow they had an ample case against Gallas if they wished to get rid of him. They knew from his intercepted letters that he had arranged to have Peterborough shadowed on his mission as ambassador to Vienna. They had had his own opinion of them set before them in terms which to men of intelligence must have appeared particularly insulting because so shrewd. They found, however, a difficulty in dismissing Count Gallas; he had already been recalled. The Emperor Charles VI had summoned him to Vienna. It was possible none the less to inflict on him an affront which travelled round Europe. On October 26 the Master of the Ceremonies announced to him that, "owing to the displeasure his conduct had caused her, the Queen had forbidden him the Court, and would explain her reasons to the Emperor. Announcements from the Emperor through another servant would be acceptable to the Queen."

Marlborough's overtures, through Stair and in his correspondence with Oxford, had lasted during the campaign. Many persons not privy to these communications believed that an effective combination between the General and the Lord Treasurer would be a supreme advantage to the public. It would afford the best chance either of "a good peace or a good war." It would secure the Hanoverian Succession beyond all question. It would furnish the Queen with a Government of a moderate character, representative of both parties and at the mercy of neither. It certainly fulfilled in home affairs what had been the consistent conviction and desire both of the General and the Treasurer. It was in principle a return to the basis of 1704, without Sarah or Godolphin. But the obstacles were now insuperable.

Marlborough, absorbed in the arduous campaign and unaware of the secret negotiations, had only responded to Oxford's peace feelers by general assurances. He was more than willing to see a broad settlement made in Europe. But that he should be a party to a separate peace behind the backs of the other signatory states never entered his mind. He was the soul of the Grand Alliance. He was enjoying far better treatment at the hands of its members than from his own countrymen. While in England savage party enmities beset him, in Europe he was trusted, admired, and venerated. Oxford, who understood this, did not venture to declare his own true position. He was sure that no common policy on these lines could be agreed between them. He meant to have peace almost at any price, and he now felt certain he had it in his grasp. As the campaign drew to a conclusion the correspondence between the two men had evaporated in civilities.

Each relied on certain forces or processes. Hanover was now Marlborough's most important stronghold. He still hoped for a friendly arrangement with the Treasurer, but he was determined to preserve his influence there. When at the beginning of October he returned to The Hague and entered its atmosphere of anxiety and suspicion he put himself in the closest contact with the Elector George Lewis. Neither knew what the British Government had done or intended. Both were sure that private negotiations were going on between England and France. How far these were operative, or whether there was a definite agreement on any particular point, was still unknown. It cannot, however, be doubted that Marlborough and the Hanoverian Court were in entire agreement, each spurring on the other, that a separate peace by England at the expense of the allies should be resisted by every means in their power.

On the other side Oxford and St John had their plan. If, as Oxford apprehended, they could not gain Marlborough to their schemes they meant to dismiss and dishonour him; and they believed they had the means to do both. If he would go forward with Ministers upon the path of a separate peace his interests would be protected in every way.

If not, then, in the words which Bolingbroke had used to Drummond earlier in the year, "such scenes will open as no victories can varnish over." Thus Marlborough's choice was either to become the military tool of a disloyal peace or to face the full malice of the Government supported by the Queen and commanding majorities in both Houses. He was somewhat slow in becoming aware of this issue.

His eyes were to some extent opened upon his arrival at The Hague. The partisan attack launched by the new Ministry upon the financial conduct of Godolphin, the fantastic tale of "thirty-five millions unaccounted for," had led to the appointment in the spring of a House of Commons "Commission of Accounts," composed of ardent Tories. Their hope and object was to unearth financial scandals and cases of peculation among their predecessors and opponents. Marlborough above all, attracted the thirsty scrutiny of the Tory-Jacobite committee. These volumes have not concealed the many good and valid reasons which the Jacobites had to seek revenge upon him. From the night in 1688 when he rode away from James's camp at Salisbury he had been their most relentless and deceitful foe. His own notorious love of wealth, the fortune he had made, the perpetual annuity voted to him for his victories, the salaries and allowances he drew from so many English military offices and as Deputy Captain-General of Holland, the ten years in which he had managed things in his own way—all proclaimed a broad and fertile field to the inquisitors. It had been known in Government circles for years past that he deducted annually a percentage from the pay of the foreign contingents serving under him and took other perquisites to form an Army fund which he said was devoted to Secret Service of all kinds. Over this, of course, he had complete control. It is the essence of Secret Service funds that no account of them can ever be presented. Thus he could be charged by his political foes with having pocketed as much as he chose of this percentage.

Marlborough does not seem to have been the least disturbed by the holding of the inquiry. He wrote to Sir Solomon Medina, the principal Government contractor, who had been summoned to England, that he was glad he was to be a witness, and would afford any documentary assistance in his power. But either Medina had some grievance about the payments made to him or he was gained to the Government interest. Whatever the cause, he certainly framed his deposition in an injurious and misleading form. He said that from 1707 to 1711 he had paid the Duke of Marlborough on bread and various contracts for the army the sum of 332,425 guilders *for his own use*, and yearly twelve or fourteen wagons gratis "for the use of the Duke himself." He mentioned also quite properly that on each contract he had presented Cardonnel with a gratuity of five hundred ducats, and paid Mr Sweet, the Deputy-Paymaster at Amsterdam, 1 per cent. on all the moneys he received.

As soon as he heard of this Marlborough wrote a full explanation to the Commissioners.

> Having been informed on my arrival here that Sir Solomon de Medina has acquainted you with my having received several sums of money from him, that it might make the less impression on you I would lose no time in letting you know that this is no more than what has been allowed as a perquisite to the general, or commander-in-chief of the army in the Low Countries, even before the Revolution, and since; and I do assure you, at the same time, that whatever sums I have received on that account have been constantly employed for the service of the public, in keeping secret correspondence, and getting intelligence of the enemy's motions and designs.

He then declared that he had also received 2½ per cent. upon the pay of the foreign auxiliaries during all these years for Secret Service, that he had himself negotiated this agreement in the capacity of plenipotentiary under King William III, and that he held Queen Anne's warrant dated July 6, 1702, for the transaction.

> And now, gentlemen [he continued], as I have laid the whole matter fairly before you, and I hope you will allow I have served my Queen and country with that faithfulness and zeal which becomes an honest man, the favour that I intreat of you is that when you make your report to the Parliament you will lay this part before them in its true light, so that they may see this necessary and important part of the war has been provided for and carried on without any other expense to the public than ten thousand pounds a year. And I flatter myself that when the accounts of the army in Flanders come under your consideration, you will be sensible the service on this side has been carried on with all the economy and good husbandry to the public that was possible.

Evidently he supposed his explanation was complete and would be accepted. Anyone considering his behaviour at this time will feel, "Here is a man with a clear conscience who cares nothing for the worst that his foes may do." And this conclusion has its force for us to-day.

Marlborough never hesitated at all in the course which he took. He rallied the whole political power of the Allies against a separate British peace. He used all his paramount influence in Hanover, both through Robethon, Secretary to the Elector, and also directly upon the Electress Sophia and the Elector, to make them dare all against it. Whatever he afterwards encountered, it was with his eyes open. He did not turn aside by a single step from the policy on which he was resolved. He faced the accusations with which he knew he would be assailed with no more unmanly shrinking than he would a cannon-ball in the field. He meant to throw his whole weight—and it might well be decisive—on the side of the immense forces gathering against the Ministry and their dishonourable negotiations.

The strongest efforts had been made by the Queen's Ministers to reconcile the Elector of Hanover to their courses. Lord Rivers was sent over with the so-called French offer of peace preliminaries. Oxford, Shrewsbury, and even Buckingham, a non-violent but undoubted Jacobite, vied with one another in their professions of devotion to the Hanoverian Succession. Abigail later on, with more comprehension than she ever showed at any other time, explained to Mesnager the root fact that the peace could only be carried under extreme asseverations of the loyalty of the Queen and of the whole Government to the Act of Settlement. This aspect was well understood at Hanover. By no one was it realized more intensely than by the aged Electress Sophia. She must be regarded as the mainspring of Hanoverian policy. That her son also held her views does not detract from this. This resolute, clear-sighted old woman revolted at the fabric of falsehood and hypocrisy which now enwrapped the policy of Britain. She never made a secret of her admiration for Marlborough. When Strafford had on one occasion twitted her "that he saw she belonged to Marlborough's party" she answered with vigour, "If the Queen had made an ape her general, and this ape had won so many victories, I should be on the side of the ape."

In answer to the laboured explanations of the peace policy of the English Government the Electress Sophia remarked to Strafford, "If you had been willing to accept peace on such terms as are printed in the English gazettes a great deal of blood and a great deal of the money of England and Holland might have been saved." The Elector too gave his opinion upon the peace proposals to the Queen, and mentioned that he would send to London a man who was in his confidence. This envoy was, of course, the Baron von Bothmar.

Following upon all this, the Hanoverian Court framed a long formal protest to the British Government against according Louis XIV

> a peace glorious to himself, ruinous to the victorious Allies, and destructive to the liberties of all Europe, in acquiring the power of giving a monarch to Spain, of imposing another on Great Britain, and of making the validity of the Crown of the Empire depend on his approbation.

Bothmar, armed with this manifesto, set out for London. He did not travel alone. At The Hague he was joined by Marlborough, and the two arrived together in the closest relations in good time for the meeting of Parliament. Bothmar presented his memorandum to the Secretary of State on November 28. The Ministers were surprised and shocked by this implacable resistance from the one quarter they were bound to respect. They were still more surprised and angered when the very next day they found this document also published and reprinted in successive editions of the *Daily Courant*. The Duchess of Somerset read the document to the Queen. Thus all along the line the struggle was openly joined. The heir to the throne, the reunited Whig Party, the weight of the Grand Alliance, and behind them all Marlborough, ranged themselves against the separate peace already agreed between England and France.

The political crisis which followed is notable in English history.

CHAPTER EIGHTY-NINE

✓ *The Political Climax*

ᕼᑯ 1711, Winter ᑯᕼ

THE disclosures by the *Daily Courant* on October 13 of the peace preliminaries said to be 'offered' by France brought the whole question before the nation. The Whig Party was instantly united against the settlement. They had recovered their poise in opposition. They began to feel again that "they had a bottom." If any issue could revive them it was surely the abandonment of the principle "No peace without Spain," which they themselves had accepted from the Tories, and to which many Tories still adhered.

At this time they gained a welcome, though hardly an exhilarating, adherent of high consequence. The Earl of Nottingham, who had been forced to cede the Secretaryship of State to Oxford in 1704, was, even more than Rochester, a High Tory, and without doubt the leader of the Church of England. He had shared in Rochester's fall, but he had not been restored when the Tories returned to power. He had always expounded the Tory strategy of leaving foreigners to cut each other's throats on the mainland, while England picked up valuable possessions in the outer seas. In 1704 this policy had expressed itself in terms of contact with Portugal and of a major English effort in Spain rather than in Flanders. In fact, though in an entirely different connotation, Nottingham was the parent of the phrase "No peace without Spain," now on all Whig lips. He could therefore, with a fine show of verbal consistency, place himself upon the Whig side on the dominating question of the hour. But as lay leader of the Church he was the champion of the Occasional Conformity Bill. The Whigs accordingly guaranteed an unopposed passage for the Bill in return for his wholehearted opposition to the proposed peace.

Rumours that Nottingham was being got at soon reached the Tory chiefs. In Whig circles there was wicked glee. Nottingham's health was drunk in bumpers at their banquets and in the Kit-cat Club. His lugubrious countenance and preternaturally solemn demeanour had long gained him a nickname. Wharton, with deplorable levity, remarked, "It is Dismal will save England at last."

Oxford and his friends, aware of the gathering storm, were full of fears for the meeting of Parliament. They could count on the Commons, where the bulk of the Tory Members would stand by them through thick and thin. Even if the parsons were placated by Nottingham the squires would not be daunted. After all, it was the squires who would have to give the votes. But in the House of Lords the forces were nicely balanced. Nottingham would certainly influence a number of peers, and even some bishops might be affected. The Scottish peers therefore acquired particular importance. It was urgent to bring them to London, and it cannot be doubted that appeals for their attendance were sustained by various inducements. Still, it took eight or nine days of hard travel for the chivalry of North Britain to reach the Metropolis. All the Whig forces, on the other hand, would be ready from the first day. Parliament was prorogued from week to week. It should normally have met early in November. People began to say that the Government did not dare to call Parliament together upon their peace terms. This talk travelled to The Hague. It was indispensable that Ministers should announce in the Queen's Speech that the States-General had agreed to a conference after the preliminaries. Strafford declared that the Dutch and other allies were becoming unmanageable. They were ceasing to pay attention to anything he said. Finally Parliament was summoned for December 7, and on this the Dutch, hoping that the Ministry would not survive the ordeal, consented to meet the French at Utrecht in February.

But an even graver anxiety oppressed Oxford and St John. They began to feel uncertain about the Queen. Deeply as she desired peace, she was aware that its dangers might affect not only her Ministers but herself. Her new Ministers were challenging all those strong forces in the nation which had brought her to the throne, and the great European combination whereby Marlborough had raised her to the head of

Europe. From all quarters forces seemed to close in upon her. Every foreign ambassador told the same tale. She knew that she was deceiving and deserting her allies, that her royal word would be a mockery throughout the world.

Abigail's soothings were a comfort to the Queen; but she had another woman friend. The Duchess of Somerset was not in contact with the Queen's person in the intimate fashion of her bedchamber woman; she was rather a trusted social companion daily at the Queen's side, matching Abigail's assurances with Whig admonitions, not easily at times to be distinguished from threats.

On top of this came Nottingham's change of sides, and the prospect that the dear Church entrusted to Anne's keeping would soon gain that safeguard against hypocrisy and blasphemy for the sake of office for which it had so long and so earnestly striven—which the Queen had always wished it should have. The combination of the Whigs with even part of the Church party seemed a strange, unnatural thing. Nevertheless, the Queen felt that for the Whigs to carry the Occasional Conformity Bill meant a sensible mitigation of those sectarian broils which had always vexed her so sorely, and a real victory for the Church.

A final effort was made to gain Marlborough and some of the Whig leaders. The peace policy must go through, but all personal issues could be smoothed over. The Queen sent for Somers, Halifax, and Cowper. Not one of the Whigs would yield; and Marlborough was bound to the Grand Alliance. When it was found that the Opposition meant to play their hand for what it was worth, Oxford resolved to match their stake—to match it and to overbid it.

Marlborough landed at Greenwich on November 17, remained during November 18 at Greenwich Hospital, and waited on the Queen only the next day. Anne gave Oxford her own account of the interview. "The Duke of Marlborough came to me yesterday as soon as I had dined, made a great many of his usiall proffessions of duty and affection to me. He seemed dejected and very uneasy about this matter of the publick accounts, stayed neare an hour and saw nobody heare but my self."

The account which St John received of this audience drew from him the following comment:

The Duke of Marlborough I have seen once, but it has been in public, so that I am very much a stranger to his Grace's sentiments. I hear however that . . . in his conversation with the Queen he has spoken against what we are doing; in short *his fate hangs heavy upon him*; and he has of late pursued every council [*sic*] which was worst for him.

But it was not only Marlborough upon whom Fate hung heavy. Three years would see a fuller unfolding. Marlborough was to pass the last decade of his life in his Oxfordshire home in honour and splendour. St John was to dwell attainted, in exile, cast off even by the Pretender to whom he had fled, and, with all his matchless abilities, never again in thirty years to speak in Parliament or hold office under the Crown.

At length the day of great debate arrived. Whatever the misgivings of Ministers, these bold and hardy men played their hand magnificently. In the Queen's Speech we discern the literary parade and polish of Bolingbroke, and also that comprehension of all the political values which he shared with Oxford. The Queen read her speech herself. Every statement, every guarding phrase, every word, should be studied by those who wish to bring back again to themselves the passions and artifices of those days in their pristine force. The whole story is there in all its truth, and with all its lies. Every appeal that the Government could make to its supporters, every affront profitable to offer to the other side, found a place in this adroit and provocative declaration. The first sentence contained what was meant to be a cut at Marlborough, and drew out the main lines of party conflict. "I am glad that I can now tell you that *notwithstanding the arts of those who delight in war*, both place and time are appointed for opening the Treaty of a general Peace." The second affirmed what was not only false, but known to be false. "Our allies, especially the States-General, whose interest I look upon as inseparable from my own, have, by *their ready concurrence, expressed their entire confidence in me*." This was followed by assurances about the Protestant religion, the succession, and by a eulogy on the blessings of Peace and Plenty in which all might concur.

After the Queen had read her Ministers' speech, which was also what she meant and wished to say herself, she took an unusual course. Laying aside her robes, she returned to the House *incognito*, as the phrase went, and sat in a special box prepared for her. Thus the Lords would debate her words in her presence, as though in Cabinet. After the Ministerial proposal of the customary address of thanks uprose—lank, sombre, cadaverous—Nottingham. High Tory, High Churchman, trusted leader of the country clergy, statesman who had now extorted the Occasional Conformity Bill from the Whigs, carrying with him in that small, narrowly balanced assembly eight or ten peers in his following, shaking the bishops where they sat, Nottingham moved his amendment to add to the Lords' reply the crucial words "that no peace could be safe or honourable to Great Britain, or Europe, if Spain and the West Indies were allotted to any branch of the house of Bourbon."

The Government speakers took the line that this was not the moment to debate the issue of Spain, for which another day would be found, but rather to thank the Queen for her Speech. Accordingly they met Nottingham's amendment by moving what is called the 'previous question'—*ie.*, that "the question be not now put." On this the Government was defeated by a single vote. Marlborough sat an impressive figure through its course. "He was at the head of the Whigs," wrote Oxford to Strafford a few days later. He was bound to speak in any case, but chance gave him an advantage. Lord Anglesey, who had hastened back with Ormonde from Ireland, spoke late, and said, "We might have enjoyed that blessing [of peace] soon after the battle of Ramillies, if the same had not been put off by some persons, whose interest it was to prolong the war." This repeated the malignant sentence of the Royal Speech, and fixed the charge directly upon Marlborough by reference to Ramillies, of which certainly he had no need to feel ashamed. He had never had much practice in speaking, but he was always able to express himself with force and dignity. In those days the weightiest speeches were often the shortest. He rose and said:

"I think myself happy, in having an opportunity given me, of vindicating myself on so material a point, which my enemies have so loudly, and so unjustly laid to my charge before a person [here he bowed to the Queen where she sat] who, knowing the integrity of my heart, and the uprightness of my conduct, will not fail to do me justice. I refer myself to the Queen whether, while I have had the honour to serve her Majesty as general and plenipotentiary, I have not constantly informed her, and her council, of all the proposals of peace that have been made: and have not desired instructions for my conduct on that subject. I can declare with a safe conscience, in the presence of her Majesty, of the illustrious assembly, and of that Supreme Being, Who is infinitely above all the powers upon earth, and before Whom, according to the ordinary course of nature, I must soon appear, to give an account of my actions, that I was ever desirous of a safe, honourable and lasting peace; and that I always have been very far from any design of prolonging the war for my own private advantage, as my enemies have most falsely insinuated. My advanced age, and the many fatigues I have undergone, make me earnestly wish for retirement and repose, to think of eternity during the remainder of my days; the rather, because I have not the least motive to desire the continuance of the war, having been so generously rewarded, and had honours and riches heaped upon me, far beyond my desert and expectation, both by her Majesty and her Parliaments. I think myself bound to this public acknowledgment to her Majesty and my country, that I shall always be ready to serve them, if I can but crawl along, to obtain an honourable and lasting peace; but at the same time, I must take the liberty to declare, that I can, by no means [join in] the measures that have lately been taken to enter into a negotiation of peace with France, upon the foot of the seven preliminary articles; for I am of the same opinion with the rest of the Allies, that the safety and liberties of Europe would be in imminent danger, if Spain and the West Indies were left to the house of Bourbon; which, with all humility, and as I think myself in duty bound, I have declared to her Majesty, whom I had the honour to wait on, after my return from Holland: and therefore, I am for inserting in the address the clause offered by the Earl of Nottingham."

It had been expected that this speech with its profound effect would finish the debate, but the division was not until the next day, and Cowper, Bishop Burnet, and Halifax flung in their discharges in Marlborough's support. Again the couriers for all Europe were waiting upon the result. They left with joyful reports from the ambassadors that the Government had been beaten. Upon the voting the next day Oxford and the Ministers, who had counted upon a majority of ten, found themselves defeated by twelve. In the sensation and stir which followed the voting of all these solid, tough, amazingly capable oligarchs, the Queen rose from her seat in her private box, and the high functionaries pressed forward to attend her. Would she, asked Shrewsbury, give her hand to him to be led from the House, or would she prefer the hereditary Lord Great Chamberlain, Lord Lindsey, to conduct her? "Neither of you," said Anne, and with a wave of her hand she beckoned the Duke of Somerset, still in a sense a Cabinet Minister, but who had voted against the Government and the address to the Crown, and who, to quote Swift, "was louder than any in the House for the clause against peace," to lead her forth.

This proceeding staggered every one. According to the rules of this intense game, upon which, be it remembered, the fortunes not only of Britain but of Europe depended, such an event betokened the fall of the Ministry.

The sequel to the vote in the Lords marks again the power of the House of Commons. Against them were the Lords, the allied princes and sovereigns of Europe, the victorious Commander, all the interest of the Whig Party, and, it must also be urged, the honour and faith of Britain to a European League which she had long led. Up to this point it had been believed that an adverse vote in the House of Lords on a major issue of confidence would overthrow the Ministry. But the Tory majority in the Commons cared nothing for all this. They meant to beat the Whigs and stop the war, and their will prevailed. Walpole, by ever-growing quality and performance now become in fact leader of the Opposition in the Commons, had moved the same amendment to the address on the same day. It was rejected by 232 to 106. Thus those Ministers who had by backstairs intrigue and royal favour insinuated themselves into office without due Parliamentary support had now exchanged this questionable, precarious foundation for a Parliamentary majority, which proved to them a rock around which all the tides, currents, and waves of political life swirled in vain. The Queen's undermining gesture after the division in the Lords revealed her to be wavering on the verge of reluctantly deserting Oxford, as she had blithely deserted Marlborough and Godolphin. But the vote of the Commons restored her nerve. The Crown and Commons together could override all other forces in the realm. This was the fact which after some delay proved decisive.

Upon Marlborough's speech and vote in the debate on December 7, Oxford resolved to proceed to all possible extremities against him. The Lord Treasurer's confidant, Drummond, now in England advising Ministers, wrote that very night to tell Heinsius that Marlborough was to be dismissed from the command of the Army, and that the Duke of Ormonde would take his place. Actually this was not effected for another three weeks. There were two reasons for the delay. The first was to gain time to blacken his character by bringing the report of the Commission of Accounts before the House of Commons. The second was the difficulty of convincing the Queen that she could break him publicly without danger to herself.

On December 15 the Commons called for the report of the Commissioners of Public Accounts, and on the 17th for the documents on which it was based. This damaging indictment, the most hostile that lifelong foes and faction could devise, was circulated under obligations of secrecy to all the Members on the 21st. The Commons were then adjourned for Christmas until January 14. Thus Oxford and St John planned to have one side of the case only under the eyes of those who would judge it for three weeks before any answer could be made. At the same time they hoped that rumours of the gravity of the charges against Marlborough and of scandalous revelations would spread far and wide in an atmosphere of mystery and suspicion.

When these tactics were discerned Marlborough himself published in the *Daily Courant* the letter of justification which he had sent from The Hague to the Commissioners. The letter made so considerable an impression in that buzzing, excited Court and in the London world that the Government thought it best to publish the report, which was accordingly done on December 29. By this the impression was created that there was a case of peculation disclosed against Marlborough, to which he had an answer, but that the matter must now go forward to a Parliamentary decision. As the Ministers were sure of their majority in the House of Commons, it was obvious that some formal censure upon the Duke was intended, and would be inflicted.

Thus armed, Oxford used all his influence with the Queen. He did not confine himself to the dismissal of Marlborough. He demanded from Anne a simultaneous extraordinary creation of peers, to be sure of a majority in both Houses. The two proposals went forward together. Anne was already inclined to the second. She had been induced to confer an English peerage—the Dukedom of Brandon—upon the Duke of Hamilton. The recipient of this honour claimed the right to sit and vote in the House of Lords as an English peer. No such case had previously arisen. The matter had been sharply debated on December 10. Where majorities were so narrow every vote counted, and the bringing in of Scottish nobles under English peerages was a serious party issue. The Whigs, using their majority, succeeded in defeating this proposal by a majority of five. The Queen, who listened to this debate as to others, took it as an attack upon her prerogative. No one had ever questioned before the power of the Crown to create peers, and the fact that a man was a Scottish peer already could be no disability to him. She therefore agreed to Oxford's plan to overcome the Whigs in the Lords by making twelve additional Tory peers at one stroke. This memorable decision was taken, and its consequences rolled forward in our history.

The Queen still shrank, though not on any grounds of compunction, from the step upon which the world waited of dismissing Marlborough while all preparations were still going forward for another campaign. Oxford and St John worked upon her fears. In this they went to all lengths in malice and mendacity. They warned the Queen that she had now reached the same parting of the ways which had confronted her grandfather over the execution of the great Lord Strafford. To Charles I's faithless surrender at that crisis they ascribed his ruin and slaughter. To desert chosen and trusted Ministers in the hour of stress was only to redouble all existing difficulties and dangers. The Ministers declared that for their protection not only must the extraordinary creation of peers be made, but that Marlborough should be publicly broken, and that the Duke and Duchess of Somerset should be dismissed from the Queen's presence. Unless this were done, and done at once, they could not guarantee that the Whigs, who were in fact, they suggested, the Cromwellians of sixty years before, with Marlborough at their head, would not thrust her from her throne, and deprive her of her liberty and perhaps of her life. Marlborough, they hinted, would reign in her stead.

Such arguments prevailed upon the Queen. Marlborough appeared at Court for the last time in Queen Anne's reign on December 30. He was still Captain-General and a member of the Cabinet. No Whigs attended, and he stood alone among his enemies. He was shunned by all. "Nobody hardly took notice of him," wrote Swift, who received an exulting account from his Ministerial friends. Such a spectacle, though entirely in accordance with the character of such tribes, is none the less unpleasant. There he stood, stared at and scorned, with no protection but his composure and his fame. The Cabinet Council on the following day, with the Queen presiding, recorded the following decision:

> Being informed that an information against the Duke of Marl-
> borough was laid before the House of Commons, by the commis-
> sioners of the public accounts, her Majesty thought fit to dismiss him

from all his employments, that the matter might undergo an impartial investigation.

That night Queen Anne wrote the letter to her servant and counsellor of thirty years, and the builder of her fame and power, which ended for ever all relations between them. We do not know the terms in which Oxford and Abigail prompted her to write, because Marlborough was so moved by reading them that he flung the letter in the fire. His answer tells the tale.

Marlborough to the Queen

Jan. 1, 1712

I am very sensible of the honour your Majesty does me in dismissing me from your service by a letter of your own hand, though I find by it that my enemies have been able to prevail with your Majesty to do it in the manner that is most injurious to me. And if their malice and inveteracy against me had not been more powerful with them than the consideration of your Majesty's honour and justice, they would not have influenced you to impute the occasion of my dismission to a false and malicious insinuation, contrived by themselves, and made public when there was no opportunity for me to give in my answer, which they must needs be conscious would fully detect the falsehood and malice of their aspersions, and not leave them that handle for bringing your Majesty to such extremities against me.

But I am much more concerned at an expression in your Majesty's letter which seems to complain of the treatment you had met with. I know not how to understand that word, nor what construction to make of it. I know I have always endeavoured to serve your Majesty faithfully and zealously through a great many undeserved mortifications. But if your Majesty does intend, by that expression, to find fault with my not coming to the Cabinet Council, I am very free to acknowledge that my duty to your Majesty and country would not give me leave to join in the counsel of a man who, in my opinion, puts your Majesty upon all manner of extremities. And it is not my opinion only, but the opinion of all mankind, that the friendship of France must needs be destructive to your Majesty, there being in that Court a root of enmity irreconcilable to your Majesty's Government and the religion of these kingdoms. I wish your Majesty may never find the want of so faithful a servant as I have always endeavoured to approve myself to you.

The New Year's Day *Gazette* announced the creation of the twelve peers (among whom was Abigail's husband), and the dismissal of Marlborough from all his offices. The most pregnant comment was made by Louis XIV: "The affair of displacing the Duke of Marlborough will do all for us we desire."

CHAPTER NINETY

The Visit of Prince Eugene

ᛋᚨ 1712, January-March ᛞᚹ

THE impact of the Hanoverian manifesto on the London world was serious. Many Tories were shaken by it. Few there were who did not ask
themselves how they would stand when this reproachful Prince was
their King and master. If they held together it was for mutual protection. Thus the crisis lasted. The Hanover complaint met its counter-
blast in Swift's *Conduct of the Allies*. This cool and massive catalogue
of all the shortcomings of the Dutch, of the Empire, of the German
states, constitutes an indictment filled with just counts. Being primed
with the secret information of Ministers, Swift was able to expose the
recent neglect of the Dutch to accept their part in Marlborough's
scheme of wintering on the frontiers. He represented the allies as a
tribe of recreants and spongers who had failed in their engagements
and thriven on the victories and subsidies of England. In many ways
the booklet was inevitably a tribute to Marlborough. But nothing could
have been better devised to create schism in the Grand Alliance at a
time when the French were still in arms and the war in progress. No
one can dispute many of Swift's reproaches against the allies. But the
Dutch at least had an overwhelming rejoinder. Although a far smaller
community, they had maintained continuously in Flanders double the
army of England. They had repeatedly desired to make peace. They
had been forced to continue the war by Queen Anne—for that was
how they could state it—upon the strange cry, "No peace without
Spain," which had arisen from English party politics. They had shed
their blood for this to please England. Now they were insulted and

(851)

about to be deserted. But to the Tories all this was the best October ale. They salved their conscience by abusing their allies.

For all his partisanship Swift was shocked at Marlborough's dismissal. "These are strong remedies," he wrote (December 31); "pray God the patient is able to bear them. The last Ministry people are utterly desperate."

Marlborough bore his graceless treatment with dignity. Apart from the flash of anger which Anne's letter had extorted from him, his bearing was serene and even cheerful. He spoke and wrote as if his affairs belonged to less dismal chapters of history. He felt himself supported by the interest of one of the great parties in the island. He knew that he had the goodwill and confidence of the whole of the Grand Alliance. He was sure the armies he had led, and particularly the British troops, thought well of him. Although no man of spirit cares to have a task of which he is master taken from his hands while still unfinished, he was unfeignedly relieved not to have to risk his military fame and long-strained luck at the beck and direction of Oxford and St John and the rest of his Tory foes. The balm of ease, after ceaseless toil and thought, flowed out upon his soul. Everything in his behaviour shows that the oft-repeated wishes of his home letters for peace and quiet were sincere.

It is remarkable that, although while in power Marlborough complained often of his treatment in his secret letters to Godolphin and Sarah, and showed himself so sensitive to the attacks of the Press and the pamphleteers, once he became a private person without responsibility for national interests, no word is ever known to have escaped him of reproach or self-pity. Up till the moment when he was dismissed from his offices we have an enormous mass of correspondence both public and private relating to the war and politics. But henceforth, except for a few farewell letters, he wrapped himself in almost complete silence. A handful of letters to Sarah in rare intervals of separation, a few on business, a few on politics (mostly to Hanover), one about the Woodstock election, and a few asking for some assistance or protection for faithful servants, or wounded or unemployed officers, are all that have been found during these years of exile and obloquy.

The Whigs raised the loudest outcry in their power, and their newspapers strove to contend with the cataract of libels and abuse which the Ministers unloosed. History was searched for a parallel to Marlborough's fall, and the name of Belisarius was now on many lips. Sarah asked Bishop Burnet to explain the allusion to her, and when he told her of the Emperor Justinian's ill-usage of his great general she inquired the cause. The Bishop is said to have replied, "It was because he had the broth of a wife." But perhaps this was only what he thought of afterwards.

The tale of Marlborough's disgrace astounded Europe. It was everywhere, even in France, regarded as a prodigy of ingratitude by a sovereign towards a servant and subject. It had been a strange experience for friend and foe to watch the Queen seemingly tearing down with both hands the whole structure of European policy, the building of which had been the task and glory of her reign. When she proceeded to strike at the architect of her own and her country's fame and power, amazement and scorn were universal.

In the armies which he had led the shock and grief at his dismissal were painful. General Kane in his *Memoirs* expressed the overwhelming opinion of British officers.

> And now, after this great Man had reduced the Common Enemy of Europe to the last Extremity, had taken the last Barrier of his Kingdom, which lay now open to the Allies, his Army dispirited, and their Courage, and his whole Nation in a most miserable Condition; I say, after he had done all these great Things so much to the Honour of the British Nation, was he ignominiously traduc'd, and turn'd out of all Employ, and even forc'd to fly his Country, of which he had been so great an Ornament; and this done by a Set of vile profligate Men, who had insinuated themselves into the Favour of the weak Queen, and were at this Time carrying on a scandalous underhand Treaty with the Grand Enemy of Europe.

This feeling was shared by every rank. Corporal Matthew Bishop was consternated. "On hearing that it was confirmed that he was no longer to command, it terrified my Soul to such a Degree, that I could not rest Night or Day."

The corporal's emotions led him into poetry, and he gave vent to the following lines—often quoted, though their author is usually forgotten.

God and a Soldier Men alike adore,
When at the Brink of Danger, not before;
The Danger past, alike are both requited,
God is forgot, and the brave Soldier slighted.

But a friend was approaching. Charles III had quitted Spain in October, and assumed his duties as the Emperor Charles VI. At Milan he heard of the French peace preliminaries, and wrote his protest at once to Queen Anne. It was not until he reached Innsbruck a week later, and met his Council of Regency, including Prince Eugene and Wratislaw, that he learned of the dismissal of Gallas. This was regarded by all as a great affront, but opinions were divided as to how it should be met. Eugene urged that no other Ambassador should be sent to London until full amends had been made. But the opposite counsels prevailed, and after two days' discussion the Emperor commanded Eugene himself to go to England and try to restore his relations with Queen Anne. This was, in fact, the plan which the luckless Gallas had urged during the whole summer Like most of the decisions of the Holy Roman Empire, it was adopted too late.

No guest could have been more unwelcome to Harley and St John than the famous warrior. They knew that his comradeship with Marlborough was proof against all shocks. They were sure that he would cross-question them about their peace negotiations. It was obvious, moreover, that his arrival would comfort and fortify the Whigs. They therefore without delay and by every channel repeatedly tried to prevent his coming. St John sent a stream of letters to Strafford at The Hague to turn him back, and to enlist the Dutch in this task. "Your Excellency is to discourage as much as possible this Prince from coming over. . . . It is high time to put a stop to this foreign influence on British councils; and we must either emancipate ourselves now, or be for ever slaves."

Eugene floated down the Rhine and reached The Hague in the middle of December. Here Strafford delivered his discouragements. Heinsius, completely cowed by the new English attitude, advised the Prince against the visit. A message was given him from St John that, owing to the ferment in men's minds in England, the Government could not be answerable for his safety. Eugene, impelled by further orders from the Emperor, replied by asking for a yacht and a frigate for a convoy. The request was presented to the Cabinet by Hoffmann. At first this was considered as a courtesy which could not be refused. But as the anxieties of Ministers grew their manners declined. Eventually they decided to refuse all assistance. Fresh instructions were sent to Strafford, who was also a member of the Admiralty Board, to deny Eugene all transport or protection on the seas. But this order took some time to reach The Hague.

Eugene pressed for transport and convoy to England. Strafford, not having received the latest Cabinet decision, left it to the captain of the frigate, to whom he sent an ambiguous note. The captain complied with alacrity; but the voyage was severe. For more than a week Eugene tossed about between Flushing and Harwich, buffeted by the waves and baffled by the winds. This was certainly the longest sea journey which this great man ever endured. The tale of his coming had outstripped him. When he reached Harwich he was told that all the towns between that port and London were crowded with people who had gathered from the countryside to welcome him and to look at him. Here we see with what attention and passion our ancestors followed the great events and heroic figures of their age. They were tough, but they nursed a strong sentiment. News travelled fast and far, and people formed their own opinions.

Eugene also learned of Marlborough's dismissal from all his offices. He was resolved to be a model of discretion; so, instead of landing at Harwich, he coasted round to the Thames. Up the Thames he sailed in the yacht. He was boarded by one of Marlborough's officers, and later by Drummond from the Court. "I had to tell him," reported Eugene to the Emperor,

> that since it was known all over the world what a firm and intimate friendship I had fostered with the Duke of Marlborough, now finding him in misfortune, I could not do otherwise than uphold my friendship with him, lest the world should say, and I leave it as an evil echo after me, that I deserted and abandoned a friend in his hour of sorrow and stress when fortune had forsaken him.

He had thought of landing at Greenwich, but there was a large gathering awaiting him there. He hoped to land at the Tower, but the wharf was black with people; so he came on with the tide as far as the Whitehall Stairs, where no one expected him. He took "the first cab he saw," and drove to Leicester House, the residence of the departed

Gallas, which was still maintained to receive him. At Leicester House Marlborough was the first to visit him. They were long together. The next morning he was to see the Queen. The Secretary of State conducted him in his own carriage to the Queen.

> She gave me audience in her Cabinet, and I found her somewhat embarrassed and aloof. I explained to her briefly my mission, and finally asked her with which Minister I should converse. I noticed, however, that she must have been primed beforehand, for she gave me as answer that she had resolved that the business already known to me by secret information should be dealt with only in Holland, and she could not depart from this.

The Prince observed that there were other matters besides, and especially the restoring of a perfect harmony between her Majesty and the Emperor. Anne was now being drawn beyond the limits of her Ministerial advice; so she said that her health would not enable her to see much of him, but her Ministers, meaning Oxford and St John, would hear all he had to say.

Eugene was two months in England. His anterooms in Leicester House were so crowded with notables, some of whom came a hundred miles to see him, that the floors cracked under their weight. Crowds surrounded the house continuously, and followed him cheering when he walked abroad "in modest dress, very thoughtful or *rêveur*," with "a way to toss his head on the right and the left to be seen of everybody." When he went to the Opera with Marlborough the spectacle of "those venerable and respectfull men sitting in a box together" attracted the eyes of the audience much more than the actors.

Shortly after his arrival tidings had come from Spain. Starhemberg, who had been reputed to be finished, had won a considerable action under the walls of Cardona. The enemy had been repulsed with the loss of his whole artillery. This news made a stir. To Oxford and St John it was most unwelcome. These Ministers, in whose eyes the Allies were "the common enemy," necessarily regarded a British and allied victory as a disaster. The Tory Party, while loyal to their leaders, had never reconciled themselves to the abandonment of the Spanish aim and catchword. Now it appeared the cause was not lost; perhaps we were winning after all. It was in this unfavourable atmosphere that the two ruling Ministers approached the formidable trial of strength involved in charging first Walpole and then Marlborough with peculation. This episode of domestic politics will be reserved for the next chapter. Both before and after it they laboured to raise the "ferment" they affected to deplore to the highest pitch.

During the month of February rumours ran rife in London that Prince Eugene and Marlborough were engaged in a plot to depose the Queen. Torcy gravely records in his memoirs how Eugene was to set London on fire, while Marlborough seized the person of the Queen. He safeguarded himself by the words, "It may be that those who tell these tales were ill-informed." This monstrous story was spread about the capital, and every effort was made by the Government to create a mood of panic which should react in their favour, both upon their majority in the Commons and still more upon the nerves of Anne.

There was, of course, no shred of truth in all this rubbish. Eugene's reports to the Emperor are preserved in the archives at Vienna, and are printed in the *Feldzüge*. They comprise dispatches written on the dates mentioned to the Cabinet by Oxford. They deal very candidly with English affairs and statesmen, but there is nothing to lend the slightest colour to the rumours of a revolutionary design.

The lie was given to all this chatter and buzz of horrible plots to stimulate the faithful and delude the vulgar when the Queen summoned Eugene to her presence on her birthday, and presented him with a diamond-hilted sword valued at £4000. If Ministerial beliefs had been on a par with their whisperings they must have expected that he would draw it and plunge it into her breast. Nothing of the kind occurred. On the contrary, during his last days in England Oxford made remarkable overtures to Eugene. His methods were characteristic. He got into touch with him through a friend who knew a friend of the Prince's, and by this devious channel arranged that he should visit Eugene up his backstairs in the dark of the night. His demeanour was most cordial, his two-hour talk discursive. But Harley had, as usual, a clear purpose behind his copious verbiage. He did not mean to make a personal enemy of Eugene, or let him leave the country with every contact broken. He exacted from the Prince a return visit. It was arranged with similar precautions, and proved equally sterile. "I entered his own house in the deepest secrecy," wrote Eugene, "through a particular door which is usually kept locked. We talked together confidentially, but as there is nothing material to report, I need not go into details."

Two of Eugene's rejoinders during his visit to London which went the rounds and have become well known are typical of the attitude which he consistently adopted. Burnet records that, he having mentioned to the Prince the remark of a Minister that Marlborough had "perhaps been once fortunate," Eugene replied, "No greater tribute could be given him, since he was always successful." When at a dinner Oxford toasted him as "the greatest general of the age," "If that be true," said Eugene, "I owe it to your lordship." Thus always did the famous Prince and warrior proclaim his friendship and admiration for his comrade of so many glorious days.

CHAPTER NINETY-ONE

The Peculation Charge

ᛃᚲ 1712, January ᚲᛃ

DURING Prince Eugene's visit the Government continued their campaign of detraction against the late Ministry, and above all against Marlborough. Next in their animosity and fear stood Walpole. They knew they had struck down the great man of their day. It was only after some years that Harley and St John realized that they had incurred the implacable vengeance of the great man of the future.

The first report of the Commission of Accounts had been presented to Parliament before the Christmas adjournment. The Commissioners were still at their task. Evidence was tendered to them which revealed an impropriety committed by Walpole a year earlier, when he was Secretary-at-War. In a contract for forage not made by him but for which he was responsible two sums of £500 had been paid to one of his personal friends, a certain Robert Mann. There was no suggestion that Walpole himself had benefited by the money. He had merely endorsed the bills and sent them to Mann. The explanation was sufficient to clear Walpole of personal corruption; but it showed a want of delicacy and propriety against which public servants would nowadays be required to keep especially on their guard.

Many of the members did not think the case very good, and deemed it unfair to use it against the Leader of the Opposition. This opinion manifested itself strongly as the party discussion proceeded. But Bromley clinched matters by saying bluntly that unless Walpole were got out of the way it would not be possible for the Government to carry through their business. His knowledge was too great, his attacks too damaging. His exclusion was, he said, the *unum necessarium*. On this appeal it was decided to go to all lengths against Walpole.

On January 17 Walpole was heard in his defence, and thereafter it was moved that he was "guilty of a high breach of trust and notorious corruption." An amendment was proposed to leave out the words "notorious corruption." The House rejected this by 207 votes to 155. It was then moved to commit him to the Tower during the pleasure of the House. On this the Opposition moved that the House should adjourn. The Government majority fell to only twelve. A further motion "that the said Robert Walpole be for the said offence expelled from this House" was carried by twenty-two. These figures tell their own tale. A majority of twelve on the crucial division was a poor showing for a Government which had a normal majority of between 100 and 150. Walpole was accordingly arrested and sent to the Tower.

Few even in the Tory Party considered Walpole at all affected in his honour. He was visited not only by the leading Whigs, and of course by Marlborough, but also by many other persons of consequence. His room in the Tower was more like the scene of a levee than a prison. The Ministers had gained their advantage in excluding their most dangerous antagonist from the House of Commons, but they were deeply concerned by the lack of support they had received from their own followers upon the critical division. It was resolved to take much greater care on the next occasion.

This was, of course, their attack upon Marlborough. Oxford and St John were by now alive to the difficulties of branding the champion of Britain in her age of glorious advance. For eight years in succession the House had passed its resolutions of thanks by overwhelming majorities and often unanimously. Every session delegations of its members had waited upon him to express their admiration and gratitude for his services. It was a sharp turn now, after he had been stripped of all office and was a private person, to inflict upon him by a purely party vote an insulting censure which sought to rank him with criminals.

Proposals were made to Marlborough's friends in the House that he should acquiesce in the report of the Commission, in which case the censures would be the mildest possible. On the other hand, if he resolved to defend himself and to oppose the Government it was hinted that severe measures would be taken. The 'gentlemen of England' in Oxford's phrase, would be used with vigour. Impeachment was their only weapon, for the Commons could not commit a peer to prison. That there was talk of impeachment is evident.

Evidently Marlborough was offered the resolutions which were afterwards passed by the House, with the threat of far worse if he resisted them. He refused point-blank. He was perhaps willing that the House should take note of the report and decline to act upon it because of his previous services. Nothing less than this would satisfy him. He would "rather lose his head."

Somers, under King William, when impeached for his share in the Partition Treaties of 1700, had appeared at the bar of the Commons, and by his eloquence and his facts had converted the assembly. Marlborough had been inclined to follow this precedent, but his friends, including certainly Godolphin, dissuaded him. Passions ran too high. The life of the Government was at stake. Every effort had been made to bring up their reserves. He would only court a greater humiliation by pleading in person. He therefore, with Godolphin's assistance, prepared a statement.

As this matter affects Marlborough so deeply it is better to record the principal features of this statement covering every point in the charges:

> The first Article in the Report is founded upon the deposition of Sir Solomon de Medina, by which you are informed of a yearly sum paid by him and his predecessor, contractors for Bread and Bread-waggons, to myself. This payment in my letter I have called a perquisite of the general or commander-in-chief in the Low Countries; and it has been constantly applied to one of the most important parts of the service there, I mean the procuring intelligence, and other secret service. . . .
>
> The commissioners are pleased to observe that these sums cannot be esteemed legal perquisites because they do not find them claimed or received by any other English general in the Low Countries. But I must take leave to affirm to this house, that this perquisite or payment has been allowed to the general or commander in chief in the Low Countries both before and ever since the Revolution, to enable him to carry on such secret services.
>
> In receiving this as an established and known perquisite, I have followed and kept up that usage, which I found in the army, when I first entered upon that service; and upon this ground alone I hope that this House will not think that I was unwarranted in taking it.
>
> Now as to the second Article in the Report. During the last war,

the allowances by parliament for the contingencies of the army, of which that of secret service is the principal, was £50,000 per ann. But this allowance fell so far short of the expense on that head, that upon the prospect of this war's breaking out, the late king assured him [calculated], that this last part of the service never cost him less than £70,000 per ann. However, the allowance of parliament for the whole contingent service during this war has been but £10,000 per annum, £3000 of which or thereabouts has generally gone for other contingencies than that of intelligence. The late king, being unwilling to come to parliament for more money, on that head of the service, proposed this allowance from the foreign troops, as an expedient to assist that part of the service, and commanded me to make the proposition to them; which I did accordingly, and it was readily consented to. By this means a new fund of about £15,000 per annum was provided for carrying on the secret service, without any expense to the public, or grievance to the troops from whom the allowance was made. . . .

This expedient being formed in the manner I have shewn, her majesty was pleased to approve it by her warrant, . . . [which] was countersigned by the secretary of state whose province it belonged to, as the only proper officer. . . .

I cannot suppose that I need to say how essential a part of the service this is, that no war can be conducted successfully, without early and good intelligence, and that such advices cannot be had but at a very great expense. Nobody can be ignorant of this, that knows anything of secret correspondence or considers the numbers of persons that must be employed in it, the great hazard they undergo, the variety of places in which the correspondence must be kept, and the constant necessity there is of supporting and feeding this service; not to mention some extraordinary expenses of a higher nature, which ought only to be hinted at. And I affirm, that whatever sums have been received on this account, have been constantly employed in procuring intelligence, in keeping correspondence, and other secret service. . . . And though the merit of our successes should be least of all attributed to the general, the many successful actions, such as have surpassed our own hopes, or the apprehensions of the enemy, in this present war in Flanders, to which our constant good intelligence has greatly contributed, must convince every gentleman, that such advices have been obtained, and consequently that this money has been rightly applied. . . .

Having given this full and faithful account of the rise and use of this deduction, it must, I flatter myself, appear to everybody that hears me, to have been a real service, as well as saving of money to the public. And though honour is due to the memory of the late king, who formed this expedient, and to her majesty, who approved of it, by her warrant, I cannot, upon this ground, apprehend any imputation to myself, who have pursued this, so much to the advantage of my country. . . .

The debate was fierce and solemn. The Members felt that in striking at Marlborough they were striking at the new greatness of their country. On the other hand, what would happen to their party if they did not strike home? But the defence was solid. Sir John Germaine, speaking from the bar, declared that he had served in the Low Countries under Prince Waldeck, and that that General had, as Marlborough declared, received the same perquisites and allowances for the purpose of military intelligence and Secret Service. Sir Charles Hedges, the Tory Secretary of State, who ten years before had countersigned the Queen's warrant under which Marlborough received the 2½ per cent., stood by his action and absolved the former Commander-in-Chief of all impropriety. There was no dispute about the warrant. Then up rose Brydges Paymaster and Accountant-General. No report of his speech is contained in the *Parliamentary History*, but Hoffmann's dispatch, unearthed by Klopp, shows that Brydges was particularly vigorous in emphasizing that the British people owed the information services to the careful expenditure of this money, and in consequence the Army had never been surprised. Brydges dared to say "that the proceedings were a scandal to the British people."

On the other side St John, Wyndham, Hanmer, and Edward Harley urged the infliction of the censure. Not only Whigs, but moderate Tories spoke on Marlborough's side. The House was full to overflowing. No fewer than 435 Members took part in the division, and it was carried by a majority of 276 against 165 that "the taking of several sums of money annually by the Duke of Marlborough from the contractor for foraging the bread and bread wagons in the Low Countries was unwarrantable and illegal." The Government, refusing a motion for adjournment which was moved by the Opposition, also carried "that the deduction of 2½ per cent. from the pay of the foreign troops in her Majesty's service is public money, and ought to be accounted for." On the two heads the sums involved were computed to amount to between £170,000 and £250,000. It remains only to be mentioned that Cardonnel's petty perquisite of 500 ducats, for which there was no excuse but custom, was made the ground for expelling him from the House, and that Mr Sweet, although it was proved that his deduction of 1 per cent. was likewise a customary fee to the Paymaster of the Forces, was ordered to be prosecuted.

It would have been natural after such resolutions for the Commons to impeach Marlborough at the bar of the Lords. However, no further steps were taken. One reason at least is obvious. The Duke of Ormonde was now Commander-in-Chief. The Ministers who had just obtained a party verdict against Marlborough authorized Ormonde to draw the same deduction upon the bread contract and bread wagons, and to receive the same 2½ per cent. on the pay of the foreign troops, and to use it for the same purposes as Marlborough had done. Thus, while inducing the House of Commons to condemn his practice, they themselves vindicated him by adopting it.

There is one final refutation of these charges, which has never yet been published. A year later at Utrecht in long procession the Princes and Courts of the Grand Alliance recorded their full approval of the deduction of the 2½ per cent., declared that it was their own money, and that it had been spent to their entire satisfaction.

The Electors of Cassel and Düsseldorf sent identical letters:

> * Although we agreed entirely that this deduction of 2½ per cent. for the Secret Services had been granted without expecting any rendering of account, the nature of the business demanding it, nevertheless we admit that we are fully satisfied and convinced that the said money has been disposed of for the above purposes, and we should think it an injury to the reputation of this great General if we did not declare that his prudent and wise handling of these sums has principally contributed, after the Grace of God, to the gain of so many glorious victories, and to the surprising successes which have accompanied the armies of the Allies during the whole course of this long war.
>
> And in order that a complete and full justice may be done from our side, we have to bear witness that we granted and accorded voluntarily the said 2½ per cent. to the said Duke of Marlborough for the above purposes and without the rendering of account.

It is to be noticed that these testimonies were recorded when Marlborough had fallen from power and was only a wanderer on the Continent. They were solemnly presented by the allied princes and states to the Peace Congress as an act of justice and as a salute to the General who had served them well.

Professor G. M. Trevelyan has declared that no one ever gave better value to England than Marlborough for every guinea he received. But this is not the point at issue. No single charge of corruption or malversation was ever proved against Marlborough, and the charges on which he was condemned were manifestly disproved. For two years all the malice of a triumphant faction and all the power of the Crown were remorselessly used to make a case against him. The Commission of Accounts ransacked the records of the Army in the confident expectation of finding that he had been accustomed to take a profit upon sales of commissions by officers to their successors, or on promotions to replace officers killed in action. This was one of the libels blatantly proclaimed against him by the Tory pamphleteers. It touched his conduct not only as Captain-General but as Colonel of the Guards. It is incredible that if such abuses had occurred they would not have been brought to light.

But the Tory lie stands upon the journals of the House of Commons. Marlborough's answers and the failure of his accusers did not bar a scandalous prosecution being set on foot against him for the recovery of all these sums expended so well in the British interests. Nor could they prevent a sneer or a smear remaining on the pages of history, and successive generations being content with the loose impression that there was something dishonest in Marlborough's conduct.

Marlborough was careful and thrifty in all he did. He saved money for himself and the public every week. His strictness about the funds, public and private, under his control descended to the smallest details. In a lavish and corrupt age he practised a severe, businesslike economy. He would take presents from the princes of the Alliance, and might even in the event of a peace and in certain circumstances have accepted the rewards of Louis XIV himself for services which were not incompatible with the interests of England. No doubt when, in the occupation of conquered territory, 'safeguards' were granted to individual owners, he took these payments as a kind of prize money. But where public money was concerned his record is impeccable. He is entitled to claim from his countrymen the declaration that he acted with strict integrity and according to his warrant in the administration of all Army funds entrusted to him. If this be challenged, let the contrary case be made.

CHAPTER NINETY-TWO

The Restraining Orders

ᘓ 1712, January-May ᘒ

THE Tories were now triumphant at home, and on January 29, 1712, their plenipotentiaries, the Bishop of Bristol and Lord Strafford, together with representatives of Holland and the Empire, met the French in conference at Utrecht. None of the Allies knew what secret understandings subsisted between England and France, but when the Marquis d'Huxelles announced the French proposals these were denounced at once as treating the allies of England as if they were vanquished states. The unconditional retention of Spain and the Indies by Philip V was claimed by the French to be finally settled. The rest of the French demands affronted the Dutch, the Germanic Princes, and the Empire. English interests alone were privileged. The anger of the allies knew no bounds, and in England outside the Court circle widespread wrath was mingled with wider shame. In the Commons the 'gentlemen' "stood by the Queen"; but in the Lords Halifax, in spite of the recent wholesale creation of peers, carried an address to continue the war rather than submit to such terms. This "ill-usage of the Queen" by war-loving factions in factious defiance of her Ministers, as St John viewed it, absolved him in his own opinion from all inconvenient obligations. He and Oxford began forthwith to negotiate a peace treaty with the French, the signature of which would bind the allies or leave them to their fate.

At this moment there occurred in the French royal family a remarkable, and many believed a sinister series of deaths. Only a sickly and infected infant now lay between the personal union of the crowns of France and Spain.

St John and Oxford proposed that Philip V should renounce the throne of Spain if he acceded to that of France, in which case France would receive compensation in Italy, and Spain would fall to the Duke of Savoy. The advantages offered to France in Italy were so substantial that Louis XIV agreed that the proposal should be made to Philip. The concession cost him little. It captivated the English Ministers, who saw themselves suddenly within reach of diverting Spain and the Indies from the house of Bourbon and vindicating after all the "No peace without Spain" cry, thus completely cutting the ground from under the Whigs. On May 28, while the messengers were riding to Madrid, Oxford told the Lords that peace upon these lines was near. But a new surprise was in store. Philip V chose at all costs to retain the Crown of Spain, which he had gained with his sword and with the love of the Spanish people through so many cruel years of war. All solutions were therefore destroyed, and Europe was confronted with the double deadlock which perhaps Louis XIV had foreseen—that Philip could not renounce the Crown of Spain. Upon this all the Allies called for the renewal of the war. No basis of peace, no treaty of any kind, was in sight. The armies were, in fact, already assembling, and such was the feeling in England that the Ministry ordered the Duke of Ormonde and the British forces to join them. Thus the only result of the Tory peace effort and intrigue with France, for the sake of which they had supplanted Marlborough and Godolphin and rendered their country odious to all its allies, had been to condemn all Europe to two more campaigns.

Ormonde reached The Hague on April 9, and assumed command of the British-paid forces, all of which, with the rest of the allies, were now marching to the points of assembly.

The allied army, concentrating beyond Tournai, amounted to 122,000 men, with 120 field cannon, apart from the siege-train. Against them stood Villars with 100,000 men, ill-equipped and with a weak artillery. When on May 17 Ormonde met Eugene at Tournai the physical ascendancy of the Allies was evident, and the purely military prospects bright. It was agreed to pass the Scheldt behind Bouchain, and to advance towards the enemy, either to attack him if he were ill posted or to lay siege to Quesnoy, a small but effective fortress ten miles south of Valenciennes.

On April 25/May 6 St John wrote desiring Ormonde to make sure that all the foreign troops paid by Britain should be kept under Ormonde's direct command—*i.e.* not merged with the similar mercenary forces in the Dutch pay.

In reply to this Ormonde reminded the Minister that in his instructions he "was ordered to act in conjunction with the Allies, in prosecuting the war with vigour; so that, should there happen a fair opportunity to attack the enemy, he could not decline it, if proposed by the Prince and States." And a few days later: "If there be a good opportunity to attack the enemy, and get into France, by the way of Champagne, I am sure the Prince and the States will press it, unless they hear from England that the peace is near being concluded."

The armies were now in presence of one another, and on May 10/21 St John wrote the following letter to Ormonde:

> Her Majesty, my Lord, has reason to believe that we shall come to an agreement upon the great article of the union of the two monarchies, as soon as a courier, sent from Versailles to Madrid, can return; it is therefore the Queen's positive command to your Grace that you avoid engaging in any siege, or hazarding a battle, till you have farther orders from her Majesty. I am, at the same time, directed to let your Grace know that the Queen would have you disguise the receipt of this order, and her Majesty thinks that you cannot want pretences for conducting yourself so as to answer her ends, without owning that which might, at present, have an ill effect if it was publicly known.

This was the notorious restraining order which later formed the principal article in St John's impeachment. But the postscript is not less remarkable:

> P.S. I had almost forgot to tell your Grace that communication is given of this order to the Court of France; so that if the Mareschal de Villars takes, in any private way, notice of it to you, your Grace will answer accordingly. If this order is changed on either side, we shall, in honour, be obliged to give notice of it to the other.

To Gaultier St John was even more explicit. "I asked Mr St John," wrote Gaultier to Torcy (May 21), "what Marshal Villars should do if by chance Prince Eugene and the Dutch attempted some offensive. He answered that there would be nothing to be done but to fall upon him *and cut him to pieces, him and his army.*"

It would have been a grievous, though a permissible, measure to tell Eugene, the States-General, and other members of the Alliance that the British forces would not fight until the peace treaty was settled one way or the other. But for an English Minister, acting in the name of the Queen, to conceal from the allies his intention, while disclosing it secretly to the enemy, was in fact to encompass the defeat of Eugene and the slaughter of the allies and comrades with whom the British troops had so long stood shoulder to shoulder. Nothing in the history of civilized peoples has surpassed this black treachery. The punishment meted out in after-years by their countrymen to the criminals concerned may lighten, but cannot efface, its indelible stain.

Ormonde, so popular and magnificent, so gallant in his youth, now showed himself the weak, base creature he was at heart. With his eyes open he lent himself to this shame; and it was no thanks to him that Eugene and the allied generals to whom Ormonde was bound in soldierly faith did not in fact suffer the fate wickedly contemplated by St John. But the Prince, who had so much experience of war and treachery, was vigilant; and the Dutch, fortunately for themselves, were wary. It was noticed that Villars, although but a league away from the superior confederate army, took no trouble to entrench his camp, and sent out no reconnaissances to test the strength of the allied forces. He lay as if to invite attack. He might well do this, for, according to St John's assurances through Gaultier and Torcy, as well as from the communications he had directly with Ormonde, he had a right to suppose that not only the redcoats but all the British-paid forces, numbering between forty and fifty thousand men, or nearly half Eugene's army, would desert at the moment of battle, and leave the rest an easy prey —in St John's words, to be "cut to pieces."

The apparent imprudence of so capable a general redoubled the suspicions of the allies. Eugene resolved to put Ormonde to the test. The Duke, though consenting to dishonour, was no adept in deceit. He failed at once as hero and as cheat. He could not meet Eugene and the allied generals as guests at his table without revealing his embarrassment. He could not withstand the hard questions which the Dutch Deputies asked in formal interviews.

When on June 7 a letter from St John came it expressed "the impatience her Majesty was in to hear whether the orders, sent on May 10, came safely and early to his hands, and the assurance she had of his punctual obedience to her commands in so nice and important a conjuncture." Ormonde had already described to St John the distrust among the allies by which he was encompassed. Now he struck a note new to the Secretary:

> There are several among them who do not hesitate to say aloud that they have been betrayed. I am afraid that if the conclusion of peace is postponed, *I shall find myself Commander only of the British national troops.* I am strengthened in this fear by the fact that the Elector of Hanover is strongly opposed to the peace, and will let his troops serve with the Dutch. I am also doubtful whether we can win over the Danes.

He ended with a belated and irresolute suggestion:

> You may guess how uneasy a situation I am in; and, if there be no prospect of action, I do not see of what use I am here; and, if it suit with her Majesty's service, I should be glad I might have leave to return to England.

He did not know how far men's minds had travelled upon the frenzy of despair which convulsed the councils at The Hague—councils secret now from those deemed "the English traitors." It was, in fact, seriously planned to disarm and arrest the twelve thousand British troops in Flanders. The famous redcoats whose martial honour stood so high in those professional camps were to be seized as hostages against the faithlessness of their Government.

This desperate project, hitherto recorded only in Continental histories, fortunately came to naught. That it was known to St John is shown by a sentence in his letter to Harley of this same date: "Some are even saucy enough to insinuate so far as to attempt seizing the British troops in Flanders." To such a point had the Queen and her new friends brought the Common Cause.

Rumours of the deadlock at headquarters travelled far and fast. Even "the gentlemen of England" were upset at the idea of a British Commander-in-Chief standing in the line with his allies but forbidden to give them true aid and succour. On May 28/June 8 Halifax brought the whole business before the Lords. He recounted the memorable victories of the Allies which had brought the "common enemy" of Christendom to extremities. He declared these prospects totally defaced by the orders given to the Queen's General not to act offensively against the enemy.

On this there was much questioning of the Government whether in fact any restraining orders had been given to Ormonde. The Lord Treasurer said

> that they who had the honour to serve the Queen could not reveal the orders she gave to her General without a particular direction from her Majesty; and that in his opinion those orders were not fit to be divulged. However, he would adventure to say that, if the Duke of Ormonde had refused to act offensively, he did not doubt, but he had followed his instructions: and it was prudence not to hazard a battle upon the point of concluding a good peace, especially considering they had to deal with an enemy so apt to break his word.

This was pretty blunt. St John in the Commons had no mind to go so far. He covered himself with denials, which were accepted by his supporters, and, as Swift said, "these all went swimmingly." In the Lords the matter was more sharply probed. "Though the Duke of Ormonde," said Oxford, "may have refused to hazard a general action, yet I can be positive he would not decline joining with the allies in a siege, orders having been sent him for that purpose." This eminently civilian idea that a siege is a compromise midway between a battle and a treaty gave Marlborough his opening. He had come to the House resolved to support or second Halifax. He now rose and said, "I do not know how to reconcile the orders not to hazard a battle and to join in a siege to the rules of war, since it is impossible to make a siege without either hazarding a battle in case the enemy attempt to relieve the place, or shamefully raising the siege." He continued:

> "Altho' the negotiations for peace may be far advanced, yet I can see no reason which should induce the Allies or ourselves to remain inactive, and not push on the war with the utmost vigour, as we have incurred the expense of recruiting the army for the service of another year. That army is now in the field, and it has often occurred that a victory or a siege has produced good effects and manifold advantages, when treaties were still farther advanced than is the present negotiation. And as I am of opinion that we should make the most we can for ourselves, the only infallible way to force France to an entire submission is to besiege and occupy Cambrai or Arras, and to carry the war into the heart of that kingdom."

Argyll, newly returned from Spain, responded to this appeal, though not in wholehearted support of Marlborough. Halifax, not relishing the prospects of a division, was now willing to withdraw his motion. This was not allowed. In the closing moments "Swallow" Poulett flung the grossest insult at Marlborough which his busy brain could frame.

> "Nobody [he said] could doubt of the Duke of Ormonde's courage and bravery; but that he was not like a certain General, who led troops to the slaughter to cause a great number of officers to be knocked on the head in a battle, or against stone walls, in order to fill his pockets by disposing of their commissions."

Finally Oxford, speaking again, gave the most positive assurances that neither he nor the Government would ever engage in a separate peace. His words were remarkable: "Nothing of that nature was ever intended; for such a peace would be so foolish, villainous, and knavish that every servant of the Queen must answer for it with his head to the nation." "The Allies," he assured the Lords, "are acquainted with our proceedings, and satisfied with our terms." Wharton, whose interventions were always pointed, besought the Lords to bear in mind these words "foolish, villainous, and knavish," and also the words "answer for it with his head." Ministers obtained a majority of sixty-eight to forty. But Parliament and the nation did not know what the Government had done, and what the allies, now paraded as in contented accord, were really thinking.

Marlborough had sat silent under Poulett's taunt. It was evident that it was not one to be answered with words. As soon as the House was up he sent Lord Mohun to Poulett with an invitation, in the style of those days, "to take the air in the country." Poulett had not been expecting such a retort. "Is this a challenge?" he asked. Mohun replied that the message explained itself. He added, "I shall accompany the Duke of Marlborough, and your lordship will do well to provide a second." A tragic episode was soon to prove that when Mohun spoke in this way he was in earnest. Affairs of this kind were usually kept by gentlemen secret from their wives. Poulett was, however, unable to conceal his agitation. Lady Poulett acted promptly and with the zeal of an affectionate spouse. She wrote no fewer than five letters to the Secretary of State, imparting the unhappy position in which her lord now found himself. Although he was twelve years younger than Marlborough, he felt politics ought not to take this unpleasant turn. In her first letter his wife begs Lord Dartmouth "to order the guards to be ready upon two noblemen's falling out; she will listen when Lord Mohun comes, and will send a more speedy and exact account." Her next note runs, "I listend and itt is my Lord Mallbouro that has challings my Lord by Lord Mohun. Pray lett him be secured immedatly." In a third note, headed "Saturday morning," Lady Poulett again urges Lord Dartmouth to send guards, and adds, "the Treasurer must make itt up with Halifax . . . that noe more quarills happens one this occasion which I hope you and the Queen will prevent for the present. Pray burn my letters and send the very next gard att hand to secure my Lord and Lord Mohun."

Thus energetically did Lady Poulett arouse Dartmouth to a just sense of the impending danger. The Secretary of State went at once to Marlborough, and personally requested him "not to stir abroad." To reassure the Pouletts two sentries were forthwith placed outside their house. These measures taken, the Queen was informed. She sent Marlborough a royal command that "this might go no further," and to require his word to that effect. Here were other "restraining orders." Eventually some sort of apology was made by Poulett. In this age of duelling, and while charges of selling commissions were actually the subject of official investigation against Marlborough, it was hardly possible to imagine a more just provocation than Poulett's words. This did not prevent Swift and his *Examiner* pack from crying out in scandalized virtue against party duels.

CHAPTER NINETY-THREE

Exile

∿ ᵼɑ 1712-13 ᴅᵹ

THE presentation of the proposed terms of a separate peace to Parliament on June 6 forced from Marlborough his last public action during the remaining life of the Queen. These terms were a shock to many supporters of the Government, but the Ministerial defence, the realization that the main issue was decided and that the Tory policy had prevailed, commanded great majorities in both Houses. Marlborough made his protest and declared, "That the measures pursued in England for a year past were directly contrary to her Majesty's engagements with the Allies, sullied the triumphs and glories of her reign, and would render the English name odious to all other nations." Strafford replied with asperity, saying "That some of the Allies [meaning the Dutch] would not show such backwardness to a peace as they had hitherto done but for a member of that illustrious assembly [meaning the Duke of Marlborough] who maintained a secret correspondence with, and endeavored to persuade them to carry on the war; feeding them with hopes that they should be supported by a strong party here." Cowper, alluding to Strafford's foreign mode of speech, rejoined "That the ex-Ambassador had been so long abroad that he had almost forgotten, not only the language, but the Constitution of his own country. That, according to our laws, it could never be suggested as a crime . . . to hold correspondence with our allies; . . . whereas it would be a hard matter to justify the conduct of some persons in treating clandestinely with the common enemy."

Nothing could, however, stem the tide, and the treaty terms were approved in the Lords by no fewer than eighty-one to thirty-six. Twenty-four lords recorded their formal protest. Among them are the names of Somerset, Godolphin, Devonshire, Haversham, Wharton, Marlborough, Nottingham, Mohun, Townshend, and Cowper. The majority ordered this to be expunged from the journals of the House, but the powerful nobles and politicians concerned, defying Parliamentary laws, had the terms of their protest circulated throughout the country, and only printers and publishers were punished for the offence.

Having thus placed himself on record, Marlborough withdrew finally to the country. Blenheim was, of course, only a skeleton, and all work upon it stopped. But he still had his house at St Albans, and Marlborough House, in London, had been open for nearly a year. He lived during the summer months in rustic pomp at Holywell, observing with impassive eye the procession of military disasters which fell upon the Allies, and the destruction of his achievements in the campaigns of 1710 and 1711. On Blenheim Day he gave a feast, which Godolphin, Cowper, Walpole, and a large company attended. He had pitched his campaigning tent upon the bowling-green. In this historic tabernacle most of the great decisions of his ten campaigns had been taken. The tent, we are told, "was magnificent, being of Arras-work, and very curious in its kind." It stood there the rest of the summer, and sightseers resorted to it in crowds from the countryside at a fee of sixpence. The hostile Press declared he was using army tents to shelter his faction and to amass greater opulence. The venom and scurrility of the attacks made upon him by the Government-paid or otherwise procured writers from Swift downward exceeded anything known before or since. If he had been the vilest criminal, if he had been guilty of cowardice or treachery in the field, if he had led the English armies to a series of shameful defeats, nothing more could have been said against him.

During the autumn Marlborough resolved to leave England. There was then, and has been since, much controversy about his reasons, and so many can be given that a certain air of mystery still shrouds the event. There are, as usual, two contradictory explanations for his action. The first is that he wished to go, that the Cabinet would have prevented him, but that Harley secured him his passport from the Queen. Alternatively, it is said that he did not wish to go, but that

Harley, fearing to have him in the country, forced him into exile by the threat of using letters or information supplied by the French Government either of Marlborough's correspondence with Saint-Germain or of his offers to make peace in 1708.

Both these theories are plausible. Marlborough would certainly have liked to live in England; but this ceaseless girding and insult directed upon him by the Court and the Ministry, with all their resources, was not calculated to make life pleasant even in the country in summertime. Winter was now drawing near, and with it the reassembly of a Parliament eager to hound him down, and ready to approve every new affront or injury which Ministers might suggest. Although the Whig nobility, the bulk of the officers who had served under him, and the mass of ordinary folk were still friendly, and as the social scale was descended, enthusiastic, a definite change had been produced during this year by the torrent of calumny unloosed and impelled against him.

In those days of brief triennial Parliaments a new election was distant but a year. If Marlborough remained in England nothing could prevent his greatness from becoming the most obvious target. Instead of the bolts and balls he was accustomed to face in the field, he would find himself in the midst of a filthy warfare of slander and abuse. The election of 1713 might well be fought on fouling his name and reputation. The worst motives would be imputed to whatever he did. If he exerted himself it would be his disappointed malice; if he remained silent it was no doubt his guilty conscience. All these long years of camp and march we have seen in his letters the longing for home and peace—the peaches ripening on the wall, the great building at Woodstock growing from day to day, rest with children and Sarah at his side. But this prospect now seemed to be defiled. He could not at this time find happiness or even peace in England.

There was a fierce spirit among the veteran officers of the Army now at home in England. Some had been forced to resign their commissions; others had seen promotion go on party grounds to their rivals, their juniors, and, as they judged, their inferiors. They felt that the fruits of the long struggle which had been won, and in which they had risked their lives, were being wantonly cast away, and that the military fame of England, till now glorious, was being dishonoured. The idea that the British Army, which had borne itself so proudly on the Continent, had become odious in all the camps for deeds of baseness and

deceit obsessed their minds. These were hard men, wrought by a lifetime of war, to whom bloodshed was a profession. Their swords were at
their sides as they paced the streets of London. At any moment—in
the park, in the coffee-houses, in the taverns—taunts might be thrown
and passions break loose, and a bloody deed be done. Whatever happened would be laid to Marlborough's account. To leave the country
was to be free from all this. The whole Continent regarded Marlborough as a prodigy. The lustre of his victories, the sagacious consistency
of his policy, the enormous changes in the relative power of nations
which had followed from his conduct, assured him a reverential welcome everywhere outside France. He was rich; money could be transferred abroad; there was Mindelheim, which he had never seen. In
England he was a prey. In Europe he was a Prince. Here, then, was
peace and a broad sanctuary. Why tarry among foes and fogs?

A more directly practical reason for his going abroad is apparent in
the State suits set on foot against him. The Attorney-General was slowly moving forward the prosecution which, pursuant to the resolution of
the Commons, required that Marlborough should repay to the Exchequer all the moneys he had expended upon the Army intelligence
service in a ten years' successful war. This might well confront him
with a judgment to find more than a quarter of a million sterling. Another suit, equally vexatious, had been started against him by the
Crown about the expenses of the "monument of national gratitude,"
Blenheim. Careful as he had been, it was alleged that when the Government payments were in arrear he had written from the front to keep
the workmen in employment for a few weeks upon his orders or
Sarah's, or otherwise had interfered. The Queen was now moved to use
this against him. A process to require him to repay at least £30,000 was
on foot. If he left England these processes might be suspended. If he
remained at home and at variance with the Ministry he might be sensibly impoverished. One could not tell the lengths which malice would
go as it fed upon triumph.

Marlborough himself wished to leave the country. There was no necessity for Oxford to put pressure upon him. The "major part of the
Ministers, particularly Mr St John, was against it, being afraid of his
Grace as well abroad as at home and thought their power would secure
them better against him here." It was Oxford who, behind their backs,
procured Marlborough's passport from the Queen, and took pains to

obtain Marlborough's personal acknowledgment to him for it. Anne was favourable to Marlborough's wish and remarked, "He did wisely." The pass permitted Marlborough to go into foreign parts,

> whithersoever he may think fit, together with his suite, and committed him to the good offices of kings, princes, republics and Her Majesty's Allies as well as to commanders etc. her own subjects.

It is dated from Windsor Castle on October 30, 1712, and countersigned "Bolingbroke." This did not prevent the Secretary of State sending the following message of November 11 through Gaultier to Torcy:

> The Duke of Marlborough has asked permission from the Queen to quit the kingdom, and that, after a good deal of contest and consideration, her Majesty has given him leave. He is to pass by Ostend, Bruges, Ghent, Brussels, and Liége to his principality [of Mindelheim], thence through the Tyrol to Venice, and finally to Naples, where he is to sojourn as long as he pleases. Such is the route which has been traced out for him without permission to pass anywhere else.

To describe Bolingbroke as a good liar would be a misstatement. He scattered his lies with such profusion that he wasted them.

Marlborough conveyed most of his settled estate to his sons-in-law. He transferred £50,000 to Cadogan at The Hague, so that, as Sarah wrote, he should not be without the means of sustenance "if the Stuart line were restored." On November 24 he set out with only a few servants for Dover. Sarah was to follow later. Contrary winds detained him for a week, but on December 1 he embarked upon the ordinary packet-boat without any attention except the salute of its captain. No record exists of his reflections upon this melancholy voyage.

Sarah in her will prescribed as the condition of any biography of her husband that no single line of poetry should be quoted in it. Nevertheless, the valedictory verses which Addison wrote deserve inclusion on every ground.

> Go, Mighty Prince, and those great Nations see,
> Which thy Victorious Arms before made free;
> View that fam'd Column, where thy Name engrav'd,
> Shall tell their Children, who their Empire sav'd.
> Point out that *Marble*, where thy Worth is shown,
> To every grateful Country, but thy own.

EXILE

O Censure undeserv'd! Unequal Fate!
Which strove to lessen *Him* who made *Her* Great;
Which pamper'd with Success, and Rich in Fame,
Extoll'd his Conquest, but condemn'd His Name,
But Virtue is a Crime, when plac'd on high;
Tho' all the Fault's in the Beholder's Eye.

The captain of the packet-boat on arriving at Ostend the next morning hoisted her ensign on the topmast-head. This was taken as a signal that Marlborough was on board. Forthwith all the cannon on the sea-front fired a salute, and on the ship entering the harbour the artillery of the ramparts fired three salvos. Cadogan and the Governor with a great crowd received Marlborough as he landed. When the next day, December 13, he set out for Antwerp not only did all the Dutch cannon fire again, but even the English ships in the harbour as well. At Antwerp he was met by the governor, the Marquis of Terracena, who had come over to the allied cause with the rest of Belgium on the morrow of Ramillies. The Marquis offered in the name of the Emperor all the honours due to sovereigns. Marlborough declined these dangerous compliments; but the mass of the people thronged about him, acclaiming him as their deliverer and champion. This, indeed, he had been, against not only the French but also the Dutch.

From Antwerp he wrote to Oxford asking again that Cadogan might be released from his duties to travel with him as his companion. The brave, generous Irish soldier, who was never found wanting in fidelity or chivalry, gladly cast away any prospects he might have under the Tories in order to accompany his old chief. "The Duke of Marlborough's ill-health," he wrote to Oxford, "the inconvenience a winter's journey exposes him to, and his being without any one friend to accompany him, make the requesting leave to wait on him an indispensable duty on me, who for so many years have been honoured with his confidence and friendship, and [owe] all I have in the world to his favour." The Ministers were not unwilling to oblige him. The Queen's permission was granted; but Cadogan was shortly afterwards dismissed from all his appointments.

So enthusiastic were the demonstrations of the Belgians that the Duke, mindful of the long arm of Queen Anne's Government, took by-roads on his journey to Maestricht. Here in Dutch territory he found the whole garrison drawn up to receive him. General Dopf attached

(879)   ·

himself to him in the name of the States-General, and with Cadogan conducted him upon what became perforce a triumphal progress. On the journey to Aix-la-Chapelle all the cavalry forces within long marches came out to ride with him; and in the town of Aix, then so small as to be described by Lediard as "a poor, obscure village," the peasants from the surrounding country crowded in, curious and wondering. A saying ran about Holland and Belgium at this time, "Better be born in Lapland than in England."

Sarah joined her husband in the New Year. He had impatiently and eagerly awaited her arrival in Maestricht. Together they wended through Germany, always being received with respect and pleasure by the inhabitants and with salutes and ceremonies by the rulers.

Sarah's letters from exile are a refreshing counterpart after forty years to the love-letters which she wrote to the young officer of the Guards. The rabid politician, bitter controversialist, fierce mentor and rebuker of the Queen, the tyrant of the Court and of society, recede. We find a mellow and philosophical personage, sometimes scornful but entirely self-possessed, content for the most part with life as it offers itself each day.

Husband and wife both stayed some time at Aix-la-Chapelle, where John had "the advantage of one month of the hot baths."

At Frankfort, which they reached in May, they were not far from the war. "I am come just now," wrote Sarah (May 14, 1713),

> from a Window from which I saw a great many Troops pass that were under the Command of P. Eugene. They paid all the Respects as they went by to the D. of Marl. as if hee had been in his old Post. The Men lookd very well. . . . To see so many brave Men marching was a very fine Sight, it gave me melancholly Reflections, and made me weep; but at the same time I was so much animated that I wishd I had been a Man that I might have ventured my Life a thousand Times in the glorious Cause of Liberty, the Loss of which will be seen and lamented too late for any Remedy; . . . The Civilitys are so great that are paid him by all sorts of People, that one can't but reflect how much a greater Claim he had to all manner of good Usage from his own ungrateful Country. It would fill a Book to give you an Account of all the Honours don him as we came to this Place by the Ellector of Solms, and in all the Towns, as if the D. of Marl. had been King of them, which in his Case is very valuable, because it

shews tis from their Hearts; and if hee had been their King hee might have been like others, a Tyrant.

From May till the end of the year Marlborough and his wife lived quietly in Frankfort. The Duke paid a visit to his principality of Mindelheim, and was received there with royal honours.

Gradually homesickness got the better of Sarah's "phylosophy," and she uttered a cry of pain more audible because of its restraint.

> The best Thing I have heard is that those Men who have been so bold in betraying this Country have been much frightnd of late, but I have heard that some of them were never counted very valiant, and tis the Nature of Cowards, I believe, never to think they have Security enough when the least Danger appeares. . . . But I am intirely of your Mind that wee shall soon bee out of the Pain of Uncertainty. I wish I could as easyly believe that I shall bee contented when I have lost all, and am forced to live the rest of my Life in these durty Countrys. I am now in some Doubt whether my Phylosophy will goe so far as that, tho it has been sufficient to support me against all that the worst of Men or Women have don, and tho I know one shall bear whatever one can't help, I pray most heartily that I may not be tryd any further, for tis quite another Thing to hear that one is never to see England nor one's Children again . . . than it is to leave a disagreeable Court, when one knows one has not deserved ill Treatment, and only to make a Sort of a Pilgrimage for a little while, hoping to see Justice don upon some of one's Enemys.

The hardest forfeit was not, however, to be exacted.

There are three aspects of Marlborough's life at this time which require scrutiny. First, his contacts with England; secondly, his relations with Saint-Germain; and, thirdly, his association with Hanover. Upon all these there has been much discussion.

Cadogan was his chief agent and most faithful friend. The rugged Irish soldier who had borne the brunt of so many serious days had been for twenty years in Marlborough's circle and for ten his right-hand man. He lost his employments; yet he still preserved connexions with Ministers to which they attached importance, and which were serviceable to Marlborough. Cadogan shared in the main Marlborough's exile, but was able to pass to and fro from Germany to England through Holland, or even through Dunkirk, being everywhere received as the honoured Quartermaster of the army in famous days.

Stanhope ranks next in Marlborough's system. The immense personal force and versatility of this man grows on all those who study his vivid career. He was as straight as a die. Sincere, ardent Whig and Protestant, warrior, diplomatist, and statesman, he was certainly one of the greatest personalities of the age of Anne. Marlborough placed full confidence in him, and he was upon the whole his foremost champion in London. Yet this attachment was not due so much to personal regard or admiration as to a conviction that Marlborough's sword and the Protestant Succession were one. All the Whigs valued Stanhope, from the ageing Lords of the Junto to the new generation of brilliant men who were now approaching their prime. They knew that in the Cause he would stop at nothing that honour allowed.

The third was Sunderland whose ties with Marlborough were those of husband of his daughter and father of his heir. Walpole was another Whig in a close intimacy with the great absentee. The able Stair, leading the Whigs in Scotland—the danger-point of Jacobite intrigue—and the younger Craggs, the faithful envoy of many missions, were also in frequent movement between Frankfort or Antwerp and London.

Nearly all these men, now in this chilly period, had sunshine days before them. Cadogan would be Captain-General, Stanhope Secretary of State and head of a Government. A similar experience awaited Sunderland. Before Walpole there spread that long reign of power which consolidated the achievements of Marlborough's wars, and laid the foundations on which the great Chatham was afterwards to build the further expansion of England. Stair was to become one of the most capable ambassadors our Island has ever sent to Paris. Craggs attained a Secretaryship of State. To all these men during the years of evil Marlborough was a figure of unfading fame, and if occasion should serve of immense importance.

It seems unnatural that, with these masterful, virile Whig associates and all that the near future seemed to hold in store, Marlborough should still have cultivated those undefined, mysterious, and to a large extent meaningless relations with Saint-Germain which never ceased from 1689, when William was enthroned, to 1716, when Marlborough sank into bowed old age. His communications with the cast-out Court, his asseverations of sympathy, his cruelty of mocking hopes, his blandishments and moonshine promises, continued in an airy way.

From Berwick's letters we see that Marlborough asked the banished Prince and circle to trust him as a friend who always cherished the hope of being of service. He suggested to them that they should use their influence, and that of the French Government, to assuage the hostility of Oxford towards him. He pointed out that the Tory Government had all his estates and property in their power, that he was pursued by a Crown lawsuit which might beggar him, and that unless they could help him he would be forced to make some bargain with Harley which would prevent him from achieving his lifelong aspirations for their good. Finally he sought a pardon from James III which would protect him in the event of a restoration. These protestations did not deceive Saint-Germain. They had endured twenty years of them. On the other hand, they were in no condition to reject any assurances of goodwill. In their forlorn plight, with the desperate project of an invasion of Britain always in their minds, it was better to be cheated again by Marlborough than to feel once and for all certain he was their foe. They nursed the illusion that a day would come when by a sweep of his arm he would undo the past. But this was but a daydream. They had little to give but words, which seemed an equitable return.

Historians have made great play with this shadow traffic. They have sought to represent it as a prodigy of infamy and deceit, and have even alleged that Marlborough was at all times ready to serve the side that won. But there is no truth in this. That Marlborough would have been glad to end his days at Blenheim Palace even if Parliament had brought back the Stuart line may be true. He did not wish to die abroad in poverty, or to be victimized and stripped at home; but he never meant to allow a Jacobite restoration if by his utmost exertions he could prevent it. This is what invests his whole relationship to Saint-Germain with an air of heartlessness and hypocrisy, which was habitual and persisted in long after his gestures had ceased to count in any effective degree.

Why did he do it? At this stage he must have realized that the risk of such correspondence far outweighed the reality of any benefits he could personally receive. It might estrange him from all his Whig colleagues. It might ruin his interests with the future Hanoverian King. It is possible only to surmise the answer. There is, however, a theory which fits all the facts of twenty years. These contacts with the Jacobite Court were to him a window of indispensable intelligence. We have seen how on the eve of the Blenheim march he was closeted with the Jacobite agents, and how he learned from them in return that Berwick was to serve in Spain and would not be sent against him in Germany. Is it certain that the Paris spy whose deadly information has been mentioned so frequently, and who clearly moved in the innermost circles of Court politics and fashion at Versailles, was a Frenchman, and not an English Jacobite of rank, busying himself in this ceaseless reporting of military and political facts? Might not such an agent have felt that he was helping his own country at the same time that he pocketed the Secret Service payments, and might he not have salved his conscience by the belief that in helping Marlborough he was helping some one who was perhaps the sole hope at once of a victorious England and a Stuart restoration?

This is, of course, pure speculation, but at this period we find Marlborough's relations with the Court of Hanover as good as those with Saint-Germain. We have seen how some of William III's Ministers maintained correspondence with James II, and showed King William the letters they sent and the answers they received. Something very similar occurred at the present juncture. Marlborough is hand-in-glove with the Hanoverian Court. All their principal personages are working in the closest confidence with him. Bernstorf, Robethon, Bothmar, ask his opinion and act on his advice. They were as sure that he was in their interests as the Jacobites were sure they were being fooled.

In these spider's webs of diplomacy and intrigue all the actors were enveloped. Oxford's and Bolingbroke's relations with Torcy, begun while they were at war and continued now, were more confidential than any which they had with the Queen, with their allies, with their colleagues, or with their own supporters in Parliament. In October 1712 Bolingbroke had asked Torcy to let him have the names of Whig leaders who were in correspondence with Saint-Germain. Torcy accordingly approached the Pretender and his Secretaries. It was vital to the banished Court that the inviolability of British confidences made to them should be preserved. Honour apart, one single breach of confidence would have fatally and for ever debased the currency of treason. The Pretender replied to the effect that he was a gentleman as well as a king. Nevertheless Torcy and the French Foreign Office, to whom the poor Jacobites were daily beholden, managed to obtain either some old letters of Marlborough's or tolerable proofs that communications had passed between him and Saint-Germain.

Some time in 1713 Harley, himself wooing both the Pretender and the Elector alternately, sent documentary evidence to Hanover which he confidently expected would blast Marlborough's dangerous credit in that quarter. When the whole tale of Marlborough's craft and stratagems is remembered, and how he was renowned for dissimulation, it is indeed astonishing that these revelations should not have achieved their aim. But they made not the slightest impression. Klopp says, "Marlborough succeeded in an astonishing way in not losing the confidence of Saint-Germain, while at the same time preserving that of Hanover."

But this dictum would be erroneously construed if it were thought that Marlborough was in fact playing a double game. On the one side all was civil sham, and known to be so; on the other, deadly earnest and rightly judged as such. The Electress Sophia reposed absolute faith in him. She regarded him with the highest admiration and regard. Her son, more sceptical, and soured by Marlborough's reticence in the Oudenarde campaign, none the less had no doubt which side he was on.

Marlborough had hardly reached Frankfort in 1713 when he became deeply leagued with the Hanover Court. "What are the steps in general which we should take here," they asked in a memorial dated March 10, for the Elector's friends in England, communicated to Marlborough through Cadogan, "after we have received the news of the Queen's death? What procurations, patents, or orders should we have ready to be sent then, wherever it will be necessary?" On the assumption that it was necessary that the Electoral Prince (the Elector's eldest son, who had fought so well at Oudenarde, and was afterwards George II) was to set forth immediately on the Queen's death for London, a whole series of searching questions were asked both of the Whigs at home and of Marlborough abroad. "What part would Marlborough choose to act? Would he go directly to London, being one of the Regents, or go along with the Elector?" Meanwhile Robethon asked that he should stay within reach, and that, instead of going to live at Frankfort, he should settle at Wesel.

Cadogan gave answers in Marlborough's name to many of the questions.

It was the Duke's opinion that the Elector should go to England immediately upon the Queen's death, with full powers from the Electress as her lieutenant-general. The kings of England frequently invested lieutenants to govern the kingdom in their absence, with all the authority and power they possessed themselves.

Marlborough intimated that when he was sure of the fidelity of the troops abroad he himself might follow the Elector into England, and leave the Electoral Prince with Cadogan to command them.

Eventually Sunderland supplied the forms of the patents. Cadogan gave Bothmar the character of some officers. The commandant at Dunkirk, a Scotsman, and two battalions of that nation were thorough Jacobites; but the eight English battalions were well affected, and "would give a very good account of the other two, and of their commandant."

Side by side with Marlborough, the Hanoverians gazed through the window which he had opened and kept open for their benefit and his own. Can we not see how very flat the exposures of the distrusted and detested Harley fell when flaunted before such close confederates? Marlborough could have revealed to the Court of Hanover every word he had spoken to the Jacobite agents without in the least affecting their relations. Indeed, it may well be that he did so.

No one can read without regret and repugnance the long, wearisome tale of the frauds and injuries which Marlborough perpetrated upon the house of Stuart. No attempt has been made in these pages to conceal or palliate them. It is enough for his fundamental integrity to prove that from the moment when he warned James II at Winchester in 1687 to the day when he welcomed King George I upon his succession in 1714, a period of nearly thirty years, he never swerved from his fidelity to the Protestant Succession. To this he devoted all the power of his sword and his statecraft, and all the network of his subterfuges and deceits. The reader is not invited to admire the seamy side of that intense period, but only to admit that Marlborough's purpose throughout was unchanged.

CHAPTER NINETY-FOUR

Utrecht and the Succession

᠊ᠥᠥ 1713-14 ᠊ᠥᠥ

THESE early months of 1713 were the brightest in Bolingbroke's career. Between the vivid years of audacity, excitement, debauchery, and intrigue and the long grey aftermath of disappointment, exclusion, and futility, they form a gleaming passage. In the state into which he had brought our affairs abroad he was the only man capable of securing any settlement with France. He and his associates had broken up the Grand Alliance, had involved its armies in defeat, and had revived not only French hopes but French ambitions. But for Bolingbroke's statecraft, gambler's-craft, and personality, we might have thrown away the victory without gaining peace. For good or ill the Treaty of Utrecht was better than an indefinite continuance of a broken-backed war. Therefore there were occasions in the spring of 1713 when Bolingbroke's gifts were serviceable to his country. At times, indeed, he seems to speak in ringing tones for that great England whose sacrifices he had mocked, whose interests he had squandered, and whose honour he had lastingly defaced.

In England Ministers did not dare meet Parliament except upon the basis of a compacted peace. There were no fewer than eleven prorogations. At last Bolingbroke realized that all his blandishments of the French and his camaraderie with Torcy were exhausted. The desperate nature of his own plight if Parliament met while war and peace were alike in chaos startled him to robust action. All his sense of values underwent a swift change. The French, so eagerly courted and praised, fell under his ban. The Dutch, so sourly viewed, so roughly treated, began to acquire a new merit. The fact that each of these Governments looked upon his transition with contempt did not strip it of its efficacy. At the end of February the Secretary of State drew up an ultimatum to the French Court prescribing the final outstanding demands of England. There were the fishing rights off Nova Scotia; there were the monopoly upon the Amazon for Portugal and the addition of Tournai to the Dutch Barrier. These must be met fully and forthwith, or England would rouse all the allies to a renewal of the war. France was neither in the condition nor temper to stand a united onslaught. The resumption by England of her place in their ranks would largely reverse the advantages they had gained by her desertion. Considering how wonderful had been their deliverance, how cruel the strain upon the French people, how worn out their martial strength, to haggle too long over details in the hopes of exploiting the confusion of the allies would be a folly and a crime from which they shrank. Accordingly, on March 31/April 11, 1713, the peace was signed at Utrecht between France and England, Holland, Portugal, Prussia, and Savoy. England and France signed first at two o'clock in the afternoon, Savoy and Prussia, with Portugal, in the evening, and the Dutch Republic at midnight.

What is called the Treaty of Utrecht is in fact a series of separate agreements between individual allied states with France and with Spain. The Empire continued the war alone. In the forefront stood the fact that the Duke of Anjou, recognized as Philip V, held Spain and the Indies, thus flouting the unreasonable declaration to which the English Parliament had so long adhered. With this out of the way, the British Government gained their special terms, most of which would long ago have been conceded, and many of which ceased to have importance after a few years. The French Court recognized the Protestant Succession in Britain; agreed to expel the Pretender from France, to demolish the fortifications of Dunkirk, and to cede various territories in North America and the West Indies—to wit, Hudson Bay, Newfoundland, Nova Scotia, and St Christopher. Perpetual amity and goodwill was declared, and both sides swore not to make war without giving six months' notice. With Spain the terms were that England should hold Minorca and Gibraltar, thus securing to her while she remained the chief sea Power the entry and control of the Mediterranean. Commercial advantages in Spanish South America were obtained, and in particular the Assiento, or the right for thirty years to import African negroes as slaves into the New World. By this it was hoped to build the South Sea Company as a Tory rival to the Bank of England. Spain covenanted not to cede any portion of her dominions to France, and as a corollary England guaranteed the integrity of the remaining Spanish Empire against all comers. A renunciation was made both by France and Spain against the union of the two Crowns. This now hung for its validity upon the health of the frail child since known to history as Louis XV.

The Dutch secured a restricted Barrier. The commercial advantages of trade with Belgium were to be shared between England and Holland. Prussia obtained Guelderland at the expense of Dutch claims. Lille was restored to France. Victor Amadeus of Savoy gained Sicily and a strong frontier on the Alps. Portugal was rewarded for feeble services with trading rights upon the Amazon. The frontiers on the Rhine and the fate of Bavaria and the Milanese were left to the decision of further war. Such were the settlements reached at Utrecht in the spring of 1713.

The Emperor Charles, indignant at the Spanish surrender, continued the war during the whole of 1713; but the French armies, though themselves exhausted, took the key fortress of Landau, and penetrated into Germany. In March 1714 the Emperor was forced to conclude the Peace of Rastadt, where he entrusted to Prince Eugene the duty of making such terms with Marshal Villars as the situation permitted. By this treaty the Elector, Max Emmanuel, was reinstated in Bavaria, incidentally extruding Marlborough from his principality of Mindelheim. On this basis Europe subsided into a long, if uneasy, peace, and although these terms were not comparable with what the Allies could have gained in 1706, in 1709, or at Gertruydenberg in 1710, they none the less ended for a while the long torment to which Christendom had been subjected.

Bolingbroke's masterly defence of the Treaty of Utrecht and its forerunner, Swift's *Conduct of the Allies*, together with the squandered opportunity of making peace in 1709, constitute a case for the policy of the Tories which, though rejected during the long period of Whig rule, has commanded the respect of later times. Bolingbroke was no doubt right in saying that if the Allies in 1712 had conformed to the new policy of Queen Anne's Government, and had cordially joined with them in making general peace, the odious events which followed in the field would have been avoided. If they had agreed with him, there would have been no need for him to go behind their backs. If they had desisted from the campaign, England would not have been forced to desert their camps. If they had not incurred the military disasters in the autumn of 1712, the united Allies could have forced France into far more satisfactory arrangements for the Dutch, the Germanic states, and the Empire than were in fact achieved. But all this reasoning stands on a false foundation. They did not conform, they did not agree, they did not desist, and the disasters followed. Was, then, England relieved from all obligations towards them? The solemn condition of the Grand Alliance was that they should make peace in common, and England was by no means absolved by the fact that she suddenly became more anxious for peace than the other signatory states. If the shortcomings of our allies in waging war were as gross as Swift pretends, that was a ground for reproach, but not for betrayal or desertion. It certainly did not lie with England, which for so long had urged the unrelenting prosecution of the war, which had imposed its formula, "No peace without Spain," upon reluctant Dutch and indifferent Germanic states, to blame them for not obediently abandoning their policy because England had a new Minister and Queen Anne a new favourite. The secret and separate negotiations of the Tory Ministers inspired our allies with distrust and anger. It was neither right nor reasonable, therefore, to expect from states smarting under the sense of having been tricked patient, loyal co-operation. If the Tory Ministers had wished to carry their policy, they should have done so straightforwardly, openly, and in concert with their allies. They did not do this, because they had to deceive their own Parliament as well as their allies, and confront them both stage by stage with new situations.

It is not, therefore, upon the terms of settlement in general that censure can found itself. The mean and treacherous manner in which the Grand Alliance had been broken up, with the shameful episodes of violated faith and desertion in the field, inflicted the stigma which was for so long visible on the face of this transaction. Forty years later William Pitt, writing to Sir Benjamin Keene, feeling the odium which still clung to England and infected her every public pledge, pronounced the stern judgment that "Utrecht was an indelible reproach of the last generation."

Marlborough had always believed that unless France was reduced, not merely to temporary exhaustion, but to a definitely restricted power, the wars of his generation would be renewed in the future. This was looking far ahead, but the fact remains that in the century that followed Europe was racked with repeated conflicts and Great Britain fought four separate wars with France, aggregating in all forty-three years of deadly strife. During these wars the first British Empire was largely ruined. Great coalitions were formed against Britain. She was stripped by war and other causes of her vast American possessions. Her existence as a world state was repeatedly in jeopardy, and finally, against Napoleon, she was at one time left alone to face the world. That these indescribable perils were surmounted by the valour and vigour of the descendants of those who fought in the age of Anne unfolds a series of new marvels and prodigies in our island story.

At the time the sense of frustration and of the casting away of the fruits of so much perseverance and good fortune rankled deeply in many bosoms. The fierce debates in Parliament cannot be read without a blush. All might so easily have been made smooth and clean; but the unending cadence of history shows that moderation and mercy in victory are no less vital than courage and skill in war. England in 1713 rejoiced that peace, no matter how, had come at last. The nation as a whole endorsed and acclaimed what Queen Anne and her Ministers had done, and even when under George I the Whigs regained the full and prolonged control of affairs they did not venture to challenge the settlements which were made.

Early in December 1713 the Queen fell ill. Her condition caused lively alarm in all quarters, but for different reasons. Neither the Court of Hanover nor the Whigs in Great Britain had made any effective preparations for the tremendous and deadly crisis which must instantly attend a demise of the Crown. No man, not the shrewdest or best-informed, could predict what would happen. The Tories had majorities in both houses; they had a newly elected Tory House of Commons. All the commands in the fleet, Army, and fortresses were in the hands of trusted Tory or Jacobite adherents. Ormonde was Warden of the Cinque Ports, and in close touch with Berwick. A Jacobite governed Edinburgh. The Whig Earl of Dorset had been ejected from Dover Castle. No attempt had been made by the Whigs to organize the nuclei of resistance. They had their Act of Settlement—the law on their side—but that was all.

A wave of fear swept through one half of political England lest they should lose the Queen, through the other lest the Protestant Succession should be subverted, and through both lest civil war, with all its uncountable horrors, should come. It was a quarrel which nobody wanted, but into which all would inexorably be drawn. The French were also on the move. Under pretext of changing garrisons several battalions and all the Irish regiments in the French service moved towards the coastal towns. Abigail's brother, Jack Hill, who was governor of Dunkirk, expatiated on its advantages to French troops as a port of embarkation for England. Faced with this peril, the Whigs looked about them for means of defence. A hurried meeting was held at Wharton's house. Strenuous appeals were made to Hanover by the Whigs in England and by Marlborough from Frankfort. The Electress and her son acted with what vigour was possible. Marlborough and Cadogan both held their provisional commissions to take command of the British forces which remained in the Low Countries. There were troops at Ghent and Bruges, there were troops at Ostend; above all, there was the garrison at Dunkirk. Two of Marlborough's trusted Lieutenants held command under Hill.

Marlborough himself travelled from Frankfort to Antwerp, where he established himself at the beginning of December. Here he was in much closer contact with events. He had sent Cadogan to The Hague to learn the "sentiments and thoughts of our friends in England, and to inform himself of the situation of things in Holland." Upon Cadogan's return from The Hague he sent a full account, and formally accepted the Elector's commission as Commander-in-Chief.

Thus we see Marlborough still in the centre of all those forces which he had previously directed, and assisting to weld together the Whigs in Britain, the army in Flanders, the Dutch and the Empire behind the house of Hanover. There can be no doubt of either his acts or his intentions.

It would, however, be a mistake to imagine him at this time as a fretful, energetic schemer impatiently awaiting a new turn of fortune's wheel. From the moment he had been relieved of his military and European responsibilities he had sensibly aged. He laid down at the same time his burdens and his strength. However painful it might be to watch the squandering of so much that he had gained, he did not despair about what could not be prevented. He yielded himself easily to his new-found leisure. The will-power which for ten years had held the whole movement of Europe upon its course first relaxed and then declined. He enjoyed the placid days as they succeeded one another. Sarah rallied him severely. He had grown, she complained, "intolerably lazy." He would hardly write a letter—not even to his well-loved daughters. But his noble air and the sense of authority and kindliness which his presence conveyed made their impression upon all who met him. Alison records a notable saying about him at this time. "The only things the Duke has forgotten are his deeds. The only things he remembers are the misfortunes of others."

Sorrow too fell upon him in these wanderings. Early in 1714 his third daughter, Elizabeth, Countess of Bridgewater, died of the smallpox scourge. She was his favourite child, and deeply attached to him. All accounts describe her sunshine nature and graceful virtues. When at Antwerp Marlborough received the news of her death his head dropped on the marble mantelpiece against which he leaned, and he is said to have become unconscious.

By the end of January the Queen was clearly better. She had recovered sufficiently to open Parliament in person on February 15. In March she fell ill again, and anxiety became intensified. In April the Whigs and the adherents of the house of Hanover persuaded the Hanoverian envoy Schütz to request a writ of summons for the Electoral Prince to take his seat in the House of Lords as Duke of Cambridge. This measure was well conceived. It exposed the Ministers to the utmost embarrassment, and it split the Tory Party. The whole bench of bishops, with two exceptions, voted with the Opposition. The Ministers escaped censure, which in this case was tantamount to an accusation of high treason, only by the twelve votes of the batch of peers created two years before.

The writ for the Electoral Prince, of course, struck the Queen in her most sensitive spot. She was convulsed with distress and wrath. A series of vehement letters in Bolingbroke's haughty style were sent to Hanover. The aged Electress, whose illuminating intelligence had long cast its light upon the European scene, was so painfully affected by their tone that she expired a few days later. The Elector George Lewis was now the direct constitutional heir. By this time Oxford and Bolingbroke had received the Pretender's answer to their invitation to change his religion. His answer was fatal to his prospects, but for ever honourable to his name. It has been well said that his sincerity and honesty should win for his memory the gratitude of the British nation. He repulsed with indignation the suggestion that he should forsake his faith for his Crown. When Oxford and Bolingbroke received his reply both realized that there was no hope of a Restoration. Oxford, with hardly a day's delay, renewed perfervid blandishments to the Court of Hanover. From this moment he seems definitely to have rallied to the Hanoverian Succession and to have endeavoured to bring the Queen to the conviction that it was inevitable. But now he found his influence gone. He had quarrelled with Abigail. He had refused her a share in the profits of the Assiento contract, for which Bolingbroke had led her to hope. She therefore threw all her weight against him, and, dreading the prospects of a Hanoverian monarchy, strove to lead the Queen into Jacobite paths. Here, however, Anne became intractable. She, like every one else, had been staggered by the Pretender's uncompromising refusal to abandon the Roman Catholic faith. She feared that his accession would fatally injure the Church of England, her rock in tribulation. She therefore allowed events to drift on their course, and implored Oxford and Bolingbroke to be reconciled to each other. This, indeed, was but one of the measures their safety required. But their mutual hatreds and charges against each other were too serious to be overridden even by the instinct of self-preservation.

On the other side nothing was now neglected. The group of war leaders, Marlborough, Cadogan, Stanhope, and Argyll, were now all acting in unity, and resolved if need be to proceed to extremities. A convention was drawn up between the States-General and Hanover for ships and troops. Stanhope privily organized the French Huguenot officers and men in London. Many veterans discharged from Marlborough's armies were enrolled in secret bands. Argyll and Stair took similar steps in Scotland. It was widely believed that the Regular Army itself, in spite of the purge of officers, would not act against the renowned Chiefs of the great war. A Whig Association was formed comprising a large number of officers who undertook to remain armed and ready at call, and a fund was created to which the merchants of the City largely contributed.

When Marlborough at Antwerp was invited to join this body he declined. His refusal excited surprise at the time, and has been criticized since. It can hardly be doubted that he was wise not to join a purely

Whig conspiracy. He was more than ever determined in his freedom not to be enrolled in the ranks of either party. By any overt action he would have presented the Government with the advantage of reviving the cry that he sought to become a second Cromwell. There is, however, no question where he stood. A more decisive step was in his mind. He had resolved to return to England. "Pray be pleased to take an opportunity," he wrote to Robethon (June 18), "of acquainting his Electoral Highness that my best friends think my being in England may be of much more use to the service than my continuing abroad, upon which I design to return as soon as the Parliament is up."

The air of meaningless mystery which surrounds Marlborough's leaving England also covers his return. It is certain that he took this decision without reference to whether the Queen was dead, dying, or about to recover, and without regard to whether Oxford or Bolingbroke emerged the winner from their struggle. The only consideration which he mentioned was that Parliament should have risen. This would free him from some minor annoyances. Parliament was prorogued on July 9/20, and Marlborough set out accordingly for Ostend.

Sarah was with him. There was no doubt about her sentiments. She was, as ever, the full-blooded Whig, hating the Pope and Pretender with equal zeal. Her motive also was simple. She was burning to get home. The longing to be back in England seemed to have taken possession of her soul. There is no doubt that the moment of Marlborough's return was influenced by this rather than by any deeply calculated plan of action. We see also that he had not the slightest fear of returning home. He asked no one's permission. He made no concealment of his intentions. He appeared perfectly sure of himself, and that he would be able to deal with the facts of his native land as he found them. He was as cool and matter-of-fact as on the morning of one of his battles.

Throughout his voluntary exile Marlborough had maintained civil relations with Oxford, and in January 1714 the Treasurer had granted a warrant of £10,000, for which the Duke thanked him, for some resumpion of the building of Blenheim. It is possible, though no correspondence exists, that Bolingbroke had also kept contact with him. But there is no truth in the widely made suggestion that his return to England was the result of any understanding or agreement with either of the quarrelling Ministers.

On the road to Ostend an incident occurred. The Royal Irish Regiment, ultra-Protestants from Northern Ireland, and Webb's were both quartered in the castle of Ghent. Captain Parker tells us that "on hearing that the Duke was to pass that way, all the officers of both Regiments went without Antwerp port, and drew up in two lines to pay him our compliments, and shew the respect we still retained for his Grace." The Duke and Sarah rode up on horseback, and spent half an hour talking to the officers "on indifferent matters before resuming their journey."

While Marlborough and his eager wife waited at Ostend for the fair wind events moved to their decision in England.

CHAPTER NINETY-FIVE

The Death of the Queen

ᘓ 1714, July ᘔ

"Good God," exclaimed the Duke of Buckingham (after he had been put out of office),

> how has this poor Nation been governed in my time! During the reign of King Charles the Second we were governed by a parcel of French whores; in King James the Second's time by a parcel of Popish Priests; in King William's time by a parcel of Dutch Footmen; and now we are governed by a dirty chambermaid, a Welsh attorney, and a profligate wretch that has neither honour nor honesty.

Many accounts converge upon the conclusion that the final scene in the long debate between Oxford and Bolingbroke at the Cabinet Council of July 27 brought about the death of Queen Anne. Already scarcely capable of standing or walking, she nevertheless followed the intense political struggles proceeding around her with absorbed attention. She notified the Lord Treasurer by gesture and utterance that he must surrender the White Staff. The sodden, indolent, but none the less tough and crafty politician, who had overthrown Marlborough and changed the history of Europe, had his final fling at his triumphant rival. For months past he had lapped up the Treasury tales of the corruption whereby the Secretary of State and Abigail were enriching themselves. Some weeks before he had submitted to the Queen a "brief account" of his own conduct, in which detailed charges of peculation were made against Bolingbroke. The swindles of the Quebec expedition in 1711, the naked abstraction at the beginning of 1714 of

Secret Service money by Bolingbroke to pay off a mortgage on his estate, the passport scandal, and the gross malversations of Arthur Moore, in which Bolingbroke was deeply involved—all these were at his fingers' ends. And this was the man who should supplant him! In savage tones across the table, both men being within six feet of the Queen, he denounced him to her as a rogue and thief, and in terms of vague but none the less impressive menace made it plain that he would denounce him to Parliament.

Anne was deeply smitten. She had made up her mind, by the processes which have been described, to get rid of this lax but formidable Minister, by whose advice and aid she had violated the friendships of her lifetime and stultified the purpose of her reign. But she knew too much about Bolingbroke, his morals, his finances, his malpractices, public and private, to feel that in quitting Harley she had another stepping-stone on which to stand. Certainly she could not appoint to the Lord Treasurership a man whose financial probity was under investigation and in general disrepute. There is little doubt that she was harassed beyond human endurance. She had taken all upon herself, and now she did not know which way to turn. She was assisted and carried from this violent confrontation, and two days later the gout which had hitherto tormented her body moved with decision towards her brain. Oxford went home to scribble doggerel to Swift about the vicissitudes of statesmen. Bolingbroke remained master of the field and of the day—but only for the day.

During forty-eight hours Bolingbroke possessed plenary power at a cardinal point in English history. What did he mean to do? Had he a clear resolve, equal to the emergency, for which he was prepared to die or kill? "Harry" was never of that stuff. There was no Cromwell in him; there was no Marlborough; there was no Stanhope. He dawdled, he wavered, he crumpled. More than that, his luck ran out.

There is a striking incident recorded of the night of July 28. Bolingbroke, who was in the position of a man charged with the royal commission to reconstitute a Government, had bidden all the rising generation of Whig leaders to dinner at his house in Golden Square. The names of those he had invited are surprising—Stanhope, Craggs, Pulteney, Walpole, Cadogan—in fact, a cluster of Marlborough's friends and adherents and of Bolingbroke's most bitter foes. All these men had been outraged by his conduct. The generals had seen the cause they had fought for cast away. Cadogan had seen his revered chief wronged, insulted, and driven into exile. Stanhope had been superseded. Craggs on Marlborough's missions had been treated with barely disguised contempt. Walpole had been sent to the Tower for five months on a charge of corruption, which at its worst was venial compared to the misdeeds of Bolingbroke. Yet they were all invited, and all except Walpole met round Bolingbroke's table on the night of July 28.

The Secretary expatiated upon his fidelity to the house of Hanover and to the Act of Settlement, and made it clear that places in his new Government would be offered to the company. But surely this was not the end to which his actions for months had seemed to point. He had purged the Army: he had begun to tamper with the Navy. Every one of these Whigs believed that he was plotting to bring in the Pretender, and place him as an avowed Papist upon the throne, in defiance of all the laws and oaths that had followed the revolution of 1688. If he did not mean this what did he mean? It is pretty plain nowadays that he meant nothing definite—certainly nothing that could become effective at that time. He wanted to build up a situation step by step, so that if his affairs prospered he could move with safety in the direction he desired. But if it became too dangerous he thought he could withdraw with equal facility, and court the Elector of Hanover as easily as the "Prince of Wales." For this he needed power and time. He gained the power, but the time was denied him.

The resolute, able men who sat at his table were not hampered by any of the balancings which obsessed their host. They meant, if it were necessary, to fight a civil war for the Protestant Succession. Their situation was incomparably stronger than when the Queen had first fallen ill at the end of 1713. They had a sworn association; they had arms; they had large funds; they had the whole force of a great party and of strong elements in the national life. For months they had been secretly recruiting Marlborough's veterans—sergeants, corporals, private men. They had several thousands of them on their lists in London, and many others in the Provinces. They had with them nearly all the officers who had led the British troops under Marlborough in ten years of victory. They were in the closest touch with Marlborough, and knew he was on his way to England—would, if need be, take the field at their head. If he could not arrive in time, Stanhope would act. Little recked they of lands or life. Finally, they had the law and the Constitution on their side.

It must have been one of the strangest dinner-parties upon record, and there are many. No one knew the Queen was going to die. No one knew how long she would live. She might live for years. She had been as ill as this at Christmas, and had recovered. At the end Stanhope spoke words of grave and fair import. He offered a soldier's terms to Bolingbroke. Let him put the fleet into the hands of admirals loyal to the Hanoverian Succession. Let him restore Marlborough to the command of the Army and of the fortified seaports. This done, let him enjoy the Queen's favour while she lived, and all would take their chance of office under the future George I without bearing him malice. If not, let him play the other hand, and put it to the test. But Bolingbroke, who had got round so many deadly difficulties in breaking Marlborough, deserting the allies, and carrying the Treaty of Utrecht, and now at last had got rid of Oxford, was by no means ready for such sharp choices. He was obviously incapable of responding with force and sincerity. He fell back on general phrases. As the party broke up Stanhope in all the bluntness of after-dinner camaraderie said, "Harry, you have only two ways of escaping the gallows. The first is to join the honest party of the Whigs; the other to give yourself up entirely to the French King and seek his help for the Pretender. If you do not choose the first, we can only imagine that you have decided for the second."

If Bolingbroke had had more time, if the Queen had lived for another six weeks, it seems very likely that he would have brought about—not for any steady purpose or conviction, for at his heart there was nothing but brilliant opportunism, but for his caprice and ambition—what might have been a civil war as cruel and bloody as has ever rent our nation. While he had made every preparation in his power, had even bargained with Torcy for French troops, yet when it came to the point he had neither the soul to decide nor the manhood to dare. We must indeed thank God that our Island story was not seared by a hideous tragedy; that Marlborough's sword and the bayonets of his veterans, were not engaged on English soil against a goodly company of sentimental Jacobites and stout-hearted country squires and their dependants; and that the old quarrel of Cavalier and Roundhead, in different forms but perhaps on a far larger scale, was not renewed again in England. To the brink of this catastrophe our national life was brought by the wickedness and inherent degeneracy of this richly gifted man.

One is surprised to find serious writers describing his actions as if they were deserving of impartial presentment. Whigs and Tories, Hanoverians and Jacobites—it was, they suggest, six of one and half a dozen of the other. Marlborough had won the war; Bolingbroke had made the peace. Great and respectable currents of opinion flowed in either cause, and the history, we are enjoined, must with a cool detachment tolerate both points of view. But this weak mood cannot be indulged in a world where the consequences of men's actions produce such frightful calamities for millions of humble folk, and may rob great nations of their destiny. By personal vices of heart and mind, by deeds of basest treachery, by violation of law and public faith, this man St John—unpurposed, unprincipled, miscreant adventurer—had brought his native land to the edge of the abyss, and in this horrid juncture he could not even clothe crime with coherency. Let the lifelong failure and suppression of his bright gifts procure no mitigation of modern censure. Let us also rejoice that poor Queen Anne was now at her last gasp. Just in the nick of time she died. She had lived long enough to strip the name of Britain of most of the glories with which it had shone. She had seen it become odious or contemptible throughout the world. She sank into her mortal collapse with her country in the jaws of measureless tribulation. But luckily she expired while there was still time to save it.

Anne allowed Oxford to take leave of her with some ceremony; but her gout increased, and she suffered from pains in the head. Her six doctors who divided the responsibility were all anxious. "On Friday morning [the 30th]," wrote one of them, Daniel Malthus, "her Majesty rose and in her dressing room between 9 and 10, had two very violent convulsions, one immediately after the other which lasted till 11." Meanwhile the Council met in the palace. They were about to transact business when the door opened, and in marched the Duke of Somerset and the Duke of Argyll. Both were Privy Councillors, but neither of them had received a summons. They declared that the dangerous illness of the Queen made it their duty to proffer their services. The Tory Ministers were taken aback at this apparition. These were not men who could easily be ejected. Somerset was the embodiment of political effrontery and violence. Argyll had been the first man in the storm of

Oudenarde. If the Tory Ministers had risen from the table, drawn their swords, and ordered the intruders to depart, they would have been at the level of the crisis. As it was, they were only flustered. Before they could recover, Shrewsbury, who had certainly planned this stroke, was uttering suave phrases of welcome and thanks to the two Dukes for the patriotic impulse which had moved them. With an adroitness which can be discerned across the interval of time, he began to speak of the Queen's health. The doctors must at once be summoned to the Council. The two stranger Dukes should hear for themselves what they had to say. The doctors came, and related at length the various professional tortures they were inflicting upon the patient. By the time they had finished Somerset and Argyll were for all intents and purposes members of the Cabinet. It is noteworthy that these were the same three Dukes, and men of middle views, who had turned the scale in 1710 against Godolphin and Marlborough. Now they acted in an even greater crisis. In each case Shrewsbury was the prime mover, and revealed in different forms the latent power and guile of his nature.

It was obvious that the great business of the day was to advise how the Queen should fill the vacant office of Lord Treasurer. Oxford had delivered up his staff. It had not yet been bestowed upon another. To whom could it go but Shrewsbury? This was no matter of finance. The Succession was at stake, and the prevention of civil war. Shrewsbury was willing to become First Minister during the emergency. What had the Tories, and, above all, what had Bolingbroke, to say? None of them had any conviction. They had no plan. They had taken no resolves. Against them were determined men. Before he knew where he was Bolingbroke was proposing that the Queen should be advised to appoint Shrewsbury Lord Treasurer.

"From near noon," says Dr Malthus, "Her Majesty had her understanding perfect, but from that time answered nothing but aye or no." The doctors were asked "whether she could be spoke to." To quote Malthus, "At the coming out of the fit the Duchess of Somerset desired from the Lords of the Council that they might propose something to her of great moment to her, which granted, some went in, of which the Dukes of Shrewsbury, Somerset, and Argyll were part." Lord Chancellor Harcourt guided her hand as she passed the White Staff to Shrewsbury, uttering, it was untruthfully asserted, the words, "Use it for the good of my people." The Queen then sank into a coma, and the Ministers returned to the council chamber with Shrewsbury at their head. By this transaction, which seemed to move so naturally and perhaps inevitably, Bolingbroke was destroyed. In the morning all power was in his hands; in the evening he was almost an outcast.

The Council sat far into the night. Vigorous measures were taken to ensure the Hanoverian Succession. Messengers were dispatched in all directions to rally to their duty every functionary and officer throughout the land. The fleet was mobilized under the Whig Earl of Berkeley, and ordered to patrol the Channel and watch the French ports. Ten battalions were recalled from Flanders. The garrisons were put under arms, and the train-bands warned. The Dutch were reminded of their treaty obligations. Everything was prepared to proclaim the accession of the Elector of Hanover as George I. These orders bore the signatures not only of Shrewsbury, Somerset, and Argyll, but of Bolingbroke and his Tory colleagues. In the circumstances they could do no less. Indeed, as the ponderous balance had now tilted, their safety lay in showing themselves especially ardent. Throughout the 31st the Council toiled and acted. On this day the Cabinet became merged in the Privy Council. Somers, Halifax, and other leading Whigs took their places at the table. It was now a national body of overwhelming power, none dissenting or daring to dissent. As the day wore on the physicians reported that the Queen could certainly not recover, and that the end was near. All preparations were made with heralds and Household troops to proclaim King George.

Queen Anne breathed her last at half-past seven on August 1. It is sad to relate that her death brought an immense relief to great masses of her subjects. By a harsh coincidence the Schism Act, by which Bolingbroke was to persecute the Dissenters, came into force on that same day. The death of the Queen was an assurance to Nonconformist England that it would be a dead letter. But above all there was the blessed certainty that there would be no Popery, no disputed succession, no French bayonets, no civil war. Without the slightest protest or resistance, the Elector of Hanover was proclaimed Sovereign of the United Kingdom of Great Britain and Ireland.

CHAPTER NINETY-SIX

Marlborough in the New Reign

ᚠᚲ 1714-16 ᚲᚠ

ALL England awaited the arrival of King George I. An epoch glorious in its prime, shameful in its close, had passed away. The famous age of Anne, the supreme manifestation of British genius, its virtues and vices, in peace and war, by land and sea, in politics, letters, and architecture, was over. A new scene opens with different patterns, lights, and values. All the old actors quit the stage—some in ignominy, some in splendour. Younger men of high gifts and proved capacity present the drama of national life after the triumphs and intense passions of the war. Milder, easier, more comfortable, less romantic themes rule in British society for many years. England had gained heights in the world that she had never reached before. She sat exhausted after prodigious exertions upon these commanding uplands, and regathered her strength and poise.

The contrary wind which had detained Marlborough for a momentous fortnight was at last changed to 'fair.' He landed at Dover on August 2, and there learned the news of the Queen's death. On this homecoming he did not attempt concealment.

He was everywhere received with demonstrations of welcome and regard. Notables and populace thronged the streets of every town and village through which he and Sarah passed, and when they entered the City they were escorted by hundreds of gentlemen on horseback, a body of grenadiers, the civic authorities, a long train of attendant coaches, and an immense concourse of all classes, who accompanied him with loud, unceasing cheers, drowned amid which, we are assured, there were also boos.

The gradations by which Bolingbroke passed from the position of the most powerful and most brilliant Minister to a culprit awaiting his trial succeeded each other with swiftness. His authority had gone. His policy, if he had one, was gone. Indeed, his only hope was to disavow the designs in which he had dabbled. He was still Secretary of State. But soon a black box in Bothmar's keeping was opened with the names of the Regents appointed by King George I to rule the realm till he could reach London. There were twenty-five Regents. Among them was not found the name of Bolingbroke. The list had been drawn up from the Hanover angle. Extreme Whigs like Somers, Sunderland, and Wharton were not included; neither were any of the Tory Ministers. Marlborough was surprised and offended not to be declared a Regent; but, considering that this Council of Regency was to come into being in England only until the King could come himself, and that Marlborough was also beyond the seas at the time the list was drawn, his complaint was ill-founded. The omission of his name, as was soon proved, was neither a slight nor intended to be one.

St John, though he put upon it the best face he could, was not slow in realizing his position. To him, it has been said, the twenty-five Regents were twenty-five Sovereigns. He was directed to send his dispatches to them. Day after day for nearly three weeks he paced the anteroom awaiting their pleasure. Swift, whose world had also clattered about his ears, and who saw the loss of all he had gained by the malice of his pen, warned the stranded Secretary to expect the worst. On August 16 there arrived from Hanover a curt dismissal and an order to deliver up his seals to Townshend. Thereupon, as an indication of what was in store, he was visited by two lords who collected and sealed up such papers as he had not already destroyed and was willing to surrender. He retired to the country, a prey to equally well-founded regrets and fears.

Oxford in misfortune was sustained by his admirable phlegm, by liquor, and by the intense inward joy with which he watched the ruin of his faithless and lately triumphant confederate. He was more concerned in bringing to light Bolingbroke's peculation in the Quebec expedition than about his own defence. He even seems to have persuaded himself at first that he would find favour in the new reign. In this he was speedily undeceived.

George I landed at Greenwich on September 18, and in the palace by the waterside received the nobility of his realm. At heart this lucky German Prince regarded them all with a comprehensive, impartial distrust and disdain. He had received the news of his accession without excitement and certainly without enthusiasm. He had accepted the British Crown as a duty entailing exile from home. He had gazed long and attentively upon the darker side of British politics without understanding the stresses which were its explanation. He had seen both parties competing year after year for his favour in order to advance their own ends. He despised them, alike for their servility and their factiousness. They had begged him to leave his Hanoverian home to rule over them. He would be graciously pleased to do so, according to the rules arising from their civil and religious fights. He brought with him a pair of ugly and rapacious German mistresses and a son whom he hated like the plague.

He trusted no English statesman. Bolingbroke and Oxford were the men who had betrayed the allied cause—the men of Utrecht. Ormonde was the general who had deserted Prince Eugene. Shrewsbury had played a part of duplicity in breaking up the Grand Alliance. Somers, Halifax, Sunderland, and the rest of the Whigs had all been ready to sell one another for the sake of office. Even the mighty Marlborough, master of war and guide of Europe, had concealed from him the plans of the Oudenarde campaign, and had certainly sought to reinsure himself with Saint-Germain. Thus our new sovereign took the poorest view of his principal subjects, and set himself to manage them with much perplexity but genuine contempt. And who was he himself, it may be asked, to be their judge? A narrow, vindictive, humdrum German martinet, with dull brains, coarse tastes, crude appetites; a commonplace and ungenerous ruler, and a sluggish and incompetent commander in the field—that was all. Surely his accession, however indispensable, was a humbling experience to the tremendous society and nation whose arm had broken the might of the France of Louis XIV. But these are the penalties of a divided national life.

The political arrangements were made with that expert skill which is best exercised under conditions of unsympathetic detachment. The King of England could not speak a word of English; but he had his own advisers, who now became the repositories of power. They decided in principle to ban the Tories from office, to put the old Whig Junto in the shade, and to bring forward a new generation. Bolingbroke had already been dismissed. When Oxford at length came forward Dorset presented him thus: "Here is the Earl of Oxford, of whom your Majesty must have heard." The King, disconcerted, allowed him to kiss his hand, gave him a frozen stare, and turned away. Ormonde, having already learned that he was stripped of his command, departed from the Court without a word.

Marlborough, on the other hand, had been received with the greatest honour and cordiality. "My lord Duke," exclaimed the King, as soon as he landed, "I hope your troubles are now all over." He was immediately granted an hour's audience, and the first warrant signed by the King reinstated him as Captain-General, Master-General of the Ordnance, and Colonel of the 1st Guards. A week later the King was entertained at a banquet at Marlborough House, and in every way showed the Captain-General countenance and favour. There was no doubt more policy than personal friendship in these demonstrations. Nothing could strengthen the new reigning house more at this moment than these proofs that Marlborough was with it. In the British Army, where the veterans had not forgotten Ormonde's desertion of Prince Eugene in 1712, the "Old Corporal" was welcomed back with warm satisfaction; and throughout Europe the States and Princes of the former allies were impressed with the power and stability of the new Government.

At first the Whigs and Hanoverians were in a mood to revive the foreign policy and European grouping so grievously broken since 1710, but these ideas faded before the realities of a new day. Utrecht was irrevocable. A Ministry was swiftly formed. All the Lords of the Junto were installed in Cabinet posts. Shrewsbury gladly yielded the Treasurer's staff, and resumed the wand of Lord Chamberlain. The Treasury was placed in commission under the Presidency of the none the less unsatisfied Halifax. But the real business of the State, subject to the supervision of the Hanoverian circle, fell increasingly to Townshend, Stanhope, and Walpole. There could be found no three abler men in the full vigour of manhood and prime. Townshend and Stanhope were the Secretaries of State. Walpole, owing to the disapprobation of Bothmar, had to console himself with the lucrative office of Paymaster of the Forces and the patronage that flowed therefrom.

Now was the hour of Whig retaliation. The Tory Parliament, lately swelling with incipient Jacobitism, had been profuse in its asseverations of loyalty to King George and had voted him munificent supplies. They were remorselessly dissolved; and from the new election an overwhelming Whig majority was returned, which, as it fell out, inaugurated nearly forty years of Whig ascendancy. As if the spell which had bound them to life had been snapped with the end of their period, Somers, Shrewsbury, Halifax, and Wharton all died within a few years. Bolingbroke alone survived for more than a generation to gaze forlornly upon the past and mock himself with vain hopes.

His immediate conduct and fortunes deserve a passing glance. The Whig Parliament proceeded to repeat the odious process of recrimination and censure in which four years earlier the Tories under Harley and St John had so wantonly indulged at the expense of Marlborough and Godolphin. A sincere loathing was felt by the political victors for the men who had made the Treaty of Utrecht. Not one of them was ever allowed to hold Ministerial office again. But against the principal authors of the desertion and separate peace the ancient processes of the Constitution were set in motion. Parliament, with the full assent of the Crown, demanded the punishment of the ex-Treasurer, who had negotiated with France behind their backs; of the ex-Secretary, who had, it was alleged, conspired to subvert the Act of Settlement and bring in a Popish prince to the prejudice of the lawful sovereign; and of the General, who had marched away from the allied camps, taking with him the pontoons which might have averted the massacre of Denain. The procedure of impeachment was invoked. The brilliant Bolingbroke's nerves collapsed hopelessly under the strain. At first jaunty and audacious, he tried to carry off all with a gay confidence. He spoke in the Lords with fire and skill. He built the largest bonfire before his house to celebrate the Coronation. He presented himself at the theatre as a patron of the arts, and kept high state in his London house. But a slow, cold fear began to gnaw his heart. He knew how much he owed. He dreaded what he would have to pay. His trepidations led him to an astonishing course. He threw himself upon the magnanimity of Marlborough.

Marlborough was no doubt surprised when the ex-Secretary of State called at his door. A long account stood between them. Marlborough had befriended him in his early career. He had made him Secretary-at-War in the great days. He had helped him pay his debts. He had almost called him his son. He had never done him any injury, and there is no record of any harsh word which he ever spoke about him. On the other hand, no one had pursued Marlborough with more malignity than Bolingbroke. He had helped in his overthrow. He had turned Swift loose upon him to traduce his character and libel his wife. In his hour of authority he had lectured and patronized him. He had written scores of letters about him in terms of hostility and contempt. He had largely destroyed his European work. He had removed him from the command of the allied armies, broken his faithful officers, and involved the British troops in the foulest dishonour. He had led and persuaded the House of Commons, in spite of truth or justice, to brand him for all time as guilty of peculation and corruption. His had been the hand that would have denied him even an asylum abroad. He had even written to Torcy that he would cut off his head, and only a few months before had threatened to send him to the Tower if he set foot in his native land. Now, in all the disreputable inconsequence of his nature, he came to beg his help and advice.

Marlborough was not a vindictive man, but, as Bolingbroke's biographer justly observes, "He would have been either much more or much less than human—he would perhaps have acted with ridiculous weakness—could he in his heart have forgiven Bolingbroke, or have performed towards him a friendly part." The Captain-General received his visitor with his usual good manners. Bolingbroke sought to know how he stood with the new régime, and what his fate was to be. He appealed for aid and pity, under the cloak of seeking advice. Marlborough read him through and through. He had had many opportunities of seeing whether a man was frightened or not; but he was all bows, consideration, and urbanity. Bolingbroke soon felt that at least he had one friend. When this impression was established, Marlborough confided to him the fact that his (Bolingbroke's) life was in danger. It was not the purpose of the new King and Government to persecute the Tory Party or punish the Tory leaders as a whole. In the new reign there must be a fair start. But it was felt that an example should be made. Speaking as one known to be deep in the secrets alike of Heinsius and of the Hanoverian circle, he hinted that Oxford and the Whigs had reached an agreement on which Bolingbroke's blood should set the seal. The sole hope for him was to fly the country. There might just be time.

Bolingbroke, already in the grip of fear, was panic-stricken not only by Marlborough's words but by his manner. That very night, after showing himself ostentatiously at the theatre, he set out for Paris disguised as the valet of the French messenger La Vigne.

By his flight Bolingbroke was held to have admitted the worst his enemies could allege. An Act of Attainder was passed upon him. In a few months he became Secretary of State to the Pretender, and held this office during the rebellion of 1715, thus making war upon the country of which he had so recently been a principal Minister. His habit of revealing secret business to his mistresses and his outspoken criticisms of the Shadow Court at Saint-Germain led to his dismissal in 1716 by the Pretender. It was eight years before he was, with some tolerance, allowed to return to England, but the Attainder, though mitigated in respect of his property, debarred him for ever from Parliamentary life.

Oxford's behaviour in adversity extorted respect from all. When it became clear that the new House of Commons would demand his impeachment, and a formidable catalogue of high crimes and misdemeanours was drawn against him with all the skill of the Whigs, guided by the deadly common sense of Walpole, he announced through his brother, Edward Harley, "that he would neither fly his country nor conceal himself, but be forthcoming whenever he should be called upon to justify his conduct." When eventually the articles of impeachment were exhibited against the ex-Treasurer in the Lords, and a resolution was carried to commit him to safe custody in the Tower, he spoke with a dignity "unconcerned with the life of an insignificant old man," and declared that with his dying breath he would vindicate the memory of Queen Anne and the measures she had pursued. Edward Harley says that "he fetched tears either of rage or compassion from the greatest of his enemies; the Duke of Marlborough himself saying that he could not but envy him that under such circumstances he could talk with so much resolution." He had much to answer for; but behind him stood the fact that his policy had received the sincere assent of the Queen, and had been affirmed by two successive elections and Parliaments. His coach was accompanied through Piccadilly and Holborn to the Tower by a great throng of the common people, and when the Whigs shouted, "Down with the Pretender!" and "Down with the traitors!" the Tory chorus overpowered them with "High

Church!" "Ormonde and Oxford for ever!" The gates of the Tower closed against this excited concourse, and Oxford remained there for a long time.

Marlborough's restoration to the highest military and political functions had been complete. He was the most august member of the Cabinet. He held once more his great military offices. His political friends occupied all the important positions, military, civil, and diplomatic. Marlborough's numerous relations were so well represented in Ministerial and Court positions as to cause jealousy. His three sons-in-law, Lord Godolphin, the Earl of Bridgewater, and the Duke of Montagu, received respectively the posts of Cofferer of the Household, Lord Chamberlain to the Prince of Wales's Household, and the command of a regiment; and his daughter, the Duchess of Montagu, was Lady-in-Waiting to the Princess of Wales. His levée was as crowded as in the famous years. Once again, affable and bland, smiling and bowing, courteous to all, he was the centre of the Antechamber, "making the same figure at Court that he did when he first came into it." Sarah seldom accompanied him to these circles where she had so long been powerful. She was disillusioned. She had urged her husband not to take any office. "I think," she wrote to Lady Cowper, "anyone that has common sense or honesty must needs be very weary of everything that one meets with in Courts."

The Duke, however, wielded an immense influence whenever he cared to use it. He had the satisfaction—and it must have been a great one—of reinstating in the Army the faithful, war-proved officers who had been the victims of Bolingbroke's purges. With Argyll and Cadogan as his two surbordinates, he rearranged and redistributed the commands of the Army, the fortresses and regiments. That this process should be severe and resented by the Tories was inevitable. It was certainly not needlessly vindictive. Marlborough, now as ever, was averse to the partisan treatment of national affairs. If he had been inclined to pursue officers of merit who had been disloyal to him he had the fullest opportunity. But there is no record of such a reproach having been made against him. None the less the control of the Army was brought into harmony with the interests of the house of Hanover and the Protestant Succession. This work, which occupied the winter of 1714 and the greater part of the next year, was soon to be put to a serious test.

In fact, during 1715 the actual Government of the country seemed to be carried on by an inner Cabinet of German and British Ministers, of whom Marlborough, though not the most active, was the foremost. "Under the cover of darkness," wrote Hoffmann, "Marlborough, Townshend, and Bernstorf meet every night at Bothmar's house." Bonet, the Prussian envoy, wrote at the same time, "This quadrumvirate settles everything." Very soon they were joined by Stanhope. This system prevailed during the whole of 1715, and Marlborough dropped out of it through the decline of his energy and the eventual breakdown of his health. He no longer made the same commanding impression upon people. Although he was the King's greatest subject, and in the greatest situations, the actual leadership and conduct of business did not lie in his hands. Nor did he seek to assert it. His life's work was done, and his genius for command and control had gradually departed.

There is ample explanation and excuse in human nature for the wrath with which the Whigs pursued the ousted Tories. But the reaction which followed was formidable. The Tory Party, undoubtedly the stronger, now saw themselves not only stripped of power and office, but censured in scathing terms by those over whom they had lately ruled. They claimed that the country had been with them in the Peace. They were sure it was with them against the renewal of the war. The Whigs, they declared, in their hearts sought to resume the foreign policy of 1710, for which a great standing army and heavy expenditure would be required. Inflamed by the impeachment of their leaders, offended by the foreign aspect of the Court and the King's hostility to them, the Tories gave way to angers which stirred in every class and every parish throughout the land. This violent mood prepared their further undoing, for the Pretender, misled by their discontents, encouraged by Bolingbroke, proceeded to claim his rights with the sword. Here is no place to describe the rebellion of 1715 in Scotland and its suppression. Marlborough as Captain-General used the whole power of the Army against the Jacobites. He was no longer fit to take the field himself, nor, indeed, were the forces and operations upon a scale requiring his presence. It seemed natural that Argyll should command King George's forces in Scotland, and thither also Marlborough sent Cadogan with the six thousand Dutch troops readily furnished by the States-General under the Succession Treaty.

Marlborough presided over, rather than conducted, the brief and petty campaign. He rightly predicted Preston as the point at which the Jacobite inroad from Scotland would be arrested. He sat daily in the Cabinet and strongly supported the exclusion of the Duke of Somerset, whose high words about the detention of a nephew in the Tower had provoked his colleagues. When Argyll's chivalrous sympathy for his fellow-countrymen in arms against the Crown made him lax and lukewarm at the head of the Royal forces in Scotland, Marlborough intervened effectively to have him superseded by Cadogan.

Political England, which in the spring and summer of 1715 had been so fiercely discontented with the Hanoverian-Whig régime, rallied to it in overwhelming decision against rebellion and invasion. Both parties—one sadly, but none the less decidedly—joined in the protestations of loyalty to King George. A price of £100,000 was set upon the Pretender, dead or alive. Hundreds of suspected notables were placed under preventive arrest. The Swedish fleet, in which Charles XII had planned to come to Scotland with twelve thousand of his veterans, was attacked and destroyed in Danish waters by British battleships, allied with the Danish squadron and under the Danish flag. Ormonde, whose popularity had been counted on to carry all before it in the south and west of Scotland, arrived in France a fugitive, and did not dare even to land again in counties, like Devonshire and Cornwall, in which he had formerly been all-powerful. The ill-starred Pretender, escaping from his flicker of sovereignty in Scotland, dismissed Bolingbroke from a phantom Secretaryship of State. The death of Louis XIV in September 1715 and the accession to power of the Duke of Orleans as Regent fundamentally altered the policy of France towards the house of Stuart, and new combinations opened in Europe which are beyond the scope of this account.

Very little blood was shed in the fighting of 1715, and—according to the modern standards—restraint was shown by the Government towards the prisoners they had taken. Two lords only suffered on the scaffold, and a few score of shootings and hangings measured the penalties among officers and the rank and file. Tory England, which had rejected the cause of a Popish prince and had adhered steadfastly to the Act of Settlement, now looked forward to a general election as the constitutional means of voicing just grievances. But in this they were forestalled by the passing of an Act which, with doubtful moral warrant, extended the life of the House of Commons to seven years. In this period the Hanoverian dynasty became consolidated upon the throne, and the Whig Party grew to such ascendancy that they could afford to fight among themselves for the control of the Government. After their able men had jostled each other for some years the scandals which followed the bursting of the South Sea Bubble opened to Walpole a long reign of peace and plenty, sustained by bribery and party management. This period of repose and growth, albeit an unheroic pendant to the glories of the age of Anne, was the necessary prelude for the renewed advance of Britain to Imperial State under the command of the great Pitt. Thus the scroll unfolds.

CHAPTER NINETY-SEVEN

At Blenheim Palace

ᴈᴅ 1716-22 ᴅᴈ

MARLBOROUGH'S daughter Anne, Sunderland's wife, who by all the records preserved of her appears in a light of kindness and charm, died of what was called a "pleuritic fever" in April 1716. Her father was broken by the blow. His love for his wife and children stood always first in his life. Sarah also gave way to deep depression. They retired to Holywell alone together. Here on May 28 the headaches and giddiness which had always dogged him culminated in a paralytic stroke. He was at first robbed of both sense and speech. Dr Garth, summoned from London, administered the bleedings and cuppings which were the remedies of those days. Gradually his mind cleared, and bit by bit his speech returned. In the summer he was well enough to be moved to Bath, where the waters did him good, and the natural strength of his constitution largely repaired the lesion in his brain. In November he had a second even more severe stroke, and it was thought by all that his end had come. But again he made a surprising recovery. He was able after a while to resume the riding which had become second nature to him and was his daily exercise almost to the end of his life. His mind, though its energies were weakened, had rapidly regained its full poise and clearness, but he never recovered the complete power of speech. He could converse agreeably on every subject, and his judgment and sagacity were unimpaired; but, as often happens in such cases, certain words were stumbling-blocks, and as he was not willing to expose this weakness to strangers, he became increasingly silent except in the family circle. He still took a keen interest in public affairs. He voted for

Oxford's impeachment in 1717. "He was at this time," says Sarah, "so ill that he could not go fifteen miles without being tired." He had in his old age developed an inveterate dislike of the opponent who had brought him down, and though stricken himself, he used all the influence he could still command to prevent the impeachment from being allowed to lapse. Perhaps his own sense of being mentally crippled embittered him. All his life he had been a humane man, whose path was free from the tiresome, baulking shadows of revenge.

On account of his infirmities he sought, as was indeed no more than proper, to give up the Captain-Generalcy. But this did not commend itself to George I. The quarrel between the King and the Prince of Wales was at its height, and the sovereign could not run the risk of the vacant office being demanded for his son. He therefore begged Marlborough to continue Captain-General, and the Duke in fact held this post, though quite unable to discharge it, until a few months before his death.

Marlborough had nearly five more years of life. He always maintained a considerable state. He attended the House of Lords regularly till November 1721, and lived at Holywell, which was well established and comfortable, or at the Lodge in Windsor Park, which Sarah had considerably enlarged, or at Marlborough House; but all his active interest was in Blenheim. One wing was finished, and the rest was rising slowly year by year. His surviving daughters and their husbands, and now grandchildren growing up, all wished to pay their court to him; but Sarah for one reason and another surrounded him instead with all kinds of quarrels, for which she has left abundant self-justifications.

It can hardly be thought strange that she fell out with her architect, Vanbrugh, as well as with several of the contractors who built Blenheim. She had always, as has been seen, disapproved of a palace on so magnificent a scale. She visited this upon Vanbrugh, whose ambitious design had been the cause of so much friction and embarrassment to Marlborough. When she saw the chaos in which the works stood in 1716 her wrath overflowed. She fought Vanbrugh with zest and zeal. He was a person of some consequence in society with a tongue and pen of venom. Here, then, was another fertile and enduring theme of strife. The building of Blenheim under all the varying relationships of Marlborough with successive Governments no doubt gave opportunity to extravagance, inefficiency, and actual fraud. On the whole, the merits lay on Sarah's side, and she certainly gained several actions against the contractors.

But the saddest quarrels, and those that rent Marlborough's heart, were with her two surviving daughters, Henrietta, Lady Godolphin, and Mary, Duchess of Montagu. Both daughters, while declaring and evincing devotion to their father, treated their mother undutifully and even cruelly. These distresses darkened Marlborough's closing years, but while he tried to soften his wife's severity he always stood by her on every occasion. And she stood by him. All the love and tenderness of her vehement, tireless nature centered upon her failing husband. She waited on him hand and foot. She watched over him night and day. She studied his every wish, except in the one matter which would have rejoiced him most. At one time a sham reconciliation with her daughters was performed in his presence; but love was dead on both sides between mother and children. Sarah prowled around his couch like a she-bear guarding its slowly dying mate, and tearing all, friend or foe, who approached.

These shadows did not, however, fill the picture of Marlborough's decline. There were happiness and pleasure as well. The new generation and their friends were welcome in the half-finished palace. Young soldiers came on visits of courtship or pleasure, or in the hope of seeing the warrior whose deeds resounded through the world. Coxe gives an agreeable account of theatricals where, after its lines had been carefully pruned by Sarah of all immodest suggestion, *All for Love* was acted with much skill. It was in this bright and innocent circle that Marlborough realized some of those pleasures of home of which he had dreamed throughout his campaigns. He himself played cards for amusement, particularly piquet and ombre; while Sarah indulged her taste for more serious stakes. He rode about his wide park and properties often twice a day, or drove behind postilions with his wife. Always he remained a centre of harmony, patience, and gentleness; and always the object of veneration and love, with which pity increasingly mingled.

In 1720 the amazing episode of the South Sea Bubble inflamed, scorched, and seared London society. Sarah, with her almost repellent common sense, forced the Duke out of the market before the collapse, and added £100,000 to the fortune which he and she had gathered. Nor was this feminine intuition. In a blistering letter she wrote, while all English society was bewitched by speculation, "Every mortal that has common sense or that knows anything of figures sees that 'tis not possible by all the arts and tricks upon earth long to carry £400,000,000 of paper credit with £15,000,000 of specie. This makes me think that this project must burst in a little while and fall to nothing." All the Ministers, her enemies, were involved in the scandals and widespread ruin which followed. Sunderland and Craggs were grievously stricken in fame and fortune. Unscathed herself, Sarah gave full rein to her honest indignation. She urged the hounds of public wrath upon the trail of the wrongdoers. But these held high places, and, although hard pressed, were able to retaliate in their own fashion. All her enemies in the Government and at Court laid their heads together. They worked upon the King. To keep her quiet or busy with her own affairs, they set on foot against her, with his connivance, the most fantastic slander that could be imagined. She was in a plot, they said, to bring back the Pretender. She had even sent him a large sum of money. Marlborough, in spite of his health, was summoned by his estranged son-in-law Sunderland, then Prime Minister, to receive this monstrous accusation against his wife.

Nothing could have been better calculated to drive Sarah into fury—she, the lifelong Whig, the foe of Popery! But when she resorted to Court aflame with injured innocence she found herself sullenly received, and her impassioned letter of protest drew from the King only the following curt reply:

St James's

December 17, 1720

Whatever I may have been told upon your account, I think I have shown, on all occasions, the value I have for the services of the Duke your husband; and I am always disposed to judge of him and you by the behaviour of each of you in regard to my service. Upon which I pray God, my lady Marlborough, to preserve you in all happiness.

George R.

None the less the old warrior lived his last spell in sedate splendour, and was not deserted by that Olympian calm which had been his shield in the great days. After all his toil he reposed in much tranquillity and contentment. He devoted to the conciliation of domestic broils those resources of tact and patience which had so long held the confederacy of Europe united. From the habitable wing at Blenheim he watched the masonry rising up with that daily interest which had in bygone years measured so many processes of battering down; and the distant chink and clang of the hammers took the place of the cannonades by which more than thirty of the strongest fortresses in Europe had been infallibly reduced to surrender. But always he was true to the Grand Alliance on which his life had been founded. Never in all the family conflicts did he allow his loyalty to stray from Sarah. There he remained at the end of the long road, on the crest of the hill, trying to bring order out of confusion and reach his just and final peace. Although the evening sky was slashed with storm-clouds, the horizon upon which the light faded was suffused with a gentle and steady glow. Those who loved him and those whom he loved bickered and snapped at one another, while he did his best for them all.

It is indeed astonishing that during all these years when he had so much leisure he should never have left any record, even in conversation, of the critical and disputed passages in his life, nor told his tales of camp and court. Had he done so, it is impossible that some account should not have been preserved. For him the past was the past, and, so far as he was concerned, it might rest in silence. He was by no means indifferent to his fame. His desire "to leave a good name to history" had always been strong within him; but as he looked back over his life he seems to have felt sure that the facts would tell their tale, and that he need not stir himself to do so. He looked to the great stones rising round him into a noble pile as one answer which would repeat itself with the generations. It is the truth that only a single remark of his about himself has survived. One day he paced with failing steps the state rooms of his palace, and stood long and intently contemplating his portrait by Kneller. Then he turned away with the words, "That was once a man."

The span of mortals is short, the end universal; and the tinge of melancholy which accompanies decline and retirement is in itself an anodyne. It is foolish to waste lamentations upon the closing phase of human life. Noble spirits yield themselves willingly to the successively falling shades which carry them to a better world or to oblivion.

Early in June 1722, at Windsor Lodge, he was attacked with further paroxysms, and though his reason was unclouded, his strength began to fail rapidly. He was aware that his end was near. Around him fierce animosities divided his wife from his daughters. Sarah unfolds a sad account of the final scene.

> * The afternoon before her father died, when I had no hopes of his recovery, I was mightily surprised and troubled at what I did not expect, that the Duchess of Montagu and my lady Godolphin were without. . . . I am sure it is impossible for any tongue to express what I felt at that time; but I believe anybody that ever loved another so tenderly as I did the Duke of Marlborough may have some feeling of what it was to have one's children come in, in those last hours who I knew did not come to comfort me but like enemies that would report to others whatever I did in a wrong way. However at the time I thought my soul was tearing from my body and that I could not say many things before them, yet I would not refuse them to come in, for fear I should repent of it. Upon which I desired Mrs Kingdom to go to them and tell them that I did not know what disorder it might give their father to go to him now, but I desired they would judge themselves and do as they liked, but I begged of them that they would not stay long in the room because I could not come in while they were there, being in so much affliction. Mrs Kingdom delivered this message and she told me that the Duchess of Montagu answered that she did not understand her but that if she meant that they were not to see their mother they were very well used to that.
>
> They staid a great while and not being able to be out of the room longer from him I went in though they were there, and kneel'd down by him. They rose up when I came in and made curtsys but did not speak to me and after some time I called for prayers. When they were over I asked the Duke of Marlborough if he heard them well and he answered *yes and he had joined in them.*
>
> After that he took several things and when it was almost dark, these ladies being all the time present, I said I believed he would be easier in his bed, the couch being too narrow, and ask'd him if he liked to go to bed. He said Yes, so we carried him upon the couch into his own room.

He lay quietly or in a coma for some hours, and died with the dawn of June 16 in the seventy-third year of his age.

His funeral was a scene of solemn splendour and martial pomp. Sarah would not accept the offers of the State, wishing to bear the expense herself; but the nobility, the Army, and the College of Heralds surrounded and followed the funeral car as it made its way through immense crowds to Westminster Abbey. Eight Dukes, Knights of the Garter, followed the Duke of Montagu, chief mourner, and in the procession walked Cadogan, now Commander-in-Chief, and a group of generals who had shared equally in Marlborough's glories and misfortunes. The coffin was lowered into the vault at the east end of Henry VII's Chapel, and rested there for some years.

Sarah survived John by twenty-two years. The story of her life would require a separate study far beyond the limits of this work. She lived entirely for her husband's memory. At sixty-two she was still remarkably handsome, and her high, keen intelligence also exercised a powerful attraction. Lord Coningsby begged her to marry him, and wrote her letters of ardent affection. But she put him aside gently, and their considerable correspondence, which had lasted over many years, comes abruptly to an end in 1723. Another suitor was found in the Duke of Somerset. To this lord of vast possessions, who had played his part in history, she returned her famous answer, "If I were young and handsome as I was, instead of old and faded as I am, and you could lay the empire of the world at my feet, you should never share the heart and hand that once belonged to John, Duke of Marlborough." Somerset respected her all the more, and she was a help to him in his later marriage.

Although hitherto she had never cared for Blenheim, she made it her duty to fulfil in letter and in spirit Marlborough's wishes for its completion. She threw herself into this task with characteristic efficiency, and the fifty thousand pounds he had left to finish it went double as far as equal sums spent by the Government in previous years. Besides this she herself built a triumphal arch at the entrance to the park from Woodstock. On the rise opposite the palace she set up a pillar of a hundred and thirty feet, surmounted by a leaden statue of the Duke, which looks from the ground no larger than human, but is actually twenty-five feet high. On three sides of the plinth of this fine monument she had inscribed the Acts of Parliament setting forth the gift of Blenheim by the nation and Queen Anne, and on the fourth an inscription recounting the ten campaigns. This inscription is said to be by the hand of Bolingbroke, and is a masterpiece of compact and majestic statement. In fact, it would serve as a history in itself, were all other records lost.

She was no doubt the richest woman alive in any country, having at least £40,000 a year in the commanding currency of those days. She used her fortune to sustain her ideas and assert her power. She lived in some state in her various homes, and even built, and rebuilt to her liking, a fifth house for herself at Wimbledon. She also gave largely to charity. She built almshouses in Woodstock and in St Albans, and helped a surprising number of people whose misfortunes or qualities appealed to her, some of whose cases have become known. She administered her estates with broad-minded capacity, and distributed her favours among her descendants according to her likes and dislikes, both of which continued to be vehement. Her most remarkable gift was the ten thousand pounds and landed property with which she presented William Pitt, then comparatively a small figure in national affairs, in order to make him independent of Court or Cabinet favour. Although her relish for his attacks upon Walpole affords one explanation of her motive, it is nevertheless an extraordinary fact that in the bloom of youth and in extreme old age her instinct discerned undiscovered genius in the two greatest builders of British imperial power.

After her death, in accordance with her wish, Marlborough's body was removed from King Henry VII's Chapel in Westminster Abbey to the tomb she had built at Blenheim. There they lie side by side in victorious peace.

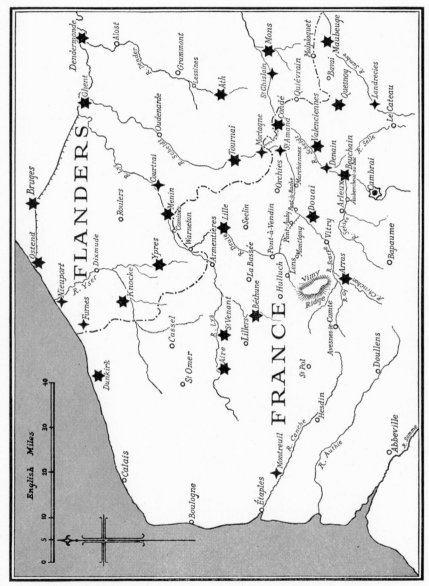

16. The Western Netherlands and Northern France

BIBLIOGRAPHY

INDEX

⟨⟨ BIBLIOGRAPHY [1] ⟩⟩

I. MANUSCRIPT SOURCES

The Public Record Office
   Secret Service Accounts (Treasury, 48).
The British Museum
   Unedited Coxe MSS.
   Additional Manuscripts, 41178 (Townshend Papers).
Blenheim Palace, Woodstock
   Marlborough Papers.
   Sarah, Duchess of Marlborough, Papers.
   Sunderland Papers.
Le Ministère des Affaires Étrangères, Quai d'Orsay, Paris
   Correspondance politique, "Angleterre," tome 265.
The Hague Archives
   Heinsius Archives.
   Archives of the States-General (Goslinga and Slingelandt letters).
The Huntington Library, San Marino, California
   Stowe Collection (Brydges Papers).
   Family papers of the Hon. Edward Cadogan.
   Family papers of Lieutenant-Colonel Gordon Halswell.

II. PRINTED SOURCES

AILESBURY, THOMAS BRUCE, EARL OF: *Memoirs*, vol. ii (Roxburgh Club, 1890).

BERWICK, JAMES FITZJAMES, DUKE OF: *Memoirs*, vol. ii (English translation, 1779).

BISHOP, MATTHEW: *Life and Adventures* (1744).

BLACKADER, LIEUTENANT-COLONEL JOHN: *Diary* (1700–28) (ed. A. Crichton, 1824).

BOLINGBROKE, HENRY ST JOHN, VISCOUNT: *Letters and Correspondence* (ed. G. Parke, four vols., 1798).

---

[1] The dates indicate neither the first nor the current editions of works, but the editions consulted.

BIBLIOGRAPHY

BOYER, ABEL: *History of the Reign of Queen Anne digested into Annals* (1709–14).

BURNET, GILBERT: *History of His Own Time*, vols. v, vi (1823).

COWPER, WILLIAM, FIRST EARL: *Private Diary* (Roxburgh Club, 1846).

EUGENE, PRINCE OF SAVOY: *Feldzüge*, Series II, vols. ii–vi (Imperial General Staff, Vienna, 1876–81).

FEUQUIÈRE, ANTOINE MANASSÈS DE PAS, MARQUIS DE: *Mémoires* (Paris, 1775).

GOSLINGA, SICCO VAN: *Mémoires* (1706–9 and 1711) (1857).

HARDWICKE, PHILIP YORKE, EARL OF: *State Papers* (two vols., 1778).

HANMER, SIR THOMAS: *Correspondence* (ed. Sir H. Bunbury, 1838).

HEARNE, THOMAS: *Collections* (ed. C. E. Doble, 1889).

KANE, COLONEL RICHARD: *Campaigns of King William and the Duke of Marlborough* (1735).

LA COLONIE, JEAN-MARTIN DE: *The Chronicles of an Old Campaigner* (translated Walter C. Horsley, 1904).

LAMBERTY, G. DE: *Mémoires pour servir à l'histoire du XVIII siècle*, vols. v, vi (1735, etc.).

MACPHERSON, JAMES: *Original Papers containing the Secret History of Great Britain* (two vols., 1775).

MANLEY, MRS: *The New Atalantis* (1720).

MARLBOROUGH, JOHN CHURCHILL, DUKE OF: *Letters and Dispatches*, vols. iv, v (ed. Sir G. Murray, 1845).

MARLBOROUGH, SARAH, DUCHESS OF: *Account of the Conduct of the Dowager Duchess of Marlborough from her First Coming to Court to the Year 1710* (1742).

—— *Private Correspondence* (two vols., 1838).

—— *Letters from Madresfield Court* (1875).

NATZMER, GENERAL: *Des General Feldmarschalls Dubislav G. von Natzmer Leben und Kriegsthaten* (1838).

PARKER, CAPTAIN ROBERT: *Memoirs* (1683–1718) (1746).

Parliamentary History of England, vol. vi (ed. William Cobbett and J. Wright, 1810) (Hansard).

PELET, J. J. G., and F. E. DE VAULT: *Mémoires militaires relatifs à la succession d'Espagne sous Louis XIV* (1850).

RALPH: *The Other Side of the Question* (1742) (answer to the Conduct).

Recueil des instructions données aux Ambassadeurs de France: Hollande, vol. ii (ed. Louis André and Émile Bourgeois, Paris, 1923).

SCHULENBURG, J. M.: *Reichsgrafen von der Leben und Denkwürdigkeiten*, vol. ii (1834).

SWIFT, DEAN: *Works* (ed. Sir W. Scott, nineteen vols, 1883).

TINDAL, N.: *Continuation of Rapin's History*, vols. v, vi (1763).

TORCY, JEAN-BAPTISTE COLBERT, MARQUIS DE: *Mémoires* (ed. Michaud and Poujoulat, 1850).

BIBLIOGRAPHY

VILLARS, CLAUDE-LOUIS-HECTOR, DUC DE: *Mémoires* (ed. de Vogüé, 1887).
WENTWORTH, THOMAS (EARL OF STRAFFORD): *The Wentworth Papers* (ed. J. J. Cartwright, 1883).

III. REPORTS OF THE HISTORICAL MANUSCRIPTS COMMISSION

Bath Papers, vols. i, iii (1904). (Harley, Shrewsbury, St John, and Marlborough correspondence.)
Dartmouth Papers (1889).
Downshire Papers (1924). (Queen's death.)
Hare Papers (1895). (Francis Hare, Chaplain-General.)
Mar Papers (1904). (Jacobite correspondence.)
Marlborough Papers (1881).
Portland Papers, vols. ii, iv, v, vii (1897). (Harley correspondence.)
Round Papers (1895). (Petkum correspondence.)
Russell-Frankland-Astley Papers (1900). (Tory correspondence.)
Seafield Papers (1894). (Godolphin letters.)
Stuart Papers, vol. i (1902). (Jacobite correspondence.)
Townshend Papers (1887).

IV. PRINCIPAL WORKS ON JOHN, DUKE OF MARLBOROUGH, AND SARAH, DUCHESS OF MARLBOROUGH

ALISON, SIR ARCHIBALD: *Life of John, Duke of Marlborough* (1852).
ATKINSON, C. T.: *Marlborough and the Rise of the British Army* (1921).
CAMPBELL, K.: *Sarah, Duchess of Marlborough* (1932).
COXE, W. C.: *Memoirs of John, Duke of Marlborough* (1820).
LEDIARD, THOMAS: *Life of John, Duke of Marlborough* (1736).
REID, S. J.: *John and Sarah, Duke and Duchess of Marlborough* (1914).
TAYLOR, F.: *The Wars of Marlborough* (1921).

V. SECONDARY AUTHORITIES

ARNETH, RITTER VON: *Prinz Eugen von Savoyen* (1864).
COXE, W. C.: *Memoirs of Sir Robert Walpole* (three vols., 1798).
FEILING, K. G.: *A History of the Tory Party* (1640–1714) (1924).
FORTESCUE, SIR JOHN: *A History of the British Army*, vol. i (1889).
GACHARD, L. P.: *Histoire de la Belgique au commencement du 18e siècle* (1880).
GEIKIE, R., and I. MONTGOMERY: *The Dutch Barrier* (1705–19) (1930).
KLOPP, O.: *Der Fall des Hauses Stuart*, vols. xii–xiv (1881–85).

(929)

BIBLIOGRAPHY

LANDAU, KARL: *Geschichte Kaiser Karls vi als König von Spanien* (1889).

LAPRADE, W. T.: *Public Opinion and Politics in Eighteenth-century England* (1936).

LEADHAM, I. S.: *Political History of England* (1702–60) (1921).

LEGG, WICKHAM: *Matthew Prior* (1921).

LEGRELLE, A.: *La Diplomatie française et la succession d'Espagne*, vols. v, vi (1892).

—— *Berwick et Marlborough: Une Négociation inconnue* (1893).

MACKNIGHT, THOMAS: *Life of Viscount Bolingbroke* (1863).

MICHAEL, WOLFGANG: *England under George I* (translated 1936).

MILLER, O. B.: *Robert Harley* (Stanhope Prize Essay, 1925).

MORGAN, W. T.: *English Political Parties and Leaders in the Reign of Queen Anne* (1920).

NICHOLSON, T. C., and A. S. TURBERVILLE: *Charles Talbot, Duke of Shrewsbury* (1930).

NOORDEN, CARL VON: *Europäische Geschichte im achtzehnten Jahrhundert*, vol. iii (1871).

PARNELL, HON. ARTHUR: *The War of the Succession in Spain* (1888).

PETRIE, SIR CHARLES: *Bolingbroke* (1937).

REESE, WERNER: *Das Ringen um Frieden und Sicherheit* (1708–9) (1933).

SAUTAI, M. T.: *La bataille de Malplaquet* (1904).

SICHEL, WALTER: *Bolingbroke and his Times* (1901).

STANHOPE, PHILIP HENRY, EARL: *History of the Reign of Queen Anne* (1872).

STRICKLAND, AGNES: *Lives of the Queens of England*, vol. viii (1852).

TREVELYAN, G. M.: *England under Queen Anne: The Peace and the Protestant Succession* (1934).

WEBER, OTTOKAR: *Der Friede von Utrecht* (1891).

WILLIAMS, BASIL: *Stanhope* (1932).

VI. ARTICLES

BURNE, A. H.: "Marlborough's Battlefields Illustrated: Malplaquet," *The Journal of the Royal Artillery*, vol. lx (1933–34).

CRA'STER, H. H. E.: "Orkney's Letters," *English Historical Review*, vol. xix, April 1904.

FIELDHOUSE, H. N.: "Bolingbroke and the D'Iberville Correspondence," *English Historical Review*, vol. lii, October 1937.

HARVEY, E. L.: "Letters and Accounts of James Brydges (1705–13)," *Huntington Library Bulletin*, No. 2 (1931).

LORD, W. F.: "Political Parties in the Reign of Queen Anne," *Transactions of the Royal Historical Society*, vol. xiv (N.S.) (1900).

BIBLIOGRAPHY

MORGAN, W. T.: "The General Election of 1710," *Political Science Quarterly,* vol. xxxvii (1922).

THORNTON, P. M.: "The Hanover Papers (1695–1719)," *English Historical Review,* vol. i (1886).

TREVELYAN, G. M.: "The Jersey Period of the Utrecht Negotiations," *English Historical Review,* vol. xlix (1934).

Review of G. W. Cooke's *Memoirs of Lord Bolingbroke in Edinburgh Review,* vol. lxii, October 1835.

INDEX

INDEX

Boufflers, Louis-François, Duke of, 315–18, 320, 327, 331, 334, 654–55, 707–8, 746–49, 767; at Enzheim, 50; at Lille, 633, 636, 638; at Malplaquet, 730, 734, 737, 742–44; along Meuse River, 285, 288–97, 300; at Mons, 722; at battle of Wynendael, 645, 649

Boulogne, 372, 711, 770

Bourbon, House of, 32, 490, 493, 544, 579, 678, 844–45, 867

Bourlon Wood, 820

Boussu Gap, 722–23

Boyle, Henry, 265, 582, 778–79, 782

Boyne, battle of, 151

Brabant, Lines of, 280, 452–53, 455, 459, 461–63, 476, 498, 509

Brabant, province of, 288, 291, 294, 313, 343, 480, 506, 528–29, 533, 578, 595, 637, 763, 768, 813, 824

Bradford, Francis Newport, Earl of, 101, 184, 186

Braine l'Alleud, 593

Brandenburg, Frederick III, Elector of. *See* Frederick I of Prussia

Brandenburg, Frederick William Hohenzollern, Great Elector of, death of, 122; battle of Fehrbellin, 31; intrigues of, 30–31; invasion of Belgium, 34

Brandon, Dukedom of, 847

Breda, English garrison at, 313, 321; Declaration of, 10; Treaty of, 29, 47

Brenner Pass, 326, 331, 541

Brentford, 186

Brest Expedition, and Marlborough, 202

Breusch River, 50

Briançon, 487, 591

Bribery, 74–75, 914; and Holland and France, 30; and Marlborough, 211, 542, 692, 696–97. *See also* Corruption

Bridges, tactical uses of, 617, 765, 816, 820, 822–23

Bridgewater, Countess of, death of, 893

Bridgewater, John Egerton, Earl of, at court, 911

Bridgwater, Monmouth at, 101–3, 106–7

Bridport, 98

Brill, the, 690

Bringfield, Colonel, 529

Brissoeil, 721

Bristol, Monmouth at, 100–1; royal garrison at, 4

Bristol, Bishop of, 866

British Isles, united, 659

British troops. *See* England, army of

Broad Church bishops, 307

Brownley, Mrs., 56

Brownley, William, 484, 859

Bruce, Thomas. *See* Ailesbury, Thomas Bruce, Earl of

Bruges, 529–30, 538, 587–88, 593, 605, 621, 623–24, 628, 644, 646, 648, 652, 654–56, 675, 878; capture of, 666; surprise of, 596–602

Bruges Canal, 627

Brunswick-Wolfenbüttel, Duke of, 276

Brussels, 97, 163, 233, 316, 442, 471, 512, 527–31, 587–88, 592–93, 597, 626–27, 631, 634, 641, 682–83, 691, 748–49, 814, 878; fall of, 466, 538–39; magistrates of, 528; Marlborough at, 464, 466–68, 599–600; siege of, 652–54

Brydges, James, 228, 863

Buckingham, George Villiers, Duke of, 24, 480, 485

Buckingham, John Sheffield, Duke of, 582, 838, 897

Bülow, General von, 740

Burgau, 390

Burgundy, Louis, Duke of, 588, 592–93, 596, 601–2, 623–24, 628, 630, 632, 651–53, 672, 675; at siege of Lille, 637–39, 641; along the Meuse River, 296, 299; at Oudenarde, 607, 609–11, 617–19, 621; peace overtures of, 702

Burnet, Gilbert, Bishop of Salisbury, cited, 24–25, 96, 103, 143–44, 226, 585, 845, 858; and Gloucester, 219; and Duchess of Marlborough, 853

Buys, William, Pensionary of Amsterdam, 476, 694, 750, 797

Byng, Admiral George, 138, 494

Cabal, the, 784; against Marlborough, 758, 774–75; and Secret Treaty of

INDEX

Church, 306, 353, 426, 479, 483, 773; despotism of, 28, 32; and Divine Right, 17, 160, 273; emotionalism in, 274; in England, 97, 115–16, 124; in France, 641; High Tories in, 575; and James II, 119, 126; patronage in, 484; politics in, 273; power of, 14, 308, 481, 485; structure of, 277; unity of, 15; vocation of, 238; and William III, 125, 143

Christian V, King of Denmark, 86

Church of England, 90, 115–16, 182, 247, 262, 267, 271–74, 308, 437, 728, 758, 840, 894, 911

Churchill, Arabella (sister), birth of, 4, 6; at court of Charles II, 21; married to Colonel Godfrey, 198; mistress to James II, 17–18, 20, 40–41

Churchill, General Charles (brother), 9, 399, 466–67; conquest of Belgium, 526, 528; and Blenheim, 348, 408, 411; at Brabant, 454; march to Danube, 363; in Ireland, 154–55; fortresses at Meuse, 299; and Monmouth's revolt, 100; storming of the Schellenberg, 376; in the Tower, 210

Churchill, Charles (son), death of, 186

Churchill, Elizabeth (daughter), Countess of Bridgewater, death of, 893

Churchill, Admiral George (brother), 581; at Cape La Hogue, 201; to Court of Madrid, 18; and Marlborough, 660–61, and Earl of Sandwich, 18; in the Tower, 210

Churchill, "Hariote" (daughter), death of, 84

Churchill, Lady Henrietta (daughter), 84, 917; married to Godolphin, 222–23

Churchill, John, Marquis of Blandford (son), death of, 224, 227, 310, 347

Churchill, John (grandfather), 4; appointed Commissioner for the King, 3; second marriage of, 5

Churchill, Lady Mary (daughter), 488, 917

Churchill, Sir Winston (father), ancestral home of, 71; loyalty to Charles I, 3–4; childhood of, 6–7; children of,

8–9; debts of, 5, 69; genealogical studies of, 6–7, 9, 11; in Ireland, 16–19; knighted, 17; and Lady Drake, 5; and Marlborough, 23, 48, 60; and rebellion of Monmouth, 98; restoration of favor of, 10, 16; and Roundheads, 4; opinion of Sarah Jennings (Duchess of Marlborough), 58; scantiness of records on, 18

Churchill, Mrs. Winston, children of, 6

Churchill family, Anglican Protestants, 111, 113; coat of arms of, 11

Churchill, Manor of, in Somersetshire, 52

Churchill River, 207

Cinque Ports, 891

Ciply-Quévy, 722

Civil List, voted by Parliament, 217, 439

Civil rights, 528

Civil War, in England, 1, 4, 26, 124

Claims, Court of, in Ireland, 16

Clarendon, Henry Hyde, second Earl of, 99, 132; and James II conspiracy, 119; and Marlborough, 102

Clement XI, Pope, 244

Clérambault, Philippe, Marquis de, at Blenheim, 408

Clergy, 441, 844; and Charles II, 12; and James II, 116, 119; and Puritanism, 2

Cleveland, Barbara, Duchess of, 58, 68, 71; and Charles II, 21–22, 24; and Marlborough, 22–25, 43, 46, 61–62, 70

Clifford, Thomas, Baron, and Secret Treaty of Dover, 38

Coalition movements, 548, 587, 666, 677, 774, 891

Coat of Arms, importance of, 14. See also Churchill family; Jennings family

Coblenz, fortress of, 314, 351–52, 360–62, 429, 432, 443, 590, 594

Cockpit Group, political machinations of, 87, 120, 132, 137–38, 149, 171, 175, 180–81, 189, 252, 262, 265, 267, 269, 285, 309, 460

Coffee Houses, and British society, 752, 834, 877

546, 548, 559–62, 565, 570, 581, 627, 648, 677, 685, 763, 801, 806, 899

Ennetières, campaign around, 638

Enzheim, battle of, 50

Episcopacy, and Catholicism, 125; and Charles II, 82

Erle, General Thomas, 591, 627, 644, 646, 649

Espionage, 77, 362, 396, 701, 813, 834, 837, 884. *See also* Intelligence

Essex, Robert Devereaux, Earl of, and Puritan Army, 2

Essex, Arthur Capel, Earl of, fate of, 84, 90

Established Church. *See* Church of England

Esthonia, and Sweden, 31

Estcourt, Sir William, 306

Estrées, Jean, Count d', 42

Eton, 306, 309

Etrun, 820

Eugene, Prince, of Savoy, 276, 279, 284, 300, 327, 343–44, 352, 367, 368–72, 392, 395–99, 420, 426, 431, 442–43, 448, 454, 479, 502–5, 575, 588, 626–32, 671, 682–83, 690, 779, 797, 800, 869; and Anne, 856–57; and Belgium, 522, 530, 535–36, 543; at Blenheim, 403–7, 410–12, 415; in Catalonia, 698; characteristics of, 237–38, 544, 599; on the Danube, 365–66; at Douai, 768; and the Dutch, 680–81, 694, 868; and the Emperor, 691, 694, 696, 723, 783, 857; and England, 851–56, 859, 907; and France, 238, 626; and Grand Alliance, 906; in Italy, 445; at Lille, 636–39, 644, 654; at Malplaquet, 731–32, 737, 741–44; and Marlborough, 226, 367, 371, 401, 403, 420, 424–27, 545, 549, 558, 579, 587, 590–96, 599–602, 627–29, 632–34, 640–41, 644–59, 666, 685, 696, 709–13, 719–30, 736, 744, 747–48, 762–71, 783–84, 807–8, 855–58; at Mons, 719, 722, 749; and Ninth Campaign, 765–66; at Oudenarde, 604, 606, 608, 612–17, 621–24; and peace negotiations, 672,

697, 703; on the Rhine River, 808; and Savoy, 561; at the Schellenberg, 375; in Spain, 576, 578, 580–81, 590; and Sunderland's dismissal, 784; at Toulon, 560, 562–65, 830–31; at Tournai, 714–16, 867; at Turin, 830–31; at Vienna, 333–45, 682, 688; and Villars, 889; wounded, 644, 647; and Wynendael, 649

Europe, 285, 302, 326–29, 347, 361, 364, 374, 398, 401, 411, 418, 424, 440–41, 445, 449, 462, 505, 709; alliances and coalitions in, 234, 262, 756, 774, 789, 846, 907, 918–19; balance of power in, 32–33, 44, 242, 359, 388, 419, 423, 434, 623, 658, 801; courts in, 34, 435, 755, 846; disarmament, 214, 267; and Electress Sophia, 893; and Emperor, 834; and England, 194, 227, 267, 345, 440, 583, 754, 780, 790–95, 841, 846; French domination of, 129, 243, 635, 913; and Hanoverian Succession, 907; and Holland, 256; liberty in, 260, 544, 634, 839, 845; and siege of Lille, 633; and Malplaquet, 746; Marlborough's influence in, 572, 646, 664–65, 676, 751, 775, 821, 826, 853, 877, 892–93, 897, 906; peace movement in, 216, 229, 659, 672–73, 682, 705, 753, 844, 867; Protestantism in, 122, 127, 137; society in, 419, 666, 763; reaction to Sunderland's dismissal, 782–84; and Treaty of Utrecht, 888–89; tyranny in, 255; wracked by war, 229, 267, 357, 466, 475, 524, 539, 891

Eutin, Danish seizure of, 500

Evance, Sir Stephen, 208

Examiner, The, 873

Exclusion Bill, aims and history of, 74–76, 89, 156, 158, 160

Exeter, William III at, 129

Exheim, 398

Exile, of James II, 166–67

Eyne, campaign around, 604–8, 611

Fagel, François Nicholaas, Baron, 637, 715–16, 733–34, 823

INDEX

Grammont's Memoirs (Hamilton), 17

Grand Alliance, 40, 206, 212, 234, 264, 267, 269, 286, 329–30, 333, 337, 353, 370, 424, 429, 435–36, 442, 449, 566, 574, 586, 630, 659, 679, 712, 750, 754, 756–57, 784, 864, 887; and Bavaria, 389; and Belgium, 530, 537, 539, 548; and Blenheim, 346, 349; and the Emperor, 238, 800–1; England in, 779, 803, 890; failure of, 163–64, 190, 833, 906; formation of, 233, 235–37, 239, 243; and France, 35; influence of Marlborough in, 260, 501, 795, 842, 852–53, 919; peace negotiations of, 671–72, 682, 690, 696, 704, 865, 890; perfidy among members, 831; power of, 209, 805, 839; and Savoy, 227; signatory members of, 239, 543–44, 665, 795, 806, 833, 835, 890; and Spain, 475, 498; treaties of, 258, 285; unity in, 483, 541, 543, 680, 797; weakness of, 545, 566, 851

Grand Battery, at Malplaquet, 735–36, 739

Grand Pensionary of Holland. *See* Heinsius, Anton

Grand Prior, 358

Grandval Conspiracy, 191

Grave, campaign around, 288, 293

Gravensbrück, castle of, 289

Gravesend, 139

Great Britain. *See* England

"Great Design," details and failure of, 316, 321

Great Frost, 682–84

Great Rebellion, and Whig Party, 80

Great Seal, and James II, 139

Greenwich, port of, 437, 843, 855, 906

Gregg, William, treachery of, 663

Grenadiers, 320, 377, 384, 457, 515, 534, 569, 724, 813, 824, 826, 904

Grey Dragoons, 743

Grey of Wark, Lord, and rebellion of Monmouth, 97, 99, 102–3, 105–6

Grimaldi, General, 465–67, 596, 609, 656

Groenendaele, campaign around, 466

Groenewald, struggle for, 610–17

Groffy, steward to Marlborough, 770

Gross Heppach, 370–71, 375, 426

Grumbkow, General Joachim Ernst von, 599, 683

Guards, Cologne Life, 458–59, 515

Guards, First, 105, 134, 160, 382–83, 438–39, 520–21; in France, 43; Grafton, commander of, 118; and James II, 166; and Marlborough, 42–43, 48, 880

Guelderland, Spanish, 329–30, 889

Guelders, province of, 299–300, 329, 350, 500

Guiscard, Louis, Marquis, 503

Guise, Colonel Sir John, 629

Gulf of Lyons, 443

Gumley, Miss, 306

Gustavus, fort of, 379

Habeas Corpus Act, suspension of, 187, 196

Hagenau, campaign near, 427, 444, 476, 503, 537

Hague, The, 21, 96–97, 238, 249, 264, 272, 286–87, 293, 299–300, 316, 320–21, 324, 327, 342–45, 350, 392, 425, 434, 436, 444, 463, 474–75, 481, 502, 528, 537–38, 560, 576, 655, 659, 670, 680, 683, 699, 710, 764–65, 790, 797, 800, 806, 808, 826–27, 847, 854, 867, 870; and Anne, 112; Cadogan in, 878, 892; conference in, 162, 580–81, 589–90, 870; English ambassador at, 74, 123; Eugene in, 854–55; and Grand Alliance, 239; and Marlborough, 83, 259, 313, 318, 505, 566–68, 799, 835–36, 839; mob scenes in, 41; and Parliament, 329; peace negotiations of, 682, 700, 750; Triple Alliance signed at, 35; and William III, 219

Haine River, 721–22

Haine-Saint-Pierre, 569

Hal, campaign around, 464, 593

Halifax, George Savile, Lord, 76, 577, 687, 693, 779, 787, 842, 845, 866, 870–72, 907–8; and Charles II, 88; and Dissenters, 110; on invasion, 139; and James II, 117, 120, 122, 167; on

INDEX

INDEX

House of Lords, political actions of, 98,
201, 217, 225, 302–4, 307–9, 336,
349, 438, 481–85, 570, 577, 580–82,
668, 687, 693, 748, 755–57, 759–60,
791, 836, 841, 843–44, 846–48, 864,
870–71, 874–75, 893, 908, 916
Household Troops, 9, 101, 190, 133,
438
Howard, Lord William. See Stafford,
Earl of
Howe, Jack, 265
Howe, Mr, 782
Hudson Bay Company, 888; and Marlborough, 206–7
Huguenots, 127, 213, 894; in Ireland,
153; at Oudenarde, 621; at Malplaquet, 728; refugees from France, 109,
215, 486, 503; and war in Spain, 486
Hulpen, Marlborough's bivouac at, 466
Hungarian Rebellion, 32, 326–27, 331,
365, 425, 442, 537, 590, 685, 830
Hungary, 445, 800, 831; and Empire,
807; and Hapsburg dynasty, 32; hus-
sar troops of, 599; Magyars of, 32;
and Vetes, 701
Hungerford, William of Orange at, 139
Hunsruck Mountains, 431
Huntington, Theophilus Hastings, Earl
of, arrest and release of, 186
Huy, fortress, siege and capture of, 318,
325, 327, 332–33, 442, 448, 455, 592
Huysse, 607, 619
Hyde, Laurence. See Rochester, Earl of
Hyde Park, review of guards at, 20
Huxelles, Nicolas du Blé, Marquis d',
866

"I Will Maintain," motto of William of
Orange, 127
Iberian peninsula, 576. See also Spain
Impeachment, threats of, 832; against
Anne, 80; against Bolingbroke, 908;
against Marlborough, 860–61; against
Oxford, 910, 916; against St John,
868; of Tory Party members, 912
Imperial Army, 281, 325, 331, 427, 442,
444–45, 589, 762, 831; in Alsace, 43;
in Belgium, 536, 546; bivouac area of,
367; and Blenheim, 343; commanders

of, 345; at Enzheim, 50–51; at Malplaquet, 737; at Mons, 727; at Naples,
559; on Ne Plus Ultra line, 807–8; at
Toulon, 548; and Turenne, 50; war
council of, 369
Imperial Government, 240, 330, 374,
390, 423, 494, 503, 542, 561, 677,
703, 740, 800–1, 914
India, colonial empire of, 29, 38, 213,
230, 243, 254, 499, 658, 677, 686,
801–2, 830, 833, 866–67, 888
Indulgence, Declaration of, and James
II, 81, 109, 118–19
Infantry, 348, 362, 366, 374–79, 382,
385, 399, 407–8, 411, 413–14, 430,
456–59, 466, 468, 509, 531, 594–95,
598, 605; Allied, 731, 817; Bavarian,
379, 384; Danish, 367, 411, 511, 522;
Dutch, 447, 511, 526, 613–14, 616,
621, 739; English, 190, 381, 382,
447, 454, 466, 494, 503, 512, 604,
608, 610–12, 617, 638–39, 644, 646–
47, 655, 729, 739–40, 742, 744, 823;
Eugene's, 600; French, 412, 424, 604,
607, 610–12, 615, 618, 625; German,
385, 412; Imperial, 377, 386, 393;
Prussian, 739; Spanish, 647
Ingoldsby, Lieutenant-General Richard,
382, 424
Ingolstadt, siege of, 389, 392, 396, 398,
505, 420–21, 427
Ingria, under Swedish rule, 31
Innocent XI, Pope, 244
Innsbrück, 854
Intelligence Service, Military, 506–7,
599, 684, 814, 861–63, 877. See also
Secret Service
Intrigue, bedchamber, 790; in England,
545, 664; French, 596; Jacobite, 166–
68, 882; against Marlborough, 774–
75; military, 795; Papist, 74; political,
287, 583, 585, 591, 784, 798, 805,
829, 836, 867, 869, 884, 894–95; Rye
House plot, 88; Secret Treaty of
Dover, 38; and William III, 177
Invasion, of England, 182–83
Ireland, 272, 307, 361, 486, 662, 728,
746, 789, 844; Cadogan in, 236;
Catholicism in, 124; and England, 27,

(955)

INDEX

INDEX

INDEX

Musgrave, 305
Musketry, 101, 612, 617

Nairne, David, and Fenwick, 202
Namur, fortress, siege and conquest of, 190, 194, 244, 280, 302, 327, 443, 452, 454–56, 462, 464, 506, 524, 527, 538, 542, 570, 601–2, 650, 810
Naples, Kingdom of, expedition against, 231, 239, 547–48, 559, 561, 678, 686, 688, 692, 695, 831, 878; and Marlborough, 256
Napoleon, lessons from, 208, 318, 372, 392, 425, 519, 544, 698, 702, 891; Wellington on, 805
Narrow Seas, English claims to, 29, 255, 278. See also Channel (English)
Nassau-Saarbrück, Prince of, 294
National Covenant, taken by John Churchill (grandfather), 3
Natzmer, General, at Bouchain, 828; at Oudenarde, 613, 615–18
Navarre, regiment of, 732–33
Nebel, stream, 400–1, 405, 407–11
Neckar River campaign, 280, 285, 363, 367, 419
Neerysche, dyke crossed at, 466, 471
Negative Oath, taken by John Churchill (grandfather), 3
Nepotism, of Duchess of Marlborough, 220
Netherlands, The, campaigns in, 285, 287, 298, 327, 333, 343–44, 347, 351, 372, 471–72, 764, 802; fortresses of, 546, 659; French driven out of, 543; Spanish, 330, 537; trade in, 633; Vice-Royalty of, offered to Marlborough, 669. See also Dutch, the; Flanders; Holland
Neuburg, 389, 398
Neutrality, 655; of England, 34, 229; of Sweden, 236
Neuville, 822
New Atalantis, The (Manley), 52
New World, colonization of, 28, 212, 234, 244, 253, 472, 659, 676, 889
Newcastle, John Holles, Duke of, 773, 779, 787

Newcastle, the, 133
Newfoundland, and English fishing rights to, 695, 888
Newmarket, Godolphin's house at, 218, 310, 428, 582, 790
Newmarket Road, 82
Newsells Park, marriage of Marlborough at, 69
Newspapers in the Seventeenth Century, 15, 336; Whig Party news-sheets, 834, 853
Nice, capture of, 562–63
Nieuport, fortress and siege of, 534, 538, 628, 644, 646, 648, 652
Nikon, monk, 31
Nimwegen, French at, 280, 286–88, 291, 298, 313; peace of, 213, 233–34
Ninove, French crossing of Dender at, 596–97
Nivelles, 593
"No Peace Without Spain," English rallying cry, 753, 840, 851, 890
Noailles, Anne-Jules, Duc de, 546, 707, 764
Nonconformists, foot soldiers of, 106; in House of Commons, 125; and James II, 110; leaders of, 118; and liberty of conscience, 108; opinions of, 274, 903; organization of, 126; vote of, 796
Nördlingen, campaigns around, 332, 346, 358, 360, 374, 387, 397, 399–400, 404
Norken stream, military campaigns around, 607–10, 612, 619
Normandy, ports of, 152, 182
Norris, Admiral Sir John, 559
Northamptonshire, riots in, 168
North Sea, 42, 124, 356, 581, 685
Northern League, and Louis XIV, 35
Northern War, and Grand Alliance, 549
Norton, St Philip, 101
Nottingham, Daniel Finch, Earl of, 115, 117–18, 139, 178, 186, 188–89, 264–65, 268, 353, 482, 484–85, 578, 840–44, 875
Nova Scotia, 888
Noyelles, Count, 456–57, 470, 559
Nuremberg, siege of, 346, 358, 360, 374, 389, 392, 397

INDEX

Pont-à-Rache, 768

Pont-à-Tressin, 645

Pont-à-Vendin, 765

Pontchartrain, Comte de, 232

Pontoons, military use of, 374, 403, 407, 604–5, 612, 762, 812, 816

Pope, Captain Richard, 362

Popery, 110, 129, 272, 903, 918; and Charles II, 88; in England, 80, 252; fear of, 109, 124, 126; in France, 232; Halifax against, 89; and James II, 126, 175; and Duchess of Marlborough, 895; and Popes, 232, 244, 402, 431, 897; and War of Spanish Succession, 232

Popish Plots, 81, 88, 97, 156, 308, 833, 908, 913

Population, Belgian, 629, 679; Dutch, 29; in London, 438

Port Mahon, capture of, 685

Portland, Hans William Bentinck, Earl of, 128, 144, 172–73, 176, 196, 247, 251, 339, 480; and Marlborough, 218; and William III, 687

Portsmouth, 80, 100, 134, 138–39, 152, 488

Portsmouth, Louise de la Kéroualle, Duchess of, 36, 92, 94

Portugal, 437, 442, 486–87, 493–94, 698, 840, 888–89; and Grand Alliance, 244; and Spain, 35, 230; troops of, 554; Wellington's opinions on, 805

Poulett, John, Baron, 1–3

Poulett, John, Earl of, 806; challenged to duel by Marlborough, 872–73

Poulett, Lady, 873

Poverty, Marlborough's fear of, 277

Powers, Maritime, 316, 324, 337, 437, 443–46, 449, 537

Prendergast, Sir Thomas, sent to Oudenarde, 597

Presbyterianism, 485, 728; and Charles II, 10; government of, 485

Press in Seventeenth Century, 15, 875. *See also* Newspapers

Preston, Richard Graham, 913; and James II, 128

Pretender, the. *See* Stuart, James Francis Edward

Prince of Wales, designation of Old Pretender, 227–28

Prisoners, 277, 295, 413, 418, 420, 447, 487, 492, 527, 530, 535, 609, 645–46, 813; of Bouchain, 826; English, 462; exchange of, 683; French, 598; at Oudenarde, 621–24; political, 391; at Tournai, 718; treatment of, 15

Privy Council, English, 187, 189, 218, 224, 247, 249, 353, 901

Privy Seal Office, English, 751, 773

Propaganda, 277, 283, 337; French, 232; of Whig Party, 484

Protestantism, 141, 230, 658, 706, 843, 882; and Anne, 86; in army, 117; and Catholicism, 124; of Charles II, 30; cause of, 166, 175, 472; coalition of, 137; conspiracies of, 126; in Dutch Republic, 122, 256; in England, 37, 121, 132, 156, 247, 338; and English line of royal succession, 92, 339, 402, 484, 687, 882, 886, 888, 892, 899, 911; in Europe, 127; in France, 237; of French-Canadians, 206; in Germany, 30; of James II, 108, 171; landlords, 326; of Marlborough, 39, 73, 75, 91, 129, 157–58, 170, 255; of Monmouth, 96; in Northern Ireland, 896; and Oath of Allegiance, 77; and Old Pretender, 227, 893–94; in Sweden, 31; William III champion of, 245; and writers, 78

Provence, 561

Prussia, and balance of power, 30; conference at The Hague, 162; envoys of, 912; and France, 32; and Grand Alliance, 236; on peace, 703; and Pomerania, 31; power of, 434, 537, 800, 807; sovereignty of, 402, 434, 436, 448, 715, 729, 739, 888; and Sweden, 31, 34; territory of, 545; and Treaty of Utrecht, 889; troops of, 122, 314, 330, 368, 434–35, 445–48, 502, 507, 679, 684; in Bavaria, 389; in Belgium, 528, 537–38; at Blenheim, 412–14; at Malplaquet, 728, 754; and Toulon, 563; with invasion army of William III, 127

(971)

INDEX

Sion House, Anne at, 180

Sirault, 721

Sixteenth Regiment of Foot, 146

Skelton's regiment, fate of, 48

Slangenberg, General, 147, 287, 319, 321–25, 464, 468–72, 474–75, 504; at Lines of Brabant, 451, 454–55, 461, 463

Sluys, port of, 37

Smallpox, deaths caused by, 310, 889, 893; and the Emperor, 800; and Duke of Gloucester, 227; and Queen Mary, 193

Smith, John, election of as Speaker, 484, 570

"Sneakers," the, 482

Sobieski, John, 30, 391

Society, English, 109, 172; French, 27; Scottish, 77

Soignies, Forest of, allied advance through, 466, 569–70, 593, 631

Sole Bay, battle of, 42, 44, 47–48

Solms, Amalia of, 158

Solms, Count, 163, 173, 216; defeat at Steinkirk, 190–91

Somers, John, Baron, political machinations of, 194, 224, 540, 579, 659–60, 662, 679–80, 687, 693, 779, 787, 789, 791, 842, 861, 905, 908

Somerset, Charles Seymour, Duke of, 70, 109, 180, 265, 353, 585, 759–60, 773–75, 787, 791, 845, 875, 902–3, 913, 921; and Harley, 776

Somerset, Elizabeth, Duchess of, 839, 842, 848, 902

Somersetshire, Churchill Manor in, 52

Somerton, 101–2

Somme River, 630, 711, 770

Sondenheim, drowning tragedy at, 413

Sophia, Electress of Hanover, 227, 391, 436, 484–85, 838, 885, 892–93

Sopwell, 84

Sorrel, favorite horse of William III, 244

South Sea Company, and bursting of the Bubble, 889, 914, 917

Southern France, invasion of, 547, 559–60

Southern Germany, defence of, 337, 405, 570

Spaar, General, Baron, 318–19; at Malplaquet, 733

Spain, alliances and treaties, 35, 47, 212, 239, 243; Allies in, 233, 544–46; Argyll to, 806; army of, 9, 421, 495, 528, 534, 542, 591, 651, 805; authoritarianism in, 28; and Barcelona, 213; Berwick in, 884; and Bourbon dynasty, 678; cautionary towns in, 749; and Charles III, 854; colonization of, 239, 275, 801, 888; and the Empire, 239, 801, 889; and England, 28–29, 496, 575–76, 578–79, 589; and Eugene, 576–77, 580, 589–90; and France, 28, 233, 486, 564, 678–79, 694, 697–99, 706–7, 888–89; and Germany, 578; and Hapsburg dynasty, 830; and Holland, 29–30, 47, 162, 238, 686; and Italy, 257; and James II, 122; and Marlborough, 487, 490–91, 537, 547; Mediterranean islands of, 239; and the peace movement, 678, 686–87, 696–98, 700–1, 753, 840, 844–45, 851, 866–67, 890; people of, 277, 319, 534, 701, 867; persecution in, 255; and Peterborough, 488–89; and Philip V, 239; and Portugal, 35; and Secret Treaty of Dover, 37; sovereignty of, 34, 232, 275, 277–78, 284, 401, 423, 487, 494, 499–500, 506, 537, 560–61, 564, 576, 579, 677, 685, 703, 871; and Starhemberg, 590; throne of, 239, 330, 694–95, 697, 699, 800–2, 866–67; and Turkey, 32; war in, 7, 22, 145, 441, 486, 497, 543, 547, 762, 833, 856

Spain, King of, 674, 701, 707, 801–2, 830

Spanish Armada, 28, 183

Spanish Flanders, 532

Spanish Guelderland, 329

Spanish Inheritance, 326, 677

Spanish Netherlands, 28, 233, 330, 421, 498–500, 658, 681, 763; authority in, 528; fortresses of the, 280; revolution in, 537

Spanish War of Succession. See War of the Spanish Succession

(976)